Basic Standard Deduction Amounts

Filing Status	Standard Deduction Amount	
	2000	2001
Single	$4,400	$4,550
Married, filing jointly	7,350	7,600
Surviving spouse	7,350	7,600
Head of household	6,450	6,650
Married, filing separately	3,675	3,800

Amount of Each Additional Standard Deduction

Filing Status	2000	2001
Single	$1,100	$1,100
Married, filing jointly	850	900
Surviving spouse	850	900
Head of household	1,100	1,100
Married, filing separately	850	900

Personal and Dependency Exemption

2000	2001
$2,800	$2,900

Income Tax Rates—Corporations

Taxable Income	Tax Rate
Not over $50,000	15%
Over $50,000 but not over $75,000	25%
Over $75,000 but not over $100,000	34%
Over $100,000 but not over $335,000	39%*
Over $335,000 but not over $10,000,000	34%
Over $10,000,000 but not over $15,000,000	35%
Over $15,000,000 but not over $18,333,333	38%**
Over $18,333,333	35%

*Five percent of this rate represents a phase-out of the benefits of the lower tax rates on the first $75,000 of taxable income.
**Three percent of this rate represents a phase-out of the benefits of the lower tax rate (34% rather than 35%) on the first $10 million of taxable income.

3 simple ways Checkpoint helps you make sense of all those taxes.

1 — Intuitive Web-based design makes it fast and simple to find what you need.

2 — A comprehensive collection of primary tax law, cases and rulings along with analytical insight you simply can't find anywhere else.

3 — Because more tax pros use Checkpoint® than any other resource today!

Checkpoint®
Look no further

For technical support call:

1 - 800 - 423 - 0487

Visit our Web site at:

w w w . R I A h o m e . c o m

RIA
A THOMSON COMPANY

West Federal Taxation

An Introduction to Business Entities

2002
EDITION

General Editors

James E. Smith
Ph.D., C.P.A.
College of William and Mary

William A. Raabe
Ph.D., C.P.A.
Capital University

David M. Maloney
Ph.D., C.P.A.
University of Virginia

Authors for West Federal Taxation Series

James H. Boyd
Ph.D., C.P.A.
Arizona State University

D. Larry Crumbley
Ph.D., C.P.A.
Louisiana State University

Jon S. Davis
Ph.D., C.P.A.
University of Wisconsin-Madison

Steven C. Dilley
J.D., Ph.D., C.P.A.
Michigan State University

William H. Hoffman, Jr.
J.D., Ph.D., C.P.A.
University of Houston

Mark B. Persellin
Ph.D., C.P.A., C.F.P.
St. Mary's University

Boyd C. Randall
J.D., Ph.D.
Brigham Young University

Debra L. Sanders
Ph.D., C.P.A.
Washington State University

W. Eugene Seago
J.D., Ph.D., C.P.A.
Virginia Polytechnic
Institute and State University

Eugene Willis
Ph.D., C.P.A.
University of Illinois at Urbana

SOUTH-WESTERN
THOMSON LEARNING

Australia · Canada · Mexico · Singapore · Spain · United Kingdom · United States

West Federal Taxation An Introduction to Business Entities, 2002 Edition
by Smith, Raabe, Maloney

Acquisitions Editor:	Scott Person
Developmental Editor:	Rebecca von Gillern
Marketing Manager:	Jennifer Codner
Production Editor:	Marcella Dechter
Manufacturing Coordinator:	Doug Wilke
Internal Design:	Carolyn Deacy Design, San Francisco
Cover Design:	Paul Neff Design, Cincinnati
Production House:	Litten Editing and Production—Peggy Shelton
Compositor:	Texterity, Inc.
Printer:	Von Hoffmann Press, Inc.

Printed in the United States of America
1 2 3 4 5 04 03 02 01

For more information contact South-Western College Publishing, 5101 Madison Road,
Cincinnati, Ohio, 45227 or find us on the Internet at http://www.swcollege.com

For permission to use material from this text or product, contact us by
• **telephone: 1-800-730-2214**
• **fax: 1-800-730-2215**
• **web: http://www.thomsonrights.com**

Library of Congress Cataloging-in-Publication Data

ISBN 0–324–11053–7

ISSN 1093–5154
2002 ANNUAL EDITION

This book is printed on acid-free paper.

Preface

The American Institute of Certified Public Accountants' Model Tax Curriculum Task Force recommended that the first tax course be taught using a business entities approach. This departure from the traditional approach in which the focal point is the individual taxpayer requires a different type of textbook and a more integrated learning orientation.

The West Federal Taxation team has responded to this recommendation and the related market need with the publication of *West Federal Taxation: An Introduction to Business Entities*. In designing a text that would reflect the Model Tax Curriculum program content for the first tax course, we responded to the changing needs of the tax education community. The outstanding traditional texts *West Federal Taxation: Individual Income Taxes* and *West Federal Taxation: Corporations, Partnerships, Estates, and Trusts* serve as source volumes for some of the content. Where appropriate material was available in these source volumes, it was adapted as necessary to meet the design objectives for an entities text. Where requisite material was unavailable, we created what our readers called for. Developing the text's content in this fashion is beneficial because the result is a text:

- Whose source material has been market-tested and widely accepted for over 20 years.
- Where organization, structure, and writing style promote readability and comprehension.
- That emphasizes tax concepts and issues, not the details of tax rules.
- Which allows professors to modify their approach for the first tax course on an incremental basis rather than on a radical basis.
- Whose ancillaries contain content that has been market-tested and used energetically for over 20 years.
- Which meets the high, professional standards of a West Federal Taxation text.
- Which meets the Model Tax Curriculum suggested program content objectives for the first tax course.
- That prepares its readers for the future, practicing in consulting and tax positions, succeeding in attaining further credentials and certifications, and demanding continuing education in tax law and policy.

Analysis of the Model Tax Curriculum suggested program content for the first tax course clearly shows that the intent is *not* to replace the first tax course with the second tax course. Much of what traditionally has been taught in the first tax course is contained in the Model Tax Curriculum suggested program content. What is significantly different is that business entities are now the focal point.

The objectives of the Model Tax Curriculum for the first tax course are as follows:

- To introduce students to a broad range of tax concepts and types of taxpayers.
- To emphasize the role of taxation in the business decision-making process.
- To provide students with the ability to conduct basic tax research and tax planning.
- To expose students to professional standards and ethics.
- To provide students with a knowledge of the interrelationship and differences between financial accounting and tax accounting.

In designing and developing *West Federal Taxation: An Introduction to Business Entities*, we have endeavored to ensure that it is characterized by the same qualities of accuracy, readability, and pedagogical design that have made the WFT series the most popular tax texts on the market, with sales surpassing one million copies.

An Introduction to Business Entities is designed for those who wish to emphasize business taxation, rather than individual taxation, in the introductory tax course. Chapters 1 and 2 cover the various types of taxes in the U.S. system, conceptual underpinnings of the Federal income tax system, a tax planning framework, and tax research methodology. These topics are applicable to all approaches to educating tax students. Tax planning concepts and tax research methodology are used as unifying themes throughout the text. Coverage of these topics provides the skills for solving tax planning and research problems contained in each of the remaining chapters in the text.

Chapters 3 through 8 focus on income, deductions, losses, and property transactions. While most of the topics covered in these chapters are relevant to both individuals and businesses, the emphasis is on the taxation of business entities. Individuals may be shareholders, partners, or proprietors in business entities, particularly in small businesses. Because of this, limited coverage of provisions relevant only to individuals is included when necessary to explain the tax impact of transactions on business owners.

Chapters 9 through 14 deal with the formation and operation of regular corporations, S corporations, partnerships, limited liability entities, and sole proprietorships. This material concludes with an innovative chapter which compares the tax consequences of the different business entity forms within a tax planning framework.

In accordance with the Model Tax Curriculum suggested program content for the first tax course, Chapters 15 and 16 cover tax concepts that relate only to individual taxpayers. These two chapters are not dependent on any of the material included in Chapters 3 through 14. After covering Chapters 1 and 2, instructors who prefer to address individual tax provisions and proprietorships before beginning the business entity approach can do so. Then, they can change the focus to business entities for the remainder of the course.

TAX RESEARCH

CHECKPOINT® STUDENT EDITION ONLINE TAX RESEARCH DATABASE

With the 2002 editions of the WFT series, South-Western is pleased to offer a student version of the renowned CheckPoint Online Federal Tax Research Database from RIA. An access code for this product is enclosed with every copy of *An Introduction to Business Entities,* 2002 edition. Available only via the Internet, this database provides students access to a combination of tax research and analysis from RIA, the leading provider of information and technology to tax, accounting, and corporate professionals. Utilizing RIA's CheckPoint Student Edition, students will complete the tax course possessing the marketable skill of knowing how to conduct tax research with the number-one tax online research system in the industry today. With CheckPoint, students can spend less of their valuable time looking for the right answers and more time applying the information.

CCH U.S. MASTER TAX GUIDE PLUS™

The *CCH U.S. Master Tax Guide Plus* online federal tax research database offers access to thousands of primary source documents with unprecedented ease and speed. With the convenience of using the Internet, the *CCH U.S. Master Tax Guide Plus* makes it easier than ever to conduct tax research. This research tool can be shrinkwrapped with the text and used by students to conduct tax research. To learn more about the *CCH U.S. Master Tax Guide Plus*, visit our Web site at **http://tax.swcollege.com.**

PEDAGOGICAL FEATURES

The pedagogy of this textbook is designed to assist the student in the learning process and to address the recommendations of the Accounting Education Change Commission (AECC) and the AICPA Model Tax Curriculum. A list of special features follows.

- **New! Bridge-Discipline Boxes** are provided throughout the text because we realize that taxation should be viewed as a part of a decision-making model that includes financial reporting, economics, finance, law, and societal needs. This material helps bridge the gap in going from one business course to another.
- **New! Bridge-Discipline Questions** in the end-of-chapter material give students the opportunity to apply concepts they've learned in the Bridge-Discipline Boxes to test their knowledge and understanding of these concepts.
- **New! Extender Problems.** Identified by an icon in the end-of-chapter material, these problems require students to go slightly beyond the material they've covered in the chapter to solve the problem. The students need to use their critical-thinking skills and a modest amount of research to solve these problems. Some of the problems can be solved using additional material provided on our Web site **http://wft-entities.swcollege.com** while others will require the use of other sources.
- **New! Tax Talk.** These tax quotes provided at the beginning of each chapter outline the importance of the tax concepts for that chapter. The quotes tie together the chapter concepts with things happening in the real world, helping to make tax issues come to life.
- **Digging Deeper** features are designed to help students go further in their knowledge of certain topics. This additional information can be found on our Web site and is identified within the chapters by an icon.
- **Tax Facts** sections are included throughout each chapter and focus on fun, relevant facts to know about that chapter's topics.
- **Suggested Further Readings** point to at least three suggestions per chapter that take students outside the text to relevant journal, newspaper, and magazine articles.
- **International Implications.** This boxed feature underscores the fact that all entities operate in a global environment and economy. They enlighten and inform the reader of international aspects of various key taxation issues and of the tax consequences of U.S. entities operating in a global environment.
- **Internet Exercises.** Included as part of the Research Problems for each chapter are questions which require the use of the tax resources of the Internet. These unique, creative exercises are identified with a "globe and computer mouse" icon.

- **Learning Objectives.** Each chapter begins with student learning objectives for the chapter. These behavioral objectives provide the students with guidance in learning the essential concepts and principles.
- **Chapter Outlines.** The learning objectives are followed by a topical outline of the material in the chapter. Page references appear in the outline to provide the student with ready access to each topic.
- **Margin Notes.** Each of the learning objectives appears in the margin when the text introduces related material.
- **Readability of the text** is enhanced with bold print to identify key terms when they are introduced. In addition, the text uses frequent examples and Concept Summaries to help students understand and synthesize important concepts.
- **Tax in the News.** Tax in the News items appear in each chapter as a boxed feature to enliven the text discussion. These items are drawn from today's business and popular press and present current issues that are relevant to the chapter material.
- **Planning Considerations.** Once knowledge of the tax law has been acquired, it needs to be used. Because we recognize the importance of applying tax rules in a business context, each chapter includes planning considerations as boxed features located throughout the chapter. These planning considerations illustrate the application of tax laws in a business environment.
- **Key Terms.** Before the Problem Materials in each chapter is a list of key terms to assist student learning. When the key term is introduced in the chapter, it appears in bold print. The list of key terms includes page references to the chapter coverage. In addition, each key term is defined in the Glossary (Appendix C).

- **Communication Assignments.** In recognition of the importance of communication in tax and accounting practice, specially-marked items in the Problem Materials include a written communication component. Selected Problems, Cumulative Problems, and Research Problems are identified as communication assignments with a "scroll" icon. These problems ask the student to prepare a tax client letter, a memorandum for the tax files, or other oral or written communications. To aid the student in preparation of these assignments, Chapter 2 includes an illustration of a client letter and memo.

- **Issue Identification Questions.** These questions, identified by a "light bulb" icon, are unstructured and open-ended. There is not enough information given in the problem to enable the student to develop a definitive answer. However, students are given sufficient information to identify the important tax issues. These problems are designed to help students develop critical thinking skills.

- **Tax Return Problems.** These problems, identified by a "computer" icon, lend themselves particularly well to computerized solutions. They can be solved using any commercially available tax preparation software.

- **Decision-Making Problems.** The Problem Materials include decision-making problems that are designed to enhance the student's analytical skills. These problems are defined with a "balance" icon.

- **Ethical Problems.** Ethical problems, identified by a "magnifying glass" icon, introduce thought-provoking ethical issues related to the chapter topics. In response to the recommendations of the AECC, they also demonstrate that many issues do not have a single correct answer. The ethical problems were selected to provoke discussion and provide opportunities for debate based on the student's value system rather than to provide a defensible answer.

SUPPLEMENTS

The 2002 instructional package includes a variety of supplements for instructor and student use. These supplements are listed below.

Instructor Supplements

- A *Solutions Manual* that has been carefully checked to ensure accuracy. A matrix is included indicating topic coverage for each problem. The solutions are also referenced to the relevant pages in the text. The *Solutions Manual* is available on disk and on the WFT Web site.
- A *Test Bank* with a comprehensive set of examination questions and solutions, with answers referenced to pages in the text. The questions are arranged in accordance with the material in the chapter. To assist the professor in selecting questions for an examination, all questions are labeled in a matrix to indicate topical coverage.
- *Examview® Testing Software* allows professors to generate tests electronically with ease.
- *PowerPoint* slides of teaching notes are also available.
- *Teaching Transparency Acetates* contain the key slides from the PowerPoint version of the Instructors' Guide for instructors who may wish to use traditional transparencies.
- *WFT Individual Practice Sets* prepared by Raymond Wacker, Southern Illinois University—Carbondale, and *WFT Corporation, S Corporation, and Partnership Practice Sets*, prepared by Donald Trippeer, East Carolina University. They are designed to cover most of the common forms that would be used by a tax practitioner for the average client.
- The *WFT Online* puts the most current information and supplements in the user's hands as soon as it is available. Adopters can log onto the Web site (**http://tax.swcollege.com** or **http://wft.swcollege.com**) and gain access to key information and supplements before they are available in print. The Web site also includes student-oriented materials, such as extra problem material and quizzes, topical news items, news about West Federal Tax supplements and publications, and more.

Student Supplements

- A valuable tool to boost student understanding, the *Student Study Guide* includes a chapter outline of key concepts, self-evaluation tests, and solutions to the self-evaluation tests with page references to the text.
- *West's Internal Revenue Code of 1986 and Treasury Regulations: Annotated and Selected, 2002 Edition* by James E. Smith, College of William and Mary. This resource, available for student purchase, provides the opportunity for the student to be exposed to the Code and the Regulations in a single-volume book that also contains useful annotations (i.e., Editorial Summaries that help the student to understand and apply the Code and Regulations).
- Powerpoint slides which give a mini-review of each chapter are available on our Web site.
- Tax legislation articles and updates are regularly posted to our Web site and can be accessed by students.
- Check out our online tutorials created to give you more information on relevant topics. You can find them on our Web site at: **http://wft.swcollege.com**.

TAX FORMS COVERAGE

Although it is not our purpose to approach the presentation and discussion of taxation from the standpoint of preparation of tax forms, some orientation to forms is beneficial. Because 2001 forms will not be available until later in the year, most tax return problems in the 2002 edition are written for the 2000 tax year. The 2000 problems can be solved manually or with any commercially available tax return preparation software.

For the reader's convenience, Appendix B contains a full reproduction of some of the 2000 tax forms frequently encountered in practice. These and other tax forms can be obtained from the IRS link on the South-Western College Publishing tax Web site at **http://tax.swcollege.com.** This textbook is published in the spring, long before tax forms for the year of publication are available from the government. Because we believe that students should be exposed to the most current tax forms, several new return problems (with solutions) and 2001 tax forms will be provided to adopters. This supplement will arrive after the beginning of 2002.

TAX LAW UPDATES

In the WFT series, we follow a policy of annually revising the text material to reflect changes in the Federal tax law. Errors and other shortcomings are also corrected annually. However, in the event of *significant* tax law changes, we will provide a timely, complete, and easy-to-use supplement to each adopter. These supplements can also be found on our Web site under **Tax Updates and Forms** at **http://wft-entities.swcollege.com.**

ACKNOWLEDGMENTS

As is the case with any literary undertaking, we welcome user comments. Such comments will not be taken lightly and, we hope, will lead to improvements in subsequent editions of *West Federal Taxation: An Introduction to Business Entities.*

We are most appreciative of the many suggestions that we have received while preparing the text, many of which have been incorporated in this edition. We particularly thank Donald Trippeer, East Carolina University, who has painstakingly assembled the Test Bank, Solutions Manual, and PowerPoint slides and Debra Sanders, Washington State University, for compiling the student Study Guide. Thanks also to James C. Young, Northern Illinois University, for continuing to provide us with his inflation adjustments, which are available prior to the release of the official amounts by the IRS.

Special thanks to Gary A. McGill, University of Florida, for his work in developing the International Implications feature. These items document that tax planning and compliance increasingly are global endeavors. They are an important addition to the pedagogy of this text.

Finally, this textbook would not have been possible without the support of Scott Person, Jennifer Codner, Rebecca von Gillern, and Marci Dechter at South-Western College Publishing and the on-going work of Peggy Shelton and Pat Lewis. Their editorial and development assistance is greatly appreciated.

James E. Smith
William A. Raabe
David M. Maloney

April 15, 2001

About the Editors

James E. Smith is the John S. Quinn Professor of Accounting at the College of William and Mary. He has been a member of the Accounting Faculty for thirty years. He received his Ph.D. degree from the University of Arizona.

Professor Smith has served as a discussion leader for Continuing Professional Education programs for the AICPA, Federal Tax Workshops, and various state CPA societies. He has conducted programs in over 40 states for approximately 25,000 CPAs. He has been the recipient of the AICPAs' Outstanding Discussion Leader Award and the American Taxation Association/Arthur Andersen Teaching Innovation Award.

Other awards received by him include the Virginia Society of CPAs' Outstanding Accounting Educator Award and the James Madison University's Outstanding Accounting Educator Award. He was the President of the Administrators of Accounting Programs Group (AAPG) in 1991–1992. He was the faculty adviser for the William and Mary teams that received first place in the Arthur Andersen Tax Challenge in 1994, 1995, 1997, and 2000.

William A. Raabe is the founding Dean of the Capital University (OH) School of Business. A graduate of Carroll College (WI) and the University of Illinois, Dr. Raabe's teaching and research interests include international and multistate taxation, technology in tax education, personal financial planning, and the economic impact of sports teams and fine arts groups. Dr. Raabe also is the author of *Federal Tax Research* and the *Multistate Corporate Tax Guide*. He coordinates the material on the West Federal Taxation Internet page, and he has written estate planning software used widely by tax professionals. Dr. Raabe has been a visiting tax faculty member for a number of public accounting firms, bar associations, and CPA societies. He has received numerous teaching awards, including the Accounting Educator of the Year award from the Wisconsin Institute of CPAs.

David M. Maloney completed his undergraduate work at the University of Richmond and his graduate work at the University of Illinois. He teaches courses in Federal taxation in the graduate and undergraduate programs at the University of Virginia's McIntire School of Commerce. Since joining the Virginia faculty in January 1984, Professor Maloney has been a recipient of major research grants from the Ernst & Young and KPMG Foundations. In addition, his work has been published in numerous professional journals, including *The Journal of Taxation*, *The Tax Adviser*, *Tax Notes*, *The Journal of Corporate Taxation*, *Accounting Horizons*, and *The Journal of Accountancy*. He is a member of several professional organizations, including the American Accounting Association and the American Taxation Association.

Contents in Brief

Contents

APPENDIXES

Introduction to Taxation

LEARNING OBJECTIVES

After completing Chapter 1, you should be able to:

1. Understand the components of a tax.

2. Identify the various taxes affecting business enterprises.

3. Understand some of the history of the Federal income tax.

4. Recall the basic tax formula for individuals and taxable business entities.

5. Understand the relationship between business entities and their owners.

6. Recognize tax planning opportunities and apply a simplified model of tax planning.

7. Recognize the economic, social, equity, and political considerations that underlie the tax law.

8. Describe the role played by the IRS and the courts in the evolution of the Federal tax system.

Outline

TAX TALK	*How many people were taxed, who was taxed, and what was taxed tell more about a society than anything else.*
	—*Charles Adams*

Taxes have a pervasive impact on our lives. They affect every individual in the United States from birth to death, and even beyond death (through taxation of the individual's estate). Taxes likewise affect every business from formation of the business entity to its operations, distribution of profits to owners, and ultimate disposition or liquidation.

Despite the wide-ranging impact of taxes, most studies of the tax law overemphasize the provisions applying to individual taxpayers and ignore much of the tax law relevant to business. That approach fails to address the role of taxes in *business decisions*, and it fails to provide the broad knowledge base necessary to succeed in today's business environment. This text adopts a more balanced approach; it introduces the tax laws that apply to all business entities and surveys the tax rules specific to each type of entity. It also recognizes that both tax and nontax considerations are important in business planning and therefore presents the tax laws within the context of the business transactions to which they relate.

LEARNING OBJECTIVE 1

Understand the components of a tax.

The Structure of Taxes

Most taxes have two components: a tax rate and a tax base (such as income, wages, value, or sales price). Tax liability is computed by multiplying these two components. Taxes vary by the structure of their rates and by the base subject to tax.

TAX RATES

Tax rates can be either progressive, proportional, or regressive. A tax rate is *progressive* if it increases as the tax base increases. The Federal income tax and the Federal estate and **gift taxes** are progressive. For example, the Federal income tax rates for corporations range from 15 to 39 percent for taxable incomes from $1 to $100,001. These rates increase with increases in taxable income.

EXAMPLE 1

Refer to the corporate Tax Rate Schedule inside the front cover of this text. If Abel Corporation has taxable income of $5,000, its income tax is $750 and its average tax rate is 15% ($750/$5,000, or the ratio of tax liability to the tax base). If, however, Abel's taxable income is $200,000, its income tax is $61,250 [$22,250 + 0.39($200,000 − $100,000)], and its average tax rate is 30.63% ($61,250/$200,000). The tax is progressive because the average tax rate increases with increases in the tax base (income). ■

A tax is *proportional* if the rate of tax is constant, regardless of the size of the tax base. State retail **sales taxes** are proportional, as is the Federal Medicare tax on salaries and wages. Proportional tax rates also underlie the various "flat tax" proposals recently in the news.[1]

EXAMPLE 2

Bob purchases an automobile for $6,000. If the sales tax on automobiles is 7% in Bob's state, he will pay a $420 tax. Alternatively, if Bob pays $20,000 for a car, his sales tax will be $1,400 (still 7% of the sales price). Because the average tax rate does not change with the tax base (sales price), the sales tax is proportional. ■

Finally, *regressive* tax rates decrease as the tax base increases. Federal **employment taxes,** such as FICA and FUTA, are regressive. When the tax base and the taxpayer's ability to pay generally are positively correlated (i.e., when they move in the same direction), many tax pundits view regressive tax rates as unfair. This is because the tax burden decreases as a *percentage* of the taxpayer's ability to pay.

EXAMPLE 3

The combined Social Security and Medicare tax rate levied on the wages of employees is 7.65% up to a maximum of $80,400 and 1.45% on all wages over $80,400. Sarah earns a salary of $30,000. She will pay FICA taxes of $2,295, with an average tax rate of 7.65%. Alternatively, if Sarah earns $100,000, she will pay $6,434.80 [(0.0765 × $80,400) + 0.0145 ($100,000 − $80,400)], with an average tax rate of 6.43%. The FICA tax is regressive since the average tax rate decreases as the tax base increases. ■

Under all three tax rate structures, the *amount* of taxes due increases as the tax base increases. The structure of tax rates only affects the *rate* of increase (i.e., progressive taxes increase at an increasing rate, proportional taxes increase at a constant rate, and regressive taxes increase at a decreasing rate).

TAX BASES

Most taxes are levied on one of four kinds of tax bases.

- Transactions (including sales or purchases of goods and services and transfers of wealth).
- Property or wealth (including ownership of specific kinds of property).
- Privileges and rights (including the ability to do business as a corporation, the right to work in a certain profession, and the ability to move goods between countries).
- Income, on a gross or net-of-expenses basis.

---

[1]Flat tax proposals call for a new tax with one low, proportional rate (usually between 15% and 20%). Such a tax would have a very broad base, taxing almost all forms of income with few deductions. To avoid taxing the poor, large personal exemptions would be provided (e.g., $30,000 for a family of four).

Because the Federal income tax usually has the most significant influence on business decisions, it is the principal focus of this text. Other taxes can play an important role, however, so it is important to have at least some familiarity with them. The next section introduces many of the taxes imposed on individuals and businesses in the United States.

LEARNING OBJECTIVE 2

Identify the various taxes affecting business enterprises.

Types of Taxes

After taxes on income, the various transaction taxes usually play the most widespread role in business (and personal) contexts. In many countries, transaction taxes are even more important than income taxes. There are three types of transaction taxes: sales and certain **excise taxes,** employment taxes, and taxes on the transfer of wealth.

TAXES ON THE PRODUCTION AND SALE OF GOODS

Sales tax and some excise taxes are imposed on the production, sale, or consumption of commodities or the use of services. Excise taxes and general sales taxes differ by the breadth of their bases. An excise tax base is limited to a specific kind of good or service while a general sales tax is broad based (e.g., it might be levied on all retail sales). All levels of government impose excise taxes while state and local governments make heavy use of the general sales tax.

Federal Excise Taxes.   Together with customs duties, excise taxes served as the principal source of revenue for the United States during its first 150 years of existence. Since World War II, the role of excise taxes in the Federal government's fund-raising efforts has steadily declined, falling from about 30 to 40 percent of revenues just prior to the war to less than 4 percent now. During this time, the Federal government came to rely upon income and employment taxes as its principal sources of funds.

Despite the decreasing contribution of excise taxes to the Federal coffers, they continue to have a significant impact on specific industries. Currently, trucks, trailers, tires, liquor, tobacco, firearms, sporting equipment, luxury automobiles, air travel, and telephone service are all subject to Federal excise taxes. In the past, the sale and manufacture of a variety of other goods, including furs, jewelry, boats, and theater tickets, have been taxed. Excise taxes extend beyond sales transactions. They are also levied on privileges and rights, as discussed below.

The bases used for Federal excise taxes are as diverse as the goods that are taxed. Fuels are taxed by the gallon, vaccines by the dose, telephone service and air travel by the price paid for the service, sport fishing equipment and bows and arrows by the sales price of the good, water travel by the passenger, coal by the ton extracted or by the sales price, insurance by the premiums paid, and the gas guzzler tax by the mileage rating on the automobile produced. Some of these taxes are levied on producers, some on resellers, and some on consumers. In almost every circumstance, the tax rate structure is proportional.

With the exception of Federal excise taxes on alcohol, tobacco, and firearms, Federal excise taxes are due at least quarterly, when the Federal excise tax return (Form 720) is filed.

State Excise Taxes.   Many states levy excise taxes on the same items taxed by the Federal government. For example, most states have excise taxes on gasoline, liquor, and tobacco. However, the tax on specific goods can vary dramatically

---

TAX IN THE NEWS

WHEN TEMPORARY BECOMES PERMANENT AND A LUXURY BECOMES A NECESSITY!

Over a century ago, Congress enacted the Federal excise tax on telephones to help finance the Spanish-American War. The tax was intended to be temporary and was justified as being imposed on a "luxury" item.

The continued existence of this tax raises some interesting (and embarrassing) policy issues.

- The reason for the tax has come and gone.
- "Temporary" should imply something less than a century.
- Telephones today are hardly luxury items.

During 2000, Congress considered this matter. One can hope that repeal of this tax is in the offing.

---

between states. Compare Alaska's $1.00 tax on each pack of cigarettes to Virginia's $0.025 tax. These differences at the state level provide ample incentive for smuggling between states and for state-line enterprises specializing in taxed goods.[2]

Other goods and services subject to state and local excise taxes include admission to amusement facilities, hotel occupancy, rental of other facilities, and sales of playing cards, oleomargarine products, and prepared foods. Most states impose a tax on transfers of property that require recording of documents (such as real estate sales and sales of stock and securities).

General Sales Tax. The broad-based general sales tax is a major source of revenue for most state and local governments. It is used in all but five states (Alaska, Delaware, Montana, New Hampshire, and Oregon). While specific rules vary from state to state, the sales tax typically employs a proportional tax rate and includes retail sales of tangible personal property (and occasionally personal services) in the base. Some states exempt medicine and food from the base, and sometimes tax rates vary with the good being sold (e.g., the sales tax rate for automobiles may differ from the rate on other goods). The sales tax is collected by the retailer and then paid to the state government.

Local general sales taxes, over and above those levied by the state, are common. It is not unusual to find taxpayers living in the same state who pay different general rates of sales taxes due to the location of their residence.

EXAMPLE 4

Pete and Sam both live in a state that has a general sales tax of 3%. Sam, however, resides in a city that imposes an additional general sales tax of 2%. Even though Pete and Sam live in the same state, one is subject to a rate of 3%, while the other pays a tax of 5%. ∎

Use Taxes. One obvious approach to avoiding state and local sales taxes is to purchase goods in a state that has little or no sales tax and then transport the goods

---

[2]Some excise taxes are referred to as "sin" taxes (because goods such as liquor and tobacco are subject to the tax). Although it is commonly believed that these taxes are imposed for the purpose of discouraging consumption, evidence frequently fails to show that sin taxes have a significant impact on consumption. Since demand for cigarettes and gasoline tends to be relatively inelastic (insensitive to price), the increase in price caused by excise taxes has little to do with rates of consumption.

WHY IS GASOLINE EXPENSIVE? IT DEPENDS ON WHERE YOU LIVE

Recent increases in the cost of gasoline and fuel oil have caused such a furor in the United States that supplies have been released from the national oil reserve. Whether this will reduce prices more than temporarily seems doubtful. But in the United States, unlike other countries, the high price of gasoline is largely attributable to the rising cost of crude oil.

In other countries (and using selected European nations as examples), the real culprit is the amount of tax imposed. Consider the following situations.

Country	Price per Gallon*	Tax as a Percentage of Total
United Kingdom	$4.29	76%
France	3.66	69
Germany	3.42	67
Sweden	3.86	66

*Converted to U.S. dollars

In the United Kingdom, for example, the price per gallon without tax would be $1.04, but with tax of $3.25, the price becomes $4.29. But why is the tax so steep? At least in the United Kingdom, the concern is global warming. The high tax is designed to discourage Britons from driving their own cars and encourage them to use mass transit facilities instead. Unfortunately, this punishes truckers, cab drivers, and farmers who have no such alternative.

SOURCE: Prices and taxes as of September 11, 2000, compiled by the Energy Information Administration.

back to one's home state. **Use taxes** exist to prevent this tax reduction ploy. The use tax is a value-based tax, usually imposed at the same rate as the sales tax, on the use, consumption, or storage of tangible property. Every state that imposes a general sales tax levied on the consumer also has a use tax.

EXAMPLE 5

Susan resides in a jurisdiction that imposes a 5% general sales tax but lives near a state that has no sales or use tax. Susan purchases an automobile for $10,000 from a dealer located in the neighboring tax-free state. Though Susan will pay no sales tax to the dealer when she purchases her car, she will be assessed a use tax when she returns to her home state and licenses the automobile. ■

The use tax is difficult to enforce for many other purchases and is therefore often avoided. In some cases, for example, it may be worthwhile to make purchases through an out-of-state mail-order business. In spite of shipping costs, the avoidance of the local sales tax that otherwise might be incurred often makes the price of such products as computer components cheaper. Some states are taking steps to curtail this loss of revenue.

Value Added Tax.   The **value added tax (VAT)** is a sales tax levied at each stage of production on value added by the producer. VAT is in widespread use

---

INTERNET SALES OFTEN GO UNTAXED

Typically, state and local sales taxes are the responsibility of the seller. Thus, these taxes are to be collected at the point of sale. Enforcement of the collection procedure, however, becomes tenuous when the seller has no physical presence (called "nexus") within the jurisdiction of the taxing authority. One computer manufacturer located in Texas, for example, does not collect sales taxes on Internet sales made out of state. Instead, the sales invoice contains the following notification: "The purchaser is responsible for remitting any additional taxes to the taxing authority." Would it come as a surprise to learn that most purchasers fail to pay any sales tax due?

The probability of Internet retailing escaping the application of sales (or use) taxes has been aggravated by Congress, which enacted the Internet Tax Freedom Act. This legislation placed a three-year ban on *new* Internet sales taxes. Although this prohibition did not affect the application of existing sales and use taxes, it did deter the implementation of various compliance procedures for their collection. It appears that Congress will further extend the moratorium. But there appears to be a groundswell of brick and mortar retail establishments that say they cannot compete against Internet businesses if e-commerce continues to avoid sales and use taxes.

in many countries around the world (most notably in the European Union and in Canada). The tax typically serves as a major source of revenue for governments that use it. Some proposals to reduce the Federal government's reliance on income tax have focused on VAT as an alternative tax system.

EXAMPLE 6

Farmer Brown sells wheat to a flour mill for $100. If the wheat cost $65 for Brown to produce and if the VAT rate is 10%, then Brown will owe a VAT of $3.50 [0.10($100 − $65)]. If the mill sells the flour for $200 to a baker and if it cost the mill $120 to make the flour (including the cost of Brown's wheat), then it will pay a VAT of $8 [0.10($200 − $120)]. If the baker sells the bread he makes from the flour for $400 and if it cost the baker $280 to make the bread, then he will pay a VAT of $12 [0.10($400 − $280)]. The consumer who buys the bread will not pay any VAT directly. It is likely, however, that some or all of the total VAT paid of $23.50 ($3.50 + $8 + $12) will be paid by the consumer in the form of higher prices for the bread.[3] ∎

EMPLOYMENT TAXES

Both Federal and state governments tax the salaries and wages paid to employees. On the Federal side, employment taxes represent a major source of funds. For example, the **FICA tax** accounts for over 34 percent of revenues in the Federal budget, second only to the income tax in its contribution.

The Federal government imposes two kinds of employment tax. The Federal Insurance Contributions Act (FICA) imposes a tax on self-employed individuals, employees, and employers. The proceeds of the tax are used to finance Social

---

[3]In the area of economics dealing with taxation (public finance), the issue of who ultimately pays a tax is known as *tax incidence*.

Security and Medicare payments. The Federal Unemployment Tax Act (FUTA) imposes a tax on employers. The **FUTA tax** provides funds to state unemployment benefit programs. Most state employment taxes are similar to the FUTA tax, with proceeds used to finance state unemployment benefit payments.

FICA Taxes.   The FICA tax has two components: old age, survivors, and disability insurance payments (commonly referred to as Social Security) and Medicare health insurance payments. The Social Security tax rate is 6.2 percent, and the Medicare tax rate is 1.45 percent. The maximum base for the Social Security tax is $76,200 for 2000 and $80,400 for 2001. There is no ceiling on the base amount for the Medicare tax. The employer must withhold the FICA tax from an employee's wages and must also pay a matching tax.

Payments are usually made through weekly or monthly deposits to a Federal depository. Employers must also file Form 941, Employer's Quarterly Federal Tax Return, by the end of the first month following each quarter of the calendar year (e.g., by July 31 for the quarter ending on June 30) and pay any remaining amount of employment taxes due for the previous quarter. Failure to pay can result in large and sometimes ruinous penalties.

EXAMPLE 7

Janet receives $90,000 in salary in 2001. She pays FICA taxes of $6,289.80 [(7.65% × $80,400) + 1.45%($90,000 − $80,400)]. Her employer is required to pay a matching FICA tax of $6,289.80. Janet's share of FICA taxes is withheld from her salary by her employer and deposited on a regular basis together with the employer's share of FICA. ∎

If an employee has two or more employers during any year, FICA tax withheld from salary may exceed the amount due. When this occurs, the employee will receive a refundable credit[4] against Federal income taxes equal to the excess FICA tax paid.

EXAMPLE 8

Miguel worked at two jobs this year. In his first job, he earned $55,000 in wages, and $4,207.50 in FICA was withheld. In his second job, his salary was $60,000, and $4,590 in FICA was withheld. Total FICA withheld for Miguel by employers during the year amounted to $8,797.50.

Since Miguel's salary and wages amounted to $115,000, he should have paid $6,652.30 [(7.65% × $80,400) + 1.45%($115,000 − $80,400)] for tax year 2001. Hence, he overpaid FICA by $2,145.20 ($8,797.50 − $6,652.30). This amount is available as a credit against Miguel's Federal income tax liability when he files his 2001 Form 1040, U.S. Individual Income Tax Return. ∎

Finally, FICA tax is not assessed on all wages paid. For example, wages paid to children under the age of 18 who are employed in a parent's trade or business are exempt from the tax.

Self-Employment Tax.   Self-employed individuals also pay FICA in the form of a self-employment (SE) tax (determined on Schedule SE, filed with Form 1040, U.S. Individual Income Tax Return). Self-employed individuals are required to pay both the employer and the employee portion of the FICA tax. Therefore, the 2001 SE tax rate is 15.3 percent (2 × 7.65%) on income up to $80,400 and 2.9 percent (2

[4]For tax purposes, it is always crucial to appreciate the difference between a deduction and a credit. A credit is a dollar-for-dollar reduction of tax liability. A deduction, however, reduces taxable income so that any benefit is limited by the taxpayer's marginal tax rate. An estate subject to a 50% tax rate, for example, would need $2 of deductions to prevent $1 of tax liability from developing; that is, if taxable income is reduced by $2, the tax is reduced by $1 ($2 × 50%). In contrast, $1 of credit completely offsets $1 of tax liability.

× 1.45%) on all additional income. Self-employed individuals deduct half of the SE tax—the amount normally deductible by an employer as a business expense. The self-employment tax is discussed in more detail in Chapter 16.

Unemployment Taxes. FUTA applies at a rate of 6.2 percent on the first $7,000 of covered wages paid during the year to each employee. As with FICA, this represents a regressive rate structure. The Federal government allows a credit for unemployment tax paid (or allowed under a merit rating system)[5] to the state. The credit cannot exceed 5.4 percent of the covered wages. Thus, the amount required to be paid to the IRS could be as low as 0.8 percent (6.2% − 5.4%).

FUTA and state unemployment taxes differ from FICA in that the tax is imposed only on the employer. A few states, however, levy a special tax on employees to provide either disability benefits or supplemental unemployment compensation, or both.

Employers must file Form 940, Employer's Annual Federal Employment Tax Return, to determine the amount of Federal unemployment taxes due in a given year. The return is due on or before January 31 of the following year.[6] Most states also require unemployment tax returns to be filed with quarterly estimated payments.

DEATH TAXES

A **death tax** is a tax on the transfer of property upon the death of the owner. If the death tax is imposed on the transferor at death, it is classified as an **estate tax.** If it taxes the recipient of the property, it is termed an **inheritance tax.** As is typical of other types of transaction taxes, the value of the property transferred provides the base for determining the amount of the death tax.

The Federal government imposes only an estate tax. State governments, however, levy inheritance taxes, estate taxes, or both.

EXAMPLE 9

At the time of her death, Wilma lived in a state that imposes an inheritance tax but not an estate tax. Mary, one of Wilma's heirs, lives in the same state. Wilma's estate is subject to the Federal estate tax, and Mary is subject to the state inheritance tax. ∎

The Federal Estate Tax. Never designed to generate a large amount of revenue, the estate tax was originally intended to prevent large concentrations of wealth from being kept within a family for many generations. Whether this objective has been accomplished is debatable, because estate taxes can be substantially reduced (or deferred for decades) through careful planning.

Determination of the estate tax base begins with the gross estate, which includes property the decedent owned at the time of death. It also includes property interests, such as life insurance proceeds paid to the estate or to a beneficiary other than the estate if the deceased-insured had any ownership rights in the policy. Most property included in the gross estate is valued at fair market value as of the date of death.

Deductions from the gross estate in arriving at the taxable estate include funeral and administration expenses, certain taxes, debts of the decedent, transfers to charitable organizations, and, in some cases, an unlimited marital deduction. The

---

[5]States follow a policy of reducing unemployment tax on employers with stable employment. Thus, an employer with no employee turnover might face state unemployment tax rates as low as 0.1% or, in some cases, zero. This *merit rating system* explicitly accounts for the savings generated by steady employment.

[6]Employers may be required to make more frequent payments of the tax (estimated payments) if their FUTA liability is sufficiently large.

marital deduction is available for amounts actually passing to a surviving spouse (a widow or widower).

Once the taxable estate has been determined and certain taxable gifts have been added to it, progressive estate tax rates ranging from 18 to 60 percent are applied to determine a tentative tax liability. The tentative liability is reduced by a variety of credits to arrive at the amount due. Although many credits are available, probably the most significant is the *unified transfer tax credit*. This credit eliminates estate tax liability for most individuals. For 2001, the amount of the credit is $220,550. Based on the estate tax rates, the credit offsets a tax base of $675,000.[7]

EXAMPLE 10

Ildiko made no taxable gifts before her death in 2001. If Ildiko's taxable estate amounts to $675,000 or less, no Federal estate tax is due because of the application of the unified transfer tax credit. Under the tax law, the tentative estate tax on a taxable estate of $675,000 is $220,550, exactly equal to the maximum unified transfer tax credit allowed. ■

State Death Taxes.   As noted earlier, states usually levy an inheritance tax, an estate tax, or both. The two forms of death taxes differ according to whether the tax is imposed on the heirs or on the estate.

Characteristically, an inheritance tax divides the heirs into classes based on their relationship to the decedent. The more closely related the heir, the lower the rates imposed and the greater the exemption allowed. Some states completely exempt amounts passing to a surviving spouse from taxation.

GIFT TAXES

Like death taxes, the gift tax is an excise tax levied on the right to transfer property. In this case, however, the tax is imposed on transfers made during the owner's life rather than at death. A gift tax applies only to transfers that are not supported by full and adequate consideration (i.e., gifts).

EXAMPLE 11

Carl sells property worth $20,000 to his daughter for $1,000. Although property worth $20,000 has been transferred, only $19,000 represents a gift, since this is the portion not supported by full and adequate consideration. ■

The Federal Gift Tax.   The Federal gift tax is intended to complement the estate tax. The gift tax base is the sum of all taxable gifts made *during one's lifetime*. Gifts are valued at the date of transfer. To compute the tax due in a year, the tax rate schedule is applied to the sum of all lifetime taxable gifts. The resulting tax is then reduced by gift taxes paid in prior years.

EXAMPLE 12

In 1995, Willie gave $700,000 of taxable gifts to his son. The gift tax paid in 1995 (before application of any credits) was $229,800. In 2001, Willie will give an additional $100,000 in taxable gifts to his son. The tax base in 2001 will be $800,000 of lifetime gifts, and the tax will be $267,800. However, the actual gift tax due in 2001 (before credits) will be $38,000 ($267,800 − $229,800 tax paid on prior-year gifts). ■

Under current law, the Federal gift tax and the Federal estate tax are *unified*. The transfer of assets by a decedent at death is effectively treated as a final gift under the tax law. Thus, the unified transfer tax credit available under the estate

---

[7]The unified transfer tax credit is scheduled to increase annually until 2006. In 2006, the credit will equal $345,800, offsetting a taxable estate of $1 million.

WILL ESTATE AND GIFT TAXES SURVIVE?

During 2000, Congress passed a bill that would have phased out the Federal transfer taxes on estates and gifts. Justification for the eventual repeal of these taxes was twofold. First, they constitute a type of double taxation. This conclusion is based on the assumption that the amounts transferred had already been subject to the income tax when earned by the decedent (or donor). Second, the estate tax in particular is threatening the continued existence of small businesses and family farms. To pay the tax, the heirs are often forced to liquidate the business.

The bill was vetoed by President Clinton. Although sympathetic to the plight of small businesses and family farms, the President felt that the bill went too far in unduly benefiting wealthy taxpayers.

An attempt by Congress to override the President's veto fell short of the number of votes needed. President Bush likely will encourage some form of estate/gift tax repeal during his term in office.

tax is also available to reduce the tax liability generated by lifetime gifts. If the credit is exhausted during one's lifetime, it will not be available to reduce the estate tax liability. In addition, the same tax rate schedule applies to both lifetime gifts and the estate tax.

EXAMPLE 13

Before his death, Gyung gives $1 million of taxable gifts. Because the unified transfer tax credit was used during his life to offset the tax due on some of these gifts, no credit is left to reduce Gyung's estate tax liability. ■

Annual taxable gifts are determined by reducing the fair market value of gifts given by an *annual exclusion* of $10,000 per donee. A married couple can elect *gift splitting*, which enables them to transfer twice the annual exclusion ($20,000) per donee per year.

EXAMPLE 14

On December 31, 2000, Vera (a widow) gives $10,000 to each of her four married children, their spouses, and her eight grandchildren. On January 3, 2001, she repeats the same procedure. Due to the annual exclusion, Vera has *not* made a taxable gift, although she transferred $160,000 [$10,000 × 16 (the number of donees)] in 2000 and $160,000 [$10,000 × 16 (the number of donees)] in 2001 for a total of $320,000 ($160,000 + $160,000). If Vera were married, she could have given twice as much ($640,000) by electing gift splitting with her husband. ■

State Gift Taxes. The states currently imposing a gift tax are Connecticut, Louisiana, North Carolina, and Tennessee. Most of the laws provide for lifetime exemptions and annual exclusions. Unlike the Federal version, the amount of state gift tax often depends on the relationship between the donor and the donee. As with state inheritance taxes, larger exemptions and lower rates apply when the donor and donee are closely related to each other.

PROPERTY TAXES

A property tax can be a tax on the ownership of property or a tax on wealth, depending on the base used. Any measurable characteristic of the property being taxed can be used as a base (e.g., weight, size, number, or value). Most property

PROPERTY TAXES CAN BE A NEGOTIABLE ITEM

After two years of controversy, Michael Dell (founder and CEO of Dell Computer Corporation) and the Travis County Appraisal District recently reached a settlement. The controversy related to the property taxes on Dell's home near Austin, Texas. Dell suggested that the property's value was between $5.5 and $6.5 million. The taxing district, however, contended that it was worth closer to $22 million. The problem confronting the taxing authorities was the lack of comparable luxury homes in this part of Texas.

The parties finally agreed on an appraisal of $12 million. One would suspect that the $250,000 in property taxes that Dell must pay each year due to this appraisal should not prove too burdensome for one of America's 10 richest individuals.

taxes in the United States are taxes on wealth since they use value as a base. These value-based property taxes are known as **ad valorem taxes**. Property taxes are generally administered by state and local governments where they serve as a significant source of revenue.

Real Property Taxes.   Property taxes on **realty** are used exclusively by states and their local political subdivisions such as cities, counties, and school districts. They represent a major source of revenue for local governments, but their importance at the state level has waned over the past few years. Some states, for example, have imposed freezes on the upward revaluations of residential housing.

How realty is defined can have an important bearing on which assets are subject to tax. This is especially true in jurisdictions that do not impose ad valorem taxes on **personalty.** Although the definition is primarily a question of state property law, realty generally includes real estate and any capital improvements that are classified as fixtures. A fixture is something so permanently attached to the real estate that its removal will cause irreparable damage. A built-in bookcase might be a fixture, whereas a movable bookcase is not. Certain items such as electrical wiring and plumbing change from personalty to realty when installed in a building.

The following are some of the characteristics of ad valorem taxes on realty.

- Property owned by the Federal government is exempt from tax. Similar immunity usually is extended to property owned by state and local governments and by certain charitable organizations.
- Some states provide for lower valuations on property dedicated to agricultural use or other special uses (e.g., wildlife sanctuaries).
- Some states partially exempt the homestead, or personal residence, portion of property from taxation. Additionally, modern homestead laws normally protect some or all of a personal residence (including a farm or ranch) from the actions of creditors pursuing claims against the owner.
- Lower taxes may apply to a residence owned by a taxpayer age 65 or older.
- Some jurisdictions extend immunity from tax for a specified period of time (a tax holiday) to new or relocated businesses.

Ad Valorem Taxes on Personalty.   Personalty includes all assets that are not realty. It may be helpful to distinguish between the classification of an asset (realty or personalty) and the use to which it is put. Both realty and personalty can

TAX IN THE NEWS

PROPERTY TAXES—IT MATTERS WHERE YOU LIVE!

A recent survey conducted by Runzheimer International (a Rochester, Wisconsin consulting firm) clearly shows that geography can cause a considerable difference in the amount of property taxes that one pays. Consider, for example, a four-bedroom, 2,200-square-foot residence appraised at $150,000. Located in Buffalo, New York, the house generates an ad valorem tax of $5,000 each year. The same house in Montgomery, Alabama, however, is taxed at $400. Based on the home's value, the effective tax rate is 3.3 percent in Buffalo but only 0.27 percent in Montgomery. Thus, real property taxes are approximately 12 times higher in Buffalo than in Montgomery.

Other high property tax areas include Rockford (Ill.), Pittsburgh (Pa.), and San Antonio (Tex.). Low-tax areas include Denver (Colo.), New Orleans (La.), and Salt Lake City (Utah).

be either business-use or personal-use property. Examples include a residence (personal-use realty), an office building (business-use realty), surgical instruments (business-use personalty), and casual clothing (personal-use personalty).

Personalty can also be classified as tangible property or intangible property. For property tax purposes, intangible personalty includes stocks, bonds, and various other securities (e.g., bank shares).

The following generalizations may be made concerning the property taxes on personalty.

- Particularly with personalty devoted to personal use (e.g., jewelry, household furnishings), taxpayer compliance ranges from poor to zero. Some jurisdictions do not even attempt to enforce the tax on these items. For automobiles devoted to personal use, many jurisdictions have converted from value as the tax base to a tax based on the weight of the vehicle. Some jurisdictions also consider the vehicle's age (e.g., automobiles six years or older are not subject to the ad valorem tax because they are presumed to have little value).
- For personalty devoted to business use (e.g., inventories, trucks, machinery, equipment), taxpayer compliance and enforcement procedures are notably better.
- Some jurisdictions impose an ad valorem property tax on intangibles.

TAXES ON PRIVILEGES AND RIGHTS

Taxes on privileges and rights are usually considered excise taxes. A few of the most important of these taxes are reviewed here.

Federal Customs Duties. Customs duties or tariffs can be characterized as a tax on the right to move goods across national borders. These taxes, together with selective excise taxes, provided most of the revenues needed by the Federal government during the nineteenth century. For example, tariffs and excise taxes alone paid off the national debt in 1835 and enabled the U.S. Treasury to pay a surplus of $28 million to the states. Today, however, customs duties account for only 1 percent of revenues in the Federal budget.

In recent years, tariffs have served the nation more as an instrument for carrying out protectionist policies than as a means of generating revenue. Thus, a particular U.S. industry might be saved from economic disaster, so the argument goes, by placing customs duties on the importation of foreign goods that can be sold at lower prices. Protectionists contend that the tariff therefore neutralizes the competitive edge held by the producer of the foreign goods.[8]

Protectionist policies seem more appropriate for less-developed countries whose industrial capacity has not yet matured. In a world where a developed country should have everything to gain by encouraging international free trade, such policies may be of dubious value since tariffs often lead to retaliatory action on the part of the nation or nations affected.

Franchise Taxes and Occupational Taxes.   A **franchise tax** is a tax on the privilege of doing business in a state or local jurisdiction. Typically, the tax is imposed by states on corporations, but the tax base varies from state to state. While some states use a measure of corporate net income as part of the base, most states base the tax on the capitalization of the corporation (with or without certain long-term debt).

Closely akin to the franchise tax are **occupational taxes** applicable to various trades or businesses, such as a liquor store license, a taxicab permit, or a fee to practice a profession such as law, medicine, or accounting. Most of these are not significant revenue producers and fall more into the category of licenses than taxes. The revenue derived is used to defray the cost incurred by the jurisdiction to regulate the business or profession for the public good.

Severance Taxes.   Severance taxes are based on the extraction of natural resources (e.g., oil, gas, iron ore, and coal). They are an important source of revenue for many states (e.g., Alaska).

INCOME TAXES

Income taxes are levied by the Federal government, most states, and some local governments. In recent years, the trend in the United States has been to place greater reliance on this method of taxation while other countries are relying more heavily on transactions taxes such as the VAT.

Income taxes are generally imposed on individuals, corporations, and certain fiduciaries (estates and trusts). Most jurisdictions attempt to assure the collection of income taxes by requiring certain pay-as-you-go procedures, including withholding requirements for employees and estimated tax prepayments for all taxpayers.

LEARNING OBJECTIVE 3

Understand some of the history of the Federal income tax.

A Brief History.   The first income tax in America was introduced by English colonists in Massachusetts Bay Colony in 1634. However, it was not until the increased revenue needs brought on by the Civil War that the U.S. government introduced an income tax (from 1861 to 1872). At its peak in 1866, the first U.S. income tax raised $376 million, or 25 percent of Federal revenue collections for the year (in contrast, the Federal income tax accounted for about 60 percent of Federal revenues in the 2001 Federal budget). The Civil War tax was levied only on the wealthy with graduated rates from 1 to 10 percent. The Confederate States of America also employed an income tax to help finance their war effort.

---

[8]The North American Free Trade Agreement (NAFTA) substantially reduced the tariffs on trade between Canada, Mexico, and the United States. General Agreement on Tariffs and Trade (GATT) legislation reduced tariffs on selected commodities among 124 countries.

TAX FACT

WHAT IS THE U.S. TAX BURDEN?

One popular measure of the burden of taxes in the U.S. economy is the Tax Foundation's "Tax Freedom Day." This statistic is a determination of the day upon which an individual has completed the entire year's obligation to governmental units (i.e., if all earnings were paid as taxes to this point, annual taxes would be paid up, and one would now begin to "work for your own account").

Being "free from taxes" may bring about a feeling of relief, but in reality tax burdens vary greatly from state to state. And as the U.S. economy has evolved and develops a more complex tax structure, adding emphasis on income and sales/use taxes, and reducing the relative reliance on tariffs and excise taxes, year-to-year comparisons become difficult. Nonetheless, as a rough measure of the presence of government in our lives, Tax Freedom Day carries some importance.

Year	Tax Freedom Day
1902	1/31
1930	2/12
1945	4/4
1960	4/15
1970	4/26
1990	5/1
1999	5/11
2000	5/3

After the Civil War, the income tax was repealed, and the Federal government returned to a reliance on tariffs and excise taxes. Following an economic depression in 1893, the Democratic Party reinstated the individual income tax in an attempt to address a deficit in the Treasury. The tax used a proportional 2 percent rate on incomes over $4,000. The tax was controversial and was found unconstitutional in *Pollock v. Farmer's Loan and Trust Co.*[9] The tax was attacked on the grounds that it was a *direct* tax that required apportionment.[10] This failed to meet a requirement of the U.S. Constitution, which stated:

> . . . No Capitation, or other direct, Tax shall be laid, unless in Proportion to the Census or Enumeration herein before directed to be taken.

Thus, any direct tax imposed by Congress was required to be apportioned among the states on the basis of their relative populations. Consequently, each state would need to have a different Federal income tax rate for its citizens because the size of each state's population differed.

---

[9]3 AFTR 2602, 157 U.S. 429 (USSC, 1895).

[10]In an earlier case, *Springer v. U.S.*, 102 U.S. 586 (USSC, 1880), the constitutionality of the Civil War era income tax was challenged on the same grounds. In *Springer*, the Supreme Court held that the income tax was indirect (and that only head taxes and real estate taxes were direct). When addressing *Pollock*, the Supreme Court distinguished the two cases, saying that *Pollock* focused on taxation of income generated from real estate; the Court then held that a tax on income from real estate was equivalent to a direct tax on real estate.

In 1909, a coalition of liberal Republicans and midwestern Populists sought relief from the ever-increasing burden of tariffs by imposing a tax on inheritances and income. President Taft successfully redirected this movement toward the enactment of a 4 percent corporate income tax. The constitutionality of this tax was challenged unsuccessfully in *Flint v. Stone Tracy Co.*[11] In this instance, the Supreme Court held the tax to be indirect and said it was essentially an excise tax on the right to do business as a corporation.

At this point, politicians, sensing that tariffs affected consumers (voters) more than an income tax on the wealthy, began to move toward individual income taxes. Finally, on February 25, 1913, the Sixteenth Amendment was passed. It provided that:

> The Congress shall have the power to lay and collect taxes on incomes from whatever source derived, without apportionment among the several States, and without regard to any census or enumeration.

Promptly after passage of the amendment, on October 3, 1913, Congress passed the first individual income tax and made it retroactive to March 1, 1913. In its original form, the income tax of 1913 had a 1 percent tax rate on incomes in excess of $3,000 ($4,000 for married couples) plus a 6 percent surtax on very high incomes (over $500,000). In 1913, the average personal income was $621; only 2 percent of the U.S. population paid income tax from 1913 to 1915, and 90 percent of Federal revenues were still collected from tariffs and excise taxes.

In 1916, as the United States became involved in World War I, all this began to change. Maximum income tax rates were raised to 15 percent. In 1917, they were raised again to 67 percent; in 1918, they were increased to 77 percent. Exemptions were reduced to $1,000 ($2,000 for married couples). At its peak, the income tax provided 60 percent of Federal revenues during World War I. These high rates remained in effect after the war to speed debt reduction. Despite the rapid increase in rates, the income tax remained steeply progressive, with the top 1 percent of taxpayers paying 70 percent of the tax bill. By 1925, as the Federal debt was eliminated, maximum individual tax rates were dropped to 25 percent.

Still, it took a second world war for the income tax to affect the average citizen. In 1939, less than 6 percent of the U.S. population paid any income tax. By 1945, over 74 percent paid income tax. In the interim, Congress introduced a pay-as-you-go system by enacting the Current Tax Payment Act of 1943, which required withholding of Federal income taxes from salaries.

The Federal government has never looked back. Since 1945, the scope of the income tax and its complexity have continued to increase, and the income tax remains every person's tax.

The Structure of the Federal Income Tax.

LEARNING OBJECTIVE 4

Recall the basic tax formula for individuals and taxable business entities

The Structure of the Federal Income Tax.   Although some variations exist, the basic Federal income tax formula is similar for all taxable entities. This formula is shown in Figure 1–1.

The income tax is based on the assumption that all income is subject to tax and that no deductions are allowed unless specifically provided for in the law. Some types of income are specifically excluded on the basis of various economic, social, equity, and political considerations. Examples include gifts, inheritance, life insurance proceeds received by reason of death, and interest income from state and local bonds. All entities are allowed to deduct business expenses from gross income, but a number of limitations and exceptions are applied. A variety of credits

[11]3 AFTR 2834, 220 U.S. 107 (USSC, 1911).

■ **FIGURE 1–1**
Basic Formula for Federal
Income Tax

Income (broadly conceived)	$xxx,xxx
Less: Exclusions (income that is not subject to tax)	(xx,xxx)
Gross income (income that is subject to tax)	$xxx,xxx
Less: Deductions	(xx,xxx)
Taxable income	$xxx,xxx
Federal income tax on taxable income (see Tax Rate Schedules inside front cover of text)	$ xx,xxx
Less: Tax credits (including Federal income tax withheld and other prepayments of Federal income taxes)	(x,xxx)
Tax owed (or refund)	$ xxx

BRIDGE DISCIPLINE

Bridge to Political Science and Sociology

The tax law and its effects on citizens and businesses of the United States are included in many other academic disciplines. Tax burdens are part of American fiction, family studies, and minority issues, as well as economics, finance, and management courses.

In the Bridge feature found in most chapters of this text, we relate the concerns of other disciplines to a more specific review of tax law, as presented here. With the topical knowledge obtained in this text, the reader can better understand the issues raised by other disciplines, sometimes to support beliefs held by others, and sometimes to refute them.

For instance, the structure of the U.S. tax system raises many issues of equity and fairness. Politicians and journalists discuss these issues freely, often without the requisite tax knowledge to draw proper conclusions.

- Should the property tax on real estate be used to finance the local public education system? Why should elderly taxpayers with grown children, or parents who send their children to private schools, continue to pay for public schools through these taxes?
- How would a repeal of the estate/gift tax affect legacy gifts made to charitable organizations? Would the lack of a charitable contribution deduction impair the ability of charities to raise operating and capital funds?
- Does a regressive sales/use tax fall harder on individuals of color?
- Why do Federal income taxes remain so high now that the threat of war has subsided?

against the tax are also allowed, again on the basis of economic, social, equity or political goals of Congress.

Income tax rates for all entities are progressive. The corporate rates range from 15 percent on the lowest level of taxable income to 35 percent on the highest level. Individual rates range from 15 percent to 39.6 percent. Estates and trusts are also subject to taxation, with rates ranging from 15 percent to 39.6 percent.

Partnerships, qualifying small business corporations, and some limited liability companies are not taxable entities, but must file information returns. Owners of these business entities then are taxed on the net taxable income of the enterprise, proportionate to their holdings.

Income (broadly conceived)	$xx,xxx
Less: Exclusions (income that is not subject to tax)	(x,xxx)
Gross income (income that is subject to tax)	$xx,xxx
Less: Certain business and investment deductions (usually referred to as deductions *for* adjusted gross income)	(x,xxx)
Adjusted gross income	$xx,xxx
Less: The greater of certain personal and employee deductions (usually referred to as *itemized deductions*) *or* The standard deduction (including any *additional* standard deduction)	(x,xxx)
Less: Personal and dependency exemptions	(x,xxx)
Taxable income	$xx,xxx
Federal income tax on taxable income (see Tax Rate Schedules inside front cover of text)	$ x,xxx
Less: Tax credits (including Federal income tax withheld and other prepayments of Federal income taxes)	(xxx)
Tax owed (or refund)	$ xxx

In the case of individuals, deductions are separated into two categories—deductions *for* adjusted gross income (AGI) and deductions *from* AGI. Generally, deductions *for* AGI are related to business activities, while deductions *from* AGI are often personal in nature (e.g., medical expenses, mortgage interest and property taxes on a personal residence, charitable contributions, and personal casualty losses) or related to investment activities. Deductions *from* AGI take the form of *itemized deductions* and personal and dependency exemptions. Individuals may take a *standard deduction* (a specified amount based on filing status) rather than itemizing actual deductions. An overview of the individual income tax formula is provided in Figure 1–2.

State Income Taxes.   Most states (except Alaska, Florida, Nevada, South Dakota, Texas, Washington, and Wyoming) impose a traditional income tax on individuals. Tennessee taxes only income from stocks and bonds, and New Hampshire taxes only dividend and interest income. Most states also impose either a corporate income tax or a franchise tax based in part on corporate income. The following additional points can be made about state income taxes.

- State income tax usually relies on Federal income tax laws to some degree—the states use Federal taxable income as a base, with a few adjustments (e.g., a few allow a deduction for Federal income taxes paid and sometimes an exclusion on interest income earned on Federal securities).
- For individuals, a few states impose a flat rate on Federal AGI.
- Several states piggyback directly on the Federal income tax system by using the Federal income tax liability as a base.
- Most states also require withholding of state income tax from salaries and wages and estimated payments by corporations and self-employed individuals.
- Most states have their own set of rates, exemptions, and credits.
- Many states also allow a credit for taxes paid to other states.

TAX IN THE NEWS

VISITORS BEWARE! THE CITY AND STATE YOU VISIT MAY NOT BE ALL THAT FRIENDLY

Even if you are not a resident, you may be subject to local and state income taxes if you earn money in that jurisdiction. Besides the nonresident who commutes (e.g., a taxpayer who lives in Connecticut but works full-time in New York City), taxpayers who perform services on an itinerant basis may be vulnerable. For example, the Dallas Cowboys are subject to the city of Philadelphia income tax every time they are hosted by the Eagles. This must be particularly distressing to Troy Aikman, who lives in a city (Dallas) and a state (Texas) that do not have an income tax.

Although these situations are often publicized as the "jock tax," other persons besides professional athletes get hit. Particularly susceptible are entertainers, doctors, lawyers, lecturers, and anyone who generates large fees and has a high profile. Ordinary professionals are not targeted because the amount of taxes involved would not justify the collection effort.

Is it any wonder that Las Vegas, which has no city or state income tax, is such a popular place to perform highly paid services like entertainment and prize fighting?

Local Income Taxes. Cities imposing an income tax include Baltimore, Cincinnati, Cleveland, Detroit, Kansas City (Mo.), New York, Philadelphia, and St. Louis. City income taxes usually apply to anyone who earns income in a city. They are designed to collect contributions for government services from those who live in the suburbs but work in the city as well as from local residents.

LEARNING OBJECTIVE 5

Understand the relationship between business entities and their owners.

Income Taxation of Business Entities

PROPRIETORSHIPS

The simplest form of business entity is a **proprietorship,** which is not a separate taxable entity. Instead, the proprietor reports the net profit of the business on his or her own individual tax return.

Individuals who own proprietorships often have specific tax goals with regard to their financial interactions with the business. Because a proprietorship is, by definition, owned by an individual, the individual has great flexibility in structuring the entity's transactions in a way that will minimize his or her income tax (or, in some cases, the income tax of the family unit).

EXAMPLE 15

Susan, a single individual, is the sole proprietor of Quality Fabrics, a retail store in which she works full-time. The business is her only source of income. Susan's taxable income in 2001 is $106,550, and her Federal income tax is $27,547 ($14,837.50 + 31% of the amount over $65,550). Thus, her *marginal tax rate* (the rate she pays on the highest *layer* of taxable income) is 31%. ■

EXAMPLE 16

Assume the same facts as in the previous example, except that Susan pays her nondependent 19-year-old son a $10,000 salary to work part-time at Quality Fabrics. This will reduce her 2001 taxable income by $10,000 and reduce her tax bill by $3,100 ($10,000 deduction × 31%

marginal tax rate). Her son will have $2,550 in taxable income (after the standard deduction and personal exemption) and will be taxed at a 15% rate, which results in Federal income tax of $382.50. In summary, Susan (the individual taxpayer) is able to operate the business entity (Quality Fabrics) in a way that will save the family unit $2,717.50 in Federal income tax ($3,100 saved by Susan − $382.50 paid by her son). ■

Examples 15 and 16 reflect the fact that a proprietorship itself is not a taxpaying entity. The owner of the proprietorship must report the income and deductions of the business on a Schedule C (Profit or Loss from Business) and must report the net profit (or loss) of the proprietorship on his or her Form 1040 (U.S. Individual Income Tax Return). Specific issues related to the taxation of sole proprietorships are reviewed in detail in Chapter 16.

CORPORATIONS

Some corporations pay tax on corporate taxable income while others pay no tax at the corporate level. Corporations that are separate taxable entities are referred to as **C corporations,** because they are governed by Subchapter C of the Internal Revenue Code. Corporations that meet certain requirements and pay no tax at the corporate level are referred to as **S corporations,** because they are governed by Subchapter S of the Code. S corporations are discussed in detail in Chapter 12. C corporations are addressed in Chapters 9 and 10.

A C corporation is required to file a tax return (Form 1120) and is subject to the Federal income tax. The shareholders then pay income tax on the dividends they receive when the corporation distributes its profits. Thus, the profits of the corporation can be seen as subject to double taxation, first at the corporate level and then at the shareholder level.

EXAMPLE 17

Joseph is single, has no dependents, and does not itemize deductions. He is the president and sole shareholder of Falcon Corporation. Falcon's taxable income for 2001 is $100,000, and its tax liability is $22,250. If Joseph has the corporation pay all of its after-tax income to him as a dividend, he will receive $77,750, have taxable income of $70,300 (after the standard deduction and personal exemption), and will pay Federal income tax of $16,310 ($14,837.50 + 31% of the amount over $65,550). The combined Federal income tax paid by Joseph and the corporation is $38,560. ■

EXAMPLE 18

Assume the same facts as in the previous example, except that Joseph has the corporation pay him a salary of $100,000, which is deductible by the corporation. Thus, the corporation will have zero taxable income and zero tax liability. Joseph's taxable income is $92,550, and his Federal income tax is $23,207.50 ($14,837.50 + 31% of the amount over $65,550). Thus, Joseph can save $15,352.50 ($38,560 − $23,207.50) in combined Federal income tax by having the corporation pay him a salary instead of a dividend. ■

PARTNERSHIPS

A partnership is not a separate taxable entity. The partnership is required to file a tax return (Form 1065) on which it summarizes the financial results of the business. Each partner then reports his or her share of the net income or loss and other special items that were reported on the partnership return.

EXAMPLE 19

Cameron and Connor form a partnership in which they are equal partners. The partnership reports a $100,000 net profit on its tax return, but is not subject to the Federal income tax.

Cameron and Connor each report $50,000 net income from the partnership on their separate individual income tax returns. ∎

S CORPORATIONS

An S corporation is like a C corporation with regard to nontax factors. Shareholders have limited liability, shares are freely transferable, there is a centralized management (vested in the board of directors), and there is continuity of life (i.e., the corporation continues to exist after the withdrawal or death of a shareholder). With regard to tax factors, however, an S corporation is more like a partnership. The S corporation is not subject to the Federal *income tax*. Like a partnership, it does file a tax return (Form 1120S), but the shareholders report their share of net income or loss and other special items on their own tax returns.

EXAMPLE 20

Kay and Dawn form a corporation and elect to have it treated as an S corporation. Kay owns 60% of the stock of the corporation, and Dawn owns 40%. The S corporation reports a $100,000 net profit on its tax return, but is not subject to the income tax. Kay will report $60,000 net income from the S corporation on her individual income tax return, and Dawn will report $40,000 on her tax return. ∎

The S corporation, limited liability company, and partnership forms of organization, which are referred to as *flow-through* entities, avoid the double taxation problem associated with the C corporation.

LIMITED LIABILITY COMPANIES AND LIMITED LIABILITY PARTNERSHIPS

Limited liability companies (LLCs) and limited liability partnerships (LLPs) have grown rapidly in popularity over the last few years. These organizations exist under state laws, and the specific rules vary somewhat from state to state. Both forms have limited liability and some (but not all) of the other nontax features of corporations. Additionally, both forms usually are treated as partnerships for tax purposes.

DEALINGS BETWEEN INDIVIDUALS AND ENTITIES

Many of the provisions in the tax law deal with the relationships between owners and the business entities they own. The following are some of the major interactions between owners and business entities.

- Owners put assets into a business when they establish a business entity (e.g., a proprietorship, partnership, or corporation).
- Owners take assets out of the business during its existence in the form of salary, dividends, withdrawals, redemptions of stock, etc.
- Through their entities, owner-employees set up retirement plans for themselves, including IRAs, Keogh plans, and qualified pension plans.
- Owners dispose of all or part of a business entity.

Every major transaction that occurs between an owner and a business entity has important tax ramifications. The following are a few of the many tax issues that arise.

- How to avoid taxation at both the owner level and the entity level (i.e., the multiple taxation problem).
- How to get assets into the business with the least adverse tax consequences.
- How to get assets out of the business with the least adverse tax consequences.
- How to dispose of the business entity with the least adverse tax consequences.

When addressing these (and other) tax issues, a common set of tax planning tools can be applied. These tax planning fundamentals are introduced in the next section.

LEARNING OBJECTIVE 6

Recognize tax planning opportunities and apply a simplified model of tax planning.

Tax Planning Fundamentals

OVERVIEW OF TAX PLANNING

Taxpayers generally attempt to minimize their tax liabilities, and it is perfectly acceptable to do so by using legal means. It is a long-standing principle that taxpayers have no obligation to pay more than their fair share of taxes. The now-classic words of Judge Learned Hand in *Commissioner v. Newman* reflect the true values a taxpayer should have.

> Over and over again courts have said that there is nothing sinister in so arranging one's affairs as to keep taxes as low as possible. Everybody does so, rich or poor; and all do right, for nobody owes any public duty to pay more than the law demands; taxes are enforced exactions, not voluntary contributions. To demand more in the name of morals is mere cant.[12]

Minimizing taxes legally is referred to as **tax avoidance.** On the other hand, some taxpayers attempt to *evade* income taxes illegally. There is a major distinction between tax avoidance and **tax evasion.** Though eliminating or reducing taxes is also a goal of tax evasion, the term *evasion* implies the use of subterfuge and fraud as a means to this end. Tax avoidance is legal, while tax evasion subjects the taxpayer to numerous civil and criminal penalties, including prison sentences.

Clients expect tax practitioners to provide advice to help them minimize their tax costs. This part of the tax practitioner's practice is referred to as *tax planning*. To structure a sound tax minimization plan, a practitioner must have a thorough knowledge of the tax law. Tax planning skill is based on a knowledge of tax saving provisions in the tax law, as well as provisions that contain pitfalls for the unwary. Thorough study of the remainder of this text will provide the knowledge required to recognize opportunities and avoid pitfalls.

THE GOAL OF TAX PLANNING

The goal of tax planning is to design a transaction so as to minimize its tax costs, while meeting the other nontax objectives of the client. Generally, this means that the client attempts to maximize the present value of its after-tax income and assets. Selecting a specific form of transaction solely for the sake of tax minimization often leads to a poor business decision. Effective tax planning requires careful consideration of the nontax issues involved in addition to tax consequences.

DETERMINING THE TAX BURDEN

To engage in effective tax planning, one must be able to identify the relevant tax rate that will be applied to a transaction. There are three kinds of tax rates. A taxpayer's *marginal* tax rate (or tax bracket) is the rate that would be paid on an additional dollar of income earned. Referring to the corporate income tax rate schedule inside the front cover of this text, a corporation's marginal tax rate on its

---

[12]47–1 USTC ¶9175, 35 AFTR 857, 159 F.2d 848 (CA–2, 1947).

first dollar of income is 15 percent. Similarly, the marginal tax rate faced by a corporation with $100,001 of income is 39 percent.[13] The *average* tax rate is the ratio of taxes paid to the tax base. Thus, a corporation with $100,000 of taxable income is subject to an average tax rate of 22.25 percent ($22,250 in tax divided by $100,000 in taxable income). A third kind of tax rate, the *effective* rate, can be seen as either (1) the ratio of taxes paid to financial net income before tax or (2) the sum of currently payable and deferred tax expense divided by net income before tax. Of these approaches to determining a taxpayer's rate, the marginal rate is most appropriate for tax planning purposes.

EXAMPLE 21

Azure Corporation has taxable income of $80,000. Azure also has $10,000 of tax-free interest income from municipal bonds. Using the corporate tax rate schedule inside the front cover of this text, one can determine that the company's tax liability is $15,450. If Azure were to earn an additional dollar in taxable income, it would pay $0.34 in tax. Thus, the company's marginal tax rate is 34%. Azure's average tax rate is the ratio of taxes paid to taxable income or 19.3% ($15,450/$80,000). Finally, the company has an effective rate of tax of 17.2% ($15,450/$90,000), the ratio of taxes paid to financial net income before tax (here, the sum of taxable income and tax-free income). ∎

The actual tax paid may not always be apparent. For example, the amount of taxes paid should include both current taxes and the present value of future taxes generated by a transaction.

EXAMPLE 22

Magenta Corporation is a publishing company that specializes in electronic media. It is a new corporation that was formed on January 1, 2000. During that year it generated a net operating loss (NOL) of $300,000. The NOL can be carried forward to offset future years' taxable income and thereby reduce Magenta's future tax liabilities. Magenta expects to earn $100,000 of income each year over the next four years. The NOL should completely offset the company's taxable income for the first three of these years.

At the beginning of 2001, Magenta must decide whether to invest in a project that will earn an additional $40,000 of taxable income during 2001 or a project that will generate $36,000 tax-free. The company's president reasons that, since the company has an NOL carryforward, the applicable tax rate is 0%, so the taxable project should be chosen.

The president's reasoning is incorrect, because an additional $40,000 of income now will result in $40,000 of taxable income in 2003 (since there will be $40,000 less NOL available in that year).

	2001	2002	2003	2004
Alternative 1 (tax-free investment)				
Pre-NOL taxable income	$ 100,000	$ 100,000	$ 100,000	$100,000
NOL carryforward (from 2000)	(300,000)	(200,000)	(100,000)	–0–
Taxable income	$ –0–	$ –0–	$ –0–	$100,000
Alternative 2 (taxable investment)				
Pre-NOL taxable income	$ 140,000	$ 100,000	$ 100,000	$100,000
NOL carryforward (from 2000)	(300,000)	(160,000)	(60,000)	–0–
Taxable income	$ –0–	$ –0–	$ 40,000	$100,000

---

[13]Corporate tax rates are steeply progressive over the first $100,000 in taxable income. Congress adopted this approach to aid small businesses.

The tax on the $40,000 project equals the discounted value of the tax due in 2003. Assuming a 10% discount rate and a 15% corporate tax rate, the present value of taxes paid in three years is $4,508, and the discounted tax rate is 11.3%. Thus, the after-tax proceeds on the taxable project will be $35,492, or $508 *less* than the $36,000 earnings on the tax-free project. ∎

Finally, the amount of tax paid should include both *explicit* taxes (paid directly to the government) and **implicit taxes** (paid through higher prices or lower returns on tax-favored investments). An implicit tax was found earlier in Example 6.

EXAMPLE 23

Ellen, an individual taxpayer with a 15% marginal tax rate, has inherited $100,000 that she wants to invest in bonds. She has the option of investing in taxable corporate bonds that yield 9% or tax-free municipal bonds that yield 6%. Assume that the bonds are identical, except for their tax status.

Ellen's tax rate on the corporate bonds is explicit at 15%. The tax rate on the municipal bonds is implicit, evidenced by the lower return on the bonds. Since the bonds are identical, if the municipal bonds were taxable, they would yield a 9% pre-tax rate. Their after-tax rate is 6% because they are tax-free. Hence, the implicit tax rate on the municipal bonds equals 33%, or the tax rate that would generate a 6% after-tax return on a 9% bond [9% − (0.33 × 9%)].

Since Ellen is in a 15% tax bracket, she should invest in the taxable bonds because she would face a higher marginal tax rate (a 33% implicit rate) if she invested in the municipal bonds. Stated another way, Ellen's after-tax return on the taxable bonds is greater than the 6% return available on the tax-free bonds. ∎

TAX MINIMIZATION STRATEGIES

Changing the Character of Income and Expense.   One approach to minimizing tax costs is to change the character of income and expenses from tax-disfavored to tax-favored categories. For individual taxpayers, the tax treatment of long-term capital gains versus ordinary income provides one example. Long-term capital gains generally are subject to a top tax rate of 20 percent, while ordinary income is subject to a top tax rate of 39.6 percent for individuals.

EXAMPLE 24

Betty, who is in the 39.6% marginal income tax bracket, has held Elk Corporation stock for 11 months. Betty paid $10,000 for the stock, which is now worth $30,000. She wants to sell the stock to buy a new sailboat. If she sells the stock now, she will have a short-term capital gain of $20,000 ($30,000 selling price − $10,000 cost). Short-term capital gains are taxed as ordinary income, so Betty will pay tax of $7,920 ($20,000 ordinary income × 39.6%). If her holding period for the stock is *more than one year*, however, she will have a long-term capital gain and will pay tax of $4,000 ($20,000 long-term capital gain × 20%). Thus, Betty can save $3,920 ($7,920 − $4,000) in income tax if she holds the stock for one more month before selling it. ∎

Many other situations present an opportunity for changing or choosing the character of income or deductions available to a taxpayer. For example, whether income is *earned* (salary, wages, commissions, etc.) or *unearned* (interest or dividends) can make a difference in computing taxable income. Whether a loss is an *active loss* or a *passive loss* similarly can make a difference. These issues will be discussed in subsequent chapters.

Shifting Tax Liability across Time.   Taxpayers must file annual tax returns. The IRS requires that both income and expenses be reported in the proper year. If not for this requirement, taxpayers could freely shift income and expenses from year to year and take advantage of tax rate differentials or could defer tax liabilities indefinitely.

EXAMPLE 25

Otter Company, a calendar year, cash basis proprietorship, mails payroll checks to its employees on the last day of each month. On December 31, 2001, Otter mailed a $2,000 payroll check to Kay, an employee who is on the cash basis. The tax law regards payment as having been made when the check was mailed, so Otter is allowed to deduct the salary payment in 2001. On the other hand, Kay is not required to report the income until 2002, the year she received the payment. Otter would not have the option of deducting the payment in 2002, nor would Kay have the option of reporting the income in 2001. ■

Although various rules limit the shifting of income and deductions across time periods, some opportunities still exist. Generally, time-shifting strategies call for income to be deferred or shifted from high-tax to low-tax years and deductions and credits to be accelerated or shifted from low-tax to high-tax years.

EXAMPLE 26

Egret Corporation, a calendar year taxpayer, is in the 34% bracket in 2001, but expects to be in the 25% bracket in 2002. The corporation, which is negotiating a $10,000 service contract with a client, decides to wait until 2002 to sign the contract and perform the services. The client is indifferent as to when the contract is completed. Thus, Egret saves $900 in income tax by deferring the service contract income to 2002, when it will be taxed at the 25% rate instead of the current 34% rate. This illustrates the use of the *income deferral strategy* to reduce taxes. ■

EXAMPLE 27

Flamingo Corporation, a calendar year taxpayer, is in the 34% bracket in 2001, but expects to be in the 25% bracket in 2002. The corporation plans to make a $20,000 charitable contribution to State University in March 2002. Flamingo's tax adviser points out that the deduction will save $6,800 in income tax if made in 2001, but will save only $5,000 if made in 2002. The president of the corporation responds that the corporation will not have the funds to make the contribution until 2002. The tax adviser informs the president that there is a tax provision that will allow the corporation to deduct the charitable contribution in 2001 if the board of directors authorizes the contribution in 2001 and payment is made before March 15, 2002. Thus, Flamingo saves $1,800 in income tax [$20,000 deduction × (34% − 25%)] by *accelerating the deduction* into 2001, when the tax rate is 9% higher. ■

The decision about whether to defer income from a high-tax to a low-tax year (or accelerate deductions or credits from a low-tax to a high-tax year) should rest on the trade-off between taxes saved and the time value of money.

EXAMPLE 28

Refer to the facts in Example 26. If Egret faces a 15% cost of capital, then the choice for the company is between $6,600 after taxes in 2001 ($10,000 − $3,400 in taxes) versus the *present value* of $7,500 after taxes in 2002, or $6,521. With a 15% discount rate, Egret would be better off signing the contract and performing the services in 2001. ■

Shifting Tax Liability between Entities. Shifting income and deductions between entities can be a very effective tool in plans to minimize tax liability. Examples 16 and 18 earlier in the chapter illustrate the effective use of this approach.

The tax law introduces numerous restrictions that limit the number of entity-shifting possibilities available to taxpayers. For example, the law provides that income from property or services cannot be assigned for tax purposes. Thus, the son in Example 16 had to work for his wages; income from the sole proprietorship could not be shifted to him otherwise. Similarly, to shift income from property from one taxpayer to another, the property must also be transferred.

EXAMPLE 29

Jack and Jill, both age 24, are married and are graduate students at State University. Their income places them in the 15% income tax bracket, and they are struggling to make ends meet. Jill's parents, the Harts, are quite wealthy, and their high income places them in the 39.6% marginal income tax bracket. To help Jack and Jill meet their financial obligations, the Harts give them stock in the family corporation. The stock pays $5,000 per year in dividends. In addition, they give Jack and Jill bond coupons that are subsequently redeemed for interest of $3,600 during the year. The dividend income is taxable to Jack and Jill, because the stock that generates the dividend income is owned by them. On the other hand, the interest income is taxable to the Harts because they gave only the interest coupons (i.e., the right to receive income) and retained ownership of the bonds. Observe that shifting the dividend income to Jack and Jill saves the family unit $1,230 [$5,000 × (39.6% − 15%)]. ∎

Shifting Tax Liability across Jurisdictions.   The state or country where income is earned (or where a deduction is incurred) can have a large impact on an entity's overall tax liability. Hence, shifting income from high-tax jurisdictions to low-tax jurisdictions or shifting deductions from low-tax jurisdictions to high-tax jurisdictions is an important tax planning strategy.

EXAMPLE 30

Gold International owns a sales subsidiary in Texas and a manufacturing subsidiary in Ireland (which imposes a 10% tax rate on certain types of business income). The Irish subsidiary makes drill presses and sells them to the Texas subsidiary for $4,000,000, which then modifies them and offers them for sale to businesses in the United States for $8,400,000. The cost of manufacturing and modifying each drill press is $3,000,000. Of the $5,400,000 of profit earned, $1,000,000 is attributable to the Irish corporation (which is subject to a 10% tax rate), and $4,400,000 is attributable to the U.S. corporation (which is subject to a 34% tax rate). Gold will have a total tax liability of $1,596,000 [($1,000,000 × 10%) + ($4,400,000 × 34%)]. ∎

EXAMPLE 31

Assume the same facts as in the previous example, except $5,000,000 of the profit is attributable to the Irish corporation and $400,000 is attributable to the U.S. corporation. In this case, Gold's total tax liability will be $636,000 [($5,000,000 × 10%) + ($400,000 × 34%)]. Thus, by altering the amount of work done in each of the two subsidiaries and the amount of income generated by each, Gold's tax liability changed by $960,000 ($1,596,000 − $636,000). ∎

LEARNING OBJECTIVE 7

Recognize the economic, social, equity, and political considerations that underlie the tax law.

Understanding the Federal Tax Law

The Federal tax law is a mosaic of statutory laws, administrative pronouncements, and court decisions. Anyone who has attempted to work with these provisions would have to admit to their complexity. For the person who has to trudge through a mass of rules to find the solution to a tax problem, it may be of some consolation to know that the law's complexity can generally be explained. Whether sound or not, there are reasons for the formulation of every rule. Knowing these reasons, therefore, is an important step toward understanding the Federal tax law.

REVENUE NEEDS

The foundation of the income tax system is the raising of revenue to cover the cost of government operations. Ideally, annual outlays should not exceed anticipated revenues, thereby leading to a balanced budget with no resulting deficit. Many

TAX FACT

WHO PAYS THE FEDERAL INCOME TAX?

A Tax Foundation study of 1998 IRS data holds that more than half of all Federal individual income taxes are paid by the top 5 percent of earners. Actually, the top 1 percent of U.S. earners pay about a third of all such taxes collected. These amounts are up from similar amounts in 1988, when the top 1 percent paid over a quarter of the Federal individual income taxes, and the top 5 percent paid over 45 percent.

Skews of this sort in the tax-payment data are consistent with the trend since 1980 to shift tax liabilities disproportionately to the top income and wealth groups. Such results likely were purposefully a part of the elder Bush and Clinton tax increases. But they also speak to the effort to relieve low-income taxpayers of all income tax liabilities, as collecting these relatively small amounts likely costs the government more than the revenues it generates.

Tax Foundation data also shows a stabilization of government expenditures at about 30 percent of annual U.S. GDP, with the Federal government accounting for roughly two-thirds of such expenditures. Prior to World War II, Federal expenditures were generally *less than* state and local amounts, except during war years. State and local expenditures roughly doubled between 1955 and 1975, while Federal expenditures increased more slowly during that period. Since 1975, expenditures have remained constant as to both total and Federal/local allocations relative to GDP growth.

Selected data from these studies follow.

Federal Individual Income Taxes

1998	Returns (000)	Tax Paid (Millions)	Income Split Point	Share of Total AGI	Share of Tax	Average Tax Rate
All taxpayers	123,776	$788,452		100.0%	100.0%	14.4%
Top 1% AGI	1,238	274,009	$269,496	18.5	34.8	27.1
Top 5%	6,189	424,506	114,729	32.9	53.8	23.6
Top 10%	12,378	512,838	83,220	43.8	65.0	21.4
Top 25%	30,944	651,984	50,607	65.0	82.7	18.2
Top 50%	61,888	755,240	25,491	86.3	95.8	16.0
Bottom 50%	61,888	33,212		13.7	4.2	4.4

1988	Returns (000)	Tax Paid (Millions)	Income Split Point	Share of Total AGI	Share of Tax	Average Tax Rate
All taxpayers	108,872	$412,761		100.0%	100.0%	13.2%
Top 1% AGI	1,089	113,841	$157,136	15.2	27.6	24.0
Top 5%	5,444	188,303	72,735	28.5	45.6	21.1
Top 10%	10,887	236,411	55,437	39.5	57.3	19.2
Top 25%	27,218	321,297	35,398	62.4	77.8	16.5
Top 50%	54,436	389,145	18,367	85.1	94.3	14.6
Bottom 50%	54,436	23,616		14.9	5.7	5.1

states have achieved this objective by passing laws or constitutional amendments precluding deficit spending.

The U.S. Constitution allows deficit spending, and politicians often find it hard to resist the temptation to spend more than the tax system collects currently. Congress uses several approaches to reduce a tax bill's net revenue loss. When tax reductions are involved, the full impact of the legislation can be phased in over a period of years. Or, as an alternative, the tax reduction can be limited to a period of years. When the period expires, Congress can then renew or not renew the provision in light of budget considerations.

ECONOMIC CONSIDERATIONS

Using the tax system in an effort to accomplish economic objectives has become increasingly popular in recent years. Generally, proponents of this approach use tax legislation to promote measures designed to help control the economy or encourage certain economic activities and businesses.

Encouragement of Certain Activities.   Without passing judgment on the wisdom of any such choices, it is quite clear that the tax law does encourage certain types of economic activity or segments of the economy. For example, the favorable treatment (immediate deduction) allowed research and development expenditures can be explained by the desire to foster technological progress.

Similarly, Congress has used depreciation deductions as a means of encouraging investment in business capital. Theoretically, shorter asset lives and accelerated methods should encourage additional investment in depreciable property acquired for business use. Conversely, longer asset lives and the required use of the straight-line method of depreciation dampen the tax incentive for capital outlays.

Is preserving the environment a desirable objective? Ecological considerations explain why the tax law permits favorable treatment for costs incurred in the installation of pollution control facilities.

Is it wise to stimulate U.S. exports of goods and services? Considering the pressing and continuing problem of a deficit in the U.S. balance of payments, the answer should be clear. Along this line, Congress has created an exclusion designed to encourage domestic exports of goods by reducing the effective tax rate. Also in an international setting, Congress has deemed it advisable to establish incentives for U.S. citizens who accept employment overseas.

Is saving desirable for the economy? Saving leads to capital formation and thereby makes funds available to finance home construction and industrial expansion. The tax law encourages saving by according preferential treatment to private retirement plans. Not only are contributions to Keogh (H.R. 10) plans and certain Individual Retirement Accounts (IRAs) deductible, but income on the contributions is not taxed until withdrawn.

Encouragement of Certain Industries.   No one can question the proposition that a sound agricultural base is necessary for a well-balanced national economy. Undoubtedly, this explains why farmers are accorded special treatment under the Federal income tax system. Among the benefits available to farmers are the election to expense rather than capitalize certain soil and water conservation expenditures and fertilizers and the election to defer the recognition of gain on the receipt of crop insurance proceeds.

Encouragement of Small Business.   At least in the United States, a consensus exists that what is good for small business is good for the economy as a whole. Whether valid or not, this assumption has led to a definite bias in the tax law favoring small business. Several income tax provisions can be explained by the desire to benefit small business, including the low marginal tax rates applied to the first dollars of the entity's income.

SOCIAL CONSIDERATIONS

Some provisions of the Federal tax law, particularly those dealing with the income tax of individuals, can be explained by a desire to encourage certain social results.

- Certain benefits provided to employees through accident and health plans financed by employers are nontaxable to employees. Encouraging such plans is considered socially desirable since they provide medical benefits in the event of an employee's illness or injury.
- A contribution made by an employer to a qualified pension or profit sharing plan for an employee may receive special treatment. The contribution and any income it generates are not taxed to the employee until the funds are distributed. Such an arrangement also benefits the employer by allowing a tax deduction when the contribution is made to the qualified plan. Various types of retirement plans are encouraged to supplement the subsistence income level the employee would otherwise have under the Social Security system.
- A deduction is allowed for contributions to qualified charitable organizations. The deduction attempts to shift some of the financial and administrative burden of socially desirable programs from the public (government) to the private (citizens) sector.
- Various tax credits, deductions, and exclusions that are designed to encourage taxpayers to obtain or extend the level of education are allowed.
- A tax credit is allowed for amounts spent to furnish care for certain minor or disabled dependents to enable the taxpayer to seek or maintain gainful employment. Who could deny the social desirability of encouraging taxpayers to provide care for their children while they work?
- A tax deduction is denied for certain expenditures deemed to be contrary to public policy. This disallowance extends to such items as fines, penalties, illegal kickbacks, bribes to government officials, and gambling losses in excess of gains. Social considerations dictate that the tax law should not encourage these activities by permitting a deduction.

EQUITY CONSIDERATIONS

The concept of equity is relative. Reasonable persons can, and often do, disagree about what is fair or unfair. In the tax area, moreover, equity is most often tied to a particular taxpayer's personal situation. To illustrate, compare the tax positions of those who rent their personal residences with those who own their homes. Renters may not take a Federal income tax deduction for the rent they pay. For homeowners, however, a large portion of the house payments they make may qualify for the Federal mortgage interest and property tax deductions. Although renters may have difficulty understanding this difference in tax treatment, the encouragement of home ownership can be justified on both economic and social grounds.

In many other parts of the law, however, equity concerns are evident. The concept of equity appears in tax provisions that alleviate the effect of multiple taxation and postpone the recognition of gain when the taxpayer lacks the ability or **wherewithal to pay** the tax. Provisions that mitigate the effect of the application of the annual accounting period concept and help taxpayers cope with the eroding results of inflation also reflect equity considerations.

Alleviating the Effect of Multiple Taxation.   The income earned by a taxpayer may be subject to taxes imposed by different taxing authorities. If, for example, the taxpayer is a resident of New York City, income might be subject to Federal,

BRIDGE DISCIPLINE

Bridge to Economics

Economists refer to taxes as a "dead weight loss," in that a tax levy of any sort withdraws money from the overall economy after it has been earned as part of the Gross Domestic Product. A more modern view of the taxing process would counter that most tax collections are recirculated through the economy as wage payments to government workers, benefit payments to retirees, and interest payments to investors.

But how much tax is too much? History is littered with tax rebellions, including the Boston Tea Party and a property tax revolt started in California in the mid-1970s. According to 2000 data from the Tax Foundation, taxes continue to rank as the highest single outlay for the U.S. family, exceeding the combined totals spent for housing and health care. A full analysis of the data is available at **www.taxfoundation.org** under the most current version of the report titled "The Price of Civilized Society."

Category		Amount
Taxes		
Federal	$7,237	
State and local	3,210	$10,447
Housing, household		5,913
Health care, medical		4,133
Food		2,713
Transportation		2,552
Recreation		1,994
Clothing		1,436

state of New York, and city of New York income taxes. To compensate for this apparent inequity, the Federal tax law allows a taxpayer to claim a deduction for state and local income taxes.

The deduction does not, however, neutralize the effect of multiple taxation, since the benefit derived depends on the taxpayer's Federal income tax rate. Only a tax credit, rather than a deduction, would completely eliminate the effects of multiple taxation on the same income. Equity considerations can also explain the Federal tax treatment of certain income from foreign sources.

The Wherewithal to Pay Concept.   The wherewithal to pay concept recognizes the inequity of taxing a transaction when the taxpayer lacks the means to pay the tax. The wherewithal to pay concept underlies a provision in the tax law dealing with the treatment of gain resulting from an involuntary conversion. An involuntary conversion occurs when property is destroyed by casualty or taken by a public authority through condemnation. If gain results from the conversion, it need not be recognized if the taxpayer replaces the property within a specified time period. The replacement property must be similar or related in service or use to that involuntarily converted.

EXAMPLE 32

Ron, a rancher, has some pasture land that is condemned by the state for use as a game preserve. The condemned pasture land cost Ron $120,000, but the state pays him $150,000 (its fair market value). Shortly thereafter, Ron buys more pasture land for $150,000.

Ron has realized gain of $30,000 [$150,000 (condemnation award) − $120,000 (cost of land)]. It would be inequitable to require Ron to pay a tax on this gain for two reasons. First, without disposing of the property acquired (the new land), Ron would be hard-pressed to pay the tax. Second, his economic position has not changed. ■

EXAMPLE 33

Assume the same facts as in Example 32, except that Ron reinvests only $140,000 of the award in new pasture land. Now, Ron has a taxable gain of $10,000. Instead of ending up with only replacement property, Ron now has $10,000 in cash. ■

Mitigating the Effect of the Annual Accounting Period Concept. For purposes of effective administration of the tax law, all taxpayers must report to and settle with the Federal government at periodic intervals. Otherwise, taxpayers would remain uncertain as to their tax liabilities, and the government would have difficulty judging revenues and budgeting expenditures. The period selected for final settlement of most tax liabilities is one year.

The application of this annual accounting period concept can lead to dissimilar tax treatment for taxpayers who are, from a long-range standpoint, in the same economic position.

EXAMPLE 34

José and Alicia, both sole proprietors, experienced the following results during the indicated three tax years.

	Profit (or Loss)	
Year	José	Alicia
2000	$50,000	$ 150,000
2001	60,000	60,000
2002	60,000	(40,000)

Although José and Alicia have the same profit of $170,000 over the period from 2000 through 2002, the annual accounting period concept places Alicia at a disadvantage for tax purposes. However, the net operating loss deduction generated in 2002 offers Alicia some relief by allowing her to carry back some or all of her 2002 loss to the earlier profitable years (in this case, 2000). Thus, with an NOL carryback, Alicia can obtain an immediate refund for some of the taxes she paid on the $150,000 profit reported for 2000. ■

The installment method of recognizing gain on the sale of property allows a taxpayer to spread tax consequences over the payout period. The harsh effect of taxing all the gain in the year of sale is thereby avoided. The installment method can also be explained by the wherewithal to pay concept, since recognition of gain is tied to the collection of the installment notes received from the sale of the property.

Coping with Inflation. Because of the progressive nature of the income tax, a wage adjustment to compensate for inflation can push the recipient into a higher income tax bracket without increasing real income. Known as *bracket creep*, this phenomenon's overall impact is an erosion of purchasing power. Congress recognized this problem and began to adjust various income tax components, such as marginal tax brackets, standard deduction amounts, and personal and dependency exemptions. Indexation usually is based upon the rise in the consumer price index over the prior year.

POLITICAL CONSIDERATIONS

A large segment of the Federal tax law is made up of statutory provisions. Since these statutes are enacted by Congress, is it any surprise that political considerations influence tax law? For purposes of discussion, the effect of political considerations on the tax law is divided into the following topics: special interest legislation, political expediency, and state and local government influences.

Special Interest Legislation.   There is no doubt that certain provisions of the tax law can largely be explained by the political influence some groups have had on Congress. For example, is there any other realistic reason that prepaid subscription and dues income is not taxed until earned, while prepaid rents are taxed to the landlord in the year received?

Special interest legislation is not necessarily to be condemned if it can be justified on economic, social, or some other utilitarian grounds. At any rate, it is an inevitable product of our political system.

Political Expediency.   Various tax reform proposals rise and fall in favor with the shifting moods of the American public. That Congress is sensitive to popular feeling is an accepted fact. Therefore, certain provisions of the tax law can be explained by the political climate at the time they were enacted.

Measures that deter more affluent taxpayers from obtaining so-called preferential tax treatment have always had popular appeal and, consequently, the support of Congress. Provisions such as the limitation on the deductibility of interest on investment indebtedness can be explained on this basis.

State and Local Government Influences.   State law has had an influence in shaping our present Federal tax law. One example of this effect is the evolution of Federal tax law in response to states with community property systems. The states with community property systems are Louisiana, Texas, New Mexico, Arizona, California, Washington, Idaho, Nevada, and Wisconsin. Spouses in Alaska can elect community property treatment. The rest of the states are common law jurisdictions. The difference between common law and community property systems centers around the property rights possessed by married persons. In a common law system, each spouse owns whatever he or she earns. Under a community property system, one-half of the earnings of each spouse is considered owned by the other spouse.

EXAMPLE 35

Al and Fran are husband and wife, and their only income is the $60,000 annual salary Al receives. If they live in New Jersey (a common law state), the $60,000 salary belongs to Al. If, however, they live in Arizona (a community property state), the $60,000 is divided equally, in terms of ownership, between Al and Fran. ■

At one time, the tax position of the residents of community property states was so advantageous that many common law states actually adopted community property systems. Needless to say, the political pressure placed on Congress to correct the disparity in tax treatment was considerable. To a large extent, this was accomplished in 1948 when the law extended many of the community property tax advantages to residents of common law jurisdictions.

The major advantage extended was the provision allowing married taxpayers to file joint returns and compute the tax liability as if the income had been earned one-half by each spouse. This result is automatic in a community property state, since half of the income earned by one spouse belongs to the other spouse. The income-splitting benefits of a joint return are now incorporated as part of the tax rates applicable to married taxpayers.

LEARNING OBJECTIVE 8

Describe the role played by
the IRS and the courts in the
evolution of the Federal tax
system.

INFLUENCE OF THE INTERNAL REVENUE SERVICE

The influence of the IRS on tax law is apparent in many areas beyond its role in issuing the administrative pronouncements that make up a considerable portion of our tax law. The IRS has been instrumental in securing the passage of much legislation designed to curtail the most flagrant tax avoidance practices (to close tax loopholes). In addition, the IRS has sought and obtained legislation to make its own job easier (to attain administrative feasibility).

Closing Perceived Tax Loopholes.   Certain tax provisions are intended to prevent a loophole from being used to avoid the tax consequences intended by Congress. Working within the letter of existing law, ingenious taxpayers and their advisers devise techniques that accomplish indirectly what cannot be accomplished directly. As a consequence, legislation is enacted to close the loopholes that taxpayers have located and exploited. Some tax law can be explained in this fashion and is discussed in the chapters to follow.

Administrative Feasibility.   Some tax law is justified on the grounds that it simplifies the task of the IRS in collecting the revenue and administering the law. With regard to collecting the revenue, the IRS long ago realized the importance of placing taxpayers on a pay-as-you-go basis. Elaborate withholding procedures apply to wages, and accrual basis taxpayers often must pay taxes on prepaid income in the year received and not when earned. The approach may be contrary to generally accepted accounting principles, but it is consistent with the wherewithal to pay concept.

Of considerable aid to the IRS in collecting revenue are the numerous provisions that impose interest and penalties on taxpayers for noncompliance with the tax law. Provisions such as the penalties for failure to pay a tax or to file a return that is due, the negligence penalty for intentional disregard of rules and regulations, and various penalties for civil and criminal fraud serve as deterrents to taxpayer noncompliance.

One of the keys to an effective administration of our tax system is the audit process conducted by the IRS. To carry out this function, the IRS is aided by provisions that reduce the chance of taxpayer error or manipulation and therefore reduce the audit effort that is necessary. An increase in the amount of the standard deduction, for example, reduces the number of individual taxpayers who will choose the alternative of itemizing their personal deductions. With fewer deductions to check, the audit function is simplified.

INFLUENCE OF THE COURTS

In addition to interpreting statutory provisions and the administrative pronouncements issued by the IRS, the Federal courts have influenced tax law in two other respects.[14] First, the courts have formulated certain judicial concepts that serve as guides in the application of various tax provisions. Second, certain key decisions have led to changes in the Internal Revenue Code.

Judicial Concepts Relating to Tax.   Particularly in dealings between related parties, the courts test transactions by looking to whether the taxpayers acted in

---

[14]A great deal of case law is devoted to ascertaining congressional
intent. The courts, in effect, ask: What did Congress have in mind
when it enacted a particular tax provision?

TAX FACT

THE COSTS OF COMPLEXITY

A tax system that is designed to accomplish so many, sometimes contradictory, goals is bound to be a complex animal. According to the University of Michigan's Office of Tax Policy Research, the current system may actually be so complex as to be self-defeating. By one measure, the costs of complying with the individual income tax portions of the Internal Revenue Code—taxpayers' time, recordkeeping systems and software, and costs for tax advisers and preparers—equal twelve cents for every dollar collected by the Treasury for the tax year. Office director Joel Slemrod says that "The U.S. personal income tax system is probably the most complicated in the world," even after years of tax reform measures have worked to decrease marginal rates and reduce the number of available deductions and credits.

an arm's length manner. The question to be asked is: Would unrelated parties have handled the transaction in the same way?

EXAMPLE 36

Rex, the sole shareholder of Silver Corporation, leases property to the corporation for a yearly rent of $6,000. To test whether the corporation should be allowed a rent deduction for this amount, the IRS and the courts will apply the arm's length concept. Would Silver Corporation have paid $6,000 a year in rent if it had leased the same property from an unrelated party (rather than from Rex)? Suppose it is determined that an unrelated third party would have paid an annual rent for the property of only $5,000. Under these circumstances, Silver Corporation will be allowed a deduction of only $5,000. The other $1,000 it paid for the use of the property represents a nondeductible dividend. Accordingly, Rex will be treated as having received rent income of $5,000 and dividend income of $1,000. ■

Judicial Influence on Statutory Provisions.   Some court decisions have been of such consequence that Congress has incorporated them into statutory tax law. For example, many years ago the courts found that stock dividends distributed to the shareholders of a corporation were not taxable as income. This result was largely accepted by Congress, and a provision in the tax statutes now addresses the issue.

On occasion, however, Congress has reacted negatively to judicial interpretations of the tax law.

EXAMPLE 37

Nora leases unimproved real estate to Wade for 40 years. At a cost of $200,000, Wade erects a building on the land. The building is worth $100,000 when the lease terminates and Nora takes possession of the property. Does Nora have any income either when the improvements are made or when the lease terminates? In a landmark decision, a court held that Nora must recognize income of $100,000 upon the termination of the lease. ■

Congress felt that the result reached in Example 37 was inequitable in that it was not consistent with the wherewithal to pay concept. Consequently, the tax law was amended to provide that a landlord does not recognize any income either when the improvements are made (unless made in lieu of rent) or when the lease terminates.

SUMMARY

In addition to its necessary revenue-raising objective, the Federal tax law has developed in response to several other factors.

- *Economic considerations.* The emphasis here is on tax provisions that help regulate the economy and encourage certain activities and types of businesses.
- *Social considerations.* Some tax provisions are designed to encourage (or discourage) socially desirable (or undesirable) practices.
- *Equity considerations.* Of principal concern in this area are tax provisions that alleviate the effect of multiple taxation, recognize the wherewithal to pay concept, mitigate the effect of the annual accounting period concept, and recognize the eroding effect of inflation.
- *Political considerations.* Of significance in this regard are tax provisions that represent special interest legislation, reflect political expediency, and reflect the effect of state and local law.
- *Influence of the IRS.* Many tax provisions are intended to aid the IRS in the collection of revenue and the administration of the tax law.
- *Influence of the courts.* Court decisions have established a body of judicial concepts relating to tax law and have, on occasion, led Congress to enact statutory provisions to either clarify or negate their effect.

Suggested Further Readings

Ellen D. Cook, "No Simple Solution for the Marriage Penalty Quandary," *Practical Tax Strategies,* March 2000, pp. 113–117.

Howard Gleckman, "Tax Reform: The Sound Bite and the Fury of Corporate Welfare," *Business Week*, January 17, 2000, p. 80.

N. Gregory Mankiw, "An Economic Lesson: Why Shouldn't We Die Tax-Free?" *Fortune*, September 6, 1999, pp. 54–55.

KEY TERMS

Ad valorem tax, 1–12	FUTA tax, 1–8	S corporation, 1–20
C corporation, 1–20	Gift tax, 1–2	Sales tax, 1–3
Death tax, 1–9	Implicit tax, 1–24	Tax avoidance, 1–22
Employment tax, 1–3	Inheritance tax, 1–9	Tax evasion, 1–22
Estate tax, 1–9	Occupational tax, 1–14	Use tax, 1–6
Excise tax, 1–4	Personalty, 1–12	Value added tax (VAT), 1–6
FICA tax, 1–7	Proprietorship, 1–19	
Franchise tax, 1–14	Realty, 1–12	Wherewithal to pay, 1–29

Problem Materials

PROBLEMS

1. Aqua Corporation believes that it will have a better distribution location for its product if it relocates the corporation to another state. What considerations (both tax and nontax) should Aqua Corporation weigh before making a decision on whether to make the move?

2. Before passage of the Sixteenth Amendment to the U.S. Constitution, there was no income tax in the United States. Please comment.

3. Give several examples of taxes that are *proportional*. That are *progressive*.

4. Jim, a resident of Washington (which imposes a general sales tax), goes to Oregon (which does not impose a general sales tax) to purchase his automobile. Will Jim successfully avoid the Washington sales tax? Explain.

5. Explain the difference between an inheritance tax and an estate tax.

6. In 2000, Horace makes a taxable gift of $250,000 upon which he pays a Federal gift tax of $70,800. In 2002, Horace makes another taxable gift of $250,000. Will the 2002 taxable gift result in the same gift tax as the 2000 gift? Why or why not?

7. How much property can Herman, a widower, give to his four married children, their spouses, and eight grandchildren over a period of 10 years without making a taxable gift?

8. When married persons elect to split a gift, what tax advantages do they enjoy?

9. The Toth family lives in a residence that they have owned for several years. They purchased the residence from St. Matthew's Catholic Church, which had used the house as a rectory for its priest. To the Toths' surprise, since they purchased the residence, they have not received any ad valorem property tax bills from either the city or the county. Is there a plausible explanation for this? Explain. What, if anything, should the Toths do about the property tax matter?

10. When Gull Company constructs a climate-controlled warehouse, it is very careful to keep as many of the components as portable as possible. Thus, the sprinkler system is detachable, window units provide air conditioning and heating, and the interior walls can be removed. What is Gull trying to accomplish?

11. John, a nationally known vocalist, lives in Nevada. John's agent has been trying to convince him to go on tour to increase his record sales. John, however, refuses to perform anywhere but in Las Vegas clubs. What might explain John's attitude?

12. The city of Bowling Green has decided to sell a parcel of unimproved land that it owns. The highest bid received is $1 million from a group that wants to build a church on the property. The second highest bid is $900,000 and is submitted by an automobile dealership. Why might it be more beneficial for the city to accept the $900,000 bid?

13. When his grandmother dies, Shawn inherits her personal residence. Shawn converts the residence to a rental house. Can Shawn anticipate that the ad valorem taxes on the property will change? Why or why not?

14. Is the Medicare component of FICA a proportional or a progressive tax? Explain.

15. Compare FICA and FUTA in connection with each of the following.
    a. Incidence of taxation.
    b. Justification for taxation.
    c. Rates and base involved.

16. Velma lives in Wilson County, which is adjacent to Grimes County. Although the retail stores in both counties are comparable, Velma drives an extra 10 miles to do all of her shopping in Grimes County. Why might she do this?

17. During a social event, Muriel and Earl are discussing the home computer each recently purchased. Although the computers are identical makes and models, Muriel is surprised to learn that she paid a sales tax, while Earl did not. Comment as to why this could happen.

18. Paul lives in a jurisdiction that imposes a general sales tax of 4%. On a recent trip to a supermarket, Paul purchased goods that cost $100 but was charged only $3.50 in sales tax. What is a possible explanation for the discrepancy?

19. Jill is a single individual. In 2001, she has total income of $175,000, credits of $18,000, exclusions of $30,000, deductions *for* AGI of $40,000, itemized deductions of $20,000 (assume no AGI limitations are applicable), a standard deduction of $4,550, a personal exemption equal to $2,900, and estimated tax payments of $3,000.
    a. What is her tax due?
    b. If Jill were a corporation instead of an individual, and if all of her deductions were business related, what would be the tax due?

20. Cory and Cynthia have decided to go into business together. They will operate a sandwich delivery business. They expect to have a loss in the first and second years of the business and subsequently expect to make a substantial profit. Both are also concerned about potential liability if a customer ever gets sick. They have called your office and asked for advice about whether they should run their business as a partnership or as a corporation. Write a letter to Cynthia Clay, at 1206 Seventh Avenue, Fort Worth, TX 76101, describing the alternative forms of business that they can select. In your letter, explain what form or forms of business you recommend and why.

21. Ashley runs a small business in Boulder, Colorado, that makes snow skis. She expects the business to grow substantially over the next three years. Because she is concerned about product liability and is planning to take the company public in the year 2001, she is currently considering incorporating the business. Financial data are as follows.

	2000	2001	2002
Sales revenue	$150,000	$320,000	$600,000
Tax-free interest income	5,000	8,000	15,000
Deductible cash expenses	30,000	58,000	95,000
Tax depreciation	25,000	20,000	40,000

Ashley expects her marginal tax rate to be 39.6% over the next three years before any profits from the business are considered. Her cost of capital is 10%.
    a. Compute the present value of the future cash flows for 2000 to 2002, assuming Ashley incorporates the business and pays all after-tax income as dividends.
    b. Compute the present value of the future cash flows for 2000 to 2002, assuming Ashley continues to operate the business as a sole proprietorship.
    c. Should Ashley incorporate the business this year? Why or why not?

22. Sienna, Inc., faces a marginal tax rate of 25%, an average tax rate of 17.5%, and an effective marginal tax rate of 16.8%. Sienna is considering investing in Kiowa County bonds, which currently pay a 5% return (equivalent taxable bonds are paying an 8% return).
    a. What is the implicit tax rate on the Kiowa County bonds?
    b. Are the Kiowa County bonds a good investment for Sienna? Why or why not?

23. Chartreuse, Inc., has a net operating loss carryforward of $100,000. If Chartreuse continues its business with no changes, it will have $50,000 of taxable income (before the NOL) in both 2001 and 2002. If Chartreuse decides to invest in a new product line instead, it expects to have taxable income of $70,000 in 2001 and $50,000 in 2002. What marginal tax rate does the new product line face in 2001?

24. Mauve Supplies, Inc., reports total income of $120,000. The corporation's taxable income is $105,000. What are Mauve's marginal, average, and effective tax rates?

25. How does the tax law foster technological progress?

26. Discuss the possible justification for the following provisions of the tax law.
    a. A change in the tax rate structure.
    b. The treatment of contributions to Keogh (H.R. 10) plans and Individual Retirement Accounts (IRAs).
    c. The immediate deduction of soil and water conservation expenditures.
    d. A deduction for charitable contributions.
    e. The disallowance of a deduction for fines.

27. What purpose is served by allowing individuals to deduct home mortgage interest and property taxes?

28. Wilma, a cattle rancher, has a pasture condemned by the State Parks Commission for use as a recreational facility. The pasture cost Wilma $30,000, and the state paid her its appraised value of $100,000. Shortly thereafter, Wilma purchases additional pasture land for $80,000. Can Wilma avoid the tax on any of the gain under the *wherewithal to pay* concept? Explain.

29. In what manner does the tax law mitigate the effect of the annual accounting period concept for installment sales?

30. How does the tax law cope with the impact of inflation?

EXTENDER 31. Chee lives in a state that imposes an income tax. His Federal income tax return for 1999 is audited in 2001, and, as a result of adjustments made by the IRS, Chee must pay an additional amount of tax, interest, and penalty. Several months later, Chee is notified that his 1999 state income tax return is to be audited. Are these two incidents a coincidence?

EXTENDER 32. Contrast a value added tax (VAT) with a national sales tax in terms of anticipated taxpayer compliance.

BRIDGE DISCIPLINE

1. Consider the Tax Foundation data in the Bridge feature on page 1–30.
   a. Convert the data to a pie chart.
   b. Redraw the pie chart, showing your own preferences for the spending patterns of a U.S. family.
   c. If you were a politician, how would you move the country's economy from the chart in (a) to the one in (b)?

CHAPTER 2

Working with the Tax Law

LEARNING OBJECTIVES

After completing Chapter 2, you should be able to:

1. Understand the statutory, administrative, and judicial sources of the tax law and the purpose of each source.

2. Locate and work with the tax law and understand the tax research process.

3. Communicate the results of the tax research process in a client letter and a tax file memorandum.

4. Have an awareness of computer-assisted tax research.

Outline

TAX TALK   *The less people know about how sausages and laws are made, the better they'll sleep at night.*

—Otto von Bismarck

LEARNING OBJECTIVE 1

Understand the statutory, administrative, and judicial sources of the tax law and the purpose of each source.

Tax Sources

Understanding taxation requires a mastery of the sources of the *rules of tax law*. These sources include not only legislative provisions in the form of the Internal Revenue Code, but also congressional Committee Reports, Treasury Department Regulations, other Treasury Department pronouncements, and court decisions. Thus, the *primary sources* of tax information include pronouncements from all three branches of government: legislative, executive, and judicial.

In addition to being able to locate and interpret the sources of the tax law, a tax professional must understand the relative weight of authority within these sources. The tax law is of little significance, however, until it is applied to a set of facts and circumstances. This chapter, therefore, both introduces the statutory, administrative, and judicial sources of the tax law *and* explains how the law is applied to individual and business transactions. It also explains how to apply research techniques effectively.

Tax research is necessary because the application of the law to a specific situation is often not clear. As complicated as the Internal Revenue Code is, it cannot clearly address every conceivable situation. Accordingly, the tax professional must search other sources (such as administrative rulings and judicial decisions) to determine the most likely tax treatment of a transaction.

Often, this search process will yield widely differing results for similar fact patterns. One of the goals of tax research is to discover which facts and which legal rules are most relevant in determining the ultimate tax consequences. Working with such knowledge, a tax professional can then advise the client about the tax consequences of several possible courses of action. Tax research, in other words, is of critical importance not only in properly characterizing completed events but also in planning proposed transactions.

STATUTORY SOURCES OF THE TAX LAW

Origin of the Internal Revenue Code. Before 1939, the statutory provisions relating to taxation were contained in the individual revenue acts enacted by Congress. The inconvenience and confusion that resulted from dealing with many separate acts led Congress to codify all of the Federal tax laws. Known as the

TAX FACT

MEASURING TAX SYSTEM COMPLEXITY

A recent report by the Joint Economic Committee (JEC) of Congress provides several measures of the complexity of the U.S. tax system. Some of these issues also were addressed in testimony to Congress by the Tax Foundation. Here are some of the JEC's observations that justify a conclusion that the U.S. tax system has become too complex.

Internal Revenue Code in 2000	2,840 pages	2.8 million words
Tax Regulations in 2000	8,920 pages	10.7 million words
CCH Federal Tax Reporter	6,900 pages in 2000	400 pages in 1913
Cost of complying with the Federal tax system, all taxpayers and forms	6.1 billion hours	$183 billion in value of such time, at $30 per hour
Individuals using paid tax preparers	53% in 1997 40% in 1990	19% in 1960
Telephone calls to IRS tax "help lines"	110 million	73% received "correct" responses
IRS budget	$8.2 billion in 2000	$12 million in 1900
IRS employees	100,000 workers in 2000	10,000 workers in 1900

Internal Revenue Code of 1939, this codification arranged all Federal tax provisions in a logical sequence and placed them in a separate part of the Federal statutes. A further rearrangement took place in 1954 and resulted in the Internal Revenue Code of 1954, which continued in effect until it was replaced by the Internal Revenue Code of 1986.[1]

Now, statutory amendments to the tax law are integrated into the existing Code. Thus, subsequent tax legislation, such as the Taxpayer Relief Act of 1997, has become part of the Internal Revenue Code of 1986.

The Legislative Process. Federal tax legislation generally originates in the House of Representatives, where it is first considered by the House Ways and Means Committee. Tax bills can originate in the Senate if they are attached as riders to other legislative proposals. If acceptable to the committee, the proposed bill is referred to the entire House of Representatives for approval or disapproval. Approved bills are sent to the Senate, where they initially are considered by the Senate Finance Committee.

---

[1]Aside from changes due to a large tax act, the organization of the Internal Revenue Code of 1986 is not substantively different from the organization of the 1954 Code. In contrast, the numbering scheme of sections in the 1939 Code differs from that used in the 1954 Code.

The next step is referral from the Senate Finance Committee to the entire Senate. Assuming no disagreement between the House and Senate, passage by the Senate means referral to the President for approval or veto. If the bill is approved or if the President's veto is overridden, the bill becomes law and part of the Internal Revenue Code.

When the Senate version of the bill differs from that passed by the House, the Conference Committee, which includes members of both the House Ways and Means Committee and the Senate Finance Committee, is called upon to resolve the differences. House and Senate versions of major tax bills frequently differ. One reason bills are often changed in the Senate is that each senator has considerable latitude to make amendments when the Senate as a whole is voting on a bill referred to it by the Senate Finance Committee. In contrast, the entire House of Representatives either accepts or rejects what is proposed by the House Ways and Means Committee, and changes from the floor are rare.

The deliberations of the Conference Committee usually produce a compromise between the two versions, which is then voted on by both the House and the Senate. If both bodies accept the revised bill, it is referred to the President for approval or veto. The typical legislative process dealing with tax bills is summarized in Figure 2–1.

Referrals from the House Ways and Means Committee, the Senate Finance Committee, and the Conference Committee are usually accompanied by *Committee Reports*. These Committee Reports often explain the provisions of the proposed legislation and are therefore a valuable source for ascertaining the *intent of Congress*. What Congress had in mind when it considered and enacted tax legislation is the key to interpreting legislation. Since Regulations interpreting new legislation normally are not issued immediately after a statute is enacted, taxpayers and the courts look to Committee Reports to determine congressional intent.

The role of the Conference Committee indicates the importance of compromise in the legislative process. As an example of the practical effect of the compromise process, consider what happened to a provision allowing the amortization of certain intangible assets in the Revenue Reconciliation Act of 1993 (see Figure 2–2).

Arrangement of the Code.   The Internal Revenue Code is found in Title 26 of the U.S. Code. Here is a partial table of contents.

Subtitle A. Income Taxes
   Chapter 1. Normal Taxes and Surtaxes
      Subchapter A. Determination of Tax Liability
         Part I. Tax on Individuals
            Sections 1–5
         Part II. Tax on Corporations
            Sections 11–12

In referring to a provision of the Code, the key is usually the Section number. In citing Section 2(a) (dealing with the status of a surviving spouse), for example, it is unnecessary to include Subtitle A, Chapter 1, Subchapter A, Part I. Merely mentioning Section 2(a) will suffice, since the Section numbers run consecutively and do not begin again with each new Subtitle, Chapter, Subchapter, or Part. Not all Code Section numbers are used, however. Part I ends with Section 5 and Part II starts with Section 11 (at present there are no Sections 6, 7, 8, 9, and 10).[2]

---

[2]When the Code was drafted, Section numbers were intentionally omitted so that later changes could be incorporated into the Code without disrupting its organization. When Congress does not leave enough space, subsequent Code Sections are given A, B, C, etc., designations. A good example is the treatment of Sections 280A through 280H.

■ **FIGURE 2–1**
Legislative Process for Tax Bills

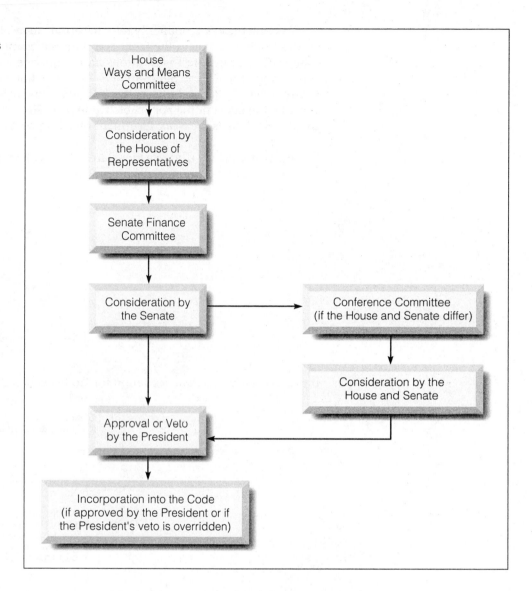

■ **FIGURE 2–2**
Example of Compromise in the
Conference Committee

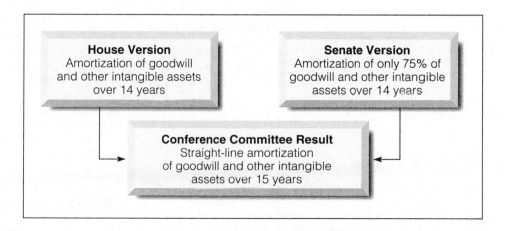

Tax practitioners commonly refer to certain areas of income tax law by Subchapter designation. Some of the more common Subchapter designations include Subchapter C ("Corporate Distributions and Adjustments"), Subchapter K ("Partners and Partnerships"), and Subchapter S ("Tax Treatment of S Corporations and Their Shareholders"). Particularly in the last situation, it is much more convenient to describe the effect of the applicable Code provisions (Sections 1361–1379) as "Subchapter S" than as the "Tax Treatment of S Corporations and Their Shareholders."

Citing the Code.   Code Sections are often broken down into subparts.[3] Section 2(a)(1)(A) serves as an example.

§   2   (a)   (1)   (A)

Abbreviation for "Section"

Section number

Subsection designation[4]

Paragraph designation

Subparagraph designation

Broken down by content, a citation for Code Section 2(a)(1)(A) appears as follows.

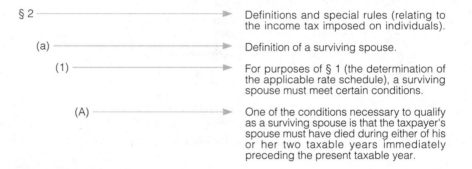

§ 2 ──────────────→ Definitions and special rules (relating to the income tax imposed on individuals).

(a) ──────────────→ Definition of a surviving spouse.

(1) ──────────────→ For purposes of § 1 (the determination of the applicable rate schedule), a surviving spouse must meet certain conditions.

(A) ──────────────→ One of the conditions necessary to qualify as a surviving spouse is that the taxpayer's spouse must have died during either of his or her two taxable years immediately preceding the present taxable year.

Throughout the text, references to the Code Sections are in the form given above. The symbols "§" and "§§" are used in place of "Section" and "Sections." The following table summarizes the format used in the text.

Complete Reference	Text Reference
Section 2(a)(1)(A) of the Internal Revenue Code of 1986	§ 2(a)(1)(A)
Sections 1 and 2 of the Internal Revenue Code of 1986	§§ 1 and 2
Section 2 of the Internal Revenue Code of 1954	§ 2 of the Internal Revenue Code of 1954
Section 12(d) of the Internal Revenue Code of 1939[5]	§ 12(d) of the Internal Revenue Code of 1939

---

[3]Some Code Sections do not have subparts. See, for example, Sections 211 and 241.

[4]Some Code Sections omit the subsection designation and use, instead, the paragraph designation as the first subpart. See, for example, Sections 212(1) and 1222(1).

[5]Section 12(d) of the Internal Revenue Code of 1939 is the predecessor to § 2 of the Internal Revenue Codes of 1954 and 1986.

INTERNATIONAL IMPLICATIONS

PROTECTION AGAINST DOUBLE TAXATION

To eliminate the double taxation that a taxpayer might incur if subject to tax in two countries, the United States has entered into treaties with most of the major countries of the world. Often there are multiple treaties with a country covering various tax issues.

Treaty provisions generally are reciprocal (apply to both treaty countries). Thus, a U.S. citizen or resident who receives income from a treaty country may refer to U.S. Treasury tables to see if a treaty might affect the tax to be paid to that foreign country. As part of the proof of entitlement to the treaty benefits, foreign countries sometimes require certification from the U.S. Government that an applicant files an income tax return as a U.S. citizen or resident.

Effect of Treaties. The United States signs certain tax treaties (sometimes called tax conventions) with foreign countries to render mutual assistance in tax enforcement and to avoid double taxation. These treaties affect transactions involving U.S. persons and entities operating or investing in a foreign country, as well as persons and entities of a foreign country operating or investing in the United States. Although these bilateral agreements are not codified in any one source, they are published in various Internal Revenue Service publications as well as in privately published tax services.

Neither a tax law nor a tax treaty automatically takes precedence. When there is a direct conflict, the most recent item will take precedence. With certain exceptions, a taxpayer must disclose on the tax return any position where a treaty overrides a tax law.[6] There is a $1,000 per *failure to disclose* penalty for individuals and a $10,000 per failure to disclose penalty for corporations.[7]

ADMINISTRATIVE SOURCES OF THE TAX LAW

The administrative sources of the Federal tax law can be grouped as follows: Treasury Department Regulations, Revenue Rulings and Revenue Procedures, and various other administrative pronouncements (see Exhibit 2–1). All are issued by either the U.S. Treasury Department or the IRS.

Treasury Department Regulations. Regulations are issued by the U.S. Treasury Department under authority granted by Congress.[8] Usually interpretive by nature, they provide taxpayers with considerable guidance on the meaning and application of the Code and often include examples. Regulations carry considerable authority as the official interpretation of tax statutes. They are an important factor to consider in complying with the tax law.

Treasury Regulations are arranged in the same sequence as the Code. A number is added at the beginning, however, to indicate the type of tax or other matter to

---

[6]§ 7852(d).
[7]§ 6712.

[8]§ 7805.

■ **EXHIBIT 2–1**
Administrative Sources

Source	Location	Authority†
Regulations	*Federal Register** *Internal Revenue Bulletin* *Cumulative Bulletin*	Force and effect of law. May be cited as precedent.
Temporary Regulations	*Federal Register** *Internal Revenue Bulletin* *Cumulative Bulletin*	May be cited as precedent.
Proposed Regulations	*Federal Register** *Internal Revenue Bulletin* *Cumulative Bulletin*	Preview of final Regulations. Not precedent.
Revenue Rulings Revenue Procedures Treasury Decisions Actions on Decisions	*Internal Revenue Bulletin*** *Cumulative Bulletin*	Do not have the force and effect of law. Not precedent.
General Counsel Memoranda Technical Advice Memoranda	Tax Analysts' *Tax Notes*; RIA's *Internal Memoranda* of the IRS; CCH's *IRS Position Reporter*	May not be cited as precedent.
Letter Rulings	Research Institute of America and Commerce Clearing House loose-leaf services**	Applicable only to taxpayer addressed. Not precedent.

*Final, Temporary, and Proposed Regulations are published in soft-cover form and on CD-ROM by several publishers (including *RIA OnPoint*).

**Revenue Rulings, Revenue Procedures, and letter rulings are also published on CD-ROM by several publishers (including *RIA OnPoint*).

†Each of these sources may be substantial authority for purposes of the accuracy-related penalty in § 6662. Notice 90–20, 1990–1 C.B. 328.

which they relate. For example, the prefix 1 designates the Regulations under the income tax law. Thus, the Regulations under Code § 2 would be cited as Reg. § 1.2, with subparts added for further identification. The numbering pattern of these subparts often has no correlation with the Code subsections. The prefix 20 designates estate tax Regulations, 25 addresses gift tax Regulations, 31 relates to employment taxes, and 301 refers to procedure and administration. This list is not all-inclusive. Reg. § 1.351–1(a)(2) is an example of a citation.

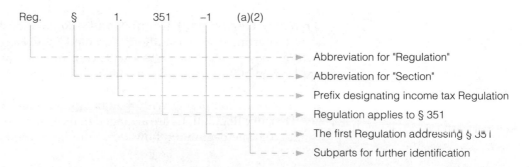

New Regulations and changes in existing Regulations are usually issued in proposed form before they are finalized. The interval between the proposal of a

Regulation and its finalization permits taxpayers and other interested parties to comment on the propriety of the proposal. These comments are usually provided in writing, but oral comments can be offered at hearings held by the IRS on the Regulations in question pursuant to a public notice. This practice of notice-and-comment is a major distinction between Regulations and other forms of Treasury guidance such as Revenue Rulings, Revenue Procedures, and the like.

Proposed Regulations under Code § 2, for example, are cited as Prop.Reg. § 1.2. The Tax Court indicates that Proposed Regulations carry little weight—no more than a position advanced in a written brief prepared by a litigating party before the Tax Court.[9]

Sometimes the Treasury Department issues **Temporary Regulations** relating to matters where immediate guidance is important. These Regulations are issued without the comment period required for Proposed Regulations. Temporary Regulations have the same authoritative value as final Regulations and may be cited as precedents. Since 1989, Temporary Regulations also are issued as Proposed Regulations and automatically expire within three years after the date of their issuance.[10]

Proposed, Temporary, and **Final Regulations** are published in the *Federal Register*, the *Internal Revenue Bulletin*, and major tax services.

Regulations may also be classified as *legislative, interpretive*, or *procedural*. This classification scheme is discussed later in the chapter.

Revenue Rulings and Revenue Procedures.

Revenue Rulings are official pronouncements of the National Office of the IRS.[11] Like Regulations, they are designed to provide interpretation of the tax law. However, they do not carry the same legal force and effect as Regulations and usually deal with more restricted problems. In addition, Regulations are approved by the Secretary of the Treasury, whereas Revenue Rulings generally are not. Both Revenue Rulings and Revenue Procedures serve an important function in providing *guidance* to IRS personnel and taxpayers in handling routine tax matters. Revenue Rulings and Revenue Procedures generally apply retroactively and may be revoked or modified by subsequent rulings or procedures, Regulations, legislation, or court decisions.

Revenue Rulings typically provide one or more examples of how the IRS would apply a law to specific fact situations. Revenue Rulings may arise from technical advice to District Offices of the IRS, court decisions, suggestions from tax practitioner groups, and various tax publications. A Revenue Ruling may also arise from a specific taxpayer's request for a letter ruling. If the IRS believes that a taxpayer's request for a letter ruling deserves official publication due to its widespread impact, the letter ruling will be converted into a Revenue Ruling and issued for the information and guidance of taxpayers, tax practitioners, and IRS personnel. Names, identifying descriptions, and money amounts are changed to conceal the identity of the requesting taxpayer.

Revenue Procedures are issued in the same manner as Revenue Rulings, but deal with the internal management practices and procedures of the IRS. Familiarity with these procedures increases taxpayer compliance and helps make the administration of the tax laws more efficient. The failure of a taxpayer to follow a Revenue Procedure can result in unnecessary delay or, in a discretionary situation, can cause the IRS to decline to act on behalf of the taxpayer. Some recent Revenue Procedures:

---

[9]*F. W. Woolworth Co.*, 54 T.C. 1233 (1970); *Harris M. Miller*, 70 T.C. 448 (1978); and *James O. Tomerlin Trust*, 87 T.C. 876 (1986).

[10]§ 7805(e).

[11]§ 7805(a).

- Released guidance on converting a qualified S corporation trust into an electing small business trust.
- Specified the procedures for requesting consent to changes in accounting methods.
- Provided a safe harbor that may be used to determine a majority of interest for a limited partnership.

Revenue Rulings and Revenue Procedures are published weekly by the U.S. Government in the *Internal Revenue Bulletin* (I.R.B.). Semiannually, the *Bulletins* for a six-month period are gathered together and published in a bound volume called the *Cumulative Bulletin* (C.B.).[12]

The proper form for citing Rulings and Procedures depends on whether the item has been published in the *Cumulative Bulletin* or is available only in I.R.B. form. Consider, for example, the following sequence.

Temporary Citation
{
Rev.Rul. 2000–48, I.R.B. No. 42, 349.
Explanation: Revenue Ruling Number 48, appearing on page 349 of the 42nd weekly issue of the *Internal Revenue Bulletin* for 2000.

Permanent Citation
{
Rev.Rul. 2000–48, 2000–2 C.B. 349.
Explanation: Revenue Ruling Number 48, appearing on page 349 of Volume 2 of the *Cumulative Bulletin* for 2000.

Until the second volume of the 2000 *Cumulative Bulletin* is published, the I.R.B. citation is used. After the publication of the *Cumulative Bulletin*, the C.B. citation is preferred. Note that the page reference of 349 is the same for both the I.R.B. (temporary) and C.B. (permanent) versions of the citation. The IRS numbers the pages of the I.R.B.'s consecutively for each six-month period so as to facilitate their conversion to C.B. form. Revenue Procedures are cited in the same manner, except that "Rev.Proc." is substituted for "Rev.Rul."

Letter Rulings.   **Letter rulings** are issued for a fee upon a taxpayer's request and describe how the IRS will treat a *proposed* transaction for tax purposes. Letter rulings can be useful to taxpayers who wish to be certain of how a transaction will be taxed before proceeding with it. Letter rulings allow taxpayers to avoid unexpected tax costs. The procedure for requesting a ruling can be quite cumbersome, although it sometimes is the most effective way to carry out tax planning. The IRS limits the issuance of individual rulings to restricted, pre-announced areas of taxation and generally will not rule on situations that are fact-intensive. Thus, a ruling may not be obtained on many of the problems that are particularly troublesome to taxpayers.[13]

Although letter rulings once were private and not available to the public, the law now requires the IRS to make such rulings available for public inspection after identifying details are deleted.[14] Published digests of private letter rulings can be found in RIA's *Private Letter Rulings*, BNA *Daily Tax Reports*, and Tax Analysts' *Tax Notes*. IRS Letter Rulings Reports (published by Commerce Clearing House) contain both digests and full texts of all letter rulings. *Letter Ruling Review* (published

---

[12]Usually, only two volumes of the *Cumulative Bulletin* are published each year. However, when Congress has enacted major tax legislation, additional volumes may be published containing the congressional Committee Reports supporting the Revenue Act.

[13]The first *Internal Revenue Bulletin* issued each year contains a list of areas in which the IRS will not issue advance rulings. This list may be modified throughout the year. See, for example, Rev.Proc. 2001–3, I.R.B. No. 1, 103.

[14]§ 6110.

by Tax Analysts), a monthly publication, selects and discusses the most important of the approximately 40 letter rulings issued each week. In addition, computerized databases of letter rulings are also available through several private publishers.

Letter rulings are issued multidigit file numbers, which indicate the year and week of issuance as well as the number of the ruling during that week. Consider, for example, Ltr.Rul. 200018052, which indicates the tax treatment for transportation costs incurred in getting to and from a temporary work location.

2000	18	052
Year 2000	18th week of issuance	52nd ruling issued during the 18th week

Other Administrative Pronouncements. *Treasury Decisions* (TDs) are issued by the Treasury Department to promulgate new Regulations, amend or otherwise change existing Regulations, or announce the position of the Government on selected court decisions. Like Revenue Rulings and Revenue Procedures, TDs are published initially in the *Internal Revenue Bulletin* and subsequently transferred to the *Cumulative Bulletin*.

The IRS publishes other administrative communications in the *Internal Revenue Bulletin*, such as Announcements, Notices, LRs (Proposed Regulations), Termination of Exempt Organization Status, Practitioner Disciplinary Actions, and Prohibited Transaction Exemptions.

Like letter rulings, **determination letters** are issued at the request of taxpayers and provide guidance on the application of the tax law. They differ from letter rulings in that the issuing source is the District Director rather than the National Office of the IRS. Further, determination letters usually involve *completed* (as opposed to proposed) transactions. Determination letters are not regularly published and are made known only to the party making the request.

EXAMPLE 1

The shareholders of Red Corporation and Green Corporation want assurance that the consolidation of their corporations into Blue Corporation will be a nontaxable reorganization. The proper approach is to ask the National Office of the IRS to issue a letter ruling concerning the income tax effect of the proposed transaction. ■

EXAMPLE 2

Chris operates a barber shop in which he employs eight barbers. To comply with the rules governing income tax and payroll tax withholdings, Chris wants to know whether the barbers working for him are employees or independent contractors. The proper procedure is to request a determination letter on their status from the appropriate District Director. ■

The National Office of the IRS releases **Technical Advice Memoranda (TAMs)** weekly. TAMs resemble letter rulings in that they give the IRS's determination of an issue. Letter rulings, however, are responses to requests by taxpayers, whereas TAMs are issued by the National Office of the IRS in response to questions raised by IRS field personnel during audits. TAMs deal with completed rather than proposed transactions and are often requested for questions relating to exempt organizations and employee plans.

The law requires that several internal memoranda that constitute the working law of the IRS be released. TAMs and General Counsel Memoranda (GCMs) are not officially published, and the IRS indicates that they may not be cited as

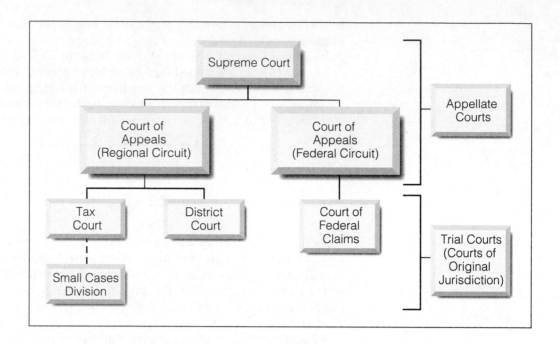

precedents by taxpayers.[15] However, these working documents do explain the IRS's position on various issues.

JUDICIAL SOURCES OF THE TAX LAW

The Judicial Process in General.   After a taxpayer has exhausted some or all of the remedies available within the IRS (no satisfactory settlement has been reached at the agent level or at the Appeals Division level), the dispute can be taken to the Federal courts. The dispute is first considered by a **court of original jurisdiction** (known as a trial court), with any appeal (either by the taxpayer or the IRS) taken to the appropriate appellate court. In most situations, the taxpayer has a choice of four trial courts: a **District Court,** the **Court of Federal Claims,** the **Tax Court,** or the **Small Cases Division** of the Tax Court. The court system for Federal tax litigation is illustrated in Figure 2–3.

The broken line between the Tax Court and the Small Cases Division indicates that there is no appeal from the Small Cases Division. Decisions from the Small Cases Division are not published and have no precedential value. They may not be relied upon by other taxpayers or even by the taxpayer in question in subsequent years. The jurisdiction of the Small Cases Division is limited to cases involving amounts of $50,000 or less.

Trial Courts.   The differences among the various trial courts (courts of original jurisdiction) can be summarized as follows.

- *Number of courts.* There is only one Court of Federal Claims and only one Tax Court, but there are many District Courts. The taxpayer does not select the District Court that will hear the dispute but must sue in the one that has jurisdiction where the taxpayer resides.

---

[15]These are unofficially published by the sources listed in Exhibit 2–1. Internal memoranda may constitute substantial authority for purposes of the § 6662 accuracy-related penalty. Notice 90–20, 1990–1 C.B. 328.

- *Number of judges.* A case tried in a District Court is heard before only 1 judge. The Court of Federal Claims has 16 judges, and the Tax Court has 19 regular judges. The entire Tax Court, however, will review a case (the case is sent to court conference) only when important or novel tax issues are involved. Most cases will be heard and decided by 1 of the 19 judges.
- *Location.* The Court of Federal Claims meets most often in Washington, D.C., while a District Court meets at a prescribed seat for the particular district. Each state has at least one District Court, and many of the populous states have more than one. Choosing the District Court usually minimizes the inconvenience and expense of traveling for the taxpayer and his or her counsel. The Tax Court is based in Washington, D.C., but various judges travel to different parts of the country and hear cases at predetermined locations and dates. This procedure eases the distance problem for the taxpayer, but it can mean a delay before the case comes to trial.
- *Jurisdiction of the Court of Federal Claims.* The Court of Federal Claims has jurisdiction over any claim against the United States that is based upon the Constitution, any Act of Congress, or any Regulation of an executive department. Thus, the Court of Federal Claims hears nontax litigation as well as tax cases.
- *Jurisdiction of the Tax Court and District Courts.* The Tax Court hears only tax cases and is the most popular forum. The District Courts hear a wide variety of nontax cases, including drug crimes and other Federal violations, as well as tax cases. For this reason, some people suggest that the Tax Court has more expertise in tax matters.
- *Jury trial.* The only court in which a taxpayer can obtain a jury trial is a District Court. Juries can decide only questions of fact and not questions of law. Therefore, taxpayers who choose the District Court route often do not request a jury trial. If a jury trial is not elected, the judge will decide all issues. Note that a District Court decision is controlling only in the district in which the court has jurisdiction.
- *Payment of deficiency.* Before the Court of Federal Claims or a District Court can have jurisdiction, the taxpayer must pay the tax deficiency assessed by the IRS and then sue for a refund. If the taxpayer wins (assuming no successful appeal by the Government), the tax paid plus appropriate interest will be recovered. Jurisdiction in the Tax Court, however, is usually obtained without first paying the assessed tax deficiency.

 1 *Find more information on this topic at our Web site: **http://wft-entities.swcollege.com**.*

- *Appeals.* Appeals from a District Court or a Tax Court decision go to the Court of Appeals for the circuit in which the taxpayer resides. Appeals from the Court of Federal Claims go to the Federal Circuit Court of Appeals.
- *Bankruptcy.* When a taxpayer files a bankruptcy petition, the IRS, like other creditors, is prevented from taking action against the taxpayer. Sometimes a bankruptcy court may settle a tax claim.

For a summary of the Federal trial courts, see Concept Summary 2–1.

Appellate Courts.   The losing party can appeal a trial court decision to a **Circuit Court of Appeals.** The 11 geographic circuits, the circuit for the District of Columbia, and the Federal Circuit[16] are shown in Figure 2–4.

---

[16]The Federal Circuit Court of Appeals was created to hear decisions appealed from the Claims Court (now the Court of Federal Claims).

CONCEPT SUMMARY 2–1

Federal Judicial System: Trial Courts

Issue	Tax Court	District Court	Court of Federal Claims
Number of judges per court	19*	1 per case	16
Payment of deficiency before trial	No	Yes	Yes
Jury trial available	No	Yes	No
Types of disputes	Tax cases only	Mostly criminal and civil issues	Claims against the United States
Jurisdiction	Nationwide	Location of taxpayer	Nationwide
Appeal route	Court of Appeals	Court of Appeals	Federal Circuit Court of Appeals

*There are also 14 special trial judges and 9 senior judges.

■ **FIGURE 2–4**
The Circuit Courts of Appeals

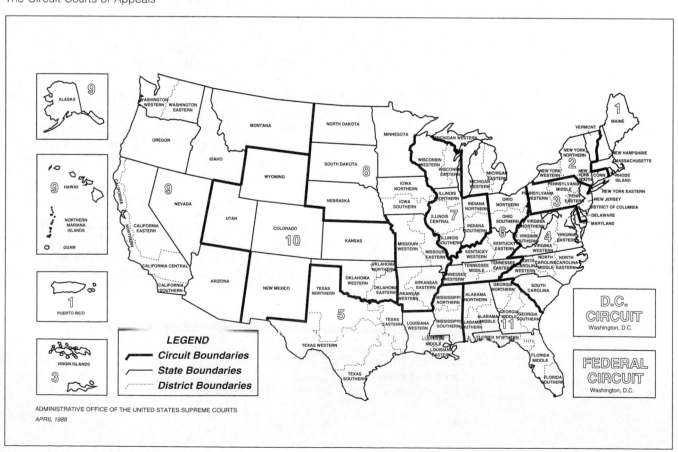

ADMINISTRATIVE OFFICE OF THE UNITED STATES SUPREME COURTS
APRIL 1988

If the Government loses at the trial court level (District Court, Tax Court, or Court of Federal Claims), it need not (and frequently does not) appeal. The fact that an appeal is not made, however, does not indicate that the IRS agrees with the result and will not litigate similar issues in the future. The IRS may decide not to appeal for a number of reasons. First, its current litigation load may be heavy. As a consequence, the IRS may decide that available personnel should be assigned to other, more important cases. Second, the IRS may not appeal for strategic reasons. For example, the taxpayer may be in a sympathetic position, or the facts may be particularly strong in his or her favor. In that event, the IRS may wait for a weaker case to test the legal issues involved. Third, if the appeal is from a District Court or the Tax Court, the Court of Appeals of jurisdiction could have some bearing on whether the IRS decides to pursue an appeal. Based on past experience and precedent, the IRS may conclude that the chance for success on a particular issue might be more promising in another Court of Appeals. If so, the IRS will wait for a similar case to arise in a different jurisdiction.

The Federal Circuit at the appellate level provides a taxpayer with an alternative forum to the Court of Appeals of his or her home circuit. When a particular circuit has issued an adverse decision, the taxpayer may prefer the Court of Federal Claims route since any appeal will be to the Federal Circuit Court of Appeals.

District Courts, the Tax Court, and the Court of Federal Claims must abide by the **precedents** set by the Court of Appeals of their jurisdiction. A particular Court of Appeals need not follow the decisions of another Court of Appeals. All courts, however, must follow decisions of the **Supreme Court.**

This pattern of appellate precedents raises an issue for the Tax Court. Because the Tax Court is a national court, it decides cases from all parts of the country. Appeals from its decisions, however, go to all of the Courts of Appeals except the Federal Circuit Court of Appeals. Accordingly, identical Tax Court cases might be appealed to different circuits with different results. As a result of the *Golsen*[17] case, the Tax Court will not follow its own precedents in a subsequent case if the Court of Appeals with jurisdiction over the taxpayer in question has previously reversed the Tax Court on the specific issue at hand.

EXAMPLE 3

Emily lives in Texas and sues in the Tax Court on Issue A. The Fifth Circuit Court of Appeals is the appellate court with jurisdiction. The Fifth Circuit has already decided, in a case involving similar facts but a different taxpayer, that Issue A should be resolved against the Government. Although the Tax Court feels that the Fifth Circuit is wrong, under its *Golsen* policy it will render judgment for Emily. Shortly thereafter, in a comparable case, Rashad, a resident of New York, sues in the Tax Court on Issue A. Assume that the Second Circuit Court of Appeals, the appellate court with jurisdiction in New York, has never expressed itself on Issue A. Presuming the Tax Court has not reconsidered its position on Issue A, it will decide against Rashad. Thus, it is entirely possible for two taxpayers suing in the same court to end up with opposite results merely because they live in different parts of the country. ■

Appeal to the Supreme Court is not automatic. It must be applied for via a **Writ of Certiorari.** If the Court agrees to hear the case, it will grant the Writ (*Cert. Granted*). Most often, it will decline to hear the case (*Cert. Denied*). In fact, the Supreme Court rarely hears tax cases. The Court usually grants certiorari to resolve a conflict among the Courts of Appeals (e.g., two or more appellate courts have opposing positions on a particular issue) or where the tax issue is extremely important. The granting of a *Writ of Certiorari* indicates that at least four members of

---

[17]*Jack E. Golsen*, 54 T.C. 742 (1970).

the Supreme Court believe that the issue is of sufficient importance to be heard by the full Court.

The *role* of appellate courts is limited to a review of the record of trial compiled by the trial courts. Thus, the appellate process usually involves a determination of whether the trial court applied the proper law in arriving at its decision, rather than a consideration of the trial court's factual findings.

An appeal can have any of a number of possible outcomes. The appellate court may approve (affirm) or disapprove (reverse) the lower court's finding, or it may send the case back for further consideration (remand). When many issues are involved, a mixed result is not unusual. Thus, the lower court may be affirmed (*aff'd.*) on Issue A and reversed (*rev'd.*) on Issue B, while Issue C is remanded (*rem'd.*) for additional fact finding.

When more than one judge is involved in the decision-making process, disagreements are not uncommon. In addition to the majority view, one or more judges may concur (agree with the result reached but not with some or all of the reasoning) or dissent (disagree with the result). In any one case, the majority view controls. But concurring and dissenting views can influence other courts or, at some subsequent date when the composition of the court has changed, even the same court.

Judicial Citations—General.   Having briefly described the judicial process, it is appropriate to consider the more practical problem of the relationship of case law to tax research. As previously noted, court decisions are an important source of tax law. The ability to locate a case and to cite it is therefore a must in working with the tax law. Judicial citations usually follow a standard pattern: case name, volume number, reporter series, page or paragraph number, court (where necessary), and the year of decision.

Judicial Citations—The Tax Court.   The Tax Court issues two types of decisions: Regular and Memorandum. The Chief Judge decides whether the opinion is issued as a Regular or Memorandum decision. The distinction between the two involves both substance and form. In terms of substance, *Memorandum* decisions deal with situations necessitating only the application of already established principles of law. *Regular* decisions involve novel issues not previously resolved by the court. In actual practice, however, this distinction is not always so clear. Be that as it may, both Regular and Memorandum decisions represent the position of the Tax Court and, as such, can be relied on.

Regular and Memorandum decisions issued by the Tax Court also differ in form. Memorandum decisions are not officially published while Regular decisions are published by the U.S. Government in a series called *Tax Court of the United States Reports* (T.C.). Each volume of these *Reports* covers a six-month period (January 1 through June 30 and July 1 through December 31) and is given a succeeding volume number. But there is usually a time lag between the date a decision is rendered and the date it appears in official form. A temporary citation may be necessary to help the researcher locate a recent Regular decision. Consider, for example, the temporary and permanent citations for *Stephen W. Williams*, a decision filed on March 1, 2000:

Temporary $\left\{\begin{array}{l}\end{array}\right.$ *Stephen W. Williams,* 114 T.C. ____, No. 8 (2000).
Citation   *Explanation:* Page number left blank because not yet known.

Permanent $\left\{\begin{array}{l}\end{array}\right.$ *Stephen W. Williams,* 114 T.C. 136 (2000).
Citation   *Explanation:* Page 136 of Vol. 114 of *Tax Court of the United States Reports.*

Both citations tell us that the case will ultimately appear in Volume 114 of the *Tax Court of the United States Reports*. Until this volume becomes available to the general public, however, the page number must be left blank. Instead, the temporary citation identifies the case as being the 8th Regular decision issued by the Tax Court since Volume 113 ended. With this information, the decision can easily be located in either of the special Tax Court services published by Commerce Clearing House and Research Institute of America (formerly by Prentice-Hall). Once Volume 114 is released, the permanent citation can be substituted and the number of the case dropped.

Before 1943, the Tax Court was called the Board of Tax Appeals, and its decisions were published as the *United States Board of Tax Appeals Reports* (B.T.A.). These 47 volumes cover the period from 1924 to 1942. For example, the citation *Karl Pauli,* 11 B.T.A. 784 (1928) refers to the 11th volume of the *Board of Tax Appeals Reports,* page 784, issued in 1928.

If the IRS loses a decision, it may indicate whether it agrees or disagrees with the results reached by the court by publishing an **acquiescence** ("A" or "Acq.") or **nonacquiescence** ("NA" or "Nonacq."), respectively. The acquiescence program is used where guidance is helpful, regardless of the court that issued the opinion. The acquiescence or nonacquiescence is published in the *Internal Revenue Bulletin* and the *Cumulative Bulletin* as an *Action on Decision.* The IRS can retroactively revoke an acquiescence.

Although Memorandum decisions are not published by the U.S. Government, they are published by Commerce Clearing House (CCH) and Research Institute of America. Consider, for example, the three different ways that *Jack D. Carr* can be cited.

Jack D. Carr, T.C.Memo. 1985–19.
> The 19th Memorandum decision issued by the Tax Court in 1985.

Jack D. Carr, 49 TCM 507.
> Page 507 of Vol. 49 of the CCH *Tax Court Memorandum Decisions.*

Jack D. Carr, RIA T.C.Mem.Dec. ¶85,019.
> Paragraph 85,019 of the RIA *T.C. Memorandum Decisions.*

The third citation contains the same information as the first. Thus, ¶85,019 indicates the following information about the case: year 1985, 19th T.C. Memo. decision. Although the RIA citation does not include a specific volume number, the paragraph citation (85,019) indicates that the decision can be found in the 1985 volume of the RIA Memorandum Decision service.

Judicial Citations—The District Courts, Court of Federal Claims, and Courts of Appeals.

District Court, Court of Federal Claims, and Court of Appeals decisions dealing with Federal tax matters are reported in both the CCH *U.S. Tax Cases* (USTC) and the RIA *American Federal Tax Reports* (AFTR) series.

District Court decisions, dealing with *both* tax and nontax issues, are also published by West Publishing Company in its *Federal Supplement Series.* A District Court case can be cited in three different forms.

Simons-Eastern Co. v. U.S., 73–1 USTC ¶9279 (D.Ct.Ga., 1972).
> *Explanation:* Reported in the first volume of the *U.S. Tax Cases* (USTC) published by Commerce Clearing House for calendar year 1973 (73–1) and located at paragraph 9279 (¶9279).

Simons-Eastern Co. v. U.S., 31 AFTR2d 73–640 (D.Ct.Ga., 1972).
> *Explanation:* Reported in the 31st volume of the second series of the *American Federal Tax Reports* (AFTR2d) published by RIA, beginning on page 640. The "73" preceding the page number indicates the year the case was published but is a designation used only in recent decisions.

Simons-Eastern Co. v. U.S., 354 F.Supp. 1003 (D.Ct.Ga., 1972).

> *Explanation:* Reported in the 354th volume of the *Federal Supplement Series* (F.Supp.) published by West Publishing Company, beginning on page 1003.

In all of the preceding citations, the name of the case is the same (Simons-Eastern Co. being the taxpayer), as are the references to the District Court of Georgia (D.Ct.Ga.) and the year the decision was rendered (1972).

Decisions of the Court of Federal Claims and the Courts of Appeals are published in the USTCs, AFTRs, and the *Federal Second Series* (F.2d). Volume 999, published in 1993, is the last volume of the *Federal Second Series*. It is followed by the *Federal Third Series* (F.3d). Beginning with October 1982, decisions of the Court of Federal Claims are published in the *Claims Court Reporter* (abbreviated as Cl.Ct.). Beginning with Volume 27 on October 30, 1992, the name of the reporter changed to the *Federal Claims Reporter* (abbreviated as Fed.Cl.).

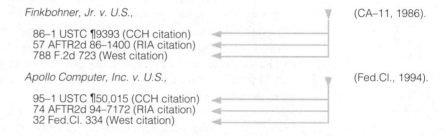

Finkbohner, Jr. v. U.S.,   (CA–11, 1986).

86–1 USTC ¶9393 (CCH citation)
57 AFTR2d 86–1400 (RIA citation)
788 F.2d 723 (West citation)

Apollo Computer, Inc. v. U.S.,   (Fed.Cl., 1994).

95–1 USTC ¶50,015 (CCH citation)
74 AFTR2d 94–7172 (RIA citation)
32 Fed.Cl. 334 (West citation)

Finkbohner, Jr. is a decision rendered by the Eleventh Circuit Court of Appeals in 1986 (CA–11, 1986), while *Apollo Computer, Inc.* was issued by the Court of Federal Claims in 1994 (Fed.Cl., 1994).

Judicial Citations—The Supreme Court.   Like all other Federal tax decisions (except those rendered by the Tax Court), Supreme Court decisions dealing with Federal tax matters are published by Commerce Clearing House in the USTCs and by RIA in the AFTRs. The U.S. Government Printing Office publishes all Supreme Court decisions in the *United States Supreme Court Reports* (U.S.), as do West Publishing Company in its *Supreme Court Reporter* (S.Ct.) and the Lawyer's Co-operative Publishing Company in its *United States Reports, Lawyer's Edition* (L.Ed.).

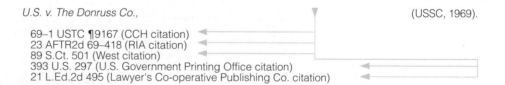

U.S. v. The Donruss Co.,   (USSC, 1969).

69–1 USTC ¶9167 (CCH citation)
23 AFTR2d 69–418 (RIA citation)
89 S.Ct. 501 (West citation)
393 U.S. 297 (U.S. Government Printing Office citation)
21 L.Ed.2d 495 (Lawyer's Co-operative Publishing Co. citation)

The parenthetical reference (USSC, 1969) identifies the decision as having been rendered by the U.S. Supreme Court in 1969. In this text, the citations of Supreme Court decisions are limited to the CCH (USTC), RIA (AFTR), and West (S.Ct.) versions.

LEARNING OBJECTIVE 2

Locate and work with the tax law and understand the tax research process.

Working with the Tax Law—Tax Research

Tax research is undertaken to determine the best available solution to a situation that has tax consequences. In the case of a completed transaction, the objective of the research is to determine the tax result of what has already taken place. For

BRIDGE DISCIPLINE

Bridge to Business Law

U.S. income tax laws change daily by the action of Congress, tax administrators, and the courts. This process matches the three-branch structure of the rest of the government, with the legislative, executive, and judicial branches each having a say in making tax law. But this distinction among the functions of government is perhaps less clear when it involves the tax law.

- Presidential vetoes of tax legislation are rare.
- The Tax Court is a creation of the Congress in the Internal Revenue Code, not of the U.S. Constitution.
- The cost of tax litigation and the time that it takes for a case to work its way through the judicial system render the courts unavailable to most taxpayers.

Under the U.S. Constitution, legislation involving government revenues must start in the House of Representatives. This provision likely was included so that the public would have greater control over those who want greater access to their pocketbooks. Several recent pieces of tax legislation, though, have been initiated as bills in the Senate. And during the years of the deepest Federal deficits, all bills introduced in both houses of Congress were required to be "revenue neutral" (i.e., they had to include provisions by which the legislation's new programs would be paid for). In both houses, this resulted in amendments to the Internal Revenue Code being attached to legislation involving clean air and water standards, child care programs, and product import and export limitations.

In a few cases, the courts considered a taxpayer challenge to the way this tax legislation was crafted. But so far the courts have failed to overturn any tax provisions solely because they were initiated in the Senate. The courts' rationale for this seemingly unconstitutional position is that (1) the House and its committees heard a full discussion of the proposal, and (2) too much time has passed since adoption of the legislation to easily un-wind it and undertake a refund procedure.

example, is the expenditure incurred by the taxpayer deductible or not deductible for tax purposes? When dealing with proposed transactions, tax research is concerned with the determination of possible alternative tax consequences to facilitate effective tax planning.

Tax research involves the following procedures.

- Identifying and refining the problem.
- Locating the appropriate tax law sources.
- Assessing the tax law sources.
- Arriving at the solution or at alternative solutions while giving due consideration to nontax factors.
- Effectively communicating the solution to the taxpayer or the taxpayer's representative.
- Following up on the solution (where appropriate) in light of new developments.

This process is depicted schematically in Figure 2–5. The broken lines indicate steps of particular interest when tax research is directed toward proposed, rather than completed, transactions.

■ **FIGURE 2–5**
Tax Research Process

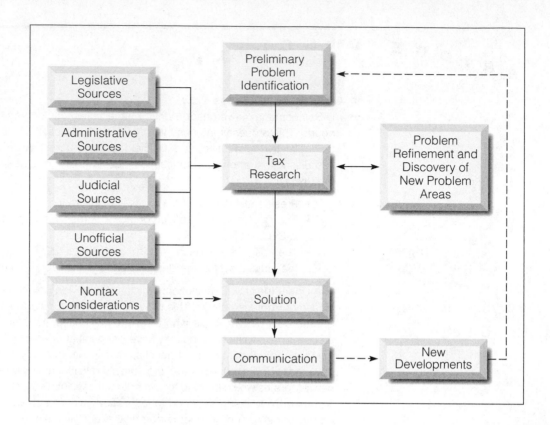

IDENTIFYING THE PROBLEM

Problem identification starts with a compilation of the relevant facts involved. In this regard, *all* of the facts that may have a bearing on the problem must be gathered, as any omission could modify the solution reached. To illustrate, consider what appears to be a very simple problem.

EXAMPLE 4

In reviewing their tax and financial situation, Fred and Megan, a married couple, notice that Fred's investment in Airways stock has declined from its purchase price of $8,000 to a current market value of $5,500. Megan wants to sell this stock now and claim the $2,500 loss ($5,500 value − $8,000 cost) as a deduction this year. Fred, however, believes that Airways Co. will yet prosper and does not want to part with its stock. Their daughter suggests that they sell the Airways Co. stock to Maple, Inc., a corporation owned equally by Fred and Megan. That way, they can claim the deduction this year while still holding the stock through their corporation. Will this suggestion work? ■

REFINING THE PROBLEM

Fred and Megan in Example 4 face three choices: (1) sell the Airways stock through their regular investment broker and get a deduction in the current year (Megan's plan); (2) continue to hold the Airways stock (Fred's plan); and (3) sell the Airways stock to a corporation owned 50–50 by Fred and Megan (their daughter's suggestion). The tax consequences of plans (1) and (2) are clear, but the question that Fred and Megan want to resolve is whether plan (3) will work as anticipated. Refining the problem further, can shareholders deduct a loss from the sale of an asset to a corporation that they control? Section 267(a)(1) indicates that losses from the sale of property between persons specified in § 267(b) are not deductible. This subsection lists 12 different relationships, including, in § 267(b)(2): "an individual and a corporation more than 50 percent in value of the outstanding stock of which is owned, directly or indirectly, by or for such individual." Thus, if Fred and Megan each own 50 percent of Maple, neither owns *more than* 50 percent, as § 267(b) requires. Accordingly, the loss disallowance rule would not apply to Fred, and their daughter's suggestion would appear to be sound.

The language of the statute, however, indicates that any stock owned *directly or indirectly* by an individual is counted toward the 50 percent test. Might Megan's stock be considered owned "indirectly" by Fred? Further research is necessary. Section 267(c) contains rules for determining "constructive ownership of stock," or when stock owned by one person will be attributed to someone else. One of the rules in this subsection declares that an individual is considered to own any stock that is owned by that person's *family*, and family is defined in § 267(c)(4) as including a person's spouse, among others. Therefore, Megan's stock will be attributed to Fred, so that Fred is treated as owning all of the stock of Maple, Inc. As a result, § 267(a) would indeed apply, and no loss would be deductible if Fred sells his Airways stock to Maple. In short, the daughter's suggestion will not work.

LOCATING THE APPROPRIATE TAX LAW SOURCES

Once the problem is clearly defined, what is the next step? While it is a matter of individual judgment, most tax research begins with the index volume of a paper-based tax service or a keyword search of an online or CD-ROM tax service. If the problem is not complex, the researcher may bypass the tax service and turn directly to the Internal Revenue Code and the Treasury Regulations. For the beginner, the latter procedure saves time and will solve many of the more basic problems. If the researcher does not have a personal copy of the Code or Regulations, resorting to the appropriate volume(s) of a tax service or a CD-ROM is necessary.[18] The major tax services and their publishers are:

Standard Federal Tax Reporter, Commerce Clearing House.

United States Tax Reporter, Research Institute of America.

Federal Tax Coordinator 2d, Research Institute of America.

Tax Management Portfolios, Bureau of National Affairs.

Mertens Law of Federal Income Taxation, Callaghan and Co.

Working with Tax Services.   In this text, it is not feasible to explain the use of any particular tax service—this ability can be obtained with experience. However, several important observations about the use of tax services cannot be overemphasized. First, always check for current developments. The main text of any paper-based service is revised too infrequently to permit reliance on that portion as the *latest* word on any subject. Where current developments can be found depends on which service is being used. Commerce Clearing House's *Standard Federal Tax Reporter* contains a special volume devoted to current matters. Both RIA's *United States Tax Reporter* and *Federal Tax Coordinator 2d* integrate the new developments

---

[18]Several of the major tax services publish paperback editions of the Code and Treasury Regulations that can be purchased at modest prices. These editions are usually revised twice each year. For an annotated and abridged version of the Code and Regulations that is published annually, see James E. Smith, *West's Internal Revenue Code of 1986 and Treasury Regulations: Annotated and Selected* (St. Paul, Minn.: West/South-Western College Publishing, 2001). The complete Code and Regulations are also available in *RIA Checkpoint*.

into the body of the service throughout the year. Second, there is no substitute for the original source. Do not base a conclusion solely on a tax service's commentary. If the Code Section, Regulation, or case is vital to the research, read it.

Tax Periodicals.   Various tax periodicals are another source of information. The easiest way to locate a journal article on a particular tax problem is through CCH's *Federal Tax Articles*. This six-volume service includes a subject index, a Code Section number index, and an author's index. In addition, RIA's tax service has a topical "Index to Tax Articles" section that is organized using the RIA paragraph index system. *The Accounting & Tax Index* also is available in three quarterly issues plus a cumulative year-end volume covering all four quarters.

The following are some of the more useful tax periodicals.

The Journal of Taxation
Warren, Gorham and Lamont
31 St. James Avenue
Boston, MA 02116

Oil, Gas, and Energy Quarterly
Matthew Bender & Co.
2 Park Avenue
New York, NY 10016

The International Tax Journal
Panel Publishers
14 Plaza Road
Greenvale, NY 11548

TAXES—The Tax Magazine
Commerce Clearing House, Inc.
2700 Lake Cook Road
Riverwood, IL 60015

The Tax Adviser
AICPA
1211 Avenue of the Americas
New York, NY 10036

Estate Planning
Warren, Gorham and Lamont
31 St. James Avenue
Boston, MA 02116

Tax Law Review
Warren, Gorham and Lamont
31 St. James Avenue
Boston, MA 02116

Practical Tax Strategies
Warren, Gorham and Lamont
31 St. James Avenue
Boston, MA 02116

The Tax Executive
1001 Pennsylvania Avenue, NW
Suite 320
Washington, D.C. 20004

Journal of Corporate Taxation
Warren, Gorham and Lamont
31 St. James Avenue
Boston, MA 02116

Journal of Taxation for Individuals
Warren, Gorham and Lamont
31 St. James Avenue
Boston, MA 02116

Journal of the American Taxation Association
American Accounting Association
5717 Bessie Drive
Sarasota, FL 34233

Tax Notes
6830 Fairfax Drive
Arlington, VA 22213

ASSESSING TAX LAW SOURCES

Once a source has been located, the next step is to assess it in light of the problem at hand. Proper assessment involves careful interpretation of the tax law and consideration of its relevance and significance.

TAX IN THE NEWS

INTERNAL REVENUE CODE: INTERPRETATION PITFALLS

One author has noted 10 common pitfalls in interpreting the Code.

1. Determine the limitations and exceptions to a provision. Do not permit the language of the Code Section to carry greater or lesser weight than was intended.
2. Just because a Section fails to mention an item does not necessarily mean that the item is excluded.
3. Read definitional clauses carefully.
4. Do not overlook small words such as *and* and *or*. There is a world of difference between these two words.
5. Read the Code Section completely; do not jump to conclusions.
6. Watch out for cross-referenced and related provisions, since many Sections of the Code are interrelated.
7. At times Congress is not careful when reconciling new Code provisions with existing Sections. Conflicts among Sections, therefore, do arise.
8. Be alert for hidden definitions; terms in a particular Code Section may be defined in the same Section or in a separate Section.
9. Some answers may not be found in the Code; therefore, a researcher may have to consult the Regulations and/or judicial decisions.
10. Take careful note of measuring words such as *less than 50 percent*, *more than 50 percent*, and *at least 80 percent*.

SOURCE: Adapted by permission from Henry G. Wong, "Ten Common Pitfalls in Reading the Internal Revenue Code," *Journal of Business Strategy* (July–August 1972): 30–33. Reprinted with permission by Faulkner & Gray, Inc., 11 Penn Plaza, New York, NY 10001.

Interpreting the Internal Revenue Code. The language of the Code is often difficult to comprehend fully. Contrary to many people's suspicions, the Code is not written deliberately to confuse. Nevertheless, it often has that effect. The Code is intended to apply to more than 275 million citizens, most of whom are willing to exploit any linguistic imprecision to their benefit—to find a "loophole," in popular parlance. Moreover, many of the Code's provisions are limitations or restrictions involving two or more variables. Expressing such concepts algebraically would be more direct; using words to accomplish this task instead is often quite cumbersome. Among the worst such attempts is § 341(e) relating to so-called collapsible corporations, which includes one sentence that has more than 450 words.

Nevertheless, the Code is the governing law, the only source of tax law (other than treaties) that has received the actual approval of Congress and the President. Accordingly, it is usually the first source to be consulted, and often it is the only source needed.

Assessing the Significance of a Treasury Regulation. Treasury Regulations are the official interpretation of the Code and are entitled to great deference. Occasionally, however, a court will invalidate a Regulation or a portion thereof on the grounds that the Regulation is contrary to the intent of Congress. Usually, courts do not question the validity of Regulations because of the belief that "the first administrative interpretation of a provision as it appears in a new act often expresses the general understanding of the times or the actual understanding of those who played an important part when the statute was drafted."[19]

Keep in mind the following observations when assessing the significance of a Regulation.

- IRS agents *must* give the Code and the Regulations issued thereunder equal weight when dealing with taxpayers and their representatives.
- Proposed Regulations provide a preview of future final Regulations, but they are not binding on the IRS or taxpayers.
- In a challenge, the burden of proof is on the taxpayer to show that a Regulation varies from the language of the statute and has no support in the Committee Reports.
- Final Regulations can be classified as procedural, interpretive, or legislative. **Procedural Regulations** neither establish tax laws nor attempt to explain tax laws. Procedural Regulations often include procedural instructions, indicating information that taxpayers should provide the IRS, as well as information about the internal management and conduct of the IRS itself.
- **Interpretive Regulations** rephrase and elaborate what Congress stated in the Committee Reports that were issued when the tax legislation was enacted. Such Regulations are *hard and solid* and almost impossible to overturn unless they do not clearly reflect the intent of Congress.
- In some Code Sections, Congress has given the *Secretary or his delegate* the specific authority to prescribe Regulations to carry out the details of administration or to otherwise create rules not included in the Code. Under such circumstances, Congress is effectively delegating its legislative powers to the Treasury Department. Regulations issued pursuant to this type of authority possess the force and effect of law and are often called **Legislative Regulations** [e.g., see § 385(a)].

Assessing the Significance of Other Administrative Sources of the Tax Law. Revenue Rulings issued by the IRS carry much less weight than Treasury Department Regulations. Revenue Rulings are important, however, in that they reflect the position of the IRS on tax matters. In any dispute with the IRS on the interpretation of tax law, taxpayers should expect agents to follow the results reached in applicable Revenue Rulings. It is not unusual, however, for courts to overturn Revenue Rulings as incorrect applications of the law to the facts presented.

Actions on Decisions further tell the taxpayer the IRS's reaction to certain court decisions. Recall that the IRS follows a practice of either acquiescing (agreeing) or nonacquiescing (not agreeing) with selected judicial decisions. A nonacquiescence does not mean that a particular court decision is of no value, but it does indicate that the IRS may choose to litigate the issue involved.

Assessing the Significance of Judicial Sources of the Tax Law. The judicial process as it relates to the formulation of tax law has been described. How much reliance can be placed on a particular decision depends upon the following factors.

- *The level of the court.* A decision rendered by a trial court (e.g., a District Court) carries less weight than one issued by an appellate court (e.g., the Fifth Circuit Court of Appeals). Unless Congress changes the Code, decisions by the U.S. Supreme Court represent the last word on any tax issue.

---

[19]*Augustus v. Comm.*, 41–1 USTC ¶9255, 26 AFTR 612, 118 F.2d 38 (CA–6, 1941).

- *The legal residence of the taxpayer.* If, for example, a taxpayer lives in Texas, a decision of the Fifth Circuit Court of Appeals means more than one rendered by the Second Circuit Court of Appeals. This is the case because any appeal from a District Court or the Tax Court would be to the Fifth Circuit Court of Appeals and not to the Second Circuit Court of Appeals.
- *The type of decision.* A Tax Court Regular decision carries more weight than a Memorandum decision because the Tax Court does not consider Memorandum decisions to have precedential value.[20]
- *The weight of the decision.* A decision that is supported by cases from other courts carries more weight than a decision that is not supported by other cases.
- *Subsequent events.* Was the decision affirmed or overruled on appeal?

In connection with the last two factors, a citator is helpful to tax research.[21] A citator lists subsequent published opinions that refer to the case being assessed. Reviewing these references enables the tax researcher to determine whether the decision in question has been reversed, affirmed, followed by other courts, or distinguished in some way. If one plans to rely on a judicial decision to any significant degree, "running" the case through a citator is imperative.

Understanding Judicial Opinions. Reading judicial opinions can be more productive if certain conventions of usage are understood. In tax cases, the taxpayer is usually the person initiating the court action and accordingly is labeled the *plaintiff.* The government generally is the party against whom the case is being brought and accordingly is called the *defendant.* Some courts, including the Tax Court, apply the terms *petitioner* and *respondent* to the plaintiff and defendant, respectively, particularly when the case is an appellate proceeding. Appellate courts often use the terms *appellant* and *appellee* instead.

It is also important to distinguish between a court's final determination, or *holding,* and passing comments made in the course of its opinion. These latter remarks, examples, and analogies, often collectively termed *dicta,* are not part of the court's conclusion and do not have precedential value. Nevertheless, they often facilitate one's understanding of the court's reasoning and can enable a tax adviser to better predict how the court might resolve some future tax case.

Assessing the Significance of Other Sources. *Primary sources* of tax law include the Constitution, legislative history materials (e.g., Committee Reports), statutes, treaties, Treasury Regulations, IRS pronouncements, and judicial decisions. In general, the IRS regards only primary sources as substantial authority. However, reference to *secondary materials* such as legal periodicals, treatises, legal opinions, General Counsel Memoranda, and written determinations may be useful. In general, secondary sources are not authority.

Although the statement that the IRS regards only primary sources as substantial authority is generally true, there is one exception. Substantial authority *for purposes of* the accuracy-related penalty in § 6662 includes a number of secondary materials (e.g., letter rulings and General Counsel Memoranda).[22] "Authority" does not include conclusions reached in treatises, legal periodicals, and opinions rendered by tax professionals.

---

[20]*Severino R. Nico, Jr.,* 67 T.C. 647 (1977).

[21]The major citators are published by Commerce Clearing House, RIA, and Shepard's Citations, Inc.

[22]Reg. § 1.6661–3(b)(2).

A letter ruling or determination letter can be relied upon *only* by the taxpayer to whom it is issued, except as noted above with respect to the accuracy-related penalty.

2 *Find more information on this topic at our Web site:* ***http://wft-entities.swcollege.com.***

ARRIVING AT THE SOLUTION OR AT ALTERNATIVE SOLUTIONS

Example 4 raises the question of whether taxpayers would be denied a loss deduction from the sale of stock to a corporation that they own. The solution depends, in part, on the relationship of the corporation's shareholders to each other. Since Fred and Megan are married to each other, § 267(c)(2) attributes Megan's stock to Fred in applying the "more than 50 percent" test of § 267(b)(2). Accordingly, Fred and Maple, Inc. are considered related parties under § 267(a), and a sale between them does not provide a deductible loss. If Fred and Megan were not related to each other, the constructive stock ownership rules would not apply, and a loss could be deducted on a sale by Fred to Maple.

If Maple, Inc., were a *partnership* instead of a corporation, § 267 would not apply, per Regulation § 1.267(b)–1(b)(1). That Regulation, however, references a different Code Section, namely § 707, which produces the same result: no deduction of the loss from a sale between a "more than 50 percent" partner and the partnership. This additional research prevents Fred and Megan from erroneously selling their Airways stock to a partnership in hopes of obtaining a loss deduction from the sale. Accordingly, Fred must sell the Airways stock to an unrelated party in order to deduct the loss.

Since Fred still wants to own Airways stock, he might consider purchasing new Airways Co. stock to replace the stock he sells. Additional research reveals that for the loss on the sale to be deductible, § 1091 requires that 30 days elapse between the purchase of the new stock and the sale of the old stock. This section applies to purchases and sales of *substantially identical stock or securities*. As a result, to deduct the loss on the Airways stock, Fred must either wait at least 30 days after selling this stock to buy new Airways stock or acquire stock in a different company at any time. This new company can even be in the same general business as is Airways.[23]

COMMUNICATING TAX RESEARCH

LEARNING OBJECTIVE 3

Communicate the results of the tax research process in a client letter and a tax file memorandum.

Once the problem has been researched adequately, a memorandum, letter, or speech setting forth the result may need to be prepared. The form the communication takes could depend on a number of considerations. For example, does an employer or instructor recommend a particular procedure or format for tax research memos? Is the memo to be given directly to the client or will it first go to the preparer's employer? If the communication is a speech, who is the audience? How long should one speak?[24] Whatever form it takes, a good research communication should contain the following elements:

- A clear statement of the issue.
- In more complex situations, a short review of the fact pattern that raises the issue.

[23]Rev.Rul. 59–44, 1959–1 C.B. 205.
[24]See W. A. Raabe and G. E. Whittenburg, "Talking Tax: How to Make a Tax Presentation," *The Tax Adviser*, March 1997, pp. 179–182.

■ **FIGURE 2–6**
Tax File Memorandum

August 26, 2001

TAX FILE MEMORANDUM

FROM: John J. Jones

SUBJECT: Fred and Megan Taxpayer
                  Engagement: Issues

Today I talked to Fred Taxpayer with respect to his August 14, 2001 letter requesting tax assistance. He wishes to know if he can sell his stock in Airways Co. to Maple, Inc., and deduct the $2,500 loss on his Airways stock.

FACTS: Maple, Inc., is owned 50% by Fred and 50% by Megan. Fred wants to continue holding Airways stock in anticipation of a rebound in its value, and that is why he has asked about a proposed sale of this stock to Maple.

ISSUE: Can shareholders deduct a loss on the sale of an asset to a corporation all of whose stock they own?

ANALYSIS: Section 267(a) provides that no loss will be deductible on a sale or exchange between certain related parties. One of these relationships involves a corporation and a shareholder who owns "more than 50 percent" of that corporation's stock [see § 267(b)(2)]. Although Fred owns only 50% of Maple, Inc., his wife, Megan, owns the other 50%. The constructive ownership rule of § 267(c)(2) attributes stock held by family members, and a spouse is part of a taxpayer's family for this purpose, according to § 267(c)(4). Consequently, Megan's stock will be attributed to Fred, who is then treated as owning 100% of Maple, Inc. The related-party disallowance rule would then apply to the loss from Fred's selling his Airways stock to Maple. Accordingly, Fred must sell this stock to an unrelated party to make his loss deductible.

Since Fred really wants to retain an investment in Airways, he can purchase replacement stock either before or after he sells his original Airways stock. Section 1091(a), however, requires that at least 30 days elapse between the purchase and the sale, or the sale and the purchase, as the case may be. Moreover, for this purpose, an option to buy the stock is treated as equivalent to the stock itself. As a result, Fred must wait at least 30 days between transactions and cannot utilize stock options in the interim to minimize his stock market exposure.

A final alternative might be to replace the Airways stock with securities of a comparable company in the same industry. Although no two companies are exactly alike, there may be another company whose management philosophy, marketing strategy, and financial data are sufficiently similar to Airways to provide an equivalent return on investment. Under this alternative, Fred could acquire the new company's shares immediately without waiting the 30 days mandated by § 1091(a). Despite the two companies' investment similarity, they would not be treated as "substantially identical" for this purpose [see Rev.Rul. 59–44, 1959–1 C.B. 205].

CONCLUSION: Fred should *not* sell his Airways stock to Maple. Instead, he should sell this stock via his regular broker and either acquire new Airways stock at least 30 days before or after the date of sale, or acquire stock of a similar company whenever he chooses.

- A review of the pertinent tax law sources (e.g., Code, Regulations, Revenue Rulings, judicial authority).
- Any assumptions made in arriving at the solution.
- The solution recommended and the logic or reasoning supporting it.
- The references consulted in the research process.

Illustrations of the memo for the tax file and the client letter associated with Example 4 appear in Figures 2–6 and 2–7.

FOLLOW-UP PROCEDURES

Because tax research may involve a proposed (as opposed to a completed) transaction, a change in the tax law (either legislative, administrative, or judicial) could alter the original conclusion. Additional research may be necessary to test the solution in light of current developments (refer to the broken lines at the right in Figure 2–5).

■ **FIGURE 2–7**
Client Letter

Smith, Raabe, and Maloney, CPAs
5101 Madison Road
Cincinnati, OH 45227

August 30, 2001

Mr. and Ms. Fred Taxpayer
111 Boulevard
Williamsburg, Virginia 23185

Dear Mr. and Ms. Taxpayer:

This letter is in response to your request for us to review your family's financial and tax situation. Our conclusions are based upon the facts as outlined in your August 14th letter. Any change in the facts may affect our conclusions.

Mr. Taxpayer owns stock in Airways Co. that has declined in value, but he would like to retain this stock in anticipation of a rebound in its worth. You have proposed a sale of this stock at its current market value to Maple, Inc., a corporation owned 50–50 by Mr. and Mrs. Taxpayer. Such a sale, however, would not permit the loss to be deducted.

A better approach would be to sell the Airways stock before year-end and repurchase this stock through your regular stockbroker. Please understand that the loss will not be deductible unless at least 30 days elapse between the sale and the repurchase of the stock. You can either sell the old stock first and then buy the new stock, or buy the new stock first and then sell the old stock. However, it is essential that at least 30 days elapse between the sale and purchase transactions. Using options during this 30-day period is ineffective and will prevent the loss from being deducted in the current taxable year.

If the 30-day requirement is unacceptable, you might consider replacing the Airways stock with securities of some other company, perhaps even a company in the same general business as is Airways. Your regular stockbroker should be able to suggest appropriate possibilities. In that situation, your loss on the Airways stock can be deducted without regard to when you buy the new stock.

Should you need more information or need to clarify our conclusions, do not hesitate to contact me.

Sincerely yours,

John J. Jones, CPA
Partner

LEARNING OBJECTIVE 4

Have an awareness of computer-assisted tax research.

COMPUTER-ASSISTED TAX RESEARCH

Computer-based tax research tools hold a prominent position in tax practice. Electronic tax resources allow the tax library to better reflect the tax law's dynamic and daily changes. Nevertheless, using a computer to locate tax law sources cannot substitute for developing and maintaining a thorough knowledge of the tax law or for careful analysis when addressing tax research issues.

Accessing tax documents electronically offers several important advantages over a paper-based approach.

- Materials generally are available to the practitioner faster through an electronic system.
- Some tax documents, such as slip opinions of trial-level court cases and interviews with policymakers, are available *only* through electronic means.
- Commercial subscriptions to electronic tax services sometimes provide, at little or no cost, additional tax law sources to which the researcher would not have access through stand-alone purchases of traditional material. For example, the full text of private letter rulings is costly to acquire in a paper-based format, but electronic publishers may bundle the rulings with other materials for a reasonable cost.

■ **EXHIBIT 2–2**
Electronic Tax Services

Electronic Service	Description
CCH	Includes the CCH tax service, primary sources including treatises, and other subscription materials. Ten to 20 discs and online.
RIA	Includes primary sources, the *Federal Tax Coordinator*, and the *United States Tax Reporter*. The citator has elaborate document-linking features. Major tax treatises and other subscription materials are provided. One to 10 discs and online.
WESTLAW	Code, Regulations, *Cumulative Bulletins*, cases, citator, and editorial material are included. Twelve discs and online.
Kleinrock's	A single disc with statutory, administrative, and judicial tax law. Another disc provides tax forms and instructions for Federal and state jurisdictions.

Strict cost comparisons of paper and electronic tax research materials are difficult to make, especially when the practitioner uses computers that are already in place and employed elsewhere in the practice. Over time, however, the convenience, cost, and reliability of electronic research tools clearly make them the dominant means of finding and analyzing tax law.

Using Electronic Tax Services. Usually, tax professionals use one of the following strategies when performing computer-based tax research.

- *Search* various databases using keywords that are likely to be found in the underlying documents, as written by Congress, the judiciary, or administrative sources.
- *Link* to tax documents for which all or part of the proper citation is known.
- *Browse* the tax databases, examining various tables of contents and indexes in a traditional manner or using cross-references in the documents to jump from one tax law source to another.

Virtually all of the major commercial tax publishers and most of the primary sources of the law itself, such as the Supreme Court and some of the Courts of Appeals, provide tax material in a variety of electronic formats, including CD-ROM services and online services. Exhibit 2–2 summarizes the most popular of the electronic tax services on the market today.

CD-ROM Services. The CD-ROM has been a medium for tax data for about a decade. CCH, RIA, WESTLAW, and others offer vast tax libraries to the practitioner, often in conjunction with a subscription to traditional paper-based resources and accompanied by newsletters, training seminars, and ongoing technical support.

At its best, a CD-ROM tax library provides the archival data that make up a permanent, core library of tax documents. For about $200 a year, a CD-ROM is updated quarterly, providing more comprehensive tax resources than the researcher is ever likely to need. The CD-ROM is comparable in scope to a paper-based library of a decade ago costing perhaps $20,000 to establish and $5,000 per year in perpetuity to maintain. If the library is contained on a small number of discs, it also can offer portability through use on notebook computers.

TAX FACT

AN ELECTRONIC IRS

The IRS is pushing for greater numbers of taxpayers to file their tax returns electronically. For tax year 1998 about 20 percent of all individuals filed their Forms 1040 using one of the available electronic formats. From the taxpayer's standpoint, electronic filing offers several advantages.

- Electronic filing better matches taxpayers' increasingly computer-oriented lifestyles. As many taxpayers use software to manage their bank and brokerage accounts, the transfer of tax data among programs becomes more effective.
- Refunds are processed and paid more quickly. Thirty percent of returns receiving significant refunds and 40 percent of those using the earned income tax credit were e-filed.

The IRS benefits from electronic filing too.

- IRS computers capture all of the data submitted by an e-filing taxpayer, but only 40 percent from those filing returns on paper.
- The error rate for data entry into IRS computers is 2 percent for e-filed returns, but it is 20 percent for paper-based returns.

Increases in the use of e-filing are obvious, and such increases may be traceable to taxpayer familiarity with computer usage, approximated by taxpayer age.

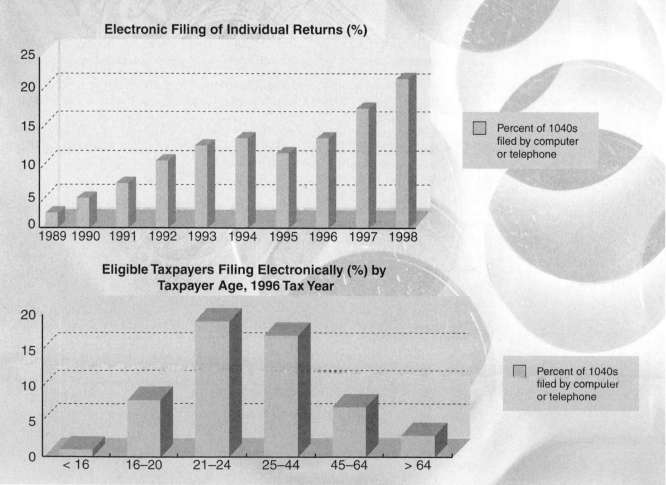

Electronic Filing of Individual Returns (%)

Legend: Percent of 1040s filed by computer or telephone

Eligible Taxpayers Filing Electronically (%) by Taxpayer Age, 1996 Tax Year

Legend: Percent of 1040s filed by computer or telephone

■ **EXHIBIT 2–3**
Online Tax Services

Online Service	Description
LEXIS/NEXIS	Includes Federal and state statutory, administrative, and judicial material. Extensive libraries of newspapers, magazines, patent records, and medical and economic databases, both U.S. and foreign-based.
RIA	Includes the RIA tax service, major tax treatises, Federal and state statutes, administrative documents, and court opinions. Extensive citator access, editorial material, and practitioner aids.
CCH	Includes the CCH tax service, primary sources including treatises, and other subscription materials. Tax and economic news sources, extensive editorial material, and practitioner support tools.
WESTLAW	Federal and state statutes, administrative documents, and court opinions. Extensive citator access, editorial material, and gateways to third-party publications. Extensive government document databases.

Online Services.   Online research systems allow practitioners to obtain virtually instantaneous use of tax law sources by accessing databases via a modem connection or via the Internet. Online services generally employ price-per-search cost structures, which can be as much as $200 per hour, significantly higher than the cost of CD materials. Thus, unless a practitioner can pass along related costs to clients or others, online searching generally is limited to the most important issues and to the researchers with the most experience and training in search techniques.

Perhaps the best combination of electronic tax resources is to conduct day-to-day work on a CD system, so that the budget for the related work is known in advance, and augment the CD search with online access where it is judged to be critical. Exhibit 2–3 provides details about the most commonly used commercial online tax services.

The Internet.   The Internet provides a wealth of tax information in several popular forms, sometimes at no direct cost to the researcher. Using web browser software and a modem, the tax professional can access information provided around the world that can aid the research process.

- *The World Wide Web (WWW)* provides access to a number of sites maintained by accounting and consulting firms, publishers, tax academics and libraries, and governmental bodies. The best sites offer links to other sites and direct contact to the site providers. Exhibit 2–4 lists some of the Web sites that may be most useful to tax researchers and their Internet addresses as of press date.
- *Newsgroups* provide a means by which information related to the tax law can be exchanged among taxpayers, tax professionals, and others who subscribe to the group's services. Newsgroup members can read the exchanges among other members and offer replies and suggestions to inquiries as desired. Discussions address the interpretation and application of existing law, analysis of proposals and new pronouncements, and reviews of tax software.

While tax information on the Internet is plentiful, freely accessed information should never be relied upon without referring to other, more reliable sources.

■ **EXHIBIT 2–4**
Tax-Related Web Sites

Web Site	WWW Address at Press Date	Description
Internal Revenue Service	http://www.irs.gov/	News releases, downloadable forms and instructions, tables, and e-mail.
Court opinions	http://www.law.emory.edu/FEDCTS/	Allows the researcher to link to the site of the jurisdiction (other than the Tax Court) that is the subject of the query.
Discussion groups moderated by Tax Analysts	http://www.tax.org/discuss/discussion.htm	Policy-oriented discussions of tax laws and proposals to change the law, links to student tax clinics, excerpts from the *Tax Notes* newsletter, and a tax calendar.
Tax Sites Directory	http://www.taxsites.com	References and links to tax sites on the Internet, including state and Federal tax sites, academic and professional pages, tax forms, and software.
Tax laws online	http://www4.law.cornell.edu/cfr/26cfrI.htm	Treasury Regulations.
	http://uscode.house.gov/title_26.htm	Internal Revenue Code.
Tax World	http://taxworld.org	References and links to tax sites on the Internet, including property tax and international tax links.
Commercial tax publishers	For example, http://www.taxlibrary.com and http://cch.com	Information about products and services available by subscription, and newsletter excerpts.
Large accounting firms and professional organizations	For example, the AICPA's page is at http://www.aicpa.org and an Ernst & Young LLP Tax Services page is at http://www.ey.com/home.asp	Tax planning newsletters, descriptions of services offered and career opportunities, and exchange of data with clients and subscribers.
South-Western College Publishing	http://www.swcollege.com/tax/tax.html	Informational updates, newsletters, support materials for students and adopters, and continuing education.
Tax Court decisions	http://www.ustaxcourt.gov/	Recent Tax Court decisions.

Caution: Addresses change frequently.

Always remember that anyone can set up a Web site and quality control is often lacking.

In many situations, solutions to research problems benefit from, or require, the use of various electronic tax research tools. A competent tax professional must become familiar and proficient with these tools and be able to use them to meet the expectations of clients and the necessities of work in the modern world.[25]

---

[25]For a more detailed discussion of the use of electronic tax research in the modern tax practice, see W. A. Raabe, G. E. Whittenburg, J. C. Bost, and D. L. Sanders, *West's Federal Tax Research*, 5th ed. (Cincinnati, OH: South-Western College Publishing, 2000).

Suggested Further Readings

Jack Baker, Randall K. Hanson, and James K. Smith, "Professions Clash on What Is 'Practice of Law,'" *Practical Tax Strategies*, May 1999, pp. 268–273.

David M. Cottrell and Ronald G. Worsham, "Internet Resources for International Tax Practitioners Are Emerging and Expanding," *Journal of International Taxation*, January 1997, pp. 10–37.

Dennis R. Schmidt, Roxanne M. Spindle, and William F. Yancey, "Tax Professional's Guide to Navigating Through Cyberspace," *Practical Tax Strategies*, June 1999, pp. 324–339.

KEY TERMS

Acquiescence, 2–17

Circuit Court of Appeals, 2–13

Court of Federal Claims, 2–12

Court of original jurisdiction, 2–12

Determination letters, 2–11

District Court, 2–12

Final Regulations, 2–9

Interpretive Regulations, 2–24

Legislative Regulations, 2–24

Letter rulings, 2–10

Nonacquiescence, 2–17

Precedents, 2–15

Procedural Regulations, 2–24

Proposed Regulations, 2–9

Revenue Procedures, 2–9

Revenue Rulings, 2–9

Small Cases Division, 2–12

Supreme Court, 2–15

Tax Court, 2–12

Technical Advice Memoranda (TAMs), 2–11

Temporary Regulations, 2–9

Writ of Certiorari, 2–15

Problem Materials

PROBLEMS

1. Judicial decisions interpreting a provision of the Internal Revenue Code of 1939 or 1954 are no longer of any value in view of the enactment of the Internal Revenue Code of 1986. Assess the validity of this statement.

2. Barbara Brown operates a small international firm named Mallard, Inc. A new treaty between the United States and Ukraine conflicts with a Section of the Internal Revenue Code. Barbara asks you for advice. If she follows the treaty position, does she need to disclose this on her tax return? If she is required to disclose, are there any penalties for failure to disclose? Prepare a letter in which you respond to Barbara. Mallard's address is 100 International Drive, Tampa, FL 33620.

3. Distinguish among legislative, interpretive, and procedural Regulations.

4. Distinguish between the following.
   a. Treasury Regulations and Revenue Rulings.
   b. Revenue Rulings and Revenue Procedures.

    c. Revenue Rulings and letter rulings.

    d. Letter rulings and determination letters.

5. Rank the following items from the highest authority to the lowest in the Federal tax law system.

    a. Interpretive Regulation.

    b. Legislative Regulation.

    c. Letter ruling.

    d. Revenue Ruling.

    e. Internal Revenue Code.

    f. Proposed Regulation.

6. Explain how Regulations are arranged. How would the following Regulations be cited?

    a. Finalized Regulations under § 61.

    b. Proposed Regulations under § 385.

    c. Temporary Regulations under § 163.

7. Interpret each of the following citations.

    a. Rev.Rul. 74–503, 1974–2 C.B. 11.

    b. Rev.Proc. 87–59, 1987–2 C.B. 764.

    c. Ltr.Rul. 8550037.

8. Which of the following would be considered advantages of the Small Cases Division of the Tax Court?

    a. Appeal to the Tax Court is possible.

    b. A hearing of a deficiency of $62,000 is considered on a timely basis.

    c. Taxpayer can handle the litigation without using a lawyer or certified public accountant.

    d. Taxpayer can use Small Cases Division decisions for precedential value.

    e. The actual hearing is conducted informally.

    f. Travel time will probably be reduced.

9. List an advantage and a disadvantage of using the Tax Court as the trial court for Federal tax litigation.

10. Carl Jensen is considering litigating a tax deficiency of approximately $274,000 in the court system. He asks you to provide him with a short description of his alternatives indicating the advantages and disadvantages of each. Prepare your response to Carl in the form of a letter. His address is 200 Mesa Drive, Tucson, AZ 85714.

11. A taxpayer lives in Michigan. In a controversy with the IRS, the taxpayer loses at the trial court level. Describe the appeal procedure for each of the following trial courts:

    a. Small Cases Division of the Tax Court.

    b. Tax Court.

    c. District Court.

    d. Court of Federal Claims.

12. Suppose the U.S. Government loses a tax case in the District Court of South Carolina and does not appeal the result. What does the failure to appeal signify?

13. For the Tax Court, District Court, and the Court of Federal Claims, indicate the following.

    a. Number of regular judges per court.

    b. Availability of a jury trial.

    c. Whether the deficiency must be paid before the trial.

14. In which of the following states could a taxpayer appeal the decision of a District Court to the Fifth Circuit Court of Appeals?

    a. Alabama.

    b. Arkansas.

    c. New York.

    d. South Carolina.

    e. Texas.

15. What is the Supreme Court's policy on hearing tax cases?

16. In assessing the validity of a prior court decision, discuss the significance of the following on the taxpayer's issue.
    a. The decision was rendered by the Central District Court of Illinois. Taxpayer lives in central Illlinois.
    b. The decision was rendered by the Court of Federal Claims. Taxpayer lives in Illinois.
    c. The decision was rendered by the Second Circuit Court of Appeals. Taxpayer lives in Illinois.
    d. The decision was rendered by the Supreme Court.
    e. The decision was rendered by the Tax Court. The IRS has acquiesced in the result.
    f. Same as (e), except that the IRS has nonacquiesced in the result.

17. What is the difference between a Regular and a Memorandum decision of the Tax Court?

18. Interpret each of the following citations.
    a. 54 T.C. 1514 (1970).
    b. 408 F.2d 117 (CA–2, 1969).
    c. 69–1 USTC ¶9319 (CA–2, 1969).
    d. 23 AFTR2d 69–1090 (CA–2, 1969).
    e. 293 F.Supp. 1129 (D.Ct.Miss., 1967).
    f. 67–1 USTC ¶9253 (D.Ct.Miss., 1967).
    g. 19 AFTR2d 647 (D.Ct.Miss., 1967).
    h. 56 S.Ct. 289 (USSC, 1935).
    i. 36–1 USTC ¶9020 (USSC, 1935).
    j. 16 AFTR 1274 (USSC, 1935).
    k. 422 F.2d 1336 (Ct.Cls., 1970).

19. Explain the following abbreviations.
    a. CA–2
    b. Fed.Cl.
    c. *aff'd.*
    d. *rev'd.*
    e. *rem'd.*
    f. *Cert. denied*
    g. *acq.*
    h. B.T.A.
    i. USTC
    j. AFTR
    k. F.3d
    l. F.Supp.
    m. USSC
    n. S.Ct.
    o. D.Ct.

20. Give the Commerce Clearing House citation for each of the following courts.
    a. Small Cases Division of the Tax Court.
    b. District Court.
    c. Supreme Court.
    d. Court of Federal Claims.
    e. Tax Court Memorandum decision.

21. Where can you locate a published decision of the Court of Federal Claims?

22. Which of the following items can probably be found in the *Cumulative Bulletin*?
    a. Action on Decision.
    b. Small Cases Division of the Tax Court decision.
    c. Letter ruling.
    d. Revenue Procedure.
    e. Final Regulation.
    f. Court of Appeals decision.
    g. Senate Finance Committee Report.
    h. Acquiescences to Tax Court decisions.
    i. U.S. Circuit Court of Appeals decision.

23. Answer the following questions based upon this citation: *United Draperies, Inc. v. Comm.*, 340 F.2d 936 (CA–7, 1964), *aff'g* 41 T.C. 457 (1963), *cert. denied* 382 U.S. 813 (1965).
    a. In which court did this decision first appear?
    b. Did the appellate court uphold the trial court?
    c. Who was the plaintiff?
    d. Did the Supreme Court uphold the appellate court decision?

24. As part of her coursework for a Masters of Tax degree, Ann is required to prepare a 30-page term paper about limited liability partnerships. Identify some relevant research steps Ann may take.

25. James has just been audited by the IRS and, as a result, has been assessed a substantial deficiency (which he has not yet paid) in additional income taxes. In preparing his defense, James advances the following possibilities.
    a. Although a resident of Texas, James plans to sue in a District Court in Oregon that appears to be more favorably inclined toward taxpayers.
    b. If (a) is not possible, James plans to take his case to a Texas state court where an uncle is the presiding judge.
    c. Since James has found a B.T.A. decision that seems to help his case, he plans to rely on it under alternative (a) or (b).
    d. If he loses at the trial court level, James plans to appeal to either the Court of Federal Claims or the Eleventh Circuit Court of Appeals because he has relatives in both Washington, D.C., and Atlanta. Staying with these relatives could save James lodging expense while his appeal is being heard by the court selected.
    e. Even if he does not win at the trial court or appeals court level, James feels certain of success on an appeal to the Supreme Court.

    Evaluate James's notions concerning the judicial process as it applies to Federal income tax controversies.

26. Using the legend provided, classify each of the following statements (more than one answer per statement may be appropriate).

    Legend

    D = Applies to the District Court
    T = Applies to the Tax Court
    C = Applies to the Court of Federal Claims
    A = Applies to the Circuit Court of Appeals
    U = Applies to the Supreme Court
    N = Applies to none of the above

    a. Decides only Federal tax matters.
    b. Decisions are reported in the F.3d Series.
    c. Decisions are reported in the USTCs.
    d. Decisions are reported in the AFTRs.
    e. Appeal is by *Writ of Certiorari*.
    f. Court meets most often in Washington, D.C.
    g. Offers the choice of a jury trial.
    h. Is a trial court.
    i. Is an appellate court.
    j. Allows appeal to the Federal Circuit Court of Appeals and bypasses the taxpayer's particular Circuit Court of Appeals.
    k. Has a Small Cases Division.
    l. Is the only trial court where the taxpayer does not have to first pay the tax assessed by the IRS.

27. Using the legend provided, classify each of the following citations as to the type of court.

    Legend

    D = Applies to the District Court
    T = Applies to the Tax Court
    C = Applies to the Court of Federal Claims
    A = Applies to the Circuit Court of Appeals
    U = Applies to the Supreme Court
    N = Applies to none of the above

    a. 388 F.2d 420 (CA–7, 1968).
    b. 79 T.C. 7 (1982).
    c. 54 S.Ct. 8 (USSC, 1933).
    d. 3 B.T.A. 1042 (1926).
    e. T.C.Memo. 1954–141.
    f. 597 F.2d 760 (Ct.Cl., 1979).
    g. Ltr.Rul. 9414051.
    h. 465 F.Supp. 341 (D.Ct.Okla., 1978).
    i. Rev.Rul. 93–1.

28. Using the legend provided, classify each of the following tax sources.

    Legend

    P = Primary tax source
    S = Secondary tax source
    B = Both
    N = Neither

    a. Sixteenth Amendment to the Constitution.
    b. Tax Treaty between the United States and Spain.
    c. Revenue Procedure.
    d. General Counsel Memoranda (1989).
    e. Tax Court memorandum decision.
    f. *Journal of Taxation* article.
    g. Temporary Regulations (2000).
    h. Tax Court regular decision.
    i. Small Cases Division of the Tax Court decision.
    j. House Ways and Means Committee Report.

29. An accountant friend of yours tells you that he "almost never" does any tax research, because he feels that "research usually reveals that some tax planning idea has already been thought up and shot down." Besides, he points out, most tax returns are never audited by the IRS. Can a tax adviser who is dedicated to reducing his client's tax liability justify the effort to engage in tax research? Do professional ethics *demand* such efforts? Which approach would a client probably prefer?

30. Another friend of yours, who is a philosophy major, has overheard the conversation described in the previous problem and declares that all tax research is "immoral." She says that tax research enables people with substantial assets to shift the burden of financing public expenditures to those who "get up every morning, go to work, play by the rules, and pay their bills." How do you respond?

31. Some politicians have suggested that the United States should replace the Federal income tax with a national sales tax or other consumption-based levy that would be collected at the point of purchase. Such a system, its advocates say, would make tax

planning unnecessary and render tax research skills obsolete. How would you respond to a client that has asked you for your evaluation of this proposal?

 32. Under what circumstances can court decisions lead to changes in the Code?

EXTENDER 33. Locate the following Code provisions and give a brief description of each.
   a. § 61(a)(13).
   b. § 643(a)(2).
   c. § 2503(g)(2)(A).

BRIDGE DISCIPLINE

1. Comment on these statements.
   a. The tax law is created and administered in the same way as other Federal provisions.
   b. Most taxpayers find it too expensive and time-consuming to sue the government in a tax dispute.

RESEARCH PROBLEMS

*Note: Solutions to Research Problems can be prepared by using the **RIA Checkpoint® Student Version Online research product,** or the **CCH U.S. Master Tax Guide Plus™** online Federal tax research database, which is available to accompany this text. It is also possible to prepare solutions to the Research Problems by using tax research materials found in a standard tax library.*

Research Problem 1.   Determine the general topics of the following subchapters in Chapter 1, Subtitle A of the Internal Revenue Code of 1986.
   a. B.
   b. D.
   c. F.
   d. K.
   e. P.

Research Problem 2.   Locate the following Code citations and give a brief topical description of each.
   a. § 708(a).
   b. § 1371(a)(1).
   c. § 2503(a).

Research Problem 3.   Locate the following Regulations and give a brief topical description of each.
   a. Reg. § 1.170A–4A(b)(2)(ii)(C).
   b. Reg. § 1.672(b)–1.
   c. Reg. § 20.2031–7(f).

Research Problem 4.   Find Rev.Rul. 78–325, 1978–2 C.B. 124 and describe its content.

Research Problem 5.   Complete the following citations.
   a. *Tupper v. U.S.*, 134 F.3d ____ (CA–1, 1998).
   b. *Corn Products Refining Co. v. Comm.*, 350 U.S. ____ (USSC, 1955).
   c. *Walter J. Nicholls*, T.C.Memo. 1995–____.
   d. Rev.Rul. 78–____, 1978–2 C.B. 124.
   e. Rev.Proc. 95–1, 1995–1 C.B. ____.
   f. *Max Sobel Wholesale Liquors*, 69 T.C. ____ (1977), aff'd 630 F.2d ____ (CA–9, 1980).
   g. *Ruhland v. U.S.*, 839 F.Supp. 993 (D.Ct. ____, 1993).

Research Problem 6.   Find *Daubert v. Merrell Dow Pharmaceuticals, Inc.*, 509 U.S. 579 (1993) and answer these questions.
   a. Who were the petitioners (plaintiffs)?
   b. Who was the respondent (defendant)?
   c. Who delivered the opinion for the Court?

      d. Who filed a concurring opinion?

      e. What was the major issue?

      f. What was the overall opinion?

Research Problem 7. Go to page 174 in the March 2000 issue of *The Tax Adviser*. Who are the authors and what is the title of the article that starts on this page? Give a short summary of this article.

Use the tax resources of the Internet to address the following questions. Do not restrict your search to the World Wide Web, but include a review of newsgroups and general reference materials, practitioner sites and resources, primary sources of the tax law, chat rooms and discussion groups, and other opportunities.

Research Problem 8. Go to each of the following Internet locations.

      a. Several primary sources of the tax law, including the U.S. Supreme Court, a Circuit Court of Appeals, the Internal Revenue Service, and final Regulations.

      b. Sources of proposed Federal tax legislation.

      c. A collection of tax rules for your state.

Research Problem 9. Go to each of the following Internet locations.

      a. Several newspapers and magazines, such as *USA Today*, the *New York Times*, the *Washington Post*, *Newsweek* magazine, your local newspaper, and a local television station.

      b. Other news sources such as *CNN Interactive*, Newspapers OnLine, and a collection of online versions of magazines.

Research Problem 10. Go to each of the following Internet locations.

      a. The American Institute of CPAs, the American Taxation Association, several tax-related newsgroups, and tax information provided by enrolled agents.

      b. *Tax World*, the *Tax Prophet*, *Taxing Times*, and *Tax Sites*.

      c. Home pages for the professor of your course, PricewaterhouseCoopers LLP, Ernst & Young LLP, Deloitte & Touche LLP, a local tax consulting firm, and a local tax law firm.

Gross Income

LEARNING OBJECTIVES

After completing Chapter 3, you should be able to:

1. Explain the concepts of gross income and realization and distinguish between the economic, accounting, and tax concepts of gross income.

2. Understand when the cash, accrual, and hybrid methods of accounting are used and how they are applied.

3. Identify who should pay the tax on an item of income.

4. Understand that statutory authority is required to exclude an item from gross income.

5. Apply the Internal Revenue Code provisions on loans made at below-market interest rates.

6. Determine the extent to which receipts can be excluded under the tax benefit rule.

7. Understand the Internal Revenue Code provision that excludes interest on state and local government obligations from gross income.

8. Understand the Internal Revenue Code provision that excludes leasehold improvements from gross income.

9. Determine the extent to which life insurance proceeds are excluded from gross income.

10. Describe the circumstances under which income must be reported from the discharge of indebtedness.

11. Describe the tax consequences of property transactions.

Outline

TAX TALK *The first nine pages of the Internal Revenue Code define income. The remaining 1,100 pages spin the web of exceptions and preferences.*

—Warren G. Magnuson

Mary purchases a number of computer components from a supplier for $500. She hires an employee to assemble them into a computer that has a market value of $1,100. Keith, one of Mary's long-time customers, has been especially effective in sending new business to Mary's operation, so Mary sells the computer to Keith for $950. Direct labor costs for the computer totaled $150, and an allocable share of Mary's overhead for the current sale was determined to be $40.

Keith called in his order on December 15, 2001. Because he was going to be out of town, though, Keith told Mary to bring the computer to his office on January 6, 2002. The computer was fully assembled on December 22, 2001, but Mary delivered the machine on January 6, 2002.

Mary does business in a storefront in the local strip mall, using the name Home-Made Computers. Home-Made is a partnership, owned equally by Mary and her sister Sherry.

Some variation of this simple scenario is carried out millions of times every day in today's global economy. Several broad tax questions, such as the following, arise as a result of these transactions.

- What: What is income?
- When: In which tax period is the income recognized?
- Who: Who is taxed on the income?

The Tax Formula

The basic income tax formula is introduced in Chapter 1 and summarized in Figure 1–1. This chapter, together with Chapters 4 through 8, examines the elements of this formula in detail. However, before embarking on a detailed study of the income tax, a brief introduction of each component of the tax formula is provided below as an overview.

COMPONENTS OF THE TAX FORMULA

Income (Broadly Conceived). This includes all of the taxpayer's income, both taxable and nontaxable. Although it is essentially equivalent to gross receipts, it does not include a return of capital or borrowed funds.

Exclusions. For various reasons, Congress has chosen to exclude certain types of income from the income tax base. The principal income exclusions that apply to all entities (e.g., life insurance proceeds received by reason of death of the insured and state and local bond interest) are discussed later in this chapter, while exclusions that are unique to individuals are addressed in Chapters 15 and 16.

Gross Income. Section 61 of Internal Revenue Code provides the following definition of **gross income.**

> Except as otherwise provided in this subtitle, gross income means all income from whatever source derived.

This language is derived from the Sixteenth Amendment to the Constitution. The "except as otherwise provided" phrase refers to exclusions.

Supreme Court decisions have made it clear that *all* sources of income are subject to tax unless Congress specifically excludes the type of income received.

> The starting point in all cases dealing with the question of the scope of what is included in "gross income" begins with the basic premise that the purpose of Congress was to use the full measure of its taxing power.[1]

While it is clear that income is to be broadly construed, the statutory law fails to provide a satisfactory definition of the term and lists only a small set of items that are specifically included in income, including:

- Compensation for services.
- Business income.
- Gains from sales and other disposition of property.
- Interest.
- Dividends.
- Rents and royalties.
- Certain income arising from discharge of indebtedness.
- Income from partnerships.

Deductions. Generally, all ordinary and necessary trade or business expenses are deductible by taxpaying entities. Such expenses include the cost of goods sold, salaries, wages, operating expenses (such as rent and utilities), research and development expenditures, interest, taxes, depreciation, amortization, and depletion.

As noted in Chapter 1, individuals can use two categories of deductions— deductions *for* AGI and deductions *from* AGI. In addition, individuals are unique among taxpaying entities in that they are permitted to deduct a variety of personal expenses (i.e., expenses unrelated to business or investment), they are allowed a standard deduction if this amount exceeds the deductible personal expenses, and they are allowed a deduction for personal and dependency exemptions.

---

[1]*James v. U.S.*, 61–1 USTC ¶9449, 7 AFTR2d 1361, 81 S.Ct. 1052 (USSC, 1961).

Determining the Tax.   Taxable income is determined by subtracting deductions (after any applicable limitations) from gross income. The tax rates (located inside the front cover of this text) are then applied to determine the tax. Finally, tax prepayments (such as Federal income tax withholding on salaries and estimated tax payments) and a wide variety of credits are subtracted from the tax to determine the amount due to the Federal government or the refund due to the taxpayer.

LEARNING OBJECTIVE 1

Explain the concepts of gross income and realization and distinguish between the economic, accounting, and tax concepts of gross income.

Gross Income—What Is It?

ECONOMIC AND ACCOUNTING CONCEPTS OF INCOME

As noted above, Congress failed to provide in the Code a clear definition of income. Instead, it was left to the judicial and administrative branches of government to thrash out the meaning of income. As the income tax law developed, two competing models of income were considered by these agencies: economic income and accounting income.

The term **income** is used in the Code but is defined very broadly. Early in the history of our tax laws, the courts were required to interpret "the commonly understood meaning of the term which must have been in the minds of the people when they adopted the Sixteenth Amendment."[2]

Economists measure income (**economic income**) by determining the change (increase or decrease) in the fair market value of the entity's net assets from the beginning to the end of the year. This focus on change in *net worth* as a measure of income (or loss) requires no disposition of assets. For *individual* taxpayers, one adds the value of the year's personal consumption of goods and services (e.g., food, the rental value of owner-occupied housing, etc.).[3]

EXAMPLE 1

Helen's economic income is calculated by comparing her net worth at the end of the year (December 31) with her net worth at the beginning of the year (January 1) and adding her personal consumption.

Fair market value of Helen's assets on December 31	$220,000	
Less liabilities on December 31	(40,000)	
Net worth on December 31		$ 180,000
Fair market value of Helen's assets on January 1	$200,000	
Less liabilities on January 1	(80,000)	
Net worth on January 1		(120,000)
Increase in net worth		$ 60,000
Consumption		
Food, clothing, and other personal expenditures	25,000	
Imputed rental value of the home Helen owns and occupies	12,000	
Total consumption		37,000
Economic income		$ 97,000

∎

---

[2]*Merchants Loan and Trust Co. v. Smietanka*, 1 USTC ¶42, 3 AFTR 3102, 41 S.Ct. 386 (USSC, 1921).

[3]See Henry C. Simons, *Personal Income Taxation* (Chicago: University of Chicago Press, 1933), Chapters 2–3.

ₐ ᵣ ᵢ ᴅ ᴳ ᴱ   ᴰ ᴵ ˢ ᶜ ᴵ ᴾ ᴸ ᴵ ₙ ₑ

Bridge to Financial Accounting

Accountants use a definition of income that relies on the realization principle.[4] **Accounting income** is not recognized until it is realized. For realization to occur:

- An exchange of goods or services must take place between the entity and some independent, external party, and
- The goods or services received by the entity must be capable of being objectively valued.[5]

Thus, an increase in the fair market value of an asset before its sale or other disposition is *not* sufficient to trigger the recognition of accounting income. Similarly, the imputed savings that arise when an entity creates assets for its own use (e.g., feed grown by a farmer for his or her livestock) do not constitute accounting income because no exchange has occurred.

Business taxpayers often reconcile their annual income computations derived for financial accounting and tax law purposes. Taxpayers required to prepare audited financial statements must explain in the footnotes to the statements (1) the most important accounting principles used in computing book income, and (2) the most important tax elections and other consequences of the tax law on earnings per share.

The tax law relies to some extent on net worth as a measure of income.[6] Potentially, anything that increases net worth is income, and anything that decreases net worth is deductible (if permitted by statute). Thus, *windfall income* such as buried treasure found in one's backyard is taxable under the theory that net worth has been increased.[7] Likewise, a lender does *not* recognize gross income on receipt of loan principal repayments. The lender's investment simply changes from a loan receivable to cash, so net worth does not change.

Because the strict application of a tax based on economic income would require taxpayers to determine the value of their assets annually, compliance would be burdensome. Controversies between taxpayers and the IRS would inevitably arise under an economic approach to income determination because of the subjective nature of valuation in many circumstances. In addition, using market values to determine income for tax purposes could result in liquidity problems. That is, a taxpayer's assets could increase in value but not be easily converted into the cash needed to pay the resulting tax (e.g., increases in the value of commercial real estate).[8] Thus, the IRS, Congress, and the courts have rejected broad application of the economic income concept as impractical.

COMPARISON OF THE ACCOUNTING AND TAX CONCEPTS OF INCOME

Although income tax rules frequently parallel financial accounting measurement concepts, differences do exist. Of major significance, for example, is the fact that

---

[4]See the American Accounting Association Committee Report on the "Realization Concept," *The Accounting Review* (April 1965): 312–322.
[5]Valuation is carried out in the local currency of the reporting entity.
[6]*Comm. v. Glenshaw Glass Co.*, 55–1 USTC ¶9308, 47 AFTR 162, 348 U.S. 426 (USSC, 1955).

[7]*Cesarini v. U.S.*, 69–1 USTC ¶9270, 23 AFTR2d 69–997, 296 F.Supp. 3 (D.Ct. Oh., 1969), *aff'd* 70–2 USTC ¶9509, 26 AFTR2d 70–5107, 428 F.2d 812 (CA–6, 1970); Rev.Rul. 61, 1953–1 C.B. 17.
[8]In Chapter 1, this was identified as a justification of the wherewithal to pay concept.

A FREE COMPUTER MAY NOT BE FREE

Ford Motor Company, American Airlines, Delta Airlines, and Intel have offered free computers to an estimated 600,000 of their workers. However, the deal may not be as good as originally anticipated. Under the broad concept of gross income, it appears that the employees must include the value of the computers in gross income. A typical employee would owe $560 in tax on the receipt of a $2,000 computer. Legislation has been introduced in Congress that would exclude the receipt of a computer from an employee's gross income if the following conditions are satisfied.

- The company offers a free computer to each employee working in the United States.
- The employee receives only one such free computer every 36 months.

The exclusion would be limited to $1,260.

SOURCE: Adapted from the Associated Press, "Tax-Free Gift to Employees a Possibility," *Roanoke Times*, May 10, 2000, pp. A5, A6.

unearned (prepaid) income received by an accrual basis taxpayer often is taxed in the year of receipt. For financial accounting purposes, such prepayments are not treated as income until earned. Because of this and other differences, many corporations report financial accounting income that is substantially different from the amounts reported for tax purposes.

The Supreme Court provided an explanation for some of the variations between accounting and taxable income in a decision involving inventory and bad debt adjustments.

> The primary goal of financial accounting is to provide useful information to management, shareholders, creditors, and others properly interested; the major responsibility of the accountant is to protect these parties from being misled. The primary goal of the income tax system, in contrast, is the equitable collection of revenue. . . . Consistently with its goals and responsibilities, financial accounting has as its foundation the principle of conservatism, with its corollary that "possible errors in measurement [should] be in the direction of understatement rather than overstatement of net income and net assets." In view of the Treasury's markedly different goals and responsibilities, understatement of income is not destined to be its guiding light. . . .
>
> Financial accounting, in short, is hospitable to estimates, probabilities, and reasonable certainties; the tax law, with its mandate to preserve the revenue, can give no quarter to uncertainty.[9]

FORM OF RECEIPT

Gross income is not limited to cash received. "It includes income realized in any form, whether in money, property, or services. Income may be realized [and recognized], therefore, in the form of services, meals, accommodations, stock or other property, as well as in cash."[10]

---

[9]*Thor Power Tool Co. v. Comm.*, 79–1 USTC ¶9139, 43 AFTR2d 79–362, 99 S.Ct. 773 (USSC, 1979).

[10]Reg. § 1.61–1(a).

EXAMPLE 2	Ostrich Corporation allows Cameron, an employee, to use a company car for his vacation. Cameron realizes income equal to the rental value of the car for the time and mileage. ■
EXAMPLE 3	Plover, Inc., owes $10,000 on a mortgage. The creditor accepts $8,000 in full satisfaction of the debt. Plover realizes income of $2,000 from retiring the debt.[11] ■
EXAMPLE 4	Donna is a CPA specializing in individual tax return preparation. Her neighbor, Jill, is a dentist. Each year, Donna prepares Jill's tax return in exchange for two dental checkups. Jill and Donna both have gross income equal to the fair market value of the services they provide. ■

Year of Inclusion

TAXABLE YEAR

The annual accounting period or **taxable year** is a basic component of our tax system. Generally, an entity must use the *calendar year* to report its income. However, a *fiscal year* (a period of 12 months ending on the last day of any month other than December) can be elected if the taxpayer maintains adequate books and records. This fiscal year option generally is not available to partnerships, S corporations, and personal service corporations.

Determining the tax year in which the income is recognized is important for determining the tax consequences of the income.

- With a progressive tax rate system, a taxpayer's marginal tax rate can change from year to year.
- Congress may change the tax rates.
- The relevant rates may change because of a change in the entity's status (e.g., a proprietorship may incorporate).
- Several provisions in the Code depend on the taxpayer's income for the year (e.g., the charitable contribution deduction).

LEARNING OBJECTIVE 2

Understand when the cash, accrual, and hybrid methods of accounting are used and how they are applied.

ACCOUNTING METHODS

The year in which an item of income is subject to tax often depends upon the **accounting method** the taxpayer employs. The three primary methods of accounting are (1) the cash receipts and disbursements method, (2) the accrual method, and (3) the hybrid method. Most individuals use the cash receipts and disbursements method of accounting, whereas most corporations use the accrual method. Because the Regulations require the accrual method for determining purchases and sales when inventory is an income-producing factor,[12] some businesses employ a hybrid method that is a combination of the cash and accrual methods.

In addition to these overall accounting methods, a taxpayer may choose to spread the gain from an installment sale of property over the collection period by using the *installment method* of income recognition. Contractors may either spread profits from contracts over the period in which the work is done (the *percentage of completion method*) or defer all profit until the year in which the project is completed (the *completed contract method*) in limited circumstances.[13]

---

[11]Reg. § 1.61–12. See *U.S. v. Kirby Lumber Co.*, 2 USTC ¶814, 10 AFTR 458, 52 S.Ct. 4 (USSC, 1931). Exceptions to this general rule exist.

[12]Reg. § 1.446–1(c)(2)(i).

[13]§§ 453 and 460.

The IRS has the power to prescribe the accounting method to be used by the taxpayer. The IRS holds broad powers to determine if the accounting method used *clearly reflects income.*

> If no method of accounting has been regularly used by the taxpayer, or *if the method used does not clearly reflect income, the computation of taxable income shall be made under such method as, in the opinion of the Secretary . . . does clearly reflect income.*[14]

Cash Receipts Method. Under the **cash receipts method,** property or services received are included in the taxpayer's gross income in the year of actual or constructive receipt by the taxpayer or agent, regardless of whether the income was earned in that year.[15] The income received need not be reduced to cash in the same year. All that is necessary for income recognition is that property or services received have a fair market value—a cash equivalent.[16] Thus, a cash basis taxpayer that receives a note in payment for services has income in the year of receipt equal to the fair market value of the note. However, a creditor's mere promise to pay (e.g., an account receivable), with no supporting note, is not usually considered to have a fair market value.[17] Thus, the cash basis taxpayer defers income recognition until the account receivable is collected.

EXAMPLE 5

Finch & Thrush, a CPA firm, uses the cash receipts method of accounting. In 2001, the firm performs an audit for Orange Corporation and bills the client for $5,000, which is collected in 2002. In 2001, the firm also performs an audit for Blue Corporation. Because of Blue's precarious financial position, Finch & Thrush requires Blue to issue an $8,000 secured negotiable note in payment of the fee. The note has a fair market value of $6,000. The firm collects $8,000 on the note in 2002. Finch & Thrush has the following gross income for the two years.

	2001	2002
Fair market value of note received from Blue	$6,000	
Cash received		
From Orange on account receivable		$ 5,000
From Blue on note receivable		8,000
Less: Recovery of capital	–0–	(6,000)
Total gross income	$6,000	$ 7,000

Generally, a check received is considered a cash equivalent. Thus, a cash basis taxpayer must recognize the income when the check is received. This is true even if the taxpayer receives the check after banking hours.[18]

Certain taxpayers are not permitted to use the cash method of accounting regardless of whether inventories are material. Specifically, the accrual basis must be used to report the income earned by (1) corporations (other than S corporations), (2) partnerships with a corporate partner, and (3) tax shelters.[19] A number of other businesses still can use the cash method. Included are:[20]

---

[14]§ 446(b).

[15]*Julia A. Strauss,* 2 B.T.A. 598 (1925). The doctrine of *constructive receipt* holds that if income is unqualifiedly available although not physically in the taxpayer's possession, it is subject to the income tax. An example is accrued interest on a savings account. Under the doctrine of constructive receipt, the interest is taxed to a depositor in the year available, rather than the year actually withdrawn. The

fact that the depositor uses the cash basis of accounting for tax purposes is irrelevant. Reg. § 1.451–2.

[16]Reg. §§ 1.446–1(a)(3) and (c)(1)(i).

[17]*Bedell v. Comm.,* 1 USTC ¶359, 7 AFTR 8469, 30 F.2d 622 (CA–2, 1929).

[18]*Charles F. Kahler,* 18 T.C. 31 (1952).

[19]§ 448(a).

[20]§ 448(b).

use cash basis

- A farming business.
- A qualified personal service corporation (e.g., a corporation performing services in health, law, engineering, architecture, accounting, actuarial science, performing arts, or consulting).
- Any entity that is not a tax shelter whose average annual gross receipts for the most recent three-year period are $5 million or less.

PLANNING CONSIDERATIONS

Cash Receipts Method

The timing of income from services can often be controlled through the cash method of accounting. Although taxpayers are somewhat constrained by the constructive receipt doctrine, seldom will customers and clients offer to pay before they are asked. The usual lag between billings and collections (e.g., December's billings collected in January) will result in a deferral of some income until the last year of operations. For example, before rendering services, a corporate officer approaching retirement may contract with the corporation to defer a portion of his or her compensation to the lower tax bracket retirement years.

Accrual Method.   Under the **accrual method,** an item generally is included in gross income for the year in which it is earned, regardless of when the income is collected. The income is earned when (1) all the events have occurred that fix the right to receive the income and (2) the amount to be received can be determined with reasonable accuracy.[21]

Generally, the taxpayer's rights to the income accrue when title to property passes to the buyer or the services are performed for the customer or client.[22] If the rights to the income have accrued but are subject to a potential refund claim (e.g., under a product warranty), the income is reported in the year of sale, and a deduction is allowed in subsequent years when actual claims accrue.[23]

Where the taxpayer's rights to the income are being contested (e.g., when a contractor fails to meet specifications), gross income is recognized only when payment has been received.[24] If the payment is received before the dispute is settled, however, the court-made **claim of right doctrine** requires the taxpayer to recognize the income in the year of receipt.[25]

EXAMPLE 6

Tangerine Construction, Inc., completes construction of a building in 2001 and presents a bill to the customer. The customer refuses to pay the bill and claims that Tangerine has not met specifications. A settlement with the customer is not reached until 2002. No income accrues to Tangerine until 2002. Alternatively, if the customer pays for the work and then files suit for damages, Tangerine cannot defer the income, and it is taxable in 2001. ■

EXAMPLE 7

Assume the same facts as in Example 5, except that Finch & Thrush uses the accrual basis of accounting. The firm must recognize $13,000 ($8,000 + $5,000) income in 2001, the year its rights to the income accrue. ■

---

[21]Reg. § 1.451–1(a).

[22]*Lucas v. North Texas Lumber Co.,* 2 USTC ¶484, 8 AFTR 10276, 50 S.Ct. 184 (USSC, 1930).

[23]*Brown v. Helvering,* 4 USTC ¶1222, 13 AFTR 851, 54 S.Ct. 356 (USSC, 1933).

[24]*Burnet v. Sanford and Brooks,* 2 USTC ¶636, 9 AFTR 603, 51 S.Ct. 150 (USSC, 1931).

[25]*North American Oil Consolidated Co. v. Burnet,* 3 USTC ¶943, 11 AFTR 16, 52 S.Ct. 613 (USSC, 1932).

Hybrid Method. The Regulations require that the accrual method be used for determining sales and cost of goods sold. To simplify record keeping, some taxpayers account for inventory using the accrual method and use the cash method for all other income and expense items. This approach, called the **hybrid method,** is used primarily by small businesses when inventory is an income-producing factor.

SPECIAL RULES FOR CASH BASIS TAXPAYERS

Constructive Receipt. Income that has not actually been received by the taxpayer is taxed as though it had been received—the income is constructively received—under the following conditions.

- The amount is made readily available to the taxpayer.
- The taxpayer's actual receipt is not subject to substantial limitations or restrictions.[26]

The rationale for the **constructive receipt** doctrine is that if the income is available, the taxpayer should not be allowed to postpone income recognition. For instance, a taxpayer is not permitted to defer income for December services by refusing to accept payment until January.

EXAMPLE 8

Rob, a physician, conducts his medical practice as a sole proprietorship. Rob is also a member of a barter club. In 2001, Rob provided medical care for other club members and earned 1,000 points. Each point entitles him to $1 in goods and services sold by other members of the club; the points can be used at any time. In 2002, Rob exchanged his points for a new color TV. Rob recognizes $1,000 of gross income in 2001 when the 1,000 points were credited to his account.[27] ■

EXAMPLE 9

On December 31, an employer issued a bonus check to an employee but asked her to hold it for a few days until the company could make deposits to cover the check. The income was not constructively received on December 31 since the issuer did not have sufficient funds in its account to pay the debt.[28] ■

EXAMPLE 10

Mauve, Inc., an S corporation, owned interest coupons that matured on December 31. The coupons can be converted to cash at any bank at maturity. Thus, the income was constructively received on December 31, even though Mauve failed to cash in the coupons until the following year.[29] ■

EXAMPLE 11

Flamingo Company mails dividend checks on December 31, 2001. The checks will not be received by the shareholders until January. The shareholders do not realize gross income until 2002.[30] ■

The constructive receipt doctrine does not reach income that the taxpayer is not yet entitled to receive even though the taxpayer could have contracted to receive the income at an earlier date.

EXAMPLE 12

Murphy offered to pay Peach Corporation (a cash basis taxpayer) $100,000 for land in December 2001. Peach Corporation refused but offered to sell the land to Murphy on January

---

[26]Reg. § 1.451–2(a).
[27]Rev.Rul. 80–52, 1980–1 C.B. 100.
[28]*L. M. Fischer,* 14 T.C. 792 (1950).

[29]Reg. § 1.451–2(b).
[30]Reg. § 1.451–2(b).

CONGRESS RESCUES LOTTERY WINNERS FROM CONSTRUCTIVE RECEIPT PROBLEMS

Under the general rules of constructive receipt, a lottery winner who elected to receive the winnings in installments could face horrendous tax problems. If the winner had the right to receive the entire amount, but elected to be paid in installments, tax was due on all the amounts to be received in the future as well as the amount received currently. Frequently, the winner made the election without being aware of the tax consequences. To protect poorly advised, or unadvised, lottery winners, Congress changed § 451(h) so that the constructive receipt doctrine will not apply to "qualified prizes," a term crafted specifically to address the lottery and prize winner's situation. Thus, lottery winnings can be received in installments and included in gross income as the installments are actually received.

1, 2002, when the corporation would be in a lower tax bracket. If Murphy accepts Peach's offer, the gain is taxed to Peach in 2002 when the sale is completed.[31] ■

Original Issue Discount. Lenders frequently make loans that require a payment at maturity of more than the amount of the original loan. The difference between the amount due at maturity and the amount of the original loan is actually interest but is referred to as **original issue discount.** Under the general rules of tax accounting, a cash basis lender would not report the original issue discount as interest income until the year the amount is collected, although an accrual basis borrower would deduct the interest as it is earned. However, the Code puts the lender and borrower on parity by requiring that the original issue discount be reported when it is earned, regardless of the taxpayer's accounting method.[32] The *interest earned* is calculated by the effective interest rate method.

EXAMPLE 13

On January 1, 2001, Blue and White, a cash basis partnership, pays $82,645 for a 24-month certificate of deposit. The certificate is priced to yield 10% (the effective interest rate) with interest compounded annually. No interest is paid until maturity, when Blue and White receives $100,000. Thus, the partnership's gross income from the certificate is $17,355 ($100,000 – $82,645). Blue and White calculates income earned each year as follows.

2001: (0.10 × $82,645) =	$ 8,264
2002: [0.10($82,645 + $8,264)] =	9,091
	$17,355

■

The original issue discount rules do not apply to U.S. savings bonds or to obligations with a maturity date of one year or less from the date of issue.[33]

Amounts Received under an Obligation to Repay. The receipt of funds with an obligation to repay that amount in the future is the essence of borrowing.

---

[31]*Cowden v. Comm.,* 61–1 USTC ¶9382, 7 AFTR2d 1160, 289 F.2d 20 (CA–5, 1961).

[32]§§ 1272(a)(3) and 1273(a).

[33]§ 1272(a)(2).

```
TAX IN THE NEWS
```

ORIGINAL ISSUE DISCOUNT RULES MAY DAMPEN ENTHUSIASM FOR INFLATION-ADJUSTED BONDS

The U.S. Treasury Department now sells inflation-adjusted bonds. The bonds are aimed at small investors looking for a hedge against inflation. The interest paid each year and the principal are adjusted to reflect the effects of inflation. These bonds present some unique tax accounting issues. In particular, while the interest payment is clearly income, how should the annual adjustment to principal be taxed?

In Temporary Regulation § 1.1275–7T, the Treasury Department concluded that the taxpayer is required to treat the adjustment to principal as original issue discount amortized during the year. For example, if a bond is issued for $1,000 when the inflation index is 100, and the index at the end of the first year is 102, the bondholder is entitled to $1,020 at maturity assuming no further changes in price level. The investor is required to include $20 in gross income for the increase in principal that will not be received until maturity. Thus, inflation adjustments can create gross income before any cash has been received.

The taxpayer's assets and liabilities increase by the same amount, so no income is realized when the borrowed funds are received.

EXAMPLE 14

A landlord receives a damage deposit from a tenant. The landlord does not recognize income until the deposit is forfeited because the landlord has an obligation to repay the deposit if no damage occurs.[34] However, if the deposit is in fact a prepayment of rent, it is taxed in the year of receipt. ■

SPECIAL RULES FOR ACCRUAL BASIS TAXPAYERS

Prepaid Income.   For financial reporting purposes, advance payments received from customers are reflected as prepaid income and as a liability of the seller. For tax purposes, however, the prepaid income often is taxed in the year of receipt.

EXAMPLE 15

In December 2001, a company pays its January 2002 rent of $1,000. The accrual basis landlord must include the $1,000 in 2001 gross income for tax purposes, although the unearned rent income is reported as a liability on the landlord's balance sheet for December 31, 2001. ■

Deferral of Advance Payments for Goods.   Generally, an accrual basis taxpayer can elect to defer recognition of income from advance payments for goods if the method of accounting for the sale is the same for tax and financial reporting purposes.[35]

EXAMPLE 16

Brown Company ships goods only after payment for the goods has been received. In December 2001, Brown receives $10,000 for goods that are not shipped until January 2002. Brown

---

[34]*John Mantell*, 17 T.C. 1143 (1952).

[35]Reg. § 1.451–5(b). See Reg. § 1.451–5(c) for exceptions to this deferral opportunity.

can elect to report the income in 2002 for tax purposes, assuming the company reports the income in 2002 for financial reporting purposes. ∎

Deferral of Advance Payments for Services. An accrual basis taxpayer can defer recognition of income for advance payments for services to be performed by the end of the tax year following the year of receipt.[36] No deferral is allowed if the taxpayer might be required, under the agreement, to perform any services after the tax year following the year of receipt of the advance payment. Prepaid rent or prepaid interest always is taxed in the year of receipt.

EXAMPLE 17

Canary Corporation, an accrual basis taxpayer, sells its services under 12-month, 18-month, and 24-month contracts. The corporation provides services to each customer every month. In April 2001, Canary sold the following customer contracts.

Length of Contract	Total Proceeds
12 months	$6,000
18 months	3,600
24 months	2,400

Fifteen hundred dollars of the $6,000 may be deferred ($3/12 \times \$6,000$), and $1,800 of the $3,600 may be deferred ($9/18 \times \$3,600$), because those amounts will not be earned until 2002. However, the entire $2,400 received on the 24-month contract is taxable in the year of receipt (2001), since a part of the income will still be unearned by the end of the tax year following the year of receipt (part will be earned in 2003). ∎

PLANNING CONSIDERATIONS

Prepaid Income

The accrual basis taxpayer who receives advance payments from customers should structure the transactions using the rules discussed above to avoid having to pay tax on income before the time the income is actually earned. In addition, both cash and accrual basis taxpayers can sometimes defer income by stipulating that the payments are deposits rather than prepaid income. For example, a landlord might consider requiring an equivalent damage deposit rather than prepayment of the last month's rent.

LEARNING OBJECTIVE 3

Identify who should pay the tax on an item of income.

Income Sources

PERSONAL SERVICES

It is a well-established principle of taxation that income from personal services must be included in the gross income of the person who performs the services. This principle was first established in a Supreme Court decision, *Lucas v. Earl*.[37] Mr. Earl entered into a binding agreement with his wife under which Mrs. Earl was to receive one-half of Mr. Earl's salary. Justice Holmes used the celebrated **fruit and tree metaphor** to explain that the fruit (income) must be attributed to

---

[36]Rev.Proc. 71–21, 1971–2 C.B. 549.

[37]2 USTC ¶496, 8 AFTR 10287, 50 S.Ct. 241 (USSC, 1930).

TAX IN THE NEWS

FAMILY TAX PLANNING: SHOULD A CHILD WORK OR PLAY?

A self-employed person who hires his or her children can reduce both the family's income taxes and self-employment taxes. When a child is paid reasonable compensation for services performed for the business, income is shifted from the parents' (typically higher) marginal tax bracket to the child's tax bracket. The kiddie tax, which taxes part of a child's unearned income at the parents' rates (if the child is under age 14), does not apply to earned income. The proprietor's self-employment income is also reduced, thus reducing his or her Social Security and Medicare taxes. If the child is under age 18, his or her earnings are not subject to Social Security and Medicare taxes.

SOURCE: Adapted from Ann Perry, "Putting Kids to Work Is Good for the Family Piggy Bank," *San Diego Union-Tribune*, July 2, 2000, p. I1.

---

the tree from which it came (Mr. Earl's services). A mere **assignment of income** does not shift the liability for the tax.

Services of an Employee. Services performed by an employee for the employer's customers are considered performed by the employer. Thus, the employer is taxed on the income from the services provided to the customer, and the employee is taxed on any compensation received from the employer.[38]

EXAMPLE 18

Dr. Shontelle incorporates her medical practice and enters into a contract to work for the corporation for a salary. All patients contract to receive their services from the corporation, and those services are provided through the corporation's employee, Dr. Shontelle. The corporation must include the patients' fees in its gross income. Dr. Shontelle must include her salary in her gross income. The corporation is allowed a deduction for a reasonable salary paid to Dr. Shontelle. ■

INCOME FROM PROPERTY

Income earned from property (interest, dividends, rent) must be included in the gross income of the owner of the property. If a shareholder clips interest coupons from bonds shortly before the interest payment date and transfers the coupons to his or her solely owned corporation, the interest still is taxed to the shareholder. Similarly, a parent who assigns rents from income-producing property to a child is taxed on the rent, since the parent retains ownership of the property.[39]

Often income-producing property is transferred after income from the property has accrued but before the income is recognized under the transferor's method of accounting. The IRS and the courts have developed rules to allocate the income between the transferor and the transferee. These allocation rules are addressed below.

---

[38]*Sargent v. Comm.*, 91–1 USTC ¶50,168, 67 AFTR2d 91–718, 929 F.2d 1252 (CA–8, 1991).

[39]*Galt v. Comm.*, 54–2 USTC ¶9457, 46 AFTR 633, 216 F.2d 41 (CA–7, 1954); *Helvering v. Horst*, 40–2 USTC ¶9787, 24 AFTR 1058, 61 S.Ct. 144 (USSC, 1940).

TAX FACT

HOW MUCH AND WHAT TYPE OF INCOME?

Of the 122.5 million individual income tax returns filed for the 1997 tax year, 85 percent included wage or salary income, and over half included some amount of taxable interest income. But except for these two categories, no other type of income was found in even a quarter of the returns filed. Sales of business assets were found on 1 percent of the returns, and they netted to zero (i.e., recognized gains and losses were about equal in magnitude for the year). Capital gains showed up on about a quarter of the returns, but only when distributions from mutual fund investments were included. About 5 percent of the returns included flow-through income or loss from partnerships and S corporations.

---

1 *Find more information on this topic at our Web site: **http://wft-entities.swcollege.com**.*

Interest.   According to the IRS, interest accrues daily. Therefore, the interest for the period that includes the date of the transfer is allocated between the transferor and the transferee based on the number of days during the period that each owned the property.

EXAMPLE 19

Floyd, a cash basis taxpayer, gives his son, Seth, bonds with a face amount of $10,000 and an 8% stated annual interest rate, payable December 31. The gift is made on January 31, 2001. Floyd recognizes $68 in interest income (8% × $10,000 × 31/365). Seth recognizes $732 in interest income ($800 − $68). ∎

When the transferor recognizes gross income from the property depends upon the method of accounting and the manner in which the property was transferred. In the case of a gift of income-producing property, the donor's share of the accrued income is recognized at the time it would have been recognized had the donor continued to own the property.[40] If the transfer is a sale, however, the transferor recognizes the accrued income at the time of the sale because the accrued interest is included in the sales proceeds.

EXAMPLE 20

Assume the same facts as in the preceding example, except that the interest payable on December 31 is not actually or constructively received by the bondholders until January 3, 2002. As a cash basis taxpayer, Floyd generally does not recognize interest income until it is received. If Floyd had continued to own the bonds, he would have included the interest in his gross income in 2002, the year he would have received it. Therefore, Floyd includes the $68 accrued income in his gross income as of January 3, 2002.

Further assume that Floyd sells identical bonds on the date of the gift. The bonds sell for $9,900, including accrued interest. On January 31, 2001, Floyd recognizes the accrued interest of $68 on the bonds sold. Thus, the selling price of the bonds is $9,832 ($9,900 − $68). ∎

Dividends.   A corporation is taxed on its earnings, and the shareholders are taxed on the dividends paid to them from the corporation's after-tax earnings. The dividend can take the form of an actual dividend or a constructive dividend (e.g., shareholder use of corporate assets).

---

[40]Rev.Rul. 72–312, 1972–1 C.B. 22.

TAX FACT

BUSINESS INCOME AND LOSS

Sole proprietors reporting net business income on the 1997 Form 1040 made up about 10 percent of all returns filed for the year. These Schedule C computations generated almost $200 billion in net income, an amount that increased greatly in nominal terms in the last decade, but essentially stayed even with inflation. Flow-through income from partnerships and S corporations is found on only half as many returns, but the income reported is essentially the same in nominal dollars. Flow-through income has increased dramatically and consistently since the 1987 tax year, when changes in marginal tax rates shifted to favor individual rather than C corporation taxpayers.

Unlike interest, dividends do not accrue on a daily basis because the declaration of a dividend is at the discretion of the corporation's board of directors. Generally, dividends are taxed to the person who is entitled to receive them—the shareholder of record as of the corporation's record date.[41] Thus, if a taxpayer sells stock after a dividend has been declared but before the record date, the dividend generally will be taxed to the purchaser.

If a donor makes a gift of stock to someone (e.g., a family member) after the declaration date but before the record date, the Tax Court has held that the donor does not shift the dividend income to the donee. The *fruit* has sufficiently ripened as of the declaration date to tax the dividend income to the donor of the stock.[42] In a similar set of facts, the Fifth Court of Appeals concluded that the dividend income should be included in the gross income of the donee (the owner at the record date). In this case, the taxpayer gave stock to a qualified charity (a charitable contribution) after the declaration date and before the record date.[43]

2 *Find more information on this topic at our Web site:* ***http://wft-entities.swcollege.com.***

EXAMPLE 21

On June 20, the board of directors of Black Corporation declares a $10 per share dividend. The dividend is payable on June 30, to shareholders of record on June 25. As of June 20, Kathleen owns 200 shares of Black Corporation's stock. On June 21, Kathleen sells 100 of the shares to Jon for their fair market value and gives 100 of the shares to Andrew (her son). Both Jon and Andrew are shareholders of record as of June 25. Jon (the purchaser) is taxed on $1,000 since he is entitled to receive the dividend. However, Kathleen (the donor) is taxed on the $1,000 received by Andrew (the donee) because the gift was made after the declaration date of the dividend. ■

INCOME RECEIVED BY AN AGENT

Income received by the taxpayer's agent is considered to be received by the taxpayer. A cash basis principal must recognize the income at the time it is received by the agent.[44]

---

[41]Reg. § 1.61–9(c). The record date is the cutoff for determining the shareholders who are entitled to receive the dividend.

[42]*M. G. Anton,* 34 T.C. 842 (1960).

[43]*Caruth Corporation v. U.S.,* 89–1 USTC ¶9172, 63 AFTR2d 89–716, 865 F.2d 644 (CA–5, 1989).

[44]Rev.Rul. 79–379, 1979–2 C.B. 204.

EXAMPLE 22

Longhorn, Inc., a cash basis corporation, delivers cattle to the auction barn in late December. The auctioneer, acting as the corporation's agent, sells the cattle and collects the proceeds in December. The auctioneer does not pay Longhorn until the following January. The corporation must include the sales proceeds in its gross income in the year the auctioneer received the funds. ■

PLANNING CONSIDERATIONS

Techniques for Reducing Gross Income

NONTAXABLE ECONOMIC BENEFITS

Home ownership is the prime example of economic income from capital that is not subject to tax. If the taxpayer uses his or her capital to purchase investments, but pays rent on a personal residence, the taxpayer would pay the rent from after-tax income. However, if the taxpayer purchases a personal residence instead of the investments, he or she would give up gross income from the forgone investments in exchange for the rent savings. The savings in rent enjoyed as a result of owning the home are not subject to tax. Thus, the homeowner will have substituted nontaxable for taxable income.

TAX DEFERRAL

General. Since deferred taxes are tantamount to interest-free loans from the government, the deferral of taxes is a worthy goal of the tax planner. However, the tax planner must also consider the tax rates for the years the income is shifted from and to. For example, a one-year deferral of income from a year in which the taxpayer's tax rate was 28 percent to a year in which the tax rate will be 39.6 percent would not be advisable if the taxpayer expects to earn less than an 11.6 percent after-tax return on the deferred tax dollars.

The taxpayer can often defer the recognition of income from appreciated property by postponing the event triggering realization (the final closing on a sale or exchange of property). If the taxpayer needs cash, obtaining a loan by using the appreciated property as collateral may be the least costly alternative. When the taxpayer anticipates reinvesting the proceeds, a sale may be inadvisable.

EXAMPLE 23

Ira owns 100 shares of Pigeon Company common stock with a cost of $20,000 and a fair market value of $50,000. Although the stock's value has increased substantially in the past three years, Ira thinks the growth days are over. If he sells the Pigeon stock, Ira will invest the proceeds from the sale in other common stock. If Ira's marginal tax rate on the sale is 20%, he will have only $44,000 [$50,000 –

.20($50,000 – $20,000)] to reinvest. The alternative investment must substantially outperform Pigeon in the future in order for the sale to be beneficial. ■

Selection of Investments. Because no tax is due until a gain has been recognized, the law favors investments that yield appreciation rather than annual income.

EXAMPLE 24

Vera can buy a corporate bond or an acre of land for $10,000. The bond pays $1,000 of interest (10%) each year, and Vera expects the land to increase in value 10% each year for the next 10 years. She is in the 40% (combined Federal and state) tax bracket for ordinary income and 26% for qualifying capital gains. If the bond would mature or the land would be sold in 10 years and Vera would reinvest the interest at a 10% before-tax return, she would accumulate the following amount at the end of 10 years.

		Bond	Land
Original investment		$10,000	$10,000
Annual income	$ 1,000		
Less tax	(400)		
	$ 600		
Compound amount reinvested for 10 years at 6% after-tax	× 13.18	7,908	
		$17,908	
Compound amount, 10 years at 10%			× 2.59
			$25,900
Less tax on sale: 26%($25,900 – $10,000)			(4,134)
			$21,766

Therefore, the value of the deferral that results from investing in the land rather than in the bond is $3,858 ($21,766 – $17,908). ■

INTERNATIONAL IMPLICATIONS

FROM "ALL SOURCES" IS A BROAD DEFINITION

When § 61 refers to "income from whatever source derived," the taxing authorities are reaching far beyond the borders of the United States. Although one interpretation of "source" in this context is type of income (wages, interest, etc.), a broader interpretation revolves around the place where the income is generated. In this context, citizens and residents of the United States are subject to taxation on income earned from sources both inside and outside the country. This "worldwide income" tax base can cause potential double taxation problems when other countries also tax income earned within their borders. Beneficially, mechanisms such as the foreign tax credit can alleviate some or all of these tax burdens.

LEARNING OBJECTIVE 4

Understand that statutory authority is required to exclude an item from gross income.

Specific Items of Gross Income

The all-inclusive principles of gross income determination as applied by the IRS and the courts have, on occasion, been expanded or modified by Congress through legislation. This legislation generally provides more specific rules for determining gross income from certain sources. Most of these special rules appear in §§ 71–90 of the Code.

In addition to provisions describing how specific sources of gross income are to be taxed, several specific rules *exclude* items from gross income. Authority for excluding specific items is provided in §§ 101–150 and in various other provisions in the Code.

Many statutory exclusions are unique to *individual taxpayers* (e.g., gifts and inheritances,[45] scholarships,[46] and a variety of fringe benefits paid to *employees*). These exclusions are discussed in Chapters 15 and 16. Other exclusions are broader and apply to all entities. These exclusions include interest on state and local bonds (§ 103), life insurance proceeds received by reason of death of the insured (§ 101), the fair market value of leasehold improvements received by the lessor when a lease is terminated (§ 109),[47] and income from discharge of indebtedness (§ 108). Some of the broadly applied statutory rules describing inclusions and exclusions are discussed below.

LEARNING OBJECTIVE 5

Apply the Internal Revenue Code provisions on loans made at below-market interest rates.

IMPUTED INTEREST ON BELOW-MARKET LOANS

As discussed earlier in the chapter, generally no income is recognized unless it is realized. Realization occurs when the taxpayer performs services or sells goods and thus becomes entitled to a payment from the other party. It follows that no income is realized if the goods or services are provided at no charge. Under this interpretation of the realization requirement, before 1984, interest-free loans were used to shift income between taxpayers.

---

[45]§ 102.
[46]§ 117.

[47]If the tenant made the improvements in lieu of rent, the value of the improvements is not eligible for exclusion.

EXAMPLE 25

Brown Corporation is in the 35% tax bracket and has $200,000 in a money market account earning 10% interest. Jack is the sole shareholder of Brown. He is in the 15% tax bracket and has no investment income. In view of the difference in tax rates, Jack believes that it would be better for him to receive and pay tax on the earnings from Brown's $200,000 investment. Jack does not wish to receive the $200,000 from Brown as a dividend because that would trigger a tax.

Before 1984, Jack could achieve his goals as follows. He could receive the money market account from Brown Corporation in exchange for a $200,000 non-interest-bearing note, payable on Brown's demand. As a result, Jack would receive the $20,000 earnings on the money market account, and the combined taxes of Brown Corporation and Jack would be decreased by $4,000.

Decrease in Brown's tax—$(0.10 \times \$200,000) \times 0.35$	($7,000)
Increase in Jack's tax—$(0.10 \times \$200,000) \times 0.15$	3,000
Overall decrease in tax liability	$4,000

Under 1984 amendments to the Code, Brown Corporation in the preceding example is deemed to have received an interest payment from Jack even though no interest was actually paid.[48] This payment of imputed interest is taxable to Brown Corporation. Jack may be able to deduct the imaginary interest payment on his return as investment interest if he itemizes deductions. To complete the fictitious series of transactions, Brown Corporation is deemed to return the interest to Jack in the form of a taxable dividend.

Imputed interest is calculated using rates the Federal government pays on new borrowings and is compounded semiannually. The Federal rates are adjusted monthly and are published by the IRS.[49] There are three Federal rates: short-term (not over three years and including demand loans), mid-term (over three years but not over nine years), and long-term (over nine years).

EXAMPLE 26

Assume the Federal rate applicable to the loan in the preceding example is 7% through June 30 and 8% from July 1 through December 31. Brown Corporation made the loan on January 1, and the loan is still outstanding on December 31. Brown must recognize interest income of $15,280, and Jack has interest expense of $15,280. Brown is deemed to have paid a $15,280 dividend to Jack.

Interest Calculations	
January 1 to June 30—$(0.07 \times \$200,000)$ (½ year)	$ 7,000
July 1 to December 31—$[0.08(\$200,000 + \$7,000)]$ (½ year)	8,280
	$15,280

If interest is charged on the loan but is less than the Federal rate, the imputed interest is the difference between the amount that would have been charged at the Federal rate and the amount actually charged.

EXAMPLE 27

Assume the same facts as in Example 26, except that Brown Corporation charged 6% interest, compounded annually.

---

[48]§ 7872(a)(1).

[49]§§ 7872(b)(2) and (f)(2).

CONCEPT SUMMARY 3–1

Effect of Certain Below-Market Loans on the Lender and Borrower

Type of Loan		Lender	Borrower
Gift	Step 1	Interest income	Interest expense
	Step 2	Gift made*	Gift received
Compensation related	Step 1	Interest income	Interest expense
	Step 2	Compensation expense	Compensation income
Corporation to shareholder	Step 1	Interest income	Interest expense
	Step 2	Dividend paid	Dividend income

*The gift may be subject to the gift tax (refer to Chapter 1).

Interest at the Federal rate	$ 15,280
Less interest charged (0.06 × $200,000)	(12,000)
Imputed interest	$ 3,280

The imputed interest rules apply to the following types of below-market loans.[50]

1. Gift loans (made out of love, affection, or generosity).
2. Compensation-related loans (employer loans to employees).
3. Corporation-shareholder loans (a corporation's loans to its shareholders, as in Example 25).
4. Tax avoidance loans and other loans that significantly affect the borrower's or lender's Federal tax liability (discussed in the following paragraphs).

The effects of the first three types of loans on the borrower and lender are summarized in Concept Summary 3–1.

Exceptions and Limitations. No interest is imputed on total outstanding *compensation-related loans* or *corporation-shareholder loans* of $10,000 or less unless the purpose of the loan is tax avoidance.[51] This vague tax avoidance standard exposes practically all compensation-related and corporation-shareholder loans to possible imputed interest problems. Nevertheless, the $10,000 exception should apply when an employee's borrowing was necessitated by personal needs (e.g., to meet unexpected expenses) rather than tax considerations.

Similarly, no interest is imputed on outstanding *gift loans* of $10,000 or less between individuals, unless the loan proceeds are used to purchase income-producing property.[52] This exemption eliminates from these complex provisions immaterial amounts that do not result in apparent shifts of income.

On loans of $100,000 or less between individuals, the imputed interest cannot exceed the borrower's net investment income for the year (gross income from all investments less the related expenses).[53] Through the gift loan provision, the imputed interest rules are designed to prevent high-income individuals from shifting

---

[50]§ 7872(c).
[51]§ 7872(c)(3).
[52]§ 7872(c)(2).
[53]§ 7872(d). The $100,000 provision applies only to gift loans.

CONCEPT SUMMARY 3–2

Exceptions to the Imputed Interest Rules for Below-Market Loans

Exception	Eligible Loans	Ineligible Loans and Limitations
De minimis—aggregate loans of $10,000 or less	Gift loans	Proceeds used to purchase income-producing assets.
	Employer-employee	Principal purpose is tax avoidance.
	Corporation-shareholder	Principal purpose is tax avoidance.
Aggregate loans of $100,000 or less	Gift loans between individuals	Principal purpose is tax avoidance. For all other loans, interest is imputed to the extent of the borrower's net investment income, if it exceeds $1,000.

income to relatives in a lower marginal bracket. This shifting of investment income is considered to occur only to the extent that the borrower has net investment income. Thus, the income imputed to the lender is limited to the borrower's net investment income. As a further limitation or exemption, if the borrower's net investment income for the year does not exceed $1,000, no interest is imputed on loans of $100,000 or less. However, these limitations for loans of $100,000 or less do not apply if a principal purpose of a loan is tax avoidance. In such a case, interest is imputed, and the imputed interest is not limited to the borrower's net investment income.[54]

These exceptions to the imputed interest rules are summarized in Concept Summary 3–2.

LEARNING OBJECTIVE 6

Determine the extent to which receipts can be excluded under the tax benefit rule.

TAX BENEFIT RULE

Generally, if a taxpayer obtains a deduction for an item in one year and in a later year recovers all or a portion of the prior deduction, the recovery is included in gross income in the year received.[55]

EXAMPLE 28

A business deducted as a loss a $1,000 receivable from a customer when it appeared the amount would never be collected. The following year, the customer paid $800 on the receivable. The business must report the $800 as gross income in the year it is received. ■

However, the § 111 **tax benefit rule** limits income recognition when a deduction does not yield a tax benefit in the year it is taken. If the taxpayer in Example 28 has no tax liability in the year of the deduction, the $800 receipt will be excluded from gross income in the year of the recovery.

EXAMPLE 29

Before deducting a $1,000 loss from an uncollectible business receivable, Tulip Company had taxable income of $200. The business bad debt deduction yields only a $200 tax benefit

---

[54]*Deficit Reduction Tax Bill of 1984: Explanation of the Senate Finance Committee* (April 2, 1984), p. 484.

[55]§ 111(a).

(assuming no loss carryback is made). That is, taxable income is reduced by only $200 (to zero) as a result of the bad debt deduction. Therefore, if the customer makes a payment on the previously deducted receivable in the following year, only the first $200 is a taxable recovery of a prior deduction. Any additional amount collected is nontaxable because only $200 of the loss yielded a reduction in taxable income (i.e., a tax benefit). ■

LEARNING OBJECTIVE 7

Understand the Internal Revenue Code provision that excludes interest on state and local government obligations from gross income.

INTEREST ON CERTAIN STATE AND LOCAL GOVERNMENT OBLIGATIONS

At the time the Sixteenth Amendment was ratified by the states, there was some question as to whether the Federal government possessed the constitutional authority to tax interest on state and local government obligations. Taxing such interest was thought to violate the doctrine of intergovernmental immunity because the tax would impair the ability of state and local governments to finance their operations.[56] Thus, interest on state and local government obligations was specifically exempted from Federal income taxation.[57] However, the Supreme Court has concluded that there is no constitutional prohibition against levying a nondiscriminatory Federal income tax on state and local government obligations.[58] Nevertheless, the statutory exclusion still exists.

The current exempt status applies solely to state and local government bonds. Thus, income received from the accrual of interest on a condemnation award or an overpayment of state tax is fully taxable.[59] Nor does the exemption apply to gains on the sale of tax-exempt securities.

DIGGING DEEPER

3 *Find more information on this topic at our Web site:* **http://wft-entities.swcollege.com.**

EXAMPLE 30

Macaw Corporation purchases State of Virginia bonds for $10,000 on July 1, 1999. The bonds pay $400 interest each June 30 and December 31. On March 31, 2001, Macaw sells the bonds for $10,500 plus $200 of accrued interest. Macaw must recognize a $500 taxable gain ($10,500 − $10,000), but the $200 accrued interest is exempt from taxation. ■

Obviously, the interest exclusion reduces the cost of borrowing for state and local governments. A taxpayer with a 36 percent marginal tax rate requires only a 5.12 percent yield on a tax-exempt bond to obtain the same after-tax income as a taxable bond paying 8 percent interest [5.12% ÷ (1 − 0.36) = 8%].

State and local governments have developed sophisticated financial schemes to attract new industry. For example, local municipalities have issued bonds to finance construction of plants to be leased to private enterprise. Because the financing could be arranged with low-interest municipal obligations, the plants could be leased at lower cost than other facilities the private business could obtain. However, Congress has placed limitations on the use of tax-exempt securities to finance private business.[60]

---

[56]*Pollock v. Farmer's Loan & Trust Co.*, 3 AFTR 2602, 15 S.Ct. 912 (USSC, 1895).

[57]§ 103(a).

[58]*South Carolina v. Baker III*, 88–1 USTC ¶9284, 61 AFTR2d 88–995, 108 S.Ct. 1355 (USSC, 1988).

[59]*Kieselbach v. Comm.*, 43–1 USTC ¶9220, 30 AFTR 370, 63 S.Ct. 303 (USSC, 1943); *U.S. Trust Co. of New York v. Anderson*, 3 USTC ¶1125, 12 AFTR 836, 65 F.2d 575 (CA–2, 1933).

[60]See § 103(b). The alternative minimum tax may apply to some of this interest income.

PLANNING CONSIDERATIONS

State and Municipal Bonds

Tax-exempt state and local bonds are almost irresistible investments for taxpayers with high marginal tax rates. To realize the maximum benefit from the exemption, the investor can purchase zero coupon bonds, which pay interest only at maturity. The advantage of the zero coupon feature is that the investor can earn tax-exempt interest on the accumulated principal and interest. If the investor purchases a tax-exempt bond that pays the interest each year, the interest received may be such a small amount that an additional tax-exempt investment cannot be made. In addition, reinvesting the interest may entail transaction costs (broker's fees). The zero coupon feature avoids these problems. However, state and municipal bond interest may increase the base of the alternative minimum tax, as discussed in Chapter 13.

LEARNING OBJECTIVE 8

Understand the Internal Revenue Code provision that excludes leasehold improvements from gross income.

IMPROVEMENTS ON LEASED PROPERTY

When a real property lease expires, the landlord regains control of both the real property and any improvements to the property (e.g., buildings and landscaping) made by the tenant during the term of the lease. In 1940, the Supreme Court held that the fair market value of improvements made by a tenant to the landlord's property should be included in the landlord's gross income upon termination of the lease.[61] Congress effectively reversed this decision by enacting § 109, which defers tax on the value of the improvements until the property is sold. More specifically, any improvements made to the leased property are excluded from the landlord's gross income unless the improvement is made to the property in lieu of rent.

if u sell improvements, claim income
no basis for depreciation either

EXAMPLE 31

Mahogany Corporation leases office space to Zink and Silver, Attorneys-at-Law. When the law firm took possession of the office space, it added wall partitions, an in-wall computer network, and a variety of other improvements to the space. The improvements were not made in lieu of rent payments to Mahogany. When the lease expires and Mahogany regains possession of the space, the improvements will be excluded from Mahogany's gross income. ■

NO income

LEARNING OBJECTIVE 9

Determine the extent to which life insurance proceeds are excluded from gross income.

LIFE INSURANCE PROCEEDS   *tax free in general when*

General Rule. Life insurance proceeds paid to the beneficiary because of the death of the insured are exempt from income tax.[62] Congress chose to exempt life insurance proceeds for the following reasons.   *someone dies ✓collect tax free*

- For family members, life insurance proceeds serve much the same purpose as a nontaxable inheritance.
- In a business context (as well as in a family situation), life insurance proceeds replace an economic loss suffered by the beneficiary.

Thus, Congress concluded that, in general, making life insurance proceeds exempt from income tax was a good policy.

Some exceptions

---

[61]*Helvering v. Bruun,* 40–1 USTC ¶9337, 24 AFTR 652, 60 S.Ct. 631 (USSC, 1940).

[62]*Estate of D. R. Daly,* 3 B.T.A. 1042 (1926).

Can't deduct premiums

| EXAMPLE 32 | Sparrow Corporation purchased an insurance policy on the life of its CEO and named itself as the beneficiary. Sparrow paid $24,000 in premiums. When the company's CEO died, Sparrow collected the insurance proceeds of $60,000. The $60,000 is excluded from Sparrow's gross income. ■ |

Exceptions to Exclusion Treatment.   The income tax exclusion applies only when the insurance proceeds are received because of the death of the insured. If the owner cancels the policy and receives the cash surrender value, he or she must recognize gain to the extent of the excess of the amount received over the cost of the policy.[63]

Another exception to exclusion treatment applies if the policy is transferred after the insurance company issues it. If the policy is transferred for valuable consideration, the insurance proceeds are includible in the gross income of the transferee to the extent the proceeds received exceed the amount paid for the policy by the transferee plus any subsequent premiums paid.

| EXAMPLE 33 | Platinum Corporation pays premiums of $5,000 for an insurance policy with a face amount of $12,000 on the life of Beth, an officer of the corporation. Subsequently, Platinum sells the policy to Beth's husband for $5,500. On Beth's death, her husband receives the proceeds of $12,000. Beth's husband can exclude from gross income $5,500 plus any premiums he paid subsequent to the transfer. ■ |

The Code, however, provides four exceptions to the rule illustrated in the preceding example.[64] These exceptions permit exclusion treatment for transfers to the following. The first three exceptions facilitate the use of insurance contracts to fund **buy-sell agreements.**

1. A partner of the insured.
2. A partnership in which the insured is a partner.
3. A corporation in which the insured is an officer or shareholder.
4. A transferee whose basis in the policy is determined by reference to the transferor's basis, such as a gift or a transfer due to a divorce.

| EXAMPLE 34 | Rick and Sam are equal partners who have a buy-sell agreement that allows either partner to purchase the interest of a deceased partner for $50,000. Neither partner has sufficient cash to actually buy the other partner's interest, but each has a life insurance policy on his own life in the amount of $50,000. Rick and Sam could exchange their policies (usually at little or no taxable gain), and upon the death of either partner, the surviving partner could collect tax-free insurance proceeds. The proceeds could then be used to purchase the decedent's interest in the partnership. ■ |

Investment earnings arising from the reinvestment of life insurance proceeds are generally subject to income tax. For example, the beneficiary may elect to collect the insurance proceeds in installments that include taxable interest income. The interest portion of each installment is included in gross income.

---

[63]*Landfield Finance Co. v. U.S.*, 69–2 USTC ¶9680, 24 AFTR2d 69–5744, 418 F.2d 172 (CA–7, 1969).

[64]§ 101(a)(2).

PLANNING CONSIDERATIONS

Life Insurance

Life insurance is a tax-favored investment. The annual increase in the cash surrender value of the policy is not taxable because it is subject to substantial restrictions (no income has been actually or constructively received). By borrowing on the policy's cash surrender value, the owner can receive the policy's increase in value in cash without recognizing income.

LEARNING OBJECTIVE 10

Describe the circumstances under which income must be reported from the discharge of indebtedness.

INCOME FROM DISCHARGE OF INDEBTEDNESS

Income is generated when appreciated property is used to pay a debt or when the creditor cancels debt. If appreciated property is used to pay a debt, the transaction is treated as a sale of the appreciated property followed by payment of the debt.[65] Foreclosure by a creditor is also treated as a sale or exchange of the property.[66]

EXAMPLE 35

Juan owed the State Bank $100,000 on an unsecured note. Juan satisfied the note by transferring to the bank common stock with a basis of $60,000 and a fair market value of $100,000. Juan recognizes a $40,000 gain on the transfer. Juan also owed the bank $50,000 on a note secured by land. When Juan's basis in the land was $20,000 and the land's fair market value was $50,000, the bank foreclosed on the loan and took title to the land. Juan recognizes a $30,000 gain on the foreclosure. ■

A creditor may cancel debt to assure the vitality of the debtor. In such cases, the debtor's net worth is increased by the amount of debt forgiven.

EXAMPLE 36

Brown Corporation is unable to meet the mortgage payments on its factory building. Both the corporation and the mortgage holder are aware of the depressed market for industrial property in the area. Foreclosure would only result in the creditor's obtaining unsellable property. To improve Brown's financial position and thus improve its chances of obtaining from other lenders the additional credit necessary for survival, the creditor agrees to forgive all amounts past due and to reduce the principal amount of the mortgage. Brown's net worth is increased by the amount of past due debt that was forgiven *plus* the reduction in the mortgage balance. ■

Generally, the debtor recognizes gross income equal to the amount of debt canceled.[67] The following two examples illustrate additional circumstances where gross income results from cancellation of indebtedness.

EXAMPLE 37

A corporation issues bonds with a face value of $500,000. Subsequently, the corporation repurchases the bonds in the market for $150,000. It has effectively canceled its $500,000 debt with a $150,000 payment, so it recognizes $350,000 in gross income.[68] ■

EXAMPLE 38

In 1995, Turquoise Corporation borrowed $60,000 from National Bank to purchase a warehouse. Turquoise agreed to make monthly principal and interest payments for 15 years. The interest rate on the note was 7%. When the balance on the note had been reduced through monthly payments to $48,000, the bank offered to accept $45,000 in full settlement of the

---

[65]Reg. § 1.1001–2(a).
[66]*Estate of Delman v. Comm.*, 73 T.C. 15 (1979).
[67]§ 61(a)(12).

[68]See *U.S. v. Kirby Lumber Co.*, 2 USTC ¶814, 10 AFTR 458, 52 S.Ct. 4 (USSC, 1931).

note. The bank made the offer because interest rates had increased to 11%. Turquoise accepted the bank's offer. As a result, Turquoise recognizes $3,000 ($48,000 − $45,000) of gross income.[69] ■

Though discharge of indebtedness generally increases the taxpayer's gross income, in the following cases, the reduction in debt is excluded from gross income.[70]

1. Creditors' gifts.
2. Discharges under Federal bankruptcy law.
3. Discharges that occur when the debtor is insolvent.
4. Discharge of the farm debt of a solvent taxpayer.
5. Discharge of **qualified real property business indebtedness.**
6. A seller's cancellation of a buyer's indebtedness.
7. A shareholder's cancellation of a corporation's indebtedness.
8. Forgiveness of certain loans to students.

Creditors' Gifts.   If the creditor reduces the debt as an act of *love, affection or generosity*, the debtor has simply received a nontaxable gift (situation 1). Such motivations generally arise only on loans between friends or family members. Rarely will a gift be found to have occurred in a business context. A businessperson may settle a debt for less than the amount due, but as a matter of business expediency (e.g., high collection costs or disputes as to contract terms) rather than generosity.[71]

Insolvency and Bankruptcy.   Cancellation of indebtedness income is excluded when the debtor is insolvent (i.e., the debtor's liabilities exceed the fair market value of the assets) or when the cancellation of debt results from a bankruptcy proceeding (situations 2 and 3). The insolvency exclusion is limited to the amount of insolvency. The tax law permits this exclusion to avoid imposing undue hardship on the debtor (wherewithal to pay) and the debtor's limited resources.

The law imposes a cost for the insolvency and bankruptcy exclusion. More specifically, the debtor must decrease certain tax benefits (capital loss carryforwards, net operating loss carryforwards, some tax credits, and suspended passive losses)[72] by the amount of income excluded. In addition, if the amount of excluded income exceeds these tax benefits, the debtor must then reduce the basis in assets.[73] Thus, excluded cancellation of indebtedness income either accelerates recognition of future income (by reducing tax benefit carryforwards) or is deferred until the debtor's assets are sold (or depreciated).

EXAMPLE 39

Before any debt cancellation, Maroon Corporation has assets with a fair market value of $500,000 and liabilities of $600,000. A creditor agrees to cancel $125,000 of liabilities. Maroon excludes $100,000 of the debt cancellation income (the amount of insolvency) and is taxed on $25,000. Maroon also reduces any tax benefits and the basis of its assets by $100,000 (the excluded income). ■

Qualified Real Property Indebtedness   Taxpayers (other than C corporations) can elect to exclude income from cancellation of indebtedness if the canceled debt is secured by real property used in a trade or business (situation 5). In addition,

---

[69]Rev.Rul. 82–202, 1982–1 C.B. 35.
[70]§§ 108 and 1017.
[71]*Comm. v. Jacobson*, 49–1 USTC ¶9133, 37 AFTR 516, 69 S.Ct. 358 (USSC, 1949).

[72]See Chapter 5 for a discussion of net operating loss carryforwards and suspended passive losses. Chapter 8 discusses capital loss carryforwards. Chapter 13 discusses tax credits.
[73]§ 108(b).

the debt must have been used to acquire or improve real property in a trade or business to qualify for the exclusion.[74] The amount of the exclusion is limited to the *lesser of* (1) the excess of the debt over the fair market value of the real property or (2) the adjusted basis of all depreciable real property held. In addition, the basis of all depreciable real property held by the debtor must be reduced by the amount excluded.

EXAMPLE 40

Blue, Inc., owns a warehouse worth $5 million, with a $3 million basis. The warehouse is subject to a $7 million mortgage that was incurred in connection with the acquisition of the warehouse. In lieu of foreclosure, the lender decides that it will reduce the mortgage to $4.5 million. Blue may elect to exclude $2 million from gross income ($7 million – $5 million). If Blue makes the election, it must reduce the aggregate basis of its depreciable realty by $2 million. ∎

EXAMPLE 41

Assume the same facts as in the preceding example, except that the basis of the warehouse is $1 million. If the warehouse is the only piece of depreciable realty that Blue owns, only $1 million of the debt cancellation income may be excluded. ∎

Seller Cancellation. When a seller of property cancels debt previously incurred by a buyer in a purchase transaction, the cancellation generally is not treated as income to the buyer (situation 6). Instead, the reduction in debt is considered to be a reduction in the purchase price of the asset. Consequently, the basis of the asset is reduced in the hands of the buyer.[75]

EXAMPLE 42

Snipe, Inc., purchases a truck from Sparrow Autos for $10,000 in cash and a $25,000 note payable. Two days after the purchase, Sparrow announces a sale on the same model truck, with a sales price of $28,000. Snipe contacts Sparrow and asks to be given the sales price on the truck. Sparrow complies by canceling $7,000 of the note payable. The $7,000 is excluded from Snipe's gross income, and the basis of the truck to Snipe is $28,000. ∎

Shareholder Cancellation. If a shareholder cancels the corporation's indebtedness to him or her (situation 7) and receives nothing in return, the cancellation usually is considered a contribution of capital to the corporation by the shareholder. Thus, the corporation recognizes no income. Instead, its paid-in capital is increased, and its liabilities are decreased by the same amount.[76]

4 *Find more information on this topic at our Web site: http://wft-entities.swcollege.com.*

Student Loans. Many states make loans to students on the condition that the loan will be forgiven if the student practices a profession in the state upon completing his or her studies. The amount of the loan that is forgiven (situation 8) is excluded from gross income.[77]

LEARNING OBJECTIVE 11

Discuss the tax consequences of property transactions.

GAINS AND LOSSES FROM PROPERTY TRANSACTIONS

In General. When property is sold or otherwise disposed of, gain or loss may result. Such gain or loss has an effect on the gross income of the party making the sale or other disposition when the gain or loss is *realized* and *recognized* for tax purposes. The concept of realized gain or loss is expressed as follows.

---

[74]§ 108(a)(1)(D).
[75]§ 108(e)(5).

[76]§ 108(e)(6).
[77]§ 108(f).

EMPLOYER-FINANCED STOCK PURCHASE LEADS TO TAX DISASTER

Conseco Corporation guaranteed $480 million in loans to its officers, who used the loans to purchase Conseco stock. Since the time when the loans were made, the value of the stock has decreased to $159 million. If the banks call the loans, horrendous tax problems could result. The corporation would be forced to pay the debt and then would become the creditor (the same as the bank). The officers would not have income at that point. But if the corporation then cancels the debt, as is likely to happen, the officers would have discharge of indebtedness income. The tax liability could exceed the value of the stock. The beneficiaries of the transactions would be the Federal government and the bank.

SOURCE: Adapted from Debra Sparks, "Conseco's Wild and Wooly Loans," *Business Week*, March 20, 2000, p. 104.

$$\begin{matrix} \text{Amount realized} \\ \text{from the sale} \end{matrix} - \begin{matrix} \text{Adjusted basis of} \\ \text{the property} \end{matrix} = \begin{matrix} \text{Realized gain} \\ \text{(or loss)} \end{matrix}$$

The amount realized is the selling price of the property less any costs of disposition (e.g., brokerage commissions) incurred by the seller. The adjusted basis of the property is determined as follows.

Cost (or other original basis) at date of acquisition[78]	
Add:	Capital additions
Subtract:	Depreciation (if appropriate) and other capital recoveries (see Chapter 4)
Equals:	Adjusted basis at date of sale or other disposition

Without realized gain or loss, generally, there can be no recognized (taxable) gain or loss. All realized gains are recognized unless some specific part of the tax law provides otherwise. Realized losses may or may not be recognized (deductible) for tax purposes, depending on the circumstances involved. For example, losses realized from the disposition of personal-use property (property held by individuals and not used for business or investment purposes) are not recognized.

EXAMPLE 43

During the current year, Ted sells his sailboat (adjusted basis of $4,000) for $5,500. Ted also sells one of his personal automobiles (adjusted basis of $8,000) for $5,000. Ted's realized gain of $1,500 from the sale of the sailboat is recognized. The $3,000 realized loss on the sale of the automobile, however, is not recognized. Thus, the gain is taxable, but the loss is not deductible. ∎

Once it has been determined that the disposition of property results in a recognized gain or loss, the next step is to classify the gain or loss as capital or ordinary.

---

[78]Cost usually means purchase price plus expenses related to the acquisition of the property and incurred by the purchaser (e.g., brokerage commissions). For the basis of property acquired by gift or inheritance and other basis rules, see Chapter 7.

Although ordinary gain is fully taxable and ordinary loss is fully deductible, the same is not true for capital gains and capital losses.

Capital Gains and Losses. Gains and losses from the disposition of capital assets receive special tax treatment. Capital assets are defined in the Code as any property held by the taxpayer *other than* property listed in § 1221. The list in § 1221 includes, among other things, inventory, accounts receivable, and depreciable property or real estate used in a business. The sale or exchange of assets in these categories usually results in ordinary income or loss treatment (see Chapter 8). The sale of any other asset generally creates a capital gain or loss.

EXAMPLE 44

Cardinal, Inc., owns a pizza parlor. During the current year, Cardinal sells an automobile. The automobile, which had been used as a pizza delivery car for three years, was sold at a loss of $1,000. Because this automobile was a depreciable asset used in its business, Cardinal has an ordinary loss of $1,000, rather than a capital loss. Cardinal also sold securities held for investment during the current year. The securities were sold for a gain of $800. The securities are capital assets. Therefore, Cardinal has a capital gain of $800. ■

Individuals and corporations are taxed differently on capital gains and losses. An individual's *net capital gain* is subject to the following *maximum* tax rates.[79]

	Maximum Rate[80]
Short-term gains (assets held for one year or less)	39.6%
Long-term gains (assets held for more than one year)	20%

A corporation's net capital gain does not receive any beneficial tax treatment.

The net capital losses of individuals can be used to offset up to $3,000 of ordinary income each year. Any remaining capital loss is carried forward indefinitely until it is exhausted. Corporations may deduct capital losses only to the extent of capital gains. Capital losses of corporations in excess of capital gains may not be deducted against ordinary income. A corporation's unused capital losses can be carried back three years and then carried forward five years to offset capital gains in those years.[81]

EXAMPLE 45

Tina has a short-term capital loss of $5,000 during 2001 and no capital gains. She can deduct $3,000 of this amount as an ordinary loss. The remaining $2,000 loss is carried over to 2002 and will continue to be carried forward until it is fully deducted.

If Tina were a corporation, none of the capital loss would be deductible in 2001. All $5,000 would be carried back and offset against capital gains in 1998, 1999, and 2000 (generating an immediate tax refund). Any unused capital loss would be carried forward and offset against capital gains in 2002 to 2006. ■

5 *Find more information on this topic at our Web site: **http://wft-entities.swcollege.com**.*

---

[79]§ 1(h). Net capital gain is defined in § 1222(11) as the excess of the net long-term capital gain over the net short-term capital loss.
[80]Certain assets, such as collectibles (e.g., art, antiques, stamps, etc.) and some real estate, receive special treatment. Collectibles gain is taxed at a maximum rate of 28%, and certain real estate gain is taxed at a maximum rate of 25%.
[81]§§ 1211 and 1212.

Suggested Further Readings

Sanford J. Aaron, "Clear as Mud: Discharge of Qualified Real Property Business Indebtedness," *Journal of Real Estate Taxation*, Winter 1998, pp. 138–164.

W. Eugene Seago, "Supreme Court Adopts Loan v. Advance Payment Test for Customer Deposits," *Journal of Taxation*, April 2000, pp. 204–210.

"Club Member's Refundable No-Interest Deposit Is Neither Income nor Below-Market Loan," *Journal of Taxation*, January 1998, p. 53.

KEY TERMS

Accounting income, 3–5

Accounting method, 3–7

Accrual method, 3–9

Assignment of income, 3–14

Buy-sell agreements, 3–24

Cash receipts method, 3–8

Claim of right doctrine, 3–9

Constructive receipt, 3–10

Economic income, 3–4

Fruit and tree metaphor, 3–13

Gross income, 3–3

Hybrid method, 3–10

Income, 3–4

Life insurance proceeds, 3–23

Original issue discount, 3–11

Qualified real property business indebtedness, 3–26

Tax benefit rule, 3–21

Taxable year, 3–7

Problem Materials

PROBLEMS

1. Jack, a cash basis taxpayer, operated Donna's farm under an arrangement whereby Jack would receive one-half of the grain crop, less the cost of seed and fertilizer. The seed and fertilizer cost $10,000, which was paid during the year. In September, Jack harvested the crop. A portion of the grain was sold for $30,000 cash in September, and Jack received $12,000 as his share of the $30,000 in October. Also in October, more of the grain was sold for $40,000. The grain was delivered to the purchaser in October, but payment was not to be received until January of the following year. Jack also used a portion of the grain for his personal use. The cost of the personal-use grain was $1,400, but it could have been sold for $3,000. In February of the following year, Jack collected the balance Donna owed to him. Identify the relevant tax issues for Jack.

2. Compute the taxpayer's (1) economic income and (2) gross income for tax purposes from the following events:
   a. The taxpayer sold stock for $10,000. The stock cost $6,000 in 1994. The fair market value of the stock at the beginning of the year was $9,000.
   b. The taxpayer used her controlled corporation's automobile for her vacation. The rental value of the automobile for the vacation period was $800.

c. The taxpayer raised vegetables in her garden. The fair market value of the vegetables was $900, and the cost of raising them was $100. She ate some of the vegetables and gave the remainder to neighbors.

d. The local government changed the zoning ordinances so that some of the taxpayer's residential property was reclassified as commercial. Because of the change, the fair market value of the taxpayer's property increased by $10,000.

e. During the year, the taxpayer borrowed $50,000 for two years at 9% interest. By the end of the year, interest rates had increased to 12%, and the lender accepted $49,000 in full satisfaction of the debt.

3. The roof of your corporation's office building recently suffered some damage as the result of a storm. You, the president of the corporation, are negotiating with a carpenter who has quoted two prices for the repair work: $600 if you pay in cash ("folding money") and $700 if you pay by check. The carpenter observes that the IRS can more readily discover his receipt of a check. Thus, he hints that he will report the receipt of the check (but not the cash). The carpenter has a full-time job and will do the work after hours and on the weekend. He comments that he should be allowed to keep all he earns after regular working hours. Evaluate what you should do.

4. Kevin, a cash basis taxpayer, received the following from his employer during 2001.

- Salary of $80,000.

- 2000 bonus of $12,000 received in 2001.

The 2000 bonus was not paid until 2001 because Kevin's employer suffered a computer crash and could not complete the bonus calculations in a timely manner. In addition, Kevin earned a 2001 bonus of $15,000 that was to be paid by the end of December 2001. However, in December, Kevin told his employer to delay the payment of the bonus until January 2002, when Kevin plans to retire.

a. Determine the effect of the above on Kevin's gross income in 2001.

b. Assume that Kevin is your client and he tells you that he now does not plan to retire until 2003. He is reasonably certain that he will be in a lower marginal tax bracket in that year. Write a memorandum explaining what you plan to advise Kevin regarding his 2002 bonus.

5. Charley visits Reno, Nevada, once each year to gamble. This year his gambling loss was $15,000. He commented to you, "At least I didn't have to pay for my airfare and hotel room. The casino paid that because I am such a good customer. That was worth at least $2,500." What are the relevant tax issues for Charley?

6. Evaluate the following alternative proposals for taxing the income from property.

a. All assets would be valued at the end of the year, any increase in value that occurred during the year would be included in gross income, and any decrease in value would be deductible from gross income.

b. No gain or loss would be recognized until the taxpayer sold or exchanged the property.

c. Increases or decreases in the value of property traded on a national exchange (e.g., the New York Stock Exchange) would be reflected in gross income for the years in which the changes in value occur. For all other assets, no gain or loss would be recognized until the owner disposes of the property.

7. Which of the following investments of $10,000 each will yield the greater after-tax value, assuming the taxpayer is in the 40% tax bracket (combined Federal and state) for ordinary income and 26% for qualifying capital gains in all years? The investments will be liquidated at the end of five years.

a. Land that will increase in value by 10% each year.

b. A taxable bond yielding 10% before tax. The interest can be reinvested at 10% before tax.

Prepare a brief speech for your tax class in which you explain why the future value of the land will exceed the future value of the taxable bond. Compound amount of $1 and compound value of annuity payments at the end of five years are given as:

Interest Rate	$1 Compounded for Five Years	$1 Annuity Compounded for Five Years
6%	$1.33	$5.64
10%	1.61	6.10

8. Determine the taxpayer's income for tax purposes in each of the following cases.
   a. Zelda borrowed $30,000 from the First National Bank. The bank required her to deliver collateral for the loan in the form of stocks with a value of $30,000 and a cost of $10,000.
   b. Zelda owned a lot on Sycamore Street that measured 100 feet by 100 feet. The cost of the lot to her is $10,000. The city condemned a 10-foot strip of the land so that it could widen the street. Zelda received a $2,000 condemnation award.
   c. Zelda owned land zoned for residential use only. The land cost $5,000 and had a market value of $7,000. Zelda spent $500 and several hundred hours petitioning the county supervisors to change the zoning to A–1 commercial. When the county approved the zoning change, the value of the property immediately increased to $20,000.

9. Al is an attorney who conducts his practice as a sole proprietor. During 2001, he received cash of $150,000 for legal services. Of the amount collected, $25,000 was for services provided in 2000. At the end of 2001, Al had accounts receivable of $45,000, all for services rendered in 2001. During the year, Al billed a client $20,000, but the client died and Al has no hope of collecting the balance due. At the end of the year, Al received $5,000 as a deposit on property a client was in the process of selling. Compute Al's gross income for 2001:
   a. Using the cash basis of accounting.
   b. Using the accrual basis of accounting.
   c. Advise Al on which method of accounting he should use.

10. Autumn Company began operating a grocery store during the year. Autumn's only books and records are based on cash receipts and disbursements, but the company president has asked you to compute the company's gross profit from the business for tax purposes.

Sale of merchandise	$480,000
Purchases of merchandise	220,000

   You determine that as of the end of the year Autumn has accounts payable for merchandise of $20,000 and accounts receivable from customers totaling $12,000. The cost of merchandise on hand at the end of the year was $9,000. Compute Autumn's accrual method gross profit for the year.

11. Color Paint Shop, Inc. (459 Ellis Avenue, Harrisburg, PA 17111), is an accrual basis taxpayer that paints automobiles. During 2001, the company painted Samuel's car and was to receive a $1,000 payment from his insurance company. Samuel was not satisfied with the work, however, and the insurance company refused to pay. In December 2001, Color and Samuel agreed that Color would receive $800 for the work, subject to final approval by the insurance company. In the past, Color had come to terms with customers only to have the insurance company negotiate an even smaller amount. In May 2002, the insurance company reviewed the claim and paid the $800 to Color. An IRS agent thinks that Color should report $1,000 of income in 2001 and deduct a $200 loss in 2002. Prepare a memo to Susan Apple, a tax partner for whom you are working, with the recommended treatment for the disputed income.

12. Dance, Inc., is a dance studio that sells dance lessons for cash, on open account, and for notes receivable. The company also collects interest on bonds held as an investment. The company's cash receipts for the year totaled $219,000.

Cash sales	$ 70,000
Collections on accounts receivable	120,000
Collections on notes receivable	20,000
Interest on bonds	9,000
	$219,000

The balances in accounts receivable, notes receivable, and accrued interest on bonds at the beginning and end of the year were as follows.

	1–1	12–31
Accounts receivable	$24,000	$24,000
Notes receivable	9,000	13,000
Accrued interest on bonds	2,500	4,000
	$35,500	$41,000

The fair market value of the notes is equal to 60% of their face amount. There were no bad debts for the year, and all notes were for services performed during the year. Compute the corporation's gross income:
a. Using the cash basis of accounting.
b. Using the accrual basis of accounting.
c. Using a hybrid method—accrual basis for lessons and cash basis for interest income.

13. Determine the effect of the following on a cash basis taxpayer's gross income for 2001.
   a. Received his paycheck for $3,000 from his employer on December 31, 2001. He deposited the paycheck on January 2, 2002.
   b. Received a bonus of $5,000 from his employer on January 10, 2002. The bonus was for the outstanding performance of his division during 2001.
   c. Received a dividend check from IBM on November 28, 2001. He mailed the check back to IBM in December requesting that additional IBM stock be issued to him under IBM's dividend reinvestment plan.

14. Swan Appliance Company, an accrual basis taxpayer, sells home appliances and service contracts. Determine the effects of each of the following transactions on the company's 2001 gross income assuming that the company uses any available options to defer its taxes.
   a. In December 2000, the company received a $1,200 advance payment from a customer for an appliance that Swan special ordered from the manufacturer. The appliance did not arrive from the manufacturer until January 2001, and Swan immediately delivered it to the customer. The sale was reported in 2001 for financial accounting purposes.
   b. In June 2001, the company sold a 12-month service contract for $240. The contract gave the customer an option to renew for an additional 12 months for $240. The company also sold a 24-month service contract for $450 in December 2001.
   c. On December 31, 2001, the company sold an appliance for $1,200. The company received $500 cash and a note from the customer for $700 and $260 interest, to be paid at the rate of $40 a month for 24 months. Because of the customer's poor credit record, the fair market value of the note was only $600. The cost of the appliance was $750.

15. Quail & Associates is a cash basis partnership. In 2001, Quail's partners negotiated with a client for services to be performed in 2002. Quail's client offered to pay $30,000 each month—a total of $360,000 for the year. Quail's partners countered that they would accept $30,000 each month for the first eight months of the year and the remaining $120,000 in January 2003. The client accepted Quail's terms.
   a. Did Quail actually or constructively receive $360,000 in 2002?
   b. What could explain Quail's willingness to spread the payments over a longer period of time?

16. The Heron Apartments requires its new tenants to pay the rent for the first and last months of the annual lease and a $400 damage deposit, all at the time the lease is signed. In December 2001, a tenant paid $800 for January 2002 rent, $800 for December 2002 rent, and $400 for the damage deposit. In January 2003, Heron refunded the tenant's damage deposit. What are the effects of these payments on Heron's taxable income for 2001, 2002, and 2003?
    a. Assume Heron is a cash basis taxpayer.
    b. Assume Heron is an accrual basis taxpayer.

17. a. Gus is a cash basis taxpayer. He sold 100 shares of Pelican, Inc., stock for $15,000. The cost to him was $1,000. Shortly before Gus sold the stock, Pelican decided to distribute unneeded assets to its shareholders. Therefore, Pelican declared a large dividend. Gus would have been entitled to a $5,000 dividend, but he sold his Pelican stock after the dividend declaration date and before the record date. What are the effects of the stock sale and the dividend on Gus's gross income?
    b. On the same day that Gus sold his Pelican stock, he gave 100 shares of Pelican stock to Jake, his son. He also gave Jake a corporate bond that had $400 of accrued interest that was not paid until after the son received the bond. What are the effects of these gifts on Gus's gross income?

18. Bethany Investment Partners is a cash basis taxpayer. It purchased a 20-year zero-coupon bond (no annual interest is paid) for $4,291 on January 1, 2001. The maturity value of the bond in 20 years is $20,000, which is the principal plus 8% interest compounded annually.
    a. What is Bethany's interest income from the bond for 2001?
    b. What is its basis for the bond on December 31, 2001?
    c. Will the interest income from the bond be greater in 2010 than it was in 2001? Explain.

19. Brad is the president of the Zinc Corporation. He and other members of his family control the corporation. Brad has a temporary need for $50,000, and the corporation has excess cash. He could borrow the money from a bank at 9%, and Zinc is earning 6% on its temporary investments. Zinc has made loans to other employees on several occasions. Therefore, Brad is considering borrowing $50,000 from the corporation. He will repay the loan principal in two years plus interest at 5%. Identify the relevant tax issues for Brad and Zinc Corporation.

20. On June 30, 2001, Ridge borrowed $52,000 from his employer. On July 1, 2001, Ridge used the money as follows.

Interest-free loan to Ridge's controlled corporation (operated by Ridge on a part-time basis)	$21,000
Interest-free loan to Tab (Ridge's son)	11,000
National Bank of Grundy 6% certificate of deposit ($14,840 due at maturity, June 30, 2002)	14,000
National Bank of Grundy 6.25% certificate of deposit ($6,773 due at maturity, June 30, 2003)	6,000
	$52,000

Ridge's employer did not charge him interest. The applicable Federal rate was 12% throughout the relevant period. Tab had investment income of $800 for the year, and he used the loan proceeds to pay medical school tuition. There were no other outstanding loans between Ridge and Tab. What are the effects of the preceding transactions on Ridge's 2001 taxable income?

21. Indicate whether the imputed interest rules apply in the following situations.
    a. Mitch is a cash basis attorney who charges his clients based on the number of hours it takes to do the job. The bill is due upon completion of the work. However, for clients who make an initial payment when the work begins, Mitch grants a discount on the final bill. The discount is equal to 10% interest on the deposit.

b. Local Telephone Company requires that customers make a security deposit. The deposit is refunded after the customer has established a good record for paying the telephone bill. The company pays 6% interest on the deposits.

c. Lynn asked Kelly for a $125,000 loan to purchase a new home. Kelly made the loan and did not charge interest. Kelly never intended to collect the loan, and at the end of the year Kelly told Lynn that the debt was forgiven.

22. Vito is the sole shareholder of Vito, Inc. The corporation also employs him. On June 30, 2001, Vito borrowed $8,000 from Vito, Inc., and on July 1, 2002, he borrowed an additional $3,000. Both loans were due on demand. No interest was charged on the loans, and the Federal rate was 10% for all relevant dates. Vito used the money to purchase stock, and he had no investment income. Determine the tax consequences to Vito and Vito, Inc., if:

a. The loans are considered employer-employee loans.

b. The loans are considered corporation-shareholder loans.

23. White and Swan Modeling is a partnership. How does the tax benefit rule apply to White and Swan in the following transactions?

a. In 2001, White and Swan paid Vera $5,000 for locating a potential client. The deal fell through, and in 2002, Vera refunded the $5,000 to the partnership.

b. In 2001, White and Swan paid an attorney $300 for services in connection with a title search. Because the attorney was negligent, the partnership incurred some additional costs in acquiring the land. In 2002, the attorney refunded his $300 fee to White and Swan.

24. Tedra is a CPA. Her clients frequently ask her for advice about investing. The current rate quoted on tax-exempt state and local government bond funds is 4.4%, and the rate on taxable U.S. government obligations is 6.6%. Both types of accounts are considered "risk-free." What is the minimum marginal tax bracket in which clients can benefit from investing in the tax-exempt funds?

25. The exclusion of state and local bond interest from Federal income tax is often criticized as creating a tax haven for the wealthy. Critics, however, often fail to take into account the effect of market forces. In recent months, the long-term tax-exempt interest rate has been 4.45% while the long-term taxable rate for bonds of comparable risk was approximately 6.4%. On the other hand, state and local governments do enjoy a savings in interest costs because of the tax-favored status of their bonds. To date, Congress has concluded that the benefits gained by the states and municipalities and their residents outweigh any damages to our progressive income tax system. Do you agree with the proponents of the exclusion? Why or why not?

26. Determine the taxable life insurance proceeds in the following cases.

a. When Monty died, his wife collected $50,000 on a group term insurance policy purchased by Monty's employer. Monty had never included the premiums in gross income.

b. The Cardinal Software Company purchased an insurance policy on the life of a key employee. The company paid $50,000 in premiums and collected $500,000 of insurance proceeds.

c. When Barbara died, she and her husband owed $15,000 on a loan. Under the terms of the loan, Barbara was required to purchase life insurance to pay the creditor the amount due at the date of Barbara's death. The creditor collected from the life insurance company the amount due at the time of Barbara's death. Is the creditor required to recognize income from the collection of the life insurance proceeds?

27. The Egret Company, which has a 40% (combined Federal and state) marginal tax rate, estimated that if its current president should die, the company would incur $200,000 in costs to find a suitable replacement. In addition, profits on various projects the president is responsible for would likely decrease by $300,000. The president has recommended that Egret purchase a $500,000 life insurance policy. How much insurance should the company carry on the life of its president to compensate for the after-tax

loss that would result from the president's death, assuming the $200,000 costs of finding a president are deductible and the lost profits would have been taxable?

28. Fay and Edward are partners in a financial consulting firm. The partners have an agreement that if either partner should die, the surviving partner will purchase the deceased partner's interest for 150% of its book value. Each partner has purchased an insurance policy on the life of the other partner as a means of funding the cross-purchase arrangement. Fay died, and Edward collected $150,000 on the life insurance policy on Fay's life. Edward had paid $40,000 in premiums on the insurance policy. What are the tax consequences to Edward of receiving the $150,000 of life insurance proceeds?

29. Hawk Industries, Inc., has experienced financial difficulties as a result of its struggling business. The corporation has been behind on its mortgage payments for the last six months. The mortgage holder has offered to accept $80,000 in full payment of the $100,000 owed on the mortgage and payable over the next 10 years. The interest rate of the mortgage is 7%, and the market rate is now 8%. What tax issues are raised by the creditor's offer?

30. Robin, who was experiencing financial difficulties, was able to adjust his debts as follows.
   a. His father agreed to cancel a $10,000 debt to help him out in his time of need. Robin's father told him, "I am not going to treat you any better than I treat your brothers and sister; therefore, the $10,000 is coming out of your inheritance from me."
   b. Robin's controlled corporation canceled a $6,000 debt he owed to the company.
   c. The Trust Land Company, which had sold Robin land, reduced the mortgage on the land by $12,000 and forgave him from paying $4,000 in accrued interest. Robin had deducted the interest on the previous year's tax return.

EXTENDER 31. During 2001, Fletcher had the following transactions involving capital assets.

Short-term gain on the sale of a stock investment	$4,000
Long-term gain on the sale of a sailing boat (used for pleasure)	2,000
Long-term loss on the sale of a power boat (used for pleasure)	(3,000)
Long-term gain on the sale of real estate held as an investment	5,000

   a. If Fletcher is in the 31% tax bracket, how much income tax do these transactions generate?
   b. What if Fletcher is in the 15% tax bracket?
   c. What if Fletcher is a C corporation in the 35% tax bracket? Assume that the power boat is used in the corporation's business.

EXTENDER 32. During 2001, Cole had the following gains and losses from the sale of capital assets.

Loss on Pigeon Corporation stock (held 9 months)	($4,000)
Gain on painting (held for 2 years as an investment)	5,000
Gain on unimproved land (held for 3 years as an investment)	3,000

   a. If Cole is in the 36% tax bracket, how much income tax do these transactions generate?
   b. What if Cole is in the 15% tax bracket?
   c. What if Cole is a C corporation in the 35% tax bracket?

EXTENDER 33. Selma opened a farm implements store in 2001. The only accounting records she maintains are her cash receipts and disbursements for the business. Cash receipts for 2001 total $600,000, and cash disbursements total $250,000. The cash receipts include the $50,000 Selma originally invested in the business and a $5,000 customer deposit on a new tractor that was to be delivered by the factory in January 2002. You determine that there were no accounts receivable at the beginning of the year. At the end of the year, receivables total $15,000. The inventory at the end of the year is $75,000, and the accounts payables are $40,000. Determine the gross income for the store for 2001 for tax purposes.

1. Using an online research service, find the audited financial statements of a major U.S. corporation.
   a. Summarize its most important financial accounting policies.
   b. Describe two elements of the Federal income tax law that significantly affected the corporation's earnings per share for the operating year.

2. Your client is a new partnership, Aspen Associates, which is an engineering consulting firm. Generally, Aspen bills clients for services at the end of each month. Client billings are about $50,000 each month. On average, it takes 45 days to collect the receivables. Aspen's expenses are primarily for salary and rent. Salaries are paid on the last day of each month, and rent is paid on the first day of each month. The partnership has a line of credit with a bank, which requires monthly financial statements. These must be prepared using the accrual method. Aspen's managing partner, Amanda Sims, has suggested that the firm should also use the accrual method for tax purposes and thus reduce accounting fees by $500. Write a letter to your client explaining why you believe it would be worthwhile for Aspen to file its tax return on the cash basis even though its financial statements are prepared on the accrual basis. Aspen's address is 100 James Tower, Denver, CO 80208.

RESEARCH PROBLEMS

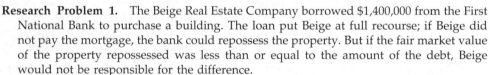

*Note: Solutions to Research Problems can be prepared by using the **RIA Checkpoint® Student Version Online research product**, or the **CCH U.S. Master Tax Guide Plus™** online Federal tax research database, which is available to accompany this text. It is also possible to prepare solutions to the Research Problems by using tax research materials found in a standard tax library.*

Research Problem 1. The Beige Real Estate Company borrowed $1,400,000 from the First National Bank to purchase a building. The loan put Beige at full recourse; if Beige did not pay the mortgage, the bank could repossess the property. But if the fair market value of the property repossessed was less than or equal to the amount of the debt, Beige would not be responsible for the difference.

When the fair market value of the property and the balance on the mortgage were $1,000,000, Beige was unable to make its monthly loan payment. After much negotiation, the bank reduced the principal to $800,000, which enabled Beige to make its payment in a timely manner. The IRS added $200,000 of income from discharge of indebtedness to Beige's taxable income for the year. Beige contends it has no gross income because the fair market value of the building is less than or equal to the reduced principal of the debt. Advise Beige on who is correct in a memo to the tax research file.

Partial list of research aids:
Rev.Rul. 91–31, 1991–1 C.B. 19.

Research Problem 2. The First Central Bank, an accrual basis taxpayer, has a credit card operation. Customers pay $30 per year for the right to use the card. If the customer decides to cancel the card during the year, the customer receives a refund of a prorated amount. The IRS position is that the amounts received are interest and thus are not eligible for deferral under Rev.Proc. 71–21. The taxpayer argues that the prepaid income is for services that are to be rendered over 12 months and thus the prepaid income can be amortized over the 12-month period. Determine the appropriate tax treatment.

Research Problem 3. Your client, the Cheyenne Golf and Tennis Club, requires its newly admitted members to purchase stock in the corporation and to make a deposit of $10,000. The deposit is to be repaid in 30 years, and no interest is charged. Is the deposit subject to the imputed interest rules for below-market loans? Outline the points you intend to make when you call the client back next week.

Partial list of research aids:
TAM 9735002.

Research Problem 4. Debra is a cash basis taxpayer. In December 2001, she purchased a used piano for $400. In 2002, she discovered $4,500 hidden inside the piano. Debra was unable to determine who placed the funds in the piano. She included the $4,500 in her 2002 gross income. When her 2002 return was examined, she explained the source of the $4,500 of other income she reported. Upon hearing the story, the IRS agent contended that Debra should have included the $4,500 on her 2001 return. Since she bought the piano in 2001, that is when her wealth actually increased. Debra was in the 36% marginal tax bracket in 2001, but was only in the 15% marginal tax bracket in 2002.

Debra has asked your advice about the correct year for reporting the $4,500. Summarize your analysis in a memo to the tax research file.

Partial list of research aids:
Cesarini v. U.S., 70–2 USTC ¶9509, 26 AFTR2d 70–5107, 428 F.2d 812 (CA–6, 1970).

Use the tax resources of the Internet to address the following questions. Do not restrict your search to the World Wide Web, but include a review of newsgroups and general reference materials, practitioner sites and resources, primary sources of the tax law, chat rooms and discussion groups, and other opportunities.

Research Problem 5. Determine the applicable Federal rate as of today for purposes of below-market loans. Use this figure to complete Problem 20.

Research Problem 6. Go to the Web page for a securities broker or mutual fund. Use a "calculator" provided there to indicate the following.

Taxable Interest Rate	Your Marginal Tax Rate	Breakeven Exempt Interest Rate
6%	36%	?
6%	15%	?
8%	28%	?
8%	39.6%	?

Research Problem 7. Summarize an article that you found about the tax and nontax advantages of a buy-sell agreement.

Business Deductions

LEARNING OBJECTIVES

After completing Chapter 4, you should be able to:

1. Understand the meaning and application of the ordinary, necessary, and reasonableness requirements for the deduction of business expenses.

2. Describe the cash and accrual methods of accounting for business deductions.

3. Apply a variety of Internal Revenue Code deduction disallowance provisions.

4. Understand the limitations applicable to the charitable contribution deduction for corporations.

5. Recognize and apply the alternative tax treatments for research and experimental expenditures.

6. Determine the amount of cost recovery under MACRS, and apply the § 179 expensing election and the deduction limitations on listed property and automobiles when making the MACRS calculation.

7. Identify intangible assets that are eligible for amortization and calculate the amount of the deduction.

8. Determine the amount of depletion expense and recognize the alternative tax treatments for intangible drilling and development costs.

Outline

TAX TALK

Last year I had difficulty with my income tax. I tried to take my analyst off as a business deduction. The Government said it was entertainment. We compromised finally and made it a religious contribution.

—*Woody Allen*

LEARNING OBJECTIVE 1

Understand the meaning and application of the ordinary, necessary, and reasonableness requirements for the deduction of business expenses.

Overview of Business Deductions

ORDINARY AND NECESSARY REQUIREMENT

Section 162(a) permits a deduction for all **ordinary and necessary** expenses paid or incurred in carrying on a trade or business. To understand the scope of this provision, it is necessary to understand the meanings of the terms ordinary and necessary.

Neither ordinary nor necessary is defined in the Code or Regulations. However, the courts have had to deal with these terms on numerous occasions and have held that an expense is necessary if a prudent business person would incur the same expense and the expense is expected to be appropriate and helpful in the taxpayer's business.[1] Many expenses that are necessary are not ordinary.

EXAMPLE 1

Welch felt that it would be helpful for the development of his new business if he repaid the debts owed by a bankrupt corporation that he had worked for. Consequently, over a

---

[1]*Welch v. Helvering*, 3 USTC ¶1164, 12 AFTR 1456, 54 S.Ct. 8 (USSC, 1933).

period of years, he took a portion of his income and repaid these debts, even though he was under no legal obligation to do so. Welch claimed these repayments as ordinary and necessary business expenses. The Supreme Court indicated that the payments were *necessary* for the development of Welch's business because they contributed toward Welch's reputation and built goodwill. However, the Court also indicated that the expenses were *not ordinary*, since the act of repaying the debts of a bankrupt company was unusual and not a normal method of doing business. Instead, the repayments were more appropriately classified as capital expenditures for goodwill.[2] ■

An expense is ordinary if it is normal, usual, or customary in the type of business conducted by the taxpayer and is not capital in nature.[3] However, an expense need not be recurring to be deductible as ordinary.

EXAMPLE 2	Zebra Corporation engaged in a mail-order business. The post office judged that Zebra's advertisements were false and misleading. Under a fraud order, the post office stamped "fraudulent" on all letters addressed to Zebra's business and returned them to the senders. Zebra spent $30,000 on legal fees in an unsuccessful attempt to force the post office to stop. The legal fees (though not recurring) were ordinary business expenses because they were normal, usual, or customary in the circumstances.[4] ■

REASONABLENESS REQUIREMENT

Although § 162 is intended to allow taxpayers to deduct a broad range of trade or business expenses, certain expenses are mentioned specifically:

- *Reasonable* salaries paid for services. *rendered*
- Expenses for the use of business property.

The Code applies the **reasonableness requirement** solely to salaries and other compensation for services.[5] However, the courts have held that for *any* business expense to be ordinary and necessary, it must also be reasonable in amount.[6]

What constitutes reasonableness is a question of fact.[7] If an expense is unreasonable, the excess amount is not allowed as a deduction. The question of reasonableness usually arises with respect to closely held corporations with no separation of ownership and management.

Transactions between shareholders and a closely held corporation may result in the disallowance of deductions for excessive salaries, rent, and other expenses paid by the corporation to the shareholders. The courts will view an unusually large salary in light of all relevant circumstances and may find that the salary is reasonable despite its size. If excessive payments for salaries, rent, and other expenses are closely related to the percentage of stock owned by the recipients, the payments are generally treated as dividends.[8] Since dividends are not deductible by the corporation, the disallowance results in an increase in corporate taxable income. Deductions for reasonable salaries will not be disallowed solely because

---

[2]*Welch v. Helvering*, 3 USTC ¶1164, 12 AFTR 1456, 54 S.Ct. 8 (USSC, 1933). For a contrasting decision, see *Dunn and McCarthy, Inc. v. Comm.*, 43–2 USTC ¶9688, 31 AFTR 1043, 139 F.2d 242 (CA–2, 1943), involving an *existing* business, where repayments to employees of a bankrupt corporation were held to be both ordinary and necessary.
[3]*Deputy v. DuPont*, 40–1 USTC ¶9161, 23 AFTR 808, 60 S.Ct. 363 (USSC, 1940).
[4]*Comm. v. Heininger*, 44–1 USTC ¶9109, 31 AFTR 783, 64 S.Ct. 249 (USSC, 1943).

[5]§ 162(a)(1).
[6]*Comm. v. Lincoln Electric Co.*, 49–2 USTC ¶9388, 38 AFTR 411, 176 F.2d 815 (CA–6, 1949).
[7]*Kennedy, Jr. v. Comm.*, 82–1 USTC ¶9186, 49 AFTR2d 82–628, 671 F.2d 167 (CA–6, 1982), *rev'g* 72 T.C. 793 (1979).
[8]Reg. § 1.162–8.

the corporation has paid insubstantial portions of its earnings as dividends to its shareholders.

EXAMPLE 3

Sparrow Corporation, a closely held corporation, is owned equally by Lupe, Carlos, and Ramon. The company has been highly profitable for several years and has not paid dividends. Lupe, Carlos, and Ramon are key officers of the company, and each receives a salary of $200,000. Salaries for similar positions in comparable companies average only $100,000. Amounts paid the owners in excess of $100,000 may be deemed unreasonable, and, if so, a total of $300,000 in salary deductions by Sparrow is disallowed. The disallowed amounts are treated as dividends rather than salary income to Lupe, Carlos, and Ramon because the payments are proportional to stock ownership. Salaries are deductible by the corporation, but dividends are not. ■

not deductible

PLANNING CONSIDERATIONS

Unreasonable Compensation

In substantiating the reasonableness of a shareholder-employee's compensation, an internal comparison test is sometimes useful. If it can be shown that nonshareholder-employees and shareholder-employees in comparable positions receive comparable compensation, it is indicative that compensation is not unreasonable.

Another possibility is to demonstrate that the shareholder-employee has been underpaid in prior years. For example, the shareholder-employee may have agreed to take a less-than-adequate salary during the unprofitable formative years

of the business. He or she would expect the "postponed" compensation to be paid in later, more profitable years. The agreement should be documented, if possible, in the corporate minutes.

Keep in mind that in testing for reasonableness, the total pay package must be considered. Compensation includes all fringe benefits or perquisites, such as contributions by the corporation to a qualified pension plan, regardless of when the funds are available to the employee.

Common Business Deductions. The language of § 162 is broad enough to permit the deduction of many different types of ordinary and necessary business expenses. Some of the more common deductions are listed in Exhibit 4–1.

LEARNING OBJECTIVE 2

Describe the cash and accrual methods of accounting for business deductions.

Timing of Expense Recognition

A taxpayer's accounting method is a major factor in determining taxable income. The method used determines *when* an item is includible in income and *when* an item is deductible on the tax return. Usually, the taxpayer's regular method of record keeping is used for income tax purposes.[9] The taxing authorities require that the method used clearly reflect income and that items be handled consistently.[10] The most common methods of accounting are the cash method and the accrual method.

Throughout the portions of the Code dealing with deductions, the phrase "paid or incurred" is used. A cash basis taxpayer is allowed a deduction only in the year an expense is *paid*. An accrual basis taxpayer is allowed a deduction in the year in which the liability for the expense is *incurred* (becomes certain).

---

[9]§ 446(a).

[10]§§ 446(b) and (e); Reg. § 1.446–1(a)(2).

■ **EXHIBIT 4–1**
Partial List of Business
Deductions

Advertising	Pension and profit sharing plans
Bad debts	Rent or lease payments
Commissions and fees	Repairs and maintenance
Depletion	Salaries and wages
Depreciation	Supplies
Employee benefit programs	Taxes and licenses
Insurance	Travel and transportation
Interest	Utilities

CASH METHOD REQUIREMENTS

The expenses of cash basis taxpayers are deductible only when they are actually paid with cash or other property. Promising to pay or issuing a note does not satisfy the actually paid requirement.[11] However, the payment can be made with borrowed funds. Thus, taxpayers are allowed to claim the deduction at the time they charge expenses on credit cards. They are deemed to have simultaneously borrowed money from the credit card issuer and constructively paid the expenses.[12]

Although the cash basis taxpayer must have actually or constructively paid the expense, payment does not assure a current deduction. The Regulations require capitalization of any expenditure that creates an asset having a useful life that extends substantially beyond the end of the tax year.[13] Thus, cash basis and accrual basis taxpayers cannot take a current deduction for capital expenditures except through amortization, depletion, or depreciation over the tax life of the asset.

EXAMPLE 4

Redbird, Inc., a cash basis taxpayer, rents property from Bluejay, Inc. On July 1, 2001, Redbird paid $24,000 rent for the 24 months ending June 30, 2003. The prepaid rent extends 18 months after the close of the tax year—substantially beyond the year of payment. Therefore, Redbird must capitalize the prepaid rent and amortize the expense on a monthly basis. Redbird's deduction for 2001 is $6,000. ■

1 *Find more information on this topic at our Web site: http://wft-entities.swcollege.com.*

PLANNING CONSIDERATIONS

Time Value of Tax Deductions

Cash basis taxpayers often have the ability to make early payments for their expenses at the end of the tax year. This may permit the payments to be deducted in the year of payment instead of in the following tax year. In view of the time value of money, a tax deduction this year may be worth more than the same deduction next year. Before employing this strategy, the taxpayer must consider next year's expected income and tax rates and whether a cash-flow problem may develop from early payments. Thus, a variety of considerations must be taken into account when planning the timing of tax deductions.

---

[11]*Page v. Rhode Island Trust Co., Exr.*, 37–1 USTC ¶9138, 19 AFTR 105, 88 F.2d 192 (CA–1, 1937).

[12]Rev.Rul. 78–39, 1978–1 C.B. 73. See also Rev.Rul. 80–335, 1980–2 C.B. 170, which applies to pay-by-phone arrangements.

[13]Reg. § 1.461–1(a).

all events test
known
earned
deductions incurred

minimize ability to get deductions

ACCRUAL METHOD REQUIREMENTS

The period in which an accrual basis taxpayer can deduct an expense is determined by applying the *all events test* and the *economic performance test*. A deduction cannot be claimed until (1) all the events have occurred to create the taxpayer's liability and (2) the amount of the liability can be determined with reasonable accuracy. Once these requirements are satisfied, the deduction is permitted only if economic performance has occurred. The economic performance test is met only when the service, property, or use of property giving rise to the liability is actually performed for, provided to, or used by the taxpayer.[14]

EXAMPLE 5

On December 22, 2001, Robin, Inc., an entertainment business, sponsored a jazz festival in a rented auditorium at City College. Robin is responsible for cleaning up the auditorium after the festival and for reinstalling seats that were removed so more people could attend the festival. Since the college is closed over the Christmas holidays, the company hired by Robin to perform the work did not begin these activities until January 2, 2002. The cost to Robin is $1,200. Robin cannot deduct the $1,200 until 2002, when the services are performed. ■

As illustrated in Examples 6 and 7, an exception to the economic performance requirement allows some *recurring* items to be deducted if certain conditions are met.[15]

2 *Find more information on this topic at our Web site: http://wft-entities.swcollege.com.*

EXAMPLE 6

Towhee Company, an accrual basis, calendar year taxpayer, entered into a monthly maintenance contract during the year. Towhee makes a monthly accrual at the end of every month for this service and pays the fee sometime between the first and fifteenth of the following month when services are performed. The December 2001 accrual is deductible even though the service is performed on January 12, 2002. ■

EXAMPLE 7

Tanager, Inc., an accrual basis, calendar year taxpayer, shipped merchandise sold on December 30, 2001, via Greyhound Van Lines on January 2, 2002, and paid the freight charges at that time. Since Tanager reported the sale of the merchandise in 2001, the shipping charge should also be deductible in 2001. This procedure results in a better matching of income and expenses. ■

Reserves for estimated expenses (frequently employed for financial accounting purposes) generally are not allowed for tax purposes because the economic performance test cannot be satisfied.

EXAMPLE 8

Oriole Airlines is required by Federal law to test its engines after 3,000 flying hours. Aircraft cannot return to flight until the tests have been conducted. An unrelated aircraft maintenance company does all of the company's tests for $1,500 per engine. For financial reporting purposes, the company accrues an expense based upon $.50 per hour of flight and credits an allowance account. The actual amounts paid for maintenance are offset against the

---

[14]§ 461(h).   [15]§ 461(h)(3)(A).

allowance account. For tax purposes, the economic performance test is not satisfied until the work has been done. Therefore, the reserve method cannot be used for tax purposes. ∎

LEARNING OBJECTIVE 3

Apply a variety of Internal Revenue Code deduction disallowance provisions.

Disallowance Possibilities

While most ordinary and necessary business expenses are deductible, the tax law contains provisions that disallow a deduction for certain expenditures. The most frequently encountered disallowance provisions are discussed below.

[handwritten: illegal payments not deductible]

PUBLIC POLICY LIMITATIONS

Justification for Denying Deductions. The courts developed the principle that a payment that is in violation of public policy is not a necessary expense and is not deductible.[16] Although a bribe or fine may be appropriate, helpful, and even contribute to the profitability of an activity, allowing a deduction for such expenses would frustrate clearly defined public policy. A deduction would effectively represent an indirect governmental subsidy for taxpayer wrongdoing.

Under legislation enacted based on this principle, deductions are disallowed for specific types of expenditures that are considered contrary to public policy:

- Bribes and kickbacks illegal under either Federal or state law, including those associated with Medicare or Medicaid.
- Two-thirds of the treble damage payments made to claimants resulting from violation of the antitrust law.[17]
- Fines and penalties paid to a government for violation of law.

EXAMPLE 9

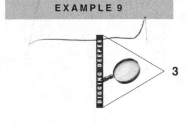

Brown Corporation, a moving company, consistently loads its trucks with weights in excess of the limits allowed by state law. The additional revenue more than offsets the fines levied. The fines are for a violation of public policy and are not deductible. ∎

3 *Find more information on this topic at our Web site: http://wft-entities.swcollege.com.*

Legal Expenses Incurred in Defense of Civil or Criminal Penalties. To deduct legal expenses as trade or business expenses, the taxpayer must be able to show that the origin and character of the claim are directly related to a trade or business. Personal legal expenses are not deductible. Thus, legal fees incurred in connection with a criminal defense are deductible only if the crime is associated with the taxpayer's trade or business.[18]

EXAMPLE 10

[handwritten: deductible win/lose]

Debra, a majority shareholder and chief financial officer of Blue Corporation, incurred legal expenses in connection with her defense in a criminal indictment for evasion of Blue's income taxes. Debra may deduct her legal expenses because she is deemed to be in the trade or business of being an executive. The legal action impairs her ability to conduct this business activity.[19] ∎

---

[16]*Tank Truck Rentals, Inc. v. Comm.,* 58–1 USTC ¶9366, 1 AFTR2d 1154, 78 S.Ct. 507 (USSC, 1958).

[17]§§ 162(c), (f), and (g).

[18]*Comm. v. Tellier,* 66–1 USTC ¶9319, 17 AFTR2d 633, 86 S.Ct. 1118 (USSC, 1966).

[19]Rev.Rul. 68–662, 1968–2 C.B. 69.

INTERNATIONAL IMPLICATIONS

TO BRIBE OR NOT TO BRIBE

Should a nation hold its companies to the same standards abroad as at home? Or, to put it another way, if a U.S. company spends money on bribes in a country where bribery is an accepted way of doing business, should it be allowed to deduct those bribes on its Federal income tax return?

According to a U.S. government report, between May 1994 and April 1998 U.S. companies paid bribes totaling $108 billion to influence 239 international contracts. About 70 percent of the bribes went to government officials and about 50 percent were for military procurement. Certain foreign countries permit such bribes as a way of doing business. Australia, Belgium, France, Luxembourg, New Zealand, Sweden, and Switzerland are among the countries that recently signed a treaty outlawing international bribery but still permit bribes to be deducted on their income tax returns. Such foreign bribes are illegal for U.S. companies under the Foreign Corrupt Practices Act of 1977. Opponents of the law argue that it forces U.S. companies to operate at a competitive disadvantage in the international business community.

Expenses Related to an Illegal Business. The usual expenses of operating an illegal business (e.g., a numbers racket) are deductible.[20] However, § 162 disallows a deduction for fines, bribes to public officials, illegal kickbacks, and other illegal payments.

EXAMPLE 11

Grizzly, Inc., owns and operates a saloon. In addition, Grizzly operates an illegal gambling establishment out of the saloon's back room. In connection with the illegal gambling activity, Grizzly had the following expenses during the year:

Rent	$ 60,000
Payoffs to police	40,000
Depreciation on equipment	100,000
Wages	140,000
Interest	30,000
Criminal fines	50,000
Illegal kickbacks	10,000
Total	$430,000

All of the usual expenses (rent, depreciation, wages, and interest) are deductible; payoffs, fines, and kickbacks are not deductible. Of the $430,000 spent, $330,000 is deductible and $100,000 is not. ■

An exception applies to expenses incurred in illegal trafficking in drugs.[21] Drug dealers are not allowed a deduction for ordinary and necessary business expenses

---

[20]*Comm. v. Sullivan*, 58–1 USTC ¶9368, 1 AFTR2d 1158, 78 S.Ct. 512 (USSC, 1958).   [21]§ 280E.

incurred in their business. In arriving at gross income from the business, however, dealers may reduce total sales by the cost of goods sold.[22]

POLITICAL CONTRIBUTIONS AND LOBBYING ACTIVITIES

Generally not deductible

Political Contributions.   Generally, no business deduction is permitted for direct or indirect payments for political purposes.[23] Historically, the government has been reluctant to extend favorable tax treatment to political expenditures by businesses. Allowing deductions might encourage abuses and enable businesses to have undue influence upon the political process.

Lobbying Expenditures.   The Code places severe restrictions on the deductibility of expenses incurred in connection with lobbying activities.[24] These provisions deny deductions for expenditures incurred in connection with:

- influencing state or Federal legislation;
- participating or intervening in any political campaign on behalf of, or in opposition to, any candidate for public office;
- attempting to influence voters with respect to elections, legislative matters, or referendums; and
- attempting to influence the actions of certain high-ranking public officials (including the President, Vice President, and cabinet-level officials).

ex local of federal

There are three exceptions to the disallowance provisions. First, an exception is provided for influencing *local* legislation (e.g., city and county governments). Second, the disallowance provision does not apply to activities devoted solely to *monitoring* legislation. Third, a *de minimis* exception allows the deduction of up to $2,000 of annual *in-house expenditures*, if the expenditures are not otherwise disallowed under the provisions discussed above. In-house lobbying expenditures do not include expenses paid to professional lobbyists or any portion of dues used by associations for lobbying. If in-house expenditures exceed $2,000, none of the in-house expenditures can be deducted.

EXAMPLE 12

Egret Company pays a $10,000 annual membership fee to the Free Trade Group, a trade association for plumbing wholesalers. The trade association estimates that 70% of its dues are allocated to lobbying activities. Thus, Egret's deduction is limited to $3,000 ($10,000 × 30%), the amount that is not associated with lobbying activities. ∎

EXCESSIVE EXECUTIVE COMPENSATION

The Code contains a *millionaires provision* that applies to compensation paid by *publicly held* corporations.[25] The provision does not limit the amount of compensation that can be *paid* to an employee. Instead, it limits the amount the employer can *deduct* for the compensation of a covered executive to $1 million annually. Covered employees include the chief executive officer and the four other most highly compensated officers. Employee compensation *excludes* the following:

CEO + 4 other highly comp officers

- Commissions based on individual performance.
- Certain performance-based compensation based on company performance according to a formula approved by a board of directors compensation

---

[22]Reg. § 1.61–3(a). Gross income is defined as sales minus cost of goods sold. Thus, while § 280E prohibits any deductions for drug dealers, it does not modify the normal definition of gross income.

[23]§ 276.
[24]§ 162(e).
[25]§ 162(m).

committee (comprised solely of two or more outside directors) and by share-holder vote. The performance attainment must be certified by this compensation committee.

- Payments to tax-qualified retirement plans.
- Payments that are excludible from the employee's gross income (e.g., certain fringe benefits).

DISALLOWANCE OF DEDUCTIONS FOR CAPITAL EXPENDITURES

The Code specifically disallows a deduction for "any amount paid out for new buildings or for permanent improvements or betterments made to increase the value of any property or estate."[26] The Regulations further define capital expenditures to include expenditures that add to the value or prolong the life of property or adapt the property to a new or different use.[27] Incidental repairs and maintenance of the property are not capital expenditures and can be deducted as ordinary and necessary business expenses. Repairing a roof is a deductible expense, but replacing a roof is a capital expenditure subject to depreciation deductions over its useful life. The tune-up of a delivery truck is an expense; a complete overhaul probably is a capital expenditure.

Capitalization versus Expense.   When an expenditure is capitalized rather than expensed, the deduction is at best deferred and at worst lost forever. Although an immediate tax benefit for a large cash expenditure is lost, the cost may be deductible in increments over a longer period of time.

If the expenditure is for a tangible asset that has an ascertainable life, it is capitalized and may be deducted as depreciation over the life of the asset or as a cost recovery allowance over a specified statutory period under either ACRS or MACRS.[28] Land is not subject to depreciation (or cost recovery) since it does not have an ascertainable life.

EXAMPLE 13

Buffalo Corporation purchases a prime piece of land and an old but usable apartment building located in an apartment-zoned area. Buffalo pays $500,000 for the property and immediately has the building demolished at a cost of $100,000. The $500,000 purchase price and the $100,000 demolition costs must be capitalized, and the tax basis of the land is $600,000. Since land is a nondepreciable asset, no deduction is allowed. More favorable tax treatment might result if Buffalo rents the apartments in the old building for a period of time to attempt to establish that there is no intent to demolish the building. If Buffalo's attempt is successful, it might be possible to allocate a substantial portion of the original purchase price of the property to the building (a depreciable asset). When the building is later demolished, any remaining adjusted basis can be deducted as an ordinary (§ 1231) loss. ∎

INVESTIGATION OF A BUSINESS

Investigation expenses are paid or incurred to determine the feasibility of entering a new business or expanding an existing business. They include such costs as travel, engineering and architectural surveys, marketing reports, and various legal and accounting services. How such expenses are treated for tax purposes depends on a number of variables, including the following:

---

[26]§ 263(a)(1).
[27]Reg. § 1.263(a)–1(b).

[28]Depreciation and cost recovery allowances are discussed later in this chapter.

legal Expense

land
against maintenance

- The current business, if any, of the taxpayer.
- The nature of the business being investigated.
- Whether or not the acquisition actually takes place.

If the taxpayer is in a business the same as or similar to that being investigated, all investigation expenses are deductible in the year paid or incurred. The tax result is the same whether or not the taxpayer acquires the business being investigated.[29]

EXAMPLE 14

Terry, an accrual basis sole proprietor, owns and operates three motels in Georgia. In the current year, Terry incurs expenses of $8,500 in investigating the possibility of acquiring several additional motels located in South Carolina. The $8,500 is deductible in the current year whether or not Terry acquires the motels in South Carolina. ■

When the taxpayer is not in a business that is the same as or similar to the one being investigated, the tax result depends on whether the new business is acquired. If the business is not acquired, all investigation expenses generally are nondeductible.[30]

EXAMPLE 15

Lynn, president and sole shareholder of Marmot Corporation, incurs expenses when traveling from Rochester, New York, to California to investigate the feasibility of acquiring several auto care centers. Marmot is in the residential siding business. If no acquisition takes place, Marmot may not deduct any of the expenses. ■

start up costs you're not carrying business year

If the taxpayer is not in a business that is the same as or similar to the one being investigated and actually acquires the new business, the expenses must be capitalized. At the election of the taxpayer, the expenses may be amortized over a period of 60 months or more, beginning with the month in which the business is acquired.[31]

EXAMPLE 16

Tina, a sole proprietor, owns and operates 10 restaurants located in various cities throughout the Southeast. She travels to Atlanta to discuss the acquisition of an auto dealership. In addition, she incurs legal and accounting costs associated with the potential acquisition. After incurring total investigation costs of $12,000, she acquires the auto dealership on October 1, 2001.

Tina must capitalize the $12,000 of investigation expenses for the auto dealership. If she elects to amortize the expenses over 60 months, she can deduct $600 ($12,000 × 3/60) in 2001. ■

TRANSACTIONS BETWEEN RELATED PARTIES

The Code places restrictions on the recognition of gains and losses from **related-party transactions.** Without these restrictions, relationships created by birth, marriage, and business would provide endless possibilities for engaging in financial transactions that produce tax savings with no real economic substance or change. For example, to create an artificial loss, a corporation could sell investment property to its sole shareholder at a loss and deduct the loss on the corporate return. The shareholder could then hold the asset indefinitely. Although title to the property has changed, there has been no real economic loss if the shareholder and corporation

---

[29]*York v. Comm.*, 58–2 USTC ¶9952, 2 AFTR2d 6178, 261 F.2d 421 (CA–4, 1958).

[30]Rev.Rul. 57–418, 1957–2 C.B. 143; *Morton Frank*, 20 T.C. 511 (1953); and *Dwight A. Ward*, 20 T.C. 332 (1953).

[31]§ 195(b).

are considered as an economic unit. A complex set of laws has been designed to eliminate such possibilities.

Losses.   The Code provides for the disallowance of any losses from sales or exchanges of property directly or indirectly between related parties.[32] In addition to specified family relationships (e.g., brothers and sisters), certain business relationships are subject to this disallowance rule. For instance, a corporation and a shareholder are considered related parties if the shareholder owns more than 50 percent of the corporation.

When the property is subsequently sold to an unrelated party, any gain recognized is reduced by the loss previously disallowed. Any disallowed loss not used by the related-party buyer to offset his or her recognized gain on a subsequent sale or exchange to an unrelated party is permanently lost.

EXAMPLE 17

Anna, sole shareholder of Leopard Corporation, sells common stock with a basis of $1,000 to the corporation for $800. Leopard sells the stock several years later for $1,100. Anna's $200 loss is disallowed upon the sale to Leopard, and only $100 of gain ($1,100 selling price − $800 basis − $200 disallowed loss) is taxable to Leopard upon the subsequent sale. ■

EXAMPLE 18

George sells common stock with a basis of $1,050 to his wholly owned corporation for $800. George's $250 loss is disallowed under the related-party rules. The corporation sells the stock eight months later to an unrelated party for $900. The corporation's gain of $100 ($900 selling price − $800 basis) is not recognized because of George's previously disallowed loss of $250. Note that the offset may result in only a partial tax benefit upon the subsequent sale (as in this case). If George had not sold the property to the corporation, he could have recognized a $150 loss upon the sale to the unrelated party ($900 selling price − $1,050 basis). ■

Unpaid Expenses and Interest.   The law prevents related taxpayers from engaging in tax avoidance schemes where one related taxpayer uses the accrual method of accounting and the other uses the cash basis. The accrual basis allows the deduction of expenses when incurred, while the cash method requires that income be reported when received. In the absence of restrictions, an accrual basis, closely held corporation, for example, could borrow funds from a cash basis individual shareholder. At the end of the year, the corporation would accrue and deduct the interest expense, but the cash basis lender would not recognize interest income since no interest had been paid. Section 267 specifically defers the accrual of an interest deduction until the lender is required to include the interest in income; that is, when it is actually received by the cash basis taxpayer. This matching provision also applies to other expenses, such as salaries and bonuses.

The deduction deferral provision does not apply if both of the related taxpayers use the accrual method or both use the cash method. Likewise, it does not apply if the related party reporting income uses the accrual method and the related party taking the deduction uses the cash method.

Relationships and Constructive Ownership.   Section 267 operates to disallow losses and defer deductions only between *related parties*. Losses or deductions generated by similar transactions with an unrelated party are allowed. Related parties include the following:

---

[32]§ 267(a)(1).

(handwritten margin notes: "Stockholder → how u are related to Corp", "treated as Owning", "Corp", "⅓ ⅓ ⅓ A B C", "Any brothers treated as if they own 100%", "ex. ABC", "if family Owns it you'll be treated as own 100%", "in value of outstanding stock", "Determining your relationship to the entity", "Donuee")

- Brothers and sisters (whether whole, half, or adopted), spouse, ancestors (parents, grandparents), and lineal descendants (children, grandchildren) of the taxpayer.
- A corporation owned more than 50 percent (directly or indirectly) by the taxpayer.
- Two corporations that are members of a controlled group.
- A series of other complex relationships between trusts, corporations, and individual taxpayers.

Constructive ownership provisions are applied to determine whether the taxpayers are related. Under these provisions, stock owned by certain relatives or related entities is deemed to be owned by the taxpayer for purposes of applying the loss and expense deduction disallowance provisions. A taxpayer is deemed to own not only his or her stock but the stock owned by his or her lineal descendants, ancestors, brothers and sisters or half-brothers and half-sisters, and spouse. The taxpayer is also deemed to own his or her proportionate share of stock owned by any partnership, corporation, estate, or trust of which he or she is a member. An individual is deemed to own any stock owned, directly or indirectly, by his or her partner. However, constructive ownership by an individual of the other partner's shares does not extend to the individual's spouse or other relatives (no double attribution).

EXAMPLE 19

The stock of Sparrow Corporation is owned 20% by Ted, 30% by Ted's father, 30% by Ted's mother, and 20% by Ted's sister. On July 1 of the current year, Ted loaned $10,000 to Sparrow Corporation at 8% annual interest, principal and interest payable on demand. For tax purposes, Sparrow uses the accrual basis, and Ted uses the cash basis. Both report on a calendar year basis. Since Ted is deemed to own the 80% owned by his parents and sister, he constructively owns 100% of Sparrow Corporation. If the corporation accrues the interest within the taxable year, no deduction can be taken until payment is made to Ted. ∎

LACK OF ADEQUATE SUBSTANTIATION

The tax law is built on a voluntary system. Taxpayers file their tax returns, report income and take deductions to which they are entitled, and pay their taxes through withholding or estimated tax payments during the year. The taxpayer has the burden of proof for substantiating expenses deducted on the returns and must retain adequate records. Upon audit, the IRS will disallow any undocumented or unsubstantiated deductions. These requirements have resulted in numerous conflicts between taxpayers and the IRS.

Some events throughout the year should be documented as they occur. For example, it is generally advisable to receive a pledge payment statement from a charity, in addition to a canceled check (if available), for proper documentation of a charitable contribution.[33] In addition, for a charitable contribution of $250 or more, a donor must obtain a *receipt* from the donee. Other types of deductible expenditures (such as travel and entertainment expenses, and depreciation on property used for both business and personal purposes) may require receipts or some other type of support.

EXPENSES AND INTEREST RELATED TO TAX-EXEMPT INCOME

Certain income, such as interest on municipal bonds, is tax-exempt.[34] The law also allows the taxpayer to deduct expenses incurred for the production of income.[35] Deduction disallowance provisions, however, make it impossible to make money

---

[33]Rev.Proc. 92–71, 1992–2 C.B. 437, addresses circumstances where checks are not returned by a financial institution or where electronic transfers are made.

[34]§ 103.
[35]§ 212.

[handwritten: Can't deduct expenses tax exempt income]

at the expense of the government by excluding interest income and deducting interest expense.[36]

EXAMPLE 20

Oriole, Inc., a corporation in the 35% bracket, purchased $100,000 of 6% municipal bonds. At the same time, Oriole used the bonds as collateral on a bank loan of $100,000 at 8% interest. A positive cash flow would result from the tax benefit as follows:

Cash paid out on loan	($8,000)
Cash received from bonds	6,000
Tax savings from deducting interest expense	2,800
Net positive cash flow	$ 800

To eliminate the possibility illustrated in the preceding example, the Code specifically disallows a deduction for the expenses of producing tax-exempt income. Interest on any indebtedness incurred or continued to purchase or carry tax-exempt obligations also is disallowed.

Judicial Interpretations. It is often difficult to show a direct relationship between borrowings and investment in tax-exempt securities. Suppose, for example, that a taxpayer borrows money, adds it to existing funds, buys inventory and stocks, then later sells the inventory and buys municipal bonds. A series of transactions such as these can completely obscure any connection between the loan and the tax-exempt investment. One solution would be to disallow interest on any debt to the extent that the taxpayer holds any tax-exempt securities. The law was not intended to go to such extremes. As a result, judicial interpretations have tried to be reasonable in disallowing interest deductions.[37]

4 *Find more information on this topic at our Web site: http://wft-entities.swcollege.com.*

EXAMPLE 21

In January of the current year, Crane Corporation borrowed $100,000 at 8% interest. Crane used the loan proceeds to purchase 5,000 shares of stock in White Corporation. In July, Crane sold the stock for $120,000 and reinvested the proceeds in City of Denver bonds, the income from which is tax-exempt. Assuming the $100,000 loan remained outstanding throughout the entire year, Crane cannot deduct the interest attributable to the period when it held the bonds. ■

LEARNING OBJECTIVE 4

Understand the limitations applicable to the charitable contribution deduction for corporations.

Charitable Contributions *[handwritten: only when paid]*

Corporations and individuals are allowed to deduct contributions made to qualified domestic charitable organizations.[38] Qualified organizations include:[39]

- A state or possession of the United States or any subdivisions thereof.
- A corporation, trust, or community chest, fund, or foundation that is situated in the United States and is organized and operated exclusively for religious, charitable, scientific, literary, or educational purposes or for the prevention of cruelty to children or animals.

[handwritten: political contributions not deductible]

[36]§ 265.
[37]See, for example, *The Wisconsin Cheeseman, Inc. v. U.S.*, 68–1 USTC ¶9145, 21 AFTR2d 383, 388 F.2d 420 (CA–7, 1968).
[38]§ 170.
[39]§ 170(c).

exceptions for accrued based corporations

5 *Find more information on this topic at our Web site:* ***http://wft-entities.swcollege.com***.

Generally, a deduction for a **charitable contribution** will be allowed only for the year in which the payment is made. However, an important exception is made for *accrual basis* corporations. They may claim the deduction in the year preceding payment if two requirements are met. First, the contribution must be *authorized* by the board of directors by the end of that year. Second, it must be *paid* on or before the fifteenth day of the third month of the following year.

EXAMPLE 22

On December 28, 2001, Blue Company, a calendar year, accrual basis partnership, authorizes a $5,000 donation to the Atlanta Symphony Association (a qualified charitable organization). The donation is made on March 14, 2002. Because Blue Company is a partnership, the contribution can be deducted only in 2002.[40] However, if Blue Company is a corporation and the December 28, 2001 authorization was made by its board of directors, Blue may claim the $5,000 donation as a deduction for calendar year 2001. ∎

PROPERTY CONTRIBUTIONS

The amount that can be deducted for a noncash charitable contribution depends on the type of property contributed. Property must be identified as long-term **capital gain property** or ordinary income property. Long-term capital gain property is property that, if sold, would result in long-term capital gain for the taxpayer. Such property generally must be a capital asset and must be held for the long-term holding period (more than one year). **Ordinary income property** is property that, if sold, would result in ordinary income for the taxpayer. Examples of ordinary income property include inventory and short-term capital assets (held one year or less). Refer to Chapter 3 for a brief introduction to the distinction between capital and ordinary assets.

The deduction for a charitable contribution of long-term capital property is generally measured by its *fair market value*.

EXAMPLE 23

In 2001, Mallard Corporation donates a parcel of land (a capital asset) to Oakland Community College. Mallard acquired the land in 1988 for $60,000, and the fair market value on the date of the contribution is $100,000. The corporation's charitable contribution deduction (subject to a percentage limitation discussed later) is measured by the asset's fair market value of $100,000, even though the $40,000 of appreciation on the land has never been included in Mallard's income. ∎

In two situations, a charitable contribution of long-term capital gain property is measured by the basis of the property, rather than fair market value. If a corporation contributes tangible personal property and the charitable organization puts the property to an *unrelated use*, the appreciation on the property is not deductible. Unrelated use is defined as use that is not related to the purpose or function that qualifies the organization for exempt status.

EXAMPLE 24

White Corporation donates a painting worth $200,000 to Western States Art Museum (a qualified charity), which exhibits the painting. White had acquired the painting in 1980 for $90,000. Because the museum put the painting to a related use, White is allowed to deduct $200,000, the fair market value of the painting. ∎

---

[40]Each calendar year partner will report an allocable portion of the charitable contribution deduction as of December 31, 2002 (the end of the partnership's tax year). See Chapter 11.

EXAMPLE 25

Assume the same facts as in the previous example, except that White Corporation donates the painting to the American Cancer Society, which sells the painting and deposits the $200,000 proceeds in the organization's general fund. White's deduction is limited to the $90,000 basis because it contributed tangible personal property that was put to an unrelated use by the charitable organization. ∎

The deduction for charitable contributions of long-term capital gain property to certain private nonoperating foundations (defined in §§ 4942 and 509) is also limited to the basis of the property.

As a general rule, the deduction for a contribution of ordinary income property is limited to the basis of the property. On certain contributions, however, corporations enjoy two special exceptions that allow a deduction for basis plus 50 percent of the appreciation on the property. The first exception concerns inventory if the property is used in a manner related to the exempt purpose of the donee. The charity must use the property solely for the care of the ill, the needy, or infants.

EXAMPLE 26

Lark Corporation, a grocery chain, donates canned goods to the Salvation Army to be used to feed the needy. Lark's basis in the canned goods is $2,000, and the fair market value (the sales price to customers) is $3,000. Lark's deduction is $2,500 [$2,000 basis + 50%($3,000 − $2,000)]. ∎

The second exception involves gifts of scientific property to colleges and certain scientific research organizations for use in research, provided certain conditions are met.[41]

LIMITATIONS IMPOSED ON CHARITABLE CONTRIBUTION DEDUCTIONS

Both corporations and individuals are subject to percentage limits on the charitable contribution deduction.[42] The complex limitations for individual taxpayers are covered in Chapter 15.

For any one year, a corporate taxpayer's contribution deduction is limited to 10 percent of taxable income. For this purpose, taxable income is computed without regard to the charitable contribution deduction, any net operating loss carryback or capital loss carryback, and the dividends received deduction. Any contributions in excess of the 10 percent limitation may be carried forward to the five succeeding tax years. Any carryforward must be added to subsequent contributions and will be subject to the 10 percent limitation. In applying this limitation, the current year's contributions must be deducted first, with excess deductions from previous years deducted in order of time.[43]

EXAMPLE 27

During 2001, Orange Corporation (a calendar year taxpayer) had the following income and expenses.

Income from operations	$140,000
Expenses from operations	110,000
Dividends received	10,000
Charitable contributions made in May 2001	5,000

---

[41] These conditions are set forth in § 170(e)(4). For the inventory exception, see § 170(e)(3).

[42] The percentage limitations applicable to individuals and corporations are set forth in § 170(b).

[43] The carryover rules relating to all taxpayers are in § 170(d).

[handwritten: R&D → 7 expense]

TAX FACT

WHAT TEN PERCENT CEILING?

Just how generous is corporate America? Based on recent data, of the $684 billion of corporate income subject to tax, contributions and gifts totaled approximately $8 billion. In other words, just over 1 percent of a corporation's income subject to tax, on average, goes to charity.

Source: 1997 Corporate Returns—Basic Tables.

[handwritten left margin: income taxable without taking charity]

For purposes of the 10% limitation only, Orange Corporation's taxable income is $40,000 ($140,000 − $110,000 + $10,000). Consequently, the allowable charitable contribution deduction for 2001 is $4,000 (10% × $40,000). The $1,000 unused portion of the contribution can be carried forward to 2002, 2003, 2004, 2005, and 2006 (in that order) until exhausted. ■

[handwritten right margin: or more, 60 months]

EXAMPLE 28

Assume the same facts as in the previous example. In 2002, Orange Corporation has taxable income (for purposes of the 10% limitation) of $50,000 and makes a charitable contribution of $4,500. The maximum deduction allowed for 2002 is $5,000 (10% × $50,000). The entire 2002 contribution of $4,500 and $500 of the 2001 charitable contribution carryforward are currently deductible. The remaining $500 of the 2001 carryforward may be carried over to 2003 (and later years, if necessary). ■

LEARNING OBJECTIVE 5

Recognize and apply the alternative tax treatments for research and experimental expenditures.

Research and Experimental Expenditures

[handwritten right margin: over, amortize, or]

Section 174 covers the treatment of **research and experimental expenditures.** The Regulations define research and experimental expenditures as follows:

> . . . all such costs incident to the development of an experimental or pilot model, a plant process, a product, a formula, an invention, or similar property, and the improvement of already existing property of the type mentioned. The term does not include expenditures such as those for the ordinary testing or inspection of materials or products for quality control or those for efficiency surveys, management studies, consumer surveys, advertising, or promotions.[44]

The law permits three alternatives for the handling of research and experimental expenditures:

- Expense in the year paid or incurred.
- Defer and amortize.
- Capitalize.

[handwritten: expense / capitalized currently]

If the costs are capitalized, a deduction is not available until the research project is abandoned or is deemed worthless. Since many products resulting from research projects do not have a definite and limited useful life, a taxpayer should ordinarily

---

[44]Reg. § 1.174–2(a)(1).

elect to write off the expenditures immediately or to defer and amortize them. It is generally preferable to elect an immediate write-off of the research expenditures because of the time value of the tax deduction.

The law also provides for a research activities credit. The credit amounts to 20 percent of certain research and experimental expenditures.[45]

EXPENSE METHOD

A taxpayer can elect to expense all of the research and experimental expenditures incurred in the current year and all subsequent years. The consent of the IRS is not required if the method is adopted for the first taxable year in which such expenditures were paid or incurred. Once the election is made, the taxpayer must continue to expense all qualifying expenditures unless a request for a change is made to, and approved by, the IRS. In certain instances, a taxpayer may incur research and experimental expenditures before actually engaging in any trade or business activity. In such instances, the Supreme Court has applied a liberal standard of deductibility and permitted a deduction in the year of incurrence.[46]

DEFERRAL AND AMORTIZATION METHOD

Alternatively, research and experimental expenditures may be deferred and amortized if the taxpayer makes an election.[47] Under the election, research and experimental expenditures are amortized ratably over a period of not less than 60 months. A deduction is allowed beginning with the month in which the taxpayer first realizes benefits from the research and experimental expenditures. The election is binding, and a change requires permission from the IRS.

EXAMPLE 29

Gold Corporation decides to develop a new line of adhesives. The project begins in 2001. Gold incurs the following expenses in 2001 and 2002 in connection with the project:

	2001	2002
Salaries	$25,000	$18,000
Materials	8,000	2,000
Depreciation and machinery	6,500	5,700

The benefits from the project will be realized starting in March 2003. If Gold Corporation elects a 60-month deferral and amortization period, there is no deduction prior to March 2003, the month benefits from the project begin to be realized. The deduction for 2003 is $10,867, computed as follows.

Salaries ($25,000 + $18,000)	$43,000
Materials ($8,000 + $2,000)	10,000
Depreciation ($6,500 + $5,700)	12,200
Total	$65,200
$65,200 × (10 months/60 months)	$10,867

■

---

[45]§ 41. See Chapter 13 for a more detailed discussion of the research activities credit.

[46]*Snow v. Comm.*, 74–1 USTC ¶9432, 33 AFTR2d 74–1251, 94 S.Ct. 1876 (USSC, 1974).

[47]§ 174(b)(2).

The option to treat research and experimental expenditures as a deferred expense is usually employed when a company does not have sufficient income to offset the research and experimental expenses. Rather than create net operating loss carryovers that might not be utilized because of the 20-year limitation on such carryovers, the deferral and amortization method may be used. The deferral of research and experimental expenditures should also be considered if the taxpayer expects higher tax rates in the future.

Other Expense Rules

In addition to the provisions related to charitable contributions and research and experimental expenditures, a variety of other expenses are subject to special rules and limitations. Some of these rules are noted briefly in the paragraphs that follow.

INTEREST EXPENSE

Generally, corporations are not limited in the amount of interest expense they may deduct. However, the deductibility of expenses (including interest) from certain activities may be limited.[48] In contrast, individuals generally may not deduct interest expense on loans used for personal purposes, unless the loan is secured by a home. Furthermore, individuals may only deduct interest expense associated with investments to the extent of net investment income.[49]

Because the deductibility of interest expense associated with certain activities is limited, the IRS provides rules for allocating interest expense among activities. Under these rules, interest is allocated in the same manner as the debt with respect to which the interest is paid, and debt is allocated by tracing disbursements of the debt proceeds to specific expenditures. The interest tracing rules are complex and depend on whether loan proceeds are commingled with other cash and the length of time the loan proceeds are held before they are spent.

TAXES

As with interest expense, tax payments in a business or investment context are generally deductible. However, most Federal taxes are not deductible. Individuals may also deduct tax payments, subject to limitations (discussed in Chapter 15). One unique problem associated with determining the deductibility of taxes relates to real estate taxes paid during a year when the real estate is sold.

Real estate taxes for the entire year are apportioned between the buyer and seller based on the number of days the property was held by each during the real property tax year. This apportionment is required whether the tax is paid by the buyer or the seller or is prorated according to the purchase agreement. It is the apportionment that determines who is entitled to deduct the real estate taxes in the year of sale. The required apportionment prevents the shifting of the deduction for real estate taxes from buyer to seller, or vice versa. In making the apportionment, the assessment date and the lien date are disregarded. The date of sale counts as a day the property is owned by the buyer.

---

[48]See, for example, the discussion of the passive activity limits in Chapter 5.

[49]See Chapter 15 for a more detailed discussion of the deductibility of interest by individuals.

TAX FACT

COST RECOVERY BY ANY OTHER NAME

Not surprisingly, the most prevalent write-off of assets used in a trade or business or in the production of income comes in the form of the cost recovery or depreciation allowances. Of the more than $585 billion of corporate deductions in a recent year, the relative use of the three broad types of write-offs is shown below.

	Percentage
Amortization	10
Cost recovery or depreciation	88
Depletion	2
	100

Source: 1997 Corporate Returns—Basic Tables.

EXAMPLE 30

A county's real property tax year runs from April 1 to March 31. Nuthatch Corporation, the owner on April 1, 2001, of real property located in the county, sells the real property to Crane, Inc., on June 30, 2001. Crane owns the real property from June 30, 2001, through March 31, 2002. The tax for the real property tax year April 1, 2001, through March 31, 2002, is $730. The portion of the real property tax treated as imposed upon Nuthatch, the seller, is $180 [(90/365) × $730, April 1 through June 29, 2001], and $550 [(275/365) × $730, June 30, 2001, through March 31, 2002] of the tax is treated as imposed upon Crane, the purchaser. ■

If the actual real estate taxes are not prorated between the buyer and seller as part of the purchase agreement, adjustments are required. The adjustments are necessary to determine the amount realized by the seller and the adjusted basis of the property to the buyer. If the buyer pays the entire amount of the tax, it effectively has paid the seller's portion of the real estate tax and has therefore paid more for the property than the actual purchase price. Thus, the amount of real estate tax that is apportioned to the seller (for Federal income tax purposes) and paid by the buyer is added to the buyer's adjusted basis. The seller must increase the amount realized on the sale by the same amount.

EXAMPLE 31

Seth sells real estate on October 3, 2001, for $50,000. The buyer, Wilma, pays the real estate taxes of $1,095 for the 2001 calendar year, which is the real estate property tax year. Of the real estate taxes, $825 (for 275 days) is apportioned to and is deductible by the seller, Seth, and $270 (for 90 days) of the taxes is deductible by Wilma. The buyer has paid Seth's real estate taxes of $825 and has therefore paid $50,825 for the property. Wilma's basis is increased to $50,825, and the amount realized by Seth from the sale is increased to $50,825. ■

The opposite result occurs if the seller (rather than the buyer) pays the real estate taxes. In this case, the seller reduces the amount realized from the sale by the amount that has been apportioned to the buyer. The buyer is required to reduce his or her adjusted basis by a corresponding amount.

TAX PACKAGE TO ATTRACT INVESTORS

The Fijian Ministry of Finance and National Planning has been authorized to prepare a comprehensive new investment package to increase private investment in Fiji's economy. The package is to include (1) a lower tax rate for all corporate taxpayers to make Fiji more regionally competitive; (2) investment and accelerated depreciation allowances for taxpayers that will allow the government to provide targeted support for particular sectors, regions, and races; and (3) an extension of loss carryforwards to ease the early years of investment.

SOURCE: Adapted from "Fiji: Finance Ministry to Prepare Package to Attract Investors," Fijilive Web site, Suva, sourced to *Fiji Daily Post*, August 16, 2000.

EXAMPLE 32

Silver Corporation sells real estate to Butch for $50,000 on October 3, 2001. While Silver held the property, it paid the real estate taxes of $1,095 for the calendar year, which is the real estate property tax year. Although Silver paid the entire $1,095 of real estate taxes, $270 of that amount is apportioned to Butch, based on the number of days he owned the property, and is therefore deductible by him. The effect is that the buyer, Butch, has paid only $49,730 for the property. The amount realized by Silver, the seller, is reduced by $270, and Butch reduces his basis in the property to $49,730. ■

LEARNING OBJECTIVE 6

Determine the amount of cost recovery under MACRS, and apply the § 179 expensing election and the deduction limitations on listed property and automobiles when making the MACRS calculation.

Cost Recovery Allowances

OVERVIEW

Taxpayers may write off the cost of certain assets that are used in a trade or business or held for the production of income. A write-off may take the form of a *cost recovery allowance* (depreciation under prior law), depletion, or amortization. Tangible assets, other than natural resources, are written off through cost recovery allowances. Natural resources, such as oil, gas, coal, and timber, are *depleted*. Intangible assets, such as copyrights and patents, are *amortized*. Generally, no write-off is allowed for an asset that does not have a determinable useful life.

The tax rules for writing off the cost of business assets differ from the accounting rules. Several methods are available for determining depreciation for accounting purposes, including the straight-line, declining balance, and sum-of-the-years' digits methods. Historically, *depreciation* for tax purposes was computed using variations of these accounting methods. The **depreciation rules** continue to apply to assets that were placed in service before 1981 and to certain post-1980 assets that do not qualify for write-off under the **cost recovery system.**

In 1981, the depreciation system was replaced by the **accelerated cost recovery system (ACRS).** Under ACRS, write-offs for tax purposes were determined using cost recovery tables provided in the tax law. These cost recovery allowances generally were determined using shorter asset lives and more accelerated depreciation methods than were available under the depreciation system.

BRIDGE DISCIPLINE

Bridge to Finance

For many business entities, success in producing goods for sale is dependent on the efficient use of fixed assets, such as machinery and equipment. An important question for such businesses to resolve is how they should gain access to the required complement of fixed assets: that is, whether the assets should be purchased or leased. To answer this question, the taxpayer must determine which alternative is more cost-effective. Critical to this assessment is quantifying the after-tax cost (including the associated tax benefits) of each option.

Purchasing productive assets for business use often necessitates an immediate cash outflow. However, the tax savings resulting from the available depreciation expense deductions mitigate the impact of that outflow, by reducing the taxpayer's taxable income and the income tax paid for the year. Consequently, the tax savings from the depreciation calculation associated with the purchase of an asset reduce the after-tax cost of employing the asset. The analysis can be refined further by evaluating the tax savings from the depreciation deductions in present value terms by quantifying the tax savings from the depreciation expense over the life of the asset. The asset's purchase also can be financed with debt.

Taxpayers who lease rather than buy an asset benefit by not giving up the use of funds that otherwise would have gone to purchase the asset. Lessees also forgo the opportunity to claim depreciation deductions; however, they reduce the cost of the leasing option by claiming the lease expense as a deduction against their tax base.

In 1986, ACRS was replaced by the **modified accelerated cost recovery system (MACRS),** which provided longer lives and less accelerated write-offs than ACRS. Cost recovery allowances for property placed in service after 1980 and before 1987 continue to be determined using ACRS tables as needed. Property placed in service after 1986 generally is subject to the MACRS rules. The MACRS rules for personal property and both ACRS and MACRS for real estate are covered in this text. Refer to IRS Publication 534 for detailed coverage of the alternative depreciation system.

MODIFIED ACCELERATED COST RECOVERY SYSTEM (MACRS)

MACRS provides separate cost recovery tables for realty (real property) and personalty (personal property). *Realty* generally includes land and buildings permanently affixed to the land. Write-offs are not available for land because it does not have a determinable useful life. Cost recovery allowances for real property, other than land, are based on recovery lives specified in the law. The IRS provides tables that specify cost recovery allowances for most types of realty.

Personalty is defined as any asset that is not realty. Personalty includes furniture, machinery, equipment, and many other types of assets. Do not confuse personalty (or personal property) with personal-use property. Personal-use property is any property (realty or personalty) that is held for personal use rather than for use in a trade or business or an income-producing activity. Cost recovery is not allowed for personal-use assets.

In summary, both realty and personalty can be either business-use/income-producing property or personal-use property. Examples include a residence (realty that is personal use), an office building (realty that is business use), a dump truck (personalty that is business use), and regular wearing apparel (personalty that is personal use). It is imperative that this distinction between the classification of an asset (realty or personalty) and the use to which the asset is put (business or personal) be understood.

ELIGIBLE PROPERTY UNDER MACRS

Assets used in a trade or business or for the production of income are eligible for cost recovery if they are subject to wear and tear, decay or decline from natural causes, or obsolescence. Assets that do not decline in value on a predictable basis or that do not have a determinable useful life (e.g., land, stock, antiques) are not eligible for cost recovery.

Cost Recovery Allowed or Allowable. The basis of cost recovery property must be reduced by the cost recovery *allowed* and by not less than the *allowable* amount. The allowed cost recovery is the cost recovery actually taken, whereas the allowable cost recovery is the amount that could have been taken under the applicable cost recovery method. If the taxpayer does not claim any cost recovery on property during a particular year, the basis of the property must still be reduced by the amount of cost recovery that should have been deducted (the *allowable* cost recovery).

EXAMPLE 33

On March 15, Heron Corporation paid $10,000 for a copier to be used in its business. The copier is five-year property. Heron elected to use the straight-line method of cost recovery, but did not take any cost recovery allowance in year 3 or 4. Therefore, the allowed cost recovery (cost recovery actually deducted) and the allowable cost recovery are as follows:[50]

	Cost Recovery Allowed	Cost Recovery Allowable
Year 1	$1,000	$ 1,000
Year 2	2,000	2,000
Year 3	–0–	2,000
Year 4	–0–	2,000
Year 5	2,000	2,000
Year 6	1,000	1,000
Totals	$6,000	$10,000

The adjusted basis of the copier at the end of year 6 is $0 ($10,000 cost – $10,000 *allowable* cost recovery). If Heron sells the copier for $800 in year 7, it will recognize an $800 gain ($800 amount realized – $0 adjusted basis). ∎

Cost Recovery Basis for Personal-Use Assets Converted to Business or Income-Producing Use. If personal-use assets are converted to business or income-producing use, the basis for cost recovery and for loss is the lower of the

---

[50]The cost recovery allowances are based on the half-year convention, which allows a half-year's cost recovery in the first and last years of the recovery period.

■ **EXHIBIT 4–2**
Cost Recovery Periods: MACRS
Personalty

Class	Examples
3-year	Tractor units for use over-the-road
	Any horse that is not a racehorse and is more than 12 years old at the time it is placed in service
	Special tools used in the manufacturing of motor vehicles, such as dies, fixtures, molds, and patterns
5-year	Automobiles and taxis Trucks
	Light and heavy general-purpose trucks
	Typewriters, calculators, and copiers
	Computers and peripheral equipment
7-year	Office furniture, fixtures, and equipment
	Agricultural machinery and equipment
	Single-purpose agricultural or horticultural structures
10-year	Vessels, barges, tugs, and similar water transportation equipment
	Assets used for petroleum refining or for the manufacture of grain and grain mill products, sugar and sugar products, or vegetable oils and vegetable oil products
15-year	Land improvements
	Assets used for industrial steam and electric generation and/or distribution systems
	Assets used in the manufacture of cement
20-year	Farm buildings except single-purpose agricultural and horticultural structures
	Water utilities

adjusted basis or the fair market value at the time the property was converted. As a result of this basis rule, losses that occurred while the property was personal-use property will not be recognized for tax purposes through the cost recovery of the property.

EXAMPLE 34

Hans acquires a personal residence for $120,000. Four years later, when the fair market value is only $100,000, he establishes a consulting company and uses the residence solely for office space. The basis for cost recovery is $100,000, since the fair market value is less than the adjusted basis. The $20,000 decline in value is deemed to be personal (since it occurred while Hans held the property for personal use). Therefore, depreciation deductions will be based on $100,000 rather than $120,000. ■

COST RECOVERY FOR PERSONAL PROPERTY

MACRS provides that the cost recovery basis of eligible personalty (and certain realty) is recovered over 3, 5, 7, 10, 15, or 20 years.[51] Examples of property in the different cost recovery categories are shown in Exhibit 4–2.[52]

Accelerated depreciation is allowed for these six MACRS classes of property. The appropriate computational methods and conventions are built into the tables, so it is not necessary to perform any calculations. To determine the amount of the cost recovery allowance, simply identify the asset by class and go to the appropriate table.[53]

---

[51]Property is classified by recovery period under MACRS based on asset depreciation range (ADR) midpoint lives provided by the IRS. Rev.Proc. 87–56, 1987–2 C.B. 674 is the source for the ADR midpoint lives.

[52]§ 168(e).
[53]§ 168(b).

The cost recovery allowance under MACRS is calculated by multiplying the cost recovery basis by the percentage that reflects the applicable cost recovery method and the applicable convention. The MACRS percentages for personalty are shown in Table 4–1 (MACRS tables begin at the end of the chapter prior to the Problem Materials).

EXAMPLE 35

Robin Corporation acquires a five-year class asset on April 10, 2001, for $30,000. Robin's cost recovery deduction for 2001 is $6,000 [$30,000 × .20 (Table 4–1)]. ■

Taxpayers may *elect* the straight-line method to compute cost recovery allowances for each of these classes of property. Certain property is not eligible for accelerated cost recovery and must be depreciated under an alternative depreciation system (ADS). Both the straight-line election and ADS are discussed later in the chapter.

MACRS views property as placed in service in the middle of the first year and allows a half-year of cost recovery in the year of acquisition and in the final year of cost recovery (the **half-year convention**).[54] Thus, for example, the statutory recovery period for three-year property begins in the middle of the year the asset is placed in service and ends three years later. In practical terms, this means the actual write-off periods cover 4, 6, 8, 11, 16, and 21 tax years. MACRS also allows for a half-year of cost recovery in the year of disposition or retirement.

EXAMPLE 36

Assume the same facts as in Example 35 and that Robin disposes of the asset on March 5, 2003. Robin's cost recovery deduction for 2003 is $2,880 [$30,000 × ½ × .192 (Table 4–1)]. ■

Mid-Quarter Convention. If more than 40 percent of the value of property other than eligible real estate[55] is placed in service during the last quarter of the year, a **mid-quarter convention** applies.[56] Under the convention, property acquisitions are grouped by the quarter they were acquired for cost recovery purposes. Acquisitions during the first quarter are allowed 10.5 months of cost recovery; the second quarter, 7.5 months; the third quarter, 4.5 months; and the fourth quarter, 1.5 months. The percentages are shown in Table 4–2.

EXAMPLE 37

Silver Corporation acquires the following five-year class property in 2001.

Acquisition Dates	Cost
February 15	$ 200,000
July 10	400,000
December 5	600,000
Total	$1,200,000

If Silver Corporation uses the statutory percentage method, the cost recovery allowances for the first two years are computed as indicated below. Because more than 40% ($600,000/ $1,200,000 = 50%) of the acquisitions are in the last quarter, the mid-quarter convention applies.

[54]§ 168(d)(4)(A).
[55]See Cost Recovery for Real Estate later in this chapter for a discussion of eligible real estate.
[56]§ 168(d)(3).

2001

February 15	[$200,000 × .35 (Table 4–2)]	$ 70,000
July 10	($400,000 × .15)	60,000
December 5	($600,000 × .05)	30,000
Total		$160,000

2002

February 15	[$200,000 × .26 (Table 4–2)]	$ 52,000
July 10	($400,000 × .34)	136,000
December 5	($600,000 × .38)	228,000
Total		$416,000

When property to which the mid-quarter convention applies is disposed of, the property is treated as though it were disposed of at the midpoint of the quarter. Hence, in the quarter of disposition, cost recovery is allowed for one-half of the quarter.

EXAMPLE 38

Assume the same facts as in Example 37, except that Silver Corporation sells the $400,000 asset on November 30, 2002. The cost recovery allowance for 2002 is computed as follows.

February 15	[$200,000 × .26 (Table 4–2)]	$ 52,000
July 10	[$400,000 × .34 × (3.5/4)]	119,000
December 5	($600,000 × .38)	228,000
Total		$399,000

COST RECOVERY FOR REAL ESTATE

Under the ACRS rules, realty that still is in use is assigned to either an 18-year or 19-year recovery period. Realty subject to ACRS must have been placed in service before January 1, 1987.

Under MACRS, the cost recovery period for residential rental real estate is 27.5 years, and the straight-line method is used for computing the cost recovery allowance. **Residential rental real estate** includes property where 80 percent or more of the gross rental revenues are from nontransient dwelling units (e.g., an apartment building). Hotels, motels, and similar establishments are not residential rental property. Nonresidential real estate has a recovery period of 39 years (31.5 years for such property placed in service before May 13, 1993) and is also depreciated using the straight-line method.[57]

Some items of real property are not treated as real estate for purposes of MACRS. For example, single-purpose agricultural structures are in the 7-year MACRS class. Land improvements are in the 15-year MACRS class.

All eligible real estate placed in service after June 22, 1984 (under both ACRS and MACRS) is depreciated using the **mid-month convention.**[58] Regardless of when during the month the property is placed in service, it is deemed to have been placed in service at the middle of the month. In the year of disposition, a mid-month convention is also used.

---

[57]§§ 168(b), (c), and (e).
[58]For ACRS property placed in service prior to June 23, 1994, a full month convention was used.

MACRS Computational Rules: Statutory Percentage and Straight-Line Methods

	Personal Property	Real Property
Convention	Half-year or mid-quarter	Mid-month
Cost recovery deduction in the year of disposition	Half-year for year of disposition or half-quarter for quarter of disposition	Half-month for month of disposition

Cost recovery is computed by multiplying the applicable rate (taken from a table) by the cost recovery basis. The MACRS real property rates are provided in Table 4–3.

EXAMPLE 39

Badger Rentals, Inc., acquired a building on April 1, 1993, for $800,000. If the building is classified as residential rental real estate, the cost recovery allowance for 2001 is $29,088 (.03636 × $800,000). If the building is classified as nonresidential real estate, the 2001 cost recovery allowance is $25,400 (.03175 × $800,000). (See the middle section of Table 4–3 for percentages.) ■

EXAMPLE 40

Assume the same facts as in Example 39, except that Badger acquired the nonresidential building on November 19, 2001. The 2001 cost recovery allowance is $2,568 [$800,000 × .00321 (Table 4–3)]. ■

An overview of MACRS rules is provided in Concept Summary 4–1.

THE MACRS STRAIGHT-LINE ELECTION

Although MACRS requires straight-line depreciation for all eligible real estate as previously discussed, the taxpayer may *elect* to use the straight-line method for personal property.[59] The property is depreciated using the class life (recovery period) of the asset with a half-year convention or a mid-quarter convention, whichever is applicable. The election is available on a class-by-class and year-by-year basis. The percentages for the straight-line election with a half-year convention appear in Table 4–4.

EXAMPLE 41

Terry acquires a 10-year class asset on August 4, 2001, for $100,000. He elects the straight-line method of cost recovery. Terry's cost recovery deduction for 2001 is $5,000 ($100,000 × .050). His cost recovery deduction for 2002 is $10,000 ($100,000 × .10). (See Table 4–4 for percentages.) ■

ELECTION TO EXPENSE ASSETS UNDER § 179

Section 179 (Election to Expense Certain Depreciable Business Assets) permits a taxpayer to elect to deduct up to $24,000 in 2001[60] of the acquisition cost of *tangible*

---

[59] § 168(b)(5).

[60] The expense amount was $10,000 for property placed in service in tax years beginning before January 1, 1993; $17,500 for property placed in service from January 1, 1993 to December 31, 1996; $18,000 for property placed in service in tax years beginning in 1997; $18,500 for property placed in service in tax years beginning in 1998; and, $19,000 for property placed in service in tax years beginning in 1999.

[handwritten: machinery equipment vehicles]

personal property used in a trade or business. The maximum first-year deduction under this provision increases to $25,000 on the following schedule.

[handwritten: doesn't carryover]

Tax Year Beginning in	Maximum Expense Deduction
2000	$20,000
2001 or 2002	24,000
2003 and thereafter	25,000

Amounts that are expensed under § 179 may not be capitalized and depreciated. The **§ 179 expensing election** is an annual election and applies to the acquisition cost of property placed in service that year. The immediate expense election is not available for real property or for property used for the production of income.[61]

EXAMPLE 42

Kodiak Corporation acquires machinery (five-year class) on February 1, 2001, at a cost of $40,000 and elects to expense $24,000 under § 179. Kodiak's statutory percentage cost recovery deduction for 2001 is $3,200 [($40,000 cost − $24,000 expensed) × .200]. (See Table 4-1 for percentage.) Kodiak's total deduction for 2001 is $27,200 ($24,000 + $3,200). ■

[handwritten: depreciate on $16,000]

Annual Limitations.   Two additional limitations apply to the amount deductible under § 179. First, the ceiling amount on the deduction is reduced dollar-for-dollar when property (other than ineligible real estate) placed in service during the taxable year exceeds $200,000. Second, the amount expensed under § 179 cannot exceed the aggregate amount of taxable income derived from the conduct of any trade or business by the taxpayer. Taxable income of a trade or business is computed without regard to the amount expensed under § 179. Any § 179 deduction in excess of taxable income is carried forward to future taxable years and added to other amounts eligible for expensing. The § 179 amount eligible for expensing in a carry-forward year is limited to the *lesser* of (1) the appropriate statutory dollar amount ($24,000 in 2002) reduced by the cost of § 179 property placed in service in excess of $200,000 in the carryforward year or (2) the business income limitation in the carryforward year.

[handwritten: over of 200,000 knocks down your $24,000 limit]

EXAMPLE 43

Jill owns a computer service and operates it as a sole proprietorship. In 2001, she will net $11,000 before considering any § 179 deduction. If Jill spends $204,000 on new equipment, her § 179 expense deduction is computed as follows.

§ 179 deduction before adjustment	$24,000
Less: Dollar limitation reduction ($204,000 − $200,000)	(4,000)
Remaining § 179 deduction	$20,000
Business income limitation	$11,000
§ 179 deduction allowed	$11,000
§ 179 deduction carryforward ($20,000 − $11,000)	$ 9,000

■

Effect on Basis.   The basis of the property for cost recovery purposes is reduced by the § 179 amount after it is adjusted for property placed in service in excess of $200,000. This adjusted amount does not reflect any business income limitation.

---

[61]§§ 179(b) and (d).

> **EXAMPLE 44**

Assume the same facts as in Example 43 and that the new equipment is five-year class property. Jill's statutory percentage cost recovery deduction for 2001 is $36,800 [($204,000 − $20,000) × .200]. (See Table 4–1 for percentage.) ■

BUSINESS AND PERSONAL USE OF AUTOMOBILES AND OTHER LISTED PROPERTY

Limits exist on MACRS deductions for automobiles and other **listed property** used for both personal and business purposes.[62] These limits would apply, for example, to an automobile used by a sole proprietor partly for business purposes and partly for personal use.

If the listed property is *predominantly* used for business, the taxpayer is allowed to use the *statutory percentage method* to recover the cost. In cases where the property is *not predominantly* used for business, the cost is recovered using the *straight-line method*. The statutory percentage method results in a faster recovery of cost than the straight-line method. Listed property includes the following:

- Any passenger automobile.
- Any other property used as a means of transportation.
- Any property of a type generally used for purposes of entertainment, recreation, or amusement.
- Any computer or peripheral equipment, with the exception of equipment used exclusively at a regular business establishment, including a qualifying home office.
- Any cellular telephone or other similar telecommunications equipment.
- Any other property specified in the Regulations.[63]

Automobiles and Other Listed Property Used Predominantly in Business. For listed property to be considered as predominantly used in business, its *business usage* must exceed 50 percent.[64] The use of listed property for production of income does not qualify as business use for purposes of the more-than-50 percent test. However, both production of income and business use percentages are used to compute the cost recovery deduction.

> **EXAMPLE 45**

On September 1, 2001, Emma places in service listed five-year recovery property. The property cost $10,000. If Emma uses the property 40% for business and 25% for the production of income, the property is not considered as predominantly used for business. The cost is recovered using straight-line cost recovery. Emma's cost recovery allowance for the year is $650 ($10,000 × 10% × 65%). If, however, Emma uses the property 60% for business and 25% for the production of income, the property is considered as used predominantly for business. Therefore, she may use the statutory percentage method. Emma's cost recovery allowance for the year is $1,700 ($10,000 × .200 × 85%). ■

The method for determining the percentage of business usage for listed property is specified in the Regulations. The Regulations provide that for automobiles a mileage-based percentage is to be used. Other listed property is to use the most appropriate unit of time (e.g., hours) the property is actually used (rather than available for use).[65]

---

[62] § 280F.
[63] § 280F(d)(4).

[64] § 280F(b)(4).
[65] Reg. § 1.280F–6T(e).

Limits on Cost Recovery for Automobiles.   The law places special limitations on the cost recovery deduction for *passenger automobiles*.[66] These statutory dollar limits were imposed on passenger automobiles because of the belief that the tax system was being used to underwrite automobiles whose cost and luxury far exceeded what was needed for their business use.

The following limits apply to the cost recovery deductions for passenger automobiles for 2001.[67]

Year of Use	Recovery Limitation
1	$3,060
2	4,900
3	2,950
Succeeding years until all cost is recovered	1,775

These limits are imposed before any percentage reduction for personal use. In addition, the limitation in the first year includes any amount the taxpayer elects to expense under § 179.[68] If the passenger automobile is used partly for personal use, the personal-use percentage is ignored for the purpose of determining the unrecovered cost available for deduction in later years.

EXAMPLE 46

On July 1, 2001, Dan places in service an automobile that cost $20,000. The car is always used 80% for business and 20% for personal use. The cost recovery for the automobile would be as follows.

2001	$2,448 [$20,000 × 20% (limited to $3,060) × 80%]
2002	$3,920 [$20,000 × 32% (limited to $4,900) × 80%]
2003	$2,360 [$20,000 × 19.2% (limited to $2,950) × 80%]
2004	$1,420 [$20,000 × 11.52% (limited to $1,775) × 80%]
2005	$1,420 [$20,000 × 11.52% (limited to $1,775) × 80%]
2006	$1,420 [$5,540 unrecovered cost ($20,000 − $14,460*) (limited to $1,775) × 80%]

*($3,060 + $4,900 + $2,950 + $1,775 + $1,775). Although the statutory percentage method appears to restrict the deduction to $922 [$20,000 × 5.76% (limited to $1,775) × 80%], the unrecovered cost of $5,540 (limited to $1,775) multiplied by the business usage percentage is deductible. At the start of 2004 (year 4), there is an automatic switch to the straight-line recovery method. Under this method, the unrecovered cost up to the maximum allowable limit ($1,775) is deductible in the last year of the recovery period (2006 or year 6). Because the limit may restrict the deduction, any remaining unrecovered cost is deductible in the next or succeeding year(s), subject to the maximum allowable yearly limit ($1,775), multiplied by the business usage percentage.

The total cost recovery for the years 2001–2006 is $12,988 ($2,448 + $3,920 + $2,360 + $1,420 + $1,420 + $1,420). The remaining cost will be recovered in future years. ∎

The cost recovery limitations are maximum amounts. If the regular calculation produces a lesser amount of cost recovery, the lesser amount is used.

EXAMPLE 47

On April 2, 2001, Gail places in service an automobile that cost $10,000. The car is always used 70% for business and 30% for personal use. The cost recovery allowance for 2001 is $1,400 ($10,000 × 20% × 70%), which is less than $2,142 ($3,060 × 70%). ∎

---

[66]§ 280F(d)(5).
[67]§ 280F(a)(2). The 2000 indexed amounts were $3,060, $4,900, $2,950, and $1,775.

[68]§ 280F(d)(1).

The cost recovery limitations apply *only* to passenger automobiles and not to other listed property.

Automobiles and Other Listed Property Not Used Predominantly in Business.

The cost of listed property that does not pass the more-than-50 percent business usage test in the year the property is placed in service must be recovered using the straight-line method.[69] The straight-line method to be used is that required under the alternative depreciation system (introduced later in the chapter). This system requires a straight-line recovery period of five years for automobiles. However, even though the straight-line method is used, the cost recovery allowance for passenger automobiles cannot exceed the dollar limitations noted above.

If the listed property fails the more-than-50 percent business usage test, the straight-line method must be used for the remainder of the property's life. This applies even if at some later date the business usage of the property increases to more than 50 percent. Even though the straight-line method must continue to be used, however, the amount of cost recovery will reflect the increase in business usage.

Change from Predominantly Business Use.

If the business-use percentage of listed property falls to 50 percent or lower after the year the property is placed in service, the property is subject to *cost recovery recapture*. The amount required to be recaptured and included in the taxpayer's return as ordinary income is the excess cost recovery. *Excess cost recovery* is the excess of the cost recovery deduction taken in prior years using the statutory percentage method over the amount that would have been allowed if the straight-line method had been used since the property was placed in service.[70]

After the business usage of the listed property drops below the more-than-50 percent level, the straight-line method must be used for the remaining life of the property.

Leased Automobiles.

A taxpayer who leases a passenger automobile for business purposes must report an *inclusion amount* in gross income. The inclusion amount is computed from an IRS table for each taxable year for which the taxpayer leases the automobile. The purpose of this provision is to prevent taxpayers from circumventing the cost recovery dollar limitations by leasing, instead of purchasing, an automobile.

The dollar amount of the inclusion is based on the fair market value of the automobile and is prorated for the number of days the auto is used during the taxable year. The prorated dollar amount is then multiplied by the business and income-producing usage percentage to determine the amount to be included in gross income.[71] The taxpayer deducts the lease payments, multiplied by the business and income-producing usage percentage. The net effect is that the annual deduction for the lease payment is reduced by the inclusion amount.

EXAMPLE 48

On April 1, 2001, Jim leases and places in service a passenger automobile worth $40,000. The lease is to be for a period of five years. During the taxable years 2001 and 2002, Jim uses the automobile 70% for business and 30% for personal use. Assuming the dollar amounts from the IRS table for 2001 and 2002 are $186 and $409, Jim must include $98 in gross income for 2001 and $286 for 2002, computed as follows.

---

[69]§ 280F(b)(2).
[70]§ 280F(b)(3).

[71]Reg. § 1.280F–7(a).

2001 $186 × (275/365) × 70% = $98
2002 $409 × (365/365) × 70% = $286

In addition, Jim can deduct 70% of the lease payments each year because this is the business-use percentage. ∎

Substantiation Requirements.   Listed property is subject to the substantiation requirements of § 274. This means that the taxpayer must prove the business usage as to the amount of expense or use, the time and place of use, the business purpose for the use, and the business relationship to the taxpayer of persons using the property. Substantiation requires adequate records or sufficient evidence corroborating the taxpayer's statement. However, these substantiation requirements do not apply to vehicles that, by reason of their nature, are not likely to be used more than a *de minimis* amount for personal purposes.[72]

ALTERNATIVE DEPRECIATION SYSTEM (ADS)

The **alternative depreciation system (ADS)** must be used in lieu of MACRS for the following:[73]

- To calculate the portion of depreciation treated as an alternative minimum tax (AMT) adjustment for purposes of the corporate and individual AMT (see Chapter 13).[74]
- To compute depreciation allowances for property for which any of the following is true:
  - Used predominantly outside the United States.
  - Leased or otherwise used by a tax-exempt entity.
  - Financed with the proceeds of tax-exempt bonds.
  - Imported from foreign countries that maintain discriminatory trade practices or otherwise engage in discriminatory acts.
- To compute depreciation allowances for earnings and profits purposes (see Chapter 10).

Tables 4–5, 4–6, and 4–7 provide cost recovery rates under the ADS method. Additional details of the ADS method are beyond the scope of this chapter.

LEARNING OBJECTIVE 7

Identify intangible assets that are eligible for amortization and calculate the amount of the deduction.

Amortization

Taxpayers can claim an **amortization** deduction on certain intangible assets. The amount of the deduction is determined by amortizing the adjusted basis of such intangibles ratably over a 15-year period beginning in the month in which the intangible is acquired.[75]

An amortizable § 197 intangible is any § 197 intangible acquired after August 10, 1993, and held in connection with the conduct of a trade or business or for the production of income. Section 197 intangibles include goodwill and going-concern value, franchises (except sports franchises), trademarks, and trade names. Covenants not to compete, copyrights, and patents are also included if they are acquired

---

[72]§§ 274(d) and (i).
[73]§ 168(g).
[74]This AMT adjustment applies for real and personal property placed in service before 1999. However, it will continue to apply for personal property placed in service after 1998, if the taxpayer uses the 200% declining-balance method for regular income tax purposes. See Chapter 13.
[75]§ 197(a).

[handwritten note: goodwill → no longer amortized in finance normally under tax, u can't amortize goodwill all ~]

in connection with the acquisition of a business. Generally, self-created intangibles are not § 197 intangibles. The 15-year amortization period applies regardless of the actual useful life of an amortizable § 197 intangible. No other depreciation or amortization deduction is permitted with respect to any amortizable § 197 intangible except those permitted under the 15-year amortization rules.

EXAMPLE 49

On June 1, 2001, Sally purchased and began operating the Falcon Cafe. Of the purchase price, $90,000 is correctly allocated to goodwill. The deduction for amortization for 2001 is $3,500 [($90,000/15) × (7/12)]. ■

PLANNING CONSIDERATIONS
Structuring the Sale of a Business

On the sale of a sole proprietorship where the sales price exceeds the fair market value of the tangible assets and stated intangible assets, a planning opportunity may exist for both the seller and the buyer.

The seller's preference is for the excess amount to be allocated to *goodwill* because goodwill is a capital asset whose sale may result in favorably taxed long-term capital gain. Amounts received for a *covenant not to compete,* however, produce ordinary income, which is not subject to favorable long-term capital gain rates.

Because a covenant and goodwill both are amortized over a statutory 15-year period, the tax results of a covenant

not to compete versus goodwill are the same for the *buyer.* However, the buyer should recognize that an allocation to goodwill rather than a covenant may provide a tax benefit to the seller. Therefore, the buyer, in negotiating the purchase price, should factor in the tax benefit to the seller of having the excess amount labeled goodwill rather than a covenant not to compete. Of course, if the noncompetition aspects of a covenant are important to the buyer, a portion of the excess amount can be assigned to a covenant.

LEARNING OBJECTIVE 8

Determine the amount of depletion expense and recognize the alternative tax treatments for intangible drilling and development costs.

Depletion

Natural resources (e.g., oil, gas, coal, gravel, timber) are subject to **depletion,** which is simply a form of depreciation applicable to natural resources. Land generally cannot be depleted.

The owner of an interest in the natural resource is entitled to deduct depletion. An owner is one who has an economic interest in the property.[76] An economic interest requires the acquisition of an interest in the resource in place and the receipt of income from the extraction or severance of that resource. Although all natural resources are subject to depletion, oil and gas wells are used as an example in the following paragraphs to illustrate the related costs and issues.

In developing an oil or gas well, the producer must make four types of expenditures.

- Natural resource costs.
- Intangible drilling and development costs.
- Tangible asset costs.
- Operating costs.

---

[76]Reg. § 1.611–1(b).

Natural resources are physically limited, and the costs to acquire them (e.g., oil under the ground) are, therefore, recovered through depletion. Costs incurred in making the property ready for drilling such as the cost of labor in clearing the property, erecting derricks, and drilling the hole are **intangible drilling and development costs (IDC).** These costs generally have no salvage value and are a lost cost if the well is not productive (dry). Costs for tangible assets such as tools, pipes, and engines are capital in nature. These costs must be capitalized and recovered through depreciation (cost recovery). Costs incurred after the well is producing are operating costs. These costs would include expenditures for such items as labor, fuel, and supplies. Operating costs are deductible when incurred (on the accrual basis) or when paid (on the cash basis).

The expenditures for depreciable assets and operating costs pose no unusual problems for producers of natural resources. The tax treatment of depletable costs and intangible drilling and development costs is quite a different matter.

INTANGIBLE DRILLING AND DEVELOPMENT COSTS (IDC)

Intangible drilling and development costs (IDC) can be handled in one of two ways at the option of the taxpayer. They can be either charged off as an expense in the year in which they are incurred or capitalized and written off through depletion. The taxpayer makes the election in the first year such expenditures are incurred either by taking a deduction on the return or by adding them to the depletable basis. No formal statement of intent is required. Once made, the election is binding on both the taxpayer and the IRS for all such expenditures in the future. If the taxpayer fails to make the election to expense IDC on the original timely filed return the first year such expenditures are incurred, an automatic election to capitalize them has been made and is irrevocable.

As a general rule, it is more advantageous to expense IDC. The obvious benefit of an immediate write-off (as opposed to a deferred write-off through depletion) is not the only advantage. Since a taxpayer can use percentage depletion, which is calculated without reference to basis, the IDC may be completely lost as a deduction if they are capitalized.

DEPLETION METHODS

There are two methods of calculating depletion: cost and percentage. **Cost depletion** can be used on any wasting asset (and is the only method allowed for timber). **Percentage depletion** is subject to a number of limitations, particularly for oil and gas deposits. Depletion should be calculated both ways, and generally the method that results in the larger deduction is used. The choice between cost and percentage depletion is an annual election.

Cost Depletion.   Cost depletion is determined by using the adjusted basis of the asset.[77] The basis is divided by the estimated recoverable units of the asset (e.g., barrels, tons) to arrive at the depletion per unit. The depletion per unit then is multiplied by the number of units sold (not the units produced) during the year to arrive at the cost depletion allowed. Cost depletion, therefore, resembles the units-of-production method of calculating depreciation.

---

[77]§ 612.

TAX IN THE NEWS

PERCENTAGE DEPLETION

In an effort to formulate a national energy policy, U.S. Representative Wes Watkins, a Republican from Oklahoma, introduced a bill aimed at reducing this country's dependence on foreign oil. Among its provisions, the bill would suspend the taxable income limit on percentage depletion for oil and gas wells.

SOURCE: Adapted from Jim Myers, "Watkins Debuts Bill for National Energy Policy," *The Tulsa World*, June 30, 2000.

EXAMPLE 50

On January 1, 2001, Pablo purchases the rights to a mineral interest for $1,000,000. At that time, the remaining recoverable units in the mineral interest are estimated to be 200,000. The depletion per unit is $5 [$1,000,000 (adjusted basis)/200,000 (estimated recoverable units)]. If during the year 60,000 units are mined and 25,000 are sold, the cost depletion is $125,000 [$5 (depletion per unit) × 25,000 (units sold)]. ∎

If the taxpayer later discovers that the original estimate was incorrect, the depletion per unit for future calculations must be redetermined based on the revised estimate.[78]

EXAMPLE 51

Assume the same facts as in Example 50. In 2002, Pablo realizes that an incorrect estimate was made. The remaining recoverable units now are determined to be 400,000. Based on this new information, the revised depletion per unit is $2.1875 [$875,000 (adjusted basis)/400,000 (estimated recoverable units)]. The adjusted basis is the original cost ($1,000,000) reduced by the depletion claimed in 2001 ($125,000). If 30,000 units are sold in 2002, the depletion for the year is $65,625 [$2.1875 (depletion per unit) × 30,000 (units sold)]. ∎

Percentage Depletion. Percentage depletion (also referred to as statutory depletion) is a specified percentage provided for in the Code. The percentage varies according to the type of mineral interest involved. A sample of these percentages is shown in Exhibit 4–3. The rate is applied to the gross income from the property, but in no event may percentage depletion exceed 50 percent of the taxable income from the property before the allowance for depletion.[79]

EXAMPLE 52

Assuming gross income of $100,000, a depletion rate of 22%, and other expenses relating to the property of $60,000, the depletion allowance is determined as follows:

Gross income	$100,000
Less: Other expenses	(60,000)
Taxable income before depletion	$ 40,000
Depreciation allowance [the lesser of $22,000 (22% × $100,000) or $20,000 (50% × $40,000)]	(20,000)
Taxable income after depletion	$ 20,000

---

[78]§ 611(a).

[79]§ 613(a). Special rules apply for certain oil and gas wells under § 613A (e.g., the 50% ceiling is replaced with a 100% ceiling, and the percentage depletion may not exceed 65% of the taxpayer's taxable income from all sources before the allowance for depletion).

■ **EXHIBIT 4–3**
Sample of Percentage Depletion
Rates

22% Depletion	
Cobalt	Sulfur
Lead	Tin

15% Depletion	
Copper	Oil and gas
Gold	Silver

10% Depletion	
Coal	Perlite

5% Depletion	
Gravel	Sand

The adjusted basis of the property is reduced by $20,000, the depletion allowed. If the other expenses had been only $55,000, the full $22,000 could have been deducted, and the adjusted basis would have been reduced by $22,000. ■

Note that percentage depletion is based on a percentage of the gross income from the property and makes no reference to cost. Thus, when percentage depletion is used, it is possible to deduct more than the original cost of the property. If percentage depletion is used, however, the adjusted basis of the property (for computing cost depletion) must be reduced by the amount of percentage depletion taken until the adjusted basis reaches zero.

PLANNING CONSIDERATIONS

Switching Depletion Methods

Since the election to use the cost or percentage depletion method is an annual election, a taxpayer can use cost depletion (if higher) until the basis is exhausted and then switch to percentage depletion in the following years.

EXAMPLE 53

Assume the following facts for Warbler Company.

Remaining depletable basis	$ 11,000
Gross income (10,000 units)	100,000
Expenses (other than depletion)	30,000
Percentage depletion rate	22%

Since cost depletion is limited to the basis of $11,000 and the percentage depletion is $22,000, Warbler would choose the latter. The company's basis is then reduced to zero. In future years, however, Warbler can continue to take percentage depletion since percentage depletion is taken without reference to the remaining basis. ■

Cost Recovery Tables

Summary of Cost Recovery Tables

Table 4–1   MACRS statutory percentage table for personalty.

Applicable depreciation methods: 200 or 150 percent declining-balance switching to straight-line.

Applicable recovery periods: 3, 5, 7, 10, 15, 20 years.

Applicable convention: half-year.

Table 4–2   MACRS statutory percentage table for personalty.

Applicable depreciation method: 200 percent declining-balance switching to straight-line.

Applicable recovery periods: 3, 5, 7 years.

Applicable convention: mid-quarter.

Table 4–3   MACRS straight-line table for realty.

Applicable depreciation method: straight-line.

Applicable recovery periods: 27.5, 31.5, 39 years.

Applicable convention: mid-month.

Table 4–4   MACRS optional straight-line table for personalty.

Applicable depreciation method: straight-line.

Applicable recovery periods: 3, 5, 7, 10, 15, 20 years.

Applicable convention: half-year.

Table 4–5   Alternative minimum tax declining-balance table for personalty.

Applicable depreciation method: 150 percent declining-balance switching to straight-line.

Applicable recovery periods: 3, 5, 7, 9.5, 10, 12 years.

Applicable convention: half-year.

Table 4–6   ADS straight-line table for personalty.

Applicable depreciation method: straight-line.

Applicable recovery periods: 5, 9.5, 12 years.

Applicable convention: half-year.

Table 4–7   ADS straight-line table for realty.

Applicable depreciation method: straight-line.

Applicable recovery period: 40 years.

Applicable convention: mid-month.

[handwritten: + 1st Year = 50% 40% × 80%]

■ TABLE 4–1
MACRS Accelerated
Depreciation for Personal
Property Assuming Half-Year
Convention

For Property Placed in Service after December 31, 1986

Recovery Year	3-Year (200% DB)	5-Year (200% DB)	7-Year (200% DB)	10-Year (200% DB)	15-Year (150% DB)	20-Year (150% DB)
1	33.33	20.00	14.29	10.00	5.00	3.750
2	44.45	32.00	24.49	18.00	9.50	7.219
3	14.81*	19.20	17.49	14.40	8.55	6.677
4	7.41	11.52*	12.49	11.52	7.70	6.177
5		11.52	8.93*	9.22	6.93	5.713
6		5.76	8.92	7.37	6.23	5.285
7			8.93	6.55*	5.90*	4.888
8			4.46	6.55	5.90	4.522
9				6.56	5.91	4.462*
10				6.55	5.90	4.461
11				3.28	5.91	4.462
12					5.90	4.461
13					5.91	4.462
14					5.90	4.461
15					5.91	4.462
16					2.95	4.461
17						4.462
18						4.461
19						4.462
20						4.461
21						2.231

[handwritten: additional 6 months missed in yr 1]

*Switchover to straight-line depreciation.

[handwritten: when Ø get larger deduction using straight line]

■ TABLE 4–2
MACRS Accelerated
Depreciation for Personal
Property Assuming Mid-Quarter
Convention

For Property Placed in Service after December 31, 1986 (Partial Table*)

3-Year

Recovery Year	First Quarter	Second Quarter	Third Quarter	Fourth Quarter
1	58.33	41.67	25.00	8.33
2	27.78	38.89	50.00	61.11

5-Year

Recovery Year	First Quarter	Second Quarter	Third Quarter	Fourth Quarter
1	35.00	25.00	15.00	5.00
2	26.00	30.00	34.00	38.00

7 Year

Recovery Year	First Quarter	Second Quarter	Third Quarter	Fourth Quarter
1	25.00	17.85	10.71	3.57
2	21.43	23.47	25.51	27.55

*The figures in this table are taken from the official tables that appear in Rev.Proc. 87–57, 1987–2 C.B. 687. Because of their length, the complete tables are not presented.

■ **TABLE 4–3**
MACRS Straight-Line
Depreciation for Real Property
Assuming Mid-Month
Convention*

½ month for Jan + rest of year (handwritten)

For Property Placed in Service after December 31, 1986: 27.5-Year Residential Real Property

| Recovery Year(s) | The Applicable Percentage Is (Use the Column for the Month in the First Year the Property Is Placed in Service): | | | | | | | | | | | |
	1	2	3	4	5	6	7	8	9	10	11	12
1	3.485	3.182	2.879	2.576	2.273	1.970	1.667	1.364	1.061	0.758	0.455	0.152
2–18	3.636	3.636	3.636	3.636	3.636	3.636	3.636	3.636	3.636	3.636	3.636	3.636
19–27	3.637	3.637	3.637	3.637	3.637	3.637	3.637	3.637	3.637	3.637	3.637	3.637
28	1.970	2.273	2.576	2.879	3.182	3.485	3.636	3.636	3.636	3.636	3.636	3.636
29	0.000	0.000	0.000	0.000	0.000	0.000	0.152	0.455	0.758	1.061	1.364	1.667

For Property Placed in Service after December 31, 1986, and before May 13, 1993: 31.5-Year Nonresidential Real Property

| Recovery Year(s) | The Applicable Percentage Is (Use the Column for the Month in the First Year the Property Is Placed in Service): | | | | | | | | | | | |
	1	2	3	4	5	6	7	8	9	10	11	12
1	3.042	2.778	2.513	2.249	1.984	1.720	1.455	1.190	0.926	0.661	0.397	0.132
2–19	3.175	3.175	3.175	3.175	3.175	3.175	3.175	3.175	3.175	3.175	3.175	3.175
20–31	3.174	3.174	3.174	3.174	3.174	3.174	3.174	3.174	3.174	3.174	3.174	3.174
32	1.720	1.984	2.249	2.513	2.778	3.042	3.175	3.175	3.175	3.175	3.175	3.175
33	0.000	0.000	0.000	0.000	0.000	0.000	0.132	0.397	0.661	0.926	1.190	1.455

For Property Placed in Service after May 12, 1993: 39-Year Nonresidential Real Property

| Recovery Year(s) | The Applicable Percentage Is (Use the Column for the Month in the First Year the Property Is Placed in Service): | | | | | | | | | | | |
	1	2	3	4	5	6	7	8	9	10	11	12
1	2.461	2.247	2.033	1.819	1.605	1.391	1.177	0.963	0.749	0.535	0.321	0.107
2–39	2.564	2.564	2.564	2.564	2.564	2.564	2.564	2.564	2.564	2.564	2.564	2.564
40	0.107	0.321	0.535	0.749	0.963	1.177	1.391	1.605	1.819	2.033	2.247	2.461

*The official tables contain a separate row for each year. For ease of presentation, certain years are grouped in these tables. In some instances, this will produce a difference of .001 for the last digit when compared with the official tables.

■ **TABLE 4–4**
MACRS Straight-Line
Depreciation for Personal
Property Assuming Half-Year
Convention*

For Property Placed in Service after December 31, 1986

| MACRS Class | Percentage First Recovery Year | Other Recovery Years | | Last Recovery Year | |
		Years	%	Year	%
3-year	16.67	2–3	33.33	4	16.67
5-year	10.00	2–5	20.00	6	10.00
7-year	7.14	2–7	14.29	8	7.14
10-year	5.00	2–10	10.00	11	5.00
15-year	3.33	2–15	6.67	16	3.33
20-year	2.50	2–20	5.00	21	2.50

*The official table contains a separate row for each year. For ease of presentation, certain years are grouped in this table. In some instances, this will produce a difference of .01 for the last digit when compared with the official table.

■ TABLE 4–5
Alternative Minimum Tax: 150%
Declining-Balance Assuming
Half-Year Convention

For Property Placed in Service after December 31, 1986 (Partial Table*)

Recovery Year	3-Year 150%	5-Year 150%	7-Year 150%	9.5-Year 150%	10-Year 150%	12-Year 150%
1	25.00	15.00	10.71	7.89	7.50	6.25
2	37.50	25.50	19.13	14.54	13.88	11.72
3	25.00**	17.85	15.03	12.25	11.79	10.25
4	12.50	16.66**	12.25**	10.31	10.02	8.97
5		16.66	12.25	9.17**	8.74**	7.85
6		8.33	12.25	9.17	8.74	7.33**
7			12.25	9.17	8.74	7.33
8			6.13	9.17	8.74	7.33
9				9.17	8.74	7.33
10				9.16	8.74	7.33
11					4.37	7.32
12						7.33
13						3.66

*The figures in this table are taken from the official table that appears in Rev.Proc. 87–57, 1987–2 C.B. 687. Because of its length, the complete table is not presented.
**Switchover to straight-line depreciation.

■ TABLE 4–6
ADS Straight-Line for Personal
Property Assuming Half-Year
Convention

For Property Placed in Service after December 31, 1986 (Partial Table*)

Recovery Year	5-Year Class	9.5-Year Class	12-Year Class
1	10.00	5.26	4.17
2	20.00	10.53	8.33
3	20.00	10.53	8.33
4	20.00	10.53	8.33
5	20.00	10.52	8.33
6	10.00	10.53	8.33
7		10.52	8.34
8		10.53	8.33
9		10.52	8.34
10		10.53	8.33
11			8.34
12			8.33
13			4.17

*The figures in this table are taken from the official table that appears in Rev.Proc. 87–57, 1987–2 C.B. 687. Because of its length, the complete table is not presented. The tables for the mid-quarter convention also appear in Rev.Proc. 87–57.

■ TABLE 4–7
ADS Straight-Line for Real
Property Assuming Mid-Month
Convention

For Property Placed in Service after December 31, 1986

Recovery Year(s)	Month Placed in Service											
	1	2	3	4	5	6	7	8	9	10	11	12
1	2.396	2.188	1.979	1.771	1.563	1.354	1.146	0.938	0.729	0.521	0.313	0.104
2–40	2.500	2.500	2.500	2.500	2.500	2.500	2.500	2.500	2.500	2.500	2.500	2.500
41	0.104	0.312	0.521	0.729	0.937	1.146	1.354	1.562	1.771	1.979	2.187	2.396

Suggested Further Readings

Karyn Bybee Friske and Darlene Pulliam Smith, "The Status of the 'Independent Investor' Test in Reasonable Compensation Determinations," *The Tax Adviser*, June 2000, pp. 406–411.

Eugene Seago, "A New Revenue Procedure Makes the Cash Method More Available, But Does It Go Far Enough?" *Journal of Taxation*, July 2000, pp. 12–17.

Steven C. Thompson and Randy Serrett, "Tax Tips for Starting Up a Sideline Business," *Taxation for Accountants*, September 1998, pp. 167–174.

Leonard G. Weld and Charles E. Price, "Capitalization vs. Expense," *The CPA Journal*, June 1999, pp. 35–39.

KEY TERMS

Accelerated cost recovery system (ACRS), 4–21

Alternative depreciation system (ADS), 4–32

Amortization, 4–32

Capital gain property, 4–15

Charitable contribution, 4–15

Cost depletion, 4–34

Cost recovery system, 4–21

Depletion, 4–33

Depreciation rules, 4–21

Half-year convention, 4–25

Intangible drilling and development costs (IDC), 4–34

Listed property, 4–29

Mid-month convention, 4–26

Mid-quarter convention, 4–25

Modified accelerated cost recovery system (MACRS), 4–22

Ordinary and necessary, 4–2

Ordinary income property, 4–15

Percentage depletion, 4–34

Reasonableness requirement, 4–3

Related-party transactions, 4–11

Research and experimental expenditures, 4–17

Residential rental real estate, 4–26

Section 179 expensing election, 4–28

Problem Materials

PROBLEMS

1. Ted is an agent for Waxwing Corporation, an airline manufacturer, and is negotiating a sale with a representative of the U.S. government and with a representative of a developing country. Waxwing has sufficient capacity to handle only one of the orders. Both orders will have the same contract price. Ted believes that if Waxwing will authorize a $500,000 payment to the representative of the foreign country, he can guarantee the sale. He is not sure that he can obtain the same result with the U.S. government. Identify the relevant tax issues for Waxwing.

2. Linda operates a drug-running operation. Which of the following expenses she incurs can reduce taxable income?
   a. Bribes paid to border guards.
   b. Salaries to employees.
   c. Price paid for drugs purchased for resale.
   d. Kickbacks to police.
   e. Rent on an office.
   f. Depreciation on office furniture and equipment.
   g. Tenant's casualty insurance.

3. Cardinal Corporation is a trucking firm that operates in the Mid-Atlantic states. One of Cardinal's major customers frequently ships goods between Charlotte and Baltimore. Occasionally, the customer sends last-minute shipments that are outbound for Europe on a freighter sailing from Baltimore. To satisfy the delivery schedule in these cases, Cardinal's drivers must substantially exceed the speed limit. Cardinal pays for any related speeding tickets. During the past year, two drivers had their licenses suspended for 30 days each for driving at such excessive speeds. Cardinal continues to pay each driver's salary during the suspension periods.

    Cardinal believes that it is necessary to conduct its business in this manner if it is to be profitable, maintain the support of the drivers, and maintain the goodwill of customers. Evaluate Cardinal's business practices.

4. Quail Corporation anticipates that being positively perceived by the individual who is elected mayor will be beneficial for business. Therefore, Quail contributes to the campaigns of both the Democratic and the Republican candidates. The Republican candidate is elected mayor. Can Quail deduct any of the political contributions it made?

5. Carmine, Inc., a tobacco manufacturer, incurs certain expenditures associated with political contributions and lobbying activities. Which of these expenditures can be deducted?

Payments to Washington, D.C. law firm to lobby members of Congress	$800,000
Payments to Washington, D.C. law firm to lobby the Vice President	200,000
Payments to Washington, D.C. law firm to lobby the head of the FDA	25,000
Payments to Richmond law firm to lobby members of the state legislature	50,000
Payments to Williamsburg law firm to lobby members of the Williamsburg City Council	5,000
Political contribution to the Democratic National Committee	300,000
Political contribution to the Republican National Committee	350,000
Political contribution to Committee to Reelect the Mayor of Williamsburg	6,000

6. Ella owns 60% of the stock of Peach, Inc. The stock has declined in value since Ella purchased it five years ago. She is going to sell 5% of the stock to a relative to pay her 12-year-old daughter's private school tuition. Ella is also going to make a gift of 10% of her stock to another relative. Identify the relevant tax issues for Ella.

7. Jake owns City of Atlanta bonds with an adjusted basis of $50,000. During the year, he receives interest payments of $2,600. Jake financed the purchase of the bonds by borrowing $30,000 at 7% interest. Jake's interest payments on the loan this year are $2,100.
   a. Should Jake report any interest income this year?
   b. Can Jake deduct any interest expense this year?

8. Drew and his wife Cassie own all of the stock of Thrush, Inc. Cassie is the president and Drew is the vice president. Cassie and Drew are paid salaries of $400,000 and $300,000, respectively, each year. They consider the salaries to be reasonable based on a comparison with salaries paid for comparable positions in comparable companies. They project Thrush's taxable income for next year, before their salaries, to be $800,000. They decide to place their four teenage children on the payroll and to pay them total salaries of $100,000. The children will each work about five hours per week for Thrush.
   a. What are Drew and Cassie trying to achieve by hiring the children?
   b. Calculate the tax consequences of hiring the children on Thrush, Inc., and on Drew and Cassie's family.

9. Edward, an attorney, is hired by a major accounting firm to represent it and its clients in dealing with members of the U.S. Congress. The accounting firm is supporting liability reform that would limit the "joint and several" liability of professionals such as attorneys and CPAs. Edward is paid a retainer of $20,000. In addition, during the year, Edward is paid $10,000 for this representation. The firm also reimburses Edward $2,500 for meal and entertainment expenses incurred in meeting with members of Congress and their staffs. In addition, the firm pays Edward $5,000 for his work in opposing legislation that would adversely affect several of its major clients. What is the amount of these payments that the firm may deduct?

10. Jenny, the owner of a very successful restaurant chain, is exploring the possibility of expanding the chain into a city in the neighboring state. She incurs $20,000 of expenses associated with this investigation. Based on the regulatory environment for restaurants in the city, she decides not to do so. During the year, she also investigates opening a hotel that will be part of a national hotel chain. Her expenses for this are $15,000. The hotel begins operations on December 1. Determine the amount that Jenny can deduct in the current year for investigating these two businesses.

11. Janet Saxon sold stock (basis of $55,000) to her brother, Fred, for $42,000.
   a. What are the tax consequences to Janet?
   b. What are the tax consequences to Fred if he later sells the stock for $60,000? For $37,000? For $50,000?
   c. Write a letter to Janet in which you inform her of the tax consequences if she sells the stock to Fred for $42,000 and explain how a sales transaction could be structured that would produce better tax consequences for her. Janet's address is 32 Country Lane, Lawrence, KS 66045.

12. Bobwhite, Inc. (a calendar year C corporation) had the following income and expenses in 2002.

Income from operations	$350,000
Expenses from operations	225,000
Dividends received (less than 20% ownership)	20,000
Charitable contribution	25,000

   a. How much is Bobwhite, Inc.'s charitable contribution deduction for 2002?
   b. What happens to the portion of the contribution not deductible in 2002?

13. Dan Simms is the president and sole shareholder of Simms Corporation, 1121 Madison Street, Seattle, WA 98121. Dan plans for the corporation to make a charitable contribution to the University of Washington, a qualified public charity. He will have the corporation donate Jaybird Corporation stock, held for five years, with a basis of $8,000 and a fair market value of $20,000. Dan projects a $200,000 net profit for Simms Corporation in

2001 and a $100,000 net profit in 2002. Dan calls you on December 5, 2001, and asks whether he should make the contribution in 2001 or 2002. Write a letter advising Dan about the timing of the contribution.

14. Blue Corporation, a manufacturing company, decided to develop a new line of merchandise. The project began in 2001. Blue had the following expenses in connection with the project.

	2001	2002
Salaries	$200,000	$300,000
Materials	80,000	90,000
Insurance	12,000	12,000
Utilities	8,000	10,000
Cost of inspection of materials for quality control	5,000	7,000
Promotion expenses	20,000	–0–
Advertising	–0–	18,000
Equipment depreciation	15,000	15,000
Cost of market survey	4,000	–0–

The new product will be introduced for sale beginning in May 2003. Determine the amount of the deduction for 2001, 2002, and 2003 if:
   a. Blue Corporation elects to expense the research and experimental expenditures.
   b. Blue Corporation elects to amortize the research and experimental expenditures over 60 months.

15. On November 4, 1999, Blue Company acquired an asset (27.5-year residential real property) for $100,000 for use in its business. In 1999 and 2000, respectively, Blue took $321 and $2,564 of cost recovery. These amounts were incorrect because Blue applied the wrong percentages (i.e., those for 39-year rather than 27.5-year property). Blue should have taken $455 and $3,636 of cost recovery in 1999 and 2000. On January 1, 2001, the asset was sold for $98,000. Calculate the gain or loss on the sale of the asset in 2001.

16. Juan, a sole proprietor, acquires a five-year class asset on March 14, 2001, for $150,000. This is the only asset acquired by Juan during the year. He does not elect immediate expensing under § 179. On July 15, 2002, Juan sells the asset.
   a. Determine Juan's cost recovery for 2001.
   b. Determine Juan's cost recovery for 2002.

17. Pat, a sole proprietor, acquires a warehouse on November 1, 2001, at a cost of $4.5 million. On January 30, 2012, Pat sells the warehouse. Calculate Pat's cost recovery for 2001 and for 2012.

18. Janice acquired an apartment building on June 4, 2001, for $1.4 million. The value of the land is $200,000. Janice sold the apartment building on November 29, 2007.
   a. Determine Janice's cost recovery for 2001.
   b. Determine Janice's cost recovery for 2007.

EXTENDER 19. On December 2, 1984, Wade purchased and placed in service a warehouse. The warehouse cost $850,000. Wade used the statutory percentage cost recovery method. On July 7, 2001, Wade sold the warehouse.
   a. Determine Wade's cost recovery for 1984.
   b. Determine Wade's cost recovery for 2001.

 20. Lori, who is single, purchased a copier (five-year class property) for $31,000 and furniture (seven-year class property) for $42,000 on May 20, 2001. Lori expects the taxable income derived from her business (without regard to the amount expensed under § 179) to be about $100,000. Lori wants to elect immediate § 179 expensing, but she doesn't know which asset she should expense under § 179.

    a. Determine Lori's total deduction if the § 179 expense is taken with respect to the copier.

    b. Determine Lori's total deduction if the § 179 expense is taken with respect to the furniture.

    c. What is your advice to Lori?

21. Jack owns a small business that he operates as a sole proprietor. In 2001, Jack will net $10,000 of business income before consideration of any § 179 deduction. Jack spends $207,000 on new equipment in 2001. If Jack also has $4,000 of § 179 deduction carryforwards from 2000, determine his § 179 expense deduction for 2001 and the amount of any carryforward.

22. Olga is the proprietor of a small business. In 2001, her business income, before consideration of any § 179 deduction, is $7,500. Olga spends $202,000 on new equipment and furniture for 2001. If Olga elects to take the § 179 deduction on a desk that cost $25,000 (included in the $202,000), determine her total cost recovery for 2001 with respect to the desk.

23. On March 10, 2001, Yoon purchased three-year class property for $20,000. On December 15, 2001, he purchased five-year class property for $52,000. Yoon has net business income of $50,000 before consideration of any § 179 deduction.

    a. Calculate Yoon's cost recovery for 2001, assuming he does not make the § 179 election or use straight-line cost recovery.

    b. Calculate Yoon's cost recovery for 2001, assuming he does elect to use § 179 and does not elect to use straight-line cost recovery.

    c. Assuming Yoon's marginal tax rate is 36%, determine his tax benefit from electing § 179.

24. John Johnson is considering acquiring an automobile at the beginning of 2001 that he will use 100% of the time as a taxi. The purchase price of the automobile is $30,000. John has heard of cost recovery limits on automobiles and wants to know how much of the $30,000 he can deduct in the first year. Write a letter to John in which you present your calculations. Also, prepare a memo for the tax files. John's address is 100 Morningside, Clinton, MS 39058.

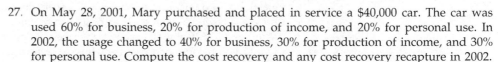

25. On February 16, 2001, Ron purchased and placed in service a new car. The purchase price was $18,000. Ron drove the car 12,000 miles during the remainder of the year, 9,000 miles for business and 3,000 miles for personal use. Ron used the statutory percentage method of cost recovery. Calculate the total deduction Ron may take for 2001 with respect to the car.

26. On June 5, 2001, Leo purchased and placed in service a $24,000 car. The business-use percentage for the car is always 100%. Compute Leo's cost recovery deduction in 2007.

EXTENDER 27. On May 28, 2001, Mary purchased and placed in service a $40,000 car. The car was used 60% for business, 20% for production of income, and 20% for personal use. In 2002, the usage changed to 40% for business, 30% for production of income, and 30% for personal use. Compute the cost recovery and any cost recovery recapture in 2002.

28. At the beginning of the current year, Abdel purchased a computer (five-year class property) for $8,000. During the year, Abdel used the computer 80% of the time for his personal investments and 20% of the time for personal use. Calculate the maximum total deduction Abdel can take with respect to the computer for the current tax year.

29. Midway through 2001, Abdel leases and places in service a passenger automobile. The lease will run for five years, and the payments are $430 per month. During 2001, Abdel uses the car 70% for business use and 30% for personal use. Assuming the inclusion dollar amount from the IRS table is $127, determine the tax consequences to Abdel from the lease for the year 2001.

30. Mike Saxon is negotiating the purchase of a business. The final purchase price has been agreed upon, but the allocation of the purchase price to the assets is still being discussed. Appraisals on a warehouse range from $1,200,000 to $1,500,000. If a value of $1,200,000

is used for the warehouse, the remainder of the purchase price, $800,000, will be allocated to goodwill. If $1,500,000 is allocated to the warehouse, goodwill will be $500,000. Mike wants to know what effect each alternative will have on cost recovery and amortization during the first year. Under the agreement, Mike will take over the business on January 1 of next year. Write a letter to Mike in which you present your calculations and recommendation. Also, prepare a memo for the tax files. Mike's address is 200 Rolling Hills Drive, Shavertown, PA 18708.

31. Sam Jones owns a granite stone quarry. When he acquired the land, Sam allocated $800,000 of the purchase price to the quarry's recoverable mineral reserves, which were estimated at 10 million tons of granite stone. Based on these estimates, the cost depletion was $.08 per ton. In April of the current year, Sam received a letter from the State Department of Highways notifying him that part of his property was being condemned so the state could build a new road. At that time, the recoverable mineral reserves had an adjusted basis of $600,000 and 7.5 million tons of granite rock. Sam estimates that the land being condemned contains about 2 million tons of granite. Therefore, for the current year, Sam has computed his cost depletion at $.11 [$600,000/(7,500,000 – 2,000,000)] per ton. Evaluate the appropriateness of what Sam is doing.

32. Wes acquired a mineral interest during the year for $5 million. A geological survey estimated that 250,000 tons of the mineral remained in the deposit. During the year, 80,000 tons were mined, and 45,000 tons were sold for $6 million. Other expenses amounted to $4 million. Assuming the mineral depletion rate is 22%, calculate Wes's lowest taxable income.

BRIDGE DISCIPLINE

1. Sparrow Corporation is considering the acquisition of an asset for use in its business over the next five years. However, Sparrow must decide whether it would be better served by leasing the asset or buying it. An appropriate asset could be purchased for $15,000, and it would qualify as a three-year asset under the MACRS classification. Assume that the election to expense assets under § 179 is not available and that the asset is not expected to have a salvage value at the end of its use by Sparrow. Alternatively, Sparrow could lease the asset for a $3,625 annual cost over the five-year period. If Sparrow is in the 34% tax bracket, would you recommend that Sparrow buy or lease the asset? In your calculations, assume that 10% is an appropriate discount factor.

2. Lark Corporation is considering the acquisition of an asset for use in its business over the next five years. However, Lark must decide whether it would be better served by leasing the asset or buying it. An appropriate asset could be purchased for $15,000, and it would qualify as a three-year asset under the MACRS classification. Assume that the election to expense assets under § 179 is made and that the asset is not expected to have a salvage value at the end of its use by Lark. Alternatively, Lark could lease the asset for a $3,625 annual cost over the five-year period. If Lark is in the 34% tax bracket, would you recommend that Lark buy or lease the asset? In your calculations, assume that 10% is an appropriate discount factor.

3. Wayside Fruit Company is a sole proprietorship owned by Neil Stephenson. The company's records reflect the following.

Sales revenue	$185,000
Operating expenses	125,000
Depreciation expense for book	10,000
Cost recovery allowance for tax	17,500
Loss on the sale of delivery truck to Neil's brother	5,000
Amount paid to fruit inspector to overlook below-standard fruit shipped to various vendors	3,000

Compute the net income before tax for book purposes and the amount of taxable income for Wayside Fruit Company.

RESEARCH PROBLEMS

*Note: Solutions to Research Problems can be prepared by using the **RIA Checkpoint®** **Student** **Version Online** research product, or the **CCH U.S. Master Tax Guide Plus**™ online Federal tax research database, which is available to accompany this text. It is also possible to prepare solutions to the Research Problems by using tax research materials found in a standard tax library.*

Research Problem 1. Amber, Inc., provides investment management services to regulated investment companies (mutual funds). During the current year, Amber created and entered into separate contracts to manage 12 new mutual funds. In launching the mutual funds, Amber incurred the following start-up costs for each fund: expenditures to develop the concept, develop the initial marketing plan, draft the management contract, form the mutual fund, obtain the board of trustees' approval of the contract, and register the new mutual fund with the Securities Exchange Commission and the various states in which the fund would be marketed. These expenditures secured for Amber the right to market the particular investment concept of each new mutual fund.

Amber deducted these expenditures as ordinary and necessary business expenses under § 162. An IRS agent has reclassified these expenditures as capital expenditures under § 263. Advise Amber on the appropriate treatment of these expenditures.

Research Problem 2. Joe and Tom are civic-minded citizens of Central City. Upon learning that Central City Hospital was filing for bankruptcy, Joe and Tom began working on a plan to reopen the hospital at some future date. They formed an LLC, created a hospital board, and began the process of dealing with all the relevant local, state, and Federal agencies.

Some time after learning of the impending closing, Joe and Tom heard that the administrator of the hospital planned to auction off the hospital's equipment. The administrator's target was to receive a bid that would exceed the costs of the auction by $74,000. Before the auction could be scheduled, Joe and Tom, acting as individuals, offered the bankruptcy court $80,000 for the equipment. The court accepted the offer. Joe and Tom each contributed $40,000 toward the purchase.

Approximately two years later, Joe and Tom donated the equipment to the hospital, which was to reopen soon. They had the property appraised, and its value was estimated at $1.5 million. Joe claimed a charitable contribution deduction of $750,000 on his tax return. The IRS audited his return and asserted that the deduction should be limited to $40,000. The agent also imposed an overvaluation penalty of approximately $50,000. Joe has asked for your advice on this issue.

Partial list of research aids:
§ 170.
Max Weitz, 56 TCM 1422, T.C.Memo. 1989–99.

Research Problem 3. Sandra purchased the following personal property during 2001.

Date	Asset	Cost
June 1	Machine A	$20,000
July 10	Machine B	10,000
November 15	Machine C	30,000

Sandra elects to take the § 179 expense on Machine C. Discuss what convention Sandra must use to determine her cost recovery deduction for 2001.

Research Problem 4. Juan owns a business that acquires exotic automobiles that are high-tech, state-of-the-art vehicles with unique design features or equipment. The exotic automobiles are not licensed nor are they set up to be used on the road. Rather, the cars are used exclusively for car shows or related promotional photography. Juan would like to know whether he can take a cost recovery deduction with respect to the exotic automobiles on his Federal income tax return.

Partial list of research aids:
Bruce Selig, 70 TCM 1125, T.C.Memo. 1995–519.

Research Problem 5.   Alfred is a 90% partner in the Allred Partnership. During the year, the partnership acquired assets and elected § 179 expensing. Before considering the § 179 expensing, the partnership had no taxable income. Advise Alfred on whether the § 179 expensing (his 90% share) can flow through the partnership to him so that he can use it as a deduction against gross income that he has from other sources.

Use the tax resources of the Internet to address the following questions. Do not restrict your search to the World Wide Web, but include a review of newsgroups and general reference materials, practitioner sites and resources, primary sources of the tax law, chat rooms and discussion groups, and other opportunities.

Research Problem 6.   The $1 million maximum compensation deduction does not seem to have deterred large corporations from remunerating their executives at very high levels. What techniques are being used to work around the millionaires provision? Are executives taking pay cuts, or are their salaries being deferred or changed in nature due to § 162(m)?

Research Problem 7.   Changes to depreciation systems often are discussed by policy makers and observers of the tax system. Outline the terms and policy objectives of one of the changes currently proposed by the Treasury, a member of Congress, or a tax policy think tank.

Losses and Loss Limitations

LEARNING OBJECTIVES

After completing Chapter 5, you should be able to:

1. Determine the amount, classification, and timing of the bad debt deduction.

2. Understand the tax treatment of worthless securities including § 1244 stock.

3. Identify a casualty and determine the amount, classification, and timing of casualty and theft losses.

4. Recognize the impact of the net operating loss carryback and carryover provisions.

5. Discuss tax shelters and the reasons for at-risk and passive loss limitations.

6. Describe how the at-risk limitation and the passive loss rules limit deductions for losses and identify taxpayers subject to these restrictions.

7. Discuss and be able to apply the definitions of activity, material participation, and rental activity under the passive loss rules.

8. Recognize the relationship between the at-risk and passive activity limitations.

9. Discuss the special treatment available to real estate activities.

Outline

TAX TALK *The income tax has made more liars out of the American people than golf has. Even when you make a tax form out on the level, you don't know when it's through if you are a crook or a martyr.*

—Will Rogers

Chapter 4 introduced rules governing the deductibility of trade and business expenses. This chapter extends the notion of deductibility to losses occurring in the course of business operations. In particular, special rules concerning the tax treatment of bad debts, casualty losses, and operating losses are reviewed. In addition, tax shelters and the rules that limit their usefulness as tax avoidance devices are discussed.

LEARNING OBJECTIVE 1

Determine the amount, classification, and timing of the bad debt deduction.

Bad Debts

If a taxpayer lends money or purchases a debt instrument and the debt is not repaid, a **bad debt** deduction is allowed. Similarly, if an accrual basis taxpayer sells goods or provides services on credit and the account receivable subsequently becomes worthless, a bad debt deduction is permitted.[1] No deduction is allowed, however, for a bad debt arising from the sale of a product or service when the taxpayer is on the cash basis because no income is reported until the cash has been collected. Permitting a bad debt deduction for a cash basis taxpayer would amount to a double deduction because the expenses of the product or service rendered are deducted when payments are made to suppliers and to employees or at the time of the sale.

EXAMPLE 1

Ella, a sole proprietor engaged in the practice of accounting, performed services for Pat for which she charged $8,000. Pat never paid the bill, and his whereabouts are unknown.

---

[1]Reg. § 1.166–1(e).

AN ALTERNATIVE TO A BAD DEBT RESERVE

ncreasingly, U.S. companies are using export credit insurance as a way of min-imizing the risk of nonpayment by foreign buyers. As companies increase their sales to foreign buyers, they incur greater risks of not being paid for the product or services provided. Because credit insurance protects accounts receivable against nonpayment, exporters can offer credit terms to foreign buyers and increase their borrowing against foreign receivables. Another benefit of export credit insurance is its tax treatment. Since the 1986 Tax Reform Act, businesses cannot take a tax deduction for bad debts based on the bad debt reserve method of accounting. Businesses can, however, take a tax deduction for export credit insurance premi-ums paid.

SOURCE: Adapted from Gordon Platt, "US Risk Managers Discover Export Credit Insurance," *Journal of Commerce*, April 26, 2000, p. 11.

If Ella is an accrual basis taxpayer, she includes the $8,000 in income when the services are performed. When she determines that Pat's account will not be collected, she deducts the $8,000 as a bad debt.

If Ella is a cash basis taxpayer, she does not include the $8,000 in income until payment is received. When she determines that Pat's account will not be collected, she cannot deduct the $8,000 as a bad debt expense because it was never recognized as income. ■

SPECIFIC CHARGE-OFF METHOD

Most taxpayers are required to use the **specific charge-off method** when accounting for bad debts. Some financial institutions are permitted to use an alternative **reserve method** for computing bad debt deductions.

A taxpayer using the specific charge-off method may claim a deduction when a specific *business* debt becomes either partially or wholly worthless or when a specific *nonbusiness* debt becomes wholly worthless.[2] For business debt, the taxpayer must satisfy the IRS that the debt is partially worthless and must demonstrate the amount of worthlessness. If a business debt previously deducted as partially worthless becomes totally worthless in a future year, only the remainder not pre-viously deducted can be deducted in the future year.

In the case of total worthlessness, a deduction is allowed for the entire amount in the year that the debt becomes worthless. The amount of the deduction depends on the taxpayer's basis in the bad debt. If the debt arose from the sale of services or products and the face amount was previously included in income, that amount is deductible. If the taxpayer purchased the debt, the deduction equals the amount the taxpayer paid for the debt instrument.

Determining when a bad debt becomes worthless can be a difficult task. Legal proceedings need not be initiated against the debtor when the surrounding facts indicate that such action will not result in collection.

EXAMPLE 2

In 1999, Partridge Company lent $1,000 to Kay, who agreed to repay the loan in two years. In 2001, Kay disappeared after the note became delinquent. If a reasonable investigation by

---

[2]§ 166(a) and Reg. § 1.166.

Partridge indicates that Kay cannot be found or that a suit against Kay would not result in collection, Partridge can deduct the $1,000 in 2001. ■

Bankruptcy is generally an indication of at least partial worthlessness of a debt. Bankruptcy may create worthlessness before the settlement date. If this is the case, the deduction may be taken in the year of worthlessness.

EXAMPLE 3

In Example 2, assume that Kay filed for personal bankruptcy in 2000 and that the debt is a business debt. At that time, Partridge learned that unsecured creditors (including Partridge) were ultimately expected to receive 20 cents on the dollar. In 2001, settlement is made and Partridge receives only $150. Partridge should deduct $800 ($1,000 loan − $200 expected settlement) in 2000 and $50 in 2001 ($200 balance − $150 proceeds). ■

If a receivable is written off as uncollectible and is subsequently collected during the same tax year, the write-off entry is reversed. If a receivable has been written off as uncollectible, collection in a later tax year may result in income being recognized. Income will result if the deduction yielded a tax benefit in the year it was taken.

BUSINESS VERSUS NONBUSINESS BAD DEBTS

The nature of a debt depends upon whether the lender is engaged in the business of lending money or whether there is a proximate relationship between the creation of the debt and the *lender's* trade or business. Where either of these conditions is true, a bad debt is classified as a **business bad debt.** If these conditions are not met, a bad debt is classified as a **nonbusiness bad debt.** The use to which the borrowed funds are put is of no consequence when making this classification decision.

EXAMPLE 4

Jamil lent his friend, Esther, $1,500. Esther used the money to start a business, which subsequently failed. Even though the proceeds of the loan were used in a business, the loan is a nonbusiness bad debt, because the business was Esther's, and not Jamil's. ■

EXAMPLE 5

Horace operates a sole proprietorship that sells premium stereo equipment. Horace uses the accrual basis to account for sales of the stereo equipment. During the year, he sold a $4,000 stereo system to Herbie on credit. Later that year, the account receivable becomes worthless. The loan is a business bad debt, because the debt was related to Horace's business. ■

CONCEPT SUMMARY 5–1

The Tax Treatment of Bad Debts Using the Specific Charge-Off Method

	Business Bad Debts	Nonbusiness Bad Debts
Timing of deduction	A deduction is allowed when the debt becomes either partially or wholly worthless.	A deduction is allowed *only* when the debt becomes wholly worthless.
Character of deduction	The bad debt may be deducted as an ordinary loss.	The bad debt is taxed as a short-term capital loss, subject to the $3,000 capital loss limitation for individuals.
Recovery of amounts previously deducted	If the account recovered was written off during the current tax year, the write-off entry is reversed. If the account was written off in a previous tax year, income is created subject to the tax benefit rule.	If the account recovered was written off during the current tax year, the write-off entry is reversed. If the account was written off in a previous tax year, income is created subject to the tax benefit rule.

Generally, nonbusiness bad debts are incurred only by individuals. It is assumed that any loans made by a corporation are related to its trade or business. Therefore, any bad debts resulting from loans made by a corporation are automatically business bad debts.

The distinction between a business bad debt and a nonbusiness bad debt is important. A business bad debt is deductible as an ordinary loss in the year incurred, whereas a nonbusiness bad debt is always treated as a short-term capital loss. Thus, regardless of the age of a nonbusiness bad debt, the deduction may be of limited benefit due to the $3,000 capital loss limitation for individuals (refer to the discussion in Chapter 3).

LOANS BETWEEN RELATED PARTIES

Loans between related parties raise the issue of whether the transaction was a *bona fide* loan or some other transfer, such as a gift, a disguised dividend payment, or a contribution to capital. The Regulations state that a bona fide debt arises from a debtor-creditor relationship based on a valid and enforceable obligation to pay a fixed or determinable sum of money. Thus, individual circumstances must be examined to determine whether advances between related parties are loans. Some considerations are these:

- Was a note properly executed?
- Was there a reasonable rate of interest?
- Was collateral provided?
- What collection efforts were made?
- What was the intent of the parties?

EXAMPLE 6

Ted, who is the sole shareholder of Penguin Corporation, lends the corporation $10,000 so that it can continue business operations. The note specifies a 2% interest rate and is payable on demand. Penguin has shown losses in each year of its five-year existence. The corporation also has liabilities greatly in excess of its assets. It is likely that Ted's transfer to the corporation

NERVES OF STEEL IN THE FACE OF A MARKET ADJUSTMENT

Although the tax law allows taxpayers to claim losses from bad investments, many taxpayers would not panic in the face of another Black Monday (October 19, 1987) on the stock market when the Dow Jones Industrials dropped by some 508 points. According to *USA Today*, investors would react as follows:

Reaction	Percentage
Do nothing	66
Buy more stocks	14
Sell some stocks	11
Sell all stocks	2
Some other reaction	7
	100

Source: *USA Today.*

would be treated as a contribution to capital rather than a liability. Consequently, no bad debt deduction would be allowed upon default by Penguin. ■

Understand the tax treatment of worthless securities including § 1244 stock.

Worthless Securities

A loss is allowed for securities that become *completely* worthless during the year (**worthless securities**).[3] Such securities are shares of stock, bonds, notes, or other evidence of indebtedness issued by a corporation or government. The losses generated are treated as capital losses (refer to Chapter 3) deemed to have occurred on the *last day* of the tax year. By treating losses as having occurred on the last day of the tax year, a loss that would otherwise have been classified as short term (if the date of worthlessness were used) may be classified as long term.

EXAMPLE 7

Falcon Company, a calendar year taxpayer, owns stock in Owl Corporation (a publicly held company). The stock was acquired as an investment on May 31, 2000, at a cost of $5,000. On April 1, 2001, the stock became worthless. Because the stock is deemed to have become worthless as of December 31, 2001, Falcon has a capital loss from an asset held for 19 months (a long-term capital loss). ■

SMALL BUSINESS STOCK

The general rule is that shareholders receive capital loss treatment for losses from sale or exchange of corporate stock. As noted in Chapter 3, the deductibility of capital losses is limited. However, it is possible to avoid capital loss limitations if the loss is sustained on **small business stock (§ 1244 stock).** Such a loss could arise

---

[3]§ 165(g).

from a sale of the stock or from the stock becoming worthless. Only *individuals*[4] who acquired the stock *from* the issuing corporation are eligible to receive ordinary loss treatment under § 1244. The ordinary loss treatment is limited to $50,000 ($100,000 for married individuals filing jointly) per year. Losses on § 1244 stock in excess of the statutory limits are treated as capital losses.

The issuing corporation must meet certain requirements for the loss on § 1244 stock to be treated as an *ordinary*—rather than a capital—loss. The principal requirement is that the total capitalization of the corporation is limited to a maximum of $1 million. This capital limit includes all money and other property received by the corporation for stock and all capital contributions made to the corporation. The $1 million test is made at the time the stock is issued. There are no requirements regarding the kind of stock issued. Section 1244 stock can be either common or preferred.

Section 1244 applies only to losses. If § 1244 stock is sold at a gain, the provision does not apply and the gain is capital gain (which, for individuals, may be subject to preferential tax treatment, as discussed in Chapter 3).

EXAMPLE 8	On July 1, 1999, Iris, a single individual, purchased 100 shares of Eagle Corporation common stock for $100,000. The Eagle stock qualifies as § 1244 stock. On June 20, 2001, Iris sells all of the Eagle stock for $20,000, which results in a loss of $80,000. Because the Eagle stock is § 1244 stock, Iris has $50,000 of ordinary loss and $30,000 of long-term capital loss. ■

PLANNING CONSIDERATIONS

Maximizing the Benefits of § 1244

Because § 1244 limits the amount of loss classified as ordinary loss on a yearly basis, a taxpayer might maximize the benefits of § 1244 by selling the stock in more than one taxable year.

EXAMPLE 9	

Mitch, a single individual, purchased small business stock in 1999 for $150,000 (150 shares at $1,000 per share). On December 20, 2001, the stock is worth $60,000 (150 shares at $400 per share). Mitch wants to sell the stock at this time. He earns a salary of $80,000 a year, has no other capital transactions, and does not expect any in the future. If Mitch sells all of the small business stock in 2001, his recognized loss will be $90,000 ($60,000 selling price – $150,000

cost). The loss will be characterized as a $50,000 ordinary loss and a $40,000 long-term capital loss. In computing taxable income for 2001, Mitch could deduct the $50,000 ordinary loss but could deduct only $3,000 of the capital loss (assuming he has no capital gains). The remainder of the capital loss could be carried over and used in future years subject to the capital loss limitations.

Alternatively, if Mitch sells 82 shares in 2001, he will recognize an ordinary loss of $49,200 [82 × ($1,000 – $400)]. If Mitch then sells the remainder of the shares in 2002, he will recognize an ordinary loss of $40,800 [68 × ($1,000 – $400)], successfully avoiding the capital loss limitation. Mitch could deduct the $49,200 ordinary loss in computing 2001 taxable income and the $40,800 ordinary loss in computing 2002 taxable income. ■

LEARNING OBJECTIVE 3	## Casualty and Theft Losses
Identify a casualty and determine the amount, classification, and timing of casualty and theft losses.	Losses on business property are deductible, whether attributable to casualty, theft, or some other cause (e.g., rust, termite damage). While all *business* property losses are generally deductible, the amount and timing of casualty and theft losses are determined using special rules. Furthermore, for individual taxpayers, who may

---

[4]The term *individuals* for this purpose includes a partnership but not a trust or an estate.

deduct casualty losses on personal-use (nonbusiness) property as well as on business and investment property (held in partnerships and S corporations or in an individual capacity), a set of special limitations applies. Casualty gains are also afforded special consideration in the tax law.

DEFINITION OF CASUALTY

The term *casualty* generally includes *fire, storm, shipwreck,* and *theft.* In addition, losses from *other casualties* are deductible. Such losses generally include any loss resulting from an event that is (1) identifiable; (2) damaging to property; and (3) sudden, unexpected, and unusual in nature. The term also includes accidental loss of property provided the loss qualifies under the same rules as any other casualty.

A *sudden event* is one that is swift and precipitous and not gradual or progressive. An *unexpected event* is one that is ordinarily unanticipated and occurs without the intent of the taxpayer who suffers the loss. An *unusual event* is one that is extraordinary and nonrecurring and does not commonly occur during the activity in which the taxpayer was engaged when the destruction occurred.[5] Examples include hurricanes, tornadoes, floods, storms, shipwrecks, fires, sonic booms, vandalism, and mine cave-ins. A taxpayer also can take a deduction for a casualty loss from an automobile accident if the accident is not attributable to the taxpayer's willful act or willful negligence. Weather that causes damage (drought, for example) must be unusual and severe for the particular region to qualify as a casualty. Furthermore, damage must be to the *taxpayer's* property to be deductible.

Events That Are Not Casualties.   Not all acts of God are treated as **casualty losses** for income tax purposes. Because a casualty must be sudden, unexpected, and unusual, progressive deterioration (such as erosion due to wind or rain) is not a casualty because it does not meet the suddenness test.

An example of an event that generally does not qualify as a casualty is insect damage. When termites caused damage over a period of several years, some courts have disallowed a casualty loss deduction.[6] On the other hand, some courts have held that termite damage over periods of up to 15 months after infestation constituted a sudden event and was, therefore, deductible as a casualty loss.[7] Despite the existence of some judicial support for the deductibility of termite damage as a casualty loss, the current position of the IRS is that termite damage is not deductible.[8]

Other examples of events that are not casualties are losses resulting from a decline in value rather than an actual loss of the property. For example, a taxpayer was allowed a loss for the actual flood damage to his property but not for the decline in market value due to the property's being flood-prone.[9] Similarly, a decline in value of an office building due to fire damage to nearby buildings is not deductible as a casualty.

DEFINITION OF THEFT

Theft includes, but is not necessarily limited to, larceny, embezzlement, and robbery.[10] Theft does not include misplaced items.[11]

---

[5]Rev.Rul. 72–592, 1972–2 C.B. 101.

[6]*Fay v. Helvering,* 41–2 USTC ¶9494, 27 AFTR 432, 120 F.2d 253 (CA–2, 1941); *U.S. v. Rogers,* 41–1 USTC ¶9442, 27 AFTR 423, 120 F.2d 244 (CA–9, 1941).

[7]*Rosenberg v. Comm.,* 52–2 USTC ¶9377, 42 AFTR 303, 198 F.2d 46 (CA–8, 1952); *Shopmaker v. U.S.,* 54–1 USTC ¶9195, 45 AFTR 758, 119 F.Supp. 705 (D.Ct. Mo., 1953).

[8]Rev.Rul. 63–232, 1963–2 C.B. 97.

[9]*S. L. Solomon,* 39 TCM 1282, T.C.Memo. 1980–87.

[10]Reg. § 1.165–8(d).

[11]*Mary Francis Allen,* 16 T.C. 163 (1951).

TAX IN THE NEWS

CHANGING THE DEFINITION OF CASUALTY

I n April 2000, Senator Mary Landrieu of Louisiana introduced a bill in Congress that would change the definition of the term *casualty loss* for Federal income tax purposes to include losses caused by Formosan termites. The Formosan termite is the world's most destructive termite. Its colonies contain up to 10 million termites and eat an average of 1,000 pounds of wood a year. A native termite colony, only one-tenth the size, eats only 7 pounds of wood a year. The Formosan termite has infested 11 states including Louisiana, causing an estimated $1 billion of damage each year.

SOURCE: Adapted from Patricia Leigh Brown, "Termites Feast in French Quarter," *The Commercial Appeal*, May 21, 2000, p. A9.

Theft losses are treated like other casualty losses, but the *timing* of recognition of the loss differs. A theft loss is deducted in the *year of discovery*, not the year of the theft (unless, of course, the discovery occurs in the same year as the theft). If, in the year of the discovery, a claim exists (e.g., against an insurance company) and there is a reasonable expectation of recovering the adjusted basis of the asset from the insurance company, no deduction is permitted.[12] If, in the year of settlement, the recovery is less than the asset's adjusted basis, a partial deduction may be available. If the recovery is greater than the asset's adjusted basis, *casualty gain* may be recognized.

EXAMPLE 10

Sakura, Inc., owned a computer that was stolen from its offices in December 1999. The theft was discovered on June 3, 2000, and the corporation filed a claim with its insurance company that was settled on January 30, 2001. Assuming there is a reasonable expectation of full recovery, no deduction is allowed in 2000. A partial deduction may be available in 2001 if the actual insurance proceeds are less than the adjusted basis of the asset. (Loss measurement rules are discussed later in this chapter.) ■

PLANNING CONSIDERATIONS

Documentation of Related-Taxpayer Loans, Casualty Losses, and Theft Losses

Since the validity of loans between related taxpayers might be questioned, adequate documentation is needed to substantiate a bad debt deduction if the loan subsequently becomes worthless. Documentation should include proper execution of the note (legal form) and the establishment of a bona fide purpose for the loan. In addition, it is desirable to stipulate a reasonable rate of interest and a fixed maturity date.

Because a theft loss deduction is not permitted for misplaced items, a police report and evidence of the value of the property (e.g., appraisals, pictures of the property, purchase receipts) are necessary to document a theft.

---

[12]Reg. §§ 1.165–1(d)(2) and 1.165–8(a)(2).

Similar documentation of the value of property should be provided to support a casualty loss deduction because the amount of loss is measured, in part, by the decline in fair market value of the property.

WHEN TO DEDUCT CASUALTY LOSSES

General Rule.   Generally, a casualty loss is deducted in the year the loss occurs. However, no casualty loss is permitted if a reimbursement claim with a reasonable *prospect of full recovery* exists.[13] If the taxpayer has a partial claim, only part of the loss can be claimed in the year of the casualty, and the remainder is deducted in the year the claim is settled.

EXAMPLE 11

Fuchsia Corporation's new warehouse was completely destroyed by fire in 2001. Its cost and fair market value were $250,000. Fuchsia's only claim against the insurance company was on a $70,000 policy that was not settled by year-end. The following year, 2002, Fuchsia settled with the insurance company for $60,000. Fuchsia is entitled to a $180,000 deduction in 2001 and a $10,000 deduction in 2002. ■

If a taxpayer receives reimbursement for a casualty loss sustained and deducted in a previous year, an amended return is not filed for that year. Instead, the taxpayer must include the reimbursement in gross income on the return for the year in which it is received to the extent that the previous deduction resulted in a tax benefit (refer to Chapter 3).

EXAMPLE 12

Golden Hawk, Inc., had a deductible casualty loss of $15,000 on its 2000 tax return. Golden Hawk's taxable income for 2000 was $60,000 after deducting the $15,000 loss. In June 2001, the corporation is reimbursed $13,000 for the prior year's casualty loss. Golden Hawk includes the entire $13,000 in gross income for 2001 because the deduction in 2000 produced a tax benefit. ■

Disaster Area Losses.   An exception to the general rule for the time of deduction is allowed for **disaster area losses,** which are casualties or disaster-related business losses sustained in an area designated as a disaster area by the President of the United States.[14] In such cases, the taxpayer may *elect* to treat the loss as having occurred in the taxable year immediately *preceding* the taxable year in which the disaster actually occurred. The rationale for this exception is to provide immediate relief to disaster victims in the form of accelerated tax benefits.

If the due date, plus extensions, for the prior year's return has not passed, a taxpayer makes the election to claim the disaster area loss on the prior year's tax return. If a disaster area is designated after the prior year's return has been filed, it is necessary to file either an amended return or a refund claim. In any case, the taxpayer must show clearly that such an election is being made.

MEASURING THE AMOUNT OF LOSS

Amount of Loss.   The rules for determining the amount of a loss depend in part on whether business, investment, or personal-use (nonbusiness) property was involved. Another factor that must be considered is whether the property was partially or completely destroyed.

---

[13]Reg. § 1.165–1(d)(2)(i).

[14]§ 165(h).

If business property or investment property (e.g., rental property) is *completely destroyed*, the loss is equal to the adjusted basis[15] (typically cost less depreciation) of the property at the time of destruction.

EXAMPLE 13

Monty's Movers owned a truck, which was used only for business purposes. The truck was destroyed by fire. Monty, the proprietor, had unintentionally allowed his insurance coverage to expire. The fair market value of the truck was $39,000 at the time of the fire, and its adjusted basis was $40,000. Monty is allowed a loss deduction of $40,000 (the adjusted basis of the truck). ■

A different measurement rule applies for *partial destruction* of business and investment property and for *partial* or *complete destruction* of personal-use property held by individuals. In these situations, the loss is the *lesser* of:

- the adjusted basis of the property, or
- the difference between the fair market value of the property before the event and the fair market value immediately after the event.

EXAMPLE 14

Wynd and Rain, a law firm, owned an airplane that was used only for business purposes. The airplane was damaged in a crash. At the date of the crash, the fair market value of the plane was $52,000, and its adjusted basis was $32,000. After the crash, the plane was appraised at $24,000. The law firm's loss deduction is $28,000 (the lesser of the adjusted basis or the decrease in fair market value). ■

Any insurance recovery reduces the loss for business, investment, and personal-use losses. In fact, a taxpayer may realize a gain if the insurance proceeds exceed the adjusted basis of the property. Chapter 8 discusses the treatment of net gains and losses on business property and income-producing property.

A special rule on insurance recovery applies to personal-use property. In particular, individuals are not permitted to deduct a casualty loss for damage to insured personal-use property unless an insurance claim is filed. This rule applies, whether the insurance provides partial or full reimbursement for the loss.[16]

Generally, an appraisal before and after the casualty is needed to measure the amount of loss. However, the *cost of repairs* to the damaged property generally is acceptable as a method of establishing the loss in value.[17]

1 *Find more information on this topic at our Web site: **http://wft-entities.swcollege.com**.*

Multiple Losses. When multiple casualty losses occur during the year, the amount of each loss is computed separately. The rules for computing loss deductions where multiple losses have occurred are illustrated in Example 15.

EXAMPLE 15

During the year, Swan Enterprises had the following business casualty losses:

Asset	Adjusted Basis	Fair Market Value of the Asset		Insurance Recovery
		Before the Casualty	After the Casualty	
A	$900	$600	$–0–	$400
B	300	800	250	150

---

[15]See Chapter 7 for a detailed discussion of basis rules.
[16]§ 165(h)(4)(E).

[17]Reg. § 1.165–7(a)(2)(ii).

The following losses are allowed:

- Asset A: $500. The complete destruction of a business asset results in a deduction of the adjusted basis of the property (reduced by any insurance recovery) regardless of the asset's fair market value.
- Asset B: $150. The partial destruction of a business asset results in a deduction equal to the lesser of the adjusted basis ($300) or the decline in value ($550), reduced by any insurance recovery ($150). ■

CASUALTY AND THEFT LOSSES OF INDIVIDUALS

Recall from Chapter 3 that the individual income tax formula distinguishes between deductions *for* AGI and deductions *from* AGI. Casualty and theft losses incurred by an individual in connection with a business or with rental and royalty activities are deductible *for* AGI and are limited only by the rules previously discussed.[18] Losses from most other investment activities and personal-use losses are generally deducted *from* AGI. Investment casualty and theft losses (e.g., the theft of a security) are classified as miscellaneous itemized deductions (subject to a 2 percent-of-AGI floor). Casualty losses of personal-use property are subject to special limitations discussed below.

Personal-Use Property.   In addition to the valuation rules discussed above, casualty loss deductions from personal-use property must be reduced by a $100 *per event* floor and a 10 percent-of-AGI *aggregate* floor.[19] The $100 floor applies separately to each casualty and applies to the entire loss from each casualty (e.g., if a storm damages both a taxpayer's residence and automobile, only $100 is subtracted from the total amount of the loss). All personal-use losses incurred during the year are then added together, and the total is reduced by 10 percent of the taxpayer's AGI. The resulting amount is the taxpayer's itemized deduction for personal-use casualty and theft losses.

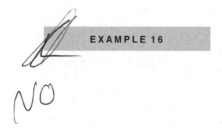

EXAMPLE 16

Rocky, who had AGI of $30,000, was involved in a motorcycle accident. His motorcycle, which was used only for personal use and had a fair market value of $12,000 and an adjusted basis of $9,000, was completely destroyed. He received $5,000 from his insurance company. Rocky's casualty loss deduction is $900 [$9,000 basis – $5,000 insurance – $100 floor – $3,000 (.10 × $30,000 AGI)]. The $900 casualty loss is an itemized deduction (*from* AGI). ■

Where there are both casualty gains and losses from personal-use property, special netting rules apply. Generally, if casualty gains exceed losses during the year, the gains and losses are treated as capital gains and losses. Alternatively, if losses exceed gains, the casualty gains (and losses to the extent of gains) are treated as ordinary gains and losses. Any excess losses are deductible as personal-use casualty losses.

2 *Find more information on this topic at our Web site: **http://wft-entities.swcollege.com**.*

Recognize the impact of the net operating loss carryback and carryover provisions.

Net Operating Losses

INTRODUCTION

The requirement that every taxpayer file an annual income tax return (whether on a calendar year or a fiscal year) can lead to inequities for taxpayers who experience

---

[18]§ 62(a)(1).

[19]§§ 165(c)(3) and (h).

CONCEPT SUMMARY 5–2

Casualty Gains and Losses

	Business-Use or Income-Producing Property	Personal-Use Property
Event creating the loss	Any event.	Casualty or theft.
Amount	The lesser of the decline in fair market value or the adjusted basis, but always the adjusted basis if the property is totally destroyed.	The lesser of the decline in fair market value or the adjusted basis.
Insurance	Insurance proceeds received reduce the amount of the loss.	Insurance proceeds received (or for which there is an unfiled claim) reduce the amount of the loss.
$100 floor	Not applicable.	Applicable per event.
Gains and losses	Gains and losses are netted (see detailed discussion in Chapter 8).	Personal casualty and theft gains and losses are netted.
Gains exceeding losses		The gains and losses are treated as gains and losses from the sale of capital assets.
Losses exceeding gains		The gains—and the losses to the extent of gains—are treated as ordinary items in computing AGI. The losses in excess of gains, to the extent that they exceed 10% of AGI, are itemized deductions (*from* AGI).

---

uneven income over a series of years. These inequities result from the application of progressive tax rates to taxable income determined on an annual basis.

EXAMPLE 17

Orange, Inc., realizes the following taxable income or loss over a five-year period: Year 1, $50,000; Year 2, ($30,000); Year 3, $100,000; Year 4, ($200,000); and Year 5, $380,000. Blue Corporation has taxable income of $60,000 every year. Note that both corporations have total taxable income of $300,000 over the five-year period. Assume there is no provision for carryback or carryover of net operating losses. Orange and Blue would have the following five-year tax liabilities:

Year	Orange's Tax	Blue's Tax
1	$ 7,500	$10,000
2	–0–	10,000
3	22,250	10,000
4	–0–	10,000
5	129,200	10,000
	$158,950	$50,000

The computation of tax is made without regard to any NOL benefit. Rates applicable to 2001 are used to compute the tax.

Even though Orange and Blue realized the same total taxable income ($300,000) over the five-year period, Orange would have to pay taxes of $158,950, while Blue would pay taxes of only $50,000. ∎

TAX FACT

THE UTILITY OF THE NOL DEDUCTION

Of the approximately 4.6 million corporate income tax returns filed in 1996, nearly 507,000 benefited from the use of the net operating loss deduction.

Source: 1996 Corporation Returns—Basic Tables.

To provide partial relief from this inequitable tax treatment, a deduction is allowed for **net operating losses (NOLs).**[20] This provision permits an NOL for any one year to be offset against taxable income in other years. The NOL provision provides relief only for losses from the operation of a trade or business or from casualty and theft.

Only C corporations and individuals are permitted an NOL deduction, since losses of partnerships and S corporations pass through to their owners. For C corporations, the NOL equals any negative taxable income for the year, with an adjustment for the dividends received deduction (see Chapter 9). In addition, deductions for prior-year NOLs are not allowed when determining a current-year NOL.

NOLs of individuals are computed by adding back to negative taxable income the excess of nonbusiness deductions (e.g., the standard deduction, charitable contributions, alimony payments) over nonbusiness income, personal and dependency exemptions, and any net capital loss deducted in calculating taxable income. Business deductions that are allowed for determining the NOL include moving expenses, losses on rental property, loss on the sale of small business stock, one-half of the self-employment tax (refer to Chapter 1), and losses from a sole proprietorship, partnership, or S corporation.

CARRYBACK AND CARRYOVER PERIODS

General Rules. A current-year NOL is usually carried back and deducted against income over the two preceding tax years.[21] It is carried back first to the second year before the loss year and then to the year immediately preceding the loss year (until it fully offsets income). If the loss is not completely used against income in the carryback period, it is carried forward for 20 years following the loss year. NOLs that are not used within the 20-year carryforward period are lost. Thus, an NOL sustained in 2001 is used first in 1999 and then 2000. Then, the loss is carried forward and offsets income in 2002 through 2021.

When an NOL is carried back, the taxpayer requests an immediate refund of prior years' taxes by filing an amended return for the previous two years. When an NOL is carried forward, the current return shows an NOL deduction for the prior year's loss. Thus, a struggling business with an NOL can receive rapid cash-flow assistance.

---

[20]§ 172.

[21]A three-year carryback period is available for any portion of an individual's NOL resulting from a casualty or theft loss. The three-year carryback rule also applies to NOLs that are attributable to presidentially declared disaster areas that are incurred by a small business or a taxpayer engaged in farming. For purposes of this provision, a small business is one whose average annual gross receipts for a three-year period are $5 million or less.

SALE OF NOLS

In January 2000, Pennsylvania Democratic lawmakers proposed tax cuts intended to stimulate the state's high-tech industries. One proposal would allow companies to sell their NOLs to the state at 80 percent of their future value. The current state law allows companies to deduct up to $2 million of their annual business losses against future taxable income for 10 years. Under the proposed plan, companies would give up the future benefits of the NOLs in exchange for a check from the state.

SOURCE: Adapted from Frank Reeves, "Democrats Bearing Tax Breaks for Business," *Pittsburgh Post-Gazette*, January 26, 2000, p. C1.

NOLs from Multiple Tax Years. When there are NOLs in two or more years, the earliest year's loss is used first. Later years' losses can then be used until they are offset against income or lost. Thus, one year's return could show NOL carryovers from two or more years. Each loss is computed and applied separately.

Election to Forgo Carryback. A taxpayer can *irrevocably elect* not to carry back an NOL. The election is made on a corporate tax return (Form 1120) by checking the appropriate box. Individuals can make the election by attaching a statement to their tax return. If the election is made, the loss can *only* be carried forward for 20 years. This election may be desirable in circumstances where marginal tax rates in future years are expected to exceed rates in prior years.

LEARNING OBJECTIVE 5

Discuss tax shelters and the reasons for at-risk and passive loss limitations.

The Tax Shelter Problem

Before Congress enacted legislation to reduce or eliminate their effectiveness, **tax shelters** were popular investments for tax avoidance purposes because they could generate losses and other benefits that could be used to offset income from other sources. Because of the tax avoidance potential of many tax shelters, they were attractive to wealthy taxpayers with high marginal tax rates. Many tax shelters merely provided an opportunity for "investors" to buy deductions and credits in ventures that were not expected to generate a profit, even in the long run.

Although it may seem odd that a taxpayer would intentionally invest in an activity that was designed to produce losses, there is a logical explanation. The typical tax shelter operated as a partnership and relied heavily on nonrecourse financing.[22] Accelerated depreciation and interest expense deductions generated large losses in the early years of the activity. At the very least, the tax shelter deductions deferred the recognition of any net income from the venture until the activity was sold. In the best of situations, the investor could realize additional tax savings by offsetting other income (e.g., salary, interest, and dividends) with losses flowing from the tax shelter. Ultimately, the sale of the investment would result

---

[22]Nonrecourse debt is an obligation for which the borrower is not personally liable. An example of nonrecourse debt is a liability on real estate acquired by a partnership without the partnership or any of the partners assuming any liability for the mortgage. The acquired property generally is pledged as collateral for the loan.

[handwritten margin notes: "→ but you don't stand to lose anything personally?", "Bank could take away your cattle"]

INTERNATIONAL IMPLICATIONS

PASSAGE OF THE OMNIBUS INVESTMENTS ACT

To make the Philippines more attractive to foreign investors, the Philippines House of Representatives has approved the new Omnibus Investments Act. The Act provides that during the period of its income tax holiday incentive, pioneer enterprises registered with the Board of Investments can carry over NOLs as a deduction from gross income for the next five consecutive taxable years. Pioneer industries and Board of Investments registered firms can also deduct any research and development expenses from taxable income during the first 10 years of their existence.

SOURCE: Adapted from Cathy Rose A. Garcia, "Omnibus Investments Act Passed on Second Reading," *Business World (Philippines)*, June 7, 2000.

in *tax-favored* capital gain. The following examples illustrate what was possible *before* Congress enacted legislation to curb tax shelter abuses.

EXAMPLE 18

[handwritten margin note: "getting losses for more than he invested"]

Bob, who earned a salary of $400,000 as a business executive and dividend income of $15,000, invested $20,000 for a 10% interest in a cattle-breeding tax shelter. He did not participate in the operation of the business. Through the use of $800,000 of nonrecourse financing and available cash of $200,000, the partnership acquired a herd of an exotic breed of cattle costing $1 million. Depreciation, interest, and other deductions related to the activity resulted in a loss of $400,000, of which Bob's share was $40,000. Bob was allowed to deduct the $40,000 loss, even though he had invested and stood to lose only $20,000 if the investment turned sour. The net effect of the $40,000 deduction from the partnership was that a portion of Bob's salary and dividend income was "sheltered," and as a result, he was required to calculate his tax liability on only $375,000 of income [$415,000 (salary and dividends) – $40,000 (deduction)] rather than $415,000. If this deduction were available under current law and if Bob was in the 39.6% income tax bracket, a tax savings of $15,840 ($40,000 × 39.6%) would be generated in the first year alone! ∎

A review of Example 18 shows that the taxpayer took a two-for-one write-off ($40,000 deduction, $20,000 investment). In the heyday of tax shelters, promoters often promised even larger write-offs for the investor.

The first major provision aimed at tax shelters is the **at-risk limitation.** Its objective is to limit a taxpayer's deductions to the amount that the taxpayer could actually lose from the investment (the amount "at risk") if it turns out to be a financial disaster.

EXAMPLE 19

Returning to the facts of the preceding example, under the current at-risk rules Bob would be allowed to deduct $20,000 (i.e., the amount that he could lose if the business failed). This deduction would reduce his other income, and as a result, Bob would report $395,000 of income ($415,000 – $20,000). The remaining nondeductible $20,000 loss and any future losses flowing from the partnership would be suspended under the at-risk rules and would be deductible in the future only as Bob's at-risk amount increased. ∎

The second major attack on tax shelters came with the passage of the **passive loss** rules. These rules were intended to halt an investor's ability to benefit from the mismatching of an entity's expenses and income that often occurs in the early

---

TAX IN THE NEWS

IS THE ATTACK ON CORPORATE TAX SHELTERS AN ATTEMPT TO CLOSE LOOPHOLES OR INCREASE TAXES?

Certain government officials wish to crack down on so-called corporate tax shelters, which, they say, cost the Treasury billions of dollars in lost revenues. In fact, in one recent estimate, the corporate tax breaks and spending subsidies translate into a $65 billion annual cost. According to these officials, the tax shelters, which are not touched by the current passive loss rules, go largely undetected by the IRS because they are buried in complex corporate tax returns.

At the heart of the issue are questions about the meaning of the term *tax shelter* and whether certain transactions are intended to produce actual economic benefit or are pursued solely for tax savings. Stated another way by Yale University professor Michael Graetz, a tax shelter is "a deal done by very smart people that, absent tax considerations, would be very stupid." On the other side, some legislators and others assert that some of the government's proposed fixes are worse than the problems they intend to solve. In addition, these opponents say that the proposed restrictions would so impede legitimate business transactions that they would be equivalent to a tax increase.

---

years of the business. Congress observed that despite the at-risk limitations, investors could still deduct losses flowing from an entity and thereby defer their tax liability on other income. These passive loss rules have, to a great degree, made the term *tax shelter* obsolete by suspending the deductibility of losses.

The passive loss rules require the taxpayer to segregate all income and losses into three categories: active, passive, and portfolio. In general, the passive loss limits *disallow* the deduction of passive losses *against active or portfolio income*, even when the taxpayer is at risk to the extent of the loss. In general, passive losses can only offset passive income.

EXAMPLE 20

Returning to the facts of Example 18, the passive activity loss rules further restrict Bob's ability to claim the $20,000 tax deduction shown in Example 19. Because Bob is a passive investor and does not materially participate in any meaningful way in the activities of the cattle-breeding operation, the $20,000 loss allowed under the at-risk rules is disallowed under the passive loss rules. The passive loss is disallowed because Bob does not generate any passive income that could absorb his passive loss. His salary (active income) and dividends (portfolio income) cannot be sheltered by any of the passive loss. Consequently, Bob's current-year taxable income is $415,000, and he receives no current benefit for his share of the partnership loss. However, all is not lost because Bob's share of the entity's loss is *suspended*. That is, it is carried forward and can be deducted in the future when he has passive income or sells his interest in the activity. ■

The following two sections explore the nature of the at-risk limits and passive activity loss rules and their impact on investors. Congress intentionally structured these rules so that investors evaluating potential investments must consider mainly the *economics* of the venture instead of the *tax benefits* or tax avoidance possibilities that an investment may generate.

BRIDGE DISCIPLINE

Bridge to Finance

An over-arching requirement to maximizing wealth is to reduce the present value cost of taxation. One way to reduce the cost of taxation in present value terms is to defer the payment of a tax into the future for as long as possible. This can be accomplished by reducing the taxpayer's tax base (i.e., taxable income) either by deferring the recognition of income or by accelerating the timing of deductions. As a result, to the extent that the tax cost associated with an investment alternative is reduced, the after-tax benefit from that investment and the investor's wealth position are enhanced.

For example, a common attribute of many tax-advantaged investments is the availability of tax losses that investors may claim on their own income tax returns. Many times, these tax losses are the result of investment-level deductions, such as interest and depreciation expenses, that are bunched in the early years of the life of the investment rather than being due to economic woes of the investment itself.

Through the at-risk limitations and the passive loss rules, the tax law works to scale back the ability of taxpayers to claim tax losses flowing from certain investments. These limitations have a direct impact on *when* investors can claim loss deductions flowing from affected investments. The typical result of these provisions is that the loss deductions are deferred. As a result, when evaluating competing investment alternatives, taxpayers must address the impact of these tax limitations in projecting the after-tax benefits that can be expected to follow.

LEARNING OBJECTIVE 6

Describe how the at-risk limitation and the passive loss rules limit deductions for losses and identify taxpayers subject to these restrictions.

At-Risk Limitations

The at-risk provisions limit the deductibility of losses from business and income-producing activities. These provisions, which apply to individuals and closely held corporations, are designed to prevent taxpayers from deducting losses in excess of their actual economic investment in an activity. In the case of an S corporation or a partnership, the at-risk limits apply at the owner level. Under the at-risk rules, a taxpayer's deductible loss from an activity for any taxable year is limited to the amount the taxpayer has at risk at the end of the taxable year (i.e., the amount the taxpayer could actually lose in the activity).

While the amount at risk generally vacillates over time, the initial amount considered at risk consists of the following:[23]

- The amount of cash and the adjusted basis of property contributed to the activity by the taxpayer.
- Amounts borrowed for use in the activity for which the taxpayer is personally liable.
- The adjusted basis of property pledged as security that is not used in the activity.

This amount generally is increased each year by the taxpayer's share of income and is decreased by the taxpayer's share of losses and withdrawals from the activity. In addition, because *general partners* are jointly and severally liable for recourse

CONCEPT SUMMARY 5–3

Calculation of At-Risk Amount

Increases to a taxpayer's at-risk amount:

- Cash and the adjusted basis of property contributed to the activity.
- Amounts borrowed for use in the activity for which the taxpayer is personally liable.
- The adjusted basis of property pledged as security that is not used in the activity.
- Taxpayer's share of amounts borrowed for use in the activity that are qualified nonrecourse financing.
- Taxpayer's share of the activity's income.

Decreases to a taxpayer's at-risk amount:

- Withdrawals from the activity.
- Taxpayer's share of the activity's loss.
- Taxpayer's share of any reductions of debt for which recourse against the taxpayer exists or reductions of qualified nonrecourse debt.

debts of the partnership, their at-risk amounts are increased when the partnership increases its debt and are decreased when the partnership reduces its debt. However, a taxpayer generally is not considered at risk with respect to borrowed amounts if either of the following is true:

- The taxpayer is not personally liable for repayment of the debt (e.g., nonrecourse debt).
- The lender has an interest (other than as a creditor) in the activity.

An important exception provides that, in the case of an activity involving the holding of real property, a taxpayer is considered at risk for his or her share of any *qualified nonrecourse financing* that is secured by real property used in the activity.[24]

Subject to the passive activity rules discussed later in the chapter, a taxpayer may deduct a loss as long as the at-risk amount is positive. However, once the at-risk amount is exhausted, any remaining loss cannot be deducted until a later year. Any losses disallowed for any given taxable year by the at-risk rules may be deducted in the first succeeding year in which the rules do not prevent the deduction—that is, when there is, and to the extent of, a positive at-risk amount.

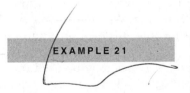

EXAMPLE 21

In 2001, Sue invests $40,000 in an oil partnership. The partnership, through the use of nonrecourse loans, spends $60,000 on deductible intangible drilling costs applicable to Sue's interest. Assume Sue's interest in the partnership is subject to the at-risk limits but is not subject to the passive loss limits. Since Sue has only $40,000 of capital at risk, she cannot deduct more than $40,000 against her other income and must reduce her at-risk amount to zero ($40,000 at-risk amount − $40,000 loss deducted). The nondeductible loss of $20,000 ($60,000 loss generated − $40,000 loss allowed) can be carried over to 2002.

In 2002, Sue has taxable income of $15,000 from the oil partnership and invests an additional $10,000 in the venture. Her at-risk amount is now $25,000 ($0 beginning balance + $15,000 taxable income + $10,000 additional investment). This enables Sue to deduct the $20,000 carryover loss and requires her to reduce her at-risk amount to $5,000 ($25,000 at-risk amount − $20,000 carryover loss allowed). ■

---

[24]§ 465(b)(6).

An additional complicating factor is that previously allowed losses must be recaptured as income to the extent the at-risk amount is reduced below zero.[25] This rule applies in situations such as when the amount at risk is reduced below zero by distributions to the taxpayer or when the status of indebtedness changes from recourse to nonrecourse.

Passive Loss Limits

CLASSIFICATION AND IMPACT OF PASSIVE INCOME AND LOSS

Classification.   The passive loss rules require income and loss to be classified into one of three categories: *active, passive,* or *portfolio.* **Active income** includes, but is not limited to, the following:

- Wages, salary, commissions, bonuses, and other payments for services rendered by the taxpayer.
- Profit from a trade or business in which the taxpayer is a material participant.

Portfolio income includes, but is not limited to, the following:

- Interest, dividends, annuities, and royalties not derived in the ordinary course of a trade or business.
- Gain or loss from the disposition of property that produces portfolio income or is held for investment purposes.

Section 469 provides that income or loss from the following activities is treated as *passive:*

- Any trade or business or income-producing activity in which the taxpayer does not materially participate.
- Subject to certain exceptions, all rental activities, whether the taxpayer materially participates or not.

Although the Code defines rental activities as passive activities, several exceptions allow losses from certain real estate rental activities to be offset against nonpassive (active or portfolio) income. The exceptions are discussed under Special Rules for Real Estate later in the chapter.

General Impact.   Losses or expenses generated by passive activities can only be deducted to the extent of income from passive activities. Any excess may not be used to offset income from active or portfolio income. Instead, any unused passive losses are suspended and carried forward to future years to offset passive income generated in those years. Otherwise, suspended losses may be used only when a taxpayer disposes of his or her entire interest in an activity. In that event, all current and suspended losses related to the activity may offset active and portfolio income.

EXAMPLE 22

Kim, a physician, earns $150,000 from her full-time practice. She also receives $10,000 in dividends and interest from various portfolio investments, and her share of a passive loss from a tax shelter not limited by the at-risk rules is $60,000. Because the loss is a passive loss, it is not deductible against her other income. The loss is suspended and is carried over to the future. If Kim has passive income from this investment or from other passive investments in the future, she can offset the suspended loss against that passive income. If she

---

[25]§ 465(e).

does not have passive income to offset this suspended loss in the future, she will be allowed to offset the loss against other types of income when she eventually disposes of the passive activity. ■

Impact of Suspended Losses.   The actual economic gain or loss from a passive investment (including any suspended losses) can be determined when a taxpayer disposes of his or her entire interest in the investment. As a result, under the passive loss rules, upon a fully taxable disposition, any overall loss realized from the activity by the taxpayer is recognized and can be offset against passive, active, and portfolio income.

A fully taxable disposition generally involves a sale of the property to a third party at arm's length and thus, presumably, for a price equal to the property's fair market value. Gain recognized upon a transfer of an interest in a passive activity generally is treated as passive and is first offset by the suspended losses from that activity.

EXAMPLE 23	Rex sells an apartment building, a passive activity, with an adjusted basis of $100,000 for $180,000. In addition, he has suspended passive losses of $60,000 associated with the building. His total gain, $80,000, and his taxable gain, $20,000, are calculated as follows:

Net sales price	$ 180,000
Less: Adjusted basis	(100,000)
Total gain	$ 80,000
Less: Suspended losses	(60,000)
Taxable gain (passive)	$ 20,000

■

If current and suspended losses of the passive activity exceed the gain realized from the sale or if the sale results in a realized loss, the amount of

- any loss from the activity for the tax year (including losses suspended in the activity disposed of)

in excess of

- net income or gain for the tax year from all passive activities (without regard to the activity disposed of)

is treated as a loss that is not from a passive activity. In computing the loss from the activity for the year of disposition, any gain or loss recognized is included in the calculation.

EXAMPLE 24	Dean sells an apartment building with an adjusted basis of $100,000 for $150,000. In addition, he has current and suspended passive losses of $60,000 associated with the building and has no other passive activities. His total gain of $50,000 and his deductible loss of $10,000 are calculated as follows:

Net sales price	$ 150,000
Less: Adjusted basis	(100,000)
Total gain	$ 50,000
Less: Suspended losses	(60,000)
Deductible loss (not passive)	($ 10,000)

The $10,000 loss can be deducted against Dean's active and portfolio income. ■

Carryovers of Suspended Losses. In the above examples, it was assumed that the taxpayer had an interest in only one passive activity, and as a result, the suspended loss was related exclusively to the activity that was disposed of. When a taxpayer owns more than one passive activity, however, any suspended losses must be allocated among the activities. The allocation to an activity is made by multiplying the disallowed passive activity loss from all activities by the following fraction:

$$\frac{\text{Loss from activity}}{\text{Sum of losses for taxable year from all activities having losses}}$$

EXAMPLE 25

Diego has investments in three passive activities with the following income and losses for 2000:

Activity A	($ 30,000)
Activity B	(20,000)
Activity C	25,000
Net passive loss	($ 25,000)
Net passive loss allocated to:	
Activity A [$25,000 × ($30,000/$50,000)]	($ 15,000)
Activity B [$25,000 × ($20,000/$50,000)]	(10,000)
Total suspended losses	($ 25,000)

Suspended losses are carried over indefinitely and are offset in the future against any passive income from the activities to which they relate.[26]

EXAMPLE 26

Assume the same facts as in the preceding example and that Activity A produces $10,000 of income in 2001. Of the suspended loss of $15,000 from 2000 for Activity A, $10,000 is offset against the income from this activity. If Diego sells Activity A in early 2002, then the remaining $5,000 suspended loss is used in determining his final gain or loss. ∎

Passive Credits. Credits arising from passive activities are limited in much the same way as passive losses. Passive credits can be utilized only against regular tax attributable to passive income,[27] which is calculated by comparing the tax on all income (including passive income) with the tax on income excluding passive income.

EXAMPLE 27

Sam owes $50,000 of tax, disregarding net passive income, and $80,000 of tax, considering both net passive and other taxable income (disregarding the credits in both cases). The amount of tax attributable to the passive income is $30,000.

Tax due (before credits) including net passive income	$ 80,000
Less: Tax due (before credits) without including net passive income	(50,000)
Tax attributable to passive income	$ 30,000

Sam in the preceding example can claim a maximum of $30,000 of passive activity credits; the excess credits are carried over. These passive activity credits (such as the low-income housing credit and rehabilitation credit) can only be used

---

[26]§ 469(b). [27]§ 469(d)(2).

against the *regular* tax attributable to passive income. If a taxpayer has a net loss from passive activities during a given year, no credits can be used.

Carryovers of Passive Credits. Tax credits attributable to passive activities can be carried forward indefinitely, much like suspended passive losses. Unlike passive losses, however, passive credits are lost forever when the activity is disposed of in a taxable transaction where loss is recognized. Credits are allowed on dispositions only when there is sufficient tax on passive income to absorb them.

EXAMPLE 28

Alicia sells a passive activity for a gain of $10,000. The activity had suspended losses of $40,000 and suspended credits of $15,000. The $10,000 gain is offset by $10,000 of the suspended losses, and the remaining $30,000 of suspended losses is deductible against Alicia's active and portfolio income. The suspended credits are lost forever because the sale of the activity did not generate any tax after considering the effect of the suspended losses. This is true even if Alicia has positive taxable income or is subject to the alternative minimum tax. ■

EXAMPLE 29

If Alicia in the preceding example had realized a $100,000 gain on the sale of the passive activity, the suspended credits could have been used to the extent of regular tax attributable to the net passive income.

Gain on sale	$100,000
Less: Suspended losses	(40,000)
Net gain	$ 60,000

If the tax attributable to the net gain of $60,000 is $15,000 or more, the entire $15,000 of suspended credits can be used. If the tax attributable to the gain is less than $15,000, the excess of the suspended credits over the tax attributable to the gain is lost forever. ■

When a taxpayer has adequate regular tax liability from passive activities to trigger the use of suspended credits, the credits lose their character as passive credits. They are reclassified as regular tax credits and made subject to the same limits as other credits (see Chapter 13).

Passive Activity Changes to Active. If a formerly passive activity becomes active, suspended losses are allowed to the extent of income from the now active business.[28] If any of the suspended loss remains, it continues to be treated as a loss from a passive activity. The excess suspended loss can be deducted against passive

---

[28]§ 469(f).

income or carried over to the next tax year and deducted to the extent of income from the now active business in the succeeding year(s).

TAXPAYERS SUBJECT TO THE PASSIVE LOSS RULES

The passive loss rules apply to individuals, estates, trusts, personal service corporations, and closely held C corporations.[29] Passive income or loss from investments in partnerships or S corporations (see Chapters 11 and 12) flows through to the owners, and the passive loss rules are applied at the owner level. Consequently, it is necessary to understand how the passive activity rules apply to both entities *and* their owners (including individual taxpayers).

Personal Service Corporations.   Application of the passive loss limitations to **personal service corporations** is intended to prevent taxpayers from sheltering personal service income by creating personal service corporations and acquiring passive activities at the corporate level.

<table>
<tr><td>

EXAMPLE 30

</td><td>

Five tax accountants, who earn a total of $1 million a year in their individual practices, form a personal service corporation. Shortly after its formation, the corporation invests in a passive activity that produces a $200,000 loss during the year. Because the passive loss rules apply to personal service corporations, the corporation may not deduct the $200,000 loss against the $1 million of active income. ■

</td></tr>
</table>

Determination of whether a corporation is a *personal service corporation* is based on rather broad definitions. A personal service corporation is a corporation that meets both of the following conditions:

- The principal activity is the performance of personal services.
- Such services are substantially performed by owner-employees.

---

[29]§ 469(a).

Generally, personal service corporations include those in the fields of health, law, engineering, architecture, accounting, actuarial science, performing arts, and consulting.[30]

3 *Find more information on this topic at our Web site: **http://wft-entities.swcollege.com**.*

Closely Held C Corporations. Application of the passive loss rules to closely held (non-personal service) corporations is also intended to prevent individuals from incorporating to avoid the passive loss limitations. A corporation is classified as a **closely held C corporation** if at any time during the taxable year, more than 50 percent of the value of its outstanding stock is owned, directly or indirectly, by or for five or fewer individuals. Closely held corporations (other than personal service corporations) may use passive losses to offset *active* income, but *not portfolio* income.

EXAMPLE 31

Silver Corporation, a closely held (non-personal service) C corporation, has a $500,000 passive loss from a rental activity, $400,000 of active income, and $100,000 of portfolio income. The corporation may offset $400,000 of the $500,000 passive loss against the $400,000 of active business income, but may not offset the remainder against the $100,000 of portfolio income. Thus, $100,000 of the passive loss is suspended ($500,000 passive loss − $400,000 offset against active income). ■

Application of the passive loss limitations to closely held corporations prevents shareholders from transferring their portfolio investments to such corporations in order to offset passive losses against portfolio income.

LEARNING OBJECTIVE 7

Discuss and be able to apply the definitions of activity, material participation, and rental activity under the passive loss rules.

ACTIVITY DEFINED

Identifying what constitutes an activity is a necessary first step in applying the passive loss limitation. The current rules used to delineate an activity state that, in general, a taxpayer can treat one or more trade or business activities or rental activities as a single activity if those activities form an *appropriate economic unit* for measuring gain or loss. The Regulations provide guidelines for identifying appropriate economic units.[31] These guidelines are designed to prevent taxpayers from arbitrarily combining different businesses in an attempt to circumvent the passive loss limitation. For example, combining a profitable active business and a passive business generating losses into one activity would allow the taxpayer to offset passive losses against active income.

4 *Find more information on this topic at our Web site: **http://wft-entities.swcollege.com**.*

To determine which ventures form an appropriate economic unit, all of the relevant facts and circumstances must be considered. However, special rules restrict the grouping of rental and nonrental activities.[32] The example below, adapted from the Regulations, illustrates the application of the activity grouping rules.[33]

EXAMPLE 32

George owns a men's clothing store and a video game parlor in Chicago. He also owns a men's clothing store and a video game parlor in Milwaukee. Reasonable methods of applying the facts and circumstances test may result in any of the following groupings:

[30]§ 448(d)(2).
[31]Reg. § 1.469–4.
[32]Reg. § 1.469–4(d).
[33]Reg. § 1.469–4(c)(3).

- All four businesses may be grouped into a single activity.
- The clothing stores may be grouped into an activity, and the video game parlors may be grouped into an activity.
- The Chicago businesses may be grouped into an activity, and the Milwaukee businesses may be grouped into an activity.
- Each of the four businesses may be treated as a separate activity. ■

Once a set of activities has been grouped by the taxpayer using the above rules, the grouping cannot be changed unless a material change in the facts and circumstances occurs or the original grouping was clearly inappropriate. In addition, the Regulations also grant the IRS the right to regroup activities when one of the primary purposes of the taxpayer's grouping is to avoid the passive loss limitation and the grouping fails to reflect an appropriate economic unit.[34]

MATERIAL PARTICIPATION

If a taxpayer materially participates in a nonrental trade or business activity, any loss from that activity is treated as an active loss that can offset active income. If a taxpayer does not materially participate, however, the loss is treated as a passive loss, which can only offset passive income. Therefore, controlling whether a particular activity is treated as active or passive is an important part of the tax strategy of a taxpayer who owns an interest in one or more businesses. Consider the following examples.

EXAMPLE 33

Cameron, a corporate executive, earns a salary of $600,000 per year. In addition, he owns a separate business in which he participates. The business produces a loss of $100,000 during the year. If Cameron materially participates in the business, the $100,000 loss is an active loss that may offset his active income from his corporate employer. If he does not materially participate, the loss is passive and is suspended. Cameron may use the suspended loss in the future only when he has passive income or disposes of the activity. ■

EXAMPLE 34

Connor, an attorney, earns $350,000 a year in his law practice. He owns interests in two activities, A and B, in which he participates. Activity A, in which he does not *materially* participate, produces a loss of $50,000. Connor has not yet met the material participation standard for Activity B, which produces income of $80,000. However, he can meet the material participation standard if he spends an additional 50 hours in Activity B during the year. Should Connor attempt to meet the material participation standard for Activity B? If he continues working in Activity B and becomes a material participant, the $80,000 of income from the activity is active, and the $50,000 passive loss from Activity A must be suspended. A more favorable tax strategy is for Connor to *not meet* the material participation standard for Activity B, thus making the income from that activity passive. This enables him to offset the $50,000 passive loss from Activity A against the passive income from Activity B. ■

It is possible to devise numerous scenarios in which the taxpayer could control the tax outcome by increasing or decreasing participation in different activities. Examples 33 and 34 demonstrate two of the possibilities. The conclusion reached in most analyses of this type is that taxpayers will benefit by having profitable activities classified as passive so that any passive losses can be used to offset that passive income. If the activity produces a loss, however, the taxpayer will benefit if it is classified as active so that the loss is not subject to the passive loss limitations.

---

[34]Reg. § 1.469–4(f).

Temporary Regulations[35] provide seven tests that are intended to help taxpayers determine when **material participation** is achieved.

Tests Based on Current Participation. The first four tests are quantitative tests that require measurement, in hours, of the individual's participation in the activity during the year.

1. *Does the individual participate in the activity for more than 500 hours during the year?*

The purpose of the 500-hour requirement is to restrict deductions from the types of trade or business activities that Congress intended to treat as passive activities. The 500-hour standard for material participation was adopted for the following reasons:[36]

- Few investors in traditional tax shelters devote more than 500 hours a year to such an investment.
- The IRS believes that income from an activity in which the taxpayer participates for more than 500 hours a year should not be treated as passive.

2. *Does the individual's participation in the activity for the taxable year constitute substantially all of the participation in the activity of all individuals (including nonowner employees) for the year?*

EXAMPLE 35

Ned, a physician, operates a separate business in which he participates for 80 hours during the year. He is the only participant and has no employees in the separate business. Ned meets the material participation standard of Test 2. If he had employees, it could be difficult to apply Test 2, because the Temporary Regulations do not define the term "substantially all." ∎

3. *Does the individual participate in the activity for more than 100 hours during the year, and is the individual's participation in the activity for the year not less than the participation of any other individual (including nonowner employees) for the year?*

EXAMPLE 36

Adam, a college professor, owns a separate business in which he participates 110 hours during the year. He has an employee who works 90 hours during the year. Adam meets the material participation standard under Test 3, but probably does not meet it under Test 2 because his participation is only 55% of the total participation. It is unlikely that 55% would meet the substantially all requirement of Test 2. ∎

Tests 2 and 3 are included because the IRS recognizes that the operation of some activities does not require more than 500 hours of participation during the year.

4. *Is the activity a significant participation activity for the taxable year, and does the individual's aggregate participation in all significant participation activities during the year exceed 500 hours?*

A **significant participation activity** is a trade or business in which the individual's participation exceeds 100 hours during the year. This test treats taxpayers as material participants if their aggregate participation in several significant participation activities exceeds 500 hours. Test 4 thus accords the same treatment to an individual who devotes an aggregate of more than 500 hours to several significant

---

[35]Temp. and Prop.Reg. § 1.469-5T(a).

[36]T.D. 8175, 1988-1 C.B. 191.

participation activities as to an individual who devotes more than 500 hours to a single activity.

EXAMPLE 37

Mike owns five different businesses. He participates in each activity during the year as follows:

Activity	Hours of Participation
A	110
B	140
C	120
D	150
E	100

Activities A, B, C, and D are significant participation activities, and Mike's aggregate participation in those activities is 520 hours. Therefore, Activities A, B, C, and D are *not* treated as passive activities. Activity E is not a significant participation activity (not more than 100 hours), so it is not included in applying the 500-hour test. Activity E is treated as a passive activity, unless Mike meets one of the other material participation tests for that activity. ■

EXAMPLE 38

Assume the same facts as in the preceding example, except that Activity A does not exist. All of the activities are now treated as passive. Activity E is not counted in applying the more-than-500-hour test, so Mike's aggregate participation in significant participation activities is 410 hours (140 in Activity B + 120 in Activity C + 150 in Activity D). He could meet the significant participation test for Activity E by participating for one more hour in the activity. This would cause Activities B, C, D, and E to be treated as nonpassive activities. However, before deciding whether to participate for at least one more hour in Activity E, Mike should assess how the participation would affect his overall tax liability. ■

Tests Based on Prior Participation. Tests 5 and 6 are based on material participation in prior years. Under these tests, a taxpayer no longer participating in an activity can continue to be *classified* as a material participant. The IRS takes the position that material participation in a trade or business for a long period of time is likely to indicate that the activity represents the individual's principal livelihood, rather than a passive investment. Consequently, withdrawal from the activity or reduction of participation to the point where it is not material does not change the classification of the activity from active to passive.

5. *Did the individual materially participate in the activity for any 5 taxable years (whether consecutive or not) during the 10 taxable years that immediately precede the taxable year?*

EXAMPLE 39

Dawn, who owns a 50% interest in a restaurant, was a material participant in the operations of the restaurant from 1995 through 1999. She retired at the end of 1999 and is no longer involved in the restaurant except as an investor. Dawn will be treated as a material participant in the restaurant in 2000. Even if she does not become involved in the restaurant as a material participant again, she will continue to be treated as a material participant in 2001, 2002, 2003, and 2004. In 2005 and later years, Dawn's share of income or loss from the restaurant will be classified as passive unless she materially participates in those years. ■

6. *Is the activity a personal service activity, and did the individual materially participate in the activity for any three preceding taxable years (whether consecutive or not)?*

As indicated above, the material participation standards for personal service activities differ from other businesses. An individual who was a material participant in a personal service activity for *any three years* prior to the taxable year continues to be treated as a material participant after withdrawal from the activity.

EXAMPLE 40

Evan, a CPA, retires from the EFG Partnership after working full-time in the partnership for 30 years. As a retired partner, he will continue to receive a share of the profits of the firm for the next 10 years, even though he will not participate in the firm's operations. Evan also owns an interest in a passive activity that produces a loss for the year. Because he continues to be treated as a material participant in the EFG Partnership, his income from the partnership is active income. Therefore, he is not allowed to offset the loss from his passive investment against the income from the EFG Partnership. ■

Test Based on Facts and Circumstances.   Test 7 assesses the facts and circumstances to determine whether the taxpayer has materially participated.

7. *Based on all the facts and circumstances, did the individual participate in the activity on a regular, continuous, and substantial basis during the year?*

5 *Find more information on this topic at our Web site:* ***http://wft-entities.swcollege.com***.

Unfortunately, the Temporary Regulations do not define what constitutes regular, continuous, and substantial participation.[37]

Participation Defined.   Participation generally includes any work done by an individual in an activity that he or she owns. Participation does not include work if it is of a type not customarily done by owners *and* if one of its principal purposes is to avoid the disallowance of passive losses or credits. Also, work done in an individual's capacity as an investor (e.g., reviewing financial reports in a non-managerial capacity) is not counted in applying the material participation tests. However, participation by an owner's spouse counts as participation by the owner.[38]

EXAMPLE 41

Tom, who is a partner in a CPA firm, owns a computer store that has operated at a loss during the year. In order to offset this loss against the income from his CPA practice, Tom would like to avoid having the computer business classified as a passive activity. Through December 15, he has worked 400 hours in the business in management and selling activities. During the last two weeks of December, he works 80 hours in management and selling activities and 30 hours doing janitorial chores. Also during the last two weeks in December, Tom's wife participates 40 hours as a salesperson. She has worked as a salesperson in the computer store in prior years, but has not done so during the current year. If any of Tom's work is of a type not customarily done by owners and if one of its principal purposes is to avoid the disallowance of passive losses or credits, it is not counted in applying the material participation tests. It is likely that Tom's 480 hours of participation in management and selling activities will count as participation, but the 30 hours spent doing janitorial chores will not. However, the 40 hours of participation by his wife will count, and as a result, Tom will qualify as a material participant under the more-than-500-hour rule (480 + 40 = 520). ■

Limited Partners.   A *limited* partner is one whose liability to third-party creditors of the partnership is limited to the amount the partner has invested in the partnership. Such a partnership must have at least one *general* partner, who is fully liable in an individual capacity for the debts of the partnership to third parties. Generally,

---

[37]Temp. and Prop.Reg. § 1.469–5T(b)(2).   [38]Temp. and Prop.Reg. § 1.469–5T(f)(3).

a *limited partner* is not considered a material participant unless he or she qualifies under Test 1, 5, or 6 in the above list. However, a *general partner* may qualify as a material participant by meeting any of the seven tests. If a general partner also owns a limited interest in the same limited partnership, all interests are treated as a general interest.[39]

Corporations.   Personal service corporations and closely held C corporations cannot directly participate in an activity. However, a corporation is deemed to materially participate if its owners materially participate in an activity of the corporation. Together, the participating owners must own directly or indirectly more than 50 percent of the value of the outstanding stock of the corporation.[40] Alternatively, a closely held C corporation may be deemed to materially participate if, during the entire year, it has at least one full-time employee actively managing the business and at least three full-time nonowner employees working for the business. In addition, the corporation's trade or business expenses must exceed its gross income by 15 percent for the year.[41]

RENTAL ACTIVITIES

The Code specifies that, subject to certain exceptions, all rental activities are to be treated as passive activities.[42] A **rental activity** is defined as any activity where payments are received principally for the use of tangible (real or personal) property.[43] Importantly, an activity that is classified as a rental activity is subject to the passive activity loss rules, even if the taxpayer involved is a material participant.

EXAMPLE 42

Sarah owns an apartment building and spends an average of 60 hours a week in its operation. Assuming that the apartment building operation is classified as a rental activity, it is automatically subject to the passive activity rules, even though Sarah spends more than 500 hours a year in its operation. ∎

Temporary Regulations, however, provide exceptions for certain situations where activities involving rentals of real and personal property are *not* to be treated as rental activities.[44] Activities covered by any of the exceptions provided by the Temporary Regulations are not *automatically* treated as passive activities because they would not be classified as rental activities. Instead, the activities are subject to the material participation tests.

6 *Find more information on this topic at our Web site: **http://wft-entities.swcollege.com.***

EXAMPLE 43

Dan owns a videocassette rental business. Because the average period of customer use is seven days or less, Dan's business is not treated as a rental activity. ∎

The fact that Dan's videocassette business in the previous example is not treated as a rental activity does not necessarily mean that it is classified as a nonpassive activity. Instead, the videocassette business is treated as a trade or business activity subject to the material participation standards. If Dan is a material participant, the business is treated as active. If he is not a material participant, it is treated as a passive activity.

---

[39]Temp. and Prop.Reg. § 1.469–5T(e)(3)(ii).
[40]Temp. and Prop.Reg. § 1.469–1T(g)(3)(i)(A).
[41]Temp. and Prop.Reg. § 1.469–1T(g)(3)(i)(B).

[42]§ 469(c)(2).
[43]§ 469(j)(8).
[44]Temp. and Prop.Reg. § 1.469–1T(e)(3)(ii).

Passive Activity Loss Rules: General Concepts

What is the fundamental passive activity rule?	Passive activity losses may be deducted only against passive activity income and gains. Losses not deducted are suspended and used in future years.
Who is subject to the passive activity rules?	Individuals. Estates. Trusts. Personal service corporations. Closely held C corporations.
What is a passive activity?	A trade or business or income-producing activity in which the taxpayer does not materially participate during the year, or rental activities, subject to certain exceptions, regardless of the taxpayer's level of participation.
What is an activity?	One or more trades or businesses or rental activities that comprise an appropriate economic unit.
How is an appropriate economic unit determined?	Based on a reasonable application of the relevant facts and circumstances.
What is material participation?	In general, the taxpayer participates on a regular, continuous, and substantial basis. More specifically, when the taxpayer meets the conditions of one of the seven tests provided in the Regulations.
What is a rental activity?	In general, an activity where payments are received for the use of tangible property. More specifically, a rental activity that does *not* meet one of the six exceptions provided in the Regulations. Special rules apply to rental real estate.

LEARNING OBJECTIVE 8

Recognize the relationship between the at-risk and passive activity limitations.

INTERACTION OF AT-RISK AND PASSIVE ACTIVITY LIMITS

The determination of whether a loss is suspended under the passive loss rules is made *after* application of the at-risk rules, as well as other provisions relating to the measurement of taxable income. A loss that is not allowed for the year because the taxpayer is not at risk with respect to it is suspended under the at-risk provision and not under the passive loss rules. Further, a taxpayer's basis is reduced by deductions (e.g., depreciation) even if the deductions are not currently usable because of the passive loss rules.

EXAMPLE 44

Jack's adjusted basis in a passive activity is $10,000 at the beginning of 2000. His loss from the activity in 2000 is $4,000. Since Jack has no passive activity income, the $4,000 cannot be deducted. At year-end, Jack has an adjusted basis and an at-risk amount of $6,000 in the activity and a suspended passive loss of $4,000. ■

EXAMPLE 45

Jack in the preceding example has a loss of $9,000 in the activity in 2001. Since the $9,000 exceeds his at-risk amount ($6,000) by $3,000, that $3,000 loss is disallowed by the at-risk rules. If Jack has no passive activity income, the remaining $6,000 is suspended under the passive activity rules. At year-end, he has:

- A $3,000 loss suspended under the at-risk rules.
- $10,000 of suspended passive losses.
- An adjusted basis and at-risk amount in the activity of zero. ■

[handwritten: couple of exemptions]

EXAMPLE 46

Jack in Example 45 realizes $1,000 of passive income in 2002. Because the $1,000 increases his at-risk amount, $1,000 of the $3,000 unused loss is reclassified as a passive loss. If he has no other passive income, the $1,000 income is offset by $1,000 of suspended passive losses. At the end of 2002, Jack has:

- No taxable passive income.
- $2,000 ($3,000 – $1,000) of unused losses under the at-risk rules.
- $10,000 of (reclassified) suspended passive losses ($10,000 + $1,000 of reclassified unused at-risk losses – $1,000 of passive losses offset against passive income).
- An adjusted basis and an at-risk amount in the activity of zero. ∎

EXAMPLE 47

In 2003, Jack has no gain or loss from the activity in Example 46. He contributes $5,000 more to the passive activity. Because the $5,000 increases his at-risk amount, the $2,000 of losses suspended under the at-risk rules is reclassified as passive. Jack gets no passive loss deduction in 2003. At year-end, he has:

- No suspended losses under the at-risk rules.
- $12,000 of suspended passive losses ($10,000 + $2,000 of reclassified suspended at-risk losses).
- An adjusted basis and an at-risk amount of $3,000 ($5,000 additional investment – $2,000 of reclassified losses). ∎

LEARNING OBJECTIVE 9

Discuss the special treatment available to real estate activities.

[handwritten: Rental activities general are passive]

SPECIAL RULES FOR REAL ESTATE

The passive loss limits contain two exceptions related to real estate activities. These exceptions allow all or part of real estate rental losses to offset active or portfolio income, even though the activity is a passive activity.

Real Estate Professionals. The first exception allows certain real estate professionals to avoid passive loss treatment for losses from real estate rental activities.[45] To qualify for nonpassive treatment, a taxpayer must satisfy both of the following requirements:

- More than half of the personal services that the taxpayer performs in trades or businesses are performed in real property trades or businesses in which the taxpayer materially participates.
- The taxpayer performs more than 750 hours of services in these real property trades or businesses as a material participant.

Taxpayers who do not satisfy the above requirements must continue to treat losses from real estate rental activities as passive losses.

EXAMPLE 48

During the current year, Della performs personal service activities as follows: 900 hours as a personal financial planner, 550 hours in a real estate development and leasing business, and 600 hours in real estate rental activities. Any loss Della incurs in either real estate activity will not be subject to the passive loss rules, since more than 50% of her personal services are devoted to real property trades or businesses and her material participation in those real estate activities exceeds 750 hours. Thus, any loss from the real estate activities can offset active and portfolio income. ∎

As discussed earlier, a spouse's work is taken into consideration in satisfying the material participation requirement. However, the hours worked by a spouse

---

[45]§ 469(c)(7).

are not taken into account when ascertaining whether a taxpayer has worked for more than 750 hours in real property trades or businesses during a year. Services performed by an employee are not treated as being related to a real estate trade or business unless the employee performing the services owns more than a 5 percent interest in the employer. Additionally, a closely held C corporation may also qualify for the passive loss relief if more than 50 percent of its gross receipts for the year are derived from real property trades or businesses in which it materially participates.[46]

Rental Real Estate Deduction.   The second exception is more significant in that it is not restricted to real estate professionals. This exception allows individuals to deduct up to $25,000 of losses on real estate rental activities against active and portfolio income. The potential annual $25,000 deduction is reduced by 50 percent of the taxpayer's adjusted gross income (AGI) in excess of $100,000. Thus, the entire deduction is phased out at $150,000. If married individuals file separately, the $25,000 deduction is reduced to zero unless they lived apart for the entire year. If they lived apart for the entire year, the loss amount is $12,500 each, and the phase-out begins at $50,000.

To qualify for the $25,000 exception, a taxpayer must:[48]

- *Actively* participate in the real estate rental activity.
- Own 10 percent or more (in value) of all interests in the activity during the entire taxable year (or shorter period during which the taxpayer held an interest in the activity).

The difference between *active participation* and *material participation* is that the former can be satisfied without regular, continuous, and substantial involvement in operations as long as the taxpayer participates in making management decisions in a significant and bona fide sense. In this context, relevant management decisions include such decisions as approving new tenants, deciding on rental terms, and approving capital or repair expenditures.

The $25,000 allowance is available after all active participation rental losses and gains are netted and applied to other passive income. If a taxpayer has a real estate rental loss in excess of the amount that can be deducted under the real estate rental exception, that excess is treated as a passive loss.

EXAMPLE 49

Brad, who has $90,000 of AGI before considering rental activities, has $85,000 of losses from a real estate rental activity in which he actively participates. He also actively participates in another real estate rental activity from which he has $25,000 of income. He has other passive income of $36,000. The net rental loss of $60,000 is offset by the $36,000 of passive income, leaving $24,000 that can be deducted against other income. ∎

The $25,000 offset allowance is an aggregate of both deductions and credits in deduction equivalents. The deduction equivalent of a passive activity credit is the amount of deductions that reduces the tax liability for the taxable year by an amount equal to the credit.[49] A taxpayer with $5,000 of credits and a marginal tax rate of 28 percent would have a deduction equivalent of $17,857 ($5,000/28%).

[46]§ 469(c)(7)(B) and Reg. § 1.469–9.
[47]§ 469(i).
[48]§ 469(i)(6).
[49]§ 469(j)(5).

If total deductions and deduction equivalents exceed $25,000, the taxpayer must allocate the benefit on a pro rata basis. First, the allowance must be allocated among the losses (including real estate rental activity losses suspended in prior years) and then to credits.

EXAMPLE 50

Kevin is an active participant in a real estate rental activity that produces $8,000 of income, $26,000 of deductions, and $1,500 of credits. Kevin, whose marginal tax rate is 28%, may deduct the net passive loss of $18,000 ($8,000 – $26,000). After deducting the loss, he has an available deduction equivalent of $7,000 ($25,000 – $18,000 passive loss). Therefore, the maximum amount of credits that he may claim is $1,960 ($7,000 × 28%). Since the actual credits are less than this amount, Kevin may claim the entire $1,500 credit. ∎

EXAMPLE 51

Kelly, whose marginal tax rate is 28%, actively participates in three separate real estate rental activities. The relevant tax results for each activity are as follows:

- Activity A: $20,000 of losses.
- Activity B: $10,000 of losses.
- Activity C: $4,200 of credits.

Kelly's deduction equivalent from the credits is $15,000 ($4,200/28%). Therefore, the total passive deductions and deduction equivalents are $45,000 ($20,000 + $10,000 + $15,000), which exceeds the maximum allowable amount of $25,000. Consequently, Kelly must allocate pro rata first from among losses and then from among credits. Deductions from losses are limited as follows:

- Activity A: $25,000 × [$20,000/($20,000 + $10,000)] = $16,667.
- Activity B: $25,000 × [$10,000/($20,000 + $10,000)] = $8,333.

Since the amount of passive deductions exceeds the $25,000 maximum, the deduction balance of $5,000 and passive credits of $4,200 must be carried forward. Kelly's suspended losses and credits by activity are as follows:

		Activity		
	Total	A	B	C
Allocated losses	$ 30,000	$ 20,000	$ 10,000	$ –0–
Allocated credits	4,200	–0–	–0–	4,200
Utilized losses	(25,000)	(16,667)	(8,333)	–0–
Suspended losses	5,000	3,333	1,667	–0–
Suspended credits	4,200	–0–	–0–	4,200

∎

DISPOSITION OF PASSIVE ACTIVITIES

Recall from an earlier discussion that if a taxpayer disposes of an entire interest in a passive activity, any suspended losses (and in certain cases, suspended credits) may be utilized when calculating the final economic gain or loss on the investment. In addition, if a loss ultimately results, that loss can offset other types of income. However, the consequences may differ if the activity is disposed of in a transaction that is not fully taxable. For example, if an interest in a passive activity is disposed of by gift, the suspended losses are added to the basis of the property.[50] Other rules apply if the activity is transferred in a nontaxable exchange, at death, or in an installment sale.

---

[50]§ 469(j)(6).

PLANNING CONSIDERATIONS

Utilizing Passive Losses

Taxpayers who have passive activity losses (PALs) should adopt a strategy of generating passive activity income that can be sheltered by existing passive losses. One approach is to buy an interest in a passive activity that is generating income (referred to as a passive income generator, or PIG). Then the PAL can offset income from the PIG. From a tax perspective, it would be foolish to buy a loss-generating passive activity (PAL) unless one has passive income to shelter or the activity is rental real estate that can qualify for the $25,000 exception or the exception available to real estate professionals.

A taxpayer with existing passive losses might consider buying rental property. If a large down payment is made and since only the straight-line method is available under MACRS (refer to Chapter 4), net income could be realized. The income would be sheltered by other passive losses, and depreciation expense would be spread out evenly and preserved for future years. Future gain realized upon the sale of the rental property could be sheltered by existing suspended passive losses.

Taxpayers with passive losses should consider all other trades or businesses in which they have an interest. If they show that they do not materially participate in the activity,

the activity becomes a passive activity. Existing passive losses and suspended losses could shelter any income generated. Family partnerships in which certain members do not materially participate would qualify. The silent partner in any general partnership engaged in a trade or business would also qualify.

The passive loss rules can have a dramatic effect on a taxpayer's ability to claim passive losses currently. However, several steps can be taken to mitigate their impact:

- Replace passive activity debt with home equity indebtedness, which provides deductible interest to individuals (see Chapter 15).
- Carefully select the year in which a passive activity is to be disposed of at a gain, as it can be to the taxpayer's advantage to wait until sufficient passive losses have been generated to completely offset the gain recognized on the asset's disposition.
- Keep accurate records of all sources of income and losses, particularly any suspended passive losses and credits and the activities to which they relate, so that their potential tax benefit will not be lost.

Suggested Further Readings

Nell Adkins, Frank Messina, and Steven C. Thompson, "New Refund Oppportunities for Prior Casualty and Theft Losses," *The Tax Adviser*, March 2000, pp. 182–187.

Richard M. Lipton, "Tax Court in *Hillman* Approves Self-Charged Rules Not Provided by the Passive Loss Regs.," *Journal of Taxation*, June 2000, pp. 342–345.

W. Eugene Seago, "Accounting for Inventory Shrinkage after TRA '97," *Journal of Taxation*, January 1998, pp. 5–13.

KEY TERMS

Problem Materials

PROBLEMS

1. Several years ago Loon Finance Company lent Scott $20,000 to help him start a new business. In May of the current year, Scott filed for bankruptcy, and Loon was notified that it could expect to receive no more than 60 cents on the dollar. As of the end of the current year, Loon has not received any payments. Loon has contacted you about the possibility of taking a bad debt deduction of $8,000 for the current year. Assume that the company uses the specific charge-off method of accounting for bad debts.

    Write a letter to Loon Finance Company that contains your advice as to whether it can claim a bad debt deduction of $8,000 for the current year. Also, prepare a memo for the tax files. Loon's address is 100 Tyler Lane, Erie, PA 16563.

2. In 1999, Tom loaned his friend $5,000 to purchase a car. In 2000, after Tom's friend had paid off $1,000 of the loan, she declared bankruptcy, and Tom was informed that he would not be able to collect any of the remaining $4,000 balance on the debt. In 2000, Tom had $50,000 of taxable income, none of which was from capital gains. In November 2001, Tom's friend paid him the $4,000 that she owed Tom, even though she was not legally obligated to do so. Determine Tom's tax treatment of the loan for 2000 and 2001.

3. Mable and Jack file a joint return. For the current year, they had the following items:

Salaries	$150,000
Loss on sale of § 1244 stock acquired two years ago	110,000
Gain on sale of § 1244 stock acquired six months ago	12,000
Nonbusiness bad debt	7,000

    Determine the impact of the above items on Mable and Jack's income for the current year.

4. A loss is allowed for securities that become worthless during the year. The loss generated is deemed to have occurred on the last day of the taxable year in which the securities become completely worthless.

    Ten years ago, Jack purchased some Green Corporation stock (§ 1244 small business stock) for $40,000. Over the ensuing years, Jack had no communications with the corporation and just sort of forgot about his investment. Earlier this year, Jack was visiting an old friend, and the topic of Green Corporation was raised. Jack asked his friend about the corporation, and his friend informed him that Green was declared bankrupt two years earlier.

    Because of this information, Jack has decided to write off the $40,000 on this year's Federal income tax return. Jack has reached this decision because he honestly did not know that the stock became worthless two years ago and because two years ago he was in a very low tax bracket. This year Jack is in the highest tax bracket.

    Evaluate what Jack is doing.

5. Mary, a single taxpayer, purchased 10,000 shares of § 1244 stock several years ago at a cost of $20 per share. In November of the current year, Mary receives an offer to sell the stock for $12 per share. She has the option of either selling all of the stock now or selling half of the stock now and half of the stock in January of next year. Mary's salary is $80,000 for the current year, and it will be $90,000 next year. Mary has long-term capital gains of $8,000 for the current year and will have $10,000 next year. If Mary's goal is to minimize her AGI for the two years, determine whether she should sell all of her stock this year or half of her stock this year and half next year.

6. Green Shop, Inc., was incorporated in 1966, and John owns all of its outstanding stock. The original cost basis in Green was $20,000. Blue Shop, Inc., was incorporated in 1968, and John owns all of its outstanding stock. Upon incorporation of Blue, John filed a § 1244 election with respect to his stock in Blue. John paid $10,000 for his § 1244 stock in Blue. Green and Blue were engaged in selling similar lines of clothing at retail. Inventory for both stores was purchased in Green's name. The costs of the transferred merchandise were entered on Blue's books as accounts payable to Green and on Green's books as accounts receivable from Blue. Blue ceased operations on January 31 of last year. At that time, Blue owed a large amount of money to Green for merchandise previously shipped to Blue. Blue transferred its remaining inventory back to Green to reduce the debt. After this transfer of inventory, Blue's remaining assets were insufficient to pay both the remaining accounts payable to Green and those to Blue's other creditors. On January 31 of last year, John assumed the obligation to pay $52,000 of Blue's debt to Green. On May 30 of the current year, John adopted a resolution directing that Blue be dissolved within 12 months. Identify the relevant tax issues for John with respect to Green and Blue.

EXTENDER

7. Paul Sanders, a married taxpayer who files a joint return with his wife, acquired stock in a corporation that qualified as a small business corporation under § 1244. The stock cost $30,000 and was acquired three years ago. A few months after he acquired the stock he gave it to his brother, Mike Sanders. The stock was worth $30,000 on the date of the gift. Mike, who is married and files a joint return with his wife, sells the stock for $10,000 in the current tax year. You represent Mike who asks you whether he can take a loss deduction on the sale of the stock. If so, how will the loss be treated for tax purposes? Prepare a letter to your client and a memo to the files. Mike's address is 2600 Riverview Drive, Plank, MO 63701.

8. Grackle Farming, Inc., owns a 500-acre farm in Minnesota. A tornado hit the area and destroyed a farm building and some farm equipment and damaged a barn. Fortunately for Grackle, the tornado occurred after the company had harvested its corn crop. Applicable information is as follows:

Asset	Basis	FMV Before	FMV After	Insurance Recovery
Building	$90,000	$ 70,000	$ –0–	$70,000
Equipment	40,000	50,000	–0–	25,000
Barn	90,000	120,000	70,000	25,000

Because of the extensive damage caused by the tornado, the President of the United States designated the area as a disaster area.

Grackle had $90,000 of taxable income last year. The company's taxable income for the current year, excluding the loss from the tornado, is $220,000. Determine the amount of the corporation's loss and the year in which it should take the loss.

9. Toucan Corporation purchased an office building many years ago. The property included a large black oak tree approximately 80 feet in height and about 100 years old. The tree was the dominant feature in the front of the building, where it stood alone next to the street. Because of the age and stature of the tree, the corporation had it inspected regularly by a tree expert. In August of the current year, the corporation's CEO noticed that the entire top or crown of the tree had turned brown. Because none of the leaves on other trees in the area had turned brown, the tree expert was called

in to inspect the tree. The inspection showed that the tree had been attacked by woodborers and was beyond saving and effectively dead. Identify the relevant tax issues for Toucan Corporation.

10. On November 1 of the current year, Sam dropped off to sleep while driving home from a business trip. Luckily, he was only slightly injured in the resulting accident, but the company car that he was driving was completely destroyed.

Sam is an employee of Snipe Industries. The corporation purchased the car new two years ago for $40,000. The automobile had a fair market value of $30,000 before the accident and $12,000 after the accident. The car was covered by an insurance policy that had a $3,000 deductible clause. The corporation is afraid that the policy will be canceled if it makes a claim for the damages. Therefore, Snipe is considering not filing a claim. The company believes that the casualty loss deduction will help mitigate the loss of the insurance reimbursement. The corporation's taxable income for the current year is $25,000.

Write a letter to Snipe Industries that contains your advice regarding the filing of an insurance claim for reimbursement for the damages to the company's car. Snipe Industries' address is 450 Colonel's Way, Warrensburg, MO 64093.

11. Mary, a single taxpayer, had the following items of income and expense during 2001:

Gross receipts from business	$70,000
Business expenses	90,000
Mary's salary as an employee of Blue, Inc.	15,000
Interest income	2,000
Itemized deductions (no casualty or theft)	14,000

a. Determine Mary's taxable income for 2001.
b. Determine Mary's NOL for 2001.

12. In the current year, Lionel invests $20,000 for an interest in a partnership in which he is a material participant. His share of the partnership loss for the year is $25,000. Discuss the tax treatment of Lionel's share of the loss, and compute his at-risk amount.

13. In the current year, Bill Parker (54 Oak Drive, St. Paul, MN 55162) is considering making an investment of $60,000 in Best Choice Partnership. The prospectus provided by Bill's broker indicates that the partnership investment is not a passive activity and that Bill's share of the entity's loss in the current year will likely be $40,000, while his share of the partnership loss next year will probably be $25,000. Write a letter to Bill in which you indicate how the losses would be treated for tax purposes in the current and next years.

14. Since his college days, Charles has developed an entrepreneurial streak. After testing his wings in his family's grocery business, he has decided to start several ventures on his own. Even though Charles is independently wealthy, he is looking forward to working, even if for a limited amount of time, in each of the ventures. He plans to "drop in" on the businesses from time to time between personal trips to Europe, the Caribbean, and the South Pacific. As of the end of the year, he has established computer software stores in Dayton, Austin, and Seattle; bagel bakeries in Albany, Athens, and Talahassee; and mountain bike and ski rental shops in small towns in Vermont, West Virginia, Colorado, and California. Identify the tax issues facing Charles.

15. Hazel has two investments in nonrental passive activities. Activity A, which was acquired seven years ago, was profitable until the current year. Activity B was acquired this year. Currently, Hazel's share of the loss from Activity A is $10,000, and her share of the loss from Activity B is $6,000. What is the total of Hazel's suspended losses from these activities as of the end of the current year?

16. Ray acquired an activity several years ago. In 2001, the loss from the activity is $50,000. Ray has AGI of $140,000 before considering the loss from the activity. The activity is

a bakery, and Ray is not a material participant. What is his AGI after considering this activity?

17. Leanne has investments in four passive activity partnerships purchased several years ago. Last year, the income and losses were as follows:

Activity	Income (Loss)
A	$ 60,000
B	(60,000)
C	(30,000)
D	(10,000)

In the current year, she sold her interest in Activity D for a $20,000 gain. Activity D, which had been profitable until last year, had a current loss of $3,000. How will the sale of Activity D affect Leanne's taxable income in the current year?

18. Leon sells his interest in a passive activity for $100,000 during the year. Determine the tax effect based on each of the following sets of independent facts:
    a. His adjusted basis in this investment is $35,000. Losses from prior years that were not deductible due to the passive loss restrictions total $40,000.
    b. His adjusted basis in this investment is $75,000. Losses from prior years that were not deductible due to the passive loss restrictions total $40,000.
    c. His adjusted basis in this investment is $75,000. Losses from prior years that were not deductible due to the passive loss restrictions total $40,000. In addition, suspended credits total $10,000.

19. Orange, Inc., a closely held personal service corporation, has $100,000 of passive losses in the current year. In addition, Orange has $80,000 of active business income and $20,000 of portfolio income. How much of the passive loss may Orange use to offset other types of income this year?

20. White, Inc., earns $400,000 from operations in the current year. White also receives $36,000 in interest on various investments. During the year, White pays $150,000 to acquire a 20% interest in a passive activity that produces a $200,000 loss.
    a. How will these facts affect White's taxable income, assuming the corporation is a personal service corporation?
    b. How will these facts affect White's taxable income, assuming the corporation is a closely held, non-personal service corporation?

21. Green Corporation, a closely held C corporation, earns active income of $50,000 in the current year. Green receives $60,000 in interest during the year. In addition, Green incurs a loss of $80,000 from an investment in a passive activity acquired last year. What is Green's net income for the current year after considering the passive investment?

22. Greg Horne (431 Maple Avenue, Cincinnati OH 45229), a syndicated radio talk show host in Cincinnati, earns a $400,000 salary in 2001. He works approximately 30 hours per week in this job, which leaves him time to participate in several businesses he acquired in 2001. He owns a movie theater and a drugstore in Cincinnati, a movie theater and a drugstore in Indianapolis, and a drugstore in Louisville. A preliminary analysis on December 1, 2001, shows projected income and losses for the various businesses as follows:

	Income (Loss)
Cincinnati movie theater (95 hours participation)	$ 56,000
Cincinnati drugstore (140 hours participation)	(89,000)
Indianapolis movie theater (90 hours participation)	34,000
Indianapolis drugstore (170 hours participation)	(41,000)
Louisville drugstore (180 hours participation)	(15,000)

Greg has full-time employees in each of the five businesses listed above. Write a letter to Greg suggesting a grouping method and other strategies that will provide the greatest tax advantage. Greg does not know much about the tax law, so provide a concise, nontechnical explanation.

23. Rene retired from public accounting after a long and successful career of 45 years. As part of her retirement package, she continues to share in the profits and losses of the firm, albeit at a lower rate than when she was working full-time. Because Rene wants to stay busy during her retirement years, she has invested and works in a local hardware business, operated as a partnership. Unfortunately, the business has recently gone through a slump and has not been generating profits. Identify relevant tax issues for Rene.

24. Kristin Graf (123 Baskerville Mill Road, Jamison, PA 18929) is trying to decide how to invest a $10,000 inheritance and comes to you for advice. One option is to make an additional investment in Rocky Road Adventures in which she has an at-risk basis of $0, suspended losses under the at-risk rules of $7,000, and suspended passive losses of $1,000. If Kristin makes this investment, her share of the expected profits this year would be $8,000. If her investment stays the same, her share of profits from Rocky Road Adventures would be $1,000. Another option is to invest $10,000 as a limited partner in the Ragged Mountain Winery; this investment would produce passive income of $9,000 to Kristin this year. Write a letter to Kristin in which you describe the current tax consequences of each alternative. Kristin is in the 31% tax bracket.

25. A number of years ago, Lee acquired a 20% interest in the ABC Partnership for $60,000. The partnership, which was profitable until 2001, is his sole investment. Lee's amount at risk in the partnership interest was $120,000 at the end of 2000. ABC incurred a loss of $400,000 in 2001 and reported income of $200,000 in 2002. Assuming Lee is not a material participant in ABC, how much of his loss from ABC Partnership is deductible in 2001 and 2002, respectively?

26. Last year, Fran invested $40,000 for an interest in a partnership in which she is a material participant. Her share of the partnership's loss for the year was $50,000. In the current year, Fran's share of the partnership's income is $30,000. What is the effect on her taxable income for the current year?

27. Soong, a physician, earns $200,000 from his practice. He also receives $18,000 in dividends and interest on various portfolio investments. During the year, he pays $45,000 to acquire a 20% interest in a partnership that produces a $300,000 loss.
   a. What is the effect of the partnership loss on Soong's income assuming he was not a material participant during the year?
   b. What is the effect of the partnership loss on Soong's income assuming he was a material participant during the year?

28. During the current year, Alan is determined to make better use of the tax losses that tend to flow from the various businesses that he owns. He is particularly sensitive to the limitations that the passive loss rules place on the deductibility of losses because of the disaster that occurred last year. His accountant informed him that he would not be able to claim any of the losses on his income tax return because of his lack of material participation. He has even suggested to his wife that she may have to put in some time at the businesses if his goals are to be accomplished. Identify the tax issues that Alan faces.

29. Ken has a $40,000 loss from an investment in a partnership in which he does not participate. He paid $30,000 for his interest in the partnership. How much of the loss is disallowed by the at-risk rules? How much is disallowed by the passive loss rules?

30. Joe Cook (125 Hill Street, Charleston, WV 25311) acquired an activity four years ago. The loss from the activity is $50,000 in the current year. He also earns a salary of $140,000 as a computer programmer in the current year. The activity is an apartment building in an exclusive part of the city, and Joe is an active participant. Joe has also informed you that he may not participate in the activity next year. Write a letter to Joe explaining

the current tax impact of the loss and the consequences of not actively participating next year.

31. During the current year, Donald worked 1,200 hours as a computer consultant, 600 hours in a real estate development business, and 500 hours in real estate rental activities. He earned $60,000 as a computer consultant, but lost $18,000 in the development business and $26,000 in the real estate rental business. How should Donald treat the losses on his Federal income tax return?

32. You have just met with Scott Myers (603 Pittsfield Dr., Champaign, IL 61821), a successful full-time real estate developer and investor. During your meeting you discussed his tax situation, because you are starting to prepare his 2001 Federal income tax return. During your meeting, Scott mentioned that he and his wife, Susan, went to great lengths to maximize their participation in an apartment complex that they own and manage. In particular, Scott included the following activities in the 540 hours of participation for the current year:

    • Time spent thinking about the rentals.

    • Time spent by Susan on weekdays visiting the apartment complex to oversee operations of the buildings (i.e., in a management role).

    • Time spent by both Scott and Susan on weekends visiting the apartment complex to assess operations. Scott and Susan always visited the complex together on weekends and both counted their hours (i.e., one hour at the complex was two hours of participation).

    • Time spent on weekends driving around the community looking for other potential rental properties to purchase. Again, both Scott's hours and Susan's hours were counted, even when they drove together.

    After reviewing Scott's records, you note that the apartment complex generated a significant loss this year. Prepare a letter to Scott describing your position on the deductibility of the loss.

33. During the current year, Maria Catanach works 1,200 hours as a computer consultant, 320 hours in a real estate development business, and 400 hours in real estate rental activities. Jorge, her husband, works 250 hours in the real estate development business and 180 hours in the real estate rental business. Maria earns $60,000 as a computer consultant; however, the Catanachs lost $18,000 in the real estate development business and $26,000 in the real estate rental business. How should they treat the losses on their joint current Federal income tax return?

34. During the current year, Gene performs services as follows: 1,800 hours as a CPA in his tax practice and 50 hours in an apartment leasing operation in which he has a 15% interest. Because of his oversight duties, Gene is considered to be an active participant in the leasing operation. He expects that his share of the loss realized from the apartment leasing operation will be $30,000 while his tax practice will show a profit of approximately $80,000. Gene is single and has no other income besides that stated above. Discuss the character of income and losses generated by these activities.

35. Last year, George and Louise purchased several rental units near the university hoping to benefit from their appreciation and expected cash flow. Because George and Louise both have full-time jobs and are unable to spend time managing the facilities, they contracted with a well-regarded property manager to attract renters, collect the rents, and respond to service calls. After the close of the year, the property manager provided George and Louise an accounting of the revenues and expenses related to the operations of the units, which showed a positive cash flow. To the couple's surprise, however, after considering the impact of the depreciation calculation and the interest expense on the properties' mortgages, a net tax loss resulted.

    Not wanting to lose the opportunity to claim a loss on their income tax return, they chose to reflect their loss as qualifying for the real estate rental activity exception. How do you feel about George and Louise's position?

36. Ida, who has AGI of $80,000 before considering rental activities, is active in three separate real estate rental activities. Ida has a marginal tax rate of 28%. She has $12,000 of losses from Activity A, $18,000 of losses from Activity B, and income of $10,000 from Activity C. She also has $2,100 of tax credits from Activity A. Calculate her deductions and credits allowed and the suspended losses and credits.

37. Ella has $105,000 of losses from a real estate rental activity in which she actively participates. She has other rent income of $25,000 and other passive income of $32,000. How much rental loss can Ella deduct against active and portfolio income (ignoring the at-risk rules)? Does she have any suspended losses to carry over?

BRIDGE DISCIPLINE

1. Marketplace, Inc., has recognized over time that a certain percentage of its customer accounts receivable will not be collected. To ensure the appropriate matching of revenues and expenditures in its financial reports, Marketplace uses the reserve method for bad debts. Records show the following pertaining to its treatment of bad debts.

Beginning allowance for bad debts	$120,000
Ending allowance for bad debts	123,000
Bad debts written off during the year	33,000

   a. What was the bad debt expense for financial accounting purposes during the year?
   b. What was the bad debt expense for income tax purposes during the year?
   c. Assuming the before-tax net income for financial accounting purposes was $545,000, what is the taxable income for the year if the treatment of bad debts is the only book/tax difference?

2. Amanda wishes to invest $40,000 in a relatively safe venture and has discovered two alternatives that would produce the following income and loss over the next three years:

Year	Alternative 1 Income (Loss)	Alternative 2 Income (Loss)
1	($ 24,000)	($48,000)
2	(24,000)	32,000
3	72,000	40,000

She is interested in the after-tax effects of these alternatives over a three-year horizon. Assume that:

• Amanda's investment portfolio produces sufficient passive income to offset any potential passive loss that may arise from these alternatives.

• Amanda's marginal tax rate is 28%, and her cost of capital is 8% (the present value factors are 0.92593, 0.85734, and 0.79383).

• Each investment alternative possesses equal growth potential and comparable financial risk.

• In the loss years for each alternative, there is no cash flow from or to the investment (i.e., the loss is due to depreciation), while in those years when the income is positive, cash flows to Amanda equal the amount of the income.

Based on these facts, compute the present value of these two investment alternatives and determine which option Amanda should choose.

3. Emily has $100,000 that she wishes to invest and is considering the following two options:

   • Option A: Investment in Redbird Equity Mutual Fund, which is expected to produce dividends of $8,000 per year.

   • Option B: Investment in Cardinal Limited Partnership (buys, sells, and operates wine vineyards). Emily's share of the partnership's income and loss over the next three years would be:

Year	Income (Loss)
1	($ 8,000)
2	(2,000)
3	34,000

   Emily is interested in the after-tax effects of these alternatives over a three-year horizon. Assume that Emily's investment portfolio produces ample passive income to offset any passive losses that may be generated. Her cost of capital is 8% (the present value factors are 0.92593, 0.85734, and 0.79383), and she is in the 31% tax bracket. The two investment alternatives possess equal growth potential and comparable financial risk. Based on these facts, compute the present value of these two investment alternatives and determine which option Emily should choose.

RESEARCH PROBLEMS

*Note: Solutions to Research Problems can be prepared by using the **RIA Checkpoint® Student Version Online research product**, or the **CCH U.S. Master Tax Guide Plus**™ online Federal tax research database, which is available to accompany this text. It is also possible to prepare solutions to the Research Problems by using tax research materials found in a standard tax library.*

Research Problem 1. George Johnson, a Minnesota resident, parked his car on a lake while he was watching an iceboat race. During the race, the ice beneath his car unexpectedly gave way, and the car sank to the bottom of the lake. Write a letter to George advising him as to whether he can claim a casualty loss for the damage to the car. Also, prepare a memo for the tax files. George's address is 100 Apple Lane, St. Paul, MN 55123.

Research Problem 2. John, a successful physician who owns 100% of his incorporated medical practice, and his wife, Samantha, are considering the purchase of a commercial office building that is located near the local community hospital. If they purchase the building, John would move his medical practice to this new location. The practice would rent the building for an arm's length price. The arrangement fits with their other financial affairs as the resulting rent income would be available to absorb passive losses generated by other passive activities. The net effect of freeing up the passive losses will be a reduction in their income tax liability. Will John and Samantha's plan work?

Research Problem 3. George and Judy Cash own a 30-foot yacht that is held for rent at Oregon Inlet on the Outer Banks of North Carolina. The yacht is offered for rent to tourists during March through November every year. George and Judy's permanent residence in a neighboring state is too far from Oregon Inlet for them to be involved in the yacht's operation and maintenance. They are, however, able to perform periodic tasks, such as its cleaning and winterizing. Routine daily management, operating, and chartering responsibilities have been contracted to "Captain Mac." George and Judy are able to document spending 120 hours on the yacht chartering activities during the year. Determine how any losses resulting from the activity are treated under the passive activity loss rules.

Use the tax resources of the Internet to address the following questions. Do not restrict your search to the World Wide Web, but include a review of newsgroups and general reference materials, practitioner sites and resources, primary sources of the tax law, chat rooms and discussion groups, and other opportunities.

Research Problem 4.   Scan several publications that are read by owners of small businesses. Some of the articles in these publications address tax-related issues such as how to structure a new business. Do these articles do an adequate job of conveying the benefits of issuing § 1244 small business stock? Prepare a short memo explaining the use of § 1244 stock and post it to a newsgroup that is frequented by inventors, engineers, and others involved in start-up corporations.

Research Problem 5.   Scan the materials offered in several newsgroups frequented by tax consultants. In what context are "tax shelters" still discussed by these professionals? Do these advisers adequately take into account the rules of §§ 465 and 469? Summarize several techniques these professionals recommend for mitigating the effect of these provisions.

Accounting Periods and Methods

LEARNING OBJECTIVES

After completing Chapter 6, you should be able to:

1. Understand the relevance of the accounting period concept, the different types of accounting periods, and the limitations on their use.

2. Outline the procedure for changing accounting methods.

3. Determine when the installment method of accounting can be used and apply the related calculation techniques.

4. Understand the alternative methods of accounting for long-term contracts (the completed contract method and the percentage of completion method).

5. Recognize when accounting for inventories is required.

Outline

TAX TALK

I recently heard a CPA remark that the only accounting principle which the Internal Revenue Service regards as "generally accepted" is "A bird in the hand is worth two in the bush." Although my friend overstates his case a bit—quite a bit—I cannot dismiss the thrust of his comment without some soul searching.

—*Sheldon S. Cohen, former IRS Commissioner*

Tax practitioners must deal with the issue of *when* particular items of income and expense are recognized as well as the basic issue of *whether* the items are includible in taxable income. Earlier chapters discussed the types of income subject to tax and allowable deductions (the *whether* issue) and explained the principal tax accounting methods available. This chapter examines in more detail the issue of the periods in which income and deductions are reported (the *when* issue). Generally, a taxpayer's income and deductions must be assigned to particular 12-month periods—calendar years or fiscal years.

Income and deductions are placed within particular years through the use of tax accounting methods. As explained in Chapters 3 and 4, the basic accounting methods are the cash method, accrual method, and hybrid method. Other special purpose methods, such as the installment method and the methods used for long-term construction contracts, are available for specific circumstances or types of transactions.

Over the long run, the accounting period used by a taxpayer will not affect the aggregate amount of reported taxable income. However, taxable income for any particular year may vary significantly due to the use of a particular reporting period. Through the choice of accounting methods or accounting periods, it is possible to accomplish one's tax goals by arranging to postpone the recognition of taxable income or accelerate an available deduction.

BRIDGE DISCIPLINE

Bridge to Financial Accounting

The determination of taxable income is governed by the Federal income tax law. Conversely, the determination of financial accounting income is based on financial accounting rules (i.e., GAAP). Differences in these two amounts for a particular year may be based on permanent differences (e.g., a dividends received deduction is allowed in calculating taxable income and is not allowed in calculating financial accounting income) and on temporary differences (e.g., revenues and expenses are reported in different periods for income tax purposes and for financial reporting purposes).

The existence of these temporary differences results in substantial complexity under SFAS No. 109 in calculating the income statement tax provision and in calculating deferred taxes on the balance sheet. This complexity could be eliminated if, as some business and accounting professionals have proposed, the FASB were to modify the current financial reporting standard and base the financial accounting tax provision on the current-period income tax liability on the income tax return.

The income tax liability on the Federal income tax return is calculated by applying the tax rates to the tax base (i.e., taxable income). Obviously, the tax rates used are the current income tax rates contained in the Internal Revenue Code. SFAS No. 109 provides that in calculating the tax provision and the deferred taxes, both current rates and future enacted rates (i.e., future enacted rates are used in calculating the deferred taxes) are used.

LEARNING OBJECTIVE 1

Understand the relevance of the accounting period concept, the different types of accounting periods, and the limitations on their use.

Accounting Periods

IN GENERAL

A taxpayer who keeps adequate books and records may be allowed to elect a **fiscal year,** a 12-month period ending on the *last day* of a month other than December, for the **accounting period.** Otherwise, a *calendar year* must be used.[1] Frequently, corporations and other business entities can satisfy the record-keeping requirements and elect to use a fiscal year.[2] Often the fiscal year conforms to a natural business year (e.g., a summer resort's fiscal year may end on September 30, after the close of the season). Individuals seldom use a fiscal year because they do not maintain the necessary books and records to do so, and because complications can arise as a result of changes in the tax law (e.g., often the transition rules and effective dates differ for fiscal year taxpayers).

Generally, a taxable year may not exceed 12 calendar months. However, if certain requirements are met, a taxpayer may elect to use an annual period that varies from 52 to 53 weeks.[3] In that case, the year-end must be on the same day of the week (e.g., the Tuesday falling closest to October 31 or the last Tuesday in October). The day of the week selected for ending the year will depend upon business considerations. For example, a retail business that is not open on Sundays may end its tax year on a Sunday so that it can take an inventory without interrupting business operations.

[1] § 441(g).
[2] Temp.Reg. § 1.441–1T(e)(2).
[3] § 441(f).

EXAMPLE 1

Wren Corporation is in the business of selling farm supplies. Its natural business year terminates at the end of October with the completion of harvesting. At the end of the fiscal year, Wren must take an inventory, which is most easily accomplished on a Tuesday. Therefore, Wren could adopt a 52–53 week tax year ending on the Tuesday closest to October 31. If Wren selects this method, the year-end date may fall in the following month if that Tuesday is closer to October 31. The tax year ending in 2001 will contain 52 weeks beginning on Wednesday, November 1, 2000, and ending on Tuesday, October 30, 2001. The tax year ending in 2002 will have 52 weeks beginning on Wednesday, October 31, 2001, and ending on Tuesday, October 29, 2002. ■

SPECIFIC PROVISIONS FOR PARTNERSHIPS, S CORPORATIONS, AND PERSONAL SERVICE CORPORATIONS

Partnerships and S Corporations.

When a partner's tax year and the partnership's tax year differ, the partner will enjoy a deferral of income. This results because the partner reports his or her share of the partnership's income and deductions for the partnership's tax year ending within or with the partner's tax year.[4] For example, if the tax year of the partnership ends on January 31, a calendar year partner will not report partnership profits for the first 11 months of the partnership tax year until the following year. Therefore, partnerships are subject to special tax year requirements.

In general, the partnership tax year must be the same as the tax year of the majority interest partners. The **majority interest partners** are the partners who own a greater-than-50 percent interest in the partnership capital and profits. If there are no majority interest partners, the partnership must adopt the same tax year as its principal partners. A **principal partner** is a partner with a 5 percent or more interest in the partnership capital or profits.[5]

EXAMPLE 2

The RST Partnership is owned equally by Rose Corporation, Silver Corporation, and Tom. The partners have the following tax years.

	Partner's Tax Year Ending
Rose	June 30
Silver	June 30
Tom	December 31

The partnership's tax year must end on June 30. If Silver Corporation's as well as Tom's year ended on December 31, the partnership would be required to adopt a calendar year. ■

If the principal partners do not all have the same tax year and no majority of partners have the same tax year, the partnership must use a year that results in the *least aggregate deferral* of income.[6] Under the **least aggregate deferral method,** the different tax years of the principal partners are tested to determine which produces the least aggregate deferral. This is calculated by first multiplying the combined percentages of the principal partners with the same tax year by the months of deferral for the last year. Once this is done for each set of principal partners with the same tax year, the resulting products are summed to produce the aggregate deferral. After calculating the aggregate deferral for each of the test

---

[4]Reg. § 1.706–1(a).
[5]§§ 706(b)(1)(B) and (b)(3).

[6]Temp.Reg. § 1.706–1T(a)(2).

Scorps - Calendar yrs

years, the test year with the smallest summation (the least aggregate deferral) is the tax year for the partnership.

EXAMPLE 3

The DE Partnership is owned equally by Dove Corporation and Egret, Inc. Dove's fiscal year ends on March 31, and Egret's fiscal year ends on August 31. The partnership must use the partner's fiscal year that will result in the least aggregate deferral of income. Therefore, the fiscal years ending March 31 and August 31 must both be tested.

	Test for Fiscal Year Ending March 31			
Partner	**Year Ends**	**Profit %**	**Months of Deferral**	**Product**
Dove	3–31	50	0	0
Egret	8–31	50	5	2.5
	Aggregate deferral months			2.5

Thus, with a year ending March 31, Egret would be able to defer its half of the income for five months. That is, Egret's share of the partnership income for the fiscal year ending March 31, 2002, would not be included in its income until August 31, 2002.

	Test for Fiscal Year Ending August 31			
Partner	**Year Ends**	**Profit %**	**Months of Deferral**	**Product**
Dove	3–31	50	7	3.5
Egret	8–31	50	0	0
	Aggregate deferral months			3.5

Thus, with a year ending August 31, Dove would be able to defer its half of the income for seven months. That is, Dove's share of the partnership income for the fiscal year ending August 31, 2002, would not be included in its income until March 31, 2003.

The year ending March 31 must be used because it results in the least aggregate deferral of income. ■

Generally, S corporations must adopt a calendar year.[7] However, partnerships and S corporations may *elect* an otherwise *impermissible year* under either of the following conditions.

- A business purpose for the year can be demonstrated.[8]
- The partnership's or S corporation's year results in a deferral of not more than three months' income, and the entity agrees to make required tax payments.[9]

Business Purpose. The only business purpose for a fiscal year that the IRS has acknowledged is the need to conform the tax year to the *natural business year* of an entity.[10] An objective *gross receipts test* is applied to determine if the entity has a natural business year. At least 25 percent of the entity's gross receipts for the 12-month period must be realized in the final 2 months of the 12-month period

---

[7]§§ 1378(a) and (b).
[8]§§ 706(b)(1)(C) and 1378(b)(2).
[9]§§ 444(b)(1) and (c)(1).

[10]Rev.Rul. 87–57, 1987–2 C.B. 117, and Rev.Proc. 87–32, 1987–1 C.B. 131.

for three consecutive years. Generally, only seasonal businesses qualify under this test.

EXAMPLE 4

A Virginia Beach motel had gross receipts as follows.

	1999	**2000**	**2001**
July–August receipts	$ 300,000	$250,000	$ 325,000
September 1–August 31 receipts	1,000,000	900,000	1,250,000
Receipts for 2 months divided by receipts for 12 months	30.0%	27.8%	26.0%

Since it satisfies the natural business year test, the motel will be allowed to use a fiscal year ending August 31. ■

Required Tax Payments.   For S corporations and partnerships that do not wish to use a required year or a business purpose year, another year-end may be elected, as long as the resulting deferral period does not exceed three months. This election is not free of costs. In particular, the electing entity must make a *required tax payment* for any year that the election is in effect.[11] The required tax payment is a refundable, non-interest-bearing deposit (not deductible for Federal tax purposes) made to the IRS. The deposit compensates the government for the interest lost on any deferred tax liability. The required tax payment is credited against future required tax payments or returned in the following year if the entity's partners or shareholders are required to pay tax on previously deferred income.

The amount due is computed by applying the highest individual tax rate plus 1 percent to an estimate of the deferral period income. The deferral period runs from the close of the fiscal year to the end of the calendar year. Estimated income for this period is based on the average monthly earnings for the previous fiscal year. The amount due is reduced by the balance of required tax payments on deposit for the previous year.[12]

EXAMPLE 5

Brown, Inc., an S corporation, elected a fiscal year ending September 30. Bob, a calendar year taxpayer, is the only shareholder. For the fiscal year ending September 30, 2001, Brown earned $100,000. Brown is permitted to have a September 30 fiscal year, since that year-end will result in only a three-month deferral of income for Bob. An annual tax payment is also required. If required tax payments for the previous year were $5,000, the corporation must pay $5,150 by April 15, 2002.

$$(\$100,000 \times \tfrac{3}{12} \times 40.6\%^*) - \$5,000 \text{ (credit from prior year)} = \$5,150.$$

*Maximum § 1 rate of 39.6% + 1%. ■

Personal Service Corporations.   A **personal service corporation (PSC)** is a corporation whose shareholder-employees provide personal services (e.g., medical, dental, legal, accounting, engineering, actuarial, consulting, or performing arts). Generally, a PSC must use a calendar year.[13] However, a PSC can *elect* a fiscal year under either of the following conditions.

---

[11]§§ 444(c) and 7519. No payment is required if the calculated amount is $500 or less.

[12]§ 7519(b).
[13]§ 441(i).

- A business purpose for the year can be demonstrated.
- The PSC year results in a deferral of not more than three months' income, the corporation pays the shareholder-employee's salary during the portion of the calendar year after the close of the fiscal year, and the salary for that period is at least proportionate to the shareholder-employee's salary received for the preceding fiscal year.[14]

1 *Find more information on this topic at our Web site: http://wft-entities.swcollege.com.*

EXAMPLE 6

Nancy's personal service corporation paid Nancy a salary of $120,000 during its fiscal year ending September 30, 2001. The corporation cannot satisfy the business purpose test for a fiscal year. The corporation can continue to use its fiscal year without any negative tax effects, provided Nancy receives at least $30,000 [(3 months/12 months) × $120,000] as salary during the period October 1 through December 31, 2001. ∎

CHOOSING A TAX YEAR

A taxpayer elects to use a calendar or fiscal year by the timely filing of the initial tax return. For all subsequent years, the taxpayer must use this same period unless approval for change is obtained from the IRS.[15]

CHANGES IN THE ACCOUNTING PERIOD

v need permission for

A taxpayer must obtain consent from the IRS before changing the tax year.[16] This consent requirement is significant in that it permits the IRS to issue authoritative administrative guidelines that must be met by taxpayers who wish to change their accounting period. An application for permission to change tax years must be made on Form 1128, Application for Change in Accounting Period. The application must be filed on or before the fifteenth day of the second calendar month following the close of the short period that results from the change in accounting period.[17]

EXAMPLE 7

Beginning in 2001, Gold Corporation, a calendar year taxpayer, would like to switch to a fiscal year ending March 31. The first period after the change in accounting period (January 1, 2001 through March 31, 2001) is less than a 12-month period and is referred to as a *short period*. Thus, the corporation must file Form 1128 by May 15, 2001. ∎

IRS Requirements. The IRS will not grant permission for the change unless the taxpayer can establish a substantial business purpose for the request. One substantial business purpose is to change to a tax year that coincides with the *natural business year* (discussed earlier).[18]

2 *Find more information on this topic at our Web site: http://wft-entities.swcollege.com.*

TAXABLE PERIODS OF LESS THAN ONE YEAR

A **short taxable year** (or **short period**) is a period of less than 12 calendar months. A taxpayer may have a short year for (1) the first income tax return, (2) the final income tax return, or (3) a change in the tax year. If the short period results from

---

[14]§§ 444(b)(1), (c)(2), and 280H.
[15]Temp.Reg. §§ 1.441–1T(b)(3) and (4).
[16]§ 442. Under certain conditions, corporations are allowed to change tax years without obtaining IRS approval. See Reg. § 1.442–1(c)(1).

[17]Reg. § 1.442–1(b)(1).
[18]Rev.Proc. 87–32, 1987–1 C.B. 131, and Rev.Rul. 87–57, 1987–2 C.B. 117.

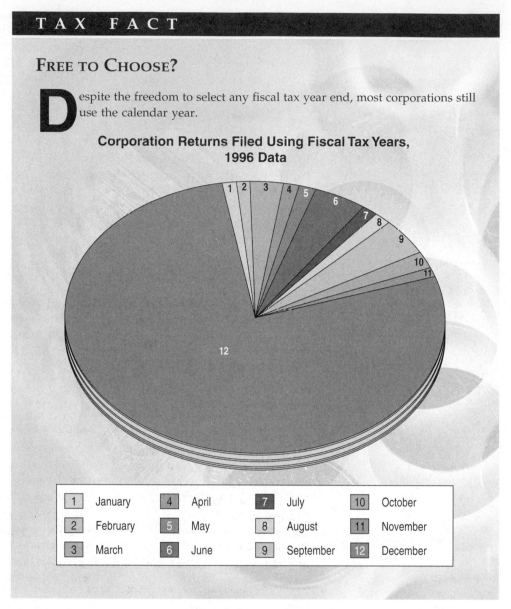

TAX FACT

FREE TO CHOOSE?

Despite the freedom to select any fiscal tax year end, most corporations still use the calendar year.

Corporation Returns Filed Using Fiscal Tax Years, 1996 Data

1	January	4	April	7	July	10	October
2	February	5	May	8	August	11	November
3	March	6	June	9	September	12	December

a change in the taxpayer's annual accounting period, the taxable income for the period must be annualized. Due to the progressive tax rate structure, taxpayers could reap benefits from a short-period return if some adjustments were not required. Thus, the taxpayer is required to complete the following.

1. Annualize the short-period income.

$$\text{Annualized income} = \text{Short-period income} \times \frac{12}{\substack{\text{Number of months} \\ \text{in the short period}}}$$

2. Compute the tax on the annualized income.
3. Convert the tax on the annualized income to a short-period tax.

$$\text{Short-period tax} = \text{Tax on annualized income} \times \frac{\substack{\text{Number of months} \\ \text{in the short period}}}{12}$$

EXAMPLE 8

Gray Corporation obtained permission to change from a calendar year to a fiscal year ending September 30, beginning in 2001. For the short period January 1 through September 30, 2001, the corporation's taxable income was $48,000. The relevant tax rates and the resultant short-period tax are computed as follows.

Amount of Taxable Income	Tax Rates
$0–$50,000	15% of taxable income
Over $50,000 to $75,000	$7,500 plus 25% of taxable income in excess of $50,000

Calculation of Short-Period Tax	
Annualized income ($48,000 × $\frac{12}{9}$) =	$64,000
Tax on annualized income [$7,500 + 0.25($64,000 − $50,000)] =	$11,000
Short-period tax = ($11,000 × $\frac{9}{12}$) =	$ 8,250
Annualizing the income increased the tax by $1,050:	
Tax with annualizing	$ 8,250
Tax without annualizing ($48,000 × 0.15)	(7,200)
Increase in tax from annualizing	$ 1,050

TAX YEAR RELIEF

Several provisions in the Code are designed to give the taxpayer relief from the harsh results that can be produced by the combined effects of an arbitrary accounting period and a progressive rate structure. For example, under the net operating loss carryback and carryover rules, a loss in one year can be carried back and offset against taxable income for the preceding 2 years. Unused net operating losses are then carried forward for 20 years.[19] In addition, the Code provides special relief provisions for casualty losses pursuant to a natural disaster and for the reporting of insurance proceeds from destruction of crops.[20]

3 *Find more information on this topic at our Web site: **http://wft-entities.swcollege.com**.*

LEARNING OBJECTIVE 2

Outline the procedure for changing accounting methods.

Change of Accounting Methods

The Code allows taxpayers to use either the cash receipts and disbursements method, the accrual method, or some combination of the two. Taxpayers with more than one business may use a different method for each business,[21] but whichever method is used must *clearly reflect* the taxpayer's income.[22]

The two principal methods are themselves very different. The **cash method** focuses on when cash or its equivalent is received or paid. The **accrual method**

[19]§ 172.
[20]§§ 165(i) and 451(d).

[21]§ 446(d).
[22]§ 446(b).

TAX IN THE NEWS

IRS Fails to Impose Accrual Method—And Pays for Trying

A nursing services corporation paid its employees before being paid by its customers for the nursing services it provided. As a result, at the end of the year, the company had nearly $250,000 in accounts receivable that had not been included in its cash basis income, even though the company had deducted the related employee expenses. The IRS claimed that this mismatching of revenues and expenses showed that the taxpayer was not entitled to use the cash method and was required to use the accrual method instead.

The Tax Court, however, concluded that the taxpayer had not intentionally prepaid its expenses or deferred its income, that it had applied the cash method consistently, and that the resulting mismatch of income and expense was simply a product of that method. The court noted further that Congress was aware of the cash method's potential for such mismatching when it authorized the method's use. Therefore, the IRS's position was not substantially supported by the law, so the IRS had to pay the taxpayer's attorney fees!

SOURCE: *Laura E. Austin*, T.C.Memo. 1997–157, 73 TCM 2470.

---

reports income when it is earned as determined by legal and economic considerations. Deductions under this method are claimed when a taxpayer's liability has been established and *economic performance* has occurred.

But what happens if a taxpayer wants to change its accounting method? Some taxpayers may not change their method; for example, if inventories are a material factor in the business (see the final section of this chapter), the accrual method is

---

BRIDGE DISCIPLINE

Bridge to Financial Accounting

The accounting method used by an entity governs when revenues and expenses are reported. Potential methods are the cash method, the accrual method, and the hybrid method.

Generally accepted accounting principles (GAAP) utilize the accrual method, and Federal income tax reporting permits all three under particular circumstances. Recognizing the opportunities available under the cash method, the Code imposes limitations on its use.

Even when the accrual method is used for both Federal income tax purposes and financial reporting purposes, differences can occur. For financial reporting purposes, the income associated with the receipt of a cash prepayment is not recognized until it is earned. For income tax purposes, the taxpayer may be required to recognize the cash prepayment as income when it is received. An entity making a cash prepayment cannot deduct it as an expense for financial reporting purposes until the expense is incurred. For income tax purposes, the taxpayer may be able to deduct the expense when paid under the "one-year rule for prepaid expenses."

TAX IN THE NEWS

ACCRUALS FOR LIABILITY UNDER RECALLS

In 2000, several manufacturers announced product recalls that will cost the companies hundreds of millions of dollars. Often it takes several months for customers to make their claims. In addition, many customers who are entitled to refunds or replacements never apply for them. While the recalls are in effect, the company must reflect the estimated expense associated with potential claims in its financial statements. However, for tax purposes, the economic performance test will not be satisfied until the company actually makes the refund or replacement.

mandatory.[23] Similarly, the cash method may not be used by corporations that have annual gross receipts in excess of $5 million or by partnerships that have a corporation as a partner.[24] Within these limitations, however, a taxpayer can change accounting methods. This section considers the process of doing so and the adjustments that are required.

A taxpayer elects a particular accounting method when it files its initial tax return using that method. To change that method, the taxpayer must obtain the permission of the IRS. A request for change is made on Form 3115, Application for Change in Accounting Method. Generally, the form must be filed within the taxable year of the desired change.[25]

The term **accounting method** encompasses not only the overall accounting method used by the taxpayer (the cash or accrual method) but also the treatment of any material item of income or deduction.[26] Thus, a change in the method of deducting property taxes from a cash basis to an accrual basis that results in a deduction for taxes in a different year constitutes a change in an accounting method. Another example of an accounting method change is a switch in the method or basis used in the valuation of inventories.

CORRECTION OF AN ERROR

A change in accounting method must be distinguished from the *correction of an error*. A taxpayer can correct an error (by filing amended returns) without permission, and the IRS can simply adjust the taxpayer's liability if an error is discovered on audit of the return. Some examples of errors are incorrect postings, errors in the calculation of tax liability or tax credits, deductions of business expense items that are actually personal, and omissions of income and deductions.[27]

CHANGE FROM AN INCORRECT METHOD

An *incorrect accounting method* is the consistent (year-after-year) use of an incorrect rule to report an item of income or expense. An incorrect accounting method generally will not affect a taxpayer's total lifetime income (unlike an error). That is, an incorrect method has a self-balancing mechanism. For example, deducting freight on inventory in the year the goods are purchased, rather than when the

[23]Reg. § 1.446–1(a)(4)(i).
[24]§§ 448(a) and (b)(3).
[25]Rev.Proc. 97–21, 1997–1 C.B. 680.
[26]Reg. § 1.446–1(a)(1).
[27]Reg. § 1.446–1(e)(2)(ii)(b).

inventory is sold, is an incorrect accounting method. The total cost of goods sold over the life of the business is not affected, but the year-to-year income is incorrect.[28]

An incorrect method is not treated as a mechanical error that can be corrected by merely filing an amended tax return. Instead, permission must be obtained from the IRS to change to a correct method.

NET ADJUSTMENTS DUE TO CHANGE IN ACCOUNTING METHOD

In the year of a change in accounting method, some items of income and expense may have to be adjusted to prevent the change from distorting taxable income.

EXAMPLE 9

In 2001, White Corporation, with consent from the IRS, switched from the cash to the accrual basis for reporting sales and cost of goods sold. The corporation's accrual basis gross profit for the year was computed as follows.

Sales		$100,000
Beginning inventory	$ 15,000	
Plus: Purchases	60,000	
Less: Ending inventory	(10,000)	
Cost of goods sold		(65,000)
Gross profit		$ 35,000

At the end of the previous year, White Corporation had accounts receivable of $25,000 and accounts payable for merchandise of $34,000. The accounts receivable from the previous year in the amount of $25,000 were never included in gross income since White was on the cash basis and did not recognize the uncollected receivables. In the current year, the $25,000 was not included in the accrual basis sales since the sales were made in a prior year. Therefore, a $25,000 adjustment to income is required to prevent the receivables from being omitted from income.

The corollary of the failure to recognize a prior year's receivables is the failure to recognize a prior year's accounts payable. The beginning of the year's accounts payable was not included in the current or prior year's purchases. Thus, a deduction for the $34,000 was not taken in either year and is therefore included as an adjustment to income for the period of change.

An adjustment is also required to reflect the $15,000 beginning inventory that White deducted (due to the use of a cash method of accounting) in the previous year. In this instance, the cost of goods sold during the year of change was increased by the beginning inventory and resulted in a double deduction.

The net adjustment due to the change in accounting method is computed as follows.

Beginning inventory (deducted in prior and current year)	$ 15,000
Beginning accounts receivable (omitted from income)	25,000
Beginning accounts payable (omitted from deductions)	(34,000)
Net increase in taxable income	$ 6,000

---

[28]But see *Korn Industries v. U.S.*, 76–1 USTC ¶9354, 37 AFTR2d 76–1228, 532 F.2d 1352 (Ct.Cls., 1976).

Disposition of the Net Adjustment.   If the IRS *requires* a taxpayer to change an accounting method, the net adjustment is added to gross income for the year of the change. If this adjustment exceeds $3,000, the taxpayer can elect to calculate the tax by spreading the adjustment over one or more previous years.[29] This election can be beneficial if the taxpayer's marginal tax rate was lower in those prior years than in the year of the change.

To encourage taxpayers to *voluntarily* change from incorrect methods and to facilitate changes from one correct method to another, the IRS generally allows a taxpayer to spread the adjustment into future years. One-fourth of the adjustment is applied to the year of the change, and one-fourth is applied to each of the next three years.[30]

EXAMPLE 10

White Corporation in the preceding example voluntarily changed from an incorrect method (the cash basis was incorrect because inventories were material to the business) to a correct method. The company must add $1,500 (¼ × $6,000 positive adjustment) to its 2001, 2002, 2003, and 2004 income. ∎

LEARNING OBJECTIVE 3

Determine when the installment method of accounting can be used and apply the related calculation techniques.

Installment Method

IN GENERAL

Under the general rule for computing gain or loss from the sale of property, a taxpayer recognizes the entire amount of gain or loss upon the sale or other disposition of the property.

EXAMPLE 11

Meadowlark, Inc., sells property to Pintail Corporation for $10,000 cash plus Pintail's note (fair market value and face amount of $90,000). Meadowlark's basis for the property was $15,000. Gain or loss is computed under either the cash or accrual basis as follows.

Cash down payment	$ 10,000
Note receivable	90,000
Amount realized	$100,000
Less: Basis in the property	(15,000)
Realized gain	$ 85,000

∎

In this example, the general rule for recognizing gain or loss requires Meadowlark to pay tax on the *entire* gain in the year of sale even though it received only $10,000 cash. Congress enacted the installment sales provisions to prevent this sort of hardship by allowing the taxpayer to spread the gain from installment sales over the collection period.

Eligibility.   The **installment method** applies only to *gains* (not losses) from the sale of property where the seller will receive at least one payment *after* the year of sale. Even when this requirement is met, the installment method may not be used for sales of the following assets.

---

[29]§ 481(b). See also Notice 98–31, 1998–2 C.B. 9.   [30]Rev.Proc. 97–27, 1997–1 C.B. 680.

- Stocks or securities traded on an established market.[31]
- Property subject to *depreciation recapture*, as explained in Chapter 8.[32]
- Property held for sale in the ordinary course of business.[33]

Still, some taxpayers may use the installment method for the sale of certain residential lots, certain time-share units, and farming business property.[34]

The Nonelective Aspect.   If a sale is eligible for the installment method, it *must* be reported on that basis. A special election is required to report such a sale by any method other than the installment method.

Computing the Gain for Each Year.   The gain reported each year on an installment sale is computed by the following formula.

$$\frac{\text{Total gain}}{\text{Contract price}} \times \text{Payments received} = \text{Recognized gain}.$$

The taxpayer computes each variable as follows.

1. *Total gain* is the selling price reduced by selling expenses and the adjusted basis of the property, usually the taxpayer's cost. The selling price is the total amount received by the seller, including notes receivable from the buyer and any seller's liabilities that are assumed by the buyer.
2. *Contract price* is the selling price less any seller's liabilities that are assumed by the buyer. Generally, the contract price is the amount, other than interest, that the seller will eventually receive from the buyer.
3. *Payments received* are the collections on the contract price received in the tax year. This generally is the cash received less any interest income collected for the period.

> **4** *Find more information on this topic at our Web site:* ***http://wft-entities.swcollege.com.***

EXAMPLE 12

Paul accounts for his sale of some investment land as follows.

Sales price (amount realized)		
Cash down payment	$ 1,000	
Paul's mortgage assumed by buyer	3,000	
Notes payable to the seller	13,000	$ 17,000
Less: Selling expenses		(500)
Less: Paul's basis		(10,000)
Total gain		$ 6,500

The contract price is $14,000 ($17,000 sales price – $3,000 mortgage assumed). If only $1,000 is received in the year of sale, the recognized gain in that year is:

$$\frac{\$6,500 \text{ (total gain)}}{\$14,000 \text{ (contract price)}} \times \$1,000 = \$464.$$

---

[31]§ 453(k)(2)(A).
[32]§ 453(i).

[33]§ 453(l).
[34]§§ 453(l)(2)(A) and (B).

PLANNING CONSIDERATIONS

The Installment Method

The installment method enables a taxpayer to defer reporting taxable gain until subsequent years. Once the method is used for a particular sale, however, that method must be continued for the duration of that transaction. While the *time value of money* generally advises deferral of tax liability, deferral is not always beneficial. A taxpayer might be in a higher tax bracket in later years due to other transactions or the expansion of that taxpayer's business. Similarly, Congress may raise tax rates in the future, and those higher rates usually apply to payments from an earlier year's installment sale, unless some special exception is created. In such circumstances, the taxpayer's increased tax liability might exceed any financial benefit obtained from deferring the tax on the original transaction, particularly if the deferral period was only a few years.

On the other hand, the installment method can be particularly useful if a taxpayer anticipates being in a *lower tax bracket* in later years. Whether due to a taxpayer's impending retirement or a significant reduction in a business's activities, this lower tax rate would mean less tax owed, in addition to the financial benefit gained by deferring taxes to a later year. Moreover, Congress also lowers tax rates from time to time, and a taxpayer might reap still further benefits from an installment sale that moves reported gain into a lower-tax rate year.

In either case, an installment sale necessarily entails the *nontax consideration* of credit risk. That is, an outright cash sale might be preferable to an installment sale if the buyer's creditworthiness is somewhat suspect. Even a creditworthy buyer, moreover, might find payment of its installment obligations difficult if general business conditions or specific industry factors cause a decline in its economic well-being. An installment sale, in other words, does not terminate a seller's exposure to the exigencies of the marketplace, and some sellers might prefer the certainty of an all-cash transaction despite its lack of deferral possibilities.

CONTINGENT SALES PRICES

Dispositions of business assets or even entire businesses sometimes employ open-ended or **contingent sales prices** to resolve disputes between the buyer and the seller about the value of the assets in question. Such transactions typically involve a portion of future receipts, profits in excess of some threshold, or some similar arrangement. Despite the absence of a specified sales price, the installment method can be used in these circumstances according to the following principles.

- If the sales contract sets forth a *maximum sales price*, that price is used.[35]
- If there is no maximum sales price but the payout is limited to a fixed number of years, divide the taxpayer's basis by that number and offset the result against the amount received each year.[36]
- If the sales agreement provides neither a maximum sales price nor a fixed payout period, use 15 years as the fixed payout term.[37]

EXAMPLE 13

Indigo, Inc., sells the rights to a newly patented blood analyzer to a major health products company for 10% of the earnings generated by this device, with a maximum sales price of $400,000. Indigo has a cost basis in this device of $100,000. In the first year after the sale, Indigo received $30,000. Since a maximum sales price is stipulated, it is used.

Maximum sales price	$ 400,000
Basis	(100,000)
Gain expected	$ 300,000

---

[35]Temp.Reg. § 15A.453–1(c)(2)(i).
[36]Temp.Reg. § 15A.453–1(c)(3)(i).

[37]Temp.Reg. § 15A.453–1(c)(4).

$$\frac{\text{Gain}}{\text{Contract price}} = \frac{\$300,000}{\$400,000} = 75\% \text{ (gross profit percentage).}$$

Of the $30,000 received in the first year after the sale, $22,500 ($30,000 × 75%) is reported as gain. In each subsequent year, 75% of the amount received is reported as gain. If the amount ultimately collected is less than the maximum sales price used, an appropriate adjustment will be made in the final year of the sales contract. ■

EXAMPLE 14

Assume the same facts as in the preceding example, except that no maximum sales price is provided and the payout is limited to eight years. Accordingly, the taxpayer's basis of $100,000 is divided by 8, and the result ($12,500) is then offset against the amount received each year. In the first year:

Amount received	$ 30,000
Prorated basis	(12,500)
Gain reported	$ 17,500

■

EXAMPLE 15

Assume the same facts as in the preceding examples, except that there is no fixed payout term. In this case, the taxpayer's basis of $100,000 is divided by 15 years, and the result ($6,667) offsets the amount received.

Amount received	$30,000
Prorated basis	(6,667)
Gain reported	$23,333

■

IMPUTED INTEREST

If a deferred payment contract for the sale of property with a selling price greater than $3,000 does not contain a reasonable interest rate, the tax law imputes a reasonable rate.[38] The imputing of interest effectively restates the selling price of the property to the sum of the payments at the date of the sale and the discounted present value of the future payments. The difference between the present value of a future payment and the payment's face amount is taxed as interest income, as discussed in the following paragraphs. Thus, the **imputed interest** rules prevent sellers of capital assets from increasing the selling price to reflect the equivalent of unstated interest on deferred payments and thereby converting ordinary (interest) income into long-term capital gains. In addition, the imputed interest rules affect the timing of income recognition.

Generally, if the contract does not charge at least the Federal rate, interest will be imputed at the Federal rate. The Federal rate is the interest rate the Federal government pays on new borrowing and is published monthly by the IRS.

As a general rule, the buyer and seller must account for interest on the accrual basis with semiannual compounding.[39] Requiring the use of the accrual basis assures that the seller's interest income and the buyer's interest expense are reported in the same tax year.

EXAMPLE 16

Partridge & Associates, LLP, a cash basis taxpayer, sold land on January 1, 2001, for $200,000 cash and $6 million due on December 31, 2002, with 5% interest payable on December 31, 2001, and December 31, 2002. At the time of the sale, the Federal rate was 8% (compounded semiannually). Because Partridge did not charge at least the Federal rate, interest is imputed at 8% (compounded semiannually).

---

[38]§§ 483 and 1274.   [39]§§ 1274(a), 1273(a), and 1272(a).

Date	Payment	Present Value (at 8%) on 1/1/2001	Imputed Interest
12/31/2001	$ 300,000*	$ 277,500	$ 22,500
12/31/2002	6,300,000**	5,386,500	913,500
	$6,600,000	$5,664,000	$936,000

*$6 million × 5% = $300,000 interest.
**$6 million + $300,000 interest.

Thus, the selling price is restated to $5,864,000 ($200,000 cash + $5,664,000) rather than $6,200,000 ($200,000 + $6,000,000), and Partridge recognizes interest income as follows.

	Beginning Balance	Interest Income (at 8%)*	Received	Ending Balance
2001	$5,664,000	$462,182	($ 300,000)	$5,826,182
2002	5,826,182	473,818	(6,300,000)	–0–

*Compounded semiannually.

Congress has created several exceptions regarding the rate at which interest is imputed and the method of accounting for the interest income and expense. The general rules and exceptions are summarized in Concept Summary 6–1.

RELATED-PARTY SALES

Special limitations apply when an installment sale involves related parties. These limitations prevent undue deferral of tax liability under circumstances that the taxpayers involved can presumably control. Different limitations and different definitions of *related parties* apply to sales of nondepreciable and depreciable property.

Nondepreciable Property. When related parties sell nondepreciable property to one another on the installment method, § 453(e) treats the proceeds of any subsequent sale within two years as if they had been received by the first seller.

EXAMPLE 17

Joan sells some vacant land worth $100,000 to her son, Ed, with payment spread over 20 years in $5,000 annual payments. If Ed sells this property one year later for $100,000 in cash, this sum is treated as if Joan had received it, and she will report her gain accordingly. ■

Had this rule not applied, the family unit (Joan and Ed) would have the entire proceeds of $100,000 in their possession, but could continue to report Joan's gain over the remaining 19 years of her original transaction with Ed. The later sale by Ed does not produce any reportable gain, because the sales price that he received ($100,000) did not exceed the price he paid his mother for the property in the earlier transaction.

If Ed had waited two years before selling the property, the related-party sale rule would not have applied, and Joan could have reported her gain over the remaining term of her contract with Ed. During those two years, however, Ed bore the economic risk that the property might *decline in value*. His obligation to make annual payments of $5,000 to Joan is not affected by the property's subsequent value.

For this purpose, related parties include the first seller's brothers, sisters, ancestors (e.g., parents and grandparents), lineal descendants (e.g., children and

CONCEPT SUMMARY 6–1

Interest on Installment Sales

	Imputed Interest Rate
General rule	Federal rate
Exceptions:	
• Principal amount not over $2.8 million.[1]	Lesser of Federal rate or 9%
• Sale of land (with a calendar year ceiling of $500,000) between family members (the seller's spouse, brothers, sisters, ancestors, or lineal descendants).[2]	Lesser of Federal rate or 6%

	Method of Accounting for Interest	
	Seller's Interest Income	Buyer's Interest Expense
General rule[3]	Accrual	Accrual
Exceptions:		
• Total payments under the contract are $250,000 or less.[4]	Taxpayer's overall method	Taxpayer's overall method
• Sale of a farm (sales price of $1 million or less).[5]	Taxpayer's overall method	Taxpayer's overall method
• Sale of a principal residence.[6]	Taxpayer's overall method	Taxpayer's overall method
• Sale for a note with a principal amount of not over $2 million, the seller is on the cash basis, the property sold is not inventory, and the buyer agrees to report expense by the cash method.[7]	Cash	Cash

[1]§ 1274A. This amount is adjusted annually for inflation. For 2001, the amount is $4,085,900.
[2]§§ 1274(c)(3)(F) and 483(e).
[3]§§ 1274(a) and 1272(a)(3).
[4]§§ 1274(c)(3)(C) and 483.
[5]§§ 1274(c)(3)(A) and 483.
[6]§§ 1274(c)(3)(B) and 483.
[7]§ 1274A(c). This amount is adjusted annually for inflation. For 2001, the amount is $2,918,500.

grandchildren), controlled corporations, and partnerships, trusts, and estates in which the seller has an interest.[40]

Depreciable Property. The installment method cannot be used to report a gain on the sale of depreciable property to a controlled entity. The purpose of this rule is to prevent the seller from deferring gain (until collections are received) while the related purchaser is enjoying a stepped-up basis for depreciation purposes.[41]

This prohibition on the use of the installment method applies to sales between the taxpayer and a partnership or corporation in which the taxpayer holds a more-than 50 percent interest. Constructive ownership rules are used in applying the ownership test (e.g., the taxpayer is considered to own stock owned by a spouse and certain other family members).[42] However, if the taxpayer can establish that tax avoidance was not a principal purpose of the transaction, the installment method can be used to report the gain.

[40]§ 453(f)(1).
[41]§ 453(g).
[42]§§ 1239(b) and (c).

EXAMPLE 18

Ali purchased an apartment building from his controlled corporation, Emerald Corporation. Ali was short of cash at the time of the purchase (December 2001), but was to collect a large cash payment in January 2002. The agreement required Ali to pay the entire arm's length price in January 2002. Ali had sound business reasons for acquiring the building. Emerald Corporation should be able to convince the IRS that tax avoidance was not a principal purpose for the installment sale because the tax benefits are not overwhelming. The corporation reports all of the gain in the year following the year of sale. ■

DISPOSITION OF INSTALLMENT NOTE

Generally, a taxpayer must recognize the deferred profit from an installment sale when the note itself later is transferred to another party or is otherwise relinquished.[43] The rationale for accelerating the gain is that deferral is no longer appropriate when the taxpayer has sold the obligation and received the proceeds (under the wherewithal to pay concept).

Moreover, a gift or cancellation of an installment note is treated as a taxable disposition by the donor. The amount realized from the cancellation is the face amount of the note if the parties (obligor and obligee) are related to each other.[44]

5 *Find more information on this topic at our Web site: **http://wft-entities.swcollege.com**.*

EXAMPLE 19

Liz cancels a note issued by Tina (Liz's daughter) that arose in connection with the sale of property. At the time of the cancellation, the note had a basis to Liz of $10,000, a face amount of $25,000, and a fair market value of $20,000. Presuming the initial sale by Liz to Tina qualified as an installment sale, the cancellation results in gain of $15,000 ($25,000 – $10,000) to Liz. ■

PLANNING CONSIDERATIONS

Terminating the Installment Method

As suggested earlier, an installment sale might look less appealing in retrospect if a taxpayer subsequently finds itself in a higher tax bracket. Whether this predicament is due to higher legislated rates or the expansion of the taxpayer's business, the taxpayer might be inclined to *terminate the installment sale method.* Disposing of the installment obligation often accomplishes this result, because any remaining deferred gain is thereby accelerated into the current year. To be sure, the taxpayer gives up the deferral benefit obtained when the transaction was set up as an installment sale, but saving taxes that would be paid in future years at higher rates may offset the loss of deferral benefits.

Disposing of an installment obligation, however, may not be easy. Financial obligations of most private businesses or other persons can often be difficult to sell at a price equal to their present value. Intermediaries may agree to purchase such obligations only at significant discounts to their face amount. If the maker of the note (i.e., the person obligated to pay the installment obligation) is experiencing any financial difficulty at the time, the note will be even harder to sell. Thus, *nontax considerations* may effectively preclude the acceleration of taxable gain by disposing of an installment obligation.

---

[43]§ 453B(a).

[44]§ 453B(f)(2).

INTEREST ON DEFERRED TAXES

With the installment method, the seller earns interest on the receivable. The receivable includes the deferred gain. In effect, the seller is earning interest on the deferred taxes. Since the installment method provides interest-free loans to those taxpayers who use it, the Code requires the taxpayers to pay interest on the deferred taxes in some situations.[45]

The taxpayer is required to pay interest on the deferred taxes only if *both* of the following requirements are met.

- The installment obligation arises from the sale of property (other than farming property) for more than $150,000.
- Such installment obligations outstanding at the close of the tax year exceed $5 million.

Interest on the deferred taxes is payable only on the portion of the taxes that relates to the installment obligations in *excess* of $5 million. The interest is calculated using the rate for underpayment of taxes and estimates.

ELECTING OUT OF THE INSTALLMENT METHOD

A taxpayer can *elect not to use* the installment method. The election is made by reporting on a timely filed return the gain computed by the taxpayer's usual method of accounting (cash or accrual).[46] The election is frequently applied to year-end sales by taxpayers who expect to be in a higher tax bracket in the following year.

 6 *Find more information on this topic at our Web site: http://wft-entities.swcollege.com.*

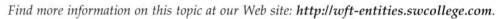

EXAMPLE 20

On December 31, 2001, Blue Corporation sold land to Orange, Inc., for $20,000 (fair market value). The cash was to be paid on January 4, 2002. Blue is a cash basis taxpayer, and its basis in the land is $8,000. Blue has a large casualty loss and very little other income in 2001. Thus, its marginal tax rate in 2001 is 15%. Blue expects its rate to increase in 2002 to 34%.

The transaction constitutes an installment sale because a payment will be received in a tax year after the tax year of disposition. Orange's promise to pay Blue is an installment obligation. If Blue elects out of the installment method, it would shift $12,000 of gain ($20,000 − $8,000) from the expected higher rate in 2002 to the 15% rate in 2001. The expected tax savings based on the rate differentials may exceed the benefit of the tax deferral available with the installment method. ■

LEARNING OBJECTIVE 4

Understand the alternative methods of accounting for long-term contracts (the completed contract method and the percentage of completion method).

Long-Term Contracts

A **long-term contract** is a building, installation, construction, or manufacturing contract that is entered into but not completed within the same tax year. However, a *manufacturing* contract is long term *only* if the contract is to manufacture (1) a unique item not normally carried in finished goods inventory or (2) items that normally require more than 12 calendar months to complete.[47] A contract to perform services (e.g., auditing or legal services) is not considered a contract for this purpose and thus cannot qualify as a long-term contract.

---

[45]§ 453A.
[46]§ 453(d) and Temp.Reg. § 15A.453–1(d). See also Rev.Rul. 82–227, 1982–2 C.B. 89.

[47]§ 460(f) and Reg. § 1.451–3(b).

TAX IN THE NEWS

IRS SAYS THE CASH METHOD DOES NOT CLEARLY REFLECT THE INCOME OF SMALL CONTRACTORS

In a 1980 Tax Court decision, *Raymond Magnon*, 73 T.C. 980, the court ruled that a small contractor could use the cash method of accounting. More recently, the IRS was unsuccessful in attempting to require a contractor to change from the cash method to the percentage of completion method. The IRS argued that the cash method did not clearly reflect income, but the Tax Court disagreed [*Ansley-Sheppard-Burgess Company*, 104 T.C. 367 (1995)].

In other recent cases, however, the IRS has been successful in requiring small contractors to change from the cash method to the accrual method (*Thompson Electric Inc.*, T.C.Memo. 1995–292, and *J. P. Sheahan Associates*, T.C.Memo. 1995–239). The IRS has successfully argued that the accumulated costs for materials and labor, whether incurred by the contractor or its subcontractors, are subject to the inventory rules. Because inventories are a material income-producing factor, the cash method does not clearly reflect income, and the IRS can require the contractor to employ the accrual method.

EXAMPLE 21

Raven & Co., Inc., a calendar year taxpayer, entered into two contracts during the year. One contract was to construct a building foundation. Work was to begin in October 2001 and be completed by June 2002. This contract is long term because it will not be entered into and completed in the same tax year. The fact that the contract requires less than 12 calendar months to complete is not relevant because the contract is not for manufacturing. The second contract was for architectural services to be performed over two years. These services will not qualify for long-term contract treatment because the taxpayer will not build, install, construct, or manufacture a product. ■

7 *Find more information on this topic at our Web site: **http://wft-entities.swcollege.com**.*

Contract costs are deducted when the revenue from the contract is recognized. Generally, two methods of accounting may be used to determine when the revenue from a contract is recognized.[48]

- The completed contract method.
- The percentage of completion method.

The *completed contract method may be used* for (1) home construction contracts (contracts in which at least 80 percent of the estimated costs are for dwelling units in buildings with four or fewer units) and (2) certain other real estate construction contracts. Other real estate contracts can qualify for the completed contract method if the following requirements are satisfied.

- The contract is expected to be completed within the two-year period beginning on the commencement date of the contract.
- The contract is performed by a taxpayer whose average annual gross receipts for the three taxable years preceding the taxable year in which the contract is entered into do not exceed $10 million.

All other contractors *must* use the percentage of completion method.

---

[48]§ 460.

COMPLETED CONTRACT METHOD

Under the **completed contract method,** no revenue from the contract is recognized or costs are deducted until the contract is completed and accepted. A taxpayer may not delay completion of a contract for the principal purpose of deferring tax.[49]

In some situations, the original contract price may be disputed, or the buyer may want additional work to be done on a long-term contract. If the disputed amount is substantial (i.e., it is not possible to determine whether a profit or loss will ultimately be realized on the contract), no income or loss is recognized until the dispute is resolved. In all other cases, the profit or loss (reduced by the amount in dispute) is recognized in the current period upon completion of the contract. However, additional work may need to be performed with respect to the disputed contract. In this case, the difference between the amount in dispute and the actual cost of the additional work is recognized in the year the work is completed, rather than in the year in which the dispute is resolved.[50]

EXAMPLE 22

Magenta Corporation, a calendar year taxpayer utilizing the completed contract method of accounting, constructed a building for Kingfisher Enterprises, Inc., under a long-term contract. The gross contract price was $500,000. Magenta finished construction in 2001 at a cost of $475,000. When Kingfisher examined the building, it insisted that the building be repainted or the contract price be reduced. The estimated cost of repainting is $10,000. Since under the terms of the contract, Magenta is assured of a profit of at least $15,000 [($500,000 − $475,000) − $10,000] even if the dispute is ultimately resolved in Kingfisher's favor, Magenta must include $490,000 ($500,000 − $10,000) in gross income and is allowed deductions of $475,000 for 2001.

In 2002, Magenta and Kingfisher resolve their dispute, and Magenta repaints certain portions of the building at a cost of $6,000. Magenta includes $10,000 in 2002 gross income and deducts the $6,000 expense in that year.

Now assume instead that the estimated cost of repainting the building is $50,000. Since the resolution of the dispute completely in Kingfisher's favor would mean a net loss on the contract for Magenta ($500,000 − $475,000 − $50,000 = $25,000 loss), Magenta does not recognize any income or loss until the year the dispute is resolved. ■

Frequently, a contractor receives payment at various stages of completion. For example, when a contract is 50 percent complete, the contractor may receive 50 percent of the contract price less a retainage. Generally, contractors are allowed to defer all tax effects from the advance payments until the payments are recognized as income under their method of accounting.

PERCENTAGE OF COMPLETION METHOD

The percentage of completion method must be used to account for long-term contracts unless the taxpayer qualifies for one of the two exceptions that allow the completed contract method to be used: home construction contracts and certain other real estate construction contracts. Under the **percentage of completion method,** a portion of the gross contract price is included in income during each period as the work progresses. The revenue accrued each period (except for the final period) is computed as follows.[51]

$$\frac{C}{T} \times P$$

---

[49]Reg. § 1.451–3(b)(2).
[50]Reg. §§ 1.451–3(d)(2)(ii)–(vii), Example (2).
[51]§ 460(b)(1)(A).

where C = Contract costs incurred during the period,
T = Estimated total cost of the contract, and
P = Contract price.

All of the costs allocated to the contract during the period are deductible from the accrued revenue. The revenue reported in the final period is simply the unreported revenue from the contract. Because T in this formula is an estimate that frequently differs from total actual costs, which are not known until the contract has been completed, the profit on a contract for a particular period may be overstated or understated.[52]

8 *Find more information on this topic at our Web site:* **http://wft-entities.swcollege.com.**

EXAMPLE 23

Tan, Inc., entered into a contract that was to take two years to complete, with an estimated cost of $2,250,000. The contract price was $3,000,000. Costs of the contract for 2001, the first year, totaled $1,350,000. The gross profit reported by the percentage of completion method for 2001 was $450,000 {[($1,350,000/$2,250,000) × $3,000,000 = $1,800,000] − $1,350,000}. The contract was completed at the end of 2002 at a total cost of $2,700,000. In retrospect, 2001 profit should have been $150,000 {[($1,350,000/$2,700,000) × $3,000,000 = $1,500,000] − $1,350,000}. Thus, taxes were overpaid for 2001. ∎

LEARNING OBJECTIVE

Recognize when accounting for inventories is required.

Inventories

Generally, tax accounting and financial accounting for inventories are much the same.

- The use of inventories is necessary to clearly reflect the income of any business engaged in the production and sale or purchase and sale of goods.[53]
- The inventories should include all finished goods, goods in process, and raw materials and supplies that will become part of the product (including containers).
- Inventory rules must give effect to the *best* accounting practice of a particular trade or business, and the taxpayer's method should be consistently followed from year to year.
- All items included in inventory should be valued at either (1) cost or (2) the lower of cost or market value.

The following are *not* acceptable methods or practices in valuing inventories.

- A reserve for anticipated price changes.
- Use of a constant price or nominal value for a so-called normal quantity of materials or goods in stock (e.g., the base stock method).
- Inclusion in inventory of stock in transit to which title is not vested in the taxpayer.
- The direct costing approach (excluding fixed indirect production costs from inventory).
- The prime costing approach (excluding all indirect production costs from inventory).

The reason for the similarities between tax and financial accounting for inventories is that § 471 sets forth what appears to be a two-prong test: "inventories shall

---

[52]Reg. § 1.451–3(c)(3).   [53]§ 471(a) and Reg. §§ 1.471–1 and –2.

INTERNATIONAL IMPLICATIONS

A TAX ADVANTAGE FROM MOVING ABROAD

While the United States requires producers to use the accrual method, with stringent capitalization requirements for inventories, some foreign countries allow such businesses to use the cash method. Thus, a U.S. manufacturing company experiences a tax windfall when it moves its production to a foreign subsidiary in a country where all production costs are deducted as incurred, and revenues are deferred until collected.

---

be taken . . . on such basis . . . as conforming as nearly as may be to the *best accounting practice* in the trade or business and as most *clearly reflecting the income.*" The best accounting practice is generally synonymous with generally accepted accounting principles (hereafter referred to as GAAP). However, the IRS determines whether an inventory method clearly reflects income.

In *Thor Power Tool Co. v. Comm.,*[54] there was a conflict between these two tests. The taxpayer's method of valuing obsolete parts was in conformity with GAAP. The IRS, however, successfully argued that the clear reflection of income test was not satisfied because the taxpayer's procedures for valuing its inventories were contrary to the Regulations. Under the taxpayer's method, inventories for parts in excess of estimated future sales were written off (expensed), although the parts were kept on hand and their asking prices were not reduced.

The taxpayer contended that conformity to GAAP creates a presumption that the method clearly reflects income. The Supreme Court disagreed, concluding that the clear reflection of income test was *paramount.* Moreover, it is the opinion of the IRS that controls in determining whether a method of inventory clearly reflects income. Thus, the best accounting practice test was rendered practically meaningless. Thus, a taxpayer's method of inventory must strictly conform to the Regulations, regardless of what GAAP may require.

DETERMINING INVENTORY COST

For merchandise purchased, cost is the invoice price less trade discounts plus freight and other handling charges.[55]

Uniform Capitalization. For inventory and property *produced* by a taxpayer, "(A) the direct cost of such property, and (B) such property's share of those indirect costs (including taxes) part or all of which are allocable to such property" must be capitalized. Congress wanted a set of capitalization rules that would apply to all types of businesses: contractors, manufacturers, farmers, wholesalers, and retailers.[56] Congress has labeled the resulting system the **uniform capitalization rules,** and tax practitioners refer to it as a *super-full absorption costing system.*

To value inventory under the uniform capitalization rules, a *producer* must.

- Classify all costs into three categories: (1) production, (2) general administrative expense, and (3) mixed services.

---

[54]79–1 USTC ¶9139, 43 AFTR2d 79–362, 99 S.Ct. 773 (USSC, 1979).
[55]Reg. § 1.471–3(b).

[56]H. Rep. 99–841, 99th Cong., 2nd Sess., 1986, pp. 302–309. § 263A. Reg. § 1.263A–1(a).

- Allocate mixed services costs to production and general administrative expenses.
- Allocate the production costs between the cost of goods sold and the ending inventory.

Mixed services costs should be allocated to production on a rational basis. For example, the costs of operating the personnel department may be allocated between production and general administration based on the number of applications processed or the number of employees. In lieu of allocating each mixed services cost, a taxpayer may elect a *simplified method* that allocates the total of all mixed services costs to production.[57]

$$MSP = \frac{TP}{TC} \times TMS$$

where MSP = Mixed services costs allocated to production,
        TP = Total production costs, other than interest and mixed services,
        TC = Total costs, other than interest, state, local or foreign income taxes, and mixed services costs, and
     TMS = Total mixed services costs.

The usual cost accounting techniques (e.g., average cost per equivalent unit) can be used to allocate production costs between the cost of goods sold and the ending inventory.

Costs included in the inventory of *wholesalers and retailers* are comparable to those of the producer. However, many of these costs are captured in the price these taxpayers pay for the goods. The following additional costs must be capitalized by wholesalers and retailers.

- All storage costs for wholesalers.
- Offsite storage costs for retailers.
- Purchasing costs (e.g., buyers' wages or salaries).
- Handling, processing, assembly, and repackaging.

The uniform capitalization rules may cause some costs to be capitalized for tax purposes but not for financial accounting purposes. For example, a wholesaler's or a manufacturer's storage costs generally are expensed for financial reporting purposes, but must be capitalized for tax purposes. A taxpayer may capitalize straight-line depreciation of production equipment for financial accounting purposes, but the actual tax depreciation must be capitalized under uniform capitalization.

Lower of Cost or Market.   Except for those taxpayers who use the LIFO method, inventories may be valued at the **lower of cost or market (replacement cost).**[58] Taxpayers using LIFO *must value inventory at cost.* However, the write-down of damaged or shopworn merchandise and goods that otherwise are unsalable at normal prices is not considered an application of the lower of cost or market method. Such items should be valued at bona fide selling price less direct cost of disposal.[59]

9 *Find more information on this topic at our Web site:* ***http://wft-entities.swcollege.com.***

In applying the lower of cost or market method, *each* item included in the inventory is valued at the lower of its cost or market value.[60]

---

[57]Reg. § 1.263A–1(h)(5).
[58]Reg. § 1.472–4.

[59]Reg. § 1.471–2(c).
[60]Reg. § 1.471–4(c).

[handwritten margin notes: "for financial acc had choice of item by item or total" "with FIFO" "LIFO costomary"]

EXAMPLE 24

The taxpayer's ending inventory is valued as follows.

Item	Cost	Market	Lower of Cost or Market
A	$5,000	$ 4,000	$4,000
B	3,000	2,000	2,000
C	1,500	6,000	1,500
	$9,500	$12,000	$7,500

Under the lower of cost or market method, the taxpayer's inventory is valued at $7,500, not $9,500. ■

Inventory Shrinkage. Because of accidents, thefts, and recording errors, a company's inventory per physical count and its inventory according to company records may differ. This difference is called *inventory shrinkage* and is typically recorded when a company completes its physical inventory. But many companies take their physical inventories at some time other than the last day of their taxable year. As a result, they need to adjust the ending inventory, per their accounting records, for the estimated shrinkage that has occurred since the last physical inventory. A taxpayer can deduct this shrinkage on its tax return.[61]

Determining Cost—Specific Identification, FIFO, and LIFO. In some cases, it is feasible to determine the cost of the particular item sold. For example, an automobile dealer can easily determine the specific cost of each automobile that has been sold. However, in most businesses it is necessary to resort to a flow of goods assumption such as *first in, first out (FIFO)*, *last in, first out (LIFO)*, or an *average cost* method. A taxpayer may use any of these methods, provided the method selected is consistently applied from year to year.

During a period of rising prices, LIFO generally produces a lower ending inventory valuation and results in a higher cost of goods sold than would be obtained under the FIFO method.

EXAMPLE 25

On January 1, the taxpayer opened a retail store to sell refrigerators. At least 10 refrigerators must be carried in inventory to satisfy customer demands. The initial investment in the 10 refrigerators is $5,000 ($500 each). During the year, 10 refrigerators were sold at $750 each and were replaced at a cost of $6,000 ($600 each). Gross profit under the LIFO and FIFO methods is computed as follows.

		FIFO		LIFO
Sales (10 × $750)		$ 7,500		$ 7,500
Beginning inventory	$ 5,000		$ 5,000	
Purchases	6,000		6,000	
	$11,000		$11,000	
Ending inventory				
10 × $600	(6,000)			
10 × $500			(5,000)	
Cost of goods sold		(5,000)		(6,000)
Gross profit		$ 2,500		$ 1,500

■

---

[61]§ 471(b).

Dollar-Value LIFO.   In the preceding example, the taxpayer was buying and selling a single product, a particular model of a refrigerator. The taxpayer employed the *specific goods LIFO* technique. Under the specific goods approach, if identical items are not on hand at the end of the period, the LIFO inventory is depleted, and all of the deferred profit is reported. Thus, taxpayers who frequently change the items carried in inventory would realize little benefit from LIFO. However, dollar-value LIFO avoids this LIFO depletion problem.

Under **dollar-value LIFO,** each inventory item is assigned to a pool. A *pool* is a collection of similar items and is treated as a separate inventory. Determining whether items are similar involves considerable judgment. In general, however, a taxpayer would prefer broad pools so that when a particular item is sold out, it can be replaced by increases in other items in the same pool. Typically, all products manufactured at a particular plant can be treated as a pool.[62] A department store may have a separate pool for each department. An automobile dealer may have separate pools for new cars, lightweight trucks, heavy-duty trucks, and car and truck parts.

At the end of the period, the ending inventory is valued at current-year prices and then at the LIFO base period (the year LIFO was adopted) prices. The ratio of the ending inventory at current prices to the ending inventory at base period prices is the *LIFO index*. If the total current inventory at base period prices is greater than the base period inventory at base period prices, a LIFO layer must be added. The LIFO index is applied to the LIFO layer to convert it to current prices.

EXAMPLE 26

Black Company adopted LIFO effective January 1, 2001. The base LIFO inventory (from December 31, 2000) was $1,000,000. On December 31, 2001, the inventory was $1,320,000 at end-of-2001 prices and $1,200,000 at end-of-2000 (the base period) prices. Thus, Black added a 2001 layer of $200,000 ($1,200,000 − $1,000,000) at base period prices. The layer must be converted to 2001 prices.

$$\text{LIFO index} = \$1,320,000/\$1,200,000 = 1.10$$

$$2001 \text{ layer} \times \text{LIFO index} = \$200,000 \times 1.10 = \$220,000$$

Therefore, the 2001 ending inventory is $1,000,000 + $220,000 = $1,220,000.

The inventory on December 31, 2002, is $1,325,000 using 2002 prices and $1,250,000 using base period prices. Thus, the LIFO index for 2002 is $1,325,000/$1,250,000 = 1.06. The LIFO inventory is $1,273,000.

	BLACK COMPANY LIFO Inventory December 31, 2002		
	Base Period Cost	LIFO Index	LIFO Layers
Base inventory	$1,000,000	1.00	$1,000,000
2001 layer	200,000	1.10	220,000
2002 layer	50,000	1.06	53,000
	$1,250,000		$1,273,000

---

[62]Reg. § 1.472–8.

THE LIFO ELECTION

A taxpayer may adopt LIFO by using the method in the tax return for the year of the change and by attaching Form 970 (Application to Use LIFO Inventory Method) to the tax return. Thus, a taxpayer need not request approval for the change. Once this election is made, it cannot be revoked. A prospective change from LIFO to any other inventory method can be made only if the consent of the IRS is obtained.[63]

10 *Find more information on this topic at our Web site:* ***http://wft-entities.swcollege.com.***

Once a LIFO election is made for tax purposes, the taxpayer's financial reports to owners and creditors must also be prepared on the basis of LIFO. The *conformity* of financial reports to tax reporting is specifically required by the Code and is strictly enforced by the IRS. However, the Regulations allow a taxpayer to make a footnote disclosure of the net income computed by another method of inventory valuation (e.g., FIFO).[64]

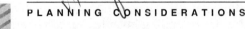

PLANNING CONSIDERATIONS

LIFO Inventory

During periods of anticipated cost increases, LIFO tends to reduce reported taxable income and thereby lowers current tax liabilities. This tendency reverses itself, however, if inventory *volumes* are not maintained. As older and therefore lower costs are matched against current income, a taxpayer's reported income will be *higher* under LIFO than under FIFO.

Taxpayers usually can avoid this phenomenon by ensuring that base inventory levels do not decrease. But *nontax considerations* often thwart this strategy. During periods of shortage, replacement goods may be unavailable. If interest rates are rising, a taxpayer may not want to increase its purchases and the corresponding cost of financing these purchases. If a recession is in progress, the taxpayer might be anticipating a slowdown in its sales and will resist acquir-

ing additional inventory beyond its expected needs. As a result of these factors, inventory levels might go down, and taxable income will then increase.

In any case, the *financial statement conformity* requirement of LIFO can make this method unappealing to corporate management. While the permitted footnote disclosures can somewhat ameliorate the impact of LIFO on a company's reported earnings, such disclosures are often more effective with sophisticated creditors than with capital markets generally. Accordingly, management may wait until a general business slowdown has dampened earnings expectations before switching to LIFO and suffering from the typical drop in earnings that occurs with the switch.

Suggested Further Readings

"Will Big Accounting Firms' Growth Blow Their Tax Deductions?" *Journal of Taxation*, December 1997, p. 378.

W. Curtis Elliott and Christopher E. Hannum, "The Chaos of *Indopco* and Value Creation: Long-Term Business Expansion of Recovery?" *Journal of Taxation*, June 1999, pp. 338–357.

Dennis I. Gaffney, Richard O. Davis, Maureen H. Smith, and James E. Wheeler, "How Retailing's 'Best' Inventory Accounting Practices Produced Distorted LIFO Pools," *Journal of Taxation*, April 1999, pp. 218–227.

[63]Reg. §§ 1.472–3(a) and –5 and Rev.Proc. 84–74, 1984–2 C.B. 736 at 742.

[64]§ 472(c), Reg. § 1.472–2(e).

Steve H. Klein, "Carrying Inventory Below Cost Can Create Tax Savings," *Taxation for Accountants*, August 1997, pp. 83–89.

W. Eugene Seago, "The IRS Issues Proposed LIFO Regulations for the 21st Century," *Journal of Taxation*, September 2000, pp. 157–165.

KEY TERMS

Accounting method, 6–11

Accounting period, 6–3

Accrual method, 6–9

Cash method, 6–9

Completed contract method, 6–22

Contingent sales prices, 6–15

Dollar-value LIFO, 6–27

Fiscal year, 6–3

Imputed interest, 6–16

Installment method, 6–13

Least aggregate deferral method, 6–4

Long-term contract, 6–20

Lower of cost or market (replacement cost), 6–25

Majority interest partner, 6–4

Percentage of completion method, 6–22

Personal service corporation (PSC), 6–6

Principal partner, 6–4

Short taxable year (short period), 6–7

Uniform capitalization rules, 6–24

Problem Materials

PROBLEMS

1. Red, White, and Blue are unrelated corporations engaged in real estate development. The three corporations formed a joint venture (treated as a partnership) to develop a tract of land. Assuming the venture does not have a natural business year, what tax year must the joint venture adopt under the following circumstances?

		Tax Year Ending	Interest in Joint Venture
a.	Red	September 30	60%
	White	June 30	20%
	Blue	March 31	20%
b.	Red	September 30	30%
	White	June 30	40%
	Blue	January 31	30%

2. The Zinnia Wholesale Company is an S corporation that began business on March 1, 2001. William, a calendar year taxpayer, owns 100% of Zinnia. He has $300,000 taxable income from other sources each year. William will work approximately 30 hours a week for the corporation. Zinnia sells swimming pool supplies, and its natural business year ends in September. Approximately 80% of Zinnia's gross receipts occur in June through September.

a. What tax year should Zinnia elect, assuming that William anticipates the company will produce a net profit for all years?

b. What tax year should Zinnia elect, assuming it will lose $10,000 a month for the first 12 months and an average of $5,000 a month for the next 12 months? In the third year, the corporation will earn taxable income.

3. Allison, a consultant, conducted her professional practice through Allison, Inc. The corporation uses a fiscal year ending September 30 even though the business purpose test for a fiscal year cannot be satisfied. For the year ending September 30, 2001, the corporation paid Allison a salary of $100,000, and during the period January through September 2001, the corporation paid her a salary of $80,000.

a. How much salary should Allison receive during the period October 1 through December 31, 2001?

b. Assume that Allison received only $20,000 salary during the period October 1 through December 31, 2001. What would be the consequences to Allison, Inc.?

4. Owl Corporation is in the business of sales and home deliveries of fuel oil and currently uses a calendar year for reporting its taxable income. However, Owl's natural business year ends May 31. For the short period, January 1 through May 31, 2001, the corporation earned $31,500. Assume the corporate tax rates are as follows: 15% on taxable income of $50,000 or less, 25% on taxable income over $50,000 but not over $75,000, and 34% on taxable income over $75,000.

a. What must Owl Corporation do to change its taxable year?

b. Compute Owl Corporation's tax for the short period.

5. Which of the following businesses must use the accrual method of accounting?

a. A corporation with annual gross receipts of $12 million from computer consulting.

b. An international accounting firm that is conducted as a partnership and has annual gross receipts in excess of $1 billion.

c. An incorporated manufacturer with annual gross receipts of $1.4 million.

d. A farming partnership with annual gross receipts of $900,000.

e. A corporation that acts as an insurance agent, with annual gross receipts of $4 million.

6. This year, the taxpayer was required to switch from the cash to the accrual basis of accounting for sales and cost of goods sold. Taxable income for this year computed under the cash basis was $60,000. Relevant account balances were as follows.

	Beginning of the Year	End of the Year
Accounts receivable	$56,000	$50,000
Accounts payable	29,000	28,000
Inventory	27,000	30,000

Compute the following:

a. The adjustment due to the change in accounting method.

b. The accrual basis taxable income for this year.

7. Moss Company is an environmental consulting business with annual gross receipts of approximately $1.8 million. Moss occasionally buys and installs equipment for its customers, but the company does not maintain an inventory of equipment. Generally, the company collects its fee within 30 days of completion of a project. An IRS agent argues that the company is selling goods and therefore must use the accrual method of accounting.

a. If the company has no ending inventory, why would the IRS require a change in accounting method? How would the change affect taxable income?

b. If a change in accounting method is required, why would Moss prefer to make a voluntary change rather than being required to do so by the IRS?

8. Rochelle, a CPA, recently obtained a new client, the Hyacinth Engineering Corporation (annual gross receipts of $2 million). The company's previous accountant had filed all returns by the accrual method of accounting, the same method that was used to prepare financial statements submitted when the company applied for a loan in its first year of operation. Rochelle recognizes that under the accrual method of accounting the company is paying tax on its accounts receivable, whereas under the cash method of accounting the income could be deferred until the cash is collected. In many cases, it takes the company three months to collect a receivable. Rochelle also recognizes that the IRS will not allow the corporation to change to the cash method.

   Rochelle is considering the following plan. A new corporation would be formed. Each shareholder in Hyacinth would own the same percentage of stock in the new corporation. The key element of the plan is that the new corporation would elect the cash method. Hyacinth would complete its contracts in progress, collect its receivables, and gradually be liquidated. Meanwhile all new business would be channeled into the new corporation. Evaluate Rochelle's plan.

9. Your client, Bluebell & Associates, is negotiating a sale of investment real estate for $24 million. Bluebell believes that the buyer would pay cash of $16 million and a note for $8 million, or $6 million cash and a note for $18 million. The notes will pay interest at slightly above the market rate. Bluebell realizes that the second option involves more risks of collection, but it is willing to accept that risk if the tax benefits of the installment sale are substantial. Write a letter advising Bluebell of the tax consequences of choosing the lower down payment and larger note option, assuming it has no other installment receivables. The company's address is 200 Jerdone, Gettysburg, PA 17325.

10. Your new client is primarily a service business, but two years ago the company began selling a few products. These sales accounted for 5% of revenues in the first year and 10% in the second year. The client consistently used the cash method of accounting for all of its income and expenses, even though it had accounts receivable from these sales and some inventory on hand at the end of each year. Accordingly, its tax returns for the two previous years were incorrect.

   The company, however, does not want to file amended returns for those previous years and pay the resulting additional tax and interest, because it is short on cash. Nor does it want to request a change in accounting method, since such a request would require a $1,250 processing fee payable to the IRS. Instead, the company wants to use the accrual method starting this year, and then correct the effect of the previous years' errors by including beginning accounts receivable collected in this year's gross income and by treating the beginning inventory balance as zero. This approach would be the least costly for your client. What do you recommend?

11. Finch Corporation, a cash basis taxpayer, has agreed to sell land to Beige, Inc., a well-established and highly profitable company. Beige is willing to (1) pay $100,000 cash or (2) pay $25,000 cash and the balance ($75,000) plus interest at 10% (the Federal rate) in two years. Finch is in the 35% marginal tax bracket (combined Federal and state) for all years and believes it can reinvest the sales proceeds and earn a 14% before-tax rate of return.
   a. Should Finch accept the deferred payments option if its basis in the land is $10,000?
   b. Do you think your results would change if Finch's basis in the land were $90,000?

12. Jasmine & Company, a cash basis taxpayer, sold a cargo temperature detector to Peacock Manufacturing for 25% of gross sales in excess of $3 million annually, with a lifetime limit of $600,000. In the first year, Jasmine received $180,000. The cost basis of this device is $200,000. What is the profit that Jasmine must report for this year?

13. Tom, a cash basis taxpayer, sold his unincorporated accounting practice for $600,000. The basis and fair market values of the assets sold were as follows.

Assets	Fair Market Value	Basis	
Office equipment	$ 50,000	Cost	$ 120,000
		Less: Depreciation	(100,000)
Office building	180,000	Cost	220,000
		Less: Depreciation	(100,000)
Land	100,000	Cost	40,000
Goodwill	270,000	Cost	–0–
Total	$600,000	Total	$ 180,000

The buyer paid $240,000 at closing and agreed to pay the balance with interest at 8% (exceeds the Federal rate) over 10 years. The office building was depreciated using the straight-line method. Thus, there is no § 1250 gain. Compute Tom's recognized gain in the year of the sale.

14. On July 1, 2000, a cash basis taxpayer sold land for $800,000 due on the date of the sale and $6 million principal and $741,600 interest (6%) due on June 30, 2002. The seller's basis in the land was $1 million. The Federal short-term rate was 8%, compounded semiannually.
    a. Compute the seller's interest income and gain in 2000, 2001, and 2002.
    b. Same as (a), except that the amount due in two years was $2 million principal and $508,800 interest and the purchaser will use the cash method to account for interest.

15. On December 30, 2001, Father sold land to Son for $10,000 cash and a 7% installment note with a face amount of $190,000. In 2002, after paying $30,000 on the principal of the note, Son sold the land. In 2003, Son paid Father $25,000 on the note principal. Father's basis in the land was $50,000. Assuming Son sold the land for $250,000, compute Father's taxable gain in 2002.

16. George sold land to an unrelated party in 2000. His basis in the land was $40,000, and the selling price was $100,000—$25,000 payable at closing and $25,000 (plus 10% interest) due January 1, 2001, 2002, and 2003. What would be the tax consequences of the following? [Treat each part independently and assume (1) George did not elect out of the installment method and (2) the installment obligations have values equal to their face amounts.]
    a. In 2001, George gave to his daughter the right to collect all future payments on the installment obligations.
    b. In 2001, after collecting the payment due on January 1, George transferred the installment obligation to his 100%-controlled corporation in exchange for additional shares of stock.
    c. On December 31, 2001, George received the payment due on January 1, 2002. On December 15, 2002, George died, and the remaining installment obligation was transferred to his estate. The estate collected the amount due on January 1, 2003.

17. The Heron Construction Company reports its income by the completed contract method. At the end of 2001, the company completed a contract to construct a building at a total cost of $1,980,000. The contract price was $2,200,000. However, the customer refused to accept the work and would not pay anything on the contract because he claimed the roof did not meet specifications. Heron's engineers estimated it would cost $150,000 to bring the roof up to the customer's standards. In 2002, the dispute was settled in the customer's favor; the roof was improved at a cost of $180,000, and the customer accepted the building and paid the $2,200,000.
    a. What would be the effects of the above on Heron's taxable income for 2001 and 2002?
    b. Same as (a), except that Heron had $2,100,000 accumulated cost under the contract at the end of 2001.

18. Daffodil Company is a real estate construction company with average annual gross receipts of $3 million. Daffodil uses the completed contract method, and the contracts require 18 months to complete. Daffodil generally builds commercial buildings under contracts with the owners and reports the income by the completed contract method. The company is considering building a series of similar stores for a retail chain. The gross profit margin would be low, but the company's gross receipts would triple. Write a letter to your client explaining the tax accounting implications of entering into these contracts. Daffodil's mailing address is P.O. Box 1000, Harrisonburg, VA 22807.

19. Rust Company is a real estate construction company with average annual gross receipts of $4 million. Rust uses the completed contract method, and the contracts require 18 months to complete. Which of the following costs would be allocated to construction in progress by Rust?
    a. The payroll taxes on direct labor.
    b. The current services pension costs for employees whose wages are included in direct labor.
    c. Accelerated depreciation on equipment used on contracts.
    d. Sales tax on materials assigned to contracts.
    e. The past service costs for employees whose wages are included in direct labor.
    f. Bidding expenses for contracts awarded.

20. The Eagle Construction Company began business on April 1 this year. The company erects prefabricated steel buildings and operates as follows. After the customer selects a building model, Eagle orders the materials from the manufacturer. Eagle then erects the building on the customer's property. Eagle prices the contract at 150% of the cost of the prefabricated building. The customer pays 70% of the price at the time the materials are ordered and the balance of the original price when the building is completed. If Eagle buys more than $1 million in materials during the year, the manufacturer will give Eagle a 2% rebate the following February. Several buildings were under construction at the end of the year. Eagle had ordered more than $1 million in materials during the year, but had paid for only about $989,000 through December. What issues involving Eagle's accounting methods are raised by these facts?

21. Indicate the accounting method that should be used to compute the income from the following contracts.
    a. A contract to build six jet aircraft.
    b. A contract to build a new home. The contractor's average annual gross receipts are $15 million.
    c. A contract to manufacture 3,000 pairs of boots for a large retail chain. The manufacturer has several contracts to produce the same boot for other retailers.
    d. A contract to pave a parking lot. The contractor's average annual gross receipts are $2 million.

22. Ostrich Company makes gasoline storage tanks. Everything produced is under contract (that is, the company does not produce until it gets a contract for a product). Ostrich makes three basic models. However, the tanks must be adapted to each individual customer's location and needs (e.g., the location of the valves, the quality of the materials and insulation). Discuss the following issues relative to Ostrich's operations.
    a. An examining IRS agent contends that each of the company's contracts is to produce a "unique product." What difference does it make whether the product is unique or a "shelf item"?
    b. What must Ostrich do with the costs of bidding on contracts?
    c. Ostrich frequently makes several cost estimates for a contract, using various estimates of materials costs. These costs fluctuate almost daily. Assuming Ostrich must use the percentage of completion method to report the income from the contract, what will be the consequence if the company uses the highest estimate of a contract's cost and the actual cost is closer to the lowest estimated cost?

23. Swallow Company is a large real estate construction company that reports its income by the percentage of completion method. In 2002, the company completed a contract at a total cost of $1,960,000. The contract price was $2,400,000. At the end of 2001, the

year the contract was begun, Swallow estimated the total cost of the contract would be $2,100,000, and total accumulated costs on the contract at the end of 2001 were $1,400,000. The relevant tax rate is 34%, and the relevant Federal interest rate is 7%. Assume that all returns were filed and taxes were paid on March 15 following the close of the calendar tax year.

a. Compute the gross profit on the contract for 2001 and 2002

b. Before bidding on a contract, Swallow generally makes three estimates of total contract costs: (1) optimistic, (2) pessimistic, and (3) most likely (based on a blending of optimistic and pessimistic assumptions). The company has asked you to write a letter explaining which of these estimates should be used for percentage of completion purposes. In writing your letter, you should consider the fact that Swallow is an S corporation; therefore, the income and deductions flow through to the shareholders who are all individuals in the 36% marginal tax bracket. The relevant Federal interest rate is 8%. Swallow's mailing address is 400 Front Avenue, Ashland, OR 97520.

24. Bluebird Company, a furniture retailer, is adding a new line of merchandise. In the current year, the company purchased merchandise with an invoice price of $700,000, less a 2% discount for early payment. Freight and handling charges totaled $60,000. The company had to lease additional storage space in a warehouse three blocks from the store. The lease on the storage space was $30,000 for the year. A buyer was added to handle the new line of merchandise, and her salary was $35,000 for the year. Also, as a result of the increase in inventory of goods on hand, the company's insurance increased by $5,000. The invoice cost of the goods on hand at the end of the year was $105,000. Compute the company's ending inventory under the FIFO method.

25. Flamingo Company produces small machinery. The company also produces parts used to repair the machinery. The parts may be sold for several years after the company has discontinued the product. Flamingo has on hand parts with an original cost of $600,000. The total offering price on these goods is $960,000. However, the company expects to sell only 80% of the parts on hand. The excess parts are kept in case the estimates are incorrect.

a. Can Flamingo deduct the excess inventory under the lower of cost or market rule?

b. Assume that Flamingo deducted the cost of the excess parts on hand. While the parts were still on hand, the company elected LIFO. What are the implications of the change in inventory method?

26. This year, Gallinule, Inc., changed from the use of the lower of cost or market FIFO method to the LIFO method. The ending inventory for last year was computed as follows.

Item	FIFO Cost	Replacement Cost	Lower of Cost or Market
A	$10,000	$ 9,000	$ 9,000
B	25,000	30,000	25,000
			$34,000

a. What is the correct beginning inventory for this year under the LIFO method?

b. What immediate tax consequences (if any) would result from the switch to LIFO?

27. Amber Company has used the dollar-value LIFO technique for the past three years. The company has only one inventory pool. Its beginning inventory for the current year was computed as follows.

	Base Period Cost	LIFO Index	LIFO Layer
Base inventory	$1,250,000	1.0	$1,250,000
Year 1 layer	450,000	1.15	517,500
Year 2 layer	100,000	1.05	105,000
	$1,800,000		$1,872,500

The ending inventory is $1,955,000 at current period prices and $1,700,000 at base period prices. Determine the company's LIFO inventory value as of the end of the current year.

28. Jeffrey Robin, the president of Robin Furniture Corporation (average annual gross receipts of $4 million), has prepared the company's financial statements and income tax return for the past 25 years. However, in July 2002, after Jeffrey had filed the 2001 return, he hired you to prepare the 2002 corporate tax return because he has not studied taxes for over 20 years and suspects that the rules may have changed. Based upon an initial examination of his trial balance and some account analyses, you have determined that the following items may require adjustments.

   - The company uses the LIFO inventory method, as valued at cost. At the end of 2001, the company has written off $25,000 for inventory items that were still on hand but probably were not marketable (because the products are obsolete). No such write-off had been taken in prior years.

   - The company expenses all freight on merchandise when the goods are received. The expensed freight allocable to the beginning inventory for 2002 was $12,000.

   - The company accrues salaries and commissions, but expenses payroll taxes in the year paid. Because of large 2001 year-end bonuses that were not paid until the beginning of 2002, the company had $24,000 in accrued payroll taxes at the beginning of 2002.

   - The company uses the accrual method and has a reserve for bad debts equal to 3% of accounts receivable, which is an accurate percentage. The balance in the account at the beginning of the year is $15,000.

   Write a letter to Mr. Robin explaining the adjustments that will be required and how the changes will be implemented. The address of Robin Furniture Corporation is 1000 East Maryland, Evansville, IL 47722.

BRIDGE DISCIPLINE

1. White Partnership is owned by the following partners who have the indicated tax years.

Partner	Percentage	Tax Year End
Robert Jones	45%	December 31
Green Partnership	10%	June 30
Bronze, Inc.	45%	June 30

   Assume that White does not have a natural business year.
   a. What are the tax year options for White for financial reporting purposes?
   b. What are the tax year options for White for Federal income tax purposes?

2. Beige Company uses the cash method of accounting for Federal income tax purposes and the accrual method for financial reporting purposes. Beige purchases an office building and land for $600,000 on July 9, 2001, with $100,000 being allocated to the land. Beige consistently follows a policy of writing off all fixed costs as rapidly as possible for Federal income tax purposes. MACRS is used in calculating depreciation for financial reporting purposes.
   a. Calculate the amount of the deduction associated with the office building for Federal income tax purposes for the current year.
   b. Calculate the depreciation expense for financial reporting purposes under MACRS for the current year.
   c. Calculate the amount of the book–tax differential.

3. Calico, Inc., an airplane manufacturer, uses the accrual method of accounting for both financial reporting and Federal income tax purposes. The spare parts inventory is

recorded at the lower of cost or market. Some spare parts in the inventory have not been needed for several years, but Calico anticipates that it will eventually sell some of these items for repair work at the current market price (i.e., no discounts required). Based on a statistical projection, the company writes down to scrap value the spare parts that it expects it will eventually have to scrap to satisfy the external auditor. An IRS agent contends that while the writedown is in accordance with GAAP, it does not "clearly reflect income," so the writedown is disallowed.

Justify the position taken by your client in response to the external auditor, and justify the position taken by the IRS agent. Are the positions reconcilable in light of the different objectives of GAAP and the Code?

RESEARCH PROBLEMS

*Note: Solutions to Research Problems can be prepared by using the **RIA Checkpoint® Student Version Online research product,** or the **CCH U.S. Master Tax Guide Plus™** online Federal tax research database, which is available to accompany this text. It is also possible to prepare solutions to the Research Problems by using tax research materials found in a standard tax library.*

Research Problem 1. Clear Corporation uses the dollar-value LIFO inventory method to report its income. In computing the ending inventory at current prices, the company uses as "current costs" the year-end cost prices of items. The Regulations require that the taxpayer use as "current costs" the prices the company paid during the current year. Thus, if 10 units are on hand, and 5 were purchased on January 1, 2001, and 5 were purchased on June 30, 2001, those prices should be used as the current costs. Clear Corporation uses the price that would have been paid on December 31, 2001. Although Clear's method is incorrect, it actually results in an overstatement of the ending inventory. Nevertheless, the IRS agent contends that Clear's method is incorrect. Because the corporation no longer has the data to determine the current cost of the items, the IRS agent has proposed that the LIFO election be terminated. Your client argues, "no harm, no foul." Will this sports analogy carry the day?

Research Problem 2. Violet Company discovered that certain equipment used in its repair operations had been accounted for as inventory rather than as fixed assets. This incorrect treatment applied to all years in which the equipment had been used, and all of those years are open under the statute of limitations. Violet filed amended returns for all years affected by the incorrect treatment to obtain a refund of overpayments of taxes for the years affected. The IRS refused to accept the amended returns. The IRS reasoned that Violet was actually changing accounting methods and this can only be accomplished through a request for change in methods. In addition, the IRS concluded that an adjustment due to a voluntary change in accounting method must be taken into income for the year of the change. Is the IRS correct? Write a letter to Agnes Boyd, the president of Violet Company, that contains your advice and prepare a memo for the tax files. Violet's address is 100 Whitaker's Mill, Fargo, ND 58105.

Research Problem 3. You recently contracted to perform tax services for a new funeral home. In preparing the initial tax return, you must decide whether the funeral home can use the cash method of accounting. When discussing this issue with the manager, the manager points out that the company is actually a service business and that the only materials involved are caskets, which average only 15% of the price of a funeral. Is the funeral home required to use the accrual method of accounting?

Research Problem 4. Your client, April Partners, is a real estate developer. Usually, April will purchase land and immediately begin development. However, for some property that it recently purchased, April has decided to wait at least one year before beginning development. April would like to know if it can deduct the costs of holding the property (insurance, taxes, and interest) while it is awaiting the appropriate time to begin development.

Partial list of research aids:
Von-Lusk, 104 T.C. 207 (1995).

Use the tax resources of the Internet to address the following questions. Do not restrict your search to the World Wide Web, but include a review of newsgroups and general reference materials, practitioner sites and resources, primary sources of the tax law, chat rooms and discussion groups, and other opportunities.

Research Problem 5. Find a solicitation for a purchase of electronic equipment or furniture that is advertised as "no payment due" until next year or thereafter. Analyze the language of the solicitation in light of applicable Federal income tax law.

Research Problem 6. Find an explanation of the impact of the 1999 legislative and administrative changes in the tax rules for installment sales. Explain who will be affected by the changes, and how 2000 tax legislation had an effect.

Research Problem 7. Join a taxpayer discussion group that is addressing issues related to the installment method. Provide statutory information concerning the method through an initial posting, then answer one or two taxpayer follow-up queries. Be sure to relate a few of the limitations on the use of the installment method to the group.

Property Transactions: Basis, Gain and Loss, and Nontaxable Exchanges

LEARNING OBJECTIVES

After completing Chapter 7, you should be able to:

1. Understand the computation of realized gain or loss on property dispositions.

2. Distinguish between realized and recognized gain or loss.

3. Explain how basis is determined for various methods of asset acquisition.

4. Describe various loss disallowance provisions.

5. Apply the nonrecognition provisions and basis determination rules for like-kind exchanges.

6. Explain the nonrecognition provisions available on the involuntary conversion of property.

7. Identify other nonrecognition provisions contained in the Code.

Outline

TAX TALK   *To base all of your decisions on tax consequences is not necessarily to maintain the proper balance and perspective on what you are doing.*

—Barber Conable

This chapter and the following chapter are concerned with the income tax consequences of property transactions, including the sale or other disposition of property. The following questions are considered with respect to the sale or other disposition of property:

- Is there a realized gain or loss?
- If so, is that gain or loss recognized for tax purposes?
- If that gain or loss is recognized, is it ordinary or capital?
- What is the basis of any replacement property that is acquired?

This chapter discusses the determination of realized and recognized gain or loss and the basis of property. The following chapter covers the classification of recognized gain or loss as ordinary or capital.

For the most part, the rules discussed in Chapters 7 and 8 apply to all types of taxpayers. Individuals, partnerships, closely held corporations, limited liability companies, and publicly held corporations all own assets for use in business activities or as investments in entities that themselves conduct business activities. Individuals, however, are unique among taxpayers because they also own assets that are used in daily life and have no significant business or investment component. Because of that possibility, some property transaction concepts apply somewhat differently to individual taxpayers depending upon how a person uses the specific asset in question. Nevertheless, the material that follows pertains to taxpayers generally except where otherwise noted.

LEARNING OBJECTIVE 1

Understand the computation of realized gain or loss on property dispositions.

Determination of Gain or Loss

REALIZED GAIN OR LOSS

For tax purposes, gain or loss is the difference between the *amount realized* from the sale or other disposition of property and the property's *adjusted basis* on the date of disposition. If the amount realized exceeds the property's adjusted basis, the result is a **realized gain.** Conversely, if the property's adjusted basis exceeds the amount realized, the result is a **realized loss.**[1]

EXAMPLE 1

Lavender, Inc., sells Swan Corporation stock with an adjusted basis of $3,000 for $5,000. Lavender's realized gain is $2,000. If Lavender had sold the stock for $2,000, it would have had a realized loss of $1,000. ∎

Sale or Other Disposition. The term *sale or other disposition* is defined broadly to include virtually any disposition of property. Thus, trade-ins, casualties, condemnations, thefts, and bond retirements are all treated as dispositions of property. The most common disposition of property is a sale or exchange. Usually, the key factor in determining whether a disposition has taken place is whether an identifiable event has occurred[2] as opposed to a mere fluctuation in the value of the property.[3]

EXAMPLE 2

Heron & Associates owns Tan Corporation stock that cost $3,000. The stock has appreciated in value by $2,000 since Heron purchased it. Heron has no realized gain since mere fluctuation in value is not a disposition or identifiable event for tax purposes. Nor would Heron have a realized loss had the stock declined in value. ∎

Amount Realized. The **amount realized** from a sale or other disposition of property is the sum of any money received plus the fair market value of other property received. The amount realized also includes any real property taxes treated as imposed on the seller that are actually paid by the buyer.[4] The reason for including these taxes in the amount realized is that by paying the taxes, the purchaser is, in effect, paying an additional amount to the seller of the property.

The amount realized also includes any liability on the property disposed of, such as a mortgage debt, if the buyer assumes the mortgage or the property is sold subject to the mortgage.[5] The amount of the liability is included in the amount realized, even if the debt is nonrecourse and even if the amount of the debt is greater than the fair market value of the mortgaged property.[6]

EXAMPLE 3

Bunting & Co. sells property to Orange, Inc., for $50,000 cash. There is a $20,000 mortgage on the property. Bunting's amount realized from the sale is $70,000 if Orange assumes the mortgage or takes the property subject to the mortgage. ∎

The **fair market value** of property received in a sale or other disposition has been defined by the courts as the price at which the property will change hands

---

[1]§ 1001(a) and Reg. § 1.1001–1(a).

[2]Reg. § 1.1001–1(c)(1).

[3]*Lynch v. Turrish*, 1 USTC ¶18, 3 AFTR 2986, 38 S.Ct. 537 (USSC, 1918).

[4]§ 1001(b) and Reg. § 1.1001–1(b). Refer to Chapter 4 for a discussion of this subject.

[5]*Crane v. Comm.*, 47–1 USTC ¶9217, 35 AFTR 776, 67 S.Ct. 1047 (USSC, 1947). Although a legal distinction exists between the direct

assumption of a mortgage and taking property subject to a mortgage, the tax consequences in calculating the amount realized are the same.

[6]*Comm. v. Tufts*, 83–1 USTC ¶9328, 51 AFTR2d 83–1132, 103 S.Ct. 1826 (USSC, 1983).

WHAT'S IT WORTH?

In an arm's length transaction, the buyer and the seller agree on what the property is worth (i.e., the fair market value). If they cannot agree, then they do not consummate the transaction.

What if the buyer and seller cannot agree on the value, but the buyer has the ability to "take the property" anyway? In an involuntary conversion of property by a governmental unit, the buyer has the authority to take the property regardless of whether or not the owner wants to sell the property.

Until recently, a visit to the Gettysburg National Military Park provided the opportunity for a panoramic view of the 5,900-acre battlefield from the top of a 320-foot tower. The tower was built in 1974 on private property as a commercial endeavor. Preservationists convinced Congress to appropriate $1.6 million to buy the tower. On the 137th anniversary of the Battle of Gettysburg (Monday, July 3, 2000), a mere 10 pounds of explosives brought down the tower. But even though the tower is gone, the battle still rages. The owners are fighting the appraised value and want more money.

SOURCE: Adapted from "Tower Is Down, but Battle Continues," *USA Today*, July 5, 2000, p. A6.

between a willing seller and a willing buyer when neither is compelled to sell or buy.[7] Fair market value is determined by considering the relevant factors in each case.[8] An expert appraiser is often required to evaluate these factors in arriving at fair market value. When the fair market value of the property received cannot be determined, the value of the property given up by the taxpayer may be used.[9]

In calculating the amount realized, selling expenses such as advertising, commissions, and legal fees relating to the disposition are deducted. The amount realized is the net amount that the taxpayer received directly or indirectly, in the form of cash or anything else of value, from the disposition of the property.

Adjusted Basis.   The **adjusted basis** of property disposed of is the property's original basis adjusted to the date of disposition.[10] Original basis is the cost or other basis of the property on the date the property is acquired by the taxpayer. Considerations involving original basis are discussed later in this chapter. *Capital additions* increase and *recoveries of capital* decrease the original basis so that on the date of disposition the adjusted basis reflects the unrecovered cost or other basis of the property.[11] Adjusted basis is determined as follows:

> Cost (or other adjusted basis) on date of acquisition
> + Capital additions
> − Capital recoveries
> = Adjusted basis on date of disposition

---

[7]*Comm. v. Marshman*, 60–2 USTC ¶9484, 5 AFTR2d 1528, 279 F.2d 27 (CA–6, 1960).

[8]*O'Malley v. Ames*, 52–1 USTC ¶9361, 42 AFTR 19, 197 F.2d 256 (CA–8, 1952).

[9]*U.S. v. Davis*, 62–2 USTC ¶9509, 9 AFTR2d 1625, 82 S.Ct. 1190 (USSC, 1962).

[10]§ 1011(a) and Reg. § 1.1011–1.

[11]§ 1016(a) and Reg. § 1.1016–1.

Capital Additions. Capital additions include the cost of capital improvements and betterments made to the property by the taxpayer. These expenditures are distinguishable from expenditures for the ordinary repair and maintenance of the property, which are neither capitalized nor added to the original basis (refer to Chapter 4). The latter expenditures are deductible in the current taxable year if they are related to business or income-producing property. Amounts representing real property taxes treated as imposed on the seller but paid or assumed by the buyer are part of the cost of the property.[12] Any liability on property that is assumed by the buyer is also included in the buyer's original basis of the property. The same rule applies if property is acquired subject to a liability. In a similar fashion, amortization of the discount on bonds increases the adjusted basis of the bonds.[13]

EXAMPLE 4

Bluebird Corporation purchased some manufacturing equipment for $25,000. Whether Bluebird uses $25,000 from the business's cash account to pay for this equipment or uses $5,000 from that account and borrows the remaining $20,000, the basis of this equipment will be the same—namely, $25,000. Moreover, it does not matter whether Bluebird borrowed the $20,000 from the equipment's manufacturer, from a local bank, or from any other lender. ∎

Capital Recoveries. Capital recoveries decrease the adjusted basis of property. The following are examples of capital recoveries:

1. *Depreciation and cost recovery allowances.* The original basis of depreciable property is reduced by the annual depreciation charges (or cost recovery allowances) while the property is held by the taxpayer. The amount of depreciation that is subtracted from the original basis is the greater of the *allowed* or *allowable* depreciation calculated on an annual basis.[14] In most circumstances, the allowed and allowable depreciation amounts are the same (refer to Chapter 4).

2. *Casualties and thefts.* A casualty or theft may result in the reduction of the adjusted basis of property.[15] The adjusted basis is reduced by the amount of the deductible loss. In addition, the adjusted basis is reduced by the amount of insurance proceeds received. However, the receipt of insurance proceeds may result in a recognized gain rather than a deductible loss. The gain increases the adjusted basis of the property.[16]

EXAMPLE 5

An insured truck owned by the Falcon Corporation is destroyed in an accident. The adjusted basis is $8,000, and the fair market value is $6,500. Falcon received insurance proceeds of $6,500. The amount of the casualty loss is $1,500 ($6,500 insurance proceeds – $8,000 adjusted basis). The adjusted basis becomes $0 ($8,000 pre-accident adjusted basis, reduced by the $1,500 casualty loss and the $6,500 of insurance proceeds received). ∎

EXAMPLE 6

Osprey, Inc., owned an insured truck that was destroyed in an accident. The adjusted basis and fair market value of the truck were $6,500 and $8,000, respectively. Osprey received insurance proceeds of $8,000. The amount of the casualty *gain* is $1,500 ($8,000 insurance proceeds – $6,500 adjusted basis). The adjusted basis is increased by the $1,500 casualty gain and is reduced by the $8,000 of insurance proceeds received ($6,500 basis before casualty + $1,500 casualty gain – $8,000 insurance proceeds = $0 basis). ∎

---

[12]Reg. §§ 1.1001–1(b)(2) and 1.1012–1(b). Refer to Chapter 4 for a discussion of this subject.

[13]See Chapter 8 for a discussion of bond discount and the related amortization.

[14]§ 1016(a)(2) and Reg. § 1.1016–3(a)(1)(i).

[15]Refer to Chapter 5 for the discussion of casualties and thefts.

[16]Reg. § 1.1016–6(a).

BRIDGE DISCIPLINE

Bridge to Financial Accounting

Certain property transactions discussed later in this chapter are treated differently for tax purposes than for financial accounting purposes. For example, the category of transactions generally referred to as "nontaxable exchanges," such as like-kind exchanges and involuntary conversions, gives taxpayers the opportunity to defer the recognition of income on the disposition of property in qualifying transactions. The gains or losses deferred under tax law, however, are not deferred for financial reporting purposes. Instead, the actual gain or loss realized is reflected in the entity's financial reports.

Identifying and calculating the book-tax differences that arise from *taxable* dispositions of certain other property may not be so easy. For example, as discussed in Chapter 4, cost recovery (i.e., depreciation) rules provided by the tax law specify various ways in which an asset's cost may be recovered over time. These methods often differ from the methods used to depreciate an asset for book purposes. Consequently, the annual book-tax differences in these depreciation expense calculations are noted in the financial reports. But, in addition, these cumulative differences, as reflected in the accumulated depreciation account, will also produce a book-tax difference on the asset's disposition. That is, because an asset's accumulated depreciation may differ for book and tax purposes, its adjusted basis will also differ. Consequently, when the asset is sold, the amount of gain or loss for book purposes will differ from that recognized for tax purposes.

3. *Certain corporate distributions.* A corporate distribution to a shareholder that is not taxable is treated as a return of capital, and it reduces the basis of the shareholder's stock in the corporation.[17] Once the basis of the stock is reduced to zero, the amount of any subsequent distributions is a capital gain if the stock is a capital asset. See Chapter 10.

4. *Amortizable bond premium.* The basis in a bond purchased at a premium is reduced by the amortizable portion of the bond premium.[18] Investors in taxable bonds may *elect* to amortize the bond premium.[19] The amount of the amortized premium on taxable bonds is permitted as an interest deduction. Therefore, the election enables the taxpayer to take an annual interest deduction to offset ordinary income in exchange for a larger capital gain or smaller capital loss on the disposition of the bond (due to the basis reduction).

1   *Find more information on this topic at our Web site: http://wft-entities.swcollege.com.*

In contrast to the treatment of taxable bonds, the premium on tax-exempt bonds *must* be amortized, and no interest deduction is permitted. Furthermore, the basis of tax-exempt bonds is reduced even though the amortization is not allowed as a deduction. No amortization deduction is permitted on tax-exempt bonds because the interest income is exempt from tax, and the amortization of the bond premium merely represents an adjustment of the effective amount of such income.

---

[17]§ 1016(a)(4) and Reg. § 1.1016–5(a).

[18]§ 1016(a)(5) and Reg. § 1.1016–5(b). The accounting treatment of bond premium amortization is the same as for tax purposes. The amortization results in a decrease in the bond investment account.

[19]§ 171(c).

CONCEPT SUMMARY 7–1

Recognized Gain or Loss

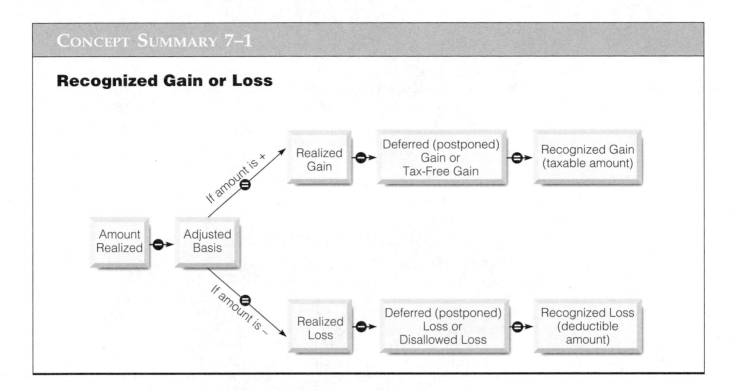

Navy, Inc., purchases Eagle Corporation taxable bonds with a face value of $100,000 for $110,000, thus paying a premium of $10,000. The annual interest rate is 7%, and the bonds mature 10 years from the date of purchase. The annual interest income is $7,000 (7% × $100,000). If Navy elects to amortize the bond premium, the $10,000 premium is deducted over the 10-year period. Navy's basis for the bonds is reduced each year by the amount of the amortization deduction. If the bonds were tax-exempt, amortization of the bond premium and the basis adjustment would be mandatory, and no deduction would be allowed for the amortization. ∎

LEARNING OBJECTIVE 2

Distinguish between realized and recognized gain or loss.

RECOGNIZED GAIN OR LOSS

Recognized gain is the amount of the realized gain that is included in the taxpayer's gross income.[20] A **recognized loss,** on the other hand, is the amount of a realized loss that is deductible for tax purposes.[21] As a general rule, the entire amount of a realized gain or loss is recognized when it is realized.[22]

Concept Summary 7–1 summarizes the realized gain or loss and recognized gain or loss concepts.

NONRECOGNITION OF GAIN OR LOSS

In certain cases, a realized gain or loss is not recognized upon the sale or other disposition of property. One such case involves nontaxable exchanges, which are covered later in this chapter. In addition, realized losses from the sale or exchange of property between certain related parties are not recognized.[23]

---

[20]§ 61(a)(3) and Reg. § 1.61–6(a).
[21]§ 165(a) and Reg. § 1.165–1(a).

[22]§ 1001(c) and Reg. § 1.1002–1(a).
[23]§ 267(a)(1).

Dispositions of Personal-Use Assets.   For individual taxpayers, special rules apply to *personal-use* assets, that is, assets such as a residence or automobile that are not used in any business or investment activity. A loss from the sale, exchange, or condemnation of such assets is not recognized for tax purposes. An exception exists for casualty or theft losses from personal-use assets (refer to Chapter 5). In contrast, any gain realized from the disposition of personal-use assets is generally taxable.

EXAMPLE 8

Freda sells an automobile, which she has held exclusively for personal use, for $6,000. The adjusted basis of the automobile is $5,000. Freda has a realized and recognized gain of $1,000. If she sold this automobile for $4,500, she would have a realized loss of $500, but the loss would not be recognized for tax purposes. ■

RECOVERY OF CAPITAL DOCTRINE

Doctrine Defined.   The **recovery of capital doctrine** pervades all the tax rules relating to property transactions. The doctrine derives its roots from the very essence of the income tax—a tax on income or profit. Because the focus of the tax is on profit, a taxpayer is entitled to recover the cost or other original basis of property acquired without being taxed on that amount.

The cost or other original basis of depreciable property is recovered through annual depreciation deductions. The basis is reduced as the cost is recovered over the period the property is held. Therefore, when property is sold or otherwise disposed of, it is the adjusted basis (unrecovered cost or other basis) that is compared with the amount realized from the disposition to determine realized gain or loss.

EXAMPLE 9

Cardinal Corporation purchased a duplicating machine for $20,000 four years ago and has deducted depreciation totaling $13,000 during those years. Since Cardinal has recovered $13,000 through depreciation, the adjusted basis of this machine is $7,000 ($20,000 − $13,000). If Cardinal sells this machine, it deducts the $7,000 adjusted basis when determining whether it realized a gain or loss upon the disposition. ■

2 *Find more information on this topic at our Web site: **http://wft-entities.swcollege.com**.*

LEARNING OBJECTIVE 3

Explain how basis is determined for various methods of asset acquisition.

Basis Considerations

DETERMINATION OF COST BASIS

As noted earlier, the basis of property is generally the property's cost. Cost is the amount paid for the property in cash or other property.[24] This general rule follows logically from the recovery of capital doctrine; that is, the cost or other basis of property is to be recovered tax-free by the taxpayer.

A *bargain purchase* of property is an exception to the general rule for determining basis. A bargain purchase may result when an employer transfers property to an employee at less than the property's fair market value (as compensation for services) or when a corporation transfers property to a shareholder at less than the property's fair market value (a dividend). These transfers create taxable income for the purchaser equal to the difference between fair market value and purchase price. The

---

[24]§ 1012 and Reg. § 1.1012–1(a).

basis of property acquired in a bargain purchase is the property's fair market value.[25] If the basis of the property were not increased by the bargain amount, the taxpayer would be taxed on this amount again at disposition.

EXAMPLE 10

Wade buys land from his employer for $10,000. The fair market value of the land is $15,000. Wade must include the $5,000 difference between the cost and the fair market value of the land in his gross income. The bargain element represents additional compensation to Wade. His basis for the land is $15,000, the land's fair market value. ∎

Identification Problems. Sometimes, it can be difficult to determine the cost of an asset being sold. This problem is frequently encountered in sales of corporate stock, because a taxpayer may purchase separate lots of a company's stock on different dates and at different prices. When the stock is sold, if the taxpayer cannot identify the specific shares being sold, the stock sold is determined on a first-in, first-out (FIFO) basis. Thus, the holding period and cost of the stock sold are determined by referring to the purchase date and cost of the first lot of stock acquired.[26] But if the stock being sold can be adequately identified, then the basis and holding period of the specific stock sold are used in determining the nature and amount of gain or loss.[27] Thus, to avoid FIFO treatment when the sold securities are held by a broker, it is often necessary to provide specific instructions and receive written confirmation of the securities being sold.

EXAMPLE 11

Pelican, Inc., purchases 100 shares of Olive Corporation stock on July 1, 1999, for $5,000 ($50 a share) and another 100 shares of Olive stock on July 1, 2000, for $6,000 ($60 a share). Pelican sells 50 shares of the stock on January 2, 2001. The cost of the stock sold, assuming Pelican cannot adequately identify the shares, is $50 a share, or $2,500. This is the cost Pelican will compare with the amount realized in determining the gain or loss from the sale. ∎

Allocation Problems. When a taxpayer acquires *several assets in a lump-sum purchase*, the total cost must be allocated among the individual assets.[28] Allocation is necessary for several reasons:

- Some of the assets acquired may be depreciable (e.g., buildings), while others may not be (e.g., land).
- Only a portion of the assets acquired may be sold.
- Some of the assets may be capital or depreciable assets that receive special tax treatment upon subsequent sale or other disposition.

The lump-sum cost is allocated on the basis of the fair market values of the individual assets acquired.

EXAMPLE 12

Magenta Corporation purchases a building and land for $800,000. Because of the depressed nature of the industry in which the seller was operating, Magenta was able to negotiate a very favorable purchase price. Appraisals of the individual assets indicate that the fair market value of the building is $600,000 and that of the land is $400,000. Magenta's basis for the building is $480,000 [($600,000/$1,000,000) × $800,000], and its basis for the land is $320,000 [($400,000/$1,000,000) × $800,000]. ∎

If a business is purchased and **goodwill** (or any other § 197 intangible asset) is involved, a special *residual allocation* rule applies. Initially, the purchase price of the business is allocated to four classes of assets in the following order:

[25]Reg. §§ 1.61–2(d)(2)(i) and 1.301–1(j).
[26]*Kluger Associates, Inc.*, 69 T.C. 925 (1978).
[27]Reg. § 1.1012–1(c)(1).
[28]Reg. § 1.61–6(a).

- Class 1—cash, demand deposits, etc.
- Class 2—marketable securities, certificates of deposit, and foreign currency.
- Class 3—all other assets, except for § 197 intangible assets.
- Class 4—goodwill and other § 197 intangible assets.

Within each class of assets, the purchase price is allocated among the assets on the basis of their respective fair market values, and the amount allocated to any specific asset cannot exceed its fair market value. Therefore, any amount paid in excess of fair market value for tangible assets (classes 1 through 3) is allocated to goodwill and other intangible assets of the acquired business (class 4). This allocation of purchase price is applicable to both the buyer and the seller.[29]

EXAMPLE 13

Roadrunner, Inc., sells its business to Coyote Corporation. The two companies agree that the values of the specific assets are as follows:

Cash	$ 10,000
Marketable securities	5,000
Inventory	35,000
Building	500,000
Land	200,000

After negotiations, Roadrunner and Coyote agree on a sales price of $1 million. Applying the residual method, the purchase price is allocated first to cash, then to marketable securities up to their fair market value. Next, the purchase price is allocated to inventory, building, and land, all on the basis of their fair market values. The residual purchase price is allocated to goodwill, resulting in the following basis of assets to Coyote Corporation:

Cash	$ 10,000
Marketable securities	5,000
Inventory	35,000
Building	500,000
Land	200,000
Goodwill	250,000

In the case of *nontaxable stock dividends*, the allocation depends on whether the dividend is a common stock dividend on common stock or a preferred stock dividend on common stock. If the dividend is common on common, the cost of the original common shares is allocated to the total shares owned after the dividend.[30]

EXAMPLE 14

Yellow, Inc., owns 100 shares of Sparrow Corporation common stock for which it paid $1,100. Yellow receives a 10% common stock dividend, giving it a new total of 110 shares. Before the stock dividend, Yellow's basis was $11 per share ($1,100 ÷ 100 shares). The basis of each share after the stock dividend is $10 ($1,100 ÷ 110 shares). ■

If the dividend is preferred stock on common, the cost of the original common shares is allocated between the common and preferred shares on the basis of their relative fair market values on the date of distribution.[31]

[29] § 1060 and Temp.Reg. § 1.338(b)–1T.
[30] §§ 305(a) and 307(a). The holding period of the new shares includes the holding period of the old shares. § 1223(5) and Reg. § 1.1223–1(e). See Chapter 8 for a discussion of the importance of the holding period.
[31] Reg. § 1.307–1(a).

EXAMPLE 15

Brown Company owns 100 shares of Cardinal Corporation common stock for which it paid $1,000. Brown receives a stock dividend of 50 shares of preferred stock on the Cardinal common stock. The fair market values on the date of distribution of the preferred stock dividend are $30 a share for common stock and $40 a share for preferred stock. Thus, the total fair market value is $3,000 ($30 × 100) for common stock and $2,000 ($40 × 50) for preferred stock. The basis of Brown's common stock after the dividend is $600, or $6 a share [($3,000/$5,000) × $1,000], and the basis of the preferred stock is $400, or $8 a share [($2,000/$5,000) × $1,000]. ■

GIFT BASIS

Although business entities can neither make nor receive gratuitous transfers, ownership interests in such entities are frequently the subject of lifetime and testamentary gifts. Partnership interests, stock in closely or publicly held corporations, and other assets are regularly passed from one generation of owners to another for a variety of family and business reasons. Special basis rules apply to such transfers.

When a taxpayer receives property as a gift, there is no cost to the donee (recipient). Thus, under the cost basis provision, the donee's basis would be zero. With a zero basis, if the donee sold the property, the entire amount realized would be treated as taxable gain. Instead, the Code[32] assigns a basis to the property received that depends upon the following:

- The date of the gift.
- The basis of the property to the donor.
- The fair market value of the property.
- The amount of the gift tax paid, if any.

Gift Basis Rules if No Gift Tax Is Paid. If a property's fair market value on the date of gift exceeds the donor's basis in the property, the donor's basis carries over to the new owner.[33] This basis is called a *carryover basis* and is used in determining the donee's gain or loss.

EXAMPLE 16

Melissa purchased stock two years ago for $10,000. She gave the stock to her son, Joe, this year, when the fair market value was $15,000. No gift tax was paid on the transfer. Joe subsequently sells the property for $15,000. Joe's basis is $10,000, and he has a realized gain of $5,000. ■

If the property's fair market value on the date of gift is *lower* than the donor's basis in the property, the donee's basis cannot be determined until the donee disposes of the property. For the purpose of determining *gain*, the donor's basis will carry over, as in the preceding example. But for determining *loss*, the property's basis will be its fair market value when the gift was made.

EXAMPLE 17

Burt purchased stock three years ago for $10,000. He gave the stock to his son, Cliff, this year, when the fair market value was $7,000. No gift tax was paid on the transfer. Cliff later sells the stock for $6,000. For determining loss, Cliff's basis is $7,000, and the realized loss from the sale is $1,000 ($6,000 amount realized − $7,000 basis). ■

---

[32]§ 1015(a).
[33]§ 1015(a) and Reg. § 1.1015–1(a)(1). See Reg. § 1.1015–1(a)(3) for cases in which the facts necessary to determine the donor's adjusted basis are unknown. See Example 22 for the effect of depreciation deductions by the donee.

Note that this loss basis rule prevents the donee from receiving a tax benefit from a decline in value that occurred while the donor held the property. Therefore, in the preceding example, Cliff has a loss of only $1,000 rather than a loss of $4,000. The $3,000 difference represents the decline in value that occurred while Burt held the property. Ironically, however, a donee might be subject to income tax on the appreciation that occurred while the donor held the property, as illustrated in Example 16.

In any case, the operation of this dual basis rule produces a curious anomaly: if the sales proceeds fall *between* the donor's adjusted basis and the property's fair market value at the date of gift, no gain or loss is recognized.

EXAMPLE 18

Assume the same facts as in the preceding example, except that Cliff sells the stock for $8,000. To calculate gain, he would use a basis of $10,000, the donor's adjusted basis. But when a $10,000 basis is compared to $8,000 of sales proceeds, a *loss* is produced. Yet in determining loss, Cliff must use the property's fair market value at the date of gift—namely, $7,000. When a $7,000 basis is compared to sales proceeds of $8,000, a *gain* is produced. Accordingly, no gain or loss is recognized on this transaction. ■

PLANNING CONSIDERATIONS

Gift Planning

Gifts of *appreciated property* can produce tax savings if the donee is in a lower tax bracket than the donor. The carryover basis rule effectively shifts the tax on the property's appreciation to the new owner, even if all of the appreciation arose while the property was owned by the donor.

On the other hand, donors should generally avoid making gifts of property that is worth less than the donor's adjusted basis (loss property). The operation of the basis rule for losses may result in either (1) a realized loss that is not deductible by either the donor or the donee or (2) reduced tax benefits when the loss is recognized by a donee facing lower marginal tax rates. Unless the property is expected to rebound in value before it is sold, a donor would be better advised to sell the property that has declined in value, deduct the resulting loss, and then transfer the proceeds to the prospective donee.

Adjustment for Gift Tax.   If gift taxes are paid by the donor, the donee's basis may exceed the donor's basis. This occurs only if the fair market value of the property at the date of the gift exceeds the donor's adjusted basis (i.e., the property has appreciated in value). The portion of the gift tax paid that is related to the appreciation is added to the donor's basis in calculating the donee's basis for the property. In this circumstance, the following formula is used for calculating the donee's basis:[34]

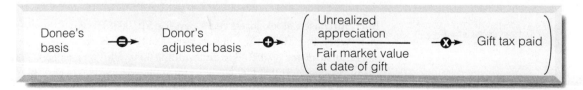

$$\text{Donee's basis} = \text{Donor's adjusted basis} + \left(\frac{\text{Unrealized appreciation}}{\text{Fair market value at date of gift}} \times \text{Gift tax paid} \right)$$

EXAMPLE 19

Bonnie made a gift of stock to Peggy earlier this year, when the fair market value of the stock was $40,000. Bonnie paid gift tax of $4,000. She had purchased the stock in 1984 for

---

[34]§ 1015(d)(6).

$10,000. Because the unrealized appreciation is $30,000 ($40,000 fair market value − $10,000 adjusted basis) and the fair market value is $40,000, three-fourths ($30,000/$40,000) of the gift tax paid is added to the basis of the property. Peggy's basis in the property (for determining both gain and loss) is $13,000 [$10,000 + $3,000 (¾ of the $4,000 gift tax)]. ■

EXAMPLE 20

Don made a gift of stock to Matt earlier this year, when the fair market value of the stock was $40,000. Don paid gift tax of $4,000. Don had purchased the stock in 1984 for $45,000. Because there is no unrealized appreciation at the date of the gift, none of the gift tax paid is added to Don's basis in calculating Matt's basis. ■

For *gifts made before 1977*, the full amount of the gift tax paid is added to the donor's basis. However, the ceiling on this total is the fair market value of the property at the date of the gift. Thus, in Example 19, if the gift had been made before 1977, the basis of the property would be $14,000 ($10,000 + $4,000). In Example 20, the donee's basis would still be $45,000 ($45,000 + $0) for gain and $40,000 for loss.

Holding Period. The **holding period** for property acquired by gift begins on the date the donor acquired the property,[35] unless the special circumstance requiring use of the property's fair market value at the date of gift applies. If so, the holding period starts on the date of the gift.[36] The significance of the holding period for capital assets is discussed in Chapter 8.

The following example summarizes the basis and holding period rules for gift property.

EXAMPLE 21

Jill acquired 100 shares of Wren Corporation stock on December 30, 1994, for $40,000. On January 3 of this year, when the stock has a fair market value of $38,000, Jill gives it to Dennis and pays gift tax of $4,000. The basis is not increased by a portion of the gift tax paid because the property has not appreciated in value at the time of the gift. Therefore, Dennis's basis for determining gain is $40,000. Dennis's basis for determining loss is $38,000 (fair market value), because the fair market value on the date of the gift is less than the donor's adjusted basis.

- If Dennis sells the stock for $45,000, he has a recognized gain of $5,000. The holding period for determining whether the capital gain is short term or long term begins on December 30, 1994, the date Jill acquired the property.
- If Dennis sells the stock for $36,000, he has a recognized loss of $2,000. The holding period for determining whether the capital loss is short term or long term begins on January 3 of this year, the date of the gift.
- If Dennis sells the property for $39,000, no gain or loss is recognized because the amount realized is between the property's fair market value when given ($38,000) and the donor's adjusted basis of $40,000. ■

Basis for Depreciation. The basis for depreciation on depreciable gift property is the donee's basis for determining gain.[37] This rule is applicable even if the donee later sells the property at a loss and uses the property's fair market value at the date of gift in calculating the amount of the realized loss.

EXAMPLE 22

Vito gave a machine to Tina earlier this year. At that time, the adjusted basis was $32,000 (cost of $40,000 − accumulated depreciation of $8,000), and the fair market value was $26,000.

---

[35]§ 1223(2) and Reg. § 1.1223–1(b).
[36]Rev.Rul. 59–86, 1959–1 C.B. 209.

[37]§ 1011 and Reg. §§ 1.1011–1 and 1.167(g)–1.

No gift tax was due. Tina's basis for determining gain is $32,000, and her loss basis is $26,000. During this year, Tina deducts depreciation (cost recovery) of $10,240 ($32,000 × 32%). At the end of this year, Tina's basis determinations are calculated as follows:

	Gain Basis	Loss Basis
Donor's basis or fair market value	$ 32,000	$ 26,000
Depreciation	(10,240)	(10,240)
	$ 21,760	$ 15,760

PROPERTY ACQUIRED FROM A DECEDENT

General Rules. The basis of property acquired from a decedent is generally the property's fair market value at the date of death (referred to as the *primary valuation amount*).[38] The property's basis is the fair market value six months after the date of death if the executor or administrator of the estate *elects* the alternate valuation date for estate tax purposes. This amount is referred to as the *alternate valuation amount*.

3 *Find more information on this topic at our Web site: **http://wft-entities.swcollege.com**.*

EXAMPLE 23

Linda and various other family members inherited stock in a closely held corporation from Linda's father, who died earlier this year. At the date of death, her father's adjusted basis for the stock Linda inherited was $35,000. The stock's fair market value at the date of death was $50,000. The alternate valuation date was not elected. Linda's basis for income tax purposes is $50,000. This is commonly referred to as a *stepped-up basis*. ■

EXAMPLE 24

Assume the same facts as in the preceding example, except that the stock's fair market value at the date of death was $20,000. Linda's basis for income tax purposes is $20,000. This is commonly referred to as a *stepped-down basis*. ■

No estate tax return must be filed for estates below a threshold amount (refer to Chapter 1). In such cases, the alternate valuation date and amount are not available. Even if an estate tax return is filed and the executor elects the alternate valuation date, the six-months-after-death date is available only for property that the executor has not distributed before this date. For any property distributed or otherwise disposed of by the executor during the six-month period preceding the alternate valuation date, the adjusted basis to the beneficiary will equal the fair market value on the date of distribution or other disposition.[39]

The alternate valuation date can be elected *only if*, as a result of the election, *both* the value of the gross estate and the estate tax liability are lower than they would have been if the primary valuation date had been used. This provision prevents the alternate valuation election from being used to increase the basis of the property to the beneficiary for income tax purposes without simultaneously increasing the estate tax liability (because of estate tax deductions or credits).[40]

EXAMPLE 25

Nancy inherited investment real estate from her father, who died earlier this year. Her father's adjusted basis for the property at the date of death was $35,000. The property's fair

[38]§ 1014(a).
[39]§ 2032(a)(1) and Rev.Rul. 56–60, 1956–1 C.B. 443.
[40]§ 2032(c).

market value was $750,000 at the date of death and $760,000 six months after death. The alternate valuation date cannot be elected because the value of the gross estate has increased during the six-month period. Nancy's basis for income tax purposes is $750,000. ■

EXAMPLE 26

Assume the same facts as in Example 25, except that the property's fair market value six months after death was $745,000. If the executor elects the alternate valuation date, Nancy's basis for income tax purposes is $745,000. ■

EXAMPLE 27

Assume the same facts as in Example 26, except that the property is distributed four months after the date of the decedent's death. At the distribution date, the property's fair market value is $747,500. Since the executor elected the alternate valuation date, Nancy's basis for income tax purposes is $747,500. ■

4 *Find more information on this topic at our Web site: **http://wft-entities.swcollege.com**.*

PLANNING CONSIDERATIONS

Property from a Decedent

If a taxpayer *retains appreciated property* until death, the property's basis will be "stepped up" to its fair market value at that time. Thus, no income tax will be paid on the property's appreciation by either the former owner (the decedent) or the new owner (the heir).

On the other hand, *depreciated property should be sold* prior to death. Otherwise, the property's basis in the heir's hands will be its declined fair market value, and neither the decedent nor the heir will be able to deduct the loss that occurred while the property was owned by the decedent.

Deathbed Gifts. The Code contains a provision designed to eliminate a tax avoidance technique occasionally described as *deathbed gifts*. This technique involves a donor making a gift of appreciated property to a dying person with the understanding that the donor (or the donor's spouse) will inherit the property on the donee's death. If a person (or that person's spouse) receives from a decedent property that this person gave to the decedent during the year before the decedent's death, the property does *not* get a stepped-up basis. Instead, the basis of that property is the donor's adjusted basis.[41]

EXAMPLE 28

Ned gives stock to his uncle, Vern, this year. Ned's basis for the stock is $1,000, and the fair market value is $9,000. No gift tax is due. Eight months later, Ned inherits the stock from Vern. At the date of Vern's death, the fair market value of the stock is $12,000. Ned's adjusted basis for the stock is $1,000. ■

Holding Period of Property Acquired from a Decedent. The holding period of property acquired from a decedent is *deemed to be long term* (held for the required long-term holding period). This provision applies regardless of whether the property is disposed of at a gain or at a loss.[42]

---

[41]§ 1014(e).   [42]§ 1223(11).

LEARNING OBJECTIVE 4

Describe various loss
disallowance provisions.

DISALLOWED LOSSES

Related Taxpayers.   Section 267 provides that realized losses from sales or exchanges of property between certain related parties are not recognized. This loss disallowance provision applies to several types of related-party transactions. The most common involve (1) members of a family and (2) an individual and a corporation in which the individual owns, directly or indirectly, more than 50 percent in value of the corporation's outstanding stock. Section 707 provides a similar loss disallowance provision where the related parties are a partner and a partnership in which the partner owns, directly or indirectly, more than 50 percent of the capital interests or profits interests in the partnership. Neither provision, however, prevents the recognition of *gains* between related parties. The rules governing the relationships covered by § 267 were discussed in Chapter 4.

If income-producing or business property is transferred to a related party and a loss is disallowed, the basis of the property to the recipient is the property's cost to the transferee. However, if a subsequent sale or other disposition of the property by the original transferee results in a realized gain, the amount of gain is reduced by the loss that was previously disallowed. This *right of offset* is not applicable if the original sale involved the sale of a personal-use asset (e.g., a personal residence). Furthermore, the right of offset is available only to the original transferee (the related-party buyer). See Example 17 and Example 18 in Chapter 4.

5 *Find more information on this topic at our Web site: http://wft-entities.swcollege.com.*

Wash Sales.   Section 1091 stipulates that in certain cases, a realized loss on the sale or exchange of stock or securities is not recognized. Specifically, if a taxpayer sells or exchanges stock or securities and within 30 days before *or* after the date of the sale or exchange acquires *substantially identical* stock or securities, any loss realized from the sale or exchange is not recognized because the transaction is a **wash sale.**[43] The term *acquire* means acquire by purchase or in a taxable exchange and includes an option to purchase substantially identical securities. *Substantially identical* means the same in all important particulars. Corporate bonds and preferred stock are normally not considered substantially identical to a corporation's common stock. However, if the bonds and preferred stock are convertible into common stock, they may be considered substantially identical under certain circumstances.[44] Attempts to avoid the application of the wash sale rules by having a related taxpayer repurchase the securities have been unsuccessful.[45] The wash sale provisions do *not* apply to gains.

Recognition of the loss is disallowed because the taxpayer is considered to be in substantially the same economic position after the sale and repurchase as before. This disallowance rule does not apply to taxpayers engaged in the business of buying and selling securities.[46] Investors, however, are not allowed to create losses through wash sales to offset income for tax purposes.

A realized loss that is not recognized is added to the *basis* of the substantially identical stock or securities whose acquisition resulted in the nonrecognition of loss.[47] In other words, the basis of the replacement stock or securities is increased by the amount of the unrecognized loss. If the loss were not added to the basis of the newly acquired stock or securities, the taxpayer would never recover the entire

---

[43]§ 1091(a) and Reg. §§ 1.1091–1(a) and (f).
[44]Rev.Rul. 56–406, 1956–2 C.B. 523.
[45]*McWilliams v. Comm.*, 47–1 USTC ¶9289, 35 AFTR 1184, 67 S.Ct. 1477 (USSC, 1947).

[46]Reg. § 1.1091–1(a).
[47]§ 1091(d) and Reg. § 1.1091–2(a).

basis of the old stock or securities. As a result, the wash sale rule operates to *defer* the recognition of the taxpayer's loss.

EXAMPLE 29

Oriole Manufacturing Company sold 50 shares of Green Corporation stock (adjusted basis of $10,000) for $8,000. Ten days later, Oriole purchased 50 shares of the same stock for $7,000. Oriole's realized loss of $2,000 ($8,000 amount realized − $10,000 adjusted basis) is not recognized because it resulted from a wash sale. Oriole's basis in the newly acquired stock is $9,000 ($7,000 purchase price + $2,000 unrecognized loss from the wash sale). ∎

The basis of the new stock or securities includes the unrecovered portion of the basis of the formerly held stock or securities. Therefore, the *holding period* of the new stock or securities begins on the date of acquisition of the old stock or securities.[48]

A taxpayer may acquire fewer shares than the number sold in a wash sale. In this case, the loss from the sale is prorated between recognized and unrecognized loss on the basis of the ratio of the number of shares acquired to the number of shares sold.[49]

PLANNING CONSIDERATIONS

Avoiding Wash Sales

The wash sale restriction can be avoided by replacing the sold security with a *similar* but not "substantially identical" security. For example, if IBM common stock is sold to claim an unrealized loss, the taxpayer could immediately acquire Intel common stock without triggering the wash sale rule.

Nontax considerations must also come into play, however, because IBM and Intel are two different companies with different investment prospects. Though both securities will be affected by many of the same factors, they will also be subject to different factors that may be even more significant than the ones they share.

CONVERSION OF PROPERTY FROM PERSONAL USE TO BUSINESS OR INCOME-PRODUCING USE

As discussed previously, losses from the sale of personal-use assets are not recognized for tax purposes, but losses from the sale of business and income-producing assets are deductible. Can a taxpayer convert a personal-use asset that has declined in value to business or income-producing use and then sell the asset to recognize a business or income-producing loss? The tax law prevents this practice by specifying that the *basis for determining loss* on personal-use assets converted to business or income-producing use is the *lower* of the property's adjusted basis or its fair market value on the date of conversion.[50] The *gain basis* for converted property is the property's adjusted basis on the date of conversion, regardless of whether property's use is business, income-producing, or personal in nature.

EXAMPLE 30

Diane's personal residence has an adjusted basis of $175,000 and a fair market value of $160,000. When she converts the personal residence to residential rental property on January 1, her basis for determining loss is $160,000 (lower of $175,000 adjusted basis and fair market

---

[48]§ 1223(4) and Reg. § 1.1223–1(d).
[49]§ 1091(b) and Reg. § 1.1091–1(c).

[50]Reg. § 1.165–9(b)(2).

value of $160,000). The $15,000 decline in value is a personal loss and can never be recognized for tax purposes. Diane's basis for determining gain is $175,000. ∎

The basis for determining loss is also the *basis for depreciating* the converted property.[51] This is an exception to the general rule that the basis for depreciation is the basis for determining gain (e.g., property received by gift). This exception prevents the taxpayer from recovering a personal loss indirectly through depreciation of the higher original basis. Once property is converted, both its basis for loss and its basis for gain are adjusted for depreciation deductions from the date of conversion to the date of disposition.

EXAMPLE 31

Assume the same facts as in Example 30. The MACRS cost recovery deduction for the current year is $5,576 ($160,000 × 3.485%). Thus, at the end of the current year, Diane's adjusted basis for gain for the rental property is $169,424 ($175,000 – $5,576), and her adjusted basis for loss is $154,424 ($160,000 – $5,576). ∎

6   *Find more information on this topic at our Web site:* ***http://wft-entities.swcollege.com.***

SUMMARY OF BASIS ADJUSTMENTS

Some of the more common items that either increase or decrease the basis of an asset appear in Concept Summary 7–2.

In discussing the topic of basis, a number of specific techniques for determining basis have been presented. Although the various techniques are responsive to and mandated by transactions occurring in the marketplace, they possess enough common characteristics to be categorized as follows:

- The basis of the asset may be determined by its cost.
- The basis of the asset may be determined by the basis of another asset.
- The basis of the asset may be determined by its fair market value.
- The basis of the asset may be determined by the basis of the asset in the hands of another taxpayer.

7   *Find more information on this topic at our Web site:* ***http://wft-entities.swcollege.com.***

General Concept of a Nontaxable Exchange

A taxpayer who is going to replace a productive asset (e.g., machinery) used in a trade or business may structure the transaction as a sale of the old asset and the purchase of a new asset. When this approach is used, any realized gain or loss on the sale of the old asset is recognized. The basis of the new asset is its cost. Alternatively, the taxpayer may be able to trade the old asset for the new asset. This exchange of assets may produce beneficial tax consequences as a nontaxable exchange.

The tax law recognizes that nontaxable exchanges result in a change in the *form* but not the *substance* of a taxpayer's relative economic position. The replacement property received in the exchange is viewed as essentially a continuation of the old investment.[52] Additional justification for nontaxable treatment is that this type

---

[51]Reg. § 1.167(g)–1.   [52]Reg. § 1.1002–1(c).

CONCEPT SUMMARY 7–2

Adjustments to Basis

Item	Effect	Refer to Chapter	Explanation
Amortization of bond discount.	Increase	7	Amortization is mandatory for certain taxable bonds and elective for tax-exempt bonds.
Amortization of bond premium.	Decrease	7	Amortization is mandatory for tax-exempt bonds and elective for taxable bonds.
Amortization of covenant not to compete.	Decrease	4	Covenant must be for a definite and limited time period. The amortization period is a statutory period of 15 years.
Amortization of intangibles.	Decrease	4	Intangibles are amortized over a 15-year period.
Bad debts.	Decrease	5	Most taxpayers must use the specific charge-off method.
Capital additions.	Increase	7	Certain items, at the taxpayer's election, can be capitalized or deducted.
Casualty.	Decrease	7	For a casualty loss, the amount of the adjustment is the sum of the deductible loss and the insurance proceeds received. For a casualty gain, the amount of the adjustment is the insurance proceeds received reduced by the recognized gain.
Condemnation.	Decrease	7	See casualty explanation.
Cost recovery.	Decrease	4	§ 168 is applicable to tangible assets placed in service after 1980 whose useful life is expressed in terms of years.
Depletion.	Decrease	4	Use the greater of cost or percentage depletion. Percentage depletion can be deducted even when the basis is zero.
Depreciation.	Decrease	4	§ 167 is applicable to tangible assets placed in service before 1981 and to tangible assets not depreciated in terms of years.
Easement.	Decrease		If the taxpayer does not retain any use of the land, all of the basis is allocable to the easement transaction. However, if only part of the land is affected by the easement, only part of the basis is allocable to the easement transaction.
Improvements by lessee to lessor's property.	Increase	3	Adjustment occurs only if the lessor is required to include the fair market value of the improvements in gross income under § 109.
Imputed interest.	Decrease	6	Amount deducted is not part of the cost of the asset.
Inventory: lower of cost or market.	Decrease	6	Not available if the LIFO method is used.
Limited expensing under § 179.	Decrease	4	Occurs only if the taxpayer elects § 179 treatment.
Medical capital expenditure deducted as a medical expense.	Decrease	15	Adjustment is the amount of the deduction (the effect on basis is to increase it by the amount of the capital expenditure net of the deduction).

Item	Effect	Refer to Chapter	Explanation
Real estate taxes: apportionment between the buyer and seller.	Increase or decrease	4	To the extent the buyer pays the seller's pro rata share, the buyer's basis is increased. To the extent the seller pays the buyer's pro rata share, the buyer's basis is decreased.
Rebate from manufacturer.	Decrease		Since the rebate is treated as an adjustment to the purchase price, it is not included in the buyer's gross income.
Stock dividend.	Decrease	7	Adjustment occurs only if the stock dividend is nontaxable. While the basis per share decreases, the total stock basis does not change.
Stock rights.	Decrease	10	Adjustment to stock basis occurs only for nontaxable stock rights and only if the fair market value of the rights is at least 15% of the fair market value of the stock or, if less than 15%, the taxpayer elects to allocate the basis between the stock and the rights.
Theft.	Decrease	5	See casualty explanation.

of transaction does not provide the taxpayer with the wherewithal to pay the tax on any realized gain.

The nonrecognition provisions for nontaxable exchanges do not apply to realized losses from the sale or exchange of personal-use assets. Such losses are never recognized (i.e., they are disallowed) because they are personal in nature.

In contrast, in a **nontaxable exchange,** recognition of gains or losses is *postponed* (i.e., deferred) until the new property received in the nontaxable exchange is subsequently disposed of in a taxable transaction. This is accomplished by assigning a carryover basis to the replacement property.

EXAMPLE 32

Starling Management Company exchanges property with an adjusted basis of $10,000 and a fair market value of $12,000 for property with a fair market value of $12,000. The transaction qualifies for nontaxable exchange treatment. Starling has a realized gain of $2,000 ($12,000 amount realized – $10,000 adjusted basis). Its recognized gain is $0. Starling's basis in the replacement property is a carryover basis of $10,000. Assume the replacement property is nondepreciable and Starling subsequently sells it for $12,000. The realized and recognized gain will be the $2,000 gain that was postponed (deferred) in the nontaxable transaction. If the replacement property is depreciable, the carryover basis of $10,000 is used in calculating depreciation. ■

In some nontaxable exchanges, only some of the property involved in the transaction qualifies for nonrecognition treatment. If the taxpayer receives cash or other nonqualifying property, part or all of the realized gain from the exchange is recognized. In these situations, gain is recognized because the taxpayer has changed or improved its relative economic position and has the wherewithal to pay income tax to the extent of cash or other property received.

It is important to distinguish between a nontaxable disposition (or nonrecognition transaction, as the term is used in the statute) and a tax-free transaction. As previously mentioned, the term *nontaxable* refers to postponement of recognition via some version of carryover basis. In a *tax-free* transaction, the nonrecognition is permanent (e.g., see the discussion later in this chapter of the exclusion of gain from the sale of a principal residence).

Either way, nontaxable and tax-free transactions must be understood as exceptions to the Code's general rule that gains and losses are recognized when they are realized. These exceptions have their own sets of requirements, limitations, and restrictions, all of which must be satisfied for a transaction to be characterized as nontaxable or tax-free. Otherwise, the general rule of recognition applies to the gain or loss at hand.

LEARNING OBJECTIVE 5

Apply the nonrecognition provisions and basis determination rules for like-kind exchanges.

Like-Kind Exchanges—§ 1031

Section 1031 provides for nontaxable exchange treatment if the following requirements are satisfied:[53]

- The form of the transaction is an exchange.
- Both the property transferred and the property received are held either for productive use in a trade or business or for investment.
- The property is like-kind property.

Qualifying **like-kind exchanges** include exchanges of business for business, business for investment, investment for business, or investment for investment property. Property held for personal use does not qualify under the like-kind exchange provisions. Thus, the purpose for which the property is held by the taxpayer in question is critical. For example, if Janet uses a small truck in her trade or business, it may qualify for like-kind treatment, but if she uses this truck as her personal-use vehicle, it is ineligible for nonrecognition treatment under § 1031.

Some assets are excluded from like-kind treatment by statute. These excluded assets include a taxpayer's inventory or "stock in trade," as well as most forms of investment other than real estate. Thus, stocks, bonds, partnership interests (whether general or limited), and other securities, even though held for investment, do not qualify for like-kind exchange treatment.

The nonrecognition provision for like-kind exchanges is *mandatory* rather than elective. A taxpayer who wants to recognize a realized gain or loss will have to structure the transaction in a form that does not satisfy the statutory requirements for a like-kind exchange.

PLANNING CONSIDERATIONS

Like-Kind Exchanges

Because nonrecognition of gain or loss is mandatory in like-kind exchanges, a taxpayer must affirmatively *avoid such exchanges* if nonrecognition treatment is not desired. If an asset is worth less than its adjusted basis, a *loss would result* from its disposition. Accordingly, the taxpayer should sell this property outright to ensure the deductibility of the loss, assuming it would otherwise be deductible.

---

[53]§ 1031(a) and Reg. § 1.1031(a)–1(a).

Even if *disposition would result in a gain*, a taxpayer might want to recognize this gain in the current taxable year. If so, a like-kind exchange should be avoided. Circumstances suggesting this strategy include:

- Unused capital loss carryovers, especially if the taxpayer is a corporation for which such carryovers are limited in duration (see Chapters 3 and 8).

- Unused net operating loss carryovers (see Chapter 5).
- Unused general business credit carryovers (see Chapter 13).
- Suspended or current passive activity losses (see Chapter 5).
- Expectations of higher tax rates in future years.

LIKE-KIND PROPERTY

The term *like-kind* is explained in the Regulations as follows: "The words 'like-kind' refer to the nature or character of the property and not to its grade or quality. One kind or class of property may not . . . be exchanged for property of a different kind or class."[54] The Regulations go on to explain that although real estate can be exchanged only for other real estate, the definition of real estate is quite broad. *Real estate* (or realty) includes principally rental buildings, office and store buildings, manufacturing plants, warehouses, and land. It is immaterial whether real estate is improved or unimproved. Thus, unimproved land can be exchanged for an apartment house. On the other hand, real property located in the United States exchanged for foreign real property (and vice versa) does not qualify as like-kind property. A similar provision applies to exchanges of foreign and domestic personalty.

In any case, real estate cannot be exchanged in a like-kind transaction for personalty. *Personalty* includes tangible assets other than real estate, such as machinery, equipment, trucks, automobiles, furniture, and fixtures. Thus, an exchange of a machine (personalty) for a small office building (realty) is not a like-kind exchange. Finally, the Code mandates that livestock of different sexes are not like-kind property.

8 *Find more information on this topic at our Web site:* **http://wft-entities.swcollege.com**.

EXAMPLE 33

Pheasant, Inc., made the following exchanges during the taxable year:

    a. Inventory for a machine used in business.
    b. Land held for investment for a building used in business.
    c. Stock held for investment for equipment used in business.
    d. A business truck for a business truck.
    e. Livestock for livestock of a different sex.
    f. Land held for investment in New York for land held for investment in London.

Exchanges (b), investment real property for business real property, and (d), business personalty for business personalty, qualify as exchanges of like-kind property. Exchanges (a), inventory; (c), stock; (e), livestock of different sexes; and (f), U.S. and foreign real estate do not qualify. ■

The Regulations dealing with § 1031 like-kind exchanges provide greater specificity when determining whether depreciable tangible personalty is of a like kind. Such property held for productive use in a business is of like kind only if the exchanged property is within the same *general business asset class* (as specified by

---

[54]Reg. § 1.1031(a)–1(b).

the IRS in Rev.Proc. 87–56) or the same *product class* (as specified by the Department of Commerce). Property included in a general business asset class is evaluated exclusively under the Revenue Procedure, rather than under the product class system.

The following are examples of general business asset classes:

- Office furniture, fixtures, and equipment.
- Information systems (computers and peripheral equipment).
- Airplanes.
- Automobiles and taxis.
- Buses.
- Light general-purpose trucks.
- Heavy general-purpose trucks.

These Regulations narrow the range of depreciable tangible personalty subject to § 1031 like-kind exchange treatment. For example, the exchange of office equipment for a computer does not qualify as an exchange of like-kind property. Even though both assets are depreciable tangible personalty, they are not like-kind property because they are in different general business asset classes. Accordingly, any realized *gain or loss* on the office equipment would be recognized currently.

 9 *Find more information on this topic at our Web site: **http://wft-entities.swcollege.com**.*

Finally, a special provision applies if the taxpayers involved in the exchange are *related parties* under § 267(b). To qualify for like-kind exchange treatment, the taxpayer and the related party must not dispose of the like-kind property received in the exchange for two years after the date of the exchange. If such a disposition does occur, the postponed gain is recognized as of that disposition. Dispositions due to death, involuntary conversions, and certain non-tax avoidance transactions are excepted from this rule.

EXCHANGE REQUIREMENT

The transaction must generally involve a direct exchange of property to qualify as a like-kind exchange. The sale of old property and the purchase of new property, even though like kind, is not an exchange. However, the Code does provide a limited procedure for real estate to be exchanged for qualifying property that is acquired subsequent to the exchange.[55]

Of course, the taxpayer may want to avoid nontaxable exchange treatment. Recognition of gain gives the taxpayer a higher basis for depreciation. To the extent that such gains would, if recognized, either receive favorable capital gain treatment or be passive activity income that could offset passive activity losses, it might be preferable to avoid the nonrecognition provisions through an indirect exchange transaction. For example, a taxpayer may sell property to one company, recognize the gain, and subsequently purchase similar property from another company. The taxpayer may also want to avoid nontaxable exchange treatment so that a realized loss can be recognized.

BOOT

If the taxpayer in a like-kind exchange gives or receives some property that is not like-kind property, recognition may occur. Property that is not like-kind property, including cash, is often referred to as **boot.** Although the term *boot* does not appear

---

[55]§ 1031(a)(3).

ARE THE CLEVELAND INDIANS STILL THE CLEVELAND INDIANS?

The Cleveland Indians were in the World Series in 1995 (losing to the Atlanta Braves) and made it to the American League playoffs (losing to the Baltimore Orioles) in 1996. Some fans were concerned, however, in March 1997, when the Indians traded one of their key players, Kenny Lofton, together with a relief pitcher to the Atlanta Braves for outfielders David Justice and Marquis Grissom. Many wondered whether the trade would help or hurt the Indians in their future bids for the championship.

General manager John Hart had an additional question when he made the deal: Did the trade qualify for § 1031 treatment? Since he made the trade, Hart must have believed that the answer to both questions was yes. Cleveland's performance in the 1997 postseason indicated that Hart knew what he was doing. The Indians came within two outs of winning game 7 of the World Series.

To show even more heart, Hart reacquired Lofton for the 1998 season, and the Indians made it to the finals of the American League playoffs, losing to the Yankees. For the 1999 season, Hart traded Grissom to Milwaukee for pitching help and signed free-agent Roberto Alomar, perhaps the best second baseman in organized baseball. Since then, Hart continues to be a frequent trader in his quest for the Indians to win the World Series.

SOURCE: Adapted from *ESPN Sportszone*.

in the Code, tax practitioners commonly use it rather than saying "property that does not qualify as like-kind property."

The *receipt* of boot will trigger recognition of gain if there is realized gain. The amount of the recognized gain is the *lesser* of the boot received or the realized gain (realized gain serves as the ceiling on recognition).

EXAMPLE 34

Blue, Inc., and White Corporation exchange machinery, and the exchange qualifies as like kind under § 1031. Since Blue's machinery (adjusted basis of $20,000) is worth $24,000 and White's machine has a fair market value of $19,000, White also gives Blue cash of $5,000. Blue's recognized gain is $4,000, the lesser of the realized gain of $4,000 ($24,000 amount realized − $20,000 adjusted basis) or the fair market value of the boot received of $5,000. ■

EXAMPLE 35

Assume the same facts as in the preceding example, except that White's machine is worth $21,000 (not $19,000). Under these circumstances, White gives Blue cash of $3,000 to make up the difference. Blue's recognized gain is $3,000, the lesser of the realized gain of $4,000 ($24,000 amount realized − $20,000 adjusted basis) or the fair market value of the boot received of $3,000. ■

The receipt of boot does not result in recognition if there is realized loss.

EXAMPLE 36

Assume the same facts as in Example 35, except that the adjusted basis of Blue's machine is $30,000. Blue's realized loss is $6,000 ($24,000 amount realized − $30,000 adjusted basis). The receipt of the boot of $5,000 does not trigger recognition of Blue's loss. ■

The *giving* of boot does not trigger recognition if the boot consists solely of cash.

EXAMPLE 37

Flicker, Inc., and Gadwall Corporation exchange equipment in a like-kind exchange. Flicker receives equipment with a fair market value of $25,000 and transfers equipment worth $21,000 (adjusted basis of $15,000) and cash of $4,000. Flicker's realized gain is $6,000 ($25,000 amount realized − $15,000 adjusted basis − $4,000 cash), none of which is recognized. ■

If, however, the boot given is appreciated or depreciated property, gain or loss is recognized to the extent of the difference between the adjusted basis and the fair market value of the boot. For this purpose, *appreciated or depreciated property* is property with an adjusted basis that differs from fair market value.

EXAMPLE 38

Assume the same facts as in the preceding example, except that Flicker transfers equipment worth $10,000 (adjusted basis of $12,000) and boot worth $15,000 (adjusted basis of $9,000). Flicker's realized gain appears to be $4,000 ($25,000 amount realized − $21,000 adjusted basis). Since realization previously has served as a ceiling on recognition, it appears that the recognized gain is $4,000 (lower of realized gain of $4,000 or amount of appreciation on boot of $6,000). However, the recognized gain actually is $6,000 (full amount of the appreciation on the boot). In effect, Flicker must calculate the like-kind and boot parts of the transaction separately. That is, the realized loss of $2,000 on the like-kind property *is not* recognized ($10,000 fair market value − $12,000 adjusted basis), but the $6,000 realized gain on the boot *is* recognized ($15,000 fair market value − $9,000 adjusted basis). ■

BASIS AND HOLDING PERIOD OF PROPERTY RECEIVED

If an exchange does not qualify as nontaxable under § 1031, gain or loss is recognized, and the basis of property received in the exchange is the property's fair market value. If the exchange qualifies for nonrecognition, the basis of property received must be adjusted to reflect any postponed (deferred) gain or loss. The *basis of like-kind property* received in the exchange is the property's fair market value less postponed gain or plus postponed loss. The *basis* of any *boot* received is the boot's fair market value.

EXAMPLE 39

Vireo Property Management Company exchanges a building (used in its business) with an adjusted basis of $30,000 and a fair market value of $38,000 for land with a fair market value of $38,000. The land is to be held as an investment. The exchange qualifies as like kind (an exchange of business real property for investment real property). Thus, the basis of the land is $30,000 (the land's fair market value of $38,000 less the $8,000 postponed gain on the building). If the land is later sold for its fair market value of $38,000, the $8,000 postponed gain is recognized. ■

EXAMPLE 40

Assume the same facts as in the preceding example, except that the building has an adjusted basis of $48,000 and a fair market value of only $38,000. The basis in the newly acquired land is $48,000 (fair market value of $38,000 plus the $10,000 postponed loss on the building). If the land is later sold for its fair market value of $38,000, the $10,000 postponed loss is recognized. ■

The Code provides an alternative approach for determining the basis of like-kind property received:

> Adjusted basis of like-kind property surrendered
> + Adjusted basis of boot given
> + Gain recognized
> − Fair market value of boot received
> − Loss recognized
> = *Basis of like-kind property received*

This approach accords with the recovery of capital doctrine. That is, the unrecovered cost or other basis is increased by additional cost (boot given) or decreased by cost recovered (boot received). Any gain recognized is included in the basis of the new property. The taxpayer has been taxed on this amount and is now entitled to recover it tax-free. Any loss recognized is deducted from the basis of the new property since the taxpayer has already received a tax benefit on that amount.

The holding period of the property surrendered in the exchange carries over and *tacks on* to the holding period of the like-kind property received.[56] This rule derives from the basic concept that the new property is a continuation of the old investment. The boot received has a new holding period (from the date of exchange) rather than a carryover holding period.

Depreciation recapture potential carries over to the property received in a like-kind exchange.[57] See Chapter 8 for a discussion of this topic.

10 *Find more information on this topic at our Web site: **http://wft-entities.swcollege.com**.*

If the taxpayer either assumes a liability or takes property subject to a liability, the amount of the liability is treated as boot given. For the taxpayer whose liability is assumed or whose property is taken subject to the liability, the amount of the liability is treated as boot received. The following example illustrates the effect of such a liability. In addition, the example illustrates the tax consequences for both parties involved in the like-kind exchange.

EXAMPLE 41

Jaeger & Company and Lark Enterprises, Inc., exchange real estate investments. Jaeger gives up property with an adjusted basis of $250,000 (fair market value of $400,000) that is subject to a mortgage of $75,000 (assumed by Lark). In return for this property, Jaeger receives property with a fair market value of $300,000 (adjusted basis of $200,000) and cash of $25,000.[58]

	Jaeger	Lark
Amount realized:		
Like-kind property received	$ 300,000	$ 400,000
Boot received:		
Cash	25,000	
Mortgage assumed	75,000	
	$ 400,000	$ 400,000
Adjusted basis:		
Like-kind property given	(250,000)	(200,000)
Boot given:		
Cash		(25,000)
Mortgage assumed		(75,000)
Realized gain	$ 150,000	$ 100,000
Recognized gain	100,000*	None**
Deferred gain	$ 50,000	$ 100,000

*Lesser of boot received ($25,000 cash + $75,000 mortgage assumed = $100,000) or gain realized ($150,000).
**No boot received.

---

[56]§ 1223(1) and Reg. § 1.1223–1(a). For like-kind exchanges after March 1, 1954, the tacked-on holding period applies only if the like-kind property surrendered was either a capital asset or § 1231 property. See Chapter 8 for the discussion of capital assets and § 1231 property.

[57]Reg. §§ 1.1245–2(a)(4) and 1.1250–2(d)(1).
[58]Example (2) of Reg. § 1.1031(d)–2 illustrates a special situation in which both the buyer and the seller transfer liabilities that are assumed by the other party or both parties acquire property that is subject to a liability.

BRIDGE DISCIPLINE

Bridge to Economics

One can assert that the "tax variable" is neutralized in nontaxable exchanges when taxable gains or losses do not arise. Neutralizing potential tax consequences can have a positive result given that tax costs tend to dampen economic activity. For example, in a like-kind exchange, a taxpayer can exchange one asset for another asset of like kind without having to recognize a gain or pay a tax. The justification for the tax deferral is that the taxpayer is viewed as having an equivalent economic investment after the transaction as before the transaction. But the tax-neutral result changes when the taxpayer receives property that is not "like kind" because the taxpayer's economic standing has changed.

If, for example, the taxpayer receives investment land *and* cash in exchange for investment land, her ownership in the land given up has, at least in part, been converted to cash, and to that degree, her investment has substantively changed. That is, the taxpayer's economic investment has changed from an ownership exclusively in land to ownership in land *and* cash. Alternatively, if the taxpayer gives up her investment land for corporate stock in a high-tech venture, the nature of her investment also would substantially change as a result of the transaction. These differences in the taxpayer's economic position after the transaction lead to the transactions being taxed.

	Jaeger	Lark
Basis of property transferred:		
Like-kind property	$ 250,000	$ 200,000
Cash		25,000
Mortgage assumed		75,000
	$ 250,000	$ 300,000
Plus: Gain recognized	100,000	
Less: Boot received	(100,000)	
Basis of new property	$ 250,000	$ 300,000

LEARNING OBJECTIVE 6

Explain the nonrecognition provisions available on the involuntary conversion of property.

Involuntary Conversions—§ 1033

Section 1033 provides that a taxpayer who suffers an involuntary conversion of property may postpone recognition of *gain* realized from the conversion, if that taxpayer *reinvests* the amount realized from the conversion in replacement property. Thus, if the amount reinvested in replacement property is *less than* the amount realized, realized gain *is recognized*, but only to the extent of the amount not reinvested. Any realized gain not recognized reduces the taxpayer's basis in the replacement property.[59] Thus, recognition of the gain is deferred until the replacement property is disposed of.

---

[59]§ 1033(b)(2).

| EXAMPLE 42 | Sandpiper, Inc., receives insurance proceeds of $29,000 when some of its manufacturing equipment (adjusted basis of $25,000) is destroyed by fire. Sandpiper purchases new equipment costing $30,000, so none of its $4,000 realized gain ($29,000 amount realized − $25,000 adjusted basis) is recognized. Sandpiper's basis in the new equipment is $26,000 ($30,000 cost − $4,000 deferred gain). ■ |

| EXAMPLE 43 | If Sandpiper, Inc., in the preceding example purchases new equipment that costs $28,000, it would recognize gain of $1,000, the difference between the $29,000 of insurance proceeds realized on the conversion and the $28,000 cost of the new equipment. The remaining $3,000 of realized gain would not be recognized; instead, it would reduce the company's basis in the new equipment to $25,000 ($28,000 cost − $3,000 deferred gain). ■ |

By its terms, § 1033 is *elective*. A taxpayer need not postpone recognition of gain, even if replacement property is acquired. In essence, a taxpayer has three options:

- Reinvest the proceeds and elect § 1033's nonrecognition of gain.
- Reinvest the proceeds and not elect § 1033, thereby triggering recognition of realized gain under the customary rules applicable to property transactions.
- Not reinvest the proceeds and recognize the realized gain accordingly.

If a *loss* occurs on an involuntary conversion, § 1033 does not apply, and the general rules for loss recognition are effective. See Chapter 5 for the discussion of the deduction of losses.

PLANNING CONSIDERATIONS

Recognizing Involuntary Conversion Gains

Sometimes, a taxpayer may prefer to *recognize a gain from an involuntary conversion* and will choose not to elect § 1033, even though replacement property is acquired. Circumstances suggesting this strategy would include:

- The taxpayer realized the gain in a low-bracket tax year, quite possibly because of the events that caused the involuntary conversion, such as a flood and its aftermath that seriously disrupted the business.
- The taxpayer has an expiring net operating loss carryover that can offset most, if not all, of the gain from the involuntary conversion.
- The replacement property is depreciable, and the taxpayer would prefer an unreduced basis for this

asset to maximize depreciation deductions in future years.

Nontax considerations might also come into play, perhaps suggesting that the property not be replaced at all. Even before the event that produced the involuntary conversion, the taxpayer might have been wanting to downsize the business or terminate it outright. In any case, the taxpayer might prefer to recognize the gain, pay the tax involved, and thereby free up the remaining proceeds for other uses—business, investment, or even personal—especially if the gain is small compared to the amount of proceeds received.

INVOLUNTARY CONVERSION DEFINED

An **involuntary conversion** results from the destruction (complete or partial), theft, seizure, requisition or condemnation, or sale or exchange under threat or imminence of requisition or condemnation of the taxpayer's property.[60] This description includes fires (other than arson),[61] tornadoes, hurricanes, earthquakes, floods, and

---

[60]§ 1033(a) and Reg. §§ 1.1033(a)–1(a) and –2(a).   [61]Rev.Rul. 82–74, 1982–1 C.B. 110.

other natural disasters. In these circumstances, *gain* can result from insurance proceeds received in an amount that exceeds the taxpayer's historical cost of the property, especially if depreciation deductions have lowered the property's adjusted basis.

For requisitions and condemnations, the amount realized includes the compensation paid by the public authority acquiring the taxpayer's property. To prove the existence of a threat or imminence of condemnation, the taxpayer must obtain confirmation that there has been a decision to acquire the property for public use. In addition, the taxpayer must have reasonable grounds to believe the property will be taken.[62] The property does not have to be sold to the authority threatening to condemn it to qualify for § 1033 postponement. If the taxpayer satisfies the confirmation and reasonable grounds requirements, he or she can sell the property to another party.[63] Likewise, the sale of property to a condemning authority by a taxpayer who acquired the property from its former owner with the knowledge that the property was under threat of condemnation also qualifies as an involuntary conversion under § 1033.[64]

11 *Find more information on this topic at our Web site: **http://wft-entities.swcollege.com**.*

REPLACEMENT PROPERTY

The requirements for replacement property generally are more restrictive than those for like-kind property under § 1031. The basic requirement is that the replacement property be similar or related in service or use to the involuntarily converted property.[65]

Different interpretations of the phrase *similar or related in service or use* apply depending on whether the involuntarily converted property is held by an *owner-user* or by an *owner-investor* (e.g., lessor). For an owner-user, the *functional use test* applies, and for an owner-investor, the *taxpayer use test* applies.

Functional Use Test. Under this test, a taxpayer's use of the replacement property and of the involuntarily converted property must be the same. Replacing a manufacturing plant with a wholesale grocery warehouse does not meet this test. Instead, the plant must be replaced with another facility of similar functional use.

Taxpayer Use Test. The taxpayer use test for owner-investors provides the taxpayer with more flexibility in terms of what qualifies as replacement property than does the functional use test for owner-users. Essentially, the properties must be used by the taxpayer (the owner-investor) in similar endeavors. For example, rental property held by an owner-investor qualifies if replaced by other rental property, regardless of the type of rental property involved. The test is met when an investor replaces a manufacturing plant with a wholesale grocery warehouse if both properties are held for the production of rental income.[66] The replacement of a rental residence with a personal residence does not meet the test.[67]

Special Real Property Test. In addition to the functional and taxpayer use tests, the Code provides a special rule for business or investment real property *that is condemned*. This rule applies the broad like-kind classification for real estate to

[62]Rev.Rul. 63–221, 1963–2 C.B. 332, and *Joseph P. Balistrieri*, 38 TCM 526, T.C.Memo. 1979–115.

[63]Rev.Rul. 81–180, 1981–2 C.B. 161.

[64]Rev.Rul. 81–181, 1981–2 C.B. 162.

[65]§ 1033(a) and Reg. § 1.1033(a)–1.

[66]*Loco Realty Co. v. Comm.*, 62–2 USTC ¶9657, 10 AFTR2d 5359, 306 F.2d 207 (CA–8, 1962).

[67]Rev.Rul. 70–466, 1970–2 C.B. 165.

A GOLD MINE VERSUS A DRY HOLE

All of us have seen movies about the California gold rush and miners who strike it rich. We have also seen movies about wildcatters who drill for oil in Texas and go broke when a dry hole results.

What do these endeavors have in common with the small town on the Virginia coast where General George Washington and his revolutionary army defeated Lord Charles Cornwallis and the British Crown? The answer is that an investor is trying to strike gold on a lot acquired along the Yorktown beachfront but may have a dry hole.

The investor initially purchased the one-acre lot for $250,000. As part of a beach development project, the city offered to purchase the property for the assessed value of $213,000. The investor thought $1.4 million was a more appropriate price. After two subsequent appraisals valued the property at $255,000 and $280,000, the city threatened to condemn the property by eminent domain. As the investor still believes that $1.4 million is the fair price, subsequent court proceedings will determine whether the investor made a wise investment.

The city has an interesting option if it loses in court. It can choose not to lose! If the fair market value is set too high, it can decide to discontinue the eminent domain proceedings.

SOURCE: Adapted from Charlotte Graham, "York Must Wait for Granger Land," *The Virginia Gazette*, July 22, 2000, p. A10 and July 29, 2000, p. A4.

such circumstances. Accordingly, improved real property can be replaced with unimproved real property.

The rules concerning the nature of replacement property are illustrated in Concept Summary 7–3.

TIME LIMITATION ON REPLACEMENT

The taxpayer normally has a two-year period after the close of the taxable year in which gain is realized from an involuntary conversion to replace the property (*the latest date*).[68] This rule affords as much as three years from the date of realization of gain to replace the property if the realization of gain took place on the first day of the taxable year.[69] If the involuntary conversion involved the condemnation of real property used in a trade or business or held for investment, the Code substitutes a three-year period for the normal two-year period. In this case, a taxpayer might have as much as four years from the date of realization of gain to replace the property.

EXAMPLE 44

Magpie, Inc.'s warehouse is destroyed by fire on December 16, 2000. The adjusted basis is $325,000. Magpie receives $400,000 from the insurance company on January 10, 2001. The company is a calendar year taxpayer. The latest date for replacement is December 31, 2003 (the end of the taxable year in which realized gain occurred plus two years). The critical

---

[68]§§ 1033(a)(2)(B) and (g)(4) and Reg. § 1.1033(a)–2(c)(3).
[69]A taxpayer can apply for an extension of this time period anytime before its expiration [Reg. § 1.1033(a)–2(c)(3)]. Also, the period for filing the application for extension can be extended if a taxpayer shows reasonable cause.

Replacement Property Tests

Type of Property and User	Like-Kind Test	Taxpayer Use Test	Functional Use Test
Land used by a manufacturing company is condemned by a local government authority.	X		
Apartment and land held by an investor are sold due to the threat or imminence of condemnation.	X		
An investor's rented shopping mall is destroyed by fire; the mall may be replaced by other rental properties (e.g., an apartment building).		X	
A manufacturing plant is destroyed by fire; replacement property must consist of another manufacturing plant that is functionally the same as the property converted.			X
Personal residence of taxpayer is condemned by a local government authority; replacement property must consist of another personal residence.			X

date is not the date the involuntary conversion occurred, but rather the date of gain realization (when the insurance proceeds are received). ■

EXAMPLE 45

Assume the same facts as in the preceding example, except that Magpie's warehouse is condemned. The latest date for replacement is December 31, 2004 (the end of the taxable year in which realized gain occurred plus three years). ■

The *earliest date* for replacement typically is the date the involuntary conversion occurs. However, if the property is condemned, it is possible to replace the condemned property before this date. In this case, the earliest date is the date of the threat or imminence of requisition or condemnation of the property. The purpose of this provision is to enable the taxpayer to make an orderly replacement of the condemned property.

LEARNING OBJECTIVE 7

Identify other nonrecognition provisions contained in the Code.

Other Nonrecognition Provisions

Several additional nonrecognition provisions are treated briefly in the remainder of this chapter.

TRANSFER OF ASSETS TO BUSINESS ENTITY—§§ 351 AND 721

Taxpayers can transfer assets to corporations in exchange for stock without recognizing gain or loss on the transfer per § 351. See Chapter 9 for the applicable restrictions and corresponding basis adjustments for the stock acquired. A similar provision (§ 721) allows the nontaxable transfer of assets to a partnership in exchange for an interest in that partnership. See Chapter 11 for a description of § 721.

EXCHANGE OF STOCK FOR PROPERTY—§ 1032

Under § 1032, a corporation does not recognize gain or loss on the receipt of money or other property in exchange for its stock (including treasury stock). In other words, a corporation does not recognize gain or loss when it deals in its own stock. This provision accords with the accounting treatment of such transactions.

CERTAIN EXCHANGES OF INSURANCE POLICIES—§ 1035

Under § 1035, no gain or loss is recognized from the exchange of certain insurance contracts or policies. The rules relating to exchanges not solely in kind (i.e., with boot) and the basis of the property acquired are the same as under § 1031. Exchanges qualifying for nonrecognition include the following:

- The exchange of life insurance contracts.
- The exchange of a life insurance contract for an endowment or annuity contract.
- The exchange of an endowment contract for another endowment contract that provides for regular payments beginning at a date not later than the date payments would have begun under the contract exchanged.
- The exchange of an endowment contract for an annuity contract.
- The exchange of annuity contracts.

EXCHANGE OF STOCK FOR STOCK OF THE SAME CORPORATION—§ 1036

Section 1036 provides that a shareholder does not recognize gain or loss on the exchange of common stock solely for common stock in the same corporation or from the exchange of preferred stock for preferred stock in the same corporation. Exchanges between individual shareholders as well as between a shareholder and the corporation are included under this nonrecognition provision. The rules relating to exchanges not solely in kind and the basis of the property acquired are the same as under § 1031. For example, a nonrecognition exchange occurs when common stock with different rights, such as voting for nonvoting, is exchanged. A shareholder usually recognizes gain or loss from the exchange of common for preferred or preferred for common even though the stock exchanged is in the same corporation.

ROLLOVERS INTO SPECIALIZED SMALL BUSINESS INVESTMENT COMPANIES—§ 1044

Section 1044 provides a postponement opportunity associated with the sale of publicly traded securities. If the amount realized is reinvested in the common stock or partnership interest of a specialized small business investment company (SSBIC), the realized gain is not recognized. Gain will be recognized, however, to the extent of any amount not reinvested. To qualify, the taxpayer must reinvest the proceeds within 60 days of the date of sale. In calculating the basis of the SSBIC stock, the amount of the purchase price is reduced by the amount of the postponed gain.

Statutory ceilings are imposed on the amount of realized gain that can be postponed for any taxable year as follows:

- For an individual taxpayer, the lesser of:
  - $50,000 ($25,000 for married filing separately).
  - $500,000 ($250,000 for married filing separately) reduced by the amount of such nonrecognized gain in all preceding taxable years.

- For a corporate taxpayer, the lesser of:
  - $250,000.
  - $1 million reduced by the amount of such nonrecognized gain in all preceding taxable years.

Investors ineligible for this postponement treatment include partnerships, S corporations, estates, and trusts.

12 *Find more information on this topic at our Web site:* ***http://wft-entities.swcollege.com.***

SALE OF A PRINCIPAL RESIDENCE—§ 121

Section 121 allows individual taxpayers to exclude gain from the sale of a *principal residence.*[70] This provision applies to the first $250,000 of realized gain, or $500,000 on a joint return. For this purpose, the residence must have been owned and used by the taxpayer as the primary residence for two of the five years preceding the date of sale. This exclusion can be prorated, however, if a taxpayer failed to meet the two-year requirement due to a change in his or her employment or health. Moreover, a surviving spouse counts the ownership and usage periods of the decedent spouse in meeting the two-year test. This provision applies only to gains; losses on residences, like those of other personal-use assets, are not recognized for tax purposes.

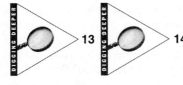

13   **14** *Find more information on these topics at our Web site:* ***http://wft-entities.swcollege.com.***

TRANSFERS OF PROPERTY BETWEEN SPOUSES OR INCIDENT TO DIVORCE—§ 1041

Section 1041 provides for nontaxable exchange treatment on property transfers *between spouses during marriage.* The basis to the recipient spouse is a carryover basis.

Section 1041 also provides that transfers of property *between spouses or former spouses incident to divorce* are nontaxable transactions. Therefore, the basis to the recipient is a carryover basis. To be treated as incident to the divorce, the transfer must be related to the cessation of marriage or must occur within one year after the date on which the marriage ceases.

Suggested Further Readings

James R. Hamill, "Build-to-Suit Exchanges," (Tax Clinic), *The Tax Adviser*, May 1999, pp. 321–322.

Richard M. Lipton, "The 'State of the Art' in Like-Kind Exchanges," *Journal of Taxation*, August 1999, pp. 78–84.

Louis S. Weller, "Early Distributions from 1031 Exchange Accounts—Another Look at a Strange Ruling," *Journal of Taxation*, August 2000, pp. 73–80.

---

[70]For an extensive explanation of this provision, see Chapter 8 of *West Federal Taxation: Advanced Taxation.*

KEY TERMS

Adjusted basis, 7–4

Amount realized, 7–3

Boot, 7–23

Fair market value, 7–3

Goodwill, 7–9

Holding period, 7–13

Involuntary conversion, 7–28

Like-kind exchange, 7–21

Nontaxable exchange, 7–20

Realized gain, 7–3

Realized loss, 7–3

Recognized gain, 7–7

Recognized loss, 7–7

Recovery of capital doctrine, 7–8

Wash sale, 7–16

Problem Materials

PROBLEMS

1. Orchid Properties, Inc., bought a rental house at the beginning of 1996 for $80,000, of which $10,000 is allocated to the land and $70,000 to the building. Early in 1998, Orchid had a tennis court built in the backyard at a cost of $5,000. The company has deducted $32,200 for depreciation on the house and $1,300 for depreciation on the court. At the beginning of this year, Orchid sells the house and tennis court for $125,000 cash.
   a. What is the company's realized gain or loss?
   b. If an original mortgage of $20,000 is still outstanding and the buyer assumes the mortgage in addition to the cash payment, what is Orchid's realized gain or loss?
   c. If the buyer takes the property subject to the mortgage, what is Orchid's realized gain or loss?

2. Black, Inc., owns a building (adjusted basis of $366,500 on January 1) that it rents to Lapwing & Longspur, which operates a restaurant in the building. The municipal health department closed the restaurant for two months this year because of health code violations. Under MACRS, the cost recovery deduction for this year would be $12,000. However, Black deducted cost recovery only for the 10 months the restaurant was open since it waived the rent income during the two-month period the restaurant was closed.
   a. What is the amount of the cost recovery deduction that Black should report on this year's income tax return?
   b. Calculate the adjusted basis of the building at the end of this year.

3. Janice owns a personal-use automobile that has an adjusted basis of $38,000. The fair market value of the automobile is $34,500.
   a. Calculate the realized and recognized loss if Janice sells the automobile for $34,500.
   b. Calculate the realized and recognized loss if Janice exchanges the automobile for another automobile worth $34,500.

4. Hubert's personal residence is condemned as part of an urban renewal project. His adjusted basis for the residence is $220,000. He receives condemnation proceeds of $175,000 and invests the proceeds in stock.
   a. Calculate Hubert's realized and recognized gain or loss.
   b. If the condemnation proceeds are $240,000, what are Hubert's realized and recognized gain or loss?
   c. What are Hubert's realized and recognized gain or loss in (a) if the house was rental property?

5. A warehouse owned by Marmot & Squirrel (a partnership) and used in its business
   (i.e., to store inventory) is being condemned by the city to provide a right of way for
   a highway. The warehouse has appreciated by $100,000 based on an estimate of fair
   market value. In the negotiations, the city is offering $40,000 less than what Marmot &
   Squirrel believes the property is worth. Alan, a real estate broker, has offered to purchase
   the property for $25,000 more than the city's offer. The partnership plans to invest the
   proceeds it will receive in an office building that it will lease to various tenants. Identify
   the relevant tax issues for Marmot & Squirrel.

6. Finch, Inc., purchases 100 shares of Bluebird Corporation stock on June 3, 2001, for
   $150,000. On August 25, 2001, Finch purchases an additional 50 shares of Bluebird stock
   for $60,000. According to market quotations, Bluebird stock is selling for $1,100 per
   share on December 31, 2001. Finch sells 60 shares of Bluebird stock on March 1, 2002,
   for $51,000.
   a. What is the adjusted basis of Finch's Bluebird stock on December 31, 2001?
   b. What is Finch's recognized gain or loss from the sale of Bluebird stock on March
      1, 2002, assuming the shares sold are from the shares purchased on June 3, 2001?
   c. What is Finch's recognized gain or loss from the sale of Bluebird stock on March
      1, 2002, assuming Finch cannot adequately identify the shares sold?

7. Randy Morgan purchases Agnes's sole proprietorship for $900,000. The assets of the
   business are as follows:

Asset	Agnes's Adjusted Basis	FMV
Accounts receivable	$ 70,000	$ 70,000
Inventory	90,000	100,000
Equipment	150,000	160,000
Furniture and fixtures	95,000	130,000
Building	190,000	250,000
Land	25,000	75,000

   Randy and Agnes agree that $50,000 of the purchase price is for Agnes's five-year
   covenant not to compete.
   a. Calculate Agnes's realized and recognized gain.
   b. Determine Randy's basis for each of the assets.
   c. Write a letter to Randy informing him of the tax consequences of the purchase.
      Randy's address is 300 Riverside Drive, Cincinnati, OH 45207.

8. Juanita has decided to dispose of the following assets that she received as gifts:
   a. In 1990, she received land worth $62,000. The donor's adjusted basis was $75,000.
      Juanita sells the land for $58,000 this year.
   b. In 1996, she received stock worth $50,000. The donor's adjusted basis was $65,000.
      Juanita sells the stock this year for $59,000.
   What is the recognized gain or loss from each of the preceding transactions? Assume
   in each transaction that no gift tax was paid.

9. Holly owns stock with an adjusted basis of $2,500 and a fair market value of $9,500.
   Holly expects the stock to continue to appreciate. Alice, Holly's best friend, has recently
   been operated on for cancer. Alice's physicians have told her that her life expectancy
   is between six months and one and a half years. One day at lunch, the two friends
   were discussing their tax situations (both feel they pay too much), when Alice mentioned
   that she had read a newspaper article about a tax planning opportunity that might be
   suitable for Holly. Holly would make a gift of the appreciated stock to Alice. In her
   will, Alice would bequeath the stock back to Holly. Since Alice is confident that she
   will live longer than a year, the basis of the stock to Holly would be the fair market
   value on the date of Alice's death. Alice would "feel good" because she had helped
   Holly "beat the tax system." You are Holly's tax adviser. How will you respond to

Alice's proposal? Would your response change if the stock were a painting that Alice could enjoy for her remaining days?

10. Barbara received a car from Samuel as a gift. Samuel paid $27,000 for the car. He had used it for business purposes and had deducted $22,000 for depreciation up to the time he gave the car to Barbara. The fair market value of the car is $23,500.
    a. Assuming Barbara uses the car for business purposes, what is her basis for depreciation?
    b. If the estimated useful life is two years (from the date of the gift), what is her depreciation deduction for each year? Use the straight-line method.
    c. If Barbara sells the car for $20,000 one year after receiving it, what is her gain or loss?
    d. If Barbara sells the car for $24,000 one year after receiving it, what is her gain or loss?

11. This year, Ron receives a gift of property that has a fair market value of $100,000 on the date of the gift. The donor's adjusted basis for the property was $32,000. Assume the donor paid gift tax of $20,000 on the gift.
    a. What is Ron's basis for gain and loss and for depreciation?
    b. If Ron had received the gift of property in 1975, what would be his basis for gain and loss and for depreciation?

12. Simon, who is retired, owns Teal, Inc., stock that has declined in value since he purchased it. He has decided either to give the stock to his nephew, Fred, who is a high school teacher, or to sell the stock and give the proceeds to Fred. Because nearly all of his wealth is invested in tax-exempt bonds, Simon faces a 15% marginal tax rate. Fred will use the cash or the proceeds from his sale of the stock to make the down payment on the purchase of a house. Based on a recent conversation, Simon is aware that Fred has a 28% marginal tax rate. Identify the tax issues relevant to Simon in deciding whether to give the stock or the sale proceeds to Fred.

13. This year, Liz receives a gift of income-producing property that has an adjusted basis of $70,000 on the date of the gift. The fair market value of the property on the date of the gift is $50,000. The donor paid gift tax of $4,000. Liz later sells the property for $54,000. Determine her recognized gain or loss.

14. Denise inherits property from Martha, her mother. Martha's adjusted basis for the property is $200,000, and the fair market value is $825,000. Six months after Martha's death, the fair market value is $840,000. Denise is the sole beneficiary of Martha's estate.
    a. Can the executor of Martha's estate elect the alternate valuation date?
    b. What is Denise's basis for the property?

15. Earl's estate includes the following assets, which are available for distribution to Robert, one of Earl's beneficiaries:

Asset	Earl's Adjusted Basis	FMV at Date of Death	FMV at Alternate Valuation Date
Cash	$10,000	$ 10,000	$ 10,000
Stock	40,000	125,000	60,000
Apartment building	60,000	300,000	325,000
Land	75,000	100,000	110,000

The fair market value of the stock six months after Earl's death was $60,000. However, believing that the stock would continue to decline in value, the executor of the estate distributed the stock to Robert one month after Earl's death. Robert immediately sold the stock for $85,000.
    a. Determine Robert's basis for the assets if the primary valuation date and amount apply.
    b. Determine Robert's basis for the assets if the executor elects the alternate valuation date and amount.

16. Susan sells land to Ellen, her sister, for $140,000. Six months later Ellen gives the land to Jerry, her son. No gift taxes are due. At the date of the gift, the land is worth $142,000. Jerry sells the land one month later for $143,000.
    a. Assuming Susan's adjusted basis for the land is $125,000, what are Susan and Jerry's recognized gain or loss on their respective sales?
    b. Assuming Susan's adjusted basis for the land is $150,000, what are Susan and Jerry's recognized gain or loss on their respective sales?

17. Peony Investors Company sells 150 shares of Lavender, Inc., stock on December 28, 2001, for $75,000. On January 10, 2002, Peony purchases 100 shares of Lavender, Inc., stock for $80,000.
    a. Assuming Peony's adjusted basis for the stock sold is $60,000, what is its recognized gain or loss, and what is its basis for the new shares?
    b. Assuming Peony's adjusted basis for the stock sold is $90,000, what is its recognized gain or loss, and what is its basis for the new shares?
    c. Advise Peony on how it can avoid any negative tax consequences encountered in (b).

18. James retires from a public accounting firm to enter private practice. He had bought a home two years earlier for $40,000. Upon opening his business, he converts one-fourth of his home into an office. The fair market value of the home on the date of conversion (January 1, 1996) is $75,000. The adjusted basis is $56,000 (ignore land). James lives and works in the home for six years (after converting it to business use) and sells it at the end of the sixth year. He deducted $2,630 of cost recovery using the statutory percentage method.
    a. How much gain or loss is recognized if James sells the property for $44,000?
    b. How much gain or loss is recognized if he sells the property for $70,000?

19. Urfan's personal residence originally cost $280,000 (ignore land). After living in the house for five years, he converts it to rental property. At the date of conversion, the fair market value of the house is $250,000.
    a. Calculate his basis for loss for the rental property.
    b. Calculate his basis for depreciation for the rental property.
    c. Calculate his basis for gain for the rental property.

20. Heron Industries, Inc., owns undeveloped land with an adjusted basis of $190,000. Heron exchanges this land for other undeveloped land worth $260,000.
    a. What are Heron's realized and recognized gain or loss?
    b. What is Heron's basis in the undeveloped land it receives?

21. Tex Wall owns undeveloped land that he is holding for investment. His adjusted basis is $175,000. On October 7, 2001, he exchanges the land with his 23-year-old daughter, Paige, for other undeveloped land that he will hold for investment. The appraised value of Paige's land is $250,000.
    a. Calculate Tex's realized and recognized gain or loss from the exchange with Paige and on a subsequent sale of the land by Tex to Baxter, a real estate broker, for $300,000 on February 15, 2002.
    b. Calculate Tex's realized and recognized gain or loss on the exchange with Paige if Tex does not sell the land received from Paige, but Paige sells the land received from Tex on February 15, 2002. Calculate Tex's basis for the land on October 7, 2001, and on February 15, 2002.
    c. Write a letter to Tex advising him on how he could avoid any recognition of gain associated with the October 7, 2001 exchange prior to his actual sale of the land. His address is The Corral, El Paso, TX 79968.

22. Starling Corporation owns a computer with an adjusted basis of $3,000. Starling exchanges the computer and cash of $5,000 for a laser printer worth $14,000.
    a. Calculate Starling's recognized gain or loss on the exchange.
    b. Calculate its basis for the printer.

23. Redfern Investments, Inc., owns land and a building with an adjusted basis of $100,000 and a fair market value of $225,000. Redfern exchanges the land and building for land

with a fair market value of $150,000 that it will use as a parking lot. In addition, Redfern receives stock worth $75,000.

a. What is the company's realized gain or loss?

b. Its recognized gain or loss?

c. The basis of the land and the stock received?

24. Tulip, Inc., would like to dispose of some land that it acquired four years ago because the land will not continue to appreciate. Its value has increased by $50,000 over the four-year period. The company also intends to sell stock that has declined in value by $50,000 during the six months since its purchase. Tulip has four offers to acquire the stock and land:

Buyer number 1:   Exchange land.

Buyer number 2:   Purchase land for cash.

Buyer number 3:   Exchange stock.

Buyer number 4:   Purchase stock for cash.

Identify the tax issues relevant to Tulip in disposing of this land and stock.

25. What is the basis of the new property in each of the following exchanges?

a. Apartment building held for investment (adjusted basis, $150,000) for office building to be held for investment (fair market value, $200,000).

b. Land and building used as a barber shop (adjusted basis, $30,000) for land and building used as a grocery store (fair market value, $350,000).

c. Office building (adjusted basis, $30,000) for bulldozer (fair market value, $42,000), both held for business use.

d. IBM common stock (adjusted basis, $14,000) for ExxonMobil common stock (fair market value, $18,000).

e. Rental house (adjusted basis, $90,000) for mountain cabin to be held for personal use (fair market value, $115,000).

26. Hyacinth Realty Company owns land in Iowa that was originally purchased for $130,000. Hyacinth has received an all-cash offer in the amount of $400,000 from a well-known shopping center developer. An international real estate broker has now offered some land located outside Florence, Italy, that is worth $400,000 in exchange for the Iowa property. Please write the company a letter analyzing these options from a tax standpoint. Hyacinth's address is 2501 Longview Lane, Des Moines, IA 50311.

27. Redbud Company owns Machine A (adjusted basis of $12,000, and fair market value of $15,000) which it uses in its business. Redbud sells Machine A for $15,000 to Oak, Inc. (a dealer). Redbud then purchases Machine B for $15,000 from Cutting Edge Company (also a dealer). Machine B would normally qualify as like-kind property.

a. What are Redbud's realized and recognized gain on the sale of Machine A?

b. What is Redbud's basis for Machine B?

c. What factors would motivate Redbud to sell Machine A and purchase Machine B rather than exchange one machine for the other?

d. Assume that the adjusted basis of Machine A is $15,000 and the fair market value of both machines is $12,000. Respond to (a) through (c).

28. Cardinal Properties, Inc., exchanges real estate held for investment plus stock for real estate to be held for investment. The stock transferred has an adjusted basis of $30,000 and a fair market value of $20,000. The real estate transferred has an adjusted basis of $30,000 and a fair market value of $90,000. The real estate acquired has a fair market value of $110,000.

a. What is Cardinal's realized gain or loss?

b. Its recognized gain or loss?

c. The basis of the newly acquired real estate?

29. Avocet Management Company exchanges a warehouse and the related land with Indigo, Inc., for an office building and the related land. Avocet's adjusted basis for the warehouse and land is $420,000. The fair market value of Indigo's office building and land is $410,000. Avocet's property has a $90,000 mortgage that Indigo assumes.
    a. Calculate Avocet's realized and recognized gain or loss.
    b. Calculate Avocet's adjusted basis for the office building and land received.
    c. As an alternative, Indigo has proposed that rather than assuming the mortgage, it will transfer cash of $90,000 to Avocet, which would use the cash to pay off the mortgage. Advise Avocet on whether this alternative would be beneficial to it from a tax perspective.

30. Determine the realized, recognized, and postponed gain or loss and the new basis for each of the following like-kind exchanges:

	Adjusted Basis of Old Asset	Boot Given	Fair Market Value of New Asset	Boot Received
a.	$ 7,000	$ –0–	$12,000	$4,000
b.	14,000	2,000	15,000	–0–
c.	3,000	7,000	8,000	500
d.	22,000	–0–	32,000	–0–
e.	10,000	–0–	11,000	1,000
f.	10,000	–0–	8,000	–0–

31. Turquoise Realty Company owns an apartment house that has an adjusted basis of $950,000 but is subject to a mortgage of $240,000. Turquoise transfers the apartment house to Dove, Inc., and receives from Dove $150,000 in cash and an office building with a fair market value of $975,000 at the time of the exchange. Dove assumes the $240,000 mortgage on the apartment house.
    a. What is Turquoise's realized gain or loss?
    b. What is its recognized gain or loss?
    c. What is the basis of the newly acquired office building?

32. For each of the following involuntary conversions, indicate whether the property acquired qualifies as replacement property:
    a. A shopping mall is destroyed by a tornado. The space in the mall was rented to various tenants. The owner of the mall uses the insurance proceeds to build a shopping mall in a neighboring community where no property has been damaged by tornadoes.
    b. A warehouse is destroyed by fire. Because of economic conditions in the area, the owner decides not to rebuild the warehouse. Instead, it uses the insurance proceeds to build a warehouse in another state.
    c. Swallow Fashions, Inc., owns a building that is destroyed by a hurricane. Because of an economic downturn in the area caused by the closing of a military base, Swallow decides to rent space for its retail outlet rather than to replace the building. It uses the insurance proceeds to buy a four-unit apartment building in another city. A realtor in that city will handle the rental of the apartments.
    d. Susan and Rick's personal residence is destroyed by a tornado. Since they would like to travel, they decide not to acquire a replacement residence. Instead, they invest the insurance proceeds in a duplex, which they rent to tenants.

33. The city of Richmond is going to condemn some buildings to build a park. Steve's principal residence is among those to be condemned. His adjusted basis for the house and land is $60,000. The appraised value of the house and land is $52,000. Steve is unaware of the future condemnation proceedings, but would like his family to move to a better neighborhood. Therefore, when Ross, a realtor, mentions that he may have a corporate client who would like to purchase the property for $65,000, Steve is ecstatic and indicates a willingness to sell.

Ross is having some "second thoughts" about his conversation with Steve. The potential corporate purchaser is a company owned by Ross and his wife. Ross is aware of the future condemnation proceedings. He considers himself a skilled negotiator and thinks he can negotiate a $130,000 price for the house. Ross is considering telling Steve that the corporate client has changed its mind. Ross would then indicate that he has learned the city will be condemning several buildings in order to create a park, but has not yet established the prices it will pay for the condemned property. He would also tell Steve that because he believes he can get more from the city than Steve would obtain, he is willing to gamble and purchase the property now from Steve for $65,000.

Ross will point out several benefits available to Steve. These include (1) not having to deal with the city, (2) receiving an amount that exceeds both the appraised value and the original purchase cost of the home, and (3) receiving the money now. While admitting that he could reap a substantial profit, Ross would emphasize that he would also be taking on substantial risks. In addition, Ross would explain that when he sells the property to the city, he will defer the taxes by reinvesting the sales proceeds (due to involuntary conversion).

Should Ross make a new proposal to Steve based on his "second thoughts"? How do you think Steve will respond?

34. Lark Corporation's office building is destroyed by a hurricane in September. The adjusted basis is $210,000. Lark receives insurance proceeds of $390,000 in October.
   a. Calculate Lark's realized gain or loss, recognized gain or loss, and basis for the replacement property if it acquires an office building for $390,000 in October.
   b. Calculate Lark's realized gain or loss, recognized gain or loss, and basis for the replacement property if it acquires a warehouse for $350,000 in October.
   c. Calculate Lark's realized gain or loss and recognized gain or loss if it does not acquire replacement property.

35. Magenta, Inc.'s warehouse, which has an adjusted basis of $325,000 and a fair market value of $490,000, is condemned by an agency of the Federal government to make way for a highway interchange. The initial condemnation offer is $450,000. After substantial negotiations, the agency agrees to transfer to Magenta a surplus warehouse that it believes is worth $490,000.
   a. What are the recognized gain or loss and the basis of the replacement warehouse if Magenta's objective is to recognize as much gain as possible?
   b. Advise Magenta regarding what it needs to do by what date in order to achieve its objective.

36. What are the *maximum* postponed gain or loss and the basis for the replacement property for the following involuntary conversions?

	Property	Type of Conversion	Amount Realized	Adjusted Basis	Amount Reinvested
a.	Drugstore (business)	Condemned	$160,000	$120,000	$100,000
b.	Apartments (investment)	Casualty	100,000	120,000	200,000
c.	Grocery store (business)	Casualty	400,000	300,000	350,000
d.	Residence (personal)	Casualty	16,000	18,000	17,000
e.	Vacant lot (investment)	Condemned	240,000	160,000	240,000
f.	Residence (personal)	Casualty	20,000	18,000	19,000
g.	Residence (personal)	Condemned	18,000	20,000	26,000
h.	Apartments (investment)	Condemned	150,000	100,000	200,000

37. Milton, who is single, listed his personal residence with a realtor on March 3, 2001, at a price of $250,000. He rejected several offers in the $200,000 range during the summer. Finally, on August 16, 2001, he and the purchaser signed a contract to sell for $245,000. The sale (i.e., closing) took place on September 7, 2001. The closing statement showed the following disbursements:

Realtor's commission	$ 14,000
Appraisal fee	500
Exterminator's certificate	300
Recording fees	400
Mortgage to First Bank	180,000
Cash to seller	49,800

Milton's adjusted basis for the house is $150,000. He owned and occupied the house for eight years. On October 1, Milton purchases another residence for $210,000.

a. Calculate Milton's recognized gain on the sale.

b. What is Milton's adjusted basis for the new residence?

c. Assume instead that the selling price is $735,000. What is Milton's recognized gain? His adjusted basis for the new residence?

EXTENDER 38. Ruth and Sal have been married for 12 years. Ruth sells Peach, Inc. stock that she has owned for four years to Sal for its fair market value of $80,000. Her adjusted basis is $35,000.

a. Calculate Ruth's recognized gain.

b. Calculate Sal's adjusted basis for the stock.

c. How would the tax consequences in (a) and (b) differ if Ruth had made a gift of the stock to Sal? Which form of the transaction would you recommend?

BRIDGE DISCIPLINE

1. In April of the current year, Blue Corporation purchased an asset to be used in its manufacturing operations for $100,000. Blue's management expects the asset to ratably provide valuable services in the production process for eight years and have a salvage value of $12,000. The asset is a five-year asset for tax purposes. Blue has adopted the half-year convention for book purposes in the year of acquisition and disposition; finally, Blue uses MACRS for tax purposes.

a. Compute the depreciation expense in the year of acquisition for book and tax purposes.

b. Identify the book-tax difference related to the depreciation expense in the year of acquisition.

2. Refer to the facts in the preceding problem. Assume Blue Corporation disposes of the manufacturing asset at the beginning of year seven for $40,000. Compute the amount of gain or loss recognized for book and tax purposes. What is the book-tax difference in the year of disposition?

3. Identify whether the taxpayer's economic position has changed in the following exchanges such that they are subject to current taxation. That is, identify whether the following qualify as like-kind exchanges under § 1031.

a. Improved for unimproved real estate.

b. Vending machine (used in business) for inventory.

c. Rental house for personal residence.

d. Business equipment for securities.

e. Warehouse for office building (both used for business).

f. Truck for computer (both used in business).

g. Rental house for land (both held for investment).

h. Ten shares of stock in Blue Corporation for 10 shares of stock in Red Corporation.

i. Office furniture for office equipment (both used in business).

j. General partnership interest in Green Partnership for general partnership interest in Brown Partnership.

RESEARCH PROBLEMS

Note: Solutions to Research Problems can be prepared by using the **RIA Checkpoint® Student Version Online research product,** *or the* **CCH U.S. Master Tax Guide Plus™** *online Federal tax research database, which is available to accompany this text. It is also possible to prepare solutions to the Research Problems by using tax research materials found in a standard tax library.*

Research Problem 1. As the result of a large inheritance from her grandmother, Beverly has a substantial investment portfolio. The securities are held in street name by her brokerage firm. Beverly's broker, Max, has standing oral instructions from her on sales transactions to sell the shares with the highest cost basis.

Three years ago, Beverly phoned Max and instructed him to sell 6,000 shares of Color, Inc. Her portfolio has 15,000 shares of Color, Inc., which were purchased in several transactions over different years. At the end of each month, the brokerage firm provides Beverly with a monthly statement that includes sales transactions. It does not identify the specific certificates transferred.

In filing her income tax return for the year of the sale, Beverly used the specific identification method to calculate the $90,000 gain on the sale of the Color shares. Now that return is being audited. The IRS has taken the position that under Reg. § 1.1012–1(c) Beverly should have used the FIFO method to report the sale of the Color shares. This would result in a recognized gain of $160,000. According to his interpretation of the Regulations, Beverly may not use the specific identification method and must use the FIFO method because the broker did not provide written confirmation of Beverly's sales instructions as required by the Regulations.

Beverly has come to you for tax advice.

Research Problem 2. For three years, Amos, a calendar year taxpayer, has owned stock that is qualified small business stock under § 1045. The stock has an adjusted basis of $10,000. On July 2, 2001, he sells the stock for $100,000. On August 3, 2001, he uses the sales proceeds of $100,000 to purchase other qualified small business stock. If possible, Amos would like to defer any recognized gain on the sale of the stock. Advise Amos on the tax consequences of the sale and the subsequent purchase and the procedure he must follow to achieve his deferral objective.

Research Problem 3. As part of its redevelopment planning, the Tucson Redevelopment Authority (TRA) proposed an auto mall for the eastern part of Tucson. Believing that this plan requires a domestic auto dealer to serve as mall anchor, the TRA suggested that Frank and Karen Ames relocate their existing Tucson auto dealership to the new mall. Frank and Karen, however, wanted to relocate their dealership to Casa Grande, which is located in a different part of Tucson.

Some months ago, officials of the TRA told Frank and Karen that TRA was prepared to condemn their auto dealership through its powers of eminent domain, unless Frank and Karen would sell their property to TRA and relocate their dealership to the auto mall. After receiving a letter from TRA to this effect, Frank and Karen entered into negotiations with TRA. Although these negotiations were often quite contentious, Frank and Karen eventually sold their property to TRA and relocated their dealership to the new mall. In doing so, they realized a substantial gain on the transaction, which they deferred by electing § 1033 treatment.

An IRS agent has now denied such deferral on the grounds that Frank and Karen did not sell their property under "threat" of condemnation, because no condemnation actually took place. What would you advise Frank and Karen?

Use the tax resources of the Internet to address the following questions. Do not restrict your search to the World Wide Web, but include a review of newsgroups and general reference materials, practitioner sites and resources, primary sources of the tax law, chat rooms and discussion groups, and other opportunities.

Research Problem 4. A number of public policy think tanks, taxpayer unions, and other private interest groups have proposed changes to the tax rules that apply to like-kind exchanges of realty. Summarize several of these proposals, including your assessment of the motivations underlying the suggested changes.

Research Problem 5. When taxpayers sell some of their mutual fund shares, they may compute their basis in the shares sold by utilizing the specific identification method. Go to the site of an investment adviser or mutual fund to find instructions on how to apply the specific identification method. What other options are described in the information you find? Illustrate each of the alternatives.

CHAPTER 8

Property Transactions: Capital Gains and Losses, Section 1231, and Recapture Provisions

LEARNING OBJECTIVES

After completing Chapter 8, you should be able to:

1. Distinguish capital assets from ordinary assets.

2. Understand the relevance of a sale or exchange to classification as a capital gain or loss.

3. Determine the applicable holding period for a capital asset.

4. Describe the tax treatment of capital gains and losses for noncorporate taxpayers.

5. Describe the tax treatment of capital gains and losses for corporate taxpayers.

6. Distinguish § 1231 assets from ordinary and capital assets, and calculate § 1231 gain or loss.

7. Determine when recapture provisions apply and their effect.

Outline

TAX TALK   *Governments likely to confiscate wealth are unlikely to find much wealth to confiscate in the long run.*

—*Thomas Sowell*

General Considerations

RATIONALE FOR SEPARATE REPORTING OF CAPITAL GAINS AND LOSSES

Since the earliest days of the Federal income tax, **capital assets** have received special treatment upon their disposition. Gains from these assets have historically received *preferential treatment* in the form of either partial exclusion of gain, lower rates, or a maximum tax rate. Losses from capital assets, however, have historically received less desirable treatment than losses from other assets. Further, because a taxpayer has complete control over the timing of dispositions, the Code imposes limitations on when capital losses can be deducted to prevent taxpayers from manipulating their tax liability excessively.

During World War II, capital asset treatment was extended to other assets. These assets are now called "§ 1231 assets" after the Code Section that prescribes their special treatment. Several years after World War II ended, Congress believed that this special treatment was no longer entirely warranted. Instead of repealing § 1231, however, Congress left that section in place but eroded many—but not all—of its benefits through *recapture provisions* in § 1245 and § 1250. Together, these Code Sections constitute one of the most complicated areas of tax law affecting both individual taxpayers and business entities.

As already intimated, one concern is that taxpayers can time the realization of gains and losses by choosing when or even whether to sell the asset in question. If Lark Enterprises, Inc., owns stock with a basis of $20 per share and a current value of $80 per share, it does not pay tax on the $60 gain until it chooses to dispose of this stock in a taxable transaction. And for the most part, Lark has complete control over that decision. When it does dispose of the stock, however, its $60 gain is taxable in full, even though this gain may have accrued over many years. To mitigate the impact of this *bunching* of income in a single year and to offset the effect of inflation over the period of Lark's ownership of the stock, preferential treatment is prescribed for this **capital gain.**

The nature of this preferential treatment is discussed later in this chapter, but the essential point for now is that preferential treatment is confined to the excess of net long-term capital gains over net short-term **capital losses.** This cumbersome description requires taxpayers to separate their capital asset transactions from their transactions involving noncapital assets. It further requires taxpayers to separate their long-term (i.e., more than one year) transactions from their short-term (i.e., one year or less) transactions. Moreover, certain types of capital assets (principally real estate and "collectibles") receive specific treatment apart from the rates generally applicable to capital assets.

As a result of the need to distinguish and separately match capital gains and losses, the tax forms include very extensive reporting requirements for capital gains and losses. This chapter explains the principles underlying the forms.

GENERAL SCHEME OF TAXATION

Recognized gains and losses must be properly classified. Proper classification depends upon three characteristics.

- The tax status of the property, including the specific type of asset.
- The manner of the property's disposition.
- The holding period of the property.

The three possible tax statuses are capital asset, § 1231 asset, and ordinary asset. Property disposition may be by sale, exchange, casualty, theft, or condemnation. The two relevant holding periods are one year or less (short term) and more than one year (long term).

LEARNING OBJECTIVE 1

Distinguish capital assets from ordinary assets.

Capital Assets

DEFINITION OF A CAPITAL ASSET

Investments comprise the most typical category of capital assets and include corporate stocks and bonds, mutual funds, partnership interests, government securities, and vacant land. These assets can be held by any type of taxpayer—individuals, partnerships, limited liability companies, and corporations, whether closely held or publicly held. In addition, individuals own certain capital assets that are part of their daily life, such as residences, automobiles, furniture, and artwork. The classification of these *personal-use* assets as capital assets is relevant only when their disposition produces a recognized gain. Losses from the disposition of personal-use assets are not recognized for tax purposes, as explained in the preceding chapter.

Capital assets are not directly defined in the Code. Instead, § 1221(a) defines what is *not* a capital asset. A capital asset is property held by the taxpayer that is *not* any of the following:

- Inventory or property held primarily for sale to customers in the ordinary course of a business. The Supreme Court, in *Malat v. Riddell*,[1] defined *primarily* as meaning *of first importance* or *principally*.
- Accounts and notes receivable acquired from the sale of inventory or acquired for services rendered in the ordinary course of business.
- Depreciable property or real estate used in a business.
- Certain copyrights; literary, musical, or artistic compositions; or letters, memoranda, or similar property held by (1) a taxpayer whose efforts created the property; (2) in the case of a letter, memorandum, or similar property, a taxpayer for whom it was produced; or (3) a taxpayer who received the property as a lifetime gift from someone described in (1) or (2).
- U.S. government publications that are (1) received by a taxpayer from the U.S. government other than by purchase at the price at which they are offered for sale to the public or (2) held by a taxpayer who received the publication as a lifetime gift from someone described in (1).
- Supplies of a type regularly used or consumed in the ordinary course of a business.

Inventory.   What constitutes inventory is determined by reference to the taxpayer's business.

EXAMPLE 1

Green Company buys and sells used cars. Its cars are inventory. Its gains from the sale of the cars are ordinary income. ■

EXAMPLE 2

Soong sells her personal-use automobile at a $500 gain. The automobile is a personal-use asset and, therefore, a capital asset. The gain is a capital gain. ■

Notice that no asset is inherently capital or ordinary. When Soong in Example 2 sells her capital asset automobile to Green Company in Example 1, that very same automobile loses its capital asset status, because it is inventory to Green Company. Similar transformations can occur if, for example, an art dealer sells a painting (inventory; *not* a capital asset) to a private collector (now a capital asset). Whether an asset is capital or ordinary, therefore, depends entirely on the relationship of *that asset* to the taxpayer who sold it. This classification dilemma is but one feature of capital asset treatment that makes this area so confused and perennially complicated.

Accounts and Notes Receivable.   Collection of an accrual basis account receivable usually does not result in a gain or loss because the amount collected equals the receivable's basis. The *sale* of an account or note receivable may generate a gain or loss, however, because it will probably be sold for more or less than its basis. That gain or loss will be ordinary because the receivable is not a capital asset. A cash basis account receivable has no basis, so sale of such a receivable generates a gain, and that gain is ordinary income. Collection of a cash basis receivable also generates ordinary income.

---

[1]66–1 USTC ¶9317, 17 AFTR2d 604, 86 S.Ct. 1030 (USSC, 1966).

AN ARTIST'S DILEMMA

Artist Peter Max was the creator of valuable paintings that had no tax basis. If he sold the paintings, the entire proceeds from the sale would be ordinary income. Instead, Max *exchanged* the paintings for valuable real estate in the United States and in several other countries. The IRS contended that the exchange of the paintings was taxable and charged Max with failing to report more than $1 million of ordinary income.

EXAMPLE 3

Oriole Company, an accrual basis taxpayer, has accounts receivable of $100,000. Revenue of $100,000 was recorded and a $100,000 basis was established when the receivable was created. Because Oriole needs working capital, it sells the receivables for $83,000 to a financial institution. Accordingly, it has a $17,000 ordinary loss. If Oriole is a cash basis taxpayer, it has $83,000 of ordinary income because it would not have recorded any revenue earlier and the receivable would have no tax basis. ∎

Business Fixed Assets. Depreciable personal property and real estate (both depreciable and nondepreciable) used by a business are not capital assets. Thus, *business fixed assets* are not capital assets. Business fixed assets can sometimes be treated as capital assets pursuant to § 1231, however, as discussed later in this chapter.

Copyrights and Creative Works. Generally, the person whose efforts led to the copyright or creative work has an ordinary asset, not a capital asset. This rule makes the creator comparable to a taxpayer whose customary activity (salary, business profits) is taxed as ordinary income. *Creative works* include the works of authors, composers, and artists. Also, the person for whom a letter, memorandum, or other similar property was created has an ordinary asset. Finally, a person receiving a copyright, creative work, letter, memorandum, or similar property by lifetime gift from the creator or the person for whom the work was created also has an ordinary asset.

EXAMPLE 4

Wanda is a part-time music composer. A music publisher purchases one of her songs for $5,000. Wanda has a $5,000 ordinary gain from the sale of an ordinary asset. ∎

EXAMPLE 5

Ed received a letter from the President of the United States in 1994. In the current year, Ed sells the letter to a collector for $300. Ed has a $300 ordinary gain from the sale of an ordinary asset (because the letter was created for Ed). ∎

EXAMPLE 6

Isabella gives a song she composed to her son. Her son sells the song to a music publisher for $5,000. Her son has a $5,000 ordinary gain from the sale of an ordinary asset. If he inherits the song from Isabella, his basis for the song is its fair market value at Isabella's death. The song is a capital asset because the son's basis is not related to Isabella's basis for the song (i.e., the song was not a *lifetime* gift). ∎

U.S. Government Publications. U.S. government publications received from the U.S. government (or its agencies) for a reduced price are not capital assets. This prevents a taxpayer from later donating the publications to charity and claiming a charitable contribution equal to the fair market value of the publications. A charitable contribution of a capital asset generally yields a deduction equal to the asset's fair market value. If such property is received by gift from the original purchaser, the property is not a capital asset to the donee. (For a more comprehensive explanation of charitable contributions of property, refer to Chapter 4.)

STATUTORY EXPANSIONS

Because of the uncertainty often associated with capital asset status, Congress has occasionally enacted Code Sections to clarify the definition in particular circumstances. These statutory expansions of the capital asset definition are discussed in this section.

1　*Find more information on this topic at our Web site:* ***http://wft-entities.swcollege.com.***

Dealers in Securities.　As a general rule, securities (stocks, bonds, and other financial instruments) held by a dealer are considered to be inventory and are, therefore, not subject to capital gain or loss treatment. A *dealer in securities* is a merchant (e.g., a brokerage firm) that regularly engages in the purchase and resale of securities to customers. However, under the following circumstances, a dealer will have capital gain or capital loss. If a dealer clearly identifies certain securities as held for investment purposes by the close of business on the acquisition date, gain from the securities' sale will be capital gain. The gain will be ordinary if the dealer ceases to hold the securities for investment prior to the sale. Losses are capital losses if at any time the securities have been clearly identified by the dealer as held for investment.[2]

2　*Find more information on this topic at our Web site:* ***http://wft-entities.swcollege.com.***

Real Property Subdivided for Sale.　Substantial real property development activities may result in the owner being considered a dealer for tax purposes. If so, income from the sale of real estate property lots will be treated as the sale of inventory and therefore will be taxed as ordinary income. However, § 1237 allows real estate investors to claim capital gain treatment if they engage *only* in *limited* development activities. To be eligible for § 1237 treatment, the following requirements must be met.

- The taxpayer is not a corporation.
- The taxpayer is not a real estate dealer.
- No substantial improvements have been made to the lots sold. *Substantial* generally means more than a 10 percent increase in the value of a lot. Shopping centers and other commercial or residential buildings are considered substantial, while filling, draining, leveling, and clearing operations are not.
- The taxpayer has held the lots sold for at least 5 years, except for inherited property. The substantial improvements test is less stringent if the property is held at least 10 years.

If the preceding requirements are met, all gain is capital gain until the taxable year in which the sixth lot is sold. Sales of contiguous lots to a single buyer in the same transaction count as the sale of one lot. Beginning with the taxable year in which the *sixth* lot is sold, 5 percent of the revenue from lot sales is potential ordinary income. That potential ordinary income is offset by any selling expenses from the lot sales. Practically, sales commissions often are at least 5 percent of the sales price, so usually none of the gain is treated as ordinary income.

---

[2]§§ 1236(a) and (b) and Reg. § 1.1236–1(a).

Section 1237 does not apply to losses. A loss from the sale of subdivided real property is ordinary loss unless the property qualifies as a capital asset under § 1221. The following example illustrates the application of § 1237.

<table>
<tr><td>**EXAMPLE 7**</td><td></td></tr>
</table>

Ahmed owns a large tract of land and subdivides it for sale. Assume Ahmed meets all the requirements of § 1237 and during the tax year sells the first 10 lots to 10 different buyers for $10,000 each. Ahmed's basis in each lot sold is $3,000, and he incurs total selling expenses of $4,000 on the sales. Ahmed's gain is computed as follows.

Selling price (10 × $10,000)	$100,000	
Less: Selling expenses (10 × $400)	(4,000)	
Amount realized		$ 96,000
Basis (10 × $3,000)		(30,000)
Realized and recognized gain		$ 66,000
Classification of recognized gain:		
Ordinary income		
Five percent of selling price (5% × $100,000)	$ 5,000	
Less: Selling expenses	(4,000)	
Ordinary gain		1,000
Capital gain		$ 65,000

LEARNING OBJECTIVE 2

Understand the relevance of a sale or exchange to classification as a capital gain or loss.

Sale or Exchange

Recognition of capital gain or loss usually requires a **sale or exchange** of a capital asset. The Code uses the term *sale or exchange,* but does not define it. Generally, a property sale involves the receipt of money by the seller and/or the assumption by the purchaser of the seller's liabilities. An exchange involves the transfer of property for other property. Thus, an involuntary conversion (casualty, theft, or condemnation) is not a sale or exchange. In several situations, the determination of whether or when a sale or exchange has taken place has been clarified by the enactment of Code Sections that specifically provide for sale or exchange treatment. These situations are discussed below.

Recognized gains or losses from the cancellation, lapse, expiration, or any other termination of a right or obligation with respect to personal property (other than stock) that is or would be a capital asset in the hands of the taxpayer are capital gains or losses.[3] See the discussion under Options later in the chapter for more details.

WORTHLESS SECURITIES AND § 1244 STOCK

Occasionally, securities such as stock and bonds may become worthless due to the insolvency of their issuer. If the security is a capital asset, the loss is deemed to have occurred as the result of a sale or exchange on the *last day* of the tax year.[4] This last-day rule may have the effect of converting a short-term capital loss into a long-term capital loss. See Capital Losses later in this chapter.

Section 1244 allows an *ordinary* deduction on disposition of stock at a loss. The stock must be that of a small business company, and the ordinary deduction is limited to $50,000 ($100,000 for married individuals filing jointly) per year.

[3]§ 1234A. [4]§ 165(g)(1).

MUTUAL FUNDS AND CAPITAL GAINS

How tax-efficient is your mutual fund? If it is a typical fund, the answer is not very efficient. Morningstar, Inc., a Chicago-based research firm, esti-mates that over the past five years investors in diversified stock mutual funds paid 15 percent of their gains in taxes each year—without even selling their shares in the fund.

The taxes were owed because funds are required to distribute to investors virtually all dividends and realized capital gains. Then the investors pay tax on the distributions.

The amount of capital gains a fund has to distribute depends on several factors. One is the number of shareholder purchases and sales. When a large numer of investors buy shares in a fund during the year, the capital gains are distributed among more shareholders, so each receives a smaller distribution. But when many investors redeem their shares, the fund may have to sell some of its stock holdings to pay them off. In the process, the fund realizes capital gains, which are then distributed to the smaller pool of remaining shareholders.

Another reason that mutual funds distribute capital gains, though, is that most fund managers are constantly buying and selling stocks. Indeed, many mutual fund have a 100 percent turnover rate each year. Every time a capital gain is realized, the shareholders must pay taxes. And if the fund has not owned the stock for the long-term holding period, the gain will be a short-term capital gain that is not eligible for the beneficial long-term rates.

For investors tired of paying tax on capital gain distributions, there are some alternatives. One is to buy individual stocks. Then the investor can decide when the capital gains are realized. Another idea is to buy index funds, which typically have less turnover than diversified mutual funds. A third is to put mutual fund holdings into an IRA or other tax-deferred account. And beware of purchasing mutual funds at the end of the year, when most funds make their distributions—you could find yourself owing tax on a large distribution from a fund that you've owned for only a few days.

SOURCE: Adapted from Jonathan Clements, "How the Taxman Dines on Your Fund," *Wall Street Journal*, August 31, 1999, p. C1.

RETIREMENT OF CORPORATE OBLIGATIONS

A debt obligation (e.g., a bond or note payable) may have a tax basis different from its redemption value because it may have been acquired at a premium or discount. Consequently, the collection of the redemption value may result in a loss or a gain. Generally, the collection of a debt obligation is *treated* as a sale or exchange.[5] Therefore, any loss or gain will be capital loss or gain because a sale or exchange has taken place

3 *Find more information on this topic at our Web site: **http://wft-entities.swcollege.com**.*

---

[5]§ 1271.

| EXAMPLE 8 | Osprey, Inc., purchases $1,000 of General Motors Corporation bonds for $1,020 in the open market. If the bonds are held to maturity, the $20 difference between Osprey's collection of the $1,000 redemption value and its cost of $1,020 is treated as capital loss. ∎ |

OPTIONS

Frequently, a potential buyer of property wants to defer a final purchase decision, but wants to control the sale and/or the sale price in the meantime. **Options** are used to achieve such control. The potential purchaser (grantee) pays the property owner (grantor) for an option on the property. The grantee then becomes the option holder. An option usually sets the price at which a grantee can buy the property and expires after a specified period of time.

Sale of an Option. In addition to exercising an option or letting it expire, a grantee can often arrange for its sale or exchange. Such a sale or exchange generally results in capital gain or loss if the option property is (or would be) a capital asset to the grantee.[6]

| EXAMPLE 9 | Robin & Associates wants to buy some vacant land for investment purposes, but cannot afford the full purchase price. Instead, the firm convinces the landowner (grantor) to sell it the right to purchase the land for $100,000 anytime in the next two years. Robin & Associates (grantee) pays $3,000 for this option to buy the land. The option is a capital asset to Robin because if the firm actually purchased the land (the option property), the land would be a capital asset. Three months after purchasing the option, Robin sells it for $7,000. The firm has a $4,000 ($7,000 − $3,000) capital gain on this sale. ∎ |

Failure to Exercise Options. If an option holder (grantee) fails to exercise the option, the lapse of the option is considered a sale or exchange on the option expiration date. Thus, the resulting loss is a capital loss if the property subject to the option is (or would be) a capital asset in the hands of the grantee.

The grantor of an option on *stocks, securities, commodities, or commodity futures* receives short-term capital gain treatment upon the expiration of the option.[7] For example, an individual investor who owns stock (a capital asset) may sell a call option, entitling the buyer of the option to acquire the stock at a specified price higher than the stock's value at the date the option is granted. The writer of the call (the grantor) receives a premium for writing the option. If the price of the stock does not increase during the option period, the option will expire unexercised. Upon the expiration of the option, the grantor must recognize a short-term capital gain equal to the premium received. These provisions do not apply to options held for sale to customers (the inventory of a securities dealer).

Options on property *other than* stocks, securities, commodities, or commodity futures result in ordinary income to the grantor when the option expires. For instance, the landowner in the preceding example would have ordinary income of $3,000 if Robin (the grantee) had allowed the option to expire.

Exercise of Options by Grantee. If an option is exercised, the amount paid for the option is added to the optioned property's selling price. This increases the gain (or reduces the loss) to the grantor resulting from the sale of the property. The grantor's gain or loss is capital or ordinary depending on the tax status of the property. The grantee adds the cost of the option to the basis of the property purchased.

---

[6]§ 1234(a) and Reg. § 1.1234–1(a)(1).   [7]§ 1234(b)(1).

CONCEPT SUMMARY 8–1

Options

Event	Effect on	
	Grantor	**Grantee**
Option is granted.	Receives value and has a contract obligation (a liability).	Pays value and has a contract right (an asset).
Option expires.	Has a short-term capital gain if the option property is stocks, securities, commodities, or commodity futures. Otherwise, gain is ordinary income.	Has a loss (capital loss if option property would have been a capital asset for the grantee). Otherwise, loss is ordinary.
Option is exercised.	Amount received for option increases proceeds from sale of the option property.	Amount paid for option becomes part of the basis of the option property purchased.
Option is sold or exchanged by grantee.	Result depends upon whether option later expires or is exercised (see above).	Could have gain or loss (capital gain or loss if option property would have been a capital asset for the grantee).

EXAMPLE 10

Several years ago, Indigo, Inc., purchased 100 shares of Eagle Company stock for $5,000. On April 1 of this year, Indigo writes a call option on the stock, giving the grantee the right to buy the stock for $6,000 during the following six-month period. Indigo (the grantor) receives a call premium of $500 for writing the call.

- If the call is exercised by the grantee on August 1, Indigo has $1,500 ($6,000 + $500 − $5,000) of long-term capital gain from the sale of the stock. The grantee has a $6,500 ($500 option premium + $6,000 purchase price) basis for the stock.
- Assume that the option expired unexercised. Indigo has a $500 short-term capital gain equal to the call premium received for writing the option. This gain is not recognized until the option expires. The grantee has a loss from expiration of the option. The nature of that loss will depend upon whether the option was a capital asset or an ordinary asset in the hands of the grantee. ■

Concept Summary 8–1 summarizes the rules for options.

PATENTS

Transfer of a **patent** is treated as the sale or exchange of a long-term capital asset when *all substantial rights* to the patent (or an undivided interest that includes all such rights) are transferred by a *holder*.[8] The transferor/holder may receive payment in virtually any form. Lump-sum or periodic payments are most common. The amount of the payments may also be contingent on the transferee/purchaser's productivity, use, or disposition of the patent. If the transfer meets these requirements, any gain or loss is automatically a long-term capital gain or loss. Whether the asset was a capital asset for the transferor, whether a sale or exchange occurred, and how long the transferor held the patent are all irrelevant.

---

[8]§ 1235.

EXAMPLE 11

Mei-Yen, a druggist, invents a pill-counting machine, which she patents. In consideration of a lump-sum payment of $200,000 plus $10 per machine sold, Mei-Yen assigns the patent to Drug Products, Inc. Assuming Mei-Yen has transferred all substantial rights, she automatically has a long-term capital gain from both the lump-sum payment and the $10 per machine royalty to the extent these proceeds exceed her basis for the patent. ■

This special long-term capital gain or loss treatment for patents is intended to encourage technological development and scientific progress. In contrast, books, songs, and artists' works may be copyrighted, but copyrights and the assets they represent are not capital assets. Thus, the disposition of these assets by their creators usually results in ordinary gain or loss.

Substantial Rights. To receive favorable capital gain treatment, all *substantial rights* to the patent (or an undivided interest in it) must be transferred. All substantial rights to a patent means all rights that are valuable at the time the patent rights (or an undivided interest in the patent) are transferred. All substantial rights have not been transferred when the transfer is limited geographically within the issuing country or when the transfer is for a period less than the remaining legal life of the patent. The circumstances of the entire transaction, rather than merely the language used in the transfer instrument, are to be considered in deciding whether all substantial rights have been transferred.[9]

EXAMPLE 12

Assume Mei-Yen, the druggist in the preceding example, only licensed Drug Products, Inc., to manufacture and sell the invention in Michigan. She retained the right to license the machine elsewhere in the United States. Mei-Yen has retained a substantial right and is not eligible for automatic long-term capital gain treatment. ■

Holder Defined. The *holder* of a patent must be an *individual* and is usually the invention's creator. A holder may also be an individual who purchases the patent rights from the creator before the patented invention has been reduced to practice. However, the creator's employer and certain parties related to the creator do not qualify as holders. Thus, in the common situation where an employer has all rights to an employee's inventions, the employer is not eligible for long-term capital gain treatment. More than likely, the employer will have an ordinary asset because the patent was developed as part of its business.

FRANCHISES, TRADEMARKS, AND TRADE NAMES

A mode of operation, a widely recognized brand name (trade name), and a widely known business symbol (trademark) are all valuable assets. These assets may be licensed (commonly known as *franchising*) by their owner for use by other businesses. Many fast-food restaurants (such as McDonald's and Taco Bell) are franchises. The franchisee usually pays the owner (franchisor) an initial fee plus a contingent fee. The contingent fee is often based upon the franchisee's sales volume.

For Federal income tax purposes, a **franchise** is an agreement that gives the franchisee the right to distribute, sell, or provide goods, services, or facilities within a specified area.[10] A franchise transfer includes the grant of a franchise, a transfer by one franchisee to another person, or the renewal of a franchise.

---

[9]Reg. § 1.1235–2(b)(1).   [10]§ 1253(b)(1).

Section 1253 provides that a transfer of a franchise, trademark, or trade name is *not* a sale or exchange of a capital asset when the transferor retains any significant power, right, or continuing interest in the property transferred.

4 *Find more information on this topic at our Web site:* ***http://wft-entities.swcollege.com.***

Significant Power, Right, or Continuing Interest.   *Significant powers, rights, or continuing interests* include control over assignment of the franchise, trademark, or trade name, as well as the quality of the transferee's products or services. The following rights also are included.

- Right to require the transferee to sell or advertise *only* the transferor's products or services.
- Right to require the transferee to purchase substantially all supplies and equipment from the transferor.
- Right to receive substantial contingent payments.
- Right to terminate the franchise, trademark, or trade name at will.

In the unusual case where no significant power, right, or continuing interest is retained by the transferor, a sale or exchange may occur, and capital gain or loss treatment may be available. For capital gain or loss treatment to be available, the asset transferred must still qualify as a capital asset.

EXAMPLE 13

Orange, Inc., a franchisee, sells the franchise to a third party. Payments to Orange are not contingent, and all significant powers, rights, and continuing interests are transferred. The gain (payments – adjusted basis) on the sale is a capital gain to Orange. ■

Noncontingent Payments.   When the transferor retains a significant power, right, or continuing interest, the transferee's noncontingent payments to the transferor are ordinary income to the transferor. The franchisee capitalizes the payments and amortizes them over 15 years. The amortization is subject to recapture under § 1245, discussed later in this chapter.

EXAMPLE 14

Grey Company signs a 10-year franchise agreement with DOH Donuts. Grey (the franchisee) makes payments of $3,000 per year for the first 8 years of the franchise agreement—a total of $24,000. Grey cannot deduct $3,000 per year as the payments are made. Instead, Grey must amortize the $24,000 total over 15 years. Thus, Grey may deduct $1,600 per year for each of the 15 years of the amortization period. The same result would occur if Grey had made a $24,000 lump-sum payment at the beginning of the franchise period. Assuming DOH Donuts (the franchisor) retains significant powers, rights, or a continuing interest, it will have ordinary income when it receives the payments from Grey. ■

Contingent Payments.   Whether or not the transferor retains a significant power, right, or continuing interest, contingent franchise payments are ordinary income for the franchisor and an ordinary deduction for the franchisee.

EXAMPLE 15

TAK, a spicy chicken franchisor, transfers an eight year franchise to Egret Corporation. TAK retains a significant power, right, or continuing interest. Egret, the franchisee, agrees to pay TAK 15% of sales. This contingent payment is ordinary income to TAK and a business deduction for Egret as the payments are made. ■

Concept Summary 8–2 summarizes the rules for franchises.

CONCEPT SUMMARY 8–2

Franchises

| Event | Effect on | |
	Franchisor	Franchisee
Franchisor Retains Significant Powers and Rights		
Noncontingent payment	Ordinary income.	Capitalized and amortized over 15 years as an ordinary deduction; if franchise is sold, amortization is subject to recapture under § 1245.
Contingent payment	Ordinary income.	Ordinary deduction.
Franchisor Does *Not* Retain Significant Powers and Rights		
Noncontingent payment	Ordinary income if franchise rights are an ordinary asset; capital gain if franchise rights are a capital asset (unlikely).	Capitalized and amortized over 15 years as an ordinary deduction; if the franchise is sold, amortization is subject to recapture under § 1245.
Contingent payment	Ordinary income.	Ordinary deduction.

LEASE CANCELLATION PAYMENTS

The tax treatment of payments received for canceling a lease depends on whether the recipient of the payments is the **lessor** or the **lessee** and whether the lease is a capital asset or not.

Lessee Treatment.   Lease cancellation payments received by a lessee (the tenant) are treated as an exchange.[11] Thus, these payments are capital gains if the lease is a capital asset. Generally, a lessee's lease is a capital asset if the property (either personalty or realty) is used for the lessee's personal use (e.g., his or her residence). A lessee's lease is an ordinary asset if the property is used in the lessee's trade or business.[12]

EXAMPLE 16

Merganser, Inc., owns an apartment building that it is going to convert into an office building. Vicki is one of the apartment tenants and receives $1,000 from Merganser to cancel the lease. Vicki has a capital gain of $1,000 (which is long term or short term depending upon how long she has held the lease). Merganser has an ordinary deduction of $1,000. ■

Lessor Treatment.   Payments received by a lessor (the landlord) for a lease cancellation are always ordinary income because they are considered to be in lieu of rental payments.[13]

EXAMPLE 17

Finch & Company owns an apartment building near a university campus. Hui-Fen is one of the tenants. Hui-Fen is graduating early and offers Finch $800 to cancel the apartment lease. Finch accepts the offer. Finch has ordinary income of $800. Hui-Fen has a nondeductible payment since the apartment was personal-use property. ■

---

[11]§ 1241 and Reg. § 1.1241–1(a).
[12]Reg. § 1.1221–1(b).

[13]*Hort v. Comm.*, 41–1 USTC ¶9354, 25 AFTR 1207, 61 S.Ct. 757 (USSC, 1941).

LOSSES FROM DAY TRADING

Many investors were caught up with "Internet stock fever" during 2000. One such investor made *15,000* trades during the year. No stock was held more than one year, so each transaction resulted in a short-term capital gain or loss. Each trade had to be documented as to the basis for the stock sold, its holding period, and the selling price net of the sales commission. Unfortunately, after accounting for all transactions, the investor had a $75,000 net short-term capital loss. Only $3,000 of this loss was deductible in 2000 because the investor had no long-term capital gains to offset the loss. The $72,000 balance of the loss is carried forward and can be deducted against capital gains of later years. Unfortunately, however, the investor has no capital left to invest. Consequently, his annual loss deduction will be limited to $3,000 for many years to come.

Determine the applicable holding period for a capital asset.

Holding Period

Property must be held more than one year to qualify for long-term capital gain or loss treatment.[14] Property not held for the required long-term period results in short-term capital gain or loss. To compute the **holding period,** start counting on the day after the property was acquired and include the day of disposition.

EXAMPLE 18

Mallard & Co. purchases a capital asset on January 15, 2000, and sells it on January 16, 2001. Mallard's holding period is more than one year. If Mallard had sold the asset on January 15, 2001, the holding period would have been exactly one year, and the gain or loss would have been short term. ∎

To be held for more than one year, a capital asset acquired on the last day of any month must not be disposed of until on or after the first day of the thirteenth succeeding month.[15]

EXAMPLE 19

Purple, Inc., purchases a capital asset on March 31, 2000. If Purple sells the asset on March 31, 2001, the holding period is one year, and Purple will have a short-term capital gain or loss. If Purple sells the asset on April 1, 2001, the holding period is more than one year, and it will have a long-term capital gain or loss. ∎

SPECIAL HOLDING PERIOD RULES

There are several special holding period rules.[16] The application of these rules depends on the type of asset and how it was acquired.

Nontaxable Exchanges. The holding period of property received in a like-kind exchange (and certain other qualified nontaxable exchanges) includes the holding

---

[14]§ 1222.
[15]Rev.Rul. 66–7, 1966–1 C.B. 188.

[16]§ 1223.

period of the former asset if the property that was exchanged was either a capital asset or a § 1231 asset.

EXAMPLE 20

Red Manufacturing Corporation exchanges some vacant real estate it owns (a capital asset) for land closer to its factory. The transaction is a like-kind exchange, so the holding period of the new land includes the holding period of the old land. ■

EXAMPLE 21

A lightning strike destroyed Vireo Company's generator (a § 1231 asset) in March. Vireo uses the entire insurance proceeds it received to acquire a comparable generator. The holding period of the new generator includes the holding period of the old generator. ■

Nontaxable Transactions Involving Carryover of Another Taxpayer's Basis.   If a transaction is nontaxable and the former owner's basis carries over to the present owner, the former owner's holding period is included in (tacked on to) the present owner's holding period.

EXAMPLE 22

Kareem acquired 100 shares of Robin Corporation stock for $1,000 on December 31, 1996. He transferred the shares by gift to Megan on December 31, 2000, when the stock was worth $2,000. Kareem's basis of $1,000 becomes the basis for determining gain or loss on a subsequent sale by Megan. Megan's holding period begins with the date the stock was acquired by Kareem. ■

EXAMPLE 23

Assume the same facts as in the preceding example, except that the fair market value of the shares was only $800 on the date of the gift. If Megan sells the stock for a loss, its value at the date of the gift is her basis. Accordingly, the tacked-on holding period rule does not apply, and Megan's holding period begins with the date of the gift. So, if she sells the shares for $500 on April 1, 2001, Megan has a $300 recognized capital loss, and the holding period is from December 31, 2000, to April 1, 2001. The loss is short term. ■

Disallowed Loss Transactions.   Under several Code provisions, realized losses are disallowed. When a loss is disallowed, there is no carryover of holding period. Losses can be disallowed under § 267 (sale or exchange between related taxpayers) and § 262 (sale or exchange of personal-use assets) as well as other Code Sections. Taxpayers who acquire property in a disallowed loss transaction will begin a new holding period and will have a basis equal to the purchase price.

EXAMPLE 24

Janet sells her personal automobile at a loss. She may not deduct the loss because it arises from the sale of personal-use property. Janet purchases a replacement automobile for more than the selling price of her former automobile. Janet has a basis equal to the cost of the replacement automobile, and her holding period begins when she acquires the replacement automobile. ■

Inherited Property.   The holding period for inherited property is treated as long term no matter how long the property is actually held by the heir. The holding period of the decedent or the decedent's estate is not relevant to the heir's holding period.

EXAMPLE 25

Shonda inherits Blue Company stock from her father. She receives the stock on April 1, 2001, and sells it on November 1, 2001. Even though Shonda did not hold the stock more than one year, she receives long-term capital gain or loss treatment on the sale. ■

TRADING ADRs ON U.S. STOCK EXCHANGES

Many non-U.S. companies now have subsidiaries that were formerly U.S. companies. For instance, Chrysler Corporation is now a subsidiary of DaimlerChrysler (formed when the German company Daimler-Benz acquired Chrysler). Shares in such foreign companies generally cannot be traded directly on American stock exchanges. Instead, the foreign companies issue instruments called American Depository Receipts (ADRs) that can be traded on U.S. stock exchanges. Purchases and sales of ADRs are treated for tax purposes as though the ADRs were shares in the corporation that issued them.

SHORT SALES

A **short sale** occurs when a taxpayer sells borrowed property and repays the lender with substantially identical property either held on the date of the sale or purchased after the sale. Short sales typically involve corporate stock. The seller's objective is to make a profit in anticipation of a decline in the stock's price. If the price declines, the seller in a short sale recognizes a profit equal to the difference between the sales price of the borrowed stock and the price paid for its replacement.

Section 1233 provides that a short sale gain or loss is a capital gain or loss to the extent that the short sale property constitutes a capital asset of the taxpayer. This gain or loss is not recognized until the short sale is closed. Generally, the holding period of the short sale property is determined by how long the property used to close the short sale was held.

EXAMPLE 26

On January 4, Green & Associates sold short 100 shares of Osprey Corporation for $1,500. Green closed the transaction on July 28 of the same year by purchasing 100 shares of Osprey for $1,000 and delivering them to the broker from whom the securities were borrowed. Because this stock was held less than one year (actually less than a day), Green's gain ($1,500 sale price – $1,000 cost) is short term. ∎

EXAMPLE 27

Assume the same facts as in the preceding example, except that the January 4 short sale was not closed until July 28 of the *following* year. The result is the same, because the stock was acquired and used to close the transaction on the same day; that is, it was not held more than a year. ∎

If a taxpayer owns securities that are "substantially identical" to those sold short, § 1259 subjects the short sale to potential *constructive sale treatment*, and the taxpayer recognizes gain (but not loss) as of that date. If the taxpayer has not closed the short sale by delivering the short sale securities to the broker from whom the securities were borrowed before January 31 of the year following the short sale, the short sale is deemed to have closed on the short sale date. The holding period in such circumstances is determined by how long the securities in question were held.

EXAMPLE 28

Assume the same facts as in Example 26, except that Green & Associates owned 100 shares of Osprey Corporation when it sold short 100 shares on January 4. Green does not close the short sale before January 31 of the following year. Green must recognize any gain on its 100 shares of Osprey as of January 4. If Green owned those shares more than one year as of that date, the gain is long term. ■

5 *Find more information on this topic at our Web site:* ***http://wft-entities.swcollege.com.***

LEARNING OBJECTIVE 4

Describe the tax treatment of capital gains and losses for noncorporate taxpayers.

Tax Treatment of Capital Gains and Losses of Noncorporate Taxpayers

This section discusses how capital gains and losses are taxed to noncorporate taxpayers, that is, individuals, noncorporate partners, trusts, and estates. The rules applicable to corporations are considered in the following section of this chapter.

CAPITAL GAINS

Gains from the sale or exchange of capital assets are taxed at various rates, depending upon the holding period, the taxpayer's regular tax rate, and the type of asset involved.

Short-Term Gains. Gains on capital assets held one year or less are taxed as *ordinary income*. Accordingly, the applicable tax rates vary from 15 percent to 39.6 percent. Although short-term capital gains receive no preferential tax treatment compared to ordinary income, they do have one advantage: they can absorb capital losses without limit. As discussed later in this section, *capital losses* are deducted first against capital gains (without limit) and then against ordinary income, but only up to $3,000 per year.[17] Thus, someone with a large capital loss will find short-term capital gains attractive, even though such gains do not qualify for lower tax rates.

PLANNING CONSIDERATIONS

Timing Capital Gains

Taxpayers have considerable control over the timing of their capital gains through the mechanism of realization. Accordingly, a taxpayer might want to defer recognizing a large capital gain in a year with *substantial itemized deductions*, such as large personal casualty losses or the purchase of a new residence with large up-front interest expenses. In so doing, the taxpayer minimizes the loss of such deductions due to AGI limitations and deduction phase-outs applicable to some high-income individuals.

Nontax considerations, of course, often dictate when assets are sold. If a particular stock is peaking in popularity, selling it might be a wise investment strategy, even if the

taxpayer's current tax situation is not optimal. Similarly, if a taxpayer needs cash to start a business, purchase a home, or pay for a child's education or medical costs, the capital asset might need to be sold at a time when investment *and* tax considerations counsel otherwise. In these circumstances, however, a taxpayer might choose to *borrow* the money required and use the capital asset as collateral for the loan, rather than sell the asset. A loan does not trigger tax consequences, and the taxpayer can continue to hold the asset until a more opportune time—albeit at the cost of paying interest, which may be nondeductible.

[17]§ 1211(b).

TAX FACT

BENEFICIAL TAX TREATMENT FOR CAPITAL GAINS

The Tax Reform Act of 1986 repealed beneficial tax treatment for capital gains. Beneficial tax treatment was reinstated for individual taxpayers through the alternative tax on net capital gain beginning in 1991. Note that while the *Internal Revenue Code of 1986* includes a Code Section [§ 1201] that provides for an alternative tax calculation for corporations, it does not now produce beneficial tax results (i.e., the § 1201 rate of 35 percent is the same as the highest statutory tax rate for corporations in § 11).

The number of individual income tax returns including net capital gain in AGI is as follows.

Year	Number of Returns (in Millions)
1975	5.8
1980	7.0
1985	10.0
1990	9.2
1995	14.8

Source: IRS Tax Stats.

Long-Term Gains.   Gains on capital assets held more than one year are classified as *long-term* gains and are eligible for a special 20 percent tax rate, or 10 percent rate for taxpayers in the 15 percent tax bracket.[18] The benefit of these long-term capital gain tax rates, therefore, is as follows.

Ordinary Income	Capital Gain	Differential
15%	10%	5
28	20	8
31	20	11
36	20	16
39.6	20	19.6

For persons in the 15 percent tax bracket, only the amount of the gain that would fall within that bracket is eligible for the 10 percent rate. Any remaining gain is taxed at 20 percent.

EXAMPLE 23

Gene is an accounting student with taxable income from summer earnings and part-time work of $15,000 after applicable personal deductions. Gene sells stock that he purchased three years ago and realizes a long-term capital gain of $20,000. His tax is determined as follows:

---

[18]Starting in 2001, taxpayers in the 15% bracket are eligible for an 8% tax rate on capital assets held more than *five years*. Taxpayers in the 28% and higher brackets will be eligible for an 18% tax rate on capital assets held more than five years if those assets were acquired *after* 2000 [§ 1(h)(2)]. Thus, this 18% rate will not apply until 2006—assuming that the law is not changed before then!

(a)	Regular tax (15%) on his earned income of $15,000	$2,250
(b)	10% on the portion of his capital gain that is within the 15% tax bracket ($27,050 in 2001 – $15,000 earnings taxed in [a] above = $12,050)	1,205
(c)	20% on the rest of his capital gain ($20,000 gain – $12,050 taxed in [b] above = $7,950)	1,590
	Tax due	$5,045

The tax on Gene's $20,000 long-term capital gain is $2,795 ($1,205 + $1,590), an effective rate of 13.98%. ∎

In point of fact, relatively few capital gains are realized by persons in the 15 percent tax bracket. Thus, the tax rate that generally applies to long-term capital gains is 20 percent.

There are two major exceptions, however, to this general treatment. The first exception is so-called *28% property*, which consists of the following items.

- **Collectibles** (works of art, rugs, antiques, gems, coins, stamps, and alcoholic beverages) held more than one year.
- The taxable half of the gain on sales of *qualified small business stock* (see the end of this section).

These assets are labeled *28% property*, because the gains that they produce are taxed at 28 percent rather than 20 percent. But this 28 percent rate is a *maximum* rate, so a taxpayer in the 15 percent bracket would pay only 15 percent. As a result, the benefit of the applicable tax rates for gains on 28% property is as follows.

Ordinary Income	Applicable Rate	Differential
15%	15%	None
28	28	None
31	28	3
36	28	8
39.6	28	11.6

In other words, these gains receive preferential tax treatment only when realized by taxpayers in the top three tax brackets.

PLANNING CONSIDERATIONS

Gifts of Appreciated Securities

Persons with appreciated securities that have been held over one year may reduce the tax due on their sale by giving the securities to someone (often a child) who is in the *lowest tax bracket*. The donor's holding period carries over, along with his or her basis, and the donee's lower tax rate applies when the securities are sold. As a result, the gain is taxed at 10 percent, rather than 20 percent. The donee should be over age 13 by year-end, however, or a *kiddie tax* will nullify most of the tax advantage being sought. The kiddie tax subjects the gain to the parents' tax rate. See Chapter 15.

Such gifts usually bear no gift tax due to the annual $10,000 exclusion. But the money received after payment of the tax belongs to the donee. It is not available to the donor, nor may it be used to pay a parent's essential support obligations. Moreover, these funds may affect a child's eligibility for need-based financial aid when applying to college.

Capital Gains of Noncorporate Taxpayers

Type of Asset	Applicable Rate
Held not more than one year.	15%–39.6%, same as ordinary income.
Collectibles held more than one year.	15% for lowest bracket taxpayers, 28% for all others.
Taxable portion (50%) of gain on qualified small business stock held more than five years.	15% for lowest bracket taxpayers, 28% for all others.
Unrecaptured § 1250 gain on depreciable real estate held more than one year.	15% for lowest bracket taxpayers, 25% for all others.
Other capital assets held more than one year.	10% for lowest bracket taxpayers, 20% for all others.

The second major exception involves depreciable real estate that has been held more than one year. Some—but not all—of the gain attributable to depreciation deductions on apartments, office buildings, shopping centers, and warehouses is taxable at 25 percent rather than 20 percent. The amount that is taxed in this manner depends upon how much depreciation is "recaptured" as ordinary income under § 1250, as explained later in this chapter. Accordingly, these gains are called *unrecaptured § 1250 gain* [§ 1(h)(7)]. In any case, the 25 percent rate is a *maximum* rate, so the benefit of the applicable tax rates for gains from the sale of depreciable real estate is as follows.

Ordinary Income	Applicable Rate	Differential
15%	15%	None
28	25	3
31	25	6
36	25	11
39.6	25	14.6

The capital gain tax rates for noncorporate taxpayers are summarized in Concept Summary 8–3.

CAPITAL LOSSES

As explained above, capital gains can be classified into four general categories.

- Short term—taxed as ordinary income.
- 28% property—taxed at 15 percent or 28 percent.
- Unrecaptured § 1250 gain—taxed at 15 percent or 25 percent.
- Regular long term—taxed at 10 percent or 20 percent.

A taxpayer can also have losses from capital assets in *three* of these four categories. The *unrecaptured § 1250 gain* category contains only gain. When both gains and losses occur in the year, they must be netted against each other in the order specified below.

Step 1. Group all gains and losses into short-term, 28% property, unrecaptured § 1250, and regular long-term categories.

Step 2. Net the gains and losses within each category to obtain net short-term, 28% property, unrecaptured § 1250, and regular long-term gain or loss.

Step 3. Offset the net 28% property and unrecaptured § 1250 amounts if they are of opposite sign. Add them if they have the same sign. Then, offset the resulting amount against the regular net long-term amount, or add the amounts if they have the same sign.

Step 4. Offset the result of step 3 with the net short-term gain or loss from step 2 if they are of opposite sign.

These netting rules offset net capital losses against the *highest taxed gain first.* Consequently, if there is a net short-term capital loss, it first offsets any net 28% property gain, any remaining loss offsets unrecaptured § 1250 gain, and then any remaining loss offsets regular long-term gain.

If the result of step 4 is *only* a short-term capital gain, the taxpayer is not eligible for a reduced tax rate. If the result of step 4 is a loss, a **net capital loss** exists, and the taxpayer may be eligible for a *capital loss deduction* (discussed later in this chapter). If there was no offsetting in step 4 because the short-term and step 3 results were both gains *or* if the result of the offsetting is either a 28% property, an unrecaptured § 1250 property, and/or a regular long-term gain, a **net capital gain** exists, and the taxpayer may be eligible for a reduced tax rate. The net capital gain may consist of regular *long-term gain, unrecaptured § 1250 gain, and/or 28% property gain.* Each of these gains may be taxed at a different rate.

EXAMPLE 30

This example shows how a net long-term capital loss is applied.

Step	Short Term	28% Property	Unrecaptured § 1250	Regular Long Term	Comment
1	$ 3,000	$ 1,000		$ 3,000	
				(8,000)	
2	$ 3,000	$ 1,000		($ 5,000)	
3		(1,000)	→	1,000	Netted because of opposite sign.
		$ –0–		($ 4,000)	
4	(3,000)	→	→	3,000	The net short-term gain is netted against the net regular long-term loss, and the remaining loss is eligible for the capital loss deduction.
	$ –0–			($ 1,000)	

EXAMPLE 31

This example shows how net short-term and regular long-term capital losses are applied.

Step	Short Term	28% Property	Unrecaptured § 1250	Regular Long Term	Comment
1	$ 3,000	$15,000	$4,000	$ 3,000	
	(5,000)	(7,000)		(8,000)	
2	($ 2,000)	$ 8,000	$4,000	($ 5,000)	
3		(5,000)	←	5,000	Net regular long-term loss is netted against 28% gain first.
		$ 3,000		$ –0–	

TAX FACT

DETRIMENTAL TAX TREATMENT FOR CAPITAL LOSSES

A corporate taxpayer cannot deduct a net capital loss against ordinary income. It can carry the loss back three years and forward five years in search of capital gains. An individual taxpayer can deduct a maximum of $3,000 of net capital loss against ordinary income in the current tax year. Any excess can be carried forward indefinitely in search of capital gains. After capital gains are exhausted in each carryforward year, a maximum of $3,000 of the remaining net capital loss can be deducted against ordinary income.

The number of individual income tax returns with a net capital loss in AGI is as follows.

Year	Number of Returns (in Millions)
1975	2.5
1980	2.0
1985	2.7
1990	5.0
1995	5.1

Source: IRS Tax Stats.

Step	Short Term	28% Property	Unrecaptured § 1250	Regular Long Term	Comment
4	2,000 →	(2,000)			Short-term loss is netted against 28% gain first.
	$ –0–	$ 1,000	$4,000		
		Net 28% gain	Net 25% gain		

If a net loss remains after applying these rules for offsetting losses, a taxpayer may deduct up to $3,000 of that loss against ordinary income.[19] Losses in excess of $3,000 are carried over to future years where they are applied first against capital gains and then deducted up to $3,000 per year. Capital loss carryovers expire, however, when the taxpayer dies.

EXAMPLE 32

James incurred a $10,000 loss on his only capital asset transaction in 2001. If he has no other capital asset transactions from that point on, his $10,000 loss is deducted as follows.

---

[19]§ 1211(b)(1). Married persons filing separate returns are limited to a $1,500 deduction per tax year.

Year	Deduction
2001	$3,000
2002	3,000
2003	3,000
2004	1,000

EXAMPLE 33

Assume the same facts as in the preceding example, except that James realizes a capital gain of $4,500 in 2003. At that time, his remaining capital loss carryover is $4,000 ($10,000 − $6,000 deducted previously). Since his capital gain in 2003 (i.e., $4,500) exceeds this loss carryforward, James can deduct the entire $4,000 against that year's capital gain. ■

EXAMPLE 34

Assume the same facts as in Example 32, except that James died in late 2002. His remaining capital loss carryforward of $4,000 ($10,000 − $6,000 deducted in 2001 and 2002) expires unused. ■

When a taxpayer's capital loss exceeds $3,000 and derives from more than one category, it is used in the following order: first, short term; then, 28% property; then, unrecaptured § 1250 property; and finally, regular long term. Unused losses are carried forward as follows: short-term losses carry forward as short-term losses, and long-term losses carry forward as long-term losses.

EXAMPLE 35

Nancy incurs a long-term capital loss of $8,500 this year, of which $3,000 is deducted against her ordinary income. The remaining $5,500 ($8,500 loss − $3,000 deducted) carries forward as a long-term capital loss. ■

PLANNING CONSIDERATIONS

Matching Gains with Losses

A taxpayer who has already realized a large capital gain may want to *match this gain* with an *offsetting capital loss*. Doing so will shelter the capital gain from taxation and will also free up an asset that has declined in value. Without the capital gain, after all, the taxpayer might hesitate to sell a loss asset, because the resulting capital loss may be deductible only in $3,000 annual increments.

Similarly, a taxpayer with a large realized capital loss might use the occasion to sell some appreciated assets. Doing so would enable the taxpayer to use the capital loss immediately and at the same time realize the benefit of the asset appreciation at little or no tax cost.

On the other hand, matching capital losses and long-term capital gains means that the taxpayer utilizes the capital loss against income that would otherwise qualify for a preferential tax rate of 10 to 28 percent. If the taxpayer's ordinary income is taxed at a higher rate, he or she might prefer to deduct the loss against that higher taxed income, even on a schedule of $3,000 per year. The *time value of money* must be considered; a current-year deduction at 10 to 28 percent might be worth more than a series of annual deductions at higher rates spread over several years.

Nontax considerations, such as investment prospects for the particular assets in question, are also important. But in the real world, future investment prospects are often unknowable or at least highly speculative, while tax impacts can be determined with relative certainty—which explains some of the late December selling activity in publicly traded securities and mutual funds.

INTERNATIONAL IMPLICATIONS

CAPITAL GAIN TREATMENT AND FOREIGN STOCK

U.S. shareholders of certain foreign corporations may find that they are denied capital gain treatment upon sale or other disposal of their stock. If a foreign corporation is considered a controlled foreign corporation (CFC) because certain U.S. shareholders as a group own more than 50 percent by vote or value, any gain recognized upon disposition of the stock will be recharacterized as dividend income to the extent of the foreign corporation's earnings and profits yet to be taxed in the United States.

U.S. persons investing in foreign corporations ultimately receive income taxable in the United States through dividends or capital gains upon disposition of the stock. If a foreign corporation pays no dividends, the U.S. shareholder's entire return from the stock investment is in the form of a gain on disposition of the stock, with the accumulated earnings of the foreign corporation reflected in that gain. This provision protects the ability of the United States to tax these accumulated earnings as ordinary dividend income when they ultimately are realized by U.S. persons.

interest relating to gains

SMALL BUSINESS STOCK

A special 50 percent *exclusion* is available to noncorporate taxpayers who derive capital gains from the sale or exchange of **qualified small business stock.**[20] Half of the gain is excluded from the taxpayer's gross income, and the other half is subjected to a maximum tax rate of 28 percent, as noted earlier in this section.

EXAMPLE 36

Yolanda realized a $100,000 gain on the sale of qualified small business stock. Assuming that Yolanda has a 36% marginal tax rate without considering this gain, $50,000 of this gain is excluded from her gross income, and the other $50,000 is taxed at a maximum tax rate of 28%. Thus, Yolanda owes tax of $14,000 ($50,000 × 28%), an effective tax rate of 14% on the entire $100,000 capital gain. ∎

This treatment is more favorable than the capital gain tax treatment explained previously. Accordingly, Congress imposed additional restrictions to ensure that the gains receiving this treatment were derived in the circumstances that Congress intended to promote. These restrictions include the following:

- The stock must have been newly issued *after* August 10, 1993.
- The taxpayer must have held the stock *more than five years.*
- The issuing corporation must use at least 80 percent of its assets, determined by their value, in the *active conduct* of a trade or business.
- When the stock was issued, the issuing corporation's assets must not have exceeded $50 million, at adjusted basis, including the proceeds of the stock issuance.
- The corporation does not engage in banking, financing, insurance, investing, leasing, farming, mineral extraction, hotel or motel operation, restaurant operation, or any business whose principal asset is the *reputation or skill* of

---

[20]§ 1202(a).

its employees (such as accounting, architecture, health, law, engineering, or financial services).

Even if each of these requirements is met, the amount of gain eligible for the exclusion is limited to the *greater* of 10 times the taxpayer's basis in the stock or $10 million per taxpayer per company,[21] computed on an aggregate basis.

EXAMPLE 37

Vanita purchased $100,000 of qualified small business stock when it was first issued in October 1995. In 2001, she sells the stock for $4 million. Her gain is $3.9 million ($4,000,000 − $100,000). Although this amount exceeds 10 times her basis ($100,000 × 10 = $1,000,000), it is *less* than $10 million, so the entire $3.9 million gain is eligible for the 50% exclusion. ■

Transactions that fail to satisfy *any one* of the applicable requirements are taxed as capital gains (and losses) realized by noncorporate taxpayers generally. See Concept Summary 8–3.

Gains are also eligible for *nonrecognition* treatment if the sale proceeds are invested in other qualified small business stock within 60 days.[22] To the extent that the sale proceeds are not so invested, gain is recognized, but the 50 percent exclusion still applies. To be eligible for this treatment, the stock sold must have been held more than six months.

EXAMPLE 38

Assume the same facts as in the preceding example, except that Vanita sold her stock in January 2001 and used $3.5 million of the sale proceeds to purchase other qualified small business stock one month later. Vanita's gain is recognized to the extent that the sale proceeds were not reinvested—namely, $500,000 ($4,000,000 sale proceeds − $3,500,000 reinvested). The 50% exclusion will apply, however, to this amount. ■

6 *Find more information on this topic at our Web site: **http://wft-entities.swcollege.com**.*

LEARNING OBJECTIVE 5
Describe the tax treatment of capital gains and losses for corporate taxpayers.

Tax Treatment of Capital Gains and Losses of Corporate Taxpayers

The treatment of a corporation's net capital gain or loss differs dramatically from the rules for noncorporate taxpayers discussed in the preceding section. Briefly, the differences are as follows.

- There is a capital gains alternative tax rate of 35 percent.[23] However, since the maximum corporate tax rate is 35 percent, the alternative tax is never beneficial. In other words, capital gains are taxed as ordinary income.
- Capital losses offset only capital gains. No deduction of capital losses is permitted against ordinary taxable income.
- There is a three-year carryback and a five-year carryover period for net capital losses.[24] Capital loss carryovers and carrybacks are always treated as short term, regardless of their original nature.

EXAMPLE 39

Sparrow Corporation has a $15,000 long-term capital loss for the current year and $57,000 of ordinary taxable income. Sparrow may not offset the $15,000 long-term capital loss against

---

[21]For married persons filing separately, the limitation is $5 million.
[22]§ 1045(a).

[23]§ 1201.
[24]§ 1212(a)(1).

its ordinary income by taking a capital loss deduction. The $15,000 long-term capital loss becomes a $15,000 short-term capital loss for carryback and carryover purposes. This amount may offset capital gains in the three-year carryback period or, if not absorbed there, offset capital gains in the five-year carryover period. Any amount remaining after this carryover period expires is permanently lost. ■

LEARNING OBJECTIVE 6

Distinguish § 1231 assets from ordinary and capital assets, and calculate § 1231 gain or loss.

Section 1231 Assets

Businesses own many assets that are used in the business rather than held for resale. In financial accounting, such assets are known as "fixed assets." For example, a foundry's 30,000-pound stamping machine is a fixed asset. It is also a depreciable asset. The building housing the foundry is another fixed asset. The remainder of this chapter largely deals with how to *classify* the gains and losses from the disposition of fixed assets. Chapter 4 discussed how to depreciate such assets. Chapter 7 discussed how to determine the adjusted basis and the amount of gain or loss from their disposition.

RELATIONSHIP TO CAPITAL ASSETS

At first glance, *classification of fixed assets* ought to be straightforward. Section 1221(a)(2) specifically excludes from the capital asset definition any property that is depreciable or that is real estate "used in a trade or business." Accordingly, the foundry's stamping machine and the building housing the foundry described above are not capital assets. Therefore, one would expect gains to be taxed as ordinary income and losses to be deductible as ordinary losses. Since World War II, however, certain business assets have received more favorable treatment.

Section 1231 provides that business assets held for more than one year can receive the best of both worlds: capital gain treatment on gains and ordinary loss treatment on losses. More specifically, this provision requires that gains and losses from **§ 1231 property** be compiled at the end of the taxable year; the *net result* is then classified as capital gain if a net gain is produced, or as ordinary loss if a net loss is produced. As a result, a particular disposition's character as capital or ordinary is not determined until the taxable year has concluded and all of the taxpayer's **§ 1231 gains and losses** are tabulated.

EXAMPLE 40

Brown & Co. sells business land and building at a $5,000 gain and equipment at a $3,000 loss. Both properties were held for more than one year. Brown's net gain is $2,000, and that net gain may be treated as a long-term capital gain under § 1231. ■

EXAMPLE 41

Chickadee, Inc., sells equipment at a $10,000 loss and business land at a $2,000 gain. Both properties were held for more than one year. Chickadee's net loss is $8,000, and that net loss is an ordinary loss. ■

7 *Find more information on this topic at our Web site:* **http://wft-entities.swcollege.com.**

Years after World War II, Congress decided that § 1231's highly favorable treatment was no longer entirely appropriate. Rather than repeal § 1231, however, Congress chose to take back some—but not all—of its benefits through the *recapture provisions* of §§ 1245 and 1250, which are discussed later in this chapter.

TAX IN THE NEWS

SALE OF "CAMPUS" LAND YIELDS POTENTIAL LONG-TERM CAPITAL GAIN

In late 2000, a large suburban Chicago insurance corporation announced that it was planning to sell 500 acres of land surrounding its headquarters "campus." The land contains lakes, a golf course, tennis courts, and a farm. All of these facilities were available for use by the corporation's employees. Now, however, the corporation has significantly downsized its workforce and moved many of its operations to other cities. Consequently, it is going to sell the 500 acres to a developer who will build luxury homes there. Since the land has been used in the corporation's business and has been held more than a year, it is a § 1231 asset. The gain from disposition of the land is a § 1231 gain.

PROPERTY INCLUDED

Section 1231 property includes the following.

- Depreciable or real property used in business (principally machinery and equipment, buildings, and land).
- Property held for the production of income if it has been involuntarily converted.
- Timber, coal, or domestic iron ore to which § 631 applies.
- Livestock held for draft, breeding, dairy, or sporting purposes.
- Unharvested crops on land used in business.
- Certain *purchased* intangible assets (such as patents and goodwill) that are eligible for amortization.

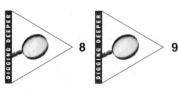 8 9 *Find more information on these topics at our Web site: **http://wft-entities.swcollege.com**.*

PROPERTY EXCLUDED

Section 1231 property does *not* include the following.

- Property not held more than one year. Livestock must be held at least 12 months (24 months in some cases). Unharvested crops do not have to be held more than one year, but the land must be so held.
- Property where casualty losses exceed casualty gains for the taxable year. If a taxpayer has a net casualty loss, the casualty gains and losses are treated as ordinary gains and losses.
- Inventory and property held primarily for sale to customers.
- Copyrights; literary, musical, or artistic compositions, etc.; and certain U.S. government publications.
- Accounts receivable and notes receivable arising in the ordinary course of the trade or business.

CASUALTY OR THEFT AND NONPERSONAL-USE CAPITAL ASSETS

When § 1231 assets are disposed of by casualty or theft, a special netting rule is applied. For simplicity, the term *casualty* is used to mean both casualty and theft dispositions. First, the casualty gains and losses from § 1231 assets *and* the casualty gains and losses from **long-term nonpersonal-use capital assets** are determined.

For business entities, virtually any capital asset is a nonpersonal-use capital asset, because partnerships, limited liability companies, and corporations are incapable of using assets *personally*. This classification, therefore, is most significant to individual taxpayers who might use certain capital assets as part of their daily life.

Once the casualty gains and losses from § 1231 assets and nonpersonal-use capital assets are determined, they are netted together. If the result is a *net gain*, the net gain is treated as § 1231 gain, but if the result is a *net loss*, the net loss is deducted outside § 1231. Thus, whether these casualties get § 1231 treatment depends on the results of the casualty netting process.

Casualties and thefts are *involuntary conversions*, it should be recalled, and gains from such conversions need not be recognized if the proceeds are timely reinvested in similar property. Thus, the netting process described above would not consider any casualty and theft gains that are being deferred because insurance proceeds were reinvested according to the requirements of § 1033 (see Chapter 7). Section 1231, in other words, has no effect on whether a *realized* gain or loss is recognized. Instead, § 1231 merely dictates how a *recognized* gain will be classified.

This special netting process for casualties and thefts does not apply to *condemnation* gains and losses. As a result, if a § 1231 asset is disposed of by condemnation, any resulting gain or loss will get § 1231 treatment.

GENERAL PROCEDURE FOR § 1231 COMPUTATION

The tax treatment of § 1231 gains and losses depends on the results of a rather complex *netting* procedure. The steps in this netting procedure are as follows.

Step 1: Casualty Netting.   Net all recognized long-term gains and losses from casualties of § 1231 assets and nonpersonal-use capital assets. This casualty netting is beneficial because if there is a net gain, the gain may receive long-term capital gain treatment. If there is a net loss, it receives ordinary loss treatment.

    a. If the casualty gains exceed the casualty losses, add the net gain to the other § 1231 gains for the taxable year.

    b. If the casualty losses exceed the casualty gains, exclude all casualty losses and gains from further § 1231 computation. The casualty gains are ordinary income and the casualty losses are deductible. For individual taxpayers, the casualty losses must be classified further. Section 1231 asset casualty losses are deductible *for* AGI, while other casualty losses are deductible *from* AGI.

Step 2: § 1231 Netting.   After adding any net casualty gain from Step 1a to the other § 1231 gains and losses (including *recognized* § 1231 asset condemnation gains and losses), net all § 1231 gains and losses.

    a. If the gains exceed the losses, the net gain is offset by the "lookback" nonrecaptured § 1231 losses (see step 3 below) from the prior five tax years. To the extent of this offset, the net § 1231 gain is classified as ordinary income. Any remaining gain is long-term capital gain.

    b. If the losses exceed the gains, the net loss is deducted against ordinary income. For individual taxpayers only, the gains are ordinary income, the § 1231 asset losses are deductible *for* AGI, and the other casualty losses are deductible *from* AGI.

Examples 42 and 43 illustrate the application of the § 1231 computation procedure.

EXAMPLE 42   Falcon Management, Inc., recognized the following gains and losses this year.

Capital Gains and Losses	
Long-term capital gain	$ 3,000
Long-term capital loss	(400)
Short-term capital gain	1,000
Short-term capital loss	(200)

Casualties	
Gain from insurance recovery on fire loss to building, owned five years	$ 1,200
Loss from theft of computer (uninsured), owned two years	(1,000)

§ 1231 Gains and Losses from Depreciable Business Assets Held Long Term	
Asset A	$ 300
Asset B	1,100
Asset C	(500)

Gains and Losses from Sale of Depreciable Business Assets Held Short Term	
Asset D	$ 200
Asset E	(300)

Falcon had no net § 1231 losses in prior tax years.

Disregarding the recapture of depreciation (discussed later in this chapter), Falcon's gains and losses receive the following tax treatment.

- The casualty netting of the § 1231 and nonpersonal-use capital assets contains two items—the $1,200 gain from the business building and the $1,000 loss from the computer. Consequently, there is a $200 net gain and that gain is treated as a § 1231 gain (added to the § 1231 gains).
- The gains from § 1231 transactions (Assets A, B, and C and the § 1231 asset casualty gain) exceed the losses by $1,100 ($1,600 − $500). This excess is a long-term capital gain and is added to Falcon's other long-term capital gains.
- Falcon's net long-term capital gain is $3,700 ($3,000 + $1,100 from § 1231 transactions − $400 long-term capital loss). Its net short-term capital gain is $800 ($1,000 − $200). The result is capital gain income of $4,500, which will be taxed at ordinary rates. If Falcon were an individual rather than a corporation, the $3,700 net long-term capital gain portion would be eligible for preferential capital gain treatment, and the $800 net short-term capital gain would be taxed as ordinary income.
- Falcon treats the gain and loss from Assets D and E as ordinary gain and loss, because § 1231 does not apply unless the assets have been held more than one year.[25]

Results of the Gains and Losses on Falcon's Tax Computation	
Net long-term capital gain	$3,700
Net short-term capital gain	800
Ordinary gain from sale of Asset D	200
Ordinary loss from sale of Asset E	(300)
Gross income	$4,400

---

[25]§ 1231(b)(1).

EXAMPLE 43

Assume the same facts as in the preceding example, except that the loss from Asset C was $1,700 instead of $500.

- The treatment of the casualty gains and losses is the same.
- The losses from § 1231 transactions now exceed the gains by $100 ($1,700 − $1,600). As a result, the net loss is deducted in full as an ordinary loss.
- Capital gain income is $3,400 ($2,600 long term + $800 short term).

Results of the Gains and Losses on Falcon's Tax Computation

Net long-term capital gain	$2,600
Net short-term capital gain	800
Net ordinary loss on Assets A, B, and C and § 1231 casualty gain	(100)
Ordinary gain from sale of Asset D	200
Ordinary loss from sale of Asset E	(300)
Gross income	$3,200

Step 3: § 1231 Lookback Provision.   The net § 1231 gain from step 2a is offset by the nonrecaptured net § 1231 losses for the five preceding taxable years.[26] For 2001, the lookback years are 1996, 1997, 1998, 1999, and 2000. To the extent of the nonrecaptured net § 1231 loss, the current-year net § 1231 gain is ordinary income. The *nonrecaptured* net § 1231 losses are those that have not already been used to offset net § 1231 gains. Only the net § 1231 gain exceeding this net § 1231 loss carryforward is given long-term capital gain treatment. The **§ 1231 lookback** provision and the other netting rules are included in Concept Summary 8–4. Examples 44 and 45 illustrate this provision.

EXAMPLE 44

Komodo Manufacturing Corporation sold various used machines and some business real estate during 2001 for a net § 1231 gain of $25,000. During 2000, Komodo had no § 1231 transactions, but in 1999, it had a net § 1231 loss of $17,000. This loss causes $17,000 of the 2001 gain to be classified as ordinary income. The remaining 2001 gain of $8,000 ($25,000 of § 1231 gain − $17,000 nonrecaptured loss) is § 1231 gain. ∎

EXAMPLE 45

Assume the same facts as in the preceding example, except that Komodo had a net § 1231 loss of $37,000 in 1999 and a net § 1231 gain of $10,000 in 2000.

- The 1999 net § 1231 loss of $37,000 would cause the net § 1231 gain of $10,000 in 2000 to be classified as ordinary income, and $27,000 ($37,000 loss − $10,000 recaptured) would carry over to 2001.
- The remaining nonrecaptured § 1231 loss of $27,000 from 1999 completely offsets the § 1231 gain of $25,000 from 2001, making that entire gain ordinary income.
- The remaining nonrecaptured § 1231 loss from 1999 is $2,000 ($27,000 carried to 2001 − $25,000 recaptured). This recapture potential carries over to 2002. ∎

LEARNING OBJECTIVE 7

Determine when recapture provisions apply and their effect.

Section 1245 Recapture

As the preceding section explained, when Congress determined that § 1231 was unduly generous, it chose to *recapture* some of § 1231's benefits rather than repeal that section altogether. This recapture phenomenon applies exclusively to the gain

---

[26]§ 1231(c).

CONCEPT SUMMARY 8–4

Section 1231 Netting Procedure

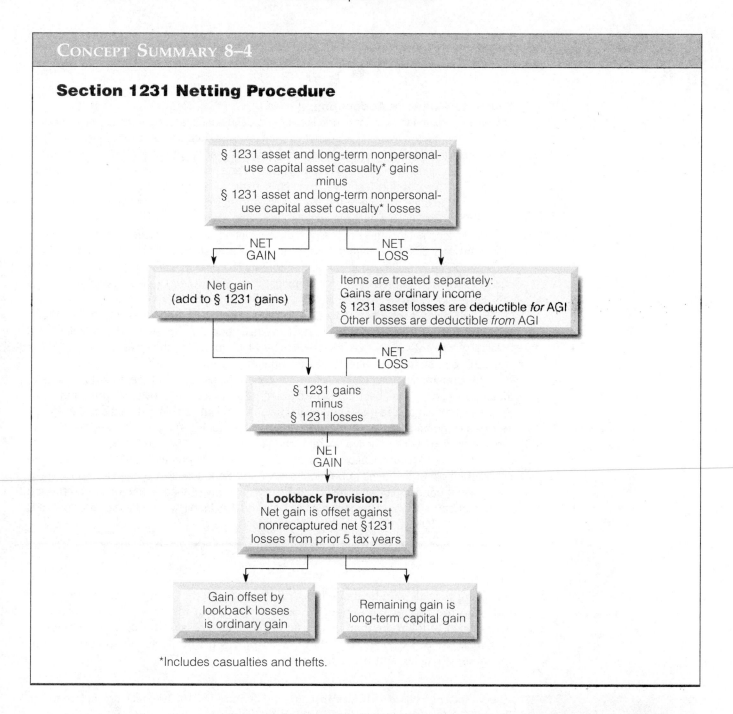

§ 1231 asset and long-term nonpersonal-use capital asset casualty* gains
minus
§ 1231 asset and long-term nonpersonal-use capital asset casualty* losses

NET GAIN

NET LOSS

Net gain
(add to § 1231 gains)

Items are treated separately:
Gains are ordinary income
§ 1231 asset losses are deductible *for* AGI
Other losses are deductible *from* AGI

NET LOSS

§ 1231 gains
minus
§ 1231 losses

NET GAIN

Lookback Provision:
Net gain is offset against
nonrecaptured net §1231
losses from prior 5 tax years

Gain offset by
lookback losses
is ordinary gain

Remaining gain is
long-term capital gain

*Includes casualties and thefts.

side of § 1231; the ordinary loss feature applicable to § 1231 property is not affected by the Code's recapture provisions. In essence, recapture takes part—often all—of the gain from the sale or exchange of a § 1231 asset and classifies it as *ordinary income* before the netting process of § 1231 begins. Accordingly, recaptured gain is computed *first*, without considering the other § 1231 transactions that occurred during the taxable year. This section discusses the § 1245 recapture rules, and the next section discusses the § 1250 recapture rules.

Section 1245 requires taxpayers to treat all gain as ordinary gain unless the property is sold for more than its original cost. This result is accomplished by

BRIDGE DISCIPLINE

Bridge to Financial Accounting

The essence of much of the tax code is to create definitions that discriminate among certain types of income or expenditure, so that special tax treatment can be afforded to one of the definitional groups. For instance, municipal bond interest might be favored over corporate bond interest income, long-term capital gains over short-term capital gains or ordinary income, and processing fees over bribes. In each case, the former generally allows a reduction of taxable income or the tax liability and helps the taxpayer to meet its goal of maximizing the available after-tax income that it generates.

Maximizing net income also is a goal of financial accounting, at least from the viewpoint of current and potential shareholders. In the long run, stock prices may advance solely because of the positive earnings that the corporation generates relative to the rest of the capital markets. The greater the net earnings, the greater the increase in stock price and private wealth.

But financial accounting makes far fewer distinctions when classifying the reporting entity's revenues and expenses. Most of the tax code's definitions and distinctions are politically or economically motivated means by which to reduce the effective tax rate of the taxpayer, perhaps without affecting its nominal rate.

The preferential treatment of long-term capital gains is one of the most long-lived of these tax fictions. The "best of both worlds" § 1231 treatment is over 60 years old itself. Whereas the gain or loss generated by the sale of a business or investment asset is merely included in the body of the income statement of the reporting entity, § 1221 and § 1231 can reduce the taxpayer's effective tax rate, and § 1245 and § 1250 can increase it.

Differences in classification of income and deductions created solely by the tax code constitute most of the items to be reconciled in the Schedule M–1 of the C corporation, S corporation, partnership, and limited liability entity. Many of these items must be reported as permanent or timing differences in the Deferred Tax Liability account regulated by APB 28 and SFAS 109.

---

requiring that all gain be treated as ordinary gain to the extent of the depreciation taken on the property disposed of. Section 1231 gain results only if the property is disposed of for more than its original cost. The excess of the sales price over the original cost is § 1231 gain. Section 1245 applies primarily to personalty such as machinery, trucks, and office furniture.

EXAMPLE 46

Avocet, Inc., purchased a $100,000 machine and deducted $70,000 depreciation before selling it for $80,000. Avocet's gain is $50,000 [$80,000 amount realized – $30,000 adjusted basis ($100,000 cost – $70,000 depreciation taken)]. Section 1245 treats as ordinary income (not as § 1231 gain) any gain to the extent of depreciation taken. In this example, the entire $50,000 gain would be ordinary income. ■

EXAMPLE 47

If Avocet, Inc., in the preceding example sold the machine for $120,000, it would have a gain of $90,000 ($120,000 amount realized – $30,000 adjusted basis). The § 1245 gain would be $70,000 (equal to the depreciation taken), and the remaining gain of $20,000 (equal to the excess of the sales price over the original cost) would be § 1231 gain. ■

EXAMPLE 48

Assume the same facts as in Example 46, except that the asset is sold for $25,000 instead of $80,000. Avocet's loss is $5,000 ($25,000 amount realized − $30,000 adjusted basis). Since there is a loss, there is no depreciation recapture. All of the loss is § 1231 loss. ■

Section 1245 recapture applies to the portion of *recognized* gain from the sale or other disposition of § 1245 property that represents depreciation, including § 167 depreciation, § 168 cost recovery, § 179 immediate expensing, and § 197 amortization. Section 1245 merely *classifies* gain as ordinary income; it does not cause gain to be recognized. Thus, in Example 46, Avocet, Inc., recaptures as ordinary income only the $50,000 of actual gain, not the entire $70,000 of depreciation taken. In other words, § 1245 recaptures the *lower* of the depreciation taken or the gain recognized.

The method of depreciation (e.g., accelerated or straight-line) does not matter. All depreciation taken is potentially subject to recapture. Thus, § 1245 recapture is often referred to as *full recapture*. Any remaining gain after subtracting the amount recaptured as ordinary income will usually be § 1231 gain. The remaining gain is casualty gain, however, if the asset is disposed of in a casualty event. For example, if the machine in Example 47 had been disposed of by casualty and the $120,000 received had been an insurance recovery, Avocet would still have a gain of $90,000, and $70,000 of that gain would still be recaptured by § 1245 as ordinary gain. The other $20,000 of gain, however, would be casualty gain.

If § 1245 property is disposed of in a transaction other than a sale, exchange, or involuntary conversion, the maximum amount recaptured is the excess of the property's fair market value over its adjusted basis. See the discussion under Exceptions to §§ 1245 and 1250 later in this chapter.

SECTION 1245 PROPERTY

Generally, § 1245 property includes all depreciable personal property (e.g., machinery and equipment), including livestock. Buildings and their structural components usually are not § 1245 property. The following property is *also* subject to § 1245 treatment.

- Amortizable personal property such as goodwill, patents, copyrights, and leaseholds of § 1245 property. Professional baseball and football player contracts are § 1245 property.
- Expensing of costs to remove architectural and transportation barriers that restrict the handicapped and/or elderly.
- Certain depreciable tangible real property (other than buildings and their structural components) employed as an integral part of certain activities such as manufacturing and production. For example, a natural gas storage tank where the gas is used in the manufacturing process is § 1245 property.
- Pollution control facilities, railroad grading and tunnel bores, on-the-job training facilities, and child care facilities on which amortization is taken.
- Single-purpose agricultural and horticultural structures and petroleum storage facilities (e.g., a greenhouse or silo).
- Although technically not § 1245 property, 15-year, 18-year, and 19-year *nonresidential real estate* for which accelerated cost recovery is used is subject to the § 1245 recapture rules. Such property would have been placed in service after 1980 and before 1987.

EXAMPLE 49

Heron & Co., Inc., acquired nonresidential rental property on January 1, 1986, for $100,000. The company used the statutory percentage method to compute the ACRS cost recovery. It sells the asset on January 15, 2001, for $120,000. The amount and nature of Heron's gain are computed as follows.

Amount realized		$120,000
Adjusted basis		
Cost	$100,000	
Less cost recovery: 1986–2000	(83,000)	
2001	(175)	
January 15, 2001, adjusted basis		(16,825)
Gain realized and recognized		$103,175

This gain is treated as ordinary income to the extent of *all* depreciation taken, because the property is 19-year nonresidential real estate for which accelerated depreciation was used. Thus, Heron reports ordinary income of $83,175 ($83,000 + $175) and § 1231 gain of $20,000 ($103,175 – $83,175). ■

OBSERVATIONS ON § 1245

- In most instances, the total depreciation taken will exceed the recognized gain. Therefore, the disposition of § 1245 property usually results in ordinary income rather than § 1231 gain. Refer to Example 46.
- Recapture applies to the total amount of depreciation allowed or allowable regardless of the depreciation method used (i.e., full recapture).
- Recapture applies regardless of the holding period of the property. Of course, the entire recognized gain would be ordinary income if the property was not held more than one year, because then § 1231 would not apply.
- Section 1245 does not apply to losses, which receive § 1231 treatment.
- Gains from the disposition of § 1245 assets may also be treated as passive activity gains (refer to Chapter 5).

EXAMPLE 50

Upon sale of some business equipment held for five years, Pink Corporation recognized a $7,500 loss. All of the $20,000 § 1245 depreciation recapture potential for the asset disappears as a result of the disposition. The transaction receives § 1231 loss treatment, and none of Pink's cost recovery deductions are recaptured into ordinary income for this asset. ■

PLANNING CONSIDERATIONS

Depreciation Recapture and § 179

Section 1245 recapture applies to all types of depreciation, including § 179 *immediate expensing*. Expensing under § 179, however, is elective and entirely within the discretion of the taxpayer. Choosing this option accelerates depreciation on the affected property but increases the potential recapture as well. Therefore, if a taxpayer anticipates that an asset will generate a gain when it is sold and that such sale will occur in the early years of the asset's life, the taxpayer might decide to forgo electing the additional depreciation under § 179.

On the other hand, electing § 179 remains attractive if little or no gain is anticipated upon an asset's disposition. After all, § 1245 recapture applies only to the extent that gain is actually realized. Moreover, even if a substantial gain is anticipated upon an asset's disposition, the *time value of money* might suggest that § 179 be elected if the disposition is expected to be many years away. In any case, the taxpayer can usually control when an asset is sold or exchanged and can thereby extend the time before the taxes saved by electing § 179 must be returned as § 1245 recapture.

Section 1250 Recapture

Depreciable property that is not subject to § 1245 recapture faces a separate recapture computation mechanism in § 1250. For the most part, § 1250 applies to *depreciable real property* (principally buildings and their structural components), such as apartments, office buildings, factories, stores, and warehouses.[27] Intangible real property, such as leaseholds of **§ 1250 property,** also is included.

Section **1250 recapture** is much less onerous than § 1245 recapture, but it is also much more complex. Section 1250 recaptures only a property's **additional depreciation,** which is the excess of the depreciation actually deducted over the amount that would have been allowed under the straight-line method of depreciation. For this reason, § 1250 recapture is often referred to as *partial recapture,* in contrast to § 1245's full recapture.

Since § 1250 recaptures only the excess over straight-line depreciation, the concept does not apply to properties that were depreciated using the straight-line method (unless they were held for one year or less). Real property placed in service *after 1986* can only be depreciated using the straight-line method, so there is *no § 1250 recapture* upon the disposition of such properties that are held for longer than one year.

But real estate is particularly long-lived, and many dispositions of such assets involve properties placed in service *before 1987,* when accelerated depreciation was often available for real estate. Accordingly, § 1250 will continue to play a major role in *classifying gain* from the disposition of real property for many years to come. Finally, § 1250 does not affect the § 1231 treatment of realized losses.

If § 1250 property is disposed of in a transaction other than a sale, exchange, or involuntary conversion, the maximum amount recaptured is the excess of the property's fair market value over its adjusted basis. For example, if a corporation distributes property to its shareholders as a dividend, a gain results if the property's fair market value is greater than its adjusted basis. The maximum amount of § 1250 recapture is the amount of that gain.

The following discussion describes the computational steps prescribed in § 1250 and reflected on Form 4797.

COMPUTING RECAPTURE ON NONRESIDENTIAL REAL PROPERTY

For § 1250 property *other than* residential rental property, the potential recapture is the amount of additional depreciation taken *since December 31, 1969.* If the property is held for one year or less (usually not the case), *all* depreciation taken, even under the straight-line method, is additional depreciation.

The following procedure is used to compute recapture on nonresidential real property under § 1250.

- Determine the recognized gain from the sale or other disposition of the property.
- Determine post-1969 additional depreciation.
- The *lower* of the recognized gain or the post-1969 additional depreciation is ordinary income.

---

[27]As previously discussed, § 1245 applies to nonresidential real estate that was placed in service after 1980 and before 1987 and was depreciated using an accelerated method.

- If any recognized gain remains (recognized gain less recapture), it is § 1231 gain. However, it would be casualty gain if the disposition was by casualty.

EXAMPLE 51

On January 3, 1980, Lark & Associates acquired a new building at a cost of $200,000 for use in the partnership's business. The building had an estimated useful life of 50 years and no estimated salvage value. Depreciation has been taken under the 150% declining-balance method through December 31, 2000. Pertinent information with respect to depreciation taken follows. Lark sold the building for $180,000 on January 2, 2001.

Year	Undepreciated Balance (Beginning of the Year)	Current Depreciation Provision	Straight-Line Depreciation	Additional Depreciation
1980–1999	$200,000	$92,118	$80,000	$12,118
2000	107,882	3,610	4,000	(390)
Total 1980–2000		$95,728	$84,000	$11,728

- Lark's recognized gain from the sale is $75,728. This is the difference between the $180,000 amount realized and the $104,272 adjusted basis ($200,000 cost – $95,728 depreciation taken).
- Post-1969 additional depreciation is $11,728. Since this amount is less than the recognized gain of $75,728, the entire gain is not recaptured.
- The remaining $64,000 ($75,728 – $11,728) gain is § 1231 gain. ■

The essence of § 1250 is that ordinary income treatment applies only to the portion of the gain realized that is attributable to depreciation taken in excess of the straight-line amount. This excess actually *diminishes over time* once the annual straight-line amount becomes greater than the amount allowed by the accelerated depreciation method.

COMPUTING RECAPTURE ON RESIDENTIAL RENTAL HOUSING

Section 1250 recapture can apply to the sale or other disposition of residential rental housing. Property qualifies as *residential rental housing* only if at least 80 percent of gross rent income is derived from dwelling units.[28] The rules are the same as for other § 1250 property, except that only the post-1975 additional depreciation need be recaptured.[29] Therefore, the additional depreciation for periods after 1975 is initially applied against the recognized gain, and such amounts may be recaptured in full as ordinary income. If any of the recognized gain is not absorbed by the recapture rules, the remaining gain is § 1231 gain.

Under § 1250, when straight-line depreciation is used, there is no § 1250 recapture potential unless the property is disposed of in the first year of use. For real

---

[28]§ 168(e)(2)(A). Note that there may be residential, nonrental housing (e.g., a bunkhouse on a cattle ranch). Such property is commonly regarded as "nonresidential real estate." The rules for such property were discussed in the preceding section.

[29]§§ 1250(a)(1) and (2) and Reg. § 1.1250–1(d)(1)(i)(c). The post-1969 through 1975 recapture percentage is 100% less one percentage

point for each full month the property is held over 100 months. This approach now yields a zero percentage no matter when the property was acquired in the 1969–1975 period.

CONCEPT SUMMARY 8–5

Comparison of § 1245 and § 1250 Depreciation Recapture

	§ 1245	§ 1250
Property affected	All depreciable personal property, but also nonresidential real property acquired after December 31, 1980, and before January 1, 1987, for which accelerated cost recovery was used. Also includes miscellaneous items such as § 179 expense and § 197 amortization of intangibles such as goodwill, patents, and copyrights.	Nonresidential real property acquired after December 31, 1969, and before January 1, 1981, on which accelerated depreciation was taken. Residential rental real property acquired after December 31, 1975, and before January 1, 1987, on which accelerated depreciation was taken.
Depreciation recaptured	Potentially all depreciation taken. If the selling price is greater than or equal to the original cost, all depreciation is recaptured. If the selling price is between the adjusted basis and the original cost, only some depreciation is recaptured.	Additional depreciation (the excess of accelerated depreciation over straight-line depreciation). All depreciation taken if property disposed of in first year.
Limit on recapture	Lower of depreciation taken or gain recognized.	Lower of additional depreciation or gain recognized.
Treatment of gain exceeding recapture gain	Usually § 1231 gain.	Usually § 1231 gain.
Treatment of loss	No depreciation recapture; loss is usually § 1231 loss.	No depreciation recapture; loss is usually § 1231 loss.

---

property placed in service after 1986, only straight-line depreciation is allowed. Therefore, the application of § 1250 is limited to first-year dispositions.

EXAMPLE 52

Sanjay Enterprises, Ltd., acquires a residential rental building on January 1, 2000, for $300,000. It receives an offer of $450,000 for the building and sells it on December 23, 2002.

- Sanjay takes $20,909 [($300,000 × .03485) + ($300,000 × .03636 × $^{11.5}/_{12}$) = $20,909] of total depreciation for 2000 and 2001. The adjusted basis of the property is $279,091 ($300,000 − $20,909).
- Sanjay's recognized gain is $170,909 ($450,000 − $279,091).
- All of the gain is § 1231 gain. ■

Concept Summary 8–5 compares and contrasts the § 1245 and § 1250 depreciation recapture rules.

UNRECAPTURED § 1250 GAINS

As noted previously, *noncorporate taxpayers* pay tax at a maximum rate of 25 percent on their **unrecaptured § 1250 gains.** These gains represent that part of the gain on § 1250 property that is attributable to depreciation that was not recaptured by § 1250. The procedure for computing this amount involves three distinct steps.

Step 1. Determine the part of the recognized gain that is attributable to *depreciation deductions* claimed in prior years.

Step 2. Apply § 1250 to determine the portion of the gain calculated in step 1 that is recaptured as ordinary income. This portion is taxable at rates of 15 percent to 39.6 percent, depending upon the seller's tax bracket, as explained previously.

Step 3. Subtract the gain recaptured under § 1250 (step 2) from the gain derived in step 1. This amount is the *unrecaptured § 1250 gain.*

EXAMPLE 53

Linda placed two apartment buildings in service during 1986 at a cost of $100,000 each. On each building, she claimed accelerated depreciation deductions of $78,000, and straight-line depreciation would have been $64,000. Thus, her adjusted basis for each building is $22,000 ($100,000 cost − $78,000 depreciation deducted), and her potential § 1250 recapture on each building is $14,000 ($78,000 accelerated depreciation − $64,000 straight-line). She now sells these buildings for $96,000 and $110,000, respectively, and computes her gain as follows.

	Building A	Building B
Amount realized	$ 96,000	$110,000
Adjusted basis	(22,000)	(22,000)
Recognized gain	$ 74,000	$ 88,000
Depreciation recaptured per § 1250	(14,000)	(14,000)
Remaining gain	$ 60,000	$ 74,000
Unrecaptured § 1250 gain	(60,000)	(64,000)
§ 1231 gain	None	$ 10,000

For property placed in service after 1986, § 1250 generally does not apply, because such property may use only straight-line depreciation under MACRS. As a result, *all* of the gain attributable to depreciation on such assets is unrecaptured § 1250 gain.

EXAMPLE 54

Assume the same facts as in the preceding example, except that Linda placed the buildings in service in 1987, so straight-line depreciation was taken. Her adjusted basis for each building, therefore, is $36,000 ($100,000 cost − $64,000 depreciation deducted). Her gains are computed as follows:

	Building A	Building B
Amount realized	$ 96,000	$110,000
Adjusted basis	(36,000)	(36,000)
Recognized gain	$ 60,000	$ 74,000
Unrecaptured § 1250 gain	(60,000)	(64,000)
§ 1231 gain	None	$ 10,000

If § 1245 applies, all of the depreciation taken is recaptured as ordinary income, and there is *no* unrecaptured § 1250 gain. So, if Building B in Example 53 were an office building, $78,000 of the gain would be ordinary income per § 1245, and the remaining $10,000 would be § 1231 gain.

Any § 1231 losses are applied *first* against the portion of the gain that is not unrecaptured § 1250 gain. So, in Example 54, if Linda had a § 1231 loss of $15,000 from another disposition, this loss would first be applied against the $10,000 of

§ 1231 gain from Building B, and the remaining $5,000 loss would then offset the unrecaptured § 1250 gain. Curiously, the five-year lookback rule of § 1231(c) operates to recharacterize unrecaptured § 1250 gain *first*. Thus, if Linda had a net § 1231 loss of $15,000 in the prior year, this loss would recharacterize $15,000 of unrecaptured § 1250 gain, rather than the $10,000 of § 1231 gain from Building B.

PLANNING CONSIDERATIONS

Selling Depreciable Real Estate

A building depreciated on an accelerated method eventually generates annual allowances that are smaller than the amount that the straight-line method would have produced. Beyond that point, the *cumulative* amount of "additional depreciation" is reduced every year the asset is operated. Doing so effectively converts gain that would otherwise be subject to § 1250 recapture into "unrecaptured § 1250 gain," enabling the taxpayer to save the difference between the applicable tax rate on ordinary income and 25 percent.

Continuing to operate the building, however, brings forth an array of important *nontax considerations*. Each year a building is used subjects it to additional maintenance expenses to keep it in operating condition. Moreover, a building's appeal to current and prospective tenants tends to decline over time as newer structures appear offering more modern amenities, such as ISDN wiring for high-speed Internet access, and other conveniences. Finally, local real estate developments might produce lower resale prices that offset much, if not all, of the tax advantage obtained by holding the property for the additional time.

ADDITIONAL RECAPTURE FOR CORPORATIONS

Although depreciation recapture is generally the same for all taxpayers, corporations that sell depreciable real estate face an additional amount of depreciation recapture. Section 291(a)(1) requires recapture of 20 percent of the excess of the amount that would be recaptured under § 1245 over the amount actually recaptured under § 1250. Buildings subject to recapture under § 1245 would have no such excess, so § 291 would not apply to these dispositions.

EXAMPLE 55

Franklin Corporation purchased an office building on January 3, 1986, for $300,000. Accelerated depreciation was taken in the amount of $236,400 before the building was sold on January 5, 2001, for $250,000. Straight-line depreciation would have been $221,400 (using a 19-year recovery period under ACRS). The corporation's depreciation recapture and § 1231 gain are computed as follows.

Sales price	$250,000
Less: Adjusted basis [$300,000 (cost of building) – $236,400 (ACRS depreciation)]	(63,600)
Recognized gain	$186,400

Because the building is 19-year real estate, it is treated as § 1245 recovery property. This gain is recaptured to the extent of all depreciation taken. Thus, all of the recognized gain is ordinary income under § 1245, and there is no additional § 291 depreciation recapture. ∎

EXAMPLE 56

Assume the building in the preceding example is residential rental property, making it § 1250 property. Gain recaptured under § 1250 is $15,000 ($236,400 depreciation taken –

$221,400 straight-line depreciation). However, for a corporate taxpayer, § 291(a)(1) causes additional § 1250 ordinary income of $34,280, computed as follows.

Ordinary income if property were § 1245 property	$186,400
Less: Gain recaptured under § 1250	(15,000)
Excess § 1245 gain	$171,400
Percentage that is ordinary gain	× 20%
Additional § 291 gain recaptured	$ 34,280
Ordinary income from depreciation recapture ($15,000 + $34,280)	$ 49,280
Section 1231 gain ($186,400 − $15,000 − $34,280)	137,120
Total recognized gain	$186,400

EXAMPLE 57

Assume the building in the preceding example is commercial property and straight-line depreciation was used. A corporate taxpayer must recapture as ordinary income 20% of the depreciation that would be ordinary income if the property were § 1245 property.

Sales price	$250,000
Less: Adjusted basis [$300,000 (cost of building) − $221,400 (straight-line depreciation)]	(78,600)
Recognized gain	$171,400
Ordinary income if property were § 1245 property	$171,400
Less: Ordinary income under § 1250	(–0–)
Excess ordinary income under § 1245	$171,400
Apply § 291 percentage	× 20%
Ordinary income under § 291	$ 34,280

For a corporate taxpayer, $34,280 of the $171,400 gain would be ordinary income, and $137,120 would be § 1231 gain. ■

Exceptions to §§ 1245 and 1250

Recapture under §§ 1245 and 1250 does not apply to the following transactions.

GIFTS

The recapture potential carries over to the donee.[30]

EXAMPLE 58

Wade gives his daughter, Helen, § 1245 property with an adjusted basis of $1,000. The amount of recapture potential is $700. Helen uses the property in her business and claims further depreciation of $100 before selling it for $1,900. Helen's recognized gain is $1,000 [$1,900 amount realized − $900 adjusted basis ($1,000 carryover basis − $100 depreciation

---

[30]§§ 1245(b)(1) and 1250(d)(1) and Reg. §§ 1.1245–4(a)(1) and 1.1250–3(a)(1).

taken by Helen)], of which $800 is recaptured as ordinary income ($100 depreciation taken by Helen + $700 recapture potential carried over from Wade). The remaining gain of $200 is § 1231 gain. Even if Helen had used the property for personal purposes, the $700 recapture potential would have carried over. ∎

DEATH

Although not an attractive tax planning approach, death eliminates all recapture potential.[31] In other words, recapture potential does not carry over from a decedent to an estate or an heir.

EXAMPLE 59

Assume the same facts as in the preceding example, except that Helen receives the property as a result of Wade's death. The $700 recapture potential from Wade is extinguished at his death. Helen has a basis in the property equal to its fair market value (assume $1,700) at Wade's death. She will have a $300 gain when the property is sold because the selling price ($1,900) exceeds the property's adjusted basis of $1,600 ($1,700 basis to Helen − $100 depreciation) by $300. Because of § 1245, Helen has ordinary income of $100. The remaining gain of $200 is § 1231 gain. ∎

CHARITABLE TRANSFERS

The recapture potential reduces the amount of the charitable contribution deduction.[32]

EXAMPLE 60

Bullfinch Corporation donates to a museum § 1245 property with a fair market value of $10,000 and an adjusted basis of $7,000. Depreciation recapture potential is $2,000 (the amount of recapture that would occur if the property were sold). The company's charitable contribution deduction (subject to the limitations discussed in Chapter 4) is $8,000 ($10,000 fair market value − $2,000 recapture potential). ∎

CERTAIN NONTAXABLE TRANSACTIONS

In certain transactions, the transferor's adjusted basis for the property carries over to the transferee.[33] The recapture potential also carries over to the transferee.[34] Included in this category are transfers of property pursuant to the following.

- Nontaxable incorporations under § 351.
- Certain liquidations of subsidiary companies under § 332.
- Nontaxable contributions to a partnership under § 721.
- Nontaxable corporate reorganizations.

Gain may be recognized in these transactions if boot is received. If gain is recognized, it is treated as ordinary income to the extent of the recapture potential or the recognized gain, whichever is lower.[35]

---

[31]§§ 1245(b)(2) and 1250(d)(2).

[32]§ 170(e)(1)(A) and Reg. § 1.170A–4(b)(1). In certain circumstances, § 1231 gain also reduces the amount of the charitable contribution. See § 170(e)(1)(B).

[33]§§ 1245(b)(3) and 1250(d)(3) and Reg. §§ 1.1245–4(c) and 1.1250–3(c).

[34]Reg. §§ 1.1245–2(a)(4) and (c)(2) and 1.1250–2(d)(1) and (3) and –3(c)(3).

[35]§§ 1245(b)(3) and 1250(d)(3) and Reg. §§ 1.1245–4(c) and 1.1250–3(c).

EXCHANGE FOR FOREIGN PROPERTY YIELDS RECOGNIZED RECAPTURE GAIN

Tangible personal property used in a trade or business may be the subject of a like-kind exchange, and the postponed gain is most likely postponed § 1245 gain. However, tangible personal property used predominantly within the United States cannot be exchanged for tangible personal property used predominantly outside the United States. Thus, such an exchange would cause recognized gain, and, as long as the fair market value of the property given up does not exceed its original cost, all of the gain is § 1245 depreciation recapture gain.

LIKE-KIND EXCHANGES AND INVOLUNTARY CONVERSIONS

As explained in Chapter 7, realized gain is recognized to the extent of boot received in a like-kind exchange. Realized gain is also recognized to the extent the proceeds from an involuntary conversion are not reinvested in similar property. Such recognized gain is subject to recapture as ordinary income under §§ 1245 and 1250. Any remaining recapture potential carries over to the property received in the exchange.

EXAMPLE 61

Crane Corporation exchanges § 1245 property with an adjusted basis of $300 for § 1245 property with a fair market value of $6,000 plus $1,000 cash (boot). The exchange qualifies as a like-kind exchange under § 1031. Crane's realized gain is $6,700 ($7,000 amount realized – $300 adjusted basis of property). Since Crane received boot of $1,000, it recognizes gain to this extent. Assuming the recapture potential is $7,500, Crane recognizes § 1245 gain of $1,000. The remaining recapture potential of $6,500 carries over to the like-kind property received. ■

10 *Find more information on this topic at our Web site: **http://wft-entities.swcollege.com**.*

Reporting Procedures

Noncapital gains and losses are reported on Form 4797, Sales of Business Property. Before filling out Form 4797, however, Form 4684, Casualties and Thefts, Part B, must be completed to determine whether any casualties will enter into the § 1231 computation procedure. Recall that gains from § 1231 asset casualties may be recaptured by § 1245 or § 1250. These gains will not appear on Form 4684. The § 1231 gains and nonpersonal-use long-term capital gains are netted against § 1231 and nonpersonal-use long-term capital losses on Form 4684 to determine if there is a net gain to transfer to Form 4797, Part I.

11 *Find more information on this topic at our Web site: **http://wft-entities.swcollege.com**.*

KEY TERMS

Additional depreciation, 8–35

Capital asset, 8–2

Capital gain, 8–3

Capital loss, 8–3

Collectibles, 8–19

Franchise, 8–11

Holding period, 8–14

Lessee, 8–13

Lessor, 8–13

Long-term nonpersonal-use capital assets, 8–27

Net capital gain, 8–21

Net capital loss, 8–21

Options, 8–9

Patent, 8–10

Qualified small business stock, 8–24

Sale or exchange, 8–7

Section 1231 gains and losses, 8–26

Section 1231 lookback, 8–30

Section 1231 property, 8–26

Section 1245 property, 8–33

Section 1245 recapture, 8–33

Section 1250 property, 8–35

Section 1250 recapture, 8–35

Short sale, 8–16

Unrecaptured § 1250 gain, 8–37

Problem Materials

PROBLEMS

1. Mariah had three property transactions during the year. She sold a vacation home used for personal purposes at a $31,000 loss. The home had been held for five years and had never been rented. Mariah also sold an antique clock for $13,500 that she had inherited from her grandmother. The clock was valued in Mariah's grandmother's estate at $12,000. Mariah owned the clock for only four months. She sold these assets to finance her full-time occupation as a song writer. Near the end of the year, Mariah sold one of the songs she had written two years earlier. She received cash of $48,000 and a royalty interest in revenues derived from the merchandising of the song. Mariah had no tax basis for the song. What is Mariah's gross income?

2. Hyacinth, Inc., is a dealer in securities. The firm has spotted a fast-rising company and would like to buy and hold its stock for investment. The stock is currently selling for $15 per share, and Hyacinth thinks it will climb to $63 a share within two years. How can Hyacinth ensure that any gain it realizes will be taxed as long-term capital gain? Draft a letter responding to Hyacinth's inquiry. The firm's address is 200 Morningside Drive, Hattisburg, MS 39406.

3. Eagle Partners has owned a large tract of land for 15 years and subdivides it for sale. Assume Eagle meets all the requirements of § 1237. During the first year of sales, Eagle sells 20 lots for $60,000 each. Its selling expenses are 7% of the sale price of each lot. Eagle has a basis of $51,000 in each lot. Compute the total gain from the sale of these lots and indicate the nature of the gain.

4. Swan Songs, Inc., is in the business of buying song copyrights from struggling songwriters, holding those copyrights, and then reselling the songs to major record companies and singers. Swan has a four-month option to purchase a song copyright. The firm paid $2,000 for this option. A famous singer has heard the song and is willing to buy the option for $10,000. Swan thinks the song may be worth $35,000 in six months. If Swan exercises the option, it will have to pay $20,000 for the song. Assuming

Swan is in the 34% tax bracket, which of these alternatives will give it a better after-tax cash flow?

5. Daffodil Enterprises Company purchased a one-year option on 20 acres of farmland for $245,000. Daffodil's plans for the property did not work out, so it let the option expire unexercised. What tax issues does the company face in determining how to treat the $245,000?

6. An investment partnership is looking for vacant land to buy. For $20,000, it is granted an 11-month option to buy 20 acres of vacant land for $400,000. The owner (who is holding the land for investment) paid $62,000 for the land several years ago.
   a. Does the landowner have gross income when $20,000 is received for granting the option?
   b. Does the partnership have an asset when the option is granted?
   c. If the option lapses, does the landowner have a recognized gain? If so, what type of gain? Does the partnership have a recognized loss? If so, what type of loss?
   d. If the option is exercised and an additional $400,000 is paid for the land, how much recognized gain does the seller have? What type of gain? What is the partnership's tax basis for the property?

7. Freys, Inc., sells a 12-year franchise to Red Company. The franchise contains many restrictions on how Red may operate its store. For instance, Red cannot use less than Grade 10 Idaho potatoes, must fry the potatoes at a constant 410 degrees, dress store personnel in Freys-approved uniforms, and have a Freys sign that meets detailed specifications on size, color, and construction. When the franchise contract is signed, Red makes a noncontingent $40,000 payment to Freys. During the same year, Red pays Freys $25,000—14% of Red's sales. How does Freys treat each of these payments? How does Red treat each of the payments?

8. Leah lives in an apartment near her college campus. Her lease runs out in July 2002, but her landlord could sell the building if he can convince all the tenants to cancel their leases and move out by the end of 2001. The landlord has offered Leah $750 to cancel her lease. Leah's lease began on August 1, 2001. What tax factors should Leah consider in deciding whether to take the landlord's offer?

9. Thrasher Corporation sells short 100 shares of ARC stock at $20 per share on January 15, 2001. It buys 200 shares of ARC stock on April 1, 2001, at $25 per share. On May 2, 2001, Thrasher closes the short sale by delivering 100 of the shares purchased on April 1.
   a. What are the amount and nature of Thrasher's loss upon closing the short sale?
   b. When does the holding period for the remaining 100 shares begin?
   c. If Thrasher sells (at $27 per share) the remaining 100 shares on January 20, 2002, what will be the nature of its gain or loss?

10. A taxpayer downloads a copy of an IRS publication from the IRS Web site. The taxpayer then makes paper copies of the IRS publication and sells them for more than the cost of copying. What is the tax status of the copies the taxpayer sells?

11. Latisha Case has the following transactions this year:

Long-term capital gain	$ 32,000
Long-term capital loss	(25,000)
Short-term capital gain	29,000
Short-term capital loss	(33,000)

What is her net capital gain or loss? Draft a letter to Latisha describing how the net capital gain or loss will be treated on her tax return. Assume Latisha's income from other sources puts her in the 36% bracket. Her address is 300 Ireland Avenue, Shepherdstown, WV 25443.

12. Sally has taxable income of $150,000 as of November 30 of this year. She wants to sell a Rodin sculpture that has appreciated $90,000 since she purchased it six years ago, but she does not want to pay more than $15,000 of additional tax on the transaction. Sally also owns various stocks, some of which are currently worth less than their basis. How can she achieve her desired result?

13. Platinum, Inc., has determined its taxable income as $215,000 before considering the results of its capital gain or loss transactions. Platinum has a short-term capital loss of $24,000, a long-term capital loss of $38,000, and a short-term capital gain of $39,000. What is Platinum's taxable income, and what (if any) are the amount and nature of its capital loss carryover?

14. The taxpayer is an antiques collector and is going to sell an antique purchased many years ago for a large gain. The facts and circumstances indicate that the taxpayer might be classified as a dealer rather than an investor in antiques. The taxpayer will save $40,000 in taxes if the gain is treated as long-term capital gain rather than as ordinary income. The taxpayer is considering the following options as ways to assure the $40,000 tax savings:

    • Give the antique to his daughter, who is an investment banker, to sell.

    • Merely assume that he has held the antique as an investment.

    • Exchange the antique in a like-kind exchange for another antique he wants.

    One of the tax preparers the taxpayer has contacted has said he would be willing to prepare the return under the second option. Would you? Why? Evaluate the other options.

15. Cheryl lives in an area that was hit hard by a hurricane. She has correctly determined that she has a $25,000 business property long-term casualty loss and a $21,000 business property long-term casualty gain. What tax issues must Cheryl deal with?

16. A painting that Tulip & Co. held for investment was destroyed in a flood. The painting was insured, and Tulip had a $30,000 gain from this casualty. It also had a $27,000 loss from an uninsured antique vase that was destroyed by the flood. The vase was also held for investment. Tulip had no other property transactions during the year and has no nonrecaptured § 1231 losses from prior years. Compute Tulip's net gain or loss and identify how it would be treated. Also, write a letter to Tulip explaining the nature of the gain or loss. Tulip's address is 2000 Meridian Road, Hannibal Point, MO 34901.

17. Jason inherited an undeveloped tract of land from his uncle three years ago. The land has a tax basis of $250,000. A real estate developer has approached Jason and would like him to contribute the land to a partnership that Jason and the developer would own. The partnership would subdivide the land, install sewers, water, electricity, cable TV, and natural gas on the land and then sell the lots to consumers. The developer estimates that Jason's share of the gain from this transaction would be $1.5 million over a total of five years. Alternatively, the developer is willing to pay Jason $500,000 for the land in its current state. What tax issues does Jason face?

18. Harold, a CPA, has a new client who recently moved to town. Harold prepares the client's current-year tax return, which shows a net § 1231 gain. Harold calls the client to request copies of the returns for the preceding five years to determine if there are any § 1231 lookback losses. The client says that the returns are "still buried in the moving mess somewhere" and cannot be found. The client also says that he does not remember any § 1231 net losses on the prior-year returns. What should Harold do? Justify your answer.

19. Geranium, Inc., has the following net § 1231 results for each of the years shown. What is the nature of the net gain in 2000 and 2001?

Tax Year	Net § 1231 Loss	Net § 1231 Gain
1996	$16,000	
1997	13,000	
1998	22,000	
1999		$11,000
2000		20,000
2001		29,000

20. Delphinium Company owns two parcels of land (§ 1231 assets). One parcel can be sold at a loss of $30,000, and the other parcel can be sold at a gain of $40,000. The company has no nonrecaptured § 1231 losses from prior years. The parcels could be sold at any time because potential purchasers are abundant. The company has a $25,000 short-term capital loss carryover from a prior tax year and no capital assets that could be sold to generate long-term capital gains. What should Delphinium do based upon these facts? (Assume tax rates are constant and ignore the present value of future cash flow.)

21. Green Industries (a sole proprietorship) sold three § 1231 assets on October 10, 2001. Data on these property dispositions are as follows.

Asset	Cost	Acquired	Depreciation	Sold for
Rack	$100,000	10/10/97	$60,000	$135,000
Forklift	35,000	10/16/98	23,000	5,000
Bin	87,000	3/12/00	34,000	60,000

a. Determine the amount and the character of the recognized gain or loss from the disposition of each asset.
b. Assuming Green has no nonrecaptured net § 1231 losses from prior years, how much of the 2001 recognized gains are treated as long-term capital gains?

22. On December 1, 1999, Gray Manufacturing Company (a corporation) purchased another company's assets, including a patent. The patent was used in Gray's manufacturing operations; $40,500 was allocated to the patent, and it was amortized at the rate of $225 per month. On June 30, 2001, Gray sold the patent for $60,000. Nineteen months of amortization had been taken on the patent. What are the amount and nature of the gain Gray recognizes on the disposition of the patent? Write a letter to Gray discussing the treatment of the gain. Gray's address is 6734 Grover Street, Back Bay Harbor, ME 23890. The letter should be addressed to Siddim Sadatha, Controller.

23. Dave is the sole proprietor of a trampoline shop. During 2001, the following transactions occurred.

- Unimproved land adjacent to the store was condemned by the city on February 1. The condemnation proceeds were $25,000. The land, acquired in 1982, had an allocable basis of $40,000. Dave has additional parking across the street and plans to use the condemnation proceeds to build his inventory.

- A truck used to deliver trampolines was sold on January 2 for $3,500. The truck was purchased on January 2, 1997, for $6,000. On the date of sale, the adjusted basis was $2,509.

- Dave sold an antique rowing machine at an auction. Net proceeds were $3,900. The rowing machine was purchased as used equipment 17 years ago for $5,200 and is fully depreciated.

- Dave sold an apartment building for $200,000 on September 1. The rental property was purchased on September 1, 1998, for $150,000 and was being depreciated over a 27.5-year life using the straight-line method. At the date of sale, the adjusted basis was $124,783.

- Dave sold a Buick on May 1 for $9,600. The vehicle had been used exclusively for personal purposes. It was purchased on September 1, 1997, for $20,800.

- An adding machine used by Dave's bookkeeper was sold on June 1. Net proceeds of the sale were $135. The machine was purchased on June 2, 1997, for $350. It was being depreciated over a five-year life employing the straight-line method. The adjusted basis on the date of sale was $95.

- Dave's trampoline stretching machine (owned two years) was stolen on May 5, but the business's insurance company will not pay any of the machine's value because Dave failed to pay the insurance premium. The machine had a fair market value of $8,000 and an adjusted basis of $6,000 at the time of theft.

- Dave had AGI of $36,000 from sources other than those described above.

- Dave has no nonrecaptured § 1231 lookback losses.

  a. For each transaction, what are the amount and nature of recognized gain or loss?
  b. What is Dave's 2001 AGI?

24. Macklin, a sole proprietor, used a drafting table in his business and completely depreciated its $3,700 cost. He now purchases a new drafting table for his business and takes the old drafting table home to use as a workbench. A similar workbench for home use would cost $450. Should Macklin report anything on his tax return regarding this conversion of his old drafting table?

25. Goshawk Corporation acquired residential rental property on January 3, 1986, for $400,000. The property was depreciated using the accelerated method and a 19-year recovery period under ACRS. Goshawk has claimed depreciation of $315,200. Straight-line depreciation during the period would have been $295,200. The corporation sold the property on January 2, 2001, for $440,000. What is the gain on the sale, and how is it taxed?

26. Assume that the property in the preceding problem was a commercial building, and that Goshawk Corporation used the straight-line method of depreciation with a 19-year recovery period under ACRS. What would be the gain, and how would it be taxed?

27. Joanne is in the 39.6% tax bracket and owns depreciable business equipment that she purchased several years ago for $135,000; she has taken $100,000 of depreciation on the equipment, and it is worth $85,000. Joanne's niece, Susan, is starting a new business and is short of cash. Susan has asked Joanne to make a gift of the equipment to her so that Susan can use it in her business. Joanne no longer needs the equipment. Identify the alternatives available to Joanne if she wishes to help Susan and the tax effects of those alternatives. (Assume all alternatives involve the business equipment in one way or another. Ignore the gift tax.)

28. Nicholas owns business equipment with a $155,000 adjusted basis; he paid $200,000 for the equipment, and it is currently worth $173,000. Nicholas dies suddenly, and his son Alvin inherits the property. What is Alvin's basis for the property, and what happens to the § 1245 depreciation recapture potential?

EXTENDER 29. Two years ago, Hsui Company (an unincorporated entity) developed a process for preserving fresh fruit that gives the fruit a much longer shelf life. The process is not patented or copyrighted, and only Hsui knows how it works. A conglomerate has approached Hsui with an offer to purchase the formula for the process. Specifically, the offer allows Hsui to choose between the following. Which option should Hsui accept?

- $850,000 cash for the formula and a 10-year covenant not to compete, paying Hsui $45,000 per year for 10 years.

- $850,000 cash for a 10-year covenant not to compete, and an annual $45,000 royalty for the formula, payable for 10 years.

EXTENDER 30. In March 1999, the Sue-Jen Partnership contracted for $30,000 to cut timber on a 100-acre tract of undeveloped Georgia land. On January 1, 2000, the timber was worth $50,000. The value in November 2000 when the timber was cut was $55,000. On January 30, 2001, the wood was sold for $48,000.

a. If Sue-Jen elects to treat the timber cutting as a sale, what is its recognized gain or loss for 1999, 2000, and 2001?

b. In each case, what is the character of this gain or loss?

c. How does the result change if the wood is sold in December 2000?

BRIDGE DISCIPLINE

1. Using an online research service, find the audited financial statements of a major U.S. corporation.

   a. List some of the items that the corporation reports as having different treatment for tax and financial accounting purposes. These items often are mentioned in the footnotes to the statements.

   b. List two or more such items that seem to increase the taxpayer's after-tax income and two or more that seem to decrease it.

RESEARCH PROBLEMS

*Note: Solutions to Research Problems can be prepared by using the **RIA Checkpoint® Student Version Online research product,** or the **CCH U.S. Master Tax Guide Plus™** online Federal tax research database, which is available to accompany this text. It is also possible to prepare solutions to the Research Problems by using tax research materials found in a standard tax library.*

Research Problem 1. Jennifer, a dentist earning $125,000 per year, purchased a commercial warehouse as an investment on January 2, 1995 at a cost of $500,000. Assume that she has claimed $80,000 of straight-line depreciation thus far. On January 3, 2001, Jennifer sold the warehouse for $600,000, consisting of a down payment of $200,000, plus annual payments of $200,000 plus interest to be received during each of the next two years. Assume that Jennifer has no other § 1231 transactions during this period. When will her gain be recognized, and what tax rate will apply?

Research Problem 2. Sidney owns a professional football franchise. He has received an offer of $80 million for the franchise, all the football equipment, the rights to concession receipts, the rights to a stadium lease, and the rights to all the player contracts he owns. Most of the players have been with the team for quite a long time and have contracts that were signed several years ago. The contracts have been substantially depreciated. Sidney is concerned about potential § 1245 recapture when the contracts are sold. He has heard about "previously unrecaptured depreciation with respect to initial contracts" and would like to know more about it. Find a definition for that phrase and write an explanation of it.

Research Problem 3. Clean Corporation runs a chain of dry cleaners. Borax is used heavily in Clean's dry cleaning process and has been in short supply several times in the past. Several years ago, Clean Corporation bought a controlling interest in Dig Corporation—a borax mining concern—to assure Clean of a continuous supply of borax if another shortage developed. Clean has just sold the stock at a loss because Dig is in difficult financial straits and because Clean has obtained an alternative source of borax. What is the nature of Clean's loss on the disposition of the Dig Corporation stock? Write a letter to the controller, Salvio Guitterez, that contains your advice and prepare a memo for the tax files. The mailing address of Clean Corporation is 4455 Whitman Way, San Mateo, CA 44589.

Research Problem 4. Walter is both a real estate developer and the owner and manager of residential rental real estate. Walter is retiring and is going to sell both the land he is holding for future development and the rental properties he owns. Straight-line depreciation was used to depreciate the rental real estate. The rental properties will be sold at a substantial loss, and the development property will be sold at a substantial gain. What is the nature of these gains and losses?

Partial list of research aids:
§§ 1221 and 1231.
Tollis v. Comm., 65 TCM 1951, T.C.Memo. 1993–63.

Use the tax resources of the Internet to address the following question. Do not restrict your search to the World Wide Web, but include a review of newsgroups and general reference materials, practitioner sites and resources, primary sources of the tax law, chat rooms and discussion groups, and other opportunities.

Research Problem 5.   Go to a newsgroup frequented by inventors and patent consultants. Answer one of the queries there relative to the tax effects of buying and selling patents, receiving royalties on patents, or otherwise investing in new technology.

Research Problem 6.   Investors are flooded with performance data and rankings of mutual funds. The "tax efficiency" of these funds is much more difficult to determine, even though this information often has an enormous impact on taxable accounts (i.e., non-retirement-oriented accounts). Examine various Web sites to determine recent distribution history of mutual funds and compare their pre-tax and after-tax performance data to assess the impact of this information on investment planning.

Research Problem 7.   Go to the IRS Web site and download a Form 4797 and its instructions. Use the form to complete Problem 21.

Corporations: Organization, Capital Structure, and Operating Rules

LEARNING OBJECTIVES

After completing Chapter 9, you should be able to:

1. Identify the tax consequences of incorporating and transferring assets to controlled corporations.

2. Understand the special rules that apply when a corporation assumes a shareholder's liability.

3. Recognize the basis issues relevant to the shareholder and the corporation.

4. Understand the tax aspects of the capital structure of a corporation.

5. Recognize the tax differences between debt and equity investments.

6. Understand the tax rules unique to corporations.

7. Compute the corporate income tax.

8. Explain the tax rules unique to multiple corporations.

9. Describe the reporting process for corporations.

Outline

TAX TALK   *Taxes owing to the Government . . . are the price that business has to pay for protection and security.*

—Benjamin N. Cardozo

Business operations may be conducted in a number of different forms. As with many business decisions, consideration must be given to the tax consequences of choosing a particular business entity. This chapter deals with the unique tax consequences of operating an entity as a regular corporation, including:

- Classification of the entity as a corporation.
- The tax consequences to the shareholders and the corporation upon the formation of the corporation.
- The capital structure of the corporation.
- Determination of the corporate income tax liability.
- Corporate tax filing requirements.

An Introduction to Corporate Tax

Corporations are governed by Subchapter C or Subchapter S of the Internal Revenue Code. Those governed by Subchapter C are referred to as **C corporations** or **regular corporations.** Corporations governed by Subchapter S are referred to as **S corporations.**

S corporations, which generally do not pay Federal income tax, are similar to partnerships in that net profit or loss flows through to the shareholders to be reported on their separate returns. Also like partnerships, S corporations do not aggregate all income and expense items in computing net profit or loss. Certain items flow through to the shareholders and retain their separate character when reported on the shareholders' returns. See Chapter 12 for detailed coverage of S corporations.

Unlike proprietorships, partnerships, and S corporations, C corporations are taxpaying entities. This results in what is known as a *double tax* effect. A C corpora-

CORPORATIONS IN CYBERSPACE—A LOOK INTO THE NEW MILLENNIUM

Advances in information technology, especially the Internet, integrated computer systems, and advanced communication capabilities, are transforming virtually every aspect of modern life. Corporations also are feeling the impact of the new technology.

The "look" of the twenty-first century corporation inevitably will change during this new century—and the process of forming a corporation will change as well. For example, how will the stock markets and capital formation centers change? With so much business being generated on the Internet, how will American corporations respond? Will capital for new corporations, be it in exchange for stock or debt, be raised online by making direct appeals to potential investors—thus avoiding bankers and brokers? Certainly, corporations will conduct their business and offer their services via the Internet to a greater extent than ever before. How will the government, including the IRS, react to the new world of electronic commerce? It is clear that with the explosion of new information and greater speed of communication transmission, corporations (and the government) must embrace the new technology or risk falling behind.

tion reports its income and expenses on Form 1120 (or Form 1120–A, the corporate short form). The corporation computes tax on the taxable income reported on the corporate tax return using the rate schedule applicable to corporations (refer to the rate schedule inside the front cover of this text). When a corporation distributes its income, the corporation's shareholders report dividend income on their own tax returns. Thus, income that has already been taxed at the corporate level is also taxed at the shareholder level.

EXAMPLE 1

Tan Corporation files Form 1120, which reports taxable income of $100,000. The corporation pays tax of $22,250. This leaves $77,750, all of which is distributed as a dividend to Carla, the sole shareholder of the corporation. Carla, who has income from other sources and has a 39.6% marginal tax rate, pays income tax of $30,789 on the distribution. The combined tax on the corporation's income is $53,039. ■

EXAMPLE 2

Assume the same facts as in Example 1, except that the business is organized as a sole proprietorship. Carla reports the $100,000 net profit from the business on her tax return and pays tax of $39,600 ($100,000 net profit × 39.6% marginal rate). Therefore, operating the business as a sole proprietorship results in a tax saving of $13,439 ($53,039 tax from Example 1 – $39,600). ■

Shareholders in closely held corporations frequently attempt to avoid double taxation by paying out all the profit of the corporation as salary to themselves.

EXAMPLE 3

Orange Corporation has net income of $180,000 during the year ($300,000 revenue – $120,000 operating expenses). Emilio is the sole shareholder of Orange Corporation. In an effort to avoid tax at the corporate level, Emilio has Orange pay him a salary of $180,000, which results in zero taxable income for the corporation. ■

TAX FACT

THE SURPRISINGLY LOW AVERAGE CORPORATE TAX RATE

According to a recent report completed by the Institute on Taxation and Economic Policy, among the nation's 250 largest corporations, the average Federal income tax rate was 20.1 percent in 1998. This is down from 22.9 percent in 1996 and is also lower than the 35 percent rate that most large corporations would typically be expected to pay. In fact, according to the report, 133 of the 250 corporations paid an effective tax rate of less than half of the 35 percent rate in at least one of the years 1996–1998.

Source: "Corporate Income Taxes in the 1990s," by Robert S. McIntyre and T. D. Coo Nguyen, Institute on Taxation and Economic Policy, October 2000.

Will the strategy described in Example 3 effectively avoid double taxation? The answer depends on whether the compensation paid to the shareholder is *reasonable*. Section 162, which covers trade or business expenses, provides that compensation is deductible only to the extent that it is reasonable in amount. The IRS is aware that many taxpayers use this strategy to bail out corporate profits and, in an audit, looks closely at compensation expense. If the IRS believes that compensation is too high based on the amount and quality of services performed by the shareholder, the compensation deduction of the corporation is reduced to a reasonable amount. Compensation that is determined to be unreasonable is usually treated as a constructive dividend to the shareholder and is not deductible by the corporation.

EXAMPLE 4

Assume the same facts as in Example 3, and that the IRS determines that $80,000 of the amount paid to Emilio is unreasonable compensation. As a result, $80,000 of the corporation's compensation deduction is disallowed and treated as a constructive dividend to Emilio. Orange has taxable income of $80,000. Emilio would report salary of $100,000 and a taxable dividend of $80,000. The net effect is that $80,000 is subject to double taxation. ∎

The unreasonable compensation issue is discussed in more detail in Chapter 10.

COMPARISON OF CORPORATIONS AND OTHER FORMS OF DOING BUSINESS

Comparison of the tax results in Examples 1 and 2 might lead to the conclusion that incorporation is not a wise tax strategy. In some cases, that would be a correct conclusion, but in others it would not. In many situations, tax and nontax factors are combined to make the corporate form of doing business the only reasonable choice.

Chapter 14 presents a detailed comparison of sole proprietorships, partnerships, S corporations, and C corporations as forms of doing business. However, it is appropriate at this point to consider some of the tax and nontax factors that favor corporations over other business entities.

Consideration of tax factors requires an examination of the corporate rate structure. The income tax rate schedule applicable to corporations is reproduced on the inside front cover of the text. As this schedule shows, corporate rates on taxable income up to $75,000 are lower than individual rates for persons in the 28 percent and higher brackets. Therefore, corporate tax will be lower than individual tax. Furthermore, there is no corporate marginal rate that is higher than the 39.6 percent top bracket for individuals. When dividends are paid, however, the double taxation problem occurs. This leads to an important question: Will incorporation ever result in Federal income tax savings? The following example illustrates a situation where this occurs.

EXAMPLE 5

Ned, an individual in the 39.6% tax bracket, owns a business that produces net profit of $50,000 each year. Ned has significant income from other sources, so he does not withdraw any of the profit from the business. If the business is operated as a proprietorship, Ned's Federal income tax on the net profit of the business is $19,800 ($50,000 × 39.6%). However, if the business is operated as a corporation and pays no dividends, the tax will be $7,500 ($50,000 × 15%). Operating as a corporation saves $12,300 of Federal income tax each year. If Ned invests this $12,300 tax savings each year for several years, it is possible that a positive cash flow will result, even though Ned will be required to pay tax on dividends distributed by the corporation some time in the future. ◼

The preceding example deals with a specific set of facts. The conclusions reached in this situation cannot be extended to all decisions about a form of business organization. Each specific set of facts and circumstances requires a thorough analysis of the tax factors.

Another tax consideration involves the nature of dividend income. All income and expense items of a proprietorship retain their character when reported on the proprietor's tax return. In the case of a partnership, several separately reported items (e.g., charitable contributions and long-term capital gains) retain their character when passed through to the partners. However, the tax attributes of income and expense items of a corporation are lost as they pass through the corporate entity to the shareholders.

Losses of a C corporation are treated differently than losses of a proprietorship, partnership, or S corporation. A loss incurred by a proprietorship may be deductible by the owner, because all income and expense items are reported by the proprietor. Partnership and S corporation losses are passed through the entity and may be deductible by the partners or shareholders. C corporation losses, however, have no effect on the taxable income of the shareholders.

EXAMPLE 6

Franco plans to start a business this year. He expects the business will incur operating losses for the first three years and then become highly profitable. Franco decides to operate as an S corporation during the loss period because the losses will flow through and be deductible on his personal return. When the business becomes profitable, he intends to switch to C corporation status. ◼

NONTAX CONSIDERATIONS

Nontax considerations will sometimes override tax considerations and lead to the conclusion that a business should be operated as a corporation. The following are some of the more important nontax considerations:

- Sole proprietors and *general* partners in partnerships face the danger of *unlimited liability*. That is, creditors of the business may file claims not only against the assets of the business but also against the *personal* assets of proprietors or general partners. Shareholders are protected from claims against their personal assets by state corporate law.
- The corporate form of business organization can provide a vehicle for raising large amounts of capital through widespread stock ownership. Most major businesses in the United States are operated as corporations.

B R I D G E   D I S C I P L I N E

Bridge to Finance

Investment brokers and promoters often try to entice individuals to invest their disposable income in ventures designed to produce handsome returns. In most situations, the type of business entity in which the funds are invested takes the form of a "flow-through" entity, such as a limited partnership. Such investment ventures rarely operate as regular corporations.

A limited partnership is the favored investment vehicle for several reasons. One of the most significant reasons is that the investors who become limited partners are protected from exposure to unlimited liability. In addition, any operating losses of the entity (which may be expected in the venture's early years) flow through to the partners and, as a result, may provide an immediate tax benefit on the partners' returns. Another major advantage of the partnership form, in contrast to the corporate form, is that the business earnings are subject to only one level of tax—at the partner or investor level. If the investments were housed in a corporation, a tax would be levied first on the corporate earnings and then at the investor level when the corporation makes distributions to the shareholders.

- Shares of stock in a corporation are freely transferable, whereas a partner's sale of his or her partnership interest is subject to approval by the other partners.
- Shareholders may come and go, but a corporation can continue to exist. Death or withdrawal of a partner, on the other hand, may terminate the existing partnership and cause financial difficulties that result in dissolution of the entity. Thus, *continuity of life* is a distinct advantage of the corporate form of doing business.
- Corporations have *centralized management*. All management responsibility is assigned to a board of directors, who appoint officers to carry out the corporation's business. Partnerships, by contrast, may have decentralized management, in which every owner has a right to participate in the organization's business decisions; **limited partnerships,** though, may have centralized management. Centralized management is essential for the smooth operation of a widely held business.

LIMITED LIABILITY COMPANIES

The **limited liability company (LLC)** has proliferated greatly in recent years, particularly since 1988 when the IRS first ruled that it would treat qualifying LLCs as partnerships for tax purposes. All 50 states and the District of Columbia have passed laws that allow LLCs, and thousands of companies have chosen LLC status. As with a corporation, operating as an LLC allows an entity to avoid unlimited liability, which is a primary *nontax* consideration in choosing this form of business organization. The tax advantage of LLCs is that qualifying businesses may be treated as partnerships for tax purposes, thereby avoiding the problem of double taxation associated with regular corporations.

Some states allow an LLC to have centralized management, but not continuity of life or free transferability of interests. Other states allow LLCs to adopt any or all of the corporate characteristics of centralized management, continuity of life, and free transferability of interests. Chapter 14's comparison of business entities includes a discussion of LLCs.

ENTITY CLASSIFICATION

[handwritten annotation: → They can choose to be corp or partnership]

In late 1996, the IRS issued its so-called **check-the-box Regulations.**[1] Effective beginning in 1997, the Regulations enable taxpayers to choose the tax status of a business entity without regard to its corporate (or noncorporate) characteristics. These rules have simplified tax administration considerably and eliminated the type of litigation that arose under prior law.

Under these rules, entities with more than one owner can elect to be classified as either a partnership or a corporation. An entity with only one owner can elect to be classified as a sole proprietorship or as a corporation. In the event of default (i.e., no election is made), multi-owned entities are classified as partnerships and single-person businesses as sole proprietorships.

The election is not available to entities that are actually incorporated under state law or to entities that are required to be corporations under Federal law (e.g., certain publicly traded partnerships). Otherwise, LLCs are not treated as being incorporated under state law. Consequently, they can elect either corporation or partnership status.

[handwritten annotation in left margin: + u don't do anything if a flow thru entity]

1 Find more information on this topic at our Web site: *http://wft-entities.swcollege.com.*

Consolidated Groups May Utilize New Regulations

The check-the-box Regulations allow a single-owner eligible entity to be treated as a corporation or a division. Since LLCs are eligible entities, a C corporation that owns 100 percent of an LLC can treat the LLC as a division. At the same time, the parent corporation can enjoy the benefit of limited liability in the LLC operations. By electing division treatment, the income of the LLC flows directly to the parent corporation for tax purposes. Consequently, the parent corporation is able to avoid detailed and complex consolidated return Regulations and filing requirements.

LEARNING OBJECTIVE 1

Identify the tax consequences of incorporating and transferring assets to controlled corporations.

Organization of and Transfers to Controlled Corporations

IN GENERAL

Property transactions normally produce tax consequences if a gain or loss is recognized. As a result, unless special provisions in the Code apply, a transfer of property to a corporation in exchange for stock is a taxable transaction. The amount of gain or loss is measured by the difference between the fair market value of the stock received and the tax basis of the property transferred.

The Code, however, does permit nonrecognition of gain or loss in limited circumstances. For example, when a taxpayer exchanges some of his or her property

---

[1]Reg. §§ 301.7701–1 through –4, and –7.

for other property of a like kind, § 1031 provides that gain (or loss) on the exchange is deferred because there has not been a substantive change in the taxpayer's investment. The deferral of gain or loss is accomplished by calculating a substituted basis for the like-kind property received. With this substituted basis, the potential gain or loss on the property given up is recognized when the property received in the exchange is sold.

In a similar fashion, § 351 provides for the nonrecognition of gain or loss upon the transfer of property to a corporation in exchange for stock. The nonrecognition of gain or loss under § 351 reflects the principle that gain should not be recognized when a taxpayer's investment has not substantively changed. When a business is incorporated, the owner's economic status remains the same; only the *form* of the investment has changed. The investment in the business assets carries over to an investment in corporate stock. When only stock in the corporation is received, the shareholder is hardly in a position to pay a tax on any realized gain. As noted later, however, when the taxpayer receives property other than stock (i.e., *boot*) from the corporation, realized gain may be recognized.

The same principles govern the nonrecognition of gain or loss under § 1031 and § 351. The concept of nonrecognition of gain or loss, present in both provisions, causes gain or loss to be deferred until a substantive change in the taxpayer's investment occurs (such as a sale to or a taxable exchange with third parties). This approach is justified under the wherewithal to pay concept discussed in Chapter 1. A further justification for the nonrecognition of gain or loss provisions under § 351 is that tax rules should not impede the exercise of sound business judgment (e.g., choice of business entity).

EXAMPLE 7

Ron is considering incorporating his donut shop. He is concerned about his personal liability for the shop's obligations. Ron realizes that if he incorporates the shop, he will be liable only for the debts of the business that he has personally guaranteed. If Ron incorporates, the following assets will be transferred to the corporation:

	Tax Basis	Fair Market Value
Cash	$10,000	$ 10,000
Furniture and fixtures	20,000	60,000
Land and building	40,000	100,000
	$70,000	$170,000

In exchange, Ron will receive stock in the newly formed corporation worth $170,000. Without the nonrecognition provisions of § 351, Ron would recognize a taxable gain of $100,000 ($170,000 − $70,000) on the transfer. Under § 351, however, Ron does not recognize any gain because his economic status has not changed. Ron's investment in the assets of his unincorporated donut shop ($70,000) carries over to his investment in the incorporated donut shop, which is now represented by his ownership of stock in the incorporated donut shop. Thus, § 351 provides for tax neutrality on the initial incorporation of Ron's donut shop. ■

When a taxpayer participates in a like-kind exchange, gain is deferred to the extent that the taxpayer receives like-kind property. The taxpayer must recognize any realized gain when receiving "boot" (i.e., property of an unlike kind). For example, if a taxpayer exchanges a truck used in a business for another truck to be used in the business and also receives cash, the taxpayer has the wherewithal to pay an income tax on the cash involved. Further, the taxpayer's economic status has changed to the extent of the cash (not like-kind property) received. Thus, any "realized" gain on the exchange is recognized to the extent of the cash received. In like manner, if a taxpayer transfers property to a corporation and receives money or property other than stock, § 351(b) provides that gain is recognized to the extent of the lesser of the gain realized or the boot received (the amount of money and the fair market value of other property received). Gain is characterized according to the type of asset transferred.[2] Loss on a § 351 transaction is never recognized. The nonrecognition of gain or loss is accompanied by a substituted basis in the shareholder's stock.[3]

EXAMPLE 8	

Abby and Bill form White Corporation. Abby transfers property with an adjusted basis of $30,000 and a fair market value of $60,000 for 50% of White's stock. Bill transfers property with an adjusted basis of $70,000 and a fair market value of $60,000 for the remaining 50% of the stock. The transfer qualifies under § 351. Abby has a deferred gain of $30,000, and Bill has a deferred loss of $10,000. Both have a substituted basis in the stock of White Corporation. Abby has a basis of $30,000 in her stock, and Bill has a basis of $70,000 in his stock. Assume instead that Abby receives stock and cash of $10,000. Abby would recognize a gain of $10,000. ∎

Section 351 is mandatory if a transaction satisfies the provision's requirements. There are three requirements for nonrecognition of gain or loss: (1) *property* is transferred (2) in exchange for *stock* and (3) the transferors must be in *control* of the transferee corporation immediately after the transfer. These three requirements are discussed below.

TRANSFER OF PROPERTY

Questions have arisen concerning what constitutes **property** for purposes of § 351. The Code specifically excludes services rendered from the definition of property. With this exception, the definition of property is comprehensive. For example, along with plant and equipment, unrealized receivables for a cash basis taxpayer and installment obligations are considered property.[4] The transfer of an installment obligation in a transaction qualifying under § 351 is not a disposition of the installment obligation. Thus, gain is not recognized to the transferor. Secret processes and formulas, as well as secret information in the general nature of a patentable invention, also qualify as property under § 351.[5]

Services are not considered to be property under § 351 for a critical reason. A taxpayer must report as income the fair market value of any consideration received as compensation for services rendered.[6] Thus, if a taxpayer receives stock in a corporation as consideration for rendering services to the corporation, the taxpayer has taxable income. In this case, the amount of income recognized by the taxpayer is equal to the fair market value of the stock received. The taxpayer's basis in the stock received is its fair market value.

---

[2]Rev.Rul. 68–55, 1968–1 C.B. 140.
[3]§ 358(a). See the discussion preceding Example 27.
[4]*Hempt Brothers, Inc. v. U.S.*, 74–1 USTC ¶9188, 33 AFTR2d 74–570, 490 F.2d 1172 (CA–3, 1974), and Reg. § 1.453–9(c)(2).

[5]Rev.Rul. 64–56, 1964–1 C.B. 133; Rev.Rul. 71–564, 1971–2 C.B. 179.
[6]§§ 61 and 83.

| EXAMPLE 9 | Ann and Bob form Brown Corporation and transfer the following consideration: |

| | Consideration Transferred | | |
	Basis to Transferor	Fair Market Value	Number of Shares Issued
From Ann:			
Personal services rendered to Brown Corporation	$ –0–	$20,000	200
From Bob:			
Installment obligation	5,000	40,000	
Inventory	10,000	30,000	800
Secret process	–0–	10,000	

The value of each share in Brown Corporation is $100.[7] Ann has taxable income of $20,000 on the transfer because services do not qualify as "property." She has a basis of $20,000 in her 200 shares of stock in Brown. Bob recognizes no gain on the transfer because all of the consideration he transferred to Brown qualifies as "property" and he has "control" of Brown after the transfer. (See the discussion concerning control below.) Bob has a substituted basis of $15,000 in the Brown stock. ■

If property is transferred to a corporation in exchange for any property other than stock, the property constitutes boot. The boot is taxable to the transferor-shareholder to the extent of any realized gain.[8]

STOCK

The Regulations state that the term "stock" does not include stock rights and stock warrants.[9] Generally, however, the term "stock" needs no clarification. It includes both common stock and most preferred stock. It does not include "nonqualified preferred stock," which possesses many of the attributes of debt.[10]

Under current law, any corporate debt or **securities** (i.e., long-term debt, such as bonds) are treated as boot because they are not an equity interest or stock. Thus, the receipt of debt in exchange for the transfer of appreciated property to a controlled corporation causes recognition of gain.

CONTROL OF THE CORPORATION

To qualify as a nontaxable transaction under § 351, the transferor(s) of the property must be in **control** of the corporation immediately after the exchange. Control means that the person or persons transferring *property* must have at least an 80 percent stock ownership in the transferee corporation. The transferor-shareholders must own stock possessing at least 80 percent of the total combined voting power of all classes of stock entitled to vote *and* at least 80 percent of the total *number* of shares of all other classes of stock.[11]

---

[7]The value of closely held stock normally is presumed to be equal to the value of the property transferred.

[8]§ 351(b).

[9]Reg. § 1.351–1(a)(1)(ii).

[10]§ 351(g). Examples of nonqualified preferred stock include preferred stock that is redeemable within 20 years of issuance and whose dividend rate is based on other than corporate performance.

Therefore, gain is recognized up to the fair market value of the nonqualified preferred stock received. Loss may be recognized when the transferor receives *only* nonqualified preferred stock (or nonqualified preferred stock and other boot) in exchange for property. See also Reg. § 1.351–1(a)(1)(ii).

[11]§ 368(c). Nonqualified preferred stock is treated as stock, and not boot, for purposes of this control test.

Control Immediately after the Transfer. Immediately after the exchange, the property transferors must control the corporation. Control can apply to a single person or to several taxpayers if they are all parties to an integrated transaction. The Regulations provide that when more than one person is involved, the exchange does not necessarily require simultaneous exchanges by two or more persons. The Regulations do, however, require that the rights of the parties (i.e., those transferring property to the corporation) be previously set out and determined. Also, the agreement to transfer property should be executed "with an expedition consistent with orderly procedure."[12]

If two or more persons transfer property to a corporation for stock, the transfers should occur close together in time and should be made in accordance with an agreement among the parties.

EXAMPLE 10

Jack exchanges property with a basis of $60,000 and a fair market value of $100,000 for 70% of the stock of Gray Corporation. The other 30% is owned by Jane, who acquired it several years ago. The fair market value of Jack's stock is $100,000. Jack recognizes a taxable gain of $40,000 on the transfer because he does not have control immediately after the exchange and his transaction cannot be integrated with Jane's for purposes of the control requirement. ∎

EXAMPLE 11

Lana, Leo, and Lori incorporate their respective businesses by forming Green Corporation. Lana exchanges her property for 300 shares in Green on January 5, 2001. Leo exchanges his property for 400 shares in Green on January 10, 2001, and Lori exchanges her property for 300 shares in Green on March 5, 2001. The three exchanges are part of a prearranged plan, so the control requirement is met. The nonrecognition provisions of § 351 apply to all of the exchanges. ∎

Stock need not be issued to the property transferors in the same proportion as the relative value of the property transferred by each. However, when stock received is not proportionate to the value of the property transferred, the actual effect of the transaction must be properly characterized. For example, in such situations one transferor may actually be making a gift of valuable consideration to another transferor.

EXAMPLE 12

Ron and Shelia, father and daughter, form Oak Corporation. Ron transfers property worth $50,000 in exchange for 100 shares of stock, while Shelia transfers property worth $50,000 for 400 shares of stock. The transfers qualify under § 351 because Ron and Shelia have control of the Oak stock immediately after the transfers of property. However, the implicit gift by Ron to Shelia must be recognized and appropriately characterized. As such, the value of the gift might be subject to the gift tax. ∎

Once control has been achieved, it is not necessarily lost if stock received by shareholders in a § 351 exchange is sold or given to persons who are not parties to the exchange shortly after the transaction. However, failure to meet the control requirement might result if a *plan* for the ultimate disposition of the stock existed *before* the exchange.[13]

---

[12]Reg. § 1.351–1(a)(1).
[13]*Wilgard Realty Co. v. Comm.*, 42–1 USTC ¶9452, 29 AFTR 325, 127 F.2d 514 (CA–2, 1942).

EXAMPLE 13

Mark and Carl form Black Corporation. They transfer appreciated property to the corporation with each receiving 50 shares of the stock. Shortly after the formation, Mark gives 25 shares to his son. Because Mark was not committed to make the gift, he is considered to own his original shares of Black Corporation stock and, along with Carl, to control Black Corporation "immediately after the exchange." The requirements of § 351 are met, and neither Mark nor Carl is taxed on the exchange. Alternatively, had Mark immediately given 25 shares to a business associate pursuant to a plan to satisfy an outstanding obligation, the formation of Black would be taxable to Mark and Carl because of their lack of control. ■

PLANNING CONSIDERATIONS

Utilizing § 351

When using § 351(a), ensure that all parties transferring property (including cash) receive control of the corporation. Simultaneous transfers are not necessary, but a long period of time between transfers makes the transaction vulnerable to taxation if the transfers are not properly documented as part of a single plan. To do this, the parties should document and preserve evidence of their intentions. Also, it is helpful to have some reasonable explanation for any delay in the transfers.

To meet the requirements of § 351, mere momentary control on the part of the transferor may not suffice if loss of control is compelled by a prearranged agreement.[14]

EXAMPLE 14

For many years, Todd operated a business as a sole proprietor employing Linda as manager. To dissuade Linda from quitting and going out on her own, Todd promised her a 30% interest in the business. To fulfill this promise, Todd transferred the business to newly formed Green Corporation in return for all its stock. Immediately thereafter, Todd transfers 30% of the stock to Linda. Section 351 probably does not apply to Todd's transfer to Green Corporation. It appears that Todd was under an obligation to relinquish control. If this is not the case and the loss of control was voluntary on Todd's part, momentary control would suffice.[15] ■

Be sure that later transfers of property to an existing corporation satisfy the control requirement if recognition of gain is to be avoided. Also with respect to later transfers, a transferor's interest cannot be counted if the value of stock received is relatively small compared with the value of stock already owned. Further, the primary purpose of the transfer may not be to qualify other transferors for § 351 treatment.[16]

Transfers for Property and Services. Section 351 treatment is lost if stock is transferred to persons who did not contribute property, causing those who did to lack control immediately after the exchange.

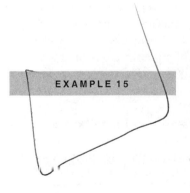

EXAMPLE 15

Kate transfers property with a value of $60,000 and a basis of $5,000 for 600 shares of stock in newly formed Wren Corporation. Brian receives 400 shares in Wren for services rendered to the corporation. Each share of stock is worth $100. Both Kate and Brian have taxable gain on the transaction. Brian is not part of the control group because he does not transfer property for stock. He has taxable income of $40,000 (400 shares × $100). Kate has a taxable gain of $55,000 [$60,000 (fair market value of the stock in Wren Corporation) − $5,000 (basis in the transferred property)]. Kate is taxed on the exchange because she receives only 60% of the stock in Wren Corporation. ■

[14]Rev.Rul. 54–96, 1954–1 C.B. 111.
[15]Compare *Fahs v. Florida Machine and Foundry Co.*, 48–2 USTC ¶9329, 36 AFTR 1161, 168 F.2d 957 (CA–5, 1948), with *John C. O'Connor*,

16 TCM 213, T.C.Memo. 1957–50, *aff'd* in 58–2 USTC ¶9913, 2 AFTR2d 6011, 260 F.2d 358 (CA–6, 1958).
[16]Reg. § 1.351–1(a)(1)(ii).

A person who performs services for the corporation in exchange for stock and also transfers some property is treated as a member of the transferring group. That person is taxed on the value of the stock issued for services but not on the stock issued for property. In such a case, all the stock received by the person transferring both property and services is counted in determining whether the transferors acquired control of the corporation.[17]

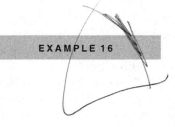

EXAMPLE 16

Assume the same facts as in Example 15, except that Brian transfers property worth $30,000 (basis of $3,000) in addition to services rendered to the corporation (valued at $10,000). Now Brian becomes a part of the control group. Kate and Brian together receive 100% of the stock in Wren Corporation. Consequently, § 351 is applicable to the exchanges. Kate has no recognized gain. Brian does not recognize gain on the transfer of the property but has taxable income to the extent of the value of the shares issued for services rendered. Thus, Brian recognizes income of $10,000. ■

Transfers for Services and Nominal Property. To be a member of the group and aid in qualifying all transferors under the 80 percent control test, the person contributing services must transfer property having more than a "relatively small value" compared to the value of services performed. Section 351 will not apply when a small amount of property is transferred and the primary purpose of the transfer is to qualify the transaction under § 351 for concurrent transferors.[18]

EXAMPLE 17

Kim and Eric transfer property to Redbird Corporation, each in exchange for one-third of the stock. Howie receives the other one third of the stock for services rendered. The transaction will not qualify under § 351 because Howie is not a member of the group transferring property and Kim and Eric together received only 66⅔% of the stock. Thus, the post-transfer control requirement is not met.

Assume instead that Howie also transfers property. Then he is a member of the group, and the transaction qualifies under § 351. Howie is taxed on the value of the stock issued for services, but the remainder of the transaction is tax-free. However, if the property transferred by Howie is of a relatively small value in comparison to the stock he receives for his services, and the primary purpose for transferring the property is to cause the transaction to be tax-free for Kim and Eric, the exchange does not qualify under § 351. Gain or loss is recognized by all parties. ■

The IRS generally requires that before a transferor who receives stock for both property and services can be included in the control group, the value of the property transferred must be at least 10 percent of the value of the services provided.[19] If the value of the property transferred is less than this amount, the IRS will not issue an advance ruling that the exchange meets the requirements of § 351.

EXAMPLE 18

Sara and Rick form White Corporation. Sara transfers land (worth $100,000, basis of $20,000) for 50% of the stock in White. Rick transfers equipment (worth $5,000, adjusted basis of $1,000) and provides services worth $95,000 for 50% of the stock. Rick's stock in White Corporation is unlikely to be counted in determining control for purposes of § 351; thus,

---

[17]Reg. § 1.351–1(a)(2), Ex. 3.
[18]Reg. § 1.351–1(a)(1)(ii).

[19]Rev.Proc. 77–37, 1977–2 C.B. 568.

INTERNATIONAL IMPLICATIONS

DOES § 351 COVER THE INCORPORATION OF A FOREIGN BUSINESS?

When a taxpayer wishes to incorporate a business overseas by moving assets across U.S. borders, the deferral mechanism of § 351 applies in certain situations, but not in others. In general, § 351 is available to defer gain recognition when starting up a new corporation outside the United States unless so-called tainted assets are involved. Under § 367, tainted assets, which include assets such as inventory and accounts receivable, are treated as having been sold by the taxpayer prior to the corporate formation; therefore, their transfer results in the current recognition of gain. The presence of tainted assets triggers gain because Congress does not want taxpayers to be able to shift the gain outside of U.S. jurisdiction. The gain recognized is ordinary or capital, depending on the nature of the asset involved.

---

the control requirement is not met. None of Rick's stock is counted in determining control because the property he transfers has a nominal value in comparison to the value of the services he renders. Sara recognizes $80,000 of gain on the transfer of the land. She has a basis of $100,000 in her White stock. Rick must recognize income of $95,000 on the transfer for services rendered and a gain of $4,000 for property transferred. Rick also has a $100,000 basis in his White stock. ■

Transfers to Existing Corporations.　Once a corporation is in operation, § 351 also applies to any later transfers of property for stock by either new or existing shareholders.

EXAMPLE 19

Sam and Beth formed Blue Corporation three years ago. Both Sam and Beth transferred appreciated property to Blue in exchange for 500 shares each in the corporation. The original transfers qualified under § 351, and neither Sam nor Beth was taxed on the exchange. In the current year, Sam transfers property (worth $100,000, adjusted basis of $5,000) for 500 additional Blue shares. Sam has a taxable gain of $95,000 on the transfer. The exchange does not qualify under § 351 because Sam does not have 80% control of Blue Corporation immediately after the transfer; he owns 1,000 shares of the 1,500 shares outstanding, or a 66⅔% interest. ■

If current shareholders transfer property with a small value relative to the value of stock already owned, a special rule applies (similar to the nominal property rule noted previously). In particular, if the purpose of the transfer is to qualify a transaction under § 351, the ownership of the current shareholders is not counted when determining control. Thus, in the preceding example, if Beth had contributed $200 for one share of stock at the time of Sam's contribution, Beth's ownership would not count toward the 80 percent control requirement and Sam would still have a taxable exchange.

ASSUMPTION OF LIABILITIES—§ 357

LEARNING OBJECTIVE 2

Understand the special rules
that apply when a corporation
assumes a shareholder's
liability.

Without the special rules of § 357, the transfer of mortgaged property to a controlled corporation could require recognition of gain by the transferor if the corporation assumed the mortgage. This would be consistent with the rule in like-kind exchanges under § 1031. Liabilities assumed by the other party are considered the equivalent of cash and treated as boot. Section 357(a) provides, however, that when the acquiring corporation **assumes a liability** in a § 351 transaction, the transfer does *not* result in boot to the transferor-shareholder. Nevertheless, liabilities assumed by the transferee corporation are treated as boot in determining the basis of the stock received. As a result, the basis of the stock received is reduced by the amount of the liabilities assumed by the corporation.

EXAMPLE 20

Vera transfers property with an adjusted basis of $60,000, fair market value of $100,000, to Gray Corporation for 100% of the stock in Gray. The property is subject to a liability of $25,000 that Gray Corporation assumes. The exchange is tax-free under §§ 351 and 357. However, the basis to Vera of the Gray stock is $35,000 [$60,000 (basis of property transferred) – $25,000 (amount of the liability assumed by Gray)]. ∎

The general rule of § 357(a) has two exceptions: (1) § 357(b) provides that if the principal purpose of the assumption of the liabilities is to avoid tax *or* if there is no bona fide business purpose behind the exchange, the liabilities are treated as boot; and (2) § 357(c) provides that if the sum of the liabilities exceeds the adjusted basis of the properties transferred, the excess is taxable gain.

Exception (1): Tax Avoidance or No Bona Fide Business Purpose.   Unless liabilities are incurred shortly before incorporation, § 357(b) generally poses few problems. A tax avoidance purpose for transferring liabilities to a controlled corporation normally is not a concern in view of the basis adjustment as noted above. Since the liabilities transferred reduce the basis of the stock received, any realized gain merely is deferred and not completely eliminated. Any postponed gain is recognized when and if the stock is disposed of in a taxable sale or exchange.

Satisfying the bona fide business purpose is not difficult if the liabilities were incurred in connection with the transferor's normal course of conducting a trade or business. But the bona fide business purpose requirement can cause difficulty if the liability is taken out shortly before the property is transferred and the proceeds are utilized for personal purposes.[20] This type of situation is analogous to a cash distribution by the corporation, which is taxed as boot.

EXAMPLE 21

Dan transfers real estate (basis of $40,000 and fair market value of $90,000) to a controlled corporation in return for stock in the corporation. Shortly before the transfer, Dan mortgages the real estate and uses the $20,000 of proceeds to meet personal obligations. Thus, along with the real estate, the mortgage is transferred to the corporation. In this case, the assumption of the mortgage lacks a bona fide business purpose. Consequently, the release of the liability is treated as boot received, and Dan has a taxable gain on the transfer of $20,000, computed as follows:[21]

---

[20]See, for example, *Campbell, Jr. v. Wheeler*, 65–1 USTC ¶9294, 15 AFTR2d 578, 342 F.2d 837 (CA–5, 1965).

[21]§ 351(b).

Stock	$ 70,000
Release of liability—treated as boot	20,000
Total amount realized	$ 90,000
Less: Basis of real estate	(40,000)
Realized gain	$ 50,000
Recognized gain	$ 20,000

The effect of the application of § 357(b) is to taint *all* liabilities transferred, even if some are supported by a bona fide business purpose.

EXAMPLE 22

Tim, an accrual basis taxpayer, incorporates his sole proprietorship. Among the liabilities transferred to the new corporation are trade accounts payable of $100,000 and a MasterCard bill of $5,000. Tim had used the MasterCard to purchase a wedding anniversary gift for his wife. Under these circumstances, the *entire* $105,000 of liabilities is boot and triggers the recognition of gain to the extent gain is realized. ■

Exception (2): Liabilities in Excess of Basis.   Section 357(c) states that, if the amount of the liabilities assumed *exceeds* the total of the adjusted bases of the properties transferred, the excess is taxable gain. Without this provision, if liabilities exceed basis in property exchanged, a taxpayer would have a negative basis in the stock received in the controlled corporation.[22] Section 357(c) precludes the negative basis possibility by treating the excess over basis as gain to the transferor.

EXAMPLE 23

Andre transfers land and equipment with adjusted bases of $35,000 and $5,000, respectively, to a newly formed corporation in exchange for 100% of the stock. The corporation assumes $50,000 of liabilities on the transferred properties. Without § 357(c), Andre's basis in the stock of the new corporation would be a negative $10,000 [$40,000 (bases of properties transferred) + $0 (gain recognized) – $0 (boot received) – $50,000 (liabilities assumed)]. Section 357(c), however, causes Andre to recognize a gain of $10,000 ($50,000 liabilities assumed – $40,000 bases of assets transferred). As a result, the stock has a zero basis in Andre's hands, determined as follows:

Bases in the properties transferred ($35,000 + $5,000)	$ 40,000
Plus: Gain recognized	10,000
Less: Boot received	(–0–)
Less: Liabilities assumed	(50,000)
Basis in the stock received	$ –0–

Thus, Andre recognizes $10,000 of gain, and a negative stock basis is avoided. ■

The definition of liabilities under § 357(c) excludes obligations that would have been deductible to the transferor had those obligations been paid before the transfer. Thus, accounts payable of a cash basis taxpayer that give rise to a deduction are

---

[22]*Easson v. Comm.*, 33 T.C. 963 (1960), *rev'd* in 61–2 USTC ¶9654, 8 AFTR2d 5448, 294 F.2d 653 (CA–9, 1961).

not considered to be liabilities for purposes of § 357(c). In addition, they are not considered in the computation of stock basis.

EXAMPLE 24

Tina, a cash basis taxpayer, incorporates her sole proprietorship. In return for all of the stock of the new corporation, she transfers the following items:

	Adjusted Basis	Fair Market Value
Cash	$10,000	$10,000
Unrealized accounts receivable (amounts due to Tina but not yet paid to her)	–0–	40,000
Trade accounts payable	–0–	30,000
Note payable	5,000	5,000

Unrealized accounts receivable and trade accounts payable have a zero basis. Under the cash method of accounting, no income is recognized until the receivables are collected, and no deduction materializes until the payables are satisfied. The note payable has a basis because it was issued for consideration received.

In this situation, the trade accounts payable are disregarded for gain recognition purposes and in determining Tina's stock basis. Thus, because the balance of the note payable does not exceed the basis of the assets transferred, Tina does not have a problem of liabilities in excess of basis (i.e., the note payable of $5,000 does not exceed the basis in the cash and accounts receivable of $10,000). ■

If §§ 357(b) and (c) both apply to the same transfer, § 357(b) dominates.[23] This could be significant because § 357(b) does not create gain on the transfer, as does § 357(c), but merely converts the liability to boot. Thus, the realized gain limitation continues to apply to § 357(b) transactions.

EXAMPLE 25

Chris owns land with a basis of $100,000 and a fair market value of $1,000,000. The land is subject to a mortgage of $300,000. One month prior to transferring the land to Robin Corporation, Chris borrows an additional $200,000 for personal purposes and gives the lender a second mortgage on the land. Therefore, upon the incorporation, Robin Corporation issues stock worth $500,000 to Chris and assumes the mortgages on the land.

Both § 357(c) and § 357(b) apply to the transfer. The mortgages on the property ($500,000) exceed the basis of the property ($100,000). Thus, Chris has a gain of $400,000 under § 357(c). Chris borrowed $200,000 just prior to the transfer and used the loan proceeds for personal purposes. Under § 357(b), Chris has boot of $500,000 in the amount of the liabilities. Note that *all* of the liabilities are treated as boot, not just the "tainted" $200,000 liability. He has realized gain of $900,000 [$1,000,000 (stock of $500,000 and assumption of liabilities of $500,000) − $100,000 (basis in the land)]. Gain is recognized to the extent of the boot of $500,000. Section 357(b) dominates over § 357(c). ■

---

[23]§ 357(c)(2)(A).

PLANNING CONSIDERATIONS

Avoiding § 351

Section 351(a) provides for the nonrecognition of gain on transfers to controlled corporations. As such, it is often regarded as a relief provision favoring taxpayers. In some situations, however, avoiding § 351(a) may produce a more advantageous tax result. The transferors might prefer to recognize gain on the transfer of property if the tax cost is low. For example, they may be in low tax brackets, or the gain may be a capital gain from which substantial capital losses can be offset. Also, recognition of gain will lead to a stepped-up basis in the transferred property in the corporation.

Another reason a particular transferor might wish to avoid § 351 concerns possible loss recognition. Recall that § 351 refers to the nonrecognition of both gains and losses. Section 351(b)(2) specifically states: "No loss to such recipient shall be recognized." A transferor who wishes to recognize loss has several alternatives:

- Sell the property to the corporation for its stock. The IRS could attempt to collapse the "sale," however, by taking the approach that the transfer really falls under § 351(a).[24]
- Sell the property to the corporation for other property or boot. Because the transferor receives no stock, § 351 is inapplicable.

- Transfer the property to the corporation in return for securities or nonqualified preferred stock. Recall that § 351 does not apply to a transferor who receives securities or nonqualified preferred stock. In both this and the previous alternatives, watch for the possible disallowance of the loss under the related-party rules.

Suppose loss property is to be transferred to the corporation and no loss is recognized by the transferor due to § 351(a). This could present an interesting problem in terms of assessing the economic realities involved.

EXAMPLE 26

Iris and Ivan form Wren Corporation with the following investment: property by Iris (basis of $40,000 and fair market value of $50,000) and property by Ivan (basis of $60,000 and fair market value of $50,000). Each receives 50% of the Wren stock. Has Ivan acted wisely in settling for only 50% of the stock? At first, it would appear so, since Iris and Ivan each invested property of the same value ($50,000). But what about tax considerations? Due to the carryover basis rules, the corporation now has a basis of $40,000 in Iris's property and $60,000 in Ivan's property. In essence, Iris has shifted a possible $10,000 gain to the corporation while Ivan has transferred a $10,000 potential loss. With this in mind, an equitable allocation of the Wren stock would call for Ivan to receive a greater percentage interest than Iris. ∎

LEARNING OBJECTIVE 3

Recognize the basis issues relevant to the shareholder and the corporation.

BASIS DETERMINATION AND OTHER ISSUES

Recall that § 351(a) postpones gain or loss recognition until the taxpayer's investment changes substantially. By virtue of the basis rules described below, the postponed gain or loss is recognized when the stock is disposed of in a taxable transaction.

Basis of Stock to Shareholder. For a taxpayer transferring property to a corporation in a § 351 transaction, the basis of *stock* received in the transaction is the same as the basis the taxpayer had in the property transferred, increased by any gain recognized on the exchange and decreased by boot received. For basis purposes, boot received includes any liabilities transferred by the shareholder to the corporation. Also note that if the shareholder receives any *other property* (i.e., boot) along with the stock, it takes a basis equal to its fair market value.[25]

---

[24]*U.S. v. Hertwig,* 68–2 USTC ¶9495, 22 AFTR2d 5249, 398 F.2d 452 (CA–5, 1968).

[25]§ 358(a).

■ **FIGURE 9–1**
Shareholder's Basis in Stock Received

Adjusted basis of property transferred	$xx,xxx
Plus: Gain recognized	x,xxx
Minus: Boot received (including any liabilities transferred)	(x,xxx)
Equals: Basis of stock received	$xx,xxx

■ **FIGURE 9–2**
Corporation's Basis in Property Received

Adjusted basis of property transferred	$xx,xxx
Plus: Gain recognized by transferor-shareholder	xxx
Equals: Basis of property to corporation	$xx,xxx

Basis of Property to Corporation.   The basis of property received by the corporation is the basis of the exchanged property in the hands of the transferor increased by the amount of any gain recognized to the transferor-shareholder.[26]

The basis rules are summarized in Figures 9–1 and 9–2 and illustrated in Examples 27 and 28.

EXAMPLE 27

Maria and Ned form Brown Corporation. Maria transfers land (basis of $30,000 and fair market value of $70,000); Ned invests cash ($60,000). They each receive 50 shares in Brown Corporation, worth $1,200 per share, but Maria also receives $10,000 cash from Brown. The transfers of property, the realized and recognized gain on the transfers, and the basis of the stock in Brown Corporation to Maria and Ned are as follows:

	A Basis of Property Transferred	B FMV of Stock Received	C Boot Received	D Realized Gain (B + C − A)	E Recognized Gain (Lesser of C or D)	F Basis of Stock in Brown (A − C + E)
From Maria:						
Land	$30,000	$60,000	$10,000	$40,000	$10,000	$30,000
From Ned:						
Cash	60,000	60,000	–0–	–0–	–0–	60,000

Brown Corporation has a basis of $40,000 in the land: Maria's basis of $30,000 plus her recognized gain of $10,000. ■

EXAMPLE 28

Assume the same facts as in Example 27 except that Maria's basis in the land is $68,000 (instead of $30,000). Because recognized gain cannot exceed realized gain, the transfer generates only $2,000 of gain to Maria. The realized and recognized gain and the basis of the stock in Brown Corporation to Maria are as follows:

---

[26]§ 362(a).

	A	B	C	D	E	F
					Recognized	Basis of
	Basis of	FMV of		Realized	Gain	Stock in
	Property	Stock	Boot	Gain	(Lesser of	Brown
	Transferred	Received	Received	(B + C − A)	C or D)	(A − C + E)
Land	$68,000	$60,000	$10,000	$2,000	$2,000	$60,000

Brown's basis in the land is $70,000 ($68,000 basis to Maria + $2,000 gain recognized by Maria). ■

Stock Issued for Services Rendered.
A corporation's disposition of stock for property is not a taxable exchange.[27] A transfer of shares for services is also not a taxable transaction to a corporation.[28] Can a corporation deduct the fair market value of the stock it issues in consideration of services as a business expense? Yes, unless the services are such that the payment is characterized as a capital expenditure.[29]

EXAMPLE 29

Carol and Carl form White Corporation. Carol transfers cash of $500,000 for 100 shares of White Corporation stock. Carl transfers property worth $400,000 (basis of $90,000) and agrees to serve as manager of the corporation for one year; in return, Carl receives 100 shares of stock in White. The value of Carl's services to White Corporation is $100,000. Carol's and Carl's transfers qualify under § 351. Neither Carol nor Carl is taxed on the transfer of their property. However, Carl has income of $100,000, the value of the services he will render to White Corporation. White has a basis of $90,000 in the property it acquired from Carl, and it may claim a business deduction under § 162 of $100,000 for the value of services Carl will render. Carl's stock basis is $190,000 ($90,000 + $100,000). ■

EXAMPLE 30

Assume, in the preceding example, that Carl receives the 100 shares of White Corporation stock as consideration for the appreciated property and for providing legal services in organizing the corporation. The value of Carl's legal services is $100,000. Carl has no gain on the transfer of the property but has income of $100,000 for the value of the services rendered. White Corporation has a basis of $90,000 in the property it acquired from Carl and must capitalize the $100,000 as an organizational expense. Carl's stock basis is $190,000 ($90,000 + $100,000). ■

Holding Period for Shareholder and Transferee Corporation.
The shareholder's holding period for stock received for a capital asset or for § 1231 property includes the holding period of the property transferred to the corporation. The holding period of the property is *tacked on* to the holding period of the stock. The holding period for stock received for any other property (e.g., inventory) begins on the day after the exchange. The transferee corporation's holding period for property acquired in a § 351 transfer is the holding period of the transferor-shareholder regardless of the character of the property to the transferor.[30]

RECAPTURE CONSIDERATIONS

In a pure § 351(a) nontaxable transfer (no boot involved) to a controlled corporation, the recapture of accelerated cost recovery rules do not apply.[31] Instead, any recapture potential of the property carries over to the corporation as it steps into the shoes

---

[27]§ 1032.
[28]Reg. § 1.1032–1(a).
[29]Rev.Rul. 62–217, 1962–2 C.B. 59, modified by Rev.Rul. 74–503, 1974–2 C.B. 117.

[30]§§ 1223(1) and (2).
[31]§§ 1245(b)(3) and 1250(d)(3).

of the transferor-shareholder for purposes of basis determination. However, to the extent that gain is recognized, the recapture rules are applied.

EXAMPLE 31

Paul transfers equipment (adjusted basis of $30,000, original cost of $120,000, and fair market value of $100,000) to a controlled corporation in return for additional stock. If Paul had sold the equipment, it would have yielded a gain of $70,000, all of which would be recaptured as ordinary income under § 1245. If the transfer comes within § 351(a), Paul has no recognized gain and no accelerated cost recovery to recapture. If the corporation later disposes of the equipment in a taxable transaction, it must take into account the § 1245 recapture potential originating with Paul.

   If Paul had received boot of $60,000 on the transfer, all of the recognized gain would be recaptured as ordinary income. The remaining $10,000 of recapture potential would carry over to the corporation. ■

PLANNING CONSIDERATIONS

Other Considerations When Incorporating a Business

When a business is incorporated, the organizers must determine which assets and liabilities should be transferred to the corporation. A transfer of assets that produce passive income (rents, royalties, dividends, and interest) can cause the corporation to be a personal holding company in a tax year when operating income is low. Thus, the corporation could be subject to the personal holding company penalty tax (see the discussion in Chapter 10).

   A transfer of the accounts payable of a cash basis taxpayer may prevent the taxpayer from taking a tax deduction when the accounts are paid. These payables should generally be retained.

   Leasing property to the corporation may be a more attractive alternative than transferring ownership. Leasing provides the taxpayer with the opportunity of withdrawing money from the corporation without the payment being characterized as a dividend. If the property is donated to a family member in a lower tax bracket, the lease income can be shifted as well. If the depreciation and other deductions available in connection with the property are larger than the lease income, a high tax rate taxpayer could retain the property until the income exceeds the deductions.

   Another way to shift income to other taxpayers is by the use of corporate debt. Shareholder debt in a corporation can be given to family members with low marginal tax rates. This technique also shifts income without a loss of control of the corporation.

LEARNING OBJECTIVE 4

Understand the tax aspects of the capital structure of a corporation.

Capital Structure of a Corporation

CAPITAL CONTRIBUTIONS

When a corporation receives money or property in exchange for capital stock (including treasury stock), neither gain nor loss is recognized by the recipient corporation.[32] The corporation's gross income also does not include shareholders' contributions of money or property to the capital of the corporation. Additional funds received from shareholders through voluntary pro-rata payments are not income to the corporation. This is the case even though there is no increase in the number of outstanding shares of stock of the corporation. The payments represent an additional price paid for the shares held by the shareholders (increasing their basis) and are treated as additions to the operating capital of the corporation.[33]

---

[32]§ 1032.   [33]§ 118 and Reg. § 1.118–1.

corp basis – your old basis + gain recognized

0 basis

Contributions by nonshareholders, such as land contributed to a corporation by a civic group or a governmental group to induce the corporation to locate in a particular community, are also excluded from the gross income of a corporation.[34] However, property that is transferred to a corporation by a nonshareholder in exchange for goods or services rendered is taxable income to the corporation.[35]

EXAMPLE 32

A cable company charges its customers an initial fee to hook up to a new cable system installed in the area. These payments are used to finance the total cost of constructing the cable facilities. The customers will make monthly payments for the cable service. The initial payments are used for capital expenditures, but they represent payments for services to be rendered by the cable company. As such, they are taxable income and not contributions to capital by nonshareholders. ∎

? isn't income to corp

The basis of property received by a corporation from a shareholder as a **capital contribution** is equal to the basis of the property in the hands of the shareholder increased by any gain recognized by the shareholder. The basis of property transferred to a corporation by a nonshareholder as a contribution to capital is zero.

you'll get more basis than what you own

If a corporation receives *money* as a contribution to capital from a nonshareholder, a special rule applies. The basis of any property acquired with the money during a 12-month period beginning on the day the contribution was received is reduced by the amount of the contribution. The excess of money received over the cost of new property is used to reduce the basis of other property held by the corporation and is applied in the following order:

- Depreciable property.
- Property subject to amortization.
- Property subject to depletion.
- All other remaining properties.

The basis of property within each category is reduced in proportion to the relative bases of the properties.[36]

EXAMPLE 33

A city donates land to Brown Corporation as an inducement for Brown to locate in the city. The receipt of the land produces no taxable income to Brown, and the land's basis to the corporation is zero. If, in addition, the city gives the corporation $10,000 in cash, the money is not taxable income to the corporation. However, if the corporation purchases property with the $10,000 within the next 12 months, the basis of the property is reduced by $10,000. Any excess cash not used is handled according to the ordering rules noted above. ∎

DEBT IN THE CAPITAL STRUCTURE

LEARNING OBJECTIVE 5

Recognize the tax differences between debt and equity investments.

Advantages of Debt.　Significant tax differences exist between debt and equity in the capital structure, and shareholders must be aware of these differences. The advantages of issuing long-term debt are numerous. Interest on debt is deductible by the corporation, while dividend payments are not. Further, the shareholders are not taxed on loan repayments unless the repayments exceed basis. An investment in stock usually cannot be withdrawn tax free as long as a corporation has earnings and profits. Withdrawals will be deemed to be taxable dividends to the extent of

---

[34] See *Edwards v. Cuba Railroad Co.*, 1 USTC ¶139, 5 AFTR 5398, 45 S.Ct. 614 (USSC, 1925).

[35] Reg. § 1.118–1. See also *Teleservice Co. of Wyoming Valley v. Comm.*, 27 T.C. 722 (1957), *aff'd* in 58–1 USTC ¶9383, 1 AFTR2d 1249, 254 F.2d 105 (CA–3, 1958), *cert. den.* 78 S.Ct. 1360 (USSC, 1958).

[36] § 362(c); Reg. §§ 1.362–2(b) and 1.118–1.

FREEDOM FROM THE TRAP OF DOUBLE TAXATION: JUST HOW SUCCESSFUL CAN THAT BE?

It seems that many taxpayers are hesitant to structure their businesses as C corporations because they want to avoid the burden of double taxation. Other taxpayers who have chosen to operate their businesses as C corporations are keenly aware of the problem and work to minimize the double taxation impact. One common way to mitigate the problem is to issue debt to the owners of the business along with stock.

Regardless of how sophisticated these tax minimization strategies may be, however, they never can be completely successful, at least according to the Tax Foundation. The Tax Foundation annually computes "Tax Freedom Day" to illustrate the degree to which the average American is burdened by our tax system and how long one must work just to pay taxes to the government. According to the foundation's 2000 calculation, the average American does not obtain freedom from taxes until he or she has worked 124 days during the year.

The foundation's calculation includes more than just income and Social Security taxes paid directly by individuals. Also included are "hidden" or "implicit" taxes that are passed on to the final consumer. For example, the typical taxpayer must work 12 days to pay corporate income taxes that are nominally paid by the corporation, but are ultimately paid by the consumer of the corporation's goods and services. So, even when entrepreneurs do not choose to operate their businesses as corporations, they still bear a corporate tax burden!

SOURCE: Tax Foundation, Washington, D.C.

earnings and profits of the distributing corporation. (The concept of earnings and profits is discussed in Chapter 10.)

EXAMPLE 34

Wade transfers cash of $100,000 to a newly formed corporation for 100% of the stock. In the first year of operations, the corporation has net income of $40,000. If the corporation distributes $9,500 to Wade, the distribution is a taxable dividend with no corresponding deduction to the corporation. Assume, instead, that Wade transfers to the corporation cash of $50,000 for stock. In addition, he lends the corporation $50,000. The note is payable in equal annual installments of $5,000 and bears interest at the rate of 9%. At the end of the year, the corporation pays Wade interest of $4,500 ($50,000 × 9%), and a note repayment of $5,000. The interest payment is taxable to Wade and deductible to the corporation. The $5,000 principal repayment on the loan is neither taxed to Wade nor deductible by the corporation. ■

Reclassification of Debt as Equity (Thin Capitalization Problem). In situations where the corporation is said to be thinly capitalized, the IRS contends that debt is really an equity interest and denies shareholders the tax advantages of debt financing. If a debt instrument has too many features of stock, it may be treated as a form of stock by the IRS. As a result, the principal and interest payments are considered dividends. Under § 385, the IRS has the authority to characterize corporate debt wholly as equity or as part debt and part equity.

For the most part, the principles used to classify debt as equity developed in connection with closely held corporations where the holders of the debt are often shareholders. The rules have often proved inadequate for dealing with large, publicly traded corporations.

Section 385 lists several factors that *may* be used to determine whether a debtor-creditor relationship or a shareholder-corporation relationship exists. The thrust of § 385 is to authorize the Treasury to prescribe Regulations that provide more definite guidelines for determining when debt should be reclassified as equity. To date, the Treasury Department has not drafted final Regulations. Consequently, taxpayers must rely on judicial decisions to determine whether a true debtor-creditor relationship exists.

The courts have identified the following factors to be considered when classifying a security as debt or equity:

- Whether the debt instrument is in proper form. An open account advance is more easily characterized as a contribution to capital than a loan evidenced by a properly written note executed by the shareholder.[37]
- Whether the debt instrument bears a reasonable rate of interest and has a definite maturity date. When a shareholder advance does not provide for interest, the return expected is that inherent in an equity interest (e.g., a share of the profits or an increase in the value of the shares).[38] Likewise, a lender unrelated to the corporation will usually be unwilling to commit funds to the corporation for an indefinite period of time (i.e., no definite due date).
- Whether the debt is paid on a timely basis. A lender's failure to insist upon timely repayment (or satisfactory renegotiation) indicates that the return sought does not depend upon interest income and the repayment of principal.
- Whether payment is contingent upon earnings. A lender ordinarily will not advance funds that are likely to be repaid only if the venture is successful.
- Whether the debt is subordinated to other liabilities. Subordination tends to eliminate a significant characteristic of the creditor-debtor relationship. Creditors should have the right to share with other general creditors in the event of the corporation's dissolution or liquidation. Subordination also destroys another basic attribute of creditor status—the power to demand payment at a fixed maturity date.[39]
- Whether holdings of debt and stock are proportionate (e.g., each shareholder owns the same percentage of debt as stock). When debt and equity obligations are held in the same proportion, shareholders are, apart from tax considerations, indifferent as to whether corporate distributions are in the form of interest or dividends.
- Whether funds loaned to the corporation are used to finance initial operations or capital asset acquisitions. Funds used to finance initial operations or to acquire capital assets the corporation needs to operate are generally obtained through equity investments.
- Whether the corporation has a high ratio of shareholder debt to shareholder equity. **Thin capitalization** occurs when shareholder debt is high relative to shareholder equity. This indicates the corporation lacks reserves to pay interest and principal on debt when corporate income is insufficient to meet

---

[37]*Estate of Mixon v. U.S.*, 72–2 USTC ¶9537, 30 AFTR2d 72–5094, 464 F.2d 394 (CA–5, 1972).

[38]*Slappey Drive Industrial Park v. U.S.*, 77–2 USTC ¶9696, 40 AFTR2d 77–5940, 561 F.2d 572 (CA–5, 1977).

[39]*Fin Hay Realty Co. v. U.S.*, 68–2 USTC ¶9438, 22 AFTR2d 5004, 398 F.2d 694 (CA–3, 1968).

current needs.[40] In determining a corporation's debt-equity ratio, courts look at the relation of the debt both to the book value of the corporation's assets and to their actual fair market value.[41]

Section 385 also authorizes the Treasury to issue Regulations classifying an instrument either as *wholly* debt or equity or as *part* debt and *part* equity. This flexible approach is important because some instruments cannot readily be classified either wholly as stock or wholly as debt. It may also provide an avenue for the IRS to address problems in publicly traded corporations.

Corporate Operations

The rules related to gross income, deductions, and losses discussed in previous chapters of this text generally apply to corporations. In a few instances, it was noted that corporations face unique limitations such as the 10 percent of taxable income limitation for charitable contributions and the limitation allowing corporate capital losses to be deductible only against capital gains. Corporations also are permitted some deductions not generally available to other entities. These special deductions and other special rules regarding the determination of corporate income tax liability are discussed in the following paragraphs.

DEDUCTIONS AVAILABLE ONLY TO CORPORATIONS

Dividends Received Deduction.   The purpose of the **dividends received deduction** is to mitigate multiple levels of taxation. Without the deduction, dividends paid between corporations could be subject to several levels of tax. For example, if Corporation A pays Corporation B a dividend, and B passes the dividend on to its shareholders, the dividend is taxed at three levels: Corporation A, Corporation B, and Corporation B's shareholders. The dividends received deduction alleviates this inequity by limiting or eliminating the amount of dividend income taxable to corporations.

As the following table illustrates, the amount of the dividends received deduction depends on the percentage of ownership the recipient corporate shareholder holds in a domestic corporation making the dividend distribution.[42]

Percentage of Ownership by Corporate Shareholder	Deduction Percentage
Less than 20%	70%
20% or more (but less than 80%)	80%
80% or more*	100%

*The payor corporation must be a member of an affiliated group with the recipient corporation.

The dividends received deduction is limited to a percentage of the taxable income of the shareholder-corporation. For this purpose, taxable income is com-

---

[40]A court held that a debt-equity ratio of approximately 14.6:1 was not excessive. See *Tomlinson v. 1661 Corp.*, 67–1 USTC ¶9438, 19 AFTR2d 1413, 377 F.2d 291 (CA–5, 1967).

[41]In *Bauer v. Comm.*, 84–2 USTC ¶9996, 55 AFTR2d 84–433, 748 F.2d 1365 (CA–9, 1984), a debt-equity ratio of 92:1 resulted when book value was used. But the ratio ranged from 2:1 to 8:1 when equity included both paid-in capital and accumulated earnings.

[42]§ 243(a).

puted without regard to the net operating loss (NOL), the dividends received deduction, and any capital loss carryback to the current tax year. The percentage of taxable income limitation corresponds to the deduction percentage. Thus, if a corporate shareholder owns less than 20 percent of the stock in the distributing corporation, the dividends received deduction is limited to 70 percent of taxable income. However, the taxable income limitation does not apply if the corporation has an NOL for the current taxable year.[43]

The following steps summarize the computation of the deduction:

1. Multiply the dividends received by the deduction percentage.
2. Multiply the taxable income by the deduction percentage.
3. The deduction is limited to the lesser of Step 1 or Step 2, unless subtracting the amount derived in Step 1 from taxable income *generates* an NOL. If so, the amount derived in Step 1 should be used. This is referred to as the *NOL rule*.

EXAMPLE 35

Red, White, and Blue Corporations, three unrelated calendar year corporations, have the following transactions for the year:

	Red Corporation	White Corporation	Blue Corporation
Gross income from operations	$ 400,000	$ 320,000	$ 260,000
Expenses from operations	(340,000)	(340,000)	(340,000)
Dividends received from domestic corporations (less than 20% ownership)	200,000	200,000	200,000
Taxable income before the dividends received deduction	$ 260,000	$ 180,000	$ 120,000

In determining the dividends received deduction, use the three-step procedure described above:

	Red	White	Blue
Step 1 (70% × $200,000)	$140,000	$140,000	$140,000
Step 2			
70% × $260,000 (taxable income)	$182,000		
70% × $180,000 (taxable income)		$126,000	
70% × $120,000 (taxable income)			$ 84,000
Step 3			
Lesser of Step 1 or Step 2	$140,000	$126,000	
Deduction generates an NOL			$140,000

White Corporation is subject to the 70% of taxable income limitation. It does not qualify for NOL rule treatment since subtracting $140,000 (Step 1) from $180,000 (100% of taxable income) does not yield a negative figure. Blue Corporation qualifies under the NOL rule because subtracting $140,000 (Step 1) from $120,000 (100% of taxable income) yields a negative figure. In summary, each corporation has a dividends received deduction for the year as follows: $140,000 for Red Corporation, $126,000 for White Corporation, and $140,000 for Blue Corporation. ■

---

[43]§ 246(b)(2).

Deduction of Organizational Expenditures.   Expenses incurred in connection with the organization of a corporation normally are chargeable to a capital account. That they benefit the corporation during its existence seems clear. But over what period should organizational expenses be amortized? The lack of a determinable and limited estimated useful life makes such a determination difficult. Section 248 was enacted to solve this problem.

Under § 248, a corporation may elect to amortize **organizational expenditures** over a period of 60 months or more. The period begins with the month in which the corporation begins business.[44] Organizational expenditures *subject to the election* include:

- Legal services incident to organization (e.g., drafting the corporate charter, bylaws, minutes of organizational meetings, terms of original stock certificates).
- Necessary accounting services.
- Expenses of temporary directors and of organizational meetings of directors or shareholders.
- Fees paid to the state of incorporation.

Expenditures that *do not qualify* include those connected with issuing or selling shares of stock or other securities (e.g., commissions, professional fees, and printing costs) or with the transfer of assets to a corporation. Such expenditures reduce the amount of capital raised and are not deductible.

To qualify for the election, the expenditure must be *incurred* before the end of the tax year in which the corporation begins business. In this regard, the corporation's method of accounting is of no consequence. Thus, an expense incurred by a cash basis corporation in its first tax year qualifies even though not paid until a subsequent year.

The election is made in a statement attached to the corporation's tax return for its first tax year. The return and statement must be filed no later than the due date of the return (including any extensions).

If the election is not made on a timely basis, organizational expenditures cannot be deducted until the corporation ceases to do business and liquidates. These expenditures will be deductible if the corporate charter limits the life of the corporation.

EXAMPLE 36

Black Corporation, an accrual basis, calendar year taxpayer, was formed and began operations on May 1, 2001. The following expenses were incurred during its first year of operations (May 1–December 31, 2001):

Expenses of temporary directors and of organizational meetings	$500
Fee paid to the state of incorporation	100
Accounting services incident to organization	200
Legal services for drafting the corporate charter and bylaws	400
Expenses incident to the printing and sale of stock certificates	300

not organizational cost

Assume Black Corporation makes a timely election under § 248 to amortize qualifying organizational expenses over a period of 60 months. The monthly amortization is $20 [($500 + $100 + $200 + $400) ÷ 60 months], and $160 ($20 × 8 months) is deductible for tax year 2001. Note that the $300 of expenses incident to the printing and sale of stock certificates

---

[44]The month in which a corporation begins business may not be immediately apparent. See Reg. § 1.248–1(a)(3). For a similar problem in the Subchapter S area, see Chapter 12.

does not qualify for the election. These expenses cannot be deducted. Instead, they reduce the amount of the capital realized from the sale of stock. ∎

Organizational expenditures are distinguished from start-up expenditures covered by § 195. Start-up expenditures include various investigation expenses involved in entering a new business, whether incurred by a corporate or a noncorporate taxpayer. Start-up expenses also include operating expenses, such as rent and payroll, that are incurred by a corporation before it actually begins to produce any gross income. At the election of the taxpayer, such expenditures (e.g., travel, market surveys, financial audits, legal fees) can be amortized over a period of 60 months or longer rather than capitalized as part of the cost of the business.

PLANNING CONSIDERATIONS

Organizational Expenditures

To qualify for the 60-month amortization procedure of § 248, only organizational expenditures incurred in the first taxable year of the corporation can be considered. This rule could prove to be an unfortunate trap for corporations formed late in the year.

EXAMPLE 37

Thrush Corporation is formed in December 2001. Qualified organizational expenditures are incurred as follows: $2,000 in December

2001 and $3,000 in January 2002. If Thrush uses the calendar year for tax purposes, only $2,000 of the organizational expenditures qualify for amortization. ∎

A solution to the problem posed by Example 37 may be for Thrush Corporation to adopt a fiscal year that ends on or beyond January 31. All organizational expenditures will then have been incurred before the close of the first tax year.

LEARNING OBJECTIVE 7

Compute the corporate income tax.

DETERMINING THE CORPORATE INCOME TAX LIABILITY

Corporate Income Tax Rates. Corporate income tax rates have fluctuated widely over past years. Refer to the inside front cover of the text for a schedule of current corporate income tax rates.

EXAMPLE 38

Gold Corporation, a calendar year taxpayer, has taxable income of $90,000 for 2001. Its income tax liability is $18,850, determined as follows:

Tax on $75,000	$13,750
Tax on $15,000 × 34%	5,100
Tax liability	$18,850

∎

For a corporation that has taxable income in excess of $100,000 for any tax year, the amount of the tax is increased by the lesser of (1) 5 percent of the excess or (2) $11,750. In effect, the additional tax means a 39 percent rate for every dollar of taxable income from $100,000 to $335,000.[45]

EXAMPLE 39

Silver Corporation, a calendar year taxpayer, has taxable income of $335,000 for 2001. Its income tax liability is $113,900, determined as follows:

---

[45]§ 11(b).

Tax on $100,000	$ 22,250
Tax on $235,000 × 39%	91,650
Tax liability	$113,900

Note that the tax liability of $113,900 is 34% of $335,000. Thus, due to the 39% rate (34% normal rate + 5% additional tax on taxable income between $100,000 and $335,000), the benefit of the lower rates on the first $75,000 of taxable income completely phases out at $335,000. Note that the normal rate drops back to 34% on taxable income between $335,000 and $10 million. ■

Section 11(b) provides that qualified **personal service corporations (PSCs)** are taxed at a flat 35 percent rate on all taxable income. Thus, PSCs do not enjoy the tax savings of being in the 15 percent to 34 percent brackets applicable to other corporations. For this purpose, a PSC is a corporation that is substantially employee owned. Also, it must engage in one of the following activities: health, law, engineering, architecture, accounting, actuarial science, performing arts, or consulting.

TAX LIABILITY OF RELATED CORPORATIONS

LEARNING OBJECTIVE 8

Explain the tax rules unique to multiple corporations.

Related corporations are subject to special rules for computing the income tax, the AMT exemption, and the § 179 election to expense certain depreciable assets.[46] If these restrictions did not exist, the shareholders of a corporation could gain significant tax advantages by splitting a single corporation into *multiple* corporations. The next two examples illustrate the potential *income tax* advantage of multiple corporations.

EXAMPLE 40

Gray Corporation annually yields taxable income of $300,000. The corporate tax on $300,000 is $100,250, computed as follows:

Tax on $100,000	$ 22,250
Tax on $200,000 × 39%	78,000
Tax liability	$100,250

■

EXAMPLE 41

Assume that Gray Corporation in the previous example is divided equally into four corporations. Each corporation would have taxable income of $75,000, and the tax for each (absent the special provisions for related corporations) would be computed as follows:

Tax on $50,000	$ 7,500
Tax on $25,000 × 25%	6,250
Tax liability	$13,750

The total liability for the four corporations would be $55,000 ($13,750 × 4). Consequently, the savings would be $45,250 ($100,250 − $55,000). ■

To preclude the advantages that could be gained by using multiple corporations, the tax law requires special treatment for *controlled groups* of corporations. A comparison of Examples 40 and 41 reveals that the income tax savings that could be achieved by using multiple corporations result from having more of the total income taxed at lower rates. To close this potential loophole, the law limits a

[46]§ 1561(a). Small corporations are not subject to the AMT for tax years beginning after 1997. See Chapter 13 for details.

controlled group's taxable income in the tax brackets below 35 percent to the amount the corporations in the group would have if they were one corporation. Thus, in Example 41, under the controlled corporation rules, only $12,500 (one-fourth of the first $50,000 of taxable income) for each of the four related corporations would be taxed at the 15 percent rate. The 25 percent rate would apply to the next $6,250 (one-fourth of the next $25,000) of taxable income of each corporation. This equal allocation of the $50,000 and $25,000 amounts is required unless all members of the controlled group consent to an apportionment plan providing for an unequal allocation.

Similar limitations apply to the § 179 expense election and to the $40,000 exemption amount for purposes of computing the AMT (see Chapter 13).

CONTROLLED GROUPS

A **controlled group** of corporations includes parent-subsidiary groups, brother-sister groups, combined groups, and certain insurance companies. Groups of the first three types are discussed in the following sections. Insurance groups are not discussed in this text.

Parent-Subsidiary Controlled Group.   A **parent-subsidiary controlled group** consists of one or more *chains* of corporations connected through stock ownership with a common parent corporation. The ownership connection can be established through either a *voting power test* or a *value test*. The voting power test requires ownership of stock possessing at least 80 percent of the total voting power of all classes of stock entitled to vote.[47] The value test requires ownership of at least 80 percent of the total value of all shares of all classes of stock of each of the corporations, except the parent corporation, by one or more of the other corporations.

EXAMPLE 42	Aqua Corporation owns 80% of White Corporation. Aqua and White Corporations are members of a parent-subsidiary controlled group. Aqua is the parent corporation and White is the subsidiary. ■

The parent-subsidiary relationship described in Example 42 is easy to recognize because Aqua Corporation is the direct owner of White Corporation. Real-world business organizations are often much more complex, sometimes including numerous corporations with chains of ownership connecting them. In these complex corporate structures, determining whether the controlled group classification is appropriate becomes more difficult. The ownership requirements can be met through direct ownership (refer to Example 42) or through indirect ownership, as illustrated in the following example.

EXAMPLE 43	Red Corporation owns 80% of the voting stock of White Corporation, and White Corporation owns 80% of the voting stock of Blue Corporation. Red, White, and Blue Corporations constitute a controlled group in which Red is the common parent and White and Blue are subsidiaries. This parent-subsidiary relationship is diagrammed in Figure 9–3. The same result would occur if Red Corporation, rather than White Corporation, owned the Blue Corporation stock. ■

Brother-Sister Corporations.   A **brother-sister controlled group** *may* exist if two or more corporations are owned by five or fewer *persons* (individuals, estates,

---

[47]§ 1563(a)(1).

■ **FIGURE 9–3**
Controlled Groups—Parent-
Subsidiary Corporations

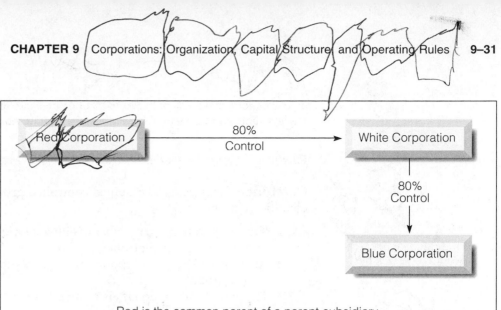

Red is the common parent of a parent-subsidiary
controlled group consisting of Red, White, and Blue Corporations.

or trusts). Brother-sister status will apply if such a shareholder group meets an 80 percent total ownership test *and* a 50 percent common ownership test.[48]

- The *total* ownership test is met if the shareholder group possesses stock representing at least 80 percent of the total combined voting power of all classes of stock entitled to vote, *or* at least 80 percent of the total value of shares of all classes of stock of *each corporation.*
- The *common* ownership test is met if the shareholder group owns more than 50 percent of the total combined voting power of all classes of stock entitled to vote, *or* more than 50 percent of the total value of shares of all classes of stock of *each corporation.*

In applying the common ownership test, the stock held by each person is considered only to the extent that the stock ownership is equivalent for each corporation. That is, if a shareholder owns 30 percent of Silver Corporation and 20 percent of Gold Corporation, such shareholder has common ownership of 20 percent of each corporation.

EXAMPLE 44

Hawk, Eagle, Crane, and Dove Corporations each have only one class of stock outstanding. The stock is owned by the following unrelated individuals:

Individuals	Corporations				Common Ownership
	Hawk	Eagle	Crane	Dove	
Allen	40%	30%	60%	60%	30%
Barton	50%	20%	30%	20%	20%
Carter	10%	30%	10%	10%	10%
Dixon		20%		10%	
Total	100%	100%	100%	100%	60%

Five or fewer individuals (Allen, Barton, and Carter) with more than a 50% common ownership (60%) own at least 80% of all classes of stock in Hawk, Eagle, Crane, and Dove. They

[48]§ 1563(a)(2).

[handwritten: have 3 ways]

own 100% of Hawk, 80% of Eagle, 100% of Crane, and 90% of Dove. Consequently, Hawk, Eagle, Crane, and Dove are regarded as members of a brother-sister controlled group. ■

[handwritten: combination of brother-sister, parent-sub]

2 *Find more information on this topic at our Web site:* ***http://wft-entities.swcollege.com.***

Combined Groups.   A combined controlled group exists if all of the following conditions are met:

- Each corporation is a member of either a parent-subsidiary controlled group or a brother-sister controlled group.
- At least one of the corporations is a parent of a parent-subsidiary controlled group.
- The parent corporation is also a member of a brother-sister controlled group.

EXAMPLE 45

Robert owns 80% of all classes of stock of Red and Orange Corporations. Red Corporation, in turn, owns 80% of all classes of stock of Blue Corporation. Orange owns all the stock of Green Corporation. Red, Blue, Orange, and Green are members of the same combined group. As a result, Red, Blue, Orange, and Green are limited to taxable income in the tax brackets below 35% as though they were one corporation. This is also the case for the election to expense certain depreciable business assets under § 179 and the $40,000 exemption for purposes of computing the AMT. ■

Application of § 482.   Congress has recognized that a parent corporation has the power to shift income among its subsidiaries. Likewise, shareholders who control brother-sister groups can shift income and deductions among the related corporations.

[handwritten: Not on test]

When the true taxable income of a subsidiary or other related corporation has been understated or overstated, the IRS can reallocate the income and deductions of the related corporations under § 482. Section 482 permits the IRS to allocate gross income, deductions, and credits between any two or more organizations, trades, or businesses that are owned or controlled by the same interests. This is appropriate when the allocation is necessary to prevent avoidance of taxes or to reflect income correctly. Controlled groups of corporations, especially multinational corporations, are particularly vulnerable to § 482.

LEARNING OBJECTIVE 9

Describe the reporting process for corporations.

Procedural Matters

FILING REQUIREMENTS FOR CORPORATIONS

A corporation must file a Federal income tax return whether or not it has taxable income.[49] A corporation that was not in existence throughout an entire annual accounting period is required to file a return for the fraction of the year during which it was in existence. In addition, a corporation must file a return even though it has ceased to do business if it has valuable claims for which it will bring suit. A corporation is relieved of filing income tax returns only when it ceases to do business and retains no assets.

3 *Find more information on this topic at our Web site:* ***http://wft-entities.swcollege.com.***

The return must be filed on or before the fifteenth day of the third month following the close of a corporation's tax year. As noted in Chapter 6, a regular corporation,

---

[49]§ 6012(a)(2).

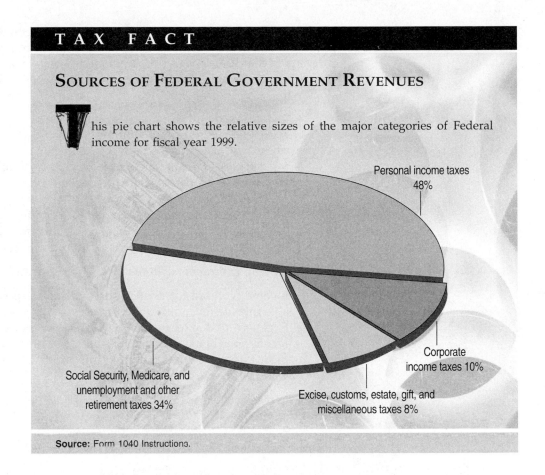

TAX FACT

SOURCES OF FEDERAL GOVERNMENT REVENUES

This pie chart shows the relative sizes of the major categories of Federal income for fiscal year 1999.

Personal income taxes 48%

Corporate income taxes 10%

Excise, customs, estate, gift, and miscellaneous taxes 8%

Social Security, Medicare, and unemployment and other retirement taxes 34%

Source: Form 1040 Instructions.

other than a PSC, can use either a calendar or a fiscal year to report its taxable income. The tax year of the shareholders has no effect on the corporation's tax year.

ESTIMATED TAX PAYMENTS

A corporation must make payments of estimated tax unless its tax liability can reasonably be expected to be less than $500. The required annual payment (which includes any estimated AMT liability) is the lesser of (1) 100 percent of the corporation's final tax or (2) 100 percent of the tax for the preceding year (if that was a 12-month tax year and the return filed showed a tax liability).[50] Estimated payments can be made in four installments due on or before the fifteenth day of the fourth month, the sixth month, the ninth month, and the twelfth month of the corporate taxable year. The full amount of the unpaid tax is due on the due date of the return without regard to extensions. A corporation failing to pay its required estimated tax payments will be subjected to a nondeductible penalty on the amount by which the installments are less than the tax due.

RECONCILIATION OF TAXABLE INCOME AND FINANCIAL NET INCOME

Schedule M–1 on the last page of Form 1120 is used to reconcile net income as computed for financial accounting purposes with taxable income reported on the

---

[50]§§ 6655(d) and (e).

corporation's income tax return. The starting point on Schedule M–1 is net income per books (financial accounting net income). Additions and subtractions are entered for items that affect net income per books and taxable income differently. The following items are entered as additions (see lines 2 through 5 of Schedule M–1 below):

- Federal income tax liability (deducted in computing net income per books but not deductible in computing taxable income).
- The excess of capital losses over capital gains (deducted for financial accounting purposes but not deductible by corporations for income tax purposes).
- Income that is reported in the current year for tax purposes that is not reported in computing net income per books (e.g., prepaid income).
- Various expenses that are deducted in computing net income per books but are not deducted in computing taxable income (e.g., charitable contributions in excess of the 10 percent ceiling applicable to corporations).

The following subtractions are entered on lines 7 and 8 of Schedule M–1:

- Income reported for financial accounting purposes but not included in taxable income (e.g., tax-exempt interest).
- Expenses deducted on the tax return but not deducted in computing net income per books (e.g., a charitable contributions carryover deducted in a prior year for financial accounting purposes but deductible in the current year for tax purposes).

The result is taxable income (before the NOL deduction and the dividends received deduction).

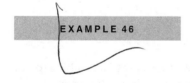

EXAMPLE 46

During the current year, Tern Corporation had the following transactions:

Net income per books (after tax)	$92,400
Taxable income	50,000
Federal income tax liability (15% × $50,000)	7,500
Interest income from tax-exempt bonds	5,000
Interest paid on loan, the proceeds of which were used to purchase the tax-exempt bonds	500
Life insurance proceeds received as a result of the death of a key employee	50,000
Premiums paid on key employee life insurance policy	2,600
Excess of capital losses over capital gains	2,000

For book and tax purposes, Tern Corporation determines depreciation under the straight-line method. Tern's Schedule M–1 for the current year is as follows:

Schedule M-1	Reconciliation of Income (Loss) per Books With Income per Return (See page 20 of instructions.)		
1 Net income (loss) per books	92,400	7 Income recorded on books this year not included on this return (itemize):	
2 Federal income tax	7,500	Tax-exempt interest $ 5,000	
3 Excess of capital losses over capital gains	2,000	Life insurance proceeds on key	
4 Income subject to tax not recorded on books this year (itemize):		employee $50,000	55,000
		8 Deductions on this return not charged against book income this year (itemize):	
5 Expenses recorded on books this year not deducted on this return (itemize):		a Depreciation $	
a Depreciation $		b Contributions carryover $	
b Contributions carryover $			
c Travel and entertainment $ Int. on tax-exempt bonds $500, Prem. on key employee ins. $2,600	3,100	9 Add lines 7 and 8	55,000
6 Add lines 1 through 5	105,000	10 Income (line 28, page 1)—line 6 less line 9	50,000

BRIDGE DISCIPLINE

Bridge to Financial Accounting

Measures of corporate income for financial reporting and income tax purposes differ because the objectives of these measures differ. Income measures for financial reporting purposes are intended to help various stakeholders have a clear view of the corporation's financial position and operational results. Income measures for Federal income tax purposes, on the other hand, must comply with the relevant provisions of the Internal Revenue Code. The tax law is intended not only to raise revenues to fund government operations, but to reflect the objectives of government fiscal policy as well.

As a consequence of these differing objectives, revenue and expense measurements used to determine taxable income may differ from those used in financial reporting. In most cases, differences between book and tax measurements are temporary in nature. Two such temporary differences relate to the different methods of calculating depreciation expense and the limits placed on the deductibility of net capital losses for tax purposes. Permanent differences between book and tax income, such as the dividends received deduction, also may exist.

Accounting standards for reporting income tax expenses and liabilities require that the tax impact of *temporary* differences be recognized currently in the financial statements. Because many temporary differences allow a firm to postpone its tax payments to later years, the financial statements must show the amount of the expense that is paid currently and that portion that is to be paid in a later period. The portion of the taxes to be paid in a later period is shown as a liability for such future income taxes. The liability for future income taxes is referred to as a deferred income tax liability.

Schedule M–2 reconciles unappropriated retained earnings at the beginning of the year with unappropriated retained earnings at year-end. Beginning balance plus net income per books, as entered on line 1 of Schedule M–1, less dividend distributions during the year equals ending retained earnings. Other sources of increases or decreases in retained earnings are also listed on Schedule M–2.

EXAMPLE 47

Assume the same facts as in the preceding example. Tern Corporation's beginning balance in unappropriated retained earnings is $125,000. During the year, Tern distributed a cash dividend of $30,000 to its shareholders. Based on these further assumptions, Tern's Schedule M–2 for the current year is as follows:

Schedule M-2	Analysis of Unappropriated Retained Earnings per Books (Line 25, Schedule L)				
1	Balance at beginning of year	125,000	5 Distributions: a Cash	30,000
2	Net income (loss) per books	92,400	b Stock	
3	Other increases (itemize):		c Property	
			6 Other decreases (itemize):	
			7 Add lines 5 and 6	30,000
4	Add lines 1, 2, and 3	217,400	8 Balance at end of year (line 4 less line 7)	187,400	■

4 *Find more information on this topic at our Web site: **http://wft-entities.swcollege.com.***

SUMMARY

The evolution of the check-the-box Regulations has provided taxpayers with a simplified method for determining an entity's tax classification. Nevertheless, taxpayers should not discount the importance of choosing the appropriate form of entity. As demonstrated in this chapter and Chapter 10, a variety of tax provisions applicable to corporations do not extend to other entities. Of particular importance are the different deductions available to corporations and the corporate income tax rate structure. Corporations must also be aware of their levels of debt to avoid equity reclassification. Such reclassification causes deductible interest paid on debt to become nondeductible dividend payments. Equally important are the timing and completeness requirements of the corporate filing provisions. Failure to comply with the appropriate filing provisions may result in heavy penalties and interest.

Suggested Further Readings

Rolf Auster, "Tax Twists on Timing Qualified Small Business Stock Sales," *Practical Tax Strategies,* February 2000, pp. 77–79.

"Creating and Using Hybrid Entities," *Tax Adviser*, August 1999, pp. 568–573.

Bruce W. McClain and Thomas Lechner, "Audit Strategies for Defending Against the Accumulated Earnings Tax," *Practical Tax Strategies*, March 2000, pp. 132–139.

KEY TERMS

Assumption of liabilities, 9–15

Brother-sister controlled group, 9–30

C corporation, 9–2

Capital contribution, 9–22

Check-the-box Regulations, 9–7

Control, 9–10

Controlled group, 9–30

Dividends received deduction, 9–25

Limited liability company (LLC), 9–6

Limited partnership, 9–6

Organizational expenditures, 9–27

Parent–subsidiary controlled group, 9–30

Personal service corporation (PSC), 9–29

Property, 9–9

Regular corporation, 9–2

Related corporations, 9–29

S corporation, 9–2

Schedule M–1, 9–33

Securities, 9–10

Thin capitalization, 9–24

Problem Materials

PROBLEMS

1. Rosita, who owns a proprietorship, has scheduled an appointment to talk with you about the advisability of incorporating. At this time, you know nothing about Rosita's business or her existing tax situation. List the questions you will need to ask during the appointment so you can help her make an informed decision.

2. On June 17, 2001, Susan and Valerie started an investment firm called B & W Investments. During 2001, both Susan and Valerie lived and conducted their business in Illinois.

B & W Investments is an unincorporated entity under Illinois state law. Neither Susan nor Valerie filed an election regarding the Federal tax classification of B & W Investments. Susan's husband, Bill, told Valerie and Susan that they must file a Form 1120 for the 2001 taxable year and will be taxed twice on B & W's earnings. Is Bill correct in his assessment?

3. Bunting Company, a computer retailer, had a net loss of $100,000 from merchandising operations in 2001. Lena, who owns Bunting, works 20 hours a week in the business. She has a large amount of income from other sources and is in the 39.6% marginal tax bracket. What is Lena's tax if Bunting Company is a proprietorship? A C corporation?

4. Indigo Company has approximately $200,000 in net income in 2001 before deducting any compensation or other payment to its sole owner, Kim. Kim is single. Her income aside from the company's profits is low and would be offset by her personal exemption and standard deduction. Discuss the tax aspects of each of the following arrangements:
   a. Kim operates Indigo Company as a proprietorship.
   b. Kim incorporates Indigo Company and pays herself a salary of $50,000 and no dividend.
   c. Kim incorporates the company and pays herself a $50,000 salary and a dividend of $108,250 ($150,000 – $41,750 corporate income tax).
   d. Kim incorporates the company and pays herself a salary of $200,000.

5. Mike owns 100% of White Company, which had net operating income of $60,000 ($100,000 operating income – $40,000 operating expenses) in 2001. In addition, White Company had a long-term capital gain of $10,000. Mike has sufficient income from other activities to place him in the 39.6% marginal tax bracket before considering the results from White Company. Using this information, explain the tax treatment if White Company is:
   a. A corporation and pays no dividends during the year.
   b. A corporation and pays Mike $70,000 of dividends during the year.
   c. A corporation and pays Mike a $70,000 salary during the year.
   d. A proprietorship and Mike withdraws $0 during the year.
   e. A proprietorship and Mike withdraws $70,000 during the year.

6. Emily incorporates her sole proprietorship, but does not transfer a building used by the business to the corporation. Instead, the building is leased to the corporation for an annual rental. What tax reasons might Emily have for not transferring the building to the corporation when the business was incorporated?

7. Cecil and Edie form Grouse Corporation with the following investments:

| | **Consideration Transferred** | | |
	Basis to Transferor	**Fair Market Value**	**Number of Shares Issued**
From Cecil—			
Cash	$ 80,000	$ 80,000	
Installment obligation	280,000	720,000	80
From Edie—			
Cash	280,000	280,000	
Equipment	240,000	360,000	
Patent	8,000	560,000	120

The installment obligation has a face amount of $720,000 and was acquired last year from the sale of land held for investment purposes (adjusted basis of $280,000).
   a. How much gain, if any, must Cecil recognize?
   b. What is Cecil's basis in the Grouse Corporation stock?
   c. What is Grouse Corporation's basis in the installment obligation?

d. How much gain, if any, must Edie recognize?

e. What is Edie's basis in the Grouse Corporation stock?

f. What is Grouse Corporation's basis in the equipment and the patent?

g. How would your answer change if Cecil received Class A common stock and Edie received Class B common stock?

h. How would your answer change if Edie were a partnership?

8. Brad, Otis, Wade, and Andrea form Teal Corporation with the following investments:

| | Consideration Transferred | | |
	Basis to Transferor	Fair Market Value	Number of Shares Issued
From Brad—			
Personal services rendered to Teal Corporation	$ –0–	$ 30,000	30
From Otis—			
Equipment	345,000	300,000	270*
From Wade—			
Cash	60,000	60,000	
Unrealized accounts receivable	–0–	90,000	150
From Andrea—			
Land & building	210,000	450,000	
Mortgage on land & building (liability)	300,000	300,000	150

*Otis receives $30,000 in cash in addition to the 270 shares.

The mortgage transferred by Andrea is assumed by Teal Corporation. The value of each share of Teal Corporation stock is $1,000.

a. What, if any, is Brad's recognized gain or loss?

b. What is Brad's basis in the Teal Corporation stock?

c. How much gain or loss must Otis recognize?

d. What is Otis's basis in the Teal Corporation stock?

e. What is Teal Corporation's basis in the equipment?

f. What, if any, is Wade's recognized gain or loss?

g. What is Wade's basis in the Teal Corporation stock?

h. What is Teal Corporation's basis in the unrealized accounts receivable?

i. How much gain or loss must Andrea recognize?

j. What is Andrea's basis in the Teal stock?

k. What is Teal Corporation's basis in the land and building?

9. Mary, Lee, and Randall transfer assets from their respective businesses to form Bluebird Corporation. On May 1, 2001, Mary transfers her property, basis of $100,000 and value of $400,000, for 200 shares. On May 10, 2001, Lee exchanges his property, basis of $140,000 and value of $600,000, for 300 shares. On December 10, 2001, Randall transfers his property, basis of $1,180,000 and value of $1 million, for 500 shares.

a. What are the tax consequences of the three transfers to all parties if the three exchanges are part of a prearranged plan?

b. What are the tax consequences to all parties if Randall's transfer is not part of a prearranged plan with Mary and Lee to incorporate their businesses?

c. Which arrangement would the parties prefer?

10. Andrew Boninti (1635 Maple Street, Syracuse, NY 13201) exchanges property, basis of $30,000 and fair market value of $600,000, for 60% of the stock of Gray Corporation. The other 40% is owned by Kendall Smith, who acquired her stock several years ago.

You represent Andrew, who asks whether he must report gain on the transfer. Prepare a letter to Andrew and a memorandum for the tax files where you document your response.

11. Lee exchanges property, basis of $20,000 and fair market value of $500,000, for 65% of the stock of Pelican Corporation. The other 35% is owned by Abby, Lee's daughter, who acquired her stock last year. What are the tax issues?

12. Dan and Vera form Crane Corporation. Dan transfers land (worth $200,000, basis of $60,000) for 50% of the stock in Crane. Vera transfers machinery (worth $150,000, adjusted basis of $30,000) and provides services worth $50,000 for 50% of the stock.
    a. Will the transfers qualify under § 351?
    b. What are the tax consequences to Dan and Vera?
    c. What is Crane Corporation's basis in the land and the machinery?

13. Carlos organized Red Corporation 10 years ago. He contributed property worth $1 million (basis of $200,000) for 2,000 shares of stock in Red (representing 100% ownership). Carlos later gave each of his children, Isabella and Marta, 500 shares of the stock. In the current year, Carlos transfers property worth $420,000 (basis of $300,000) to Red for 500 more shares in the corporation. What gain, if any, will Carlos recognize on the transfer?

14. Ann and Bob form Robin Corporation. Ann transfers property worth $420,000 (basis of $150,000) for 70 shares in Robin Corporation. Bob receives 30 shares for property worth $165,000 (basis of $30,000) and for legal services in organizing the corporation; the services are worth $15,000.
    a. What gain, if any, will the parties recognize on the transfer?
    b. What basis do Ann and Bob have in the stock in Robin Corporation?
    c. What is Robin Corporation's basis in the property and services it received from Ann and Bob?

15. Assume in Problem 14 that the property Bob transfers to Robin Corporation is worth $15,000 (basis of $3,000) and his services in organizing the corporation are worth $165,000. What are the tax consequences to Ann, Bob, and Robin Corporation?

16. Kim is an employee of Azure Corporation. In the current year, she receives a salary of $30,000 and is also given 10 shares of Azure stock for services she renders to the corporation. The shares in Azure Corporation are worth $1,000 each. How will the transfer of the 10 shares to Kim be handled for tax purposes by Kim and by Azure Corporation?

17. Brady transfers property with an adjusted basis of $50,000, fair market value of $400,000, to Swift Corporation for 100% of the stock. The property is subject to a liability of $60,000, which Swift assumes. What is the basis of the Swift stock to Brady? What is the basis of the property to Swift Corporation?

18. Three years ago, Chris exchanged an apartment building worth $1,500,000 (basis of $300,000), which was subject to a mortgage of $200,000, for land worth $1,150,000, subject to a mortgage of $150,000, and cash of $300,000. In the current year, Chris transfers the land that he received in the exchange to newly formed Amber Corporation for all of the stock in Amber. Amber Corporation assumes the original mortgage on the land, currently in the amount of $100,000, and another mortgage in the amount of $20,000 that Chris later placed on the land to secure his purchase of some equipment that he uses in this business. What are the tax issues?

19. Lori, a sole proprietor, was engaged in a service business and reported her income on the cash basis. On February 1, 2001, she incorporated her business and transferred the assets of the business to the corporation in return for all the stock plus the corporation's assumption of her proprietorship's liabilities. All the receivables and the unpaid trade payables were transferred to the newly formed corporation. The balance sheet of the corporation immediately following its formation was as follows:

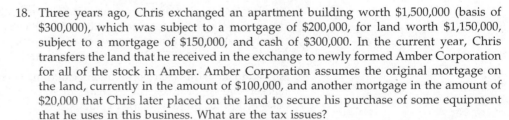

GREEN CORPORATION
BALANCE SHEET
FEBRUARY 1, 2001

Assets

	Basis to Green	Fair Market Value
Cash	$ 80,000	$ 80,000
Accounts receivable	–0–	240,000
Equipment (cost $180,000; depreciation claimed $60,000)	120,000	320,000
Building (straight-line depreciation)	160,000	400,000
Land	40,000	160,000
Total	$400,000	$1,200,000

Liabilities and Stockholder's Equity

Liabilities:	
Accounts payable—trade	$ 120,000
Notes payable—bank	360,000
Stockholder's equity:	
Common stock	720,000
Total	$1,200,000

Discuss the tax consequences of the incorporation of the business to Lori and to Green Corporation.

20. Several entrepreneurs plan to form a corporation to construct a housing project. Travis, the party who will be contributing the land for the project, wants more security than shareholder status provides. He is contemplating two possibilities: receive corporate bonds for his land, or take out a mortgage on the land before transferring it to the corporation for stock. Comment on the tax effects of the choices Travis is considering. What other alternatives can you suggest?

21. David organized White Corporation and transferred land with a basis of $200,000, fair market value of $600,000, and subject to a mortgage of $150,000. A month before incorporation, David borrowed $100,000 for personal purposes and gave the bank a lien on the land. White Corporation issued stock worth $350,000 to David and assumed the loans in the amount of $150,000 and $100,000. What are the tax consequences of the incorporation to David and White Corporation?

22. Jean incorporates her sole proprietorship. Inadvertently, she transfers to the new corporation a credit charge for a family dinner she hosted. After the corporation pays the bill, she realizes her mistake and issues a note payable to the corporation for the charge. Has Jean avoided § 357(c)? Has she acted properly?

23. Sara and Jane form Wren Corporation. Sara transfers property, basis of $25,000 and fair market value of $200,000, for 50 shares in Wren Corporation. Jane transfers property, basis of $10,000 and fair market value of $185,000, and agrees to serve as manager of Wren for one year; in return Jane receives 50 shares in Wren. The value of Jane's services to Wren is $15,000.
   a. What gain will Sara and Jane recognize on the exchange?
   b. What basis will Wren Corporation have in the property transferred by Sara and Jane? How should Wren treat the value of the services Jane renders?

24. Assume in Problem 23, that Jane receives the 50 shares of Wren Corporation stock in consideration for the appreciated property and for providing legal services in organizing the corporation. The value of Jane's services is $15,000.

a. What gain does Jane recognize?

b. What is Wren Corporation's basis in the property transferred by Jane? How should Wren treat the value of the services Jane renders?

25. On January 10, 2001, Carol transferred machinery worth $100,000 (adjusted basis of $20,000) to a controlled corporation, Lark. The transfer qualified under § 351. Carol had deducted $85,000 of depreciation on the machinery while it was used in her proprietorship. On November 15, 2001, Lark Corporation sells the machinery for $95,000. What are the tax consequences to Carol and to Lark Corporation on the sale of the machinery?

26. Tan Corporation desires to set up a manufacturing facility in one of the southern states. After considerable negotiations with the city of Alexandria, Louisiana, Tan accepts the following offer from the city: land (fair market value of $3 million) and cash of $1 million.

a. How much gain, if any, must Tan Corporation recognize?

b. What basis will Tan Corporation have in the land?

c. Within one year of the donation, Tan constructs a building for $800,000 and purchases inventory for $300,000. What basis will Tan Corporation have in each of these assets?

27. Emily Patrick (36 Paradise Road, Northampton, MA 01060) formed Teal Corporation a number of years ago with an investment of $200,000 of cash, for which she received $20,000 in stock and $180,000 in bonds bearing interest of 8% and maturing in nine years. Several years later, Emily lent the corporation an additional $50,000 on open account. In the current year, Teal Corporation becomes insolvent and is declared bankrupt. During the corporation's existence, Emily was paid an annual salary of $60,000. Write a letter to Emily in which you explain how she should treat her losses for tax purposes.

28. In each of the following independent situations, determine the dividends received deduction. Assume that none of the corporate shareholders owns 20% or more of the stock in the corporations paying the dividends.

	Red Corporation	White Corporation	Blue Corporation
Income from operations	$ 700,000	$ 800,000	$ 700,000
Expenses from operations	(600,000)	(900,000)	(740,000)
Qualifying dividends	100,000	200,000	200,000

29. Owl Corporation was formed on December 1, 2001. Qualifying organizational expenses were incurred and paid as follows:

Incurred and paid in December 2001	$12,000
Incurred in December 2001 but paid in January 2002	6,000
Incurred and paid in February 2002	3,600

Assume Owl Corporation makes a timely election under § 248 to amortize its organizational expenditures over a period of 60 months. What amount may be amortized in the corporation's first tax year under each of the following assumptions?

a. Owl Corporation adopts a calendar year and the cash basis of accounting for tax purposes.

b. Same as (a), except that Owl Corporation chooses a fiscal year of December 1–November 30.

c. Owl Corporation adopts a calendar year and the accrual basis of accounting for tax purposes.

d. Same as (c), except that Owl Corporation chooses a fiscal year of December 1–November 30.

30. Falcon Corporation, a cash basis and calendar year taxpayer, was formed and began operations on July 1, 2001. Falcon incurred the following expenses during its first year of operations (July 1–December 31, 2001):

Expenses of temporary directors and of organizational meetings	$ 3,600
Fee paid to the state of incorporation	1,800
Expenses in printing and sale of stock certificates	1,350
Legal services for drafting the corporate charter and bylaws (not paid until January of 2002	5,400
Total	$12,150

If Falcon Corporation makes a timely election under § 248 to amortize qualifying organizational expenses, how much may the corporation deduct for tax year 2001?

31. In each of the following independent situations, determine the corporation's income tax liability. Assume that all corporations use a calendar year for tax purposes and that the tax year involved is 2001.

	Taxable Income
Violet Corporation	$ 46,000
Indigo Corporation	260,000
Blue Corporation	1,620,000
Green Corporation	24,000,000

32. The outstanding stock in Black and White Corporations, each of which has only one class of stock, is owned by the following unrelated individuals:

	Corporations	
Shareholders	Black	White
Ahmad	20	16
Luis	5	54
Sara	75	30
Total	100	100

Determine if a brother-sister controlled group exists.

33. The outstanding stock of Wren, Robin, Finch, and Jay is owned by the following unrelated individual and corporate shareholders as follows:

	Corporations			
Shareholders	Wren	Robin	Finch	Jay
Ann	30%	20%	30%	10%
Bob	50%		50%	5%
Carl	20%		20%	
Wren Corporation		80%		

Which corporations, if any, are members of a controlled group?

34. Eagle and Cardinal Corporations both have 100 shares of stock outstanding. Each shareholder paid $500 for his stock in each corporation, and the fair market value of the stock of each corporation is $800 per share. The stock is owned by the following unrelated individuals:

Shareholders	Eagle Shares	Cardinal Shares
George	30	15
Sam	5	50
Tom	65	35
Total	100	100

a. Does a brother-sister controlled group exist?
b. Will a brother-sister controlled group exist if Tom sells 10 of his shares in Cardinal Corporation to Sam?
c. Discuss any tax advantages that will result if Tom sells 10 of his Cardinal shares to Sam.
d. Sam has suggested to Tom that they complete the transaction in (c). Tom asks your advice and says that he has a 31% marginal tax rate. Write a letter to Tom Roland at 3435 Grand Avenue, South Point, OH 45680, explaining the tax advantages that will result if he sells 10 of his Cardinal shares to Sam. Also, identify any problems, both tax and nontax, that the sale could cause for Tom.

EXTENDER 35. The outstanding stock in corporations Amber, Sand, Tan, Beige, and Purple, which have only one class of stock outstanding, is owned by the following unrelated individuals:

	Corporations				
Individuals	Amber	Sand	Tan	Beige	Purple
Anna	55%	51%	55%	55%	55%
Bill	45%	49%			
Carol			45%		
Don				45%	
Eve					45%
Total	100%	100%	100%	100%	100%

Determine if a brother-sister controlled group exists.

EXTENDER 36. Indicate in each of the following independent situations whether the corporation may file Form 1120–A:

	Jay Corporation	Shrike Corporation	Martin Corporation
Sales of merchandise	$600,000	$400,000	$300,000
Total assets	200,000	360,000	400,000
Total income (gross profit plus other income, including gains)	480,000	490,000	380,000
Member of controlled group	no	yes	no
Ownership in foreign corporation	no	no	no

37. The following information for 2001 relates to Martin Corporation, a calendar year, accrual basis taxpayer. You are to determine the amount of Martin's taxable income for the year using this information. You may use Schedule M–1 if provided by your instructor.

Net income per books (after tax)	$209,710
Federal income tax liability	30,050
Interest income from tax-exempt bonds	12,000
Interest paid on loan incurred to purchase tax-exempt bonds	1,200
Life insurance proceeds received as a result of the death of the president of the corporation	120,000
Premiums paid on policy on the life of the president of the corporation	6,240
Excess of capital losses over capital gains	4,800

38. For 2000, Rose Corporation, an accrual basis, calendar year taxpayer, had net income per books of $172,750 and the following special transactions:

Life insurance proceeds received on the death of the corporation president	$100,000
Premiums paid on the life insurance policy on the president	10,000
Prepaid rent received and properly taxed in 1999 but credited as rent income in 2000	15,000
Rent income received in 2000 ($10,000 is prepaid and relates to 2001)	25,000
Interest income on tax-exempt bonds	5,000
Interest on loan to carry tax-exempt bonds	3,000
MACRS depreciation in excess of straight-line (straight-line was used for book purposes)	4,000
Capital loss in excess of capital gains	6,000
Federal income tax liability and accrued tax provision for 2000	22,250

Using Schedule M–1 of Form 1120 (the most recent version available), compute Rose Corporation's taxable income for 2000.

39. In January, Don and Steve each invested $100,000 of cash to form a corporation to conduct business as a retail golf equipment store. On January 5, they paid Bill, an attorney, to draft the corporate charter, file the necessary forms with the state, and write the bylaws. They leased a store building and began to acquire inventory, furniture, display equipment, and office equipment in February. They hired a sales staff and clerical personnel in March and conducted training sessions during the month. They had a successful opening on April 1, and sales increased steadily throughout the summer. The weather turned cold in October, and all local golf courses closed by October 15, which resulted in a drastic decline in sales. Don and Steve expect business to be very good during the Christmas season and then to taper off significantly from January 1 through February 28. The corporation accrued bonuses to Don and Steve on December 31, payable on April 15 of the following year. The corporation made timely estimated tax payments throughout the year. The corporation hired a book-keeper in February, but he does not know much about taxation. Don and Steve have hired you as a tax consultant and have asked you to identify the tax issues that they should consider.

COMPREHENSIVE TAX RETURN PROBLEM

40. On May 8, 1994, Michael Keeling and David Dill formed Home Movies Corporation to sell home theatre equipment. Pertinent information regarding Home Movies is summarized as follows:

- The business address is 4010 Lakeview, Battle Creek, MI 49016.

- The employer identification number is 75–3392543; the principal business activity code is 451110.

- Michael and David each own one-half of the outstanding common stock; no other class of stock is authorized. Michael is president of the company, and David is secretary-treasurer. Both are full-time employees of the corporation, and each receives a salary of $189,500. Michael's Social Security number is 288–50–2953; David's Social Security number is 220–30–4495.

- The corporation uses the accrual method of accounting and reports on a calendar year basis. Inventories are determined using the lower of cost or market method. For book and tax purposes, the straight-line method of depreciation is used.

- During 2000, the corporation distributed a cash dividend of $72,000.

Selected portions of Home Movies' profit and loss statement for 2000 reflect the following debits and credits:

Account	Debit	Credit
Gross sales		$2,556,000
Sales returns and allowances	$ 72,000	
Cost of goods sold	925,000	
Dividends received from stock investments in less-than-20%-owned U.S. corporations		108,000
Interest income		
State bonds	$12,600	
Certificates of deposit	23,000	35,600
Premiums on term life insurance policies on the lives of Michael and David; Home Movies Corporation is the designated beneficiary	14,000	
Salaries—officers	379,000	
Salaries—clerical and sales	350,000	
Taxes (state, local, and payroll)	92,000	
Repairs	58,000	
Interest expense		
Loan to purchase state bonds	$ 7,200	
Other business loans	16,800	24,000
Advertising	83,400	
Rental expense	177,700	
Depreciation	36,000	

A comparative balance sheet for Home Movies Corporation reveals the following:

Assets	January 1, 2000	December 31, 2000
Cash	$ 369,000	$ 251,194
Trade notes and accounts receivable	790,560	956,140
Inventories	540,000	640,800
Federal bonds	127,000	154,000
State bonds	143,000	186,000
Prepaid Federal tax	–0–	1,620

Assets	January 1, 2000	December 31, 2000
Buildings and other depreciable assets	$ 216,000	$ 216,000
Accumulated depreciation	(79,920)	(115,920)
Land	18,500	18,500
Other assets	2,740	1,300
Total assets	$2,126,880	$2,309,634

Liabilities and Equity		
Accounts payable	$ 208,000	$ 214,004
Other current liabilities	134,270	69,600
Mortgages	214,000	205,000
Capital stock	425,000	425,000
Retained earnings	1,145,610	1,396,030
Total liabilities and equity	$2,126,880	$2,309,634

Net income per books (before any income tax accrual) is $454,000. During 2000, Home Movies Corporation made estimated tax payments of $133,200 to the IRS. Prepare a Form 1120 for Home Movies Corporation for tax year 2000.

BRIDGE DISCIPLINE

1. Charles is planning to invest $10,000 in a venture whose management is undecided as to whether it should be structured as a regular corporation or as a partnership. Charles will hold a 10% interest in the entity. Determine the treatment to Charles if the entity is a corporation or if it is a partnership. In the analysis, assume Charles is in the 36% marginal tax bracket, and the entity, if operating as a corporation, is in the 34% marginal tax bracket. Also, assume that the passive activity rules do not apply to Charles.
   a. If the entity incurs an $80,000 loss in year 1, what is Charles's cash outflow if the entity is a corporation? A partnership?
   b. In year 2, the entity earns $200,000 and makes no distribution to any of the owners. What is the tax burden on Charles if the entity is a corporation? A partnership?
   c. In year 3, the entity earns $200,000 and distributes all of that year's after-tax proceeds to the owners. What amount of cash is available to Charles if the entity operates as a corporation? A partnership?

2. On your review of the books and records of Ridge Corporation, you note the following information pertaining to its tax provision.

Net income per books	$525,400
Book income tax expense	234,600
Dividends received deduction	70,000
Capital gains	50,000
Capital losses	(60,000)
MACRS depreciation	80,000
Book depreciation	65,000

   a. Calculate Ridge's taxable income and Federal income tax liability for the year.
   b. Calculate Ridge's deferred income tax liability.

RESEARCH PROBLEMS

*Note: Solutions to Research Problems can be prepared by using the **RIA Checkpoint® Student Version Online research product,** or the **CCH U.S. Master Tax Guide Plus™** online Federal tax research database, which is available to accompany this text. It is also possible to prepare solutions to the Research Problems by using tax research materials found in a standard tax library.*

Research Problem 1. Joe and Tom are civic-minded citizens of Central City. Upon learning that Central City Hospital was filing for bankruptcy, Joe and Tom began working on a plan to reopen the hospital at some future date. They formed an LLC, created a hospital board, and began the process of dealing with all the relevant local, state, and Federal agencies.

Some time after learning of the impending closing, Joe and Tom heard that the administrator of the hospital planned to auction off the hospital's equipment. The administrator's target was to receive a bid that would exceed the costs of the auction by $74,000. Before the auction could be scheduled, Joe and Tom, acting as individuals, offered the bankruptcy court $80,000 for the equipment. The court accepted the offer. Joe and Tom each contributed $40,000 toward the purchase.

Approximately two years later, Joe and Tom donated the equipment to the hospital, which was to reopen soon. They had the property appraised, and the value was estimated at $1.5 million. Joe claimed a charitable contribution deduction of $750,000 on his tax return. The IRS audited his return and asserted that the deduction should be limited to $40,000. The agent also imposed an overvaluation penalty of approximately $50,000. Joe has asked for your advice on this issue.

Partial list of research aids:
§ 170.
Max Weitz, 56 TCM 1422, T.C.Memo. 1989–99.

Research Problem 2. John Hunter, the president and sole shareholder of Hunter, Inc., has asked you to assist him in obtaining the maximum charitable contribution deduction for his corporation. The corporation has 36 desktop computers that are almost two years old. Due to recent advances in technology, Hunter has decided to replace all of these computers with new, more powerful models. Each computer cost $5,000 and has a market value of $3,400 and a basis of $2,600. Hunter plans to donate the computers to a qualified charitable organization, but has not decided which charity will be the beneficiary of the corporation's generosity. Draft a letter to John Hunter at Hunter, Inc., 1200 West Madison, Bellwood, IL 60104 and advise him on the issue he has raised.

Research Problem 3. Joel has operated his business as a sole proprietorship for many years but has decided to incorporate the business this year in order to limit his exposure to personal liability. The balance sheet of his business is as follows:

	Adjusted Basis	Fair Market Value
Assets:		
Cash	$ 50,000	$ 50,000
Accounts receivable	40,000	40,000
Inventory	30,000	60,000
Fixed assets	10,000	200,000
	$130,000	$350,000
Liabilities:		
Trade accounts payable	$ 25,000	$ 25,000
Notes payable	175,000	175,000
Owner's equity	(70,000)	150,000
	$130,000	$350,000

One problem with this plan is that the liabilities of his sole proprietorship exceed the basis of the assets to be transferred to the corporation by $70,000 ($200,000 − $130,000). Joel would be required to recognize a gain of $70,000. He is not pleased with this result and asks you about the effect of drawing up a $70,000 note that he would then transfer to the corporation. Would the transfer of this note promising a $70,000 future payment to the corporation enable Joel to avoid recognition of the gain?

Partial list of research aids:
§ 357(c).

Use the tax resources of the Internet to address the following questions. Do not restrict your search to the World Wide Web, but include a review of newsgroups and general reference materials, practitioner sites and resources, primary sources of the tax law, chat rooms and discussion groups, and other opportunities.

Research Problem 4.   Download the forms used to compute a corporation's estimated tax payments and to transmit the payment to an approved bank. Complete the forms for a corporation that must make quarterly estimated payments of $11,000 this year.

Research Problem 5.   The U.S. stock market has seen a record number of initial public offerings (IPOs) in the last few years, some of which have involved issuances of tracking stock. Investigate the market's reaction to this new type of equity interest.

Corporations: Earnings & Profits and Dividend Distributions

LEARNING OBJECTIVES

After completing Chapter 10, you should be able to:

1. Understand the role that earnings and profits play in determining the tax treatment of distributions.

2. Compute a corporation's earnings and profits.

3. Apply the rules for allocating earnings and profits to distributions.

4. Understand the tax impact of property dividends on the recipient shareholder and the corporation making the distribution.

5. Understand the nature and treatment of constructive dividends.

6. Distinguish between taxable and nontaxable stock dividends.

7. Discuss the tax treatment of stock redemptions.

Outline

TAX TALK   *The relative stability of profits after taxes is evidence that the corporation profits tax is, in effect, almost entirely shifted; the government simply uses the corporation as a tax collector.*

—K. E. Boulding

Generally, a corporation cannot deduct distributions made to its shareholders. In contrast, shareholders may be required to treat distributions as ordinary income, a nontaxable recovery of capital, or capital gain.

Since distributions provide no deduction to the paying corporation and often require income recognition by the shareholders, a double tax results (i.e., at both the corporate and the shareholder levels). Because of the possibility of a double tax when dealing with corporations, the tax treatment of distributions often raise issues such as the following.

- The availability of earnings to be distributed.
- The basis of the stock in the hands of the shareholder.
- The character of the property being distributed.
- Whether the shareholder gives up ownership in return for the distribution.
- Whether the distribution is liquidating or nonliquidating in character.

LEARNING OBJECTIVE 1

Understand the role that earnings and profits play in determining the tax treatment of distributions.

Taxable Dividends—In General

To the extent that a distribution is made from corporate earnings and profits (E & P), the shareholder is deemed to receive a dividend, taxed as ordinary income.[1] Generally, corporate distributions are presumed to be paid out of E & P (defined later in this chapter) and are treated as dividends, *unless* the parties to the transaction can show otherwise.

The portion of a corporate distribution that is not taxed as a dividend (because of insufficient E & P) is nontaxable to the extent of the shareholder's basis in the stock. The stock basis is reduced accordingly. The excess of the distribution over the shareholder's basis is treated as a capital gain if the stock is a capital asset.[2]

---

[1]§ 316(a).

[2]§ 301(c).

TAX IN THE NEWS

THE CASE FOR DIVIDENDS

As stock prices soared to unprecedented levels in recent years, investors poured money into high-growth, high-tech stocks that rarely pay dividends. Certainly, these aggressive investors were rewarded—at least until Nasdaq's recent downturn—but some investment advisers have suggested all along that investors might want to make room in their portfolios for some dividend-paying stocks.

For one thing, dividend-paying companies are likely to have stable earnings. When the economy turns down, they can provide a safe haven for investors. Especially for young investors who reinvest their dividends, dividend-paying stocks can increase their returns significantly. Between 1988 and 1998, for example, the S&P 500 rose 318 percent, but with reinvested dividends, the gain was 451 percent.

Further, elderly taxpayers receive a greater degree of psychological security when they invest in dividend-paying stocks. Even though dividends are taxed at ordinary income rates, and not at the lower capital gains rates that a growth-stock strategy produces, the certainty of a cash dividend still appeals to many.

EXAMPLE 1

At the beginning of the year, Amber Corporation (a calendar year taxpayer) has accumulated E & P of $30,000. The corporation has no current E & P. During the year, the corporation distributes $40,000 to its *equal* shareholders, Bob and Bonnie. Only $30,000 of the $40,000 distribution is a taxable dividend. Suppose Bob's basis in his stock is $8,000, while Bonnie's basis is $4,000. Under these conditions, Bob recognizes a taxable dividend of $15,000 and reduces the basis of his stock from $8,000 to $3,000. The $20,000 Bonnie receives from Amber Corporation is accounted for as follows.

- Taxable dividend of $15,000.
- Reduction in stock basis from $4,000 to zero.
- Capital gain of $1,000. ∎

LEARNING OBJECTIVE 2

Compute a corporation's earnings and profits.

Earnings and Profits (E & P)—§ 312

The notion of **earnings and profits** is similar in many respects to the accounting concept of retained earnings. Both are measures of the firm's capital accumulation. However, these two concepts differ in one fundamental way. Retained earnings are based on financial accounting rules, while E & P is determined using rules specified in the tax law.

E & P fixes the upper limit on the amount of dividend income that shareholders must recognize as a result of a distribution by the corporation. In this sense, E & P represents the corporation's economic ability to pay a dividend without impairing its capital. Thus, the effect of a specific transaction on the E & P account can be determined by considering whether the transaction increases or decreases the corporation's capacity to pay a dividend.

COMPUTATION OF E & P

The Code does not explicitly define the term *earnings and profits*. Instead, the corporation keeps at least two E & P accounts.[3] In general, E & P determinations are applied in the same manner for cash and accrual basis taxpayers.

Accumulated **E & P** is fixed as of the beginning of the tax year, which is the sum of the undistributed earnings of the entity since February 28, 1913. **Current E & P** is that portion of E & P attributable to the current tax year's operations. It is computed by using the corporation's Federal taxable income and then applying a series of adjustments to more closely approximate the cash flow of the entity.[4]

Additions to Taxable Income. It is necessary to add certain previously excluded income items back to taxable income to determine current E & P. Included among these positive adjustments are interest income on municipal bonds, excluded life insurance proceeds (in excess of cash surrender value), Federal income tax refunds from taxes paid in prior years, and the dividends received deduction.

EXAMPLE 2

A corporation collects $100,000 on a key employee life insurance policy (the corporation is the owner and beneficiary of the policy). At the time the policy matured on the death of the insured employee, it possessed a cash surrender value of $30,000. None of the $100,000 is included in the corporation's taxable income, but $70,000 is added to taxable income when computing current E & P. ■

Subtractions from Taxable Income. Some of the corporation's nondeductible expenditures are subtracted from taxable income to arrive at E & P. These negative adjustments include related-party losses, excess capital losses, expenses incurred to produce tax-exempt income, Federal income taxes paid, nondeductible key employee life insurance premiums (net of increases in cash surrender value), and nondeductible fines and penalties.

EXAMPLE 3

A corporation sells property (basis of $10,000) to its sole shareholder for $8,000. Because of § 267 (disallowance of losses on sales between related parties), the $2,000 loss cannot be deducted in arriving at the corporation's taxable income. But since the overall economic effect of the transaction is a decrease in the corporation's assets by $2,000, the loss reduces the current E & P for the year of the sale. ■

EXAMPLE 4

A corporation pays a $10,000 premium on a key employee life insurance policy covering the life of its president. As a result of the payment, the cash surrender value of the policy is increased by $7,000. Although none of the $10,000 premium is deductible for tax purposes, current E & P is reduced by $3,000. ■

Timing Adjustments. Some E & P adjustments shift the effect of a transaction from the year of its inclusion in taxable income to the year in which it has an economic effect on the corporation. Charitable contribution carryovers, net operating loss carryovers, and capital loss carryovers all give rise to this kind of adjustment.

---

[3]Reg. § 1.312–6(a).

[4]Section 312 describes most of the adjustments to taxable income necessary to determine E & P. Regulations relating to E & P begin at Reg. § 1.312–6.

EXAMPLE 5

During 2001, Raven Corporation makes charitable contributions, $12,000 of which cannot be deducted in arriving at the taxable income for the year because of the 10% taxable income limitation. Consequently, the $12,000 is carried forward to 2002 and fully deducted in that year. The excess charitable contribution reduces the corporation's current E & P for 2001 by $12,000 and increases its current E & P for 2002, when the deduction is allowed, by a like amount. The increase in E & P in 2002 is necessary because the charitable contribution carryover reduces the taxable income for that year (the starting point for computing E & P) and already has been taken into account in determining the E & P for 2001. ∎

Gains and losses from property transactions generally affect the determination of E & P only to the extent that they are recognized for tax purposes. Thus, gains and losses deferred under the like-kind exchange provision and deferred involuntary conversion gains do not affect E & P until recognized. Accordingly, no adjustment is required for these items.

Accounting Method Adjustments. In addition to the above adjustments, accounting methods used for determining E & P are generally more conservative than those allowed under the income tax. For example, the installment method is not permitted for E & P purposes even though, in some cases, it is allowed when computing taxable income. Thus, an adjustment is required for the deferred gain attributable to sales of property made during the year under the installment method. Specifically, all principal payments are treated as having been received in the year of sale.[5]

EXAMPLE 6

In 2001, Cardinal Corporation, a calendar year taxpayer, sells unimproved real estate (basis of $20,000) for $100,000. Under the terms of the sale, beginning in 2002, Cardinal will receive two annual payments of $50,000 each with interest of 9%. Cardinal Corporation does not elect out of the installment method. Since Cardinal's taxable income for 2001 will not reflect any of the gain from the sale, the corporation must make an $80,000 positive adjustment for 2001 (the deferred profit component) in computing E & P. Similarly, negative adjustments will be required in 2002 and 2003 when the deferred profit is recognized under the installment method. ∎

The alternative depreciation system (ADS) must be used for purposes of computing E & P.[6] This method requires straight-line depreciation over a recovery period equal to the Asset Depreciation Range (ADR) midpoint life.[7] Thus, if MACRS cost recovery is used for income tax purposes, a positive or negative adjustment equal to the difference between MACRS and ADS must be made each year. Likewise, when assets are disposed of, an additional adjustment to taxable income is required to allow for the difference in gain or loss resulting from the difference in income tax basis and E & P basis.[8] The adjustments arising from depreciation are illustrated in the following example.

EXAMPLE 7

On January 2, 1999, White Corporation purchased equipment with an alternative recovery period of 10 years for $30,000. The equipment was then depreciated under MACRS. The asset was sold on July 2, 2001, for $27,000. For purposes of determining taxable income and E & P, cost recovery claimed on the equipment is summarized below.

[5]§ 312(n)(5).
[6]§ 312(k)(3)(A).
[7]See § 168(g)(2). The ADR midpoint life for most assets is set out in Rev.Proc. 87–56, 1987–2 C.B. 674. The recovery period is 5 years for automobiles and light-duty trucks and 40 years for real property. For assets with no class life, the recovery period is 12 years.
[8]§ 312(f)(1).

Year	Cost Recovery Computation	MACRS	ADS	Adjustment Amount
1999	$30,000 × 14.29%	$ 4,287		
	$30,000 ÷ 10-year ADR recovery period × ½ (half-year for first year of service)		$1,500	$2,787
2000	$30,000 × 24.49%	7,347		
	$30,000 ÷ 10-year ADR recovery period		3,000	4,347
2001	$30,000 × 17.49% × ½ (half-year for year of disposal)	2,624		
	$30,000 ÷ 10-year ADR recovery period × ½ (half-year for year of disposal)		1,500	1,124
Total cost recovery		$14,258	$6,000	$8,258

Each year White Corporation increases its taxable income by the adjustment amount indicated above to determine E & P. In addition, when computing E & P for 2001, White reduces taxable income by $8,258 to account for the excess gain recognized for income tax purposes, as shown below.

	Income Tax	E & P
Amount realized	$ 27,000	$ 27,000
Adjusted basis for income tax ($30,000 cost – $14,258 MACRS)	(15,742)	
Adjusted basis for E & P ($30,000 cost – $6,000 ADS)		(24,000)
Gain on sale	$ 11,258	$ 3,000
Adjustment amount ($3,000 – $11,258)	($ 8,258)	

In addition to more conservative depreciation methods, the E & P rules impose limitations on the deductibility of § 179 expense.[9] In particular, this expense is deducted over a period of five years for E & P purposes. Thus, in any year that § 179 is elected, 80 percent of the resulting expense is added back to taxable income to determine current E & P. In each of the following four years, a negative adjustment equal to 20 percent of the § 179 expense is made.

A variety of other accounting method adjustments are also required to determine current E & P. For example, cost depletion is required for E & P purposes, so an adjustment must be made to taxable income in cases where percentage depletion is used. Similarly, the percentage of completion method is required for E & P purposes when accounting for long-term contracts, so an adjustment is required when the completed contract method is employed. Intangible drilling costs and mine exploration and development costs may be deducted currently for income tax purposes, but must be capitalized for E & P. Once capitalized, these expenditures can be amortized under the E & P rules over 60 months for intangible drilling costs and over 120 months for mine exploration and development costs.[10]

---

[9] § 312(k)(3)(B).   [10] § 312(n)(2).

CONCEPT SUMMARY 10–1

Computing E & P

Transaction	Adjustment to Taxable Income in Arriving at Current E & P	
	Addition	Subtraction
Tax-exempt income	X	
Dividends received deduction	X	
Collection of proceeds from insurance policy on life of corporate officer (in excess of cash surrender value)	X	
Deferred gain on installment sale (all gain is added to E & P in year of sale)	X	
Future recognition of installment sale gross profit		X
Excess capital loss and excess charitable contribution (over 10% limitation) in year incurred		X
Deduction of charitable contribution, NOL, or capital loss carryovers in succeeding taxable years (increase E & P because deduction reduces taxable income while E & P was reduced in a prior year)	X	
Federal income taxes paid		X
Federal income tax refund	X	
Loss on sale between related parties		X
Nondeductible fines and penalties		X
Payment of premiums on insurance policy on life of corporate officer (in excess of increase in cash surrender value of policy)		X
Realized gain (not recognized) on an involuntary conversion	No effect	
Realized gain or loss (not recognized) on a like-kind exchange	No effect	
Percentage depletion (only cost depletion can reduce E & P)	X	
Accelerated depreciation (E & P is reduced only by straight-line, units-of-production, or machine hours depreciation)	X	
§ 179 expense in year elected (80%)	X	
§ 179 expense in four years following election (20% each year)		X
Intangible drilling costs deducted currently (reduce E & P in future years by amortizing costs over 60 months)	X	
Mine exploration and development costs (reduce in future years by amortizing costs over 120 months)	X	

SUMMARY OF E & P ADJUSTMENTS

E & P serves as a measure of the earnings of the corporation that are available for distribution as taxable dividends to the shareholders. Current E & P is determined by making a series of adjustments to the corporation's taxable income. These adjustments are reviewed in Concept Summary 10–1.

ALLOCATING E & P TO DISTRIBUTIONS

LEARNING OBJECTIVE 3

Apply the rules for allocating earnings and profits to distributions.

When a positive balance exists in both the current and the accumulated E & P accounts, corporate distributions are deemed to be made first from current E & P and then from accumulated E & P. When distributions exceed the amount of current

CONCEPT SUMMARY 10–2

Allocating E & P to Distributions

1. Current E & P is allocated first to distributions on a pro rata basis; then, accumulated E & P is applied (to the extent necessary) in chronological order beginning with the earliest distribution. See Example 8.
2. Unless and until the parties can show otherwise, it is presumed that current E & P covers all distributions. See Example 9.
3. When a deficit exists in accumulated E & P and a positive balance exists in current E & P, distributions are regarded as dividends to the extent of current E & P. See Example 10.
4. When a deficit exists in current E & P and a positive balance exists in accumulated E & P, the two accounts are netted at the date of distribution. If the resulting balance is zero or a deficit, the distribution is treated as a return of capital, first reducing the basis of the stock to zero, then generating capital gain. If a positive balance results, the distribution is a dividend to the extent of the balance. Any loss in current E & P is allocated ratably during the year unless the parties can show otherwise. See Example 11.

BRIDGE DISCIPLINE

Bridge to Finance

Investors often have tried to read the dividend policies of a corporation as indicators of the strength of the entity: Constant dividend payments indicated a stable financial structure for the corporation, while dividend increases were a predictor of good times and triggered stock price increases. Reductions in historic dividend payment patterns foreshadowed financial difficulties and often caused a quick and sizable drop in share price.

Nobel Prize winners Merton Miller, University of Chicago, and Franco Modigliani, MIT, disagreed. They viewed dividends as a remnant of various financing sources available to the corporation: If it was cheaper to finance future growth by retaining profits and decreasing or eliminating dividend payments, so be it. The entity must reduce its cost of capital wherever possible, and, under this interpretation, a dividend decrease might indicate the internal financial strength of the corporation. Conversely, the payment of a dividend reduces the capital available to the entity, thereby forcing the entity to finance its operations and growth from some third-party source and risking future weakness if the cost of that capital increases.

Miller and Modigliani held that stock price and dividend policy were unrelated, and that changes in dividend patterns should not affect the capitalized value of the business. Their original studies are more than 40 years old, but the market seems to have adopted them. No one complains today that Microsoft never pays dividends.

E & P, it becomes necessary to allocate current and accumulated E & P to each distribution made during the year. Current E & P is allocated on a pro rata basis to each distribution. Accumulated E & P is applied in chronological order, beginning with the earliest distribution. As can be seen in the following example, this allocation is important if any shareholder sells stock during the year.

EXAMPLE 8

As of January 1 of the current year, Black Corporation has accumulated E & P of $10,000. Current E & P for the year amounts to $30,000. Megan and Matt are sole *equal* shareholders of Black from January 1 to July 31. On August 1, Megan sells all of her stock to Helen. Black makes two distributions to shareholders during the year: $40,000 to Megan and Matt ($20,000 to each) on July 1, and $40,000 to Matt and Helen ($20,000 to each) on December 1. Current and accumulated E & P are allocated to the two distributions as follows.

	Source of Distribution		
	Current E & P	Accumulated E & P	Return of Capital
July 1 distribution ($40,000)	$15,000	$10,000	$15,000
December 1 distribution ($40,000)	15,000	—	25,000

Thus, since 50% of the total distributions are made on July 1 and December 1, respectively, one-half of current E & P is allocated to each of the two distributions. Accumulated E & P is applied in chronological order, so the entire amount is attributed to the July 1 distribution. The tax consequences to the shareholders are presented below.

	Shareholder		
	Megan	Matt	Helen
July distribution ($40,000)			
Dividend income—			
From current E & P ($15,000)	$ 7,500	$ 7,500	$ –0–
From accumulated E & P ($10,000)	5,000	5,000	–0–
Return of capital ($15,000)	7,500	7,500	–0–
December distribution ($40,000)			
Dividend income—			
From current E & P ($15,000)	–0–	7,500	7,500
From accumulated E & P ($0)	–0–	–0–	–0–
Return of capital ($25,000)	–0–	12,500	12,500
Total dividend income	$12,500	$20,000	$ 7,500
Nontaxable return of capital (presuming sufficient basis in the stock investment)	$ 7,500	$20,000	$12,500

Because the balance in the accumulated E & P account is exhausted when it is applied to the July 1 distribution, Megan has more dividend income than Helen, even though both receive equal distributions during the year. In addition, each shareholder's basis is reduced by the nontaxable return of capital; any excess over basis results in capital gain. ∎

When the tax years of the corporation and its shareholders are not the same, it may be impossible to determine the amount of current E & P on a timely basis. For example, if shareholders use a calendar year and the corporation uses a fiscal year, then current E & P may not be ascertainable until after the shareholders' tax returns have been filed. To address this timing problem, the allocation rules presume that current E & P is sufficient to cover every distribution made during the year unless or until the parties can show otherwise.

EXAMPLE 9	Green Corporation uses the fiscal year of July 1 through June 30 for tax purposes. Carol, Green's only shareholder, uses a calendar year. As of July 1, 2001, Green Corporation has a zero balance in its accumulated E & P account. For fiscal year 2001–2002, the corporation incurs a $5,000 deficit in current E & P. On August 1, 2001, Green distributed $10,000 to Carol. The distribution is dividend income to Carol and is reported when she files her income tax return for the 2001 calendar year, on or before April 15, 2002. Because Carol cannot prove until June 30, 2002, that the corporation has a deficit for the 2001–2002 fiscal year, she must assume the $10,000 distribution is fully covered by current E & P. When Carol learns of the deficit, she can file an amended return for 2001 showing the $10,000 as a return of capital. Alternatively, Carol can file for an extension on April 15, 2002, while she awaits Green Corporation's fiscal year-end. ∎

Additional difficulties arise when either the current or the accumulated E & P account has a deficit balance. In particular, when current E & P is positive and accumulated E & P has a deficit balance, accumulated E & P is *not* netted against current E & P. Instead, the distribution is deemed to be a taxable dividend to the extent of the positive current E & P balance.

EXAMPLE 10	At the beginning of the current year, Brown Corporation has a deficit of $30,000 in accumulated E & P. For the year, it has current E & P of $10,000 and distributes $5,000 to its shareholders. The $5,000 distribution is treated as a taxable dividend since it is deemed to have been made from current E & P. This is the case even though Brown Corporation still has a deficit in accumulated E & P at the end of the year. ∎

In contrast to the above rule, when a deficit exists in current E & P and a positive balance exists in accumulated E & P, the accounts are netted at the date of distribution. If the resulting balance is zero or negative, the distribution is a return of capital. If a positive balance results, the distribution is a dividend to the extent of the balance. Any current E & P deficit is allocated ratably during the year unless the parties can show otherwise.

EXAMPLE 11	At the beginning of the current year, Gray Corporation (a calendar year taxpayer) has accumulated E & P of $10,000. During the year, the corporation incurs a $15,000 deficit in current E & P that accrues ratably. On July 1, Gray Corporation distributes $6,000 in cash to Hal, its sole shareholder. To determine how much of the $6,000 cash distribution represents dividend income to Hal, the balances of both accumulated and current E & P as of July 1 are determined and netted. This is necessary because of the deficit in current E & P.

	Source of Distribution	
	Current E & P	**Accumulated E & P**
January 1		$10,000
July 1 (½ of $15,000 deficit in current E & P)	($7,500)	2,500
July 1 distribution—$6,000:		
Dividend income: $2,500		
Return of capital: $3,500		

The balance in E & P on July 1 is $2,500. Thus, of the $6,000 distribution, $2,500 is taxed as a dividend, and $3,500 represents a return of capital. ∎

PLANNING CONSIDERATIONS

Corporate Distributions

In connection with the discussion of corporate distributions, the following points need reinforcement.

- Because E & P is the measure of dividend income, its periodic determination is essential to corporate planning. Thus, an E & P account should be established and maintained, particularly if the possibility exists that a corporate distribution might be a return of capital.
- Accumulated E & P is the sum of all past years' current E & P. There is no statute of limitations on the computation of E & P. The IRS can, for example, redetermine a corporation's current E & P for a tax year long since passed. Such a change affects accumulated E & P and has a direct impact on the taxability of current distributions to shareholders.
- Distributions can be planned to avoid or minimize dividend exposure.

EXAMPLE 12

Flicker Corporation has accumulated E & P of $100,000 as of January 1 of the current year. During the year, it expects to have earnings from operations of $80,000 and to make a cash distribution of $60,000. Flicker Corporation also expects to sell an asset for a loss of $100,000. Thus, it anticipates a current E & P deficit of $20,000. The best approach is to recognize the loss as soon as possible and immediately thereafter make the cash distribution to the shareholders. Suppose these two steps take place on January 1. Because the current E & P has a deficit, the accumulated E & P account must be brought up to date (refer to Example 11). Thus, at the time of the distribution, the combined E & P balance is zero [$100,000 (beginning balance in accumulated E & P) – $100,000 (existing deficit in current E & P)], and the $60,000 distribution to the shareholders constitutes a return of capital. Current deficits are allocated pro rata throughout the year unless the parties can prove otherwise. Here they can. ∎

EXAMPLE 13

After several unprofitable years, Darter Corporation has a deficit in accumulated E & P of $100,000 as of January 1, 2001. Starting in 2001, Darter expects to generate annual E & P of $50,000 for the next four years and would like to distribute this amount to its shareholders. The corporation's cash position (for dividend purposes) will correspond to the current E & P generated. Compare the following possibilities.

1. On December 31 of 2001, 2002, 2003, and 2004, Darter Corporation distributes a cash dividend of $50,000.
2. On December 31 of 2002 and 2004, Darter Corporation distributes a cash dividend of $100,000.

The two alternatives are illustrated as follows.

Year	Accumulated E & P (First of Year)	Current E & P	Distribution	Amount of Dividend
Alternative 1				
2001	($100,000)	$50,000	$50,000	$50,000
2002	(100,000)	50,000	50,000	50,000
2003	(100,000)	50,000	50,000	50,000
2004	(100,000)	50,000	50,000	50,000
Alternative 2				
2001	($100,000)	$50,000	$ –0–	$ –0–
2002	(50,000)	50,000	100,000	50,000
2003	(50,000)	50,000	–0–	–0–
2004	–0–	50,000	100,000	50,000

Alternative 1 produces $200,000 of dividend income because each $50,000 distribution is fully covered by current E & P. Alternative 2, however, produces only $100,000 of dividend income to the shareholders. The remaining $100,000 is a return of capital. Why? At the time Darter Corporation made its first distribution of $100,000 on December 31, 2002, it had a deficit of $50,000 in accumulated E & P (the original deficit of $100,000 is reduced by the $50,000 of current E & P from 2001). Consequently, the $100,000 distribution yields a $50,000 dividend (the current E & P for 2002), and $50,000 is treated as a return of capital. As of January 1, 2003, Darter's accumulated E & P now has a deficit balance of $50,000, since a distribution cannot increase a deficit in E & P. Adding the remaining $50,000 of current E & P from 2003, the balance as of January 1, 2004, is zero. Thus, the second distribution of $100,000 made on December 31, 2004, also yields $50,000 of dividends (the current E & P for 2004) and a $50,000 return of capital. ∎

LEARNING OBJECTIVE 4

Understand the tax impact of property dividends on the recipient shareholder and the corporation making the distribution.

Property Dividends

The previous discussion assumed that all distributions by a corporation to its shareholders are in the form of cash. Although most corporate distributions are paid in cash, a corporation may distribute a **property dividend** for various reasons. The shareholders may want a particular property that is held by the corporation.

BRIDGE DISCIPLINE

Bridge to Investments

Most investors look to the stocks of utilities, real estate investment trusts, and tobacco companies as the source of steady dividend payments. This is a prudent decision on the investor's part, as the typical S&P 500 stock offers a dividend yield of just over 1 percent. But an investor could put together a fairly diversified portfolio using only stocks that regularly produce dividend yields of at least 4 percent. Using recent data, these companies include the following.

- Bank One
- Dow Chemical
- Hong Kong Telecommunications
- JC Penney
- Telefonos de Mexico
- Weyerhauser

Dividends can be important to the investor because:

- They can be used in a tax-sheltered account, like a § 401(k) plan, such that the tax inefficiency of the dividends is not recognized immediately by the investor.
- Even today, about 40 percent of the total return from an investment can be traced to holding stocks that make regular distributions.
- Generally, a dividend-paying company is a profitable company, and lately corporate profits have been hard to come by.
- Earning and reinvesting dividends is an easy way to put into place an investment policy of dollar-cost averaging, a technique that forces the investor to buy more shares when prices are low and fewer shares when prices are high. Dollar-cost averaging often implements a contrarian investment strategy.

Or a corporation that is strapped for cash may want to distribute a dividend to its shareholders.

Property distributions have the same tax impact as distributions of cash except for effects attributable to any difference between the basis and the fair market value of the distributed property. In most situations, distributed property is appreciated, so its sale would result in a gain to the corporation. Distributions of property with a basis that differs from fair market value raise several tax questions.

- For the shareholder:
  - What is the amount of the distribution?
  - What is the basis of the property in the shareholder's hands?
- For the corporation:
  - Is a gain or loss recognized as a result of the distribution?
  - What is the effect of the distribution on E & P?

PROPERTY DIVIDENDS—EFFECT ON THE SHAREHOLDER

When a corporation distributes property rather than cash to a shareholder, the amount distributed is measured by the fair market value of the property on the date

TAX FACT

THE DOWNWARD TRAJECTORY OF DIVIDENDS

Clearly, in recent years most investors in the U.S. stock market have been more interested in capital gains than in dividends. Although the S&P 500 index has risen significantly over the last two decades, the percentage of S&P 500 companies paying dividends has declined. Furthermore, as companies' stock prices have risen, their dividends have not kept pace. The dividend yield of the S&P 500 has declined from over 4 percent to only a little more than 1 percent.

Percentage of S&P 500 Companies Paying Dividends

Dividend Yield of the S&P 500

of distribution.[11] As with a cash distribution, the portion of a property distribution covered by existing E & P is a dividend, and any excess is treated as a return of capital. If the fair market value of the property distributed exceeds the corporation's E & P and the shareholder's basis in the stock investment, a capital gain usually results.

The amount distributed is reduced by any liabilities to which the distributed property is subject immediately before and immediately after the distribution and by any liabilities of the corporation assumed by the shareholder. The basis in the distributed property to the shareholder is the fair market value of the property on the date of the distribution.

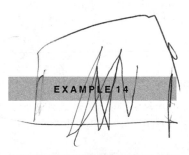

EXAMPLE 14

Robin Corporation has E & P of $60,000. It distributes land with a fair market value of $50,000 (adjusted basis of $30,000) to its sole shareholder, Charles. The land is subject to a liability of $10,000, which Charles assumes. Charles has a taxable dividend of $40,000 [$50,000 (fair market value) − $10,000 (liability)]. The basis of the land to Charles is $50,000. ■

EXAMPLE 15

Ten percent of Tan Corporation is owned by Red Corporation. Tan has ample E & P to cover any distributions made during the year. One distribution made to Red consists of a vacant lot with a basis of $5,000 and a fair market value of $3,000. Red recognizes a taxable dividend of $3,000, and its basis in the lot becomes $3,000. ■

---

[11]§ 301.

THE STORY OF DISAPPEARING DIVIDENDS

Fifty years ago, nine out of ten American companies paid dividends. In the 1950s, a low dividend yield was seen as an indication that the market was overvalued. Today, only one in five American companies pays dividends. Furthermore, while America's largest companies paid out roughly half of their profits in dividends in 1990, they pay out only one-third now. Why are dividends disappearing?

The change is likely attributable to a number of factors. The emergence of Nasdaq in the 1970s allowed access to capital markets to small, innovative companies that could not have met the New York Stock Exchange listing requirements. Listings soared during the 1980s and 1990s, and most of the new listings were on the Nasdaq exchange. However, many of these new companies were not initially profitable and, therefore, ill-advised to pay a dividend. Even a profitable company may retain earnings to invest in new technologies, or if it believes its own investment opportunities are better than those of its shareholders.

Taxes may also play a role in the disappearance of the dividend. Dividends are taxed to shareholders at a top Federal rate of 39.6 percent. In contrast, a long-term capital gain is taxed at only 20 percent. Dividends may have been replaced, in part, by "stock buybacks," a company's repurchase of its own shares. Stock buybacks, which represented only 3 to 5 percent of annual corporate profits in the 1970s, accounted for 26 percent of annual corporate profits in the 1980s and 1990s.

Some technology companies, notably Microsoft, do not pay dividends, but do have extensive buyback programs. Microsoft buys back shares primarily to reissue them to employees and managers when they cash in their stock options. The goal of the buyback is not to distribute profits, but to avoid diluting the stock of existing shareholders.

Distributing property that has depreciated in value as a property dividend may reflect poor planning. Note what happens in Example 15. Basis of $2,000 disappears due to the loss (basis $5,000, fair market value $3,000). As an alternative, if Tan Corporation sells the lot, it could use the loss to reduce its taxes. Then Tan could distribute the $3,000 of proceeds to its shareholders.

PROPERTY DIVIDENDS—EFFECT ON THE CORPORATION

As noted earlier, the distribution of a property dividend raises two questions related to the corporation's tax position: Is a gain or loss recognized? What is the effect on E & P?

Recognition of Gain or Loss. All distributions of appreciated property generate gain to the distributing corporation.[12] In effect, a corporation that distributes appreciated property is treated as if it had sold the property to the shareholder

---

[12]§ 311.

for its fair market value. However, the distributing corporation does *not* recognize loss on distributions of property.[13]

EXAMPLE 16

A corporation distributes land (basis of $10,000 and fair market value of $30,000) to a shareholder. The corporation recognizes a gain of $20,000.

EXAMPLE 17

Assume the property in Example 16 has a basis of $30,000 and a fair market value of $10,000. The corporation does not recognize a loss on the distribution.

If the distributed property is subject to a liability in excess of basis or the shareholder assumes such a liability, a special rule applies. The fair market value of the property for purposes of determining gain on the distribution is treated as not being less than the amount of the liability.[14]

EXAMPLE 18

Assume the land in Example 16 is subject to a liability of $35,000. The corporation recognizes gain of $25,000 on the distribution ($35,000 – $10,000). ■

Effect of Corporate Distributions on E & P. Corporate distributions reduce E & P by the amount of money distributed or by the greater of the fair market value or the adjusted basis of property distributed, less the amount of any liability on the property.[15] E & P is increased by gain recognized on appreciated property distributed as a property dividend.

EXAMPLE 19

Crimson Corporation distributes property (basis of $10,000 and fair market value of $20,000) to Brenda, its shareholder. Crimson Corporation recognizes a gain of $10,000, which is added to its E & P. E & P is then reduced by $20,000, the fair market value of the property. Brenda has dividend income of $20,000 (presuming sufficient E & P). ■

EXAMPLE 20

Assume the same facts as in Example 19, except that the property's adjusted basis in the hands of Crimson Corporation is $25,000. Because loss is not recognized and the property's adjusted basis is greater than its fair market value, E & P is reduced by $25,000. Brenda reports dividend income of $20,000 (the fair market value of the property received. ■

EXAMPLE 21

Assume the same facts as in Example 20, except that the property is subject to a liability of $6,000. E & P is now reduced by $19,000 [$25,000 (adjusted basis) – $6,000 (liability)]. Brenda has a dividend of $14,000 [$20,000 (amount of the distribution) – $6,000 (liability)], and her basis in the property is $20,000. ■

Under no circumstances can a distribution, whether cash or property, either generate a deficit in E & P or add to a deficit in E & P. Deficits can arise only through recognized corporate losses.

EXAMPLE 22

Teal Corporation has accumulated E & P of $10,000 at the beginning of the current tax year. During the year, it has current E & P of $15,000. At the end of the year, it distributes cash of $30,000 to its sole shareholder, Walter. Teal's E & P at the end of the year is zero. The accumulated E & P of $10,000 is increased by current E & P of $15,000 and reduced $25,000 by the dividend distribution. The remaining $5,000 of the distribution to Walter does not reduce E & P because a distribution cannot generate a deficit in E & P. ■

---

[13]A corporation contributed appreciated land to a limited partnership in exchange for limited partnership units. The corporation then distributed the limited partnership units to its shareholders. The court treated the corporation as though it had distributed the land, which triggered gain under § 311. *Pope & Talbot, Inc. v. Comm.*, 83 AFTR2d 99–364, 162 F.3d 1236 (CA–9, 1999).

[14]§ 311(b)(2).

[15]§§ 312(a), (b), and (c).

Constructive Dividends

Any measurable economic benefit conveyed by a corporation to its shareholders can be treated as a dividend for Federal income tax purposes even though it is not formally declared or designated as a dividend. A distribution need not be issued pro rata to all shareholders.[16] Nor must the distribution satisfy the legal requirements of a dividend as set forth by applicable state law. This benefit, often described as a **constructive dividend,** is distinguishable from actual corporate distributions of cash and property in form only.

Constructive dividend situations usually arise in closely held corporations. Here, the dealings between the parties are less structured, and frequently, formalities are not preserved. The constructive dividend serves as a substitute for actual distributions. Usually, it is intended to accomplish some tax objective not available through the use of direct dividends. The shareholders may be attempting to distribute corporate profits in a form deductible to the corporation, like compensation.[17] Alternatively, the shareholders may be seeking benefits for themselves while avoiding the recognition of income. Some constructive dividends are, in reality, disguised dividends. But not all constructive dividends are deliberate attempts to avoid actual and formal dividends; many are inadvertent. Thus, an awareness of the various constructive dividend situations is essential to protect the parties from unanticipated, undesirable tax consequences.

TYPES OF CONSTRUCTIVE DIVIDENDS

The most frequently encountered types of constructive dividends are summarized below.

Shareholder Use of Corporate-Owned Property. A constructive dividend can occur when a shareholder uses the corporation's property for personal purposes at no cost. Personal use of corporate-owned automobiles, airplanes, yachts, fishing camps, hunting lodges, and other entertainment facilities is commonplace in some closely held corporations. The shareholder has dividend income to the extent of the fair rental value of the property for the period of its personal use.

Bargain Sale of Corporate Property to a Shareholder. Shareholders often purchase property from a corporation at a cost below the fair market value of the property. These bargain sales produce dividend income to the extent that the property's fair market value on the date of sale differs from the amount the shareholder paid for the property.[18] These situations might be avoided by appraising the property on or about the date of the sale. The appraised value should become the price to be paid by the shareholder.

Bargain Rental of Corporate Property. A bargain rental of corporate property by a shareholder also produces dividend income. Here the measure of the constructive dividend is the excess of the property's fair rental value over the rent actually paid. Again, appraisal data should be used to avoid any questionable situations.

---

[16]See *Lengsfield v. Comm.,* 57–1 USTC ¶9437, 50 AFTR 1683, 241 F.2d 508 (CA–5, 1957).

[17]Recall that dividend distributions do not provide the distributing corporation with an income tax deduction, although they do reduce E & P.

[18]Reg. § 1.301–1(j).

TAX FACT

EXECUTIVE COMPENSATION: AMOUNT AND COMPOSITION

Median executive compensation exceeds $1 million in the following five industries: insurance, communications, telecommunications, energy, and financial services. While stock options accounted for less than 20 percent of a CEO's direct pay in 1980, long-term compensation—mostly from exercised stock options—made up 80 percent of the average CEO's pay package by 1998.

Source: Fay Hansen, "Executive Compensation is Still Rising," *Compensation and Benefits Review*, January 1999, p. 7; Dennis Lyons and Spencer Stuart, "CEO Compensation: The Whole Truth," *Chief Executive*, July 1, 1999, p. 44.

Payments for the Benefit of a Shareholder.   If a corporation pays an obligation of a shareholder, the payment is treated as a constructive dividend. The obligation involved need not be legally binding on the shareholder; it may, in fact, be a moral obligation.[19] Forgiveness of shareholder indebtedness by the corporation creates an identical problem.[20] Excessive rentals paid by a corporation for the use of shareholder property also are treated as constructive dividends.

Unreasonable Compensation.   A salary payment to a shareholder-employee that is deemed to be **unreasonable compensation** is frequently treated as a constructive dividend. As a consequence, it is not deductible by the corporation. In determining the reasonableness of salary payments, the following factors are considered.

- The employee's qualifications.
- A comparison of salaries with dividend distributions.
- The prevailing rates of compensation for comparable positions in comparable business concerns.
- The nature and scope of the employee's work.
- The size and complexity of the business.
- A comparison of salaries paid with both gross and net income.
- The taxpayer's salary policy toward all employees.
- For small corporations with a limited number of officers, the amount of compensation paid the employee in question in previous years.[21]

Loans to Shareholders.   Advances to shareholders that are not bona fide loans are constructive dividends. Whether an advance qualifies as a bona fide loan is a question of fact to be determined in light of the particular circumstances. Factors considered in determining whether the advance is a bona fide loan include the following.[22]

- Whether the advance is on open account or is evidenced by a written instrument.

---

[19]*Montgomery Engineering Co. v. U.S.*, 64–2 USTC ¶9618, 13 AFTR2d 1747, 230 F.Supp. 838 (D.Ct. N.J., 1964), *aff'd* in 65–1 USTC ¶9368, 15 AFTR2d 746, 344 F.2d 996 (CA–3, 1965).
[20]Reg. § 1.301–1(m).

[21]*Mayson Manufacturing Co. v. Comm.*, 49–2 USTC ¶9467, 38 AFTR 1028, 178 F.2d 115 (CA–6, 1949).
[22]*Fin Hay Realty Co. v. U.S.*, 68–2 USTC ¶9438, 22 AFTR2d 5004, 398 F.2d 694 (CA–3, 1968).

HARD WORK PAYS OFF!

By 1985, William Rogers, a pharmacist with 25 years of experience in health care, had successfully developed and sold two businesses—a pharmacy chain and a medical supply company. In 1986, after turning down a $1 million offer to manage the home health care division of a large corporation, Rogers founded Alpha Medical, Inc., with a $1,000 contribution. Over the next four years, Rogers built Alpha Medical into a business with 60 employees, a taxable income of almost $7 million, and a 1990 return on equity of almost 100 percent. The business provided both financial management and medical consulting services to hospitals and home health care companies. Rogers was the company's sole shareholder and president. He regularly worked 12 hours a day and was on call 24 hours a day. Rogers made all major decisions for Alpha Medical, acquired all of the company's clients, and personally negotiated all of the company's contracts. In addition, he personally developed many of the company's products and collaborated with programmers to develop proprietary software used by the company.

In 1986, Rogers received only $67,000 in compensation. The amount increased to $431,000 in 1988 and $928,000 in 1989. In 1990, Rogers was paid over $4.4 million, 64 percent of the company's taxable income, while the company paid only a $1,500 dividend.

During an audit of Alpha Medical, the IRS argued that only $400,000 of Rogers's compensation in 1990 was reasonable and that the remaining $4 million was not deductible. As a result, the IRS assessed a $1.3 million tax deficiency and an accuracy-related penalty.

The Tax Court split the difference between the IRS and the taxpayer, holding that $2.3 million of Rogers's pay was reasonable. On appeal, however, the Sixth Circuit Court of Appeals ruled that all $4.4 million of the compensation paid to Rogers was reasonable. In its decision, the Court of Appeals said that "in light of Rogers's record of accomplishment, risks he assumed, and amazing growth, reasonable shareholders would have gladly agreed to Rogers's level of compensation." The Court of Appeals also explicitly noted that Rogers had been undercompensated in prior years and that he had incurred a substantial opportunity cost when he refused the $1 million job offer so that he could start Alpha Medical.

SOURCE: *Alpha Medical, Inc. v. Comm.*, 99–1 USTC ¶50,461, 83 AFTR2d 99–697, 172 F.3d 942 (CA–6, 1999).

- Whether the shareholder furnished collateral or other security for the advance.
- How long the advance has been outstanding.
- Whether any repayments have been made.
- The shareholder's ability to repay the advance.
- The shareholder's use of the funds (e.g., payment of routine bills versus nonrecurring, extraordinary expenses).
- The regularity of the advances.
- The dividend-paying history of the corporation.

Even when a corporation makes a bona fide loan to a shareholder, a constructive dividend may be triggered, equal to the amount of any imputed (forgone) interest on the loan.[23] Imputed interest equals the amount of interest (using the rate the Federal government pays on new borrowings, compounded semiannually) that exceeds the interest charged on the loan. When the imputed interest provision applies, the shareholder is deemed to have made an interest payment to the corporation equal to the amount of imputed interest, and the corporation is deemed to have repaid the imputed interest to the shareholder through a constructive dividend. As a result, the corporation receives interest income and makes a nondeductible dividend payment, and the shareholder has taxable dividend income that may be offset with an interest deduction.

EXAMPLE 23

Mallard Corporation lends its principal shareholder, Henry, $100,000 on January 2 of the current year. The loan is interest-free and payable on demand. On December 31, the imputed interest rules are applied. Assuming the Federal rate is 6%, compounded semiannually, the amount of imputed interest is $6,090. This amount is deemed paid by Henry to Mallard in the form of interest. Mallard is then deemed to return the amount to Henry as a constructive dividend. Thus, Henry has dividend income of $6,090, which may be offset with a deduction for the interest paid to Mallard. Mallard has interest income of $6,090 for the interest received, with no offsetting deduction for the dividend payment. ■

Loans to a Corporation by Shareholders.   Shareholder loans to a corporation may be reclassified as equity because the debt has too many features of stock. Any interest and principal payments made by the corporation to the shareholder are then treated as constructive dividends. This topic was covered more thoroughly in the discussion of "thin capitalization" in Chapter 9.

TAX TREATMENT OF CONSTRUCTIVE DIVIDENDS

Constructive distributions are treated the same for tax purposes as actual distributions.[24] Thus, a corporate shareholder is entitled to the dividends received deduction (refer to Chapter 9). The constructive distribution is taxable as a dividend only to the extent of the corporation's current and accumulated E & P. The burden of proving that the distribution constitutes a return of capital because of inadequate E & P rests with the taxpayer.[25]

PLANNING CONSIDERATIONS

Constructive Dividends

Tax planning can be particularly effective in avoiding constructive dividend situations. Shareholders should try to structure their dealings with the corporation on an arm's length basis. For example, reasonable rent should be paid for the use of corporate property, and a fair price should be paid for its purchase. The parties should make every effort to support the amount involved with appraisal data or market information obtained from reliable sources at or near the time of the transaction. Dealings between shareholders and a closely held corporation should be as formal as possible. In the case of loans to shareholders, for example, the parties should provide for an adequate rate of interest and written evidence of the debt. Shareholders also should establish and follow a realistic repayment schedule.

---

[23]See § 7872. A more detailed discussion of imputed interest is found in Chapter 3.

[24]*Simon v. Comm.,* 57–2 USTC ¶9989, 52 AFTR 698, 248 F.2d 869 (CA–8, 1957).

[25]*DiZenzo v. Comm.,* 65–2 USTC ¶9518, 16 AFTR2d 5107, 348 F.2d 122 (CA–2, 1965).

If shareholders wish to distribute corporate profits in a form deductible to the corporation, a balanced mix of the possible alternatives lessens the risk of constructive dividend treatment. Rent for the use of shareholder property, interest on amounts borrowed from shareholders, or salaries for services rendered by shareholders are all feasible substitutes for dividend distributions. But overdoing any one approach may attract the attention of the IRS. Too much interest, for example, may mean the corporation is thinly capitalized, and some of the debt may be reclassified as equity.

Much can be done to protect against the disallowance of unreasonable compensation. Example 24 is an illustration, all too common in a family corporation, of what *not* to do.

EXAMPLE 24

Bob Cole wholly owns Eagle Corporation. Corporate employees and annual salaries include Mrs. Cole ($30,000), Cole, Jr. ($20,000), Bob Cole ($160,000), and Ed ($80,000). The operation of Eagle Corporation is shared about equally between Bob Cole and Ed, who is an unrelated party. Mrs. Cole performed significant services for Eagle during its formative years but now merely attends the annual meeting of the board of directors. Cole, Jr., Bob Cole's son, is a full-time student and occasionally signs papers for the corporation in his capacity as treasurer. Eagle Corporation has not distributed a dividend for 10 years, although it has accumulated substantial E & P. Mrs. Cole, Cole, Jr., and Bob Cole run the risk of a finding of unreasonable compensation, based on the following factors.

- Mrs. Cole's salary is vulnerable unless proof is available that some or all of her $30,000 annual salary is payment for services rendered to the corporation in prior years, if she was underpaid for those years.[26]
- Cole, Jr.'s salary is also vulnerable; he does not appear to earn the $20,000 paid to him by the corporation. Although neither Cole, Jr., nor Mrs. Cole is a shareholder, each one's relationship to Bob Cole is enough of a tie-in to raise the unreasonable compensation issue.
- Bob Cole's salary appears susceptible to challenge. Why is he receiving $80,000 more than Ed when it appears that they share equally in the operation of the corporation?
- The fact that Eagle Corporation has not distributed dividends over the past 10 years, even though it is capable of doing so, increases the likelihood of a constructive dividend. ■

What could have been done to improve the tax position of the parties in Example 24? Mrs. Cole and Cole, Jr., are not entitled to a salary as neither seems to be performing any

services for the corporation. Paying them a salary simply aggravates the problem. The IRS is more apt to consider *all* the salaries to members of the family as being excessive under the circumstances. Bob Cole should probably reduce his compensation to correspond to that paid Ed. He can then attempt to distribute corporate earnings to himself in some other form.

Paying some dividends to Bob Cole would also help alleviate the problems raised in Example 24. The IRS has been successful in denying a deduction for salary paid to a shareholder-employee, even when the payment was reasonable, in a situation where the corporation had not distributed any dividends.[27] Most courts, however, have not denied deductions for compensation solely because a dividend was not paid. A better approach is to compare an employee's compensation with the level of compensation prevalent in the particular industry.

The corporation can substitute *indirect* compensation for Bob Cole by paying expenses that benefit him personally but are nevertheless deductible to the corporation. For example, premiums paid by the corporation for sickness, accident, and hospitalization insurance for Bob Cole are deductible to the corporation and generally nontaxable to him.[28] Any payments under the policy are not taxable to Bob Cole unless they exceed his medical expenses.[29] The corporation can also pay for travel and entertainment expenses incurred by Cole on behalf of the corporation. If these expenditures are primarily for the benefit of the corporation, Bob Cole will not recognize any taxable income and the corporation will receive a deduction.[30] The tax treatment of these benefits is discussed in more detail in Chapter 16.

When testing for reasonableness, the IRS looks at the total compensation package, including indirect compensation payments to a shareholder-employee. Thus, indirect payments must not be overlooked.

EXAMPLE 25

Cora, the president and sole shareholder of Willet Corporation, is paid an annual salary of $100,000 by the corporation. Cora would like to draw funds from the corporation but is concerned that additional salary payments might cause the IRS to contend her salary is unreasonable. Cora does not want Willet to pay any dividends. She also wishes to donate $50,000 to her alma mater to establish scholarships for needy students. Willet Corporation could make the

---

[26]See, for example, *R. J. Nicoll Co.*, 59 T.C. 37 (1972).

[27]*McCandless Tile Service v. U.S.*, 70–1 USTC ¶9284, 25 AFTR2d 70–870, 422 F.2d 1336 (Ct.Cls., 1970). The court in *McCandless* concluded that a return on equity of 15% of net profits was reasonable.

[28]Reg. § 1.162–10.

[29]The medical reimbursement plan must meet certain nondiscrimination requirements of § 105(h)(2).

[30]Reg. § 1.62–2(c)(4).

contribution on Cora's behalf. The payment clearly benefits Cora, but the amount of the contribution will not be taxed to her.[31] Willet can take a charitable contribution deduction for the payment. ∎

EXAMPLE 26

Assume in Example 25 that Cora has made an individual pledge to the university to provide $50,000 for scholarships for needy students. Willet Corporation satisfies Cora's pledge by paying the $50,000 to

the university. The $50,000 will be taxed to Cora.[32] In this context, the $50,000 payment to the university may be treated as *indirect* compensation to Cora. In determining whether Cora's salary is unreasonable, both the *direct* payment of $100,000 and the *indirect* $50,000 payment will be considered. Cora's total compensation package is $150,000. Cora may be eligible for a charitable contribution deduction, up to 50% of her adjusted gross income. However, the phase-out of itemized deductions for high-income individuals may limit the deduction. ∎

LEARNING OBJECTIVE 6

Distinguish between taxable and nontaxable stock dividends.

Stock Dividends

As a general rule, **stock dividends** are excluded from income if they are pro rata distributions of stock or stock rights, paid on common stock.[33] However, there are five exceptions to this general rule. These exceptions to nontaxability of stock dividends deal with various disproportionate distribution situations.

1 *Find more information on this topic at our Web site: **http://wft-entities.swcollege.com**.*

If a stock dividend is not taxable, the corporation's E & P is not reduced.[34] If a stock dividend is taxable, the distributing corporation treats the distribution in the same manner as any other taxable property dividend.

If a stock dividend is taxable, the basis of the newly received shares to the shareholder-distributee is fair market value, and the holding period starts on the date of receipt. If a stock dividend is not taxable, the basis of the stock on which the dividend is distributed is reallocated.[35] If the dividend shares are identical to these formerly held shares, basis in the old stock is reallocated by dividing the taxpayer's cost in the old stock by the total number of shares. If the dividend stock is not identical to the underlying shares (e.g., a stock dividend of preferred on common), basis is determined by allocating the basis of the formerly held shares between the old and new stock according to the fair market value of each. The holding period includes the holding period of the previously held stock.[36]

EXAMPLE 27

Gail bought 1,000 shares of stock two years ago for $10,000. In the current tax year, Gail receives 10 shares of common stock as a nontaxable stock dividend. Gail's basis of $10,000 is divided by 1,010. Consequently, each share of stock has a basis of $9.90 instead of the pre-dividend $10 basis. ∎

EXAMPLE 28

Assume instead, Gail received a nontaxable preferred stock dividend of 100 shares. The preferred stock has a fair market value of $1,000, and the common stock, on which the preferred is distributed, has a fair market value of $19,000. After the receipt of the stock dividend, the basis of the common stock is $9,500, and the basis of the preferred is $500, computed as follows.

---

[31]*Henry J. Knott*, 67 T.C. 681 (1977).
[32]*Schalk Chemical Co. v. Comm.*, 62–1 USTC ¶9496, 9 AFTR2d 1579, 304 F.2d 48 (CA–9, 1962).
[33]Companies often issue stock dividends or authorize stock splits in order to keep the stock price in an affordable range. Stock splits do not change the total value of an investment. For example, 100

shares at $100 will become 200 shares at $50 after the split. However, some studies show that a stock split often leads to an upward price trend over the year following the split.
[34]§ 312(d)(1).
[35]§ 307(a).
[36]§ 1223(5).

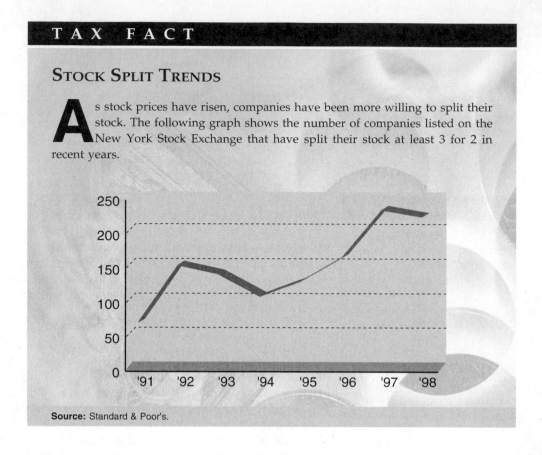

TAX FACT

STOCK SPLIT TRENDS

As stock prices have risen, companies have been more willing to split their stock. The following graph shows the number of companies listed on the New York Stock Exchange that have split their stock at least 3 for 2 in recent years.

Source: Standard & Poor's.

Fair market value of common	$19,000
Fair market value of preferred	1,000
	$20,000
Basis of common: $\frac{19}{20} \times \$10,000$	$ 9,500
Basis of preferred: $\frac{1}{20} \times \$10,000$	$ 500

2 *Find more information on this topic at our Web site: http://wft-entities.swcollege.com.*

Stock Redemptions

Many investors are tempted to use a "no dividends" strategy in working with a healthy corporation whose accumulated profits and market value continue to rise over time.

EXAMPLE 29

Sally invests $100,000 in the new Cream Corporation. Cream is successful in generating operating profits, and it reinvests its accumulated profits in the business rather than paying dividends. Fifteen years later, Sally's shares are worth $300,000, and her share of Cream's E & P exceeds $1 million. Sally sells the shares for a $200,000 long-term capital gain, taxed at a rate of only 20%, not at the higher marginal tax rate that Sally would use if she had received ordinary income from Cream in the form of a dividend. By using a capital asset transaction, Sally seems to have converted ordinary income to long-term capital gain, resulting in a significant tax savings to her, at no detriment to Cream. ∎

A similar strategy would seem to convert ordinary income into tax-favored long-term capital gain where several shareholders can act in concert. Using a **stock redemption** to carry out this strategy, the corporation buys back shares from its shareholders in a market transaction.

EXAMPLE 30

Mike and Cheryl are husband and wife, and each owns 100 shares in Mauve Corporation, the total of all of Mauve's outstanding stock. Mauve's operations have produced a sizable aggregated operating profit over the years, such that its E & P exceeds $5 million. Mike and Cheryl both have a realized gain of $600,000 on their original investment of $100,000 each, and they would like to enjoy some of the cash that Mauve has accumulated during their holding period. At Mike's request, instead of paying a dividend which would be taxed at his 36% marginal tax rate, Mauve buys back one-half of Mike's shares for $350,000. This seems to produce a $300,000 long-term capital gain [$350,000 (sales proceeds) – $50,000 (basis in 50 shares of Mauve stock)], rather than a $350,000 dividend for Mike. ∎

Stock redemptions, however, generally result in dividend income for the shareholder whose stock is redeemed, rather than a capital asset transaction, unless the shareholder surrenders significant control in the entity as a result of the redemption. Section 302 allows capital asset treatment where either:

- All of the shareholder's stock is redeemed.[37]
- The investor is a minority shareholder after the redemption and surrendered at least 20 percent of his or her holdings in the transaction.[38]

3 *Find more information on this topic at our Web site: **http://wft-entities.swcollege.com**.*

When the transaction is treated as a dividend, the investor's basis in the redeemed shares *does not disappear* but attaches to any remaining shares that he or she owns.

Other provisions also allow capital asset treatment for a stock redemption.[39] In measuring the investor's stock holdings before and after the redemption, shares owned by related taxpayers also are counted.[40]

4 *Find more information on this topic at our Web site: **http://wft-entities.swcollege.com**.*

Stock redemptions occur for numerous reasons, including the following.

- To acquire the holdings of a retiring or deceased shareholder.
- To carry out a property settlement related to a divorce.
- To increase the per-share price of the stock as it trades in a market.

The tax consequences for the redeeming corporation are summarized as follows.

- If noncash property is used to acquire the redeemed shares, the corporation recognizes any realized gain (but not loss) on the distributed assets.[41]
- E & P of the redeeming corporation *disappears* to the extent of the number of shares redeemed as a percentage of the shares outstanding before the buyback.[42]

---

[37]§ 302(b)(3).
[38]§ 302(b)(2).
[39]For example, see §§ 302(b)(1), 302(b)(4), and 303.

[40]§ 318 is used for this purpose.
[41]§ 311.
[42]§ 312(n)(7).

TAX IN THE NEWS

STOCK REDEMPTIONS, DIVORCE, AND TAX AVOIDANCE

Under § 1041, property transfers pursuant to a divorce result in (1) nonrecognition of gain (loss) to the transferor and (2) no gross income and a carryover basis in the property to the transferee. Two court cases illustrate the importance of tax planning in divorce proceedings. In *Carol M. Read* [114 T.C. 14 (2000)] and *Linda K. B. Craven* [2000–2 USTC ¶50,541, 85 AFTR2d 2229, 215 F.3d 1201 (CA–11, 2000)], a family-owned corporation redeemed all the stock of a taxpayer pursuant to the terms of a divorce decree. Such transactions typically result in recognized gain to the shareholder. However, the courts held that the redemptions were transfers pursuant to a divorce and on behalf of the taxpayers' former spouses. As such, the stock redemptions were tax-free to the taxpayers under § 1041.

Thus, a dividend likely results in Example 30. The strategy illustrated in Example 29, though, can be effective in avoiding dividend income and converting it instead into a tax-favored long-term capital gain. To restrict the taxpayer's ability to avoid dividend treatment, the taxes discussed in the following section were enacted.

Restrictions on Corporate Accumulations

Two provisions of the Code are designed to prevent corporations and their shareholders from avoiding the double tax on dividend distributions. Both provisions impose a penalty tax on undistributed income retained by the corporation. The rules underlying these provisions are complex and beyond the scope of this text. However, a brief description is provided as an introduction.

The *accumulated earnings tax* (in §§ 531–537) imposes a 39.6 percent tax on the current year's corporate earnings that have been accumulated without a reasonable business need. The burden of proving what constitutes a reasonable need is borne by the taxpayer. In determining accumulated income, most businesses are allowed a $250,000 minimum credit. Thus, most corporations can accumulate $250,000 in earnings over a series of years without fear of an accumulated earnings tax. Beyond the minimum credit, earnings can be accumulated for:

- Working capital needs (to purchase inventory),
- Retirement of debt incurred in connection with the business,
- Investment or loans to suppliers or customers (if necessary to maintain the corporation's business), or
- Realistic business contingencies, including lawsuits or self-insurance.

The *personal holding company (PHC) tax* (described in §§ 541–547) was enacted to discourage the sheltering of certain kinds of passive income in corporations owned by individuals with high marginal tax rates. Historically, the tax was aimed at "incorporated pocketbooks" that were frequently found in the entertainment and construction industries. For example, a taxpayer could shelter income from securities in a corporation, which would pay no dividends, and allow the corporation's stock to increase in value. Like the accumulated earnings tax, the PHC tax employs a 39.6 percent rate and is designed to force a corporation to distribute

earnings to shareholders. However, in any single year, the IRS cannot impose both the PHC tax and the accumulated earnings tax. Generally, a company is considered a PHC and may be subject to the tax if:

- More than 50 percent of the value of the outstanding stock was owned by five or fewer individuals at any time during the last half of the year, and
- A substantial portion (60 percent or more) of the corporation's income is composed of passive types of income, including dividends, interest, rents, royalties, or certain personal service income.

Suggested Further Readings

Stephanie Heilborn, "Taxpayer Who Diverted Income from Corporation with no Earnings and Profits Not Guilty of Criminal Tax Evasion: *United States v. D'Agostino*," *The Tax Lawyer*, Winter 1999, pp. 407–415.

Edward J. Schnee, "Calculating Gain on Corporate Distributions," *Journal of Accountancy*, December 1, 1999, p. 90.

KEY TERMS

Accumulated earnings and profits, 10–4	Earnings and profits (E & P), 10–3	Stock dividends, 10–21
Constructive dividend, 10–16	Property dividend, 10–11	Stock redemption, 10–23
Current earnings and profits, 10–4		Unreasonable compensation, 10–17

Problem Materials

PROBLEMS

1. At the start of the current year, Swan Corporation (a calendar year taxpayer) has accumulated E & P of $200,000. Its current E & P is $60,000. During the year, Swan distributes $280,000 ($140,000 each) to its equal shareholders, George and Albert. George has a basis of $48,000 in his stock, and Albert has a basis of $8,000 in his stock. How is the distribution treated for tax purposes?

2. During the year, Vireo Corporation received dividend income of $300,000 from a corporation in which it holds a 10% interest. Vireo also received interest income of $50,000 from municipal bonds. The municipality used the proceeds from the sale of the bonds to construct a needed facility to house county documents and to provide office space for several county officials. Vireo borrowed funds to purchase the municipal bonds and paid $25,000 in interest on the loan this year. Vireo's taxable income exclusive of the items noted above was $225,000.
   a. What is Vireo Corporation's taxable income after considering the dividend income, the interest from the municipal bonds, and the interest paid on the indebtedness to purchase the municipals?

b. What is Vireo Corporation's E & P as of December 31 if its E & P account balance was $80,000 as of January 1?

3. In 1993, Beige Corporation made a cash distribution to its shareholders, one of whom was Steve Jordan. At that time, the parties involved believed that the distribution was a return of capital because Beige had no E & P. Accordingly, none of the shareholders reported dividend income. In Steve's case, he reduced the $200,000 original basis of his stock investment by $40,000, his share of the distribution. In 2000, it is discovered that E & P had been incorrectly computed. The 1993 distribution was fully covered by E & P and *should not have been treated as a return of capital.*

   In 2001, Steve sells his stock in Beige Corporation for $350,000. He plans to report a gain of $150,000 [$350,000 (selling price) − $200,000 (original basis)] on the sale. Although Steve realizes that he should have recognized dividend income of $40,000 for 1993, the statute of limitations has made this a closed year.

   Comment on Steve's situation.

4. On November 15, 2001, Red Corporation sold a parcel of land. The land had a basis of $350,000, and Red received a $900,000 note as consideration in the sale. The note is to be paid in five installments, the first of which is due on December 15, 2002. Because Red did not elect out of the installment method, none of the $550,000 gain is included in taxable income for 2001.

   Red Corporation had a deficit in accumulated E & P of $280,000 on January 1, 2001. For 2001, before considering the effect of the land sale, Red had a deficit in current E & P of $120,000.

   Buck, the sole shareholder in Red, has a basis of $100,000 in his stock. If Red distributes $300,000 to Buck on December 31, 2001, how much gross income must Buck report on the distribution for tax purposes?

5. In determining Oriole Corporation's current E & P for 2001, how should taxable income be adjusted by the following transactions?
   a. Sale of land on installment in 2001, with the first payment due in 2002.
   b. A capital loss carryover from 2000 fully used in 2001.
   c. Excess charitable contributions carried forward to 2002.
   d. Gain deferred in a qualifying involuntary conversion that occurred in 2001.
   e. Federal income taxes paid in 2001.
   f. Section 179 expenses elected and deducted in 1999.

6. Gadwall Corporation is a calendar year taxpayer. At the beginning of the current year, Gadwall has accumulated E & P of $350,000. The corporation incurs a current E & P deficit of $400,000 that accrues ratably throughout the year. On September 30, Gadwall distributes $200,000 to its sole individual shareholder, Richard. If Richard has a basis in his stock of $15,000, how is the distribution taxed to him?

7. Complete the following schedule. For each case, assume the shareholder has ample basis in the stock investment.

	Accumulated E & P Beginning of Year	Current E & P	Cash Distributions (All on Last Day of Year)	Amount Taxable	Return of Capital
a.	$ 100,000	($ 30,000)	$150,000	$	$
b.	(200,000)	40,000	90,000		
c.	90,000	140,000	220,000		
d.	140,000	(60,000)	120,000		
e.	Same as (d), except the distribution of $120,000 is made on June 30 and the corporation uses the calendar year for tax purposes.				

8. Complete the following schedule. For each case, assume that there is one shareholder whose basis in the corporate stock is $20,000. Any current losses accrue ratably throughout the year.

	Accumulated E & P Beginning of Year	Current E & P	Cash Distributions (All on Last Day of Year)	Amount Taxable	Capital Gain
a.	($ 100,000)	$120,000	$150,000	$ _____	$ _____
b.	70,000	30,000	110,000	_____	_____
c.	(100,000)	80,000	70,000	_____	_____
d.	210,000	(160,000)	90,000	_____	_____
e.	Same as (d), except the distribution of $90,000 is made on June 30 and the corporation uses the calendar year for tax purposes.			_____	_____

9. Carrie Lynn, the sole shareholder of Junco Corporation, had a basis of $50,000 in Junco stock that she sold to Rajib on July 30 for $200,000. Junco had accumulated E & P of $95,000 on January 1 and current E & P of $80,000. During the year, Junco made the following distributions: $150,000 of cash to Carrie Lynn on July 1, and $150,000 of cash to Rajib on December 30. How will the distributions be taxed to Carrie Lynn and Rajib? What gain will Carrie Lynn recognize on the sale of her stock to Rajib?

10. In each of the following *independent* situations, indicate the effect on taxable income and E & P, stating the amount of any increase (or decrease) as a result of the transaction. Assume E & P has already been increased by the taxable amount.

	Transaction	Taxable Income Increase (Decrease)	E & P Increase (Decrease)
a.	Recognition of $20,000 gain from payment received on installment note from sale in prior year.	_____	_____
b.	Payment of $27,000 in Federal income taxes.	_____	_____
c.	$8,000 in premiums paid for insurance on corporate officer's life. As a result of premium payment, cash surrender value of policy increased $500.	_____	_____
d.	Capital loss, $43,000. No capital gains were recognized in the current year.	_____	_____
e.	Disallowed portion (50%) of meals and entertainment expenses, $8,500.	_____	_____
f.	Realized gain on involuntary conversion of $175,000 ($25,000 of gain is recognized).	_____	_____

11. In each of the following *independent* situations, indicate the effect on taxable income and E & P, stating the amount of any increase (or decrease) as a result of the transaction. Assume E & P has already been increased by the taxable income.

Transaction	Taxable Income Increase (Decrease)	E & P Increase (Decrease)
a. Sale of unimproved real estate to the sole shareholder of the corporation at a realized loss of $40,000.		
b. Intangible drilling costs incurred on May 1 of the current year; $30,000 is deductible from current-year taxable income.		
c. Sale of unimproved real estate to unrelated third party; basis is $200,000, fair market value is $400,000 (no election out of installment method; payments in year of sale total $100,000).		
d. Dividends of $10,000 received from 10%-owned corporation, together with dividends received deduction (assume taxable income limit does not apply).		
e. Realized gain of $150,000 from qualifying like-kind exchange ($30,000 of gain is recognized).		
f. Section 179 expense deduction of $12,000 in current year.		
g. Impact of current-year § 179 expense deduction in succeeding year.		
h. MACRS depreciation of $80,000. ADS depreciation would have been $50,000.		
i. A $60,000 refund of Federal income taxes paid in previous year.		

12. Vireo Corporation distributes property (basis of $120,000, fair market value of $160,000) to its sole shareholder, Pete. The property is subject to a liability of $195,000, which Pete assumes. Vireo has E & P of $210,000 prior to the distribution.
    a. What gain, if any, does Vireo recognize on the distribution?
    b. What is the amount of Pete's dividend income on the distribution?

13. Penguin Corporation, with E & P of $500,000, distributes land worth $110,000, adjusted basis of $150,000, to Orca, a corporate shareholder. The land is subject to a liability of $30,000, which Orca assumes.
    a. What is the amount of dividend income to Orca?
    b. What is Orca's basis in the land it received?
    c. How does the distribution affect Penguin Corporation's E & P account?

14. At the beginning of the current year, Dove Corporation (a calendar year taxpayer) has accumulated E & P of $40,000. During the year, Dove incurs a $30,000 loss from operations that accrued ratably. On July 1, Dove distributes $35,000 in cash to Marv, its sole shareholder. How will the $35,000 be taxed to Marv?

15. Amethyst Corporation pays its president and sole shareholder, Fiona, an annual salary of $300,000. Fiona wishes to avoid dividends because of the presumed double tax on Amethyst's income. She is concerned that if she were to receive any more salary, the

IRS might treat it as a constructive dividend. Each year, Fiona gives her favorite charity $50,000. This year, if she makes a pledge for the usual amount, would Fiona have a problem if Amethyst paid the pledge on her behalf? Explain.

16. Gold Corporation distributes land with an adjusted basis of $100,000 and a fair market value of $60,000 to its shareholder, Homer. What are the tax consequences to Gold Corporation and to Homer?

17. Copper Corporation has two equal shareholders, Cybil and Sally. Cybil acquired her Copper stock three years ago by transferring property worth $600,000, basis of $200,000, for 60 shares of the stock. Sally acquired 60 shares in Copper Corporation two years ago by transferring property worth $620,000, basis of $70,000. Copper Corporation's accumulated E & P as of January 1 of the current year is $300,000. On March 1 of the current year, the corporation distributed to Cybil property worth $100,000, basis to Copper of $30,000. It distributed cash of $200,000 to Sally. On July 1 of the current year, Sally sold her stock to Dana for $800,000. On December 1 of the current year, Copper distributed cash of $80,000 each to Dana and to Cybil. What are the tax issues?

18. Redwing Corporation is a closely held company with accumulated E & P of $500,000 and current E & P of $55,000. Mike and Royce are brothers, and each owns a 50% share in Redwing. On a day-to-day basis, Mike and Royce share management responsibilities equally. What are the tax consequences of the following independent transactions involving Redwing, Mike, and Royce? How does each transaction affect Redwing's E & P?
    a. Redwing sells a parking lot (adjusted basis $33,000, fair market value $18,000) to Mike for $5,000.
    b. Redwing lends Royce $200,000 on July 1 of this year. The loan, evidenced by a note, is due on demand. No interest is charged on the loan. The current applicable Federal interest rate is 9%.
    c. Redwing owns a yacht in Miami, Florida. It rents the yacht to vacationers throughout the year. During the current year, Mike and Royce each use the yacht for one month and pay no rent to Redwing. The rental value of the yacht is $7,500 per week. Mike has indicated that the average maintenance cost per week for the rental is $500.
    d. Mike leases equipment to Redwing for $20,000 per year. If the corporation were to lease the same equipment from another company, the rent would be $13,000.

19. Whether compensation paid to a corporate employee is reasonable is a question of fact to be determined from the surrounding circumstances. How would the resolution of this problem be affected by each of the following factors?
    a. The employee is not a shareholder but is related to the sole owner of the corporate employer.
    b. The shareholder-employee never completed high school.
    c. The shareholder-employee is a full-time college student.
    d. The shareholder-employee was underpaid for her services during the formative period of the corporate employer.
    e. The corporate employer pays only a nominal dividend each year.
    f. Year-end bonuses are paid to all shareholder-employees, but not to non-shareholder-employees.

20. Plover Corporation has beginning E & P of $51,000. Its current-year taxable income is $320,000. On December 31, Plover distributed business property worth $100,000, adjusted basis of $300,000, to Lea, its sole shareholder. Lea assumes an $80,000 liability on the property. Included in the determination of Plover's current taxable income is $10,000 of income recognized from an installment sale in a previous year. In addition, the corporation incurred a Federal income tax liability of $108,050, paid life insurance premiums of $2,000, and received term life insurance proceeds of $46,400 on the death of an officer in the current year.
    a. What is the amount of taxable income to Lea?
    b. What is the E & P of Plover Corporation after the property distribution?

    c. What is Lea's tax basis in the property received?

    d. How would your answers to (a) and (b) change if Plover had sold the property at its fair market value, used $80,000 of the proceeds to pay off the liability, and then distributed the remaining cash and any tax savings to Lea?

21. Verdigris Corporation owns 25% of the stock of Rust Corporation. Rust Corporation, with E & P of $150,000 on December 20, distributes land with a fair market value of $60,000 and a basis of $90,000 to Verdigris. The land is subject to a liability of $50,000, which Verdigris assumes.

    a. How is Verdigris Corporation taxed on the distribution?

    b. What is Rust Corporation's E & P after the distribution?

22. At the beginning of its taxable year, Bunting Corporation had E & P of $175,000. Bunting Corporation sold an asset at a loss of $175,000 on June 30. Bunting incurred a deficit in current E & P of $195,000, which includes the $175,000 loss on the sale of the asset, for the calendar year. Assume Bunting made a distribution of $40,000 to its sole individual shareholder on July 1. How will the shareholder be taxed on the $40,000?

23. Becard Corporation is a calendar year taxpayer. At the beginning of the current year, Becard had a deficit in accumulated E & P of $120,000. Its net profits for the period January 1 through September 30 were $150,000, but its E & P for the entire taxable year was only $10,000. Becard made a distribution of $30,000 to its sole individual shareholder on December 31. How will the shareholder be taxed on the distribution?

24. Your client, Cormorant Corporation, declares a dividend permitting its common stockholders to elect to receive 8 shares of cumulative preferred stock or 2 additional shares of common stock for every 10 shares of common stock currently held. Cormorant currently has only common stock outstanding, with a fair market value of $50 per share. Two shareholders elect to receive preferred stock, and all the remaining shareholders elect to receive common stock. Cormorant asks you whether the shareholders must recognize any taxable income on the receipt of the stock. Prepare a letter to Cormorant and a memo to the file. Cormorant's address is 6730 Pima Drive, Madison, WI 53708.

25. Hiro purchased 5,000 shares of Canary Corporation common stock five years ago for $25,000. In the current year, Hiro receives a nontaxable preferred stock dividend of 250 shares. The preferred stock has a fair market value of $5,000. Hiro's common stock in Canary has a fair market value of $45,000. What is Hiro's basis in the preferred and common stock after the stock dividend is received?

26. Sarah Beckert bought 3,000 shares of Grebe Corporation stock two years ago for $10,000. Last year, Sarah received a nontaxable stock dividend of 1,000 shares in Grebe. In the current tax year, Sarah sold all of the stock received as a dividend for $8,000. Prepare a letter to Sarah and a memo to the file describing the tax consequences of the stock sale. Sarah's address is 1822 N. Sarnoff Road, Tucson, AZ 85710.

 **EXTENDER**

27. Lark Corporation declares a nontaxable dividend payable in rights to subscribe to common stock. One right and $60 entitle the holder to subscribe to one share of stock. One right is issued for each share of stock owned. At the date of distribution of the rights, the market value of the stock was $80 per share, and the market value of the rights was $20 per right. Karen, a shareholder, owns 100 shares of stock that she purchased two years ago for $3,000. Karen received 100 rights, of which she exercises 60 to purchase 60 additional shares. She sells the remaining 40 rights for $750. What are the tax consequences of these transactions to Karen?

28. Partridge Corporation has accumulated E & P of $300,000 as of January 1 of the current year. It expects to have earnings from operations of $240,000 and to make a cash

distribution of $180,000 during the year. Partridge Corporation also expects to sell an asset for a loss of $300,000. Thus, it anticipates incurring a current E & P deficit of $60,000 for the year. What can Partridge do to cause its shareholders to have the least amount of dividend income?

29. Shonda owns 110 shares of the 200 outstanding shares of Hawk Corporation. Shonda paid $1,000 per share for the stock five years ago. The remaining Hawk stock is owned by several unrelated individuals. In the current year, Hawk redeems 20 of Shonda's shares for $60,000 ($3,000 per share). Hawk's E & P at the time of the redemption was $200,000.
    a. How does Shonda report the $60,000?
    b. What is Shonda's basis in her remaining shares?
    c. What is Hawk's E & P after the redemption?

EXTENDER

30. Stork Corporation has 1,000 shares of common stock outstanding. The shares are owned as follows.

    • Leo Jones, 700 shares

    • Lori Johnson, 100 shares

    • Lana Pierce, 200 shares

    Lori is Lana's mother. Leo is not related to the two other shareholders. Stork redeems 100 of Lana's shares for $45,000. Lana paid $100 per share for her stock two years ago. On the date of the redemption, Stork's E & P was $400,000.
    Prepare a memo to the tax research file and a letter to Lana (1000 Main Street, Oldtown, MN 55166) outlining the tax effects of the redemption to her.

EXTENDER

31. In the current year, Red Corporation transfers land to Adair's estate to carry out a redemption treated under § 303. The redeemed stock represents 20% of the corporation's total outstanding shares. Information about the transaction includes the following.

    • Red's E & P is $4 million.

    • Basis of the land to Red is $1.2 million.

    • Value of the land on the redemption date is $1 million.

    The estate sold the land for $1 million nine months after receiving it. The estate incurred $2 million in estate taxes and in funeral and administration expenses. Detail the tax consequences to the estate and to Red Corporation attributable to these events.

EXTENDER

32. Teal Corporation's 100 shares of outstanding common stock are held equally by Ann and Bonnie. The shareholders are not related to each other. Each paid $1,000 per share for the Teal stock 10 years ago. Teal shows $20,000 of current E & P and $100,000 of accumulated E & P. Teal distributes $80,000 of cash to Ann in exchange for 25 of her shares.
    a. What are the tax consequences of the exchange for Ann?
    b. What is Teal's E & P balance after the exchange?

BRIDGE DISCIPLINE

1. Using an online research service, find the audited financial statements of five major U.S. corporations, each in a different operating industry (e.g., manufacturing, energy, financial services, health care).
    a. Compute the total return on each corporation's stock for the past two years.
    b. Compute the dividend yield of the stock for the past two years.

RESEARCH PROBLEMS

Note: Solutions to Research Problems can be prepared by using the **RIA Checkpoint® Student Version Online research product,** *or the* **CCH U.S. Master Tax Guide Plus**™ *online Federal tax research database, which is available to accompany this text. It is also possible to prepare solutions to the Research Problems by using tax research materials found in a standard tax library.*

Research Problem 1. Spifficar, Inc., owns and operates several car washes in Tucson, Arizona. A married couple, Joe and Simone Simpson, are the sole shareholders of Spifficar, and they have been your clients for the last decade. Over the course of several years, Joe and Simone made weekly deposits of their receipts from the car washes to corporate and personal bank accounts. In a recent phone conversation with Joe, he told you some very disturbing news. It turns out that the Simpsons regularly took a portion of the weekly collections home rather than depositing them at the bank. These amounts were hidden in shoe boxes under the Simpsons' bed and were not reported as taxable income by them. The total hidden under their bed amounts to approximately $250,000. Joe says that the IRS notified them that criminal tax evasion charges under § 7201 are being brought against them. The IRS believes that the Simpsons' actions provide prima facie evidence that they intended to defraud the government.

As Joe and Simone's accountant, you recognize that Spifficar has a deficit in its current and accumulated E & P accounts and that a deficit has existed over the period at issue with the IRS. In addition, your records indicate that the Simpsons' basis in the Spifficar stock is $300,000 (before taking into consideration the money hidden under their bed). You believe that these facts may have some bearing on the evasion charges being made against them. Investigate the tax law related to this situation and prepare a letter to the Simpsons' attorney reporting the results of your research. Their attorney is Monty Davis, 1212 S. Camino Seco, Tucson, AZ 85710.

Research Problem 2. Your client, Preston Legal Sevices, Inc. (PLS), was formed in 1989 by Julie Preston with a capital contribution of $1,000. PLS is a law firm specializing in product liability litigation. Since its formation, the company has been principally involved in one class action lawsuit. In 1999, a $40 million settlement was finally reached in the suit. As part of the settlement, the court awarded $6 million of legal fees to PLS, to be paid between 1999 and 2001. Julie is the only attorney employed by PLS and its sole shareholder. In addition, the corporation employs a secretary. A summary of the company's financial situation for 1999 and 2000 is provided below.

	1999	2000
Legal fees received	$ 4,000,000	$ 1,500,000
Compensation to Preston	(1,900,000)	(1,450,000)
Other expenses	(100,000)	(50,000)
Taxable income	$ 2,000,000	$ –0–
Approximate Federal tax paid	(700,000)	–0–
Cash for future expenses	$ 1,300,000	$ –0–

Every year since the corporation's formation, the board of directors has held an annual meeting to establish the level of compensation to be paid to Julie. The typical formula used by the board sets compensation equal to the legal fees she earned on behalf of PLS, less expenses and funds needed for future operations.

In 2001, PLS expects to receive the remaining $500,000 in legal fees from the class action lawsuit. No other revenues will be received during the year. At the 2001 board meeting, Julie proposes that her salary be set at $2.5 million. She suggests that the salary payment be funded by (1) the legal fees to be received in 2001, (2) the $1.3 million cash balance remaining in the corporation (there is no longer any anticipated need for the cash), and (3) the $700,000 tax refund that PLS will receive as a result of the $2 million net operating loss [$500,000 (legal fees) – $2,500,000 (compensation expense)] generated in 2001 and carried back to 1999. To help the corporation's cash flow, Julie further proposes that she loan the corporation $700,000 until the tax refund is received. As the company's tax adviser, you have been asked to ascertain the tax consequences of the plan. Prepare a letter to Julie reporting on the results of your research. Her address is 1803 E. Monroe Street, Madison, WI 53706. When drafting your letter, remember that Julie is an attorney and she prefers that you provide her with legal authority supporting your conclusions.

Research Problem 3. Aqua Corporation wholly owns Egret Corporation. Aqua formed Egret four years ago with the transfer of several assets to the corporation, together with a substantial amount of cash. Aqua's basis in Egret stock is $5.5 million. Since it was formed, Egret has been a very profitable software company and currently has accumulated E & P of $4 million. The company's principal assets are software patents currently worth $5 million and cash and marketable securities of approximately $4.5 million (a total fair market value of $9.5 million).

Aqua and Egret are members of an affiliated group and have made the election under § 243(b) so that Aqua is entitled to a 100% dividends received deduction. From a strategic perspective, Aqua is no longer interested in the software industry and so is considering a sale of Egret. In anticipation of a sale in the next year or two, the management of Aqua has contacted you for advice. If Egret is sold outright, then Aqua Corporation will have a capital gain of $4 million ($9.5 million fair market value less a basis of $5.5 million). As an alternative, it has been suggested that taxes on a future sale would be minimized if Egret pays Aqua a dividend (using existing cash and securities) equal to its E & P. With the 100% dividends received deduction, this payment would be a tax-free transfer from Egret to Aqua. Subsequent to the dividend payment, Egret could be sold for its remaining value of $5.5 million ($5 million in software patents plus $500,000 in cash), generating no additional loss or gain to Aqua.

a. Prepare a letter to the president of Aqua Corporation describing the results of your research on the proposed plan. The president's name and address is Bill Gateson, 601 Pittsfield Dr., Champaign, IL 61821.

b. Prepare a memo for your firm's client files.

Partial list of research aids:
Waterman Steamship Corp. v. Comm., 70–2 USTC ¶9514, 26 AFTR2d 70–5185, 430 F.2d 1185 (CA–5, 1970).

Research Problem 4. Corey Gray is the sole shareholder and CEO of NetBiz, Inc., an information systems and e-commerce consulting firm. NetBiz and Corey have been your clients since NetBiz started business six years ago. NetBiz has corporate offices in San Jose and San Francisco, California. Corey lives between the two offices, in Palo Alto. On a typical day, Corey works about 14 hours. Excluding commuting, he averages 200 business miles per day, traveling back and forth between the two offices and to clients.

Corey personally owns two cars: a 1999 Saab 9-5 and a Ford Expedition. Corey's wife usually drives the Expedition, while Corey drives the Saab. During a lunch with Corey in January of this year, he mentioned that NetBiz had just purchased a new exotic car (a Ferrari 550 Maranello) at a price of $235,000 for his use. During lunch, Corey indicated that NetBiz purchased the Ferrari as a "promotional tool" to help him acquire new business. The company had considered renting a Ferrari when needed (instead of purchasing one), but no auto agencies in the Bay area rent Ferrari 550s.

In early December, you met with Corey to discuss a variety of year-end tax planning issues. At that time, Corey said that he had driven the car only about 5,000 miles (about half for business) since it was acquired. He attributed the low usage to his belief that the Ferrari might seem ostentatious to many of his clients, who have modest incomes. After questioning Corey further, you discovered that his use of the Ferrari was confined to occasional commutes to work, trips to meetings with large corporate clients, or trips to the dealership for maintenance (NetBiz spent about $9,500 on maintenance this year for the car and plans to use MACRS depreciation). When the Ferrari was not being driven, Corey kept it garaged at home.

After reflecting on your meeting with Corey, you have decided that there are two tax issues associated with the Ferrari. Determine (a) whether the expenses associated with the Ferrari will be deductible by NetBiz and (b) the value of the constructive dividend received by Corey.

 Use the tax resources of the Internet to address the following questions. Do not restrict your search to the World Wide Web, but include a review of newsgroups and general reference materials, practitioner sites and resources, primary sources of the tax law, chat rooms and discussion groups, and other opportunities.

Research Problem 5.   Just how common are dividend distributions? Are dividends concentrated in the companies traded on the New York Stock Exchange, or do closely held corporations pay dividends with the same frequency and at the same rates? Financial institutions and observers are acutely interested in these issues. Search for comments on such questions at various commercial Web sites as well as one or two academic journals or newsgroups.

Research Problem 6.   The last few years have seen the rise of a new security, called "trust preferred stock." Search for Web sites dealing with trust preferred stock. Briefly describe the security and identify its key tax and financial reporting characteristics.

Partnerships and Limited Liability Entities

LEARNING OBJECTIVES

After completing Chapter 11, you should be able to:

1. Discuss governing principles and theories of partnership taxation.

2. Describe the tax effects of forming a partnership with cash and property contributions.

3. Examine the tax treatment of expenditures of a newly formed partnership and identify elections available to the partnership.

4. Calculate partnership taxable income and describe how partnership items affect a partner's income tax return.

5. Determine a partner's basis in the partnership interest.

6. Describe the limitations on deducting partnership losses.

7. Review the treatment of transactions between a partner and the partnership.

8. Describe the application of partnership tax law provisions to limited liability companies (LLCs) and limited liability partnerships (LLPs).

Outline

TAX TALK   *Today is the first day of the rest of your taxable year.*

—*Jeffrey L. Yablon*

Overview of Partnership Taxation

Much of the new business in today's world of commerce is conducted in what the Internal Revenue Code would classify as *partnerships*. As evidence of their popularity, almost 2 million partnership tax returns are filed with the IRS annually.

Whether termed a *joint venture, working agreement, shared operating arrangement,* or some other designation, a partnership is formed when individuals or separate business entities get together for the specific purpose of earning profits by jointly operating a trade or business. For example, a partnership likely exists when a U.S. business enters into a joint venture with a foreign distributor to gain access to an overseas consumer market. Or a number of businesses located in a blighted downtown area might work together to boost sales and customer traffic by forming a group that unifies and improves the appearance of the storefronts in the area, conducts joint advertising, and coordinates sales and coupon activities.

Partnerships allow a great degree of flexibility in the conduct of business: for example, a group can limit its goals to a specific list of agreed-to projects or to a given time period, or businesses can work together without altering any of their underlying capital structures. In many service professions, such as law, medicine, and accounting, state laws prohibit the owners from using a corporation to limit their liability to clients or patients, so the partnership form prevails.

The tax law addressing the transactions of partners and partnerships is found in Subchapter K of the Code. These provisions comprise only a few short pages in the Code, however. Most of the details of partnership tax law have evolved through extensive Regulations and a healthy number of court cases.

TAX FACT

PARTNERSHIP POWER

Partnerships represent a sizable number of tax entities, and they generate a significant part of the net income of the economy, especially in the investment sectors.

Partnership Activities, Tax Year 1997	
Number of partnerships	1,750,000
Number of partners	16,185,000
Reported partnership net income—total	$168 billion
Reported partnership business income	$94 billion
Reported partnership portfolio income	$57 billion
Reported partnership rental real estate income	$17 billion

everything just flows to u

FORMS OF DOING BUSINESS—FEDERAL TAX CONSEQUENCES

This chapter and the next chapter analyze business forms that offer certain advantages over C corporations. These entities are partnerships and S corporations, which are called *flow-through* or *pass-through* entities because the owners of the trade or business elect to avoid treating the enterprise as a separate taxable entity. Instead, the owners are taxed on a proportionate share of the firm's taxable income at the end of each of its taxable years, regardless of the amount of cash or property distributions the owners receive during the year. The entity serves as an information provider to the IRS and its owners with respect to the proportionate income shares, and the tax falls directly upon the owners of those shares.

A partnership may be especially advantageous in many cases. A partnership's income is subject to only a single level of taxation, whereas C corporation income is subject to *double taxation*. Corporate income is taxed at the entity level at rates up to 35 percent. Any after-tax income that is distributed to corporate owners is taxed again as a dividend at the owner level. Though partnership income may be subject to high individual rates (currently up to 39.6 percent), the resulting tax will likely be lower than a combined corporate-level tax and a second tax on dividends.

In addition, administrative and filing requirements are relatively simple for a partnership, and the entity offers certain planning opportunities not available to other entities. Both C and S corporations are subject to rigorous allocation and distribution requirements (generally, each allocation or distribution is proportionate to the ownership interest of the shareholder). A partnership, though, may adjust its allocations of income and cash flow among the partners each year according to their needs, as long as certain standards are met. Any previously unrealized income (such as appreciation of corporate assets) of a C corporation is taxed at the entity level when the corporation liquidates, but a partnership generally may liquidate tax-free. Finally, many states impose reporting and licensing requirements on corporate entities, including S corporations. These include franchise or capital stock tax returns that may require annual assessments and costly professional preparation assistance. Partnerships, on the other hand, often have no reporting requirements beyond Federal and state informational tax returns.

B R I D G E   D I S C I P L I N E

Bridge to Finance

As movies have become more expensive to produce, many production studios have turned to limited partnerships as a lucrative source of investment capital. For example, DreamWorks and the Walt Disney Company have sold limited partnership or LLC interests in entities formed to produce specific movies.

The sponsoring studio usually injects capital for a small (1–5 percent) general partnership interest, and the limited partners contribute the remaining capital—hundreds of millions of dollars or more. The partnership agreement spells out the number and types of films the partnership intends to produce and provides a formula for allocating cash flows to the partners. The partnership agreement includes various benefits for the general partner (studio), such as a preferred allocation of cash flows (the first $1 million per year, for example), distribution fees for marketing the movies, and/or reimbursement of specified amounts of corporate overhead. Any cash remaining after these expenses is allocated under a fixed formula between the general and limited partners (for example, the limited partners may receive 90 percent of remaining cash flows).

These film-financing partnerships are not necessarily private operations. A layperson with a well-connected tax or investment adviser can become a partner in the next Julia Roberts project, perhaps financed by Silver Screen Partners XXII. Partnership shares sell for multiples of $100,000 or more, and in return the investor can become part-owner in an entity that is certain to throw off operating losses for many years to come.

Especially interested in movie financing of this type can be non-U.S. investors. The use of partnerships and limited liability entities is a common way to attract cross-border investment, as many developed countries treat such joint ventures favorably under their tax laws, allowing deferral of income recognition and lower tax withholding on the income of these entities. U.S. investors are attracted to joint venture financing of film projects in several countries, including Canada, that offer generous tax credits for projects that are filmed and processed chiefly within their borders. The partnership tax regime can offer an immediate flow-through of these tax benefits.

Think about traditional bank financing of manufacturing or distribution activities in comparison, and you will see why the movie studio finds partnerships so appealing: How many banks would allow the general partner to receive reimbursements and allocations before debt principal and interest are paid?

This capital-raising technique has proved so advantageous to the studios that some related industries, such as movie lighting contractors and special effects companies, have also used limited partnerships to raise capital. The next time you go to a movie, watch the credits at the end and think about the large number of people who invested cash in the movie hoping for a blockbuster!

Although partnerships may avoid many of the income tax and reporting burdens faced by other entities, they are subject to all other taxes in the same manner as any other business. Thus, the partnership files returns and pays the outstanding amount of pertinent sales taxes, property taxes, and payroll taxes.

In summary, partnerships offer advantages to both large and small businesses. For smaller business operations, a partnership enables several owners to combine their resources at low cost. It also offers simple filing requirements, the taxation of income only once, and the ability to discontinue operations relatively inexpensively. For larger business operations, a partnership offers a unique ability to raise capital with low filing and reporting costs (compared to corporate bond issuances, for example).

WHAT IS A PARTNERSHIP?

A partnership is an association of two or more persons to carry on a trade or business, with each contributing money, property, labor, or skill, and with all expecting to share in profits and losses. A "person" can be an individual, a corporation, or another partnership. For Federal income tax purposes, a partnership includes a syndicate, group, pool, joint venture, or other unincorporated organization, through which any business, financial operation, or venture is carried on. The entity must not be otherwise classified as a corporation, trust, or estate.[1]

An eligible entity can "check the box" on the partnership tax return indicating that the entity wants to be taxed as a partnership.[2] A partnership must have at least two owners, so a sole proprietor or one-shareholder corporation cannot "check the box" and be taxed as a partnership.[3]

Businesses operating in several forms are taxed as partnerships. Provisions controlling these legal forms of doing business typically are dictated by the laws of the states in which the businesses operate.

- In a **general partnership,** the partners share profits and losses in some specified manner, as dictated by the partnership agreement. Creditors can reach the assets of the business and the personal assets of the general partners to satisfy any outstanding debts. A general partner can be bankrupted by a judgment against the entity, even though the partner did not cause the violation triggering the damages.
- In a **limited partnership,** profits and losses are shared as the partners agree, but ownership interests are either general (creditors can reach the personal assets of the partner) or limited (a partner's exposure to entity liabilities is limited to the partner's own capital contributions). Usually, the general partners conduct most of the partnership business, and they have a greater say in making decisions that affect the entity operations.
- The **limited liability partnership (LLP)** is used chiefly in the service professions, such as accounting and consulting. The primary difference between an LLP and a general partnership is that an LLP partner is not liable for acts of negligence, fraud, or malpractice committed by other partners.
- The **limited liability company (LLC)** is discussed in more detail later in this chapter. This entity is taxed as a partnership, but its capital structure resembles that of a corporation, with shares for sale and an owner's liability limited almost strictly to the extent of capital contributions. Some states allow LLCs to be owned solely by one person.

greater liability protection

LEARNING OBJECTIVE 1

Discuss governing principles and theories of partnership taxation.

PARTNERSHIP TAXATION AND REPORTING

A partnership is not a taxable entity.[4] Rather, the taxable income or loss of the partnership flows through to the partners at the end of the entity's tax year.[5] Partners report their allocable share of the partnership's income or loss for the year on their tax returns. As a result, the partnership itself pays no Federal income tax

---

[1] § 7701(a)(2).
[2] Reg. §§ 301.7701–1 to 301.7701–3, as discussed in Chapter 9 of this text.
[3] § 761(a).
[4] § 701.
[5] § 702.

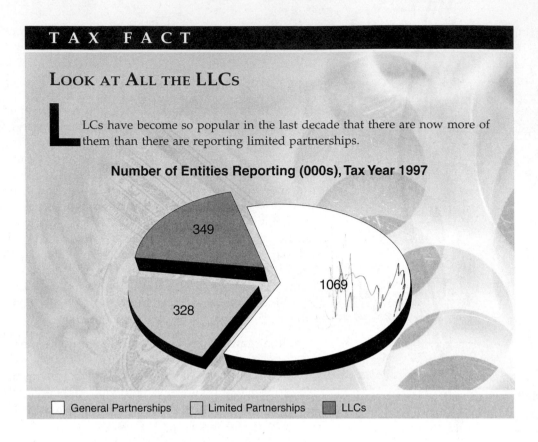

TAX FACT

LOOK AT ALL THE LLCs

LCs have become so popular in the last decade that there are now more of them than there are reporting limited partnerships.

Number of Entities Reporting (000s), Tax Year 1997

349

1069

328

☐ General Partnerships   ☐ Limited Partnerships   ■ LLCs

on its income; instead, the partners' individual tax liabilities are affected by the activities of the entity.

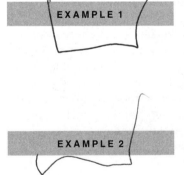

EXAMPLE 1

Adam is a 40% partner in the ABC Partnership. Both Adam's and the partnership's tax years end on December 31. This year, the partnership generates $200,000 of ordinary taxable income. However, because the partnership needs capital for expansion and debt reduction, Adam makes no cash withdrawals during the year. He meets his living expenses by reducing his investment portfolio. Adam is taxed on his $80,000 allocable share of the partnership's income ($200,000 × 40%), even though he received no distributions from the entity during the year. This allocated income is included in Adam's gross income. ∎

EXAMPLE 2

Assume the same facts as in Example 1, except that the partnership realizes a taxable loss of $100,000. Adam's adjusted gross income is reduced by $40,000 because his proportionate share of the loss flows through to him from the partnership. As a result, he deducts a $40,000 partnership loss for the year. (Note: Loss limitation rules discussed later in the chapter may result in some or all of this loss being deducted in a later year.) ∎

Many items of partnership income, expense, gain, or loss retain their tax identity as they flow through to the partners. These **separately stated items** include those items that may affect any two partners' tax liability computations differently.[6] For example, the § 179 expense of a partnership is separately stated because one partner might be able to deduct his or her share of the expense completely, while another's deduction might be limited. Separately stated items include recognized gains and

---

[6]§ 703(a)(1). Certain large partnerships can elect to limit the number of separately stated items.

losses from property transactions, dividend income, preferences and adjustments for the alternative minimum tax (see Chapter 13), foreign tax payments, and expenditures that individual partners would treat as itemized deductions (e.g., charitable contributions).

Items that are not separately stated, because all partners will treat them the same on their individual tax returns, are aggregated and form the *ordinary income* of the partnership. Thus, profits from product sales, advertising expenses, and depreciation recapture amounts are combined to form the entity's ordinary income. This amount is then allocated among the partners and flows through to their tax returns. The ordinary income that flows through to a general partner, as well as any salary-like guaranteed payments (discussed in a later section) received, usually is subject to self-employment tax, as well as Federal income tax.[7]

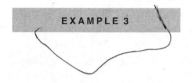

EXAMPLE 3

Beth is a 25% partner in the BR Partnership. The cash basis entity collected sales income of $60,000 during 2001 and incurred $15,000 in business expenses. In addition, it sold a corporate bond for a $9,000 long-term capital gain. Finally, the partnership made a $1,000 contribution to the local Performing Arts Fund drive. The fund is a qualifying charity. BR and all of its partners use a calendar tax year.

For 2001, Beth is allocated ordinary taxable income of $11,250 [($60,000 − $15,000) × 25%] from the partnership. She also is allocated a flow-through of a $2,250 long-term capital gain and a $250 charitable contribution deduction. The ordinary income increases Beth's gross income, and the capital gain and charitable contribution are combined with her other similar activities for the year as though she had incurred them herself. These items could be treated differently on the tax returns of the various partners (e.g., because a partner may be subject to a percentage limitation on charitable contribution deductions for 2001), so they are not included in the computation of ordinary partnership income. Instead, the items flow through to the partners separately. ∎

1 *Find more information on this topic at our Web site:* **http://wft-entities.swcollege.com**.

Even though it is not a taxpaying entity, the partnership files an information tax return, Form 1065. Look at Form 1065 in Appendix B, and refer to it during the following discussion. The ordinary income and expense items generated by the partnership's trade or business activities are netted to produce a single income or loss amount. The partnership reports this ordinary income or loss from its trade or business activities on Form 1065, page 1. Schedule K (page 3 of Form 1065) accumulates all items that must be separately reported to the partners, including net trade or business income or loss (from page 1). The amounts on Schedule K are allocated to all the partners. Each partner receives a Schedule K–1, which shows that partner's share of partnership items.

EXAMPLE 4

The BR Partnership in Example 3 reports its $60,000 of sales income on Form 1065, page 1, line 1. The $15,000 of business expenses are reported in the appropriate amounts on page 1, line 2 or lines 9–20. Partnership ordinary income of $45,000 is shown on page 1, line 22, and on Schedule K, line 1. The $9,000 capital gain and the $1,000 charitable contribution are reported only on Schedule K, on lines 4e and 8, respectively.

Beth receives a Schedule K–1 from the partnership that shows her shares of partnership ordinary income of $11,250, long-term capital gain of $2,250, and charitable contributions of $250 on lines 1, 4e, and 8, respectively.

She combines these amounts with similar items from other sources on her personal tax return. For example, if she has a $5,000 long-term capital loss from a stock transaction during

---

[7]§ 1402(a).

the year, her overall net capital loss is $2,750. She then evaluates this net amount to determine the amount she may deduct on her Form 1040. ■

Thus, one must look at both page 1 and Schedule K to get complete information regarding a partnership's operations for the year. Schedule K accumulates all partnership tax items and arrives at a total amount on line 25a. Schedule M–1, page 4, reconciles accounting income with this total of partnership tax items on Schedule K (line 25a). Schedule L generally shows an accounting-basis balance sheet, and Schedule M–2 reconciles beginning and ending partners' capital accounts.

PARTNER'S OWNERSHIP INTEREST IN A PARTNERSHIP

Each partner typically owns both a **capital interest** and a **profits (loss) interest** in the partnership. A capital interest is measured by a partner's **capital sharing ratio,** which is the partner's percentage ownership of the capital of the partnership. A partner's capital interest can be determined in several ways. The most widely accepted method measures the capital interest as the percentage of net asset value (asset value remaining after payment of all partnership liabilities) a partner would receive on immediate liquidation of the partnership.

A profits (loss) interest is simply the partner's percentage allocation of current partnership operating results. **Profit and loss sharing ratios** usually are specified in the partnership agreement. They are used to determine each partner's allocation of partnership ordinary taxable income and separately stated items.[8] The partnership can change its profit and loss allocations at any time by amending the partnership agreement.

The partnership agreement may, in some cases, provide for a **special allocation** of certain items to specified partners, or it may allocate items in a different proportion from the general profit and loss sharing ratios. These items are separately reported to the partner receiving the allocation. For a special allocation to be recognized for tax purposes, it must produce nontax economic consequences to the partners receiving the allocation.[9]

EXAMPLE 5

When the George-Helen Partnership was formed, George contributed cash and Helen contributed some City of Iuka bonds that she had held for investment purposes. The partnership agreement allocates all of the tax-exempt interest income from the bonds to Helen as an inducement for her to remain a partner. This is an acceptable special allocation for income tax purposes; it reflects the differing economic circumstances that underlie the partners' contributions to the capital of the entity. Since Helen would have received the tax-exempt income if she had not joined the partnership, she can retain the tax-favored treatment via the special allocation. ■

EXAMPLE 6

Assume the same facts as in Example 5. Three years after it was formed, the George-Helen Partnership purchased some City of Butte bonds. The municipal bond interest income of $15,000 flows through to the partners as a separately stated item, so it retains its tax-exempt status. The partnership agreement allocates all of this income to George because he is subject to a higher marginal income tax bracket than is Helen. The partnership then allocates $15,000 more of the partnership's ordinary income to Helen than to George. These allocations are not effective for income tax purposes because they have no purpose other than a reduction of the partners' combined income tax liability. ■

---

[8] § 704(a).   [9] § 704(b).

BRIDGE DISCIPLINE

Beth ~ Capital account will be FMV even though basis is

Bridge to Financial Accounting

The equivalent in financial accounting to the partner's basis in his or her partnership interest is the **capital account.** A partner's ending balance in the capital account rarely is the same as his or her basis in the partnership interest. Just as the tax and accounting bases of a specific asset may differ, a partner's capital account and basis in the partnership interest usually are not equal.

Whereas contributions and most distributions from the partnership do not create financial accounting income, the capital account is "written up" or down to aggregate fair market value when the entity is formed. For most partnerships with simple financial transactions, *changes* to the capital account parallel closely the annual changes to the partner's basis in the partnership. Basis in one's partnership interest cannot be a negative number, but the capital account can become negative.

Oddly, the Schedules K–1 for the partners require an accounting for their capital accounts, but there is no required reconciliation for the partner's tax basis on the Schedule K–1. As a result, the tax adviser may find that a new partnership client has poor records with respect to the basis amounts of the partners, and a reconstruction must take place so that future computations will be correct. Sometimes, lacking adequate information with which to make this computation, the capital account is used because it is "close enough" and forms a good surrogate for the partner's basis in the partnership.

A partner has a **basis in the partnership interest,** just as he or she would have a tax basis in any asset owned. When income flows through to a partner from the partnership, the partner's basis in the partnership interest increases accordingly. When a loss flows through to a partner, basis is reduced.[10] A partner's basis is important when determining the treatment of distributions from the partnership to the partner, establishing the deductibility of partnership losses, and calculating gain or loss on the disposition of the partnership interest.

EXAMPLE 7

Paul contributes $20,000 of cash to acquire a 30% capital and profits interest in the Red Robin Partnership. In its first year of operations, the partnership earns ordinary income of $40,000 and makes no distributions to Paul. Paul's initial basis is the $20,000 he paid for the interest. He reports ordinary income of $12,000 (30% × $40,000 partnership income) on his individual return and increases his basis by the same amount, to $32,000. ■

The Code provides for increases and decreases in a partner's basis so that the income or loss from partnership operations is taxed only once. In Example 7, if Paul sold his interest at the end of the first year for $32,000, he would have no gain or loss. If the Code did not provide for an adjustment of a partner's basis, Paul's basis would still be $20,000, and he would be taxed on the gain of $12,000 in addition to being taxed on his $12,000 share of income.

2 *Find more information on this topic at our Web site:* ***http://wft-entities.swcollege.com.***

DIGGING DEEPER

---

[10]§§ 705, 722, and 723.

Describe the tax effects of
forming a partnership with
cash and property
contributions.

Formation of a Partnership: Tax Effects

GAIN OR LOSS ON CONTRIBUTIONS TO THE PARTNERSHIP

When a taxpayer transfers property to an entity in exchange for valuable consideration, a taxable exchange usually results. Typically, both the taxpayer and the entity realize and recognize gain or loss on the exchange.[11] The gain or loss recognized by the transferor is the difference between the fair market value of the consideration received and the adjusted basis of the property transferred.[12]

In most situations, however, neither the partner nor the partnership recognizes the gain or loss that is realized when a partner contributes property to a partnership in exchange for a partnership interest. Instead, recognition of any realized gain or loss is deferred.[13]

There are two reasons for this nonrecognition treatment. First, forming a partnership allows investors to combine their assets toward greater economic goals than could be achieved separately. Only the form of ownership, rather than the amount owned by each investor, has changed. Requiring that gain be recognized on such transfers would make the formation of some partnerships economically unfeasible. Second, because the partnership interest received is typically not a liquid asset, the partner may not be able to generate the cash to pay the tax. Thus, deferral of the gain recognizes the economic realities of the business world and follows the wherewithal to pay principle.

EXAMPLE 8

Alicia transfers two assets to the Wren Partnership on the day the entity is created, in exchange for a 60% profit and loss interest worth $60,000. She contributes cash of $40,000 and retail display equipment (basis to her as a sole proprietor, $8,000; fair market value, $20,000). Since an exchange has occurred between two parties, Alicia *realizes* a $12,000 gain on this transaction. The gain realized is the fair market value of the partnership interest of $60,000 less the basis of the assets that Alicia surrendered to the partnership [$40,000 (cash) + $8,000 (equipment)].

Under § 721, Alicia *does not recognize* the $12,000 realized gain in the year of contribution. Alicia might not have had sufficient cash if she had been required to pay tax on the $12,000 gain. All that she received from the partnership was an illiquid partnership interest; she received no cash with which to pay any resulting tax liability. ■

EXAMPLE 9

Assume the same facts as in Example 8, except that the equipment Alicia contributes to the partnership has an adjusted basis of $25,000. She has a $5,000 *realized* loss [$60,000 − ($40,000 + $25,000)], but she cannot deduct the loss. Realized losses, as well as realized gains, are deferred by § 721.

Unless it was essential that the partnership receive Alicia's display equipment rather than similar equipment purchased from an outside supplier, Alicia should have considered selling the equipment to a third party. This would have allowed her to deduct a $5,000 loss in the year of the sale. Alicia then could have contributed $60,000 cash (including the proceeds from the sale) for her interest in the partnership, and the partnership would have funds to purchase similar equipment. ■

EXAMPLE 10

Five years after the Wren Partnership (Examples 8 and 9) was created, Alicia contributes another piece of equipment to the entity. This property has a basis of $35,000 and a fair market value of $50,000. Alicia will defer the recognition of the $15,000 realized gain. Section

---

[11]§ 1001(c).
[12]§ 1001(a).

[13]§ 721.

721 is effective *whenever* a partner makes a contribution to the capital of the partnership, not just when the partnership is formed. ∎

EXCEPTIONS TO NONRECOGNITION

The nonrecognition provisions of § 721 do *not* apply where:

- the transaction is essentially a taxable exchange of properties;
- the transaction is a disguised sale of properties; or
- the partnership interest is received in exchange for services rendered to the partnership by the partner.[14]

Exchange. If a transaction is essentially a taxable exchange of properties, the tax is not deferred under the nonrecognition provisions of § 721.[15]

EXAMPLE 11

Sara owns land, and Bob owns stock. Sara would like to have Bob's stock, and Bob wants Sara's land. If Sara and Bob both contribute their property to newly formed SB Partnership in exchange for interests in the partnership, the tax on the transaction appears to be deferred under § 721. The tax on a subsequent distribution by the partnership of the land to Bob and the stock to Sara also appears to be deferred under § 731. According to a literal interpretation of the statutes, no taxable exchange has occurred. Sara and Bob will find, however, that this type of tax subterfuge is not permitted. The IRS will disregard the passage of the properties through the partnership and will hold, instead, that Sara and Bob exchanged the land and stock directly. Thus, the transactions will be treated as any other taxable exchange. ∎

Disguised Sale. A similar result (i.e., recognition) occurs in a **disguised sale** of properties. A disguised sale is deemed to occur when a partner contributes property to a partnership and soon thereafter receives a distribution from the partnership. This distribution could be viewed as a payment by the partnership for purchase of the property.[16]

EXAMPLE 12

Kim transfers property to the KLM Partnership. The property has an adjusted basis of $10,000 and a fair market value of $30,000. Two weeks later, the partnership makes a distribution of $30,000 of cash to Kim. Under the rules of § 731, the distribution would not be taxable to Kim if the basis for her partnership interest prior to the distribution was greater than the $30,000 of cash distributed. However, the transaction appears to be a disguised purchase-sale transaction, rather than a contribution and distribution. Therefore, Kim must recognize gain of $20,000 on transfer of the property, and the partnership is deemed to have purchased the property for $30,000. ∎

A disguised sale is presumed to exist when a contribution by one partner is followed within two years by a specified distribution to him or her from the partnership.

Services. Another exception to the nonrecognition provision of § 721 occurs when a partner receives an interest in the partnership as compensation for services rendered to the partnership. This is not a tax-deferred transaction because services are not treated as "property" that can be transferred to a partnership on a tax-free basis. Instead, the partner performing the services recognizes ordinary compensation income equal to the fair market value of the partnership interest received.[17]

---

[14]§ 721(b). A few other exceptions to § 721 treatment also exist.
[15]Reg. § 1.731–1(c)(3).

[16]§ 707(a)(2)(B).
[17]§ 83(a).

The partnership may deduct the amount included in the *service partner's* income if the services are of a deductible nature. If the services are not deductible by the partnership, they must be capitalized. For example, architectural plans created by a partner are capitalized to the structure built with those plans. Alternatively, day-to-day management services performed by a partner for the partnership usually are deductible by the partnership.

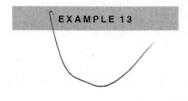

EXAMPLE 13

Bill, Carol, and Dave form the BCD Partnership, with each receiving a one-third interest in the entity. Dave receives his one-third interest as compensation for the accounting and tax planning services he rendered during the formation of the partnership. The value of a one-third interest in the partnership (for each of the parties) is $20,000. The partnership deducts $20,000 for Dave's services in computing ordinary income. Dave recognizes $20,000 of compensation income, and he has a $20,000 basis in his partnership interest. The same result would occur if the partnership had paid Dave $20,000 for his services and he immediately contributed that amount to the entity for a one-third ownership interest. ∎

TAX ISSUES RELATED TO CONTRIBUTED PROPERTY

When a partner makes a tax-deferred contribution of an asset to the capital of a partnership, the entity assigns a *carryover basis* to the property.[18] The partnership's basis in the asset is equal to the basis the partner held in the property prior to its transfer to the partnership. The partner's basis in the new partnership interest equals the prior basis in the contributed asset. The tax term for this basis concept is *substituted basis*. Thus, two assets are created out of one when a partnership is formed, namely, the property in the hands of the new entity and the new asset (the partnership interest) in the hands of the partner. Both assets are assigned a basis that is derived from the partner's basis in the contributed property.

The holding period of a partner's interest includes that of the contributed property when the property was a § 1231 asset or capital asset in the partner's hands. Otherwise, the holding period starts on the day the interest is acquired. The holding period of an interest acquired by a cash contribution starts at acquisition.

To understand the logic of these rules, consider what Congress was attempting to accomplish in this deferral transaction. For both parties, realized gain is deferred, under the wherewithal to pay concept, until the asset or ownership interest is subsequently disposed of in a taxable transaction. The deferral is accomplished through the use of a substituted basis by the partner and a carryover basis by the partnership. This treatment is similar to the treatment of assets transferred to a controlled corporation and the treatment of like-kind exchanges.[19]

EXAMPLE 14

On June 1, José transfers property to the JKL Partnership in exchange for a one-third interest in the partnership. The property has an adjusted basis to José of $10,000 and a fair market value of $30,000. José has a $20,000 realized gain on the exchange ($30,000 − $10,000), but he does not recognize any of the gain. José's basis for his partnership interest is the amount necessary to recognize the $20,000 deferred gain if his partnership interest is subsequently sold for its $30,000 fair market value. This amount, $10,000, is the substituted basis. The basis of the property contributed to the partnership is the amount necessary to allow for the recognition of the $20,000 deferred gain if the property is subsequently sold for its $30,000 fair market value. This amount, also $10,000, is the carryover basis. ∎

---

[18]§ 723.   [19]§§ 351 and 1031.

The holding period for the contributed asset also carries over to the partnership. Thus, the partnership's holding period for the asset includes the period during which the partner owned the asset individually.

Depreciation Method and Period. If depreciable property is contributed to the partnership, the partnership usually is required to use the same cost recovery method and life used by the partner. The partnership merely "steps into the shoes" of the partner and continues the same cost recovery calculations. Thus, the partnership may not expense any part of the basis of depreciable property it receives from the transferor partner under § 179.

Receivables, Inventory, and Losses. To prevent ordinary income from being converted into capital gain, gain or loss is treated as ordinary when the partnership disposes of either of the following.[20]

- Contributed receivables that were unrealized in the contributing partner's hands at the contribution date. Such receivables include the right to receive payment for goods or services.
- Contributed property that was inventory in the contributor's hands on the contribution date, if the partnership disposes of the property within *five years of the contribution*. For this purpose, inventory includes all tangible property except capital and real or depreciable business assets.

EXAMPLE 15

Tyrone operates a cash basis retail electronics and television store as a sole proprietor. Ramon is an enterprising individual who likes to invest in small businesses. On January 2 of the current year, Tyrone and Ramon form the TR Partnership. Their partnership contributions are listed below.

	Adjusted Basis	Fair Market Value
From Tyrone:		
Receivables	$ –0–	$ 2,000
Inventory	2,500	5,000
Land used as parking lot*	1,200	5,000
From Ramon:		
Cash	12,000	12,000

*The parking lot had been held for nine months at the contribution date.

Within 30 days of formation, TR collects the receivables and sells the inventory for $5,000. It uses the land for the next 10 months as a parking lot, then sells it for $3,500. TR realized the following income in the current year from these transactions.

- Ordinary income of $2,000 from collecting receivables.
- Ordinary income of $2,500 from sale of inventory.
- § 1231 gain of $2,300 from the sale of land.

Since the land takes a carryover holding period, it is treated as having been held 19 months at the sale date. ∎

---

[20]§ 724. For this purpose, § 724(d)(2) waives the holding period requirement in defining § 1231 property.

A similar rule is designed to prevent a capital loss from being converted into an ordinary loss. Under the rule, if contributed property is disposed of at a loss and the property had a "built-in" capital loss on the contribution date, the loss is treated as a capital loss if the partnership disposes of the property *within five years of the contribution*. The capital loss is limited to the "built-in" loss on the date of contribution.[21]

EXAMPLE 16

Assume the same facts as Example 15, except for the following.

- Tyrone held the land as an investment. It had a fair market value of $800 at the contribution date.
- TR used the land as a parking lot for 10 months and sold it for $650.

TR realizes the following income and loss from these transactions.

- Ordinary income of $2,000 from collecting the receivables.
- Ordinary income of $2,500 from the sale of inventory.
- Capital loss of $400 from the sale of land ($800 − $1,200).
- § 1231 loss of $150 from the sale of land ($650 − $800).

Since the land was sold within five years of the contribution date, the $400 built-in loss is a capital loss. The postcontribution loss of $150 is a § 1231 loss since TR used the property in its business. ∎

INSIDE AND OUTSIDE BASES

In this chapter, reference is made to the partnership's inside basis and the partners' outside basis. **Inside basis** refers to the adjusted basis of each partnership asset, as determined from the partnership's tax accounts. **Outside basis** represents each partner's basis in the partnership interest. Each partner "owns" a share of the partnership's inside basis for all its assets and should maintain a record of the outside basis.

In many cases—especially on formation of the partnership—the total of all the partners' outside bases equals the partnership's inside bases for all its assets. Differences between inside and outside basis arise when a partner's interest is sold to another person for more or less than the selling partner's share of the inside basis of partnership assets. The buying partner's outside basis equals the price paid for the interest, but the buyer's share of the partnership's inside basis is the same amount as the seller's share of the inside basis.

Concept Summary 11–1 reviews the rules that apply to partnership asset contribution and basis adjustments.

TAX ACCOUNTING ELECTIONS

LEARNING OBJECTIVE 3

Examine the tax treatment of expenditures of a newly formed partnership and identify elections available to the partnership.

A newly formed partnership must make numerous tax accounting elections. These elections are formal decisions on how a particular transaction or tax attribute should be handled. Most of these elections must be made by the partnership rather than by the partners individually.[22] The *partnership* makes the elections involving the following items.

- Inventory method.
- Cost or percentage depletion method, excluding oil and gas wells.
- Accounting method (cash, accrual, or hybrid).

[21]§ 724(c).   [22]§ 703(b).

> **CONCEPT SUMMARY 11–1**
>
> ## Partnership Formation and Basis Computation
>
> 1. Generally, partners or partnerships do not recognize gain or loss when property is contributed for capital interests.
> 2. Partners contributing property for partnership interests take the contributed property's adjusted basis for their *outside basis* in their partnership interest. The partners are said to take a substituted basis in their partnership interest.
> 3. The partnership will continue to use the contributing partner's basis for the *inside basis* in property it receives. The contributed property is said to take a carryover basis.
> 4. The partnership's holding period for contributed property may include the contributing partner's holding period.
> 5. Gain is recognized by a contributing partner when services are contributed or when the capital contribution is a disguised sale or exchange.
> 6. Special rules may apply when the partnership disposes of contributed receivables, inventory, or loss assets.

- Cost recovery methods and assumptions.
- Tax year.
- Amortization of organization costs and amortization period.
- Amortization of start-up expenditures and amortization period.
- Section 179 deductions for certain tangible personal property.
- Nonrecognition treatment for gains from involuntary conversions.

Each partner is bound by the decisions made by the partnership relative to the elections. If the partnership fails to make an election, a partner cannot compensate for the error by making the election individually.

Though most elections are made by the partnership, each *partner* individually makes a specific election on the following relatively narrow tax issues.

- Whether to take a deduction or a credit for taxes paid to foreign countries.
- Whether to claim the cost or percentage depletion method for oil and gas wells.
- Whether to reduce the basis of depreciable property first when excluding income from discharge of indebtedness.

INITIAL COSTS OF A PARTNERSHIP

In its initial stages, a partnership incurs expenses relating to some or all of the following: forming the partnership (organization costs), admitting partners to the partnership, marketing and selling partnership units to prospective partners (**syndication costs**), acquiring assets, starting business operations (start-up costs), negotiating contracts, and other items. Many of these expenditures are not currently deductible. However, the Code permits straight-line amortization of "organization" and "start-up" costs; acquisition costs incurred to acquire depreciable assets are included in the initial basis of the acquired assets; and costs related to some intangible assets may be amortized. "Syndication costs" may be neither amortized nor deducted.[23]

Organization Costs.   Organization costs are incident to the creation of the partnership and are capital in nature. Such costs include accounting and legal fees

---

[23]§ 709(a).

associated with the partnership formation.[24] Costs incurred for the following purposes are *not* organization costs.

- Acquiring assets for the partnership.
- Transferring assets to the partnership.
- Admitting partners, other than at formation.
- Removing partners, other than at formation.
- Negotiating operating contracts.

A partnership can elect to amortize organization costs over a period of 60 months or more, starting with the month in which it begins business. The election must be made by the due date of the partnership's first tax return.[25] To qualify for amortization, organization costs must be incurred within a period that starts at a reasonable time before the partnership begins business and ends with the unextended due date of the partnership's first tax return. Cash method partnerships may not deduct amortization on organization costs in the year incurred if they are not paid by the end of the first year.

EXAMPLE 17

The calendar year Bluejay Partnership is formed on May 1 of the current year and immediately starts business. Bluejay incurs $720 in legal fees for drafting the partnership agreement and $480 in accounting fees for tax advice of an organizational nature. The legal fees are paid in October of the current year. The accounting fees are paid in January of the following year. The partnership selects the cash method of accounting and elects to amortize its organization costs.

On its first tax return, Bluejay deducts $96 of organization costs [($720 legal fees/60 months) × 8 months]. No deduction is taken for the accounting fees because the partnership selected the cash method and the fees were paid the following year. On its tax return for next year, Bluejay deducts organization costs of $304 {[($720 legal fees/60 months) × 12 months] + [($480 accounting fees/60 months) × 20 months]}. This amount includes the $64 of accounting fees [($480/60) × 8] that could have been deducted on Bluejay's first tax return if they had been paid by the end of that year. ∎

Start-up Costs.   Operating costs that are incurred after the entity is formed but before it begins business are known as start-up costs. Like organization costs, start-up costs are capitalized and may be amortized over a period of 60 months or more, starting with the month in which the partnership begins business.[26] Such costs include marketing surveys prior to conducting business, pre-operating advertising expenses, costs of establishing an accounting system, and salaries paid to executives and employees before the start of business.

3   *Find more information on this topic at our Web site: **http://wft-entities.swcollege.com.***

Operations of the Partnership

A key consideration in the taxation of partnerships is that a variety of entities can be partners and each may be affected differently by the partnership's operations. In particular, any combination of individuals, corporations, trusts, estates, or other partnerships may be partners. Furthermore, at the end of each year, every partner

---

[24]§ 709(b)(2).
[25]§ 709(b)(1).

[26]§ 195.

receives a share of the partnership's income, deductions, credits, and alternative minimum tax (AMT) preferences and adjustments.[27] These flow-through items ultimately may be reported and taxed on a wide variety of income tax returns [e.g., Forms 1040 (Individuals), 1041 (Fiduciaries), 1120 (C corporations), and 1120S (S corporations)], each facing different limitations and rules. Thus, the ultimate tax treatment of partnership operations is directly affected by how the partnership reports its operating results.

REPORTING OPERATING RESULTS

Form 1065 is due on the fifteenth day of the fourth month following the close of the partnership's tax year; for a calendar year partnership, this is April 15.

Classifying Income and Deductions. The measurement and reporting of partnership income require a two-step approach. Some items are not reported separately. These are netted at the partnership level and flow through to the partners as an aggregate number. Other items must be segregated and reported separately on the partnership return and each partner's Schedule K–1. Items passed through separately include the following.[28]

- Short- and long-term capital gains and losses.
- Section 1231 gains and losses.
- Charitable contributions.
- Portfolio income items (dividends, interest, and royalties).
- Immediately expensed tangible personal property (§ 179).
- Items allocated differently from the general profit and loss ratio.
- Recovery of items previously deducted (tax benefit items).
- AMT preference and adjustment items.
- Self-employment income.
- Passive activity items (e.g., rental real estate income or loss).
- Expenses related to portfolio income.
- Intangible drilling and development costs.
- Taxes paid to foreign countries and U.S. possessions.
- Nonbusiness and personal items (e.g., alimony, medical, dental).

A partnership is not allowed the following deductions.

- Net operating loss.
- Dividends received deduction.

In addition, items that are allowed only to individuals, such as standard deductions or personal exemptions, are not allowed to the partnership.

EXAMPLE 18

Tiwanda is a one-third partner in the TUV Partnership. The partnership experienced a $20,000 net loss from operations last year, its first year of business. The partnership's transactions for the year are summarized below.

Fees received	$100,000
Salaries paid	30,000
Cost recovery deductions	10,000
Supplies, repairs	3,000

---

[27]§ 702(a). [28]§ 702(b).

Payroll taxes paid	$ 9,000
Contribution to art museum	6,000
Short-term capital gain	12,000
Passive income (rental operations)	7,500
Portfolio income (dividends received)	1,500
Tax-exempt income (bond interest)	2,100
AMT adjustment (private activity bond interest)	3,600
Payment of partner Vern's alimony obligations	4,000

The two-step computational process that is used to determine partnership income is applied in the following manner.

Nonseparately Stated Items (Ordinary Income)	
Fee income	$100,000
Salaries paid	(30,000)
Cost recovery deductions	(10,000)
Supplies, repairs	(3,000)
Payroll taxes paid	(9,000)
Ordinary income	$ 48,000

Separately Stated Items	
Contribution to art museum	$ 6,000
Short-term capital gain	12,000
Passive income (rental operations)	7,500
Portfolio income (dividends received)	1,500
Tax-exempt income (bond interest)	2,100
AMT adjustment (private activity bond interest)	3,600

Each of the separately stated items passes through proportionately to each partner and is included on the appropriate schedule or netted with similar items that the partner generated for the year. Thus, in determining what her tax liability will be on her Form 1040, Tiwanda includes a $2,000 charitable contribution, a $4,000 short-term capital gain, $2,500 of passive rent income, $500 of dividend income, and a $1,200 positive adjustment in computing alternative minimum taxable income. Tiwanda treats these items as if she had generated them herself. She must disclose her $700 share of tax-exempt interest on the first page of her Form 1040. In addition, Tiwanda reports $16,000 as her share of the partnership's ordinary income, the net amount of the nonseparately stated items.

The partnership is not allowed a deduction for last year's $20,000 net operating loss—this item was passed through to the partners in the previous year. Moreover, the partnership is not allowed a deduction for personal expenditures (payment of Vern's alimony). ∎

Withdrawals.   Capital withdrawals by partners during the year do not affect the partnership's income classification and reporting process.[29] These items usually are treated as distributions made on the last day of the partnership's tax year. In Example 10, the payment of Vern's alimony by the partnership is probably treated as a distribution from the partnership to Vern.

---

[29]§ 731(a).

CHAPTER 11 Partnerships and Limited Liability Entities

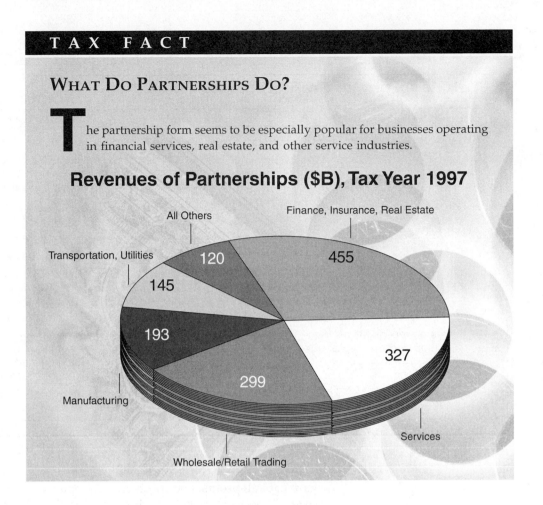

TAX FACT

WHAT DO PARTNERSHIPS DO?

The partnership form seems to be especially popular for businesses operating in financial services, real estate, and other service industries.

Revenues of Partnerships ($B), Tax Year 1997

All Others — 120
Finance, Insurance, Real Estate — 455
Transportation, Utilities — 145
Manufacturing — 193
Services — 327
Wholesale/Retail Trading — 299

PLANNING CONSIDERATIONS

Drafting the Partnership Agreement

Although a written partnership agreement is not required, many rules governing the tax consequences to partners and their partnerships refer to such an agreement. Remember that a partner's distributive share of income, gain, loss, deduction, or credit is determined in accordance with the partnership agreement. Consequently, if taxpayers operating a business in partnership form want a measure of certainty as to the tax consequences of their activities, a carefully drafted partnership agreement is crucial. An agreement that sets forth the obligations, rights, and powers of the partners should prove invaluable in settling controversies among them and provide some degree of certainty as to the tax consequences of the partners' actions.

4 *Find more information on this topic at our Web site: **http://wft-entities.swcollege.com.***

PARTNERSHIP ALLOCATIONS

Two key special allocation rules also can affect a partner's Schedule K–1 results.[30]

---

[30]The Code requires certain other allocations not discussed here.

Concept Summary 11–2

Tax Reporting of Partnership Activities

Event	Partnership Level	Partner Level
1. Compute partnership ordinary income.	Form 1065, line 22, page 1. Schedule K, Form 1065, line 1, page 3.	Schedule K–1 (Form 1065), line 1, page 1. Each partner's share is passed through for separate reporting. Each partner's basis is increased.
2. Compute partnership ordinary loss.	Form 1065, line 22, page 1. Schedule K, Form 1065, line 1, page 3.	Schedule K–1 (Form 1065), line 1, page 1. Each partner's share is passed through for separate reporting. Each partner's basis is decreased. The amount of a partner's loss deduction may be limited. Losses that may not be deducted are carried forward for use in future years.
3. Separately reported items like portfolio income, capital gain and loss, and § 179 deductions.	Schedule K, Form 1065, various lines, page 3.	Schedule K–1 (Form 1065), various lines, pages 1 and 2. Each partner's share of each item is passed through for separate reporting.
4. Net earnings from self-employment.	Schedule K, Form 1065, line 15, page 3.	Schedule K–1 (Form 1065), line 15, page 2.

Economic Effect. The partnership agreement can provide that any partner may share capital, profits, and losses in different ratios.[31] For example, a partner could have a 25 percent capital sharing ratio, yet be allocated 30 percent of the profits and 20 percent of the losses of the partnership, or, as in Examples 5 and 6, a partner could be allocated a specific amount or items of income, deduction, gain, or loss. Such special allocations are permissible if they meet the **economic effect test.**[32] The rules prevent partners from shifting income and loss items merely to reduce current taxes.

5 *Find more information on this topic at our Web site: **http://wft-entities.swcollege.com.***

Precontribution Gain or Loss. Certain income, gain, loss, and deductions relative to contributed property may not be allocated under the economic effect rules.[33] Instead, **precontribution gain or loss** is allocated among the partners to take into account the variation between the basis of the property and its fair market value on the date of contribution.[34] For nondepreciable property, this means that *built-in* gain or loss on the date of contribution is allocated to the contributing partner when the property is eventually disposed of by the partnership in a taxable transaction.

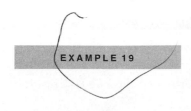

EXAMPLE 19

Seth and Tim form the equal profit and loss sharing ST Partnership. Seth contributes cash of $10,000, and Tim contributes land purchased two years ago and held for investment. The land has an adjusted basis of $6,000 and fair market value of $10,000 at the contribution

---

[31]§ 704(a).
[32]Reg. § 1.704–1(b).

[33]§ 704(b).
[34]§ 704(c)(1)(A).

[handwritten notes in top margin: "1st 4 in gain got by tim because of built in gain"]

date. For accounting purposes, the partnership records the land at its fair market value of $10,000. For tax purposes, the partnership takes a carryover basis of $6,000 in the land. After using the land as a parking lot for five months, ST sells it for $10,600. No other transactions have taken place.

The accounting and tax gain from the land sale are computed as follows.

	Accounting	Tax
Amount realized	$ 10,600	$10,600
Less: Adjusted basis	(10,000)	(6,000)
Gain realized	$ 600	$ 4,600
Gain at contribution date to Tim	(–0–)	(4,000)
Remaining gain (split equally)	$ 600	$ 600

Seth recognizes $300 of the gain ($600 remaining gain ÷ 2), and Tim recognizes $4,300 [$4,000 built-in gain + ($600 remaining gain ÷ 2)]. ∎

BASIS OF A PARTNERSHIP INTEREST

A partner's adjusted basis in the newly formed partnership usually equals (1) the adjusted basis in any property contributed to the partnership plus (2) the fair market value of any services the partner performed for the partnership (i.e., the amount of ordinary income reported by the partner for services rendered to the partnership).

A partnership interest also can be acquired after the partnership has been formed. The method of acquisition controls how the partner's initial basis is computed. If the partnership interest is purchased from another partner, the purchasing partner's basis is the amount paid (cost basis) for the partnership interest. The basis of a partnership interest acquired by gift is the donor's basis for the interest plus, in certain cases, some or all of the transfer (gift) tax paid by the donor. The basis of a partnership interest acquired through inheritance generally is the fair market value of the interest on the date the partner dies.

After the partnership begins its activities, or after a new partner is admitted to the partnership, the partner's basis is adjusted for numerous items. The following operating results *increase* a partner's adjusted basis.

- The partner's proportionate share of partnership income (including capital gains and tax-exempt income).
- The partner's proportionate share of any increase in partnership liabilities.

The following operating results *decrease* the partner's adjusted basis in the partnership. A partner's adjusted basis for the partnership interest cannot be reduced below zero.

- The partner's proportionate share of partnership deductions and losses (including capital losses).
- The partner's proportionate share of nondeductible expenses.
- The partner's proportionate share of any reduction in partnership liabilities.[35]

Increasing the adjusted basis for the partner's share of partnership taxable income is logical since the partner has already been taxed on the income. By

---

[35]§§ 705 and 752.

increasing the partner's basis, the Code ensures that the partner is not taxed again on the income when he or she sells the interest or receives a distribution from the partnership.

It is also logical that the tax-exempt income should increase the partner's basis. If the income is exempt in the current period, it should not contribute to the recognition of gain when the partner either sells the interest or receives a distribution from the partnership.

Decreasing the adjusted basis for the partner's share of deductible losses, deductions, and noncapitalizable, nondeductible expenditures is logical for the same reasons.

Flow thru of income increases, basis

EXAMPLE 20

Yuri is a one-third partner in the XYZ Partnership. His proportionate share of the partnership income during the current year consists of $20,000 of ordinary taxable income and $10,000 of tax-exempt income. None of the income is distributed to Yuri. The adjusted basis of Yuri's partnership interest before adjusting for his share of income is $35,000, and the fair market value of the interest before considering the income items is $50,000.

The unrealized gain inherent in Yuri's investment in the partnership is $15,000 ($50,000 − $35,000). Yuri's proportionate share of the income items should increase the fair market value of the interest to $80,000 ($50,000 + $20,000 + $10,000). By increasing the adjusted basis of Yuri's partnership interest to $65,000 ($35,000 + $20,000 + $10,000), the Code ensures that the unrealized gain inherent in Yuri's partnership investment remains at $15,000. This makes sense because the $20,000 of ordinary taxable income is taxed to Yuri this year and should not be taxed again when Yuri either sells his interest or receives a distribution. Similarly, the tax-exempt income is exempt this year and should not increase Yuri's gain when he either sells his interest or receives a distribution from the partnership. ■

Partnership Liabilities. A partner's adjusted basis is affected by the partner's share of partnership debt.[36] Partnership debt includes most debt that is considered a liability under financial accounting rules except for accounts payable of a cash basis partnership and certain contingent liabilities.

Two major types of partnership debt exist.[37] **Recourse debt** is partnership debt for which the partnership or at least one of the partners is personally liable. This liability can exist, for example, through the operation of state law or through personal guarantees that a partner makes to the creditor. Personal liability of a party related to a partner (under attribution rules) is treated as the personal liability of the partner. **Nonrecourse debt** is debt for which no partner (or party related to a partner) is personally liable. Lenders of nonrecourse debt generally require that collateral be pledged against the loan. Upon default, the lender can claim only the collateral, not the partners' personal assets.

EXAMPLE 21

The Bay Partnership financed its asset acquisitions with debt. If the partnership defaults on the debt, the lender can place a lien on the partners' salaries and personal assets. This constitutes recourse debt. ■

EXAMPLE 22

The Tray Partnership financed its asset acquisitions with debt. If the partnership defaults on the debt, the lender can repossess the equipment purchased with the loan proceeds. This constitutes nonrecourse debt. ■

EXAMPLE 23

When Ray bought into the Sleigh Partnership, the entity was in the midst of settling litigation as to its liability to those who had purchased its products and were making warranty claims

---

[36]§ 752.   [37]Reg. § 1.752–1(a).

against the entity. Ray's basis in his partnership interest does not include his share of these contingent liabilities. ■

A partner's share of entity-level debt usually increases as a result of increases in outstanding partnership debt.

EXAMPLE 24

Jim and Becky contribute property to form the JB Partnership. Jim contributes cash of $30,000. Becky contributes land with an adjusted basis and fair market value of $45,000, subject to a liability of $15,000. The partnership borrows $50,000 to finance construction of a building on the contributed land. At the end of the first year, the accrual basis partnership owes $3,500 in trade accounts payable to various vendors. No other operating activities occurred. If Jim and Becky share equally in liabilities, the partners' bases in their partnership interests are determined as follows.

Jim's Basis		Becky's Basis	
Contributed cash	$30,000	Basis in contributed land	$ 45,000
Share of debt on land (assumed by partnership)	7,500	Less: Debt assumed by partnership	(15,000)
Share of construction loan	25,000	Share of debt on land (assumed by partnership)	7,500
Share of trade accounts payable	1,750	Share of construction loan	25,000
		Share of trade accounts payable	1,750
	$64,250		$ 64,250

In this case, it is reasonable that the parties have an equal basis after contributing their respective properties, because each is a 50% owner and they contributed property with identical net bases and identical *net* fair market values. ■

A decrease in a partner's share of partnership debt decreases the partner's basis. A partner's share of partnership debt decreases as a result of (1) decreases in total partnership debt and (2) assumption of a partner's debt by the entity. This limits the partner's ability to deduct current-year flow-through losses.

6 *Find more information on this topic at our Web site: http://wft-entities.swcollege.com.*

Other Factors Affecting Basis Calculations. The partner's basis is also affected by (1) postacquisition contributions of cash or property to the partnership and (2) postacquisition distributions of cash or property from the partnership.[38]

EXAMPLE 25

Ed is a one-third partner in the ERM Partnership. On January 1, 2001, Ed's basis in his partnership interest was $50,000. During 2001, the calendar year, accrual basis partnership generated ordinary taxable income of $210,000. It also received $60,000 of tax-exempt interest income from City of Buffalo bonds. It paid $3,000 in nondeductible bribes to local law enforcement officials, so that the police would not notify the Federal government about the products that the entity had imported without paying the proper tariffs. On July 1, 2001, Ed contributed $20,000 cash and a computer (zero basis to him) to the partnership. Ed's monthly draw from the partnership is $3,000; this is not a guaranteed payment. The only liabilities that the partnership has incurred are trade accounts payable. On January 1, 2001,

---

[38]§ 733.

Operations of the Partnership

> **Basis is generally adjusted in the following order.**
> Initial basis. Amount paid for partnership interest, or gift or inherited basis (including share of partnership debt).
>
> \+ Partner's subsequent asset contributions
> \+ Since interest acquired, partner's share of the partnership's
>
> - Debt increase
> - Income items
> - Tax-exempt income items
> - Excess of depletion deductions over adjusted basis of property subject to depletion
>
> \- Partner's distributions and withdrawals
> \- Since interest acquired, partner's share of the partnership's
>
> - Debt decrease
> - Nondeductible items not chargeable to a capital account
> - Special depletion deduction for oil and gas wells
> - Loss items
>
> **The basis of a partner's interest can never be negative.**

the trade accounts payable totaled $45,000; this account balance was $21,000 on December 31, 2001. Ed shares in one-third of the partnership liabilities for basis purposes.

Ed's basis in the partnership on December 31, 2001, is $115,000, computed as follows.

Beginning balance	$ 50,000
Share of ordinary partnership income	70,000
Share of tax-exempt income	20,000
Share of nondeductible expenditures	(1,000)
Ed's basis in noncash capital contribution (computer)	–0–
Additional cash contributions	20,000
Capital withdrawal ($3,000 per month)	(36,000)
Share of net decrease in partnership liabilities [⅓ × ($45,000 − $21,000)]	(8,000)
	$115,000

EXAMPLE 26

Assume the same facts as in Example 25. If Ed withdraws cash of $115,000 from the partnership on January 1, 2002, the withdrawal is tax-free to him and reduces his basis to zero. The distribution is tax-free because Ed has recognized his share of the partnership's net income throughout his association with the entity via the annual flow-through of his share of the partnership's income and expense items to his personal tax return. Note that the $20,000 cash withdrawal of his share of the municipal bond interest retains its nontaxable character in this distribution. Ed receives the $20,000 tax-free because his basis was increased in 2001 when the partnership received the interest income. ■

Entity-level liabilities, and thus a partner's interest basis, change from day to day, but the partner's interest basis generally needs to be computed only once or twice a year. When a partnership interest is sold, exchanged, or retired, however, the partner must compute the adjusted basis as of the date the transaction occurs. Computation of gain or loss requires an accurate calculation of the partner's adjusted basis on the transaction date.

Figure 11–1 summarizes the rules for computing a partner's basis in a partnership interest.

LOSS LIMITATIONS

Partnership losses flow through to the partners for use on their tax returns. However, the amount and nature of the losses that may be used in a partner's tax computations may be limited. When limitations apply, all or a portion of the losses is suspended and carried forward until the rules allow them to be used. Only then can the losses decrease the partner's tax liability.

Three different limitations may apply to partnership losses that are passed through to a partner. The first allows the deduction of *losses* only to the extent the partner has adjusted basis for the partnership interest. Losses that are deductible under this basis limitation may then be subject to the *at-risk* limitations. Losses are deductible under this provision only to the extent the partner is at risk for the partnership interest. Any losses that survive this second limitation may be subject to a third limitation, the *passive* loss rules. Only losses that make it through all of these applicable limitations are eligible to be deducted on the partner's tax return.

EXAMPLE 27

Meg is a partner in a partnership that does not invest in real estate. On January 1, Meg's adjusted basis for her partnership interest is $50,000, and her at-risk amount is $35,000. Her share of losses from the partnership for the year is $60,000, all of which is passive. She has one other passive income-producing investment that produced $25,000 of passive income during the year. Meg can deduct $25,000 of partnership losses on her Form 1040.

Applicable Provision	Deductible Loss	Suspended Loss
Basis limitation	$50,000	$10,000
At-risk limitation	35,000	15,000
Passive loss limitation	25,000	10,000

Meg can deduct only $50,000 under the basis limitation. Of this $50,000, only $35,000 is deductible under the at-risk limitation. Under the passive loss limitation, passive losses can only be deducted against passive income. Thus, Meg can deduct only $25,000 on her return. The remaining $35,000 of losses is suspended. ∎

Basis Limitation. A partner may only deduct losses flowing through from the partnership to the extent of the partner's adjusted basis in the partnership.[39] A partner's adjusted basis in the partnership is determined at the end of the partnership's taxable year. It is adjusted for distributions and any partnership gains during the year, but it is determined *before considering any losses for the year*.

Losses that cannot be deducted because of this rule are suspended and carried forward (never back) for use against future increases in the partner's adjusted basis. Such increases might result from additional capital contributions, from sharing in additional partnership debts, or from future partnership income.

EXAMPLE 28

Carol and Dan do business as the CD Partnership, sharing profits and losses equally. All parties use the calendar year. At the start of the current year, the basis of Carol's partnership interest is $25,000. The partnership sustains an operating loss of $80,000 in the current year. Only $25,000 of Carol's $40,000 allocable share of the partnership loss can be deducted under the basis limitation. As a result, the basis of Carol's partnership interest is zero as of January 1 of the following year, and Carol must carry forward the remaining $15,000 of partnership losses. ∎

---

[39]§ 704(d).

EXAMPLE 29	Assume the same facts as in Example 28, and that the partnership earns a profit of $70,000 for the next calendar year. Carol reports net partnership income of $20,000 ($35,000 distributive share of income − $15,000 carryforward loss). The basis of Carol's partnership interest becomes $20,000. ∎

PLANNING CONSIDERATIONS

Make Your Own Tax Shelter

In Example 28, Carol's entire $40,000 share of the current-year partnership loss could have been deducted under the basis limitation in the current year if she had contributed an additional $15,000 or more in capital by December 31. Alternatively, if the partnership had incurred additional debt by the end of the current year, Carol's basis might have been increased to permit some or all of the loss to be deducted in that year. Thus, if partnership losses are projected for a given year, careful tax planning can ensure their deductibility under the basis limitation.

Notice that, in Figure 11–1, contributions to capital, distributions from the partnership, and partnership income items are taken into account before loss items. This *losses last* rule can produce some unusual results in taxation of partnership distributions and deductibility of losses.

| EXAMPLE 30 | The Ellen-Glenn Partnership is owned equally by partners Ellen and Glenn. At the beginning of the year, Ellen's basis in her partnership interest is exactly $0. Her share of partnership income is $10,000 for the year, and she receives a $10,000 distribution from the partnership.

Under the basis adjustment ordering rules of Figure 11–1, Ellen's basis is first increased by the $10,000 of partnership income; then it is decreased by her $10,000 distribution. She reports her $10,000 share of partnership taxable income on her personal tax return. Her basis at the end of the year is exactly $0 ($0 + $10,000 income − $10,000 distribution). ∎ |
|---|---|

| EXAMPLE 31 | Assume the same facts as in Example 30, except that Ellen's share of partnership operating results is a $10,000 loss instead of $10,000 income. She again receives a $10,000 distribution.

A distribution of cash in excess of basis in the partnership interest results in a gain to the distributee partner to the extent of the excess. Ellen's distribution is considered before the deductibility of the loss is evaluated under the basis limitation.

Therefore Ellen recognizes gain on the $10,000 distribution because she has no basis in her partnership interest. The gain effectively ensures that she still has a $0 basis after the distribution. The loss cannot be deducted under the basis limitation rule because Ellen has no basis in her partnership interest. ∎ |
|---|---|

Given this $20,000 difference in partnership earnings in the two examples ($10,000 income versus $10,000 loss), does income taxed to Ellen differ in the same way? Actually, she reports $10,000 of income (gain) in each case: ordinary income in Example 30, and (probably) a capital gain from the distribution in Example 31. In Example 31, she also has a $10,000 suspended loss carryforward. These results are due solely to the basis adjustment ordering rules.

At-Risk Limitation.   Under the at-risk rules, the partnership losses from business and income-producing activities that individual partners and closely held C corporation partners can deduct are limited to amounts that are economically invested in the partnership. Invested amounts include the cash and the adjusted basis of property contributed by the partner and the partner's share of partnership earnings that has not been withdrawn.[40] A closely held C corporation exists when five or fewer individuals own more than 50 percent of the entity's stock under appropriate attribution and ownership rules.

When some or all of the partners are personally liable for partnership recourse debt, that debt is included in the adjusted basis of those partners. Usually, those partners also include the debt in their amount at risk.

No partner, however, carries any financial risk on nonrecourse debt. Therefore, as a general rule, partners cannot include nonrecourse debt in their amount at risk even though that debt is included in the adjusted basis of their partnership interest. This rule has an exception, however, that applies in many cases. Real estate nonrecourse financing provided by a bank, retirement plan, or similar party or by a Federal, state, or local government generally is deemed to be at risk.[41] Such debt is termed **qualified nonrecourse debt.** In summary, although the general rule provides that nonrecourse debt is not at risk, the overriding exception may provide that it is deemed to be at risk.

EXAMPLE 32

Kelly invests $5,000 in the Kelly Green Limited Partnership as a 5% general partner. Shortly thereafter, the partnership acquires the master recording of a well-known vocalist for $250,000 ($50,000 from the partnership and $200,000 secured from a local bank via a *recourse* mortgage). Kelly's share of the recourse debt is $10,000, and her basis in her partnership interest is $15,000 ($5,000 cash investment + $10,000 debt share). Since the debt is recourse, Kelly's at-risk amount also is $15,000. Kelly's share of partnership losses in the first year of operations is $11,000. Kelly is entitled to deduct the full $11,000 of partnership losses under both the basis and the at-risk limitations because this amount is less than both her outside basis and at-risk amount. ■

EXAMPLE 33

Assume the same facts as in Example 32, except the bank loan is nonrecourse (the partners have no direct liability under the terms of the loan in the case of a default). Kelly's basis in her partnership interest still is $15,000, but she can deduct only $5,000 of the flow-through loss. The amount she has at risk in the partnership does not include the nonrecourse debt. (The debt does not relate to real estate so it is not qualified nonrecourse debt.) ■

deduct 5 & carry 6

Passive Activity Rules.   A partnership loss share may also be disallowed under the passive activity rules. Recall from Chapter 5 that an activity is considered passive if the taxpayer (in this case, a partner) does not materially participate or if the activity is considered a rental activity. Losses from passive partnership activities are aggregated by each partner with his or her other passive income and losses. Any net loss is suspended and carried forward to future years. Thus, the passive activity limitation applies at the partner level and is computed after the basis and at-risk limitations.

[40]§ 465(a).   [41]§ 465(b)(6).

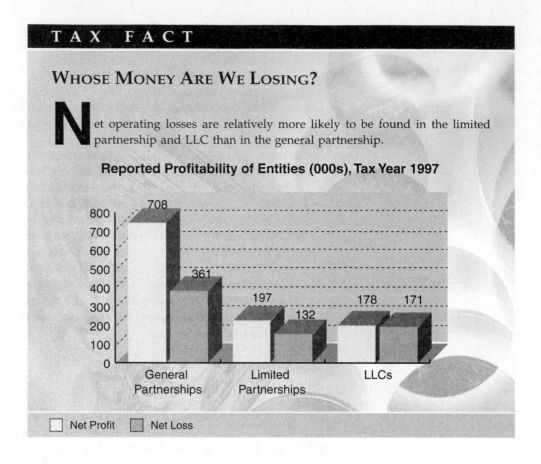

TAX FACT

WHOSE MONEY ARE WE LOSING?

Net operating losses are relatively more likely to be found in the limited partnership and LLC than in the general partnership.

Reported Profitability of Entities (000s), Tax Year 1997

General Partnerships: Net Profit 708, Net Loss 361
Limited Partnerships: Net Profit 197, Net Loss 132
LLCs: Net Profit 178, Net Loss 171

☐ Net Profit   ☐ Net Loss

PLANNING CONSIDERATIONS

Formation and Operation of a Partnership

In transferring assets to a partnership, potential partners should be cautious to ensure that they are not required to recognize any gain upon the creation of the entity. The non-recognition provisions of § 721 are relatively straightforward and resemble the provisions under § 351. However, any partner can make a tax-deferred contribution of assets to the entity either at the inception of the partnership or later. This possibility is not available to less-than-controlling shareholders in a corporation.

The partners should anticipate the tax benefits and pitfalls that are presented in Subchapter K and should take appropriate actions to resolve any resulting problems. Typically, all that is needed is an appropriate provision in the partnership agreement (e.g., with respect to differing allocation percentages for gains and losses). Recall, however, that a special allocation of income, expense, or credit items in the partnership agreement must satisfy certain requirements before it is acceptable to the IRS.

LEARNING OBJECTIVE 7

Review the treatment of transactions between a partner and the partnership.

Transactions between Partner and Partnership

Many types of transactions occur between a partnership and one of its partners. The partner may contribute property to the partnership, perform services for the partnership, or receive distributions from the partnership. The partner may borrow money from or lend money to the partnership. Property may be bought and sold between the partner and the partnership. Several of these transactions were

[handwritten margin notes: "doesn't do anything to basis", "not determined with reference to partnership income", "partner deduction include", "ex- salary from partnership", "withdrawal reduces basis"]

discussed earlier in the chapter. The remaining types of partner-partnership transactions are the focus of this section.

GUARANTEED PAYMENTS

If a partnership makes a payment to a partner in his or her capacity as a partner, the payment may be a draw against the partner's share of partnership income; a return of some or all of the partner's original capital contribution; or a guaranteed payment, among other treatments. A **guaranteed payment** is a payment for services performed by the partner or for the use of the partner's capital. The payment may not be determined by reference to partnership income. Guaranteed payments are usually expressed as a fixed-dollar amount or as a percentage of capital that the partner has invested in the partnership. Whether the partnership deducts or capitalizes the guaranteed payment depends on the nature of the payment.

EXAMPLE 34	David, Donald, and Dale formed the accrual basis DDD Partnership. According to the partnership agreement, David is to manage the partnership and receive a $21,000 distribution from the entity every year, payable in 12 monthly installments. Donald is to receive an amount that is equal to 18% of his capital account, as it is computed by the firm's accountant at the beginning of the year, payable in 12 monthly installments. Dale is the partnership's advertising specialist. He withdraws about 3% of the partnership's net income every month for his personal use. David and Donald receive guaranteed payments from the partnership, but Dale does not. ∎

Guaranteed payments resemble the salary or interest payments of other businesses and receive somewhat similar income tax treatment.[42] In contrast to the provision that usually applies to withdrawals of assets by partners from their partnerships, guaranteed payments are deductible (or capitalized) by the entity. Deductible guaranteed payments, like any other deductible expenses of a partnership, can create an ordinary loss for the entity. Partners receiving a guaranteed payment report ordinary income, treated as paid on the last day of the entity's tax year.

EXAMPLE 35	Continue with the situation introduced in Example 34. For calendar year 2001, David receives the $21,000 as provided by the partnership agreement, Donald's guaranteed payment for 2001 is $17,000, and Dale withdraws $20,000 under his personal expenditures clause. Before considering these amounts, the partnership's ordinary income for 2001 is $650,000. The partnership can deduct its payments to David and Donald, so the final amount of its 2001 ordinary income is $612,000 ($650,000 − $21,000 − $17,000). Thus, each of the equal partners is allocated $204,000 of ordinary partnership income for their 2001 individual income tax returns ($612,000 ÷ 3). In addition, David reports the $21,000 guaranteed payment as income, and Donald includes the $17,000 guaranteed payment in his 2001 income. Dale's partnership draw is deemed to have come from his allocated $204,000 (or from the accumulated partnership income that was taxed to him in prior years) and is not taxed separately to him. ∎

EXAMPLE 36	Assume the same facts as in Example 35, except that the partnership's tax year ends on March 31, 2002. The total amount of the guaranteed payments is taxable to the partners on that date. Thus, even though David received 9 of his 12 payments for fiscal 2002 in the 2001 calendar year, all of his guaranteed payments are taxable to him in 2002. Similarly, all of Donald's guaranteed payments are taxable to him in 2002, rather than when they are received. The deduction for, and the gross income from, guaranteed payments is allowed on the same date that all of the other income and expense items relative to the partnership are allocated to the partners (i.e., on the last day of the entity's tax year). ∎

---

[42]§ 707(c).

CONCEPT SUMMARY 11–3

Partner-Partnership Transactions

1. Partners can transact business with their partnerships in a nonpartner capacity. These transactions include the sale and exchange of property, rentals, loans of funds, etc.
2. A payment to a partner may be classified as a guaranteed payment if it is for services or use of the partner's capital and is not based on partnership income. A guaranteed payment usually is deductible by the partnership and is included in the partner's income on the last day of the partnership's tax year.
3. A payment to a partner may be treated as being to an outside (though related) party. Such a payment is deductible or capitalizable by the partnership at the time it must be included in income under the partner's method of accounting.
4. Guaranteed payments and payments to a partner that are treated as being to an outside party are deductible if the payment constitutes an ordinary and necessary (rather than capitalizable) business expense.
5. Losses are disallowed between a partner or related party and a partnership when the partner or related party owns more than a 50% interest in the partnership's capital or profits.
6. Income from a related-party sale is treated as ordinary income if the property is not a capital asset to both the transferor and the transferee.
7. Partners are not employees of their partnership, so the entity cannot deduct payments for partner fringe benefits, nor need it withhold or pay any payroll tax for payments to partners.

OTHER TRANSACTIONS BETWEEN A PARTNER AND A PARTNERSHIP

Certain transactions between a partner and the partnership are treated as if the partner were an outsider, dealing with the partnership at arm's length.[43] Loan transactions, rental payments, and sales of property between the partner and the partnership are generally treated in this manner.

EXAMPLE 37

Emilio, a one-third partner in the ABC Partnership, owns a tract of land that the partnership wishes to purchase. The land has a fair market value of $30,000 and an adjusted basis to Emilio of $17,000. If Emilio sells the land to the partnership, he recognizes a $13,000 gain on the sale, and the partnership takes a $30,000 cost basis in the land. If the land has a fair market value of $10,000 on the sale date, Emilio recognizes a $7,000 loss. ∎

7 *Find more information on this topic at our Web site: **http://wft-entities.swcollege.com**.*

Sales of Property.   No loss is recognized on a sale of property between a person and a partnership when the person owns, directly or indirectly, more than 50 percent of partnership capital or profits.[44] The disallowed loss may not vanish entirely, however. If the person eventually sells the property at a gain, the disallowed loss reduces the gain that would otherwise be recognized.[45]

EXAMPLE 38

Barry sells land (adjusted basis, $30,000; fair market value, $45,000) to a partnership in which he controls a 60% capital interest. The partnership pays him $20,000 for the land. Barry cannot deduct his $10,000 realized loss. The sale apparently was not at arm's length, but the taxpayer's intentions are irrelevant. Barry and the partnership are related parties, and the loss is disallowed.

---

[43]§ 707(a).
[44]§ 707(b).

[45]This is similar to treatment under § 267.

When the partnership sells the land to an outsider at a later date, it receives a sales price of $44,000. The partnership can offset the recognition of its $24,000 realized gain on the subsequent sale ($44,000 sales proceeds − $20,000 adjusted basis) by the amount of the $10,000 prior disallowed loss ($20,000 − $30,000). Thus, the partnership recognizes a $14,000 gain on its sale of the land. ■

Using a similar rationale, any gain that is realized on a sale or exchange between a partner and a partnership in which the partner controls a capital or profit interest of more than 50 percent is recognized as ordinary income, unless the asset is a capital asset to both the seller and the purchaser.[46]

EXAMPLE 39

Kristin purchases some land (adjusted basis, $30,000; fair market value, $45,000) for $45,000 from a partnership in which she controls a 90% profit interest. The land was a capital asset to the partnership. If Kristin holds the land as a capital asset, the partnership recognizes a $15,000 capital gain. However, if Kristin is a land developer and the property is not a capital asset to her, the property must recognize $15,000 of ordinary income from the sale, even though the property was a capital asset to the partnership. ■

PARTNERS AS EMPLOYEES

A partner usually does not qualify as an employee for tax purposes. For example, a partner receiving guaranteed payments is not regarded as an employee of the partnership for purposes of payroll taxes (e.g., FICA or FUTA). Moreover, since a partner is not an employee, the partnership cannot deduct its payments for the partner's fringe benefits. Nonetheless, a general partner's distributive share of ordinary partnership income and guaranteed payments for services are generally subject to the Federal self-employment tax.[47]

PLANNING CONSIDERATIONS

Transactions between Partners and Partnerships

Partners should be careful when engaging in transactions with the partnership to ensure that no negative tax results occur. A partner who owns a majority of the partnership generally should not sell property at a loss to the partnership because the loss is disallowed. Similarly, a majority partner should not sell a capital asset to the partnership at a gain, if the asset is to be used by the partnership as other than a capital asset. The gain on this transaction is taxed as ordinary income to the selling partner rather than as capital gain.

As an alternative to selling property to a partnership, the partner may lease it to the partnership. The partner recognizes rent income, and the partnership has a rent expense.

A partner who needs more cash immediately can sell the property to an outside third party; then the third party can lease the property to the partnership for a fair rental.

The timing of the deduction for payments by accrual basis partnerships to cash basis partners varies depending on whether the payment is a guaranteed payment or is treated as a payment to an outsider. If the payment is a guaranteed payment, the deduction occurs when the partnership properly accrues the payment. If the payment is treated as a payment to an outsider, the actual date the payment is made controls the timing of the deduction.

---

[46]§ 707(b)(2).   [47]§ 1402(a).

CONCEPT SUMMARY 11–4

Advantages and Disadvantages of the Partnership Form

The partnership form may be attractive when one or more of the following factors is present:

- The entity is generating net taxable losses and/or valuable tax credits, which will be of use to the owners.
- The owners want to avoid complex corporate administrative and filing requirements.
- Other means of reducing the effects of the double taxation of corporate business income (e.g., compensation to owners, interest, and rental payments) have been exhausted.
- The entity does not generate material amounts of tax preference and adjustment items, which increase the alternative minimum tax liabilities of its owners.
- The entity is generating net passive income, which its owners can use to claim immediate deductions for net passive losses that they have generated from other sources.
- Given the asset holdings and distribution practices of the entity, the possibility of liability under the accumulated earnings and personal holding company taxes is significant.
- The owners wish to make special allocations of certain income or deduction items that are not possible under the C or S corporation forms.
- The owners have adequate bases in their partnership interests to facilitate the deduction of flow-through losses and the assignment of an adequate basis to assets distributed in-kind to the partners.

The partnership form may be less attractive when one or more of the following factors is present:

- The maximum marginal tax rate applicable to individual owners is higher than the rate applicable to C corporations, and the income is not expected to be distributed soon. (If distributed by a C corporation, double taxation would likely occur.)
- The entity is generating net taxable income without distributing any cash to the owners. The owners would not receive any funds from the entity with which to pay the tax on the entity's earnings.
- The type of income that the entity is generating (e.g., business and portfolio income) is not as attractive to its owners as net passive income would be because the owners could use net passive income to offset the net passive losses that they have generated on their own.
- The entity is in a high-exposure business, and the owners desire protection from personal liability. An LLC or LLP structure may be available, however, to limit personal liability.
- The owners want to avoid Federal self-employment tax.

LEARNING OBJECTIVE 8

Describe the application of partnership tax law provisions to limited liability companies (LLCs) and limited liability partnerships (LLPs).

Limited Liability Entities

LIMITED LIABILITY COMPANIES

The *limited liability company (LLC)* combines partnership taxation with limited personal liability for all owners of the entity. All states and the District of Columbia have passed legislation permitting the establishment of LLCs.

Taxation of LLCs. A properly structured LLC may be taxed as a partnership under the "check-the-box" rules. Because LLC members are not personally liable for the debts of the entity, the LLC is effectively treated as a limited partnership with no general partners. This may result in unusual application of partnership taxation rules. The IRS has not specifically ruled on most aspects of LLC taxation, so several of the following comments are based on speculation about how a partnership with no general partners would be taxed.

TAX IN THE NEWS

PARTNERSHIPS AROUND THE WORLD—AND BEYOND

Technology continues to act as a catalyst—and incentive—for the creation of joint ventures. From Web kiosks at gas stations to global satellite networks, high-tech companies are forging alliances to bring technology to consumers. Microsoft has teamed up with Amoco to provide news, weather, and other content for customers to watch while they fill up at the gas station. America Online (AOL) and Radiant Systems, Inc., formed their own venture to offer programming at other gas stations, pizza parlors, and numerous other retail outlets. Later, AOL orchestrated a takeover of entertainment giant Time Warner. These ventures appear to be spurred by a desire to capture larger shares of the ever-expanding global market.

Meanwhile, AT&T and WorldCom are continuing to align themselves with partners in foreign telecommunications markets: each wants to have the widest possible service coverage area so it can offer efficient communications and computer networking to business clients with a global presence.

Primestar is a partnership formed by several media and cable companies to offer digital satellite television services on numerous channels to customers for a monthly rental fee. And several partnerships have been formed to establish satellite-based Web communications around the world.

- Formation of a new LLC is treated in the same manner as formation of a partnership. Generally, no gain or loss is recognized by the LLC member or the LLC, the member takes a substituted basis in the LLC interest, and the LLC takes a carryover basis in the assets it receives.
- An LLC's income and losses are allocated proportionately. Special allocations are permitted, as long as they demonstrate economic effect.
- Contributed property with built-in gains can be subject to tax on certain distributions within five years of the contribution.
- A loss must meet the basis, at-risk, and passive loss limitations to be currently deductible. Because the debt is considered nonrecourse to each of the members, it may not be included in the at-risk limitation unless it is "qualified nonrecourse financing." The IRS has not issued rulings as to whether a member is treated as a material or active participant of an LLC for passive loss purposes. Presumably, passive or active status will be based on the time the member spends in LLC activities.
- The initial accounting period and accounting method elections are available to an LLC.
- An LLC member's share of partnership income is *not* subject to self-employment taxes.
- Property takes a carryover or substituted basis when distributed from an LLC.

Advantages of an LLC. An LLC offers certain advantages over a limited partnership.

- Generally, none of the members of an LLC is personally liable for the entity's debts. General partners in a limited partnership have personal liability for partnership recourse debts.

- Limited partners cannot participate in the management of a partnership. All owners of an LLC have the legal right to participate in the entity's management.

An LLC also offers certain advantages over an S corporation (see Chapter 12), including the following.

- An LLC can have an unlimited number of owners, while an S corporation is limited to 75 shareholders.
- Any taxpayers, including corporations, nonresident aliens, other partnerships, and trusts, can be owners of an LLC. S corporation shares can be held only by specified parties.
- The transfer of property to an LLC in exchange for an ownership interest in the entity is governed by partnership tax provisions rather than corporate tax provisions. Thus, the transfers need not satisfy the 80 percent control requirement needed for tax-free treatment under the corporate tax statutes.
- The S corporation taxes on built-in gains and passive income do not apply to LLCs.
- An owner's basis in an LLC includes the owner's share of almost all LLC liabilities under § 752. Only certain entity liabilities are included in the S corporation shareholder's basis.
- An LLC may make special allocations, whereas S corporations must allocate income, loss, etc., only on a per share/per day basis.

Disadvantages of an LLC. The disadvantages of an LLC stem primarily from the entity's relative newness. There is no established body of case law interpreting the various state statutes, so the application of specific provisions is uncertain. An additional uncertainty for LLCs that operate in more than one jurisdiction is which state's law will prevail and how it will be applied.

Among other factors, statutes differ from state to state as to the type of business an LLC can conduct—primarily the extent to which a service-providing firm can operate as an LLC. A service entity may find it cannot operate as an LLC in several jurisdictions where it conducts business. Despite these uncertainties and limitations, LLCs are being formed at increasing rates, and the ranks of multistate LLCs are rising quickly.

LIMITED LIABILITY PARTNERSHIPS

In 1991, Texas began to allow professional practices to organize as registered *limited liability partnerships (LLPs)*. Since then, other states have adopted similar legislation. The difference between a general partnership and an LLP is small, but very significant. Recall that general partners are jointly and severally liable for all partnership debts. Partners in a registered LLP are jointly and severally liable for contractual liability (i.e., they are treated as general partners for commercial debt). They are also personally liable for their own malpractice or other torts. They are not, however, personally liable for the malpractice and torts of their partners. As a result, the exposure of their personal assets to lawsuits filed against other partners and the partnership is considerably reduced.

An LLP must have formal documents of organization and register with the state. LLPs are taxed as partnerships under Federal tax rules.

SUMMARY

Partnerships are popular among business owners because formation of the entity is relatively simple and tax-free. The Code places very few restrictions on who can be a partner. Partnerships are especially attractive when operating losses are anticipated, or when marginal rates that would apply to partnership income are less than those that would be paid by a C corporation. Partnerships do not offer the limited liability of a corporate entity, but the use of limited partnerships, LLCs, and LLPs can offer some protection to the owners.

Partnerships are tax-reporting, not taxpaying, entities. Distributive shares of ordinary income and separately stated items are taxed to the partners on the last day of the tax year. Special allocations and guaranteed payments are allowed and offer partners the ability to tailor the cash-flow and taxable amounts that are distributed by the entity to its owners. Deductions for flow-through losses may be limited by the passive activity, related-party, and at-risk rules, as well as by the partner's interest basis. The flexibility of the partnership rules makes this form continually attractive to new businesses, especially in a global setting.

Suggested Further Readings

"Can Limited Partnerships Elect Out of Subchapter K?" *Journal of Taxation*, August 1999, p. 125.

Bruce P. Ely and Christopher R. Grissom, "State Taxation of LLCs and LLPs," *Business Entities*, March/April 1999, pp. 24–32.

Charles I. Middleton, "Use of a Partnership in International Dealings Can Be Beneficial for Both Inbound and Outbound Transactions," *Journal of Partnership Taxation*, Winter 1999, pp. 306–334.

Jay A. Soled, "Gifts of Partnership Interests: An Income Tax Perspective," *Business Entities*, May/June 1999, pp. 30–34.

KEY TERMS

Basis in partnership interest, 11-9

Capital account, 11–9

Capital interest, 11–8

Capital sharing ratio, 11–8

Disguised sale, 11–11

Economic effect test, 11–20

General partnership, 11–5

Guaranteed payment, 11–29

Inside basis, 11–14

Limited liability company (LLC), 11–5

Limited liability partnership (LLP), 11–5

Limited partnership, 11–5

Nonrecourse debt, 11–22

Outside basis, 11–14

Precontribution gain or loss, 11–20

Profit and loss sharing ratios, 11–8

Profits (loss) interest, 11–8

Qualified nonrecourse debt, 11–27

Recourse debt, 11–22

Separately stated item, 11–6

Special allocation, 11-8

Syndication costs, 11–15

Problem Materials

PROBLEMS

1. Justin and Tiffany will contribute property to form the equal TJ Partnership. Justin will contibute cash of $20,000 plus land with a fair market value of $80,000 and an adjusted basis of $65,000. Tiffany currently operates a sole proprietorship with assets valued at $100,000 and an adjusted basis of $125,000. Tiffany will contribute these assets in-kind to the partnership. Describe the tax consequences of the formation to Tiffany, Justin, and the partnership.

2. Larry and Ken form an equal partnership with a cash contribution of $50,000 from Larry and a property contribution (adjusted basis of $30,000 and a fair market value of $50,000) from Ken.
   a. How much gain, if any, must Larry recognize on the transfer? Must Ken recognize any gain?
   b. What is Larry's basis in his partnership interest?
   c. What is Ken's basis in his partnership interest?
   d. What basis does the partnership take in the property transferred by Ken?

3. Tom and Katie form an equal partnership with a $80,000 cash contribution from Tom and a contribution of property (basis of $100,000, fair market value of $80,000) from Katie.
   a. Compute Katie's realized and recognized gain or loss from the contribution.
   b. Compute Tom's basis in his partnership interest.
   c. Compute Katie's basis in her partnership interest.
   d. What basis does the partnership take in Katie's contributed asset?
   e. Are there more tax-effective ways to structure the transaction?

4. Three years after the S&P Partnership is formed, Sylvia, a 25% partner, contributes an additional $50,000 of cash and land she has held for investment. Sylvia's basis in the land is $60,000, and its fair market value is $100,000. Her basis in the partnership interest was $50,000 before this contribution. The partnership uses the land as a parking lot for four years and then sells it for $120,000.
   a. How much gain or loss does Sylvia recognize on the contribution?
   b. What is Sylvia's basis in her partnership interest immediately following this contribution?
   c. How much gain or loss does S&P recognize on this contribution?
   d. What is S&P's basis in the property it receives from Sylvia?
   e. How much gain or loss does the partnership recognize on the later sale of the land, and what is the character of the gain or loss? How much is allocated to Sylvia?

5. Block, Inc., a calendar year general contractor, and Strauss, Inc., a development corporation with a July 31 year-end, formed the equal SB Partnership on January 1 of the current year. Both partners are C corporations. The partnership was formed to construct and lease shopping centers in Wilmington, Delaware. Block contributed equipment (basis of $650,000, fair market value of $650,000), building permits, and architectural designs that had been created by Block's employees (basis of $0, fair market value of $100,000).

   Strauss contributed land (basis of $50,000, fair market value of $250,000) and cash of $500,000. The cash was used as follows.

Legal fees for drafting partnership agreement	$ 10,000
Materials and labor costs for construction in progress on shopping center	400,000
Office expense (utilities, rent, overhead, etc.)	90,000

   What issues must the partnership address in preparing its initial tax return?

6. Craig and Beth are equal members of the CB Partnership, formed on June 1 of the current year. Craig contributed land that he inherited from his father three years ago. Craig's father purchased the land in 1946 for $6,000. The land was worth $50,000 when the father died. The fair market value of the land was $75,000 at the date it was contributed to the partnership.

    Beth has significant experience developing real estate. After the partnership is formed, she will prepare a plan for developing the property and secure zoning approvals for the partnership. She would normally bill a third party $25,000 for these efforts. Beth will also contribute $50,000 of cash in exchange for her 50% interest in the partnership. The value of her 50% interest is $75,000.
    a. How much gain or income will Craig recognize on his contribution of the land to the partnership? What is the character of any gain or income recognized?
    b. What basis will Craig take in his partnership interest?
    c. How much gain or income will Beth recognize on the formation of the partnership? What is the character of any gain or income recognized?
    d. What basis will Beth take in her partnership interest?
    e. Construct an opening balance sheet for the partnership reflecting the partnership's basis in the assets and the fair market value of these assets.
    f. Outline any planning opportunities that may minimize current taxation to any of the parties.

7. Continue with the facts presented in Problem 6. At the end of the first year, the partnership distributes the $50,000 of cash to Craig. No distribution is made to Beth.
    a. Under general tax rules, how would the payment to Craig be treated?
    b. How much income or gain would Craig recognize as a result of the payment?
    c. Under general tax rules, what basis would the partnership take in the land Craig contributed?
    d. What alternate treatment might the IRS try to impose?
    e. Under the alternate treatment, how much income or gain would Craig recognize?
    f. Under the alternate treatment, what basis would the partnership take in the land contributed by Craig?
    g. How can the transaction be restructured to minimize risk of IRS recharacterization?

8. The SJ Partnership was formed to acquire land and subdivide it as residential housing lots. On July 1, 2001, Sarah contributed land valued at $200,000 to the partnership in exchange for a 50% interest. She had purchased the land in 1997 for $160,000 and held it for investment purposes (capital asset). The partnership holds the land as inventory.

    On the same date, Joe contributed land valued at $200,000 that he had purchased in 1996 for $240,000. He also became a 50% owner in SJ. Joe is a real estate developer, but he held this land personally for investment purposes. The partnership holds this land as inventory.

    In 2002, the partnership sells the land contributed by Sarah for $220,000.

    In 2003, the partnership sells half of the subdivided real estate contributed by Joe for $88,000. The other half is finally sold in 2008 for $108,000.
    a. What is each partner's initial basis in his or her partnership interest?
    b. What is the amount of gain or loss recognized on the sale of the land contributed by Sarah? What is the character of this gain or loss?
    c. What is the amount of gain or loss recognized each year on the sale of the land contributed by Joe? What is the character of this gain or loss?

9. The partnership agreement for the SJ Partnership in Problem 8 provides that all gains and losses are allocated equally between the partners unless otherwise required under the tax law.
    a. How will the gains or losses determined in (b) and (c) in Problem 8 be allocated to each of the partners?
    b. Calculate each partner's basis in his or her partnership interest at December 31, 2008. Assume the partnership has no transactions through the end of the year 2008 other than the transactions described in Problem 8. Why are these balances the same or different?

10. The cash basis Sparrow Partnership incurred the following costs in 2001, the partner-ship's initial year of operations.

Legal fees for preparing partnership agreement	$ 3,000
Printing costs for preparing documents used to help sell the partnership interests	16,000
Accounting fees for tax advice of an organizational nature	5,000
Pre-opening expenses to establish office, set up accounting systems, advertise for business, etc.	20,000

All of these costs were paid in 2001, except for $1,000 of the legal fees, which were not paid until 2002. If the partnership begins business in July 2001, how much can Sparrow deduct in that year? In 2002? What elections must the partnership make in its initial tax return to secure the deductions?

11. Lisa and Lori are equal members of the Redbird Partnership. They are real estate investors who formed the partnership several years ago with equal cash contributions. Redbird then purchased a piece of land.

On January 1 of the current year, to acquire a one-third interest in the entity, Lana contributed some land she had held for investment to the partnership. Lana purchased the land three years ago for $30,000; its fair market value at the contribution date was $40,000. No special allocation agreements were in effect before or after Lana was admit-ted to the partnership. The Redbird Partnership holds all land for investment.

Immediately before Lana's property contribution, the balance sheet of the Redbird Partnership was as follows.

	Basis	FMV		Basis	FMV
Land	$5,000	$80,000	Lisa, capital	$2,500	$40,000
			Lori, capital	2,500	40,000
	$5,000	$80,000		$5,000	$80,000

a. At the contribution date, what is Lana's basis in her interest in the Redbird Partnership?
b. When does the partnership's holding period begin for the contributed land?
c. On June 30 of the current year, the partnership sold the land contributed by Lana for $40,000. How much is the recognized gain or loss, and how is it allocated among the partners?
d. Prepare a balance sheet reflecting basis and fair market value for the partnership immediately after the land sale.

12. Assume the same facts as in Problem 11, with the following exceptions.

- Lana purchased the land three years ago for $50,000. Its fair market value was $40,000 when it was contributed to the partnership.

- Redbird sold the land contributed by Lana for $34,000.

a. How much is the recognized gain or loss, and how is it allocated among the partners?
b. Prepare a balance sheet reflecting basis and fair market value for the partnership immediately after the land sale. Complete schedules that support the amount in each partner's capital account.

13. Carrie and Matt are equal partners in the accrual basis CM Partnership. At the beginning of the current year, Carrie's capital account has a balance of $60,000, and the partnership has recourse debts of $80,000 payable to unrelated parties. All partnership recourse debt is shared equally between the partners. The following information about CM's operations for the current year is obtained from the partnership's records.

Taxable income	$80,000
Tax-exempt interest income	5,000
§ 1231 gain	6,000
Long-term capital gain	500
Short-term capital loss	4,000
IRS penalty	3,000
Charitable contribution to Red Cross	1,000
Cash distribution to Carrie	14,000
Payment of Carrie's medical expenses	2,000

Assume that year-end partnership debt payable to unrelated parties is $100,000.
a. If all transactions are reflected in her beginning capital account and basis in the same manner, what is Carrie's basis in the partnership interest at the beginning of the year?
b. What is Carrie's basis in the partnership interest at the end of the current year?

14. Harlen will contribute $50,000 of cash to the HJ Partnership. Jane currently operates a sole proprietorship with assets valued at $50,000. Jane's tax basis in these assets is $75,000. Jane will either contribute these assets to the partnership in exchange for a 50% interest, or she will sell the assets to Brady Salvage (a third party) for their $50,000 fair market value and contribute that cash to the partnership. The partnership needs assets similar to those Jane owns, but it can purchase new assets from a third party for $60,000. Describe the tax consequences of each alternative to both Jane and the partnership.

15. The RUB Partnership reported the following items during the current tax year.

Taxable income	$120,000
Municipal bond interest income	10,000
Gain on sale of real estate	60,000

Taxable income includes $20,000 of income from the collection of cash basis accounts receivable contributed by 25% partner Rolfe at the beginning of the year.

The municipal bond income was earned on bonds contributed by 50% partner Una. None of the interest was accrued on the contribution date. The partnership agreement provides that all this income will be specially allocated to Una this year, and no offsetting allocation will be made now or later.

The real estate gain resulted from the sale of a parcel of land contributed by 25% partner Bart. When the property was contributed, it was valued at $100,000 and Bart's basis was $80,000. The real estate is a capital asset to both Bart and the partnership.

Prepare a schedule showing how each item is allocated to each of the three partners. The partnership will maintain capital account balances and perform all other record keeping required to meet the substantial economic effect requirements.

16. The KB Partnership is owned equally by Kay and Bob. Bob's basis is $20,000 at the beginning of the tax year. Kay's basis is $12,000 at the beginning of the year. KB reported the following income and expenses for the current tax year.

Sales revenue	$200,000
Cost of sales	110,000
Guaranteed payment to Kay	30,000
Depreciation expense	15,000
Utilities	20,000
Rent	16,000
Interest income	3,000
Tax-exempt interest income	6,000

| Long-term capital loss | $ 4,000 |
| Payment to Mount Vernon Hospital for Bob's medical expenses | 10,000 |

a. Determine the ordinary partnership income and separately stated items for the partnership.

b. Calculate Bob's basis in his partnership interest at the end of the tax year. What items should Bob report on his Federal income tax return?

c. Calculate Kay's basis in her partnership interest at the end of the tax year. What items should Kay report on her Federal income tax return?

17. Assume the same facts as in Problem 16, except for the following.

• Partnership revenues were $160,000 instead of $200,000.

• Kay received a distribution of $20,000 cash.

a. Redetermine the ordinary income and separately stated items for the partnership.

b. Calculate Bob's basis in his partnership interest at the end of the tax year. How much income or loss should Bob report on his Federal income tax return?

c. Calculate Kay's basis in her partnership interest at the end of the tax year. How much income or loss should Kay report on her Federal income tax return?

18. Your client, the Williams Institute of Technology (WIT), is a 60% partner in the Research Industries Partnership (RIP). WIT is located at 76 Bradford Lane, St. Paul, MN 55164. The controller, Jeanine West, has sent you the following note and a copy of WIT's 2000 Schedule K–1 from the partnership.

Excerpt from client's note
"RIP" expects its 2001 operations to include the following.

| Net loss from operations | $200,000 |
| Capital gain from sale of land | 100,000 |

The land was contributed by DASH, the other partner, when its value was $260,000. The partnership sold the land for $300,000. The partnership used this cash to repay all the partnership debt and pay for research and development expenditures, which a tax partner in your firm has said RIP can deduct this year.

We want to be sure we can deduct our full share of this loss, but we do not believe we will have enough basis. We are a material participant in this partnership's activities."

Items Reported on the 2000 Schedule K–1	
WIT's share of partnership recourse liabilities	$90,000
WIT's ending capital account balance	30,000

Draft a letter to the controller that describes the following.

• WIT's allocation of partnership items.

• WIT's basis in the partnership interest following the allocation.

• Any limitations on loss deductions.

• Any recommendations you have that would allow WIT to claim the full amount of losses in 2001.

WIT's 2000 Schedule K–1 accurately reflects the information needed to compute its basis in the partnership interest. The research expenditures are fully deductible this year, as the partner said.

Your client has experience researching issues in the Internal Revenue Code, so you may use some citations. However, be sure that the letter is written in layperson's terms and that legal citations are minimized.

19. Lee, Brad, and Rick form the LBR Partnership on January 1 of the current year. In return for a 25% interest, Lee transfers property (basis of $15,000, fair market value of $17,500) subject to a nonrecourse liability of $10,000. The liability is assumed by the partnership. Brad transfers property (basis of $16,000, fair market value of $7,500) for a 25% interest, and Rick transfers cash of $15,000 for the remaining 50% interest.
    a. How much gain must Lee recognize on the transfer?
    b. What is Lee's basis in his interest in the partnership?
    c. How much loss may Brad recognize on the transfer?
    d. What is Brad's basis in his interest in the partnership?
    e. What is Rick's basis in his interest in the partnership?
    f. What basis does the LBR Partnership take in the property transferred by Lee?
    g. What is the partnership's basis in the property transferred by Brad?

20. Assume the same facts as in Problem 19, except that the property contributed by Lee has a fair market value of $27,500 and is subject to a nonrecourse mortgage of $20,000.
    a. What is Lee's basis in his partnership interest?
    b. How much gain must Lee recognize on the transfer?
    c. What is Brad's basis in his partnership interest?
    d. What is Rick's basis in his partnership interest?
    e. What basis does the LBR Partnership take in the property transferred by Lee?

21. Sam has operated a microbrewery (sole proprietorship) in southern Oregon for the past 15 years. The business has been highly profitable lately, and demand for the product will soon exceed the amount Sam can produce with his present facilities. Marcie, a long-time fan of the brewery, has offered to invest $1,500,000 for equipment to expand production. The assets and goodwill of the brewery are currently worth $1,000,000 (tax basis is only $200,000). Sam will continue to manage the business. He is not willing to own less than 50% of whatever arrangement they arrive at. What issues should Sam and Marcie address and document before finalizing their venture?

22. The BCD Partnership plans to distribute cash of $20,000 to partner Brad at the end of the tax year. The partnership reported a loss for the year, and Brad's share of the loss is $10,000. Brad has a basis of $15,000 in the partnership interest, including his share of partnership liabilities. The partnership expects to report substantial income in future years.
    a. What rules are used to calculate Brad's ending basis in his partnership interest?
    b. How much income or loss will Brad report for the tax year?
    c. Will any of the $10,000 be suspended?
    d. Could any planning opportunities be used to minimize the tax ramifications of the distribution?

23. The Owl Partnership was formed on May 1 of the current year and admitted Harry and Ron as equal partners on that date. The partners contributed $150,000 of cash each and borrowed $300,000 from a local bank to establish a specialty book store. The partners spent May and June buying inventory, equipment, supplies, and advertising for their "Grand Opening" on July 1. The partnership will use the accrual method of accounting. The partnership incurred the following costs during its first year of operations.

    • Purchased all assets of Floomish & Botts of New York, including:

Trade name and logo	$ 30,000
Inventory	120,000
Shop fixtures, racks, shelves, etc.	50,000
Store building	200,000

    • Other costs:

Additional inventory	$400,000
Transfer tax to acquire building	10,000
Building renovation costs	50,000

Legal fees to form partnership	$12,000
Advertising for "Grand Opening"	9,000
Advertising after opening	5,000
Consulting fees for establishing accounting system	8,000
Additional equipment rental, eight months at $3,000/month	24,000
Utilities at $500 per month	4,000
Salaries to sales clerks	40,000
Payments to Harry and Ron for services ($3,500/month each for six months, beginning in July)	42,000
Tax return preparation expense	6,000

- Revenues during the year included the following.

Sales revenues	$750,000
Interest income on bank balances	2,000

- Inventory remaining at the end of the year was valued at $80,000 on a FIFO basis.

a. Determine how each of the above costs and revenues is treated by the partnership, and identify the period over which the costs can be deducted, if any.

b. Calculate the amortization deduction for any amortizable costs.

c. Identify any elections the partnership should make on its initial tax return.

24. Fred and Fran are equal partners in the calendar year F & F Partnership. Fred uses a fiscal year ending June 30, and Fran uses a calendar year. Fred receives an annual guaranteed payment of $50,000 from F & F. F & F's taxable income (after deducting Fred's guaranteed payment) was $40,000 for 2001 and $50,000 for 2002.

a. What is the aggregate amount of income from the partnership that Fred must report for his tax year ending June 30, 2002?

b. What is the aggregate amount of income from the partnership that Fran must report for her tax year ending December 31, 2002?

c. If Fred's annual guaranteed payment is increased to $60,000 starting on January 1, 2002, and the partnership's taxable income for 2001 and 2002 is the same (i.e., $40,000 and $50,000, respectively), what is the aggregate amount of income from the partnership that Fred must report for his tax year ending June 30, 2002?

25. Ned, a 50% partner in the MN Partnership, is to receive a payment of $35,000 for services. He will also be allocated 50% of the partnership's profits or losses. After deducting the payment to Ned, the partnership has a loss of $25,000. Ned's basis in his partnership interest was $10,000 before these items.

a. How much, if any, of the $25,000 partnership loss is allocated to Ned?

b. What is the net income from the partnership that Ned must report on his Federal income tax return?

c. What is Ned's basis in his partnership interest following the guaranteed payment and loss allocation?

26. Four Lakes Partnership is owned by four sisters. Anne holds a 70% interest; each of the others owns 10%. Anne sells investment property to the partnership for its fair market value of $100,000. Her tax basis was $150,000.

a. How much loss, if any, may Anne recognize?

b. If the partnership later sells the property for $160,000, how much gain must it recognize?

c. If Anne's basis in the investment property was $20,000 instead of $150,000, how much, if any, capital gain would she recognize on the sale?

27. Comment on the validity of each of the following statements.

a. Since a partnership is not a taxable entity, it is not required to file any type of tax return.

    b. Each partner can choose a different method of accounting and depreciation computation in determining the gross income from the entity.

    c. Generally, a transfer of appreciated property to a partnership results in recognized gain to the contributing partner at the time of the transfer.

    d. A partner can carry forward, for an unlimited period of time, the partner's share of any partnership operating losses that exceed the partner's basis in the entity, provided the partner retains an ownership interest in the partnership.

    e. When a partner renders services to the entity in exchange for an unrestricted interest, that partner does not recognize any gross income.

    f. Losses on sales between a partner and the partnership always are nondeductible.

    g. A partnership may choose a year that results in the least aggregate deferral of tax to the partners, unless the IRS requires the use of a natural business year.

    h. A partner's basis in a partnership interest includes that partner's share of partnership recourse and nonrecourse liabilities.

    i. Built-in loss related to nondepreciable property contributed to a partnership must be allocated to the contributing partner to the extent the loss is eventually recognized by the partnership.

    j. Property that was held as inventory by a contributing partner, but is a capital asset in the hands of the partnership, results in a capital gain if the partnership immediately sells the property.

 28. Melinda, Gabe, and Pat each contributed $10,000 cash to start up the MGP General Partnership on January 1 this year. Each partner shares equally in partnership income, losses, deductions, gains, and credits. At the end of the year, the partnership balance sheet reads as follows.

	Basis	FMV		Basis	FMV
Assets	$60,000	$75,000	Recourse debt	$30,000	$30,000
			Melinda, capital	14,000	19,000
			Gabe, capital	14,000	19,000
			Pat, capital	2,000	7,000
				$60,000	$75,000

How will the basis computations of the partners' interests be affected by the partnership debt?

 29. The Cardinal Partnership leases apartments to individuals. Chris is a 15% partner in Cardinal, and her share of this year's operating losses totals $70,000. Before accounting for this loss, Chris reported the following amounts.

- Share of partnership recourse liabilities $10,000
- Share of partnership nonrecourse liabilities   6,000
- Capital account in Cardinal   40,000

    Chris also is a partner in the Bluebird Partnership, which earns income from equipment rentals of more than 30 days. Chris's share of Bluebird's income this year is $23,000.

    Chris performs substantial services for Bluebird and spends several hundred hours a year working for Cardinal. Chris's AGI before accounting for the partnership investments totals $100,000.

    Your manager has asked you to determine how much of the Cardinal loss Chris can deduct this year. Draft a memo to the tax research file describing the various loss limitations that apply to Chris.

COMPREHENSIVE TAX RETURN PROBLEM

30. Myron M. Fox (297–19–4567), Rhonda R. Fiori (284–74–1234), Cassandra P. Martin (257–62–3395), and Henrietta Q. Pasquale (219–75–4967) are equal general partners in

FFMP, a small business management consulting partnership whose Federal ID number is 67–9580874. The partnership uses the cash basis and the calendar year and began operations on January 1, 1995. Since that time, it has experienced significant growth each year. Its current address is 2835 Harbor View Drive, Freetown, ME 04469. The following information was taken from the partnership's income statement for the current year.

Revenues	
Fees collected	$300,000
Dividend income	3,600
Taxable interest	1,400
Tax-exempt interest	2,600
Short-term capital loss	(4,000)
Total revenues	$303,600
Expenses	
Accounting fees	$ 5,000
Advertising	5,000
Contribution to United Fund	2,000
Depreciation expense	6,600
Employee salaries	50,000
Guaranteed payment, Myron M. Fox, office manager	20,000
Entertainment, subject to 50% disallowance	2,000
Travel (meals = $600)	2,600
Equipment rental	6,000
Office rentals paid	24,000
Interest expense	4,000
Insurance premiums	2,200
Office expense	12,000
Payroll taxes	8,600
Utilities	5,700
Total expenses	$155,700

The partnership claimed $6,600 of depreciation expense for both tax and financial accounting purposes. The depreciation creates an adjustment of $1,000 for alternative minimum tax purposes.

Net income per books is $147,900. On January 1, the partners' capital accounts equaled $60,000 each. No additional capital contributions were made this year, and each partner made total withdrawals of $40,000 during the year. The partnership's balance sheet as of December 31 is as follows.

	Beginning	**Ending**
Cash	$ 42,000	$??
Tax-exempt securities	52,000	52,000
Marketable securities	160,000	120,000
Office furniture and equipment	05,000	65,000
Accumulated depreciation	(32,000)	??
Total assets	$287,000	$??

	Beginning	Ending
Nonrecourse debt payable on equipment	$ 47,000	$32,000
Capital, Fox	60,000	??
Capital, Fiori	60,000	??
Capital, Martin	60,000	??
Capital, Pasquale	60,000	??
Total liabilities and capital	$287,000	$??

Assume all debt is shared by the partners.

None of the partners, all of whom are U.S. citizens, sold any portion of their interests in FFMP during the year. All of the entity's financial operations are concentrated in Maine although consulting contracts were secured during the year in other states. The partnership had no foreign bank accounts or operations and no interest in any foreign trusts or any other partnerships. The partnership is not publicly traded and is not a statutory tax shelter. The partnership is not subject to consolidated audit procedures and does not have a designated tax matters partner.

The business code for FFMP's operations is 541600. FFMP itself is not a partner in any other partnership. The partnership's Form 1065 was prepared by Fox and sent to the Andover, MA IRS Service Center. All partners are active in partnership operations.

a. Prepare Form 1065 and Schedule K for the FFMP Partnership, leaving blank any items where insufficient information has been provided.

b. Prepare Schedule K–1 for Myron M. Fox, 415 Knight Court, Freetown, ME 04469.

BRIDGE DISCIPLINE

1. Jim Dunn, Amy Lauersen, and Tony Packard have agreed to form a partnership. In return for a 30% capital interest, Dunn transferred machinery (basis $268,000, fair market value $400,000), subject to a liability of $100,000. The liability was assumed by the partnership. Lauersen transferred land (basis $450,000, fair market value $300,000) for a 30% capital interest. Packard transferred cash of $400,000 for the remaining 40% interest. Compute the initial values of Dunn's basis and capital account.

RESEARCH PROBLEMS

Note: Solutions to Research Problems can be prepared by using the **RIA Checkpoint® Student Version Online research product,** *or the* **CCH U.S. Master Tax Guide Plus™** *online Federal tax research database, which is available to accompany this text. It is also possible to prepare solutions to the Research Problems by using tax research materials found in a standard tax library.*

Research Problem 1. Your clients, Mark Henderson and John Burton, each contributed $10,000 of cash to form the Realty Management Partnership, a limited partnership. Mark is the general partner, and John is the limited partner. The partnership used the $20,000 of cash to make a down payment on a building. The rest of the building's $200,000 purchase price was financed with an interest-only nonrecourse loan of $180,000, which was obtained from an independent third-party bank. The partnership allocates all partnership items equally between the partners except for the MACRS deductions and building maintenance, which are allocated 70% to John and 30% to Mark. The partnership definitely wishes to satisfy the "economic effect" requirements of Reg. § 1.704–1 and Reg. § 1.704–2 and will reallocate MACRS, if necessary, to satisfy the requirements of the Regulations.

Under the partnership agreement, liquidation distributions will be paid in proportion to the partners' positive capital account balances. Capital accounts are maintained as required in the Regulations. Mark has an unlimited obligation to restore his capital account while John is subject to a qualified income offset provision.

All partnership items, except for MACRS, net to zero throughout the first three years of the partnership operations. Each year's MACRS deduction is $10,000 (to simplify the calculations).

Draft a letter to the partnership evaluating the allocation of MACRS in each of the three years under Reg. § 1.704–1 and Reg. § 1.704–2. The partnership's address is 53 East Marsh Ave., Smyrna, Georgia 30082. Do not address the "substantial" test.

Research Problem 2. Harrison has considerable experience as a leasing agent for residential rental properties. He is disappointed, though, that his salary with his present employer does not reflect the effort he puts forth.

Alameda Properties has offered Harrison a position handling leasing activities for a new limited partnership that is being formed to construct and manage three apartment complexes in southern California. Alameda is willing to hire Harrison for two years to lease the properties, but is unable to pay the $60,000 salary Harrison requires without impairing its ability to pay necessary cash distributions to the limited partners.

Alameda is willing to pay a $30,000 salary for two years, increasing to a market salary thereafter. Alameda is also willing to allow Harrison to purchase a 10% interest in the partnership, but Harrison cannot afford the required $20,000 capital contribution.

The partnership expects to distribute cash flows from operations of approximately $150,000 per year, for an estimated seven-year holding period (taxable income will be much lower because depreciation and interest deductions will be greater than mortgage payments).

Harrison and Alameda Properties have approached you for assistance in structuring a mutually satisfactory arrangement. You are aware that a partner can be awarded an interest in the future profits of a partnership and have learned from a colleague that in 1993 the IRS issued a Revenue Procedure that outlines the types of profits interests that will not be subject to current taxation. Present a structure to Harrison and Alameda Properties that meets their respective goals, and outline the advantages and disadvantages to each party.

Research Problem 3. Fred and Grady have formed the FG Partnership to operate a retail establishment selling antique household furnishings. Fred is the general partner, and Grady is the limited partner. Both partners contribute $15,000 to form the partnership. The partnership uses the $30,000 contributed by the partners and a recourse loan of $100,000 obtained from an unrelated third-party lender to acquire $130,000 of initial inventory.

The partners believe they will have extensive losses in the first year due to advertising and intial cash-flow requirements. Fred and Grady have agreed to share losses equally. To make sure the losses can be allocated to both partners, they have included a provision in the partnership agreement requiring each partner to restore any deficit balance in the partnership capital account upon liquidation of the partnership.

Fred also was willing to include a provision that requires him to make up any deficit balance within 90 days of liquidation of the partnership. As a limited partner, Grady argued that he should not be subject to such a time requirement. The partners compromised and included a provision that requires Grady to restore a deficit balance in his capital account within two years of liquidation of the partnership. No interest is owed on the deferred restoration payment.

Determine how FG allocates the $100,000 recourse debt to the two partners to ensure that they can deduct their respective shares of partnership losses.

Use the tax resources of the Internet to address the following questions. Do not restrict your search to the World Wide Web, but include a review of newsgroups and general reference materials, practitioner sites and resources, primary sources of the tax law, chat rooms and discussion groups, and other opportunities.

Research Problem 4. Find a solicitation for funds posted by investors in a film or play. Summarize the partner's rights to profits and any tax implications discussed in the prospectus.

Research Problem 5. Find a discussion group that concentrates on the taxation of partners and partnerships. Post to the group a message defining the terms "inside and outside basis" and illustrating why the distinction between them is important. Respond to any replies you receive. Print your message and one or two of the replies.

Research Problem 6. Find the home page of a partnership that seems to be soliciting financing from new partners. Comment on the portrayal of the pertinent tax law that is included in the materials, especially with respect to the at-risk rules and the passive activity limitations.

Research Problem 7. Print an article posted by a law firm that comments on pitfalls to avoid in drafting partnership agreements. Ideally, use the home page of a firm that has offices in your state.

S Corporations

LEARNING OBJECTIVES

After completing Chapter 12, you should be able to:

1. Explain the tax effects associated with S corporation status.

2. Identify corporations that qualify for the S election.

3. Understand how to make and terminate an S election.

4. Compute nonseparately stated income and allocate income, deductions, and credits to shareholders.

5. Understand how distributions to S corporation shareholders are taxed.

6. Calculate a shareholder's basis in S corporation stock.

7. Explain the tax effects of losses on S shareholders.

8. Compute the entity-level taxes on S corporations.

Outline

TAX TALK	*In levying taxes and in shearing sheep it is well to stop when you get down to the skin.*
	—*Austin O'Malley*

> actual corp make special election for tax purposes.

LEARNING OBJECTIVE 1

Explain the tax effects associated with S corporation status.

The **S corporation** rules were enacted to minimize the role of tax considerations in the entity choice that many small businesses face. S corporation status provides a compromise for small businesses: they can avoid the double taxation and loss limitations inherent in the regular corporate form while still enjoying many of the nontax benefits extended to C corporations. Thus, S status combines the legal environment of C corporations with taxation similar to that applying to partnerships.

S corporations are treated as corporations under state law. They are recognized as separate legal entities and generally provide shareholders with the same liability protection afforded by C corporations. Some states (such as Michigan) treat S corporations as C corporations for tax purposes, resulting in a state corporate income or franchise tax liability. For Federal income tax purposes, however, taxation of S corporations resembles that of partnerships. As with partnerships, the income, deductions, and tax credits of an S corporation flow through to shareholders annually, regardless of whether dividends are paid. Thus, income generally is taxed at the shareholder level and not at the corporate level. Dividends paid by the corporation are distributed tax-free to shareholders to the extent that the distributed earnings were previously taxed to the shareholders.

Although the tax treatment of S corporations and partnerships is similar, it is not identical. For example, liabilities affect an owner's basis differently, and S corporations may incur a tax liability at the corporate level. In addition, a variety of C corporation provisions apply to S corporations. For example, the liquidation of C and S corporations is taxed in the same way. As a rule, where the S corporation provisions are silent, C corporation rules apply.

S corporation status must be elected by a *qualifying* corporation and consented to by its shareholders. Rules related to the S election and the tax treatment of S corporations are addressed in **Subchapter S** of the Internal Revenue Code (§§ 1361–1379).

An Overview of S Corporations

Since the inception of S corporations in 1958, their popularity has waxed and waned with changes in the tax law. Before the Tax Reform Act of 1986, their ranks grew

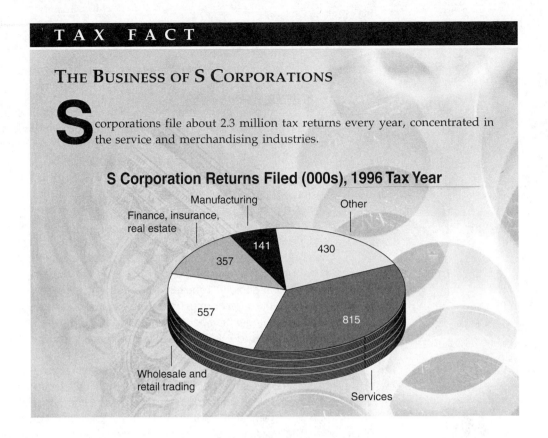

THE BUSINESS OF S CORPORATIONS

S corporations file about 2.3 million tax returns every year, concentrated in the service and merchandising industries.

S Corporation Returns Filed (000s), 1996 Tax Year

Manufacturing 141
Finance, insurance, real estate 357
Other 430
Wholesale and retail trading 557
Services 815

slowly. In contrast, in the two years following the 1986 law change, the number of S corporations increased by 52 percent. By 1993, more than 1.9 million businesses were filing S corporation returns—48 percent of all corporate returns filed in that year.

This rapid growth was driven by a change in the relationship of individual and corporate tax rates. Prior to 1986, maximum individual rates were higher than maximum corporate rates. Following the 1986 tax act, the relationship reversed. After 1993, maximum individual income tax rates were increased to 39.6 percent, again exceeding the maximum corporate rate (by 4.6 percentage points). Consequently, S corporations declined in popularity, although they remain the preferred business form of a wide range of enterprises. Today, about half of all of the five million U.S. corporations have elected S status. S corporations still can be advantageous even when the top individual tax rate exceeds the top corporate tax rate.

EXAMPLE 1

An S corporation earns $300,000, and all after-tax income is distributed currently. The marginal individual tax rate applicable to shareholders is 39.6%, and the applicable marginal corporate tax rate is 34%. The entity's available after-tax earnings, compared with those of a similar C corporation, are computed below.

	C Corporation	S Corporation
Earnings	$ 300,000	$ 300,000
Less: Corporate income tax	(102,000)	(–0–)
Amount available for distribution	$ 198,000	$ 300,000
Less: Income tax at owner level	(78,408)	(118,800)
Available after-tax earnings	$ 119,592	$ 181,200

BRIDGE DISCIPLINE

Bridge to Business Law

An S corporation is a corporation for all purposes other than its Federal and state income tax law treatment. The entity registers as a corporation with the secretary of state of the state of its incorporation. It issues shares and may hold some treasury stock. Dealings in its own stock are not taxable to the S corporation.

The corporation itself is attractive as a form of business ownership because it offers limited liability to all shareholders from the claims of customers, employees, and others. This is not the case for any type of partnership, where there always is at least one general partner bearing the ultimate personal liability for the operations of the entity. Forming an entity as an S corporation facilitates the raising of capital for the business, as an infinite number of shares can be divided in any way imaginable, so as to pass income and deductions, gains, losses, and credits through to the owners, assuming that the fairly generous "type of shareholder" requirements continue to be met.

An S corporation must comply with all licensing and registration requirements of its home state under the rules applicable to corporate entities. Some states levy privilege taxes on the right to do business in the corporate form, and the S corporation typically is not exempted from this tax.

Because an S corporation is a separate legal entity from its owners, shareholders can be treated as employees and receive qualified retirement and fringe benefits under the Code, as well as unemployment and worker's compensation protection through the corporation. Some limitations apply to the deductibility of fringe benefits, though.

The tax fiction of the S corporation is attractive to investors, as about one-half of all U.S. corporations have an S election in effect.

The S corporation generates an extra $61,608 of after-tax earnings ($181,200 − $119,592), when compared with a similar C corporation. The C corporation might be able to reduce this disadvantage, however, by paying out its earnings as compensation, rents, or interest to its owners. Tax at the owner level can also be deferred or avoided by not distributing after-tax earnings. ∎

EXAMPLE 2

A new corporation elects S status and incurs a net operating loss (NOL) of $300,000. The shareholders of the corporation may use their proportionate shares of the NOL to offset other taxable income in the current year, providing an immediate tax savings. In contrast, a newly formed C corporation is required to carry the NOL forward for up to 20 years and receives no tax benefit in the current year. Hence, an S corporation can accelerate the use of NOL deductions and thereby provide a greater present value for the tax savings generated by the loss. ∎

Limited liability companies (LLCs) can provide tax results similar to those of an S corporation, while avoiding some of the key restrictions that are imposed on S corporations and their shareholders. In addition, recent changes to a number of S corporation election and operating rules provide greater flexibility in using S corporations as a viable alternative to LLCs.

When to Elect S Corporation Status

Effective planning with S corporations begins with determining whether an S election is appropriate for the entity. The following factors should be considered.

- If shareholders are subject to high marginal rates relative to C corporation rates, it may be desirable to avoid S corporation status. Although a C corporation may be subject to double taxation, any double tax can be minimized by paying compensation to employee-shareholders. Likewise, profits of the corporation may be taken out by the shareholders through compensation arrangements, as interest, or as rent income. Corporate profits can be transferred to shareholders as capital gain income through capital structure charges, such as stock redemptions, liquidations, or sales of stock to others. Alternatively, profits may be paid out as dividends in low tax years. Any distribution of profits or sale of stock can be deferred to a later year, thereby reducing the present value of shareholder taxes. Finally, shareholder-level tax on corporate profits can be eliminated by a step-up in basis of the stock upon the shareholder's death.

- S corporation status allows shareholders to realize tax benefits from corporate losses immediately—an important consideration in new business enterprises where operating losses are common. Thus, if corporate NOLs are anticipated and there is unlikely to be corporate income over the near term to offset with the NOLs, S corporation status is advisable. However, the deductibility of the losses to shareholders must also be considered. The at-risk and passive loss limitations (refer to Chapter 5) apply to losses generated by an S corporation. In addition, as discussed later in this chapter, shareholders may not deduct losses in excess of the tax basis in their S stock. Together with the time value of money considerations of deferring any loss deduction, these limits may significantly reduce the benefits of an S election in a loss setting.

- If the entity electing S corporation status is currently a C corporation, any NOL carryovers from prior years (refer to Chapter 5) generally cannot be used in an S corporation year. Even worse, S corporation years use up the 20-year carryover period.

- Distributions of earnings from C corporations are usually taxed as ordinary income. In contrast, because S corporations are flow-through entities, all deduction and income items retain any special tax characteristics when they are reported on shareholders' returns. Whether this consideration favors S status depends upon the character of income and deductions of the S corporation.

- The S corporation rules impose significant requirements for qualifying as an S corporation. When electing S status, one should consider whether any of these requirements are likely to be violated at some point in the future.

- State and local tax laws should also be considered when making the S election. Although an S corporation usually escapes Federal income tax, it may not be immune from all state and local income taxes.

LEARNING OBJECTIVE 2

Identify corporations that qualify for the S election.

Qualifying for S Corporation Status

DEFINITION OF A SMALL BUSINESS CORPORATION

To achieve S corporation status, a corporation must *first* qualify as a **small business corporation.** A small business corporation:

- Is a domestic corporation (incorporated and organized in the United States).
- Is eligible to elect S corporation status.
- Issues only one class of stock.
- Is limited to a maximum of 75 shareholders.
- Has only individuals, estates, and certain trusts as shareholders.
- Has no nonresident alien shareholders.

[handwritten: can't have corps + partnerships as partners]

[handwritten margin note: flow thru treatment went up for losses]

Unlike other small business provisions in the tax law (e.g., § 1244), no maximum or minimum dollar sales or capitalization restrictions apply to S corporations.

Ineligible Corporations. S status is not permitted for foreign corporations, certain banks, or insurance companies. S corporations are permitted to have wholly owned C and S corporation subsidiaries.[1]

[handwritten margin note: it's okay to have some stock to have some vote to others not]

One Class of Stock. A small business corporation may have only one class of stock issued and outstanding.[2] This restriction permits differences in voting rights, but not differences in distribution or liquidation rights.[3] Thus, two classes of common stock that are identical except that one class is voting and the other is nonvoting would be treated as a single class of stock for small business corporation purposes. In contrast, voting common stock and voting preferred stock (with a preference on dividends) would be treated as two classes of stock. Authorized and unissued stock or treasury stock of another class does not disqualify the corporation. Likewise, unexercised stock options, phantom stock, stock appreciation rights, warrants, and convertible debentures usually do not constitutes a second class of stock.[4]

1 *Find more information on this topic at our Web site: http://wft-entities.swcollege.com.*

Although the one-class-of-stock requirement seems straightforward, it is possible for debt to be reclassified as stock, resulting in an unexpected loss of S corporation status.[5] To mitigate concern over possible reclassification of debt as a second class of stock, the law provides a set of *safe harbor* provisions. Neither straight debt[6] nor short-term advances[7] constitute a second class of stock.

2 *Find more information on this topic at our Web site: http://wft-entities.swcollege.com.*

Number of Shareholders. A small business corporation is limited to 75 shareholders. If shares of stock are owned jointly by two individuals, they will generally be treated as separate shareholders. However, a husband and wife are considered one shareholder. Similarly, a widower or widow and his or her spouse's estate are treated as a single shareholder.[8]

EXAMPLE 3

Fred and Wilma (husband and wife) jointly own 10 shares in Oriole, Inc., an S corporation, with the remaining 90 shares outstanding owned by 74 other shareholders. Fred and Wilma get divorced; pursuant to the property settlement approved by the court, the 10 shares held by Fred and Wilma are divided between them, five to each. Before the divorce settlement, Oriole had 75 shareholders under the small business corporation rules. After the settlement, it has 76 shareholders and no longer qualifies as a small business corporation. ∎

Type of Shareholder Limitation. Small business corporation shareholders may be individuals, estates, or certain trusts.[9] This limitation prevents partnerships, corporations, LLCs, LLPs, and IRAs from owning S corporation stock. Without this rule, partnership and corporate shareholders could easily circumvent the 75-shareholder limitation.

---

[1] Other eligibility rules exist. § 1361(b).
[2] § 1361(b)(1)(D).
[3] § 1361(c)(4).
[4] Reg. § 1.1361–1(l)(2).
[5] Refer to the discussion of debt-versus-equity classification in Chapter 9.

[6] § 1361(c)(5)(A).
[7] Reg. § 1.1361–1(l)(4).
[8] § 1361(c)(1).
[9] § 1361(b)(1)(B).

EXAMPLE 4

Paul and 80 other individuals wish to form an S corporation. Paul reasons that if the group forms a partnership, the partnership can then form an S corporation and act as a single shareholder, thereby avoiding the 75-shareholder rule. Paul's plan will not work, because partnerships cannot own stock in a small business corporation. ■

PLANNING CONSIDERATIONS

Beating the 75-Shareholder Limit

Although partnerships and corporations cannot own small business corporation stock, S corporations themselves can be partners in a partnership or shareholders in a corporation. In this way, the 75-shareholder requirement can be bypassed in a limited sense. For example, if two small business corpo-rations, each with 75 shareholders, form a partnership, then the shareholders of both corporations can enjoy the limited liability conferred by S corporation status and a single level of tax on the resulting profits.

Nonresident Aliens.   Nonresident aliens cannot own stock in a small business corporation.[10] Thus, individuals who are not U.S. citizens *must live in the United States* to own S corporation stock. Shareholders with nonresident alien spouses in community property states[11] cannot own S corporation stock because the nonresident alien spouse is treated as owning half of the stock.[12] Similarly, if a resident alien shareholder moves outside the United States, the S election is terminated.

MAKING THE ELECTION

To become an S corporation, the entity must file a valid election with the IRS. The election is made on Form 2553. For the election to be valid, it must be filed on a timely basis and all shareholders must consent. For S corporation status to apply in the current tax year, the election must be filed either in the previous year or on or before the fifteenth day of the third month of the current year.[13]

EXAMPLE 5

In 2001, a calendar year C corporation decides to become an S corporation beginning January 1, 2002. The S corporation election can be made at any time in 2001 or by March 15, 2002. An election after March 15, 2002, will not be effective until the 2003 tax year. ■

Even if the 2½-month deadline is met, a current election is not valid unless the corporation qualifies as a small business corporation for the *entire* tax year. Otherwise, the election will be effective for the following tax year. Late current-year elections, after the 2½-month deadline, may be considered timely if there is reasonable cause for the late filing.

A corporation that does not yet exist cannot make an S corporation election.[14] Thus, for new corporations, a premature election may not be effective. A new

---

[10]§ 1362(b)(1)(C).

[11]Assets acquired by a married couple are generally considered community property in these states: Alaska (by election), Arizona, California, Idaho, Louisiana, Nevada, New Mexico, Texas, Washington, and Wisconsin.

[12]See *Ward v. U.S.*, 81–2 USTC ¶9674, 48 AFTR2d 81–5942, 661 F.2d 226 (Ct.Cls., 1981), where the court found that the stock was owned as community property. Since the taxpayer-shareholder (a U.S.

citizen) was married to a citizen and resident of Mexico, the nonresident alien prohibition was violated. If the taxpayer-shareholder had held the stock as separate property, the S election would have been valid.

[13]§ 1362(b).

[14]See, for example, *T.H. Campbell & Bros., Inc.*, 34 TCM 695, T.C.Memo. 1975–149, Ltr.Rul. 8807070.

corporation's 2½-month election period begins at the earliest occurrence of any of the following events.

- When the corporation has shareholders.
- When it acquires assets.
- When it begins doing business.[15]

SHAREHOLDER CONSENT

A qualifying election requires the consent of all of the corporation's shareholders.[16] Consent must be in writing, and it must generally be filed by the election deadline. However, although no statutory authority exists for obtaining an extension of time for filing an S election (Form 2553), a shareholder may receive an extension of time to file a consent. Both husband and wife must consent if they own their stock jointly (as joint tenants, tenants in common, tenants by the entirety, or community property).[17]

EXAMPLE 6

Vern and Yvonne decide to convert their C corporation into a calendar year S corporation for 2002. At the end of February 2002 (before the election is filed), Yvonne travels to Ukraine and forgets to sign a consent to the election. Yvonne will not return to the United States until June and cannot be reached by fax or e-mail. Vern files the S election on Form 2553 and also requests an extension of time to file Yvonne's consent to the election. Vern indicates that there is a reasonable cause for the extension: a shareholder is out of the country. Since the government's interest is not jeopardized, the IRS probably will grant Yvonne an extension of time to file the consent. Vern must file the election on Form 2553 on or before March 15, 2002, for the election to be effective for the 2002 calendar year. ■

PLANNING CONSIDERATIONS

Making a Proper Election

- Because S corporation status is *elected*, strict compliance with the requirements is demanded by both the IRS and the courts. Any failure to meet a condition in the law may lead to loss of the S election and raise the specter of double tax.
- Make sure all shareholders consent. If any doubt exists concerning the shareholder status of an individual, it would be wise to request that he or she sign a consent anyway.[18] Missing consents are fatal to the election; the same cannot be said for too many consents.
- Be sure that the election is timely and properly filed. Either deliver the election to an IRS office in person, or send it by certified or registered mail or via a major overnight delivery service. The date used to determine timeliness is the postmark date, not the date the IRS receives the election.

LOSS OF THE ELECTION

An S election remains in force until it is revoked or lost. Election or consent forms are not required for future years. However, an S election can terminate if any of the following occurs.[19]

---

[15]Reg. § 1.1372–2(b)(1). Also see, for example, *Nick A. Artukovich*, 61 T.C. 100 (1973).

[16]§ 1362(a)(2).

[17]Rev.Rul. 60–183, 1960–1 C.B. 625; *William Pestcoe*, 40 T.C. 195 (1963); Reg. § 1.1362–6(b)(3)(iii).

[18]See *William B. Wilson*, 34 TCM 463, T.C.Memo. 1975–92.

[19]§ 1362(d).

- Shareholders owning a majority of shares (voting and nonvoting) voluntarily revoke the election.
- A new shareholder owning more than one-half of the stock affirmatively refuses to consent to the election.
- The corporation no longer qualifies as a small business corporation.
- The corporation does not meet the passive investment income limitation.

Voluntary Revocation. A voluntary revocation of the S election requires the consent of shareholders owning a majority of shares on the day that the revocation is to be made.[20] A revocation filed up to and including the fifteenth day of the third month of the tax year is effective for the entire tax year, unless a later date is specified. Similarly, unless an effective date is specified, revocation made after the first 2½ months of the current tax year is effective for the following tax year.

EXAMPLE 7	The shareholders of Petunia Corporation, a calendar year S corporation, voluntarily revoke the S election on January 5, 2001. They do not specify a future effective date in the revocation. Assuming the revocation is properly executed and timely filed, Petunia will be a C corporation for the entire 2001 tax year. If the revocation is not made until June 2001, Petunia will remain an S corporation in 2001 and become a C corporation at the beginning of 2002. ∎

A corporation can revoke its S status *prospectively* by specifying a future date when the revocation is to be effective. A revocation that designates a future effective date splits the corporation's tax year into a short S corporation year and a short C corporation year. The day on which the revocation occurs is treated as the first day of the C corporation year. The corporation allocates income or loss for the entire year on a pro rata basis, based on the number of days in each short year.

EXAMPLE 8	Assume the same facts as in the preceding example, except that Petunia designates July 1, 2001, as the revocation date. Accordingly, June 30, 2001, is the last day of the S corporation's tax year. The C corporation's tax year runs from July 1, 2001, to December 31, 2001. Any income or loss for the 12-month period is allocated equally between the two short years, because the two short years lasted an equal number of days. ∎

Rather than using pro rata allocation, the corporation can elect to compute the actual income or loss attributable to the two short years. This election requires the consent of everyone who was a shareholder at any time during the S corporation's short year and everyone who owns stock on the first day of the C corporation's year.[21]

transfer to corp or partnership 1

Loss of Small Business Corporation Status. If an S corporation fails to qualify as a small business corporation at any time after the election has become effective, its status as an S corporation ends. The termination occurs on the day that the corporation ceases to be a small business corporation.[22] Thus, if the corporation ever has more than 75 shareholders, a second class of stock, or a nonqualifying shareholder, or otherwise fails to meet the definition of a small business corporation, the S election is terminated immediately.

EXAMPLE 9	Peony Corporation has been a calendar year S corporation for three years. On August 13, 2001, one of its 75 shareholders sells *some* of her stock to an outsider. Peony now has 76

---

[20]§ 1362(d)(1)(B).   [22]§ 1362(d)(2)(B).
[21]§ 1362(e)(3).

shareholders, and it ceases to be a small business corporation. Peony is an S corporation through August 12, 2001, and a C corporation from August 13 to December 31, 2001. ■

Passive Investment Income Limitation.   The Code provides a **passive investment income (PII)** limitation for S corporations that were previously C corporations or for S corporations that have merged with C corporations. If an S corporation has C corporation E & P and passive income in excess of 25 percent of its gross receipts for three consecutive taxable years, the S election is terminated as of the beginning of the fourth year.[23]

EXAMPLE 10

For 1998, 1999, and 2000, Chrysanthemum Corporation, a calendar year S corporation, derived passive income in excess of 25% of its gross receipts. If Chrysanthemum holds accumulated E & P from years in which it was a C corporation, its S election is terminated as of January 1, 2001. ■

PII includes dividends, interest, rents, gains and losses from sales of securities, and royalties net of investment deductions. Rents are not considered PII if the corporation renders significant personal services to the occupant.

EXAMPLE 11

Violet Corporation owns and operates an apartment building. The corporation provides utilities for the building, maintains the lobby, and furnishes trash collection for tenants. These activities are not considered significant personal services, so any rent income earned by the corporation will be considered PII.

Alternatively, if Violet also furnishes maid services to its tenants (personal services beyond what normally would be expected from a landlord in an apartment building), the rent income would no longer be PII. ■

Reelection after Termination.   After an S election has been terminated, the corporation must wait five years before reelecting S corporation status. The five-year waiting period is waived if:

- there is a more-than-50-percent change in ownership of the corporation after the first year for which the termination is applicable, or
- the event causing the termination was not reasonably within the control of the S corporation or its majority shareholders.

PLANNING CONSIDERATIONS

Preserving the S Election

Unexpected loss of S corporation status can be costly to a corporation and its shareholders. Given the complexity of the rules facing these entities, constant vigilance is necessary to preserve the S election.

- As a starting point, the corporation's management and shareholders should be made aware of the various transactions that can lead to the loss of an election.
- Watch for possible violation of the PII limitation. Avoid a consecutive third year with excess passive income when

the corporation has accumulated E & P from C corporation years. In this connection, assets that produce passive income (e.g., stocks and bonds, certain rental assets) might be retained by the shareholders in their individual capacities and kept out of the corporation.

- Prevent violations of the small business corporation limitations. Since most such violations result from transfers of stock, the corporation and its shareholders should consider adopting a set of stock transfer restrictions.

---

[23]§ 1362(d)(3)(A)(ii).

A carefully designed set of restrictions could prevent sale of stock to nonqualifying entities or violation of the 75-shareholder rule. Similarly, stock could be repurchased by the corporation under a buy-sell agreement upon the death of a shareholder, thereby preventing nonqualifying trusts from becoming shareholders.[24]

LEARNING OBJECTIVE 4

Compute nonseparately stated income and allocate income, deductions, and credits to shareholders.

Operational Rules

S corporations are treated much like partnerships for tax purposes. With a few exceptions, S corporations generally make tax accounting and other elections at the corporate level.[25] Each year, the S corporation determines nonseparately stated income or loss and separately stated income, deductions, and credits. These items are taxed only once, as they pass through to shareholders. All items are allocated to each shareholder based on average ownership of stock throughout the year.[26] The flow-through of each item of income, deduction, and credit from the corporation to the shareholder is illustrated in Figure 12–1.

COMPUTATION OF TAXABLE INCOME

Subchapter S taxable income or loss is determined in a manner similar to the tax rules that apply to partnerships, except that S corporations recognize gains (but not losses) on distributions of appreciated property to shareholders.[27] Other special provisions affecting only the computation of C corporation income, such as the dividends received deduction, do not extend to S corporations.[28] Finally, as with partnerships, certain deductions of individuals are not permitted, including alimony payments, personal moving expenses, certain dependent care expenses, the personal exemption, and the standard deduction.

In general, S corporation items are divided into (1) nonseparately stated income or loss and (2) separately stated income, losses, deductions, and credits that could uniquely affect the tax liability of any shareholder. In essence, nonseparate items are aggregated into an undifferentiated amount that constitutes Subchapter S taxable income or loss.

EXAMPLE 12

The following is the income statement for Larkspur, Inc., an S corporation.

Sales		$ 40,000
Less: Cost of sales		(23,000)
Gross profit on sales		$ 17,000
Less: Interest expense	$1,200	
Charitable contributions	400	
Advertising expenses	1,500	
Other operating expenses	2,000	(5,100)
		$ 11,900

---

[24]Most such agreements do not create a second class of stock. Rev.Rul. 85–161, 1985–2 C.B. 191; *Portage Plastics Co. v. U.S.*, 72–2 USTC ¶9567, 30 AFTR2d 72–5229, 470 F.2d 308 (CA–7, 1973).

[25]Certain elections are made at the shareholder level (e.g., the choice between a foreign tax deduction or credit).

[26]§§ 1366(a), (b), and (c).
[27]§ 1363(d).
[28]§ 703(a)(2).

Add: Tax-exempt interest	$ 300	
Dividend income	200	
Long-term capital gain	500	1,000
Less: Short-term capital loss		(150)
Net income per books		$ 12,750

Subchapter S taxable income for Larkspur is calculated as follows, using net income for book purposes as a starting point.

Net income per books		$12,750
Separately stated items		
Deduct: Tax-exempt interest	$300	
Dividend income	200	
Long-term capital gain	500	(1,000)
		$11,750
Add: Charitable contributions	$400	
Short-term capital loss	150	550
Subchapter S taxable income		$12,300

The $12,300 of Subchapter S taxable income, as well as each of the five separately stated items, are divided among the shareholders based upon their stock ownership. ∎

ALLOCATION OF INCOME AND LOSS

Each shareholder is allocated a pro rata portion of nonseparately stated income or loss and all separately stated items. The pro rata allocation method assigns an equal amount of each of the S items to each day of the year. If a shareholder's

∎ **FIGURE 12–1**
Flow-Through of Separate Items of Income and Loss
to S Corporation Shareholders

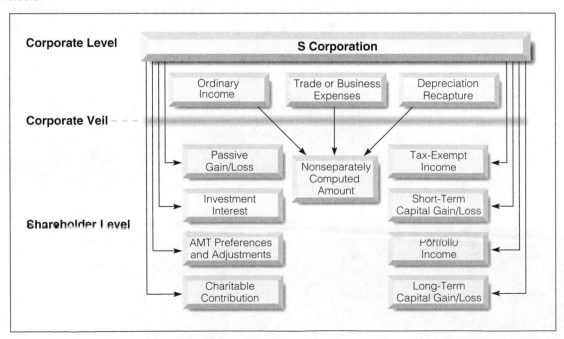

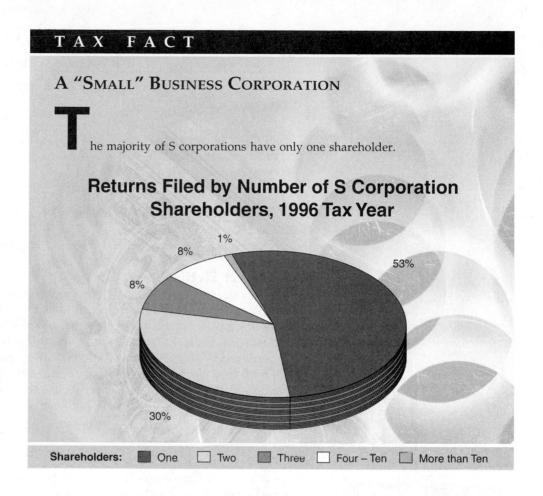

TAX FACT

A "SMALL" BUSINESS CORPORATION

The majority of S corporations have only one shareholder.

Returns Filed by Number of S Corporation Shareholders, 1996 Tax Year

Shareholders: ■ One □ Two ■ Three □ Four – Ten □ More than Ten

stock holding changes during the year, this allocation assigns the shareholder a pro rata share of each item for each day the stock is owned. On the date of transfer, the transferor (not the transferee) is considered to own the stock.[29]

S Corporation item ⊗→ Percentage of shares owned ⊗→ Percentage of year shares were owned ⊜→ Amount of item to be reported

The per-day allocation must be used, unless the shareholder disposes of his or her entire interest in the entity.[30] In case of a complete termination, a short year may result, as discussed below. If a shareholder dies during the year, his or her share of the pro rata items up to the date of death is reported on the final individual income tax return.

EXAMPLE 13

Pat, a shareholder, owned 10% of Larkspur's stock (from Example 12) for 100 days and 12% for the remaining 265 days. Using the required per-day allocation method, Pat's share of the S corporation items is computed below.

---

[29]Reg. § 1.1377–1(a)(2)(ii).   [30]§§ 1366(a)(1) and 1377(a)(1).

	Schedule K Totals	Pat's Share		Pat's Schedule K–1 Totals
		10%	12%	
Subchapter S taxable income	$12,300	$337	$1,072	$1,409
Tax-exempt interest	300	8	26	34
Dividend income	200	5	17	22
Long-term capital gain	500	14	44	58
Charitable contributions	400	11	35	46
Short-term capital loss	150	4	13	17

Pat's share of the Subchapter S taxable income is the total of $12,300 \times [0.10 \times (100/365)]$ plus $12,300 \times [0.12 \times (265/365)]$, or $1,409. All of Pat's Schedule K–1 totals flow through to the corresponding lines on his individual income tax return (Form 1040). ■

The Short-Year Election.   If a shareholder's interest is completely terminated during the tax year by disposition or death, all shareholders owning stock during the year and the corporation may elect to treat the S taxable year as two taxable years. The first year ends on the date of the termination. Under this election, an interim closing of the books is undertaken, and the shareholders report their shares of the S corporation items as they occurred during the short tax year.[31]

The short-year election provides an opportunity to shift income, losses, and credits among shareholders. The election is desirable in circumstances where more loss can be allocated to taxpayers with higher marginal rates.

3 *Find more information on this topic at our Web site: **http://wft-entities.swcollege.com**.*

Alicia, the owner of all of the shares of an S corporation, transfers her stock to Cindy halfway through the tax year. There is a $100,000 NOL for the entire tax year, but $30,000 of the loss occurs during the first half of the year. Without a short-year election, $50,000 of the loss would be allocated to Alicia and $50,000 would be allocated to Cindy. If the corporation makes the short-year election, Cindy is allocated $70,000 of the loss. The sales price of the stock probably would be increased to recognize the tax benefits being transferred from Alicia to Cindy. ■

PLANNING CONSIDERATIONS

Salary Structure

The amount of salary paid to a shareholder-employee of an S corporation can have varying tax consequences and should be considered carefully. Larger amounts might be advantageous if the maximum contribution allowed under the retirement plan has not been reached. Smaller amounts may be beneficial if the parties are trying to shift taxable income to lower-bracket shareholders, reduce payroll taxes,

curtail a reduction of Social Security benefits, or restrict losses that do not pass through because of the basis limitation.

A strategy of decreasing compensation and correspondingly increasing distributions to shareholder-employees often results in substantial savings in employment taxes. However, a shareholder of an S corporation cannot always

---

[31]§ 1377(a)(2).

perform substantial services and arrange to receive distributions rather than compensation so that the corporation may avoid paying employment taxes. The shareholder may be deemed an employee, and any distributions will be recharacterized as wages subject to FICA and FUTA taxes.[32] For planning purposes, some level of compensation should be paid to all shareholder-employees to avoid any recharacterization of distributions as deductible salaries—especially in personal service corporations.

Use of S corporations as an income-shifting device within a family (e.g., through a gift of stock from a high-marginal-rate taxpayer to a low-marginal-rate taxpayer) may be ineffective. The IRS can ignore such transfers unless the stock is purchased at fair market value.[33] Effectively, the IRS can require that reasonable compensation be paid to family members who render services or provide capital to the S corporation.

TAX TREATMENT OF DISTRIBUTIONS TO SHAREHOLDERS

S corporations do not generate earnings and profits (E & P) while the S election is in effect. Indeed, all profits are taxed in the year earned, as though they were distributed on a pro rata basis to the shareholders. Thus, distributions from S corporations do not constitute dividends in the traditional sense—there is no corporate E & P to distribute.

It is possible, however, for S corporations to have an accumulated E & P (AEP) account. This can occur when:

- the S corporation was previously a C corporation, or
- a C corporation with its own AEP merged into the S corporation.

Distributions from S corporations are measured as the cash received plus the fair market value of any other distributed property. The tax treatment of distributions differs, depending upon whether the S corporation has AEP.

S Corporation with No AEP. If the S corporation has no AEP, the distribution is a tax-free recovery of capital to the extent that it does not exceed the adjusted basis of the shareholder's stock. When the amount of the distribution exceeds the adjusted basis of the stock, the excess is treated as a gain from the sale or exchange of property (capital gain in most cases).

EXAMPLE 15

Hyacinth, Inc., a calendar year S corporation, has no AEP. During the year, Juan, an individual shareholder of the corporation, receives a cash distribution of $12,200 from Hyacinth. Juan's basis in his stock is $9,700. Juan recognizes a capital gain of $2,500, the excess of the distribution over the stock basis ($12,200 − $9,700). The remaining $9,700 is tax-free, but it reduces Juan's basis in his stock to zero. ■

S Corporation with AEP. For S corporations with AEP, a more complex set of rules applies. These rules blend the entity and conduit approaches to taxation, treating distributions of pre-election (C corporation) and postelection (S corporation) earnings differently. Distributions of C corporation AEP are taxed as dividends, while distributions of previously taxed S corporation earnings are tax-free to the extent of the shareholder's adjusted basis in the stock.

The treatment of distributions is determined by their order. In particular, distributions are deemed to be first from previously taxed, undistributed earnings of

[32]Rev.Rul. 74–44, 1974–1 C.B. 287; *Spicer Accounting, Inc. v. U.S.*, 91–1 USTC ¶50,103, 66 AFTR2d 90–5806, 918 F.2d 90 (CA–9, 1990); *Radtke v. U.S.*, 90–1 USTC ¶50,113, 65 AFTR2d 90–1155, 895 F.2d 1196 (CA–7, 1990).

[33]§ 1366(e) and Reg. § 1.1373–1(a).

the S corporation. Such distributions are tax-free and are determined by reference to a special account, the **accumulated adjustments account (AAA).**[34] Next, AEP is distributed as taxable dividends. Remaining amounts of the distribution are received tax-free to the extent of the shareholder's remaining stock basis,[35] with any excess being treated as capital gain.

EXAMPLE 16

Salvia, a calendar year S corporation, distributes $1,300 of cash to its only shareholder, Otis, on December 31. Otis's basis in his stock is $1,400, AAA is $500, and the corporation has AEP of $750 on December 31.

　　The first $500 of the distribution is a tax-free recovery of basis from the AAA. The next $750 is a taxable dividend distribution from AEP. Finally, the remaining $50 of cash is a tax-free recovery of basis. Immediately after the distribution, Salvia has no AAA or AEP. Otis's stock basis now is $850.

	Corporate AAA	Corporate AEP	Otis's Stock Basis
Beginning balance	$ 500	$ 750	$1,400
Distribution from AAA	(500)		(500)
Distribution from AEP		(750)	
Distribution of capital			(50)
Ending balance	$ –0–	$ –0–	$ 850

EXAMPLE 17

Assume the same facts as in the preceding example. The next year, Salvia has no earnings and distributes $1,000 to Otis. Of the distribution, $850 is a tax-free recovery of the S stock basis, and then $150 is taxed to Otis as a capital gain. ■

　　With the consent of all of its shareholders, an S corporation can elect to have a distribution treated as if it were made from AEP rather than from the AAA. This mechanism is known as an *AAA bypass election*. This election may be desirable when making distributions in years when S corporation shareholders have low marginal tax rates or for moving the entity to the no-AEP system of accounting for distributions.

EXAMPLE 18

Rotor is a valid S corporation. It has $50 of AEP. An AAA bypass election for Rotor's next shareholder distribution would eliminate the need to track the AAA and would greatly simplify the accounting for future distributions. The cost for this simplification is the tax on $50 of dividend income. ■

The Accumulated Adjustments Account.　　The AAA is the cumulative total of undistributed nonseparately and separately stated income and deduction items for S corporation years beginning after 1982. As noted above, it provides a mechanism to ensure that earnings of an S corporation are taxed only once. Changes to the AAA are reported annually in Schedule M–2 on page 4 of the Form 1120S.

　　AAA is computed at the end of each tax year rather than at the time of a distribution. First, add to the year's beginning balance any current nonseparately computed income and positive separately stated items (except tax-exempt income). Next, account for distributions *prior* to subtracting the negative items.

---

[34]For S corporations in existence prior to 1983, an account similar to the AAA was used. This account, called *previously taxed income* (PTI), can be distributed in cash tax-free to shareholders after AAA has been distributed. See §§ 1368(c)(1) and (e)(1).

[35]§ 1368(c).

CONCEPT SUMMARY 12–1

Distributions from an S Corporation

Where Earnings and Profits Exist	Where No Earnings and Profits Exist
1. Distributions are tax-free to the extent of the AAA.*	1. Distributions are nontaxable to the extent of adjusted basis in stock.
2. Any PTI from pre-1983 tax years can be distributed tax-free.	2. Excess is treated as gain from a sale or exchange of stock (capital gain in most cases).
3. The remaining distribution constitutes ordinary dividend from AEP.†	
4. Any residual amount is applied as a tax-free reduction in basis of stock.	
5. Excess is treated as gain from a sale or exchange of stock (capital gain in most cases).	

*A shareholder's stock basis serves as a limit on the amount that may be received tax-free.
†The AAA bypass election is available to pay out AEP before reducing the AAA [§ 1368(e)(3)].

AAA is applied to the distributions made during the year on a pro rata basis (in a fashion similar to the application of current E & P, discussed in Chapter 10). The determination of AAA is summarized in Exhibit 12–1.

Although adjustments to AAA and stock basis adjustments are similar, there are some important differences between the two amounts. In particular,

- The AAA is not affected by tax-exempt income and related expenses.
- Unlike stock basis, the AAA can have a negative balance. All losses decrease the AAA balance, even those in excess of the shareholder's basis. However, distributions may not make the AAA negative or increase a negative balance in the account.
- Every shareholder has a proportionate interest in the AAA, regardless of the amount of his or her stock basis.[36] In fact, AAA is a corporate account, so there is no connection between the amount and any specific shareholder.[37] Thus, the benefits of AAA can be shifted from one shareholder to another. For example, when an S corporation shareholder sells stock to another party, any AAA balance on the purchase date can be distributed tax-free to the purchaser.

Schedule M–2.   Schedule M–2 (reproduced on the next page) also contains a column labeled *Other adjustments account (OAA)*. This account includes items that

■ **EXHIBIT 12–1**
Adjustments to AAA

Increase by:
1. Positive separately stated items other than tax-exempt income.
2. Nonseparately computed income.

Decrease by:
3. Distribution(s) from AAA (but not below zero).
4. Negative separately stated items other than distributions (e.g., losses, deductions).

---

[36]§ 1368(c).   [37]§ 1368(e)(1)(A).

affect basis but not the AAA, such as tax-exempt income and any related nondeductible expenses. Distributions are made from the OAA after AEP and the AAA are reduced to zero. Since the OAA represents adjustments to stock basis, distributions from this account are tax-free recoveries of capital.

EXAMPLE 19

Poinsettia, an S corporation, records the following items.

AAA, beginning of the year	$ 8,500
Ordinary income	25,000
Tax-exempt interest	4,000
Key employee life insurance proceeds received	5,000
Payroll penalty expense	2,000
Charitable contributions	3,000
Unreasonable compensation	5,000
Premiums on key employee life insurance	2,100
Distributions to shareholders	16,000

Poinsettia's Schedule M–2 appears as follows.

Schedule M-2	Analysis of Accumulated Adjustments Account, Other Adjustments Account, and Shareholders' Undistributed Taxable Income Previously Taxed	(a) Accumulated adjustments account	(b) Other adjustments account
1	Balance at beginning of tax year . . .	8,500	
2	Ordinary income from page 1, line 21 . .	25,000	
3	Other additions		9,000**
4	Loss from page 1, line 21	( )	
5	Other reductions	(10,000*)	(2,100)
6	Combine lines 1 through 5	23,500	6,900
7	Distributions other than dividend distributions .	16,000	
8	Balance at end of tax year. Subtract line 7 from line 6	7,500	6,900

* $2,000 (payroll penalty) + $3,000 (charitable contributions) + $5,000 (unreasonable compensation).
** $4,000 (tax-exempt interest) + $5,000 (life insurance proceeds).

Effect of Terminating the S Election.   Normally, distributions to shareholders from a C corporation are taxed as dividends to the extent of E & P. However, any distribution of *cash* by a C corporation to shareholders during a one-year period[38] following an S election termination receives special treatment. Such a distribution is treated as a tax-free recovery of stock basis to the extent that it does not exceed the AAA.[39] Since *only* cash distributions reduce the AAA during this *postelection termination period*, a corporation should not make property distributions during this time. Instead, the entity should sell property and distribute the proceeds to shareholders.

EXAMPLE 20

Quinn, the sole shareholder of Azalea, Inc., a calendar year S corporation, decides during 2001 to terminate the S election, effective January 1, 2002. As of the end of 2001, Azalea has an AAA of $1,300. Quinn can receive a nontaxable distribution of cash during the post-termination period to the extent of Azalea's AAA. Although a cash distribution of $1,300 during 2002 would be nontaxable to Quinn, it would reduce the adjusted basis of his stock. ∎

---

[38]§ 1377(b).
[39]§ 1371(e). Termination-period distributions from the OAA are taxed as capital gains.

The Accumulated Adjustments Account

The AAA is needed to determine the tax treatment of distributions from S corporations with AEP *and* distributions made during the post-termination election period. Therefore, it is important for all S corporations (even those with no AEP) to maintain the AAA balance. Without an accurate AAA balance, distributions could needlessly be classified as taxable dividends. Alternatively, it will be costly to reconstruct the AAA after the S election terminates. Other observations about the AAA follow.

- Because tax-exempt income does not increase AAA, it may impose a tax cost on S corporations with AEP. In particular, distributions of tax-exempt income may hasten the use of any balance in the AAA, with no corresponding increase in the account. As a result, dividend distributions from AEP will be accelerated, resulting in more rapid recognition of tax liability.
- When AEP is present, a negative balance in the AAA may cause double taxation of S corporation income. With a negative AAA, a distribution of current income restores the negative AAA balance to zero, but is considered to be a distribution in excess of AAA and is taxable as a dividend to the extent of AEP.
- Distributions should be made when AAA is positive. If future years bring operating losses, AAA is reduced, and shareholder exposure to AEP and taxable dividends increases.

TAX TREATMENT OF PROPERTY DISTRIBUTIONS BY THE CORPORATION

An S corporation recognizes a gain on any distribution of appreciated property (other than in a reorganization) in the same manner as if the asset had been sold to the shareholder at its fair market value.[40] The corporate gain is passed through to the shareholders. There is an important reason for this rule. Without it, property might be distributed tax-free (other than for certain recapture items) and later sold without income recognition to the shareholder because the shareholder's basis equals the asset's fair market value. The character of the gain—capital gain or ordinary income—depends upon the type of asset being distributed.

The S corporation does not recognize a loss when distributing assets that are worth less than their basis. As with gain property, the shareholder's basis is equal to the asset's fair market value. Thus, the potential loss is postponed until the shareholder sells the stock of the S corporation. Since loss property receives a step-down in basis without any loss recognition by the S corporation, distributions of loss property should be avoided. See Concept Summary 12–2.

EXAMPLE 21

Yarrow, Inc., an S corporation for 10 years, distributes a tract of land held as an investment to one of its shareholders. The land was purchased for $22,000 many years ago and is currently worth $82,000. Yarrow recognizes a capital gain of $60,000, which increases the AAA by $60,000. The gain flows through proportionately to Yarrow's shareholders and is taxed to them.

Then a tax-free property distribution reduces AAA and shareholder stock basis by $82,000 (fair market value). The tax consequences are the same for appreciated property, whether it is distributed to the shareholders and they dispose of it, or the corporation sells the property and distributes the proceeds to the shareholders. ∎

---

[40]§ 311(b).

CONCEPT SUMMARY 12–2

Distribution of Property In-Kind

	Appreciated Property	Depreciated Property
S corporation	Realized gain is recognized by the corporation, which passes it through to the shareholders. Such gain increases a shareholder's stock basis, generating a basis in the property equal to FMV. On the distribution, the shareholder's stock basis is reduced by the FMV of the property (but not below zero).	Realized loss is not recognized. The shareholder assumes an FMV basis in the property.
C corporation	Realized gain is recognized under § 311(b) and increases E & P (net of tax). The shareholder has a taxable dividend to the extent of E & P.	Realized loss is not recognized. The shareholder assumes an FMV basis in the property.
Partnership	No gain to the partnership or partner. Basis to the partner is limited to the partner's basis in the partnership.	Realized loss is not recognized. The partner takes a carryover basis in the asset.

EXAMPLE 22

Continue with the facts of Example 21. If the land had been purchased for $80,000 many years ago and was currently worth $30,000, the $50,000 realized loss would not be recognized at the corporate level, and the shareholder would take a $30,000 basis in the land. Since loss is not recognized on the distribution of property that has declined in value, the AAA is not reduced by the unrecognized loss. For the loss on the property to be recognized, the S corporation must sell the property to an unrelated party. ■

EXAMPLE 23

Assume the same facts as in Examples 21 and 22, except that Yarrow is a C corporation or a partnership. Assume the partner's basis in the partnership is $25,000 and ignore any corporate-level taxes. Compare the results.

	Appreciated Property		
	S Corporation	C Corporation	Partnership
Entity gain/loss	$60,000	$60,000	$ –0–
Owner's gain/loss/dividend	60,000	82,000*	–0–
Owner's basis in land	82,000	82,000	22,000

	Property That Has Declined in Value		
	S Corporation	C Corporation	Partnership
Entity gain/loss	$ –0–	$ –0–	$ –0–
Owner's gain/loss/dividend	–0–	30,000*	–0–
Owner's basis in land	30,000	30,000	25,000**

*Assume sufficient E & P.
**Basis in property cannot exceed basis in partnership interest. ■

LEARNING OBJECTIVE 6

Calculate a shareholder's
basis in S corporation stock.

SHAREHOLDER'S BASIS

The calculation of the initial tax basis of stock in an S corporation is similar to that for the basis of stock in a C corporation and depends upon the manner in which the shares are acquired (e.g., gift, inheritance, purchase, exchange under § 351). Once the initial tax basis is determined, various transactions during the life of the corporation affect the shareholder's basis in the stock. Although each shareholder is required to compute his or her own basis in the S shares, neither Form 1120S nor Schedule K–1 provides a place for tracking this amount.

A shareholder's basis is increased by stock purchases and capital contributions. Operations during the year cause the following additional upward adjustments to basis.[41] *goes up by any income*

- Nonseparately computed income.
- Separately stated income items (e.g., nontaxable income).

Basis then is reduced by distributions not reported as income by the shareholder (e.g., an AAA or PTI distribution). Next, the following items reduce basis (but not below zero).

- Nondeductible expenses of the corporation (e.g., fines, penalties, illegal kickbacks).
- Nonseparately computed loss.
- Separately stated loss and deduction items.

As under the partnership rules, basis first is increased by income items; then it is decreased by distributions and finally by losses.[42] In most cases, this *losses last* rule is advantageous.

EXAMPLE 24

In its first year of operations, Iris, Inc., a calendar year S corporation, earns income of $2,000. On February 2 in its second year of operations, Iris distributes $2,000 to Marty, its sole shareholder. During the remainder of the second year, the corporation incurs a $2,000 loss.

Under the S corporation ordering rules, the $2,000 distribution is tax-free AAA to Marty. The distribution is accounted for before the loss. The $2,000 loss is *not* passed through, though, because stock basis cannot be reduced below zero. ∎

A shareholder's basis in S corporation stock can never be reduced below zero. Once stock basis is zero, any additional basis reductions (losses or deductions, but *not* distributions) decrease (but not below zero) the shareholder's basis in loans made to the S corporation. Any excess of losses or deductions over both stock and loan bases is not deductible in the current year. Losses can be deducted only to the extent that they offset stock or loan basis. Thus, until additional basis is created due to capital contributions or flow-through income, the loss deductions are suspended.

When there is a capital contribution or an item of flow-through income, then basis is first restored to the shareholder loans, up to the original principal amount.[43] Then, basis in the stock is restored.

EXAMPLE 25

Stacey, a sole shareholder, has a $7,000 stock basis and a $2,000 basis in a loan that she made to a calendar year S corporation at the beginning of the year. Subchapter S net income for the year is $8,200. The corporation also received $2,000 of tax-exempt interest income.

---

[41]§ 1367(a).
[42]Reg. § 1.1367–1(f).

[43]§ 1367(b)(2).

Cash of $17,300 is distributed to Stacey on November 15. As a result, Stacey's basis in her stock is zero, and her loan basis is still $2,000 at the end of the year, because only losses and deductions (and not distributions) reduce the loan basis. Stacey recognizes a $100 capital gain because the distribution exceeds her stock basis ($17,300 − $17,200).

	Corporate AAA	Stacey's Stock Basis	Stacey's Loan Basis
Beginning balance	$ –0–	$ 7,000	$2,000
Subchapter S net income	8,200	8,200	–0–
Tax-exempt income	–0–	2,000	–0–
Subtotal	$ 8,200	$ 17,200	$2,000
Distribution ($17,300)	(8,200)	(17,200)	–0–
Ending balance	$ –0–	$ –0–	$2,000

The basis rules for S corporation stock are similar to the rules for determining a partner's basis in a partnership interest. However, a partner's basis in the partnership interest includes the partner's direct investment plus a *ratable share* of partnership liabilities.[44] If a partnership borrows from a partner, the partner receives a basis increase as if the partnership had borrowed from an unrelated third party.[45] In contrast, except for loans from the shareholder to the corporation, corporate borrowing has no effect on S corporation shareholder basis. Loans from a shareholder to the S corporation have a tax basis only for the shareholder making the loan.

If a loan's basis has been reduced and is not restored, income is recognized when the corporation repays the loan. If the corporation issued a note as evidence of the debt, repayment constitutes an amount received in exchange for a capital asset, and the amount that exceeds the shareholder's basis is capital gain.[46] However, if the loan is made on open account, the repayment constitutes ordinary income to the extent that it exceeds the shareholder's basis in the loan. Thus, a note should be given to ensure capital gain treatment for the income that results from a loan's repayment.

EXAMPLE 26

Phil is the sole shareholder of Falcon, a valid S corporation. At the beginning of 2001, Phil's basis in his stock was $10,000. During 2001, he made a $4,000 loan to the corporation, using a written debt instrument and market interest rates. Falcon has no other outstanding debt.

Falcon generated a $13,000 taxable loss for 2001. Thus, at the beginning of 2002, Phil's stock basis was zero, and the basis in his loan to Falcon was $1,000.

Falcon repaid the loan in full on March 1, 2002. Phil recognized a $3,000 capital gain on the repayment. ■

4 *Find more information on this topic at our Web site: **http://wft-entities.swcollege.com**.*

---

[44]§ 752(a).
[45]Reg. § 1.752–1(e).
[46]*Joe M. Smith*, 48 T.C. 872 (1967), *aff'd* and *rev'd* in 70–1 USTC ¶9327, 25 AFTR2d 70–936, 424 F.2d 219 (CA–9, 1970), and Rev.Rul. 64–162, 1964–1 C.B. 304.

PLANNING CONSIDERATIONS

Working with Suspended Losses

Distributions made to shareholders with suspended losses usually create capital gain income because there is no stock or debt basis to offset. Usually, distributions should be deferred until the shareholder creates stock basis in some form. In this way, no gross income is recognized until the suspended losses are fully used.

EXAMPLE 27

Continue with the facts of Example 26 except that Falcon's loss cannot be deducted by Phil because of the lack of basis. Phil purchases $5,000 of additional stock in Falcon. Phil gets an immediate deduction for his investment, due to his $13,000 in suspended losses. Alternatively, if Falcon shows a $5,000 profit for the year, Phil pays no tax on the flow-through income, due to his $13,000 in suspended losses.

However, if Falcon distributes $5,000 to Phil in 2002 without earning any profit for the year, and prior to any capital contribution by him, Phil recognizes a $5,000 capital gain, because his stock basis is zero. ∎

---

corp has loss it flows to shareholder

LEARNING OBJECTIVE 7

Explain the tax effects of losses on S shareholders.

TREATMENT OF LOSSES

Net Operating Loss. One major advantage of an S election is the ability to pass through any net operating loss (NOL) of the corporation directly to the shareholders. A shareholder can deduct an NOL for the year in which the S corporation's tax year ends. The corporation is not entitled to any deduction for the NOL. A shareholder's basis in the stock is reduced to the extent of any pass-through of the NOL, and the shareholder's AAA is reduced by the same deductible amount.[47]

Deductions for an S corporation's NOL pass-through cannot exceed a shareholder's adjusted basis in the stock *plus* the basis of any loans made by the shareholder to the corporation.[48] A shareholder is entitled to carry forward a loss to the extent that the loss for the year exceeds basis. Any loss carried forward may be deducted *only* by the *same* shareholder if and when the basis in the stock of or loans to the corporation is restored.[49]

5 *Find more information on this topic at our Web site: **http://wft-entities.swcollege.com**.*

EXAMPLE 28

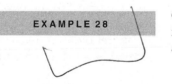

Ginny owns 10% of the stock of Pilot, a calendar year S corporation. Her basis in the shares is $10,000 at the beginning of 2001. The indicated events are accounted for under the S rules as follows.

Tax Year	Event	Tax Consequences
2001	Ginny's share of Pilot's operating loss is $15,000.	Ginny deducts $10,000. Her stock basis is reduced to zero. She holds a $5,000 suspended loss.
2002	Ginny's share of Pilot's operating loss is $4,000.	No deduction for the loss, as Ginny has no stock basis to offset. Her suspended loss is now $9,000.

---

[47]§§ 1368(a)(1)(A) and (e)(1)(A).
[48]See *Donald J. Sauvigne*, 30 TCM 123, T.C.Memo. 1971–30.

[49]§ 1366(d).

ex (borrowing from bank) loan S corp made; individual can't get that as basis; but u can for partnership

Tax Year	Event	Tax Consequences
2003	Ginny's share of Pilot's operating loss is $7,000. She purchases an additional $10,000 of stock from Pilot.	The purchase creates $10,000 stock basis. Ginny deducts $10,000—the current $7,000 loss and $3,000 of the suspended loss. Stock basis again is zero, and the new suspended loss is $6,000.
2004	Ginny sells all of her Pilot shares to Christina on January 1.	The $6,000 suspended loss disappears—it cannot be transferred to Christina. ∎

PLANNING CONSIDERATIONS

Loss Considerations

A loss in excess of tax basis may be carried forward and deducted only by the same shareholder in succeeding years. Thus, before disposing of the stock, a shareholder should increase stock/loan basis to flow through the loss. The next shareholder cannot acquire the loss carryover.

The NOL provisions create a need for sound tax planning during the last election year and the post-termination transition period. If it appears that the S corporation is going to sustain an NOL or use up any loss carryover, each shareholder's basis should be analyzed to determine if it can absorb the owner's share of the loss. If basis is insufficient to absorb the loss, further investments should be considered before the end of the post-termination period. Such investments can be accomplished through additional stock purchases from the corporation, or from other shareholders, to increase basis.

EXAMPLE 29

A calendar year C corporation has an NOL of $20,000 in 2000. The corporation makes a valid S election in 2001 and has another $20,000 NOL in that year. At all times during 2001, the stock of the corporation was owned by the same 10 shareholders, each of whom owned 10% of the stock. Tim, one of the shareholders, has an adjusted basis in his stock of $1,800 at the beginning of 2001. None of the 2000 NOL may be carried forward into the S year. Although Tim's share of the 2001 NOL is $2,000, his deduction for the loss is limited to $1,800 in 2001 with a $200 carryover to 2002. ∎

Passive Losses and Credits.   Net passive losses and credits are not deductible when incurred and must be carried over to a year when there is passive income. Thus, one must be aware of three major classes of income, losses, and credits— active, portfolio, and passive. S corporations are not directly subject to the passive activity limits, but corporate rental activities are inherently passive, and other activities of an S corporation may be passive unless the shareholder(s) materially participate(s) in operating the business. An S corporation may engage in more than one such activity.

If the corporate activity is rental or the shareholders do not materially participate, any passive losses or credits flow through. The shareholders are able to apply the losses or credits only against their income from other passive activities. An S shareholder's stock basis is reduced by passive losses that flow through to the shareholder, even though the shareholder may not be entitled to a current deduction due to the passive loss limitations.

At-Risk Rules.   S corporation shareholders, like partners, are limited in the amount of NOL they may deduct by their "at-risk" amounts. The rules for determining at-risk amounts are similar, but not identical, to the partnership at-risk rules.

An amount at risk is determined separately for each shareholder. The amount of the corporate losses that are passed through and deductible by the shareholders

---

CONCEPT SUMMARY 12–3

Treatment of S Corporation Losses

Step 1. Allocate total loss to the shareholder on a daily basis, based upon stock ownership.

Step 2. If the shareholder's loss exceeds his or her stock basis, apply any excess to the adjusted basis of indebtedness to the shareholder. Distributions do not reduce stock or debt basis below zero.

Step 3. Where a flow-through loss exceeds the stock and debt basis, any excess is suspended and carried over to succeeding tax years.

Step 4. In succeeding tax years, any net increase in basis restores the debt basis first, up to its original amount.

Step 5. Once debt basis is restored, any remaining net increase restores stock basis.

Step 6. Any suspended loss from a previous year now reduces stock basis first and debt basis second.

Step 7. If the S election terminates, any suspended loss carryover may be deducted during the post-termination period to the extent of the stock basis at the end of this period. Any loss remaining at the end of this period is lost forever.

---

is not affected by the amount the corporation has at risk. A shareholder usually is considered at risk with respect to an activity to the extent of cash and the adjusted basis of other property contributed to the electing corporation, any amount borrowed for use in the activity for which the taxpayer has personal liability for payment from personal assets, and the net fair market value of personal assets that secure nonrecourse borrowing. Any losses that are suspended under the at-risk rules are carried forward and are available during the post-termination period. The S stock basis limitations and at-risk limitations are applied before the passive activity limitations.

EXAMPLE 30

Carl has a basis of $35,000 in his S corporation stock. He takes a $15,000 nonrecourse loan from a relative and lends the proceeds to the S corporation. Carl now has a stock basis of $35,000 and a debt basis of $15,000. However, due to the at-risk limitation, he can deduct only $35,000 of losses from the S corporation. ∎

LEARNING OBJECTIVE 8

Compute the entity-level taxes on S corporations.

TAX ON PRE-ELECTION BUILT-IN GAIN

Normally, an S corporation does *not* pay an income tax, since all items flow through to the shareholders. But an S corporation that was previously a C corporation may be required to pay a built-in gains tax, a LIFO recapture tax, or a passive investment income tax.

Without the **built-in gains tax,** it would be possible to avoid the corporate double tax on disposition of appreciated property by electing S corporation status.

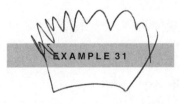

EXAMPLE 31

Zinnia, Inc., a C corporation, owns a single asset with a basis of $100,000 and a fair market value of $500,000. If Zinnia sells this asset and distributes the cash to its shareholders, there are two levels of tax, one at the corporate level and one at the shareholder level. Alternatively, if Zinnia distributes the asset to its shareholders as a dividend, a double tax still results. In an attempt to avoid the double tax, Zinnia elects S corporation status. It then sells the asset and distributes the proceeds to shareholders. Without the built-in gains tax, the gain would be taxed only once, at the shareholder level. The distribution of the sales proceeds would be a tax-free reduction of the AAA. ∎

The built-in gains tax generally applies to C corporations converting to S status after 1986. It is a *corporate-level* tax on any built-in gain recognized when the S corporation disposes of an asset in a taxable disposition within 10 calendar years after the date on which the S election took effect. The steps in computing the tax are summarized in Concept Summary 12–4.

General Rules. The base for the built-in gains tax includes any unrealized gain on appreciated assets (e.g., real estate, cash basis receivables, goodwill) held by a corporation on the day it elects S status. The highest corporate tax rate (currently 35 percent) is applied to the unrealized gain when any of the assets are sold. Any gain from the sale (net of the § 1374 tax)[50] also passes through as a taxable gain to shareholders.

EXAMPLE 32

Assume the same facts as in the preceding example. Section 1374 imposes a corporate-level tax that must be paid by Zinnia if it sells the asset after electing S status. Upon sale of the asset, the corporation owes a tax of $140,000 (35% × $400,000). In addition, the shareholders report a $260,000 taxable gain ($400,000 − $140,000). Hence, the built-in gains tax effectively imposes a double tax on Zinnia and its shareholders. ■

6 *Find more information on this topic at our Web site: http://wft-entities.swcollege.com.*

The amount of built-in gain recognized in any year is limited to an *as if* taxable income for the year, computed as if the corporation were a C corporation. Any built-in gain that escapes taxation due to the taxable income limitation is carried forward and recognized in future tax years. Thus, a corporation can defer a built-in gains tax liability whenever it has a low or negative taxable income.

EXAMPLE 33

Vinca's recognized built-in gain for 2001 is $400. If Vinca were a C corporation, its 2001 taxable income would be $300. The amount of built-in gain subject to tax in 2001 is $300. The excess built-in gain of $100 is carried forward and taxed in 2002 (assuming adequate C corporation taxable income in that year). There is no statutory limit on the carryforward period, but the gain would effectively expire at the end of the 10-year recognition period applicable to all built-in gains.[51] ■

Normally, tax attributes of a C corporation do not carry over to a converted S corporation. For purposes of the built-in gains tax, however, certain carryovers are allowed. In particular, an S corporation can offset built-in gains with unexpired NOLs or capital losses from C corporation years.

EXAMPLE 34

An S corporation has a built-in gain of $100,000 and taxable income of $90,000. The built-in gains tax liability is calculated as follows, applying the indicated loss carryforwards.

Lesser of taxable income or built-in gain	$ 90,000
Less: NOL carryforward from C year	(12,000)
Capital loss carryforward from C year	(8,000)
Tax base	$ 70,000
Highest corporate income tax rate	× 0.35
Tentative tax	$ 24,500
Less: Business credit carryforward from C year	(4,000)
Built-in gains tax liability	$ 20,500

---

[50]§ 1366(f)(2).

[51]§ 1374(d)(7); Notice 90–27, 1990–1 C.B. 336.

CONCEPT SUMMARY 12–4

Calculation of the Built-in Gains Tax Liability

Step 1.   Select the smaller of built-in gain or taxable income.*
Step 2.   Deduct unexpired NOLs and capital losses from C corporation tax years.
Step 3.   Multiply the tax base obtained in step 2 by the top corporate income tax rate.
Step 4.   Deduct any business credit carryforwards and AMT credit carryforwards arising in a C corporation tax year from the amount obtained in step 3.
Step 5.   The corporation pays any tax resulting in step 4.
*Any net recognized built-in gain in excess of taxable income is carried forward to the next year within the 10-year recognition period.

The $10,000 realized (but not taxed) built-in gain in excess of taxable income is carried forward to the next year, as long as the next year is within the 10-year recognition period. ∎

PLANNING CONSIDERATIONS

Managing the Built-in Gains Tax

Although limitations exist on contributions of loss property to the corporation before electing S status, it still is possible for a corporation to minimize built-in gains and maximize built-in losses prior to the S election. A cash basis S corporation can accomplish this by reducing receivables, accelerating payables, and accruing compensation costs.

To further reduce or defer the tax, the corporation may take advantage of the taxable income limitation by shifting income and deductions to minimize taxable income in years when built-in gain is recognized. Although the postponed built-in gain is carried forward to future years, the time value of money makes the postponement beneficial. For example, paying compensation to shareholder-employees in place of a distribution creates a deduction that reduces taxable income and postpones the built-in gains tax.

If Tulip pays at least $120,000 in salaries to the shareholders (rather than making a distribution), taxable income drops to zero, and the built-in gains tax is postponed. Thus, Tulip needs to keep the salaries as high as possible to postpone the built-in gains tax in future years and reap a benefit from the time value of money. Of course, paying the salaries may increase the payroll tax burden if the salaries are initially below FICA and FUTA limits. ∎

Giving built-in gain property to a charitable organization does not trigger the built-in gains tax. Built-in *loss* property may be sold in the same year that built-in gain property is sold to reduce or eliminate the built-in gains tax. Generally, the taxpayer should sell built-in loss property in a year when an equivalent amount of built-in gain property is sold. Otherwise, the built-in loss could be wasted.

EXAMPLE 35

Tulip, Inc., an S corporation, has built-in gain of $110,000 and taxable income of $120,000 before payment of salaries to its shareholders.

LIFO Recapture Tax.   When a corporation uses the FIFO method for its last year before making the S election, any built-in gain is recognized and taxed as the inventory is sold. A LIFO-basis corporation does not recognize this gain unless the corporation invades the LIFO layer during the 10-year built-in gains tax period. To preclude deferral of gain recognition under LIFO, any LIFO recapture amount at the time of the S election is subject to a corporate-level tax.

The taxable LIFO recapture amount equals the excess of the inventory's value under FIFO over the LIFO value. The resulting tax is payable in four equal installments, with the first payment due on or before the due date for the corporate return for the last C corporation year (without regard to any extensions). The remaining three installments must be paid on or before the due dates of the succeeding corporate returns. No interest is due if payments are made by the due dates, and no estimated taxes are due on the four tax installments. No refund is allowed if the LIFO value is higher than the FIFO value.

EXAMPLE 36

Daffodil Corporation converts from a C corporation to an S corporation at the beginning of 2001. Daffodil used the LIFO inventory method in 2000 and had an ending LIFO inventory of $110,000 (FIFO value of $190,000). Daffodil must add $80,000 of LIFO recapture amount to its 2000 taxable income, resulting in an increased tax liability of $28,000 ($80,000 × 35%). Daffodil must pay one-fourth of the tax (or $7,000) with its 2000 corporate tax return. The three succeeding installments of $7,000 each are paid with Daffodil's 2001–2003 tax returns. ■

PASSIVE INVESTMENT INCOME PENALTY TAX

A tax is imposed on the excess passive income of S corporations that possess AEP from C corporation years. The tax rate is the highest corporate income tax rate for the year. The rate is applied to excess net passive income (ENPI), which is determined using the following formula.

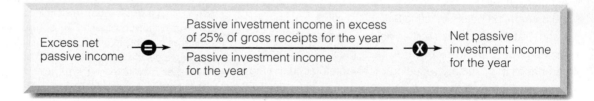

Passive investment income (PII) includes gross receipts derived from royalties, rents, dividends, interest, annuities, and sales and exchanges of stocks and securities.[52] Only the net gain from the disposition of capital assets (other than stocks and securities) is taken into account in computing gross receipts. Net passive income is passive income reduced by any deductions directly connected with the production of that income. Any passive income tax reduces the amount the shareholders must take into income.

The excess net passive income cannot exceed a hypothetical C corporate taxable income for the year, before considering special C corporation deductions (like the dividends received deduction) or an NOL carryover.[53]

EXAMPLE 37

Lilac Corporation, an electing S corporation, has gross receipts totaling $264,000 (of which $110,000 is PII). Expenditures directly connected to the production of the PII total $30,000. Therefore, Lilac has net PII of $80,000 ($110,000 – $30,000), and its PII exceeds 25% of its gross receipts by $44,000 [$110,000 PII – (25% × $264,000)]. Excess net passive income (ENPI) is $32,000, calculated as follows.

---

[52]§ 1362(d)(3)(D)(i).   [53]§§ 1374(d)(4), and 1375(a) and (b).

self employment *tax*

FICA

$$\text{ENPI} = \frac{\$44,000}{\$110,000} \times \$80,000 = \$32,000$$

Lilac's PII tax is $11,200 ($32,000 × 35%). ∎

OTHER OPERATIONAL RULES

Several other points may be made about the possible effects of various Code provisions on S corporations.

- An S corporation must make estimated tax payments with respect to any recognized built-in gain and excess passive investment income tax.
- An S corporation may own stock in another corporation, but an S corporation may not have a C corporation shareholder. An S corporation is *not* eligible for a dividends received deduction.
- An S corporation is *not* subject to the 10 percent of taxable income limitation applicable to charitable contributions made by a C corporation.
- Any family member who renders services or furnishes capital to an S corporation must be paid reasonable compensation. Otherwise, the IRS can make adjustments to reflect the value of the services or capital. This rule may make it more difficult for related parties to shift Subchapter S taxable income to children or other family members.
- Although § 1366(a)(1) provides for a flow-through of S items to a shareholder, this amount is not self-employment income and is not subject to the self-employment tax.[54] Compensation for services rendered to an S corporation is, however, subject to FICA taxes.

EXAMPLE 38

Cody and Dana each own one-third of a fast-food restaurant, and their 14-year-old son owns the other shares. Both parents work full-time in the restaurant operations, but the son works infrequently. Neither parent receives a salary this year, when the taxable income of the S corporation is $160,000. The IRS can require that reasonable compensation be deemed as paid to the parents to prevent the full one-third of the $160,000 from being taxed to the son. Otherwise, this would be an effective technique to shift earned income to a family member to reduce the total family tax burden. Furthermore, low or zero salaries can reduce FICA taxes due to the Federal government. ∎

- An S corporation is placed on the cash method of accounting for purposes of deducting business expenses and interest owed to a cash basis related party.[55] Thus, the timing of the shareholder's income and the corporate deduction must match.
- The S election is not recognized by the District of Columbia and several states, including Connecticut, New Hampshire, and Tennessee. Thus, some or all of the entity's income may be subject to a state-level income tax.
- An S corporation may issue § 1244 stock to its shareholders to obtain ordinary loss treatment.
- Losses may be disallowed due to a lack of a profit motive. If the activities at the corporate level are not profit motivated, the losses may be disallowed under the hobby loss rules of § 183 (see Chapter 16).[56]

---

[54]Rev.Rul. 59–221, 1959–1 C.B. 225. Recall from Chapter 11 that flow-through ordinary income is self-employment income to a partner or LLC member.

[55]§ 267(b).

[56]*Michael J. Houston*, T.C.Memo. 1995–159; *Mario G. De Mendoza, III*, T.C.Memo. 1994–314.

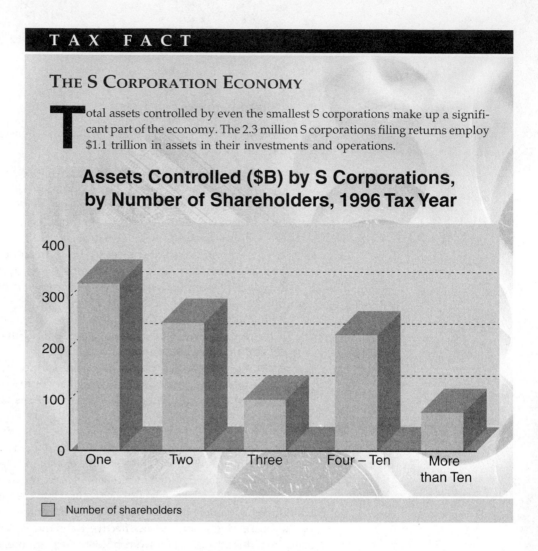

TAX FACT

THE S CORPORATION ECONOMY

Total assets controlled by even the smallest S corporations make up a significant part of the economy. The 2.3 million S corporations filing returns employ $1.1 trillion in assets in their investments and operations.

Assets Controlled ($B) by S Corporations, by Number of Shareholders, 1996 Tax Year

Number of shareholders

Summary

The S corporation rules are elective and can be used to benefit a number of owners of small businesses.

- When the business is profitable, the S corporation election removes the threat of double taxation on corporate profits.
- When the business is generating losses, deductions for allocable losses are immediately available to the shareholders.

About one-half of all U.S. corporations operate under the S rules. Flow-through income is taxed to the shareholders, who increase basis in their corporate stock accordingly. In this manner, subsequent distributions to shareholders can be made tax-free. Flow-through losses reduce stock and debt basis, but loss deductions are suspended when basis reaches zero. Flow-through items that could be treated differently by various shareholders are separately stated on Schedule K–1 of the Form 1120S.

Corporate-level taxes are seldom assessed on S corporations, but they guard against abuses of the S rules, such as shifting appreciated assets from higher C corporation rates to lower individual rates (the built-in gains tax) or doing the same with investment assets (the tax on excessive PII).

The S rules are designed for closely held businesses with simple capital structures. Eligibility rules are not oppressive, and they do not include any limitations on the corporation's capitalization value, sales, number or distribution of employees, or other operating measures. The S election process can be complex, though, and maintenance of S status must be monitored on an ongoing basis.

Suggested Further Readings

Ronald G. Caso, "Tax Planning Pays for the S Corporation Buyer and Seller," *Practical Tax Strategies*, August 1999, pp. 96–100.

Bruce Korbesmeyer, "Inadequate Compensation to 1120S Corporate Officers," *IRS Research Bulletin*, 1999, p. 89.

John B. Truskowski, "Capitalizing the S Corporation: Tax Consequences of Financing with Equity and Financing with Debt," *Business Entities*, March/April 1999, pp. 34–41.

KEY TERMS

Accumulated adjustments account (AAA), 12–16	Passive investment income (PII), 12–10	Small business corporation, 12–5
Built-in gains tax, 12–25	S corporation, 12–2	Subchapter S, 12–2

Problem Materials

PROBLEMS

1. On March 2, 2001, the two 50% shareholders of a calendar year corporation decide to elect S status. One of the shareholders, Terry, had purchased her stock from a previous shareholder (a nonresident alien) on January 18, 2001. Identify any potential problems for Terry or the corporation.

2. Burt is the custodian at Quaker Inn, an S corporation that has paid him bonuses over the years in the form of shares in the corporation. Burt now holds 276 shares in Quaker Inn.

   While listening to a television debate about a national health care plan, Burt decides that the company's health coverage is unfair. He is concerned about this because his wife, Dora, is seriously ill.

   During the second week in December, Burt informs Quaker's president that he would like a Christmas bonus of $75,000 cash, or else he will sell 10 shares of his stock to one of his relatives, a nonresident alien. The resulting loss of the S election would trigger about $135,000 in Federal corporate income taxes for the current year alone. Comment.

3. Seventy-four individuals own all of the shares of Woodpecker Corporation. Hal and Mary Jones want to buy into the corporation, and then to direct the entity to make an S election. Can Woodpecker so elect? How many signatures must appear on the consent form making the S election?

4. GoldCo has operated successfully as an S corporation for the last eight years, saving about $280,000 in Federal income taxes because of the election. The company currently has 75 shareholders, including Morrie and Kristy, a married couple who count as one shareholder for purposes of § 1361.

   Morrie and Kristy now announce that they are planning to be divorced. GoldCo's board of directors responds with the following list of suggestions. Comment.

   • Postpone the divorce for a year, during which the board will attempt to buy out the shares of one of the other shareholders.

   • Morrie and Kristy should remain married indefinitely for the good of the company.

   • The board will encourage two of the other shareholders to marry each other for the good of the company.

   • After Morrie and Kristy divorce, GoldCo should continue to file a Form 1120S, stating that they are still married and that the limitation on the number of shareholders is met.

5. Lynch's share of her S corporation's net operating loss is $41,000, but her stock basis is only $29,000. Point out any tax consequences to Lynch.

6. Zebra, Inc., a calendar year S corporation, incurred the following items for 2001. Sammy is a 40% shareholder in Zebra throughout the year.

Operating income	$100,000
Cost of goods sold	40,000
Depreciation expense	10,000
Administrative expenses	5,000
§ 1231 gain	21,000
§ 1250 gain	20,000
Short-term capital loss from stock sale	6,000
Long-term capital loss from stock sale	4,000
Long-term capital gain from stock sale	15,000
Charitable contributions	4,500

   a. Calculate Sammy's share of nonseparately computed income.
   b. Calculate Sammy's share of any net long-term capital gain.

7. An S corporation's profit and loss statement shows net profits of $90,000 (book income). The corporation has three equal shareholders. From supplemental data, you obtain the following information about the corporation. All of the indicated items are included in book income.

Selling expenses	$21,200
Tax-exempt interest	2,000
Dividends received	9,000
§ 1231 gain	6,000
§ 1250 gain	12,000
Recovery of bad debts	4,000
Long-term capital losses	6,000
Salary to owners (each)	10,000
Cost of goods sold	95,000

    a. Compute Subchapter S taxable income or loss.

    b. What would be the portion of taxable income or loss for Chang, one of the shareholders?

8. Ramos, Inc., a calendar year S corporation, incurred the following items this year.

Municipal bond interest	$ 7,000
Sales	130,000
§ 1250 gain	12,000
Short-term capital gain	30,000
Cost of goods sold	42,000
Administrative expenses	15,000
Depreciation expense	17,000
Charitable contributions	14,000

    Calculate Ramos's nonseparately computed income.

9. Polly has been the sole shareholder of a calendar year S corporation since its inception. Polly's stock basis is $15,500, and she receives a distribution of $19,000. Corporate-level accounts are as follows.

    AAA $6,000   AEP $500

    How is Polly taxed on the distribution?

10. Dave, the sole shareholder of a calendar year S corporation in Cut-N-Shot, Texas, received a distribution of $16,000. Dave's stock basis at the beginning of the tax year was $4,000. The corporation earned $11,000 of ordinary income during the year. Calculate the amount and type of income Dave recognizes.

11. Goblins, Inc., a calendar year S corporation, has $90,000 of AEP. Tobias, the sole shareholder, has an adjusted basis of $80,000 in his stock with a zero balance in the AAA. Determine the tax aspects if a $90,000 salary is paid to Tobias.

12. Assume the same facts as in Problem 11, except that Tobias receives a dividend of $90,000.

13. Indicate whether each of the following items increases or decreases an S corporation's AAA or OAA (e.g., by responding "AAA+" or "OAA–"). Enter "*NE*" if the item has no effect on the entity's Schedule M–2.

    a. Receipt of tax-exempt interest income.

    b. Unreasonable compensation determined.

    c. Section 1250 recapture income.

    d. Distribution of nontaxable income (PTI) from 1981.

    e. Nontaxable life insurance proceeds.

    f. Expenses related to tax-exempt securities.

    g. Charitable contributions.

    h. Business gifts in excess of $25.

    i. Nondeductible fines and penalties.

    j. Administrative expenses.

14. Adam and Bonnie form an S corporation, with Adam contributing cash of $100,000 for a 50% interest and Bonnie contributing appreciated ordinary income property with an adjusted basis of $20,000 and an FMV of $100,000.

    a. Determine Bonnie's initial basis in her stock, assuming that she receives a 50% corporate ownership interest.

    b. The S corporation sells the property for $120,000. Determine Adam's and Bonnie's stock basis after the sale.

15. Bip Wallace is the only shareholder in Corso, a valid S corporation. Bip's stock basis at the beginning of the year is $100,000. Corso produces a $55,000 operating loss for the year. On November 1, it distributed $70,000 to Wallace. Show your computations as to the tax consequences in spreadsheet form and include them in a memo to your manager.

16. Shelley asks your advice. Should she raise new funds for her existing S corporation by issuing stock or debt? Draft a memo for the file outlining what you will tell Shelley.

17. Collett's S corporation has a small amount of accumulated earnings and profits (AEP), requiring the use of the more complex distribution rules. His accountant tells him that this AEP forces the maintenance of the AAA figure each year. Identify relevant tax issues facing Collett.

18. Caleb Hudson owns 10% of an S corporation. He is confused with respect to the AAA and his stock basis. Write a brief memo to Caleb identifying the key differences between AAA and his stock basis.

19. Compute the ending AAA and AEP balances for Faber, a valid S corporation.

Beginning AAA balance	$100,000
Beginning AEP balance	55,000
Operating loss	60,000
Shareholder distribution, May 1	70,000

20. Money, Inc., a calendar year S corporation, has two unrelated shareholders, each owning 50% of the stock. Both shareholders have a $400,000 stock basis as of January 1, and Money has AAA of $300,000 and AEP of $600,000. During the year, Money has operating income of $100,000. At the end of the year, Money distributes securities worth $1 million, with an adjusted basis of $800,000. Determine the tax effects of these transactions.

21. Assume the same facts as in Problem 20, except that the two shareholders consent under § 1368(e)(3) (the AAA bypass election) to distribute AEP first.

22. An S corporation's Form 1120S shows taxable income of $88,000 for the year. Daniel owns 40% of the stock throughout the year. The following information is obtained from the corporate records.

Salary paid to Daniel	$52,000
Tax-exempt interest income	3,000
Charitable contributions	6,000
Dividends received from a foreign corporation	5,000
Long-term capital loss	6,000
§ 1245 gain	11,000
Refund of prior state income taxes	5,000
Cost of goods sold	72,000
Short-term capital loss	7,000
Administrative expenses	18,000
Short-term capital gain	14,000
Selling expenses	11,000
Daniel's beginning stock basis	32,000
Daniel's additional stock purchases	9,000
Beginning AAA	31,000
Daniel's loan to corporation	20,000

a. Compute book income or loss.
b. Compute Daniel's ending stock basis.
c. Calculate ending corporate AAA.

23. At the beginning of the year, Malcolm, a 50% shareholder of a calendar year S corporation, has a stock basis of $22,000. During the year, the corporation has taxable income of $32,000. The following data are obtained from supplemental sources.

Dividends received	$12,000
Tax-exempt interest	18,000
Short-term capital gain	6,000
§ 1245 gain	10,000
§ 1231 gain	7,000
Charitable contributions	5,000
Political contributions	8,000
Short-term capital loss	12,000
Dividends to Malcolm	6,000
Selling expense	14,000
Beginning AAA	40,000

   a. Compute Malcolm's ending stock basis.
   b. Compute ending AAA.

24. For each of the following independent statements, indicate whether the transaction will increase (+), decrease (–), or have no effect (*NE*) on the adjusted basis of a shareholder's stock in an S corporation.
   a. Expenses related to tax-exempt income.
   b. Short-term capital gain.
   c. Nonseparately computed loss.
   d. Section 1231 gain.
   e. Cost recovery deductions on plant and equipment.
   f. Separately computed income.
   g. Nontaxable return-of-capital distribution by the corporation.
   h. Administrative expenses.
   i. Business gifts in excess of $25.
   j. Section 1245 gain.
   k. Dividends received by the S corporation.
   l. LIFO recapture tax at S election.
   m. Recovery of state income tax.
   n. Long-term capital loss.
   o. Corporate dividends out of AAA.

25. Cloris owns 35% of the stock of an S corporation and lends the corporation $7,000 during the year. Her stock basis in the corporation at the end of the year is $25,000. If the corporation sustains a $110,000 operating loss during the year, what amount, if any, can Cloris deduct with respect to the operating loss?

26. Candy owns 40% of the stock of Park, a valid S corporation. Her stock basis is $25,000, and she loaned $8,000 to the corporation during the year. How much of Park's $110,000 operating loss can Candy deduct for this year? Show your computation of the tax consequences in spreadsheet form and include them in a memo to your manager.

27. Crew Corporation elected S status effective for tax year 2001. As of January 1, 2001, Crew's assets were appraised as follows.

	Adjusted Basis	Fair Market Value
Cash	$ 16,010	$ 16,010
Accounts receivable	–0–	55,400
Investment in land	110,000	215,000
Building	220,000	275,000
Goodwill	–0–	93,000

In each of the following situations, calculate any built-in gains tax, assuming that the highest corporate rate is 35%.

a. During 2001, Crew collects $40,000 of the accounts receivable.

b. In 2002, Crew sells the land held for investment for $223,000.

c. In 2003, the building is sold for $270,000.

28. Chris Valletta, the sole shareholder of Taylor, Inc., elects during 2001 to terminate the S election, effective January 1, 2002. As of the end of 2001, Taylor, Inc., has AAA of $120,000 and OAA of $13,000. Chris receives a cash dividend of $130,000 on January 15, 2001. If his stock basis is $220,000 before the distribution, calculate his taxable amount and his ending stock basis.

29. Opal, the owner of *all* of the shares of an S corporation in Richmond, Virginia, transfers all of the stock to Will at the middle of the tax year. There is a $200,000 NOL for the entire year, but $130,000 of the loss occurs during the first half of the year. With a short-year election, how much of the loss is allocated to Will?

30. Claude sells his shares in Ditta, a valid S corporation for $8,000. His basis in the shares is $122,000. The shares were issued under § 1244. Claude is single and the original owner of the shares. Determine his tax treatment for the sale.

31. Bryan, a cash basis S corporation, has the following assets and liabilities on January 1, 2001, the date the S election is made.

	Adjusted Basis	Fair Market Value
Cash	$ 200,000	$ 200,000
Accounts receivable	–0–	105,000
Equipment	110,000	100,000
Land	1,800,000	2,500,000
Accounts payable	–0–	110,000

During 2001, Bryan collects the accounts receivable and pays the accounts payable. The land is sold for $3 million, and the taxable income for the year is $590,000. Calculate any built-in gains tax.

32. Ruff Ltd., an S corporation in Flint, Michigan, recognizes an $80,000 built-in gain and a $10,000 built-in loss. Ruff also holds an $8,000 unexpired NOL from a C corporation year. Currently, Ruff generates taxable income of $65,000. Calculate any built-in gains tax.

33. Lejeune, Inc., an S corporation in Boone, North Carolina, has operating revenues of $400,000, taxable interest of $380,000, operating expenses of $250,000, and deductions attributable to the interest income of $140,000. Lejeune's accumulated E & P amounts to $2 million. Calculate any penalty tax payable by this S corporation or its shareholders.

34. Brew, an S corporation, has gross receipts of $190,000 and gross income of $170,000. Brew has $22,000 of accumulated earnings and profits and taxable income of $30,000. It reports passive investment income of $100,000, with $40,000 of expenses directly related to the production of passive investment income. Calculate Brew's excess net passive income and any penalty tax liability.

35. Bonnie and Clyde each own one-third of a fast-food restaurant, and their 15-year old daughter owns the other shares. Both parents work full-time in the restaurant, but the daughter works infrequently. Neither Bonnie nor Clyde receives a salary during the year, when the taxable income of the S corporation is $180,000. An IRS agent estimates that reasonable salaries for Bonnie, Clyde, and the daughter are $30,000, $35,000, and

$10,000, respectively. What adjustments would you expect the IRS to impose upon these taxpayers?

EXTENDER 36. One of your clients, Sweet Tea Corporation, is considering electing S status. Both of Sweet Tea's equal shareholders paid $30,000 for their stock. As of the beginning of 2001, Sweet Tea's subchapter C NOL carryforward is $110,000. Its taxable income projections for the next few years are as follows.

2001	$40,000
2002	25,000
2003	25,000
2004	25,000

Will you counsel Sweet Tea to make the S election?

EXTENDER 37. C&C Properties is an S corporation and owns two rental real estate undertakings: Carrot Plaza and Cantaloupe Place. Both properties produce an annual $10,000 operating loss. C&C's Schedule K aggregates the results of the two locations into one number.

Dan and Marta, C&C's two equal shareholders, both hold a $7,000 stock basis in C&C as of the beginning of the year. Marta actively participates in the Cantaloupe location, but not at Carrot. Dan actively participates at neither location. Determine the amount of the available loss pass-throughs for both shareholders.

COMPREHENSIVE TAX RETURN PROBLEM

38. John Martin (Social Security number 234–10–5214) and Stan Mitchell (Social Security number 244–58–8695) are 55% and 45% owners of Ram, Inc. (74–8265910), a textile manufacturing company located at 1011 Wright Avenue, Kannapolis, NC 28083. The company's first S election was on January 1, 1984. The following information was taken from the income statement for 2000.

Other income (active)	$ 380
Interest income	267
Gross sales	1,376,214
Beginning inventory	7,607
Direct labor	303,102
Direct materials purchased	278,143
Direct other costs	149,356
Ending inventory	13,467
Taxes	39,235
Contributions to United Fund	445
Contribution to Senator Brown's campaign	5,000
Fines on illegal activities	34
Life insurance premiums (the corporation is the beneficiary)	98
Compensation to shareholder/officers (proportionate to ownership)	34,934
Salaries and wages	62,103
Interest	17,222
Repairs	16,106
Depreciation	16,154
Advertising	3,246
Pension plan contributions	6,000
Employee benefit program	2,875
Other deductions	63,784
Net income	384,884

A comparative balance sheet appears below.

	January 1, 2000	December 31, 2000
Cash	$ 47,840	$ 61,242
Accounts receivable	93,100	153,136
Inventories	7,607	13,467
Prepaid expenses	10,333	7,582
Loans to shareholders	313	727
Building and trucks	138,203	244,348
Accumulated depreciation	(84,235)	(100,389)
Land	1,809	16,513
Life insurance	11,566	18,344
	$226,536	$ 414,970
Accounts payable	$ 52,404	$ 82,963
Notes payable (less than one year)	5,122	8,989
Loans from shareholders	155,751	191,967
Notes payable (more than one year)	21,821	33,835
Loan on life insurance	5,312	16,206
Capital stock	1,003	1,003
Paid-in capital	9,559	9,559
Retained earnings (unappropriated)	(8,314)	?
Accumulated adjustments account	–0–	?
Other adjustments account	–0–	?
Treasury stock	(16,122)	(16,122)
	$226,536	$ 414,970

The accounting firm provides the following additional information.

Dividends paid to shareholders	$290,000
AMT depreciation adjustment	(1,075)
AMT interest on private activity bonds preference	11,070

From the above information, prepare a complete Form 1120S and Schedule K–1 for John Martin (596 Lane Street, Kannapolis, NC 28083). If any information is missing, make realistic assumptions.

BRIDGE DISCIPLINE

1. Using an online research service, determine whether your state:
   a. Allows flow-through treatment for Federal S corporations.
   b. Requires any state-specific form to elect or elect out of S treatment at the state level.
   c. Places any additional withholding tax burdens on out-of-state U.S. shareholders or on non-U.S. shareholders of an S corporation.
   d. Requires any additional information disclosures or compliance deadlines for S corporations operating in the state *other than* to the revenue department (e.g., a report that must be filed with the secretary of state).

RESEARCH PROBLEMS

*Note: Solutions to Research Problems can be prepared by using the **RIA Checkpoint® Student Version Online research product,** or the **CCH U.S. Master Tax Guide Plus™** online Federal tax research database, which is available to accompany this text. It is also possible to prepare solutions to the Research Problems by using tax research materials found in a standard tax library.*

Research Problem 1.   Eel Corporation, in Spivey Corners, North Carolina, has filed a Form 1120S for six years, and the local office of the IRS has sent the company a letter requesting an audit next month. Carrie, who is in charge of tax matters at Eel, cannot find a copy of the original S election, Form 2553.

   The original shareholders and officers all agree that a local accountant filed the form, but he passed away last year. Several of the shareholders instruct Carrie to prepare a backdated Form 2553, which they will sign. Carrie could then copy the form and tell the agent that this was a copy of the original Form 2553. What should Carrie do? She estimates that any proposed deficiency would be in the range of $625,000.

Partial list of research aids:
§§ 1362(b)(5) and (f).
Rev.Proc. 97–48, 1997–2 C.B. 521.
Ltr.Rul. 9748033.

Research Problem 2.   Opal is a major shareholder of Nations, Inc., an electing S corporation. As an incentive to persuade Hugo to work for the corporation, Opal sells Hugo some of her stock at a 20% discount below fair market value. The reason for the discount was to compensate Hugo for accepting a salary from Nations below the market rate. Hugo paid the bargain price for the stock directly to Opal in the form of cash and a promissory note. Hugo is personally liable for the promissory note.

   In acquiring the Nations' stock from Opal, Hugo entered into an agreement restricting the transferability of the shares. Does this transaction create a second class of stock, thereby terminating the S election? Write a memo for the tax research file, analyzing the S election after the agreement is executed.

Partial list of research aids:
§ 1361(b)(1)(D).
Reg. § 1.1361–1(l)(2)(i).
Ltr.Rul. 9525035.

Research Problem 3.   Paul and Jane Dingy own an S corporation that operates several restaurants in Santa Cruz, California. Paul and Jane provide various services for the S corporation. On their individual tax return, the couple reported negative net earnings for self-employment because of a large loss from the S corporation. Can S corporation pass-through items be included in calculating the self-employment tax liability of the owners? Prepare a memo for the tax research file, indicating what you told the Dingys over the phone.

Partial list of research aids:
§ 1402(a).
§ 1366.

Use the tax resources of the Internet to address the following questions. Do not restrict your search to the World Wide Web, but include a review of newsgroups and general reference materials, practitioner sites and resources, primary sources of the tax law, chat rooms and discussion groups, and other opportunities.

Research Problem 4.   Find a question about S corporation tax planning that has been posted to a newsgroup. Submit to the group your answer to the query. Make a copy of the question and answer.

Research Problem 5.   Go to the sites of both the U.S. Tax Court and the U.S. Court of Appeals for your circuit and find a recent decision involving an S corporation. Prepare a summary of the decision.

Research Problem 6.   Summarize the rules put forth by Reg. § 1.1366–1, TD 8852 (issued December 21, 1999, and corrected March 8, 2000).

Business Tax Credits and Corporate Alternative Minimum Tax

LEARNING OBJECTIVES

After completing Chapter 13, you should be able to:

1. Explain how tax credits are used as a tool of Federal tax policy.

2. Work with various business-related tax credits.

3. Explain the reason for the alternative minimum tax.

4. Identify and calculate the tax preferences that are included in determining the AMT.

5. Identify and calculate AMT adjustments.

6. Understand the function of adjusted current earnings (ACE).

7. Compute the AMT liability for corporations.

Outline

TAX TALK   *A government which robs Peter to pay Paul can always count on the support of Paul.*
—George Bernard Shaw

LEARNING OBJECTIVE 1

Explain how tax credits are used as a tool of Federal tax policy.

Tax Policy and Tax Credits

Federal tax law often serves other purposes besides merely raising revenue for the government. Evidence of equity, social, and economic considerations, among others, is found throughout the tax law. These considerations also have considerable import in the area of **tax credits.** Congress has generally used tax credits to promote social or economic objectives or to work toward greater tax equity among different types of taxpayers. For example, the disabled access credit was enacted to accomplish a social objective: to encourage taxpayers to renovate older buildings so they would be in compliance with the Americans with Disabilities Act. This Act requires businesses and institutions to make their facilities more accessible to persons with various types of disabilities. As another example, the foreign tax credit, which has been a part of the law for decades, has as its chief purpose the economic and equity objectives of mitigating the burden of multiple taxation on a single stream of income.

A tax credit should not be confused with an income tax deduction. Certain expenditures (e.g., business expenses) are permitted as deductions from gross income in arriving at taxable income. While the tax benefit received from a tax deduction depends on the tax rate, a tax credit is not affected by the tax rate of the taxpayer. All taxpayers can benefit equally when a tax credit is used.

EXAMPLE 1

Assume Congress wishes to encourage a certain type of expenditure. One way to accomplish this objective is to allow a tax credit of 25% for such expenditures. Another way is to allow a deduction for the expenditures. Assume Red Corporation's tax rate is 15%, while Blue Corporation's tax rate is 34%. The following tax benefits are available to each corporation for a $1,000 expenditure.

	Red	Blue
Tax benefit if a 25% credit is allowed	$250	$250
Tax benefit if a deduction is allowed	150	340

As these results indicate, tax credits can provide benefits on a more equitable basis than tax deductions often do. ■

TAX FACT

WHERE HAVE ALL THE CREDITS GONE?

The number of individual income tax returns claiming tax credits has fluctuated substantially over the years as indicated below.

Year	Returns Claiming Credits (in Millions)
1975	65.9
1980	19.7
1985	21.0
1990	12.5
1995	15.2

The probable cause of the decline between 1975 and 1980 was tax reform legislation enacted in 1976. Likewise the probable cause of the decline between 1985 and 1990 was tax reform legislation enacted in 1986.

Source: IRS Tax Stats.

LEARNING OBJECTIVE 2

Work with various business-related tax credits.

Specific Business-Related Tax Credit Provisions

GENERAL BUSINESS CREDIT

As shown in Exhibit 13–1, the **general business credit** is comprised of a number of other credits, each of which is computed separately under its own set of rules. The general business credit combines these credits into one amount to limit the annual credit that can be used to offset a taxpayer's income tax liability. The idea behind combining the credits is to prevent a taxpayer from completely avoiding an income tax liability in any one year by offsetting it with several business credits that would otherwise be available.

Two special rules apply to the general business credit. First, any unused credit must be carried back 1 year, then forward 20 years. Second, for any tax year, the general business credit is limited to the taxpayer's *net income tax* reduced by the greater of:[1]

- The *tentative minimum tax* (see the discussion of AMT later in this chapter).
- 25 percent of *net regular tax liability* that exceeds $25,000.[2]

To understand these general business credit limitations, several terms need defining.

- *Net income tax* is the sum of the regular tax liability and the alternative minimum tax reduced by certain nonrefundable tax credits.
- *Tentative minimum tax* (discussed later in this chapter) is reduced by any foreign tax credit allowed, as specified in Exhibit 13–2.
- *Regular tax liability* is determined from the appropriate tax table or tax rate schedule, based on taxable income. However, the regular tax liability does not include certain taxes (e.g., alternative minimum tax).

---

[1] § 38(c). This rule works to keep the general business credit from completely eliminating the tax liability for many taxpayers.

[2] § 38(c)(3)(B). The $25,000 amount is apportioned among the members of a controlled group.

A CREDIT THAT WENT UP IN SMOKE

I n 1997, Congress passed a special $50 billion tax credit for the tobacco industry to subsidize the cost of a proposed multibillion dollar national settlement between tobacco companies and the 50 states. Several state attorneys general had previously sued tobacco companies in an attempt to recover billions of state Medicaid dollars spent on tobacco-related health problems. Once tobacco industry foes became aware of the significant savings that would accrue to tobacco companies from the tobacco tax credit, Congress was under considerable pressure to cut out the tax break. Less than a month after the credit's passage, legislation was introduced to repeal the controversial credit. As a result, the tobacco credit goes on record as one of the shortest-lived credits in tax history.

As several news reports suggested, repeal of the tobacco tax credit may have signaled a change in congressional sentiment concerning special interest legislation for the tobacco industry. In fact, subsequent budget proposals included provisions that would increase the price of tobacco products.

• *Net regular tax liability* is the regular tax liability reduced by certain nonrefundable credits (e.g., foreign tax credit).

EXAMPLE 2

Tanager Corporation's general business credit for the current year is $70,000. Tanager's net income tax is $150,000, tentative minimum tax is $130,000, and net regular tax liability is $150,000. Tanager has no other tax credits. The general business credit allowed for the tax year is computed as follows.

Net income tax	$ 150,000
Less: The greater of—	
• $130,000 (tentative minimum tax)	
• $31,250 [25% × ($150,000 – $25,000)]	(130,000)
Amount of general business credit allowed for tax year	$ 20,000

Tanager then has $50,000 ($70,000 – $20,000) of unused general business credits that may be carried back or forward. ■

■ **EXHIBIT 13–1**
Principal Components of the
General Business Credit

The general business credit combines (but is not limited to) the following.
• Tax credit for rehabilitation expenditures
• Business energy credits
• Work opportunity tax credit*
• Welfare-to-work credit*
• Research activities credit
• Low-income housing credit
• Disabled access credit

---

*Not available for employees hired after December 31, 2001.
**Scheduled to expire after June 30, 2004.

BRIDGE DISCIPLINE

Bridge to Finance

When calculating the cash flow benefit of particular tax attributes and making a decision based on this analysis, an inappropriate decision can be made unless present value analysis is incorporated into the calculation.

The general business credit and the related carryback and carryover provisions can be used to illustrate the cash flow impact.

Blonde, Inc.'s general business credit for 2001 is $400,000. However, the amount that may be used to reduce the current-year tax liability is only $280,000. None can be used in 2000 (the carryback year), so the $120,000 is carried forward. The $120,000 of unused general business credit is offset against tax liability as follows.

2002	$20,000
2003	40,000
2004	60,000

It appears that the cash flow benefit to Blonde is $400,000. In nominal dollars, this result is correct. However, when the present value concept is applied, the cash flow benefit is only $376,280 (assuming Blonde's discount rate is 10%).

2001	$280,000 × 1.0	=	$280,000
2002	20,000 × .909	=	18,180
2003	40,000 × .826	=	33,040
2004	60,000 × .751	=	45,060
			$376,280

The carryforward period for the general business credit is 20 years. Using a 10 percent discount rate, one dollar in 20 years is worth $.149 ($1 × .149) today. So it behooves the taxpayer to use the general business credit to offset tax liability as rapidly as possible.

Treatment of Unused General Business Credits. Unused general business credits are initially carried back one year and reduce the tax liability of that year. Thus, the taxpayer may receive a tax refund as a result of the carryback. Any remaining unused credits are then carried forward 20 years.[3]

A FIFO method is applied to the carryback, carryovers, and utilization of credits earned during a particular year. The oldest credits are used first in determining the amount of the general business credit. The FIFO method minimizes the potential for loss of a general business credit benefit due to the expiration of credit carryovers and generally works to the taxpayer's benefit.

---

[3]§ 39(a)(1).

TAX IN THE NEWS

WHAT BEHAVIOR SHOULD TAX CREDITS INCLUDE?

Many of the tax credits enacted by Congress are intended to influence taxpayer behavior. For example, the work opportunity tax credit is designed to encourage the employment of individuals who historically have difficulty finding jobs. These credits have been a part of our tax law for many years and are generally recognized as pursuing worthy tax policy goals. However, other credits, or proposed credits, are frequently criticized for too narrowly targeting particular groups of taxpayers.

For example, one tax credit, recently proposed by Representative Patrick J. Kennedy of Rhode Island, is designed to encourage the construction of luxury yachts in the United States. Such a credit would boost the U.S. boat building industry by stimulating demand, and as a result, would keep skilled workers gainfully employed. This proposal, which has been referred to congressional committees, would allow a personal tax credit of up to $2 million for the purchase of a new U.S.-made luxury yacht. It will be interesting to watch Congress's reaction to this proposal as Representative Kennedy pushes for its passage.

EXAMPLE 3

This example illustrates the use of general business credit carryovers for the taxpayer's 2001 tax year.

General business credit carryovers (unused in prior tax years)		
1998	$ 4,000	
1999	6,000	
2000	2,000	
Total carryovers	$12,000	
2001 general business credit		$ 40,000
Total credit allowed in 2001 based on tax liability)	$50,000	
Less: Carryovers used		
1998	(4,000)	
1999	(6,000)	
2000	(2,000)	
Remaining credit allowed in 2001	$38,000	
2001 general business credit used		(38,000)
2001 unused amount carried forward to 2002		$ 2,000 ∎

Most of the various credits that make up the general business credit are discussed in the paragraphs below.

TAX CREDIT FOR REHABILITATION EXPENDITURES

Taxpayers are allowed a tax credit for expenditures incurred to rehabilitate older industrial and commercial buildings and certified historic structures. The **rehabilitation expenditures credit** is intended to discourage businesses from moving from economically distressed areas (e.g., an inner city) to outlying locations and to encourage the preservation of historic structures. The current operating features of this credit follow.[4]

Rate of the Credit for Rehabilitation Expenses	Nature of the Property
10%	Nonresidential buildings and residential rental property, other than certified historic structures, originally placed in service before 1936
20%	Nonresidential and residential certified historic structures

Taxpayers who claim the rehabilitation credit must reduce the basis of the rehabilitated building by the credit allowed.[5]

<table>
<tr><td>**EXAMPLE 4**</td><td>Grosbeak, Inc., spent $60,000 to rehabilitate a building (adjusted basis of $40,000) that originally had been placed in service in 1932. Grosbeak is allowed a credit of $6,000 (10% × $60,000) for rehabilitation expenditures. The corporation then increases the basis of the building by $54,000 [$60,000 (rehabilitation expenditures) − $6,000 (credit allowed)]. If the building were a historic structure, the credit allowed would be $12,000 (20% × $60,000), and the building's depreciable basis would increase by $48,000 [$60,000 (rehabilitation expenditures) − $12,000 (credit allowed)]. ■</td></tr>
</table>

To qualify for the credit, buildings must be substantially rehabilitated. A building has been *substantially rehabilitated* if qualified rehabilitation expenditures exceed the *greater of*:

- the adjusted basis of the property before the rehabilitation expenditures, or
- $5,000.

Qualified rehabilitation expenditures do not include the cost of acquiring a building, the cost of facilities related to a building (such as a parking lot), and the cost of enlarging an existing building. Stringent rules apply concerning the retention of the building's original internal and external walls.

Recapture of Tax Credit for Rehabilitation Expenditures.

The rehabilitation credit taken is recaptured if the rehabilitated property is disposed of prematurely or if it ceases to be qualifying property. The **rehabilitation expenditures credit recapture** is added to the taxpayer's regular tax liability in the recapture year. The recapture amount also is *added* to the adjusted basis of the building.

The portion of the credit recaptured is a specified percentage of the credit that was taken by the taxpayer. This percentage is based on the period the property was held by the taxpayer, as shown in Table 13–1. If the property is held at least five years, no recapture can result.

<table>
<tr><td>**EXAMPLE 5**</td><td>On March 15, 1998, Chickadee Corporation rehabilitated a building qualifying for the 10% credit. The company spent $30,000 in qualifying rehabilitation expenditures and claimed a $3,000 credit ($30,000 × 10%). The basis of the building was increased by $27,000 ($30,000 − $3,000).

Chickadee sold the building on December 15, 2001. Chickadee recaptures a portion of the rehabilitation credit based on the schedule in Table 13–1. Because Chickadee held the rehabilitated property for more than three years but less than four, 40% of the credit, or</td></tr>
</table>

---

[4]§ 47.   [5]§ 50(c).

■ **TABLE 13–1**
Recapture Calculation for
Rehabilitation Expenditures
Credit

If the Property Is Held for	The Recapture Percentage Is
Less than 1 year	100
One year or more but less than 2 years	80
Two years or more but less than 3 years	60
Three years or more but less than 4 years	40
Four years or more but less than 5 years	20
Five years or more	0

$1,200, is added to the company's 2001 tax liability. The adjusted basis of the building is increased by the $1,200 recapture amount. ■

WORK OPPORTUNITY TAX CREDIT

The **work opportunity tax credit** was enacted to encourage employers to hire individuals from a variety of targeted and economically disadvantaged groups. The employer must hire the individual by December 31, 2001. Examples of such targeted persons include qualified ex-felons, high-risk youths, food stamp recipients, veterans, summer youth employees, and persons receiving certain welfare benefits.[6]

Computation of the Work Opportunity Tax Credit: General. The credit generally is equal to 40 percent of the first $6,000 of wages (per eligible employee) for the first 12 months of employment. The credit is not available for wages paid to an employee after the *first year* of employment. If the employee's first year overlaps two of the employer's tax years, however, the employer may take the credit over two tax years. If the credit is claimed, the employer's tax deduction for wages is reduced by the amount of the credit.

To qualify an employer for the 40 percent credit, the employee must (1) be certified by a designated local agency as being a member of one of the targeted groups and (2) have completed at least 400 hours of service to the employer. If an employee meets the first condition but not the second, the credit is reduced to 25 percent, provided the employee has completed a minimum of 120 hours of service to the employer.

1 *Find more information on this topic at our Web site: http://wft-entities.swcollege.com.*

EXAMPLE 6

In January 2001, Green hires four individuals who are certified to be members of a qualifying targeted group. Each employee works 1,000 hours and is paid wages of $8,000 during the year. Green's work opportunity credit is $9,600 [($6,000 × 40%) × 4 employees]. If the tax credit is taken, Green reduces its deduction for wages paid by $9,600. No credit is available for wages paid to these employees after their first year of employment. ■

EXAMPLE 7

On June 1, 2001, Maria, a calendar year taxpayer, hires Joe, a member of a targeted group and obtains the required certification to qualify Maria for the work opportunity credit. During his seven months of work in 2001, Joe is paid $3,500 for 500 hours of work. Maria is allowed a credit of $1,400 ($3,500 × 40%) for 2001.

[6]§ 51.

TAX IN THE NEWS

TAX CREDITS—AND THE BOOMING ECONOMY— BRING ABOUT SUCCESS STORIES

Ex-convicts have never been the most sought after persons to fill available jobs. In fact, many employers have historically preferred keeping a position open rather than hiring a murderer or a thief. Therefore, to give employers an incentive to hire individuals with less than glowing backgrounds, the work opportunity tax credit was enacted. This credit provides incentives to employers who hire ex-felons. Questions, however, as to the credit's effectiveness have been raised.

Recent reports suggest that good things are happening to ex-cons in our current economy. In New York, for example, about 40 percent of offenders on parole are employed, up from 33 percent from several years earlier. Once employers resort to filling their ranks from this pool, they often find that, despite their preconceived notions, the workers sometimes end up being "superstars."

What is the reason for this turnaround in the fortunes of such historically unemployable persons? Proponents of the work opportunity tax credit claim that this tax provision is due the credit. But others will argue that the current strong economy with its diminished unemployment rate deserves some, if not most, of the spotlight.

SOURCE: Adapted from Mark Tatge, "With Unemployment Low, a New Group Is in Demand: Ex-Cons," *Wall Street Journal*, April 24, 2000, p. A1.

Joe continues to work for Maria in 2002 and is paid $7,000 through May 31, 2002. Because up to $6,000 of first-year wages are eligible for the credit, Maria is also allowed a 40% credit on $2,500 [$6,000 − $3,500 (wages paid in 2001)] of 2002 wages paid, or $1,000 ($2,500 × 40%). None of Joe's wages paid after May 31, 2002, the end of the first year of employment, is eligible for the credit. ■

WELFARE-TO-WORK CREDIT

The **welfare-to-work credit**[7] is available to employers hiring individuals who have been long-term recipients of family assistance welfare benefits. In general, *long-term recipients* are those individuals who are certified by a designated local agency as being members of a family receiving assistance under a public aid program for the 18-month period ending on the hiring date. Unlike the work opportunity credit, which applies only to first-year wages paid to qualified individuals, the welfare-to-work credit is available for qualified wages paid in the first *two years* of employment. If an employee's first and second work years overlap two or more of the employer's tax years, the employer may take the credit during the applicable tax years. If the welfare-to-work credit is taken, the employer's tax deduction for wages is reduced by the amount of the credit.

An employer is prohibited from taking both the work opportunity credit and the welfare-to-work credit for wages paid to a qualified employee in a given tax year. The welfare-to-work credit is not available for employees hired after December 31, 2001.

---

[7]§ 51A.

Maximum Credit.   The credit is equal to 35 percent of the first $10,000 of qualified wages paid to an employee in the first year of employment, plus 50 percent of the first $10,000 of qualified wages in the second year of employment, resulting in a maximum credit per qualified employee of $8,500 [$3,500 (year 1) + $5,000 (year 2)]. The credit rate is higher for second-year wages to encourage employers to retain qualified individuals, thereby promoting the overall welfare-to-work goal.

EXAMPLE 8

In April 2001, Blue hired three individuals who are certified as long-term family assistance recipients. Each employee is paid $12,000 during 2001. Two of the three individuals continue to work for Blue in 2002, earning $9,000 each during the year. Blue's welfare-to-work credit is $10,500 [(35% × $10,000) × 3 employees] for 2001 and $9,000 [(50% × $9,000) × 2 employees] for 2002. ■

RESEARCH ACTIVITIES CREDIT

To encourage research and development (R & D) in the U.S. business community, a credit is allowed for certain qualifying expenditures paid or incurred not later than June 30, 2004. The **research activities credit** is the *sum* of two components: (1) an incremental research activities credit and (2) a basic research credit.[8]

Incremental Research Activities Credit.   The incremental research activities credit applies at a 20 percent rate to the *excess* of qualified research expenses for the taxable year (the credit year) over a base amount.

In general, *research expenditures* qualify if the research relates to discovering technological information that is intended for use in the development of a new or improved business component of the taxpayer. Such expenses qualify fully if the research is performed in-house (by the taxpayer or its employees). If the research is conducted by persons outside the taxpayer's business (under contract), only 65 percent of the amount paid qualifies for the credit.[9]

EXAMPLE 9

Bobwhite Company incurs the following research expenditures for the tax year.

In-house wages, supplies, computer time	$50,000
Payment to Cutting Edge Scientific Foundation for research	30,000

Bobwhite's qualified research expenditures are $69,500 [$50,000 + ($30,000 × 65%)]. ■

Beyond the general guidelines described above, the Code does not give specific examples of qualifying research. However, the credit is *not* allowed for research that falls into certain categories, including the following.[10]

- Research conducted after the beginning of commercial production of the business component.
- Surveys and studies such as market research, testing, and routine data collection.
- Research conducted *outside* the United States (other than research undertaken in Puerto Rico and possessions of the United States).
- Research in the social sciences, arts, or humanities.

---

[8]§ 41. It is likely that this date will be extended by Congress.   [10]§ 41(d).

[9]§ 41(b)(3)(A). In the case of payments to a qualified research consortium, 75% of the amount paid qualifies for the credit.

Determining the *base amount* involves a relatively complex series of computations, meant to approximate recent historical levels of research activity by the taxpayer. Thus, the credit is allowed only for increases in research expenses.

EXAMPLE 10

Hawk, Inc., a calendar year taxpayer, incurs qualifying research expenditures of $200,000 during the tax year. If the base amount is $100,000, the incremental research activities credit is $20,000 [($200,000 − $100,000) × 20%]. ∎

Qualified research and experimentation expenditures are not only eligible for the 20 percent credit, but can also be *expensed* in the year incurred. In this regard, a taxpayer has two choices.[11]

- Use the full credit and reduce the expense deduction for research expenses by 100 percent of the credit.
- Retain the full expense deduction and reduce the credit by the product of 100 percent of the credit times the maximum corporate tax rate.

As an alternative to the expense deduction, the taxpayer may *capitalize* the research expenses and *amortize* them over 60 months or more. In this case, the amount capitalized and subject to amortization is reduced by the full amount of the credit *only* if the credit exceeds the amount allowable as a deduction.

EXAMPLE 11

This year, Thin Corporation's potential incremental research activities credit is $20,000. The amounts that Thin can deduct and the credit amount are computed as follows.

	Credit Amount	Deduction Amount
• Full credit and reduced deduction		
$20,000 − $0	$20,000	
$200,000 − $20,000		$180,000
• Reduced credit and full deduction		
$20,000 − [(1.00 × $20,000) × .35]	13,000	
$200,000 − $0		200,000
• Full credit and capitalize and elect to amortize costs over 60 months		
$20,000 − $0	20,000	
($200,000/60) × 12		40,000

The value of the deduction depends on Thin's marginal tax rates. ∎

Basic Research Credit. Corporations (other than S corporations or personal service corporations) are allowed an additional 20 percent credit for basic research expenditures incurred not later than June 30, 2004, in *excess* of a base amount.[12] This credit is not available to individual taxpayers. *Basic research expenditures* are defined as amounts paid in cash to a qualified basic research organization, such as a college or university or a tax-exempt organization operated primarily to conduct scientific research.

---

[11]§§ 174 and 280C(c). Recall the discussion of rules for deducting research and experimental expenditures in Chapter 4.

[12]§ 41(e).

Basic research is defined generally as any original investigation for the advancement of scientific knowledge not having a specific commercial objective. The definition excludes basic research conducted outside the United States and basic research in the social sciences, arts, or humanities.

DISABLED ACCESS CREDIT

The **disabled access credit** is designed to encourage small businesses to make their facilities more accessible to disabled individuals. The credit is available for any eligible access expenditures paid or incurred by an eligible small business. The credit is calculated at the rate of 50 percent of the eligible expenditures that exceed $250 but do not exceed $10,250. Thus, the maximum amount for the credit is $5,000 ($10,000 × 50%).[13]

An *eligible small business* is one that during the previous year either had gross receipts of $1 million or less or had no more than 30 full-time employees. A sole proprietorship, partnership, regular corporation, or S corporation can qualify as such an entity.

Eligible access expenditures generally include any reasonable and necessary amounts that are paid or incurred to make certain changes to facilities. These changes must involve the removal of architectural, communication, physical, or transportation barriers that would otherwise make a business inaccessible to disabled and handicapped individuals. Examples of qualifying projects include installing ramps, widening doorways, and adding raised markings on elevator control buttons. However, the improved facility must have been placed into service prior to the enactment (November 5, 1990) of the credit.

To the extent a disabled access credit is available, no deduction or credit is allowed under any other provision of the tax law. The asset's adjusted basis is reduced by the amount of the credit.

EXAMPLE 12

This year Red, Inc., an eligible business, makes $11,000 of capital improvements to business realty that had been placed in service in June 1990. The expenditures are intended to make Red's business more accessible to the disabled and are considered eligible expenditures for purposes of the disabled access credit. The amount of the credit is $5,000 [($10,250 maximum − $250 floor) × 50%]. The depreciable basis of the capital improvement is $6,000 [$11,000 (cost) − $5,000 (amount of the credit)]. ■

2 *Find more information on this topic at our Web site: **http://wft-entities.swcollege.com**.*

FOREIGN TAX CREDIT

Both individual taxpayers and corporations may claim a credit for foreign income tax paid on income earned and subject to tax in another country or a U.S. possession.[14] The purpose of the **foreign tax credit (FTC)** is to reduce the possibility of double taxation of foreign income.

⬤ *Find more information on this topic at our Web site: **http://wft-entities.swcollege.com**.*

---

[13] § 44.

[14] § 27 provides for the credit, but the qualifications and calculation procedure for the credit are contained in §§ 901–908. Alternatively, the taxpayer can *deduct* the foreign taxes paid.

EXAMPLE 13

Ace Tools, Inc., a U.S. corporation, has a branch operation in Mexico, from which it earns taxable income of $750,000 for the current year. Ace pays income tax of $150,000 on these earnings to the Mexican tax authorities. Ace must also include the $750,000 in gross income for U.S. tax purposes. Assume that, before considering the FTC, Ace would owe $255,000 in U.S. income taxes on this foreign-source income. Thus, total taxes on the $750,000 could equal $405,000 ($150,000 + $255,000), a 54% effective rate. But Ace takes the FTC of $150,000 against its U.S. tax liability on the foreign-source income. Ace Tools' total taxes on the $750,000 now are $255,000 ($150,000 + $105,000), a 34% effective rate. ■

The tax year's FTC equals the *lesser* of the foreign taxes imposed or the *U.S. rate limitation* determined according to the following formula. Thus, where applicable foreign tax rates exceed those of the United States, the credit offsets no more than the marginal U.S. tax on the double-taxed income.

$$\frac{\text{Foreign-source taxable income}}{\text{Worldwide taxable income}} \times \text{U.S. tax before FTC}$$

Foreign taxes paid but not allowed as a credit due to the U.S. rate limitation are carried back two tax years and then forward five years.

EXAMPLE 14

Oriole, Inc., a U.S. corporation, conducts business in a foreign country. Oriole's worldwide taxable income for the tax year is $120,000, consisting of $100,000 in income from U.S. operations and $20,000 of income from the foreign source. Foreign tax of $6,000 was paid to foreign tax authorities on the $20,000. Before the FTC, Oriole's U.S. tax on the $120,000 is $30,050. The corporation's FTC is $5,008 {lesser of $6,000 paid or $5,008 limitation [$30,050 × ($20,000/$120,000)]}. Oriole's net U.S. tax liability is $25,042 ($30,050 – $5,008). Thus, Oriole carries over (back two years and forward five years) $992 FTC ($6,000 – $5,008) because of the U.S. rate limitation. ■

LEARNING OBJECTIVE 3

Explain the reason for the alternative minimum tax.

Corporate Alternative Minimum Tax

A perception that many large corporations were not paying their fair share of Federal income tax was especially widespread in the early 1980s. A study released in 1986 reported that 130 of the 250 largest corporations in the United States (e.g., Reynolds Metals, General Dynamics, Georgia Pacific, and Texas Commerce Bankshares) paid no Federal tax, or received refunds, in at least one year between 1981 and 1985. Political pressure subsequently led to the adoption of an **alternative minimum tax (AMT)** to ensure that corporations with substantial economic income pay at least a minimum amount of Federal taxes.

The AMT limits the tax savings for some taxpayers who are seen as gaining "too much" from exclusions, deductions, and credits available under the law. A separate tax system with a proportional tax rate is applied each year to a corporation's economic income. If the tentative AMT is greater than the regular corporate income tax, then the corporation must pay the regular tax plus this excess, the AMT.

Since its inception, the AMT has been vulnerable to criticisms that it is too complex. Smaller corporations especially find that the imposition of a second tax structure unduly increases their compliance burdens. Thus, proposals to cut back or even repeal the AMT were considered by Congress throughout the 1990s. A special exemption from the AMT finally was adopted in 1997. For tax years beginning after 1997, most smaller corporations are not subject to the AMT at all. A corporation is exempted from the AMT if it meets the following tests.

CONCEPT SUMMARY 13–1

Tax Credits

Credit	Computation	Comments
General business (§ 38)	May not exceed net income tax minus the greater of tentative minimum tax or 25% of net regular tax liability that exceeds $25,000.	Components include tax credit for rehabilitation expenditures, business energy credits, work opportunity tax credit, welfare-to-work credit, research activities credit, low-income housing credit, and disabled access credit. Unused credit may be carried back 1 year and forward 20 years. FIFO method applies to carrybacks, carryovers, and credits earned during current year.
Investment (§ 46)	Qualifying investment times energy percentage or rehabilitation percentage, depending on type of property. Part of general business credit and subject to its limitations.	Part of general business credit and therefore subject to same carryback, carryover, and FIFO rules. Energy percentage is 10%. Regular rehabilitation rate is 10%; rate for certified historic structures is 20%.
Work opportunity (§ 51)	Credit is limited to 40% of the first $6,000 of wages paid to each eligible employee. The employee must begin work by December 31, 2001.	Part of the general business credit and therefore subject to the same carryback, carryover, and FIFO rules. Purpose is to encourage employment of members of economically disadvantaged groups.
Welfare-to-work (§ 51A)	Credit is limited to 35% of first $10,000 of wages paid to eligible employee in first year of employment, plus 50% of first $10,000 of wages paid to same employee in second year of employment. The employment must begin work by December 31, 2001.	Part of general business credit and therefore subject to same carryback, carryover, and FIFO rules. Purpose is to encourage employment of long-term recipients of family assistance welfare benefits.
Research activities (§ 41)	Incremental credit is 20% of excess of computation-year expenditures minus a base amount. Basic research credit is allowed to certain corporations for 20% of cash payments to qualified organizations that exceed a specially calculated base amount. To qualify for the credit, research expenditures must be made not later than June 30, 2004.	Part of general business credit and therefore subject to same carryback, carryover, and FIFO rules. Purpose is to encourage high-tech research in the United States.
Low-income housing (§ 42)	Appropriate rate times eligible basis (portion of project attributable to low-income units).	Part of general business credit and therefore subject to same carryback, carryover, and FIFO rules. Credit is available each year for 10 years. Recapture may apply. Purpose is to encourage construction of housing for low-income individuals.
Disabled access (§ 44)	Credit is 50% of eligible access expenditures that exceed $250, but do not exceed $10,250. Maximum credit is $5,000.	Part of general business credit and therefore subject to same carryback, carryover, and FIFO rules. Available only to eligible small businesses. Purpose is to encourage small businesses to become more accessible to disabled individuals.
Foreign tax (§ 27)	Foreign income/total worldwide taxable income × U.S. tax = overall limitation. Lesser of foreign taxes imposed or U.S. rate limitation.	Unused credits may be carried back two years and forward five years. Purpose is to reduce double taxation of foreign income.

TAX FACT

THE REACH OF THE AMT

The relative number of taxpayers subject to the AMT for the tax year 1995 was as follows.

Type of Taxpayer	AMT Returns	Total Returns Filed
C Corporation	26,000	2,000,000
Individual	414,000	102,000,000

Source: IRS Tax Stats.

- *Initial test.* The corporation must report average annual gross receipts of no more than $5 million for the three-year period beginning after December 1993.
- *Ongoing test.* If the initial test is passed, the corporation is exempt from the AMT as long as its average annual gross receipts for the three-year period preceding the current tax year and any intervening three-year periods do not exceed $7.5 million.

A corporation that fails the initial test *never* (other than the first year exception below) can be exempt from the AMT. Furthermore, if the ongoing test is failed, the taxpayer is subject to the AMT provisions for that year and all subsequent tax years. Congress estimates that this provision will exempt up to 95 percent of all C corporations from the AMT. A corporation *automatically* is classified as a small corporation in the first tax year of existence.

THE AMT FORMULA

The AMT is imposed in addition to the regular corporate income tax, but is computed in a manner wholly separate and independent from it.[15] The AMT is a parallel income tax system that generally uses more conservative accounting methods than the regular income tax. Typically, more items are subject to tax under AMT rules, some gross income items are accelerated, and some deductions are deferred.

The formula for determining the AMT liability of corporate taxpayers appears in Exhibit 13–2 and follows the format of Form 4626 (Alternative Minimum Tax—Corporations).

The base for the AMT, **alternative minimum taxable income (AMTI),** begins with regular taxable income before any deductions for net operating losses (NOLs). A series of adjustments are then made. Most AMT adjustments relate to *timing differences* that arise because of separate regular income tax and AMT treatments. Adjustments that are caused by timing differences eventually reverse; that is, positive adjustments are offset by negative adjustments in the future, and vice versa.

The adjustments related to *circulation expenditures* illustrate this concept. Circulation expenditures include expenses incurred to establish, maintain, or increase the circulation of a newspaper, magazine, or other periodical.

---

[15]The AMT provisions are contained in §§ 55 through 59.

few credits don't help u . for AMT purposes

■ EXHIBIT 13–2
AMT Formula for Corporations

Regular taxable income before NOL deduction

Plus/minus: AMT adjustments (except ACE adjustment)

Plus: Tax preferences

Equals: AMTI before AMT NOL deduction and ACE adjustment

Plus/minus: ACE adjustment

Equals: AMTI before AMT NOL deduction

Minus: AMT NOL deduction (limited to 90%)

Equals: Alternative minimum taxable income (AMTI)

Minus: Exemption

Equals: AMT base

Times: 20% rate

Equals: Tentative AMT before AMT foreign tax credit

Minus: AMT foreign tax credit (limited to 90% or less)

Equals: Tentative minimum tax

Minus: Regular tax liability before credits minus regular foreign tax credit

Equals: Alternative minimum tax (AMT) if positive

In computing *taxable income*, corporations that are personal holding companies are allowed to deduct circulation expenditures in the year incurred. In computing AMTI, however, these expenditures must be capitalized and amortized ratably over the three-year period beginning with the year in which the expenditures were made.

EXAMPLE 15

Bobwhite, Inc., a personal holding company, incurred circulation expenditures of $30,000 in 2001. For regular income tax purposes, Bobwhite deducts $30,000 in 2001. For AMT purposes, the corporation is required to capitalize the expenditures and amortize them over a three-year period. Therefore, the deduction for AMT purposes is only $10,000. The AMT adjustment for 2001 is computed as follows.

Circulation expenditures deducted for regular income tax purposes	$30,000
Circulation expenditures deducted for AMT purposes	10,000
AMT adjustment (positive)	$20,000

EXAMPLE 16

Assume the same facts as in Example 15. The timing difference that gave rise to the positive adjustment in 2001 will reverse in the future. For AMT purposes, Bobwhite will deduct $10,000 in 2002 and $10,000 in 2003. The regular income tax deduction for circulation expenditures in each of those years will be $0, because the entire $30,000 expenditure was deducted in 2001. This results in a negative AMT adjustment of $10,000 each in 2002 and 2003. The AMT adjustments over the three-year period are summarized below.

Year	Regular Income Tax Deduction	AMT Deduction	AMT Adjustment
2001	$30,000	$10,000	$ 20,000
2002	–0–	10,000	(10,000)
2003	–0–	10,000	(10,000)
Totals	$30,000	$30,000	$ –0–

MUNICIPAL BONDS AND THE AMT

A number of investment and tax advisers are warning investors who have municipal bonds in their portfolios (either directly or through mutual funds) that the bonds may not be as tax-exempt as they think.

More and more taxpayers are likely to become subject to the AMT in the future, with municipal bond investors being among the hardest hit. Private activity bond interest that is tax-exempt for regular income tax purposes is subject to taxation under the AMT. A prime reason investors are attracted to private activity bonds is that they offer a higher yield than other municipal bonds. But if the interest results in the taxpayer paying the AMT, this seemingly higher yield might actually be lower.

Timing differences eventually reverse. Thus, positive AMT adjustments can be offset later by negative adjustments. ∎

LEARNING OBJECTIVE 4

Identify and calculate the tax preferences that are included in determining the AMT.

TAX PREFERENCES

AMTI includes designated **tax preference items.** In many cases, this part of the AMT formula has the effect of subjecting otherwise nontaxable income to the AMT. Tax preferences always increase AMTI. Some of the principal tax preferences are discussed below.

Percentage Depletion.   Congress originally enacted the percentage depletion rules to provide taxpayers with incentives to invest in the development of specified natural resources. Percentage depletion is computed by multiplying a rate specified in the Code times the gross income from the property (refer to Chapter 4). The percentage rate is based on the type of mineral involved. The basis of the property is reduced by the amount of depletion taken until the basis reaches zero. However, once the basis of the property reaches zero, taxpayers are allowed to continue taking percentage depletion deductions. Thus, over the life of the property, depletion deductions may greatly exceed the cost of the property.

The percentage depletion preference is equal to the excess of the regular income tax deduction for percentage depletion over the adjusted basis of the property at the end of the taxable year.[16] Basis is determined without regard to the depletion deduction for the taxable year. This preference item is figured separately for each piece of property for which the taxpayer is claiming depletion.

EXAMPLE 17

Finch, Inc., owns a mineral property that qualifies for a 22% depletion rate. The basis of the property at the beginning of the year is $10,000. Gross income from the property for the year is $100,000. For regular income tax purposes, Finch's percentage depletion deduction (assume it is not limited by taxable income from the property) is $22,000. For AMT purposes, Finch has a tax preference of $12,000 ($22,000 − $10,000). ∎

---

[16]§ 57(a)(1). Percentage depletion on oil and gas wells taken by independent producers and royalty owners does not create an AMT preference. See § 613A(c).

Interest on Private Activity Bonds.   Income from private activity bonds is not included in taxable income, and expenses related to carrying such bonds are not deductible for regular income tax purposes. However, interest on private activity bonds is included as a preference in computing AMTI. Expenses incurred in carrying the bonds are offset against the interest income in computing the tax preference.[17]

The Code contains a lengthy, complex definition of **private activity bonds.**[18] In general, such debt is issued by states or municipalities, but more than 10 percent of the proceeds are used to benefit private business. For example, a bond issued by a city whose proceeds are used to construct a factory that is leased to a private business at a favorable rate is a private activity bond.

 4 *Find more information on this topic at our Web site: http://wft-entities.swcollege.com.*

LEARNING OBJECTIVE 5

Identify and calculate AMT adjustments.

AMT ADJUSTMENTS

As Exhibit 13–2 indicates, the starting point for computing AMTI is the taxable income of the corporation before any NOL deduction. Certain *adjustments* must be made to this amount. Unlike tax preference items, which always increase AMTI, the adjustments may be either increases or decreases to taxable income.

Although NOLs are separately stated in Exhibit 13–2, they are actually negative adjustments. They are separately stated in Exhibit 13–2 and on Form 4626 because they may not exceed more than 90 percent of AMTI. Thus, such adjustments cannot be determined until all other adjustments and tax preference items are considered.

Computing Adjustments.   It is necessary to determine not only the amount of an adjustment, but also whether the adjustment is positive or negative. Careful study of Examples 15 and 16 reveals the following pattern with regard to *deductions*.

- If the deduction allowed for regular income tax purposes exceeds the deduction allowed for AMT purposes, the difference is a positive adjustment.
- If the deduction allowed for AMT purposes exceeds the deduction allowed for regular income tax purposes, the difference is a negative adjustment.

Conversely, the direction of an adjustment attributable to an *income* item can be determined as follows.

- If the income reported for regular income tax purposes exceeds the income reported for AMT purposes, the difference is a negative adjustment.
- If the income reported for AMT purposes exceeds the income reported for regular income tax purposes, the difference is a positive adjustment.

The principal AMT adjustments are discussed below. The adjustment for circulation expenditures was discussed previously.

Depreciation of Post-1986 Real Property.   Tax legislation enacted in 1997 eliminated the AMT depreciation adjustment for real property by providing that the MACRS recovery periods (see Table 4–3) used in calculating the regular income tax apply in calculating the AMT. Note, however, that this AMT recovery period conformity provision applies only to property placed in service after December 31, 1998.[19] Thus, the AMT depreciation adjustment discussed below does apply for real property placed in service before January 1, 1999.

---

[17]§ 57(a)(5).
[18]§ 141.

[19]§ 56(a)(1)(A)(i).

For real property placed in service after 1986 (MACRS property) and before January 1, 1999, AMT depreciation is computed under the alternative depreciation system (ADS), which uses the straight-line method over a 40-year life. The depreciation lives for regular income tax purposes are 27.5 years for residential rental property and 39 years for all other real property.[20] The difference between AMT depreciation and regular income tax depreciation is treated as an adjustment in computing the AMT. The differences will be positive during the regular income tax life of the asset because the cost is written off over a shorter period for regular income tax purposes. For example, during the 27.5-year income tax life of residential real property, the regular income tax depreciation will exceed the AMT depreciation because AMT depreciation is computed over a 40-year period.

Table 4–3 is used to compute regular income tax depreciation on real property placed in service after 1986. For AMT purposes, depreciation on real property placed in service after 1986 and before January 1, 1999, is computed under the ADS (refer to Table 4–7).

EXAMPLE 18

In January 1998, Robin Rentals placed in service a residential building that cost $100,000. Depreciation for 1998 for regular income tax purposes is $3,485 ($100,000 cost × 3.485% from Table 4–3). For AMT purposes, depreciation is $2,396 ($100,000 cost × 2.396% from Table 4–7). In computing AMTI for 1998, Robin Rentals has a positive adjustment of $1,089 ($3,485 regular income tax depreciation − $2,396 AMT depreciation). For 1999, 2000, and 2001, the regular income tax depreciation is $3,636 ($100,000 × 3.636%). For AMT purposes, depreciation is $2,500 ($100,000 × 2.500%). Robin Rentals has a positive adjustment of $1,136 ($3,636 regular income tax depreciation − $2,500 AMT depreciation) for each of these years.

If the building had been placed in service after 1998, there would have been no AMT depreciation adjustment for the tax year it is placed in service or for subsequent years. The depreciation for 1999, 2000, or 2001 (whichever year the building is placed in service) for both regular income tax purposes and AMT purposes would have been $3,485 ($100,000 × 3.485%). ∎

After real property placed in service before 1999 has been held for the entire depreciation period for regular income tax purposes, the asset will be fully depreciated. However, the depreciation period under the ADS is 41 years due to application of the half-year convention, so depreciation will continue for AMT purposes. This causes negative adjustments after the property has been fully depreciated for regular income tax purposes.

EXAMPLE 19

Assume the same facts as in the previous example. Regular income tax depreciation in the year 2026 (the twenty-ninth year of the asset's life) is zero (refer to Table 4–3). AMT depreciation is $2,500 ($100,000 cost × 2.500% from Table 4–7). Therefore, Robin has a negative AMT adjustment of $2,500 ($0 regular income tax depreciation − $2,500 AMT depreciation). ∎

After real property is fully depreciated for both regular income tax and AMT purposes, the positive and negative adjustments that have been made for AMT purposes will net to zero.

Depreciation of Post-1986 Personal Property. For most personal property placed in service after 1986 (MACRS property), the MACRS deduction for regular income tax purposes is based on the 200 percent declining-balance method with

[20]The 39-year life generally applies to nonresidential real property placed in service on or after May 13, 1993.

a switch to straight-line when that method produces a larger depreciation deduction for the asset. Refer to Table 4–1 for computing regular income tax depreciation.

For AMT purposes, the taxpayer must use the ADS for such property placed in service before 1999. This method is based on the 150 percent declining-balance method with a similar switch to straight-line for all personal property.[21] Refer to Table 4–5 for percentages to be used in computing AMT depreciation.

The MACRS deduction for personal property is larger than the ADS deduction in the early years of an asset's life. However, the ADS deduction is larger in the later years. This is so because ADS lives are sometimes longer than MACRS lives and useless accelerated depreciation methods.[22] Over the ADS life of the asset, the same amount of depreciation is deducted for both regular income tax and AMT purposes. In the same manner as other timing adjustments, the AMT adjustments for depreciation will net to zero over the ADS life of the asset.

The taxpayer may elect to use the ADS for regular income tax purposes. If this election is made, no AMT adjustment is required because the depreciation deduction is the same for regular income tax and for the AMT. The election eliminates the burden of maintaining two sets of tax depreciation records at the cost of a higher regular tax liability.

Tax legislation enacted in 1997 either reduces or eliminates the AMT adjustment for the depreciation of personal property. Prior to the effective date of this provision, the difference between regular income tax depreciation and AMT depreciation was caused by longer recovery periods for the AMT (class life versus MACRS recovery periods) and more accelerated depreciation methods for the regular income tax (200 percent declining balance rather than 150 percent declining balance).

MACRS recovery periods are used in calculating AMT depreciation. Thus, if the taxpayer elects to use the 150 percent declining-balance method for regular income tax purposes, there are no AMT adjustments. Conversely, if the taxpayer uses the 200 percent declining-balance method for regular income tax purposes, there is an AMT adjustment for depreciation. This AMT recovery period conformity provision applies only to property placed in service after 1998. Thus, the adjustment continues to apply for personal property placed in service before 1999.

Pollution Control Facilities.   For regular income tax purposes, the cost of certified pollution control facilities may be amortized over a period of 60 months. For AMT purposes, the cost of these facilities placed in service after 1986 and before 1999, is depreciated under the ADS over the appropriate class life, determined as explained above for depreciation of post-1986 property.[23] The required adjustment for AMTI is the difference between the amortization deduction allowed for regular income tax purposes and the depreciation deduction computed under the ADS. The adjustment may be positive or negative.

The AMT adjustment for pollution control facilities is reduced for property placed in service after 1998. This reduction is achieved by providing conformity in the recovery periods used for regular income tax purposes and AMT purposes (MACRS recovery periods).

---

[21]§ 56(a)(1).

[22]Class lives and recovery periods are established for all assets in Rev.Proc. 87–56, 1987–2 C.B. 674.

[23]§ 56(a)(5).

5 *Find more information on this topic at our Web site:* ***http://wft-entities.swcollege.com.***

Use of Completed Contract Method of Accounting.   For a long-term contract, taxpayers are required to use the percentage of completion method for AMT purposes.[24] However, in limited circumstances, taxpayers can use the completed contract method for regular income tax purposes.[25] The resulting AMT adjustment is equal to the difference between income reported under the percentage of completion method and the amount reported using the completed contract method.[26] The adjustment can be either positive or negative, depending on the amount of income recognized under the different methods.

A taxpayer can avoid an AMT adjustment on long-term contracts by using the percentage of completion method for regular income tax purposes rather than the completed contract method.

Adjusted Gain or Loss.   When property is sold during the year or a casualty occurs to business or income-producing property, gain or loss reported for regular income tax may be different than gain or loss determined for the AMT. This difference occurs because the adjusted basis of the property for AMT purposes must reflect any current and prior AMT adjustments for the following.[27]

- Depreciation.
- Circulation expenditures.
- Amortization of certified pollution control facilities.

A negative gain or loss adjustment is required if:

- the gain for AMT purposes is less than the gain for regular income tax purposes;
- the loss for AMT purposes is more than the loss for regular income tax purposes; or
- a loss is computed for AMT purposes and a gain is computed for regular income tax purposes.

Otherwise, the AMT gain or loss adjustment is positive.

EXAMPLE 20

In January 1998, Cardinal Corporation paid $100,000 for a duplex acquired for rental purposes. Regular income tax depreciation in 1998 was $3,485 ($100,000 cost × 3.485% from Table 4–3). AMT depreciation was $2,396 ($100,000 cost × 2.396% from Table 4–7). For AMT purposes, Cardinal made a positive adjustment for 1998 of $1,089 ($3,485 regular income tax depreciation – $2,396 AMT depreciation). Regular income tax depreciation for 1999 and for 2000 is $3,636 ($100,000 cost × 3.636% from Table 4–3). AMT depreciation for 1999 and for 2000 is $2,500 ($100,000 cost × 2.500% from Table 4–7). For AMT purposes, Cardinal made a positive adjustment for 1999 and for 2000 of $1,136 ($3,636 regular income tax depreciation – $2,500 AMT depreciation).

Cardinal then sold the duplex on December 20, 2001, for $105,000. Regular income tax depreciation for 2001 is $3,485 [($100,000 cost × 3.636% from Table 4–3) × ($^{11.5}/_{12}$)]. AMT depreciation for 2001 is $2,396 [($100,000 cost × 2.500% from Table 4–7) × ($^{11.5}/_{12}$)]. Cardinal's positive AMT adjustment for 2001 is $1,089 ($3,485 regular income tax depreciation – $2,396 AMT depreciation).

---

[24]§ 56(a)(3).

[25]See Chapter 6 for a detailed discussion of the completed contract and percentage of completion methods of accounting.

[26]§ 56(a)(3).

[27]§ 56(a)(6).

Because depreciation on the duplex differs for regular income tax and AMT purposes, Cardinal's adjusted basis for the property is different for regular income tax and AMT purposes. Consequently, the gain or loss on disposition of the duplex is different for regular income tax and AMT purposes.

The adjusted basis for Cardinal's duplex for regular income tax purposes is $85,758 and for AMT purposes is $90,208.

	Regular Income Tax	AMT
Cost	$100,000	$100,000
Depreciation		
1998	(3,485)	(2,396)
1999	(3,636)	(2,500)
2000	(3,636)	(2,500)
2001	(3,485)	(2,396)
Adjusted basis	$ 85,758	$ 90,208

The regular income tax gain is $19,242 and the AMT gain is $14,792.

	Regular Income Tax	AMT
Amount realized	$105,000	$105,000
Adjusted basis	(85,758)	(90,208)
Recognized gain	$ 19,242	$ 14,792

Because the regular income tax and AMT gain on the sale of the duplex differ, Cardinal makes a negative AMT adjustment of $4,450 ($19,242 regular income tax gain – $14,792 AMT gain). The negative adjustment matches the $4,450 total of the four positive adjustments for depreciation ($1,089 in 1998 + $1,136 in 1999 + $1,136 in 2000 + $1,089 in 2001). ∎

Passive Activity Losses. Net losses on passive activities are not deductible in computing either the regular income tax or the AMT for closely held C corporations (cannot offset portfolio income) and personal service corporations (cannot offset either active income or portfolio income). This does not, however, eliminate the possibility of adjustments attributable to passive activities.

The rules for computing taxable income differ from the rules for computing AMTI. It follows, then, that the rules for computing a loss for regular income tax purposes differ from the AMT rules for computing a loss. Therefore, any *passive loss* computed for regular income tax purposes may differ from the passive loss computed for AMT purposes.

EXAMPLE 21

Robin, Inc., a personal service corporation, acquired two passive activities in 2001. Robin received net passive income of $10,000 from Activity A and had no AMT adjustments or preferences in connection with the activity. Activity B had gross income of $27,000 and operating expenses (not affected by AMT adjustments or preferences) of $19,000. Robin claimed MACRS depreciation of $20,000 for Activity B; depreciation under the ADS would have been $15,000. In addition, Robin deducted $10,000 of percentage depletion in excess of basis. The following comparison illustrates the differences in the computation of the passive loss for regular income tax and AMT purposes for Activity B.

	Regular Income Tax	**AMT**
Gross income	$ 27,000	$ 27,000
Deductions:		
Operating expenses	($ 19,000)	($ 19,000)
Depreciation	(20,000)	(15,000)
Depletion	(10,000)	–0–
Total deductions	($ 49,000)	($ 34,000)
Passive loss	($ 22,000)	($ 7,000)

Because the adjustment for depreciation ($5,000) applies and the preference for depletion ($10,000) is not taken into account in computing AMTI, the regular income tax passive activity loss of $22,000 for Activity B is reduced by these amounts, resulting in a passive activity loss of $7,000 for AMT purposes.

For regular income tax purposes, Robin would offset the $10,000 of net passive income from Activity A with $10,000 of the passive loss from Activity B. For AMT purposes, the corporation would offset the $10,000 of net passive income from Activity A with the $7,000 passive activity loss allowed from Activity B, resulting in passive activity income of $3,000. Thus, in computing AMTI, Robin makes a positive passive loss adjustment of $3,000 [$10,000 (passive activity loss allowed for regular income tax) – $7,000 (passive activity loss allowed for the AMT)].[28]

For regular income tax purposes, Robin, Inc., has a suspended passive loss of $12,000 [$22,000 (amount of loss) – $10,000 (used in 2001)]. This suspended passive loss can offset passive income in the future or can offset active or portfolio income when the corporation disposes of the loss activity (refer to Chapter 5). For AMT purposes, Robin's suspended passive loss is $0 [$7,000 (amount of loss) – $7,000 (amount used in 2001)]. ■

PLANNING CONSIDERATIONS

Avoiding Preferences and Adjustments

Investments in state and local bonds are attractive for income tax purposes because the interest is not included in gross income. Some of these bonds (private activity bonds) are issued to generate funds that are not used for an essential function of the government (e.g., to provide infrastructure for shopping malls or industrial parks or to build sports facilities). The interest on such bonds is a tax preference item and could lead to the imposition of the AMT. When the AMT applies, investors should take this factor into account. Perhaps an investment in regular tax-exempt bonds or even fully taxed private-sector bonds might yield a higher after-tax rate of return.

For a corporation anticipating AMT problems, capitalizing rather than expensing certain costs can avoid generating preferences and adjustments. The decision should be based on the present discounted value of after-tax cash flows under the available alternatives. Costs that may be capitalized and amortized, rather than expensed, include circulation expenditures, mining exploration and development costs, and research and experimentation expenditures.

---

[28]The depreciation adjustment and depletion preference are combined as part of the passive loss adjustment and are *not* reported separately.

■ FIGURE 13–1
Determining the ACE
Adjustment*

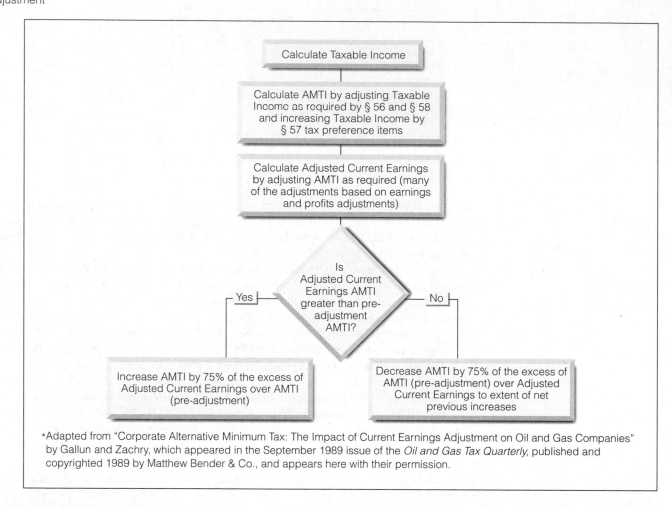

*Adapted from "Corporate Alternative Minimum Tax: The Impact of Current Earnings Adjustment on Oil and Gas Companies"
by Gallun and Zachry, which appeared in the September 1989 issue of the *Oil and Gas Tax Quarterly*, published and
copyrighted 1989 by Matthew Bender & Co., and appears here with their permission.

Understand the function of
adjusted current earnings
(ACE).

ADJUSTED CURRENT EARNINGS (ACE)

The **adjusted current earnings (ACE)** rules make up a third, separate tax system,
parallel to both AMT and taxable income. S corporations, real estate investment
trusts, regulated investment companies, and real estate mortgage investment conduits are not subject to the ACE provisions.

The purpose of the ACE adjustment is to ensure that the mismatching of
financial statement income and taxable income will not produce inequitable results.
ACE represents another attempt by Congress to assure that large corporations
with significant financial accounting income pay a fair share of Federal corporate
income tax.

The ACE adjustment is tax-based and can be negative or positive. AMTI is
increased by 75 percent of the excess of ACE over unadjusted AMTI, or AMTI is
reduced by 75 percent of the excess of unadjusted AMTI over ACE. Any negative
ACE adjustment is limited to the aggregate of the positive adjustments under ACE
for prior years reduced by the previously claimed negative adjustments (see Figure
13–1).[29] Any unused negative adjustment is lost forever.

---

[29]§§ 56(g)(1) and (2). *Unadjusted AMTI* is AMTI before the ACE adjustment and the AMT NOL deduction.

CONCEPT SUMMARY 13–2

Impact of Various Transactions on ACE and E & P

	Effect on Unadjusted AMTI in Arriving at ACE	Effect on Taxable Income in Arriving at E & P
Tax-exempt income (net of expenses)	Add	Add
Federal income tax	No effect	Subtract
Dividends received deduction (80% and 100% rules)	No effect	Add
Dividends received deduction (70% rule)	Add	Add
Exemption amount of $40,000	No effect	No effect
Key employee insurance proceeds	Add	Add
Excess charitable contribution	No effect	Subtract
Excess capital losses	No effect	Subtract
Disallowed travel and entertainment expenses	No effect	Subtract
Penalties and fines	No effect	Subtract
Intangible drilling costs deducted currently	Add	Add
Deferred gain on installment sales	Add	Add
Realized (not recognized) gain on an involuntary conversion	No effect	No effect
Loss on sale between related parties	Subtract	Subtract
Gift received	No effect	No effect
Net buildup on life insurance policy	Add	Add
Organization expense amortization	Add	Add

EXAMPLE 22

A calendar year corporation reports the following.

	2000	2001	2002
Unadjusted AMTI	$3,000,000	$3,000,000	$3,100,000
Adjusted current earnings	4,000,000	3,000,000	2,000,000

In 2000, since ACE exceeds unadjusted AMTI by $1 million, $750,000 (75% × $1,000,000) is the positive ACE adjustment. No adjustment is necessary for 2001. Unadjusted AMTI exceeds ACE by $1,100,000 in 2002, so there is a potential negative ACE adjustment of $825,000. Since the total increases to AMTI for prior years equal $750,000 (and there are no negative adjustments), only $750,000 of the potential negative ACE adjustment reduces AMTI for 2002. Further, $75,000 of negative ACE is lost forever. ■

The starting point for computing ACE is AMTI, which is regular taxable income after AMT adjustments (other than the NOL and ACE adjustments) and tax preferences.[30] Pre-NOL AMTI is adjusted for certain items to determine ACE. See Concept Summary 13–2.

6 *Find more information on this topic at our Web site: **http://wft-entities.swcollege.com**.*

---

[30]§ 56(g)(3).

EXAMPLE 23

Crimson Corporation makes the ACE adjustment calculation as follows.

AMTI		$ 5,780,000
Plus:		
Municipal bond interest	$210,000	
Installment gain	140,000	
70% dividends received deduction	300,000	
Income element in cash surrender life insurance	60,000	
Organization expense amortization	70,000	780,000
Subtotal		$ 6,560,000
Less:		
Related-party loss disallowance	240,000	(240,000)
Adjusted current earnings		$ 6,320,000
AMTI		(5,780,000)
Base amount		$ 540,000
Times		.75
ACE adjustment (positive)		$ 405,000 ■

ACE should not be confused with current E & P. Many items are treated in the same manner, but certain items that are deductible in computing E & P (but are not deductible in calculating taxable income) generally are not deductible in computing ACE (e.g., Federal income taxes). Concept Summary 13–2 compares the impact various transactions will have on the determination of ACE and E & P.

LEARNING OBJECTIVE 7

Compute the AMT liability for corporations.

COMPUTING ALTERNATIVE MINIMUM TAXABLE INCOME

The following example illustrates the effect of tax preferences and adjustments in arriving at AMTI.

EXAMPLE 24

For 2001, Tan Corporation (a calendar year company) had the following transactions.

Taxable income	$4,250,000
Income deferred by using completed contract method (versus percentage of completion method)	450,000
Percentage depletion claimed (the property has a zero adjusted basis)	1,575,000
Interest on City of Elmira (Michigan) private activity bonds	1,175,000

Tan Corporation's AMTI for 2001 is determined as follows.

Taxable income		$4,250,000
Adjustments		
Income deferred by using completed contract method (versus percentage of completion method)		100,000
Tax preferences		
Excess depletion deduction	$1,575,000	
Interest on private activity municipal bonds	1,175,000	2,750,000
AMTI		$7,450,000 ■

PLANNING CONSIDERATIONS

Optimum Use of the AMT and Regular Corporate Income Tax Rate Difference

A corporation that cannot avoid the AMT in a particular year often can save taxes by taking advantage of the difference between the AMT and the regular income tax rates. In general, a corporation that expects to be subject to the AMT should consider accelerating income and deferring deductions for the remainder of the year. Since the difference between the regular income tax rate and the AMT rate may be as much as 14 or 15 percentage points, this strategy may result in the income being taxed at less than it would be if reported in the next year (a non-AMT year). If the same corporation expects to be subject to the AMT for the next year (or years) and is not subject to AMT this year, this technique should be reversed.

Falcon is contemplating selling a tract of unimproved land (basis of $200,000 and fair market value of $1 million). Under these circumstances, it may be preferable to sell the land in 2001. The gain of $800,000 ($1,000,000 – $200,000) generates a tax of $160,000 [$800,000 (recognized gain) × 20% (AMT rate)]. However, if the land is sold in 2002, the resulting tax is $272,000 [$800,000 (recognized gain) × 34% (regular corporate income tax rate)]. A nominal savings of $112,000 ($272,000 – $160,000) materializes by making the sale in 2001. ■

Whenever one accelerates income or defers deductions, a present value analysis should be conducted. This technique to accelerate gross income is attractive only if it reduces the present value of tax liabilities.

EXAMPLE 25

Falcon Corporation expects to be in the 34% regular income tax bracket in 2002, but is subject to the AMT in 2001. In late 2001,

---

AMT RATE AND EXEMPTION

The AMT rate is 20 percent. The rate is applied to the *AMT base*, which is AMTI reduced by the *AMT exemption*. The exemption amount for a corporation is $40,000 reduced by 25 percent of the amount by which AMTI exceeds $150,000. The exemption phases out entirely when AMTI reaches $310,000.

EXAMPLE 26

Beige Corporation has AMTI of $180,000. Since the exemption amount is reduced by $7,500 [25% × ($180,000 – $150,000)], the amount remaining is $32,500 ($40,000 – $7,500). Thus, Beige Corporation's alternative minimum tax base (refer to Exhibit 13–2) is $147,500 ($180,000 – $32,500). ■

PLANNING CONSIDERATIONS

Controlling the Timing of Preferences and Adjustments

In many situations, corporations with modest levels of income may be able to avoid the AMT by making use of the exemption. To maximize the exemption, taxpayers should attempt to avoid bunching positive adjustments and tax preferences in any one year. Rather, net these items against negative adjustments to keep AMTI low. When the expenditure is largely within the control of the taxpayer, timing to avoid bunching is more easily accomplished.

MINIMUM TAX CREDIT

The **minimum tax credit** acts to make the AMT merely a *prepayment of tax* for corporations. Essentially, the AMT paid in one tax year may be carried forward indefinitely and used as a credit against the corporation's future *regular* tax liability that exceeds its tentative minimum tax. The minimum tax credit may not be carried back and may not be offset against any future AMT liability.

EXAMPLE 27

Return to the facts of Example 24. AMTI exceeds $310,000, so there is no exemption amount. The tentative minimum tax is $1,490,000 (20% of $7,450,000). Since Tan's regular income tax liability for 2001 is $1,445,000, the AMT liability is $45,000 ($1,490,000 − $1,445,000). The minimum tax credit carried forward is $45,000, the current year's AMT. The credit can be used to reduce regular income tax liability in future years (but not below the tentative alternative minimum tax). ■

OTHER ASPECTS OF THE AMT

In addition to paying their regular income tax liability, corporations must make estimated tax payments of the AMT liability. Even corporations that prepare quarterly financial statements may find this requirement adds to compliance costs.

The only credit that can be used to offset the AMT is the foreign tax credit (FTC). The general business credit and other credits discussed earlier in the chapter are unavailable in AMT years. The AMT FTC can reduce the tax by only 90 percent, reduced by the percentage of AMTI that was offset by the AMT NOL.

EXAMPLE 28

An AMT taxpayer can use both the NOL and the FTC to reduce the year's AMT liability, but only to a maximum 90% reduction. Lake Corporation's AMTI before the AMT NOL deduction is $1 million. It applies a $400,000 AMT NOL to reduce its tax base. As a result, the maximum AMT FTC that Lake can claim is $100,000 (20% AMT rate × $500,000 AMTI remaining of the 90% possible reduction). AMT taxpayers can use both the NOL deduction and the FTC to reduce the liability payable for a tax year, but the NOL is applied first, and the two provisions "share" the 90% tax reduction that they can create. ■

The AMT is computed and reported by completing Form 4626.

PLANNING CONSIDERATIONS

The Subchapter S Option

Corporations that make the S election are not subject to the corporate AMT. As noted in Chapter 12, however, various AMT adjustments and preferences pass through to the individual shareholders. But one troublesome adjustment, the one involving the ACE adjustment, is eliminated since it does not apply to individual taxpayers.

B R I D G E   D I S C I P L I N E

Bridge to Finance

For entities other than C corporations, each year the number of taxpayers to which the AMT applies increases. In addition, for taxpayers who are paying the AMT, the amount of AMT increases annually, assuming the total Federal taxable income is constant and the tentative AMT is constant.

Rose, Inc., an S corporation, has one shareholder, Jack, who is single. Rose has taxable income in 2000 and 2001 of $100,000, which is reported to Jack each year on a Schedule K-1. Jack's taxable income, excluding the $100,000 from Rose, is $300,000 each year. Jack's tentative AMT each year is $150,000.

Jack's regular income tax liability, AMT, and total Federal income tax liability for 2000 and 2001 are as follows.

2000		
Regular income tax liability		
Tax on $288,350	=	$ 91,857
111,650 × 39.6%	=	44,213
$400,000		$136,070
AMT ($150,000 − $136,070)		$ 13,930
Regular income tax		$136,070
AMT		13,930
Total tax liability		$150,000

2001		
Regular income tax liability		
Tax on $297,300	=	$ 94,708
102,700 × 39.6%	=	40,669
$400,000		$135,377
AMT ($150,000 − $135,377)		$ 14,623
Regular income tax		$135,377
AMT		14,623
Total tax liability		$150,000

When Jack's taxable income remains the same each year, why does the AMT increase by $693 ($14,623 − $13,930)? The reason is that the tax rates used in calculating the regular income tax (§ 1) are indexed for the effect of inflation each year, while the AMT tax rates (§ 55) are not subject to indexing.

A simple solution to fix these effects would be to index the AMT tax rates. Inflation-caused effects are not present for C corporations because neither the regular income tax rates (§ 11) nor the AMT rates (§ 55) are indexed.

The Individual Alternative Minimum Tax

The AMT applicable to individuals is similar to the corporate AMT. Most of the adjustments and preferences discussed above apply equally to individuals and corporations. However, there are several important differences.

- The individual AMT rate is slightly progressive, with rates at 26 percent on the first $175,000 of AMTI and at 28 percent on any additional AMTI.
- The alternative rate on net capital gain of 20 percent applies.
- The AMT exemption and phase-out amounts are tied to the individual's filing status for the year. The exemption phases out at a rate of $1 for every $4 of AMTI.

Filing Status	Initial Exemption Amount	Phase-Out Range	
		Begins at	Ends at
Married, joint	$45,000	$150,000	$330,000
Married, separate	22,500	75,000	165,000
Single, head of household	33,750	112,500	247,500

- Individuals make no AMT adjustment for ACE.
- Some additional adjustments apply to individual taxpayers. Taxes and miscellaneous itemized deductions subject to the 2 percent-of-AGI floor are not allowed as deductions for AMTI. Medical expenses are allowed only to the extent that they exceed 10 percent of AGI (instead of a 7.5 percent limitation for regular income tax purposes). Interest expense deductions are limited to qualified residence interest, interest on certain student loans, and investment interest (subject to limitations). Finally, the standard deduction and personal and dependency exemptions are not allowed as deductions when computing AMTI. Other individual-specific adjustments also exist, including an adjustment accelerating the taxation of incentive stock options.
- Determination of the minimum tax credit is more complex for individual taxpayers. The credit applies only to AMT generated as a result of *timing* differences.

Although there are several computational differences, the individual AMT and the corporate AMT have the same objective: to force taxpayers who have more economic income than that reflected in taxable income to pay a fair share of Federal income tax.

Suggested Further Readings

David M. Cronin, "Lack of Certification Not a Bar to Targeted Jobs Tax Credit," (Tax Clinic), *The Tax Adviser*, October 1999, pp. 691–695.

John O. Everett and Cherie J. O'Neil, "AMT Planning Strategies," *The Tax Adviser*, November 2000, pp. 788–799.

Sara McClelland and David Hudson, "CIP Addresses 'Qualified Research' Definition," (Tax Clinic), *The Tax Adviser*, January 2000, pp. 8–9.

KEY TERMS

Adjusted current earnings (ACE), 13–24

Alternative minimum tax (AMT), 13–13

Alternative minimum taxable income (AMTI), 13–15

Disabled access credit, 13–12

Foreign tax credit (FTC), 13–12

General business credit, 13–3

Minimum tax credit, 13–28

Private activity bonds, 13–18

Rehabilitation expenditures credit, 13–6

Rehabilitation expenditures credit recapture, 13–7

Research activities credit, 13–10

Tax credits, 13–2

Tax preference items, 13–17

Welfare-to-work credit, 13–9

Work opportunity tax credit, 13–8

Problem Materials

PROBLEMS

1. Canary, Inc., has a tentative general business credit of $110,000 for 2001. Canary's net regular tax liability before the general business credit is $125,000, and its tentative minimum tax is $100,000. Compute Canary's allowable general business credit for the year.

2. Burt Corporation has the following general business credit carryovers.

1997	$ 5,000
1998	15,000
1999	5,000
2000	20,000
Total carryovers	$45,000

   If the general business credit generated by activities during 2001 equals $45,000 and the total credit allowed during the current year is $80,000 (based on tax liability), what amounts of the current general business credit and carryovers can Burt use against its 2001 income tax liability? What is the amount of unused credit carried forward to 2002?

3. In January 2000, Iris Corporation purchased and placed into service a 1933 building that houses retail businesses. The cost was $200,000, of which $25,000 applied to the land. In modernizing the facility, Iris Corporation incurred $250,000 of renovation costs of the type that qualify for the rehabilitation credit. These improvements were placed into service in October 2001.
   a. Compute Iris Corporation's rehabilitation tax credit for 2001.
   b. Calculate the cost recovery deductions for the building and the renovation costs for 2001.

4. In the current year, Diane Lawson (127 Peachtree Drive, Savannah, GA 31419) acquires a qualifying historic structure for $250,000 (excluding the cost of land) with full intentions of substantially rehabilitating the building. Write a letter to Diane and a memo to the

tax files explaining the computation that determines the rehabilitation tax credit available to her and the impact on the depreciable basis, assuming either $200,000 or $400,000 is incurred for the rehabilitation project.

5. The tax credit for rehabilitation expenditures is available to help offset the costs related to substantially rehabilitating certain buildings. The credit is calculated on the rehabilitation expenditures incurred and not on the acquisition cost of the building itself.

You are a developer who buys, sells, and does construction work on real estate in the inner city of your metropolitan area. A potential customer approaches you about acquiring one of your buildings that easily could qualify for the 20% rehabilitation credit on historic structures. The stated sales price of the structure is $100,000 (based on appraisals ranging from $80,000 to $120,000), and the rehabilitation expenditures, if the job is done correctly, would be about $150,000.

Your business has been slow recently due to the sluggish real estate market in your area, and the potential customer makes the following proposal: if you reduce the sales price of the building to $75,000, he will pay you $175,000 to perform the rehabilitation work. Although the buyer's total expenditures would be the same, he would benefit from this approach by obtaining a larger tax credit ($25,000 increased rehabilitation costs × 20% = $5,000).

It has been a long time since you have sold any of your real estate. How will you respond?

6. Red Company hires six individuals on January 15, 2001, qualifying Red for the work opportunity tax credit. Three of these individuals receive wages of $7,000 each during 2001, for working 700 hours each. The other three receive wages of $4,000 each, for working 300 hours each.
   a. Calculate the amount of Red's work opportunity tax credit for 2001.
   b. Assume Red pays total wages of $120,000 to its employees during the year. How much of this amount is deductible in 2001 if the work opportunity tax credit is taken?

7. In March 2001, Wren Corporation hired three individuals, Trent, Bernice, and Benita, all of whom are certified as long-term family assistance recipients. Each employee is paid $11,000 during 2001. Only Bernice continued to work for Wren in 2002, earning $13,500. In February 2002, Wren hired Cassie, who was also certified as a long-term family assistance recipient. During 2002, Cassie earned $12,000. Wren does not claim the work opportunity credit with respect to any employees hired in 2001 or 2002.
   a. Compute Wren's welfare-to-work credit for 2001 and 2002.
   b. Wren pays total wages of $325,000 to its employees during 2001 and $342,000 during 2002. How much may Wren claim as a wage deduction for 2001 and 2002 if the welfare-to-work credit is claimed in both years?

8. Martin, Inc., a calendar year taxpayer, informs you that during the year it incurs expenditures of $30,000 that qualify for the incremental research activities credit. In addition, it is determined that the corporation's base amount for the year is $22,800.
   a. Determine Martin's incremental research activities credit for the year.
   b. Martin is in the 25% tax bracket. Determine which approach to the research expenditures and the research activities credit would provide the greatest tax benefit to Martin.

9. Ahmed Zinna (16 Southside Drive, Charlotte, NC 28204), one of your clients, owns two retail establishments in downtown Charlotte, North Carolina, and has come to you seeking advice concerning the tax consequences of complying with the Americans with Disabilities Act. He understands that he needs to install various features at his stores (e.g., ramps, doorways, and restrooms that are handicapped accessible) to make them more accessible to disabled individuals. He inquires whether any tax credits are available to help offset the cost of the necessary changes. He estimates the cost of the planned changes to his facilities as follows.

Location	Projected Cost
Oak Street	$20,000
Maple Avenue	9,000

He reminds you that the Oak Street store was constructed in 1995 while the Maple Avenue store is in a building that was constructed in 1902. Ahmed operates his business as a sole proprietorship and has approximately eight employees at each location. Write a letter to Ahmed in which you summarize your conclusions concerning the tax consequences of his proposed capital improvements.

10. Zinnia Corporation is an international wholesaler headquartered in the United States. Of its worldwide taxable income of $3 billion, $1.25 billion is foreign-sourced. Before any credits, Zinnia's U.S. income tax liability is $1.05 billion. If income taxes paid to foreign countries total $600 million, what is Zinnia's U.S. income tax liability after benefiting from the foreign tax credit?

11. Aqua, Inc., a calendar year corporation, has the following gross receipts and taxable income for 1994–2001.

Year	Gross Receipts	Taxable Income
1993	$11,000,000	$3,000,000
1994	4,800,000	900,000
1995	5,300,000	1,500,000
1996	4,600,000	700,000
1997	8,200,000	1,200,000
1998	8,500,000	1,900,000
1999	5,200,000	1,300,000
2000	8,000,000	1,500,000
2001	10,000,000	1,400,000

   a. When is Aqua first exempt from the AMT as a small corporation?
   b. Is Aqua subject to the AMT for 2001?

12. Quail, Inc., owns a mineral deposit that qualifies for percentage depletion. In 2001, the corporation deducts $30,000 of depletion for regular income tax purposes. Cost depletion for the year would have been only $18,000.
   a. Does the fact that Quail's percentage depletion exceeds what its cost depletion would have been produce an AMT preference?
   b. Under what circumstances would Quail have an AMT preference for depletion?

13. In March 2001, Grackle, Inc., acquired equipment for its business at a cost of $300,000. The equipment is five-year class property for regular income tax purposes and for AMT purposes.
   a. If Grackle depreciates the equipment using the method that will produce the greatest deduction for 2001 for regular income tax purposes, what is the amount of the AMT adjustment?
   b. How can Grackle reduce the AMT adjustment to $0? What circumstances would motivate Grackle to do so?
   c. Draft a letter to Helen Carlon, Grackle's controller, regarding the choice of depreciation methods. Helen's address is 500 Monticello Avenue, Glendale, AZ 85306.

14. Josepi's construction company builds personal residences that qualify for the use of the completed contract method. During the three-year period 2001–2003, Josepi recognized the following income on his two construction contracts.

Year	Contract 1	Contract 2
2001	$600,000*	$ –0–
2002	–0–	–0–
2003	–0–	700,000**

*Construction completed in 2001.
**Construction completed in 2003.

If Josepi had used the percentage of completion method, he would have recognized the following gross income from the contracts.

Year	Contract 1	Contract 2
2001	$40,000	$175,000
2002	–0–	225,000
2003	–0–	300,000

Calculate Josepi's AMT adjustments for 2001, 2002, and 2003.

15. Allie, who was an accounting major in college, is the controller of a medium-size construction corporation. She prepares the corporate tax return each year. Due to reporting a home construction contract using the completed contract method, the corporation is subject to the AMT in 2001. Allie files the 2001 corporate tax return in early February 2002. The total tax liability is $58,000 ($53,000 regular income tax liability + $5,000 AMT).

In early March, Allie reads an article on minimizing income taxes. Based on this article, she decides that it would be beneficial for the corporation to report the home construction contract using the percentage of completion method on its 2001 return. Although this will increase the corporation's 2001 income tax liability, it will minimize the total income tax liability over the two-year construction period. Therefore, Allie files an amended return on March 14, 2002. Evaluate Allie's actions from both a tax avoidance and an ethical perspective.

16. Sparrow, Inc., owns two investment properties that it acquired several years ago. The corporation's adjusted basis for each of the assets is as follows.

	Regular Income Tax	AMT
Land	$100,000	$100,000
Apartment building	450,000	490,000

Sparrow sells the land for $250,000 and the building for $800,000.
a. Calculate Sparrow's recognized gain or loss on the sale of each asset for both the regular income tax and the AMT.
b. Calculate the AMT adjustment on the sale of each asset.

17. Pheasant, Inc., is going to be subject to the AMT in 2001. The corporation owns an investment building and is considering disposing of it and investing in other realty. Based on an appraisal of the building's value, the realized gain would be $20,000. Ed has offered to purchase the building from Pheasant with the closing date being December 29, 2001. Ed wants to close the transaction in 2001 because certain beneficial tax consequences will result only if the transaction is closed prior to the beginning of 2002. Abby has offered to purchase the building with the closing date being January 2, 2002. The

building has a $25,000 greater AMT adjusted basis. For regular income tax purposes, Pheasant expects to be in the 34% tax bracket. What are the relevant tax issues that Pheasant faces in making its decision?

18. Flicker, Inc., a closely held corporation, acquired a passive activity in 2001. Gross income from operations of the activity was $160,000. Operating expenses, not including depreciation, were $122,000. Regular income tax depreciation of $49,750 was computed under MACRS. AMT depreciation, computed under ADS, was $41,000. Compute Flicker's passive loss deduction and passive loss suspended for regular income tax purposes and for AMT purposes.

19. Rock Corporation (a calendar year corporation) reports the following information for the years listed. Assume the company is not in small corporation status.

	2000	2001	2002
Unadjusted AMTI	$3,000,000	$8,000,000	$7,000,000
Adjusted current earnings	5,000,000	8,000,000	3,000,000

Compute the ACE adjustment for each year.

20. Based upon the following facts, calculate adjusted current earnings (ACE).

Alternative minimum taxable income (AMTI)	$5,120,000
Municipal bond interest	630,000
Expenses related to municipal bonds	50,000
Key employee life insurance proceeds in excess of cash surrender value	2,000,000
Organization expense amortization	100,000
Cost of goods sold	6,220,000
Advertising expenses	760,000
Loss between related parties	260,000
Life insurance expense	300,000

21. Orange Corporation, a calendar year taxpayer, reported the following amounts. Calculate Orange's positive and negative ACE adjustments.

	Preadjusted AMTI	ACE
2000	$80,000	$70,000
2001	60,000	90,000
2002	50,000	40,000
2003	50,000	10,000

22. Determine whether each of the following transactions is a preference (P), an adjustment (A), or not applicable (NA) for purposes of the corporate AMT.
    a. Depletion in excess of basis taken by Giant Oil Company.
    b. Accelerated depreciation on property.
    c. Charitable contributions of cash
    d. Adjusted current earnings.
    e. Tax-exempt interest on private activity bonds.
    f. Untaxed appreciation on property donated to charity.
    g. Dividends received deduction.

23. In each of the following independent situations, determine the tentative minimum tax. Assume the company is not in small corporation status.

	AMTI (Before the Exemption Amount)
Crane Corp.	$120,000
Rider Corp.	170,000
Mallard Corp.	340,000

24. For 2001, Peach Corporation (a calendar year company) had the following transactions.

Taxable income	$5,000,000
Regular tax depreciation on realty in excess of ADS (placed in service in 1989)	1,700,000
Amortization of certified pollution control facilities (in excess of ADS amortization)	200,000
Tax-exempt interest on private activity bonds	300,000
Percentage depletion in excess of the property's adjusted basis	700,000

    a. Determine Peach Corporation's AMTI.
    b. Determine the tentative minimum tax base (refer to Exhibit 13–2).
    c. Determine the tentative minimum tax.
    d. What is the amount of the AMT?

25. Included in Alice's regular taxable income and in her AMT base is a $100,000 capital gain on the sale of stocks that she owned for three years. Alice is in the 31% tax bracket for regular income tax purposes. In calculating her regular income tax liability, she uses the appropriate alternative tax rate on net capital gain of 20%.
    a. What rate should Alice use in calculating her tentative AMT?
    b. What is Alice's AMT adjustment?
    c. How would your answers in (a) and (b) change if the taxpayer were a C corporation in the 34% tax bracket for regular income tax purposes?

 26. Calculate the AMT for the following cases. The taxpayer reports regular taxable income of $500,000 and no tax credits.

	Tentative AMT	
Filing Status	Case 1	Case 2
Single	$190,000	$175,000
Married, filing jointly	190,000	175,000

 27. Jack, who is single with no dependents and does not itemize, provides you with the following information for 2001.

Short-term capital loss	$ 5,000
Long-term capital gain	25,000
Municipal bond interest received on private activity bonds acquired in 1993	9,000
Dividends from General Motors	1,500
Excess of FMV over cost for Incentive Stock Options (the rights became freely transferable and not subject to a substantial risk of forfeiture in 2001)	35,000

What are Jack's tax preference items and AMT adjustments for 2001?

B R I D G E   D I S C I P L I N E

1. Balm, Inc., has a general business credit for 2001 of $90,000. Balm's regular income tax liability before credits is $140,000, and its tentative AMT is $132,000.
   a. Calculate the amount of general business credit that Balm can use in 2001 and calculate its general business credit carryback and carryforward, if any.
   b. Balm projects a $140,000 regular 2002 income tax liability. Its tentative AMT will be $132,000. Balm is considering making an investment early in 2002 that annually will produce $45,000 tax-exempt income. Balm is trying to decide between two alternatives. The first alternative is a tax-exempt bond that is a private activity bond. The second alternative is a tax-exempt bond that is not a private activity bond. Advise Balm on the preferable investment.

2. Cooper Partnership, a calendar year partnership, made qualifying rehabilitation expenditures to a building that it has used in its business for eight years. These improvements were placed in service on January 5, 2000. The amount of the rehabilitation expenditures credit was $40,000.

   Cooper is negotiating to sell the building in either December 2001 or January 2002. The sales price will be $400,000, and the recognized gain will be $100,000. Provide support for the CFO's position that Cooper should delay the sale until 2002.

3. For many years, Saul's sole proprietorship and his related Form 1040 have had a number of AMT tax preferences and AMT adjustments. He has made the AMT calculation each year, but the calculated amount always has been $0. Saul's regular taxable income and the AMT adjustments and preferences for the current year are the same as for last year. Yet he must pay AMT this year. Explain how this could happen.

RESEARCH PROBLEMS

*Note: Solutions to Research Problems can be prepared by using the **RIA Checkpoint® Student Version Online research product,** or the **CCH U.S. Master Tax Guide Plus™** online Federal tax research database, which is available to accompany this text. It is also possible to prepare solutions to the Research Problems by using tax research materials found in a standard tax library.*

Research Problem 1. Miriam, an admirer of early twentieth-century architecture, discovers a 1920s-era house in the countryside outside Mobile, Alabama, during a recent Sunday excursion. She desires not only to purchase and renovate this particular house, but also to move the structure into Mobile so her community can enjoy its architectural features. Being aware of the availability of the tax credit for rehabilitation expenditures, she wishes to maximize her use of the provision, if it is available in this case, once the renovation work begins in Mobile. However, Miriam also informs you that she will pursue the purchase, relocation, and renovation of the house only if the tax credit is available. Comment on Miriam's decision and whether any renovation expenditures incurred will qualify for the tax credit for rehabilitation expenditures.

Partial list of research aids:
George S. Nalle, III, 99 T.C. 187 (1992).

Research Problem 2. Oriole Corporation is a large wholesaler of office products. To remain successful in a fiercely competitive industry, Oriole has automated and computerized many of its business operations. Specifically, the corporation has developed several new software programs to:

- Maintain files of customer histories.

- Create a paperless invoicing system.

- Develop a computer-to-computer order entry system.

- Monitor inventory levels more closely.

Oriole estimates that it spent more than $1 million to develop and test the new software programs that are used throughout the business. To date, Oriole has not sold the software programs to the public, but it is contemplating doing so. Oriole has claimed a research and experimentation deduction for the costs associated with developing the software programs. The corporation also wants to claim the research activities credit relating to the software development. Can Oriole do so? Write a memo to the tax research file summarizing your conclusions.

Research Problem 3. Parrot, Inc., receives tax-exempt interest of $20,000 on bonds that are classified as private activity bonds. The corporation appropriately excludes the $20,000 from its gross income for regular income tax purposes under § 103(a) and § 103(b)(1). Parrot has asked you for advice on the treatment of the $20,000 for AMT purposes. Find the Code Section that addresses the AMT treatment for private activity bond interest. Provide Parrot with the advice it has requested.

Use the tax resources of the Internet to address the following questions. Do not restrict your search to the World Wide Web, but include a review of newsgroups and general reference materials, practitioner sites and resources, primary sources of the tax law, chat rooms and discussion groups, and other opportunities.

Research Problem 4. The foreign tax credit is especially valuable when a U.S. business earns income in a country whose income tax rates exceed those of the United States. List five countries whose tax rates on business income exceed those of the United States, and five where the corresponding U.S. rates are higher.

Research Problem 5. Locate an outstanding proposal to modify the structure or scope of the AMT for corporations. Describe the proposal, the entity making the proposal, and potential motivations for submitting the modification to Congress.

CHAPTER 14

Comparative Forms of Doing Business

LEARNING OBJECTIVES

After completing Chapter 14, you should be able to:

1. Identify the principal legal and tax forms for conducting a business.

2. Appreciate the relative importance of nontax factors in business decisions.

3. Distinguish between the forms for conducting a business according to whether they are subject to single taxation or double taxation.

4. Identify techniques for avoiding double taxation.

5. Understand and apply the conduit and entity concepts as they affect operations, capital changes, and distributions.

6. Analyze the effects of the disposition of a business on the owners and the entity for each of the forms for conducting a business.

Outline

TAX TALK

[My law firm] had a rule—at least it seemed to be a rule—that everybody that came had to spend at least a year working on taxes. The general rationale for the rule as I could understand it was that taxes were so important to everything that you do, whatever the kind of case you are handling, you have to know something about the tax consequences of things.

—*Charles A. Horsky*

A variety of factors, both tax and nontax, can affect the choice of the form of business entity. The form that is appropriate at one point in the life of an entity and its owners may not be appropriate at a different time.

EXAMPLE 1

Eva is a tax practitioner in Kentwood, the Dairy Center of the South. Many of her clients are dairy farmers. She recently had tax planning discussions with two of her clients, Jesse, a Line Creek dairy farmer, and Larry, a Spring Creek dairy farmer.

Jesse recently purchased his dairy farm. He is 52 years old and just retired after 30 years of service as a chemical engineer at an oil refinery in Baton Rouge. Eva recommended that he incorporate his dairy farm and elect S corporation status for Federal income tax purposes.

Larry has owned his dairy farm since 1990. He inherited it from his father. At that time, Larry retired after 20 years of service in the U.S. Air Force. He has a master's degree in Agricultural Economics from LSU. His farm is incorporated, and shortly after the date of incorporation, Eva had advised him to elect S corporation status. She now advises him to revoke the S election. ■

Example 1 raises a number of interesting questions. Does Eva advise all of her dairy farmer clients to elect S corporation status initially? Why has she advised Larry to revoke his S election? Will she advise Jesse to revoke his S election at some time in the future? Will she advise Larry to make another S election at some time in the future? Why did she not advise Larry to dissolve his corporation

TAX IN THE NEWS

SHOULD YOU CHECK THAT BOX?

The check-the-box rules have been evolving since their introduction into the Regulations in late 1996. They are designed to remove tax considerations from the owners' choice of the legal form in which to conduct business. These provisions act to reduce the owners' exposure to the double taxation of taxable business profits. But taxpayers considering the use of these rules have run into several complications.

- Changing tax entity classifications from year to year comes at a cost. Changing the business form from a corporation to a partnership might trigger taxes for both the entity and its owners, defeating the purpose of the entity change.
- State income tax laws do not always match those of the Code. Several states have been slow to adopt the check-the-box rules, and others have modified the rules in some way. For instance, in several states a one-member limited liability company does not receive the expected tax treatment as a partnership, but is reclassified as a corporation or sole proprietorship. Uncertainty as to the state income tax treatment of a check-the-box selection alone may keep the owners from exercising their supposed freedom of choice of tax entity.

outright? Could Larry and Jesse have achieved the same tax consequences for their dairy farms if they had operated the farms as limited liability entities or partnerships instead of incorporating? Does the way the farm is acquired (e.g., purchase versus inheritance) affect the choice of business entity for tax purposes?

This chapter provides the basis for comparing and analyzing the tax consequences of business decisions for various types of tax entities (sole proprietorship, partnership, corporation, limited liability entity, and S corporation). Understanding the comparative tax consequences for the different types of entities and being able to apply them effectively to specific fact patterns will result in effective tax planning, which is exactly what Eva was doing with her two clients. As the following discussion illustrates, a variety of potential answers may exist for each of the questions raised by Eva's advice.

LEARNING OBJECTIVE 1

Identify the principal legal and tax forms for conducting a business.

Forms of Doing Business

PRINCIPAL FORMS

The principal *legal* forms for conducting a business entity are the sole proprietorship, partnership, limited liability entity, and corporation.[1] From a *Federal income tax* perspective, these same forms are available, but the corporate form can be taxed in either of two ways (S corporation and C or regular corporation). In most instances, the legal form and the tax form are the same.

The taxpayer generally is bound for tax purposes by the legal form that is selected. A major statutory exception to this is the ability of an S corporation to

---

[1]A business entity can also be conducted in the form of a trust or estate. These two forms are addressed in *West Federal Taxation: Advanced Taxation.*

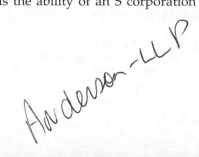

BIG 5 PARTNERSHIPS REORGANIZE AS LLPs

All of the Big 5 accounting firms have changed their organizational structure from general partnerships to limited liability partnerships (LLPs). These firms include Arthur Andersen, Deloitte & Touche, Ernst & Young, KPMG Peat Marwick, and PricewaterhouseCoopers. Many other CPA firms are doing likewise.

An LLP helps to provide protection for the *personal* assets of the partners. Under the LLP organizational structure, the only partners whose personal assets are at risk are those actually involved in the negligence or wrongdoing in question. However, the accounting firm is still responsible for the full judgment. Thus, the capital of the firm is still at risk.

receive tax treatment similar to that of a partnership.[2] In addition, taxpayers sometimes can control which set of tax rules will apply to their business operations. The "check-the-box" Regulations provide an elective procedure that enables certain entities to be classified as partnerships for Federal income tax purposes even though they have corporate characteristics.[3] These Regulations have greatly simplified the determination of entity classification. See Chapter 9 for a more detailed discussion of the check-the-box provisions.

An individual conducting a sole proprietorship files Schedule C of Form 1040. If more than one trade or business is conducted, a separate Schedule C is filed for each trade or business. A partnership files Form 1065. A corporation files Form 1120, and an S corporation files Form 1120S.

About 4.5 million corporations file U.S. income tax returns every year, and about 2 million of these use S corporation status. About 1.5 million partnership returns are filed every year, and more than 16 million individuals report sole proprietorship activities on Schedule C in a typical tax year.[4] The business entity forms that are growing in number the fastest are the sole proprietorship (twice as many as 15 years ago) and the partnership (perhaps due to the popularity of the new limited liability entities).

LIMITED LIABILITY COMPANIES

A **limited liability company (LLC)** is a hybrid business form that combines the corporate characteristic of limited liability for the owners with the tax characteristics of a partnership.[5] All of the states now permit this legal form for conducting a business.

The most frequently cited nontax benefit of an LLC is the limited liability of the owners. Compared to the other forms of ownership, LLCs offer additional benefits over other forms of business, including the following.

Advantages over S corporations

- Greater flexibility in terms of the number of owners, types of owners, special allocation opportunities, and capital structure.
- Inclusion of entity debt in the owner's basis for an ownership interest.

---

[2]§§ 1361 and 1362. See Chapter 12.
[3]Reg. §§ 301.7701–1 through –4, and –6.
[4]*Statistics of Income Bulletin*, Summer 1998.

[5]Depending on state law, an LLC may be organized as a limited liability corporation or a limited liability partnership.

TAX FACT

REVENUE RELEVANCE OF CORPORATE VERSUS INDIVIDUAL TAXPAYERS

Federal income taxes (FIT) provide over half of the Federal budget receipts. As indicated below, the portion provided by individual taxpayers (which includes the effect of flow-through entities) far exceeds that provided by corporate taxpayers.

	1996	1997	1998	1999	2000
% of budget receipts from FIT	49%	50%	52%	57%	58%
% of FIT from individual taxpayers	80%	78%	79%	81%	83%
% of FIT from corporate taxpayers	20%	22%	21%	19%	17%

Source: Federal Budget of the United States.

- More liberal deferral of gain recognition on contributions of appreciated property by an owner (determined under § 721 rather than § 351).
- For securities law purposes, an ownership interest in an LLC is not necessarily a security.

Advantages over C corporations

- Ability to pass tax attributes through to the owners.
- Absence of double taxation.

Advantages over limited partnerships

- Right of all owners to participate in the management of the business.
- Ability of all owners to have limited liability (no need for a general partner).
- For securities law purposes, an ownership interest in an LLC is not necessarily a security (the interest of a limited partner normally is classified as a security).

Advantages over general partnerships

- Limited liability for owners.
- Greater continuity of life.
- Limitation on an owner's ability to withdraw from the business.

Among the disadvantages associated with LLCs are the following.

- Absence of a developed body of case law on LLCs.
- Requirement in most states that there be at least two owners.
- Inability to qualify for § 1244 ordinary loss treatment.

Appreciate the relative importance of nontax factors in business decisions.

Nontax Factors

Taxes are only one of many factors to consider when making a business decision. Above all, any business decision should make economic sense.

EXAMPLE 2

Walter is considering investing $10,000 in a limited partnership. He projects that he will be able to deduct the $10,000 capital contribution within the next two years (as his share of partnership losses). Since Walter's marginal tax rate is 36%, the deductions will produce a positive cash-flow effect of $3,600 ($10,000 × 36%). However, there is a substantial risk that he will not recover any of his original investment. If this occurs, his negative cash flow from the investment in the limited partnership is $6,400 ($10,000 – $3,600). Walter must decide if the investment makes economic sense. ∎

CAPITAL FORMATION

The ability of an entity to raise capital is a factor that must be considered. A sole proprietorship has the narrowest capital base. Compared to the sole proprietorship, the partnership has a greater opportunity to raise funds through the pooling of owner resources.

EXAMPLE 3

Adam and Beth decide to form a partnership, AB. Adam contributes cash of $200,000, and Beth contributes land with an adjusted basis of $60,000 and a fair market value of $200,000. The partnership is going to construct an apartment building at a cost of $800,000. AB pledges the land and the building to secure a loan of $700,000. ∎

The limited partnership offers even greater potential than the general partnership form because a limited partnership can secure funds from investors (i.e., future limited partners).

EXAMPLE 4

Carol and Dave form a limited partnership, CD. Carol contributes cash of $200,000, and Dave contributes land with an adjusted basis of $60,000 and a fair market value of $200,000. The partnership is going to construct a shopping center at a cost of $5 million. Included in this cost is the purchase price of $800,000 for land adjacent to that contributed by Dave. Thirty limited partnership interests are sold for $100,000 each to raise $3 million. CD then pledges the shopping center (including the land) and obtains nonrecourse creditor financing of another $2 million. ∎

Both the at-risk limitations and the passive activity loss provisions reduce the tax attractiveness of investments in real estate, particularly in the limited partnership form. In effect, the tax rules themselves place a severe curb on the economic consequences. Chapter 5 presents these loss rules and their critical interaction.

Of the different business entities, the corporate form offers the greatest ease and potential for obtaining owner financing because it can issue additional shares of stock. The ultimate examples of this form are the large public companies that are listed on the stock exchanges.

LIMITED LIABILITY

A corporation offers its owners limited liability under state law. This absence of personal liability on the part of the owners is the most frequently cited advantage of the corporate form.

■ **FIGURE 14–1**
Limited Partnership with a
Corporate General Partner

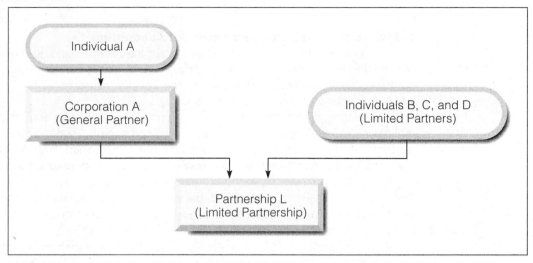

EXAMPLE 5

Ed, Fran, and Gabriella each invest $25,000 for all the shares of stock of Brown Corporation. Brown obtains creditor financing of $100,000. Brown is the defendant in a personal injury suit resulting from an accident involving one of its delivery trucks. The court awards a judgment of $2.5 million to the plaintiff. The award exceeds Brown's insurance coverage by $1.5 million. Even though the judgment probably will result in Brown's bankruptcy, the shareholders will have no personal liability for the unpaid corporate debts. ■

Limited liability is not available to all corporations. For many years, state laws did not permit professional individuals (e.g., accountants, attorneys, architects, and physicians) to incorporate. Even though professionals now are allowed to incorporate, the statutes do not provide limited liability for the performance of professional services.

Even if state law provides for limited liability, the shareholders of small corporations may forgo this benefit. Quite often, a corporation may be unable to obtain external financing (e.g., a bank loan) at reasonable interest rates unless the shareholders guarantee the loan.

The limited partnership form provides limited liability to the limited partners. Their liability is limited to the amount invested. In contrast, a general partner has unlimited liability.

EXAMPLE 6

Hazel, the general partner, invests $250,000 in HIJ, a limited partnership. Iris and Jane, the limited partners, each invest $50,000. While the potential loss for Iris and Jane is limited to $50,000 each, Hazel's liability is unlimited. ■

Indirectly, it may be possible to provide the general partner with limited liability by establishing a corporation as the general partner (see Figure 14–1). When a venture is structured this way, the general partner (the corporation) has limited its liability under the corporate statutes. In the figure, individual A is protected from personal liability by being merely the shareholder of Corporation A.

BRIDGE DISCIPLINE

Bridge to Business Law and Financial Accounting

When a business entity is created and assets are transferred to the business entity by the owners, the tax balance sheet and the financial accounting balance sheet generally will contain different amounts for the assets. The balance sheet amounts are a function of whether conduit theory or entity theory is applied.

Conduit theory, also referred to as aggregate theory or proprietary theory, assumes that the business entity is merely an extension of the owners. Therefore, the transfer of the assets by the owners to the entity is not a taxable event. The owners' basis for their ownership interests is a carryover basis. The business entity's basis for its assets is a carryover basis.

Entity theory assumes that the business entity is separate and apart for the owners. Therefore, the transfer of assets by the owners to the entity is a taxable event. The owners' basis for their ownership interests is a new basis (i.e., fair market value). The business entity's basis for its assets is a new basis (i.e., fair market value).

Financial accounting uses entity theory. Thus, the critical value is the fair market value of each asset contributed by an owner to the business entity. Tax generally uses conduit theory. Thus, the critical value is the owner's adjusted basis for the contributed assets.

OTHER FACTORS

Other nontax factors may be significant in selecting an organization form, such as:

- Estimated life of the business.
- Number of owners and their roles in the management of the business.
- Freedom of choice in transferring ownership interests.
- Organizational formality, including the related cost and extent of government regulation.

LEARNING OBJECTIVE 3

Distinguish between the forms for conducting a business according to whether they are subject to single taxation or double taxation.

Single versus Double Taxation

OVERALL IMPACT ON ENTITY AND OWNERS

The sole proprietorship, limited liability entity, and partnership are subject to *single* taxation. This result occurs because the owner(s) and the business generally are not considered separate entities for tax purposes. Therefore, the tax liability is levied at the owner level rather than at the entity level.

In contrast, a corporation and its owners can be subject to *double* taxation. This is frequently cited as the major tax disadvantage of the corporate form. The entity is taxed on the earnings of the corporation, and the owners are taxed on distributions to the extent they are made from corporate earnings.

The S corporation provides a way to avoid double taxation and possibly subject corporate earnings to a lower tax rate (the individual tax rate may be lower than the corporate tax rate). However, the ownership structure of an S corporation is restricted in both the number and type of shareholders. In addition, statutory exceptions subject the entity to taxation in certain circumstances.[6] To the extent

---

[6]Recall the Chapter 12 discussions of the taxes on an S corporation's built-in gains, LIFO recapture, and investment income.

these corporate-level taxes apply, double taxation results. Finally, the distribution policy of the S corporation may create difficulties under the *wherewithal to pay* concept.

<table>
<tr><td>**EXAMPLE 7**</td><td>Hawk Corporation has been operating as an S corporation since it began its business two years ago. For both of the prior years, Hawk incurred a tax loss. Hawk has taxable income of $75,000 this year and expects that its earnings will increase each year in the foreseeable future. Part of this earnings increase results from Hawk's expansion into other communities in the state. Since most of this expansion will be financed internally, no dividend distributions will be made to Hawk's shareholders.</td></tr>
</table>

Assuming all of Hawk's shareholders are in the 31% tax bracket, their tax liability on corporate earnings will be $23,250 ($75,000 × 31%). Even though Hawk will not distribute any cash to the shareholders, they still will be required to pay the tax liability. This creates a wherewithal to pay problem. In addition, the corporate tax liability would have been less if Hawk had not been an S corporation [(15% × $50,000) + (25% × $25,000) = $13,750].

The shareholders' wherewithal to pay problem could be resolved by terminating the S corporation election. The tax liability would then be imposed at the corporate level. Since Hawk does not intend to make any dividend distributions, double taxation at the present time would be avoided. Terminating the election also reduces the overall shareholder-corporation tax liability by $9,500 ($23,250 − $13,750).[7]

In making the decision about the form of business entity, Hawk's shareholders should consider more than the current taxable year. If the S election is terminated, another election might not be available for five years. Thus, the decision to revoke the election should be made using at least a five-year planning horizon. Perhaps a better solution would be to retain the election and distribute enough dividends to the S corporation shareholders to enable them to pay the shareholder tax liability. ■

Two other variables that relate to the adverse effect of double taxation are the timing and form of corporate distributions. If no distributions are made, then only single taxation occurs in the short run.[8] To the extent that double taxation does occur in the future, the cash-flow effect should be discounted to its present value. Second, when the distribution is made, is it in the form of a dividend or a return of capital?[9] The owners likely would prefer to receive long-term capital gain (subject to lower tax rates) instead of ordinary income. Proper structuring of the distribution can accomplish this result.

ALTERNATIVE MINIMUM TAX

All of the forms of business are directly or indirectly subject to the alternative minimum tax (AMT).[10] For the sole proprietorship and the C corporation, the effect is direct (the AMT liability calculation is attached to the tax form that reports the entity's taxable income—Form 1040 or Form 1120). For the partnership, limited liability entity, and S corporation, the effect is indirect; the tax preferences and adjustments pass through from the entity to the owners, and the AMT liability

---

[7]The absence of distributions to shareholders could create an accumulated earnings tax (AET) problem under § 531. However, as long as earnings are used to finance expansion, the "reasonable needs" provision will be satisfied, and the corporation will avoid any AET. Refer to the discussion of the AET in Chapter 10.

[8]This assumes there is no accumulated earnings tax problem. See especially Example 10 in the subsequent discussion of distributions in Minimizing Double Taxation.

[9]Redemptions of stock and corporate liquidations may be taxed as a sale of stock to shareholders (i.e., as capital gain or loss). See § 302 and Chapter 1 of *West Federal Taxation: Advanced Taxation*.

[10]§ 55.

calculation is *not* assessed on the tax form that reports the entity's taxable income—Form 1065 or Form 1120S.

When compared to other entities, the C corporation appears to have a slight advantage. The corporate AMT rate of 20 percent is less than the individual AMT rates of 26 and 28 percent. An even better perspective is provided by comparing the maximum AMT rate with the maximum regular rate for both the individual and the corporation. For the individual, the AMT rate is 71 percent (28%/39.6%) of the maximum regular rate. The AMT rate for the corporation is 57 percent (20%/35%) of the maximum regular rate. Therefore, on the basis of comparative rates, the C corporation appears to offer lower AMT tax burdens. In addition, as presented below, under certain circumstances, a C corporation is exempt from the AMT.

The apparent corporate AMT rate advantage may be more than offset by the ACE adjustment, which applies only to C corporations.[11] If the ACE adjustment continually causes the C corporation to be subject to the AMT, the owners should consider electing S corporation status (if eligibility requirements can be satisfied). Since the S corporation does not compute an ACE adjustment, it may be possible to reduce the tax liability.

The AMT does not apply to modest-sized C corporations. To be exempt from the tax, the corporation must meet both of the following tests.

- Average annual gross receipts of not more than $5 million for the three tax years after 1993.
- Average annual gross receipts of not more than $7.5 million for every subsequent three-tax-year period.

A corporation automatically is classified as a small corporation in the first year of existence. About 95 percent of all C corporations are likely to meet these tests and be exempt from the AMT in the future.

PLANNING CONSIDERATIONS

Planning for the AMT

If the AMT will apply in the current year, the entity should consider accelerating income and delaying deductions, so that current-year taxable income is taxed at the lower AMT rate. For a C corporation, the potential rate differential is 15 percentage points (20 percent AMT rate versus 35 percent regular tax rate). For an individual (i.e., either as a sole propri-etor or as a partner), the potential tax rate differential is 11.6 percentage points (28 percent highest AMT rate versus 39.6 percent regular tax rate). A present value analysis should be used to assure that the income acceleration and deduction deferral do not increase actual tax liabilities.

STATE TAXATION

In selecting a form for doing business, the determination of the tax consequences should not be limited to Federal income taxes. Consideration also should be given to state income taxes and, if applicable, local income taxes.

The S corporation provides a good illustration of this point. Suppose that the forms of business being considered are a limited partnership or a corporation. An operating loss is projected for the next several years. The owners decide to operate

---

[11]§§ 56(c)(1) and (f). Refer to the discussion of the corporate AMT in Chapter 13.

TAX IN THE NEWS

WHO PAYS CORPORATE AMT?

One of the issues often raised in debates over tax legislation is whether the corporate AMT should be repealed. Among the topics discussed are the revenue generated, the related compliance costs, and the number of corporations subject to the AMT.

According to a General Accounting Office (GAO) report, only about 30,000 of the 2.1 million corporations potentially subject to the AMT paid any AMT (i.e., less than 1.5 percent) between 1987 and 1992. Approximately 2,000 corporations accounted for 85 percent of the corporate AMT paid during that period.

Proponents of the corporate AMT argue that these statistics show that the AMT is being paid by corporations targeted by the law (i.e., large corporations). Opponents argue that the same statistics show that the compliance costs borne by the mass of corporations do not justify the continuation of this tax system.

The exemption from the AMT for small corporations may provide the needed solution. Large corporations must make minimal Federal income tax payments when the AMT applies. Most C corporations no longer need to compute the tax.

the business in the corporate form. The principal nontax criterion for the decision is the limited liability attribute of the corporation. The owners consent to an S corporation election, so the corporate losses can be passed through to the shareholders to deduct on their individual tax returns. However, assume that state law does not permit the S corporation election. Thus, the owners will not receive the tax benefits of the loss deductions that would have been available on their state income tax returns if they had chosen the limited partnership form. As a result of providing limited liability to the owner who would have been the general partner for the limited partnership, the loss deduction at the state level is forgone.

LEARNING OBJECTIVE 4

Identify techniques for avoiding double taxation.

Minimizing Double Taxation

Only the corporate form is potentially subject to double taxation. Several techniques are available for eliminating or at least reducing the second layer of taxation.

- Making distributions to the shareholders that are deductible to the corporation.
- Not making distributions to the shareholders.
- Making distributions that qualify for return of capital treatment at the shareholder level.
- Making the S corporation election.

MAKING DEDUCTIBLE DISTRIBUTIONS

The following are typical distribution forms that will result in a deduction to the corporation.

- Salary payments to shareholder-employees.
- Lease or rental payments to shareholder-lessors.
- Interest payments to shareholder-creditors.

Recognizing the potential for abuse, the IRS scrutinizes these types of distributions carefully. All three forms are evaluated in terms of *reasonableness*.[12] In addition, interest payments to shareholders may lead to reclassification of some or all of the debt as equity.[13] IRS success with either approach raises the specter of double taxation.

EXAMPLE 8

Donna owns all the stock of Green Corporation and is also the chief executive officer. Green's taxable income before salary payments to Donna is as follows.

1999	2000	2001
$80,000	$50,000	$250,000

During the year, Donna receives a monthly salary of $3,000. In December of each year, Donna reviews the operations for the year and determines the year-end bonus she is to receive. Donna's yearly bonuses are as follows.

1999	2000	2001
$44,000	$14,000	$214,000

The apparent purpose of Green's bonus program is to reduce the corporate taxable income to zero and thereby avoid double taxation. An examination of Green's tax return by the IRS would likely result in a deduction disallowance for **unreasonable compensation**. ■

EXAMPLE 9

Tom and Vicki each contribute $20,000 to TV Corporation for all of its stock. In addition, they each lend $80,000 to TV. The loan is documented by formal notes, the interest rate is 12%, and the maturity date is 10 years from the date of the loan.

The notes provide the opportunity for the corporation to make payments of $9,600 each year to both Tom and Vicki and for the payments not to be subject to double taxation. This happens because the interest payments are includible in the gross income of Tom and Vicki, but are deductible by TV in calculating its taxable income. At the time of repayment in 10 years, neither Tom nor Vicki recognizes gross income from the repayment; the $80,000 amount realized is equal to the basis for the note of $80,000.

If the IRS succeeded in reclassifying the notes as equity, Tom and Vicki still would have gross income of $9,600, but the interest would be reclassified as dividend income. Because dividend payments are not deductible by TV, the corporation's taxable income would increase by $19,200 ($9,600 × 2). To make matters worse, the repayment of the notes in 10 years would not qualify as a recovery of capital, resulting in additional dividend income for Tom and Vicki. ■

NOT MAKING DISTRIBUTIONS

Double taxation will not occur unless the corporation makes (actual or deemed) distributions to the shareholders. A closely held corporation that does not make distributions may eventually encounter an accumulated earnings tax problem unless the reasonable needs requirement is satisfied. When making distribution decisions each year, the board of directors should be apprised of any potential accumulated earnings tax problem and take the appropriate steps to eliminate it.

---

[12]§ 162(a)(1). *Mayson Manufacturing Co. v. Comm.*, 49–2 USTC ¶9467, 38 AFTR 1028, 178 F.2d 115 (CA–6, 1949); *Harolds Club v. Comm.*, 65–1 USTC ¶9198, 15 AFTR2d 241, 340 F.2d 861 (CA–9, 1965).

[13]§ 385; Rev.Rul. 83–98, 1983–2 C.B. 40; *Bauer v. Comm.*, 84–2 USTC ¶9996, 55 AFTR2d 85–433, 748 F.2d 1365 (CA–9, 1984).

The accumulated earnings tax rate of 39.6 percent is the same as the maximum marginal tax rate for individual taxpayers.[14]

EXAMPLE 10

According to an internal calculation made by Dolphin Corporation, its accumulated taxable income is $400,000. The board of directors would prefer not to declare any dividends, but is considering a dividend declaration of $400,000 to avoid the accumulated earnings tax. All of the shareholders are in the 36% bracket.

If a dividend of $400,000 is declared, the tax cost to the shareholders is $144,000 ($400,000 × 36%). If a dividend is not declared and the IRS assesses the accumulated earnings tax, the tax cost to the corporation for the accumulated earnings tax would be $158,400 ($400,000 × 39.6%).

To make matters worse, Dolphin will have incurred the accumulated earnings tax cost without getting any funds out of the corporation to the shareholders. If the unwise decision were now made to distribute the remaining $241,600 ($400,000 – $158,400) to the shareholders, the additional tax cost at the shareholder level would be $86,976 ($241,600 × 36%). Therefore, the combined shareholder-corporation tax cost would be $245,376 ($158,400 + $86,976). This is 170% ($245,376/$144,000) of the tax cost that would have resulted from an initial dividend distribution of $400,000. ∎

Assuming that the accumulated earnings tax can be avoided (e.g., a growth company whose reasonable needs justify its failure to pay dividends), a policy of no distributions to shareholders can avoid the second layer of taxation on corporate earnings. The retained earnings will drive the value of the shares upward, equal to the accumulated after-tax cash. As a result of the step-up in basis rules for inherited property, the basis of the stock for the beneficiaries will be the fair market value at the date of the decedent's death rather than the decedent's basis.

RETURN OF CAPITAL DISTRIBUTIONS

The exposure to double taxation can be reduced if the corporate distributions to the shareholders can qualify for return of capital rather than dividend treatment. This can occur when the corporation's earnings and profits (E & P) are low or negative in amount. Review Example 1 in Chapter 10. In some cases, the stock redemption provisions offer an opportunity to avoid dividend treatment altogether. Under these rules, the distribution may be treated as a sale of the shareholder's stock, resulting in a tax-free recovery of basis and then recognition of low-tax long-term capital gain.

ELECTING S CORPORATION STATUS

Electing S corporation status generally eliminates double taxation. Several factors, listed below, should be considered when making this election.

- Are all the shareholders willing to consent to the election?
- Can the qualification requirements under § 1361 be satisfied at the time of the election?
- Can the S corporation requirements continue to be satisfied?
- For what period will the conditions that make the election beneficial continue to prevail?
- Will the corporate distribution policy create wherewithal to pay problems at the shareholder level?

---

[14]§ 531. Refer to the discussion of the accumulated earnings tax in Chapter 10.

Bridge to Economics

Corporations such as General Motors, IBM, Microsoft, Wal-Mart, and ExxonMobil are major players not only in their industries, but also in the world economy. However, people are also attracted to "mom and pop type stores," which cumulatively play a major role in the economy.

In recognition of the important role of small businesses and their size competitive disadvantage at times, Congress has provided small businesses with beneficial tax treatment that is not available to major business entities. Included among such beneficial treatments are the following.

- § 11 beneficial tax rates.
- § 44 disabled access credit.
- § 55(e) exemption from the AMT for small corporations.
- § 179 limited expensing for tangible personal property.
- § 1244 ordinary loss treatment.

Each of these provisions defines, "small" in a different way. Sometimes, however, when beneficial tax treatment is provided for a business entity, the term "small" may be used inappropriately. The classic example is the small business corporation of Subchapter S. Some S corporations hold billions of dollars of assets. The only relationship to "small" is that the number of shareholders cannot exceed 75.

EXAMPLE 11

Emerald Corporation commenced business in January 2001. The two shareholders, Diego and Jaime, are both in the 31% tax bracket. The following operating results are projected for the first five years of operations.

2001	2002	2003	2004	2005
($50,000)	$400,000	$600,000	$800,000	$1,000,000

The corporation plans to expand rapidly. Therefore, no distributions will be made to shareholders. In addition, beginning in 2002, preferred stock will be offered to a substantial number of investors to help finance the expansion.

If the S corporation election is made for 2001, the $50,000 loss can be passed through to Diego and Jaime. The loss will generate a positive cash-flow effect of $15,500 ($50,000 × 31%). Assume that the election is either revoked or is involuntarily terminated at the beginning of 2002 as a result of the issuance of the preferred stock. The corporate tax liability for 2002 is $136,000 ($400,000 × 34%).

If the S corporation election is not made for 2001, the $50,000 loss is a net operating loss. The amount can be carried forward to reduce the 2002 corporate taxable income to $350,000 ($400,000 − $50,000). The resultant tax liability is $119,000 ($350,000 × 34%).

Should the S corporation election be made for just the one-year period? The answer is unclear. With an assumed after-tax rate of return to Diego and Jaime of 10%, the value of the $15,500 one year hence is $17,050 ($15,500 × 110%). Even considering the time value of money, the combined corporation-shareholder negative cash-flow effect of $118,950 ($136,000 − $17,050) in the case of an S election is about the same as the $119,000 corporate tax liability that would result for a C corporation. ■

TAX FACT

NUMBER OF INCOME TAX RETURNS FILED BY DIFFERENT TYPES OF TAXPAYERS (IN MILLIONS)

Type of Taxpayer	1975	1980	1985	1990	1995	2000
Individual	83.9	93.1	99.5	112.3	116.1	126.9
Partnership	1.1	1.4	1.8	1.8	1.6	2.1
C corporation	1.8	2.1	2.4	2.3	2.2	2.2
S corporation	.4	.5	.7	1.5	2.2	2.8

The number of S corporation returns has increased dramatically during the 25-year period. In addition, the number of S corporation returns now exceeds the number of C corporation returns. Since LLCs normally file as partnerships, it will be interesting to see what effect the popularity of this entity form will have on the number of partnership returns filed.

Source: IRS Tax Stats.

LEARNING OBJECTIVE 5

Understand and apply the conduit and entity concepts as they affect operations, capital changes, and distributions.

Conduit versus Entity Treatment

Under the **conduit concept,** the entity is viewed as merely an extension of the owners. Under the **entity concept,** the entity is regarded as being separate and distinct from its owners. The effects of the conduit and entity concepts extend to a variety of tax rules, including the following.

- Recognition at time of contribution to the entity.
- Basis of ownership interest.
- Results of operations.
- Recognition at time of distribution.
- Passive activity losses.
- At-risk rules.
- Special allocations.

The sole proprietorship is not analyzed separately because the owner and the business are the same tax entity. In one circumstance, however, a tax difference can result. Income recognition does not occur when an owner contributes an asset to a sole proprietorship. Thus, the business generally takes a carryover basis. However, if the asset is a personal-use asset, the sole proprietorship's basis is the *lower of* the adjusted basis or the fair market value at the date of contribution. If a personal-use asset is contributed to a partnership or corporation, this same *lower-of* rule applies.

EFFECT ON RECOGNITION AT TIME OF CONTRIBUTION TO THE ENTITY

Since the conduit approach applies to partnerships, § 721 provides for no recognition on the contribution of property to a partnership in exchange for a partnership interest. Section 721 protects both a contribution associated with the formation of the partnership and later contributions. The partnership takes a carryover basis in the contributed property, and the partners have a carryover basis in their partnership interests.[15]

Since the entity approach applies to corporations, the transfer of property to a corporation in exchange for its stock is a taxable event. However, if the § 351 control requirement is satisfied, no gain or loss is recognized. In this case, both the corporate property and the shareholders' stock have a carryover basis.[16] This control requirement makes it possible for shareholders who contribute appreciated property to the corporation *after* its formation to recognize gain.

To the extent that the fair market value of property contributed to the entity at the time of formation is not equal to the property's adjusted basis, a special allocation may be desirable. With a special allocation, the owner contributing the property receives the tax benefit or detriment for any recognized gain or loss that subsequently results because of the initial difference between the adjusted basis and the fair market value. For the partnership, this special allocation treatment is mandatory. No such allocation is available for a C corporation because the gain or loss is recognized at the corporation level rather than at the shareholder level. As with a C corporation, no such allocation is available for an S corporation. The recognized gain or loss is reported on the shareholders' tax returns according to their stock ownership.

EXAMPLE 12

Khalid contributes land with an adjusted basis of $10,000 and a fair market value of $50,000 for a 50% ownership interest. At the same time, Tracy contributes cash of $50,000 for the remaining 50% ownership interest. Because the entity is unable to obtain the desired zoning, it subsequently sells the land for $50,000.

If the entity is a C corporation, Khalid has a realized gain of $40,000 ($50,000 − $10,000) and a recognized gain of $0 resulting from the contribution. His basis in the stock is $10,000, and the corporation has a basis in the land of $10,000. The corporation realizes and recognizes a gain of $40,000 ($50,000 − $10,000) when it sells the land. Thus, what should have been Khalid's recognized gain is now the corporation's taxable gain. There is no way that the corporation can allocate the recognized gain directly to Khalid. The corporation could distribute the land to Khalid and let him sell it, but such a distribution is likely to be taxable to Khalid as a dividend, and gain on the distribution is also recognized at the corporate level.

If the entity is a partnership or limited liability entity, the tax consequences are the same as for the C corporation, except for the $40,000 recognized gain on the sale of the land. The partnership realizes and recognizes a gain of $40,000 ($50,000 − $10,000). However, even though Khalid's share of profits and losses is only 50%, all of the $40,000 recognized gain is allocated to him. If the entity is an S corporation, the tax consequences are the same as for the C corporation, except that Khalid reports $20,000 of the recognized gain on his tax return and Tracy reports $20,000. ∎

EFFECT ON BASIS OF OWNERSHIP INTEREST

In a partnership or limited liability entity, since the owner is the taxpayer, profits and losses of the partnership affect the owner's basis in the entity interest. Likewise, the owner's basis is increased by the share of entity liability increases and is decreased by the share of liability decreases. Accordingly, ownership basis changes frequently.[17]

Because a C corporation is a taxpaying entity, the shareholder's basis for the stock is not affected by corporate profits and losses or corporate liability changes.

---

[15]Refer to the pertinent discussion in Chapter 11.
[16]Refer to the pertinent discussion in Chapter 9.

[17]§§ 705 and 752.

The treatment of an S corporation shareholder falls between that of the partner and the C corporation shareholder. The S corporation shareholder's stock basis is increased by the share of profits and decreased by the share of losses, but it usually is not affected by corporate liability increases or decreases.[18]

EXAMPLE 13

Peggy contributes cash of $100,000 to an entity for a 30% ownership interest. The entity borrows $50,000 and repays $20,000 of this amount by the end of the taxable year. The profits for the year are $90,000.

If the entity is a partnership or limited liability entity, Peggy's basis at the end of the period is $136,000 ($100,000 investment + $9,000 share of net liability increase + $27,000 share of profits). If Peggy is a C corporation shareholder instead, her stock basis is $100,000 ($100,000 original investment). If the corporation is an S corporation, Peggy's stock basis is $127,000 ($100,000 + $27,000). ■

EFFECT ON RESULTS OF OPERATIONS

The entity concept is responsible for producing potential double taxation for the C corporation if the corporation is taxed on its earnings, and the shareholders are taxed on the distribution of earnings. Thus, from the perspective of taxing the results of operations, the entity concept appears to provide a disadvantage to corporations. However, whether the entity concept actually produces disadvantageous results depends on the following.

- Whether the corporation generates positive taxable income.
- The tax rates that apply to the corporation and to the shareholders.
- The distribution policy of the corporation.

As discussed previously, techniques exist for getting cash out of the corporation to the shareholders without incurring double taxation (e.g., compensation payments to shareholder-employees, lease payments to shareholder-lessors, and interest payments to shareholder-creditors). Since these payments are deductible to the corporation, they reduce corporate taxable income. If the payments can be used to reduce corporate taxable income to zero, the corporation will have no tax liability.

The maximum individual tax rate (39.6 percent) currently exceeds the maximum corporate tax rate (35 percent). However, at some income levels, the corporate tax rate that applies is less than the applicable individual rate.

Double taxation occurs only if distributions are made to the shareholders. Thus, if no distributions (actual or constructive) are made and if the entity can avoid the accumulated earnings tax (e.g., based on the statutory credit or the reasonable needs adjustment) and the personal holding company tax (e.g., the corporation primarily generates active income), only one current level of taxation will occur. If the distribution can qualify for return of capital rather than dividend treatment, the shareholder tax liability is decreased. Finally, taxation of the earnings at the shareholder level can be avoided permanently if the stock passes through the decedent shareholder's estate.[19]

Application of the entity concept causes income and deductions to lose any unique tax characteristics when they are passed through to shareholders in the form of dividends. This may produce a negative result for net long-term capital gains, because potential beneficial treatment is lost. Since capital gains lose their identity when passed through in the form of dividends, they cannot be used to offset capital losses at the shareholder level. An even more negative result is

---

[18]Recall from Chapter 12 that pass-through S losses can reduce a *shareholder's* basis in loans to the entity.

[19]Recall Chapter 7's analysis of the basis step-up rules for property acquired from a decedent.

produced when dividends are paid out of tax-exempt income. Tax-exempt income is excludible in calculating corporate taxable income, but is included in calculating current earnings and profits. Thus, exclusions from income may be taxed because of the entity concept.

Partnerships, limited liability entities, and S corporations use the conduit concept in reporting the results of operations. Any item that is subject to special treatment on the taxpayer-owner's tax return is reported separately to the owner. Other items are aggregated and reported as taxable income. Thus, taxable income merely represents the sum of income and deductions that are not subject to special treatment.[20]

Many of the problems that the entity concept may produce for the C corporation form are not present in pass-through entities. In particular, pass-through entities are not subjected to double taxation, problems with the reasonableness requirement, or loss of identity of the income or expense item at the owner level.

Only partnerships and limited liability entities completely apply the conduit concept when reporting the results of operations. In several circumstances, the S corporation is subject to taxation at the corporate level, including the tax on built-in gains. This limited application of the entity concept necessitates additional planning to attempt to avoid taxation at the corporate level.

EFFECT ON RECOGNITION AT TIME OF DISTRIBUTION

The application of the conduit concept results in distributions not being taxed to the owners. The application of the entity concept produces the opposite result. Therefore, tax-free distributions can be made to owners of flow-through entities, whereas distributions to C corporation shareholders may be taxable.

A combination entity/conduit concept applies to property distributions from S corporations. The conduit concept applies with respect to the shareholder. However, if the distributed property has appreciated in value, any realized gain is recognized at the corporate level.[21] This is the same treatment received by C corporations. Thus, corporate-level gain recognition is an application of the entity concept, whereas the pass-through of the gain to shareholders is an application of the conduit concept.

EXAMPLE 14

Tan, an S corporation, is equally owned by Leif and Matt. Tan distributes two parcels of land to Leif and Matt. Tan has a basis of $10,000 for each parcel. Each parcel has a fair market value of $15,000. The distribution results in a $10,000 ($30,000 − $20,000) recognized gain for Tan. Leif and Matt each report $5,000 of the gain on their individual income tax returns. ■

Stock redemptions and complete liquidations receive identical treatment whether a C or an S corporation is involved.[22]

EFFECT ON PASSIVE ACTIVITY LOSSES

The passive activity loss rules apply to flow-through entities, personal service corporations, and closely held C corporations. A *closely held C corporation* exists when more than 50 percent of the value of the outstanding stock at any time during the last half of the taxable year is owned by or for not more than five individuals.

20§§ 701, 702, 1363, and 1366.
21§ 311(b).

22§§ 302, 331, and 336.

TAX FACT

PARTNERSHIP INCOME TAX RETURNS: PROFITS VERSUS LOSSES

During the period from 1980 to 2000, the number of partnership income tax returns increased by 50 percent (i.e., from 1.4 million returns to 2.1 million returns). The beneficial tax treatment of LLCs is expected to cause this trend to continue. While the partnership provides a tax shelter opportunity by passing losses through to the partner, a majority of partnerships are profitable.

	1980	1985	1990	1995	1997
% of returns with profits	57%	53%	56%	63%	61%
% of returns with losses	43%	47%	44%	37%	39%

Source: IRS Tax Stats.

A corporation is classified as a *personal service corporation* if the following requirements are satisfied.[23]

- The principal activity of the corporation is the performance of personal services.
- The services are substantially performed by owner-employees.
- Owner-employees own more than 10 percent in value of the stock of the corporation.

The general passive activity loss rules apply to personal service corporations. Therefore, passive activity losses can be offset only against passive activity income. For closely held corporations, the application of the passive activity rules is less harsh. Passive activity losses can be offset against both active and passive income.

Since the conduit concept applies to partnerships, S corporations, and limited liability entities, the passive activity results are separately stated at the entity level and are passed through to the owners with their passive character maintained.

EFFECT OF AT-RISK RULES

The at-risk rules apply to all flow-through entities and to closely held C corporations. The rules produce a harsher result for partnerships and limited liability entities than for S corporations. This occurs because of the way liabilities affect partners' basis.

EXAMPLE 15

Walt is the general partner, and Ira and Vera are the limited partners in the WIV limited partnership. Walt contributes land with an adjusted basis of $40,000 and a fair market value of $50,000 for his partnership interest, and Ira and Vera each contribute cash of $100,000 for their partnership interests. They agree to share profits and losses equally. To finance construction of an apartment building, the partnership obtains $600,000 of nonrecourse financing [not qualified nonrecourse financing under § 465(b)(6)] using the land and the building as the pledged assets. Each partner's basis for the partnership interest is as follows.

---

[23]§ 469, derived from the definition in § 269A.

	Walt	Ira	Vera
Contribution	$ 40,000	$100,000	$100,000
Share of nonrecourse debt	200,000	200,000	200,000
Basis	$240,000	$300,000	$300,000

Without the at-risk rules, Ira and Vera could pass through losses up to $300,000 each even though they invested only $100,000 and have no personal liability for the nonrecourse debt. However, the at-risk rules limit the loss pass-through to the at-risk basis, which is $100,000 for Ira and $100,000 for Vera.

The at-risk rules also affect the general partner. Since Walt is not at risk for the nonrecourse debt, his at-risk basis is $40,000. If the mortgage were recourse debt, his at-risk basis would be $640,000 ($40,000 + $600,000).

If, instead, the entity were an S corporation and Walt received 20% of the stock and Ira and Vera each received 40%, the basis for their stock would be as follows.

Walt	Ira	Vera
$40,000	$100,000	$100,000

In S corporations, nonrecourse debt does not affect the calculation of stock basis. The stock basis for each shareholder would remain the same even if the debt were recourse debt. Only direct loans by the shareholders increase the ceiling on loss pass-through. ■

EFFECT OF SPECIAL ALLOCATIONS

An advantage of the conduit concept over the entity concept is the ability to make special allocations. Special allocations are not permitted in C corporations. Indirectly, however, the corporate form may be able to achieve results similar to those produced by special allocations through payments to owners (e.g., salary payments, lease rental payments, and interest payments) and through different classes of stock (e.g., preferred and common). However, even in these cases, the breadth of the treatment and the related flexibility are far less than that achievable under the conduit concept.

Although S corporations generally operate as conduits, they are treated more like C corporations than partnerships with respect to special allocations. This treatment results from the application of the per-share and per-day allocation rule in § 1377(a). Although S corporations are limited to one class of stock, they still can use salary, interest, and rental payments to owners to shift income to the desired recipient. However, the IRS has the authority to reallocate income among members of a family if fair returns are not provided for services rendered or capital invested.[24]

EXAMPLE 16

The stock of an S corporation is owned by Debra (50%), Helen (25%), and Joyce (25%). Helen and Joyce are Debra's adult children. Debra is subject to a 36% marginal tax rate, and Helen and Joyce have a 15% marginal tax rate. Only Debra is an employee of the corporation. She is paid an annual salary of $20,000, whereas employees with similar responsibilities in other corporations earn $100,000. The corporation generates earnings of approximately $200,000 each year.

It appears that the reason Debra is paid a low salary is to enable more of the earnings of the S corporation to be taxed to Helen and Joyce, who are in lower tax brackets. Thus, the IRS could use its statutory authority to allocate a larger salary to Debra. ■

---

[24]§ 1366(e).

Partnerships and limited liability entities have many opportunities to use special allocations, including the following (refer to Chapter 11).

- The ability to share profits and losses differently from the share in capital.
- The ability to share profits and losses differently.
- A required special allocation for the difference between the adjusted basis and the fair market value of contributed property.
- The special allocation of some items if a substantial economic effect rule is satisfied.

LEARNING OBJECTIVE 6

Analyze the effects of the disposition of a business on the owners and the entity for each of the forms for conducting a business.

Disposition of a Business or an Ownership Interest

A key factor in evaluating the tax consequences of a business disposition is whether the disposition is viewed as the sale of an ownership interest or as a sale of assets. Generally, the tax consequences are more favorable to the seller if the transaction is treated as a sale of the ownership interest.

SOLE PROPRIETORSHIPS

Regardless of the form of the transaction, the sale of a sole proprietorship is treated as the sale of individual assets. Thus, gains and losses must be calculated separately for each asset. Classification as capital gain or ordinary income depends on the nature and holding period of the individual assets. Ordinary income property such as inventory will result in ordinary gains and losses. Section 1231 property such as land, buildings, and machinery used in the business will produce § 1231 gains and losses (subject to depreciation recapture under §§ 1245 and 1250). Capital assets such as investment land and stocks qualify for capital gain or loss treatment.

If the amount realized exceeds the fair market value of the identifiable assets, the excess is allocated to goodwill, which produces capital gain for the seller. If instead the excess payment is allocated to a covenant not to compete, the related gain is classified as ordinary income rather than capital gain. Both goodwill and covenants are amortized over a 15-year statutory period.[25]

EXAMPLE 17

Seth, who is in the 36% tax bracket, sells his sole proprietorship to Wilma for $600,000. The identifiable assets are as follows.

	Adjusted Basis	**Fair Market Value**
Inventory	$ 20,000	$ 25,000
Accounts receivable	40,000	40,000
Machinery and equipment*	125,000	150,000
Buildings**	175,000	250,000
Land	40,000	100,000
	$400,000	$565,000

*Potential § 1245 recapture of $50,000.
**Potential § 1250 recapture of $20,000.

[25]§ 197.

The sale produces the following results for Seth.

	Gain (Loss)	Ordinary Income	§ 1231 Gain	Capital Gain
Inventory	$ 5,000	$ 5,000		
Accounts receivable	–0–			
Machinery and equipment	25,000	25,000		
Buildings	75,000	20,000	$ 55,000	
Land	60,000		60,000	
Goodwill	35,000			$35,000
	$200,000	$50,000	$115,000	$35,000

If the sale is structured this way, Wilma can deduct the $35,000 paid for goodwill over a 15-year period. If instead Wilma paid the $35,000 to Seth for a covenant not to compete for a period of seven years, she still would amortize the $35,000 over a 15-year period. However, Seth's $35,000 capital gain would now be taxed to him as ordinary income. If the covenant has no legal relevance to Wilma, in exchange for treating the payment as a goodwill payment, she should negotiate for a price reduction that reflects Seth's benefit from the lower capital gains tax. ■

PARTNERSHIPS AND LIMITED LIABILITY ENTITIES

The sale of a partnership or limited liability entity can be structured as the sale of assets or as the sale of an ownership interest. If the transaction takes the form of an asset sale, it is treated the same as for a sole proprietorship. The sale of an ownership interest is treated as the sale of a capital asset, although ordinary income potential exists for unrealized receivables and substantially appreciated inventory. Thus, if capital gain treatment can produce beneficial results for the taxpayer (e.g., he or she has capital losses to offset or has beneficially treated net capital gain), the sale of an ownership interest is preferable.

From a buyer's perspective, tax consequences are not affected by the form of the transaction. If the transaction is an asset purchase, the basis for the assets equals the amount paid. If a buyer intends to continue to operate as an LLC or a partnership, the assets can be contributed to the entity under § 721. Therefore, the owner's basis in the entity interest is equal to the purchase price for the assets. Likewise, if ownership interests are purchased, the owner's basis is the purchase price paid. The partnership's basis for the assets is the purchase price since the original partnership will have terminated.[26]

When the inside and outside basis of a partner's ownership interest differ (see Chapter 9), an election can be made to step up the partner's share of the entity's asset bases.[27] This tax-free basis step-up applies to all such exchanges by all of the partners as long as the election is in effect. The election allows asset basis to reflect increases in fair market value and the goodwill that a new partner has purchased.

---

[26]§ 708(b)(1)(B).   [27]§ 754.

EXAMPLE 18

Roz buys a one-third interest in the RST Partnership for $50,000 (outside basis). All of the entity's assets are depreciable, and their basis to the partnership (inside basis) is $90,000. If a § 754 election is in effect, the partnership can step up the basis of its depreciable assets by $20,000, the difference between Roz's outside and inside basis amounts [$50,000 – (⅓ × $90,000)]. All of the "new" asset basis is allocated to Roz. ■

C CORPORATIONS

The sale of a business held by a C corporation can be structured as either an asset sale or a stock sale. The stock sale has the dual advantage to the seller of being less complex both as a legal transaction and as a tax transaction. It also has the advantage of providing a way to avoid double taxation. Finally, any gain or loss on the sale of the stock is treated as a capital gain or loss to the shareholder.

EXAMPLE 19

Jane and Zina each own 50% of the stock of Purple Corporation. They have owned the business for 10 years. Jane's basis in her stock is $40,000, and Zina's basis in her stock is $60,000. They agree to sell the stock to Rex for $300,000. Jane recognizes a long-term capital gain of $110,000 ($150,000 – $40,000), and Zina recognizes a long-term capital gain of $90,000 ($150,000 – $60,000). Rex has a basis in his stock of $300,000. Purple's basis in its assets does not change as a result of the stock sale. ■

PLANNING CONSIDERATIONS

Selling Stock or Assets

Structuring the sale of the business as a stock sale may produce detrimental tax results for the purchaser. As Example 19 illustrates, the basis of the corporation's assets is not affected by the stock sale. If the fair market value of the stock exceeds the corporation's adjusted basis for its assets, the purchaser is denied the opportunity to step up the basis of the assets to reflect the amount in effect paid for them through the stock acquisition—no § 754 election is available to C corporations.

For an asset sale, the seller of the business can be either the corporation or its shareholders. If the seller is the corporation, the corporation sells the business (the assets), pays any debts not transferred, and makes a liquidating distribution to the shareholders. If the sellers are the shareholders, the corporation pays any debts that will not be transferred and makes a liquidating distribution to the shareholders; then the shareholders sell the business.

Regardless of the approach used for an asset sale, double taxation will occur. The corporation is taxed on the actual sale of the assets and is taxed as if it had sold the assets when it makes the liquidating distribution to the shareholders

who then sell the distributed assets. The shareholders are taxed when they receive cash or assets distributed in-kind by the corporation.

The asset sale resolves the purchaser's problem of not being able to step up the basis of the assets to their fair market value. The basis for each asset is its purchase price. To operate in corporate form (assuming the purchaser is not a corporation), the purchaser needs to transfer the property to a corporation in a § 351 transaction.

From the perspective of the seller, the ideal form of the transaction is a stock sale. Conversely, from the purchaser's perspective, the ideal form is an asset purchase. Double taxation seldom can be avoided in either case. Therefore, the bargaining ability of the seller and the purchaser to structure the sale as a stock sale or an asset sale, respectively, is critical.

Rather than selling the entire business, an owner may sell only his or her ownership interest. Since the form of the transaction is a stock sale, the results for the selling shareholder will be the same as if all the shareholders had sold their stock (i.e., capital gain or capital loss).

IS THE STATE OF INCORPORATION SIGNIFICANT IN DETERMINING INVESTOR VALUE?

Many variables affect the value of a company's stock. Research by Robert Daines, a law professor at New York University, raises the issue of the state of incorporation as a variable.

A corporation can incorporate in any state regardless of the location of its corporate headquarters. More than 50 percent of publicly held companies are incorporated in Delaware.

Professor Daines concludes that companies incorporated in Delaware are valued more by the stock market than companies incorporated elsewhere. His study suggests that this results from Delaware's anti-takeover laws being less stringent (i.e., easier to complete a hostile takeover) than those in other states (e.g., Ohio, Pennsylvania, Massachusetts).

According to Professor Daines, among the reasons Delaware companies are more valuable is the higher likelihood of receiving a takeover bid. Delaware companies receive more takeover bids than those incorporated elsewhere. Companies incorporated in states with more significant barriers to hostile takeover are both worth less and receive fewer takeover bids.

Some readers of Professor Daines' study raise "the chicken and the egg" issue. That is, do highly valued companies choose to incorporate in Delaware, or is the value of companies higher because they are incorporated in Delaware?

SOURCE: Adapted from Steven Lipin, "Firms Incorporated in Delaware Are Valued More by Investors," *Wall Street Journal*, February 28, 2000, p. C21.

S CORPORATIONS

Since the S corporation is a corporation, it is subject to the provisions for a C corporation discussed previously. Either an asset sale at the corporate level or a liquidating distribution of assets produces recognition at the corporate level. However, under the conduit concept applicable to the S corporation, the recognized amount is taxed at the shareholder level. Therefore, double taxation is avoided directly (only the shareholder is involved) for a stock sale and indirectly (the conduit concept ignores the involvement of the corporation) for an asset sale.

Double taxation might seem to be avoided by making an S corporation election prior to the liquidation of a C corporation, but the built-in gains tax closes this loophole; taxation occurs at the corporate level, and double taxation results.

Concept Summary 14–1 summarizes the tax consequences of business dispositions.

Overall Comparison of Forms of Doing Business

Concept Summary 14–2 provides a detailed comparison of the tax consequences of the various forms of doing business.

CONCEPT SUMMARY 14–1

Tax Treatment of Disposition of a Business

Form of Entity	Form of Transaction	Tax Consequences	
		Seller	Buyer
Sole proprietorship	Sale of individual assets.	Gain or loss is calculated separately for the individual assets. Classification as capital or ordinary depends on the nature and holding period of the individual assets. If amount realized exceeds the fair market value of the identifiable assets, the excess is allocated to goodwill (except to the extent identified with a covenant not to compete), which is a capital asset.	Basis for individual assets is the allocated cost. Prefers that any excess of purchase price over the fair market value of identifiable assets be identified with a covenant not to compete if the covenant has legal utility. Otherwise, the buyer is neutral since both goodwill and covenants are amortized over a 15-year statutory period.
	Sale of the business.	Treated as a sale of the individual assets (as above).	Treated as a purchase of the individual assets (as above).
Partnership and limited liability entity	Sale of individual assets.	Treatment is the same as for the sole proprietorship.	Treatment is the same as for the sole proprietorship. If the intent is to operate in partnership form, the assets can be contributed to a partnership under § 721.
	Sale of ownership interest.	Entity interest is treated as the sale of a capital asset (subject to ordinary income potential for unrealized receivables and substantially appreciated inventory).	Basis for new owner's ownership interest is the cost. The new entity's basis for the assets is also the pertinent cost (i.e., contributed to the entity under § 721), since the original entity will have terminated.
C corporation	Sale of corporate assets by corporation (i.e., corporation sells assets, pays debts, and makes liquidating distribution to the shareholders).	Double taxation occurs. Corporation is taxed on the sale of the assets with the gain or loss determination and the classification as capital or ordinary treated the same as for the sole proprietorship. Shareholders calculate gain or loss as the difference between the stock basis and the amount received from the corporation in the liquidating distribution. Capital gain or loss usually results, since stock typically is a capital asset.	Basis for individual assets is the allocated cost. If the intent is to operate in corporate form, the assets can be contributed to a corporation under § 351.
	Sale of corporate assets by the shareholders (i.e., corporation pays debts and makes liquidating distribution to the shareholders).	Double taxation occurs. At the time of the liquidating distribution to the shareholders, the corporation is taxed as if it had sold the assets. Shareholders calculate gain or loss as the difference between the stock basis and the fair market value of the assets received from the corporation in the liquidating distribution. Capital gain or loss usually results, since stock typically is a capital asset.	Same as corporate asset sale.

Form of Entity	Form of Transaction	Tax Consequences	
		Seller	Buyer
C corporation (continued)	Sale of corporate stock.	Enables double taxation to be avoided. Since the corporation is not a party to the transaction, there are no tax consequences at the corporate level. Shareholders calculate gain or loss as the difference between the stock basis and the amount received for the stock. Capital gain or loss usually results, since stock typically is a capital asset.	Basis for the stock is its cost. The basis for the corporate assets is not affected by the stock purchase.
S corporation	Sale of corporate assets by corporation.	Recognition occurs at the corporate level on the sale of the assets, with the gain or loss determination and the classification as capital or ordinary treated the same as for the sole proprietorship. Conduit concept applicable to the S corporation results in the recognized amount being taxed at the shareholder level. Double taxation associated with the asset sale is avoided, because the shareholder's stock basis is increased by the amount of gain recognition and decreased by the amount of loss recognition. Shareholders calculate gain or loss as the difference between the stock basis and the amount received from the corporation in the liquidating distribution. Capital gain or loss usually results, since stock typically is a capital asset.	Basis for individual assets is the allocated cost. If the intent is to operate in corporate form (i.e., as an S corporation), the assets can be contributed to a corporation under § 351.
	Sale of corporate assets by the shareholders.	At the time of the liquidating distribution to the shareholders, recognition occurs at the corporation level as if the corporation had sold the assets. The resultant tax consequences for the shareholders and the corporation are the same as for the sale of corporate assets by the S corporation.	Same as corporate asset sale by the corporation.
	Sale of corporate stock.	Same as the treatment for the sale of stock of a C corporation.	Same as the treatment for the purchase of stock of a C corporation.

CONCEPT SUMMARY 14–2

Tax Attributes of Different Forms of Business (Assume Partners and Shareholders Are All Individuals)

	Sole Proprietorship	Partnership/Limited Liability Entity	S Corporation	C Corporation
Restrictions on type or number of owners	One owner. The owner must be an individual.	Must have at least 2 owners.	Only individuals, estates, and certain trusts can be owners. Maximum number of shareholders limited to 75.	None, except some states require a minimum of 2 shareholders.
Incidence of tax	Sole proprietorship's income and deductions are reported on Schedule C of the individual's Form 1040. A separate Schedule C is prepared for each business.	Entity not subject to tax. Owners in their separate capacity subject to tax on their distributive share of income. Entity files Form 1065.	Except for certain built-in gains and passive investment income when earnings and profits are present from C corporation tax years, entity not subject to Federal income tax. S corporation files Form 1120S. Shareholders are subject to tax on income attributable to their stock ownership.	Income subject to double taxation. Entity subject to tax, and shareholder subject to tax on any corporate dividends received. Corporation files Form 1120.
Highest tax rate	39.6% at individual level.	39.6% at owner level.	39.6% at shareholder level.	35% at corporate level plus 39.6% on any corporate dividends at shareholder level.
Choice of tax year	Same tax year as owner.	Selection generally restricted to coincide with tax year of majority owners or principal owners, or to tax year determined under the least aggregate deferral method.	Restricted to a calendar year unless IRS approves a different year for business purposes or other exceptions apply.	Unrestricted selection allowed at time of filing first tax return.
Timing of taxation	Based on owner's tax year.	Owners report their share of income in their tax year within which the entity's tax year ends. Owners in their separate capacities are subject to payment of estimated taxes.	Shareholders report their shares of income in their tax year within which the corporation's tax year ends. Generally, the corporation uses a calendar year, but see "Choice of tax year." Shareholders may be subject to payment of estimated taxes. Corporation may be subject to payment of estimated taxes for the taxes imposed at the corporate level.	Corporation subject to tax at close of its tax year. May be subject to payment of estimated taxes. Dividends are subject to tax at the shareholder level in the tax year received.

	Sole Proprietorship	Partnership/Limited Liability Entity	S Corporation	C Corporation
Basis for allocating income to owners	Not applicable (only one owner).	Profit and loss sharing agreement. Cash basis items of cash basis entities are allocated on a daily basis. Other entity items are allocated after considering varying interests of owners.	Pro rata share based on stock ownership. Shareholder's pro rata share is determined on a daily basis, according to the number of shares of stock held on each day of the corporation's tax year.	Not applicable.
Contribution of property to the entity	Not a taxable transaction.	Generally not a taxable transaction.	Is a taxable transaction unless the § 351 requirements are satisfied.	Is a taxable transaction unless the § 351 requirements are satisfied.
Character of income taxed to owners	Retains source characteristics.	Conduit—retains source characteristics.	Conduit—retains source characteristics.	All source characteristics are lost when income is distributed to owners.
Basis for allocating a net operating loss to owners	Not applicable (only one owner).	Profit and loss sharing agreement. Cash basis items of cash basis entities are allocated on a daily basis. Other entity items are allocated after considering varying interests of owners.	Prorated among shareholders on a daily basis.	Not applicable.
Limitation on losses deductible by owners	Investment plus liabilities.	Owner's investment plus share of liabilities.	Shareholder's investment plus loans made by shareholder to corporation.	Not applicable.
Subject to at-risk rules?	Yes, at the owner level. Indefinite carryover of excess loss.	Yes, at the owner level. Indefinite carryover of excess loss.	Yes, at the shareholder level. Indefinite carryover of excess loss.	Yes, for closely held corporations. Indefinite carryover of excess loss.
Subject to passive activity loss rules?	Yes, at the owner level. Indefinite carryover of excess loss.	Yes, at the owner level. Indefinite carryover of excess loss.	Yes, at the shareholder level. Indefinite carryover of excess loss.	Yes, for closely held corporations and personal service corporations. Indefinite carryover of excess loss.
Tax consequences of earnings retained by entity	Taxed to owner when earned and increases his or her investment in the sole proprietorship.	Taxed to owners when earned and increases their respective interest bases in the entity.	Taxed to shareholders when earned and increases their respective interest bases in stock.	Taxed to corporation when earned and may be subject to penalty tax if accumulated unreasonably.

	Sole Proprietorship	Partnership/Limited Liability Entity	S Corporation	C Corporation
Nonliquidating distributions to owners	Not taxable.	Not taxable unless money received exceeds recipient owner's basis in entity interest. Existence of § 751 assets may cause recognition of ordinary income.	Generally not taxable unless the distribution exceeds the shareholder's AAA or stock basis. Existence of accumulated earnings and profits could cause some distributions to be dividends.	Taxable in year of receipt to extent of earnings and profits or if exceeds basis in stock.
Capital gains	Taxed at owner level using maximum rate of 20%, 25%, or 28%.	Conduit—owners must account for their respective shares. Taxed at owner level.	Conduit, with certain exceptions (a possible penalty tax)—shareholders must account for their respective shares. Tax treatment determined at shareholder level.	Taxed at corporate level with a maximum 35% rate. No other benefits.
Capital losses	Only $3,000 of capital losses can be offset each tax year against ordinary income. Indefinite carryover.	Conduit—owners must account for their respective shares. Tax treatment determined at owner level.	Conduit—shareholders must account for their respective shares. Tax treatment determined at shareholder level.	Carried back three years and carried forward five years. Deductible only to the extent of capital gains.
§ 1231 gains and losses	Taxable or deductible at owner level. Five-year lookback rule for § 1231 losses.	Conduit—owners must account for their respective shares. Tax treatment determined at owner level.	Conduit—shareholders must account for their respective shares. Tax treatment determined at shareholder level.	Taxable or deductible at corporate level only. Five-year lookback rule for § 1231 losses.
Foreign tax credits	Available at owner level.	Conduit—tax payments passed through to owners.	Generally conduit—tax payments passed through to shareholders.	Available at corporate level only.
§ 1244 treatment of loss on sale of interest	Not applicable.	Not applicable.	Available.	Available.
Basis treatment of entity liabilities	Not applicable.	Includible in interest basis.	Not includible in stock basis.	Not includible in stock basis.
Built-in gains	Not applicable.	Not applicable.	Possible corporate tax.	Not applicable.
Special allocations to owners	Not applicable (only one owner).	Available if supported by substantial economic effect.	Not available.	Not applicable.
Availability of fringe benefits to owners	None.	None.	None unless a 2% or less shareholder.	Available within antidiscrimination rules.
Effect of liquidation/ redemption/ reorganization on basis of entity assets	Not applicable.	Usually carried over from entity to owner.	Taxable step-up to fair market value.	Taxable step-up to fair market value.

	Sole Proprietorship	Partnership/Limited Liability Entity	S Corporation	C Corporation
Sale of ownership interest	Treated as the sale of individual assets. Classification of recognized gain or loss depends on the nature of the individual assets.	Treated as the sale of an entity interest. Recognized gain or loss is classified as capital, although appreciated inventory and receivables are subject to ordinary income treatment.	Treated as the sale of corporate stock. Recognized gain is classified as capital gain. Recognized loss is classified as capital loss, subject to ordinary loss treatment under § 1244.	Treated as the sale of corporate stock. Recognized gain is classified as capital gain. Recognized loss is classified as capital loss, subject to ordinary loss treatment under § 1244.
Distribution of appreciated property	Not taxable.	No recognition at the entity level.	Recognition at the corporate level to the extent of the appreciation. Conduit—amount of recognized gain is passed through to shareholders.	Taxable at the corporate level to the extent of the appreciation.
Splitting of income among family members	Not applicable (only one owner).	Difficult—IRS will not recognize a family member as an owner unless certain requirements are met.	Rather easy—gift of stock will transfer tax on a pro rata share of income to the donee. However, IRS can make adjustments to reflect adequate compensation for services.	Same as an S corporation, except that donees will be subject to tax only on earnings actually or constructively distributed to them. Other than unreasonable compensation, IRS generally cannot make adjustments to reflect adequate compensation for services and capital.
Organizational costs	Start-up expenditures are amortizable over 60 months.	Amortizable over 60 months.	Same as partnership.	Same as partnership.
Charitable contributions	Limitations apply at owner level.	Conduit—owners are subject to deduction limitations in their own capacities.	Conduit—shareholders are subject to deduction limitations in their own capacities.	Limited to 10% of taxable income before certain deductions.
Alternative minimum tax	Applies at owner level. AMT rates are 26% and 28%.	Applies at the owner level rather than at the entity level. AMT preferences and adjustments are passed through from the entity to the owners.	Applies at the shareholder level rather than at the corporate level. AMT preferences and adjustments are passed through from the S corporation to the shareholders.	Applies at the corporate level. AMT rate is 20%. Modest-sized C corporations are exempt.
ACE adjustment	Does not apply.	Does not apply.	Does not apply.	The adjustment is made in calculating AMTI. The adjustment is 75% of the excess of adjusted current earnings over unadjusted AMTI. If the unadjusted AMTI exceeds adjusted current earnings, the adjustment may be negative.

PLANNING CONSIDERATIONS

Choosing a Business Form: Case Study

The chapter began with an example that illustrated the relationship between tax planning and the choice of business form; it also raised a variety of questions about the advice given by the tax practitioner. By this time, one should be able to develop various scenarios supporting the tax advice given. The actual fact situations that produced the tax adviser's recommendations were as follows.

- Jesse's experience in the dairy industry consists of raising a few heifers during the final five years of his employment. Eva anticipates that Jesse will generate tax losses for the indeterminate future. In addition, Jesse indicated that he and his wife must have limited liability associated with the dairy farm.
- Larry was born and raised on his father's dairy farm. Both his education and his Air Force managerial experience provide him with useful tools for managing his business. However, Larry inherited his farm when milk prices were at a low for the modern era. Since none of her dairy farm clients were profitable, Eva anticipated Larry would operate his dairy farm at a loss. Larry, like Jesse, felt that limited liability was imperative. Thus, he incorporated the dairy farm and made the S corporation election.
- For the first two years, Larry's dairy farm produced tax losses. Since then, the dairy farm has produced tax

profits large enough to absorb the losses. Larry anticipates that his profits will remain relatively stable in the $50,000 to $75,000 range in the future. Since he is subject to a 31 percent marginal tax rate and anticipates that no dividend distributions will be made, his tax liability associated with the dairy farm will be reduced if he terminates the S corporation election.

As Jesse and Larry's example illustrates, selection of the proper business form can result in both nontax and tax advantages. Both of these factors should be considered in making the selection decision. Furthermore, this choice should be reviewed periodically, since a proper business form at one point in time may not be the proper form at a different time. Note that another business form Eva could have considered for Jesse is the limited liability entity.

In looking at the tax attributes, consideration should be given to the tax consequences of the following.

- Contribution of assets to the entity by the owners at the time the entity is created and at later dates.
- Taxation of the results of operations.
- Distributions to owners.
- Disposition of an ownership interest.
- Termination of the entity.

Suggested Further Readings

Hughlene A. Burton and Stewart S. Karlinsky, "S Corporations: Current Developments," *The Tax Adviser*, October 2000, pp. 722–731.

Gary L. Maydew, "Determining Reasonable Compensation: A Review of *Alpha Medical* and Other Recent Decisions," *Taxes: The Tax Magazine*, December 1999, pp. 23–29.

Ed Rigby, "Significance of the 'Choice of Entity' Decision for Business Owners," (Tax Clinic), *The Tax Adviser*, August 1999, pp. 557–558.

KEY TERMS

Conduit concept, 14–15

Entity concept, 14–15

Limited liability company (LLC), 14–4

Unreasonable compensation, 14–12

Problem Materials

PROBLEMS

1. Using the legend provided, indicate which form of business entity each of the following characteristics describes. Some of the characteristics may apply to more than one form of business entity.

Legend	
SP =	Applies to sole proprietorship
P =	Applies to partnership and LLC
S =	Applies to S corporation
C =	Applies to C corporation

   a. Has limited liability.
   b. Greatest ability to raise capital.
   c. Subject to double taxation.
   d. Subject to accumulated earnings tax.
   e. Limit on types and number of shareholders.
   f. Has unlimited liability.
   g. Sale of the business can be subject to double taxation.
   h. Contribution of property to the entity in exchange for an ownership interest can result in the nonrecognition of realized gain.

2. Using the legend provided, indicate which form of business entity each of the following characteristics describes. Some of the characteristics may apply to more than one form of business entity.

Legend	
P =	Applies to partnership and LLC
S =	Applies to S corporation
C =	Applies to C corporation

   a. Basis for an ownership interest is increased by an investment by the owner.
   b. Basis for an ownership interest is decreased by a distribution to the owner.
   c. Basis for an ownership interest is increased by entity profits.
   d. Basis for an ownership interest is decreased by entity losses.
   e. Basis for an ownership interest is increased as the entity's liabilities increase.
   f. Basis for an ownership interest is decreased as the entity's liabilities decrease.

3. A business entity has the following assets and liabilities on its balance sheet.

	Net Book Value	Fair Market Value
Assets	$675,000	$950,000
Liabilities	100,000	100,000

   The business entity has just lost a product liability suit with damages of $5 million being awarded to the plaintiff. Although the business entity will appeal the judgment, legal counsel indicates the judgment is highly unlikely to be overturned by the appellate court. The product liability insurance carried by the business has a policy ceiling of $3 million. What is the amount of liability of the entity and its owners if the form of the business entity is:
   a. A sole proprietorship?
   b. A partnership or LLC?

c. A C corporation?

d. An S corporation?

4. Ted is the managing partner of a regional accounting firm. Like many accounting firms, Ted's firm has expended considerable resources in defending itself against various liability claims, many of which are spurious.

   Ted is meeting with the firm's management committee this afternoon. On the agenda is a continuing discussion of ways to deal with liability issues. Ted has held private discussions with several members of the committee about changing the ownership form from a partnership to a Delaware limited liability company. All of the partners except Albert regard an LLC as a positive option. Albert, a founding partner of the firm who is approaching retirement, has vehemently argued that a professional accounting firm serves the public interest and that operation as an LLC is in conflict with that objective and the related public perception. As a member of the management committee, what position will you take? Why?

5. Red, White, Blue, and Orange generate taxable income as follows.

Corporation	Taxable Income
Red	$ 95,000
White	300,000
Blue	700,000
Orange	30,000,000

   a. Calculate the marginal and effective tax rates for each of the C corporations.
   b. Explain why the marginal tax rate for a C corporation can exceed 35%, but the effective tax rate cannot do so.

6. Amy and Jeff Barnes are going to operate their florist shop as a partnership or as an S corporation. Their mailing address is 5700 Richmond Highway, Alexandria, VA 22300. After paying salaries of $45,000 to each of the owners, the shop's earnings are projected to be about $60,000. The earnings are to be invested in the growth of the business. Write a letter to Amy and Jeff advising them of which of the two entity forms they should select.

7. Gary is an entrepreneur who likes to be actively involved in his business ventures. He is going to invest $400,000 in a business that he projects will produce a tax loss of approximately $75,000 per year in the short run. However, once consumers become aware of the new product being sold by the business and the quality of the service it provides, he is confident the business will generate a profit of at least $100,000 per year. Gary has substantial other income (from both business ventures and investment activities) each year. Advise Gary on the business form he should select for the short run. He will be the sole owner.

8. Jack, an unmarried taxpayer, is going to establish a manufacturing business. He anticipates that the business will be profitable immediately due to a patent that he holds. He anticipates that profits for the first year will be about $200,000 and will increase at a rate of about 20% per year for the foreseeable future. He will be the sole owner of the business. Advise Jack on the form of business entity he should select. Jack will be in the 36% tax bracket.

9. Silver Corporation will begin operations on January 1. Earnings for the next five years are projected to be relatively stable at about $100,000 per year. The shareholders of Silver are in the 31% tax bracket.

   a. Silver will reinvest its after-tax earnings in the growth of the company. Should Silver operate as a C corporation or as an S corporation?
   b. Silver will distribute its after-tax earnings each year to its shareholders. Should Silver operate as a C corporation or as an S corporation?

10. Mabel and Alan, who are in the 36% tax bracket, recently acquired a fast-food franchise. Both of them will work in the business and receive a salary of $100,000. They anticipate

that the annual profits of the business, after deducting salaries, will be approximately $500,000. The entity will distribute enough cash each year to Mabel and Alan to cover their Federal income taxes associated with the franchise.

   a. What amount will the entity distribute if the franchise operates as a C corporation?

   b. What amount will the entity distribute if the franchise operates as an S corporation?

   c. What will be the amount of the combined entity/owner tax liability in (a) and (b)?

11. Cardinal is a closely held corporation owned by 10 shareholders (each has 10% of the stock). Selected financial information provided by Cardinal follows.

Taxable income	$7,000,000
Positive AMT adjustments (excluding ACE adjustment)	250,000
Negative AMT adjustments	(15,000)
Tax preferences	6,000,000
Retained earnings	750,000
Accumulated E & P	615,000
ACE adjustment	590,000

   a. Calculate Cardinal's tax liability as a C corporation.

   b. Calculate Cardinal's tax liability as an S corporation.

   c. How would your answers in (a) and (b) change if Cardinal is not closely held (e.g., 5,000 shareholders with no shareholder owning more than 2% of the stock)?

12. Pelican Corporation, an offshore drilling company, is going to sell land and an equipment warehouse that it no longer needs. The real estate is located at 200 Brando Row, Grand Isle, LA 70535. The adjusted basis for the real estate is $400,000 ($700,000 – $300,000 straight-line depreciation), and the fair market value is $500,000. ADS straight-line depreciation would have been $275,000. The buyer of the real estate would like to close the transaction prior to the end of the calendar year. Pelican is uncertain whether the tax consequences would be better if it sold the real estate this year or next year and is considering the following options.

- $500,000 in cash payable on December 31, 2001.

- The sale will be closed on December 31, 2001, with the consideration being a $500,000 note issued by the buyer. The maturity date of the note is January 2, 2002, with the real estate being pledged as security.

Pelican projects its taxable income for 2001 and 2002 to be $600,000 (gross receipts of $8.5 million) without the sale of the real estate. Pelican's accounting period is the calendar year. Determine the tax consequences to Pelican under either option and recommend which option Pelican should select. Send your recommendation to Corey Longwell, Pelican's tax director, whose office is at the warehouse.

13. Heron Corporation has been in operation for 10 years. Since Heron's creation, all of the stock has been owned by Andy, who initially invested $200,000 in the corporation. Heron has been successful far beyond Andy's expectations, and the current fair market value of the stock is $10 million. While he has been paid a salary of $200,000 per year by the corporation, all of Heron's earnings have been reinvested in the growth of the corporation.

Heron is currently being audited by the IRS. One of the issues raised by the IRS agent is the possibility of the assessment of the accumulated earnings tax. Andy is not concerned about this issue because he believes Heron can easily justify the accumulations based on its past rapid expansion by opening new outlets. The expansion program is fully documented in the minutes of Heron's board of directors. Andy has provided this information to the IRS agent.

Two years ago, Andy decided that he would curtail any further expansion into new markets by Heron. In his opinion, further expansion would exceed his ability to manage the corporation effectively. Since the tax year under audit is three years ago, Andy sees no reason to provide the IRS agent with this information.

Heron will continue its policy of no dividend payments into the foreseeable future. Andy believes that if the accumulated earnings issue is satisfactorily resolved on this audit, it probably will not be raised again on any subsequent audits. Thus, double taxation in the form of the tax on dividends at the shareholder level or the accumulated earnings tax at the corporate level can be avoided.

What is Heron's responsibility to disclose to the IRS agent the expected change in its growth strategy? Are Andy's beliefs regarding future accumulated earnings tax issues realistic?

14. Two unmarried brothers own and operate a farm. They live on the farm and take their meals on the farm for the "convenience of the employer." The fair market value of their lodging is $20,000, and the fair market value of their meals is $12,000. The meals are prepared for them by the farm cook who prepares their meals along with those of the five other farm employees.
    a. Determine the tax consequences of the meals and lodging to the brothers if the farm is incorporated.
    b. Determine the tax consequences of the meals and lodging to the brothers if the farm is not incorporated.

15. A business entity's taxable income before the cost of certain fringe benefits paid to owners and other employees is $400,000. The amounts paid for these fringe benefits are as follows.

	Owners	**Other Employees**
Group term life insurance	$20,000	$40,000
Meals and lodging incurred for the convenience of the employer	50,000	75,000
Pension plan	30,000*	90,000

*H.R. 10 (Keogh) plan for partnership and S corporation.

The business entity is equally owned by four owners.
    a. Calculate the taxable income of the business entity if the entity is a partnership, a C corporation, or an S corporation.
    b. Determine the effect on the owners for each of the three business forms.

16. Fawn, a C corporation, has taxable income of $400,000 before paying salaries to the two shareholder-employees, Gus and Janet. Fawn follows a policy of distributing all after-tax earnings to the shareholders.
    a. Determine the tax consequences for Fawn, Gus, and Janet if the corporation pays salaries to Gus and Janet as follows.

Option 1		**Option 2**	
Gus	$240,000	Gus	$90,000
Janet	160,000	Janet	60,000

    b. Is Fawn likely to encounter any tax problems associated with either option?

17. Swallow, a C corporation, is owned by Sandra (50%) and Fran (50%). Sandra is the president, and Fran is the vice president for sales. Late in 2000, Swallow encounters working capital difficulties. Thus, Sandra and Fran each loan the corporation $200,000 on a 9% note that is due in five years with interest payable annually.
    a. Determine the tax consequences to Swallow, Sandra, and Fran for 2001 if the notes are classified as debt.
    b. Determine the tax consequences to Swallow, Sandra, and Fran for 2001 if the notes are classified as equity.

18. Liane owns land and a building that she has been using in her sole proprietorship. She is going to incorporate her sole proprietorship as a C corporation. Liane must decide whether to contribute the land and building to the corporation or to lease them to the corporation. The net income of the sole proprietorship for the past five years has averaged $200,000. Advise Liane on the tax consequences. Summarize your analysis in a memo to the tax file.

19. Marci and Jennifer each own 50% of the stock of Lavender, a C corporation. After paying each of them a "reasonable" salary of $125,000, the taxable income of Lavender is normally around $600,000. The corporation is about to purchase a $2,000,000 shopping mall ($1,500,000 allocated to the building and $500,000 allocated to the land). The mall will be rented to tenants at a net rental rate (including rental commissions, depreciation, etc.) of $500,000 annually. Marci and Jennifer will contribute $1 million each to the corporation to provide the cash required for the acquisition. Their CPA has suggested that Marci and Jennifer purchase the shopping mall as individuals and lease it to Lavender for a fair rental of $300,000. Both Marci and Jennifer are in the 39.6% tax bracket. The acquisition will occur on January 2, 2001. Determine whether the shopping mall should be acquired by Lavender or by Marci and Jennifer in accordance with their CPA's recommendation. Depreciation on the shopping mall in 2001 is $37,000.

20. Rose, Inc., has taxable income of $400,000. Rose has been in business for many years and long ago used up the accumulated earnings credit. Rose has no additional "reasonable needs of the business" for the current tax year.
    a. Determine the total potential tax liability for Rose if it declares no dividends.
    b. Determine the total potential tax liability for Rose if it declares and pays dividends equal to the after-tax earnings.

21. Pigeon, Inc., distributes land to Tim in a transaction that qualifies as a stock redemption. Pigeon's basis for the land is $10,000, and the fair market value is $75,000. Tim surrenders shares of stock that have a basis of $30,000. After the redemption, Tim owns 10% of the stock of Pigeon, Inc.
    a. Determine the tax consequences to Pigeon, Inc., and Tim if Pigeon, Inc., is a C corporation.
    b. Determine the tax consequences to Pigeon, Inc., and Tim if Pigeon, Inc., is an S corporation.

22. Tan, Inc., a C corporation that has been in existence for five years, has accumulated E & P of $990,000. It projects future earnings to continue at about $200,000 per year. David, Tan's sole shareholder and CEO, receives an annual salary of $400,000. David would like Tan to continue its current dividend policy. What issues do David and Tan need to consider if their objective is to avoid double taxation?

23. Tammy and Arnold own 40% of the stock of Roadrunner, an S corporation. The other 60% is owned by 74 other family members. Tammy and Arnold have agreed to a divorce and are in the process of negotiating a property settlement. Identify the relevant tax issues for Tammy and Arnold.

24. Eagle Corporation has been an electing S corporation since its incorporation 10 years ago. During the first three years of operations, it incurred total losses of $250,000. Since then Eagle has generated earnings of approximately $150,000 each year. None of the earnings have been distributed to the three equal shareholders, Claire, Lynn, and Todd, because the corporation has been in an expansion mode. At the beginning of 2001, Claire sells her stock to Nell for $400,000. Nell has reservations about the utility of the S election. Therefore, Lynn, Todd, and Nell are discussing whether the election should be continued. They expect the earnings to remain at approximately $150,000 each year. However, since they perceive that the company's expansion period is over and Eagle has adequate working capital, they may start distributing the earnings to the shareholders. All of the shareholders are in the 31% tax bracket. Advise the three shareholders on whether the S election should be maintained.

25. Bob and Carl Pierce each own 50% of the stock of Deer, Inc., a C corporation. When the corporation was organized, Bob contributed cash of $90,000, and Carl contributed land with an adjusted basis of $60,000 and a fair market value of $115,000. Deer assumed Carl's $25,000 mortgage on the land. In addition to the capital contributions, Bob and Carl each loaned the corporation $50,000. The maturity date of the loan is in 10 years, and the interest rate is 12%, the same as the Federal rate.
    a. Determine the tax consequences to Bob, Carl, and Deer of the initial contribution of assets, the shareholder loans, and the annual interest payments if the loans are classified as debt.
    b. Determine the tax consequences if the loans are reclassified as equity.
    c. You met with Bob at lunch to discuss the tax consequences of the capital contributions and loans made by Carl and him to Deer, Inc. Prepare a memo for the files on your discussion.

26. Buddy and Bobby form a business entity with each contributing the following property.

	Buddy	Bobby
Cash	$100,000	
Land		$100,000*

*Fair market value. Adjusted basis is $80,000.

    Four months later, the land is sold for $110,000 because the local commission refused to rezone the land from residential to commercial. The proceeds are to be applied toward the purchase of another parcel of land to be used for real estate development. Determine the tax consequences to the entity and to the owners from the formation of the business entity and the sale of the land if the entity is:
    a. A partnership.
    b. An S corporation.
    c. A C corporation.
    d. Is it possible to structure the disposition of the land and the subsequent acquisition of other land so that the realized gain on the disposition can be deferred?

27. Alicia contributes $25,000 to a business entity in exchange for a 20% ownership interest. During the first year of operations, the entity earns a profit of $150,000. At the end of that year, the entity has liabilities of $60,000.
    a. Calculate Alicia's basis for her stock if the entity is a C corporation.
    b. Calculate Alicia's basis for her stock if the entity is an S corporation.
    c. Calculate Alicia's basis for her partnership interest if the entity is a partnership.

28. An entity engages in the following transactions during the taxable year.

    • Sells stock held for three years as an investment for $30,000. The adjusted basis of the stock is $20,000.

    • Sells land used in the business for $65,000. The land had been used as a parking lot and originally cost $40,000.

    • Receives tax-exempt interest on municipal bonds of $5,000.

    • Receives dividends on IBM stock of $8,000.

    Describe the effect of these transactions on the entity and the owners of the entity if the entity is:
    a. A partnership.
    b. A C corporation.
    c. An S corporation.

29. Amber holds a 20% interest in a business to which she contributed $100,000 as part of the initial ownership group. During the life of the business, the following have occurred.

   • $200,000 cumulative losses, first three tax years.

   • $150,000 operating profit in the fourth tax year.

   • $75,000 distribution to owners at the end of the third tax year.

   • $60,000 payment to redeem 25% of Amber's ownership interest at the end of the fourth year. No other ownership redemptions have occurred.

   Determine the tax consequences to Amber if the entity is:
   a. A partnership.
   b. An S corporation.
   c. A C corporation.

30. On January 1, 2001, John contributes assets with an adjusted basis of $40,000 and a fair market value of $106,000 for a 40% ownership interest in an interior design business. Maria contributes $150,000 cash for a 60% ownership interest. The entity assumes a $6,000 mortgage attributable to one of the assets contributed by John. During 2001, the business earns $100,000. In addition, the entity makes a $30,000 cash distribution to John and a $45,000 cash distribution to Maria during the year. John and Maria are each in the 31% tax bracket.
   a. If the business entity is a C corporation, determine each of the following.

      • Recognized gain to the owners and the business entity on the creation of the business entity.

      • Original basis for John's and Maria's ownership interests.

      • Effect of the business entity earnings on the entity, John, and Maria.

      • Effect of the distributions on John and Maria.

      • Adjusted basis for John's and Maria's ownership interest at the end of the year.

   b. Determine each of the above if the business entity is an S corporation.
   c. If the objective is to minimize the income tax liability, should the business entity be a C corporation or an S corporation? Assume 2001 is a representative year.

31. A computer retailer has been in existence for five years. Annual profits have been approximately $100,000, and no distributions have been made to the owners. Anita and Hector each own a 50% interest and have the following bases for their ownership interests:

Anita	$200,000
Hector	150,000

   The company distributes a undivided interest in a parcel of investment land to Anita and Hector. The adjusted basis of the land is $280,000, and the fair market value is $360,000. Determine the tax consequences of the distribution to Anita and Hector if the entity is:
   a. A partnership.
   b. An S corporation (assume the S election has been in effect for five years).
   c. A C corporation.
   d. A limited liability company.

32. Yellow, a personal service corporation, has the following types of income and losses.

Active income	$150,000
Portfolio income	25,000
Passive activity losses	100,000

   a. Calculate Yellow's taxable income.
   b. Assume that instead of being a personal service corporation, Yellow is a closely held corporation. Calculate Yellow's taxable income.

33. Rosa contributes $50,000 to a business entity in exchange for a 10% ownership interest. The business entity incurs a loss of $900,000 for 2001. The entity liabilities at the end of 2001 are $700,000. Of this amount, $150,000 is for recourse debt, and $550,000 is for nonrecourse debt.
    a. Assume the business entity is a partnership. How much of Rosa's share of the loss can be deducted on her 2001 individual tax return? What is Rosa's basis for her partnership interest at the end of 2001?
    b. Assume the business entity is a C corporation. How much of Rosa's share of the loss can be deducted on her 2001 individual tax return? What is Rosa's basis for her stock at the end of 2001?

34. Megan owns 60% of a business entity, and Vern owns 40%. For 2001, the entity has a tax loss of $100,000. The owners would like to share profits with 60% for Megan and 40% for Vern and to share losses with 90% for Vern and 10% for Megan. Determine the tax consequences for 2001 if the entity is:
    a. A partnership.
    b. A C corporation.
    c. An S corporation.

35. Abby and Velma are equal owners of the AV Partnership. Abby invests $75,000 cash in the partnership. Velma contributes land and a building (basis to her of $50,000, fair market value of $75,000). The entity then borrows $200,000 cash using recourse financing and $100,000 using nonrecourse financing.
    a. Compute the outside basis in the partnership interest for Abby and Velma.
    b. Compute the at-risk amount for Abby and Velma.

36. Indicate which of the following special allocations are available for a partnership (P), a C corporation (C), and an S corporation (S).
    a. Share profits and losses differently from the share in capital.
    b. Share profits in a different percentage than losses.
    c. Special allocation of precontribution gain.
    d. Special allocation supported by substantial economic effect.
    e. Allocation to eliminate difference between inside and outside basis.

37. Sanjay contributes land to a business entity in January 2001 for a 30% ownership interest. Sanjay's basis for the land is $60,000, and the fair market value is $100,000. The business entity was formed three years ago by Polly and Rita, who have equal ownership. The entity is unsuccessful in getting the land rezoned from agricultural to residential. In October 2001, the land is sold for $110,000.
    Determine the tax consequences of the sale of the land for the entity and its owners if the entity is:
    a. A C corporation.
    b. An S corporation.
    c. A partnership.

38. Emily and Freda are negotiating with George to purchase the business that he operates in corporate form (Pelican, Inc.). The assets of Pelican, Inc., a C corporation, are as follows.

Asset	Basis	FMV
Cash	$ 20,000	$ 20,000
Accounts receivable	50,000	50,000
Inventory	100,000	110,000
Furniture and fixtures	150,000	170,000*
Building	200,000	250,000**
Land	40,000	150,000

*Potential depreciation recapture under § 1245 is $45,000.
**The straight-line method was used to depreciate the building. Accumulated depreciation is $340,000.

George's basis for the stock of Pelican, Inc., is $560,000. George is subject to a 31% marginal tax rate, and Pelican, Inc., faces a 34% marginal tax rate.

a. Emily and Freda purchase the *stock* of Pelican, Inc., from George for $908,000. Determine the tax consequences to Emily and Freda, Pelican, Inc., and George.

b. Emily and Freda purchase the *assets* from Pelican, Inc., for $908,000. Determine the tax consequences to Emily and Freda, Pelican, Inc., and George.

c. The purchase price is $550,000 because the fair market value of the building is $150,000, and the fair market value of the land is $50,000. No amount is assigned to goodwill. Emily and Freda purchase the *stock* of Pelican, Inc., from George. Determine the tax consequences to Emily and Freda, Pelican, Inc., and George.

39. Linda is the owner of a sole proprietorship. The entity has the following assets.

Asset	Basis	FMV
Cash	$10,000	$10,000
Accounts receivable	–0–	25,000
Office furniture and fixtures*	15,000	17,000
Building**	75,000	90,000
Land	60,000	80,000

*Potential depreciation recapture under § 1245 of $5,000.
**The straight-line method has been used to depreciate the building.

Linda sells the business for $260,000 to Juan.

a. Determine the tax consequences to Linda, including the classification of any recognized gain or loss.

b. Determine the tax consequences to Juan.

c. Advise Juan on how the purchase agreement could be modified to produce more beneficial tax consequences for him.

40. Gail and Harry own the GH Partnership. They have conducted the business as a partnership for 10 years. The bases for their partnership interests are as follows.

Gail	Harry
$100,000	$150,000

GH Partnership holds the following assets.

Asset	Basis	FMV
Cash	$ 10,000	$ 10,000
Accounts receivable	30,000	28,000
Inventory	25,000	26,000
Building*	100,000	150,000
Land	250,000	400,000

*The straight-line method has been used to depreciate the building. Accumulated depreciation is $70,000.

Gail and Harry sell their partnership interests to Keith and Liz for $307,000 each.

a. Determine the tax consequences of the sale to Gail, Harry, and GH Partnership.

b. From a tax perspective, should it matter to Keith and Liz whether they purchase Gail and Harry's partnership interests or the partnership assets from GH Partnership?

41. Ted and Skip are going to purchase the Carp Partnership, as equal partners, from Jan and Gail for $400,000. Because of your negotiations on behalf of Ted and Skip, the transaction will be structured as a purchase of the partnership, not of its individual assets. Carp's inside basis in its assets is $350,000. Write a letter to Ted at 50 Lake Shore Drive, Erie, PA 16501, explaining the following.
    a. What outside basis do Ted and Skip take in the partnership?
    b. Can Carp change its inside asset basis as a result of the purchase of the entity?

42. Vladimir owns all the stock of Ruby Corporation. The fair market value of the stock (and Ruby's assets) is about four times his adjusted basis for the stock. Vladimir is negotiating with an investor group for the sale of the corporation. Identify the relevant tax issues for Vladimir.

43. Bill Evans will purchase either the stock or the assets of Dane Corporation. All of the Dane stock is owned by Chuck. Bill and Chuck agree that Dane is worth $500,000. The tax basis for Dane's assets is $350,000. Write a letter to Bill advising him on whether he should negotiate to purchase the stock or the assets. Bill's address is 100 Village Green, Chattanooga, TN 37403.

BRIDGE DISCIPLINE

1. Parchment, Inc., is created with the following asset and liability contributions. Jake and Fran each receive 100 shares of Parchment common stock.

Shareholder	Assets	Basis	Fair Market Value
Jake	Cash	$100,000	$100,000
Fran	Land	40,000	120,000*

*The land has a mortgage of $20,000 that Parchment assumes.

   a. Prepare a financial accounting balance sheet. Discuss the relevance of conduit theory and entity theory.
   b. Prepare a tax balance sheet. Discuss the relevance of conduit theory and entity theory.
   c. Assume Parchment sells the land four months after the creation of the corporation for $150,000. Discuss the effect on the financial accounting balance sheet and the tax balance sheet.

2. Assume that Parchment in the preceding problem elects S corporation status at the time of its creation. Respond to (a), (b), and (c).

3. Assume that Parchment in (1) is a general partnership rather than a corporation. Respond to (a), (b), and (c). Would your answer change if Parchment were an LLC that "checked the box" to be taxed as a partnership?

4. Teal, Inc., has total assets of $100 million and annual revenues of $700 million. Lavender, Inc., has total assets of $12 million and annual revenues of $900,000. Both have been in existence for three years.
   a. Explain why neither Teal nor Lavender need make an AMT calculation for its first tax year.
   b. Explain why Teal must make an AMT calculation and why Lavender is not required to do so.
   c. Do you think that this different tax treatment for Teal and Lavender is equitable?

RESEARCH PROBLEMS

 Use the tax resources of the Internet to address the following questions. Do not restrict your search to the World Wide Web, but include a review of newsgroups and general reference materials, practitioner sites and resources, primary sources of the tax law, chat rooms and discussion groups, and other opportunities.

Research Problem 1.   Find an anecdote about a professional consulting firm that recently converted to LLP status. Are the firm and its competition and clients agreeable to the conversion of operating status?

Research Problem 2.   When did your state adopt LLC legislation? When did it receive IRS approval to apply partnership tax law to the entities?

Research Problem 3.   Find an article describing how a specific business put together its employee fringe benefit package in light of the limitations presented by the tax law and its form of operation.

Introduction to the Taxation of Individuals

LEARNING OBJECTIVES

After completing Chapter 15, you should be able to:

1. Understand and apply the components of the Federal income tax formula for individuals.

2. Apply the rules for arriving at personal and dependency exemptions.

3. Use the proper method for determining the tax liability.

4. Identify and work with kiddie tax situations.

5. Recognize filing requirements and proper filing status.

6. Identify specific inclusions and exclusions applicable to individuals.

7. Determine an individual's allowable itemized deductions.

8. Understand the adoption expenses credit, child tax credit, education tax credits, credit for child and dependent care expenses, and earned income credit.

Outline

TAX TALK   *I'm proud of paying taxes in the United States. The only thing is—I could be just as proud for half the money.*

—*Arthur Godfrey*

The he individual income tax accounts for approximately 48 percent of Federal budget receipts, compared to approximately 10 percent for the corporate income tax. The tax laws affecting individuals have become increasingly more complex in recent years as the government adds new laws to protect or increase this important source of revenue. Taxpayers respond to each new tax act with techniques to exploit loopholes, and the government responds with loophole-closing provisions, making the individual income tax law even more complex.[1]

LEARNING OBJECTIVE 1

Understand and apply the components of the Federal income tax formula for individuals.

The Individual Tax Formula

Individuals are subject to Federal income tax based on taxable income. This chapter explains how taxable income and the income tax of an individual taxpayer are determined. To compute taxable income, it is necessary to understand the tax formula in Figure 15–1 on the following page.

---

[1]Refer to the discussion of tax complexity in Chapter 1.

TAX FACT

THE GOVERNMENT'S INTEREST IN OUR WORK

How much of the typical American's eight-hour work day goes to pay Federal, state, and local taxes? According to the Tax Foundation, the answer is 2 hours and 42 minutes. However, the required effort also depends on where the individual lives. In high tax jurisdictions such as Connecticut and New York, people need to work on average more than 3 hours, while in Mississippi, only about 2 hours are required.

Source: Tax Foundation.

Although the tax formula is rather simple, determining an individual's taxable income can be quite complex because of the numerous provisions that govern the determination of gross income and allowable deductions.

After computing taxable income, the appropriate rates must be applied. This requires a determination of the individual's filing status, since different rates apply for single taxpayers, married taxpayers, and heads of household. The individual tax rate structure is progressive, with rates ranging from 15 percent to 39.6 percent.[2] For comparison, the lowest rate structure, which was in effect from 1913 to 1915, ranged from 1 to 7 percent, and the highest, in effect during 1944–1945, ranged from 23 to 94 percent.

Once the individual's tax has been computed, prepayments and credits are subtracted to determine whether the taxpayer owes additional tax or is entitled to a refund.

COMPONENTS OF THE TAX FORMULA

Before illustrating the application of the tax formula, a brief discussion of each of its components is helpful.

■ **FIGURE 15–1**
Individual Income Tax Formula

Income (broadly conceived)	$xx,xxx
Less: Exclusions	(x,xxx)
Gross income	$xx,xxx
Less: Deductions *for* adjusted gross income	(x,xxx)
Adjusted gross income (AGI)	$xx,xxx
Less: The greater of—	
Total itemized deductions *or*	
Standard deduction	(x,xxx)
Less: Personal and dependency exemptions	(x,xxx)
Taxable income	$xx,xxx

---

[2]The Tax Table for 2000 is available at **http://wft-entities. swcollege.com.** The Tax Rate Schedules for 2000 and 2001 are reproduced in Appendix A. The Tax Rate Schedules are also reproduced inside the front cover of this text.

Accident and health insurance proceeds

Annuity payments (to the extent proceeds represent a recovery of the taxpayer's investment)

Child support payments

Damages for personal injury or sickness

Fringe benefits of employees:

- Educational assistance payments provided by employer
- Employer-provided accident and health insurance
- Group term life insurance (for coverage up to $50,000)
- Meals and lodging (if furnished for convenience of employer)
- Tuition reductions for employees of educational institutions
- Miscellaneous benefits

Gains from sale of principal residence (subject to statutory ceiling)

Gifts and inheritances received

Interest from state and local bonds

Life insurance paid on death of insured

Scholarship grants (to a limited extent)

Social Security benefits (to a limited extent)

Workers' compensation benefits

Income (Broadly Conceived). This includes all the taxpayer's income, both taxable and nontaxable. Although it is essentially equivalent to gross receipts, it does not include a return of capital or receipt of borrowed funds. Nor does gross income include unrealized appreciation in the value of a taxpayer's assets.

EXAMPLE 1 Dave needed money to purchase a house. He sold 5,000 shares of stock for $100,000. He had paid $40,000 for the stock. In addition, he borrowed $75,000 from a bank. Dave has income that is taxable of $60,000 from the sale of the stock ($100,000 selling price − $40,000 return of capital). He has no income from the $75,000 borrowed from the bank because he has an obligation to repay that amount. ■

Exclusions. For various reasons, Congress has chosen to exclude certain types of income from the income tax base. The principal income exclusions are listed in Exhibit 15–1. The exclusions most commonly encountered by individual taxpayers (employee fringe benefits) are discussed in detail in Chapter 16.

Gross Income. The Internal Revenue Code defines gross income broadly as "except as otherwise provided . . . , all income from whatever source derived."[3] The "except as otherwise provided" refers to exclusions. Gross income includes, but is not limited to, the items in Exhibit 15–2.

EXAMPLE 2 Beth received the following amounts during the year:

Salary	$30,000
Interest on savings account	900
Gift from her aunt	10,000

---

[3]§ 61(a).

■ EXHIBIT 15–2
Partial List of Gross Income
Items

Alimony	Interest
Bargain purchase from employer	Jury duty fees
Bonuses	Partnership income
Breach of contract damages	Pensions
Business income	Prizes (with some exceptions)
Commissions	Professional fees
Compensation for services	Punitive damages
Debts forgiven (with some exceptions)	Rents
Dividends	Rewards
Embezzled funds	Royalties
Farm income	Salaries
Fees	Severance pay
Gains from illegal activities	Strike and lockout benefits
Gains from sale of property	Supplemental unemployment benefits
Gambling winnings	Tips and gratuities
Hobby income	Wages

Prize won in state lottery	$ 1,000
Alimony from ex-husband	12,000
Child support from ex-husband	6,000
Damages for injury in auto accident	25,000
Increase in the value of stock held for investment	5,000

[handwritten:] 30 900 / 31,900 / 12,000 / 43,9000

Review Exhibits 15–1 and 15–2 to determine the amount Beth must include in the computation of taxable income and the amount she may exclude. Then check your answer in footnote 4.[4] ■

Deductions for Adjusted Gross Income.   Individual taxpayers have two categories of deductions: (1) deductions *for* adjusted gross income (deductions to arrive at adjusted gross income) and (2) deductions *from* adjusted gross income. Deductions *for* adjusted gross income (AGI) include, but are not limited to, the following:[5]

- Ordinary and necessary expenses incurred in a trade or business.
- One-half of self-employment tax paid.
- Alimony paid.
- Certain payments to traditional Individual Retirement Accounts and Medical Savings Accounts.
- Moving expenses.
- The capital loss deduction (limited to $3,000).

The principal deductions *for* AGI are discussed later in this chapter.

Adjusted Gross Income (AGI).   AGI is an important subtotal that serves as the basis for computing percentage limitations on certain itemized deductions, such as medical expenses and charitable contributions. For example, medical expenses are deductible only to the extent they exceed 7.5 percent of AGI, and charitable

---

[4]Beth must include $43,900 in computing taxable income ($30,000 salary + $900 interest + $1,000 lottery prize + $12,000 alimony). She can exclude $41,000 ($10,000 gift from aunt + $6,000 child support + $25,000 damages). The unrealized gain on the stock held for invest- ment is not included in gross income. Such gain will be included in gross income only when it is realized upon disposition of the stock.
[5]See § 62 for a comprehensive list of items that are deductible *for* AGI.

INTERNATIONAL IMPLICATIONS

CITIZENSHIP IS NOT TAX-FREE

Gross income from "whatever source derived" includes income from both U.S. and foreign sources. This approach to taxation, where the government taxes its citizens and residents on their worldwide income regardless of where earned, is referred to as a *global* system. Income earned by U.S. citizens outside the United States can be subject to additional taxes, however, because all countries maintain the right to tax income earned within their borders. Consequently, the U.S. tax law includes various mechanisms to alleviate the double taxation that arises when income is subject to tax in multiple jurisdictions. These mechanisms include the foreign tax deduction, the foreign tax credit, the foreign earned income exclusion for U.S. citizens and residents working abroad, and various tax treaty provisions.

Most industrialized countries use variants of the global system. An alternative approach is the *territorial* system, where a government taxes only the income earned within its borders. Hong Kong and Guatemala, for example, use a territorial approach.

---

contribution deductions may not exceed 50 percent of AGI. These limitations might be described as a 7.5 percent *floor* under the medical expense deduction and a 50 percent *ceiling* on the charitable contribution deduction.

EXAMPLE 3

Keith earned a salary of $23,000 in the current tax year. He contributed $2,000 to his traditional Individual Retirement Account (IRA) and sustained a $1,000 capital loss on the sale of Wren Corporation stock. His AGI is computed as follows:

Gross income		
Salary		$23,000
Less: Deductions *for* AGI		
IRA contribution	$2,000	
Capital loss	1,000	(3,000)
AGI		$20,000

EXAMPLE 4

Assume the same facts as in Example 3, and that Keith also had medical expenses of $1,800. Medical expenses may be included in his itemized deductions to the extent they exceed 7.5% of AGI. In computing his itemized deductions, Keith may include medical expenses of $300 [$1,800 medical expenses – $1,500 (7.5% × $20,000 AGI)]. ■

Itemized Deductions.   As a general rule, personal expenditures are disallowed as deductions in arriving at taxable income. However, Congress has chosen to allow specific personal expenses as **itemized deductions.** Such expenditures include medical expenses, certain taxes and interest, and charitable contributions. Itemized deductions are discussed in detail later in this chapter.

EXAMPLE 5

Leo is the owner and operator of a video game arcade. All allowable expenses he incurs in connection with the arcade business are deductions *for* AGI. In addition, Leo paid medical expenses, mortgage interest, state income tax, and charitable contributions. These personal expenses are allowable as itemized deductions. ■

■ **TABLE 15–1**
Basic Standard Deduction
Amounts

Filing Status	2000	2001
Single	$4,400	$4,550
Married, filing jointly	7,350	7,600
Surviving spouse	7,350	7,600
Head of household	6,450	6,650
Married, filing separately	3,675	3,800

Standard Deduction.   The **standard deduction** is used by taxpayers who do not have itemized deductions in excess of the allowable standard deduction amount. The standard deduction is a specified amount that depends on the filing status of the taxpayer (e.g., single, married filing jointly, married filing separately). In the past, Congress has attempted to set the amount of the standard deduction at a level that would exempt poverty-level taxpayers from the income tax,[6] but it has not always been consistent in doing so.

The standard deduction is the sum of two components: a *basic* standard deduction and an *additional* standard deduction.[7] Taxpayers who are allowed a *basic* standard deduction are entitled to the applicable amount listed in Table 15–1. The standard deduction amounts are subject to adjustment for inflation each year. Currently, about 70 percent of all individual taxpayers choose to use the standard deduction in lieu of itemizing deductions. However, certain taxpayers are not allowed to claim *any* standard deduction, and the standard deduction is *limited* for others.[8]

A taxpayer who is age 65 or over *or* blind qualifies for an *additional standard deduction* of $900 or $1,100, depending on filing status (see amounts in Table 15–2). Two additional standard deductions are allowed for a taxpayer who is age 65 or over *and* blind. The additional standard deduction provisions also apply for a qualifying spouse who is age 65 or over or blind, but a taxpayer may not claim an additional standard deduction for a dependent.

To determine whether to itemize, the taxpayer compares the *total* standard deduction (the sum of the basic standard deduction and any additional standard deductions) to total itemized deductions. Taxpayers are allowed to deduct the *greater* of itemized deductions or the standard deduction. Taxpayers whose itemized deductions are less than the standard deduction compute their taxable income using the standard deduction rather than itemizing.

■ **TABLE 15–2**
Amount of Each Additional
Standard Deduction

Filing Status	2000	2001
Single	$1,100	$1,100
Married, filing jointly	850	900
Surviving spouse	850	900
Head of household	1,100	1,100
Married, filing separately	850	900

[6]S.Rep. No. 92–437, 92nd Cong., 1st Sess., 1971, p. 54. Another purpose of the standard deduction was discussed in Chapter 1 under Influence of the Internal Revenue Service—Administrative Feasibility. The size of the standard deduction has a direct bearing on the number of taxpayers who are in a position to itemize deductions.

Reducing the number of taxpayers who itemize also reduces the audit effort required from the IRS.
[7]§ 63(c)(1).
[8]§ 63(c)(6).

EXAMPLE 6

Sara, who is single, is 66 years old. She had total itemized deductions of $5,100 during 2001. Her total standard deduction is $5,650 ($4,550 basic standard deduction plus $1,100 additional standard deduction). Sara should compute her taxable income for 2001 using the standard deduction ($5,650), since it exceeds her itemized deductions ($5,100). ■

Personal and Dependency Exemptions.   Exemptions are allowed for the taxpayer, for the taxpayer's spouse, and for each dependent of the taxpayer. The exemption amount is $2,800 in 2000 and $2,900 in 2001.

APPLICATION OF THE TAX FORMULA

The tax formula shown in Figure 15–1 is illustrated in Example 7.

EXAMPLE 7

Grace, age 25, is single and has no dependents. She is a high school teacher and earned a $30,000 salary in 2001. Her other income consisted of a $1,000 prize won in a sweepstakes contest and $500 of interest on municipal bonds received as a graduation gift in 1998. During 2001, she sustained a deductible capital loss of $1,000. Her itemized deductions are $5,400. Grace's taxable income for the year is computed as follows:

Income (broadly conceived)		
Salary		$30,000
Prize		1,000
Interest on municipal bonds		500
Total income		$31,500
Less: Exclusion—		
Interest on municipal bonds		(500)
Gross income		$31,000
Less: Deduction *for* adjusted gross income—		
Capital loss		(1,000)
Adjusted gross income (AGI)		$30,000
Less: The greater of—		
Total itemized deductions	$5,400	
or the standard deduction	4,550	(5,400)
Personal and dependency exemptions (1 × $2,900)		(2,900)
Taxable income		$21,700

■

1   *Find more information on this topic at our Web site:* ***http://wft-entities.swcollege.com.***

SPECIAL LIMITATIONS FOR INDIVIDUALS WHO CAN BE CLAIMED AS DEPENDENTS

Special rules apply to the standard deduction and personal exemption of an individual who can be claimed as a dependent on another person's tax return.

When filing his or her own tax return, a *dependent's* basic standard deduction in 2001 is limited to the greater of $750 or the sum of the individual's earned income for the year plus $250.[9] However, if the sum of the individual's earned income plus

---

[9] § 63(c)(5). Both the $750 amount and the $250 amount are subject to adjustment for inflation each year. The amounts were $700 and $250, respectively, for 2000.

$250 exceeds the normal standard deduction, the standard deduction is limited to the appropriate amount shown in Table 15–1. These limitations apply only to the basic standard deduction. A dependent who is 65 or over or blind or both is also allowed the additional standard deduction amount on his or her own return (refer to Table 15–2). These provisions are illustrated in Examples 8 through 11.

EXAMPLE 8

Susan, who is 17 years old and single, is claimed as a dependent on her parents' tax return. During 2001, she received $1,200 of interest (unearned income) on a savings account. She also earned $300 from a part-time job. When Susan files her own tax return, her standard deduction is $750 (the greater of $750 or the sum of earned income of $300 plus $250). ■

EXAMPLE 9

Assume the same facts as in Example 8, except that Susan is 67 years old and is claimed as a dependent on her son's tax return. In this case, when Susan files her own tax return, her standard deduction is $1,850 [$750 (the greater of $750 or the sum of earned income of $300 plus $250) + $1,100 (the additional standard deduction allowed because Susan is 65 or over)]. ■

EXAMPLE 10

Peggy, who is 16 years old and single, earned $600 from a summer job and had no unearned income during 2001. She is claimed as a dependent on her parents' tax return. Her standard deduction is $850 (the greater of $750 or the sum of earned income of $600 plus $250). ■

EXAMPLE 11

Jack, who is a 20-year-old, single, full-time college student, is claimed as a dependent on his parents' tax return. He worked as a musician during the summer of 2001, earning $4,600. Jack's standard deduction is $4,550 (the greater of $750 or the sum of earned income of $4,600 plus $250, but limited to the $4,550 standard deduction for a single taxpayer). ■

A taxpayer who claims an individual as a dependent is allowed to claim an exemption for the dependent. The dependent cannot claim a personal exemption on his or her own return. Based on the tax formula, Jack in Example 11 would have taxable income of $50, determined as follows:

Gross income	$ 4,600
Less: Standard deduction	(4,550)
Personal exemption	(–0–)
Taxable income	$ 50

LEARNING OBJECTIVE 2

Apply the rules for arriving at personal and dependency exemptions.

Personal and Dependency Exemptions

The use of exemptions in the tax system is based in part on the idea that a taxpayer with a small amount of income should be exempt from income taxation. An exemption frees a specified amount of income from tax ($2,800 in 2000 and $2,900 in 2001). The exemption amount is indexed (adjusted) annually for inflation. An individual who is not claimed as a dependent by another taxpayer is allowed to claim his or her own personal exemption. In addition, a taxpayer may claim an exemption for each dependent.

EXAMPLE 12

Bonnie, who is single, supports her mother and father, who have no income of their own, and claims them as dependents on her tax return. Bonnie may claim a personal exemption for herself plus an exemption for each dependent. On her 2001 tax return, Bonnie may deduct $8,700 for exemptions ($2,900 per exemption × 3 exemptions). ■

PERSONAL EXEMPTIONS

The Code provides a **personal exemption** for the taxpayer and an exemption for the spouse if a joint return is filed. However, when separate returns are filed, a married taxpayer cannot claim an exemption for his or her spouse *unless* the spouse has no gross income and is not claimed as the dependent of another taxpayer.

The determination of marital status generally is made at the end of the taxable year, except when a spouse dies during the year. Spouses who enter into a legal separation under a decree of divorce or separate maintenance before the end of the year are considered to be unmarried at the end of the taxable year. The following summary illustrates the effect of death or divorce upon marital status:

Description	Marital Status and Personal Exemptions
• Walt is the widower of Helen who died on January 3, 2001.	Walt and Helen are considered to be married for purposes of filing the 2001 return. Walt may claim two exemptions on his 2001 return.
• Bill and Jane entered into a divorce decree that becomes effective on December 31, 2001.	Bill and Jane are considered to be unmarried for purposes of filing the 2001 return. Bill and Jane each may claim a personal exemption on their separate returns.

DEPENDENCY EXEMPTIONS

As indicated in Example 12, the Code allows a taxpayer to claim a **dependency exemption** for each eligible individual. A dependency exemption may be claimed for each individual for whom the following five tests are met:[10]

- Support.
- Relationship or member of the household.
- Gross income.
- Joint return.
- Citizenship or residency.

Support Test.   Over one-half of the support of the individual must be furnished by the taxpayer. Support includes food, shelter, clothing, medical and dental care, education, etc. However, a scholarship received by a student is not included for purposes of determining whether the taxpayer furnished more than half of the child's support.[11]

EXAMPLE 13

Hal contributed $3,400 (consisting of food, clothing, and medical care) toward the support of his son, Sam, who earned $1,500 from a part-time job and received a $2,000 scholarship to attend a local university. Assuming that the other dependency tests are met, Hal can claim Sam as a dependent since he has contributed more than half of Sam's support. The $2,000 scholarship is not included as support for purposes of this test. ■

If an individual does not spend funds that have been received from any source, the unspent amounts are not counted for purposes of the support test.

---

[10]§§ 151 and 152.   [11]Reg. § 1.152–1(c).

EXAMPLE 14

Emily contributed $3,000 to her father's support during the year. In addition, her father received $2,400 in Social Security benefits, $200 of interest, and wages of $600. Her father deposited the Social Security benefits, interest, and wages in his own savings account and did not use any of the funds for his support. Thus, the Social Security benefits, interest, and wages are not considered to be support provided by Emily's father. Emily may claim her father as a dependent if the other tests are met. ■

Capital expenditures for items such as furniture, appliances, and automobiles are included for purposes of the support test if the item does, in fact, constitute support.[12]

EXAMPLE 15

Norm purchased a television set costing $150 and gave it to his minor daughter. The television set was placed in the child's bedroom and was used exclusively by her. Norm should include the cost of the television set in determining the support of his daughter. ■

EXAMPLE 16

Mark paid $6,000 for an automobile that was titled and registered in his name. Mark's minor son is permitted to use the automobile equally with Mark. Since Mark did not give the automobile to his son, the $6,000 cost is not includible as a support item. However, out-of-pocket operating expenses incurred by Mark for the benefit of his son are includible as support. ■

One exception to the support test involves a **multiple support agreement.** A multiple support agreement permits one of a group of taxpayers who furnish more than half of the support of an individual to claim a dependency exemption for that individual even if no one person provides more than 50 percent of the support.[13] Any person who contributed *more than 10 percent* of the support is entitled to claim the exemption if each person in the group who contributed more than 10 percent files a written consent. This provision frequently enables one of the children of aged dependent parents to claim an exemption when none of the children meets the 50 percent support test. Each person who is a party to the multiple support agreement must meet all other requirements (except the support requirement) for claiming the exemption. A person who does not meet the relationship or member-of-the-household test, for instance, cannot claim the dependency exemption under a multiple support agreement. It does not matter if he or she contributes more than 10 percent of the individual's support.

EXAMPLE 17

Wanda, who resides with her son, Adam, received $6,000 from various sources during the year. This constituted her entire support for the year. She received support from the following individuals:

	Amount	Percentage of Total
Adam, a son	$2,880	48
Bob, a son	600	10
Carol, a daughter	1,800	30
Diane, a friend	720	12
	$6,000	100

---

[12]Rev.Rul. 57–344, 1957–2 C.B. 112; Rev.Rul. 58–419, 1958–2 C.B. 57.   [13]§ 152(c).

If Adam and Carol file a multiple support agreement, either may claim the dependency exemption for Wanda. Bob may not claim Wanda because he did not contribute more than 10% of her support. Bob's consent is not required in order for Adam and Carol to file a multiple support agreement. Diane does not meet the relationship or member-of-the-household test and cannot be a party to the agreement. The decision as to who claims Wanda rests with Adam and Carol. It is possible for Carol to claim Wanda, even though Adam furnished more of Wanda's support. ■

2 *Find more information on this topic at our Web site: **http://wft-entities.swcollege.com**.*

PLANNING CONSIDERATIONS

Multiple Support Agreements and the Medical Expense Deduction

Generally, medical expenses are deductible only if they are paid on behalf of the taxpayer, his or her spouse, and their dependents.[14] Since deductibility may rest on dependency status, planning is important in arranging multiple support agreements.

EXAMPLE 18

During the year, Zelda will be supported by her two sons (Vern and Vito) and her daughter (Maria). Each will furnish approximately one-third of the required support. If the parties decide that the depen-

dency exemption should be claimed by Maria under a multiple support agreement, any medical expenses incurred by Zelda should be paid by Maria. ■

In planning a multiple support agreement, take into account which of the parties is most likely to exceed the 7.5 percent limitation. In Example 18, for instance, Maria might be a poor choice if she and her family do not expect to incur many medical expenses of their own.

A second exception to the 50 percent support requirement can occur for a child of parents who are divorced or separated under a decree of separate maintenance. For decrees executed after 1984, the custodial parent is allowed to claim the exemption unless that parent agrees in writing not to claim a dependency exemption for the child.[15] Thus, claiming the exemption is dependent on whether a written agreement exists, *not* on meeting the support test.

EXAMPLE 19

Ira and Rita obtained a divorce decree in 1994. In 2001, their two children are in Rita's custody. Ira contributed over half of the support for each child. In the absence of a written agreement on the dependency exemptions, Rita (the custodial parent) is entitled to the exemptions in 2001. However, Ira may claim the exemptions if Rita agrees in writing. ■

3 *Find more information on this topic at our Web site: **http://wft-entities.swcollege.com**.*

---

[14]See the discussion of medical expenses later in this chapter.   [15]§ 152(e).

Relationship or Member-of-the-Household Test.   To be claimed as a dependent, an individual must be either a relative of the taxpayer or a member of the taxpayer's household. The Code contains a detailed listing of the various blood and marriage relationships that qualify. Note, however, that the relationship test is met if the individual is a qualifying relative of either spouse. Once established by marriage, a relationship continues regardless of subsequent changes in marital status.[16]

4 *Find more information on this topic at our Web site:* ***http://wft-entities.swcollege.com.***

Gross Income Test.   The dependent's gross income must be less than the exemption amount ($2,900 in 2001).[17] The gross income test is measured by income that is taxable. In the case of scholarships, for example, it excludes the nontaxable portion (e.g., amounts received for books and tuition) but includes the taxable portion (e.g., amounts received for room and board).

A parent may claim a dependency exemption for his or her child, even when the child's gross income exceeds $2,900, if the parent provided over half of the child's support and the child, at year-end, is under age 19 or is a full-time student under age 24. If the parent claims a dependency exemption, the dependent child may *not* claim a personal exemption on his or her own income tax return.

A child is defined as a son, stepson, daughter, stepdaughter, adopted son, or adopted daughter and may include a foster child.[18] For the child to qualify as a student for purposes of the dependency exemption, he or she must be a full-time student at an educational institution during some part of five calendar months of the year.[19] This exception to the gross income test for dependent children who are under age 19 or full-time students under age 24 permits a child or college student to earn money from part-time or summer jobs without penalizing the parent with the loss of the dependency exemption.

Joint Return Test.   If a dependent is married, the supporting taxpayer (e.g., the parent of a married child) generally is not permitted a dependency exemption if the married individual files a joint return with his or her spouse.[20] The joint return rule does not apply, however, if the following conditions are met:

- The reason for filing is to claim a refund for tax withheld.
- No tax liability would exist for either spouse on separate returns.
- Neither spouse is required to file a return.

EXAMPLE 20

Paul provides over half of the support of his son, Quinn. He also provides over half of the support of Vera, who is Quinn's wife. During the year, both Quinn and Vera had part-time jobs. To recover the taxes withheld, they file a joint return. If Quinn and Vera have income low enough that they are not *required* to file a return, Paul is allowed to claim both as dependents. ■

---

[16]§ 152(a). However, under § 152(b)(5), a taxpayer may not claim someone who is a member of his or her household as a dependent if their relationship is in violation of local law. For example, the dependency exemption was denied because the taxpayer's relationship to the person claimed as a dependent constituted *cohabitation*, a crime under applicable state law. *Cassius L. Peacock, III*, 37 TCM 177, T.C.Memo. 1978–30.

[17]§ 151(c)(1).
[18]Reg. § 1.151–3(a).
[19]Reg. §§ 1.151–3(b) and (c).
[20]§ 151(c)(2).

PLANNING CONSIDERATIONS

Problems with a Joint Return

A married person who files a joint return cannot be claimed as a dependent by another taxpayer. If a joint return has been filed, the damage may be undone if separate returns are substituted on a timely basis (on or before the due date of the return).

EXAMPLE 21

While preparing a client's 2000 income tax return on April 9, 2001, a tax practitioner discovered that the client's daughter had filed a joint return with her husband in late January of 2001. Presuming the daughter otherwise qualifies as the client's dependent, the exemption is not lost if she and her husband file separate returns on or before April 16, 2001. ■

Citizenship or Residency Test. To be a dependent, the individual must be either a U.S. citizen, a U.S. resident, or a resident of Canada or Mexico for some part of the calendar year in which the taxpayer's tax year begins.

PHASE-OUT OF EXEMPTIONS

Several provisions of the tax law are intended to increase the tax liability of more affluent taxpayers who might otherwise enjoy some benefit from having some of their taxable income subject to the lower income tax brackets (e.g., 15 percent, 28 percent). One such provision phases out personal and dependency exemptions as AGI exceeds specified threshold amounts. For 2000 and 2001, the phase-out *begins* at the following threshold amounts (which are indexed annually for inflation):

Filing Status	2000	2001
Joint return/surviving spouse	$193,400	$199,450
Head of household	161,150	166,200
Single	128,950	132,950
Married, filing separately	96,700	99,725

Exemptions are phased out by 2 percent for each $2,500 (or fraction thereof) by which the taxpayer's AGI exceeds the threshold amounts. For a married taxpayer filing separately, the phase-out is 2 percent for each $1,250 or fraction thereof.

The allowable exemption amount can be determined with the following steps:

1. AGI – threshold amount = excess amount.
2. Excess amount/$2,500 = reduction factor [rounded up to the next whole increment (e.g., 18.1 = 19)] × 2 = phase-out percentage.
3. Phase-out percentage (from step 2) × exemption amount = amount of exemptions phased out.
4. Exemption amount – phase-out amount = allowable exemption deduction.

EXAMPLE 22

Frederico is married but files a separate return. His 2001 AGI is $119,725. He is entitled to one personal exemption.

1. $119,725 – $99,725 = $20,000 excess amount.
2. [($20,000/$1,250) × 2] = 32% (phase-out percentage).
3. 32% × $2,900 = $928 amount of exemption phased out.
4. $2,900 – $928 = $1,972 allowable exemption deduction.

■ **TABLE 15–3**
2001 Tax Rate Schedule for
Single Taxpayers

If Taxable Income Is . . .		The Tax Is:	Of the Amount Over
Over	**But Not Over**		
$ –0–	$ 27,050	15%	$ –0–
27,050	65,550	$4,057.50 + 28%	27,050
65,550	136,750	$14,837.50 + 31%	65,550
136,750	297,350	$36,909.50 + 36%	136,750
297,350		$94,725.50 + 39.6%	297,350

Note that the exemption amount is completely phased out when the taxpayer's AGI exceeds the threshold amount by more than $122,500 ($61,250 for a married taxpayer filing a separate return), calculated as follows:

$122,501/$2,500 = 49.0004, rounded to 50 and multiplied by 2 = 100% (phase-out percentage). ■

LEARNING OBJECTIVE 3

Use the proper method for determining the tax liability.

Tax Determination

TAX TABLE METHOD

The tax liability is computed using either the Tax Table method or the Tax Rate Schedule method. Most taxpayers compute their tax using the Tax Table. Eligible taxpayers compute taxable income (as shown in Figure 15–1) and *must* determine their tax by reference to the **Tax Table**.[21]

5 *Find more information on this topic at our Web site: http://wft-entities.swcollege.com.*

Although the Tax Table is derived by using the Tax Rate Schedules (discussed below), the tax calculated using the two methods may vary slightly. This variation occurs because the tax for a particular income range in the Tax Table is based on the midpoint amount.

EXAMPLE 23

Linda is single and has taxable income of $30,000 for calendar year 2000. To determine Linda's tax using the Tax Table, find the $30,000 to $30,050 income line. The tax of $4,995 is actually the tax the Tax Rate Schedules would yield on taxable income of $30,025 (i.e., the midpoint amount between $30,000 and $30,050). ■

TAX RATE SCHEDULE METHOD

The **Tax Rate Schedules** contain rates of 15, 28, 31, 36, and 39.6 percent. Separate schedules are provided for the following filing statuses: single, married filing jointly, married filing separately, and head of household. The rate schedules for 2000 and 2001 are reproduced inside the front cover of this text and also in Appendix A. The rate schedules are adjusted for inflation each year.

The 2001 rate schedule for single taxpayers is reproduced in Table 15–3. This schedule is used to illustrate the tax computations in Examples 24, 25, and 26.

---

[21]The 2000 Tax Table is located at **http://wft-entities.swcollege.com**. This table will be used to illustrate the tax computation. The 2001 Tax Table was not available at the date of publication of this text.

EXAMPLE 24

Pat is single and had $18,000 of taxable income in 2001. His tax is $2,700 ($18,000 × 15%). ■

EXAMPLE 25

Chris is single and had taxable income of $50,000 in 2001. Her tax is $10,483.50 [$4,057.50 + 28% ($50,000 − $27,050)]. ■

Note that $4,057.50, which is the starting point in the tax computation in Example 25, is 15 percent of the $27,050 taxable income in the first bracket. Income in excess of $27,050 is taxed at a 28 percent rate. This reflects the *progressive* (or graduated) rate structure on which the U.S. income tax system is based. A tax is progressive if a higher rate of tax applies as the tax base increases.

EXAMPLE 26

Carl is single and had taxable income of $80,000 in 2001. His tax is $19,317 [$14,837.50 + 31% ($80,000 − $65,550)]. Note that the effect of this computation is to tax part of Carl's income at 15%, part at 28%, and part at 31%. An alternative computational method provides a clearer illustration of the progressive rate structure of the individual income tax:

Tax on $27,050 at 15%	$ 4,057.50
Tax on $65,550 − $27,050 at 28%	10,780.00
Tax on $80,000 − $65,550 at 31%	4,479.50
Total	$19,317.00

Carl's marginal rate (refer to Chapter 1) is 31%, and his average rate is 24.1% ($19,317 tax/$80,000 taxable income). ■

A special computation limits the effective tax rate on long-term capital gain. This beneficial tax treatment of long-term capital gain is discussed in detail in Chapter 8.

PLANNING CONSIDERATIONS

Shifting Income and Deductions across Time

It is natural for taxpayers to be concerned about the tax rates they are paying. How does a tax practitioner communicate information about rates to clients? There are several possibilities. For example, a taxpayer who is in the 15 percent bracket this year and expects to be in the 31 percent bracket next year should, if possible, defer payment of deductible expenses until next year to maximize the tax benefit of the deduction.

A note of caution is in order with respect to shifting income and expenses between years. Congress has recognized the tax planning possibilities of such shifting and has enacted many provisions to limit a taxpayer's ability to do so. Some of these limitations on the shifting of income and deductions are discussed in Chapters 3 through 6.

COMPUTATION OF NET TAXES PAYABLE OR REFUND DUE

The pay-as-you-go feature of the Federal income tax system requires payment of all or part of the taxpayer's income tax liability during the year. These payments take the form of Federal income tax withheld by employers or estimated tax paid by the taxpayer or both.[22] The payments are applied against the tax from the Tax Table or Tax Rate Schedules to determine whether the taxpayer will get a refund or pay additional tax.

Employers are required to withhold income tax on compensation paid to their employees and to pay this tax over to the government. The employer notifies the employee of the amount of income tax withheld on Form W–2 (Wage and Tax Statement). The employee should receive this form by January 31 after the year in which the income tax is withheld.

If taxpayers receive income that is not subject to withholding or income from which not enough tax is withheld, they must pay estimated tax. These individuals must file Form 1040–ES (Estimated Tax for Individuals) and pay in quarterly installments the income tax and self-employment tax estimated to be due.

The income tax from the Tax Table or the Tax Rate Schedules also is reduced by the individual's tax credits. There is an important distinction between tax credits and tax deductions. Tax credits (including tax withheld) reduce the tax liability dollar-for-dollar. Tax deductions reduce taxable income on which the tax liability is based.

EXAMPLE 27

Gail is a taxpayer in the 28% tax bracket. As a result of incurring $1,000 in child care, she is entitled to a $200 credit for child and dependent care expenses ($1,000 child care expenses × 20% credit rate). She also contributed $1,000 to the American Cancer Society and included this amount in her itemized deductions. The credit for child and dependent care expenses results in a $200 reduction of Gail's tax liability for the year. The contribution to the American Cancer Society reduces taxable income by $1,000 and results in a $280 reduction in Gail's tax liability ($1,000 reduction in taxable income × 28% tax rate). ■

Selected tax credits for individuals are discussed later in this chapter. The following are some of the more common credits available to individuals:

- Child tax credit.
- Credit for child and dependent care expenses.
- Earned income credit.

EXAMPLE 28

Kelly, age 30, is a head of household whose disabled dependent mother lives with him. During 2001, Kelly had the following: taxable income, $30,000; income tax withheld, $3,950; estimated tax payments, $600; and credit for child and dependent care expenses, $200. Kelly's net tax payable (refund due) is computed as follows:

[22]See § 3402 for withholding and § 6654 for estimated payments.

Income tax (from 2001 Tax Rate Schedule)		$ 4,500
Less: Tax credits and prepayments—		
Credit for dependent care expenses	$ 200	
Income tax withheld	3,950	
Estimated tax payments	600	(4,750)
Net taxes payable (refund due if negative)		($ 250)

LEARNING OBJECTIVE 4

Identify and work with kiddie tax situations.

UNEARNED INCOME OF CHILDREN UNDER AGE 14 TAXED AT PARENTS' RATE

Most individuals compute taxable income using the tax formula shown in Figure 15–1. Special provisions govern the computation of taxable income and the tax liability for children under age 14 who have **unearned income** in excess of specified amounts.

Recall that individuals who are claimed as dependents by other taxpayers cannot claim an exemption on their own return. This prevents parents from shifting the tax on investment income (such as interest and dividends) to a child by transferring ownership of the assets producing the income. Without this provision, the child would pay no tax on the income to the extent that it was sheltered by the child's exemption.

Current tax law also reduces or eliminates the possibility of saving taxes by shifting income from parents to children by taxing the net unearned of children under age 14 as if it were the parents' income.[23] Unearned income includes such income as taxable interest, dividends, capital gains, rents, royalties, pension and annuity income, and income (other than earned income) received as the beneficiary of a trust.

This provision, commonly referred to as the **kiddie tax,** applies to any child for any taxable year if the child has not reached age 14 by the close of the taxable year, has at least one living parent, and has unearned income of more than $1,500. The kiddie tax provision does not apply to a child age 14 or older. However, the limitation on the use of the standard deduction and the unavailability of the personal exemption do apply to such a child as long as he or she is eligible to be claimed as a dependent by a parent.

Net Unearned Income.   Net unearned income of a dependent child is computed as follows:

> Unearned income
> Less: $750
> Less: The *greater* of
>> $750 of the standard deduction *or*
>> The amount of allowable itemized deductions directly connected with the production of the unearned income
> Equals: Net unearned income

If net unearned income is zero (or negative), the child's tax is computed without using the parents' rate. If the amount of net unearned income (regardless of source) is positive, the net unearned income will be taxed at the parents' rate. The $750 amounts in the preceding formula are subject to adjustment for inflation each year.

6 *Find more information on this topic at our Web site:* ***http://wft-entities.swcollege.com***.

---

[23]§ 1(g).

Election to Report Certain Unearned Income on Parent's Return. If a child under age 14 is required to file a tax return and meets all of the following requirements, the parent may elect to report the child's unearned income that exceeds $1,500 on the parent's own tax return:

- Gross income is from interest and dividends only.
- Gross income is more than $750 but less than $7,500.
- No estimated tax has been paid in the name and Social Security number of the child, and the child is not subject to backup withholding.

If the parental election is made, the child is treated as having no gross income and then is not required to file a tax return.

The parent(s) must also pay an additional tax equal to the smaller of $112.50 or 15 percent of the child's gross income over $750. Parents who have substantial itemized deductions based on AGI may find that making the parental election increases total taxes for the family unit. Taxes should be calculated both with the parental election and without it to determine the appropriate choice.

PLANNING CONSIDERATIONS

Income of Minor Children

Taxpayers can use several strategies to avoid or minimize the effect of the rules that tax the unearned income of certain minor children at the parents' rate. The kiddie tax rules do not apply once a child reaches age 14. Parents should consider giving a younger child assets that defer the inclusion in gross income until the child reaches age 14. For example, U.S. government Series EE savings bonds can be used to defer income until the bonds are cashed in.

Growth stocks typically pay little in the way of dividends. However, the unrealized appreciation on an astute investment may more than offset the lack of dividends. The child can hold the growth stock until he or she reaches age 14. If the stock is sold then at a profit, the profit is taxed at the child's low rates.

Taxpayers in a position to do so can employ their children in their business and pay them a reasonable wage for the work they actually perform (e.g., light office help, such as filing). The child's earned income is sheltered by the standard deduction, and the parents' business is allowed a deduction for the wages. The kiddie tax rules have no effect on earned income, even if it is earned from the parents' business.

Filing Considerations

Under the category of filing considerations, the following questions need to be resolved:

- Is the taxpayer required to file an income tax return?
- If so, which form should be used?
- When and how should the return be filed?
- In computing the tax liability, which column of the Tax Table or which Tax Rate Schedule should be used?

The first three questions are discussed under Filing Requirements, and the last is treated under Filing Status.

AN IRS DILEMMA THAT WILL NOT GO AWAY

Many tax relief measures often are enacted for only a limited period of time. Congress uses this temporary approach because permanent measures could impair potential revenue sources. Most often, these provisions are renewed by an "extender law" when the original effective period expires.

Unfortunately, Congress frequently fails to enact these extender laws on a timely basis. Thus, as the expiration date comes and goes, no one knows for sure whether the extension will occur. Even worse, extender laws often apply retroactively.

Besides leaving taxpayers uncertain as to what the law is, Congress's procrastination puts the IRS in a real bind. Tax forms for the year must be printed and disseminated, so the IRS must "guess" whether the extender laws will be forthcoming. If its guess is wrong, replacement forms will compound everyone's confusion. Without doubt, irate taxpayers will regard the IRS as the culprit.

FILING REQUIREMENTS

General Rules.   An individual must file a tax return if certain minimum amounts of gross income have been received. The general rule is that a tax return is required for every individual who has gross income that equals or exceeds the sum of the exemption amount plus the applicable standard deduction.[24] For example, a single taxpayer under age 65 must file a tax return in 2001 if gross income equals or exceeds $7,450 ($2,900 exemption plus $4,550 standard deduction).[25]

7 *Find more information on this topic at our Web site: **http://wft-entities.swcollege.com**.*

The additional standard deduction for being age 65 or older is considered in determining the gross income filing requirements. For example, the 2001 filing requirement for a single taxpayer age 65 or older is $8,550 ($4,550 basic standard deduction + $1,100 additional standard deduction + $2,900 exemption).

A self-employed individual with net earnings of $400 or more from a business or profession must file a tax return regardless of the amount of gross income.

Even though an individual has gross income below the filing level amounts and therefore does not owe any tax, he or she must file a return to obtain a tax refund of amounts withheld by employers. A return is also necessary to obtain the benefits of the earned income credit allowed to taxpayers with little or no tax liability.

Filing Requirements for Dependents.   Computation of the gross income filing requirement for an individual who can be claimed as a dependent on another person's tax return is subject to more complex rules. For example, such an individual must file a return if he or she has earned income only and it is more than the

---

[24]The exemption and standard deduction amounts for determining whether a tax return must be filed are adjusted for inflation each year.

[25]§ 6012(a)(1).

TAX FACT

WHAT TAX FORM IS RIGHT FOR YOU?

Based on recent projections from the IRS, of the nearly 130 million individual income tax returns expected to be filed in 2001, taxpayers will be using the following forms and methods for reporting their income.

Form	Percentage
1040	50.8
1040A	11.3
1040EZ	8.1
Electronically filed returns	29.3
Other*	.5
	100.0

*Includes Forms 1040NR, 1040PR, and 1040SS.

Source: Number of Returns Filed, or To Be Filed With the Internal Revenue Service, Calendar Years 1998–2006.

---

total standard deduction (including any additional standard deduction) that the individual is allowed for the year.

8 *Find more information on this topic at our Web site: **http://wft-entities.swcollege.com**.*

Selecting the Proper Form. Although a variety of forms are available to individual taxpayers, the use of some of these forms is restricted. For example, Form 1040EZ cannot be used if the:

- Taxpayer claims any dependents;
- Taxpayer (or spouse) is 65 or older or blind; or
- Taxable income is $50,000 or more.

Taxpayers who desire to itemize deductions *from* AGI cannot use Form 1040A, but must file Form 1040 (the long form).

The E-File Approach. In addition to traditional paper returns, the **e-file** program is an increasingly popular alternative. Here, the required tax information is transmitted to the IRS electronically either directly from the taxpayer (i.e., an "e-file online return") or indirectly through an electronic return originator (ERO). EROs are tax professionals who have been accepted into the electronic filing program by the IRS. Such parties hold themselves out to the general public as "authorized IRS e-file providers." Providers often are also the preparers of the return.

The e-file approach has two major advantages. First, compliance with the format required by the IRS eliminates many errors that would otherwise occur. Second, the time required for processing a refund usually is reduced to three weeks or less.

When and Where to File. Tax returns of individuals are due on or before the fifteenth day of the fourth month following the close of the tax year. For the calendar

---

year taxpayer, the usual filing date is on or before April 15 of the following year.[26] When the due date falls on a Saturday, Sunday, or legal holiday, the last day for filing falls on the next business day.

If a taxpayer is unable to file the return by the specified due date, an automatic four-month extension of time can be obtained.[27] Further extensions may be granted by the IRS upon a showing of good cause by the taxpayer.

Although obtaining an extension excuses a taxpayer from a penalty for failure to file, it does not insulate against the penalty for failure to pay. If more tax is owed, the extension request should be accompanied by an additional payment to cover the balance due. The return should be sent or delivered to the Regional Service Center listed in the instructions for each type of return or contained in software applications.[28]

Mode of Payment.   Usually, payment is made by check. However, the IRS may now accept debit, credit, or charge cards for the payment of Federal income taxes. The entity providing the credit will charge the taxpayer a fee based on the size of the payment.

FILING STATUS

The amount of tax will vary considerably depending on which filing status is used. This is illustrated in the following example.

EXAMPLE 29

The following amounts of tax (rounded to the nearest dollar) are computed using the 2001 Tax Rate Schedules (inside the front cover of this text). The taxpayer (or taxpayers in the case of a joint return) is assumed to have $40,000 of taxable income.

Filing Status	Amount of Tax
Single	$7,684
Married, filing joint return	6,000
Married, filing separate return	8,262
Head of household	6,488

---

[26]§ 6072(a).

[27]Reg. § 1.6081–4.

[28]The Regional Service Centers and the geographic area each covers can also be found in *Your Federal Income Tax*, IRS Publication 17 for 2000 or at **http://www.irs.gov**.

BRIDGE DISCIPLINE

Bridge to Equity or Fairness

Much has been made in the press and in political circles in recent years concerning the so-called marriage penalty tax. This marriage penalty refers to the additional income tax that married couples pay over and above the aggregate amount two single individuals would pay with equal amounts of income. The marriage penalty arises because of the nature of the income tax rate structure that applies to individual taxpayers.

Relevant policy and ethical issues related to this dilemma are:

- Should the income tax system contain a bias against marriage?
- Should the income tax system require two people of economic means equal to that of two other people to pay a different amount of income taxes?
- Should the income tax system encourage two individuals to cohabit outside the commitment of marriage?

Congress has been struggling to design a "fix" for this problem for a number of years. However, despite all of the analysis and debate, legislation has not been enacted that will mitigate this inequity.

Rates for Single Taxpayers. A taxpayer who is unmarried or separated from his or her spouse by a decree of divorce or separate maintenance and does not qualify for another filing status must use the rates for single taxpayers. Marital status is determined as of the last day of the tax year, except when a spouse dies during the year. In that case, marital status is determined as of the date of death.

Rates for Married Individuals. The joint filing status was originally enacted to establish equity between married taxpayers in common law states and those in community property states. Before the joint return rates were enacted, taxpayers in community property states were in an advantageous position relative to taxpayers in common law states because they could split their income.

Taxpayers in common law states did not have this income-splitting option, so their taxable income was subject to higher marginal rates. This inconsistency in treatment was remedied by the joint return provisions. The progressive rates in the joint return Tax Rate Schedule are constructed based on the assumption that income is earned equally by the two spouses.

If married individuals elect to file separate returns, each reports only his or her own income, exemptions, deductions, and credits, and each must use the Tax Rate Schedule applicable to married taxpayers filing separately. It is generally advantageous for married individuals to file a joint return, since the combined amount of tax is lower. However, special circumstances (e.g., significant medical expenses incurred by one spouse subject to the 7.5 percent limitation) may warrant the election to file separate returns. It may be necessary to compute the tax under both assumptions to determine the most advantageous filing status.

When Congress enacted the joint return filing status, the result was to favor married taxpayers. In certain situations, however, the parties would incur less tax if they were not married and filed separate returns. The additional tax that a joint return can cause, commonly called the **marriage penalty,** can develop when *both* spouses have significant taxable incomes.

EXAMPLE 30

John and Betty are employed, and each earns taxable income of $55,000 in 2001. If they *are not married* and file separate returns, each has a tax liability of $11,884, or a total of $23,768 ($11,884 × 2). If they are married to each other, the filing of a joint return produces a tax of $24,947 on taxable income of $110,000 ($55,000 + $55,000). Thus, being married results in $1,179 ($24,947 − $23,768) more tax! ■

Although some have suggested changes to lessen the impact of the marriage penalty, any remedy is apt to make the tax law more complex.

9 *Find more information on this topic at our Web site: **http://wft-entities.swcollege.com**.*

The joint return rates also apply for two years following the death of one spouse, if the **surviving spouse** maintains a household for a dependent child.[29] This is referred to as surviving spouse status.

EXAMPLE 31

Fred dies in 2000 leaving Ethel with a dependent child. For the year of Fred's death (2000), Ethel files a joint return with Fred (presuming the consent of Fred's executor is obtained). For the next two years (2001 and 2002), Ethel, as a surviving spouse, may use the joint return rates. In subsequent years, Ethel may use the head-of-household rates if she continues to maintain a household as her home that is the domicile of the child. ■

Rates for Heads of Household.   Unmarried individuals who maintain a household for a dependent (or dependents) are entitled to use the **head-of-household** rates.[30] The tax liability resulting from the head-of-household rates falls between the liability using the joint return Tax Rate Schedule and the liability using the Tax Rate Schedule for single taxpayers.

To qualify for head-of-household rates, a taxpayer must pay more than half the cost of maintaining a household as his or her home. The household must also

---

[29]§ 2(a).   [30]§ 2(b).

be the principal home of a dependent relative.[31] As a general rule, the dependent must live in the taxpayer's household for over half the year.

10 *Find more information on this topic at our Web site: http://wft-entities.swcollege.com.*

LEARNING OBJECTIVE 6

Identify specific inclusions and exclusions applicable to individuals.

Overview of Income Provisions Applicable to Individuals

As indicated earlier in this chapter, the definition of gross income is broad enough to include almost all receipts of money, property, or services. However, the tax law provides for exclusion of many types of income. The following income provisions, which apply to all taxpayers (including individuals), were discussed in Chapter 3:

- Interest from state and local bonds.
- Life insurance paid on death of the insured.
- Imputed interest on below-market loans.
- Income from discharge of indebtedness.
- Income included under the tax benefit rule.

Most *exclusions* available only to individuals are for *fringe benefits* received by *employees* (refer to Exhibit 15–1). Fringe benefits are discussed in Chapter 16. Other specific inclusions and exclusions for individuals are discussed below.

Specific Inclusions Applicable to Individuals

The general principles of gross income determination as applied by the IRS and the courts have on occasion yielded results Congress found unacceptable. Consequently, Congress has provided more specific rules for determining the amount of gross income from certain sources. Some of these special rules appear in §§ 71–90 of the Code. The following provisions applicable to individuals are covered in this chapter:

- Alimony and separate maintenance payments.
- Prizes and awards.
- Unemployment compensation.
- Social Security benefits.

ALIMONY AND SEPARATE MAINTENANCE PAYMENTS

When a married couple divorce or become legally separated, state law generally requires a division of the property accumulated during the marriage. In addition, one spouse may have a legal obligation to support the other spouse. The Code distinguishes between the support payments (alimony or separate maintenance) and the property division in terms of the tax consequences.

Alimony and separate maintenance payments are deductible by the party making the payments and are includible in the gross income of the party receiving the payments.[32] Thus, taxation of the income is shifted from the income earner to the income beneficiary.

---

[31]As defined in § 152(a). See § 2(b)(1)(A)(i).   [32]§§ 71 and 215.

B R I D G E   D I S C I P L I N E

Bridge to Economics and Finance

As is the case for business entities, a primary financial goal for individual taxpayers should entail maximizing the *after-tax value* of their assets over time. This approach requires not only selecting the best investment alternatives, but also choosing those investments with the most favorable tax attributes. Fundamental to this notion is recognizing the key role that the government plays in all economic activity through its taxing authority. As a result, an investor should consider economically sound strategies that minimize the extent to which government can stake a claim to his or her success. For example, taxpayers can reduce the government's share of their wealth accumulations by deferring the payment of taxes until future years and by taking advantage of investment strategies for which tax incentives are available. Taxpayers should choose the investment alternatives that provide the best after-tax return over time and not necessarily the ones that lead to the least amount of taxation.

These points can be illustrated by examining two classic strategies. One of the best ways for individuals to maximize their personal wealth is to invest to the extent possible in qualifying retirement savings programs (e.g., traditional individual retirement accounts, § 401(k) accounts). Not only do current additions to such accounts provide a current tax deduction, but earnings within the account are not subject to taxation until they are withdrawn, which, in most cases, is during the retirement years of the owner. Postponing the tax in these two ways reduces the present value of the tax cost, which increases the after-tax value of the investment. Another strategy involves investing in tax-free municipal bonds, which produce interest income that is free of Federal income tax. The returns from such investments, however, should be compared with the after-tax returns flowing from available taxable debt securities. For example, a relevant question is how the implicit tax (see Chapter 1) associated with a municipal bond compares with the explicit tax associated with a taxable bond.

EXAMPLE 32

Pete and Tina are divorced, and Pete is required to pay Tina $15,000 of alimony each year. Pete earns $50,000 a year. Therefore, Tina must include the $15,000 in her gross income, and Pete is allowed to deduct $15,000 from his gross income. ∎

A transfer of property other than cash to a former spouse under a divorce decree or agreement is not a taxable event. The transferor is not entitled to a deduction and does not recognize gain or loss on the transfer. The transferee does not recognize income and has a cost basis equal to the transferor's basis.[33]

EXAMPLE 33

Paul transfers stock to Rosa as part of a 2001 divorce settlement. The cost of the stock to Paul is $12,000, and the stock's fair market value at the time of the transfer is $15,000. Rosa later sells the stock for $16,000. Paul is not required to recognize gain from the transfer of the stock to Rosa, and Rosa has a realized and recognized gain of $4,000 ($16,000 – $12,000) when she sells the stock. ∎

---

[33]Section 1041 was added to the Code in 1984 to repeal the rule of *U.S. v. Davis*, 62–2 USTC ¶9509, 9 AFTR2d 1625, 82 S.Ct. 1190 (USSC, 1962). Under the *Davis* rule, which applied to pre-1985 divorces, a property transfer incident to divorce was a taxable event.

In the case of cash payments, however, it is often difficult to distinguish between support payments (alimony) and property settlements. In 1984, Congress developed objective rules to classify these payments.[34]

11 *Find more information on this topic at our Web site: **http://wft-entities.swcollege.com**.*

Child Support. While alimony is taxable, a taxpayer does *not* report income from the receipt of child support payments made by his or her former spouse. This result occurs because the money is received subject to the duty to use the money for the child's benefit. The payor is not allowed to deduct the child support payments because the payments are made to satisfy the payor's legal obligation to support the child.

In many cases, it is difficult to determine whether an amount received is alimony or child support. If the amount of the payments would be reduced upon the happening of a contingency related to a child (e.g., the child attains age 21 or dies), the amount of the future reduction in the payment is deemed child support.[35]

EXAMPLE 34

A divorce agreement provides that Matt is required to make periodic alimony payments of $500 per month to Grace. However, when Matt and Grace's child reaches age 21, marries, or dies (whichever occurs first), the payments will be reduced to $300 per month. Child support payments are $200 each month, and alimony is $300 each month. ■

PRIZES AND AWARDS

The fair market value of prizes and awards must be included in gross income.[36] Therefore, TV giveaway prizes, magazine publisher prizes, door prizes, and awards from an employer to an employee in recognition of performance are fully taxable to the recipient.

A narrow exception permits a prize or award to be excluded from gross income if *all* of the following requirements are satisfied:

- The prize or award is received in recognition of religious, charitable, scientific, educational, artistic, literary, or civic achievement (e.g., Nobel Prize, Pulitzer Prize).
- The recipient was selected without taking any action to enter the contest or proceeding.
- The recipient is not required to render substantial future services as a condition for receiving the prize or award.[37]
- The recipient arranges for the prize or award to be paid *directly* to a qualified governmental unit or nonprofit organization.

Another exception is provided to allow exclusion of certain employee achievement awards in the form of tangible personal property (e.g., a gold watch). The awards must be made in recognition of length of service or safety achievement. Generally, the ceiling on the excludible amount for an employee is $400 per taxable year. However, if the award is a *qualified plan award*, the ceiling on the exclusion is $1,600 per taxable year.[38]

---

[34]More complex rules existed for determining the nature of payments under pre-1985 agreements.
[35]§ 71(c)(2).

[36]§ 74.
[37]§ 74(b).
[38]§§ 74(c) and 274(j).

UNEMPLOYMENT COMPENSATION

The unemployment compensation program is sponsored and operated by the states and Federal government to provide a source of income for people who have been employed and are temporarily out of work. In a series of rulings over a period of 40 years, the IRS exempted unemployment benefits from tax. These payments were considered social benefit programs for the promotion of the general welfare. After experiencing dissatisfaction with the IRS's treatment of unemployment compensation, Congress amended the Code to provide that the benefits are taxable.[39]

SOCIAL SECURITY BENEFITS

If a taxpayer's income exceeds a specified base amount, as much as 50 or 85 percent of Social Security retirement benefits must be included in gross income. The taxable amount of benefits is determined through the application of one of two complex formulas described in § 86.

12 *Find more information on this topic at our Web site:* ***http://wft-entities.swcollege.com.***

Specific Exclusions Applicable to Individuals

GIFTS AND INHERITANCES

Beginning with the Income Tax Act of 1913 and continuing to the present, Congress has allowed the recipient of a **gift** to exclude the value of the property from gross income. The exclusion applies to gifts made during the life of the donor (*inter vivos* gifts) and transfers that take effect upon the death of the donor (bequests and inheritances).[40] However, the recipient of a gift of income-producing property is subject to tax on the income subsequently earned from the property. Also, as discussed in Chapter 1, the donor or the decedent's estate may be subject to gift or estate taxes on such transfers.

In numerous cases, gifts are made in a business setting. For example, a salesperson gives a purchasing agent free samples; an employee receives cash from his or her employer on retirement; a corporation makes payments to employees who were victims of a natural disaster; a corporation makes a cash payment to a deceased employee's spouse. In these and similar instances, it is frequently unclear whether the payment was a gift or whether it represents compensation for past, present, or future services.

The courts have defined a gift as "a voluntary transfer of property by one to another without adequate consideration or compensation therefrom."[41] If the payment is intended to be for services rendered, it is not a gift, even though the payment is made without legal or moral obligation and the payor receives no economic benefit from the transfer. To qualify as a gift, the payment must be made "out of affection, respect, admiration, charity or like impulses."[42] Thus, the cases on this issue have been decided on the basis of the donor's intent.[43]

[39]§ 85.
[40]§ 102.
[41]*Estate of D. R. Daly*, 3 B.T.A. 1042 (1926).
[42]*Robertson v. U.S.*, 52–1 USTC ¶9343, 41 AFTR 1053, 72 S.Ct. 994 (USSC, 1952).

[43]See, for example, *Comm. v. Duberstein*, 60–2 USTC ¶9515, 5 AFTR2d 1626, 80 S.Ct. 1190 (USSC, 1960).

BEGGING AS A TAX-DISFAVORED OCCUPATION

In five recent decisions, the Tax Court ruled that amounts received from begging are nontaxable gifts. In a reversal of the normal roles, the beggars contended that the amounts received were earned income while the IRS argued that the taxpayers had merely received gifts. The beggars wanted the fruit of their efforts to be treated as earned income in order to qualify them for the earned income credit.

In the case of cash or other property received by an employee from his or her employer, Congress has eliminated any ambiguity. Transfers from an employer to an employee cannot be excluded as a gift.[44]

13 *Find more information on this topic at our Web site:* ***http://wft-entities.swcollege.com***.

SCHOLARSHIPS

General Information. Payments or benefits received by a student at an educational institution may be (1) compensation for services, (2) a gift, or (3) a scholarship. If the payments or benefits are received as compensation for services (past or present), the fact that the recipient is a student generally does not render the amounts received nontaxable.[45]

EXAMPLE 35

State University waives tuition for all graduate teaching assistants. The tuition waived is intended as compensation for services and is therefore included in the graduate assistant's gross income. ■

The **scholarship** rules are intended to provide exclusion treatment for education-related benefits that cannot qualify as gifts but are not compensation for services. According to the Regulations, "a scholarship is an amount paid or allowed to, or for the benefit of, an individual to aid such individual in the pursuit of study or research."[46] The recipient must be a candidate for a degree (either undergraduate or graduate) at an educational institution.[47]

EXAMPLE 36

Terry enters a contest sponsored by a local newspaper. Each contestant is required to submit an essay on local environmental issues. The prize is one year's tuition at State University. Terry wins the contest. The newspaper has a legal obligation to Terry (as contest winner). Thus, the benefits are not a gift. However, since the tuition payment aids Terry in pursuing her studies and is not compensation for services, the payment is a scholarship. ■

A scholarship recipient may exclude from gross income the amount used for tuition and related expenses (fees, books, supplies, and equipment required for courses), provided the conditions of the grant do not require that the funds be

---

[44]§ 102(c).
[45]Reg. § 1.117–2(a). See *C. P. Bhalla*, 35 T.C. 13 (1960), for a discussion of the distinction between a scholarship and compensation. See also *Bingler v. Johnson*, 69–1 USTC ¶9348, 23 AFTR2d 1212, 89

S.Ct. 1439 (USSC, 1969). For potential exclusion treatment, see the subsequent discussion of qualified tuition reductions.
[46]Prop.Reg. § 1.117–6(c)(3)(i).
[47]§ 117(a).

used for other purposes.[48] Amounts received for room and board are taxable and are treated as earned income for purposes of calculating the standard deduction for a taxpayer who is another taxpayer's dependent.[49]

EXAMPLE 37

Kelly receives a scholarship of $9,500 from State University to be used to pursue a bachelor's degree. She spends $4,000 on tuition, $3,000 on books and supplies, and $2,500 for room and board. Kelly may exclude $7,000 ($4,000 + $3,000) from gross income. The $2,500 spent for room and board is includible in Kelly's gross income.

    The scholarship is Kelly's only source of income. Her parents provide more than 50% of Kelly's support and claim her as a dependent. Kelly's standard deduction of $2,750 ($2,500 + $250) exceeds her $2,500 gross income. Thus, she has no taxable income. ∎

Timing Issues.   Frequently, the scholarship recipient is a cash basis taxpayer who receives the money in one tax year but pays the educational expenses in a subsequent year. The amount eligible for exclusion may not be known at the time the money is received. In that case, the transaction is held open until the educational expenses are paid.[50]

EXAMPLE 38

In August 2001, Sanjay received $10,000 as a scholarship for the academic year 2001–2002. Sanjay's expenditures for tuition, books, and supplies were as follows:

August–December 2001	$3,000
January–May 2002	4,500
	$7,500

Sanjay's gross income for 2002 includes $2,500 ($10,000 − $7,500) that is not excludible as a scholarship. None of the scholarship is included in his gross income in 2001. ∎

Disguised Compensation.   Some employers make scholarships available solely to the children of key employees. The tax objective of these plans is to provide a nontaxable fringe benefit to the executives by making the payment to the child in the form of an excludible scholarship. However, the IRS has ruled that the payments are generally includible by the parent-employee as compensation for services.[51]

DAMAGES

A person who suffers harm caused by another is often entitled to **compensatory damages.** The tax consequences of the receipt of damages depend on the type of harm the taxpayer has experienced. The taxpayer may seek recovery for (1) a loss of income, (2) expenses incurred, (3) property destroyed, or (4) personal injury.

    Generally, reimbursement for a loss of income is taxed in the same manner as the income replaced. Damages that are a recovery of expenses previously deducted by the taxpayer are generally taxable under the tax benefit rule (refer to Chapter 3).

    A payment for damaged or destroyed property is treated as an amount received in a sale or exchange of the property. Thus, the taxpayer has a realized gain if the damage payments received exceed the property's basis. Damages for personal injuries receive special treatment under the Code.

---

[48]§ 117(b).
[49]Prop.Reg. § 1.117–6(h).
[50]Prop.Reg. § 1.117–6(b)(2).

[51]Rev.Rul. 75–448, 1975–2 C.B. 55, and *Richard T. Armantrout*, 67 T.C. 996 (1977).

SPECIAL LEGISLATION IS REQUIRED FOR HOLOCAUST REPARATIONS

The governments of Germany and Switzerland and some corporations have agreed to pay reparations to Holocaust victims who suffered losses as a result of seizures of property during the period 1933–1945. In addition to the awards for the taking of property, the victims will receive interest for more than 50 years. Because the payments are for the taking of property and not for personal injury, the income and estate tax consequences of receiving the reparations could be substantial. Under present U.S. tax law, the amount received in excess of basis would be included in gross income.

The governments of Switzerland and Germany have agreed to exempt the payments from tax. Legislation has been introduced in the U.S. Congress that would likewise exempt the awards from U.S. tax.

SOURCE: Joint Committee on Taxation, *Description of Tax Provisions in President's FY2001 Budget*, March 6, 2000.

Personal Injury. The legal theory of personal injury damages is that the amount received is intended "to make the plaintiff [the injured party] whole as before the injury."[52] It follows that if the damage payments received were subject to tax, the after-tax amount received would be less than the actual damages incurred and the injured party would not be "whole as before the injury."

With regard to personal injury damages, a distinction is made between compensatory damages and **punitive damages.** Under specified circumstances, compensatory damages may be excluded from gross income. Under no circumstances may punitive damages be excluded from gross income.

Compensatory damages are intended to compensate the taxpayer for the damages incurred. Only those compensatory damages received on account of *physical personal injury or sickness* can be excluded from gross income.[53] Compensatory damages awarded on account of emotional distress are not received on account of physical injury or sickness and thus cannot be excluded from gross income (except to the extent of any amount received for medical care). Likewise, any amounts received for age discrimination or injury to one's reputation cannot be excluded.

Punitive damages are amounts the party that caused the harm must pay to the victim as punishment for outrageous conduct. Punitive damages are not intended to compensate the victim, but rather to punish the party that caused the harm. Thus, it follows that amounts received as punitive damages may actually place the victim in a better economic position than before the harm was experienced. Logically, punitive damages are thus included in gross income.

EXAMPLE 39

Tom, a television announcer, was dissatisfied with the manner in which Ron, an attorney, was defending the television station in a libel case. Tom stated on the air that Ron was botching the case. Ron sued Tom for slander, claiming damages for loss of income from clients and potential clients who heard Tom's statement. Ron's claim is for damages to his business reputation, and the amounts received are taxable.

---

[52]*C. A. Hawkins*, 6 B.T.A. 1023 (1928).   [53]§ 104(a)(2).

CONCEPT SUMMARY 15–1

Taxation of Damages

Type of Claim	Taxation of Award or Settlement
Breach of contract (generally loss of income)	Taxable.
Property damages	Recovery of cost; gain to the extent of the excess over basis. A loss is deductible for business property and investment property to the extent of basis over the amount realized. A loss may be deductible for personal-use property (see discussion of casualty losses in Chapter 5).
Personal injury	
Physical	All compensatory amounts are excluded unless previously deducted (e.g., medical expenses). Amounts received as punitive damages are included in gross income.
Nonphysical	Compensatory damages and punitive damages are included in gross income.

Ron collected on the suit against Tom and was on his way to a party to celebrate his victory when a negligent driver, Norm, drove a truck into Ron's automobile, injuring Ron. Ron filed suit for the physical personal injuries and claimed as damages the loss of income for the period he was unable to work as a result of the injuries. Ron also collected punitive damages that were awarded because of Norm's extremely negligent behavior. Ron's wife also collected damages for the emotional distress she experienced as a result of the accident. Ron may exclude the amounts he received for damages, except the punitive damages. Ron's wife must include the amounts she received for damages in gross income because the amounts were not received because of physical personal injuries or sickness. ∎

WORKERS' COMPENSATION

State workers' compensation laws require the employer to pay fixed amounts for specific job-related injuries. The state laws were enacted so that the employee will not have to go through the ordeal of a lawsuit (and possibly not collect damages because of some defense available to the employer) to recover the damages. Although the payments are intended, in part, to compensate for a loss of future income, Congress has specifically exempted workers' compensation benefits from inclusion in gross income.[54]

ACCIDENT AND HEALTH INSURANCE BENEFITS

The income tax treatment of **accident and health insurance benefits** depends on whether the policy providing the benefits was purchased by the taxpayer or the taxpayer's employer. Benefits collected under an accident and health insurance policy purchased by the taxpayer are excludible. In this case, benefits collected under the taxpayer's insurance policy are excluded even though the payments are a substitute for income.[55]

---

[54]§ 104(a)(1).

[55]§ 104(a)(3).

EXAMPLE 40

Bonnie purchases a medical and disability insurance policy. The insurance company pays Bonnie $200 per week to replace wages she loses while in the hospital. Although the payments serve as a substitute for income, the amounts received are tax-exempt benefits collected under Bonnie's insurance policy. ■

EXAMPLE 41

Joe's injury results in a partial paralysis of his left foot. He receives $5,000 for the injury from his accident insurance company under a policy he had purchased. The $5,000 accident insurance proceeds are tax-exempt. ■

A different set of rules applies if the accident and health insurance protection was purchased by the individual's employer, as discussed in Chapter 16.

EDUCATIONAL SAVINGS BONDS

The cost of a college education has risen dramatically during the past 15 years. The U.S. Department of Education estimates that by the year 2007, the cost of attending a publicly supported university for four years will exceed $60,000. For a private university, the cost is expected to exceed $200,000. Consequently, Congress has attempted to assist low- to middle-income parents in saving for their children's college education.

The assistance is in the form of an interest income exclusion on **educational savings bonds.**[56] The interest on U.S. government Series EE savings bonds may be excluded from gross income if the bond proceeds are used to pay qualified higher education expenses. The exclusion applies only if both of the following requirements are satisfied:

- The savings bonds are issued after December 31, 1989.
- The savings bonds are issued to an individual who is at least 24 years old at the time of issuance.

The redemption proceeds must be used to pay qualified higher education expenses. Qualified higher education expenses consist of tuition and fees paid to an eligible educational institution for the taxpayer, spouse, or dependent. In calculating qualified higher education expenses, the tuition and fees paid are reduced by excludible scholarships and veterans' benefits received. If the redemption proceeds (both principal and interest) exceed the qualified higher education expenses, only a pro rata portion of the interest will qualify for exclusion treatment.

EXAMPLE 42

Tracy's redemption proceeds from qualified savings bonds during the taxable year are $6,000 (principal of $4,000 and interest of $2,000). Tracy's qualified higher education expenses are $5,000. Since the redemption proceeds exceed the qualified higher education expenses, only $1,667 [($5,000/$6,000) × $2,000] of the interest is excludible. ■

The exclusion is limited by the application of the wherewithal to pay concept. That is, once the *modified AGI (MAGI)* exceeds a threshold amount, the phase-out of the exclusion begins. The threshold amounts are adjusted for inflation each year. For 2001, the phase-out begins at $55,750 ($83,650 on a joint return).[57] The phase-out is completed when MAGI exceeds the threshold amount by more than $15,000 ($30,000 on a joint return). The otherwise excludible interest is reduced by the amount calculated as follows:

---

[56]§ 135.

[57]The indexed amounts for 2000 are $54,100 and $81,100.

$$\frac{\text{MAGI} - \$55,750}{\$15,000} \times \frac{\text{Excludible interest}}{\text{before phase-out}} = \frac{\text{Reduction in}}{\text{excludible interest}}$$

On a joint return, $83,650 is substituted for $55,750 (in 2001), and $30,000 is substituted for $15,000.

EXAMPLE 43

Assume the same facts as in Example 42, except that Tracy's MAGI for 2001 is $60,000. The phase-out results in Tracy's interest exclusion being reduced by $472 {[($60,000 − $55,750)/ $15,000] × $1,667}. Therefore, Tracy's exclusion is $1,195 ($1,667 − $472). ∎

LEARNING OBJECTIVE 7

Determine an individual's allowable itemized deductions.

Itemized Deductions

Taxpayers are allowed to deduct specified expenditures as itemized deductions. Itemized deductions, which are reported on Schedule A, can be classified as follows:

- Expenses that are purely *personal* in nature.
- Expenses incurred by *employees* in connection with their employment activities.
- Expenses related to (1) the *production or collection of income* and (2) the *management of property* held for the production of income.[58]

Expenses in the third category, sometimes referred to as *nonbusiness expenses*, differ from trade or business expenses (discussed previously). Trade or business expenses, which are deductions *for* AGI, must be incurred in connection with a trade or business. Nonbusiness expenses, on the other hand, are expenses incurred in connection with an income-producing activity that does not qualify as a trade or business. If the nonbusiness expense is incurred in connection with rent or royalty property, it is classified as a deduction *for* AGI. Otherwise, it is classified as a deduction *from* AGI. Itemized deductions include, but are not limited to, the expenses listed in Exhibit 15–3.

Allowable itemized deductions are deductible *from* AGI in arriving at taxable income if the taxpayer elects to itemize. The election to itemize is appropriate when total itemized deductions exceed the standard deduction based on the taxpayer's filing status. The more important itemized deductions are discussed below.

MEDICAL EXPENSES

Medical Expenses Defined. **Medical expenses** paid for the care of the taxpayer, spouse, and dependents are allowed as an itemized deduction to the extent the expenses are not reimbursed. The medical expense deduction is limited to the amount by which such expenses exceed 7.5 percent of the taxpayer's AGI.

EXAMPLE 44

During the year, Iris had medical expenses of $4,800, of which $1,000 was reimbursed by her insurance company. If her AGI for the year is $40,000, the itemized deduction for medical expenses is limited to $800 [$4,800 − $1,000 = $3,800 − (7.5% × $40,000)]. ∎

The term *medical care* includes expenditures incurred for the "diagnosis, cure, mitigation, treatment, or prevention of disease, or for the purpose of affecting any

---

[58]Section 212 allows itemized deductions for these types of activities. However, expenses related to the production of *rental or royalty* income are deductions *for* AGI, not itemized deductions, under § 62(a)(4).

■ **EXHIBIT 15-3**
Partial List of Itemized
Deductions

Personal Expenditures

Medical expenses (in excess of 7.5% of AGI)

State and local income taxes

Real estate taxes

Personal property taxes

Interest on home mortgage

Charitable contributions (limited to a maximum of 50% of AGI)

Casualty and theft losses (in excess of 10% of AGI)

Tax return preparation fee (in excess of 2% of AGI)

Expenditures Related to Employment (in Excess of 2% of AGI)

Union dues

Professional dues and subscriptions

Certain educational expenses

Unreimbursed employee business expenses

Expenditures Related to Income-Producing Activities

Investment interest (to the extent of investment income)

Investment counsel fees (in excess of 2% of AGI)

Other investment expenses (in excess of 2% of AGI)

---

structure or function of the body."[59] Medical expense also includes premiums paid for health care insurance, prescribed drugs and insulin, and lodging while away from home for the purpose of obtaining medical care. Examples of deductible and nondeductible medical expenses appear in Exhibit 15–4.

Cosmetic Surgery. Amounts paid for unnecessary cosmetic surgery are not deductible medical expenses. However, if cosmetic surgery is deemed necessary, it is deductible as a medical expense. Cosmetic surgery is necessary when it ameliorates (1) a deformity arising from a congenital abnormality, (2) a personal injury, or (3) a disfiguring disease.

Nursing Home Care. The cost of care in a nursing home or home for the aged, including meals and lodging, can be included in deductible medical expenses if the primary reason for being in the home is to get medical care. If the primary reason for being there is personal, any costs for medical or nursing care can be included in deductible medical expenses, but the cost of meals and lodging must be excluded.

Capital Expenditures. The treatment of certain illnesses may require expenditures for equipment, special structures, or modification of the taxpayer's residence. Some examples of capital expenditures for medical purposes are swimming pools if the taxpayer does not have access to a neighborhood pool and air conditioners if they do not become permanent improvements (e.g., window units).[60] Other examples include dust elimination systems,[61] elevators,[62] and a room built to house an

---

[59]§ 213(d).
[60]Rev.Rul. 55–261, 1955–1 C.B. 307, modified by Rev.Rul. 68–212, 1968–1 C.B. 91.

[61]*F. S. Delp*, 30 T.C. 1230 (1958).
[62]*Riach v. Frank*, 62–1 USTC ¶9419, 9 AFTR2d 1263, 302 F.2d 374 (CA–9, 1962).

AVERAGE ITEMIZED DEDUCTIONS

Are your itemized deductions close to average for your income level? Actually, if you're a typical taxpayer, you take the standard deduction instead of itemizing. Approximately 70 percent of individual taxpayers take the standard deduction each year.

The IRS recently released statistics on the approximately 30 percent of individual taxpayers who did itemize in 1998—a year that saw itemized deductions rise 4 percent over 1997. Statistics for the most popular deductions are listed in the following table. The table omits medical expenses because few taxpayers (approximately 5 percent) have medical expenses in excess of the 7.5 percent floor. Similarly, casualty losses (subject to a 10 percent floor) and miscellaneous itemized deductions (subject to a 2 percent floor) are omitted. For comparison, the standard deduction in 1998 was $4,250 for single taxpayers, $7,100 for married taxpayers filing jointly, and $6,250 for heads of household.

AGI	Taxes	Contributions	Interest	Total
$ 15,000–29,999	$ 2,160	$ 1,565	$ 5,815	$ 9,540
30,000–49,999	3,025	1,635	6,129	10,789
50,000–99,999	4,957	2,163	7,564	14,684
100,000–199,999	9,344	3,618	10,995	23,957
200,000+	36,385	19,471	21,760	77,616

These statistics reveal some interesting aspects of the U.S. lifestyle. For one thing, taxpayers at all income levels—even those with AGI of more than $200,000—pay interest on borrowed funds. For another, as AGI increases, the percentage given to charity decreases. Those with AGI of $15,000 to $29,999 contribute 6.95 percent of their median income; least generous are taxpayers with AGI of $100,000 to $199,999, who contribute only 2.41 percent of their median income.

Finally, consider what taxpayers have left after meeting the expenses reflected in the table. For example, a single taxpayer with AGI of $25,000 in 1998, would have only $15,460 left after paying typical itemized deductions for that income level ($25,000 − $9,540 itemized deductions). After paying $1,914 of this amount as Federal income taxes, the taxpayer would have $13,546 left for other expenses.

SOURCE: Information from "Tax Report: Charitable Gifts and Other Itemized Deductions Continue to Rise," *Wall Street Journal*, July 19, 2000.

iron lung. These expenditures are medical in nature if they are incurred as a medical necessity upon the advice of a physician, the facility is used primarily by the patient alone, and the expense is reasonable.

Capital expenditures normally are adjustments to basis and are deductible only through depreciation. However, both a capital expenditure for a permanent improvement and expenditures made for the operation or maintenance of the improvement may qualify as medical expenses. If a capital expenditure qualifies as a medical expense, the allowable cost is deductible in the *year incurred*.

Medical Expenses for Spouse and Dependents.   In computing the medical expense deduction, a taxpayer may include medical expenses for a spouse and for

Deductible	Nondeductible
Medical (including dental, mental, and hospital) care	Funeral, burial, or cremation expenses
Prescription drugs	Nonprescription drugs (except insulin)
Special equipment	Bottled water
Wheelchairs	Diaper service, maternity clothes
Crutches	Programs for the general improvement of health
Artificial limbs	Weight reduction
Eyeglasses (including contact lenses)	Health spas
Hearing aids	Social activities (e.g., dancing and swimming lessons)
Transportation for medical care	Unnecessary cosmetic surgery
Medical and hospital insurance premiums	
Cost of alcohol and drug rehabilitation	
Certain costs to stop smoking	

a person who was a dependent at the time the expenses were paid or incurred. Of the five requirements that normally apply in determining dependency status, neither the gross income nor the joint return test applies in determining dependency status for medical expense deduction purposes.

Transportation and Lodging.   Payments for transportation to and from a hospital or other medical facility for medical care are deductible as medical expenses (subject to the 7.5 percent floor). Transportation expenses for medical care include bus, taxi, train, or plane fare, charges for ambulance service, and out-of-pocket expenses for the use of an automobile. A mileage allowance of 12 cents per mile[63] may be used instead of actual out-of-pocket automobile expenses. Whether the taxpayer chooses to claim out-of-pocket automobile expenses or the 12 cents per mile automatic mileage option, related parking fees and tolls can also be deducted. The cost of meals while en route to obtain medical care is not deductible.

14 *Find more information on this topic at our Web site:* ***http://wft-entities.swcollege.com***.

Medical Savings Accounts.   Medical Savings Accounts (MSAs) were created as a pilot project, effective for tax years beginning after December 31, 1996. The pilot project was scheduled to end on December 31, 2000, but it has been extended for two additional years. The primary tax advantage of an MSA is that contributions made by the taxpayer are deductible from gross income. Other tax considerations are discussed below.

When coupled with a *high-deductible* medical insurance policy, an MSA provides an opportunity for taxpayers to decrease the overall cost of medical coverage. The high-deductible policy provides coverage for extraordinary medical expenses (in excess of the deductible), and expenses not covered by the policy can be paid with funds withdrawn from the MSA. High-deductible policies are less expensive than low-deductible policies, so taxpayers with low medical costs can benefit from the lower premiums and use funds from the MSA to pay costs not covered by the high-deductible policy.

[63]Rev.Proc. 2000-48, I.R.B. No. 49, 570.

■ **EXHIBIT 15–5**
Deductible and Nondeductible
Taxes

Deductible	Nondeductible
State, local, and foreign real property taxes	Federal income taxes
	FICA taxes imposed on employees
State and local personal property taxes	Employer FICA taxes paid on domestic household workers
State, local, and foreign income taxes	Estate, inheritance, and gift taxes
	General sales taxes
The environmental tax	Federal, state, and local excise taxes (e.g., gasoline, tobacco, spirits)
	Taxes on real property to the extent such taxes are to be apportioned and treated as imposed on another taxpayer
	Special assessments for streets, sidewalks, curbing, and other similar improvements

MSAs can be established by employers with 50 or fewer employees, self-employed individuals, and individuals without insurance coverage. Individuals whose employers contribute to MSAs may exclude the contributions from gross income. Individuals who contribute to MSAs may deduct the contributions (within limits) as deductions *for* AGI. Earnings on MSAs are not included in gross income of the current year. MSA distributions that are used to pay for medical expenses not covered by a high-deductible policy are excluded from gross income. However, distributions for purposes other than the payment of medical expenses are included in gross income and are subject to an additional 15 percent penalty if made before age 65, death, or disability.

TAXES

A deduction is allowed for certain state and local taxes paid or accrued by a taxpayer.[64] The deduction was created to relieve the burden of multiple taxes upon the same source of revenue.

Deductible taxes must be distinguished from nondeductible fees. Fees for special privileges or services are not deductible as itemized deductions if personal in nature. Examples include fees for dog licenses, automobile inspection, automobile titles and registration, hunting and fishing licenses, bridge and highway tolls, drivers' licenses, parking meter deposits, postage, etc. These items, however, could be deductible if incurred as a business expense or for the production of income (refer to Chapter 4). Deductible and nondeductible taxes for purposes of computing itemized deductions are summarized in Exhibit 15–5.

Personal Property Taxes. Deductible personal property taxes must be *ad valorem* (assessed in relation to the value of the property). Therefore, a motor vehicle tax based on weight, model, year, or horsepower is not an ad valorem tax. In contrast, a motor vehicle tax based on the value of the car is deductible.

EXAMPLE 45

A state imposes a motor vehicle registration tax on 4% of the value of the vehicle plus 40 cents per hundredweight. Belle, a resident of the state, owns a car having a value of $4,000

---

[64]Most deductible taxes are listed in § 164, while the nondeductible items are included in § 275.

and weighing 3,000 pounds. Belle pays an annual registration fee of $172. Of this amount, $160 (4% of $4,000) is deductible as a personal property tax. The remaining $12, based on the weight of the car, is not deductible. ∎

Real Estate Taxes.   Real estate taxes of individuals are generally deductible. Taxes on personal-use property and investment property are deductible as itemized deductions. Taxes on business property are deductible as business expenses. Real property taxes on property that is sold during the year must be allocated between the buyer and the seller (refer to Chapter 4).

State and Local Income Taxes.   The position of the IRS is that state and local *income* taxes imposed upon an individual are deductible only as itemized deductions, even if the taxpayer's sole source of income is from a business, rents, or royalties.

Cash basis taxpayers are entitled to deduct state income taxes withheld by the employer in the year the taxes are withheld. In addition, estimated state income tax payments are deductible in the year the payment is made by cash basis taxpayers even if the payments relate to a prior or subsequent year.[65] If the taxpayer overpays state income taxes because of excessive withholdings or estimated tax payments, the refund received is included in gross income of the following year to the extent that the deduction reduced the taxable income in the prior year.

EXAMPLE 46

Leona, a cash basis, unmarried taxpayer, had $800 of state income tax withheld during 2001. Additionally in 2001, Leona paid $100 that was due when she filed her 2000 state income tax return and made estimated payments of $300 on her 2001 state income tax. When Leona files her 2001 Federal income tax return in April 2002, she elects to itemize deductions, which amount to $5,500, including the $1,200 of state income tax payments and withholdings. The itemized deductions reduce her taxable income.

As a result of overpaying her 2001 state income tax, Leona receives a refund of $200 early in 2002. She will include this amount in her 2002 gross income in computing her Federal income tax. It does not matter whether Leona received a check from the state for $200 or applied the $200 toward her 2002 state income tax. ∎

PLANNING CONSIDERATIONS

Timing the Payment of Deductible Taxes

It is sometimes possible to defer or accelerate the payment of certain deductible taxes, such as state income tax, real property tax, and personal property tax. For instance, the final installment of estimated state income tax is generally due after the end of a given tax year. Accelerating the payment of the final installment could result in larger itemized deductions for the current year.

INTEREST

For Federal income tax purposes, interest must be divided into five categories: business interest, personal interest, interest on qualified education loans, qualified residence interest, and investment interest. Business interest is fully deductible as an ordinary

---

[65]Rev.Rul. 71–190, 1971–1 C.B. 70. See also Rev.Rul. 82–208, 1982–2 C.B. 58, where a deduction is not allowed when the taxpayer cannot, in good faith, reasonably determine that there is additional state income tax liability.

and necessary expense. Personal (consumer) interest is not deductible. This includes credit card interest, interest on car loans, and any other interest that is not interest on qualified education loans, business interest, qualified residence interest, or investment interest. Interest on qualified education loans, investment interest, and qualified residence (home mortgage) interest are deductible, subject to limits discussed below.

Interest on Qualified Education Loans.   Taxpayers who pay interest on a qualified education loan may deduct the interest, subject to limits, as a deduction *for* AGI. A qualified education loan does not include indebtedness to certain related parties.

The deduction applies to interest paid during the first 60 months during which payments are required, thus providing a tax incentive for timely payment of student loans. The maximum deduction, which is $2,500 for taxable years beginning in 2001 and thereafter, is phased out for taxpayers with modified AGI (MAGI) between $40,000 and $55,000 ($60,000 and $75,000 on joint returns).[66]

Investment Interest.   Taxpayers frequently borrow funds that they use to acquire investment assets. When the interest expense is large relative to the income from the investments, substantial tax benefits could result. Congress has therefore limited the deductibility of interest on funds borrowed for the purpose of purchasing or continuing to hold investment property. **Investment interest** expense is limited to **net investment income** for the year.[67]

Investment income is gross income from interest, dividends, annuities, and royalties not derived in the ordinary course of a trade or business. Income from a passive activity and income from a real estate activity in which the taxpayer actively participates are not included in investment income (see Chapter 5).

Net capital gain attributable to the disposition of property producing the types of income just identified or from property held for investment purposes may be included as investment income at the taxpayer's election. To make this election, the taxpayer must agree to reduce capital gains qualifying for the alternative tax computation for net capital gain (see Chapter 8) by an equivalent amount.

EXAMPLE 47

Terry incurred $13,000 of interest expense related to her investments during the year. Her investment income included $4,000 of interest, $2,000 of dividends, and a $5,000 net capital gain on the sale of securities. Her investment income for purposes of computing the investment income limitation is $6,000 ($4,000 interest + $2,000 dividends). If she elects to treat the net capital gain as investment income, her investment income for purposes of computing the limitation is $11,000. ∎

Net investment income is the excess of investment income over investment expenses. Investment expenses are those deductible expenses directly connected with the production of investment income. Investment expenses do not include investment interest expense.

15 *Find more information on this topic at our Web site:* ***http://wft-entities.swcollege.com.***

Qualified Residence Interest.   **Qualified residence interest** is interest paid or accrued during the taxable year on indebtedness (subject to limitations) secured by any property that is a qualified residence of the taxpayer. Qualified residence

---

[66]§ 221. See § 221(b)(2)(C) for the definition of MAGI. The phase-out amounts will be adjusted for inflation for tax years beginning after 2002.

[67]§ 163(d).

interest falls into two categories: (1) interest on **acquisition indebtedness** and (2) interest on **home equity loans.** Before discussing each of these categories, however, the term *qualified residence* must be defined.

A qualified residence includes the taxpayer's principal residence and one other residence of the taxpayer or spouse. The principal residence is one that meets the requirement for nonrecognition of gain upon sale under § 121 (see Chapter 7). The one other residence, or second residence, refers to one that is used as a residence if not rented or, if rented, meets the requirements for a personal residence under the rental of vacation home rules. A taxpayer who has more than one second residence can make the selection each year of which one is the qualified second residence. A residence includes, in addition to a house in the ordinary sense, cooperative apartments, condominiums, and mobile homes and boats that have living quarters (sleeping accommodations and toilet and cooking facilities).

Although in most cases interest paid on a home mortgage is fully deductible, there are limitations.[68] Interest paid or accrued during the tax year on aggregate acquisition indebtedness of $1 million or less ($500,000 for married persons filing separate returns) is deductible as qualified residence interest. Acquisition indebtedness refers to amounts incurred in acquiring, constructing, or substantially improving a qualified residence of the taxpayer.

Qualified residence interest also includes interest on home equity loans. These loans utilize the personal residence of the taxpayer as security. Because the funds from home equity loans can be used for personal purposes (e.g., auto purchases, medical expenses), what would otherwise have been nondeductible consumer interest becomes deductible qualified residence interest. However, interest is deductible only on the portion of a home equity loan that does not exceed the lesser of:

- The fair market value of the residence, reduced by the acquisition indebtedness, or
- $100,000 ($50,000 for married persons filing separate returns).

EXAMPLE 48

Larry owns a personal residence with a fair market value of $150,000 and an outstanding first mortgage of $120,000. Therefore, his equity in his home is $30,000 ($150,000 – $120,000). Larry issues a lien on the residence and in return borrows $15,000 to purchase a new family automobile. All interest on the $135,000 of debt is treated as qualified residence interest. ■

EXAMPLE 49

Leon and Pearl, married taxpayers, took out a mortgage on their home for $200,000 in 1983. In March of the current year, when the home has a fair market value of $400,000 and they owe $195,000 on the mortgage, Leon and Pearl take out a home equity loan for $120,000. They use the funds to purchase an airplane to be used for recreational purposes. On a joint return, Leon and Pearl can deduct all of the interest on the first mortgage since it is acquisition indebtedness. Of the $120,000 home equity loan, only the interest on the first $100,000 is deductible. The interest on the remaining $20,000 is not deductible because it exceeds the statutory ceiling of $100,000. ■

Interest Paid for Services. Mortgage loan companies commonly charge a fee for finding, placing, or processing a mortgage loan. Such fees are often called **points** and are expressed as a percentage of the loan amount. Borrowers often have to pay points to obtain the necessary financing. To qualify as deductible interest, the points must be considered compensation to a lender solely for the use or forbearance of money. The points cannot be a form of service charge or payment for specific services if they are to qualify as deductible interest.[69]

---

[68]§ 163(h)(3).

[69]Rev.Rul. 67–297, 1967–2 C.B. 87.

Points must be capitalized and are amortized and deductible ratably over the life of the loan. A special exception permits the purchaser of a personal residence to deduct qualifying points in the year of payment.[70] The exception also covers points paid to obtain funds for home improvements.

EXAMPLE 50

During 2001, Thelma purchases a new residence for $130,000 and pays points of $2,600 to obtain mortgage financing. At Thelma's election, the $2,600 can be claimed as an interest deduction for 2001. ■

Points paid to refinance an existing home mortgage cannot be immediately expensed, but must be capitalized and amortized as interest expense over the life of the new loan.[71]

EXAMPLE 51

Sandra purchased her residence four years ago, obtaining a 30-year mortgage at an annual interest rate of 12%. In the current year, Sandra refinances the mortgage in order to reduce the interest rate to 9%. To obtain the refinancing, she has to pay points of $2,600. The $2,600 paid comes under the usual rule applicable to points. That is, the $2,600 must be capitalized and amortized over the life of the mortgage. ■

Prepayment Penalty.   When a mortgage or loan is paid off in full in a lump sum before its term, the lending institution may require an additional payment of a certain percentage applied to the unpaid amount at the time of prepayment. This is known as a prepayment penalty and is considered to be interest (e.g., personal, qualified residence, investment) in the year paid. The general rules for deductibility of interest also apply to prepayment penalties.

Interest Paid to Related Parties.   Nothing prevents the deduction of interest paid to a related party as long as the payment actually took place and the interest meets the requirements for deductibility. Recall from Chapter 6 that a special rule for related taxpayers applies when the debtor uses the accrual basis and the related creditor is on the cash basis. If this rule is applicable, interest that has been accrued but not paid at the end of the debtor's tax year is not deductible until payment is made and the income is reportable by the cash basis recipient.

Tax-Exempt Securities.   The tax law provides that no deduction is allowed for interest on debt incurred to purchase or carry tax-exempt securities.[72] A major problem for the courts has been to determine what is meant by the words "to purchase or carry." Refer to Chapter 4 for a detailed discussion of these issues.

Prepaid Interest.   Accrual method reporting is imposed on cash basis taxpayers for interest prepayments that extend beyond the end of the taxable year.[73] Such payments must be allocated to the tax years to which the interest payments relate. These provisions are intended to prevent cash basis taxpayers from *manufacturing* tax deductions before the end of the year by prepaying interest.

Classification of Interest Expense.   Whether interest is deductible *for* AGI or as an itemized deduction depends on whether the indebtedness has a business, investment, or personal purpose. If the indebtedness is incurred in relation to a business (other than performing services as an employee) or for the production of rent or royalty income, the interest is deductible *for* AGI. If the indebtedness is

---

[70]§ 461(g)(2).
[71]Rev.Rul. 87–22, 1987–1 C.B. 146.

[72]§ 265(a)(2).
[73]§ 461(g)(1).

CONCEPT SUMMARY 15–2

Deductibility of Personal, Education, Investment, and Mortgage Interest

Type	Deductible	Comments
Personal (consumer) interest	No	Includes any interest that is not home mortgage interest, interest on qualified education loans, investment interest, or business interest. Examples include car loans, credit cards, etc.
Qualified education interest	Yes	Deduction *for* AGI; subject to limitations.
Investment interest (*not* related to rental or royalty property)	Yes	Itemized deduction; limited to net investment income for the year; disallowed interest can be carried over to future years.
Investment interest (related to rental or royalty property)	Yes	Deduction *for* AGI; limited to net investment income for the year; disallowed interest can be carried over to future years.
Qualified residence interest on acquisition indebtedness	Yes	Deductible as an itemized deduction; limited to indebtedness of $1 million.
Qualified residence interest on home equity indebtedness	Yes	Deductible as an itemized deduction; limited to indebtedness equal to lesser of $100,000 or FMV of residence minus acquisition indebtedness.

---

incurred for personal use, such as qualified residence interest, any deduction allowed is reported on Schedule A of Form 1040 if the taxpayer elects to itemize. If the taxpayer is an employee who incurs debt in relation to his or her employment, the interest is considered to be personal, or consumer, interest. Business expenses appear on Schedule C of Form 1040, and expenses related to rents or royalties are reported on Schedule E.

CHARITABLE CONTRIBUTIONS

As noted in Chapter 4, individuals are allowed to deduct contributions made to qualified domestic organizations.[74] Contributions to qualified charitable organizations serve certain social welfare needs and thus relieve the government of the cost of providing these needed services to the community.

Criteria for a Gift. A **charitable contribution** is defined as a gift made to a qualified organization.[75] The major elements needed to qualify a contribution as a gift are a donative intent, the absence of consideration, and acceptance by the donee. Consequently, the taxpayer has the burden of establishing that the transfer was made from motives of disinterested generosity as established by the courts.[76] This test is quite subjective and has led to problems of interpretation (refer to the discussion of gifts in Chapter 3).

Benefit Received Rule. When a donor derives a tangible benefit from a contribution, he or she cannot deduct the value of the benefit.

---

[74]§ 170.
[75]§ 170(c).

[76]*Comm. v. Duberstein*, 60–2 USTC ¶9515, 5 AFTR2d 1626, 80 S.Ct. 1190 (USSC, 1960).

INTERNATIONAL IMPLICATIONS

CHOOSE THE CHARITY WISELY

Ibrahim, a U.S. citizen of Turkish descent, was distressed by the damage caused by a major earthquake in Turkey. He donated $100,000 to the Earthquake Victim's Relief Fund, a Turkish charitable organization that was set up to help victims of the earthquake. Ahmed, also a U.S. citizen of Turkish descent, donated $200,000 to help with the relief effort. However, Ahmed's contribution went to his church, which sent the proceeds of a fund drive to the Earthquake Victim's Relief Fund in Turkey. Ibrahim's contribution is not deductible, but Ahmed's is. Why? Contributions to charitable organizations are not deductible unless the organization is a U.S. charity.

EXAMPLE 52

Ralph purchases a ticket at $100 for a special performance of the local symphony (a qualified charity). If the price of a ticket to a symphony concert is normally $35, Ralph is allowed only $65 as a charitable contribution. ∎

An exception to this benefit rule provides for the deduction of an automatic percentage of the amount paid for the right to purchase athletic tickets from colleges and universities.[77] Under this exception, 80 percent of the amount paid to or for the benefit of the institution qualifies as a charitable contribution deduction.

Contribution of Services. No deduction is allowed for the value of one's services contributed to a qualified charitable organization. However, unreimbursed expenses related to the services rendered may be deductible. For example, the cost of a uniform (without general utility) that is required to be worn while performing services may be deductible, as are certain out-of-pocket transportation costs incurred for the benefit of the charity. In lieu of these out-of-pocket costs for an automobile, a standard mileage rate of 14 cents per mile is allowed.[78] Deductions are permitted for transportation, reasonable expenses for lodging, and the cost of meals while away from home incurred in performing the donated services. The travel may not involve a significant element of personal pleasure, recreation, or vacation.[79]

Nondeductible Items. In addition to the benefit received rule and the restrictions placed on contribution of services, the following items may not be deducted as charitable contributions:

- Dues, fees, or bills paid to country clubs, lodges, fraternal orders, or similar groups.
- Cost of raffle, bingo, or lottery tickets.
- Cost of tuition.
- Value of blood given to a blood bank.
- Donations to homeowners associations.
- Gifts to individuals.
- Rental value of property used by a qualified charity.

---

[77]§ 170(l).
[78]§ 170(i).
[79]§ 170(j).

Time of Deduction.   A charitable contribution generally is deducted in the year the payment is made. This rule applies to both cash and accrual basis individuals. A contribution is ordinarily deemed to have been made on the date of delivery of the property to the donee. A contribution made by check is considered delivered on the date of mailing. Thus, a check mailed on December 31, 2001, is deductible on the taxpayer's 2001 tax return. If the contribution is charged on a bank credit card, the date the charge is made determines the year of deduction.

Record-Keeping Requirements.   No deduction is allowed for contributions of $250 or more unless the taxpayer obtains written substantiation of the contribution from the charitable organization.[80] Additional information is required if the value of the donated property is over $500 but not over $5,000. For noncash contributions with a claimed value in excess of $5,000 ($10,000 in the case of nonpublicly traded stock), the taxpayer must obtain a qualified appraisal. Failure to comply with these reporting rules may result in disallowance of the charitable contribution deduction.

16 *Find more information on this topic at our Web site: **http://wft-entities.swcollege.com**.*

Valuation Requirements.   Property donated to a charity is generally valued at fair market value at the time the gift is made. The Code and Regulations give very little guidance on the measurement of the fair market value except to say, "The fair market value is the price at which the property would change hands between a willing buyer and a willing seller, neither being under any compulsion to buy or sell and both having reasonable knowledge of relevant facts."

Generally, charitable organizations do not attest to the fair market value of the donated property. Nevertheless, the taxpayer must maintain reliable written evidence as to its value.

17 *Find more information on this topic at our Web site: **http://wft-entities.swcollege.com**.*

Limitations on Charitable Contribution Deduction.   The potential charitable contribution deduction is the total of all donations, both money and property, that qualify for the deduction. After this determination is made, the actual amount of the charitable contribution deduction that is allowed for individuals for the tax year is limited as follows:

- If the qualifying contributions for the year total 20 percent or less of AGI, they are fully deductible.
- If the qualifying contributions are more than 20 percent of AGI, the deductible amount may be limited to either 20 percent, 30 percent, or 50 percent of AGI, depending on the type of property given and the type of organization to which the donation is made.
- In any case, the maximum charitable contribution deduction may not exceed 50 percent of AGI for the tax year.

To understand the complex rules for computing the amount of a charitable contribution, it is necessary to understand the distinction between **capital gain property** and **ordinary income property**. These rules, which were discussed in Chapter 4, are summarized in Concept Summary 15–3.

In addition, it is necessary to understand when the 50 percent, 30 percent, and 20 percent limitations apply. If a taxpayer's contributions for the year exceed the

---

[80]§ 170(f)(8).

CONCEPT SUMMARY 15–3

Determining the Deduction for Contributions of Property by Individuals

If the Type of Property Contributed Is:	And the Property Is Contributed to:	The Contribution Is Measured by:	But the Deduction Is Limited to:
Capital gain property	A 50% organization	Fair market value of the property	30% of AGI
Ordinary income property	A 50% organization	The basis of the property*	50% of AGI
Capital gain property (and the property is tangible personal property put to an unrelated use by the donee)	A 50% organization	The basis of the property*	50% of AGI
Capital gain property (and the reduced deduction is elected)	A 50% organization	The basis of the property	50% of AGI
Capital gain property	A private nonoperating foundation that is not a 50% organization	The basis of the property*	The lesser of 1. 20% of AGI 2. 50% of AGI minus other contributions to 50% organizations
Ordinary income property	A private nonoperating foundation that is not a 50% organization	The basis of the property*	30% of AGI

*If the FMV of the property is less than the adjusted basis (i.e., the property has declined in value instead of appreciating), the FMV is used.

applicable percentage limitations, the excess contributions may be carried forward and deducted during a five-year carryover period. These topics are discussed in the sections that follow.

Fifty Percent Ceiling.　Contributions made to public charities may not exceed 50 percent of an individual's AGI for the year. Excess contributions may be carried over to the next five years.[81] The 50 percent ceiling on contributions applies to the following types of public charities:

- A church or a convention or association of churches.
- An educational organization that maintains a regular faculty and curriculum.
- A hospital or medical school.
- An organization supported by the government that holds property or investments for the benefit of a college or university.
- A Federal, state, or local governmental unit.
- An organization normally receiving a substantial part of its support from the public or a governmental unit.

In the remaining discussion of charitable contributions, public charities and private foundations (both operating and nonoperating) that qualify for the 50 percent ceiling will be referred to as 50 percent organizations.

---

[81]§ 170(d); Reg. § 1.170A–10.

The 50 percent ceiling also applies to contributions to the following organizations:

- All private operating foundations.
- Certain private nonoperating foundations that distribute the contributions they receive to public charities and private operating foundations within two and one-half months following the year they receive the contribution.
- Certain private nonoperating foundations in which the contributions are pooled in a common fund and the income and principal sum are paid to public charities.

Thirty Percent Ceiling.   A 30 percent ceiling applies to contributions of cash and ordinary income property to private nonoperating foundations that are not 50 percent organizations. The 30 percent ceiling also applies to contributions of appreciated capital gain property to 50 percent organizations unless the taxpayer makes a special election (see Example 54 below).

In the event the contributions for any one tax year involve both 50 percent and 30 percent property, the allowable deduction comes first from the 50 percent property.

EXAMPLE 53

During the year, Lisa makes the following donations to her church: cash of $2,000 and unimproved land worth $30,000. Lisa had purchased the land four years ago for $22,000 and held it as an investment. Therefore, it is long-term capital gain property. Lisa's AGI for the year is $50,000. Disregarding percentage limitations, Lisa's potential deduction is $32,000 [$2,000 (cash) + $30,000 (fair market value of land)].

In applying the percentage limitations, however, the current deduction for the land is limited to $15,000 [30% (limitation applicable to long-term capital gain property) × $50,000 (AGI)]. Thus, the total deduction is $17,000 ($2,000 cash + $15,000 land). Note that the total deduction does not exceed $25,000, which is 50% of Lisa's AGI. ■

Under a special election, a taxpayer may choose to forgo a deduction of the appreciation on capital gain property. Referred to as the reduced deduction election, this enables the taxpayer to move from the 30 percent limitation to the 50 percent limitation.

EXAMPLE 54	Assume the same facts as in Example 53, except that Lisa makes the reduced deduction election. Now the deduction becomes $24,000 [$2,000 (cash) + $22,000 (basis in land)] because both donations fall under the 50% limitation. Thus, by making the election, Lisa has increased her current charitable contribution deduction by $7,000 [$24,000 − $17,000 (Example 53)]. ∎

Although the reduced deduction election appears attractive, it should be considered carefully. The election sacrifices a deduction for the appreciation on long-term capital gain property that might eventually be allowed. Note that in Example 53, the potential deduction was $32,000, yet in Example 54 only $24,000 is allowed. The reason the potential deduction is decreased by $8,000 ($32,000 − $24,000) is that no carryover is allowed for the amount sacrificed by the election.

Twenty Percent Ceiling.   A 20 percent ceiling applies to contributions of appreciated long-term capital gain property to private nonoperating foundations that are not 50 percent organizations. Also, recall from Chapter 4 that only the basis of the contributed property is allowed as a deduction.

Contribution Carryovers.   Contributions that exceed the percentage limitations for the current year can be carried over for five years. In the carryover process, such contributions do not lose their identity for limitation purposes. Thus, if the contribution originally involved 30 percent property, the carryover will continue to be classified as 30 percent property in the carryover year.

EXAMPLE 55	Assume the same facts as in Example 53. Because only $15,000 of the $30,000 value of the land is deducted in the current year, the balance of $15,000 may be carried over to the following year. But the carryover will still be treated as long-term capital gain property and will be subject to the 30%-of-AGI limitation. ∎

In applying the percentage limitations, current charitable contributions must be claimed first before any carryovers can be considered. If carryovers involve more than one year, they are utilized in a first-in, first-out order.

MISCELLANEOUS ITEMIZED DEDUCTIONS SUBJECT TO TWO PERCENT FLOOR

No deduction is allowed for personal, living, or family expenses.[82] However, a taxpayer may incur a number of expenditures related to employment. If an employee or outside salesperson incurs unreimbursed business expenses or expenses that are reimbursed under a nonaccountable plan (see Chapter 16), including travel and transportation, the expenses are deductible as **miscellaneous itemized deductions.**[83] Certain other expenses also fall into the special category of miscellaneous itemized deductions. Some are deductible only to the extent they exceed 2 percent of the taxpayer's AGI. These miscellaneous itemized deductions include (but are not limited to) the following:

- Professional dues to membership organizations.
- Uniforms or other clothing that cannot be used for normal wear.

---

[82]§ 262.
[83]Actors and performing artists who meet certain requirements are not subject to this rule.

A TAX INCREASE IN DISGUISE

According to IRS reports, the number of taxpayers who were affected by the 3 percent floor on itemized deductions on 1998 returns increased to 4.8 million, up 8 percent from 1997. The limitation reduced the itemized deductions of these taxpayers by $25.9 billion, up 14 percent from 1997.

SOURCE: Adapted from Tom Herman, "Tax Report: Backdoor Tax Increases Hit Growing Numbers of People," *Wall Street Journal,* July 5, 2000, p. A1.

- Fees incurred for the preparation of one's tax return or fees incurred for tax litigation before the IRS or the courts.
- Job-hunting costs.
- Fee paid for a safe deposit box used to store papers and documents relating to taxable income-producing investments.
- Investment expenses that are deductible under § 212 as discussed previously in this chapter.
- Appraisal fees to determine the amount of a casualty loss or the fair market value of donated property.
- Hobby losses up to the amount of hobby income (see Chapter 16).
- Unreimbursed employee expenses (see Chapter 16).
- Certain employee business expenses that are reimbursed are not itemized deductions, but are deducted *for* AGI. Employee business expenses are discussed in depth in Chapter 16.

OTHER MISCELLANEOUS DEDUCTIONS

Certain expenses and losses do not fall into any category of itemized deductions already discussed but are nonetheless deductible. The following expenses and losses are deductible on Schedule A as Other Miscellaneous Deductions:

- Gambling losses up to the amount of gambling winnings.
- Impairment-related work expenses of a handicapped person.
- Federal estate tax on income in respect of a decedent.
- Deduction for repayment of amounts under a claim of right if more than $3,000.

Unlike the expenses and losses discussed previously under Miscellaneous Itemized Deductions, the above expenses and losses are not subject to the 2 percent-of-AGI floor.

OVERALL LIMITATION ON CERTAIN ITEMIZED DEDUCTIONS

Congress has enacted several provisions limiting tax benefits for high-income taxpayers. These limitations include the exemption phase-out (discussed earlier in this chapter) and a phase-out of itemized deductions. For 2001, the phase-out of itemized deductions (also referred to as a *cutback* adjustment) applies to taxpayers whose AGI exceeds $132,950 ($66,475 for married taxpayers filing separately).[84] The limitation applies to the following frequently encountered itemized deductions:[85]

- Taxes.
- Home mortgage interest, including points.
- Charitable contributions.
- Unreimbursed employee expenses subject to the 2 percent-of-AGI floor.
- All other expenses subject to the 2 percent-of-AGI floor.

The following deductions are *not* subject to the limitation on itemized deductions:

- Medical and dental expenses.
- Investment interest expense.
- Nonbusiness casualty and theft losses.
- Gambling losses.

Taxpayers subject to the limitation must reduce itemized deductions by the lesser of:

- 3 percent of the amount by which AGI exceeds $132,950 ($66,475 if married filing separately).
- 80 percent of itemized deductions that are affected by the limit.

The overall limitation is applied after applying all other limitations to itemized deductions that are affected by the overall limitation. Other limitations apply to charitable contributions, certain meals and entertainment expenses, and certain miscellaneous itemized deductions.

EXAMPLE 56

Herman, who is single, had AGI of $200,000 for 2001. He incurred the following expenses and losses during the year:

Medical expenses before the 7.5%-of-AGI limitation	$16,000
State and local income taxes	3,200
Real estate taxes	2,800
Home mortgage interest	7,200
Charitable contributions	2,000
Casualty loss (after $100 floor, before 10%-of-AGI limitation)	21,500
Unreimbursed employee expenses subject to 2%-of-AGI limitation	4,300
Gambling losses (Herman had $3,000 gambling income)	7,000

Herman's itemized deductions before the overall limitation are computed as follows:

Medical expenses [$16,000 − (7.5% × $200,000)]	$ 1,000
State and local income taxes	3,200
Real estate taxes	2,800
Home mortgage interest	7,200
Charitable contributions	2,000
Casualty loss [$21,500 − (10% × $200,000)]	1,500
Unreimbursed employee expenses [$4,300 − (2% × $200,000)]	300
Gambling losses (limited to $3,000 gambling income)	3,000
Total itemized deductions before overall limitation	$21,000

---

[84]For 2000, the limitation applied if AGI exceeded $128,950 ($64,475 for married taxpayers filing separately).

[85]Other deductions subject to the limitation include Federal estate tax on income in respect of a decedent, certain amortizable bond premiums, the deduction for repayment of certain amounts, certain unrecovered investments in an annuity, and impairment-related work expenses.

Herman's itemized deductions subject to the overall limitation are as follows:

State and local income taxes	$ 3,200
Real estate taxes	2,800
Home mortgage interest	7,200
Charitable contributions	2,000
Unreimbursed employee expenses	300
Total itemized deductions before overall limitation	$15,500

Herman must reduce this amount by the smaller of the following:

• 3% ($200,000 AGI – $132,950)	$ 2,012
• 80% of itemized deductions subject to limitation ($15,500 × 80%)	12,400

Therefore, the amount of the reduction is $2,012, and Herman has $18,988 of deductible itemized deductions, computed as follows:

Deductible itemized deductions subject to overall limitation ($15,500 – $2,012)	$13,488
Itemized deductions not subject to overall limitation:	
Medical expenses	1,000
Casualty loss	1,500
Gambling losses	3,000
Deductible itemized deductions	$18,988

PLANNING CONSIDERATIONS

Effective Utilization of Itemized Deductions

An individual may use the standard deduction in one year and itemize deductions in another year. Therefore, it is frequently possible to obtain maximum benefit by shifting itemized deductions from one year to another. For example, if a taxpayer's itemized deductions and the standard deduction are approximately the same for each year of a two-year period, the taxpayer should use the standard deduction in one year and shift itemized deductions (to the extent permitted by law) to the other year. The individual could, for example, prepay a church pledge for a particular year or avoid paying end-of-the-year medical expenses to shift the deduction to the following year.

LEARNING OBJECTIVE 8

Understand the adoption expenses credit, child tax credit, education tax credits, credit for child and dependent care expenses, and earned income credit.

Individual Tax Credits

ADOPTION EXPENSES CREDIT

Adoption expenses paid or incurred by a taxpayer may give rise to the **adoption expenses credit.**[86] The provision is intended to assist taxpayers who incur nonrecurring costs directly associated with the adoption process, such as adoption fees, attorney fees, court costs, social service review costs, and transportation costs.

---

[86] § 23.

Up to $5,000 of costs incurred to adopt an eligible child qualify for the credit. An eligible child is one who is:

- under 18 years of age at the time of the adoption, or
- physically or mentally incapable of taking care of himself or herself.

A taxpayer may claim the credit in the year qualifying expenses were paid or incurred if they were paid or incurred during or after the tax year in which the adoption was finalized. For qualifying expenses paid or incurred in a tax year prior to the year when the adoption was finalized, the credit must be claimed in the tax year following the tax year during which the expenses are paid or incurred. A married couple must file a joint return in order to claim the credit.

EXAMPLE 57

In late 2001, Sam and Martha pay $2,300 in legal fees, adoption fees, and other expenses directly related to the adoption of an infant daughter, Susan. In 2002, they pay an additional $1,000, and in 2003, the year in which the adoption becomes final, they pay $3,000. Sam and Martha are eligible for a $2,300 credit in 2002 (for expenses paid in 2001) and a $2,700 credit in 2003. ■

The amount of the credit that is otherwise available is subject to phase-out for taxpayers whose AGI (modified for this purpose) exceeds $75,000, and is phased out completely when AGI reaches $115,000. The resulting credit is calculated by reducing the allowable credit (determined without this reduction) by the amount determined using the following formula:

$$\text{Allowable credit} \times \frac{\text{AGI} - \$75,000}{\$40,000}$$

EXAMPLE 58

Assume the same facts as in the previous example, except that Sam and Martha's AGI is $100,000 in each of the relevant years. As a result, their available credit in 2002 is reduced from $2,300 to $863 {$2,300 − [$2,300 × ($25,000/$40,000)]}, and in 2003 it is reduced from $2,700 to $1,013 {$2,700 − [$2,700 × ($25,000/$40,000)]}. ■

The credit is nonrefundable and is available to taxpayers only in a year in which this credit and the other nonrefundable credits do not exceed the taxpayer's liability. However, any unused adoption expenses credit may be carried over for up to five years, being utilized on a first-in, first-out basis.

CHILD TAX CREDIT

The **child tax credit** provision allows individual taxpayers to take a tax credit based solely on the *number* of their eligible dependent children.[87] This credit is one of several "family-friendly" provisions that currently are part of our tax law. To be eligible for the credit, the child must be under age 17, a U.S. citizen, and claimed as a dependent on the taxpayer's return.

Maximum Credit and Phase-Outs.   The maximum credit available is $500 per child. The available credit is phased out for higher-income taxpayers beginning when AGI reaches $110,000 for joint filers ($55,000 for married taxpayers filing separately) and $75,000 for single taxpayers. The credit is phased out by $50 for each $1,000 (or part thereof) of AGI above the threshold amounts. Since the maximum credit available to taxpayers depends on the number of qualifying children,

[87]§ 24.

the income level at which the credit is phased out completely also depends on the number of children qualifying for the credit.

EXAMPLE 59

Juanita and Alberto are married and file a joint tax return claiming their two children, ages six and eight, as dependents. Their AGI for 2001 is $122,400. Juanita and Alberto's available child tax credit is $350, computed as their maximum credit of $1,000 ($500 × 2 children) reduced by a $650 phase-out. Since Juanita and Alberto's AGI is in excess of the $110,000 threshold, the maximum credit must be reduced by $50 for every $1,000 (or part thereof) above the threshold amount {$50 × [($122,400 − $110,000)/$1,000]}. Thus, the credit reduction equals $650 [$50 × 13 (rounded up from 12.4)]. Therefore, Juanita and Alberto's child tax credit is $350. ∎

CREDIT FOR CHILD AND DEPENDENT CARE EXPENSES

A credit is allowed to taxpayers who incur employment-related expenses for child or dependent care.[88] The **credit for child and dependent care expenses** is a specified percentage of expenses incurred to enable the taxpayer to work or to seek employment. Expenses on which the credit for child and dependent care expenses is based are subject to limitations.

Eligibility.   To be eligible for the credit, an individual must maintain a household for either of the following:

- A dependent under age 13.
- A dependent or spouse who is physically or mentally incapacitated.

Generally, married taxpayers must file a joint return to obtain the credit.

Eligible Employment-Related Expenses.   Eligible expenses include amounts paid for household services and care of a qualifying individual that are incurred to enable the taxpayer to be employed. Child and dependent care expenses include expenses incurred in the home, such as payments for a housekeeper. Out-of-the-home expenses incurred for the care of a dependent under the age of 13 also qualify for the credit. In addition, out-of-the-home expenses incurred for an older dependent or spouse who is physically or mentally incapacitated qualify for the credit if that person regularly spends at least eight hours each day in the taxpayer's household. This makes the credit available to taxpayers who keep handicapped older children and elderly relatives in the home instead of institutionalizing them. Out-of-the-home expenses incurred for services provided by a dependent care center will qualify only if the center complies with all applicable laws and regulations of a state or unit of local government.

Child care payments to a relative are eligible for the credit unless the relative is a dependent of the taxpayer or the taxpayer's spouse or is a child (under age 19) of the taxpayer.

Earned Income Ceiling.   The total for qualifying employment-related expenses is limited to an individual's earned income. For married taxpayers, this limitation applies to the spouse with the lesser amount of earned income. Special rules are provided for taxpayers with nonworking spouses who are disabled or are full-time students. If a nonworking spouse is physically or mentally disabled or is a full-time student, he or she is deemed to have earned income for purposes of this limitation.

---

[88]§ 21.

THE IRS COMES TO THE RESCUE—SOMETIMES

O n the surface, the child tax credit seems fairly simple: a credit of $500 is available for each eligible dependent child of the taxpayer under age 17. Some taxpayers, however, have had difficulty communicating to the IRS on their income tax forms that they have a qualifying child.

Recently, the IRS reported that more than 30,000 taxpayers who may qualify for the child tax credit completed their returns improperly. Some taxpayers failed to complete the line for the credit, even though they indicated that they had a qualifying child. Fortunately, the IRS can correct this error and include the correct amount of the credit if the child's age can be verified from Social Security records. If verification is not possible, the IRS will write to the taxpayer and suggest that an amended return be filed if the child tax credit actually is available. Such efforts can go a long way toward enhancing the IRS's new "customer-friendly" image. However, such rescue efforts will be of no help to those unfortunate taxpayers who inadvertently fail to provide any indication that they may qualify for the credit.

The deemed amount is $200 per month if there is one qualifying individual in the household or $400 per month if there are two or more qualifying individuals in the household. In the case of a student-spouse, the student's income is deemed to be earned only for the months that the student is enrolled on a full-time basis at an educational institution.

Calculation of the Credit. In general, the credit is equal to a percentage of unreimbursed employment-related expenses up to $2,400 for one qualifying individual and $4,800 for two or more individuals. The credit rate varies between 20 percent and 30 percent, depending on the taxpayer's AGI. The following chart shows the applicable percentage for taxpayers as AGI increases:

Adjusted Gross Income		Applicable Credit Rate
Over	But Not Over	
$ –0–	$10,000	30%
10,000	12,000	29%
12,000	14,000	28%
14,000	16,000	27%
16,000	18,000	26%
18,000	20,000	25%
20,000	22,000	24%
22,000	24,000	23%
24,000	26,000	22%
26,000	28,000	21%
28,000	No limit	20%

EXAMPLE 60

Nancy, who has two children under age 13, worked full-time while her spouse, Ron, attended college for 10 months during the year. Nancy earned $21,000 and incurred $5,000 of child care expenses. Ron is deemed to be fully employed and to have earned $400 for each of the

10 months (or a total of $4,000). Since Nancy and Ron have AGI of $21,000, they are allowed a credit rate of 24%. Nancy and Ron are limited to $4,000 in qualified child care expenses (the lesser of $4,800 or $4,000). Therefore, they are entitled to a tax credit of $960 (24% × $4,000) for the year. ■

EDUCATION TAX CREDITS

The **HOPE scholarship credit** and the **lifetime learning credit**[89] are available to help qualifying low- and middle-income individuals defray the cost of higher education. The credits, both of which are nonrefundable, are available for qualifying tuition and related expenses incurred by students pursuing undergraduate or graduate degrees or vocational training. Room, board, and book costs are ineligible for the credits.

Maximum Credit. The HOPE scholarship credit permits a maximum credit of $1,500 per year (100 percent of the first $1,000 of tuition expenses plus 50 percent of the next $1,000 of tuition expenses) for the *first two years* of postsecondary education. The lifetime learning credit permits a credit of 20 percent of qualifying expenses (up to $5,000 per year) incurred in a year in which the HOPE scholarship credit is not claimed with respect to a given student. Generally, the lifetime learning credit is used for individuals who are beyond the first two years of postsecondary education. Beginning in 2003, the lifetime learning credit will be available on up to $10,000 of qualifying costs incurred per year.

Eligible Individuals. Both education credits are available for qualified expenses incurred by a taxpayer, taxpayer's spouse, or taxpayer's dependent. The HOPE scholarship credit is available per eligible student, while the lifetime learning credit is calculated per taxpayer. To be eligible for the HOPE scholarship credit, a student must take at least one-half the full-time course load for at least one academic term at a qualifying educational institution. No comparable requirement exists for the lifetime learning credit. Therefore, taxpayers who are seeking new job skills or maintaining existing skills through graduate training or continuing education are eligible for the lifetime learning credit. Taxpayers who are married must file joint returns in order to claim either education credit.

Income Limitations. Both education credits are subject to income limitations and are combined for purposes of the limitation calculation. The allowable credit amount is phased out, beginning when the taxpayer's AGI reaches $40,000 ($80,000 for married taxpayers filing jointly). The reduction is equal to the extent to which AGI exceeds $40,000 ($80,000 for married filing jointly) as a percentage of the $10,000 ($20,000 for married filing jointly) phase-out range. The credits are completely eliminated when AGI reaches $50,000 ($100,000 for married filing jointly).

EXAMPLE 61

Dean and Audry are married, file a joint tax return, have modified AGI under $80,000 and have two children, Raymond and Kelsey. During fall 2001, Raymond is beginning his freshman year at State University, and Kelsey is beginning her senior year. During the prior semester, Kelsey completed her junior year. Both Raymond and Kelsey are full-time students and may be claimed as dependents on their parents' tax return. Raymond's qualifying expenses total $2,300 for the fall semester while Kelsey's qualifying expenses total $5,200 for the prior and current semesters. For 2001, Dean and Audry may claim a $1,500 HOPE

---

[89]§ 25A.

scholarship credit [(100% × $1,000) + (50% × $1,000)] relating to Raymond's expenses and a $1,000 lifetime learning credit (20% × $5,000) relating to Kelsey's expenses. Kelsey's tuition expenses are ineligible for the HOPE scholarship credit because she is beyond her first two years of postsecondary education. ■

EXAMPLE 62

Assume the same facts as in Example 61, except that Dean and Audry's modified AGI for 2001 is $92,000. Dean and Audry are eligible to claim $1,000 in total education credits for 2001. Their available credits totaling $2,500 ($1,500 HOPE scholarship credit + $1,000 lifetime learning credit) must be reduced because their AGI exceeds the $80,000 limit for married taxpayers. The percentage reduction is computed as the amount by which modified AGI exceeds the limit, expressed as a percentage of the phase-out range, or [($92,000 − $80,000)/$20,000], resulting in a 60% reduction. Therefore, the maximum available credit for 2001 is $1,000 ($2,500 × 40% allowable portion). ■

Restrictions on Double Tax Benefit.   Taxpayers are prohibited from receiving a double tax benefit associated with qualifying educational expenses. Therefore, taxpayers who claim an education credit may not deduct the expenses, nor may they claim the credit for amounts that are otherwise excluded from gross income (e.g., scholarships, employer-paid educational assistance).

EARNED INCOME CREDIT

The **earned income credit,** which has been a part of the law for many years, has been justified as a means of providing tax equity to the working poor. In addition, the credit has been designed to help offset regressive taxes that are a part of our tax system, such as the gasoline and Social Security taxes. Further, the credit is intended to encourage economically disadvantaged individuals to become contributing members of the workforce.[90]

Eligibility Requirements.   Eligibility for the credit may depend not only on the taxpayer meeting the earned income and AGI thresholds, but also on whether he or she has a qualifying child. A qualifying child must meet the following tests:

- *Relationship test.* The individual must be a son, daughter, descendant of the taxpayer's son or daughter, stepson, stepdaughter, or an eligible foster child of the taxpayer. A legally adopted child of the taxpayer is considered the same as a child by blood.
- *Residency test.* The qualifying child must share the taxpayer's principal place of abode, which must be located within the United States, for more than one-half of the tax year of the taxpayer. Temporary absences (e.g., due to illness or education) are disregarded for purposes of this test. For foster children, however, the child must share the taxpayer's home for the entire year.
- *Age test.* The child must not have reached the age of 19 (24 in the case of a full-time student) as of the end of the tax year. In addition, a child who is permanently and totally disabled at any time during the year is considered to meet the age test.

In addition to being available for taxpayers with qualifying children, the earned income credit is also available to certain workers without children. However, this

---

[90]§ 32. This credit is subject to indexation.

provision is available only to such taxpayers aged 25 through 64 who cannot be claimed as a dependent on another taxpayer's return.

Amount of the Credit. In 2001, the earned income credit is determined by multiplying a maximum amount of earned income by the appropriate credit. Generally, earned income includes employee compensation and net earnings from self-employment but excludes items such as interest, dividends, pension benefits, and alimony. If a taxpayer has children, the credit percentage used in the calculation depends on the number of qualifying children. Thus, in 2001, the maximum earned income credit for a taxpayer with one qualifying child is $2,428 ($7,140 × 34%) and $4,008 ($10,020 × 40%) for a taxpayer with two or more qualifying children. However, the maximum earned income credit is phased out completely if the taxpayer's earned income or AGI exceeds certain thresholds. To the extent that the greater of earned income or AGI exceeds $13,090 in 2001, the difference, multiplied by the appropriate phase-out percentage, is subtracted from the maximum earned income credit.

It is not necessary for the taxpayer to actually compute the earned income credit. To simplify the compliance process, the IRS issues an Earned Income Credit Table for the determination of the appropriate amount of the credit. This table and a worksheet are included in the instructions available to individual taxpayers.

Advance Payment. The earned income credit is a form of negative income tax (a refundable credit for taxpayers who do not have a tax liability). An eligible individual may elect to receive advance payments of the earned income credit from his or her employer (rather than receiving the credit from the IRS upon filing the tax return). The amount that can be received in advance is limited to 60 percent of the credit that is available to a taxpayer with only one qualifying child. If this election is made, the taxpayer must file a certificate of eligibility (Form W–5) with his or her employer and must file a tax return for the year the income is earned.

Suggested Further Readings

Paul Bohrer and Terri Gutierrez, "Considerations When Using Education Credits," *The Tax Adviser*, January 2000, pp. 34–43.

Julia K. Brazelton, "The Tax Treatment of Damages Awarded in the Context of Employment Discrimination," *Taxes—The Tax Magazine*, May 1999, pp. 15–25.

Delton L. Chesser, Michael J. Gulig, and Danny P. Hollingsworth, "Why Give an IRA to Charity?" *The Tax Adviser*, March 1999, pp. 162–167.

Ellen D. Cook, "No Simple Solution for the Marriage Penalty Quandary," *Practical Tax Strategies*, March 2000, pp. 160–166.

Richard I. Newmark and Ted D. Englebrecht, "Courts Split on Individuals' Deficiency Interest Deduction," *Practical Tax Strategies*, February 1999, pp. 87–96.

Jay A. Soled and Priscilla Lestz, "Tax Deductions Can Lighten the Cost of Assisted Living Arrangements," *Practical Tax Strategies*, April 2000, pp. 233–236.

Ron West, "Diagnose Payments for Bigger Medical Expense Deductions," *Practical Tax Strategies*, May 1999, pp. 289–300.

KEY TERMS

Accident and health insurance benefits, 15–32

Acquisition indebtedness, 15–41

Adoption expenses credit, 15–51

Alimony and separate maintenance payments, 15–25

Capital gain property, 15–45

Charitable contribution, 15–43

Child tax credit, 15–52

Compensatory damages, 15–30

Credit for child and dependent care expenses, 15–53

Dependency exemption, 15–10

Earned income credit, 15–56

Educational savings bonds, 15–33

e-file, 15–21

Gift, 15–28

Head of household, 15–24

Home equity loans, 15–41

HOPE scholarship credit, 15–55

Investment interest, 15–40

Itemized deductions, 15–6

Kiddie tax, 15–18

Lifetime learning credit, 15–55

Marriage penalty, 15–23

Medical expenses, 15–34

Miscellaneous itemized deductions, 15–48

Multiple support agreement, 15–11

Net investment income, 15–40

Ordinary income property, 15–45

Personal exemption, 15–10

Points, 15–41

Punitive damages, 15–31

Qualified residence interest, 15–40

Scholarship, 15–29

Standard deduction, 15–7

Surviving spouse, 15–24

Tax Rate Schedules, 15–15

Tax Table, 15–15

Unearned income, 15–18

Problem Materials

PROBLEMS

1. Compute the taxpayer's taxable income for 2001 in each of the following cases:
   a. Jack is married and files a joint return with his wife, Alice. Jack and Alice have two dependent children. They have AGI of $50,000 and $8,300 of itemized deductions.
   b. Pete is an unmarried head of household with two dependents. He has AGI of $45,000 and itemized deductions of $5,200.
   c. Iris, age 22, is a full-time college student who is claimed as a dependent by her parents. She earns $4,400 from a part-time job and has interest income of $1,500.
   d. Matt, age 20, is a full-time college student who is claimed as a dependent by his parents. He earns $2,500 from a part-time job and has interest income of $4,100. His itemized deductions related to the investment income are $800.

2. Compute the taxable income for 2001 for Pierce on the basis of the following information. His filing status is head of household.

Salary	$51,000
Cash dividends from GMC stock	2,500
Contribution to a traditional IRA	2,000

Interest income on City of Reno bonds	$ 1,000
Capital loss from sale of stock investment	4,000
Gift of cash from mother	20,000
Number of dependents (children, ages 18 and 20)	2
Age	65

3. Compute the taxable income for 2001 for Courtney on the basis of the following information. Her filing status is head of household.

Salary	$59,000
Alimony	3,600
Child support	4,800
Inheritance from uncle	40,000
Proceeds of life insurance policy paid by reason of uncle's death (Courtney was the designated beneficiary)	50,000
Property taxes on home	3,600
Interest paid on home mortgage	4,800
Charitable contributions	1,200
Number of dependents (children, ages 7 and 8; mother, age 66)	3
Age	40

4. Determine the amount of the standard deduction allowed for 2001 in the following independent situations. In each case, assume the taxpayer is claimed as another person's dependent.
   a. Corey, age 18, has income as follows: $800 in cash dividends from stock investments and $400 of wages from a part-time job.
   b. Molly, age 20, has income as follows: $1,100 in interest from a savings account and $1,200 of wages from a part-time job.
   c. Jacob, age 19, has income from a part-time job of $5,000.
   d. Odette, age 21, has income from a part-time job of $4,200.
   e. Mona, age 65, has income from a part-time job of $2,000.

5. Determine the number of personal and dependency exemptions in each of the following independent situations:
   a. Petula, age 48, provides 70% of the support of Trent, her 20-year-old son who lives with her. The son earns $3,200 from a part-time job. She also provides all of the support of her 70-year-old mother, who is blind and lives in a nursing home.
   b. Rhett, age 66, is married to Penny, age 64, who is institutionalized. Rhett provides all of her support. Penny has no income, files no return, and is not claimed by anyone else as a dependent.
   c. Liza, age 32, is single and provides more than 50% of the support of two cousins, Zoe and Jerold. Zoe lives with Liza, but Jerold does not.
   d. Kurt (age 52) and Nadia (age 49) are husband and wife and furnish more than 50% of the support of their two children, Rosalyn (age 17) and Hector (age 23). Both Rosalyn and Hector earn in excess of $3,000 from part-time work. Hector is a full-time graduate student at a local college.

6. Martha, a widow, lives with her only son, Roland, and his family. Martha's only income consists of $70,000 in interest from tax-exempt bonds. She invests all of the income in stocks in her name. The stocks do not pay dividends. Martha's will provides that all of her property is to pass to Roland upon her death. Because of this expectation, Roland provides all of his mother's support, although she is in a position to provide her own support had she chosen to do so. On his tax return, Roland claims a dependency exemption for his mother. Is this proper procedure?

7. Irving and Maureen Hirt are married and file a joint return. Transactions for 2001 are as follows:

Salaries (Irving, $48,000; Maureen, $51,000)	$99,000
Interest on bonds issued by General Electric Corporation	1,300
Inheritance received from the estate of Maureen's uncle	15,000
Contribution by Irving to a traditional IRA	2,000

The Hirts provide more than half of the support of their son (Randall, age 23). Randall is a senior in law school and earns $3,200 from a part-time job. They also provide more than half of the support of Maureen's mother (Yvette, age 70), who does not live with them. Yvette's only income is $7,000 of Social Security benefits. If the Hirts have itemized deductions of $8,300, what is their taxable income for 2001?

8. Don is a wealthy executive who has taxable income of $200,000 in 2001. He is considering transferring title in a duplex he owns to his son Sam, age 16. Sam has no other income and is claimed as a dependent by Don. Net rent income from the duplex is $10,000 a year, which Sam will be encouraged to place in a savings account. Will the family save income taxes in 2001 if Don transfers title in the duplex to Sam? Explain.

9. Using the Tax Rate Schedules, compute the 2001 tax liability for each of the following taxpayers:
   a. Hollis (age 66) and Kelsey (age 59 and blind) Wynn file a joint return. They furnish more than half of the support of Brandon (age 23). Brandon, Kelsey's son by a former marriage, earns $5,000 during the year and is a full-time graduate student at a local university. The Wynns have taxable retirement income of $40,000 and itemized deductions of $9,000.
   b. Carrie, age 40 and unmarried, maintains the home where her dependent parents (ages 70 and 68) live. Carrie's income is as follows: wages of $75,000 and interest on City of Philadelphia bonds of $4,000. Carrie has itemized deductions of $6,500.
   c. Omar, age 32 and unmarried, provides more than half of the support of Nash (a 15-year-old cousin) and Jeri (a 16-year-old niece). Neither Nash nor Jeri lives with him. Omar has wages of $60,000 and a short-term capital loss of $2,000. His itemized deductions are $3,800.
   d. Faith, age 40 and widowed, provides all of the support of her children (ages 11 and 12), who live with her. She has wages of $40,000 and itemized deductions of $7,000. Faith's husband died two years ago.

10. Bruce Smith and Wanda Brown are young professionals who are employed in well-paying jobs. They have been dating each other for several years and are considering getting married in December 2001 or January 2002. For 2001, their respective AGIs are $65,000 and $68,000. They anticipate having the same AGI in 2002. In both years, they will claim the standard deduction.

    Bruce and Wanda solicit your tax advice. Specifically, they wish to know what Federal income tax results from their getting married in 2001 or in 2002. Prepare a letter to Wanda (4339 Elm Street, Apt. 39A, Cincinnati, OH 45221) setting forth the tax determination under each choice. In making your analysis, use the Tax Rate Schedules and other data (e.g., standard deduction) applicable in year 2001.

11. Gina, a cash basis taxpayer, is single and has no dependents. She provides you with the following estimates for 2000 and 2001:

	2000	2001
Adjusted gross income	$56,000	$60,000
Charitable contributions	2,200	2,400
Interest on home mortgage	1,000	850
Property taxes	700	700

Can Gina decrease her taxable income over the two-year period by prepaying her 2001 charitable contributions in 2000?

12. Under the terms of their divorce agreement, Barry is to transfer common stock (cost of $25,000, market value of $60,000) to Sandra. Barry and Sandra have a 14-year-old child. Sandra will have custody of the child, and Barry is to pay $300 per month as child support. In addition, Sandra is to receive $1,000 per month for 10 years. However, the payments will be reduced to $750 per month when their child reaches age 21. In the first year under the agreement, Sandra receives the common stock and the correct cash payments for six months. How will the terms of the agreement affect Sandra's gross income?

13. For each of the following, determine the amount that should be included in gross income:
    a. Joe was selected as the most valuable player in the Super Bowl. In recognition of this, he was awarded a sports car worth $60,000 plus $50,000 in cash.
    b. Wanda won the Mrs. America beauty contest. She received various prizes valued at $75,000.
    c. George was awarded the Nobel Peace Prize. He directed the Nobel committee to pay the $950,000 prize to State University, his alma mater.

14. Linda and Don are married and file a joint return. In 2001, they received $9,000 in Social Security benefits and $29,000 taxable pension benefits, interest, and dividends.
    a. Compute the couple's adjusted gross income on a joint return.
    b. Don would like to know whether they should sell for $100,000 a corporate bond (at no gain or loss) that pays 8% in interest each year and use the proceeds to buy a $100,000 nontaxable State of Virginia bond that will pay $6,000 in interest each year.
    c. If Linda in (a) works part-time and earns $30,000, how much would Linda and Don's adjusted gross income increase?

15. Alejandro was awarded an academic scholarship to State University. He received $5,000 in August and $6,000 in December 2001. Alejandro had enough personal savings to pay all expenses as they came due. Alejandro's expenditures for the relevant period were as follows:

Tuition, August 2001	$3,100
Tuition, December 2001	3,200
Room and board	
August–December 2001	3,000
January–May 2002	2,400
Books and educational supplies	
August–December 2001	900
January–May 2002	1,100

Determine the effect on Alejandro's gross income for 2001 and 2002.

16. Liz sued an overzealous bill collector and received the following settlement:

Damage to her automobile the collector attempted to repossess	$ 1,000
Physical damage to her arm caused by the collector	8,000
Loss of income while her arm was healing	6,000
Punitive damages	30,000

    a. What effect does the settlement have on Liz's gross income?
    b. Assume Liz also collected $40,000 of damages for slander to her personal reputation caused by the bill collector misrepresenting the facts to Liz's employer and other creditors. Is this $40,000 included in Liz's gross income?

17. Sid and Andrea Peterson are married and together have AGI of $90,000 in 2001. They have two dependents and file a joint return. During the year, they paid $2,400 for medical insurance, $10,000 in doctor bills and hospital expenses, and $1,500 for prescribed medicine and drugs.

a. In December 2001, the Petersons received an insurance reimbursement of $1,800 for hospitalization expenses. Determine the deduction allowable for medical expenses paid during the year.

b. Assume instead that the Petersons received the $1,800 insurance reimbursement in January 2002. Determine the deduction allowable for medical expenses incurred in 2001.

c. Assume again that the Petersons received the $1,800 insurance reimbursement in January 2002. Discuss whether the reimbursement will be included in their gross income for 2002.

18. Steven, age 37, had his nose broken in a high school football game 20 years ago. As a result, his nose is slightly crooked. In addition, he thinks his nose is too long. In March, he scheduled an appointment with Dr. Keane to discuss surgery to improve his appearance, primarily to shorten his nose. Dr. Keane presented him with computer simulations showing several different possibilities for the size and shape of his nose. Steven selected a nose that was much shorter and completely straight.

Steven called his CPA to ask if the cost of the surgery would be deductible. His CPA told him that unnecessary cosmetic surgery is not deductible, but hinted that most doctors can come up with a medical reason that would make such surgery deductible.

Steven discussed the tax issue with Dr. Keane on his next visit, and the doctor indicated that the surgery would be necessary to repair Steven's deviated septum, which was caused by his football injury. Dr. Keane said that he would be willing to write a letter for Steven's files, stating that the surgery was medically necessary. Is Steven justified in taking a deduction for the cosmetic surgery?

19. A local opthalmologist's advertising campaign included a certificate for a free radial keratotomy for the lucky winner of a drawing. Ahmad held the winning ticket, which was drawn in December 2000. Ahmad had no vision problems and was uncertain what he should do with the prize. In February 2001, Ahmad's daughter, who lives with his former wife, was diagnosed with a vision problem that could be treated with either prescription glasses or a radial keratotomy. The divorce decree requires that Ahmad pay for all medical expenses incurred for his daughter. Identify the relevant tax issues for Ahmad.

20. Manny developed a severe heart condition, and his physician advised him to install an elevator in his home. The cost of installing the elevator was $15,000, and the increase in the value of the residence was determined to be $5,800. Manny's AGI for the year was $52,000.

a. How much of the expenditure can Manny deduct as a medical expense?

b. Assume the same facts as in (a), except that Manny was paralyzed in an automobile accident and the expenditures were incurred to build entrance and exit ramps and widen the hallways in his home to accommodate his wheelchair. How much of the expenditure can Manny deduct as a medical expense?

21. Andrea, who uses the cash method of accounting, lives in a state that imposes an income tax. In April 2001, she files her state return for 2000 and pays an additional $1,000 in state income taxes. During 2001, her withholdings for state income tax purposes amount to $7,400, and she pays estimated state income tax of $700. In April 2002, she files her state return for 2001, claiming a refund of $1,800. Andrea receives the refund in August 2002.

a. Assuming Andrea itemized deductions in 2001, how much may she claim as a deduction for state income taxes on her Federal return for calendar year 2001 (filed in April 2002)?

b. Assuming Andrea itemized deductions in 2001, how will the refund of $1,800 that she received in 2002 be treated for Federal income tax purposes?

c. Assume that Andrea itemized deductions in 2001, and that she elects to have the $1,800 refund applied toward her 2002 state income tax liability. How will the $1,800 be treated for Federal income tax purposes?

d. Assuming Andrea did not itemize deductions in 2001, how will the refund of $1,800 received in 2002 be treated for Federal income tax purposes?

22. Irina Gray incurred $58,500 of interest expense related to her investments in 2001. Her investment income included $15,000 of interest, $9,000 of dividends, and a $22,500 net capital gain on the sale of securities. Irina has asked you to compute the amount of her deduction for investment interest, taking into consideration any options she might have. In addition, she has asked for your suggestions as to any tax planning alternatives that might be available. Write a letter to her that contains your advice. Irina lives at 432 Clinton Circle, Rochester, NY 14604.

23. Veronica borrowed $200,000 to acquire a parcel of land to be held for investment purposes. During 2001, she pays interest of $20,000 on the loan. She has AGI of $50,000 for the year. Other items related to Veronica's investments include the following:

Investment income	$10,200
Long-term capital gain on sale of stock	4,000

Veronica is unmarried and elects to itemize her deductions. She has no miscellaneous itemized deductions. Determine Veronica's investment interest deduction for 2001.

24. John and Mary Brown, married taxpayers, took out a mortgage on their home for $80,000 in 1990. In October of the current year, when the home had a fair market value of $100,000 and they owed $62,500 on the mortgage, the Browns took out a home equity loan for $55,000. They used the funds to purchase an airplane to be used for recreational purposes. What is the maximum amount on which the Browns can deduct home equity interest?

25. Pedro contributes a painting to an art museum in 2001. He has owned the painting for 12 years, and it is worth $120,000 at the time of the donation. Pedro's adjusted basis for the painting is $80,000, and his AGI for 2001 is $230,000. Pedro has asked you whether he should make the reduced deduction election for this contribution. Write a letter to Pedro Valdez, 1289 Greenway Avenue, Foster City, CA 94404 and advise him on this matter.

26. In December each year, Alice Young contributes 10% of her gross income to the United Way (a 50% organization). Alice, who is in the 36% marginal tax bracket, is considering the following alternatives as charitable contributions in December 2001:

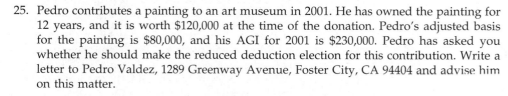

	Fair Market Value
(1) Cash donation	$21,000
(2) Unimproved land held for six years ($3,000 basis)	21,000
(3) Blue Corporation stock held for eight months ($3,000 basis)	21,000
(4) Gold Corporation stock held for two years ($26,000 basis)	21,000

Alice has asked you to help her decide which of the potential contributions listed above will be most advantageous taxwise. Evaluate the four alternatives, and write a letter to Alice to communicate your advice to her. Her address is 2622 Bayshore Drive, Berkeley, CA 94709.

27. The Skins Game, which involves four of the top golfers on the PGA Tour, is held each year on the weekend after Thanksgiving. Total prize money amounts to more than $500,000, and the leading money winner also receives an automobile as a prize. The announcers point out that 10% of the money won by each player goes to charity. In addition, on some holes, the winner of the hole receives the keys to an automobile, which goes to the player's favorite charity. Identify the relevant tax issues for the players. Consider the following possibilities with respect to the car won by the leading money winner: (1) he might keep the car for his own use and sell his present car; (2) he might sell the new car; (3) he might give the car to a friend or relative; (4) he might donate the car to charity; or (5) he might give the car to his caddy.

28. Ken, who is single, had an AGI of $300,000 during 2001. He incurred the following expenses and losses during the year:

Medical expenses before 7.5%-of-AGI limitation	$24,750
State and local income taxes	3,900
Real estate taxes	2,400
Home mortgage interest	3,200
Charitable contributions	3,900
Casualty loss before 10% limitation (after $100 floor)	33,000
Unreimbursed employee expenses subject to 2%-of-AGI limitation	7,400
Gambling losses (Ken had $5,800 of gambling income)	8,200

Compute Ken's itemized deductions before and after the overall limitation.

29. Ann and Bill were on the list of a local adoption agency for several years seeking to adopt a child. Finally, in 2001, good news comes their way and an adoption seems imminent. They pay qualified adoption expenses of $2,000 in 2001 and $4,000 in 2002. Assume the adoption becomes final in 2002. Ann and Bill always file a joint income tax return.
    a. Determine the amount of the adoption expenses credit available to Ann and Bill assuming their combined annual income is $50,000. In what year(s) will they benefit from the credit?
    b. Assuming Ann and Bill's modified AGI in 2001 and 2002 is $100,000, calculate the amount of the adoption expenses credit.

30. Pat and Jeri are husband and wife, and both are gainfully employed. They have three children under the age of 13. During the year, Pat earns $60,000, while Jeri earns $4,900. In order for them to work, they pay $5,800 to various unrelated parties to care for their children. Assuming Pat and Jeri file a joint return, what, if any, is their credit for child and dependent care expenses for the year?

31. Jim and Jill are husband and wife, and they have two dependent children under the age of 13. Both parents are gainfully employed and during the current year earn salaries as follows: $12,000 (Jim) and $4,500 (Jill). To care for their children while they work, they pay Megan (Jim's mother) $5,600. Megan does not qualify as a dependent of Jim and Jill. Assuming Jim and Jill file a joint return, what, if any, is their credit for child and dependent care expenses?

32. Colin has requested information concerning the availability of the HOPE scholarship credit and lifetime learning credit. Colin has two college-age children, Eliza, a freshman at State University, and Rhett, a senior at Out-of-State University. Both Eliza and Rhett are full-time students. Eliza's expenses for the 2001–2002 academic year are as follows: $4,500 tuition ($2,250 per semester), $800 for books and supplies, and $3,000 room and board. Rhett's expenses for the 2001–2002 academic year are as follows: $8,000 tuition ($4,000 per semester), $900 for books and supplies, and $3,500 room and board. Tuition and the applicable room and board costs are paid at the beginning of each semester. For Rhett's spring 2001 term, tuition was $4,000, books and supplies were $450, and room and board were $1,750. Colin is married, files a joint tax return, claims both children as dependents, and has a combined AGI with his wife of $95,000 for 2001. Determine Colin's education tax credit for 2001.

33. Bernadette, a long-time client of yours is an architect and president of the local Rotary chapter. To keep up to date with the latest developments in her profession, she attends continuing education seminars offered by the architecture school at State University. During 2001, Bernadette spends $2,000 on course tuition to attend such seminars. She also spends another $400 on architecture books during the year. Bernadette's son is a senior majoring in engineering at the University of the Midwest. During the 2001 calendar year, Bernadette's son incurs the following expenses: $4,200 tuition ($2,100 per semester) and $750 for books and supplies. Bernadette's son, whom she claims as a

dependent, lives at home while attending school full-time. Bernadette is married, files a joint return, and has a combined AGI with her husband of $88,000.

   a. Calculate Bernadette's education tax credit for 2001.

   b. In her capacity as president of the local Rotary chapter, Bernadette has asked you to make a 30–45 minute speech outlining the different ways the tax law helps defray (1) the cost of higher education and (2) the cost of continuing education once someone is in the workforce. Prepare an outline of possible topics for presentation. A tentative title for your presentation is "How the Tax Law Can Help Pay for College and Continuing Professional Education."

34. Briefly discuss the requirements that must be satisfied for a taxpayer to qualify for the earned income tax credit.

35. Joyce, a widow, lives in an apartment with her two minor children (ages 8 and 10) whom she supports. Joyce earns $30,000 during 2001. She uses the standard deduction.

   a. Calculate the amount, if any, of Joyce's earned income credit.

   b. During the year, Joyce is offered a new job that has greater future potential than her current job. If she accepts the job offer, her earnings for the year would be $33,000; however, she will not qualify for the earned income credit. Using after-tax cash-flow calculations, determine whether Joyce should accept the new job offer.

CUMULATIVE PROBLEMS

36. Logan and Florence Reading, 4620 San Andres Lane, Flamingo, FL 33548, file a joint return for 2001. Logan, age 60 and Social Security number 344–99–7642, is the manager of an IHOP restaurant. Florence, age 58 and Social Security number 354–55–7890, is the office manager for the Flamingo Internal Medicine Clinic. Transactions for 2001 are as follows:

Salaries ($45,000 for Logan; $51,000 for Florence)		$96,000
Interest income—		
General Electric bonds	$1,200	
City of Flamingo bonds	700	
First State Bank CD account	600	2,500
Cash dividends from stock investments		1,300
Cash gift from Logan's mother		20,000
Insurance proceeds received from Guardian Life Insurance Company (the policy was on the life of Florence's uncle, and she was the designated beneficiary)		50,000
Proceeds from the sale of capital assets—		
Sailboat (used for pleasure)		11,000
ADM stock (held as an investment)		7,000
Recovery of loan Logan made to his sister two years ago (includes interest of $1,440)		13,440
Itemized deductions paid—		
Charitable contributions	$2,400	
Interest on home mortgage	3,600	
Property taxes on home	4,000	10,000

The Readings purchased the sailboat on October 1, 1999, for $10,500 and sold it on April 13, 2001. The ADM stock was purchased on March 5, 1999, for $8,200 and was sold on October 2, 2001.

The Readings provided more than half of the support of their daughter, Ginny (age 18; Social Security number 371–85–0033), and son, Derrick (age 23; Social Security number 361–42–4610). Ginny attends junior college on a part-time basis and earns

$13,500 from a job (most of which is saved). Derrick graduated from law school on May 10, 2001. During the year, he had earned income of $6,400.

Compute the Readings' taxable income for 2001. Suggested software: Any commercially available tax preparation software.

37. Alice and Bruce Byrd are married taxpayers, ages 47 and 45, who file a joint return. Their Social Security numbers are 034–48–4382 and 016–50–9556, respectively. They live at 473 Revere Avenue, Ames, MA 01850. Alice is the office manager for a dental clinic and earns an annual salary of $50,000. Bruce is the manager of a fast-food outlet owned and operated by Plymouth Corporation. His annual salary is $40,000.

The Byrds have two children, Cynthia (age 23 and Social Security number 017–44–9126) and John (age 22 and Social Security number 017–27–4148), who live with them. Both children are full-time students at a nearby college. Alice's mother, Myrtle Jones (age 74 and Social Security number 016–15–8266), also lives with them. Her sole source of income is from Social Security benefits, which she deposits in a savings account.

During 2000, the Byrds furnished one-third of the total support of Bruce's widower father, Sam Byrd (age 70 and Social Security number 034–82–8583). Sam lived alone and received the rest of his support from Bruce's sister and brother (one-third each). They have signed a multiple support agreement allowing Bruce to claim Sam as a dependent for 2000. Sam died in November, and Bruce received life insurance proceeds of $300,000 on December 28.

The Byrds had the following expenses relating to their personal residence during 2000:

Property taxes	$2,600
Interest on home mortgage	7,500
Repairs to roof	4,200
Utilities	2,100
Fire and theft insurance	1,800

Medical expenses for 2000 include:

Medical insurance premiums	$5,100
Doctor bill for Sam incurred in 1999 and not paid until 2000	2,900
Operation for Sam	5,300

The operation for Sam represents the one-third Bruce contributed toward his father's support.

Other relevant information follows:

- Alice and Bruce had $2,900 ($1,600 for Alice and $1,300 for Bruce) withheld from their salaries for state income taxes. When they filed their 1999 state return in 2000, they paid additional state income tax of $600.

- During 2000, Alice and Bruce attended a dinner dance sponsored by the Ames Police Disability Association (a qualified charitable organization). The Byrds paid $200 for the tickets. Cost of comparable entertainment would normally be $80. The Byrds contributed $2,100 to their church and gave used clothing (cost of $700 and fair market value of $300) to the Salvation Army. All donations are supported by receipts.

- In 2000, the Byrds received interest income of $1,950 from a savings account they maintained.

- Alice's employer required that all employees wear uniforms to work. During 2000, Alice spent $470 on new uniforms and $132 on laundry charges. Bruce paid $150 for an annual subscription to the *Journal of Franchise Management*. Neither Alice's nor Bruce's employer reimburses for employee expenses.

- Alice and Bruce had $9,400 ($4,900 for Alice and $4,500 for Bruce) of Federal income tax withheld in 2000, and they paid no estimated Federal income tax. Neither Alice nor Bruce wishes to designate $3 to the Presidential Election Campaign Fund.

Part 1—Tax Computation

Compute net tax payable or refund due for Alice and Bruce Byrd for 2000. If they have overpaid, the amount is to be refunded. If you use tax forms for your computations, you will need Form 1040 and Schedules A and B. Suggested software: Any commercially available tax preparation software.

Part 2—Tax Planning

Alice and Bruce are planning some significant changes for 2001. They have provided you with the following information and asked you to project their taxable income and tax liability for 2001.

- Myrtle became seriously ill in December 2000 and is no longer able to care for herself. As a result, Alice plans to take a one-year leave of absence from work during 2001 to care for her.

- The Byrds will use $100,000 of the life insurance proceeds they received as a result of Sam's death and pay off their mortgage in early January 2001. They will invest the remaining $200,000 in short-term certificates of deposit (CDs) and use the interest for living expenses during 2001.

- They expect to earn total interest of $9,000 on the CDs. Bruce has been awarded a 5% raise for 2001, and state and Federal tax withholdings on his salary will increase accordingly.

- The Byrds will not incur any additional costs related to Sam's medical problem.

- Alice will not work at all during 2001, so none of her job-related expenses or withholdings will continue.

- The Byrds do not expect to owe additional state income tax when they file their 2000 return, but they do expect their charitable contributions and medical insurance premiums to continue at the 2000 level.

- Assume all other income and deduction items will continue at the same level in 2001 unless you have information that indicates otherwise.

38. Paul and Donna Decker are married taxpayers, ages 44 and 42, who file a joint return for 2001. The Deckers live at 1121 College Avenue, Carmel, IN 46032. Paul is an assistant manager at Carmel Motor Inn, and Donna is a teacher at Carmel Elementary School. They present you with W–2 Forms that reflect the following information:

	Paul	**Donna**
Salary	$54,000	$50,000
Federal tax withheld	9,400	8,800
State income tax withheld	800	700
FICA (Social Security and Medicare) withheld	4,131	3,825
Social Security numbers	222–11–4567	333–11–9872

Donna is the custodial parent of two children from a previous marriage who reside with the Deckers through the school year. The children, Larry and Jane Parker, reside with their father, Bob, during the summer. Relevant information for the children follows:

	Larry	**Jane**
Age	11	9
Social Security numbers	305–11–4567	303–11–9872
Months spent with Deckers	9	9

Under the divorce decree, Bob pays child support of $150 per month per child during the nine months the children live with the Deckers. Bob says he spends $200 per month per child during the three summer months they reside with him. Donna and Paul can document that they provide $1,800 of support per child per year. The divorce decree is silent as to which parent can claim the exemption for the children.

In August, Paul and Donna added a suite to their home to provide more comfortable accommodations for Hannah Snyder (263–33–4738), Donna's mother, who had moved in with them in February 2000 after the death of Donna's father. Not wanting to borrow money for this addition, Paul sold 300 shares of Acme Corporation stock for $55 per share on May 3, 2001, and used the proceeds of $16,500 to cover construction costs. The Deckers had purchased the stock on April 29, 1998, for $27 per share. They received dividends of $750 on the jointly owned stock a month before the sale.

Hannah, who is 66 years old, received $7,200 in Social Security benefits during the year, of which she gave the Deckers $1,700 to use toward household expenses and deposited the remainder in her personal savings account. The Deckers determine that they have spent $1,500 of their own money for food, clothing, medical expenses, and other items for Hannah. They do not know what the rental value of Hannah's suite would be, but they estimate it would be at least $300 per month.

Interest paid during the year included the following:

Home mortgage interest (paid to Carmel Federal Savings and Loan)	$7,460
Interest on an automobile loan (paid to Carmel National Bank)	1,490
Interest on Citibank Visa card	870

In July, Paul hit a submerged rock while boating. Fortunately, he was thrown from the boat, landed in deep water, and was uninjured. However, the boat, which was uninsured, was destroyed. Paul had paid $25,000 for the boat in June 2000, and its value was appraised at $19,000 on the date of the accident.

The Deckers paid doctor and hospital bills of $6,700 and were reimbursed $1,800 by their insurance company. They spent $940 for prescription drugs and medicines and $1,810 for premiums on their health insurance policy. They have filed additional claims of $900 with their insurance company and have been told they will receive payment for that amount in January 2002. Included in the amounts paid for doctor and hospital bills were payments of $380 for Hannah and $850 for the children.

Additional information of potential tax consequence follows:

Real estate taxes paid	$2,400
Cash contributions to church	1,300
Appraised value of books donated to public library	620
Paul's unreimbursed employee expenses to attend hotel management convention:	
Airfare	440
Hotel	170
Meals	95
Registration fee	240
Refund of state income tax for 2000 (the Deckers itemized on their 2000 Federal tax return)	1,220

Compute net tax payable or refund due for the Deckers for 2001. If they have overpaid, the amount is to be credited toward their taxes for 2002. Suggested software: Any commercially available tax preparation software.

BRIDGE DISCIPLINE

1. Wayne and Brenda each earn a salary of $50,000. They are contemplating marriage, but before making the commitment, they inquire about the marriage penalty they have heard their married friends discuss. Calculate any difference in the aggregate income

tax liability for 2001 if they remain single as compared to the amount they would owe if they marry. Assume, that their only income consists of salary and that they would claim the standard deduction in all cases.

2. George comes to you asking for your advice. He wishes to invest $10,000 either in a debt security or in an equity investment. His choices are as shown below:

   • Redbreast Corporation bond, annual coupon rate of 7.50%.

   • City of Philadelphia general obligation bond, coupon rate of 6.00%.

   • Blue Corporation 7.50% preferred stock.

   These alternatives are believed to carry comparable risk. Assuming George is in the 36% marginal tax bracket, which investment alternative could be expected to produce the superior annual after-tax rate of return?

3. Assume the same facts as in Problem 2, except that George is a C corporation rather than an individual and is in the 34% marginal tax bracket. Which investment strategy would maximize George, Inc.'s annual return?

RESEARCH PROBLEMS

*Note: Solutions to Research Problems can be prepared by using the **RIA Checkpoint® Student Version Online** research product, or the **CCH U.S. Master Tax Guide Plus**™ online Federal tax research database, which is available to accompany this text. It is also possible to prepare solutions to the Research Problems by using tax research materials found in a standard tax library.*

Research Problem 1. John and Marge Hudgens were married 26 years ago and have one child, Monica. Sometime in January 2001, after a particularly fierce argument, John packed his clothes and left for parts unknown. Marge has neither seen nor heard from him since.

Marge is employed and maintains the house where she and Monica live. Monica was a full-time student until she graduated from law school on May 9, 2001. During the year, Monica (age 23) earned $9,100 from part-time jobs. She deposited part of her earnings in a savings account under her name and used the rest for her support. The remainder of Monica's support was provided by Marge.

Marge contacts you regarding tax advice. Specifically, she is interested in the answers to the following questions for tax year 2001:

   • What is her filing status?

   • Can she claim Monica as a dependent?

   a. Write a letter to Marge addressing her concerns. Marge lives at 1349 Center Street, Warrensburg, MO 64093.
   b. Also prepare a memo for your firm's client files.

Research Problem 2. Priscilla is married and lives in a community property state. In late 2000, her husband, Layton, left for parts unknown, and she has not seen or heard from him since. The laws of the state where Priscilla lives provide certain protections for spouses who have been abandoned. Under these laws, Priscilla's income becomes separate, but Layton's income remains community. The purpose of these laws is to preclude the abandoning spouse from claiming half of the income earned by the abandoned spouse. The laws also prevent the abandoning spouse from defeating the abandoned spouse's right to half of his income.

When Priscilla learns about the state laws that purport to protect her, she is appalled at the apparent income tax consequences. Does this mean that Priscilla must recognize all of her income and half of Layton's income? What relief, if any, does the Internal Revenue Code provide in Priscilla's situation?

Research Problem 3. After several years of a difficult marriage, Donald and Marla agreed to a divorce. As part of the property settlement, Marla transferred to Donald corporate stock, a commercial building, and a personal residence. Donald transferred other property to Marla, but the fair market value of the property was $600,000 less than the fair market value of the property Marla had transferred to him. To make the settlement equal, Donald agreed to pay Marla $600,000, payable over 10 years at 8% interest. For several years, Donald deducted the interest on his Federal income tax return as investment interest. Upon audit, the IRS disallowed the interest deduction, classifying it as nondeductible personal interest. Donald believes the interest is deductible and has asked you to find support for the deduction. Write a letter indicating your findings to Donald Jansen, 104 South Fourth Street, Dalton, GA 30720.

Partial list of research aids:
Don Gilmore, 63–1 USTC ¶9285, 11 AFTR2d 758, 372 U.S. 39 (USSC, 1963).
John L. Seymour, 109 T.C. 279 (1997).

Research Problem 4. Under the terms of a post-1986 divorce agreement, Al is to receive payments from Karen as follows: $90,000 in Year 1, $60,000 in Year 2, and $20,000 each year for Years 3 through 10. Al is also to receive custody of their minor son. The payments will decrease by $5,000 per year if the son dies or when he attains age 21 and will cease upon Al's death.
a. What will be Al's taxable alimony in Year 1?
b. What will be the effect of the Years 2 and 3 payments on Al's taxable income?

Use the tax resources of the Internet to address the following questions. Do not restrict your search to the World Wide Web, but include a review of newsgroups and general reference materials, practitioner sites and resources, primary sources of the tax law, chat rooms and discussion groups, and other opportunities.

Research Problem 5. Many tax advisers with materials on the Internet propose tax planning techniques for minimizing liabilities under the kiddie tax. Summarize the most effective of these proposals, and cite the providers of the information.

Research Problem 6. Find several news reports concerning the government's effort to curb the fraudulent use of the earned income credit by taxpayers who do not qualify for it.

Individuals as Employees and Proprietors

LEARNING OBJECTIVES

After completing Chapter 16, you should be able to:

1. Distinguish between employee and self-employed status.

2. Understand the exclusions from income available to employees who receive fringe benefits.

3. Apply the rules for computing deductible expenses of employees including transportation, travel, moving, education, and entertainment expenses.

4. Appreciate the difference between accountable and nonaccountable employee plans.

5. Understand the tax provisions applicable to proprietors.

6. Distinguish between business and hobby activities and apply the rules limiting the deduction of hobby losses.

Outline

TAX TALK
The taxpayer—that's someone who works for the Federal government but doesn't have to take a civil service examination.

—*Ronald Reagan*

An individual may be an employee or may be self-employed. The terms *proprietor* and *independent contractor* are both used to describe self-employed individuals. These terms are used interchangeably throughout this chapter.

In many cases, it is difficult to distinguish between employees and self-employed individuals. This chapter begins with a discussion of the factors that must be considered in determining whether an individual is an employee or is self-employed. This is followed by a discussion of tax provisions applicable to employees and then by a discussion of tax provisions related to self-employed individuals.

LEARNING OBJECTIVE 1

Distinguish between employee and self-employed status.

Employee versus Self-Employed

When one person performs services for another, the person performing the service is either an employee or self-employed (i.e., an **independent contractor**). Failure to recognize employee status can have serious consequences. Not only can interest and penalties result, but career opportunities, such as possible political opportunities or elected positions, can disappear in the wake of extensive negative media coverage.

The determination of employment status is already controversial and can be expected to become an even greater problem in the future. As a means for achieving greater flexibility and cost control, businesses are increasingly relying on self-employed persons (i.e., independent contractors) rather than employees for many services.

The IRS is very much aware that businesses have a tendency to wrongly classify workers as self-employed rather than as employees. In some cases, misclassification is unintentional and results from difficulty in applying the complex set of rules related to employee versus independent contractor status. In other cases, misclassification may be an intentional strategy to avoid certain costs that are associated with employees. Unlike employees, self-employed persons do not have to be included in various fringe benefit programs and retirement plans. Furthermore, employers are not required to pay FICA and unemployment taxes (refer to Chapter 1) on compensation paid to independent contractors.

In terms of tax consequences, employment status also makes a great deal of difference to the worker. Allowable business expenses of self-employed taxpayers are classified as deductions *for* AGI and are reported on Schedule C (Profit or Loss from Business) of Form 1040.[1] On the other hand, unreimbursed business expenses incurred by employees are classified as itemized deductions and are deductible on Schedule A (as itemized deductions) only to the extent that the sum of certain miscellaneous itemized deductions exceeds 2 percent of the taxpayer's AGI. Unreimbursed employee expenses are reported on Form 2106 (Employee Business Expenses) and Schedule A (Itemized Deductions) of Form 1040.

Employee expenses that are reimbursed under an **accountable plan** (covered later in this chapter) are also reported as deductions *for* AGI. Employee expenses that are not reimbursed under an accountable plan are treated in the same way as unreimbursed expenses—deductible *from* AGI and limited to the excess over 2 percent of AGI.[2]

FACTORS CONSIDERED IN CLASSIFICATION

The pivotal issue in classifying an individual as an independent contractor or an employee is whether an employer-employee relationship exists. The IRS has created a complex *20-factor test* for determining whether a worker is an employee or an independent contractor. The courts, which have focused on a small number of these factors, generally hold that an individual is an employee if the individual or business acquiring the services:[3]

- has the right to specify the end result and the ways and means by which that result is to be attained,
- can exert will and control over the person providing the services with respect not only to *what* shall be done but also to *how* it shall be done,
- has the right to discharge, without legal liability, the person performing the service,
- furnishes tools or a place to work, and
- bases payment on time spent rather than the task performed.

Each case is tested on its own merits, and the right to control the means and methods of accomplishment is the definitive test. Generally, physicians, lawyers, dentists, contractors, subcontractors, and others who offer services to the public are not classified as employees.

1 *Find more information on this topic at our Web site: **http://wft-entities.swcollege.com**.*

---

[1]§§ 62(a)(1) and 162(a).
[2]§ 67(a).

[3]Reg. § 31.3401(c)–(1)(b).

BRIDGE DISCIPLINE

Bridge to Equity or Fairness and Business Law

Max performs services for Calico, Inc. Amy performs services for Amber, Inc. They perform basically the same service. Yet Max is classified as an employee, and Amy is classified as an independent contractor. Does such a legal classification produce equitable results in terms of the effects it has on Max and Amy?

Employee status produces a number of potential perks. Included are coverage in the employer's fringe benefits programs such as medical insurance, group term life insurance, and § 132 fringe benefits. For an employee, the tax rate for Social Security is 6.2 percent, and for Medicare, the rate is 1.45 percent (i.e., the employer is responsible for matching the employee amounts). For a self-employed person, the tax rates for Social Security and Medicare are 12.4 percent and 2.9 percent, respectively.

In distinguishing between an employee and an independent contractor, the overriding theme of common law is that the employee is subject to the will and control of the employer, both as to what is to be done and as to how it is to be done. Put in more legal terminology, an employer has the right to control and direct the individual who performs the services, not only as to the result to be accomplished by the work but also as to the details and means by which the result is accomplished. Among the factors generally considered in determining whether this right exists are the following:

- Degree of control exercised over the details of the work.
- Provision of facilities used in the work.
- Opportunity for profit or loss.
- Right to discharge.
- Whether work is part of regular business.
- Permanency of the relationship.
- Relationship the parties believe they are creating.
- Manner of payment, by the job or by the hour.
- Skill required.
- Offering of the services to the general public rather than to one individual or entity.
- Distinct occupation or recognized trade or calling involved.
- Custom in the trade.

EXAMPLE 1

Arnold is a lawyer whose major client accounts for 60% of his billings. He does the routine legal work and income tax returns at the client's request. He is paid a monthly retainer in addition to amounts charged for extra work. Arnold is a self-employed individual. Even though most of his income comes from one client, he still has the right to determine *how* the end result of his work is attained. ■

EXAMPLE 2

Ellen is a lawyer hired by Arnold to assist him in the performance of services for the client mentioned in Example 1. Ellen is under Arnold's supervision; he reviews her work and pays her an hourly fee. Ellen is Arnold's employee. ■

2   *Find more information on this topic at our Web site: http://wft-entities.swcollege.com.*

PLANNING CONSIDERATIONS

Self-Employed Individuals

Some taxpayers have the flexibility to be classified as either employees or self-employed individuals. Examples include real estate agents and direct sellers. These taxpayers should carefully consider all factors and not automatically assume that self-employed status is preferable.

It is advantageous to deduct one's business expenses *for* AGI and avoid the 2 percent floor for miscellaneous itemized deductions. However, a self-employed individual may incur additional expenses, such as local gross receipts taxes, license fees, franchise fees, personal property taxes, and occupation taxes. Record-keeping and filing requirements can also be quite burdensome.

One of the most expensive considerations is the **self-employment tax** imposed on independent contractors

and other self-employed individuals. For an employee in 2001, for example, the Social Security tax applies at a rate of 6.2 percent on a base amount of wages of $80,400, and the Medicare tax applies at a rate of 1.45 percent with no limit on the base amount. For self-employed persons, the rate, but not the base amount, for each tax doubles. Even though a deduction *for* AGI is allowed for one-half of the self-employment tax paid, an employee and a self-employed individual are not in the same tax position on equal amounts of earnings. For the applicability of these taxes to workers, see Chapter 1.

After analyzing all these factors, taxpayers in many cases may decide that employee status is preferable to self-employed status.

LEARNING OBJECTIVE 2

Understand the exclusions from income available to employees who receive fringe benefits.

Exclusions Available to Employees

Several exclusions that are available to *all taxpayers* were discussed in Chapter 3; these include interest on obligations of state and local governments, life insurance proceeds, and income from discharge of indebtedness. Other exclusions, available only to *individuals*, were discussed in Chapter 15; these exclusions include gifts and inheritances, scholarships, and compensation for injuries and sickness. Exclusions available only to *employees* are discussed below.

ADVANTAGES OF QUALIFIED FRINGE BENEFITS

Exclusions available only to *employees* are generally referred to as *qualified fringe benefits*. The popularity of fringe benefits is attributable to the fact that the cost of such benefits is deductible by employers and excludible by employees.

EXAMPLE 3

Cardinal Corporation, which has a marginal tax rate of 35%, provides health insurance coverage to employees at a cost of $1,000 per employee. Because Cardinal can deduct the health insurance premiums paid to provide this coverage, the net cost to the corporation is $650 per employee ($1,000 cost – $350 tax savings). The employee is allowed to exclude the value of this fringe benefit, so there is no tax cost to the employee.

The average employee of Cardinal Corporation is in the 28% bracket. If Cardinal did not provide the health insurance coverage and the employee paid a $1,000 premium, the employee would have to use after-tax dollars to acquire the coverage. The employee would have to earn $1,389 to pay for the coverage [$1,389 wages – ($1,389 × 28% tax)]. The after-tax cost to the corporation of $1,389 in wages is $903 ($1,389 wages – $486 corporate tax savings). Thus, the cost of health insurance coverage is $253 less per employee ($903 – $650) because it is both deductible by the corporation and excludible by the employee. ■

BRIDGE DISCIPLINE

Bridge to Economic and Societal Needs

The media frequently report on the plight of our "senior citizens." Organizations such as the AARP effectively lobby for the rights of senior citizens through direct lobbying in Washington and through grassroots efforts throughout the country. With the graying of America, these concerns and lobbying efforts are likely to be magnified.

Congress, in the 1930s, enacted Social Security to partially provide for the retirement needs of our senior citizens. In the 1960s, Congress enacted Medicare to partially provide for the medical needs of our senior citizens.

The Internal Revenue Code contains a number of provisions that are "senior citizen friendly." Among these are the following:

- General exclusion, except for the "rich," of Social Security benefits from gross income (§ 86).
- Exclusion of life insurance proceeds from the gross income of the recipient (§ 101).
- Exclusion of medical insurance premiums and benefits from gross income (§ 105 and § 106).
- Limited exclusion from gross income of gain on sale of a principal residence (§ 121).
- Limited exclusion from gross income of long-term care insurance premiums and benefits (§ 7702B).
- Beneficial treatment of retirement plans (Subchapter D).

EMPLOYER-SPONSORED ACCIDENT AND HEALTH PLANS

Congress encourages employers to provide employees, retired former employees, and their dependents with accident and health benefits, disability insurance, and long-term care plans. The *premiums* are deductible by the employer and are excluded from the employee's gross income.[4] Although § 105(a) provides the general rule that the employee has includible income when he or she collects the insurance *benefits*, two exceptions are provided.

Section 105(b) generally excludes payments received for medical care of the employee, spouse, and dependents. However, if the payments are for expenses that do not meet the Code's definition of medical care,[5] the amount received must be included in gross income. In addition, the taxpayer must include in gross income any amounts received for medical expenses that were deducted by the taxpayer on a prior return.

EXAMPLE 4

In 2001, Tab's employer-sponsored health insurance plan paid $4,000 for hair transplants that did not meet the Code's definition of medical care. Tab must include the $4,000 in his gross income for 2001. ■

Section 105(c) excludes payments for the permanent loss or the loss of the use of a member or function of the body or the permanent disfigurement of the employee, spouse, or a dependent. However, payments that are a substitute for salary (e.g., related to the period of time absent) are included in income.

---

[4]§ 106, Reg. § 1.106–1, and Rev.Rul. 82–196, 1982–1 C.B. 106.   [5]See the discussion of medical care in Chapter 15.

<table>
<tr><td>

EXAMPLE 5

</td><td>

Jill lost an eye in an automobile accident unrelated to her work. As a result of the accident, Jill incurred $2,000 of medical expenses, which she deducted on her return. She collected $10,000 from an accident insurance policy carried by her employer. The benefits were paid according to a schedule of amounts that varied with the part of the body injured (e.g., $10,000 for loss of an eye, $20,000 for loss of a hand). Because the payment was for loss of a *member or function of the body*, the $10,000 is excluded from Jill's gross income. Jill was absent from work for a week as a result of the accident. Her employer also provided her with insurance that reimbursed her for the loss of income due to illness or injury. Jill collected $500, which is includible in her gross income. ■

</td></tr>
</table>

MEDICAL REIMBURSEMENT PLANS

As noted above, the amounts received through the insurance coverage (insured plan benefits) are excluded from gross income under § 105. Unfortunately, because of cost considerations, the insurance companies that issue this type of policy usually require a broad coverage of employees. An alternative is to have a plan that is not funded with insurance (a self-insured arrangement). Under a self-insured plan, the employer reimburses employees directly for any medical expenses. The benefits received under a self-insured plan can be excluded from the employee's gross income, if the plan does not discriminate in favor of highly compensated employees.

Small employers (50 or fewer employees) have an alternative means of accomplishing a medical reimbursement plan. The employer can purchase a medical insurance plan with a high deductible (e.g., the employee is responsible for the first $2,000 of medical expenses) and then make contributions to the employee's **medical savings account (MSA).** The employer can make contributions each year up to the maximum contribution of 65 percent of the deductible amount for an individual or 75 percent of the deductible amount in the case of family coverage. Withdrawals from the MSA must be used to reimburse the employee for the medical expenses paid by the employee that are not covered under the high-deductible plan. The employee is not taxed on the employer's contributions to the MSA, the earnings on the funds in the account, or the withdrawals made for medical expenses.[6]

LONG-TERM CARE BENEFITS

Generally, long-term care insurance, which covers expenses such as the cost of care in a nursing home, is treated the same as accident and health insurance benefits. Thus, the employee does not recognize income when the employer pays the premiums. When benefits are received from the policy, whether the employer or the individual purchased the policy, the exclusion from gross income is limited to the *greater* of the following amounts:

- $200 (indexed amount for 2001) for each day the patient receives the long-term care.
- The actual cost of the care.

The excludible amount is reduced by any amounts received from other third parties (e.g., damages received).[7]

<table>
<tr><td>

EXAMPLE 6

</td><td>

Hazel, who suffers from Alzheimer's disease, was a patient in a nursing home for the last 30 days of 2001. While in the nursing home, she incurred total costs of $6,500. Medicare

</td></tr>
</table>

---

[6]§§ 105(h), 106(b), and 220. Medical savings accounts (MSAs) were created as a pilot project, effective for tax years beginning after December 31, 1996. The pilot project was scheduled to end December 31, 2000; however, legislation enacted late in 2000 extended MSAs for an additional two years.

[7]§ 7702B.

paid $3,200 of the costs. Hazel received $3,600 from her long-term care insurance policy (which paid $120 per day while she was in the facility). The amount Hazel may exclude is calculated as follows:

Greater of:		
Daily statutory amount of $200 ($200 × 30 days)	$6,000	
Actual cost of the care	6,500	$ 6,500
Less: Amount received from Medicare		(3,200)
Amount of exclusion		$ 3,300

Therefore, Hazel must include $300 ($3,600 – $3,300) of the long-term care benefits received in her gross income. ∎

The exclusion for long-term care insurance is not available if it is provided as part of a cafeteria plan or a flexible spending plan (discussed later in this chapter).

MEALS AND LODGING FURNISHED FOR THE CONVENIENCE OF THE EMPLOYER

Income can take any form, including meals and lodging. However, § 119 excludes from gross income the value of meals and lodging provided to the employee and the employee's spouse and dependents under the following conditions:[8]

- The meals and/or lodging are *furnished by the employer*, on the employer's *business premises*, for the *convenience of the employer*.
- In the case of lodging, the *employee is required* to accept the lodging as a condition of employment.

The courts have construed these requirements strictly, as discussed below.

Furnished by the Employer.   The following two questions have been raised with regard to the *furnished by the employer* requirement:

- Who is considered an *employee*?
- What is meant by *furnished*?

For the employee issue, the IRS and some courts have reasoned that because a partner is not an employee, the exclusion does not apply to a partner. However, the Tax Court and the Fifth Circuit Court of Appeals have ruled in favor of the taxpayer on this issue.[9]

On the issue of whether meals and lodging are *furnished* by the employer, the Supreme Court held that a *cash meal allowance* was ineligible for the exclusion because the employer did not actually furnish the meals.[10] Similarly, one court denied the exclusion where the employer paid for the food and supplied the cooking facilities but the employee prepared the meal.[11]

---

[8]§ 119(a). The meals and lodging are also excluded from FICA and FUTA tax. *Rowan Companies, Inc. v. U.S.*, 81–1 USTC ¶9479, 48 AFTR2d 81–5115, 101 S.Ct. 2288 (USSC, 1981).

[9]Rev.Rul. 80, 1953–1 C.B. 62; *Comm. v. Doak*, 56–2 USTC ¶9708, 49 AFTR 1491, 234 F.2d 704 (CA–4, 1956); but see *G. A. Papineau*, 16 T.C. 130 (1951); *Armstrong v. Phinney*, 68–1 USTC ¶9355, 21 AFTR2d 1260, 394 F.2d 661 (CA–5, 1968).

[10]*Comm. v. Kowalski*, 77–2 USTC ¶9748, 40 AFTR2d 6128, 98 S.Ct. 315 (USSC, 1977).

[11]*Tougher v. Comm.*, 71–1 USTC ¶9398, 27 AFTR2d 1301, 441 F.2d 1148 (CA–9, 1971).

On the Employer's Business Premises. The *on the employer's business premises* requirement, applicable to both meals and lodging, has resulted in much litigation. The Regulations define business premises as simply "the place of employment of the employee."[12] Thus, the Sixth Circuit Court of Appeals held that a residence, owned by the employer and occupied by an employee, located two blocks from the motel that the employee managed was not part of the business premises.[13] However, the Tax Court considered an employer-owned house located across the street from the hotel that was managed by the taxpayer to be on the business premises of the employer.[14] Perhaps these two cases can be reconciled by comparing the distance from the lodging facilities to the place where the employer's business was conducted. The closer the lodging to the business operations, the more likely the convenience of the employer is served.

For the Convenience of the Employer. The *convenience of the employer* test is intended to focus on the employer's motivation for furnishing the meals and lodging rather than on the benefits received by the employee. If the employer furnishes the meals and lodging primarily to enable the employee to perform his or her duties properly, it does not matter that the employee considers these benefits to be a part of his or her compensation.

The Regulations give the following examples in which the tests for excluding meals are satisfied:[15]

- A waitress is required to eat her meals on the premises during the busy lunch and breakfast hours.
- A bank furnishes a teller meals on the premises to limit the time the employee is away from his or her booth during the busy hours.
- A worker is employed at a construction site in a remote part of Alaska. The employer must furnish meals and lodging due to the inaccessibility of other facilities.

In 1998, Congress liberalized the convenience of the employer requirement. If more than half of the meals provided to employees are furnished for the convenience of the employer, then all such employee meals are treated as provided for the convenience of the employer.

EXAMPLE 7

Allison's Restaurant has a restaurant area and a bar. Nine employees work in the restaurant and three work in the bar. All of the employees are provided one meal per day. In the case of the restaurant workers, the meals are provided for the convenience of the employer. The meals provided to the bar employees do not satisfy the convenience of the employer requirement. Because more than half of the employees receive their meal for the convenience of the employer, all 12 employees qualify for exclusion treatment. ■

The 1998 changes were directed at assuring that all employees of an organization will receive the same tax treatment. Therefore, either all of the employees are allowed the exclusion treatment, or none of the employees can exclude the meals from gross income.

Required as a Condition of Employment. The *required as a condition of employment* test applies only to lodging. If the employee's use of the housing would serve

[12]Reg. § 1.119 1(c)(1).
[13]*Comm. v. Anderson*, 67–1 USTC ¶9136, 19 AFTR2d 318, 371 F.2d 59 (CA–6, 1966).
[14]*J. B. Lindeman*, 60 T.C. 609 (1973).
[15]Reg. § 1.119–1(f).

the convenience of the employer, but the employee is not required to use the housing, the exclusion is not available.

EXAMPLE 8

VEP, a utilities company, has all of its service personnel on 24-hour call for emergencies. The company encourages its employees to live near the plant so they can respond quickly to emergency calls. Company-owned housing is available rent-free. Only 10 of the employees live in the company housing because it is not suitable for families.

Although the company-provided housing serves the convenience of the employer, it is not required. Therefore, the employees who live in the company housing must include its value in gross income. ■

In addition, if the employee has the option of cash or lodging, the employer-required test is not satisfied.

EXAMPLE 9

Khalid is the manager of a large apartment complex. The employer gives Khalid the option of rent-free housing (value of $6,000 per year) or an additional $5,000 per year. Khalid selects the housing option. Therefore, he must include $6,000 in gross income. ■

Other housing exclusions are available for certain employees of educational institutions, ministers of the gospel, and military personnel.

GROUP TERM LIFE INSURANCE

For many years, the IRS did not attempt to tax the value of life insurance protection provided to an employee by the employer. Some companies took undue advantage of the exclusion by providing large amounts of insurance protection for key executives. In response, Congress enacted § 79, which created a limited exclusion for group term life insurance. Current law allows an exclusion of premiums on the first $50,000 of group term life insurance protection.

The benefits of this exclusion are available only to employees. Proprietors and partners are not considered employees. Moreover, the Regulations generally require broad-scale coverage of employees to satisfy the group requirement (e.g., shareholder-employees would not constitute a qualified group). The exclusion applies only to term insurance (protection for a period of time but with no cash surrender value) and not to ordinary life insurance (lifetime protection plus a cash surrender value that can be drawn upon before death).

As mentioned, the exclusion applies to the first $50,000 of group term life insurance protection. For each $1,000 of coverage in excess of $50,000, the employee must include the amounts indicated in Table 16–1 in gross income.[16]

 3 *Find more information on this topic at our Web site: **http://wft-entities.swcollege.com**.*

EXAMPLE 10

Finch Corporation has a group term life insurance policy with coverage equal to the employee's annual salary. Keith, age 52, is president of the corporation and receives an annual salary of $75,000. Keith must include $69 in gross income from the insurance protection for the year.

$$[(\$75,000 - \$50,000)/\$1,000] \times \$0.23 \times 12 \text{ months} = \$69$$ ■

---

[16]Reg. § 1.79–3(d)(2).

■ TABLE 16–1
Uniform Premiums for $1,000 of Group Term Life Insurance Protection

5-Year Age Bracket	Cost of $1,000 of Protection for a One-Month Period*
Under 25	$ .05
25–29	.06
30–34	.08
35–39	.09
40–44	.10
45–49	.15
50–54	.23
55–59	.43
60–64	.66
65–69	1.27
70 and above	2.06

*Reg. § 1.79–3, effective for coverage after June 30, 1999.

If the plan discriminates in favor of certain key employees (e.g., officers), the key employees are not eligible for the exclusion. In such a case, the key employees must include in gross income the *greater* of actual premiums paid by the employer or the amount calculated from the Uniform Premiums table in Table 16–1. The other employees are still eligible for the $50,000 exclusion and continue to use the Uniform Premiums table to compute the income from excess insurance protection.[17]

QUALIFIED TUITION REDUCTION PLANS

Employees (including retired and disabled former employees) of nonprofit educational institutions are allowed to exclude a tuition waiver from gross income, if the waiver is pursuant to a qualified tuition reduction plan.[18] The plan may not discriminate in favor of highly compensated employees. The exclusion applies to the employee, the employee's spouse, and the employee's dependent children. The exclusion also extends to tuition reductions granted by any nonprofit educational institution to employees of any other nonprofit educational institution (reciprocal agreements).

EXAMPLE 11

ABC University allows the dependent children of XYZ University employees to attend ABC University with no tuition charge. XYZ University grants reciprocal benefits to the children of ABC University employees. The dependent children can also attend tuition-free the university where their parents are employed. Employees who take advantage of these benefits are not required to recognize gross income. ■

Generally, the exclusion is limited to undergraduate tuition waivers. However, in the case of teaching or research assistants, graduate tuition waivers may also qualify for exclusion treatment. According to the Proposed Regulations, the exclusion is limited to the value of the benefit in excess of the employee's reasonable compensation.[19] Thus, a tuition reduction that is a substitute for cash compensation cannot be excluded.

[17]§ 79(d).
[18]§ 117(d).

[19]Prop.Reg. § 1.117–6(d).

EXAMPLE 12

Susan is a graduate research assistant. She receives a $5,000 salary for 500 hours of service over a nine-month period. This pay, $10 per hour, is reasonable compensation for Susan's services. In addition, Susan receives a waiver of $6,000 for tuition. Susan may exclude the tuition waiver from gross income. ∎

OTHER SPECIFIC EMPLOYEE FRINGE BENEFITS

Congress has enacted exclusions to encourage employers to (1) finance and make available child care facilities, (2) provide athletic facilities for employees, (3) finance certain education expenses of employees, and (4) assist employees who adopt children. These provisions are summarized as follows:

- The employee can exclude from gross income the value of child and dependent care services paid for by the employer and incurred to enable the employee to work. The exclusion cannot exceed $5,000 per year ($2,500 if married and filing separately). For a married couple, the annual exclusion cannot exceed the earned income of the spouse who has the lesser amount of earned income. For an unmarried taxpayer, the exclusion cannot exceed the taxpayer's earned income.[20]
- The value of the use of a gymnasium or other athletic facilities by employees, their spouses, and their dependent children may be excluded from an employee's gross income. The facilities must be on the employer's premises, and substantially all of the use of the facilities must be by employees and their family members.[21]
- Qualified employer-provided educational assistance (tuition, fees, books, and supplies) at the undergraduate level is excludible from gross income. The exclusion is limited to a maximum of $5,250 annually.[22]
- The employee can exclude from gross income up to $5,000 of expenses incurred to adopt a child where the adoption expenses are paid or reimbursed by the employer under a qualified adoption assistance program.[23] The limit on the exclusion is increased to $6,000 if the child has special needs (is not physically or mentally capable of caring for himself or herself). The exclusion is phased out over the AGI range from $75,000 to $115,000.

CAFETERIA PLANS

Generally, if an employee is offered a choice between cash and some other form of compensation, the employee is deemed to have constructively received the cash even when the noncash option is elected. Thus, the employee has gross income regardless of the option chosen.

An exception to this constructive receipt treatment is provided under the cafeteria plan rules. Under such a plan, the employee is permitted to choose between cash and nontaxable benefits (e.g., group term life insurance, health and accident protection, and child care). If the employee chooses the otherwise nontaxable benefits, the cafeteria plan rules allow the benefits to be excluded from the employee's gross income.[24] **Cafeteria plans** provide tremendous flexibility in tailoring the employee pay package to fit individual needs. Some employees (usually the younger group) prefer cash, while others (usually the older group) will opt for

---

[20]§ 129. The exclusion applies to the same types of expenses that, if paid by the employee (and not reimbursed by the employer), would be eligible for the credit for child and dependent care expenses, discussed in Chapter 15.
[21]§ 132(j)(4).

[22]§ 127. Exclusion treatment applies for tax years beginning before January 1, 2002.
[23]§ 137.
[24]§ 125.

the fringe benefit program. However, long-term care insurance cannot be part of a cafeteria plan. Thus, an employer that wishes to provide long-term care benefits must provide such benefits separate from the cafeteria plan.[25]

EXAMPLE 13

Hawk Corporation offers its employees (on a nondiscriminatory basis) a choice of any one or all of the following benefits:

Benefit	Cost
Group term life insurance	$ 200
Hospitalization insurance for family members	2,400
Child care payments	1,800
	$4,400

If a benefit is not selected, the employee receives cash equal to the cost of the benefit.

Kay, an employee, has a spouse who works for another employer that provides hospitalization insurance but no child care payments. Kay elects to receive the group term life insurance, the child care payments, and $2,400 of cash. Only the $2,400 must be included in Kay's gross income. ■

FLEXIBLE SPENDING PLANS

Flexible spending plans (often referred to as flexible benefit plans) operate much like cafeteria plans. Under these plans, the employee accepts lower cash compensation in return for the employer's agreement to pay certain costs that the employer can pay without the employee recognizing gross income. For example, assume the employer's health insurance policy does not cover dental expenses. The employee could estimate his or her dental expenses for the upcoming year and agree to a salary reduction equal to the estimated dental expenses. The employer then pays or reimburses the employee for the actual dental expenses incurred, up to the amount of the salary reduction. If the employee's actual dental expenses are less than the reduction in cash compensation, the employee cannot recover the difference. Hence, these plans are often referred to as *use or lose* plans. As is the case for cafeteria plans, flexible spending plans cannot be used to pay long-term care insurance premiums.

GENERAL CLASSES OF EXCLUDED BENEFITS

An employer can provide a variety of economic benefits to employees. Under the all-inclusive concept of income, the benefits are taxable unless one of the provisions previously discussed specifically excludes the item from gross income. The amount of the income is the fair market value of the benefit. This reasoning can lead to results that Congress considers unacceptable, as illustrated in the following example.

EXAMPLE 14

Vern is employed in New York as a ticket clerk for Trans National Airlines. Vern would like to visit his mother, who lives in Miami, Florida, but he has no money for plane tickets. Trans National has daily flights from New York to Miami that often leave with empty seats. The cost of a round-trip ticket is $400, and Vern is in the 28% tax bracket. If Trans National allows Vern to fly without charge to Miami, under the general gross income rules, Vern

---

[25]§ 125(f).

EMPLOYEES LOSE SOME UNDER "USE OR LOSE PLANS"

Over 21 million Americans lose between $125 and $200 every year as a result of overfunding their flexible benefit accounts. If the employee overestimates the amount required to provide the flexible benefits, and thus the reduction in the employee's salary, the unused portion of the fund is forfeited to the employer. The total forfeited amounts exceed $2 billion annually. Thus, employees appear to be substantial losers under these "use-it-or-lose-it" plans. Even though employees can still be net beneficiaries from the portion of the accounts that is actually used, the employees simply are not maximizing the benefits.

Tax legislation has been proposed on several occasions recently to allow any unused amount in a flexible benefit account to be transferred to various types of employee retirement accounts or to otherwise carry over for the employee's benefit. To date, none of these proposals has been enacted.

has income equal to the value of a ticket. Therefore, Vern must pay $112 tax (.28 × $400) on a trip to Miami. Because Vern does not have $112, he cannot visit his mother, and the airplane flies with another empty seat. ■

If Trans National in Example 14 will allow employees to use resources that would otherwise be wasted, why should the tax laws interfere with the employee's decision to take advantage of the available benefit? Thus, to avoid the economic inefficiency that occurs in Example 14 and in similar situations, as well as to create uniform rules for fringe benefits, Congress established six broad classes of nontaxable employee benefits:[26]

- No-additional-cost services.
- Qualified employee discounts.
- Working condition fringes.
- *De minimis* fringes.
- Qualified transportation fringes.
- Qualified moving expense reimbursements.

No-Additional-Cost Services. Example 14 illustrates a no-additional-cost fringe benefit. **No-additional-cost services** are excluded from an employee's gross income if all of the following conditions are satisfied:

- The employee receives services, as opposed to property.
- The employer does not incur substantial additional costs, including forgone revenue, in providing the services to the employee.
- The services must be from the same line of business in which the employee works.
- The services are offered to customers in the ordinary course of the business in which the employee works.[27]

EXAMPLE 15

Assume that Vern in Example 14 can fly without charge only if the airline cannot fill the seats with paying customers. That is, Vern must fly on standby. Although the airplane may

---

[26]See, generally, § 132.   [27]Reg. § 1.132–2.

burn slightly more fuel because Vern is aboard and Vern may receive the same meal as paying customers, the additional costs would not be substantial. Thus, the trip could qualify as a no-additional-cost service.

On the other hand, assume that Vern is given a reserved seat on a flight that is frequently full. The employer would be forgoing revenue to allow Vern to fly. This forgone revenue would be a substantial additional cost, and thus the benefit would be taxable to Vern. ■

4 *Find more information on this topic at our Web site:* ***http://wft-entities.swcollege.com.***

The no-additional-cost exclusion extends to the employee's spouse and dependent children and to retired and disabled former employees. In the Regulations, the IRS has conceded that partners who perform services for the partnership are employees for purposes of the exclusion.[28] However, the exclusion is not extended to highly compensated employees unless the benefit is available on a nondiscriminatory basis.

Qualified Employee Discounts. When the employer sells goods or services (other than no-additional-cost benefits just discussed) to the employee for a price that is less than the price charged regular customers, the employee ordinarily recognizes income equal to the discount. However, **qualified employee discounts** can be excluded from the gross income of the employee, subject to the following conditions and limitations:

- The exclusion is not available for discounted sales of real property (e.g., a house) or for personal property of the type commonly held for investment (e.g., common stocks).
- The property or services must be from the same line of business in which the employee works.
- In the case of property, the exclusion cannot exceed the gross profit component of the price to customers.
- In the case of services, the exclusion is limited to 20 percent of the customer price.[29]

EXAMPLE 16

Silver Corporation, which operates a department store, sells a television set to a store employee for $300. The regular customer price is $500, and the gross profit rate is 25%. The corporation also sells the employee a service contract for $100. The regular customer price for the contract is $150. The employee must recognize income of $95, computed as follows:

Customer price for property	$ 500	
Less: Qualifying discount (25% gross profit × $500 price)	(125)	
	$ 375	
Employee price	(300)	
Excess discount recognized as income		$75
Customer price for service	$ 150	
Less: Qualifying discount (20%)	(30)	
	$ 120	
Employee price	(100)	
Excess discount recognized as income		20
Total income recognized		$95

■

---

[28]Reg. § 1.132–1(b).   [29]§ 132(c).

EXAMPLE 17

Assume the same facts as in Example 16, except that the employee is a clerk in a hotel operated by Silver Corporation. Because the line of business requirement is not met, the employee must recognize $200 of income ($500 − $300) from the discount on the television and $50 of income ($150 − $100) from the service contract. ∎

As in the case of no-additional-cost benefits, the exclusion applies to employees, their spouses and dependent children, and retired and disabled former employees. However, the exclusion does not extend to highly compensated individuals unless the discount is available on a nondiscriminatory basis.

Working Condition Fringes.   Generally, an employee may exclude the cost of property or services provided by the employer if the employee could deduct the cost of those items if he or she had actually paid for them.[30] These benefits are called **working condition fringes.**

EXAMPLE 18

Mitch is a certified public accountant employed by an accounting firm. The employer pays Mitch's annual dues to professional organizations. Mitch is not required to include the payment of the dues in gross income because if he had paid the dues, he would have been allowed to deduct the amount as an employee business expense (as discussed later in this chapter). ∎

In many cases, this exclusion merely avoids reporting income and an offsetting deduction. However, in two specific situations, the working condition fringe benefit rules allow an exclusion where the expense would not be deductible if paid by the employee:

- Some automobile salespeople are allowed to exclude the value of certain personal use of company demonstrators (e.g., commuting to and from work).[31]
- The employee business expense would be eliminated by the 2 percent floor on miscellaneous itemized deductions under § 67 (refer to Chapter 15).

Unlike the other fringe benefits discussed previously, working condition fringes can be made available on a discriminatory basis and still qualify for the exclusion.

De Minimis **Fringes.**   As the term suggests, *de minimis* **fringe benefits** are so small that accounting for them is impractical. The House Report contains the following examples of *de minimis* fringes:

- The typing of a personal letter by a company secretary, occasional personal use of a company copying machine, occasional company cocktail parties or picnics for employees, occasional supper money or taxi fare for employees because of overtime work, and certain holiday gifts of property with a low fair market value are excluded.
- The value of meals consumed in a subsidized eating facility (e.g., an employees' cafeteria) operated by the employer is excluded if the facility is located on or near the employer's business premises, if revenue equals or exceeds direct operating costs, and if nondiscrimination requirements are met.

When taxpayers venture beyond the specific examples contained in the House Report and the Regulations, there is obviously much room for disagreement as to what is *de minimis*. However, note that except in the case of subsidized eating

---

[30] § 132(d).   [31] § 132(j)(3).

facilities, *de minimis* fringe benefits can be granted in a manner that favors highly compensated employees.

Qualified Transportation Fringes. The intent of the exclusion for **qualified transportation fringes** is to encourage the use of mass transit for commuting to and from work. Qualified transportation fringes encompass the following transportation benefits provided by the employer to the employee:[32]

1. Transportation in a commuter highway vehicle between the employee's residence and the place of employment.
2. A transit pass.
3. Qualified parking.

Statutory dollar limits are placed on the amount of the exclusion. Categories (1) and (2) above are combined for purposes of applying the limit. In this case, the limit on the exclusion for 2001 is $65 per month. Category (3) has a separate limit. For qualified parking, the limit on the exclusion for 2001 is $180 per month. Both of these dollar limits are indexed annually for inflation.

A commuter highway vehicle is any highway vehicle with a seating capacity of at least six adults (excluding the driver). In addition, at least 80 percent of the vehicle's use must be for transporting employees between their residences and place of employment.

Qualified parking includes the following:

- Parking provided to an employee on or near the employer's business premises.
- Parking provided to an employee on or near a location from which the employee commutes to work via mass transit, in a commuter highway vehicle, or in a carpool.

Qualified transportation fringes may be provided directly by the employer or may be in the form of cash reimbursements.

EXAMPLE 19

Gray Corporation's offices are located in the center of a large city. The company pays for parking spaces to be used by the company officers. Steve, a vice president, receives $250 of such benefits each month. The parking space rental qualifies as a qualified transportation fringe. Of the $250 benefit received each month by Steve, $180 is excludible from gross income. The balance of $70 is included in his gross income. The same result would occur if Steve paid for the parking and was reimbursed by his employer. ■

Qualified Moving Expense Reimbursements. Qualified moving expenses that are reimbursed or paid by the employer are excludible from gross income. A qualified moving expense is one that would be deductible under § 217. See the discussion of moving expenses later in this chapter.

Nondiscrimination Provisions. For no-additional-cost services and qualified employee discounts, if the plan is discriminatory in favor of *highly compensated employees*,[33] these key employees are denied exclusion treatment. However, any non-highly compensated employees who receive these benefits can still enjoy exclusion treatment.[34]

---

[32]§ 132(f).
[33]See § 414(q) for the definition of highly compensated employee.

[34]§ 132(j)(1).

EXAMPLE 20

Dove Company's officers are allowed to purchase goods from the company at a 25% discount. Other employees are allowed only a 15% discount. The company's gross profit margin on these goods is 30%.

Peggy, an officer in the company, purchased goods from the company for $750 when the price charged to customers was $1,000. Peggy must include $250 in gross income because the plan is discriminatory.

Leo, an employee of the company who is not an officer, purchased goods for $850 when the customer price was $1,000. Leo is not required to recognize income because he received a qualified employee discount. ∎

De minimis fringe benefits (except for subsidized eating facilities) and working condition fringe benefits can be provided on a discriminatory basis. Likewise, the qualified transportation fringe and the qualified moving expense reimbursement can be provided on a discriminatory basis.

5 *Find more information on this topic at our Web site: http://wft-entities.swcollege.com.*

TAXABLE FRINGE BENEFITS

If fringe benefits cannot qualify for any of the specific exclusions or do not fit into any of the general classes of excluded benefits, the employee must recognize gross income equal to the fair market value of the benefits received. Obviously, problems are frequently encountered in determining values. To help taxpayers cope with these problems, the IRS has issued extensive Regulations addressing the valuation of personal use of an employer's automobiles and meals provided at an employer-operated eating facility.[35]

If a fringe benefit plan discriminates in favor of highly compensated employees, generally those employees are not allowed to exclude the benefits they receive that other employees do not enjoy. However, the highly compensated employees, as well as the other employees, are generally allowed to exclude the nondiscriminatory benefits.[36]

EXAMPLE 21

MED Company has a medical reimbursement plan that reimburses officers for 100% of their medical expenses, but reimburses all other employees for only 80% of their medical expenses. Cliff, the president of the company, was reimbursed $1,000 during the year for medical expenses. Cliff must include $200 in gross income [(1 − .80) × $1,000 = $200]. Mike, an employee who is not an officer, received $800 (80% of his actual medical expenses) under the medical reimbursement plan. None of the $800 is includible in his gross income. ∎

LEARNING OBJECTIVE 3

Apply the rules for computing deductible expenses of employees including transportation, travel, moving, education, and entertainment expenses.

Employee Expenses

Once the employment relationship is established, employee expenses fall into one of the following categories:

- Transportation.
- Travel.
- Moving.

---

[35]Reg. § 1.61–2T(j). Generally, the income from the personal use of the employer's automobile is based on the lease value of the automobile (what it would have cost the employee to lease the automobile).

Meals are valued at 150% of the employer's direct costs (e.g., food and labor) of preparing the meals.
[36]§§ 79(d), 105(h), 127(b)(2), and 132(j)(1).

CONCEPT SUMMARY 16–1

General Classes of Fringe Benefits

Benefit	Description and Examples	Coverage Allowed	Effect of Discrimination
1. No-additional-cost services	The employee takes advantage of the employer's excess capacity (e.g., free passes for airline employees).	Current, retired, and disabled employees; their spouses and dependent children; spouses of deceased employees. Partners are treated as employees.	No exclusion for highly compensated employees.
2. Qualified discounts on goods	The employee is allowed a discount no greater than the gross profit margin on goods sold to customers.	Same as (1) above.	Same as (1) above.
3. Qualified discounts on services	The employee is allowed a discount (maximum of 20%) on services the employer offers to customers.	Same as (1) above.	Same as (1) above.
4. Working condition fringes	Expenses paid by the employer that would be deductible if paid by the employee (e.g., a mechanic's tools). Also, includes auto salesperson's use of a car held for sale.	Current employees, partners, directors, and independent contractors.	No effect.
5. *De minimis* items	Expenses so immaterial that accounting for them is not warranted (e.g., occasional supper money, personal use of the copy machine).	*Any recipient* of a fringe benefit.	No effect.
6. Qualified transportation fringes	Transportation benefits provided by the employer to employees, including commuting in a commuter highway vehicle, a transit pass, and qualified parking.	Current employees.	No effect.
7. Qualified moving expense reimbursements	Qualified moving expenses that are paid or reimbursed by the employer. A qualified moving expense is one that would be deductible under § 217.	Current employees.	No effect.

- Education.
- Entertainment.
- Other.

These expenses are discussed below in the order presented. Keep in mind, however, that these expenses are not necessarily limited to employees. A deduction for business transportation, for example, is equally available to taxpayers who are self-employed.

TRANSPORTATION EXPENSES

Qualified Expenditures.   An employee may deduct unreimbursed employment-related **transportation expenses** as an itemized deduction *from* AGI. Transportation expenses include only the cost of transporting the employee from one place to another when the employee is not away from home in travel status. Such costs include taxi fares, automobile expenses, tolls, and parking.

Commuting Expenses.   Commuting between home and one's place of employment is a personal, nondeductible expense. The fact that one employee drives 30 miles to work and another employee walks six blocks is of no significance.[37]

EXAMPLE 22

Geraldo is employed by Sparrow Corporation. He drives 22 miles each way to work. The 44 miles he drives each workday are nondeductible commuting expenses. ■

The expenses of getting from one job to another job or from one work station to another work station are deductible transportation expenses rather than nondeductible commuting expenses.

6 *Find more information on this topic at our Web site: http://wft-entities.swcollege.com.*

EXAMPLE 23

In the current year, Cynthia holds two jobs, a full-time job with Blue Corporation and a part-time job with Wren Corporation. During the 250 days that she works (adjusted for weekends, vacation, and holidays), Cynthia customarily leaves home at 7:30 A.M. and drives 30 miles to the Blue Corporation plant, where she works until 5:00 P.M. After dinner at a nearby café, Cynthia drives 20 miles to Wren Corporation and works from 7:00 to 11:00 P.M. The distance from the second job to Cynthia's home is 40 miles. Her deduction is based on 20 miles (the distance between jobs). ■

Computation of Automobile Expenses.   A taxpayer has two choices in computing deductible automobile expenses. The actual operating cost, which includes depreciation (refer to Chapter 4), gas, oil, repairs, licenses, and insurance, may be used. Records must be kept that detail the automobile's personal and business use. Only the percentage allocable to business transportation and travel is allowed as a deduction.

Use of the **automatic mileage method** is the second alternative. For 2001, the deduction is based on 34.5 cents per mile for business miles.[38] Parking fees and tolls are allowed in addition to expenses computed using the automatic mileage method.

---

[37]*Tauferner v. U.S.*, 69–1 USTC ¶9241, 23 AFTR2d 69–1025, 407 F.2d 243 (CA–10, 1969).

[38]Rev.Proc. 2000–48, I.R.B. No. 49, 570. For 2000, the rate was 32.5 cents per mile for business miles.

Generally, a taxpayer may elect either method for any particular year. However, the following restrictions apply:

- The vehicle must be owned or leased by the taxpayer.
- If two or more vehicles are in use (for business purposes) at the same time (not alternately), a taxpayer may not use the automatic mileage method.
- Use of the automatic mileage method in the first year the auto is placed in service is considered an election not to use the MACRS method of depreciation (refer to Chapter 4).
- A taxpayer may not switch to the automatic mileage method if the MACRS statutory percentage method or the election to expense under § 179 has been used.

7 *Find more information on this topic at our Web site: **http://wft-entities.swcollege.com**.*

TRAVEL EXPENSES

Definition of Travel Expenses. An itemized deduction is allowed for *unreimbursed* **travel expenses** related to a taxpayer's employment. Travel expenses are more broadly defined in the Code than are transportation expenses. Travel expenses include transportation expenses and meals and lodging while away from home in the pursuit of a trade or business. Meals cannot be lavish or extravagant. A deduction for meals and lodging is available only if the taxpayer is away from his or her tax home. Deductible travel expenses also include reasonable laundry and incidental expenses.

8 *Find more information on this topic at our Web site: **http://wft-entities.swcollege.com**.*

Away-from-Home Requirement. The crucial test for the deductibility of travel expenses is whether the employee is away from home overnight. "Overnight" need not be a 24-hour period, but it must be a period substantially longer than an ordinary day's work and must require rest, sleep, or a relief-from-work period.[39] A one-day business trip is not travel status, and meals and lodging for such a trip are not deductible.

Temporary Assignments. The employee must be away from home for a temporary period. If the taxpayer-employee is reassigned to a new post for an indefinite period of time, that new post becomes his or her tax home. Temporary indicates that the assignment's termination is expected within a reasonably short period of time. The position of the IRS is that the tax home is the business location, post, or station of the taxpayer. Thus, travel expenses are not deductible if a taxpayer is reassigned for an indefinite period and does not move his or her place of residence to the new location.

EXAMPLE 24

Malcolm's employer opened a branch office in San Diego. Malcolm was assigned to the new office for three months to train a new manager and to assist in setting up the new office. He tried commuting from his home in Los Angeles for a week and decided that he could not continue driving several hours a day. He rented an apartment in San Diego, where he lived during the week. He spent weekends with his wife and children at their home in Los Angeles. Malcolm's rent, meals, laundry, incidentals, and automobile expenses in San Diego are deductible. To the extent that Malcolm's transportation expense related to his

---

[39]*U.S. v. Correll*, 68–1 USTC ¶9101, 20 AFTR2d 5845, 88 S.Ct 445 (USSC, 1967); Rev.Rul. 75–168, 1975–1 C.B. 58.

weekend trips home exceeds what his cost of meals and lodging would have been, the excess is personal and nondeductible. ∎

EXAMPLE 25

Assume that Malcolm in Example 24 was transferred to the new location to become the new manager permanently. His wife and children continued to live in Los Angeles until the end of the school year. Malcolm is no longer "away from home" because the assignment is not temporary. His travel expenses are not deductible. ∎

To curtail controversy in this area, the Code specifies that a taxpayer "shall not be treated as temporarily away from home during any period of employment if such period exceeds 1 year."[40]

Determining the Tax Home.   Under ordinary circumstances, determining the location of a taxpayer's tax home does not present a problem. The tax home is the area in which the taxpayer derives his or her principal source of income; when the taxpayer has more than one place of employment, the tax home is based on the amount of time spent in each area.

It is possible for a taxpayer never to be away from his or her tax home. In other words, the tax home follows the taxpayer.[41] Under such circumstances, all meals and lodging remain personal and are not deductible.

EXAMPLE 26

Bill is employed as a long-haul truck driver. He is single, stores his clothes and other belongings at his parents' home, and stops there for periodic visits. Most of the time, Bill is on the road, sleeping in his truck and in motels. It is likely that Bill is never in travel status, as he is not away from home. Consequently, none of his meals and lodging are deductible. ∎

Combined Business and Pleasure Travel.   To be deductible, travel expenses need not be incurred in the performance of specific job functions. Travel expenses incurred to attend a professional convention are deductible by an employee if attendance is connected with services as an employee. For example, an employee of a law firm can deduct travel expenses incurred to attend a meeting of the American Bar Association.

Travel deductions have been used in the past by persons who claimed a tax deduction for what was essentially a personal vacation. As a result, several provisions have been enacted to restrict deductions associated with combined business and pleasure trips. If the business/pleasure trip is from one point in the United States to another point in the United States (*domestic travel*), the transportation expenses are deductible only if the trip is primarily for business.[42] If the trip is primarily for pleasure, no transportation expenses qualify as a deduction. Meals, lodging, and other expenses are allocated between business and personal days.

9 *Find more information on this topic at our Web site: **http://wft-entities.swcollege.com.***

EXAMPLE 27

In the current year, Hana travels from Seattle to New York primarily for business. She spends five days conducting business and three days sightseeing and attending shows. Her plane and taxi fare amounts to $560. Her meals amount to $100 per day, and lodging and incidental expenses are $150 per day. She can deduct the transportation expenses of $560, since the trip is primarily for business (five days of business versus three days of sightseeing). Deductible meals are limited to five days and are subject to the 50% cutback (discussed

---

[40]§ 162(a).
[41]*Moses Mitnick*, 13 T.C. 1 (1949).

[42]Reg. § 1.162–2(b)(1).

later in the chapter) for a total of $250 [5 days × ($100 × 50%)], and other deductions are limited to $750 (5 days × $150). If Hana is an employee, the unreimbursed travel expenses are miscellaneous itemized deductions subject to the 2%-of-AGI floor. ■

When the trip is outside the United States (*foreign travel*), special rules apply.[43] Transportation expenses must be allocated between business and personal days *unless* (1) the taxpayer is away from home for seven days or less or (2) less than 25 percent of the time was for personal purposes. No allocation is required if the taxpayer has no substantial control over arrangements for the trip or the desire for a vacation is not a major factor in taking the trip. If the trip is primarily for pleasure, no transportation charges are deductible. Days devoted to travel are considered business days. Weekends, legal holidays, and intervening days are considered business days, provided that both the preceding and succeeding days were business days.

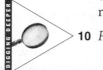

10 *Find more information on this topic at our Web site: **http://wft-entities.swcollege.com**.*

EXAMPLE 28

In the current year, Robert takes a trip from New York to Japan primarily for business purposes. He is away from home from June 10 through June 19. He spends three days vacationing and seven days conducting business (including two travel days). His airfare is $2,500, his meals amount to $100 per day, and lodging and incidental expenses are $160 per day. Since Robert is away from home for more than seven days and more than 25% of his time is devoted to personal purposes, only 70% (7 days business/10 days total) of the transportation is deductible. His deductions are as follows:

Transportation (70% × $2,500)		$1,750
Lodging ($160 × 7)		1,120
Meals ($100 × 7)	$ 700	
Less: 50% cutback (discussed later in this chapter)	(350)	350
Total deductions		$3,220

If Robert is gone the same period of time but spends only two days (less than 25% of the total) vacationing, no allocation of transportation is required. Since the pleasure portion of the trip is less than 25% of the total, all of the airfare qualifies for the travel deduction. ■

The foreign convention rules do not operate to bar a deduction to an employer if the expense is *compensatory* in nature. For example, a trip to Rome won by a top salesperson is included in the gross income of the employee and is fully deductible by the employer.

PLANNING CONSIDERATIONS

Transportation and Travel Expenses

Adequate detailed records of all transportation and travel expenses should be kept. Since the regular mileage allow-ance often is modest in amount, a new, expensive automobile used primarily for business may generate a higher expense

---

[43]§ 274(c) and Reg. § 1.274–4.

based on actual cost. The election to expense part of the cost of the automobile under § 179, MACRS depreciation, insurance, repairs and maintenance, automobile club dues, and other related costs may result in automobile expenses greater than the automatic mileage allowance.

If a taxpayer wishes to sightsee or vacation on a business trip, it would be beneficial to schedule business on both a Friday and a Monday to turn the weekend into business days for allocation purposes. It is especially crucial to schedule appropriate business days when foreign travel is involved.

MOVING EXPENSES

Moving expenses are deductible for moves in connection with the commencement of work at a new principal place of work.[44] Both employees and self-employed individuals can deduct these expenses. To be eligible for a moving expense deduction, a taxpayer must meet two basic tests: distance and time.

Distance Test.   To meet the distance test, the taxpayer's new job location must be at least 50 miles farther from the taxpayer's old residence than the old residence was from the former place of employment. In this regard, the location of the new residence is not relevant. This eliminates a moving expense deduction for (1) taxpayers who purchase a new home in the same general area without changing their place of employment and (2) taxpayers who accept a new job in the same area as their old job.

EXAMPLE 29

Harry is permanently transferred to a new job location. The distance from Harry's former home to his new job (80 miles) exceeds the distance from his former home to his old job (30 miles) by at least 50 miles. Harry has met the distance test for a moving expense deduction.

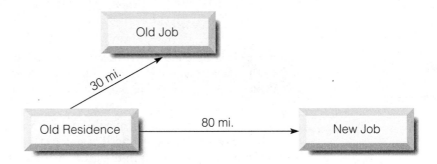

If Harry is not employed before the move, his new job must be at least 50 miles from his former residence. In this instance, Harry has also met the distance test if he was not previously employed. ∎

Time Test.   To meet the time test, an employee must be employed on a full-time basis at the new location for 39 weeks in the 12-month period following the move. If the taxpayer is a self-employed individual, he or she must work in the new location for 78 weeks during the two years following the move. The first 39 weeks

---

[44]§ 217(a).

must be in the first 12 months. The time test is suspended if the taxpayer dies, becomes disabled, or is discharged or transferred by the new employer through no fault of the employee.

11 *Find more information on this topic at our Web site: **http://wft-entities.swcollege.com**.*

Treatment of Moving Expenses. *Qualified moving expenses* include reasonable expenses of:

- Moving household goods and personal effects.
- Traveling from the former residence to the new place of residence.

For this purpose, traveling includes lodging, but not meals, for the taxpayer and members of the household.[45] It does not include the cost of moving servants or others who are not members of the household. The taxpayer can elect to use actual auto expenses (no depreciation is allowed) or the automatic mileage method. In this case, moving expense mileage is limited in 2001 to 12 cents per mile (10 cents in 2000) for each car. These expenses are also limited by the reasonableness standard. For example, if one moves from Texas to Florida via Maine and takes six weeks to do so, the transportation and lodging must be allocated between personal and moving expenses.

EXAMPLE 30	Jill is transferred by her employer from the Atlanta office to the San Francisco office. In this connection, she spends the following amounts:

Cost of moving furniture	$2,800
Transportation	700
Meals	200
Lodging	300

Jill's total qualified moving expense is $3,800 ($2,800 + $700 + $300). ∎

The moving expense deduction is allowed regardless of whether the employee is transferred by the existing employer or is employed by a new employer. It is allowed if the employee moves to a new area and obtains employment or switches from self-employed status to employee status (and vice versa). The moving expense deduction is also allowed if an individual is unemployed before obtaining employment in a new area.

12 *Find more information on this topic at our Web site: **http://wft-entities.swcollege.com**.*

PLANNING CONSIDERATIONS

Moving Expenses

Persons who retire and move to a new location incur personal nondeductible moving expenses. If the retired person accepts a full-time job in the new location before moving and meets the time and distance requirements, the moving expenses are deductible.

---

[45]§ 217(b).

EXAMPLE 31

At the time of his retirement from the national office of a major accounting firm, Gordon had an annual salary of $220,000. He moves from New York City to Seattle to retire, and accepts a full-time teaching position at a Seattle junior college at an annual salary of $15,000. If Gordon satisfies the 39-week test, his moving expenses are deductible. The disparity between the two salaries (previous and current) is of no consequence. ■

EDUCATION EXPENSES

General Requirements.   Employees *and* self-employed individuals can deduct expenses incurred for education as ordinary and necessary business expenses, provided the expenses are incurred to maintain or improve existing skills required in the present job. An employee can also deduct expenses incurred to meet the express requirements of the employer or the requirements imposed by law to retain his or her employment status.

   Education expenses are not deductible if the education is for either of the following purposes:

- To meet the minimum educational standards for qualification in the taxpayer's existing job.
- To qualify the taxpayer for a new trade or business.[46]

Thus, fees incurred for professional exams (the bar exam, for example) and fees for review courses (such as a CPA review course) are not deductible.[47] If the education incidentally results in a promotion or raise, the deduction still can be taken as long as the education maintained and improved existing skills and did not qualify the person for a new trade or business. A change in duties is not always fatal to the deduction if the new duties involve the same general work. For example, the IRS has ruled that a practicing dentist's education expenses incurred to become an orthodontist are deductible.[48]

Requirements Imposed by Law or by the Employer for Retention of Employment.   Taxpayers are permitted to deduct education expenses if additional courses are required by the employer or are imposed by law. Many states require a minimum of a bachelor's degree and a specified number of additional courses to retain a teaching job. In addition, some public school systems have imposed a master's degree requirement and require teachers to make satisfactory progress toward a master's degree in order to keep their positions. If the required education is the minimum degree required for the job, no deduction is allowed.

   Professionals (such as physicians, attorneys, and CPAs) may deduct expenses incurred to meet continuing professional education requirements imposed by states as a condition for retaining a license to practice.

EXAMPLE 32

In order to meet continuing professional education requirements imposed by the State Board of Public Accountancy for maintaining her CPA license, Nancy takes an auditing course sponsored by a local college. The cost of the education is deductible. ■

13 *Find more information on this topic at our Web site:* ***http://wft-entities.swcollege.com.***

---

[46]Reg. §§ 1.162–5(b)(2) and (3).
[47]Reg. § 1.212–1(f) and Rev.Rul. 69–292, 1969–1 C.B. 84.

[48]Rev.Rul. 74–78, 1974–1 C.B. 44.

INTERNATIONAL IMPLICATIONS

EXPATRIATES AND THE MOVING EXPENSE DEDUCTION

Expatriates, U.S. persons who accept work assignments overseas, enjoy several favorable tax advantages regarding foreign moves. First, the cost of storing household goods qualifies as a moving expense. This could lead to a major tax saving since expatriates do not ship most of their household effects to the foreign location. Furthermore, the cost of storage, particularly in a climate-controlled facility, is not insignificant.

The second advantage expatriates may enjoy is an exemption from the time test. Those who return to the United States to retire are absolved from the 39-week or 78-week work requirement. Thus, the return home expenses are treated as qualified moving expenses.

Maintaining or Improving Existing Skills.   The *maintaining or improving existing skills* requirement in the Code has been difficult for both taxpayers and the courts to interpret. For example, a business executive is permitted to deduct the costs of obtaining an MBA on the grounds that the advanced management education is undertaken to maintain and improve existing management skills. The executive is eligible to deduct the costs of specialized, nondegree management courses that are taken for continuing education or to maintain or improve existing skills. Expenses incurred by the executive to obtain a law degree are not deductible, however, because the education constitutes training for a new trade or business. The Regulations deny a self-employed accountant a deduction for expenses relating to law school.[49]

PLANNING CONSIDERATIONS

Education Expenses

Education expenses are treated as nondeductible personal items unless the individual is employed or is engaged in a trade or business. A temporary leave of absence for further education is one way to assure that the taxpayer is still treated as being engaged in a trade or business. An individual was permitted to deduct education expenses even though he resigned from his job, returned to school full-time for two years, and accepted another job in the same field upon graduation. The Court held that the student had merely suspended active participation in his field.[50]

If the time out of the field is too long, education expense deductions will be disallowed. For example, a teacher who left the field for four years to raise her child and curtailed her employment searches and writing activities was denied a deduction for education expenses. She was no longer actively engaged in the trade or business of being an educator.[51]

To secure the deduction, an individual should arrange his or her work situation to preserve employee or business status.

---

[49]Reg. § 1.162–5(b)(3)(ii) Example (1).
[50]*Stephen G. Sherman*, 36 TCM 1191, T.C.Memo. 1977–301.

[51]*Brian C. Mulherin*, 42 TCM 834, T.C.Memo. 1981–454; *George A. Baist*, 56 TCM 778, T.C.Memo. 1988–554.

Classification of Specific Items.   Education expenses include books, tuition, typing, transportation (e.g., from the office to night school), and travel (e.g., meals and lodging while away from home at summer school).

<table>
<tr><td>**EXAMPLE 33**</td></tr>
</table>

Bill, who holds a bachelor of education degree, is a secondary education teacher in the Los Angeles school system. The school board recently raised its minimum education requirement for new teachers from four years of college training to five. A grandfather clause allows teachers with only four years of college to continue to qualify if they show satisfactory progress toward a graduate degree. Bill enrolls at the University of Washington during the summer and takes three graduate courses. His unreimbursed expenses for this purpose are as follows:

Books and tuition	$2,600
Lodging while in travel status (June–August)	1,150
Meals while in travel status	800
Laundry while in travel status	220
Transportation	600

Bill has an itemized deduction as follows:

Books and tuition	$2,600
Lodging	1,150
Meals less 50% cutback (discussed later in this chapter)	400
Laundry	220
Transportation	600
	$4,970

■

ENTERTAINMENT EXPENSES

Many taxpayers attempt to deduct personal **entertainment expenses** as business expenses. For this reason, the tax law restricts the deductibility of entertainment expenses. The Code contains strict record-keeping requirements and provides restrictive tests for the deduction of certain types of entertainment expenses.

The Fifty Percent Cutback.   Only 50 percent of meal and entertainment expenses is deductible.[52] The limitation applies to employees, employers, and self-employed individuals. Although the 50 percent cutback can apply to either the employer or the employee, it will not apply twice. The cutback applies to the one who really pays (economically) for the meals or entertainment.

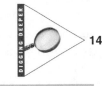

14 *Find more information on this topic at our Web site:* ***http://wft-entities.swcollege.com.***

<table>
<tr><td>**EXAMPLE 34**</td></tr>
</table>

Jane, an employee of Pelican Corporation, entertains one of her clients. If Pelican Corporation does not reimburse Jane, she is subject to the cutback. If, however, Pelican Corporation reimburses Jane (or pays for the entertainment directly), Pelican suffers the cutback. ■

Transportation expenses are not affected by the cutback rule—only meals and entertainment expenses are reduced. The cutback also applies to taxes and tips relating to meals and entertainment. Cover charges, parking fees at an entertainment

---

[52]§ 274(n).

How Permanent Is the Cutback Adjustment?

Considerable disaffection exists regarding the harsh tax consequences of the cutback adjustment. Many feel, for example, that it is unfair to small businesses when it is applied to business *meals* (as opposed to business *entertainment*).

In the Taxpayer Relief Act of 2000, Congress proposed to increase the business meals deduction from 50 percent to 70 percent, effective after December 31, 2000. For the DOT (Department of Transportation) exception, the phase-in period would be eliminated, and the full 80 percent deduction allowances would take immediate effect after year 2000.

Because the Taxpayer Relief Act *did not* become law, the cutback adjustment *has not* been changed. However, the fact that change has been proposed is indicative that it may take place in the future.

location, and room rental fees for a meal or cocktail party are also subject to the 50 percent cutback.

15 *Find more information on this topic at our Web site: http://wft-entities.swcollege.com.*

EXAMPLE 35

Joe pays a $30 cab fare to meet his client for dinner. The meal costs $120, and Joe leaves a $20 tip. His deduction is $100 [($120 + $20) × 50% + $30 cab fare]. ■

Classification of Expenses. Entertainment expenses are classified either as *directly related* to business or *associated with* business.[53] Directly related expenses are related to an actual business meeting or discussion. These expenses are distinguished from entertainment expenses that are incurred to promote goodwill, such as maintaining existing customer relations. To obtain a deduction for directly related entertainment, it is not necessary to show that actual benefit resulted from the expenditure as long as there was a reasonable expectation of benefit. To qualify as directly related, the expense should be incurred in a business setting. If there is little possibility of engaging in the active conduct of a trade or business due to the nature of the social facility, it is difficult to qualify the expenditure as directly related to business.

Expenses associated with, rather than directly related to, business entertainment must serve a specific business purpose, such as obtaining new business or continuing existing business. These expenditures qualify only if the expenses directly precede or follow a bona fide business discussion. Entertainment occurring on the same day as the business discussion is considered associated with business.

EXAMPLE 36

Jerry, a manufacturers' representative, took his client to play a round of golf during the afternoon. They had dinner the same evening, during which time business was discussed. After dinner, they went to a nightclub to have drinks and listen to a jazz band. The business dinner qualifies as directly related entertainment. The golf outing and the visit to the nightclub qualify as associated with entertainment. ■

---

[53]§ 274(a)(1)(A).

PLANNING CONSIDERATIONS

Entertainment Expenses

Taxpayers should maintain detailed records of amounts, time, place, business purpose, and business relationships. A credit card receipt details the place, date, and amount of the expense. A notation made on the receipt of the names of the person(s) attending, the business relationship, and the topic of discussion should constitute sufficient documentation.[54] Failure to provide sufficient documentation could lead to disallowance of entertainment expense deductions.

Associated with or goodwill entertainment requires a business discussion to be conducted immediately before or after the entertainment. Furthermore, a business purpose must exist for the entertainment. Taxpayers should arrange for a business discussion before or after such entertainment. They also must document the business purpose, such as obtaining new business from a prospective customer.

Restrictions upon Deductibility of Business Meals.   Business meals are deductible only if:[55]

- the meal is directly related to or associated with the active conduct of a trade or business,
- the expense is not lavish or extravagant under the circumstances, and
- the taxpayer (or an employee) is present at the meal.

A business meal with a business associate or customer is not deductible unless business is discussed before, during, or after the meal. This requirement does not apply to meals consumed while away from home in travel status.

EXAMPLE 37

Lacy travels to San Francisco for a business convention. She pays for dinner with three colleagues and is not reimbursed by her employer. They do not discuss business. She can deduct 50% of the cost of her meal. However, she cannot deduct the cost of her colleagues' meals. ■

EXAMPLE 38

Lance, a party to a contract negotiation, buys dinner for other parties to the negotiation but does not attend the dinner. No deduction is allowed because Lance was not present. ■

Restrictions upon Deductibility of Club Dues.   The Code provides that "No deduction shall be allowed . . . for amounts paid or incurred for membership in any club organized for business, pleasure, recreation, or other social purpose."[56] Although this prohibition seems quite broad, it does not apply to clubs whose primary purpose is public service and community volunteerism (e.g., Kiwanis, Lions, Rotary). Although *dues* are not deductible, actual entertainment at a club may qualify.

EXAMPLE 39

During the current year, Vincent spent $1,400 on business lunches at the Lakeside Country Club. The annual membership fee was $6,000, and Vincent used the facility 60% of the time for business. Presuming the lunches meet the business meal test, Vincent may claim $700 (50% cutback × $1,400) as a deduction. None of the club dues are deductible. ■

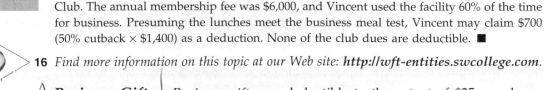

16 *Find more information on this topic at our Web site:* ***http://wft-entities.swcollege.com.***

Business Gifts.   Business gifts are deductible to the extent of $25 per donee per year.[57] An exception is made for gifts costing $4 or less (e.g., pens with the

---

[54]*Kenneth W. Guenther,* 54 TCM 382, T.C.Memo. 1987–440.
[55]§ 274(k).

[56]§ 274(a)(3).
[57]§ 274(b)(1).

employee's or company's name on them) or promotional materials. Such items are not treated as business gifts subject to the $25 limitation. In addition, incidental costs such as engraving of jewelry and nominal charges for gift-wrapping, mailing, and delivery are not included in the cost of the gift in applying the limitation. Gifts to superiors and employers are not deductible. Records must be maintained to substantiate business gifts.

OTHER EMPLOYEE EXPENSES

Office in the Home.   Employees and self-employed individuals are not allowed a deduction for **office in the home expenses** unless a portion of the residence is used *exclusively and on a regular basis* as either:

- The principal place of business for any trade or business of the taxpayer.
- A place of business used by clients, patients, or customers.

Employees must meet an additional test: The use must be for the convenience of the employer rather than merely being "appropriate and helpful."[58]

The precise meaning of "principal place of business" has been the subject of considerable controversy.[59] Congress ultimately resolved the controversy by amending the Code.[60]

For taxable years beginning after December 31, 1998, the term "principal place of business" includes a place of business that satisfies the following requirements:

- The office is used by the taxpayer to conduct administrative or management activities of a trade or business.
- There is no other fixed location of the trade or business where the taxpayer conducts these activities.

EXAMPLE 40

Dr. Smith is a self-employed anesthesiologist. During the year, he spends 30 to 35 hours per week administering anesthesia and postoperative care to patients in three hospitals, none of which provides him with an office. He also spends two or three hours per day in a room in his home that he uses exclusively as an office. He does not meet patients there, but he performs a variety of tasks related to his medical practice (e.g., contacting surgeons, bookkeeping, reading medical journals). A deduction will be allowed since he uses the office in the home to conduct administrative or management activities of his trade or business, and there is no other fixed location where these activities can be carried out. ■

The exclusive use requirement means that a specific part of the home must be used solely for business purposes. A deduction, if permitted, requires an allocation of total expenses of operating the home between business and personal use based on floor space or number of rooms.

Even if the taxpayer meets the above requirements, the allowable home office expenses cannot exceed the gross income from the business less all other business expenses attributable to the activity. That is, the home office deduction cannot create a loss. Furthermore, the home office expenses that are allowed as itemized deductions anyway (e.g., mortgage interest and real estate taxes) must be deducted first. All home office expenses of an employee are miscellaneous itemized deductions, except those (such as interest and taxes) that qualify as other personal itemized

---

[58]§ 280A(c)(1).
[59]See the restrictive interpretation arrived at in *Comm. v. Soliman*, 93–1 USTC ¶50,014, 71 AFTR2d 93–463, 113 S.Ct. 701 (USSC, 1993).

[60]§ 280A(c)(1) as modified by TRA of 1997.

deductions. Home office expenses of a self-employed individual are trade or business expenses and are deductible *for* AGI. Any disallowed home office expenses are carried forward and used in future years subject to the same limitations.

17 *Find more information on this topic at our Web site:* ***http://wft-entities.swcollege.com***.

EXAMPLE 41

Rick is a certified public accountant employed by a regional CPA firm as a tax manager. He operates a separate business in which he refinishes furniture in his home. For this business, he uses two rooms in the basement of his home exclusively and regularly. The floor space of the two rooms constitutes 10% of the floor space of his residence. Gross income from the business totals $8,000. Expenses of the business (other than home office expenses) are $6,500. Rick incurs the following home office expenses:

Real property taxes on residence	$4,000
Interest expense on residence	7,500
Operating expenses of residence	2,000
Depreciation on residence (related to 10% business use)	250

Rick's deductions are determined as follows:

Business income		$ 8,000
Less: Other business expenses		(6,500)
		$ 1,500
Less: Allocable taxes ($4,000 × 10%)	$400	
Allocable interest ($7,500 × 10%)	750	(1,150)
		$ 350
Less: Allocable operating expenses of the residence ($2,000 × 10%)		(200)
		$ 150
Less: Allocable depreciation ($250, limited to remaining income)		(150)
		$ –0–

Rick has a carryover deduction of $100 (the unused excess depreciation). Because he is self-employed, the allocable taxes and interest ($1,150), the other deductible office expenses ($200 + $150), and $6,500 of other business expenses are deductible *for* AGI. ■

Miscellaneous Employee Expenses. Deductible miscellaneous employee expenses include special clothing and its upkeep, union dues, and professional expenses. Also deductible are professional dues, professional meetings, and employment agency fees for seeking new employment in the taxpayer's current trade or business, whether or not a new job is secured.

To be deductible, *special clothing* must be both specifically required as a condition of employment and not adaptable for regular wear. For example, a police officer's uniform is not suitable for off-duty activities. An exception is clothing used to the extent that it takes the place of regular clothing (e.g., some military uniforms).

EXAMPLE 42

Captain Roberts is on active duty in the U.S. Army. The cost of his regular uniforms is not deductible since such clothing is suitable for regular wear. Captain Roberts, however, spends over $1,100 to purchase "dress blues." Under military regulations, dress uniforms may be worn only during ceremonial functions (e.g., official events, parades). The $1,100 cost, to the extent it exceeds any clothing allowance, qualifies as a deduction. ■

The current position of the IRS is that expenses incurred in *seeking employment* are deductible if the taxpayer is seeking employment in the same trade or business. The deduction is allowed whether or not the attempts to secure employment are successful. An unemployed taxpayer can take a deduction providing there has been no substantial lack of continuity between the last job and the search for a new one. No deduction is allowed for persons seeking their first job or seeking employment in a new trade or business.

CLASSIFICATION OF EMPLOYEE EXPENSES

If employee expenses are reimbursed by the employer under an accountable plan, they are not reported by the employee at all. In effect, this result is equivalent to reporting the reimbursement as income and treating the expenses as deductions *for* AGI.[61] Alternatively, if the expenses are reimbursed under a nonaccountable plan or are not reimbursed at all, then they are classified as deductions *from* AGI and can only be claimed if the taxpayer itemizes (subject to the 2 percent-of-AGI floor). Exceptions are made for moving expenses and the employment-related expenses of a qualified performing artist, where a deduction *for* AGI is allowed. Thus, the tax treatment of reimbursements under accountable and nonaccountable plans differs significantly.

Accountable Plans. An accountable plan requires the employee to:

- Adequately account for (substantiate) the expenses. An employee renders an *adequate accounting* by submitting a record, with receipts and other substantiation, to the employer.[62]
- Return any excess reimbursement or allowance. An "excess reimbursement or allowance" is any amount that the employee does not adequately account for as an ordinary and necessary business expense.

The law provides that no deduction is allowed for any travel, entertainment, business gift, or listed property (automobiles, computers) expenditure unless properly substantiated by adequate records. The records should contain the following information:[63]

- The amount of the expense.
- The time and place of travel or entertainment (or date of gift).
- The business purpose of the expense.
- The business relationship of the taxpayer to the person entertained (or receiving the gift).

This means the taxpayer must maintain an account book or diary in which the above information is recorded at the time of the expenditure. Documentary evidence, such as itemized receipts, is required to support any expenditure for lodging while traveling away from home and for any other expenditure of $75 or more. If a taxpayer fails to keep adequate records, each expense must be established by a written or oral statement of the exact details of the expense and by other corroborating evidence.[64]

18 *Find more information on this topic at our Web site: **http://wft-entities.swcollege.com**.*

---

[61]§ 62(a)(2).
[62]Reg. § 1.162–17(b)(4).
[63]§ 274(d).
[64]Reg. § 1.274–5T(c)(3).

TAX IN THE NEWS

WHAT HAPPENS WHEN AN EXCESS REIMBURSEMENT IS NOT REPORTED AS INCOME?

In July 2000, NBA referee Bennett Salvatore pleaded guilty to tax fraud before a Federal District Court in Connecticut. Over several years, the accused had failed to recognize the $39,000 of income he had obtained from downgrading first-class airline tickets received from the National Basketball Association. Mr. Salvatore was just one of approximately a dozen NBA referees prosecuted by the IRS. None of the referees had been required to render an adequate accounting to the NBA for the expenses reimbursed.

EXAMPLE 43

Bertha has travel expenses substantiated only by canceled checks. The checks establish the date, place, and amount of the expenditure. Because neither the business relationship nor the business purpose is established, the deduction is disallowed.[65] ■

EXAMPLE 44

Dwight has travel and entertainment expenses substantiated by a diary showing the time, place, and amount of the expenditure. His oral testimony provides the business relationship and business purpose; however, since he has no receipts, any expenditures of $75 or more are disallowed.[66] ■

Nonaccountable Plans.   A **nonaccountable plan** is one in which an adequate accounting or return of excess amounts, or both, is not required. All reimbursements of expenses are reported in full as wages on the employee's Form W–2. Any allowable expenses are deductible in the same manner as are unreimbursed expenses.

An employer may have an accountable plan and require employees to return excess reimbursements or allowances, but an employee may fail to follow the rules of the plan. In that case, the expenses and reimbursements are subject to nonaccountable plan treatment.

Unreimbursed Expenses.   Unreimbursed employee expenses are treated in a straightforward manner. Meals and entertainment expenses are subject to the 50 percent limit. Total unreimbursed employee business expenses are usually reported as miscellaneous itemized deductions subject to the 2 percent-of-AGI floor (refer to Chapter 15). If the employee could have received, but did not seek, reimbursement for whatever reason, none of the employment-related expenses are deductible.

19 *Find more information on this topic at our Web site: http://wft-entities.swcollege.com*

---

[65]*William T. Whitaker*, 56 TCM 47, T.C.Memo. 1988–418.   [66]*W. David Tyler*, 43 TCM 927, T.C.Memo. 1982–160.

Unreimbursed Employee Business Expenses

The 2 percent floor for unreimbursed employee business expenses offers a tax planning opportunity for married couples. If one spouse has high miscellaneous expenses subject to the floor, it may be beneficial for the couple to file separate returns. If they file jointly, the 2 percent floor is based on the adjusted gross incomes of both. Filing separately lowers the reduction to 2 percent of only one spouse's adjusted gross income.

Other provisions of the law should be considered, however. For example, filing separately could cost a couple

losses of up to $25,000 from self-managed rental units under the passive activity loss rules (discussed in Chapter 5).

Another possibility is to negotiate a salary reduction with one's employer in exchange for the 100 percent reimbursement of employee expenses. The employee is better off because the 2 percent floor does not apply. The employer is better off because certain expense reimbursements are not subject to Social Security and other payroll taxes.

CONTRIBUTIONS TO INDIVIDUAL RETIREMENT ACCOUNTS

Traditional IRAs. Employees not covered by another qualified plan can establish their own tax-deductible **Individual Retirement Accounts (IRAs).** The contribution ceiling is the smaller of $2,000 (or $4,000 for spousal IRAs) or 100 percent of compensation. If the taxpayer is an active participant in another qualified plan, the traditional IRA deduction limitation is phased out *proportionately* between certain AGI ranges, as shown in Table 16–2.

AGI is calculated taking into account any § 469 passive losses and § 86 taxable Social Security benefits and ignoring any § 911 foreign income exclusion, § 135 savings bonds interest exclusion, and the IRA deduction. There is a $200 floor on the IRA deduction limitation for individuals whose AGI is not above the phase-out range.

EXAMPLE 45

Daniel, who is single, has compensation income of $39,000 in 2001. He is an active participant in his employer's qualified retirement plan. Dan contributes $600 to an IRA. The deductible amount is reduced from $2,000 by $1,200 because of the phase-out mechanism:

$$\frac{\$6,000}{\$10,000} \times \$2,000 = \$1,200 \text{ reduction.}$$

EXAMPLE 46

Ben, an unmarried individual, is an active participant in his employer's qualified retirement plan. With AGI of $42,500, he would normally have an IRA deduction limit of $100 {$2,000 − [($42,500 − $33,000)/$10,000 × $2,000]}. However, because of the special floor provision, Ben is allowed a $200 IRA deduction. ■

■ **TABLE 16–2**
Phase-Out of IRA Deduction of an Active Participant in 2001

AGI Filing Status	Phase-Out Begins*	Phase-Out Ends
Single and head of household	$33,000	$43,000
Married, filing joint return	53,000	63,000
Married, filing separate return	–0–	10,000

*The starting point for the phase-out is increased each year through 2007 for married filing jointly and through 2005 for other filing statuses.

An individual is not considered an active participant in a qualified plan merely because the individual's spouse is an active participant in such a plan for any part of a plan year. Thus, most homemakers may take a full $2,000 deduction regardless of the participation status of their spouse, unless the couple has AGI above $150,000. If their AGI is above $150,000, the phase-out of the deduction begins at $150,000 and ends at $160,000 (phase-out over the $10,000 range).

EXAMPLE 47

Nell is covered by a qualified employer retirement plan at work. Her husband, Nick, is not an active participant in a qualified plan. If Nell and Nick's combined AGI is $135,000, Nell cannot make a deductible IRA contribution because she exceeds the income threshold for an active participant. However, since Nick is not an active participant, and their combined AGI does not exceed $150,000, he can make a deductible contribution of $2,000 to an IRA. ∎

To the extent that an individual is ineligible to make a deductible contribution to an IRA, *nondeductible contributions* can be made to separate accounts. The nondeductible contributions are subject to the same dollar limits as deductible contributions ($2,000 of earned income, $4,000 for a spousal IRA). Income in the account accumulates tax-free until distributed. Only the account earnings are taxed upon distribution because the account basis equals the contributions made by the taxpayer. A taxpayer may elect to treat deductible IRA contributions as nondeductible. If an individual has no taxable income for the year after taking into account other deductions, the election would be beneficial. The election is made on the individual's tax return for the taxable year to which the designation relates.

Roth IRAs.   A Roth IRA is a *nondeductible* alternative to the traditional deductible IRA. Introduced by Congress to encourage individual savings, earnings inside a Roth IRA are not taxable, and all qualified distributions from a Roth IRA are tax-free.[67] The maximum allowable annual contribution to a Roth IRA is the smaller of $2,000 ($4,000 for spousal IRAs) or 100 percent of the individual's compensation for the year. Contributions to a Roth IRA must be made by the due date (excluding extensions) of the taxpayer's tax return. Roth IRAs are not subject to the minimum distribution rules that apply to traditional IRAs.

A taxpayer can make tax-free withdrawals from a Roth IRA after an initial five-year holding period if any of the following requirements is satisfied:

- The distribution is made on or after the date on which the participant attains age 59½.
- The distribution is made to a beneficiary (or the participant's estate) on or after the participant's death.
- The participant becomes disabled.
- The distribution is used to pay for qualified first-time homebuyer's expenses.

EXAMPLE 48

Edith establishes a Roth IRA at age 42 and contributes $2,000 per year for 20 years. The account is now worth $96,400, consisting of $40,000 of nondeductible contributions and $56,400 in accumulated earnings that have not been taxed. Edith may withdraw the $96,400 tax-free from the Roth IRA because she is over age 59½ and has met the five-year holding period requirement. ■

If the taxpayer receives a distribution from a Roth IRA and does not satisfy the aforementioned requirements, the distribution may be taxable. If the distribution represents a return of capital, it is not taxable. Conversely, if the distribution represents a payout of earnings, it is taxable. Under the ordering rules for Roth IRA distributions, distributions are treated as first made from contributions (return of capital).

EXAMPLE 49

Assume the same facts as in Example 48, except that Edith is only age 50 and receives a distribution of $12,000. Since her adjusted basis for the Roth IRA is $16,000 (contributions of $2,000 each year made over an 8-year period), the distribution is tax-free, and her adjusted basis is reduced to $4,000 ($16,000 − $12,000). ■

Roth IRAs are subject to income limits. The maximum annual contribution of $2,000 is phased out beginning at AGI of $95,000 for single taxpayers and $150,000 for married couples who file a joint return. The phase-out range is $10,000 for married filing jointly and $15,000 for single taxpayers. For a married taxpayer filing separately, the contribution is phased out over a range beginning with AGI of $0 and ending with $10,000.

EXAMPLE 50

Bev, who is single, would like to contribute $2,000 to her Roth IRA. However, her AGI is $105,000, so her contribution is limited to $667 ($2,000 − $1,333) calculated as follows:

$$\frac{\$10,000}{\$15,000} \times \$2,000 = \$1,333 \text{ reduction.}$$

■

Education IRAs. Distributions from an IRA to pay for qualified higher education expenses receive favorable tax treatment.[68] Qualified higher education expenses include tuition, fees, books, supplies, and related equipment. Room and board qualify if the student's course load is at least one-half of the full-time course load. If the education IRA is used to pay the qualified higher education expenses of the designated beneficiary, the withdrawals are tax-free. To the extent the distributions

---

[67]§ 408A.   [68]§ 530.

during a tax year exceed qualified higher education expenses, part of the excess is treated as a return of capital (the contributions), and part is treated as a distribution of earnings under the § 72 annuity rules. Thus, the distribution is presumed to be pro rata from each category. The exclusion for the distribution of earnings part is calculated as follows:

$$\frac{\text{Qualified higher education expenses}}{\text{Total distributions}} \times \text{Earnings} = \text{Exclusion.}$$

EXAMPLE 51

Meg receives a $2,500 distribution from her education IRA. She uses $2,000 to pay for qualified higher education expenses. On the date of the distribution, Meg's IRA balance is $10,000, $6,000 of which represents her contributions. Since 60% ($6,000/$10,000) of her account balance represents her contributions, $1,500 ($2,500 × 60%) of the distribution is a return of capital, and $1,000 ($2,500 × 40%) is a distribution of earnings. The excludible amount of the earnings is calculated as follows:

$$\frac{\$2,000}{\$2,500} \times \$1,000 = \$800$$

Thus, Meg must include $200 ($1,000 – $800) in her gross income. ∎

The maximum amount that can be contributed annually to an education IRA for a beneficiary is $500. A beneficiary must be an individual and cannot be a group of children or an unborn child. The contributions are not deductible. Education IRAs are subject to income limits. The maximum annual contribution is phased out beginning at $95,000 for single taxpayers and $150,000 for married couples who file a joint return. The phase-out range is $10,000 for married filing jointly and $15,000 for single taxpayers. Contributions cannot be made to an education IRA after the date on which the designated beneficiary attains age 18. Thus, a total of up to $9,000 can be contributed for each beneficiary—$500 in the year of birth and in each of the 17 following years.

A 6 percent excise tax is imposed on excess contributions to an education IRA. A 10 percent excise tax is imposed on any distributions that are included in gross income.

The balance in an educational IRA must be distributed within 30 days after the death of a beneficiary or within 30 days after a beneficiary reaches age 30. Any balance at the close of either 30-day period is considered to be distributed at such time, and the earnings portion is included in the beneficiary's gross income. Before a beneficiary reaches age 30, any balance can be rolled over tax-free into another education IRA for a member of the beneficiary's family who is under age 30.

The education IRA exclusion is not available in any tax year in which the beneficiary claims the HOPE credit or the lifetime learning credit (see Chapter 15). Likewise, contributions cannot be made to a beneficiary's education IRA during any year in which contributions are made to a qualified state tuition program on behalf of the same beneficiary.

LEARNING OBJECTIVE 5

Understand the tax provisions applicable to proprietors.

Individuals as Proprietors

THE PROPRIETORSHIP AS A BUSINESS ENTITY

A sole proprietorship is *not* a taxable entity separate from the individual who owns the proprietorship. A sole proprietor reports the results of business operations of the proprietorship on Schedule C of Form 1040. The net profit or loss from the proprietorship is then transferred from Schedule C to Form 1040, which is used by the taxpayer to determine tax liability. The proprietor reports all of the net profit or net loss from the business, regardless of the amount actually withdrawn from the proprietorship during the year.

Income and expenses of the proprietorship retain their character when reported by the proprietor. For example, ordinary income of the proprietorship is treated as ordinary income when reported by the proprietor, and capital gain of the proprietorship is treated as capital gain by the proprietor.

EXAMPLE 52

George is the sole proprietor of George's Record Shop. Gross income of the business in 2001 is $200,000, and operating expenses are $110,000. George also sells a capital asset held by the business for a $10,000 long-term capital gain. During 2001, he withdraws $60,000 from the business for living expenses. George reports the operating income and expenses of the business on Schedule C, resulting in net profit (ordinary income) of $90,000 ($200,000 − $110,000). Even though he withdrew only $60,000, George reports all of the $90,000 net profit from the business on Form 1040, where he computes taxable income and tax liability for the year. He also reports a $10,000 long-term capital gain on his personal tax return (Schedule D of Form 1040). ■

INCOME OF A PROPRIETORSHIP

The broad definition of gross income in § 61(a) applies equally to individuals and business entities, including proprietorships, corporations, and partnerships. Thus, it is assumed that asset inflows into a proprietorship are to be treated as income. Certain items may be excluded from gross income. Many of the exclusions available to an individual are related to the individual as an employee. Refer to Chapter 3 for a detailed discussion of gross income.

DEDUCTIONS RELATED TO A PROPRIETORSHIP

Ordinary and Necessary Business Expenses. The provisions that govern business deductions also are general, and not entity specific. The § 162 requirement that trade or business expenses be *ordinary and necessary* (refer to Chapter 4) applies to proprietorships as well as corporations, partnerships, and other business entities. However, certain specific deductions are available only to self-employed taxpayers. These deductions are covered in detail below.

Health Insurance Premiums. A self-employed taxpayer may deduct 60 percent of insurance premiums paid for medical coverage in 2001 as a deduction *for* AGI.[69] The deduction is allowed for premiums paid on behalf of the taxpayer, the taxpayer's spouse, and dependents of the taxpayer. The deduction is not allowed to any taxpayer who is eligible to participate in a subsidized health plan maintained by any employer of the taxpayer or of the taxpayer's spouse.

This deduction is reported in the Adjustments to Income section of Form 1040 rather than on Schedule C. Premiums paid for medical coverage of the *employees* of a self-employed taxpayer are deductible as business expenses on Schedule C, however.

EXAMPLE 53

Ellen, a sole proprietor of a restaurant, has two dependent children. During 2001, she paid health insurance premiums of $1,800 for her own coverage and $1,000 for coverage of her two children. Ellen can deduct $1,680 ($2,800 × 60%) as a deduction *for* AGI. She can include the remaining $1,120 ($2,800 − $1,680) as a medical expense (subject to the 7.5% floor) when computing itemized deductions. ■

---

[69] § 162(l). The rate was 60% in tax year 2000. It will be 70% in 2002 and 100% in 2003 and thereafter.

Self-Employment Tax.   The tax on self-employment income is levied to provide Social Security and Medicare benefits (old age, survivors, and disability insurance and hospital insurance) for self-employed individuals. Individuals with net earnings of $400 or more from self-employment are subject to the self-employment tax.[70] For 2001, the self-employment tax is 12.4 percent of self-employment earnings up to a $80,400 *ceiling amount* (for the Social Security portion) plus 2.9 percent of the *total* amount of self-employment earnings (for the Medicare portion). Thus, the combined self-employment tax rate on earnings up to $80,400 is 15.3 percent. The ceiling amount is adjusted periodically for inflation.

For purposes of computing the *self-employment tax*, self-employed taxpayers are allowed a deduction from net earnings equal to one-half of the self-employment tax rate.[71] This deduction of 7.65 percent (one-half of the 15.3 percent rate) is reflected by multiplying net earnings from self-employment by 92.35 percent (100% − 7.65%), as shown in Example 54. For purposes of computing *taxable income,* an income tax deduction is allowed for one-half the amount of self-employment tax paid.[72]

Example 54 illustrates the computation of the self-employment tax, as well as the income tax deduction for one-half of self-employment tax paid. For income tax purposes, the amount to be reported on Schedule C is net earnings from self-employment *before* the deduction for one-half of the self-employment tax. The deduction of one-half of the self-employment tax paid is reported separately on Form 1040 as a deduction *for* AGI.

EXAMPLE 54

Computation of the self-employment tax is determined using the steps below. The self-employment tax is determined for two taxpayers with net earnings from self-employment for 2001 as follows: Ned, $55,000 and Terry, $100,000.

Computation of Self-Employment Tax for Ned

1. Net earnings	$55,000.00
2. Multiply line 1 by 92.35%.	$50,792.50
3. If the amount on line 2 is $80,400 or less, multiply the line 2 amount by 15.3%. This is the self-employment tax.	$ 7,771.25
4. If the amount on line 2 is more than $80,400, multiply the excess over $80,400 by 2.9% and add $12,301.20. This is the self-employment tax.	

Computation of Self-Employment Tax for Terry

1. Net earnings	$100,000.00
2. Multiply line 1 by 92.35%.	$ 92,350.00
3. If the amount on line 2 is $80,400 or less, multiply the line 2 amount by 15.3%. This is the self-employment tax.	
4. If the amount on line 2 is more than $80,400, multiply the excess over $80,400 by 2.9% and add $12,301.20. This is the self-employment tax.	$ 12,647.75

For income tax purposes, Ned has net earnings from self-employment of $55,000 and a deduction *for* AGI of $3,885.63 (one-half of $7,771.25). Terry has net earnings from

---

[70]§ 6017.
[71]§ 1402(a)(12).

[72]§ 164(f).

self-employment of $100,000 and a deduction *for* AGI of $6,323.88 (one-half of $12,647.75). Both taxpayers benefit from the deduction for one-half of the self-employment tax paid. ∎

Wages of employees also are subject to Social Security and Medicare taxes. The total tax rate is also 15.3 percent, with 7.65 percent being withheld from the employee's wages and the employer paying at a 7.65 percent rate. If an individual who is self-employed also receives wages from working as an employee of another organization, the ceiling amount of the Social Security portion on which the self-employment tax is computed is reduced. Thus, the self-employment tax may be reduced if a self-employed individual also receives Social Security wages in excess of the ceiling amount.

Net earnings from self-employment include gross income from a trade or business less allowable trade or business deductions, the distributive share of any partnership income or loss derived from a trade or business activity, and net income from rendering personal services as an independent contractor. Gain or loss from the disposition of property (including involuntary conversions) is excluded from the computation of self-employment income unless the property involved is inventory.

RETIREMENT PLANS FOR SELF-EMPLOYED INDIVIDUALS

Self-employed individuals have several options for retirement funding. Individual Retirement Accounts (discussed earlier in this chapter) are available to both employees and self-employed individuals. Other options for self-employed individuals include, but are not limited to, H.R. 10 (Keogh) plans and SIMPLE plans, both of which are discussed below.

Keogh Plans.   Self-employed individuals (e.g., partners and sole proprietors) are eligible to establish and receive qualified retirement benefits under **Keogh plans** (also known as H.R. 10 plans). Self-employed individuals who establish Keogh plans for themselves are also required to cover their *employees* under the plan.

Keogh investments can include a variety of funding vehicles, such as mutual funds, annuities, real estate shares, certificates of deposit, debt instruments, commodities, securities, and personal properties. When an individual decides to make all investment decisions, a *self-directed retirement plan* is established. Investment in most collectibles is not allowed in a self-directed plan.

A Keogh plan may be either a *defined contribution* plan or a *defined benefit* plan. In a defined contribution plan, the amount that can be contributed each year is subject to limitations. Retirement benefits depend on the amount contributed and the amount earned by the plan. In a defined benefit plan, the amount of retirement income is fixed and is determined on the basis of the employee's compensation while working, the number of years in the plan, and age on retirement.

A self-employed individual may annually contribute the smaller of $35,000 or 25 percent of earned income to a defined contribution Keogh plan.[73] If the defined contribution plan is a profit sharing plan, however, a 15 percent deduction limit applies. Under a defined benefit Keogh plan, the annual benefit is limited to the smaller of $140,000 (in 2001) or 100 percent of the average net earnings for the three highest years.[74]

Earned income refers to net earnings from self-employment.[75] Net earnings from self-employment means the gross income derived by an individual from any trade or business carried on by that individual, less appropriate deductions, plus

---

[73]§ 415(c)(1).
[74]§ 415(b)(1). The amount is indexed annually.

[75]§ 401(c)(2).

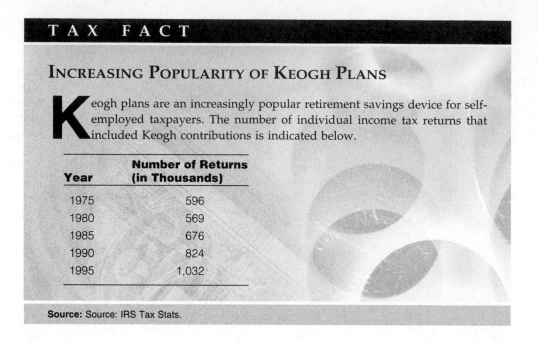

INCREASING POPULARITY OF KEOGH PLANS

Keogh plans are an increasingly popular retirement savings device for self-employed taxpayers. The number of individual income tax returns that included Keogh contributions is indicated below.

Year	Number of Returns (in Thousands)
1975	596
1980	569
1985	676
1990	824
1995	1,032

Source: Source: IRS Tax Stats.

the distributive share of income or loss from a partnership.[76] Earned income is reduced by contributions to a Keogh plan on the individual's behalf and by 50 percent of any self-employment tax.[77]

EXAMPLE 55

Pat, a partner, has earned income of $130,000 in 2001 (after the deduction for one-half of self-employment tax, but before any Keogh contribution). The maximum contribution to a defined contribution plan is $26,000, calculated from the following formula: $130,000 - .25X = X$, where X is earned income reduced by Pat's Keogh contribution. Solving this equation, $X = $104,000$; thus, the contribution limit is $.25 \times $104,000 = $26,000$. In essence, a self-employed individual can contribute 20% of gross earned income. Pat could contribute only 13.043% of self-employment gross earned income if this were a profit sharing plan. ∎

Although a Keogh plan must be established before the end of the year in question, contributions may be made up to the normal filing date for that year.

PLANNING CONSIDERATIONS

Important Dates Related to IRAs and Keogh Plans

A Keogh or IRA participant may make a deductible contribution for a tax year up to the time prescribed for filing the individual's tax return for that tax year. A Keogh plan must have been *established* by the end of the *prior* tax year (e.g., December 31, 2000) to obtain a deduction on the 2000 income tax return for the contribution made in the *current* year (2001). An individual can establish an IRA during the *current* tax year (up to the normal filing date) and still receive a deduction on the prior-year income tax return for the contribution made in the *current* year.

---

[76]§ 1402(a).   [77]§§ 401(c)(2)(A)(v) and 164(f).

↗ small employer

SIMPLE Plans.   Employers with 100 or fewer employees who do not maintain another qualified retirement plan may establish a *savings incentive match plan for employees* (SIMPLE plan).[78] The plan can be in the form of a § 401(k) plan or an IRA. The SIMPLE plan is not subject to the nondiscrimination rules that are normally applicable to § 401(k) plans.

All employees who received at least $5,000 in compensation from the employer during any two preceding years and who reasonably expect to receive at least $5,000 in compensation during the current year must be eligible to participate in the plan. The decision to participate is up to the employee. A *self-employed individual* may also participate in the plan.

The contributions made by the employee (a salary reduction approach) must be expressed as a percentage of compensation rather than as a fixed dollar amount. The plan must not permit the elective employee contribution for the year to exceed $6,500 (in 2001). Generally, the employer must either match elective employee contributions up to 3 percent of the employee's compensation or provide nonmatching contributions of 2 percent of compensation for each eligible employee. Thus, the maximum amount that may be contributed to the plan for 2001 is $11,600 [$6,500 employee contributions + $5,100 ($170,000 compensation ceiling × 3%) employer match].

No other contributions may be made to the plan other than the employee elective contribution and the required employer matching contribution (or nonmatching contribution under the 2 percent rule). All contributions are fully vested. An employer is required to make contributions to a SIMPLE § 401(k) plan once it is established, whereas an employer's contributions to a traditional § 401(k) plan are optional.

An employer's deduction for contributions to a SIMPLE § 401(k) plan is limited to the greater of 15 percent of the compensation paid or accrued or the amount that the employer is required to contribute to the plan. Thus, an employer may deduct contributions to a SIMPLE § 401(k) plan in excess of 15 percent of the $170,000 salary cap. A traditional § 401(k) plan is limited to 15 percent of the total compensation of plan participants for the year.

An employer is allowed a deduction for matching contributions only if the contributions are made by the due date (including extensions) for the employer's tax return. Contributions to a SIMPLE plan are excludible from the employee's gross income, and the SIMPLE plan is tax-exempt.

EXAMPLE 56	The Mauve Company has a SIMPLE plan for its employees under which it provides non-matching contributions of 2% of compensation for each eligible employee. The maximum amount that can be added to each participant's account in 2001 is $9,900, composed of the $6,500 employee salary reduction plus an employer contribution of $3,400 ($170,000 × 2%). ∎

Distributions from a SIMPLE plan are taxed under the IRA rules. Tax-free rollovers can be made from one SIMPLE account to another. A SIMPLE account can be rolled over to an IRA tax-free after the expiration of a two-year period since the individual first participated in the plan. Withdrawals of contributions during the two-year period beginning on the date an employee first participates in the SIMPLE plan are subject to a 25 percent early withdrawal tax rather than the 10 percent early withdrawal tax that otherwise would apply.

---

[78]§ 408(p).

PLANNING CONSIDERATIONS

Factors Affecting Retirement Plan Choices

An IRA might not be the best retirement plan option for many self-employed taxpayers. The maximum amount that can be deducted is $2,000 per year ($4,000 for a spousal plan), which may be too low to provide funding for an adequate level of retirement income. Other options such as Keogh plans and SIMPLE plans allow larger contributions and larger deductions. However, a self-employed individual who establishes either a Keogh or a SIMPLE plan is required to cover employees under such plans. This can result in substantial expenditures, not only for the required contributions, but also for expenses of administering the plan. An advantage of an IRA is that coverage of employees is not required.

ACCOUNTING PERIODS AND METHODS

Proprietors may choose among accounting methods, just as other business entities do (refer to Chapter 6). The cash method is commonly used by proprietorships that provide services, while the accrual or hybrid method generally is required if inventory is a material income-producing factor.

The accounting period rules for proprietorships generally are much simpler than the rules for partnerships and S corporations. Because a proprietorship is not an entity separate from the proprietor, the proprietorship must use the same tax year-end as the proprietor. This does not preclude the use of a fiscal year for a proprietorship, but most proprietorships use the calendar year.

ESTIMATED TAX PAYMENTS

Although the following discussion largely centers on self-employed taxpayers, some of the procedures may be applicable to employed persons. In many cases, for example, employed persons may be required to pay estimated tax if they have income that is not subject to withholding (e.g., income from rentals, dividends, or interest).

Estimated Tax for Individuals.   **Estimated tax** is the amount of tax (including alternative minimum tax and self-employment tax) an individual expects to owe for the year after subtracting tax credits and income tax withheld. Any individual who has estimated tax for the year of $1,000 or more and whose withholding does not equal or exceed the required annual payment (discussed below) must make quarterly payments.[79] Otherwise, a penalty may be assessed. No quarterly payments are required, and no penalty will apply on an underpayment, if the taxpayer's estimated tax is under $1,000. No penalty will apply if the taxpayer had no tax liability for the preceding tax year, the preceding tax year was a taxable year of 12 months, and the taxpayer was a citizen or resident for the entire preceding tax year. In this regard, having no tax liability is not the same as having no additional tax to pay.

The required annual payment must first be computed. This is the smaller of the following amounts:

- Ninety percent of the tax shown on the current year's return.
- One hundred percent of the tax shown on the preceding year's return (the return must cover the full 12 months of the preceding year). In 2001, if the AGI on the preceding year's return (2000) exceeds $150,000 ($75,000 if married filing separately), the 100 percent requirement is increased to 110 percent.

---

[79]§ 6654(c)(1).

In general, one-fourth of this required annual payment is due on April 15, June 15, and September 15 of the tax year and January 15 of the following year. Thus, the quarterly installment of the required annual payment reduced by the applicable withholding is the estimated tax to be paid. An equal part of withholding is deemed paid on each due date, even if a taxpayer's earnings fluctuate widely during the year. Payments are to be accompanied by the payment voucher from Form 1040–ES for the appropriate date.

Penalty on Underpayments.   A nondeductible penalty is imposed on the amount of underpayment of estimated tax. The rate for this penalty is the same as the rate for underpayments of tax and is adjusted quarterly to reflect changes in the average prime rate.

An *underpayment* occurs when any quarterly payment (the sum of estimated tax paid and income tax withheld) is less than 25 percent of the required annual payment. The penalty is applied to the amount of the underpayment for the period of the underpayment.[80]

EXAMPLE 57

Marta made the following payments of estimated tax for 2001 and had no income tax withheld:

April 16, 2001	$1,400
June 15, 2001	2,300
September 17, 2001	1,500
January 15, 2002	1,800

Marta's actual tax for 2001 is $8,000, and her tax in 2000 was $10,000. Therefore, each installment should have been at least $1,800 [($8,000 × 90%) × 25%]. Of the payment on June 15, $400 will be credited to the unpaid balance of the first quarterly installment due on April 16,[81] thereby effectively stopping the underpayment penalty for the first quarterly period. Of the remaining $1,900 payment on June 15, $100 is credited to the September 17 payment, resulting in this third quarterly payment being $200 short. Then $200 of the January 15 payment is credited to the September 17 shortfall, ending the period of underpayment for that portion due. The January 15, 2002, installment is now underpaid by $200, and a penalty will apply from January 15, 2002, to April 15, 2002 (unless paid sooner). Marta's underpayments for the periods of underpayment are as follows:

1st installment due:	$400 from April 16 to June 15
2nd installment due:	Paid in full
3rd installment due:	$200 from September 17, 2001 to January 15, 2002
4th installment due:	$200 from January 15, 2002 to April 15, 2002

■

If a possible underpayment of estimated tax is indicated, Form 2210 should be filed to compute the penalty due or to justify that no penalty applies.

LEARNING OBJECTIVE 6

Distinguish between business and hobby activities and apply the rules limiting the deduction of hobby losses.

Hobby Losses

Employee deductions and deductions related to a proprietorship were discussed in previous sections of this chapter. Employees are allowed to deduct certain expenditures incurred in connection with their work activities. Expenses incurred

---

[80]§ 6654(b)(2).
[81]Payments are credited to unpaid installments in the order in which the installments are required to be paid. § 6654(b)(3).

by a self-employed taxpayer are deductible only if the taxpayer can show that the activity was entered into for the purpose of making a profit.

Certain activities may have either profit-seeking or personal attributes, depending upon individual circumstances. Examples include raising horses and operating a farm that is also used as a weekend residence. While personal losses are not deductible, losses attributable to profit-seeking activities may be deducted and used to offset a taxpayer's other income. For this reason, losses generated by hobbies are not deductible.

GENERAL RULES

If an individual can show that an activity has been conducted with the intent to earn a profit, losses from the activity are fully deductible. The hobby loss rules apply only if the activity is not engaged in for profit. Hobby expenses are deductible only to the extent of hobby income.[82]

The Regulations stipulate that the following nine factors should be considered in determining whether an activity is profit-seeking or a hobby:[83]

- Whether the activity is conducted in a businesslike manner.
- The expertise of the taxpayers or their advisers.
- The time and effort expended.
- The expectation that the assets of the activity will appreciate in value.
- The taxpayer's previous success in conducting similar activities.
- The history of income or losses from the activity.
- The relationship of profits earned to losses incurred.
- The financial status of the taxpayer (e.g., if the taxpayer does not have substantial amounts of other income, this may indicate that the activity is engaged in for profit).
- Elements of personal pleasure or recreation in the activity.

The presence or absence of a factor is not by itself determinative of whether the activity is profit seeking or a hobby. Rather, the decision is a subjective one that is based on an analysis of the facts and circumstances.

PRESUMPTIVE RULE OF § 183

The Code provides a rebuttable presumption that an activity is profit seeking if the activity shows a profit in at least three of any five prior consecutive years.[84] If the activity involves horses, a profit in at least two of seven consecutive years meets the presumptive rule. If these profitability tests are met, the activity is presumed to be a trade or business rather than a personal hobby. In this situation, the burden of proof shifts from the taxpayer to the IRS. That is, the IRS bears the burden of proving that the activity is personal rather than trade or business related.

EXAMPLE 58

Camille, an executive for a large corporation, is paid a salary of $200,000. Her husband is a collector of antiques. Several years ago, he opened an antique shop in a local shopping center and spends most of his time buying and selling antiques. He occasionally earns a small profit from this activity but more frequently incurs substantial losses. If the losses are business related, they are fully deductible against Camille's salary income on a joint return. The following approach should be considered in resolving this issue:

---

[82]§ 183(b)(2).
[83]Reg. §§ 1.183–2(b)(1) through (9).

[84]§ 183(d).

- Initially determine whether the antique activity has met the three-out-of-five-years profit test.
- If the presumption is not met, the activity may nevertheless qualify as a business if the taxpayer can show that the intent is to engage in a profit-seeking activity. It is not necessary to show actual profits.
- Attempt to fit the operation within the nine criteria prescribed in the Regulations and listed above. These criteria are the factors considered in trying to rebut the § 183 presumption. ■

DETERMINING THE AMOUNT OF THE DEDUCTION

If an activity is deemed to be a hobby, the expenses are deductible only to the extent of the gross income from the hobby. These expenses must be deducted in the following order:

- Amounts deductible under other Code Sections without regard to the nature of the activity, such as property taxes and home mortgage interest.
- Amounts deductible under other Code Sections if the activity had been engaged in for profit, but only if those amounts do not affect adjusted basis. Examples include maintenance, utilities, and supplies.
- Amounts that affect adjusted basis and would be deductible under other Code Sections if the activity had been engaged in for profit.[85] Examples include depreciation, amortization, and depletion.

These deductions are deductible *from* AGI as itemized deductions to the extent they exceed 2 percent of AGI.[86] If the taxpayer uses the standard deduction rather than itemizing, all hobby loss deductions are wasted.

EXAMPLE 59

Jim, the vice president of an oil company, has AGI of $80,000. He decides to pursue painting in his spare time. He uses a home studio, comprising 10% of the home's square footage. During the current year, Jim incurs the following expenses:

Frames	$ 350
Art supplies	300
Fees paid to models	1,000
Expenses related to home:	
Total property taxes	900
Total home mortgage interest	10,000
Total home maintenance and utilities	3,600
Depreciation on 10% of home used as studio	500

During the year, Jim sold paintings for a total of $3,200. If the activity is held to be a hobby, Jim is allowed deductions as follows:

Gross income	$ 3,200
Deduct: Taxes and interest (10% of $10,900)	(1,090)
Remainder	$ 2,110

---

[85]Reg. § 1.183–1(b)(1).

[86]Reg. § 1.67–1T(a)(1)(iv) and Rev.Rul. 75–14, 1975–1 C.B. 90.

Deduct: Frames	$ 350	
Art supplies	300	
Models' fees	1,000	
Maintenance and utilities (10%)	360	(2,010)
Remainder		$ 100
Depreciation ($500, but limited to $100)		(100)
Net income		$ –0–

Jim includes the $3,200 of income in AGI, making his AGI $83,200. The taxes and interest are itemized deductions, deductible in full. Assuming Jim has no other miscellaneous itemized deductions, the remaining expenses of $2,110 are reduced by 2% of his AGI ($1,664); so the net deduction is $446. Since the property taxes and home mortgage interest are deductible anyway, the net effect is a $2,754 ($3,200 less $446) increase in taxable income. ■

EXAMPLE 60

If Jim's activity in Example 59 were held to be a business, he could deduct expenses totaling $3,600 *for* AGI, as shown below. All these expenses would be trade or business expenses. His reduction in AGI would be as follows:

Gross income		$ 3,200
Deduct: Taxes and interest	$1,090	
Other business expenses	2,010	
Depreciation	500	(3,600)
Reduction in AGI		($ 400)

As in Example 59, Jim can deduct the remaining property taxes and home mortgage interest of $9,810 ($10,900 – $1,090) as itemized deductions. ■

Suggested Further Readings

Marina L. Ferrone, "Telecommuting Employees and the Amended Home Office Deduction," (Tax Clinic), *The Tax Adviser*, February 2000, pp. 83–86.

Nancy J. Foran and Jeffrey J. Bryant, "Roth IRA Final Regs. Offer Clarity and Guidance," *The Tax Adviser*, September 1999, pp. 654–663.

Susan Kalinka, "Tax Breaks for Self-Employed not without Obstacles," *Taxes: The Tax Magazine*, November 1999, pp. 7–11.

Tamarka K. Kowalczyk, "Gaming Industry Victorious on Employee Meal Issue," *Taxes: The Tax Magazine*, October 1999, pp. 39–44.

Tim Krumwiede, "The Expanded Home Office Deduction," *Taxes: The Tax Magazine*, December 1999, pp. 13–21.

KEY TERMS

Accountable plan, 16–3	*De minimis* fringe benefits, 16–16	Entertainment expenses, 16–28
Automatic mileage method, 16–20	Education expenses, 16–26	Estimated tax, 16–44
Cafeteria plan, 16–12		Flexible spending plan, 16–13

Problem Materials

PROBLEMS

1. In determining whether someone who performs services for another is an employee or is self-employed, a number of factors are considered. In each of the independent situations appearing below, which classification is indicated? In all cases, assume Heath performs services for Melvin.
   a. Melvin pays Heath based on units produced.
   b. Melvin sets Heath's working hours.
   c. Heath has his own tools.
   d. At any time he desires, Melvin has the right to terminate Heath's services.

2. Rex, age 49, is an officer of Blue Company, which provided him with the following nondiscriminatory fringe benefits in 2001:
   a. Hospitalization insurance for Rex and his dependents. The cost of coverage for Rex was $450, and the additional cost for Rex's dependents was $400.
   b. Reimbursement of $1,500 from an uninsured medical reimbursement plan available to all employees.
   c. Group term life insurance protection of $130,000. (Each employee received coverage equal to twice his or her annual salary.)
   d. Salary continuation payments of $3,000 while Rex was hospitalized for an illness.

   While Rex was ill, he collected $2,000 on a salary continuation insurance policy he had purchased. Determine the amounts Rex must include in gross income.

3. The UVW Union and HON Corporation are negotiating contract terms. Assume the union members are in the 28% marginal tax bracket and all benefits are provided on a nondiscriminatory basis. Write a letter to the UVW Union members explaining the tax consequences of the options discussed below. The union's address is 905 Spruce Street, Washington, D.C. 20227.
   a. The company would impose a $100 deductible on medical insurance benefits. Most employees incur more than $100 each year in medical expenses.
   b. Employees would get an additional paid holiday with the same annual income (the same pay but less work).
   c. An employee who did not need health insurance (because the employee's spouse works and receives family coverage) would be allowed to receive the cash value of the coverage.

4. Bertha spent the last 60 days of 2001 in a nursing home. The cost of the services provided to her was $11,300. Medicare paid $5,600 toward the cost of her stay. Bertha also received $6,500 of benefits under a long-term care insurance policy she purchased. What is the effect on Bertha's gross income?

5. Does the taxpayer recognize gross income in the following situations?

    a. Ann is a registered nurse working in a community hospital. She is not required to take her lunch on the hospital premises, but she can eat in the cafeteria at no charge. The hospital adopted this policy to encourage employees to stay on the premises and be available in case of emergencies. During the year, Ann ate most of her meals on the premises. The total value of those meals was $750.

    b. Ira is the manager of a hotel. His employer will allow him to live in one of the rooms rent-free or receive a $600 per month cash allowance for rent. Ira elected to live in the hotel.

    c. Seth is a forest ranger and lives in his employer's cabin in the forest. He is required to live there, and because there are no restaurants nearby, the employer supplies Seth with groceries that he cooks and eats on the premises.

    d. Rocky is a partner in the BAR Ranch (a partnership). He is the full-time manager of the ranch. BAR has a business purpose for Rocky's living on the ranch.

6. Sally and Bill are married and file joint returns. In 2001, Bill, an accountant, has a salary of $75,000, and Sally receives a salary of $25,000 as an apartment manager. What are the tax consequences of the following benefits that Bill and Sally's employers provide?

    a. Bill receives a reimbursement of $5,000 for child care expenses. Sally and Bill have three children who are not yet school age.

    b. Bill and Sally are provided a free membership at a local fitness and exercise club that allows them to attend three aerobic exercise sessions per week. The value of this type of membership is $1,600 per year.

    c. Bill is provided free parking at work. The value of the parking is $1,800 per year.

    d. Sally is provided with a free apartment. Living in this apartment is a condition of her employment. Similar apartments rent for $1,200 per month.

7. Sparrow, Inc., has a wide variety of fringe benefits available to its employees. However, not all of the employees actually need the benefits. For example, some employees have working spouses whose employers provide health insurance benefits for the employee's families. In addition, Sparrow reimburses up to $5,000 for child care costs, but not all of the employees have children. Some employees have expressed a strong interest in long-term care insurance. Sparrow's management has asked you to write a memo explaining how the company can accommodate the varying needs of its employees at the lowest after-tax cost to the employee. Sparrow's address is 300 Harbor Drive, Vermilion, SD 57069.

8. Tara's employer provides a flexible benefits plan. Under the plan, medical and dental expenses incurred during the year that are not covered by the company's group health insurance plan will be paid by the flexible benefits plan. At the first of each year, the employee must set the amount to be covered by the plan. The employee's monthly salary is reduced by one-twelfth of the identified flexible benefit amount for the year. Tara thinks it is highly unlikely that she can accurately estimate her medical and dental expenses not covered by the company's group health insurance plan, but she feels these costs will probably be in the range of $1,500 to $2,500. She expects to be in the 28% marginal tax bracket. Tara would like your advice regarding how much she should reduce her salary in exchange for the expanded dental and medical benefits.

9. Snowbird Corporation would like you to review its employee fringe benefits program with regard to the tax effects of the plan on the company's president (Polly), who is also the majority shareholder:

    a. All employees receive free tickets to State University football games. Polly is seldom able to attend the games and usually gives her tickets to her nephew. The cost of Polly's tickets for the year was $75.

    b. The company pays all parking fees for its officers but not for other employees. The company paid $1,200 for Polly's parking for the year.

    c. Employees are allowed to use the copy machine for personal purposes as long as the privilege is not abused. Polly is president of a trade association and made extensive use of the copy machine to prepare mailings to members of the association. The cost of the copies was $900.

d. The company is in the household moving business. Employees are allowed to ship goods without charge whenever there is excess space on a truck. Polly purchased a dining room suite for her daughter. Company trucks delivered the furniture to the daughter. Normal freight charges would have been $600.

e. The company has a storage facility for household goods. Officers are allowed a 20% discount on charges for storing their goods. All other employees are allowed a 10% discount. Polly's discounts for the year totaled $400.

10. Tom works for Roadrunner Motors, a company that manufactures automobiles. Tom purchased a new automobile from Roadrunner at the company's cost of $10,000. The retail selling price for the automobile is $15,000. Sue works for Coyote, Inc., an auto dealership, which sells the car manufactured by Roadrunner. Sue purchased an automobile identical to Tom's from Coyote. The price Sue pays is equal to Coyote's cost of the automobile ($13,500). Tom and Sue each receive a salary of $40,000 per year. Considering only the above information, do Tom and Sue have equal ability to pay income taxes for the year, and does equitable treatment occur? If not, how should the tax law be changed to produce equitable treatment?

11. Several of Egret Company's employees have asked the company to create a hiking trail that employees could use during their lunch hours. The company owns vacant land that is being held for future expansion, but would have to spend approximately $50,000 if it were to make a trail. Nonemployees would be allowed to use the facility as part of the company's effort to build strong community support. What are the relevant tax issues for the employees?

12. Redbird, Inc., does not provide its employees with any tax-exempt fringe benefits. The company is considering adopting a hospital and medical benefits insurance plan that will cost approximately $6,000 per employee. In order to adopt this plan, the company may have to reduce salaries and/or lower future salary increases. Redbird is in the 35% (combined Federal and state rates) income tax bracket. Redbird is also responsible for matching the Social Security and Medicare taxes withheld on employees' salaries. The benefits insurance plans will not be subject to the Social Security and Medicare taxes. The employees generally fall into three marginal tax rate groups:

Income Tax	Social Security and Medicare Tax	Total
.15	.0765	.2265
.28	.0765	.3565
.36	.0145	.3745

The company has asked you to assist in its financial planning for the benefits insurance plan by computing the following:

a. How much taxable compensation is the equivalent to $6,000 of exempt compensation for each of the three classes of employees?

b. What is the company's after-tax cost of the taxable compensation computed in (a) above?

c. What is the company's after-tax cost of the exempt compensation?

d. Briefly explain your conclusions from the above analysis.

13. Dena is the regional sales manager for the Burger Hut fast-food chain. Generally, she drives her personal automobile from her residence to the regional office, works for eight hours, and returns home. On many occasions, however, she leaves the office early and visits the four local outlets (starting with No. 1 through No. 4) as part of the workday. Relevant mileage is as follows:

	Miles
Residence to regional office	20
Regional office to Burger Hut No. 1	10
Burger Hut No. 1 to Burger Hut No. 2	15
Burger Hut No. 2 to Burger Hut No. 3	12
Burger Hut No. 3 to Burger Hut No. 4	16
Burger Hut No. 4 to residence	30

Dena works 230 days in 2001. Of these, 60 days involve visits to the outlets. If she uses the automatic mileage method, what is her deduction for the year?

14. Larry went from Cleveland to New York on business. His time was spent as follows:

Thursday	Travel
Friday	Business
Saturday and Sunday	Sightseeing
Monday and Tuesday	Business
Wednesday	Travel

During the trip, Larry incurred and paid expenses of $180 per day for lodging from Thursday night through Tuesday night and $110 per day for meals from Friday through Tuesday. Round-trip airfare was $400. Larry is a self-employed attorney who practices law in Cleveland.
a. How much can Larry deduct for the New York trip?
b. How will any deduction be classified?

15. Barney and Nadia Horton own and operate a fabric store. During the year, they attended the annual convention of the National Textiles Association and incurred the following expenses:

Airfare	$1,120
Hotel room	450
Meals	420
Registration fee and program materials	740
Airport limousine	80

The hotel room charge does not include $46 for valet service. How much may the Hortons deduct, and how is the deduction classified?

16. Monica travels from her office in Boston to Lisbon, Portugal, on business. Her absence of 13 days was spent as follows:

Thursday	Depart for and arrive at Lisbon
Friday	Business transacted
Saturday and Sunday	Vacationing
Monday through Friday	Business transacted
Saturday and Sunday	Vacationing
Monday	Business transacted
Tuesday	Depart Lisbon and return to office in Boston

a. For tax purposes, how many days has Monica spent on business?
b. What difference does it make?
c. Could Monica have spent more time than she did vacationing on the trip without loss of existing tax benefits? Explain.

17. Cole is both a CPA and an attorney. For several years, he has practiced law as an employee of a large law firm in Dallas. In 2001, Cole decides to quit his job and move to El Paso, Texas. Four months after arriving in El Paso, Cole establishes a private practice as a CPA. Expenses in moving from Dallas to El Paso are as follows:

Cost of moving household effects	$5,100
Meals	120
Lodging	240

Mileage on two personal autos involved in the move is 1,400.
    a. How much, if any, can Cole deduct as a moving expense?
    b. How is the deduction, if any, classified (*for* or *from* AGI)?

18. After graduating from college with a degree in marketing, Doris accepted a job with a large department store as an assistant department manager. During the year, Doris enrolled in an evening MBA program at a local university. Her expenses for the program are as follows:

Books and tuition	$3,100
Transportation	210
Meals (before and after classes)	330

Doris also took a correspondence course (cost of $180) entitled "How to Cultivate Customer Loyalty."
    Presuming no reimbursement, which of these expenses qualify as deductions?

19. Elvis is a salesman who works for Crane Sales, Inc. Typically, Elvis spends several days out of town each week. Crane provides Elvis with a travel allowance of $1,100 per month, but requires no accountability. For the current year, Elvis had the following job-related travel expenses:

Meals	$ 5,040
Lodging	10,080
Transportation	1,400

    a. What amount qualifies as a deductible travel expense?
    b. What is the classification of any such deduction?

20. Hunter is an accountant who works for a major oil company. He also maintains a consulting practice that he operates from his home. Gross income from the consulting activity is $14,000 for the year. For the business, he devoted one room exclusively that comprised 15% of the floor space of his home. Expenses of the business (other than home office expenses) are $4,500. Hunter's home expenses are as follows:

Real property taxes	$5,000
Interest on home mortgage	6,000
Operating expenses of home	1,500
Depreciation (based on 15% business use)	1,200

    a. Compute Hunter's office in the home deduction.
    b. How are these items classified?

21. Paige incurred the following expenses related to her employment as a chief executive officer:

Lodging while away from home	$2,800
Meals while away from home	1,200
Entertainment while away from home	2,000
Dues, subscriptions, and books	1,000
Transportation expenses	4,000

Her AGI was $100,000, and she received $6,600 in reimbursements under her employer's accountable plan. What are Paige's deductions *for* and *from* AGI?

22. Molly is unmarried and is an active participant in a qualified deductible (traditional) IRA plan. Her modified AGI is $39,000 in 2001.
    a. Calculate the amount that Molly can contribute to the IRA and the amount she can deduct.
    b. Assume instead that Molly is a participant in a SIMPLE IRA and that she elects to contribute 4% of her compensation to the account, while her employer contributes 3%. What amount will be contributed for 2001? What amount will be vested?

23. Jane and Bill, who have been married for six years, are both active participants in qualified retirement plans. Their total AGI for 2001 is $156,000. Each is employed and earns a salary of $75,000.
    a. What amount, if any, may Jane and Bill contribute to traditional IRAs?
    b. What amount, if any, may Jane and Bill contribute to Roth IRAs?

24. Monica establishes a Roth IRA at age 40 and contributes $2,000 per year to the Roth IRA for 25 years. The account is now worth $99,000, consisting of $50,000 in contributions plus $49,000 in accumulated earnings. How much of these funds may Monica withdraw tax-free?

25. In 2013, Joyce receives a $4,000 distribution from her education IRA, which has a fair market value of $10,000. Total contributions to her education IRA have been $7,000. Joyce's AGI is $25,000.
    a. Joyce uses the entire $4,000 to pay for qualified higher education expenses. What amount should she include in her gross income?
    b. Assume instead that Joyce uses only $2,500 of the $4,000 distribution for qualified higher education expenses. What amount should she include in her gross income?

26. In 2001, Susan's sole proprietorship earns $220,000 of self-employment net income (after the deduction for one-half of self-employment tax).
    a. Calculate the maximum amount that Susan can deduct for contributions to a defined contribution Keogh plan.
    b. Suppose Susan contributes more than the allowable amount to the Keogh plan. What are the tax consequences to her?
    c. Can Susan retire and begin receiving Keogh payments at age 55?

27. In 2001, Fran has self-employed earnings of $125,000. Compute Fran's self-employment tax liability and the allowable income tax deduction for the self-employment tax paid.

EXTENDER

28. In each of the following independent situations, determine the amount of FICA (Social Security and Medicare) that should be withheld from the employee's 2001 salary by the employer.
    a. Harry earns a $50,000 salary, files a joint return, and claims four withholding allowances.
    b. Hazel earns a $90,000 salary, files a joint return, and claims four withholding allowances.
    c. Tracey earns a $150,000 salary, files a joint return, and claims four withholding allowances.
    d. Alicia's 17-year-old son, Carlos, earns $10,000 at the family business.

EXTENDER

29. During 2001, Helen, the owner of a store, has the following income and expenses:

Gross profit on sales	$63,000
Income from part-time job (subject to FICA)	40,000
Business expenses (related to store)	15,000
Fire loss on store building	1,200
Dividend income	200
Long-term capital gain on the sale of a stock investment	2,000

Compute Helen's self-employment tax and allowable income tax deduction for the self-employment tax paid.

30. Sandra, an orthodontist, is single and has net earnings of $90,000 from her orthodontic practice. In addition, she acquires antique books that she sells at antique shows. She participates in six to eight weekend antique shows per year. Her income and expenses for the current year are as follows:

Revenue from sale of antique books	$22,000
Expenses:	
Cost of goods sold	12,000
Show registration costs	3,000
Advertising	1,000
Dealer's license—annual fee	500
Insurance	900
Depreciation of display cases	1,200

Sandra has no other items that would affect her AGI. Itemized deductions from taxes, interest, and charitable contributions are $19,000.
a. Calculate Sandra's taxable income if the antique book activity is classified as a hobby.
b. Calculate Sandra's taxable income if the antique book activity is classified as a business.

COMPREHENSIVE TAX RETURN PROBLEMS

31. Beth R. Jordan lives at 2322 Skyview Road, Mesa, AZ 85202. She is a tax accountant with Mesa Manufacturing Company. She also writes computer software programs for tax practitioners and has a part-time tax practice. Beth, age 35, is single and has no dependents. Her Social Security number is 111–35–2222. She wants to contribute $3 to the Presidential Election Campaign Fund.

During 2000, Beth earned a salary of $50,000 from her employer. She received interest of $290 from Home Federal Savings and Loan and $335 from Home State Bank. She received dividends of $500 from Gray Corporation, $400 from Blue Corporation, and $300 from Orange Corporation.

Beth received a $1,200 income tax refund from the state of Arizona on May 12, 2000. On her 1999 Federal income tax return, she reported total itemized deductions of $6,700, which included $2,000 of state income tax withheld by her employer.

Fees earned from her part-time tax practice in 2000 totaled $3,800. She paid $400 to have the tax returns processed by a computerized tax return service.

On February 1, 2000, Beth bought 500 shares of Gray Corporation common stock for $17.60 a share. On July 16, she sold the stock for $15 a share.

Beth bought a used utility vehicle for $3,000 on June 5, 2000. She purchased the vehicle from her brother-in-law, who was unemployed and was in need of cash. On November 2, 2000, she sold the vehicle to a friend for $3,400.

On January 2, 2000, Beth acquired 100 shares of Blue Corporation common stock for $30 a share. She sold the stock on December 19, 2000, for $75 a share.

During 2000, Beth received royalties of $14,000 on a software program she had written. Beth incurred the following expenditures in connection with her software-writing activities:

Cost of microcomputer (100% business use)	$7,000
Cost of printer (100% business use)	2,000
Office furniture	3,000
Supplies	650
Fee paid to computer consultant	3,500

Beth elected to expense the maximum portion of the cost of the microcomputer, printer, and furniture allowed under the provisions of § 179. This equipment and furniture were placed in service on January 15, 2000.

Although her employer suggested that Beth attend a convention on current developments in corporate taxation, Beth was not reimbursed for the travel expenses of $1,420 she incurred in attending the convention. The $1,420 included $200 for the cost of meals.

During 2000, Beth paid $300 for prescription medicines and $2,875 in doctor bills, hospital bills, and medical insurance premiums. Her employer withheld state income tax of $1,954. Beth paid real property taxes of $1,766 on her home. Interest on her home mortgage was $3,845, and interest to credit card companies was $320. Beth contributed $20 each week to her church and $10 each week to the United Way. Professional dues and subscriptions totaled $350.

Beth's employer withheld Federal income taxes of $9,500 during 2000. Beth paid estimated taxes of $500. What is the amount of Beth's net tax payable or refund due for 2000? If Beth has a tax refund due, she wants to have it credited toward her 2001 income tax. If you use tax forms for your solution, you will need Forms 1040, 2106, and 4562 and Schedules A, B, C, D, and SE. Suggested software: Any commercially available tax preparation software.

32. George M. and Martha J. Jordan have no dependents and are both under age 65. George is a statutory employee of Consolidated Jobbers (business code is 421400), and his Social Security number is 582–99–4444. Martha is an executive with General Corporation, and her Social Security number is 241–88–6642. The Jordans live at 321 Oak Street, Lincoln, NV 89553. They both want to contribute to the Presidential Election Campaign Fund.

In 2000, George earned $48,900 in commissions. His employer withholds FICA but not Federal income taxes. George paid $9,700 in estimated taxes. Martha earned $62,500, from which $8,250 was withheld for Federal income taxes. Neither George nor Martha received any expense reimbursements.

George uses his car (purchased on January 3, 1998) on sales calls and keeps a log of all miles driven. In 2000, he drove 37,000 miles, 25,200 of them for business. He made several out-of-state sales trips, incurring transportation costs of $1,700, meals of $900, and lodging costs of $850. During the year, he also spent $1,500 taking customers to lunch.

Martha incurred the following expenses related to her work: taxi fares of $126, business lunches of $715, and a yearly commuter train ticket of $700. During the year, Martha received $1,300 in interest from the employees' credit union, $100,000 life insurance proceeds upon the death of her mother in December, and $500 in dividends from General Motors. She contributed $2,000 to her traditional Individual Retirement Account. Neither George nor Martha is covered by an employee retirement plan. Martha gave a gift valued at $100 to the president of her firm upon his promotion to that position. The Jordans had additional expenditures as follows:

Charitable contributions (cash)	$1,300
Medical and dental expenses	1,500
Real property taxes	1,100
Home mortgage interest	9,400
Tax return preparation fee	250

Part 1—Tax Computation

Compute the Jordans' Federal income tax payable or refund due, assuming they file a joint income tax return for 2000. If they have overpaid, they want the amount refunded. You will need Form 1040 and Schedules A, B, and C. Suggested software: Any commercially available tax preparation software.

Part 2—Tax Planning

Martha and George ask your help in deciding what to do with the $100,000 Martha inherited in 2000. They are considering two conservative investment alternatives:

• Invest in 8% long-term U.S. bonds.

• Invest in 6.5% municipal bonds.

a. Calculate the best alternative for next year. Assume that Martha and George will have the same income and deductions in 2001, except for the income from the investment they choose. In computing the tax, use the tax rate schedules for 2001.

b. What other factors should the Jordans take into account?

c. Write a memo to the Jordans, explaining their alternatives.

Suggested software: Any commercially available tax preparation software.

BRIDGE DISCIPLINE

1. Justin performs services for Partridge, Inc., and receives compensation of $75,000 for the year. Determine the tax consequences of Social Security and Medicare on Justin's take-home pay if:

   a. Justin is classified as an employee of Partridge.

   b. Justin is classified as an independent contractor.

2. Amanda has been an employee of Robin, Inc., for almost 5 years. She is a participant in Robin's defined contribution pension plan (money purchase plan). The total contributions made by Robin to the money purchase plan for Amanda are $50,000, and the balance in Amanda's account is $72,000. Amanda is considering accepting a job with a competitor of Robin's at an annual salary $6,000 higher than that received from Robin. Her boss, who is trying to convince her to stay, points out that she will not be vested in the money purchase plan until she has been employed by Robin for at least 5 years. In addition, she will have to start a new vesting schedule with the competitor.

   a. What is vesting, and how does it affect Amanda and her decision based on the information provided?

   b. What have been the tax consequences to Amanda of Robin's annual contribution of $10,000 to its money purchase plan for her?

   c. What effect would it have on Amanda's decision if the competitor does not provide retirement benefits?

3. The Code contains provisions that are "friendly" to specific groups of taxpayers. Among these are the following:

   • Seniors.

   • Married taxpayers.

   • Employed taxpayers.

   • Taxpayers with children.

   Provide justification for the special treatment for each of the above groups, and give an example of such special treatment for each group.

RESEARCH PROBLEMS

*Note: Solutions to Research Problems can be prepared by using the **RIA Checkpoint® Student Version Online** research product, or the **CCH U.S. Master Tax Guide Plus**™ online Federal tax research database, which is available to accompany this text. It is also possible to prepare solutions to the Research Problems by using tax research materials found in a standard tax library.*

Research Problem 1.   Tom Roberts, a chemical engineer, is a long-time employee of Teal Chemical Corporation. Tom's specialty is the design and construction of special-purpose chemical processing plants. Teal has decided to expand its presence in France and plans to transfer Tom to Paris on a three-year assignment. The planned foreign assignment will take Tom to age 65, Teal's normal retirement age.

Tom has been advised regarding the major income tax ramifications of working abroad. He has not, however, been told about the treatment of moving expenses. Since Teal Corporation pays its employees a substantial foreign service salary increment, it reimburses for moving expenses. In connection with the move, Tom plans to sell his residence and place most of his furniture in storage. Probabilities are good that the sale of the residence will result in a loss.

a. Write a letter to Tom regarding the income tax treatment of his moving expenses. Tom's address is 1389 Wilson Drive, Trent, NJ 08102. Be sure to include in the discussion the move from France back to the United States.

b. Prepare a memo for your firm's client files.

Research Problem 2.   Rick Beam has been an independent sales representative for various textile manufacturers for many years. His products consist of soft goods, such as tablecloths, curtains, and drapes. Rick's customers are clothing store chains, department stores, and smaller specialty stores. The employees of these companies who are responsible for purchasing merchandise are known as buyers. These companies generally prohibit their buyers from accepting gifts from manufacturers' sales representatives.

Each year Rick gives cash gifts (never more than $25) to most of the buyers who are his customers. Generally, he cashes a large check in November and gives the money personally to the buyers around Christmas. Rick says, "This is one of the ways that I maintain my relationship with my buyers." He maintains adequate substantiation of all the gifts.

Rick's deductions for these gifts have been disallowed by the IRS, based on § 162(c)(2). Rick is confused and comes to you, a CPA, for advice.

a. Write a letter to Rick concerning his tax position on this issue. Rick's address is 948 Octavia Street, New Orleans, LA 70113.

b. Prepare a memo for your files supporting the advice you have given.

Research Problem 3.   After graduating from high school, Joe attended various colleges, earning degrees in business (B.B.A.) and law (JD). He accepted employment with Eagle Associates, a regional accounting firm. Soon thereafter, Joe took and passed the CPA exam. While at Eagle, his usual work assignment was as follows: 30% to 40% preparing tax returns, 40% to 50% researching the tax law, and the remainder consulting with clients about tax matters.

Several years later, Joe quit his job with Eagle and pursued, on a full-time basis, a master of laws degree with a specialization in taxation. Upon graduation, Joe accepted a position as a trust officer at Finch Trust Company. At Finch, Joe manages clients' assets, acquires new clients, and prepares and files the fiduciary income tax returns that are the responsibility of the branch office where he works.

When Joe files his own income tax return, he claims a deduction for the education expenses incurred in obtaining the master of laws degree. In the event of audit by the IRS, assess Joe's chances of sustaining the deduction.

Partial list of research aids:
Harold Haft, 40 T.C. 2 (1963).
Stephen G. Sherman, 36 TCM 1191, T.C.Memo. 1977–301.
Kenneth C. Davis, 65 T.C. 1014 (1976).
John H. Hudgens III, 73 TCM 1790, T.C.Memo. 1997–33.

Research Problem 4.   Frank and Polly were married, but Frank died on February 25, 2001. During 2001, Frank earned $5,226 in wages, but Polly had no earned income. Neither had contributed any money to an IRA during 2001. What amount, if any, can be contributed to Frank's IRA and/or Polly's spousal IRA?

Use the tax resources of the Internet to address the following questions. Do not restrict your search to the World Wide Web, but include a review of newsgroups and general reference materials, practitioner sites and resources, primary sources of the tax law, chat rooms and discussion groups, and other opportunities.

Research Problem 5.   In the last few years, the IRS has been diligent in applying existing rules to classify self-employed individuals as employees of those who engage their services. What are the current criteria that the IRS utilizes in resolving the employee versus independent contractor issue? Were any changes in these criteria proposed during the formulation of TRA of 1997? In this regard, what eventually happened?

Research Problem 6.   Locate and read a recent judicial or administrative ruling regarding the deductibility of hobby losses. Look for rulings that deal with horse breeding, professional sports teams, or art collecting activities. Which criteria did the ruling emphasize in upholding or reversing the taxpayer's deduction for such losses?

Tax Rate Schedules and Tables

2000 Tax Rate Schedules

Single—Schedule X

If taxable income is: Over—	But not over—	The tax is:		of the amount over—
$0	$ 26,250	. . . . . . .15%		$0
26,250	63,550	$3,937.50 +	28%	26,250
63,550	132,600	14,381.50 +	31%	63,550
132,600	288,350	35,787.00 +	36%	132,600
288,350	. . . . . .	91,857.00 +	39.6%	288,350

Head of household—Schedule Z

If taxable income is: Over—	But not over—	The tax is:		of the amount over—
$0	$ 35,150	. . . . . . .15%		$0
35,150	90,800	$5,272.50 +	28%	35,150
90,800	147,050	20,854.50 +	31%	90,800
147,050	288,350	38,292.00 +	36%	147,050
288,350	. . . . . .	89,160.00 +	39.6%	288,350

Married filing jointly or Qualifying widow(er)—Schedule Y–1

If taxable income is: Over—	But not over—	The tax is:		of the amount over—
$0	$ 43,850	. . . . . . .15%		$0
43,850	105,950	$6,577.50 +	28%	43,850
105,950	161,450	23,965.50 +	31%	105,950
161,450	288,350	41,170.50 +	36%	161,450
288,350	. . . . . .	86,854.50 +	39.6%	288,350

Married filing separately—Schedule Y–2

If taxable income is: Over—	But not over—	The tax is:		of the amount over—
$0	$ 21,925	. . . . . . .15%		$0
21,925	52,975	$3,288.75 +	28%	21,925
52,975	80,725	11,982.75 +	31%	52,975
80,725	144,175	20,585.25 +	36%	80,725
144,175	. . . . . .	43,427.25 +	39.6%	144,175

2001 Tax Rate Schedules

Single—Schedule X

If taxable income is: Over—	But not over—	The tax is:		of the amount over—
$0	$ 27,050	. . . . . . .15%		$0
27,050	65,550	$4,057.50 +	28%	27,050
65,550	136,750	14,837.50 +	31%	65,550
136,750	297,350	36,909.50 +	36%	136,750
297,350	. . . . . .	94,725.50 +	39.6%	297,350

Head of household—Schedule Z

If taxable income is: Over—	But not over—	The tax is:		of the amount over—
$0	$ 36,250	. . . . . . .15%		$0
36,250	93,650	$5,437.50 +	28%	36,250
93,650	151,650	21,509.50 +	31%	93,650
151,650	297,350	39,489.50 +	36%	151,650
297,350	. . . . . .	91,941.50 +	39.6%	297,350

Married filing jointly or Qualifying widow(er)—Schedule Y–1

If taxable income is: Over—	But not over—	The tax is:		of the amount over—
$0	$ 45,200	. . . . . . .15%		$0
45,200	109,250	$6,780.00 +	28%	45,200
109,250	166,500	24,714.00 +	31%	109,250
166,500	297,350	42,461.50 +	36%	166,500
297,350	. . . . . .	89,567.50 +	39.6%	297,350

Married filing separately—Schedule Y–2

If taxable income is: Over—	But not over—	The tax is:		of the amount over—
$0	$ 22,600	. . . . . . .15%		$0
22,600	54,625	$3,390.00 +	28%	22,600
54,625	83,250	12,357.00 +	31%	54,625
83,250	148,675	21,230.75 +	36%	83,250
148,675	. . . . . .	44,783.75 +	39.6%	148,675

2000 Tax Table

Use if your taxable income is less than $100,000.
If $100,000 or more, use the Tax Rate Schedules.

Example. Mr. and Mrs. Brown are filing a joint return. Their taxable income on line 39 of Form 1040 is $25,300. First, they find the $25,300–25,350 income line. Next, they find the column for married filing jointly and read down the column. The amount shown where the income line and filing status column meet is $3,799. This is the tax amount they should enter on line 40 of their Form 1040.

Sample Table

At least	But less than	Single	Married filing jointly *	Married filing separately	Head of a household
			Your tax is—		
25,200	25,250	3,784	3,784	4,213	3,784
25,250	25,300	3,791	3,791	4,227	3,791
25,300	25,350	3,799	(3,799)	4,241	3,799
25,350	25,400	3,806	3,806	4,255	3,806

If line 39 (taxable income) is— At least	But less than	And you are— Single	Married filing jointly *	Married filing separately	Head of a household
		Your tax is—			
0	5	0	0	0	0
5	15	2	2	2	2
15	25	3	3	3	3
25	50	6	6	6	6
50	75	9	9	9	9
75	100	13	13	13	13
100	125	17	17	17	17
125	150	21	21	21	21
150	175	24	24	24	24
175	200	28	28	28	28
200	225	32	32	32	32
225	250	36	36	36	36
250	275	39	39	39	39
275	300	43	43	43	43
300	325	47	47	47	47
325	350	51	51	51	51
350	375	54	54	54	54
375	400	58	58	58	58
400	425	62	62	62	62
425	450	66	66	66	66
450	475	69	69	69	69
475	500	73	73	73	73
500	525	77	77	77	77
525	550	81	81	81	81
550	575	84	84	84	84
575	600	88	88	88	88
600	625	92	92	92	92
625	650	96	96	96	96
650	675	99	99	99	99
675	700	103	103	103	103
700	725	107	107	107	107
725	750	111	111	111	111
750	775	114	114	114	114
775	800	118	118	118	118
800	825	122	122	122	122
825	850	126	126	126	126
850	875	129	129	129	129
875	900	133	133	133	133
900	925	137	137	137	137
925	950	141	141	141	141
950	975	144	144	144	144
975	1,000	148	148	148	148

1,000

At least	But less than	Single	Married filing jointly *	Married filing separately	Head of a household
1,000	1,025	152	152	152	152
1,025	1,050	156	156	156	156
1,050	1,075	159	159	159	159
1,075	1,100	163	163	163	163
1,100	1,125	167	167	167	167
1,125	1,150	171	171	171	171
1,150	1,175	174	174	174	174
1,175	1,200	178	178	178	178
1,200	1,225	182	182	182	182
1,225	1,250	186	186	186	186
1,250	1,275	189	189	189	189
1,275	1,300	193	193	193	193

If line 39 (taxable income) is— At least	But less than	And you are— Single	Married filing jointly *	Married filing separately	Head of a household
		Your tax is—			
1,300	1,325	197	197	197	197
1,325	1,350	201	201	201	201
1,350	1,375	204	204	204	204
1,375	1,400	208	208	208	208
1,400	1,425	212	212	212	212
1,425	1,450	216	216	216	216
1,450	1,475	219	219	219	219
1,475	1,500	223	223	223	223
1,500	1,525	227	227	227	227
1,525	1,550	231	231	231	231
1,550	1,575	234	234	234	234
1,575	1,600	238	238	238	238
1,600	1,625	242	242	242	242
1,625	1,650	246	246	246	246
1,650	1,675	249	249	249	249
1,675	1,700	253	253	253	253
1,700	1,725	257	257	257	257
1,725	1,750	261	261	261	261
1,750	1,775	264	264	264	264
1,775	1,800	268	268	268	268
1,800	1,825	272	272	272	272
1,825	1,850	276	276	276	276
1,850	1,875	279	279	279	279
1,875	1,900	283	283	283	283
1,900	1,925	287	287	287	287
1,925	1,950	291	291	291	291
1,950	1,975	294	294	294	294
1,975	2,000	298	298	298	298

2,000

At least	But less than	Single	Married filing jointly *	Married filing separately	Head of a household
2,000	2,025	302	302	302	302
2,025	2,050	306	306	306	306
2,050	2,075	309	309	309	309
2,075	2,100	313	313	313	313
2,100	2,125	317	317	317	317
2,125	2,150	321	321	321	321
2,150	2,175	324	324	324	324
2,175	2,200	328	328	328	328
2,200	2,225	332	332	332	332
2,225	2,250	336	336	336	336
2,250	2,275	339	339	339	339
2,275	2,300	343	343	343	343
2,300	2,325	347	347	347	347
2,325	2,350	351	351	351	351
2,350	2,375	354	354	354	354
2,375	2,400	358	358	358	358
2,400	2,425	362	362	362	362
2,425	2,450	366	366	366	366
2,450	2,475	369	369	369	369
2,475	2,500	373	373	373	373
2,500	2,525	377	377	377	377
2,525	2,550	381	381	381	381
2,550	2,575	384	384	384	384
2,575	2,600	388	388	388	388
2,600	2,625	392	392	392	392
2,625	2,650	396	396	396	396
2,650	2,675	399	399	399	399
2,675	2,700	403	403	403	403

If line 39 (taxable income) is— At least	But less than	And you are— Single	Married filing jointly *	Married filing separately	Head of a household
		Your tax is—			
2,700	2,725	407	407	407	407
2,725	2,750	411	411	411	411
2,750	2,775	414	414	414	414
2,775	2,800	418	418	418	418
2,800	2,825	422	422	422	422
2,825	2,850	426	426	426	426
2,850	2,875	429	429	429	429
2,875	2,900	433	433	433	433
2,900	2,925	437	437	437	437
2,925	2,950	441	441	441	441
2,950	2,975	444	444	444	444
2,975	3,000	448	448	448	448

3,000

At least	But less than	Single	Married filing jointly *	Married filing separately	Head of a household
3,000	3,050	454	454	454	454
3,050	3,100	461	461	461	461
3,100	3,150	469	469	469	469
3,150	3,200	476	476	476	476
3,200	3,250	484	484	484	484
3,250	3,300	491	491	491	491
3,300	3,350	499	499	499	499
3,350	3,400	506	506	506	506
3,400	3,450	514	514	514	514
3,450	3,500	521	521	521	521
3,500	3,550	529	529	529	529
3,550	3,600	536	536	536	536
3,600	3,650	544	544	544	544
3,650	3,700	551	551	551	551
3,700	3,750	559	559	559	559
3,750	3,800	566	566	566	566
3,800	3,850	574	574	574	574
3,850	3,900	581	581	581	581
3,900	3,950	589	589	589	589
3,950	4,000	596	596	596	596

4,000

At least	But less than	Single	Married filing jointly *	Married filing separately	Head of a household
4,000	4,050	604	604	604	604
4,050	4,100	611	611	611	611
4,100	4,150	619	619	619	619
4,150	4,200	626	626	626	626
4,200	4,250	634	634	634	634
4,250	4,300	641	641	641	641
4,300	4,350	649	649	649	649
4,350	4,400	656	656	656	656
4,400	4,450	664	664	664	664
4,450	4,500	671	671	671	671
4,500	4,550	679	679	679	679
4,550	4,600	686	686	686	686
4,600	4,650	694	694	694	694
4,650	4,700	701	701	701	701
4,700	4,750	709	709	709	709
4,750	4,800	716	716	716	716
4,800	4,850	724	724	724	724
4,850	4,900	731	731	731	731
4,900	4,950	739	739	739	739
4,950	5,000	746	746	746	746

(Continued on next page)

* This column must also be used by a qualifying widow(er).

2000 Tax Table —Continued

If line 39 (taxable income) is —		And you are —				If line 39 (taxable income) is —		And you are —				If line 39 (taxable income) is —		And you are —			
At least	But less than	Single	Married filing jointly *	Married filing sepa-rately	Head of a house-hold	At least	But less than	Single	Married filing jointly *	Married filing sepa-rately	Head of a house-hold	At least	But less than	Single	Married filing jointly *	Married filing sepa-rately	Head of a house-hold
		Your tax is —						Your tax is —						Your tax is —			
5,000						**8,000**						**11,000**					
5,000	5,050	754	754	754	754	8,000	8,050	1,204	1,204	1,204	1,204	11,000	11,050	1,654	1,654	1,654	1,654
5,050	5,100	761	761	761	761	8,050	8,100	1,211	1,211	1,211	1,211	11,050	11,100	1,661	1,661	1,661	1,661
5,100	5,150	769	769	769	769	8,100	8,150	1,219	1,219	1,219	1,219	11,100	11,150	1,669	1,669	1,669	1,669
5,150	5,200	776	776	776	776	8,150	8,200	1,226	1,226	1,226	1,226	11,150	11,200	1,676	1,676	1,676	1,676
5,200	5,250	784	784	784	784	8,200	8,250	1,234	1,234	1,234	1,234	11,200	11,250	1,684	1,684	1,684	1,684
5,250	5,300	791	791	791	791	8,250	8,300	1,241	1,241	1,241	1,241	11,250	11,300	1,691	1,691	1,691	1,691
5,300	5,350	799	799	799	799	8,300	8,350	1,249	1,249	1,249	1,249	11,300	11,350	1,699	1,699	1,699	1,699
5,350	5,400	806	806	806	806	8,350	8,400	1,256	1,256	1,256	1,256	11,350	11,400	1,706	1,706	1,706	1,706
5,400	5,450	814	814	814	814	8,400	8,450	1,264	1,264	1,264	1,264	11,400	11,450	1,714	1,714	1,714	1,714
5,450	5,500	821	821	821	821	8,450	8,500	1,271	1,271	1,271	1,271	11,450	11,500	1,721	1,721	1,721	1,721
5,500	5,550	829	829	829	829	8,500	8,550	1,279	1,279	1,279	1,279	11,500	11,550	1,729	1,729	1,729	1,729
5,550	5,600	836	836	836	836	8,550	8,600	1,286	1,286	1,286	1,286	11,550	11,600	1,736	1,736	1,736	1,736
5,600	5,650	844	844	844	844	8,600	8,650	1,294	1,294	1,294	1,294	11,600	11,650	1,744	1,744	1,744	1,744
5,650	5,700	851	851	851	851	8,650	8,700	1,301	1,301	1,301	1,301	11,650	11,700	1,751	1,751	1,751	1,751
5,700	5,750	859	859	859	859	8,700	8,750	1,309	1,309	1,309	1,309	11,700	11,750	1,759	1,759	1,759	1,759
5,750	5,800	866	866	866	866	8,750	8,800	1,316	1,316	1,316	1,316	11,750	11,800	1,766	1,766	1,766	1,766
5,800	5,850	874	874	874	874	8,800	8,850	1,324	1,324	1,324	1,324	11,800	11,850	1,774	1,774	1,774	1,774
5,850	5,900	881	881	881	881	8,850	8,900	1,331	1,331	1,331	1,331	11,850	11,900	1,781	1,781	1,781	1,781
5,900	5,950	889	889	889	889	8,900	8,950	1,339	1,339	1,339	1,339	11,900	11,950	1,789	1,789	1,789	1,789
5,950	6,000	896	896	896	896	8,950	9,000	1,346	1,346	1,346	1,346	11,950	12,000	1,796	1,796	1,796	1,796
6,000						**9,000**						**12,000**					
6,000	6,050	904	904	904	904	9,000	9,050	1,354	1,354	1,354	1,354	12,000	12,050	1,804	1,804	1,804	1,804
6,050	6,100	911	911	911	911	9,050	9,100	1,361	1,361	1,361	1,361	12,050	12,100	1,811	1,811	1,811	1,811
6,100	6,150	919	919	919	919	9,100	9,150	1,369	1,369	1,369	1,369	12,100	12,150	1,819	1,819	1,819	1,819
6,150	6,200	926	926	926	926	9,150	9,200	1,376	1,376	1,376	1,376	12,150	12,200	1,826	1,826	1,826	1,826
6,200	6,250	934	934	934	934	9,200	9,250	1,384	1,384	1,384	1,384	12,200	12,250	1,834	1,834	1,834	1,834
6,250	6,300	941	941	941	941	9,250	9,300	1,391	1,391	1,391	1,391	12,250	12,300	1,841	1,841	1,841	1,841
6,300	6,350	949	949	949	949	9,300	9,350	1,399	1,399	1,399	1,399	12,300	12,350	1,849	1,849	1,849	1,849
6,350	6,400	956	956	956	956	9,350	9,400	1,406	1,406	1,406	1,406	12,350	12,400	1,856	1,856	1,856	1,856
6,400	6,450	964	964	964	964	9,400	9,450	1,414	1,414	1,414	1,414	12,400	12,450	1,864	1,864	1,864	1,864
6,450	6,500	971	971	971	971	9,450	9,500	1,421	1,421	1,421	1,421	12,450	12,500	1,871	1,871	1,871	1,871
6,500	6,550	979	979	979	979	9,500	9,550	1,429	1,429	1,429	1,429	12,500	12,550	1,879	1,879	1,879	1,879
6,550	6,600	986	986	986	986	9,550	9,600	1,436	1,436	1,436	1,436	12,550	12,600	1,886	1,886	1,886	1,886
6,600	6,650	994	994	994	994	9,600	9,650	1,444	1,444	1,444	1,444	12,600	12,650	1,894	1,894	1,894	1,894
6,650	6,700	1,001	1,001	1,001	1,001	9,650	9,700	1,451	1,451	1,451	1,451	12,650	12,700	1,901	1,901	1,901	1,901
6,700	6,750	1,009	1,009	1,009	1,009	9,700	9,750	1,459	1,459	1,459	1,459	12,700	12,750	1,909	1,909	1,909	1,909
6,750	6,800	1,016	1,016	1,016	1,016	9,750	9,800	1,466	1,466	1,466	1,466	12,750	12,800	1,916	1,916	1,916	1,916
6,800	6,850	1,024	1,024	1,024	1,024	9,800	9,850	1,474	1,474	1,474	1,474	12,800	12,850	1,924	1,924	1,924	1,924
6,850	6,900	1,031	1,031	1,031	1,031	9,850	9,900	1,481	1,481	1,481	1,481	12,850	12,900	1,931	1,931	1,931	1,931
6,900	6,950	1,039	1,039	1,039	1,039	9,900	9,950	1,489	1,489	1,489	1,489	12,900	12,950	1,939	1,939	1,939	1,939
6,950	7,000	1,046	1,046	1,046	1,046	9,950	10,000	1,496	1,496	1,496	1,496	12,950	13,000	1,946	1,946	1,946	1,946
7,000						**10,000**						**13,000**					
7,000	7,050	1,054	1,054	1,054	1,054	10,000	10,050	1,504	1,504	1,504	1,504	13,000	13,050	1,954	1,954	1,954	1,954
7,050	7,100	1,061	1,061	1,061	1,061	10,050	10,100	1,511	1,511	1,511	1,511	13,050	13,100	1,961	1,961	1,961	1,961
7,100	7,150	1,069	1,069	1,069	1,069	10,100	10,150	1,519	1,519	1,519	1,519	13,100	13,150	1,969	1,969	1,969	1,969
7,150	7,200	1,076	1,076	1,076	1,076	10,150	10,200	1,526	1,526	1,526	1,526	13,150	13,200	1,976	1,976	1,976	1,976
7,200	7,250	1,084	1,084	1,084	1,084	10,200	10,250	1,534	1,534	1,534	1,534	13,200	13,250	1,984	1,984	1,984	1,984
7,250	7,300	1,091	1,091	1,091	1,091	10,250	10,300	1,541	1,541	1,541	1,541	13,250	13,300	1,991	1,991	1,991	1,991
7,300	7,350	1,099	1,099	1,099	1,099	10,300	10,350	1,549	1,549	1,549	1,549	13,300	13,350	1,999	1,999	1,999	1,999
7,350	7,400	1,106	1,106	1,106	1,106	10,350	10,400	1,556	1,556	1,556	1,556	13,350	13,400	2,006	2,006	2,006	2,006
7,400	7,450	1,114	1,114	1,114	1,114	10,400	10,450	1,564	1,564	1,564	1,564	13,400	13,450	2,014	2,014	2,014	2,014
7,450	7,500	1,121	1,121	1,121	1,121	10,450	10,500	1,571	1,571	1,571	1,571	13,450	13,500	2,021	2,021	2,021	2,021
7,500	7,550	1,129	1,129	1,129	1,129	10,500	10,550	1,579	1,579	1,579	1,579	13,500	13,550	2,029	2,029	2,029	2,029
7,550	7,600	1,136	1,136	1,136	1,136	10,550	10,600	1,586	1,586	1,586	1,586	13,550	13,600	2,036	2,036	2,036	2,036
7,600	7,650	1,144	1,144	1,144	1,144	10,600	10,650	1,594	1,594	1,594	1,594	13,600	13,650	2,044	2,044	2,044	2,044
7,650	7,700	1,151	1,151	1,151	1,151	10,650	10,700	1,601	1,601	1,601	1,601	13,650	13,700	2,051	2,051	2,051	2,051
7,700	7,750	1,159	1,159	1,159	1,159	10,700	10,750	1,609	1,609	1,609	1,609	13,700	13,750	2,059	2,059	2,059	2,059
7,750	7,800	1,166	1,166	1,166	1,166	10,750	10,800	1,616	1,616	1,616	1,616	13,750	13,800	2,066	2,066	2,066	2,066
7,800	7,850	1,174	1,174	1,174	1,174	10,800	10,850	1,624	1,624	1,624	1,624	13,800	13,850	2,074	2,074	2,074	2,074
7,850	7,900	1,181	1,181	1,181	1,181	10,850	10,900	1,631	1,631	1,631	1,631	13,850	13,900	2,081	2,081	2,081	2,081
7,900	7,950	1,189	1,189	1,189	1,189	10,900	10,950	1,639	1,639	1,639	1,639	13,900	13,950	2,089	2,089	2,089	2,089
7,950	8,000	1,196	1,196	1,196	1,196	10,950	11,000	1,646	1,646	1,646	1,646	13,950	14,000	2,096	2,096	2,096	2,096

* This column must also be used by a qualifying widow(er).

(Continued on next page)

2000 Tax Table—Continued

If line 39 (taxable income) is —		And you are —			
At least	But less than	Single	Married filing jointly *	Married filing separately	Head of a household
		Your tax is —			
14,000					
14,000	14,050	2,104	2,104	2,104	2,104
14,050	14,100	2,111	2,111	2,111	2,111
14,100	14,150	2,119	2,119	2,119	2,119
14,150	14,200	2,126	2,126	2,126	2,126
14,200	14,250	2,134	2,134	2,134	2,134
14,250	14,300	2,141	2,141	2,141	2,141
14,300	14,350	2,149	2,149	2,149	2,149
14,350	14,400	2,156	2,156	2,156	2,156
14,400	14,450	2,164	2,164	2,164	2,164
14,450	14,500	2,171	2,171	2,171	2,171
14,500	14,550	2,179	2,179	2,179	2,179
14,550	14,600	2,186	2,186	2,186	2,186
14,600	14,650	2,194	2,194	2,194	2,194
14,650	14,700	2,201	2,201	2,201	2,201
14,700	14,750	2,209	2,209	2,209	2,209
14,750	14,800	2,216	2,216	2,216	2,216
14,800	14,850	2,224	2,224	2,224	2,224
14,850	14,900	2,231	2,231	2,231	2,231
14,900	14,950	2,239	2,239	2,239	2,239
14,950	15,000	2,246	2,246	2,246	2,246
15,000					
15,000	15,050	2,254	2,254	2,254	2,254
15,050	15,100	2,261	2,261	2,261	2,261
15,100	15,150	2,269	2,269	2,269	2,269
15,150	15,200	2,276	2,276	2,276	2,276
15,200	15,250	2,284	2,284	2,284	2,284
15,250	15,300	2,291	2,291	2,291	2,291
15,300	15,350	2,299	2,299	2,299	2,299
15,350	15,400	2,306	2,306	2,306	2,306
15,400	15,450	2,314	2,314	2,314	2,314
15,450	15,500	2,321	2,321	2,321	2,321
15,500	15,550	2,329	2,329	2,329	2,329
15,550	15,600	2,336	2,336	2,336	2,336
15,600	15,650	2,344	2,344	2,344	2,344
15,650	15,700	2,351	2,351	2,351	2,351
15,700	15,750	2,359	2,359	2,359	2,359
15,750	15,800	2,366	2,366	2,366	2,366
15,800	15,850	2,374	2,374	2,374	2,374
15,850	15,900	2,381	2,381	2,381	2,381
15,900	15,950	2,389	2,389	2,389	2,389
15,950	16,000	2,396	2,396	2,396	2,396
16,000					
16,000	16,050	2,404	2,404	2,404	2,404
16,050	16,100	2,411	2,411	2,411	2,411
16,100	16,150	2,419	2,419	2,419	2,419
16,150	16,200	2,426	2,426	2,426	2,426
16,200	16,250	2,434	2,434	2,434	2,434
16,250	16,300	2,441	2,441	2,441	2,441
16,300	16,350	2,449	2,449	2,449	2,449
16,350	16,400	2,456	2,456	2,456	2,456
16,400	16,450	2,464	2,464	2,464	2,464
16,450	16,500	2,471	2,471	2,471	2,471
16,500	16,550	2,479	2,479	2,479	2,479
16,550	16,600	2,486	2,486	2,486	2,486
16,600	16,650	2,494	2,494	2,494	2,494
16,650	16,700	2,501	2,501	2,501	2,501
16,700	16,750	2,509	2,509	2,509	2,509
16,750	16,800	2,516	2,516	2,516	2,516
16,800	16,850	2,524	2,524	2,524	2,524
16,850	16,900	2,531	2,531	2,531	2,531
16,900	16,950	2,539	2,539	2,539	2,539
16,950	17,000	2,546	2,546	2,546	2,546

If line 39 (taxable income) is —		And you are —			
At least	But less than	Single	Married filing jointly *	Married filing separately	Head of a household
		Your tax is —			
17,000					
17,000	17,050	2,554	2,554	2,554	2,554
17,050	17,100	2,561	2,561	2,561	2,561
17,100	17,150	2,569	2,569	2,569	2,569
17,150	17,200	2,576	2,576	2,576	2,576
17,200	17,250	2,584	2,584	2,584	2,584
17,250	17,300	2,591	2,591	2,591	2,591
17,300	17,350	2,599	2,599	2,599	2,599
17,350	17,400	2,606	2,606	2,606	2,606
17,400	17,450	2,614	2,614	2,614	2,614
17,450	17,500	2,621	2,621	2,621	2,621
17,500	17,550	2,629	2,629	2,629	2,629
17,550	17,600	2,636	2,636	2,636	2,636
17,600	17,650	2,644	2,644	2,644	2,644
17,650	17,700	2,651	2,651	2,651	2,651
17,700	17,750	2,659	2,659	2,659	2,659
17,750	17,800	2,666	2,666	2,666	2,666
17,800	17,850	2,674	2,674	2,674	2,674
17,850	17,900	2,681	2,681	2,681	2,681
17,900	17,950	2,689	2,689	2,689	2,689
17,950	18,000	2,696	2,696	2,696	2,696
18,000					
18,000	18,050	2,704	2,704	2,704	2,704
18,050	18,100	2,711	2,711	2,711	2,711
18,100	18,150	2,719	2,719	2,719	2,719
18,150	18,200	2,726	2,726	2,726	2,726
18,200	18,250	2,734	2,734	2,734	2,734
18,250	18,300	2,741	2,741	2,741	2,741
18,300	18,350	2,749	2,749	2,749	2,749
18,350	18,400	2,756	2,756	2,756	2,756
18,400	18,450	2,764	2,764	2,764	2,764
18,450	18,500	2,771	2,771	2,771	2,771
18,500	18,550	2,779	2,779	2,779	2,779
18,550	18,600	2,786	2,786	2,786	2,786
18,600	18,650	2,794	2,794	2,794	2,794
18,650	18,700	2,801	2,801	2,801	2,801
18,700	18,750	2,809	2,809	2,809	2,809
18,750	18,800	2,816	2,816	2,816	2,816
18,800	18,850	2,824	2,824	2,824	2,824
18,850	18,900	2,831	2,831	2,831	2,831
18,900	18,950	2,839	2,839	2,839	2,839
18,950	19,000	2,846	2,846	2,846	2,846
19,000					
19,000	19,050	2,854	2,854	2,854	2,854
19,050	19,100	2,861	2,861	2,861	2,861
19,100	19,150	2,869	2,869	2,869	2,869
19,150	19,200	2,876	2,876	2,876	2,876
19,200	19,250	2,884	2,884	2,884	2,884
19,250	19,300	2,891	2,891	2,891	2,891
19,300	19,350	2,899	2,899	2,899	2,899
19,350	19,400	2,906	2,906	2,906	2,906
19,400	19,450	2,914	2,914	2,914	2,914
19,450	19,500	2,921	2,921	2,921	2,921
19,500	19,550	2,929	2,929	2,929	2,929
19,550	19,600	2,936	2,936	2,936	2,936
19,600	19,650	2,944	2,944	2,944	2,944
19,650	19,700	2,951	2,951	2,951	2,951
19,700	19,750	2,959	2,959	2,959	2,959
19,750	19,800	2,966	2,966	2,966	2,966
19,800	19,850	2,974	2,974	2,974	2,974
19,850	19,900	2,981	2,981	2,981	2,981
19,900	19,950	2,989	2,989	2,989	2,989
19,950	20,000	2,996	2,996	2,996	2,996

If line 39 (taxable income) is —		And you are —			
At least	But less than	Single	Married filing jointly *	Married filing separately	Head of a household
		Your tax is —			
20,000					
20,000	20,050	3,004	3,004	3,004	3,004
20,050	20,100	3,011	3,011	3,011	3,011
20,100	20,150	3,019	3,019	3,019	3,019
20,150	20,200	3,026	3,026	3,026	3,026
20,200	20,250	3,034	3,034	3,034	3,034
20,250	20,300	3,041	3,041	3,041	3,041
20,300	20,350	3,049	3,049	3,049	3,049
20,350	20,400	3,056	3,056	3,056	3,056
20,400	20,450	3,064	3,064	3,064	3,064
20,450	20,500	3,071	3,071	3,071	3,071
20,500	20,550	3,079	3,079	3,079	3,079
20,550	20,600	3,086	3,086	3,086	3,086
20,600	20,650	3,094	3,094	3,094	3,094
20,650	20,700	3,101	3,101	3,101	3,101
20,700	20,750	3,109	3,109	3,109	3,109
20,750	20,800	3,116	3,116	3,116	3,116
20,800	20,850	3,124	3,124	3,124	3,124
20,850	20,900	3,131	3,131	3,131	3,131
20,900	20,950	3,139	3,139	3,139	3,139
20,950	21,000	3,146	3,146	3,146	3,146
21,000					
21,000	21,050	3,154	3,154	3,154	3,154
21,050	21,100	3,161	3,161	3,161	3,161
21,100	21,150	3,169	3,169	3,169	3,169
21,150	21,200	3,176	3,176	3,176	3,176
21,200	21,250	3,184	3,184	3,184	3,184
21,250	21,300	3,191	3,191	3,191	3,191
21,300	21,350	3,199	3,199	3,199	3,199
21,350	21,400	3,206	3,206	3,206	3,206
21,400	21,450	3,214	3,214	3,214	3,214
21,450	21,500	3,221	3,221	3,221	3,221
21,500	21,550	3,229	3,229	3,229	3,229
21,550	21,600	3,236	3,236	3,236	3,236
21,600	21,650	3,244	3,244	3,244	3,244
21,650	21,700	3,251	3,251	3,251	3,251
21,700	21,750	3,259	3,259	3,259	3,259
21,750	21,800	3,266	3,266	3,266	3,266
21,800	21,850	3,274	3,274	3,274	3,274
21,850	21,900	3,281	3,281	3,281	3,281
21,900	21,950	3,289	3,289	3,289	3,289
21,950	22,000	3,296	3,296	3,303	3,296
22,000					
22,000	22,050	3,304	3,304	3,317	3,304
22,050	22,100	3,311	3,311	3,331	3,311
22,100	22,150	3,319	3,319	3,345	3,319
22,150	22,200	3,326	3,326	3,359	3,326
22,200	22,250	3,334	3,334	3,373	3,334
22,250	22,300	3,341	3,341	3,387	3,341
22,300	22,350	3,349	3,349	3,401	3,349
22,350	22,400	3,356	3,356	3,415	3,356
22,400	22,450	3,364	3,364	3,429	3,364
22,450	22,500	3,371	3,371	3,443	3,371
22,500	22,550	3,379	3,379	3,457	3,379
22,550	22,600	3,386	3,386	3,471	3,386
22,600	22,650	3,394	3,394	3,485	3,394
22,650	22,700	3,401	3,401	3,499	3,401
22,700	22,750	3,409	3,409	3,513	3,409
22,750	22,800	3,416	3,416	3,527	3,416
22,800	22,850	3,424	3,424	3,541	3,424
22,850	22,900	3,431	3,431	3,555	3,431
22,900	22,950	3,439	3,439	3,569	3,439
22,950	23,000	3,446	3,446	3,583	3,446

* This column must also be used by a qualifying widow(er).

(Continued on next page)

2000 Tax Table —Continued

23,000 – 26,000 (left panel)

At least	But less than	Single	Married filing jointly *	Married filing separately	Head of a household
23,000					
23,000	23,050	3,454	3,454	3,597	3,454
23,050	23,100	3,461	3,461	3,611	3,461
23,100	23,150	3,469	3,469	3,625	3,469
23,150	23,200	3,476	3,476	3,639	3,476
23,200	23,250	3,484	3,484	3,653	3,484
23,250	23,300	3,491	3,491	3,667	3,491
23,300	23,350	3,499	3,499	3,681	3,499
23,350	23,400	3,506	3,506	3,695	3,506
23,400	23,450	3,514	3,514	3,709	3,514
23,450	23,500	3,521	3,521	3,723	3,521
23,500	23,550	3,529	3,529	3,737	3,529
23,550	23,600	3,536	3,536	3,751	3,536
23,600	23,650	3,544	3,544	3,765	3,544
23,650	23,700	3,551	3,551	3,779	3,551
23,700	23,750	3,559	3,559	3,793	3,559
23,750	23,800	3,566	3,566	3,807	3,566
23,800	23,850	3,574	3,574	3,821	3,574
23,850	23,900	3,581	3,581	3,835	3,581
23,900	23,950	3,589	3,589	3,849	3,589
23,950	24,000	3,596	3,596	3,863	3,596
24,000					
24,000	24,050	3,604	3,604	3,877	3,604
24,050	24,100	3,611	3,611	3,891	3,611
24,100	24,150	3,619	3,619	3,905	3,619
24,150	24,200	3,626	3,626	3,919	3,626
24,200	24,250	3,634	3,634	3,933	3,634
24,250	24,300	3,641	3,641	3,947	3,641
24,300	24,350	3,649	3,649	3,961	3,649
24,350	24,400	3,656	3,656	3,975	3,656
24,400	24,450	3,664	3,664	3,989	3,664
24,450	24,500	3,671	3,671	4,003	3,671
24,500	24,550	3,679	3,679	4,017	3,679
24,550	24,600	3,686	3,686	4,031	3,686
24,600	24,650	3,694	3,694	4,045	3,694
24,650	24,700	3,701	3,701	4,059	3,701
24,700	24,750	3,709	3,709	4,073	3,709
24,750	24,800	3,716	3,716	4,087	3,716
24,800	24,850	3,724	3,724	4,101	3,724
24,850	24,900	3,731	3,731	4,115	3,731
24,900	24,950	3,739	3,739	4,129	3,739
24,950	25,000	3,746	3,746	4,143	3,746
25,000					
25,000	25,050	3,754	3,754	4,157	3,754
25,050	25,100	3,761	3,761	4,171	3,761
25,100	25,150	3,769	3,769	4,185	3,769
25,150	25,200	3,776	3,776	4,199	3,776
25,200	25,250	3,784	3,784	4,213	3,784
25,250	25,300	3,791	3,791	4,227	3,791
25,300	25,350	3,799	3,799	4,241	3,799
25,350	25,400	3,806	3,806	4,255	3,806
25,400	25,450	3,814	3,814	4,269	3,814
25,450	25,500	3,821	3,821	4,283	3,821
25,500	25,550	3,829	3,829	4,297	3,829
25,550	25,600	3,836	3,836	4,311	3,836
25,600	25,650	3,844	3,844	4,325	3,844
25,650	25,700	3,851	3,851	4,339	3,851
25,700	25,750	3,859	3,859	4,353	3,859
25,750	25,800	3,866	3,866	4,367	3,866
25,800	25,850	3,874	3,874	4,381	3,874
25,850	25,900	3,881	3,881	4,395	3,881
25,900	25,950	3,889	3,889	4,409	3,889
25,950	26,000	3,896	3,896	4,423	3,896

26,000 – 29,000 (middle panel)

At least	But less than	Single	Married filing jointly *	Married filing separately	Head of a household
26,000					
26,000	26,050	3,904	3,904	4,437	3,904
26,050	26,100	3,911	3,911	4,451	3,911
26,100	26,150	3,919	3,919	4,465	3,919
26,150	26,200	3,926	3,926	4,479	3,926
26,200	26,250	3,934	3,934	4,493	3,934
26,250	26,300	3,945	3,941	4,507	3,941
26,300	26,350	3,959	3,949	4,521	3,949
26,350	26,400	3,973	3,956	4,535	3,956
26,400	26,450	3,987	3,964	4,549	3,964
26,450	26,500	4,001	3,971	4,563	3,971
26,500	26,550	4,015	3,979	4,577	3,979
26,550	26,600	4,029	3,986	4,591	3,986
26,600	26,650	4,043	3,994	4,605	3,994
26,650	26,700	4,057	4,001	4,619	4,001
26,700	26,750	4,071	4,009	4,633	4,009
26,750	26,800	4,085	4,016	4,647	4,016
26,800	26,850	4,099	4,024	4,661	4,024
26,850	26,900	4,113	4,031	4,675	4,031
26,900	26,950	4,127	4,039	4,689	4,039
26,950	27,000	4,141	4,046	4,703	4,046
27,000					
27,000	27,050	4,155	4,054	4,717	4,054
27,050	27,100	4,169	4,061	4,731	4,061
27,100	27,150	4,183	4,069	4,745	4,069
27,150	27,200	4,197	4,076	4,759	4,076
27,200	27,250	4,211	4,084	4,773	4,084
27,250	27,300	4,225	4,091	4,787	4,091
27,300	27,350	4,239	4,099	4,801	4,099
27,350	27,400	4,253	4,106	4,815	4,106
27,400	27,450	4,267	4,114	4,829	4,114
27,450	27,500	4,281	4,121	4,843	4,121
27,500	27,550	4,295	4,129	4,857	4,129
27,550	27,600	4,309	4,136	4,871	4,136
27,600	27,650	4,323	4,144	4,885	4,144
27,650	27,700	4,337	4,151	4,899	4,151
27,700	27,750	4,351	4,159	4,913	4,159
27,750	27,800	4,365	4,166	4,927	4,166
27,800	27,850	4,379	4,174	4,941	4,174
27,850	27,900	4,393	4,181	4,955	4,181
27,900	27,950	4,407	4,189	4,969	4,189
27,950	28,000	4,421	4,196	4,983	4,196
28,000					
28,000	28,050	4,435	4,204	4,997	4,204
28,050	28,100	4,449	4,211	5,011	4,211
28,100	28,150	4,463	4,219	5,025	4,219
28,150	28,200	4,477	4,226	5,039	4,226
28,200	28,250	4,491	4,234	5,053	4,234
28,250	28,300	4,505	4,241	5,067	4,241
28,300	28,350	4,519	4,249	5,081	4,249
28,350	28,400	4,533	4,256	5,095	4,256
28,400	28,450	4,547	4,264	5,109	4,264
28,450	28,500	4,561	4,271	5,123	4,271
28,500	28,550	4,575	4,279	5,137	4,279
28,550	28,600	4,589	4,286	5,151	4,286
28,600	28,650	4,603	4,294	5,165	4,294
28,650	28,700	4,617	4,301	5,179	4,301
28,700	28,750	4,631	4,309	5,193	4,309
28,750	28,800	4,645	4,316	5,207	4,316
28,800	28,850	4,659	4,324	5,221	4,324
28,850	28,900	4,673	4,331	5,235	4,331
28,900	28,950	4,687	4,339	5,249	4,339
28,950	29,000	4,701	4,346	5,263	4,346

29,000 – 32,000 (right panel)

At least	But less than	Single	Married filing jointly *	Married filing separately	Head of a household
29,000					
29,000	29,050	4,715	4,354	5,277	4,354
29,050	29,100	4,729	4,361	5,291	4,361
29,100	29,150	4,743	4,369	5,305	4,369
29,150	29,200	4,757	4,376	5,319	4,376
29,200	29,250	4,771	4,384	5,333	4,384
29,250	29,300	4,785	4,391	5,347	4,391
29,300	29,350	4,799	4,399	5,361	4,399
29,350	29,400	4,813	4,406	5,375	4,406
29,400	29,450	4,827	4,414	5,389	4,414
29,450	29,500	4,841	4,421	5,403	4,421
29,500	29,550	4,855	4,429	5,417	4,429
29,550	29,600	4,869	4,436	5,431	4,436
29,600	29,650	4,883	4,444	5,445	4,444
29,650	29,700	4,897	4,451	5,459	4,451
29,700	29,750	4,911	4,459	5,473	4,459
29,750	29,800	4,925	4,466	5,487	4,466
29,800	29,850	4,939	4,474	5,501	4,474
29,850	29,900	4,953	4,481	5,515	4,481
29,900	29,950	4,967	4,489	5,529	4,489
29,950	30,000	4,981	4,496	5,543	4,496
30,000					
30,000	30,050	4,995	4,504	5,557	4,504
30,050	30,100	5,009	4,511	5,571	4,511
30,100	30,150	5,023	4,519	5,585	4,519
30,150	30,200	5,037	4,526	5,599	4,526
30,200	30,250	5,051	4,534	5,613	4,534
30,250	30,300	5,065	4,541	5,627	4,541
30,300	30,350	5,079	4,549	5,641	4,549
30,350	30,400	5,093	4,556	5,655	4,556
30,400	30,450	5,107	4,564	5,669	4,564
30,450	30,500	5,121	4,571	5,683	4,571
30,500	30,550	5,135	4,579	5,697	4,579
30,550	30,600	5,149	4,586	5,711	4,586
30,600	30,650	5,163	4,594	5,725	4,594
30,650	30,700	5,177	4,601	5,739	4,601
30,700	30,750	5,191	4,609	5,753	4,609
30,750	30,800	5,205	4,616	5,767	4,616
30,800	30,850	5,219	4,624	5,781	4,624
30,850	30,900	5,233	4,631	5,795	4,631
30,900	30,950	5,247	4,639	5,809	4,639
30,950	31,000	5,261	4,646	5,823	4,646
31,000					
31,000	31,050	5,275	4,654	5,837	4,654
31,050	31,100	5,289	4,661	5,851	4,661
31,100	31,150	5,303	4,669	5,865	4,669
31,150	31,200	5,317	4,676	5,879	4,676
31,200	31,250	5,331	4,684	5,893	4,684
31,250	31,300	5,345	4,691	5,907	4,691
31,300	31,350	5,359	4,699	5,921	4,699
31,350	31,400	5,373	4,706	5,935	4,706
31,400	31,450	5,387	4,714	5,949	4,714
31,450	31,500	5,401	4,721	5,963	4,721
31,500	31,550	5,415	4,729	5,977	4,729
31,550	31,600	5,429	4,736	5,991	4,736
31,600	31,650	5,443	4,744	6,005	4,744
31,650	31,700	5,457	4,751	6,019	4,751
31,700	31,750	5,471	4,759	6,033	4,759
31,750	31,800	5,485	4,766	6,047	4,766
31,800	31,850	5,499	4,774	6,061	4,774
31,850	31,900	5,513	4,781	6,075	4,781
31,900	31,950	5,527	4,789	6,089	4,789
31,950	32,000	5,541	4,796	6,103	4,796

* This column must also be used by a qualifying widow(er).

(Continued on next page)

If line 39 (taxable income) is — At least	But less than	Single	Married filing jointly*	Married filing separately	Head of a household
32,000					
32,000	32,050	5,555	4,804	6,117	4,804
32,050	32,100	5,569	4,811	6,131	4,811
32,100	32,150	5,583	4,819	6,145	4,819
32,150	32,200	5,597	4,826	6,159	4,826
32,200	32,250	5,611	4,834	6,173	4,834
32,250	32,300	5,625	4,841	6,187	4,841
32,300	32,350	5,639	4,849	6,201	4,849
32,350	32,400	5,653	4,856	6,215	4,856
32,400	32,450	5,667	4,864	6,229	4,864
32,450	32,500	5,681	4,871	6,243	4,871
32,500	32,550	5,695	4,879	6,257	4,879
32,550	32,600	5,709	4,886	6,271	4,886
32,600	32,650	5,723	4,894	6,285	4,894
32,650	32,700	5,737	4,901	6,299	4,901
32,700	32,750	5,751	4,909	6,313	4,909
32,750	32,800	5,765	4,916	6,327	4,916
32,800	32,850	5,779	4,924	6,341	4,924
32,850	32,900	5,793	4,931	6,355	4,931
32,900	32,950	5,807	4,939	6,369	4,939
32,950	33,000	5,821	4,946	6,383	4,946
33,000					
33,000	33,050	5,835	4,954	6,397	4,954
33,050	33,100	5,849	4,961	6,411	4,961
33,100	33,150	5,863	4,969	6,425	4,969
33,150	33,200	5,877	4,976	6,439	4,976
33,200	33,250	5,891	4,984	6,453	4,984
33,250	33,300	5,905	4,991	6,467	4,991
33,300	33,350	5,919	4,999	6,481	4,999
33,350	33,400	5,933	5,006	6,495	5,006
33,400	33,450	5,947	5,014	6,509	5,014
33,450	33,500	5,961	5,021	6,523	5,021
33,500	33,550	5,975	5,029	6,537	5,029
33,550	33,600	5,989	5,036	6,551	5,036
33,600	33,650	6,003	5,044	6,565	5,044
33,650	33,700	6,017	5,051	6,579	5,051
33,700	33,750	6,031	5,059	6,593	5,059
33,750	33,800	6,045	5,066	6,607	5,066
33,800	33,850	6,059	5,074	6,621	5,074
33,850	33,900	6,073	5,081	6,635	5,081
33,900	33,950	6,087	5,089	6,649	5,089
33,950	34,000	6,101	5,096	6,663	5,096
34,000					
34,000	34,050	6,115	5,104	6,677	5,104
34,050	34,100	6,129	5,111	6,691	5,111
34,100	34,150	6,143	5,119	6,705	5,119
34,150	34,200	6,157	5,126	6,719	5,126
34,200	34,250	6,171	5,134	6,733	5,134
34,250	34,300	6,185	5,141	6,747	5,141
34,300	34,350	6,199	5,149	6,761	5,149
34,350	34,400	6,213	5,156	6,775	5,156
34,400	34,450	6,227	5,164	6,789	5,164
34,450	34,500	6,241	5,171	6,803	5,171
34,500	34,550	6,255	5,179	6,817	5,179
34,550	34,600	6,269	5,186	6,831	5,186
34,600	34,650	6,283	5,194	6,845	5,194
34,650	34,700	6,297	5,201	6,859	5,201
34,700	34,750	6,311	5,209	6,873	5,209
34,750	34,800	6,325	5,216	6,887	5,216
34,800	34,850	6,339	5,224	6,901	5,224
34,850	34,900	6,353	5,231	6,915	5,231
34,900	34,950	6,367	5,239	6,929	5,239
34,950	35,000	6,381	5,246	6,943	5,246

If line 39 (taxable income) is — At least	But less than	Single	Married filing jointly*	Married filing separately	Head of a household
35,000					
35,000	35,050	6,395	5,254	6,957	5,254
35,050	35,100	6,409	5,261	6,971	5,261
35,100	35,150	6,423	5,269	6,985	5,269
35,150	35,200	6,437	5,276	6,999	5,280
35,200	35,250	6,451	5,284	7,013	5,294
35,250	35,300	6,465	5,291	7,027	5,308
35,300	35,350	6,479	5,299	7,041	5,322
35,350	35,400	6,493	5,306	7,055	5,336
35,400	35,450	6,507	5,314	7,069	5,350
35,450	35,500	6,521	5,321	7,083	5,364
35,500	35,550	6,535	5,329	7,097	5,378
35,550	35,600	6,549	5,336	7,111	5,392
35,600	35,650	6,563	5,344	7,125	5,406
35,650	35,700	6,577	5,351	7,139	5,420
35,700	35,750	6,591	5,359	7,153	5,434
35,750	35,800	6,605	5,366	7,167	5,448
35,800	35,850	6,619	5,374	7,181	5,462
35,850	35,900	6,633	5,381	7,195	5,476
35,900	35,950	6,647	5,389	7,209	5,490
35,950	36,000	6,661	5,396	7,223	5,504
36,000					
36,000	36,050	6,675	5,404	7,237	5,518
36,050	36,100	6,689	5,411	7,251	5,532
36,100	36,150	6,703	5,419	7,265	5,546
36,150	36,200	6,717	5,426	7,279	5,560
36,200	36,250	6,731	5,434	7,293	5,574
36,250	36,300	6,745	5,441	7,307	5,588
36,300	36,350	6,759	5,449	7,321	5,602
36,350	36,400	6,773	5,456	7,335	5,616
36,400	36,450	6,787	5,464	7,349	5,630
36,450	36,500	6,801	5,471	7,363	5,644
36,500	36,550	6,815	5,479	7,377	5,658
36,550	36,600	6,829	5,486	7,391	5,672
36,600	36,650	6,843	5,494	7,405	5,686
36,650	36,700	6,857	5,501	7,419	5,700
36,700	36,750	6,871	5,509	7,433	5,714
36,750	36,800	6,885	5,516	7,447	5,728
36,800	36,850	6,899	5,524	7,461	5,742
36,850	36,900	6,913	5,531	7,475	5,756
36,900	36,950	6,927	5,539	7,489	5,770
36,950	37,000	6,941	5,546	7,503	5,784
37,000					
37,000	37,050	6,955	5,554	7,517	5,798
37,050	37,100	6,969	5,561	7,531	5,812
37,100	37,150	6,983	5,569	7,545	5,826
37,150	37,200	6,997	5,576	7,559	5,840
37,200	37,250	7,011	5,584	7,573	5,854
37,250	37,300	7,025	5,591	7,587	5,868
37,300	37,350	7,039	5,599	7,601	5,882
37,350	37,400	7,053	5,606	7,615	5,896
37,400	37,450	7,067	5,614	7,629	5,910
37,450	37,500	7,081	5,621	7,643	5,924
37,500	37,550	7,095	5,629	7,657	5,938
37,550	37,600	7,109	5,636	7,671	5,952
37,600	37,650	7,123	5,644	7,685	5,966
37,650	37,700	7,137	5,651	7,699	5,980
37,700	37,750	7,151	5,659	7,713	5,994
37,750	37,800	7,165	5,666	7,727	6,008
37,800	37,850	7,179	5,674	7,741	6,022
37,850	37,900	7,193	5,681	7,755	6,036
37,900	37,950	7,207	5,689	7,769	6,050
37,950	38,000	7,221	5,696	7,783	6,064

If line 39 (taxable income) is — At least	But less than	Single	Married filing jointly*	Married filing separately	Head of a household
38,000					
38,000	38,050	7,235	5,704	7,797	6,078
38,050	38,100	7,249	5,711	7,811	6,092
38,100	38,150	7,263	5,719	7,825	6,106
38,150	38,200	7,277	5,726	7,839	6,120
38,200	38,250	7,291	5,734	7,853	6,134
38,250	38,300	7,305	5,741	7,867	6,148
38,300	38,350	7,319	5,749	7,881	6,162
38,350	38,400	7,333	5,756	7,895	6,176
38,400	38,450	7,347	5,764	7,909	6,190
38,450	38,500	7,361	5,771	7,923	6,204
38,500	38,550	7,375	5,779	7,937	6,218
38,550	38,600	7,389	5,786	7,951	6,232
38,600	38,650	7,403	5,794	7,965	6,246
38,650	38,700	7,417	5,801	7,979	6,260
38,700	38,750	7,431	5,809	7,993	6,274
38,750	38,800	7,445	5,816	8,007	6,288
38,800	38,850	7,459	5,824	8,021	6,302
38,850	38,900	7,473	5,831	8,035	6,316
38,900	38,950	7,487	5,839	8,049	6,330
38,950	39,000	7,501	5,846	8,063	6,344
39,000					
39,000	39,050	7,515	5,854	8,077	6,358
39,050	39,100	7,529	5,861	8,091	6,372
39,100	39,150	7,543	5,869	8,105	6,386
39,150	39,200	7,557	5,876	8,119	6,400
39,200	39,250	7,571	5,884	8,133	6,414
39,250	39,300	7,585	5,891	8,147	6,428
39,300	39,350	7,599	5,899	8,161	6,442
39,350	39,400	7,613	5,906	8,175	6,456
39,400	39,450	7,627	5,914	8,189	6,470
39,450	39,500	7,641	5,921	8,203	6,484
39,500	39,550	7,655	5,929	8,217	6,498
39,550	39,600	7,669	5,936	8,231	6,512
39,600	39,650	7,683	5,944	8,245	6,526
39,650	39,700	7,697	5,951	8,259	6,540
39,700	39,750	7,711	5,959	8,273	6,554
39,750	39,800	7,725	5,966	8,287	6,568
39,800	39,850	7,739	5,974	8,301	6,582
39,850	39,900	7,753	5,981	8,315	6,596
39,900	39,950	7,767	5,989	8,329	6,610
39,950	40,000	7,781	5,996	8,343	6,624
40,000					
40,000	40,050	7,795	6,004	8,357	6,638
40,050	40,100	7,809	6,011	8,371	6,652
40,100	40,150	7,823	6,019	8,385	6,666
40,150	40,200	7,837	6,026	8,399	6,680
40,200	40,250	7,851	6,034	8,413	6,694
40,250	40,300	7,865	6,041	8,427	6,708
40,300	40,350	7,879	6,049	8,441	6,722
40,350	40,400	7,893	6,056	8,455	6,736
40,400	40,450	7,907	6,064	8,469	6,750
40,450	40,500	7,921	6,071	8,483	6,764
40,500	40,550	7,935	6,079	8,497	6,778
40,550	40,600	7,949	6,086	8,511	6,792
40,600	40,650	7,963	6,094	8,525	6,806
40,650	40,700	7,977	6,101	8,539	6,820
40,700	40,750	7,991	6,109	8,553	6,834
40,750	40,800	8,005	6,116	8,567	6,848
40,800	40,850	8,019	6,124	8,581	6,862
40,850	40,900	8,033	6,131	8,595	6,876
40,900	40,950	8,047	6,139	8,609	6,890
40,950	41,000	8,061	6,146	8,623	6,904

* This column must also be used by a qualifying widow(er).

(Continued on next page)

2000 Tax Table —Continued

Column headings used in all tables below:

If line 39 (taxable income) is —		And you are —			
At least	But less than	Single	Married filing jointly *	Married filing separately	Head of a household
		Your tax is —			

41,000

At least	But less than	Single	Married filing jointly	Married filing separately	Head of a household
41,000	41,050	8,075	6,154	8,637	6,918
41,050	41,100	8,089	6,161	8,651	6,932
41,100	41,150	8,103	6,169	8,665	6,946
41,150	41,200	8,117	6,176	8,679	6,960
41,200	41,250	8,131	6,184	8,693	6,974
41,250	41,300	8,145	6,191	8,707	6,988
41,300	41,350	8,159	6,199	8,721	7,002
41,350	41,400	8,173	6,206	8,735	7,016
41,400	41,450	8,187	6,214	8,749	7,030
41,450	41,500	8,201	6,221	8,763	7,044
41,500	41,550	8,215	6,229	8,777	7,058
41,550	41,600	8,229	6,236	8,791	7,072
41,600	41,650	8,243	6,244	8,805	7,086
41,650	41,700	8,257	6,251	8,819	7,100
41,700	41,750	8,271	6,259	8,833	7,114
41,750	41,800	8,285	6,266	8,847	7,128
41,800	41,850	8,299	6,274	8,861	7,142
41,850	41,900	8,313	6,281	8,875	7,156
41,900	41,950	8,327	6,289	8,889	7,170
41,950	42,000	8,341	6,296	8,903	7,184

42,000

At least	But less than	Single	Married filing jointly	Married filing separately	Head of a household
42,000	42,050	8,355	6,304	8,917	7,198
42,050	42,100	8,369	6,311	8,931	7,212
42,100	42,150	8,383	6,319	8,945	7,226
42,150	42,200	8,397	6,326	8,959	7,240
42,200	42,250	8,411	6,334	8,973	7,254
42,250	42,300	8,425	6,341	8,987	7,268
42,300	42,350	8,439	6,349	9,001	7,282
42,350	42,400	8,453	6,356	9,015	7,296
42,400	42,450	8,467	6,364	9,029	7,310
42,450	42,500	8,481	6,371	9,043	7,324
42,500	42,550	8,495	6,379	9,057	7,338
42,550	42,600	8,509	6,386	9,071	7,352
42,600	42,650	8,523	6,394	9,085	7,366
42,650	42,700	8,537	6,401	9,099	7,380
42,700	42,750	8,551	6,409	9,113	7,394
42,750	42,800	8,565	6,416	9,127	7,408
42,800	42,850	8,579	6,424	9,141	7,422
42,850	42,900	8,593	6,431	9,155	7,436
42,900	42,950	8,607	6,439	9,169	7,450
42,950	43,000	8,621	6,446	9,183	7,464

43,000

At least	But less than	Single	Married filing jointly	Married filing separately	Head of a household
43,000	43,050	8,635	6,454	9,197	7,478
43,050	43,100	8,649	6,461	9,211	7,492
43,100	43,150	8,663	6,469	9,225	7,506
43,150	43,200	8,677	6,476	9,239	7,520
43,200	43,250	8,691	6,484	9,253	7,534
43,250	43,300	8,705	6,491	9,267	7,548
43,300	43,350	8,719	6,499	9,281	7,562
43,350	43,400	8,733	6,506	9,295	7,576
43,400	43,450	8,747	6,514	9,309	7,590
43,450	43,500	8,761	6,521	9,323	7,604
43,500	43,550	8,775	6,529	9,337	7,618
43,550	43,600	8,789	6,536	9,351	7,632
43,600	43,650	8,803	6,544	9,365	7,646
43,650	43,700	8,817	6,551	9,379	7,660
43,700	43,750	8,831	6,559	9,393	7,674
43,750	43,800	8,845	6,566	9,407	7,688
43,800	43,850	8,859	6,574	9,421	7,702
43,850	43,900	8,873	6,585	9,435	7,716
43,900	43,950	8,887	6,599	9,449	7,730
43,950	44,000	8,901	6,613	9,463	7,744

44,000

At least	But less than	Single	Married filing jointly	Married filing separately	Head of a household
44,000	44,050	8,915	6,627	9,477	7,758
44,050	44,100	8,929	6,641	9,491	7,772
44,100	44,150	8,943	6,655	9,505	7,786
44,150	44,200	8,957	6,669	9,519	7,800
44,200	44,250	8,971	6,683	9,533	7,814
44,250	44,300	8,985	6,697	9,547	7,828
44,300	44,350	8,999	6,711	9,561	7,842
44,350	44,400	9,013	6,725	9,575	7,856
44,400	44,450	9,027	6,739	9,589	7,870
44,450	44,500	9,041	6,753	9,603	7,884
44,500	44,550	9,055	6,767	9,617	7,898
44,550	44,600	9,069	6,781	9,631	7,912
44,600	44,650	9,083	6,795	9,645	7,926
44,650	44,700	9,097	6,809	9,659	7,940
44,700	44,750	9,111	6,823	9,673	7,954
44,750	44,800	9,125	6,837	9,687	7,968
44,800	44,850	9,139	6,851	9,701	7,982
44,850	44,900	9,153	6,865	9,715	7,996
44,900	44,950	9,167	6,879	9,729	8,010
44,950	45,000	9,181	6,893	9,743	8,024

45,000

At least	But less than	Single	Married filing jointly	Married filing separately	Head of a household
45,000	45,050	9,195	6,907	9,757	8,038
45,050	45,100	9,209	6,921	9,771	8,052
45,100	45,150	9,223	6,935	9,785	8,066
45,150	45,200	9,237	6,949	9,799	8,080
45,200	45,250	9,251	6,963	9,813	8,094
45,250	45,300	9,265	6,977	9,827	8,108
45,300	45,350	9,279	6,991	9,841	8,122
45,350	45,400	9,293	7,005	9,855	8,136
45,400	45,450	9,307	7,019	9,869	8,150
45,450	45,500	9,321	7,033	9,883	8,164
45,500	45,550	9,335	7,047	9,897	8,178
45,550	45,600	9,349	7,061	9,911	8,192
45,600	45,650	9,363	7,075	9,925	8,206
45,650	45,700	9,377	7,089	9,939	8,220
45,700	45,750	9,391	7,103	9,953	8,234
45,750	45,800	9,405	7,117	9,967	8,248
45,800	45,850	9,419	7,131	9,981	8,262
45,850	45,900	9,433	7,145	9,995	8,276
45,900	45,950	9,447	7,159	10,009	8,290
45,950	46,000	9,461	7,173	10,023	8,304

46,000

At least	But less than	Single	Married filing jointly	Married filing separately	Head of a household
46,000	46,050	9,475	7,187	10,037	8,318
46,050	46,100	9,489	7,201	10,051	8,332
46,100	46,150	9,503	7,215	10,065	8,346
46,150	46,200	9,517	7,229	10,079	8,360
46,200	46,250	9,531	7,243	10,093	8,374
46,250	46,300	9,545	7,257	10,107	8,388
46,300	46,350	9,559	7,271	10,121	8,402
46,350	46,400	9,573	7,285	10,135	8,416
46,400	46,450	9,587	7,299	10,149	8,430
46,450	46,500	9,601	7,313	10,163	8,444
46,500	46,550	9,615	7,327	10,177	8,458
46,550	46,600	9,629	7,341	10,191	8,472
46,600	46,650	9,643	7,355	10,205	8,486
46,650	46,700	9,657	7,369	10,219	8,500
46,700	46,750	9,671	7,383	10,233	8,514
46,750	46,800	9,685	7,397	10,247	8,528
46,800	46,850	9,699	7,411	10,261	8,542
46,850	46,900	9,713	7,425	10,275	8,556
46,900	46,950	9,727	7,439	10,289	8,570
46,950	47,000	9,741	7,453	10,303	8,584

47,000

At least	But less than	Single	Married filing jointly	Married filing separately	Head of a household
47,000	47,050	9,755	7,467	10,317	8,598
47,050	47,100	9,769	7,481	10,331	8,612
47,100	47,150	9,783	7,495	10,345	8,626
47,150	47,200	9,797	7,509	10,359	8,640
47,200	47,250	9,811	7,523	10,373	8,654
47,250	47,300	9,825	7,537	10,387	8,668
47,300	47,350	9,839	7,551	10,401	8,682
47,350	47,400	9,853	7,565	10,415	8,696
47,400	47,450	9,867	7,579	10,429	8,710
47,450	47,500	9,881	7,593	10,443	8,724
47,500	47,550	9,895	7,607	10,457	8,738
47,550	47,600	9,909	7,621	10,471	8,752
47,600	47,650	9,923	7,635	10,485	8,766
47,650	47,700	9,937	7,649	10,499	8,780
47,700	47,750	9,951	7,663	10,513	8,794
47,750	47,800	9,965	7,677	10,527	8,808
47,800	47,850	9,979	7,691	10,541	8,822
47,850	47,900	9,993	7,705	10,555	8,836
47,900	47,950	10,007	7,719	10,569	8,850
47,950	48,000	10,021	7,733	10,583	8,864

48,000

At least	But less than	Single	Married filing jointly	Married filing separately	Head of a household
48,000	48,050	10,035	7,747	10,597	8,878
48,050	48,100	10,049	7,761	10,611	8,892
48,100	48,150	10,063	7,775	10,625	8,906
48,150	48,200	10,077	7,789	10,639	8,920
48,200	48,250	10,091	7,803	10,653	8,934
48,250	48,300	10,105	7,817	10,667	8,948
48,300	48,350	10,119	7,831	10,681	8,962
48,350	48,400	10,133	7,845	10,695	8,976
48,400	48,450	10,147	7,859	10,709	8,990
48,450	48,500	10,161	7,873	10,723	9,004
48,500	48,550	10,175	7,887	10,737	9,018
48,550	48,600	10,189	7,901	10,751	9,032
48,600	48,650	10,203	7,915	10,765	9,046
48,650	48,700	10,217	7,929	10,779	9,060
48,700	48,750	10,231	7,943	10,793	9,074
48,750	48,800	10,245	7,957	10,807	9,088
48,800	48,850	10,259	7,971	10,821	9,102
48,850	48,900	10,273	7,985	10,835	9,116
48,900	48,950	10,287	7,999	10,849	9,130
48,950	49,000	10,301	8,013	10,863	9,144

49,000

At least	But less than	Single	Married filing jointly	Married filing separately	Head of a household
49,000	49,050	10,315	8,027	10,877	9,158
49,050	49,100	10,329	8,041	10,891	9,172
49,100	49,150	10,343	8,055	10,905	9,186
49,150	49,200	10,357	8,069	10,919	9,200
49,200	49,250	10,371	8,083	10,933	9,214
49,250	49,300	10,385	8,097	10,947	9,228
49,300	49,350	10,399	8,111	10,961	9,242
49,350	49,400	10,413	8,125	10,975	9,256
49,400	49,450	10,427	8,139	10,989	9,270
49,450	49,500	10,441	8,153	11,003	9,284
49,500	49,550	10,455	8,167	11,017	9,298
49,550	49,600	10,469	8,181	11,031	9,312
49,600	49,650	10,483	8,195	11,045	9,326
49,650	49,700	10,497	8,209	11,059	9,340
49,700	49,750	10,511	8,223	11,073	9,354
49,750	49,800	10,525	8,237	11,087	9,368
49,800	49,850	10,539	8,251	11,101	9,382
49,850	49,900	10,553	8,265	11,115	9,396
49,900	49,950	10,567	8,279	11,129	9,410
49,950	50,000	10,581	8,293	11,143	9,424

* This column must also be used by a qualifying widow(er).

(Continued on next page)

2000 Tax Table —*Continued*

If line 39 (taxable income) is —		And you are —				If line 39 (taxable income) is —		And you are —				If line 39 (taxable income) is —		And you are —			
At least	But less than	Single	Married filing jointly *	Married filing separately	Head of a house-hold	At least	But less than	Single	Married filing jointly *	Married filing separately	Head of a house-hold	At least	But less than	Single	Married filing jointly *	Married filing separately	Head of a house-hold
		Your tax is —						Your tax is —						Your tax is —			
50,000						**53,000**						**56,000**					
50,000	50,050	10,595	8,307	11,157	9,438	53,000	53,050	11,435	9,147	11,998	10,278	56,000	56,050	12,275	9,987	12,928	11,118
50,050	50,100	10,609	8,321	11,171	9,452	53,050	53,100	11,449	9,161	12,014	10,292	56,050	56,100	12,289	10,001	12,944	11,132
50,100	50,150	10,623	8,335	11,185	9,466	53,100	53,150	11,463	9,175	12,029	10,306	56,100	56,150	12,303	10,015	12,959	11,146
50,150	50,200	10,637	8,349	11,199	9,480	53,150	53,200	11,477	9,189	12,045	10,320	56,150	56,200	12,317	10,029	12,975	11,160
50,200	50,250	10,651	8,363	11,213	9,494	53,200	53,250	11,491	9,203	12,060	10,334	56,200	56,250	12,331	10,043	12,990	11,174
50,250	50,300	10,665	8,377	11,227	9,508	53,250	53,300	11,505	9,217	12,076	10,348	56,250	56,300	12,345	10,057	13,006	11,188
50,300	50,350	10,679	8,391	11,241	9,522	53,300	53,350	11,519	9,231	12,091	10,362	56,300	56,350	12,359	10,071	13,021	11,202
50,350	50,400	10,693	8,405	11,255	9,536	53,350	53,400	11,533	9,245	12,107	10,376	56,350	56,400	12,373	10,085	13,037	11,216
50,400	50,450	10,707	8,419	11,269	9,550	53,400	53,450	11,547	9,259	12,122	10,390	56,400	56,450	12,387	10,099	13,052	11,230
50,450	50,500	10,721	8,433	11,283	9,564	53,450	53,500	11,561	9,273	12,138	10,404	56,450	56,500	12,401	10,113	13,068	11,244
50,500	50,550	10,735	8,447	11,297	9,578	53,500	53,550	11,575	9,287	12,153	10,418	56,500	56,550	12,415	10,127	13,083	11,258
50,550	50,600	10,749	8,461	11,311	9,592	53,550	53,600	11,589	9,301	12,169	10,432	56,550	56,600	12,429	10,141	13,099	11,272
50,600	50,650	10,763	8,475	11,325	9,606	53,600	53,650	11,603	9,315	12,184	10,446	56,600	56,650	12,443	10,155	13,114	11,286
50,650	50,700	10,777	8,489	11,339	9,620	53,650	53,700	11,617	9,329	12,200	10,460	56,650	56,700	12,457	10,169	13,130	11,300
50,700	50,750	10,791	8,503	11,353	9,634	53,700	53,750	11,631	9,343	12,215	10,474	56,700	56,750	12,471	10,183	13,145	11,314
50,750	50,800	10,805	8,517	11,367	9,648	53,750	53,800	11,645	9,357	12,231	10,488	56,750	56,800	12,485	10,197	13,161	11,328
50,800	50,850	10,819	8,531	11,381	9,662	53,800	53,850	11,659	9,371	12,246	10,502	56,800	56,850	12,499	10,211	13,176	11,342
50,850	50,900	10,833	8,545	11,395	9,676	53,850	53,900	11,673	9,385	12,262	10,516	56,850	56,900	12,513	10,225	13,192	11,356
50,900	50,950	10,847	8,559	11,409	9,690	53,900	53,950	11,687	9,399	12,277	10,530	56,900	56,950	12,527	10,239	13,207	11,370
50,950	51,000	10,861	8,573	11,423	9,704	53,950	54,000	11,701	9,413	12,293	10,544	56,950	57,000	12,541	10,253	13,223	11,384
51,000						**54,000**						**57,000**					
51,000	51,050	10,875	8,587	11,437	9,718	54,000	54,050	11,715	9,427	12,308	10,558	57,000	57,050	12,555	10,267	13,238	11,398
51,050	51,100	10,889	8,601	11,451	9,732	54,050	54,100	11,729	9,441	12,324	10,572	57,050	57,100	12,569	10,281	13,254	11,412
51,100	51,150	10,903	8,615	11,465	9,746	54,100	54,150	11,743	9,455	12,339	10,586	57,100	57,150	12,583	10,295	13,269	11,426
51,150	51,200	10,917	8,629	11,479	9,760	54,150	54,200	11,757	9,469	12,355	10,600	57,150	57,200	12,597	10,309	13,285	11,440
51,200	51,250	10,931	8,643	11,493	9,774	54,200	54,250	11,771	9,483	12,370	10,614	57,200	57,250	12,611	10,323	13,300	11,454
51,250	51,300	10,945	8,657	11,507	9,788	54,250	54,300	11,785	9,497	12,386	10,628	57,250	57,300	12,625	10,337	13,316	11,468
51,300	51,350	10,959	8,671	11,521	9,802	54,300	54,350	11,799	9,511	12,401	10,642	57,300	57,350	12,639	10,351	13,331	11,482
51,350	51,400	10,973	8,685	11,535	9,816	54,350	54,400	11,813	9,525	12,417	10,656	57,350	57,400	12,653	10,365	13,347	11,496
51,400	51,450	10,987	8,699	11,549	9,830	54,400	54,450	11,827	9,539	12,432	10,670	57,400	57,450	12,667	10,379	13,362	11,510
51,450	51,500	11,001	8,713	11,563	9,844	54,450	54,500	11,841	9,553	12,448	10,684	57,450	57,500	12,681	10,393	13,378	11,524
51,500	51,550	11,015	8,727	11,577	9,858	54,500	54,550	11,855	9,567	12,463	10,698	57,500	57,550	12,695	10,407	13,393	11,538
51,550	51,600	11,029	8,741	11,591	9,872	54,550	54,600	11,869	9,581	12,479	10,712	57,550	57,600	12,709	10,421	13,409	11,552
51,600	51,650	11,043	8,755	11,605	9,886	54,600	54,650	11,883	9,595	12,494	10,726	57,600	57,650	12,723	10,435	13,424	11,566
51,650	51,700	11,057	8,769	11,619	9,900	54,650	54,700	11,897	9,609	12,510	10,740	57,650	57,700	12,737	10,449	13,440	11,580
51,700	51,750	11,071	8,783	11,633	9,914	54,700	54,750	11,911	9,623	12,525	10,754	57,700	57,750	12,751	10,463	13,455	11,594
51,750	51,800	11,085	8,797	11,647	9,928	54,750	54,800	11,925	9,637	12,541	10,768	57,750	57,800	12,765	10,477	13,471	11,608
51,800	51,850	11,099	8,811	11,661	9,942	54,800	54,850	11,939	9,651	12,556	10,782	57,800	57,850	12,779	10,491	13,486	11,622
51,850	51,900	11,113	8,825	11,675	9,956	54,850	54,900	11,953	9,665	12,572	10,796	57,850	57,900	12,793	10,505	13,502	11,636
51,900	51,950	11,127	8,839	11,689	9,970	54,900	54,950	11,967	9,679	12,587	10,810	57,900	57,950	12,807	10,519	13,517	11,650
51,950	52,000	11,141	8,853	11,703	9,984	54,950	55,000	11,981	9,693	12,603	10,824	57,950	58,000	12,821	10,533	13,533	11,664
52,000						**55,000**						**58,000**					
52,000	52,050	11,155	8,867	11,717	9,998	55,000	55,050	11,995	9,707	12,618	10,838	58,000	58,050	12,835	10,547	13,548	11,678
52,050	52,100	11,169	8,881	11,731	10,012	55,050	55,100	12,009	9,721	12,634	10,852	58,050	58,100	12,849	10,561	13,564	11,692
52,100	52,150	11,183	8,895	11,745	10,026	55,100	55,150	12,023	9,735	12,649	10,866	58,100	58,150	12,863	10,575	13,579	11,706
52,150	52,200	11,197	8,909	11,759	10,040	55,150	55,200	12,037	9,749	12,665	10,880	58,150	58,200	12,877	10,589	13,595	11,720
52,200	52,250	11,211	8,923	11,773	10,054	55,200	55,250	12,051	9,763	12,680	10,894	58,200	58,250	12,891	10,603	13,610	11,734
52,250	52,300	11,225	8,937	11,787	10,068	55,250	55,300	12,065	9,777	12,696	10,908	58,250	58,300	12,905	10,617	13,626	11,748
52,300	52,350	11,239	8,951	11,801	10,082	55,300	55,350	12,079	9,791	12,711	10,922	58,300	58,350	12,919	10,631	13,641	11,762
52,350	52,400	11,253	8,965	11,815	10,096	55,350	55,400	12,093	9,805	12,727	10,936	58,350	58,400	12,933	10,645	13,657	11,776
52,400	52,450	11,267	8,979	11,829	10,110	55,400	55,450	12,107	9,819	12,742	10,950	58,400	58,450	12,947	10,659	13,672	11,790
52,450	52,500	11,281	8,993	11,843	10,124	55,450	55,500	12,121	9,833	12,758	10,964	58,450	58,500	12,961	10,673	13,688	11,804
52,500	52,550	11,295	9,007	11,857	10,138	55,500	55,550	12,135	9,847	12,773	10,978	58,500	58,550	12,975	10,687	13,703	11,818
52,550	52,600	11,309	9,021	11,871	10,152	55,550	55,600	12,149	9,861	12,789	10,992	58,550	58,600	12,989	10,701	13,719	11,832
52,600	52,650	11,323	9,035	11,885	10,166	55,600	55,650	12,163	9,875	12,804	11,006	58,600	58,650	13,003	10,715	13,734	11,846
52,650	52,700	11,337	9,049	11,899	10,180	55,650	55,700	12,177	9,889	12,820	11,020	58,650	58,700	13,017	10,729	13,749	11,860
52,700	52,750	11,351	9,063	11,913	10,194	55,700	55,750	12,191	9,903	12,835	11,034	58,700	58,750	13,031	10,743	13,765	11,874
52,750	52,800	11,365	9,077	11,927	10,208	55,750	55,800	12,205	9,917	12,851	11,048	58,750	58,800	13,045	10,757	13,781	11,888
52,800	52,850	11,379	9,091	11,941	10,222	55,800	55,850	12,219	9,931	12,866	11,062	58,800	58,850	13,059	10,771	13,796	11,902
52,850	52,900	11,393	9,105	11,955	10,236	55,850	55,900	12,233	9,945	12,882	11,076	58,850	58,900	13,073	10,785	13,812	11,916
52,900	52,950	11,407	9,119	11,969	10,250	55,900	55,950	12,247	9,959	12,897	11,090	58,900	58,950	13,087	10,799	13,827	11,930
52,950	53,000	11,421	9,133	11,983	10,264	55,950	56,000	12,261	9,973	12,913	11,104	58,950	59,000	13,101	10,813	13,843	11,944

* This column must also be used by a qualifying widow(er).

(Continued on next page)

2000 Tax Table—Continued

If line 39 (taxable income) is — At least	But less than	Single	Married filing jointly *	Married filing separately	Head of a household
59,000					
59,000	59,050	13,115	10,827	13,858	11,958
59,050	59,100	13,129	10,841	13,874	11,972
59,100	59,150	13,143	10,855	13,889	11,986
59,150	59,200	13,157	10,869	13,905	12,000
59,200	59,250	13,171	10,883	13,920	12,014
59,250	59,300	13,185	10,897	13,936	12,028
59,300	59,350	13,199	10,911	13,951	12,042
59,350	59,400	13,213	10,925	13,967	12,056
59,400	59,450	13,227	10,939	13,982	12,070
59,450	59,500	13,241	10,953	13,998	12,084
59,500	59,550	13,255	10,967	14,013	12,098
59,550	59,600	13,269	10,981	14,029	12,112
59,600	59,650	13,283	10,995	14,044	12,126
59,650	59,700	13,297	11,009	14,060	12,140
59,700	59,750	13,311	11,023	14,075	12,154
59,750	59,800	13,325	11,037	14,091	12,168
59,800	59,850	13,339	11,051	14,106	12,182
59,850	59,900	13,353	11,065	14,122	12,196
59,900	59,950	13,367	11,079	14,137	12,210
59,950	60,000	13,381	11,093	14,153	12,224
60,000					
60,000	60,050	13,395	11,107	14,168	12,238
60,050	60,100	13,409	11,121	14,184	12,252
60,100	60,150	13,423	11,135	14,199	12,266
60,150	60,200	13,437	11,149	14,215	12,280
60,200	60,250	13,451	11,163	14,230	12,294
60,250	60,300	13,465	11,177	14,246	12,308
60,300	60,350	13,479	11,191	14,261	12,322
60,350	60,400	13,493	11,205	14,277	12,336
60,400	60,450	13,507	11,219	14,292	12,350
60,450	60,500	13,521	11,233	14,308	12,364
60,500	60,550	13,535	11,247	14,323	12,378
60,550	60,600	13,549	11,261	14,339	12,392
60,600	60,650	13,563	11,275	14,354	12,406
60,650	60,700	13,577	11,289	14,370	12,420
60,700	60,750	13,591	11,303	14,385	12,434
60,750	60,800	13,605	11,317	14,401	12,448
60,800	60,850	13,619	11,331	14,416	12,462
60,850	60,900	13,633	11,345	14,432	12,476
60,900	60,950	13,647	11,359	14,447	12,490
60,950	61,000	13,661	11,373	14,463	12,504
61,000					
61,000	61,050	13,675	11,387	14,478	12,518
61,050	61,100	13,689	11,401	14,494	12,532
61,100	61,150	13,703	11,415	14,509	12,546
61,150	61,200	13,717	11,429	14,525	12,560
61,200	61,250	13,731	11,443	14,540	12,574
61,250	61,300	13,745	11,457	14,556	12,588
61,300	61,350	13,759	11,471	14,571	12,602
61,350	61,400	13,773	11,485	14,587	12,616
61,400	61,450	13,787	11,499	14,602	12,630
61,450	61,500	13,801	11,513	14,618	12,644
61,500	61,550	13,815	11,527	14,633	12,658
61,550	61,600	13,829	11,541	14,649	12,672
61,600	61,650	13,843	11,555	14,664	12,686
61,650	61,700	13,857	11,569	14,680	12,700
61,700	61,750	13,871	11,583	14,695	12,714
61,750	61,800	13,885	11,597	14,711	12,728
61,800	61,850	13,899	11,611	14,726	12,742
61,850	61,900	13,913	11,625	14,742	12,756
61,900	61,950	13,927	11,639	14,757	12,770
61,950	62,000	13,941	11,653	14,773	12,784
62,000					
62,000	62,050	13,955	11,667	14,788	12,798
62,050	62,100	13,969	11,681	14,804	12,812
62,100	62,150	13,983	11,695	14,819	12,826
62,150	62,200	13,997	11,709	14,835	12,840
62,200	62,250	14,011	11,723	14,850	12,854
62,250	62,300	14,025	11,737	14,866	12,868
62,300	62,350	14,039	11,751	14,881	12,882
62,350	62,400	14,053	11,765	14,897	12,896
62,400	62,450	14,067	11,779	14,912	12,910
62,450	62,500	14,081	11,793	14,928	12,924
62,500	62,550	14,095	11,807	14,943	12,938
62,550	62,600	14,109	11,821	14,959	12,952
62,600	62,650	14,123	11,835	14,974	12,966
62,650	62,700	14,137	11,849	14,990	12,980
62,700	62,750	14,151	11,863	15,005	12,994
62,750	62,800	14,165	11,877	15,021	13,008
62,800	62,850	14,179	11,891	15,036	13,022
62,850	62,900	14,193	11,905	15,052	13,036
62,900	62,950	14,207	11,919	15,067	13,050
62,950	63,000	14,221	11,933	15,083	13,064
63,000					
63,000	63,050	14,235	11,947	15,098	13,078
63,050	63,100	14,249	11,961	15,114	13,092
63,100	63,150	14,263	11,975	15,129	13,106
63,150	63,200	14,277	11,989	15,145	13,120
63,200	63,250	14,291	12,003	15,160	13,134
63,250	63,300	14,305	12,017	15,176	13,148
63,300	63,350	14,319	12,031	15,191	13,162
63,350	63,400	14,333	12,045	15,207	13,176
63,400	63,450	14,347	12,059	15,222	13,190
63,450	63,500	14,361	12,073	15,238	13,204
63,500	63,550	14,375	12,087	15,253	13,218
63,550	63,600	14,389	12,101	15,269	13,232
63,600	63,650	14,405	12,115	15,284	13,246
63,650	63,700	14,420	12,129	15,300	13,260
63,700	63,750	14,436	12,143	15,315	13,274
63,750	63,800	14,451	12,157	15,331	13,288
63,800	63,850	14,467	12,171	15,346	13,302
63,850	63,900	14,482	12,185	15,362	13,316
63,900	63,950	14,498	12,199	15,377	13,330
63,950	64,000	14,513	12,213	15,393	13,344
64,000					
64,000	64,050	14,529	12,227	15,408	13,358
64,050	64,100	14,544	12,241	15,424	13,372
64,100	64,150	14,560	12,255	15,439	13,386
64,150	64,200	14,575	12,269	15,455	13,400
64,200	64,250	14,591	12,283	15,470	13,414
64,250	64,300	14,606	12,297	15,486	13,428
64,300	64,350	14,622	12,311	15,501	13,442
64,350	64,400	14,637	12,325	15,517	13,456
64,400	64,450	14,653	12,339	15,532	13,470
64,450	64,500	14,668	12,353	15,548	13,484
64,500	64,550	14,684	12,367	15,563	13,498
64,550	64,600	14,699	12,381	15,579	13,512
64,600	64,650	14,715	12,395	15,594	13,526
64,650	64,700	14,730	12,409	15,610	13,540
64,700	64,750	14,746	12,423	15,625	13,554
64,750	64,800	14,761	12,437	15,641	13,568
64,800	64,850	14,777	12,451	15,656	13,582
64,850	64,900	14,792	12,465	15,672	13,596
64,900	64,950	14,808	12,479	15,687	13,610
64,950	65,000	14,823	12,493	15,703	13,624
65,000					
65,000	65,050	14,839	12,507	15,718	13,638
65,050	65,100	14,854	12,521	15,734	13,652
65,100	65,150	14,870	12,535	15,749	13,666
65,150	65,200	14,885	12,549	15,765	13,680
65,200	65,250	14,901	12,563	15,780	13,694
65,250	65,300	14,916	12,577	15,796	13,708
65,300	65,350	14,932	12,591	15,811	13,722
65,350	65,400	14,947	12,605	15,827	13,736
65,400	65,450	14,963	12,619	15,842	13,750
65,450	65,500	14,978	12,633	15,858	13,764
65,500	65,550	14,994	12,647	15,873	13,778
65,550	65,600	15,009	12,661	15,889	13,792
65,600	65,650	15,025	12,675	15,904	13,806
65,650	65,700	15,040	12,689	15,920	13,820
65,700	65,750	15,056	12,703	15,935	13,834
65,750	65,800	15,071	12,717	15,951	13,848
65,800	65,850	15,087	12,731	15,966	13,862
65,850	65,900	15,102	12,745	15,982	13,876
65,900	65,950	15,118	12,759	15,997	13,890
65,950	66,000	15,133	12,773	16,013	13,904
66,000					
66,000	66,050	15,149	12,787	16,028	13,918
66,050	66,100	15,164	12,801	16,044	13,932
66,100	66,150	15,180	12,815	16,059	13,946
66,150	66,200	15,195	12,829	16,075	13,960
66,200	66,250	15,211	12,843	16,090	13,974
66,250	66,300	15,226	12,857	16,106	13,988
66,300	66,350	15,242	12,871	16,121	14,002
66,350	66,400	15,257	12,885	16,137	14,016
66,400	66,450	15,273	12,899	16,152	14,030
66,450	66,500	15,288	12,913	16,168	14,044
66,500	66,550	15,304	12,927	16,183	14,058
66,550	66,600	15,319	12,941	16,199	14,072
66,600	66,650	15,335	12,955	16,214	14,086
66,650	66,700	15,350	12,969	16,230	14,100
66,700	66,750	15,366	12,983	16,245	14,114
66,750	66,800	15,381	12,997	16,261	14,128
66,800	66,850	15,397	13,011	16,276	14,142
66,850	66,900	15,412	13,025	16,292	14,156
66,900	66,950	15,428	13,039	16,307	14,170
66,950	67,000	15,443	13,053	16,323	14,184
67,000					
67,000	67,050	15,459	13,067	16,338	14,198
67,050	67,100	15,474	13,081	16,354	14,212
67,100	67,150	15,490	13,095	16,369	14,226
67,150	67,200	15,505	13,109	16,385	14,240
67,200	67,250	15,521	13,123	16,400	14,254
67,250	67,300	15,536	13,137	16,416	14,268
67,300	67,350	15,552	13,151	16,431	14,282
67,350	67,400	15,567	13,165	16,447	14,296
67,400	67,450	15,583	13,179	16,462	14,310
67,450	67,500	15,598	13,193	16,478	14,324
67,500	67,550	15,614	13,207	16,493	14,338
67,550	67,600	15,629	13,221	16,509	14,352
67,600	67,650	15,645	13,235	16,524	14,366
67,650	67,700	15,660	13,249	16,540	14,380
67,700	67,750	15,676	13,263	16,555	14,394
67,750	67,800	15,691	13,277	16,571	14,408
67,800	67,850	15,707	13,291	16,586	14,422
67,850	67,900	15,722	13,305	16,602	14,436
67,900	67,950	15,738	13,319	16,617	14,450
67,950	68,000	15,753	13,333	16,633	14,464

* This column must also be used by a qualifying widow(er).

(Continued on next page)

2000 Tax Table —*Continued*

If line 39 (taxable income) is — At least	But less than	Single	Married filing jointly *	Married filing separately	Head of a household
68,000					
68,000	68,050	15,769	13,347	16,648	14,478
68,050	68,100	15,784	13,361	16,664	14,492
68,100	68,150	15,800	13,375	16,679	14,506
68,150	68,200	15,815	13,389	16,695	14,520
68,200	68,250	15,831	13,403	16,710	14,534
68,250	68,300	15,846	13,417	16,726	14,548
68,300	68,350	15,862	13,431	16,741	14,562
68,350	68,400	15,877	13,445	16,757	14,576
68,400	68,450	15,893	13,459	16,772	14,590
68,450	68,500	15,908	13,473	16,788	14,604
68,500	68,550	15,924	13,487	16,803	14,618
68,550	68,600	15,939	13,501	16,819	14,632
68,600	68,650	15,955	13,515	16,834	14,646
68,650	68,700	15,970	13,529	16,850	14,660
68,700	68,750	15,986	13,543	16,865	14,674
68,750	68,800	16,001	13,557	16,881	14,688
68,800	68,850	16,017	13,571	16,896	14,702
68,850	68,900	16,032	13,585	16,912	14,716
68,900	68,950	16,048	13,599	16,927	14,730
68,950	69,000	16,063	13,613	16,943	14,744
69,000					
69,000	69,050	16,079	13,627	16,958	14,758
69,050	69,100	16,094	13,641	16,974	14,772
69,100	69,150	16,110	13,655	16,989	14,786
69,150	69,200	16,125	13,669	17,005	14,800
69,200	69,250	16,141	13,683	17,020	14,814
69,250	69,300	16,156	13,697	17,036	14,828
69,300	69,350	16,172	13,711	17,051	14,842
69,350	69,400	16,187	13,725	17,067	14,856
69,400	69,450	16,203	13,739	17,082	14,870
69,450	69,500	16,218	13,753	17,098	14,884
69,500	69,550	16,234	13,767	17,113	14,898
69,550	69,600	16,249	13,781	17,129	14,912
69,600	69,650	16,265	13,795	17,144	14,926
69,650	69,700	16,280	13,809	17,160	14,940
69,700	69,750	16,296	13,823	17,175	14,954
69,750	69,800	16,311	13,837	17,191	14,968
69,800	69,850	16,327	13,851	17,206	14,982
69,850	69,900	16,342	13,865	17,222	14,996
69,900	69,950	16,358	13,879	17,237	15,010
69,950	70,000	16,373	13,893	17,253	15,024
70,000					
70,000	70,050	16,389	13,907	17,268	15,038
70,050	70,100	16,404	13,921	17,284	15,052
70,100	70,150	16,420	13,935	17,299	15,066
70,150	70,200	16,435	13,949	17,315	15,080
70,200	70,250	16,451	13,963	17,330	15,094
70,250	70,300	16,466	13,977	17,346	15,108
70,300	70,350	16,482	13,991	17,361	15,122
70,350	70,400	16,497	14,005	17,377	15,136
70,400	70,450	16,513	14,019	17,392	15,150
70,450	70,500	16,528	14,033	17,408	15,164
70,500	70,550	16,544	14,047	17,423	15,178
70,550	70,600	16,559	14,061	17,439	15,192
70,600	70,650	16,575	14,075	17,454	15,206
70,650	70,700	16,590	14,089	17,470	15,220
70,700	70,750	16,606	14,103	17,485	15,234
70,750	70,800	16,621	14,117	17,501	15,248
70,800	70,850	16,637	14,131	17,516	15,262
70,850	70,900	16,652	14,145	17,532	15,276
70,900	70,950	16,668	14,159	17,547	15,290
70,950	71,000	16,683	14,173	17,563	15,304

If line 39 (taxable income) is — At least	But less than	Single	Married filing jointly *	Married filing separately	Head of a household
71,000					
71,000	71,050	16,699	14,187	17,578	15,318
71,050	71,100	16,714	14,201	17,594	15,332
71,100	71,150	16,730	14,215	17,609	15,346
71,150	71,200	16,745	14,229	17,625	15,360
71,200	71,250	16,761	14,243	17,640	15,374
71,250	71,300	16,776	14,257	17,656	15,388
71,300	71,350	16,792	14,271	17,671	15,402
71,350	71,400	16,807	14,285	17,687	15,416
71,400	71,450	16,823	14,299	17,702	15,430
71,450	71,500	16,838	14,313	17,718	15,444
71,500	71,550	16,854	14,327	17,733	15,458
71,550	71,600	16,869	14,341	17,749	15,472
71,600	71,650	16,885	14,355	17,764	15,486
71,650	71,700	16,900	14,369	17,780	15,500
71,700	71,750	16,916	14,383	17,795	15,514
71,750	71,800	16,931	14,397	17,811	15,528
71,800	71,850	16,947	14,411	17,826	15,542
71,850	71,900	16,962	14,425	17,842	15,556
71,900	71,950	16,978	14,439	17,857	15,570
71,950	72,000	16,993	14,453	17,873	15,584
72,000					
72,000	72,050	17,009	14,467	17,888	15,598
72,050	72,100	17,024	14,481	17,904	15,612
72,100	72,150	17,040	14,495	17,919	15,626
72,150	72,200	17,055	14,509	17,935	15,640
72,200	72,250	17,071	14,523	17,950	15,654
72,250	72,300	17,086	14,537	17,966	15,668
72,300	72,350	17,102	14,551	17,981	15,682
72,350	72,400	17,117	14,565	17,997	15,696
72,400	72,450	17,133	14,579	18,012	15,710
72,450	72,500	17,148	14,593	18,028	15,724
72,500	72,550	17,164	14,607	18,043	15,738
72,550	72,600	17,179	14,621	18,059	15,752
72,600	72,650	17,195	14,635	18,074	15,766
72,650	72,700	17,210	14,649	18,090	15,780
72,700	72,750	17,226	14,663	18,105	15,794
72,750	72,800	17,241	14,677	18,121	15,808
72,800	72,850	17,257	14,691	18,136	15,822
72,850	72,900	17,272	14,705	18,152	15,836
72,900	72,950	17,288	14,719	18,167	15,850
72,950	73,000	17,303	14,733	18,183	15,864
73,000					
73,000	73,050	17,319	14,747	18,198	15,878
73,050	73,100	17,334	14,761	18,214	15,892
73,100	73,150	17,350	14,775	18,229	15,906
73,150	73,200	17,365	14,789	18,245	15,920
73,200	73,250	17,381	14,803	18,260	15,934
73,250	73,300	17,396	14,817	18,276	15,948
73,300	73,350	17,412	14,831	18,291	15,962
73,350	73,400	17,427	14,845	18,307	15,976
73,400	73,450	17,443	14,859	18,322	15,990
73,450	73,500	17,458	14,873	18,338	16,004
73,500	73,550	17,474	14,887	18,353	16,018
73,550	73,600	17,489	14,901	18,369	16,032
73,600	73,650	17,505	14,915	18,384	16,046
73,650	73,700	17,520	14,929	18,400	16,060
73,700	73,750	17,536	14,943	18,415	16,074
73,750	73,800	17,551	14,957	18,431	16,088
73,800	73,850	17,567	14,971	18,446	16,102
73,850	73,900	17,582	14,985	18,462	16,116
73,900	73,950	17,598	14,999	18,477	16,130
73,950	74,000	17,613	15,013	18,493	16,144

If line 39 (taxable income) is — At least	But less than	Single	Married filing jointly *	Married filing separately	Head of a household
74,000					
74,000	74,050	17,629	15,027	18,508	16,158
74,050	74,100	17,644	15,041	18,524	16,172
74,100	74,150	17,660	15,055	18,539	16,186
74,150	74,200	17,675	15,069	18,555	16,200
74,200	74,250	17,691	15,083	18,570	16,214
74,250	74,300	17,706	15,097	18,586	16,228
74,300	74,350	17,722	15,111	18,601	16,242
74,350	74,400	17,737	15,125	18,617	16,256
74,400	74,450	17,753	15,139	18,632	16,270
74,450	74,500	17,768	15,153	18,648	16,284
74,500	74,550	17,784	15,167	18,663	16,298
74,550	74,600	17,799	15,181	18,679	16,312
74,600	74,650	17,815	15,195	18,694	16,326
74,650	74,700	17,830	15,209	18,710	16,340
74,700	74,750	17,846	15,223	18,725	16,354
74,750	74,800	17,861	15,237	18,741	16,368
74,800	74,850	17,877	15,251	18,756	16,382
74,850	74,900	17,892	15,265	18,772	16,396
74,900	74,950	17,908	15,279	18,787	16,410
74,950	75,000	17,923	15,293	18,803	16,424
75,000					
75,000	75,050	17,939	15,307	18,818	16,438
75,050	75,100	17,954	15,321	18,834	16,452
75,100	75,150	17,970	15,335	18,849	16,466
75,150	75,200	17,985	15,349	18,865	16,480
75,200	75,250	18,001	15,363	18,880	16,494
75,250	75,300	18,016	15,377	18,896	16,508
75,300	75,350	18,032	15,391	18,911	16,522
75,350	75,400	18,047	15,405	18,927	16,536
75,400	75,450	18,063	15,419	18,942	16,550
75,450	75,500	18,078	15,433	18,958	16,564
75,500	75,550	18,094	15,447	18,973	16,578
75,550	75,600	18,109	15,461	18,989	16,592
75,600	75,650	18,125	15,475	19,004	16,606
75,650	75,700	18,140	15,489	19,020	16,620
75,700	75,750	18,156	15,503	19,035	16,634
75,750	75,800	18,171	15,517	19,051	16,648
75,800	75,850	18,187	15,531	19,066	16,662
75,850	75,900	18,202	15,545	19,082	16,676
75,900	75,950	18,218	15,559	19,097	16,690
75,950	76,000	18,233	15,573	19,113	16,704
76,000					
76,000	76,050	18,249	15,587	19,128	16,718
76,050	76,100	18,264	15,601	19,144	16,732
76,100	76,150	18,280	15,615	19,159	16,746
76,150	76,200	18,295	15,629	19,175	16,760
76,200	76,250	18,311	15,643	19,190	16,774
76,250	76,300	18,326	15,657	19,206	16,788
76,300	76,350	18,342	15,671	19,221	16,802
76,350	76,400	18,357	15,685	19,237	16,816
76,400	76,450	18,373	15,699	19,252	16,830
76,450	76,500	18,388	15,713	19,268	16,844
76,500	76,550	18,404	15,727	19,283	16,858
76,550	76,600	18,419	15,741	19,299	16,872
76,600	76,650	18,435	15,755	19,314	16,886
76,650	76,700	18,450	15,769	19,330	16,900
76,700	76,750	18,466	15,783	19,345	16,914
76,750	76,800	18,481	15,797	19,361	16,928
76,800	76,850	18,497	15,811	19,376	16,942
76,850	76,900	18,512	15,825	19,392	16,956
76,900	76,950	18,528	15,839	19,407	16,970
76,950	77,000	18,543	15,853	19,423	16,984

* This column must also be used by a qualifying widow(er).

(Continued on next page)

2000 Tax Table—*Continued*

77,000 / 80,000 / 83,000

At least	But less than	Single	Married filing jointly *	Married filing separately	Head of a household	At least	But less than	Single	Married filing jointly *	Married filing separately	Head of a household	At least	But less than	Single	Married filing jointly *	Married filing separately	Head of a household
77,000						**80,000**						**83,000**					
77,000	77,050	18,559	15,867	19,438	16,998	80,000	80,050	19,489	16,707	20,368	17,838	83,000	83,050	20,419	17,547	21,413	18,678
77,050	77,100	18,574	15,881	19,454	17,012	80,050	80,100	19,504	16,721	20,384	17,852	83,050	83,100	20,434	17,561	21,431	18,692
77,100	77,150	18,590	15,895	19,469	17,026	80,100	80,150	19,520	16,735	20,399	17,866	83,100	83,150	20,450	17,575	21,449	18,706
77,150	77,200	18,605	15,909	19,485	17,040	80,150	80,200	19,535	16,749	20,415	17,880	83,150	83,200	20,465	17,589	21,467	18,720
77,200	77,250	18,621	15,923	19,500	17,054	80,200	80,250	19,551	16,763	20,430	17,894	83,200	83,250	20,481	17,603	21,485	18,734
77,250	77,300	18,636	15,937	19,516	17,068	80,250	80,300	19,566	16,777	20,446	17,908	83,250	83,300	20,496	17,617	21,503	18,748
77,300	77,350	18,652	15,951	19,531	17,082	80,300	80,350	19,582	16,791	20,461	17,922	83,300	83,350	20,512	17,631	21,521	18,762
77,350	77,400	18,667	15,965	19,547	17,096	80,350	80,400	19,597	16,805	20,477	17,936	83,350	83,400	20,527	17,645	21,539	18,776
77,400	77,450	18,683	15,979	19,562	17,110	80,400	80,450	19,613	16,819	20,492	17,950	83,400	83,450	20,543	17,659	21,557	18,790
77,450	77,500	18,698	15,993	19,578	17,124	80,450	80,500	19,628	16,833	20,508	17,964	83,450	83,500	20,558	17,673	21,575	18,804
77,500	77,550	18,714	16,007	19,593	17,138	80,500	80,550	19,644	16,847	20,523	17,978	83,500	83,550	20,574	17,687	21,593	18,818
77,550	77,600	18,729	16,021	19,609	17,152	80,550	80,600	19,659	16,861	20,539	17,992	83,550	83,600	20,589	17,701	21,611	18,832
77,600	77,650	18,745	16,035	19,624	17,166	80,600	80,650	19,675	16,875	20,554	18,006	83,600	83,650	20,605	17,715	21,629	18,846
77,650	77,700	18,760	16,049	19,640	17,180	80,650	80,700	19,690	16,889	20,570	18,020	83,650	83,700	20,620	17,729	21,647	18,860
77,700	77,750	18,776	16,063	19,655	17,194	80,700	80,750	19,706	16,903	20,585	18,034	83,700	83,750	20,636	17,743	21,665	18,874
77,750	77,800	18,791	16,077	19,671	17,208	80,750	80,800	19,721	16,917	20,603	18,048	83,750	83,800	20,651	17,757	21,683	18,888
77,800	77,850	18,807	16,091	19,686	17,222	80,800	80,850	19,737	16,931	20,621	18,062	83,800	83,850	20,667	17,771	21,701	18,902
77,850	77,900	18,822	16,105	19,702	17,236	80,850	80,900	19,752	16,945	20,639	18,076	83,850	83,900	20,682	17,785	21,719	18,916
77,900	77,950	18,838	16,119	19,717	17,250	80,900	80,950	19,768	16,959	20,657	18,090	83,900	83,950	20,698	17,799	21,737	18,930
77,950	78,000	18,853	16,133	19,733	17,264	80,950	81,000	19,783	16,973	20,675	18,104	83,950	84,000	20,713	17,813	21,755	18,944
78,000						**81,000**						**84,000**					
78,000	78,050	18,869	16,147	19,748	17,278	81,000	81,050	19,799	16,987	20,693	18,118	84,000	84,050	20,729	17,827	21,773	18,958
78,050	78,100	18,884	16,161	19,764	17,292	81,050	81,100	19,814	17,001	20,711	18,132	84,050	84,100	20,744	17,841	21,791	18,972
78,100	78,150	18,900	16,175	19,779	17,306	81,100	81,150	19,830	17,015	20,729	18,146	84,100	84,150	20,760	17,855	21,809	18,986
78,150	78,200	18,915	16,189	19,795	17,320	81,150	81,200	19,845	17,029	20,747	18,160	84,150	84,200	20,775	17,869	21,827	19,000
78,200	78,250	18,931	16,203	19,810	17,334	81,200	81,250	19,861	17,043	20,765	18,174	84,200	84,250	20,791	17,883	21,845	19,014
78,250	78,300	18,946	16,217	19,826	17,348	81,250	81,300	19,876	17,057	20,783	18,188	84,250	84,300	20,806	17,897	21,863	19,028
78,300	78,350	18,962	16,231	19,841	17,362	81,300	81,350	19,892	17,071	20,801	18,202	84,300	84,350	20,822	17,911	21,881	19,042
78,350	78,400	18,977	16,245	19,857	17,376	81,350	81,400	19,907	17,085	20,819	18,216	84,350	84,400	20,837	17,925	21,899	19,056
78,400	78,450	18,993	16,259	19,872	17,390	81,400	81,450	19,923	17,099	20,837	18,230	84,400	84,450	20,853	17,939	21,917	19,070
78,450	78,500	19,008	16,273	19,888	17,404	81,450	81,500	19,938	17,113	20,855	18,244	84,450	84,500	20,868	17,953	21,935	19,084
78,500	78,550	19,024	16,287	19,903	17,418	81,500	81,550	19,954	17,127	20,873	18,258	84,500	84,550	20,884	17,967	21,953	19,098
78,550	78,600	19,039	16,301	19,919	17,432	81,550	81,600	19,969	17,141	20,891	18,272	84,550	84,600	20,899	17,981	21,971	19,112
78,600	78,650	19,055	16,315	19,934	17,446	81,600	81,650	19,985	17,155	20,909	18,286	84,600	84,650	20,915	17,995	21,989	19,126
78,650	78,700	19,070	16,329	19,950	17,460	81,650	81,700	20,000	17,169	20,927	18,300	84,650	84,700	20,930	18,009	22,007	19,140
78,700	78,750	19,086	16,343	19,965	17,474	81,700	81,750	20,016	17,183	20,945	18,314	84,700	84,750	20,946	18,023	22,025	19,154
78,750	78,800	19,101	16,357	19,981	17,488	81,750	81,800	20,031	17,197	20,963	18,328	84,750	84,800	20,961	18,037	22,043	19,168
78,800	78,850	19,117	16,371	19,996	17,502	81,800	81,850	20,047	17,211	20,981	18,342	84,800	84,850	20,977	18,051	22,061	19,182
78,850	78,900	19,132	16,385	20,012	17,516	81,850	81,900	20,062	17,225	20,999	18,356	84,850	84,900	20,992	18,065	22,079	19,196
78,900	78,950	19,148	16,399	20,027	17,530	81,900	81,950	20,078	17,239	21,017	18,370	84,900	84,950	21,008	18,079	22,097	19,210
78,950	79,000	19,163	16,413	20,043	17,544	81,950	82,000	20,093	17,253	21,035	18,384	84,950	85,000	21,023	18,093	22,115	19,224
79,000						**82,000**						**85,000**					
79,000	79,050	19,179	16,427	20,058	17,558	82,000	82,050	20,109	17,267	21,053	18,398	85,000	85,050	21,039	18,107	22,133	19,238
79,050	79,100	19,194	16,441	20,074	17,572	82,050	82,100	20,124	17,281	21,071	18,412	85,050	85,100	21,054	18,121	22,151	19,252
79,100	79,150	19,210	16,455	20,089	17,586	82,100	82,150	20,140	17,295	21,089	18,426	85,100	85,150	21,070	18,135	22,169	19,266
79,150	79,200	19,225	16,469	20,105	17,600	82,150	82,200	20,155	17,309	21,107	18,440	85,150	85,200	21,085	18,149	22,187	19,280
79,200	79,250	19,241	16,483	20,120	17,614	82,200	82,250	20,171	17,323	21,125	18,454	85,200	85,250	21,101	18,163	22,205	19,294
79,250	79,300	19,256	16,497	20,136	17,628	82,250	82,300	20,186	17,337	21,143	18,468	85,250	85,300	21,116	18,177	22,223	19,308
79,300	79,350	19,272	16,511	20,151	17,642	82,300	82,350	20,202	17,351	21,161	18,482	85,300	85,350	21,132	18,191	22,241	19,322
79,350	79,400	19,287	16,525	20,167	17,656	82,350	82,400	20,217	17,365	21,179	18,496	85,350	85,400	21,147	18,205	22,259	19,336
79,400	79,450	19,303	16,539	20,182	17,670	82,400	82,450	20,233	17,379	21,197	18,510	85,400	85,450	21,163	18,219	22,277	19,350
79,450	79,500	19,318	16,553	20,198	17,684	82,450	82,500	20,248	17,393	21,215	18,524	85,450	85,500	21,178	18,233	22,295	19,364
79,500	79,550	19,334	16,567	20,213	17,698	82,500	82,550	20,264	17,407	21,233	18,538	85,500	85,550	21,194	18,247	22,313	19,378
79,550	79,600	19,349	16,581	20,229	17,712	82,550	82,600	20,279	17,421	21,251	18,552	85,550	85,600	21,209	18,261	22,331	19,392
79,600	79,650	19,365	16,595	20,244	17,726	82,600	82,650	20,295	17,435	21,269	18,566	85,600	85,650	21,225	18,275	22,349	19,406
79,650	79,700	19,380	16,609	20,260	17,740	82,650	82,700	20,310	17,449	21,287	18,580	85,650	85,700	21,240	18,289	22,367	19,420
79,700	79,750	19,396	16,623	20,275	17,754	82,700	82,750	20,326	17,463	21,305	18,594	85,700	85,750	21,256	18,303	22,385	19,434
79,750	79,800	19,411	16,637	20,291	17,768	82,750	82,800	20,341	17,477	21,323	18,608	85,750	85,800	21,271	18,317	22,403	19,448
79,800	79,850	19,427	16,651	20,306	17,782	82,800	82,850	20,357	17,491	21,341	18,622	85,800	85,850	21,287	18,331	22,421	19,462
79,850	79,900	19,442	16,665	20,322	17,796	82,850	82,900	20,372	17,505	21,359	18,636	85,850	85,900	21,302	18,345	22,439	19,476
79,900	79,950	19,458	16,679	20,337	17,810	82,900	82,950	20,388	17,519	21,377	18,650	85,900	85,950	21,318	18,359	22,457	19,490
79,950	80,000	19,473	16,693	20,353	17,824	82,950	83,000	20,403	17,533	21,395	18,664	85,950	86,000	21,333	18,373	22,475	19,504

* This column must also be used by a qualifying widow(er).

(Continued on next page)

If line 39 (taxable income) is — At least	But less than	Single	Married filing jointly *	Married filing separately	Head of a household
86,000					
86,000	86,050	21,349	18,387	22,493	19,518
86,050	86,100	21,364	18,401	22,511	19,532
86,100	86,150	21,380	18,415	22,529	19,546
86,150	86,200	21,395	18,429	22,547	19,560
86,200	86,250	21,411	18,443	22,565	19,574
86,250	86,300	21,426	18,457	22,583	19,588
86,300	86,350	21,442	18,471	22,601	19,602
86,350	86,400	21,457	18,485	22,619	19,616
86,400	86,450	21,473	18,499	22,637	19,630
86,450	86,500	21,488	18,513	22,655	19,644
86,500	86,550	21,504	18,527	22,673	19,658
86,550	86,600	21,519	18,541	22,691	19,672
86,600	86,650	21,535	18,555	22,709	19,686
86,650	86,700	21,550	18,569	22,727	19,700
86,700	86,750	21,566	18,583	22,745	19,714
86,750	86,800	21,581	18,597	22,763	19,728
86,800	86,850	21,597	18,611	22,781	19,742
86,850	86,900	21,612	18,625	22,799	19,756
86,900	86,950	21,628	18,639	22,817	19,770
86,950	87,000	21,643	18,653	22,835	19,784
87,000					
87,000	87,050	21,659	18,667	22,853	19,798
87,050	87,100	21,674	18,681	22,871	19,812
87,100	87,150	21,690	18,695	22,889	19,826
87,150	87,200	21,705	18,709	22,907	19,840
87,200	87,250	21,721	18,723	22,925	19,854
87,250	87,300	21,736	18,737	22,943	19,868
87,300	87,350	21,752	18,751	22,961	19,882
87,350	87,400	21,767	18,765	22,979	19,896
87,400	87,450	21,783	18,779	22,997	19,910
87,450	87,500	21,798	18,793	23,015	19,924
87,500	87,550	21,814	18,807	23,033	19,938
87,550	87,600	21,829	18,821	23,051	19,952
87,600	87,650	21,845	18,835	23,069	19,966
87,650	87,700	21,860	18,849	23,087	19,980
87,700	87,750	21,876	18,863	23,105	19,994
87,750	87,800	21,891	18,877	23,123	20,008
87,800	87,850	21,907	18,891	23,141	20,022
87,850	87,900	21,922	18,905	23,159	20,036
87,900	87,950	21,938	18,919	23,177	20,050
87,950	88,000	21,953	18,933	23,195	20,064
88,000					
88,000	88,050	21,969	18,947	23,213	20,078
88,050	88,100	21,984	18,961	23,231	20,092
88,100	88,150	22,000	18,975	23,249	20,106
88,150	88,200	22,015	18,989	23,267	20,120
88,200	88,250	22,031	19,003	23,285	20,134
88,250	88,300	22,046	19,017	23,303	20,148
88,300	88,350	22,062	19,031	23,321	20,162
88,350	88,400	22,077	19,045	23,339	20,176
88,400	88,450	22,093	19,059	23,357	20,190
88,450	88,500	22,108	19,073	23,375	20,204
88,500	88,550	22,124	19,087	23,393	20,218
88,550	88,600	22,139	19,101	23,411	20,232
88,600	88,650	22,155	19,115	23,429	20,246
88,650	88,700	22,170	19,129	23,447	20,260
88,700	88,750	22,186	19,143	23,465	20,274
88,750	88,800	22,201	19,157	23,483	20,288
88,800	88,850	22,217	19,171	23,501	20,302
88,850	88,900	22,232	19,185	23,519	20,316
88,900	88,950	22,248	19,199	23,537	20,330
88,950	89,000	22,263	19,213	23,555	20,344
89,000					
89,000	89,050	22,279	19,227	23,573	20,358
89,050	89,100	22,294	19,241	23,591	20,372
89,100	89,150	22,310	19,255	23,609	20,386
89,150	89,200	22,325	19,269	23,627	20,400
89,200	89,250	22,341	19,283	23,645	20,414
89,250	89,300	22,356	19,297	23,663	20,428
89,300	89,350	22,372	19,311	23,681	20,442
89,350	89,400	22,387	19,325	23,699	20,456
89,400	89,450	22,403	19,339	23,717	20,470
89,450	89,500	22,418	19,353	23,735	20,484
89,500	89,550	22,434	19,367	23,753	20,498
89,550	89,600	22,449	19,381	23,771	20,512
89,600	89,650	22,465	19,395	23,789	20,526
89,650	89,700	22,480	19,409	23,807	20,540
89,700	89,750	22,496	19,423	23,825	20,554
89,750	89,800	22,511	19,437	23,843	20,568
89,800	89,850	22,527	19,451	23,861	20,582
89,850	89,900	22,542	19,465	23,879	20,596
89,900	89,950	22,558	19,479	23,897	20,610
89,950	90,000	22,573	19,493	23,915	20,624
90,000					
90,000	90,050	22,589	19,507	23,933	20,638
90,050	90,100	22,604	19,521	23,951	20,652
90,100	90,150	22,620	19,535	23,969	20,666
90,150	90,200	22,635	19,549	23,987	20,680
90,200	90,250	22,651	19,563	24,005	20,694
90,250	90,300	22,666	19,577	24,023	20,708
90,300	90,350	22,682	19,591	24,041	20,722
90,350	90,400	22,697	19,605	24,059	20,736
90,400	90,450	22,713	19,619	24,077	20,750
90,450	90,500	22,728	19,633	24,095	20,764
90,500	90,550	22,744	19,647	24,113	20,778
90,550	90,600	22,759	19,661	24,131	20,792
90,600	90,650	22,775	19,675	24,149	20,806
90,650	90,700	22,790	19,689	24,167	20,820
90,700	90,750	22,806	19,703	24,185	20,834
90,750	90,800	22,821	19,717	24,203	20,848
90,800	90,850	22,837	19,731	24,221	20,862
90,850	90,900	22,852	19,745	24,239	20,878
90,900	90,950	22,868	19,759	24,257	20,893
90,950	91,000	22,883	19,773	24,275	20,909
91,000					
91,000	91,050	22,899	19,787	24,293	20,924
91,050	91,100	22,914	19,801	24,311	20,940
91,100	91,150	22,930	19,815	24,329	20,955
91,150	91,200	22,945	19,829	24,347	20,971
91,200	91,250	22,961	19,843	24,365	20,986
91,250	91,300	22,976	19,857	24,383	21,002
91,300	91,350	22,992	19,871	24,401	21,017
91,350	91,400	23,007	19,885	24,419	21,033
91,400	91,450	23,023	19,899	24,437	21,048
91,450	91,500	23,038	19,913	24,455	21,064
91,500	91,550	23,054	19,927	24,473	21,079
91,550	91,600	23,069	19,941	24,491	21,095
91,600	91,650	23,085	19,955	24,509	21,110
91,650	91,700	23,100	19,969	24,527	21,126
91,700	91,750	23,116	19,983	24,545	21,141
91,750	91,800	23,131	19,997	24,563	21,157
91,800	91,850	23,147	20,011	24,581	21,172
91,850	91,900	23,162	20,025	24,599	21,188
91,900	91,950	23,178	20,039	24,617	21,203
91,950	92,000	23,193	20,053	24,635	21,219
92,000					
92,000	92,050	23,209	20,067	24,653	21,234
92,050	92,100	23,224	20,081	24,671	21,250
92,100	92,150	23,240	20,095	24,689	21,265
92,150	92,200	23,255	20,109	24,707	21,281
92,200	92,250	23,271	20,123	24,725	21,296
92,250	92,300	23,286	20,137	24,743	21,312
92,300	92,350	23,302	20,151	24,761	21,327
92,350	92,400	23,317	20,165	24,779	21,343
92,400	92,450	23,333	20,179	24,797	21,358
92,450	92,500	23,348	20,193	24,815	21,374
92,500	92,550	23,364	20,207	24,833	21,389
92,550	92,600	23,379	20,221	24,851	21,405
92,600	92,650	23,395	20,235	24,869	21,420
92,650	92,700	23,410	20,249	24,887	21,436
92,700	92,750	23,426	20,263	24,905	21,451
92,750	92,800	23,441	20,277	24,923	21,467
92,800	92,850	23,457	20,291	24,941	21,482
92,850	92,900	23,472	20,305	24,959	21,498
92,900	92,950	23,488	20,319	24,977	21,513
92,950	93,000	23,503	20,333	24,995	21,529
93,000					
93,000	93,050	23,519	20,347	25,013	21,544
93,050	93,100	23,534	20,361	25,031	21,560
93,100	93,150	23,550	20,375	25,049	21,575
93,150	93,200	23,565	20,389	25,067	21,591
93,200	93,250	23,581	20,403	25,085	21,606
93,250	93,300	23,596	20,417	25,103	21,622
93,300	93,350	23,612	20,431	25,121	21,637
93,350	93,400	23,627	20,445	25,139	21,653
93,400	93,450	23,643	20,459	25,157	21,668
93,450	93,500	23,658	20,473	25,175	21,684
93,500	93,550	23,674	20,487	25,193	21,699
93,550	93,600	23,689	20,501	25,211	21,715
93,600	93,650	23,705	20,515	25,229	21,730
93,650	93,700	23,720	20,529	25,247	21,746
93,700	93,750	23,736	20,543	25,265	21,761
93,750	93,800	23,751	20,557	25,283	21,777
93,800	93,850	23,767	20,571	25,301	21,792
93,850	93,900	23,782	20,585	25,319	21,808
93,900	93,950	23,798	20,599	25,337	21,823
93,950	94,000	23,813	20,613	25,355	21,839
94,000					
94,000	94,050	23,829	20,627	25,373	21,854
94,050	94,100	23,844	20,641	25,391	21,870
94,100	94,150	23,860	20,655	25,409	21,885
94,150	94,200	23,875	20,669	25,427	21,901
94,200	94,250	23,891	20,683	25,445	21,916
94,250	94,300	23,906	20,697	25,463	21,932
94,300	94,350	23,922	20,711	25,481	21,947
94,350	94,400	23,937	20,725	25,499	21,963
94,400	94,450	23,953	20,739	25,517	21,978
94,450	94,500	23,968	20,753	25,535	21,994
94,500	94,550	23,984	20,767	25,553	22,009
94,550	94,600	23,999	20,781	25,571	22,025
94,600	94,650	24,015	20,795	25,589	22,040
94,650	94,700	24,030	20,809	25,607	22,056
94,700	94,750	24,046	20,823	25,625	22,071
94,750	94,800	24,061	20,837	25,643	22,087
94,800	94,850	24,077	20,851	25,661	22,102
94,850	94,900	24,092	20,865	25,679	22,118
94,900	94,950	24,108	20,879	25,697	22,133
94,950	95,000	24,123	20,893	25,715	22,149

* This column must also be used by a qualifying widow(er).

(Continued on next page)

2000 Tax Table —*Continued*

If line 39 (taxable income) is —		And you are —				If line 39 (taxable income) is —		And you are —			
At least	But less than	Single	Married filing jointly *	Married filing sepa-rately	Head of a house-hold	At least	But less than	Single	Married filing jointly *	Married filing sepa-rately	Head of a house-hold
		Your tax is —						Your tax is —			

95,000

At least	But less than	Single	Jointly	Separately	HoH	At least	But less than	Single	Jointly	Separately	HoH
95,000	95,050	24,139	20,907	25,733	22,164	98,000	98,050	25,069	21,747	26,813	23,094
95,050	95,100	24,154	20,921	25,751	22,180	98,050	98,100	25,084	21,761	26,831	23,110
95,100	95,150	24,170	20,935	25,769	22,195	98,100	98,150	25,100	21,775	26,849	23,125
95,150	95,200	24,185	20,949	25,787	22,211	98,150	98,200	25,115	21,789	26,867	23,141
95,200	95,250	24,201	20,963	25,805	22,226	98,200	98,250	25,131	21,803	26,885	23,156
95,250	95,300	24,216	20,977	25,823	22,242	98,250	98,300	25,146	21,817	26,903	23,172
95,300	95,350	24,232	20,991	25,841	22,257	98,300	98,350	25,162	21,831	26,921	23,187
95,350	95,400	24,247	21,005	25,859	22,273	98,350	98,400	25,177	21,845	26,939	23,203
95,400	95,450	24,263	21,019	25,877	22,288	98,400	98,450	25,193	21,859	26,957	23,218
95,450	95,500	24,278	21,033	25,895	22,304	98,450	98,500	25,208	21,873	26,975	23,234
95,500	95,550	24,294	21,047	25,913	22,319	98,500	98,550	25,224	21,887	26,993	23,249
95,550	95,600	24,309	21,061	25,931	22,335	98,550	98,600	25,239	21,901	27,011	23,265
95,600	95,650	24,325	21,075	25,949	22,350	98,600	98,650	25,255	21,915	27,029	23,280
95,650	95,700	24,340	21,089	25,967	22,366	98,650	98,700	25,270	21,929	27,047	23,296
95,700	95,750	24,356	21,103	25,985	22,381	98,700	98,750	25,286	21,943	27,065	23,311
95,750	95,800	24,371	21,117	26,003	22,397	98,750	98,800	25,301	21,957	27,083	23,327
95,800	95,850	24,387	21,131	26,021	22,412	98,800	98,850	25,317	21,971	27,101	23,342
95,850	95,900	24,402	21,145	26,039	22,428	98,850	98,900	25,332	21,985	27,119	23,358
95,900	95,950	24,418	21,159	26,057	22,443	98,900	98,950	25,348	21,999	27,137	23,373
95,950	96,000	24,433	21,173	26,075	22,459	98,950	99,000	25,363	22,013	27,155	23,389

96,000   ### 99,000

At least	But less than	Single	Jointly	Separately	HoH	At least	But less than	Single	Jointly	Separately	HoH
96,000	96,050	24,449	21,187	26,093	22,474	99,000	99,050	25,379	22,027	27,173	23,404
96,050	96,100	24,464	21,201	26,111	22,490	99,050	99,100	25,394	22,041	27,191	23,420
96,100	96,150	24,480	21,215	26,129	22,505	99,100	99,150	25,410	22,055	27,209	23,435
96,150	96,200	24,495	21,229	26,147	22,521	99,150	99,200	25,425	22,069	27,227	23,451
96,200	96,250	24,511	21,243	26,165	22,536	99,200	99,250	25,441	22,083	27,245	23,466
96,250	96,300	24,526	21,257	26,183	22,552	99,250	99,300	25,456	22,097	27,263	23,482
96,300	96,350	24,542	21,271	26,201	22,567	99,300	99,350	25,472	22,111	27,281	23,497
96,350	96,400	24,557	21,285	26,219	22,583	99,350	99,400	25,487	22,125	27,299	23,513
96,400	96,450	24,573	21,299	26,237	22,598	99,400	99,450	25,503	22,139	27,317	23,528
96,450	96,500	24,588	21,313	26,255	22,614	99,450	99,500	25,518	22,153	27,335	23,544
96,500	96,550	24,604	21,327	26,273	22,629	99,500	99,550	25,534	22,167	27,353	23,559
96,550	96,600	24,619	21,341	26,291	22,645	99,550	99,600	25,549	22,181	27,371	23,575
96,600	96,650	24,635	21,355	26,309	22,660	99,600	99,650	25,565	22,195	27,389	23,590
96,650	96,700	24,650	21,369	26,327	22,676	99,650	99,700	25,580	22,209	27,407	23,606
96,700	96,750	24,666	21,383	26,345	22,691	99,700	99,750	25,596	22,223	27,425	23,621
96,750	96,800	24,681	21,397	26,363	22,707	99,750	99,800	25,611	22,237	27,443	23,637
96,800	96,850	24,697	21,411	26,381	22,722	99,800	99,850	25,627	22,251	27,461	23,652
96,850	96,900	24,712	21,425	26,399	22,738	99,850	99,900	25,642	22,265	27,479	23,668
96,900	96,950	24,728	21,439	26,417	22,753	99,900	99,950	25,658	22,279	27,497	23,683
96,950	97,000	24,743	21,453	26,435	22,769	99,950	100,000	25,673	22,293	27,515	23,699

97,000

At least	But less than	Single	Jointly	Separately	HoH
97,000	97,050	24,759	21,467	26,453	22,784
97,050	97,100	24,774	21,481	26,471	22,800
97,100	97,150	24,790	21,495	26,489	22,815
97,150	97,200	24,805	21,509	26,507	22,831
97,200	97,250	24,821	21,523	26,525	22,846
97,250	97,300	24,836	21,537	26,543	22,862
97,300	97,350	24,852	21,551	26,561	22,877
97,350	97,400	24,867	21,565	26,579	22,893
97,400	97,450	24,883	21,579	26,597	22,908
97,450	97,500	24,898	21,593	26,615	22,924
97,500	97,550	24,914	21,607	26,633	22,939
97,550	97,600	24,929	21,621	26,651	22,955
97,600	97,650	24,945	21,635	26,669	22,970
97,650	97,700	24,960	21,649	26,687	22,986
97,700	97,750	24,976	21,663	26,705	23,001
97,750	97,800	24,991	21,677	26,723	23,017
97,800	97,850	25,007	21,691	26,741	23,032
97,850	97,900	25,022	21,705	26,759	23,048
97,900	97,950	25,038	21,719	26,777	23,063
97,950	98,000	25,053	21,733	26,795	23,079

$100,000 or over — use the Tax Rate Schedules on page A-2

* This column must also be used by a qualifying widow(er).

Income Tax Rates—Estates and Trusts

TAX YEAR 2000

Taxable Income		The Tax Is:	Of the Amount
Over—	But Not Over—		Over—
$ 0	$1,750	15%	$ 0
1,750	4,150	$ 262.50 + 28%	1,750
4,150	6,300	934.50 + 31%	4,150
6,300	8,650	1,601.00 + 36%	6,300
8,650	....	2,447.00 + 39.6%	8,650

TAX YEAR 2001

Taxable Income		The Tax Is:	Of the Amount
Over—	But Not Over—		Over—
$ 0	$1,800	15%	$ 0
1,800	4,250	$ 270.00 + 28%	1,800
4,250	6,500	956.00 + 31%	4,250
6,500	8,900	1,653.50 + 36%	6,500
8,900	....	2,517.50 + 39.6%	8,900

Income Tax Rates—Corporations

Taxable Income		The Tax Is:	Of the Amount
Over—	But Not Over—		Over—
$ 0	$ 50,000	15%	$ 0
50,000	75,000	$ 7,500 + 25%	50,000
75,000	100,000	13,750 + 34%	75,000
100,000	335,000	22,250 + 39%	100,000
335,000	10,000,000	113,900 + 34%	335,000
10,000,000	15,000,000	3,400,000 + 35%	10,000,000
15,000,000	18,333,333	5,150,000 + 38%	15,000,000
18,333,333	....	35%	0

Unified Transfer Tax Rates

FOR GIFTS MADE AND FOR DEATHS AFTER 1983

If the Amount with Respect to Which the Tentative Tax to Be Computed Is:	The Tentative Tax Is:
Not over $10,000	18 percent of such amount.
Over $10,000 but not over $20,000	$1,800, plus 20 percent of the excess of such amount over $10,000.
Over $20,000 but not over $40,000	$3,800, plus 22 percent of the excess of such amount over $20,000.
Over $40,000 but not over $60,000	$8,200, plus 24 percent of the excess of such amount over $40,000.
Over $60,000 but not over $80,000	$13,000, plus 26 percent of the excess of such amount over $60,000.
Over $80,000 but not over $100,000	$18,200, plus 28 percent of the excess of such amount over $80,000.
Over $100,000 but not over $150,000	$23,800, plus 30 percent of the excess of such amount over $100,000.
Over $150,000 but not over $250,000	$38,800, plus 32 percent of the excess of such amount over $150,000.
Over $250,000 but not over $500,000	$70,800, plus 34 percent of the excess of such amount over $250,000.
Over $500,000 but not over $750,000	$155,800, plus 37 percent of the excess of such amount over $500,000.
Over $750,000 but not over $1,000,000	$248,300, plus 39 percent of the excess of such amount over $750,000.
Over $1,000,000 but not over $1,250,000	$345,800, plus 41 percent of the excess of such amount over $1,000,000.
Over $1,250,000 but not over $1,500,000	$448,300, plus 43 percent of the excess of such amount over $1,250,000.
Over $1,500,000 but not over $2,000,000	$555,800, plus 45 percent of the excess of such amount over $1,500,000.
Over $2,000,000 but not over $2,500,000	$780,800, plus 49 percent of the excess of such amount over $2,000,000.
Over $2,500,000 but not over $3,000,000	$1,025,800, plus 53 percent of the excess of such amount over $2,500,000.
Over $3,000,000*	$1,290,800, plus 55 percent of the excess of such amount over $3,000,000.

*For large taxable transfers (generally in excess of $10 million), there is a phase-out of the graduated rates and the unified tax credit.

Table For Computation of Maximum Credit for State Death Taxes

(A) Adjusted Taxable Estate* Equal to or More Than	(B) Adjusted Taxable Estate* Less Than	(C) Credit on Amount in Column (A)	(D) Rate of Credit on Excess Over Amount in Column (A) (Percentage)
0	$ 40,000	0	None
$ 40,000	90,000	0	0.8
90,000	140,000	$ 400	1.6
140,000	240,000	1,200	2.4
240,000	440,000	3,600	3.2
440,000	640,000	10,000	4.0
640,000	840,000	18,000	4.8
840,000	1,040,000	27,600	5.6
1,040,000	1,540,000	38,800	6.4
1,540,000	2,040,000	70,800	7.2
2,040,000	2,540,000	106,800	8.0
2,540,000	3,040,000	146,800	8.8
3,040,000	3,540,000	190,800	9.6
3,540,000	4,040,000	238,800	10.4
4,040,000	5,040,000	290,800	11.2
5,040,000	6,040,000	402,800	12.0
6,040,000	7,040,000	522,800	12.8
7,040,000	8,040,000	650,800	13.6
8,040,000	9,040,000	786,800	14.4
9,040,000	10,040,000	930,800	15.2
10,040,000		1,082,800	16.0

*Adjusted Taxable Estate = Taxable Estate – $60,000

Tax Forms

(Tax forms can be obtained from the IRS web site: **http://www.irs.gov**)

Form **1040**

Department of the Treasury—Internal Revenue Service

U.S. Individual Income Tax Return **2000**   (99)   IRS Use Only—Do not write or staple in this space.

For the year Jan. 1–Dec. 31, 2000, or other tax year beginning   , 2000, ending   , 20   OMB No. 1545-0074

Label (See instructions on page 19.) **Use the IRS label. Otherwise, please print or type.**	L A B E L H E R E	Your first name and initial	Last name	Your social security number
		If a joint return, spouse's first name and initial	Last name	Spouse's social security number
		Home address (number and street). If you have a P.O. box, see page 19.	Apt. no.	▲ **Important!** ▲
		City, town or post office, state, and ZIP code. If you have a foreign address, see page 19.		You **must** enter your SSN(s) above.

Presidential Election Campaign (See page 19.) ▶

Note. Checking "Yes" will not change your tax or reduce your refund.

Do you, or your spouse if filing a joint return, want $3 to go to this fund? . . . . ▶

You: ☐ Yes ☐ No   Spouse: ☐ Yes ☐ No

Filing Status

Check only one box.

1 ☐ Single
2 ☐ Married filing joint return (even if only one had income)
3 ☐ Married filing separate return. Enter spouse's social security no. above and full name here. ▶ _____
4 ☐ Head of household (with qualifying person). (See page 19.) If the qualifying person is a child but not your dependent, enter this child's name here. ▶ _____
5 ☐ Qualifying widow(er) with dependent child (year spouse died ▶   ). (See page 19.)

Exemptions

If more than six dependents, see page 20.

6a ☐ **Yourself.** If your parent (or someone else) can claim you as a dependent on his or her tax return, **do not** check box 6a . . . .

b ☐ **Spouse** . . . .

c Dependents:

(1) First name Last name	(2) Dependent's social security number	(3) Dependent's relationship to you	(4) ✓ if qualifying child for child tax credit (see page 20)
			☐
			☐
			☐
			☐
			☐
			☐

No. of boxes checked on 6a and 6b _____

No. of your children on 6c who:
• lived with you _____
• did not live with you due to divorce or separation (see page 20) _____

Dependents on 6c not entered above _____

Add numbers entered on lines above ▶ ☐

d Total number of exemptions claimed . . . .

Income

Attach Forms W-2 and W-2G here. Also attach Form(s) 1099-R if tax was withheld.

If you did not get a W-2, see page 21.

Enclose, but do not attach, any payment. Also, please use Form 1040-V.

7	Wages, salaries, tips, etc. Attach Form(s) W-2	7	
8a	**Taxable** interest. Attach Schedule B if required	8a	
b	**Tax-exempt** interest. **Do not** include on line 8a . . .	8b	
9	Ordinary dividends. Attach Schedule B if required	9	
10	Taxable refunds, credits, or offsets of state and local income taxes (see page 22) . .	10	
11	Alimony received	11	
12	Business income or (loss). Attach Schedule C or C-EZ	12	
13	Capital gain or (loss). Attach Schedule D if required. If not required, check here ▶ ☐	13	
14	Other gains or (losses). Attach Form 4797	14	
15a	Total IRA distributions . 15a ____ b Taxable amount (see page 23)	15b	
16a	Total pensions and annuities 16a ____ b Taxable amount (see page 23)	16b	
17	Rental real estate, royalties, partnerships, S corporations, trusts, etc. Attach Schedule E	17	
18	Farm income or (loss). Attach Schedule F	18	
19	Unemployment compensation	19	
20a	Social security benefits . 20a ____ b Taxable amount (see page 25)	20b	
21	Other income. List type and amount (see page 25) ----------------	21	
22	Add the amounts in the far right column for lines 7 through 21. This is your **total income** ▶	22	

Adjusted Gross Income

23	IRA deduction (see page 27)	23	
24	Student loan interest deduction (see page 27)	24	
25	Medical savings account deduction. Attach Form 8853 .	25	
26	Moving expenses. Attach Form 3903	26	
27	One-half of self-employment tax. Attach Schedule SE	27	
28	Self-employed health insurance deduction (see page 29)	28	
29	Self-employed SEP, SIMPLE, and qualified plans . .	29	
30	Penalty on early withdrawal of savings	30	
31a	Alimony paid b Recipient's SSN ▶ _____	31a	
32	Add lines 23 through 31a		32
33	Subtract line 32 from line 22. This is your **adjusted gross income** . . . . . ▶		33

For Disclosure, Privacy Act, and Paperwork Reduction Act Notice, see page 56.   Cat. No. 11320B   Form **1040** (2000)

Form 1040 (2000)   Page **2**

Tax and Credits

34	Amount from line 33 (adjusted gross income)	34	
35a	Check if: ☐ **You** were 65 or older, ☐ Blind; ☐ **Spouse** was 65 or older, ☐ Blind. Add the number of boxes checked above and enter the total here . . . ▶ **35a**		
b	If you are married filing separately and your spouse itemizes deductions, or you were a dual-status alien, see page 31 and check here . . . . . . ▶ **35b** ☐		

Standard Deduction for Most People

Single: $4,400

Head of household: $6,450

Married filing jointly or Qualifying widow(er): $7,350

Married filing separately: $3,675

36	Enter your **itemized deductions** from Schedule A, line 28, **or standard deduction** shown on the left. **But** see page 31 to find your standard deduction if you checked any box on line 35a or 35b **or** if someone can claim you as a dependent	36	
37	Subtract line 36 from line 34	37	
38	If line 34 is $96,700 or less, multiply $2,800 by the total number of exemptions claimed on line 6d. If line 34 is over $96,700, see the worksheet on page 32 for the amount to enter .	38	
39	**Taxable income.** Subtract line 38 from line 37. If line 38 is more than line 37, enter -0-	39	
40	**Tax** (see page 32). Check if any tax is from **a** ☐ Form(s) 8814 **b** ☐ Form 4972 . . .	40	
41	Alternative minimum tax. Attach Form 6251	41	
42	Add lines 40 and 41 . . . . ▶	42	

43	Foreign tax credit. Attach Form 1116 if required	43	
44	Credit for child and dependent care expenses. Attach Form 2441	44	
45	Credit for the elderly or the disabled. Attach Schedule R . .	45	
46	Education credits. Attach Form 8863	46	
47	Child tax credit (see page 36)	47	
48	Adoption credit. Attach Form 8839	48	
49	Other. Check if from **a** ☐ Form 3800 **b** ☐ Form 8396 **c** ☐ Form 8801 **d** ☐ Form (specify) _____	49	
50	Add lines 43 through 49. These are your **total credits**	50	
51	Subtract line 50 from line 42. If line 50 is more than line 42, enter -0- . . . . . ▶	51	

Other Taxes

52	Self-employment tax. Attach Schedule SE	52	
53	Social security and Medicare tax on tip income not reported to employer. Attach Form 4137	53	
54	Tax on IRAs, other retirement plans, and MSAs. Attach Form 5329 if required . . .	54	
55	Advance earned income credit payments from Form(s) W-2	55	
56	Household employment taxes. Attach Schedule H	56	
57	Add lines 51 through 56. This is your **total tax** . . . . ▶	57	

Payments

If you have a qualifying child, attach Schedule EIC.

58	Federal income tax withheld from Forms W-2 and 1099 . .	58	
59	2000 estimated tax payments and amount applied from 1999 return	59	
60a	**Earned income credit (EIC)**	60a	
b	Nontaxable earned income: amount . . . ▶ _____ and type ▶		
61	Excess social security and RRTA tax withheld (see page 50)	61	
62	Additional child tax credit. Attach Form 8812	62	
63	Amount paid with request for extension to file (see page 50)	63	
64	Other payments. Check if from **a** ☐ Form 2439 **b** ☐ Form 4136	64	
65	Add lines 58, 59, 60a, and 61 through 64. These are your **total payments** . . . . ▶	65	

Refund

Have it directly deposited! See page 50 and fill in 67b, 67c, and 67d.

66	If line 65 is more than line 57, subtract line 57 from line 65. This is the amount you **overpaid**	66	
67a	Amount of line 66 you want **refunded to you** . . . . ▶	67a	
▶ **b**	Routing number [_____] ▶ **c** Type: ☐ Checking ☐ Savings		
▶ **d**	Account number [_____]		
68	Amount of line 66 you want **applied to your 2001 estimated tax** . ▶	68	

Amount You Owe

69	If line 57 is more than line 65, subtract line 65 from line 57. This is the **amount you owe**. For details on how to pay, see page 51 . . . . ▶	69	
70	Estimated tax penalty. Also include on line 69 . .	70	

Sign Here

Joint return? See page 19.

Keep a copy for your records.

Under penalties of perjury, I declare that I have examined this return and accompanying schedules and statements, and to the best of my knowledge and belief, they are true, correct, and complete. Declaration of preparer (other than taxpayer) is based on all information of which preparer has any knowledge.

Your signature	Date	Your occupation	Daytime phone number ( )
Spouse's signature. If a joint return, **both** must sign.	Date	Spouse's occupation	May the IRS discuss this return with the preparer shown below (see page 52)? ☐ Yes ☐ No

Paid Preparer's Use Only

Preparer's signature ▶	Date	Check if self-employed ☐	Preparer's SSN or PTIN
Firm's name (or yours if self-employed), address, and ZIP code ▶		EIN	
		Phone no. ( )	

Form **1040** (2000)

SCHEDULE C
(Form 1040)

Department of the Treasury
Internal Revenue Service (99)

Profit or Loss From Business
(Sole Proprietorship)

► **Partnerships, joint ventures, etc., must file Form 1065 or Form 1065-B.**

► **Attach to Form 1040 or Form 1041.**   ► **See Instructions for Schedule C (Form 1040).**

OMB No. 1545-0074

20**00**

Attachment
Sequence No. **09**

Name of proprietor

Social security number (SSN)

A Principal business or profession, including product or service (see page C-1 of the instructions)

B Enter code from pages C-7 & 8
►

C Business name. If no separate business name, leave blank.

D Employer ID number (EIN), if any

E Business address (including suite or room no.) ► ....
City, town or post office, state, and ZIP code

F Accounting method: **(1)** ☐ Cash   **(2)** ☐ Accrual   **(3)** ☐ Other (specify) ► ....

G Did you "materially participate" in the operation of this business during 2000? If "No," see page C-2 for limit on losses . ☐ Yes ☐ No

H If you started or acquired this business during 2000, check here . . . . ► ☐

Part I Income

1	Gross receipts or sales. **Caution.** If this income was reported to you on Form W-2 and the "Statutory employee" box on that form was checked, see page C-2 and check here . . . . . . ► ☐	**1**	
2	Returns and allowances	**2**	
3	Subtract line 2 from line 1	**3**	
4	Cost of goods sold (from line 42 on page 2)	**4**	
5	**Gross profit.** Subtract line 4 from line 3	**5**	
6	Other income, including Federal and state gasoline or fuel tax credit or refund (see page C-2) . . .	**6**	
7	**Gross income.** Add lines 5 and 6 . . . . ►	**7**	

Part II Expenses. Enter expenses for business use of your home **only** on line 30.

8	Advertising	**8**	**19** Pension and profit-sharing plans	**19**	
9	Bad debts from sales or services (see page C-3) . .	**9**	**20** Rent or lease (see page C-4):		
			a Vehicles, machinery, and equipment .	**20a**	
10	Car and truck expenses (see page C-3)	**10**	**b** Other business property . .	**20b**	
11	Commissions and fees . .	**11**	**21** Repairs and maintenance . .	**21**	
12	Depletion	**12**	**22** Supplies (not included in Part III) .	**22**	
13	Depreciation and section 179 expense deduction (not included in Part III) (see page C-3) . .	**13**	**23** Taxes and licenses	**23**	
			24 Travel, meals, and entertainment:		
			a Travel	**24a**	
14	Employee benefit programs (other than on line 19) . . .	**14**	**b** Meals and entertainment		
15	Insurance (other than health) .	**15**	**c** Enter nondeduct-ible amount in-cluded on line 24b (see page C-5) .		
16	Interest:				
a	Mortgage (paid to banks, etc.) .	**16a**	**d** Subtract line 24c from line 24b .	**24d**	
b	Other	**16b**	**25** Utilities	**25**	
17	Legal and professional services	**17**	**26** Wages (less employment credits) .	**26**	
18	Office expense	**18**	**27** Other expenses (from line 48 on page 2)	**27**	

28	**Total expenses** before expenses for business use of home. Add lines 8 through 27 in columns . ►	**28**	
29	Tentative profit (loss). Subtract line 28 from line 7	**29**	
30	Expenses for business use of your home. Attach **Form 8829**	**30**	
31	**Net profit or (loss).** Subtract line 30 from line 29.		
	● If a profit, enter on **Form 1040, line 12,** and **also** on **Schedule SE, line 2** (statutory employees, see page C-5). Estates and trusts, enter on Form 1041, line 3.	**31**	
	● If a loss, you **must** go to line 32.		
32	If you have a loss, check the box that describes your investment in this activity (see page C-5).		
	● If you checked 32a, enter the loss on **Form 1040, line 12,** and **also** on **Schedule SE, line 2** (statutory employees, see page C-5). Estates and trusts, enter on Form 1041, line 3.	**32a** ☐ All investment is at risk.	
	● If you checked 32b, you **must** attach **Form 6198.**	**32b** ☐ Some investment is not at risk.	

For Paperwork Reduction Act Notice, see Form 1040 instructions.   Cat. No. 11334P   Schedule C (Form 1040) 2000

Schedule C (Form 1040) 2000

Page **2**

Part III Cost of Goods Sold (see page C-6)

33 Method(s) used to value closing inventory: **a** ☐ Cost **b** ☐ Lower of cost or market **c** ☐ Other (attach explanation)

34 Was there any change in determining quantities, costs, or valuations between opening and closing inventory? If "Yes," attach explanation . . . . ☐ Yes ☐ No

35 Inventory at beginning of year. If different from last year's closing inventory, attach explanation	35	
36 Purchases less cost of items withdrawn for personal use	36	
37 Cost of labor. Do not include any amounts paid to yourself	37	
38 Materials and supplies	38	
39 Other costs	39	
40 Add lines 35 through 39	40	
41 Inventory at end of year	41	
42 **Cost of goods sold.** Subtract line 41 from line 40. Enter the result here and on page 1, line 4	42	

Part IV Information on Your Vehicle. Complete this part **only** if you are claiming car or truck expenses on line 10 and are not required to file Form 4562 for this business. See the instructions for line 13 on page C-3 to find out if you must file.

43 When did you place your vehicle in service for business purposes? (month, day, year) ▶ ...... / ...... / ....

44 Of the total number of miles you drove your vehicle during 2000, enter the number of miles you used your vehicle for:

a Business .... **b** Commuting .... **c** Other ....

45 Do you (or your spouse) have another vehicle available for personal use? . . . . ☐ Yes ☐ No

46 Was your vehicle available for use during off-duty hours? . . . . ☐ Yes ☐ No

47a Do you have evidence to support your deduction? . . . . ☐ Yes ☐ No

 b If "Yes," is the evidence written? . . . . ☐ Yes ☐ No

Part V Other Expenses. List below business expenses not included on lines 8–26 or line 30.

48 **Total other expenses.** Enter here and on page 1, line 27	48	

Schedule C (Form 1040) 2000

Form 1065

Department of the Treasury
Internal Revenue Service

U.S. Return of Partnership Income

For calendar year 2000, or tax year beginning .... , 2000, and ending .... , 20.... .
▶ See separate instructions.

OMB No. 1545-0099

2000

A Principal business activity	Use the IRS label. Other-wise, print or type.	Name of partnership
B Principal product or service		Number, street, and room or suite no. If a P.O. box, see page 13 of the instructions.
C Business code number		City or town, state, and ZIP code

D Employer identification number

E Date business started

F Total assets (see page 13 of the instructions)
$

G Check applicable boxes: **(1)** ☐ Initial return **(2)** ☐ Final return **(3)** ☐ Change in address **(4)** ☐ Amended return

H Check accounting method: **(1)** ☐ Cash **(2)** ☐ Accrual **(3)** ☐ Other (specify) ▶ ....

I Number of Schedules K-1. Attach one for each person who was a partner at any time during the tax year ▶ ....

Caution: Include **only** trade or business income and expenses on lines 1a through 22 below. See the instructions for more information.

Income (see page 14 of the instructions for limitations)

1a Gross receipts or sales	**1a**	
b Less returns and allowances	**1b**	**1c**
2 Cost of goods sold (Schedule A, line 8)		**2**
3 Gross profit. Subtract line 2 from line 1c		**3**
4 Ordinary income (loss) from other partnerships, estates, and trusts (attach schedule)		**4**
5 Net farm profit (loss) (attach Schedule F (Form 1040))		**5**
6 Net gain (loss) from Form 4797, Part II, line 18		**6**
7 Other income (loss) (attach schedule)		**7**
8 **Total income (loss).** Combine lines 3 through 7		**8**

Deductions (see page 14 of the instructions for limitations)

9 Salaries and wages (other than to partners) (less employment credits)		**9**
10 Guaranteed payments to partners		**10**
11 Repairs and maintenance		**11**
12 Bad debts		**12**
13 Rent		**13**
14 Taxes and licenses		**14**
15 Interest		**15**
16a Depreciation (if required, attach Form 4562)	**16a**	
b Less depreciation reported on Schedule A and elsewhere on return	**16b**	**16c**
17 Depletion **(Do not deduct oil and gas depletion.)**		**17**
18 Retirement plans, etc.		**18**
19 Employee benefit programs		**19**
20 Other deductions (attach schedule)		**20**
21 **Total deductions.** Add the amounts shown in the far right column for lines 9 through 20		**21**
22 **Ordinary income (loss)** from trade or business activities. Subtract line 21 from line 8		**22**

Sign Here

Under penalties of perjury, I declare that I have examined this return, including accompanying schedules and statements, and to the best of my knowledge and belief, it is true, correct, and complete. Declaration of preparer (other than general partner or limited liability company member) is based on all information of which preparer has any knowledge.

▶ _____   ▶ _____
Signature of general partner or limited liability company member   Date

Paid Preparer's Use Only

Preparer's signature ▶		Date	Check if self-employed ▶ ☐	Preparer's SSN or PTIN
Firm's name (or yours if self-employed), address, and ZIP code ▶		EIN ▶	
		Phone no. ( )	

For Paperwork Reduction Act Notice, see separate instructions.   Cat. No. 11390Z   Form **1065** (2000)

Form 1065 (2000)   Page **2**

Schedule A   Cost of Goods Sold (see page 17 of the instructions)

1	Inventory at beginning of year	**1**
2	Purchases less cost of items withdrawn for personal use	**2**
3	Cost of labor.	**3**
4	Additional section 263A costs *(attach schedule)*	**4**
5	Other costs *(attach schedule)*	**5**
6	**Total.** Add lines 1 through 5	**6**
7	Inventory at end of year	**7**
8	**Cost of goods sold.** Subtract line 7 from line 6. Enter here and on page 1, line 2	**8**

9a Check all methods used for valuing closing inventory:

　　(i) ☐ Cost as described in Regulations section 1.471-3

　　(ii) ☐ Lower of cost or market as described in Regulations section 1.471-4

　　(iii) ☐ Other (specify method used and attach explanation) ▶ --

　b Check this box if there was a writedown of "subnormal" goods as described in Regulations section 1.471-2(c). . . . ▶ ☐

　c Check this box if the LIFO inventory method was adopted this tax year for any goods *(if checked, attach Form 970)* . . ▶ ☐

　d Do the rules of section 263A (for property produced or acquired for resale) apply to the partnership? . . ☐ **Yes** ☐ **No**

　e Was there any change in determining quantities, cost, or valuations between opening and closing inventory? ☐ **Yes** ☐ **No**
　　If "Yes," attach explanation.

Schedule B   Other Information

		Yes	No
1	What type of entity is filing this return? Check the applicable box:		
a ☐ Domestic general partnership 　**b** ☐ Domestic limited partnership			
c ☐ Domestic limited liability company 　**d** ☐ Domestic limited liability partnership			
e ☐ Foreign partnership 　**f** ☐ Other ▶ ------------------------------------			
2	Are any partners in this partnership also partnerships?.		
3	During the partnership's tax year, did the partnership own any interest in another partnership or in any foreign entity that was disregarded as an entity separate from its owner under Regulations sections 301.7701-2 and 301.7701-3? If yes, see instructions for required attachment		
4	Is this partnership subject to the consolidated audit procedures of sections 6221 through 6233? If "Yes," see **Designation of Tax Matters Partner** below		
5	Does this partnership meet **all three** of the following requirements?		
a The partnership's total receipts for the tax year were less than $250,000;			
b The partnership's total assets at the end of the tax year were less than $600,000; **and**			
c Schedules K-1 are filed with the return and furnished to the partners on or before the due date (including extensions) for the partnership return.			
If "Yes," the partnership is not required to complete Schedules L, M-1, and M-2; Item F on page 1 of Form 1065; or Item J on Schedule K-1			
6	Does this partnership have any foreign partners?		
7	Is this partnership a publicly traded partnership as defined in section 469(k)(2)?		
8	Has this partnership filed, or is it required to file, **Form 8264,** Application for Registration of a Tax Shelter? . .		
9	At any time during calendar year 2000, did the partnership have an interest in or a signature or other authority over a financial account in a foreign country (such as a bank account, securities account, or other financial account)? See page 19 of the instructions for exceptions and filing requirements for Form TD F 90-22.1. If "Yes," enter the name of the foreign country. ▶ --		
10	During the tax year, did the partnership receive a distribution from, or was it the grantor of, or transferor to, a foreign trust? If "Yes," the partnership may have to file Form 3520. See page 19 of the instructions		
11	Was there a distribution of property or a transfer (e.g., by sale or death) of a partnership interest during the tax year? If "Yes," you may elect to adjust the basis of the partnership's assets under section 754 by attaching the statement described under **Elections Made By the Partnership** on page 7 of the instructions . . . . . . ▶		
12	Enter the number of Forms 8865 attached to this return . . . . ▶ -------------		

Designation of Tax Matters Partner (see page 19 of the instructions)

Enter below the general partner designated as the tax matters partner (TMP) for the tax year of this return:

Name of designated TMP ▶		Identifying number of TMP ▶
Address of designated TMP ▶		

Form **1065** (2000)

Schedule K   Partners' Shares of Income, Credits, Deductions, etc.

	(a) Distributive share items	(b) Total amount
1	Ordinary income (loss) from trade or business activities (page 1, line 22)	**1**
2	Net income (loss) from rental real estate activities (attach Form 8825)	**2**
3a	Gross income from other rental activities . . . . [3a]	
b	Expenses from other rental activities (attach schedule) . . . . [3b]	
c	Net income (loss) from other rental activities. Subtract line 3b from line 3a	**3c**
4	Portfolio income (loss): **a** Interest income	**4a**
b	Ordinary dividends	**4b**
c	Royalty income	**4c**
d	Net short-term capital gain (loss) (attach Schedule D (Form 1065))	**4d**
e	Net long-term capital gain (loss) (attach Schedule D (Form 1065)):	
	(1) 28% rate gain (loss) ▶ .... **(2)** Total for year . . . . . ▶	**4e(2)**
f	Other portfolio income (loss) (attach schedule)	**4f**
5	Guaranteed payments to partners	**5**
6	Net section 1231 gain (loss) (other than due to casualty or theft) (attach Form 4797) . . .	**6**
7	Other income (loss) (attach schedule)	**7**
8	Charitable contributions (attach schedule)	**8**
9	Section 179 expense deduction (attach Form 4562)	**9**
10	Deductions related to portfolio income (itemize)	**10**
11	Other deductions (attach schedule)	**11**
12a	Low-income housing credit:	
	(1) From partnerships to which section 42(j)(5) applies for property placed in service before 1990 .	**12a(1)**
	(2) Other than on line 12a(1) for property placed in service before 1990	**12a(2)**
	(3) From partnerships to which section 42(j)(5) applies for property placed in service after 1989	**12a(3)**
	(4) Other than on line 12a(3) for property placed in service after 1989	**12a(4)**
b	Qualified rehabilitation expenditures related to rental real estate activities (attach Form 3468)	**12b**
c	Credits (other than credits shown on lines 12a and 12b) related to rental real estate activities	**12c**
d	Credits related to other rental activities	**12d**
13	Other credits	**13**
14a	Interest expense on investment debts	**14a**
b	**(1)** Investment income included on lines 4a, 4b, 4c, and 4f above	**14b(1)**
	(2) Investment expenses included on line 10 above.	**14b(2)**
15a	Net earnings (loss) from self-employment	**15a**
b	Gross farming or fishing income	**15b**
c	Gross nonfarm income	**15c**
16a	Depreciation adjustment on property placed in service after 1986	**16a**
b	Adjusted gain or loss	**16b**
c	Depletion (other than oil and gas)	**16c**
d	**(1)** Gross income from oil, gas, and geothermal properties	**16d(1)**
	(2) Deductions allocable to oil, gas, and geothermal properties	**16d(2)**
e	Other adjustments and tax preference items (attach schedule)	**16e**
17a	Name of foreign country or U.S. possession ▶	
b	Gross income sourced at partner level	**17b**
c	Foreign gross income sourced at partnership level:	
	(1) Passive ▶ .... **(2)** Listed categories (attach schedule) ▶ .... **(3)** General limitation ▶	**17c(3)**
d	Deductions allocated and apportioned at partner level:	
	(1) Interest expense ▶ .... **(2)** Other . . . . . . ▶	**17d(2)**
e	Deductions allocated and apportioned at partnership level to foreign source income:	
	(1) Passive .... **(2)** Listed categories (attach schedule) .... **(3)** General limitation ▶	**17e(3)**
f	Total foreign taxes (check one): ▶ Paid ☐ Accrued ☐	**17f**
g	Reduction in taxes available for credit and gross income from all sources (attach schedule) .	**17g**
18	Section 59(e)(2) expenditures: **a** Type ▶ .... **b** Amount ▶	**18b**
19	Tax-exempt interest income	**19**
20	Other tax-exempt income	**20**
21	Nondeductible expenses	**21**
22	Distributions of money (cash and marketable securities)	**22**
23	Distributions of property other than money	**23**
24	Other items and amounts required to be reported separately to partners (attach schedule) . . .	

Left margin category labels:
Income (Loss) — Deductions — Credits — Investment Interest — Self-Employment — Adjustments and Tax Preference Items — Foreign Taxes — Other

Form 1065 (2000)   Page **4**

Analysis of Net Income (Loss)

1 Net income (loss). Combine Schedule K, lines 1 through 7 in column (b). From the result, subtract the sum of Schedule K, lines 8 through 11, 14a, 17f, and 18b	**1**

2 Analysis by partner type:	**(i)** Corporate	**(ii)** Individual (active)	**(iii)** Individual (passive)	**(iv)** Partnership	**(v)** Exempt organization	**(vi)** Nominee/Other
a General partners						
b Limited partners						

Schedule L — Balance Sheets per Books (Not required if Question 5 on Schedule B is answered "Yes.")

Assets	Beginning of tax year (a)	(b)	End of tax year (c)	(d)
1 Cash				
2a Trade notes and accounts receivable				
b Less allowance for bad debts				
3 Inventories				
4 U.S. government obligations				
5 Tax-exempt securities				
6 Other current assets (attach schedule) . . .				
7 Mortgage and real estate loans				
8 Other investments (attach schedule) . . .				
9a Buildings and other depreciable assets . . .				
b Less accumulated depreciation				
10a Depletable assets				
b Less accumulated depletion				
11 Land (net of any amortization)				
12a Intangible assets (amortizable only)				
b Less accumulated amortization				
13 Other assets (attach schedule)				
14 **Total** assets				
Liabilities and Capital				
15 Accounts payable				
16 Mortgages, notes, bonds payable in less than 1 year .				
17 Other current liabilities (attach schedule) . . .				
18 All nonrecourse loans				
19 Mortgages, notes, bonds payable in 1 year or more .				
20 Other liabilities (attach schedule)				
21 Partners' capital accounts				
22 **Total** liabilities and capital				

Schedule M-1 — Reconciliation of Income (Loss) per Books With Income (Loss) per Return
(Not required if Question 5 on Schedule B is answered "Yes." See page 30 of the instructions.)

1 Net income (loss) per books		**6** Income recorded on books this year not included on Schedule K, lines 1 through 7 (itemize):	
2 Income included on Schedule K, lines 1 through 4, 6, and 7, not recorded on books this year (itemize):		**a** Tax-exempt interest $	
3 Guaranteed payments (other than health insurance)		**7** Deductions included on Schedule K, lines 1 through 11, 14a, 17f, and 18b, not charged against book income this year (itemize):	
4 Expenses recorded on books this year not included on Schedule K, lines 1 through 11, 14a, 17f, and 18b (itemize):		**a** Depreciation $	
a Depreciation $		....	
b Travel and entertainment $		**8** Add lines 6 and 7	
		9 Income (loss) (Analysis of Net Income (Loss), line 1). Subtract line 8 from line 5	
5 Add lines 1 through 4			

Schedule M-2 — Analysis of Partners' Capital Accounts (Not required if Question 5 on Schedule B is answered "Yes.")

1 Balance at beginning of year		**6** Distributions: **a** Cash	
2 Capital contributed during year		**b** Property	
3 Net income (loss) per books		**7** Other decreases (itemize):	
4 Other increases (itemize):		....	
....		**8** Add lines 6 and 7	
5 Add lines 1 through 4		**9** Balance at end of year. Subtract line 8 from line 5	

✹

Form **1065** (2000)

SCHEDULE K-1
(Form 1065)
Department of the Treasury
Internal Revenue Service

Partner's Share of Income, Credits, Deductions, etc.

See separate instructions.

For calendar year 2000 or tax year beginning   , 2000, and ending   , 20

OMB No. 1545-0099

2000

Partner's identifying number ▶

Partnership's identifying number ▶

Partner's name, address, and ZIP code

Partnership's name, address, and ZIP code

A This partner is a ☐ general partner   ☐ limited partner
☐ limited liability company member

B What type of entity is this partner? ▶ ....

C Is this partner a ☐ domestic or a ☐ foreign partner?

D Enter partner's percentage of:

F Partner's share of liabilities (see instructions):
Nonrecourse . . . . $ ....
Qualified nonrecourse financing . $ ....
Other . . . . $ ....

G Tax shelter registration number . ▶ ....

H Check here if this partnership is a publicly traded partnership as defined in section 469(k)(2) . . . . . ☐

	(i) Before change or termination	**(ii)** End of year
Profit sharing	.... %	.... %
Loss sharing	.... %	.... %
Ownership of capital . . .	.... %	.... %

E IRS Center where partnership filed return:

I Check applicable boxes: **(1)** ☐ Final K-1   **(2)** ☐ Amended K-1

J   **Analysis of partner's capital account:**

(a) Capital account at beginning of year	(b) Capital contributed during year	(c) Partner's share of lines 3, 4, and 7, Form 1065, Schedule M-2	(d) Withdrawals and distributions	(e) Capital account at end of year (combine columns (a) through (d))
			( )	

	(a) Distributive share item		**(b)** Amount	**(c)** 1040 filers enter the amount in column (b) on:
Income (Loss)	**1** Ordinary income (loss) from trade or business activities . . .	**1**		See page 6 of Partner's Instructions for Schedule K-1 (Form 1065).
	2 Net income (loss) from rental real estate activities	**2**		
	3 Net income (loss) from other rental activities	**3**		
	4 Portfolio income (loss):			
	a Interest	**4a**		Sch. B, Part I, line 1
	b Ordinary dividends	**4b**		Sch. B, Part II, line 5
	c Royalties	**4c**		Sch. E, Part I, line 4
	d Net short-term capital gain (loss)	**4d**		Sch. D, line 5, col. (f)
	e Net long-term capital gain (loss):			
	(1) 28% rate gain (loss)	**4e(1)**		Sch. D, line 12, col. (g)
	(2) Total for year.	**4e(2)**		Sch. D, line 12, col. (f)
	f Other portfolio income (loss) *(attach schedule)*	**4f**		Enter on applicable line of your return.
	5 Guaranteed payments to partner	**5**		See page 6 of Partner's Instructions for Schedule K-1 (Form 1065).
	6 Net section 1231 gain (loss) (other than due to casualty or theft) .	**6**		
	7 Other income (loss) *(attach schedule)*	**7**		Enter on applicable line of your return.
Deductions	**8** Charitable contributions (see instructions) *(attach schedule)* . .	**8**		Sch. A, line 15 or 16
	9 Section 179 expense deduction.	**9**		See pages 7 and 8 of Partner's Instructions for Schedule K-1 (Form 1065).
	10 Deductions related to portfolio income *(attach schedule)* . . .	**10**		
	11 Other deductions *(attach schedule)*.	**11**		
Credits	**12a** Low-income housing credit:			
	(1) From section 42(j)(5) partnerships for property placed in service before 1990	**12a(1)**		Form 8586, line 5
	(2) Other than on line 12a(1) for property placed in service before 1990	**12a(2)**		
	(3) From section 42(j)(5) partnerships for property placed in service after 1989	**12a(3)**		
	(4) Other than on line 12a(3) for property placed in service after 1989	**12a(4)**		
	b Qualified rehabilitation expenditures related to rental real estate activities	**12b**		See page 8 of Partner's Instructions for Schedule K-1 (Form 1065).
	c Credits (other than credits shown on lines 12a and 12b) related to rental real estate activities.	**12c**		
	d Credits related to other rental activities	**12d**		
	13 Other credits	**13**		

For Paperwork Reduction Act Notice, see Instructions for Form 1065.   Cat. No. 11394R   **Schedule K-1 (Form 1065) 2000**

Tax Forms

Schedule K-1 (Form 1065) 2000   Page **2**

	(a) Distributive share item		(b) Amount	(c) 1040 filers enter the amount in column (b) on:
Investment Interest	**14a** Interest expense on investment debts	**14a**		Form 4952, line 1
	b **(1)** Investment income included on lines 4a, 4b, 4c, and 4f . .	**14b(1)**		See page 9 of Partner's Instructions for Schedule K-1 (Form 1065).
	(2) Investment expenses included on line 10	**14b(2)**		
Self-employment	**15a** Net earnings (loss) from self-employment	**15a**		Sch. SE, Section A or B
	b Gross farming or fishing income	**15b**		See page 9 of Partner's Instructions for Schedule K-1 (Form 1065).
	c Gross nonfarm income	**15c**		
Adjustments and Tax Preference Items	**16a** Depreciation adjustment on property placed in service after 1986	**16a**		See page 9 of Partner's Instructions for Schedule K-1 (Form 1065) and Instructions for Form 6251.
	b Adjusted gain or loss	**16b**		
	c Depletion (other than oil and gas)	**16c**		
	d **(1)** Gross income from oil, gas, and geothermal properties . .	**16d(1)**		
	(2) Deductions allocable to oil, gas, and geothermal properties	**16d(2)**		
	e Other adjustments and tax preference items *(attach schedule)*	**16e**		
Foreign Taxes	**17a** Name of foreign country or U.S. possession ▶ - - - - - - - - - - - - - - -			
	b Gross income sourced at partner level	**17b**		
	c Foreign gross income sourced at partnership level:			Form 1116, Part I
	(1) Passive	**17c(1)**		
	(2) Listed categories *(attach schedule)*	**17c(2)**		
	(3) General limitation	**17c(3)**		
	d Deductions allocated and apportioned at partner level:			
	(1) Interest expense	**17d(1)**		
	(2) Other	**17d(2)**		
	e Deductions allocated and apportioned at partnership level to foreign source income:			
	(1) Passive	**17e(1)**		
	(2) Listed categories *(attach schedule)*	**17e(2)**		
	(3) General limitation	**17e(3)**		
	f Total foreign taxes (check one): ▶ ☐ Paid ☐ Accrued . .	**17f**		Form 1116, Part II
	g Reduction in taxes available for credit and gross income from all sources *(attach schedule)*	**17g**		See Instructions for Form 1116.
Other	**18** Section 59(e)(2) expenditures: **a** Type ▶ - - - - - - - - - - - - - - -			See page 9 of Partner's Instructions for Schedule K-1 (Form 1065).
	b Amount	**18b**		
	19 Tax-exempt interest income	**19**		Form 1040, line 8b
	20 Other tax-exempt income	**20**		See pages 9 and 10 of Partner's Instructions for Schedule K-1 (Form 1065).
	21 Nondeductible expenses	**21**		
	22 Distributions of money (cash and marketable securities) . . .	**22**		
	23 Distributions of property other than money	**23**		
	24 Recapture of low-income housing credit:			Form 8611, line 8
	a From section 42(j)(5) partnerships	**24a**		
	b Other than on line 24a	**24b**		
Supplemental Information	**25** Supplemental information required to be reported separately to each partner *(attach additional schedules if more space is needed):*			

Schedule K-1 (Form 1065) 2000

Form 1120

Department of the Treasury
Internal Revenue Service

U.S. Corporation Income Tax Return

OMB No. 1545-0123

2000

For calendar year 2000 or tax year beginning .... , 2000, ending .... , 20 ....
▶ Instructions are separate. See page 1 for Paperwork Reduction Act Notice.

A Check if a:
1 Consolidated return (attach Form 851) ☐
2 Personal holding co. (attach Sch. PH) ☐
3 Personal service corp. (as defined in Temporary Regs. sec. 1.441-4T— see instructions) ☐

Use IRS label. Otherwise, print or type.

Name

Number, street, and room or suite no. (If a P.O. box, see page 7 of instructions.)

City or town, state, and ZIP code

B Employer identification number

C Date incorporated

D Total assets (see page 8 of instructions)
$

E Check applicable boxes: (1) ☐ Initial return   (2) ☐ Final return   (3) ☐ Change of address

Income

1a	Gross receipts or sales [____] **b** Less returns and allowances [____] **c** Bal ▶	1c
2	Cost of goods sold (Schedule A, line 8)	2
3	Gross profit. Subtract line 2 from line 1c	3
4	Dividends (Schedule C, line 19)	4
5	Interest	5
6	Gross rents	6
7	Gross royalties	7
8	Capital gain net income (attach Schedule D (Form 1120))	8
9	Net gain or (loss) from Form 4797, Part II, line 18 (attach Form 4797)	9
10	Other income (see page 8 of instructions—attach schedule)	10
11	**Total income.** Add lines 3 through 10 ▶	11

Deductions (See instructions for limitations on deductions.)

12	Compensation of officers (Schedule E, line 4)	12
13	Salaries and wages (less employment credits)	13
14	Repairs and maintenance	14
15	Bad debts	15
16	Rents	16
17	Taxes and licenses	17
18	Interest	18
19	Charitable contributions (see page 11 of instructions for 10% limitation)	19
20	Depreciation (attach Form 4562) 20 [____]	
21	Less depreciation claimed on Schedule A and elsewhere on return 21a [____]	21b
22	Depletion	22
23	Advertising	23
24	Pension, profit-sharing, etc., plans	24
25	Employee benefit programs	25
26	Other deductions (attach schedule)	26
27	**Total deductions.** Add lines 12 through 26 ▶	27
28	Taxable income before net operating loss deduction and special deductions. Subtract line 27 from line 11	28
29	**Less:** **a** Net operating loss (NOL) deduction (see page 13 of instructions) 29a [____]	
	b Special deductions (Schedule C, line 20) 29b [____]	29c

Tax and Payments

30	**Taxable income.** Subtract line 29c from line 28	30
31	**Total tax** (Schedule J, line 11)	31
32	**Payments: a** 1999 overpayment credited to 2000 32a [____]	
b	2000 estimated tax payments 32b [____]	
c	Less 2000 refund applied for on Form 4466 32c ([____]) **d** Bal ▶ 32d [____]	
e	Tax deposited with Form 7004 32e [____]	
f	Credit for tax paid on undistributed capital gains (attach Form 2439) 32f [____]	
g	Credit for Federal tax on fuels (attach Form 4136). See instructions 32g [____]	32h
33	Estimated tax penalty (see page 14 of instructions). Check if Form 2220 is attached ▶ ☐	33
34	**Tax due.** If line 32h is smaller than the total of lines 31 and 33, enter amount owed	34
35	**Overpayment.** If line 32h is larger than the total of lines 31 and 33, enter amount overpaid	35
36	Enter amount of line 35 you want: **Credited to 2001 estimated tax** ▶ **Refunded** ▶	36

Sign Here

Under penalties of perjury, I declare that I have examined this return, including accompanying schedules and statements, and to the best of my knowledge and belief, it is true, correct, and complete. Declaration of preparer (other than taxpayer) is based on all information of which preparer has any knowledge.

▶ _____ Signature of officer   Date ▶ _____   Title

Paid Preparer's Use Only

Preparer's signature ▶	Date	Check if self-employed ☐ Preparer's SSN or PTIN
Firm's name (or yours if self-employed), address, and ZIP code ▶		EIN ▶
		Phone no. ( )

Cat. No. 11450Q   Form **1120** (2000)

Form 1120 (2000)
Page **2**

Schedule A — Cost of Goods Sold (See page 14 of instructions.)

1	Inventory at beginning of year	**1**
2	Purchases	**2**
3	Cost of labor	**3**
4	Additional section 263A costs (attach schedule)	**4**
5	Other costs (attach schedule)	**5**
6	**Total.** Add lines 1 through 5	**6**
7	Inventory at end of year	**7**
8	**Cost of goods sold.** Subtract line 7 from line 6. Enter here and on line 2, page 1	**8**

9a Check all methods used for valuing closing inventory:

    (i) ☐ Cost as described in Regulations section 1.471-3

    (ii) ☐ Lower of cost or market as described in Regulations section 1.471-4

    (iii) ☐ Other (Specify method used and attach explanation.) ▶ --

    b Check if there was a writedown of subnormal goods as described in Regulations section 1.471-2(c) . . . . ▶ ☐

    c Check if the LIFO inventory method was adopted this tax year for any goods (if checked, attach Form 970) . . . . . ▶ ☐

    d If the LIFO inventory method was used for this tax year, enter percentage (or amounts) of closing inventory computed under LIFO **9d**

    e If property is produced or acquired for resale, do the rules of section 263A apply to the corporation? . . . . . ☐ Yes ☐ No

    f Was there any change in determining quantities, cost, or valuations between opening and closing inventory? If "Yes," attach explanation . . . . ☐ Yes ☐ No

Schedule C — Dividends and Special Deductions (See page 15 of instructions.)

		(a) Dividends received	(b) %	(c) Special deductions (a) × (b)
1	Dividends from less-than-20%-owned domestic corporations that are subject to the 70% deduction (other than debt-financed stock)		70	
2	Dividends from 20%-or-more-owned domestic corporations that are subject to the 80% deduction (other than debt-financed stock)		80	
3	Dividends on debt-financed stock of domestic and foreign corporations (section 246A)		see instructions	
4	Dividends on certain preferred stock of less-than-20%-owned public utilities		42	
5	Dividends on certain preferred stock of 20%-or-more-owned public utilities		48	
6	Dividends from less-than-20%-owned foreign corporations and certain FSCs that are subject to the 70% deduction		70	
7	Dividends from 20%-or-more-owned foreign corporations and certain FSCs that are subject to the 80% deduction		80	
8	Dividends from wholly owned foreign subsidiaries subject to the 100% deduction (section 245(b))		100	
9	**Total.** Add lines 1 through 8. See page 16 of instructions for limitation	/////	/////	
10	Dividends from domestic corporations received by a small business investment company operating under the Small Business Investment Act of 1958		100	
11	Dividends from certain FSCs that are subject to the 100% deduction (section 245(c)(1))		100	
12	Dividends from affiliated group members subject to the 100% deduction (section 243(a)(3))		100	
13	Other dividends from foreign corporations not included on lines 3, 6, 7, 8, or 11		/////	/////
14	Income from controlled foreign corporations under subpart F (attach Form(s) 5471)		/////	/////
15	Foreign dividend gross-up (section 78)		/////	/////
16	IC-DISC and former DISC dividends not included on lines 1, 2, or 3 (section 246(d))		/////	/////
17	Other dividends		/////	/////
18	Deduction for dividends paid on certain preferred stock of public utilities	/////	/////	
19	**Total dividends.** Add lines 1 through 17. Enter here and on line 4, page 1 ▶		/////	/////
20	**Total special deductions.** Add lines 9, 10, 11, 12, and 18. Enter here and on line 29b, page 1 ▶			

Schedule E — Compensation of Officers (See instructions for line 12, page 1.)

Note: *Complete Schedule E only if total receipts (line 1a plus lines 4 through 10 on page 1, Form 1120) are $500,000 or more.*

	(a) Name of officer	(b) Social security number	(c) Percent of time devoted to business	Percent of corporation stock owned (d) Common	Percent of corporation stock owned (e) Preferred	(f) Amount of compensation
1			%	%	%	
			%	%	%	
			%	%	%	
			%	%	%	
			%	%	%	

2	Total compensation of officers	
3	Compensation of officers claimed on Schedule A and elsewhere on return	
4	Subtract line 3 from line 2. Enter the result here and on line 12, page 1	

Form **1120** (2000)

Form 1120 (2000)   Page **3**

Schedule J   Tax Computation (See page 17 of instructions.)

1	Check if the corporation is a member of a controlled group (see sections 1561 and 1563) . . . . . ▶ ☐	
	Important: Members of a controlled group, see instructions on page 17.	
2a	If the box on line 1 is checked, enter the corporation's share of the $50,000, $25,000, and $9,925,000 taxable income brackets (in that order):	
	(1) ⌊$_____⌋ **(2)** ⌊$_____⌋ **(3)** $_____	
b	Enter the corporation's share of: **(1)** Additional 5% tax (not more than $11,750) $_____	
	(2) Additional 3% tax (not more than $100,000) $_____	
3	Income tax. Check if a qualified personal service corporation under section 448(d)(2) (see page 17) . . ▶ ☐	3
4	Alternative minimum tax (attach Form 4626)	4
5	Add lines 3 and 4	5
6a	Foreign tax credit (attach Form 1118) **6a**	
b	Possessions tax credit (attach Form 5735) **6b**	
c	Check: ☐ Nonconventional source fuel credit ☐ QEV credit (attach Form 8834) **6c**	
d	General business credit. Enter here and check which forms are attached: ☐ 3800	
	☐ 3468 ☐ 5884 ☐ 6478 ☐ 6765 ☐ 8586 ☐ 8830 ☐ 8826	
	☐ 8835 ☐ 8844 ☐ 8845 ☐ 8846 ☐ 8820 ☐ 8847 ☐ 8861 **6d**	
e	Credit for prior year minimum tax (attach Form 8827) **6e**	
f	Qualified zone academy bond credit (attach Form 8860) **6f**	
7	**Total credits.** Add lines 6a through 6f	7
8	Subtract line 7 from line 5	8
9	Personal holding company tax (attach Schedule PH (Form 1120))	9
10	Recapture taxes. Check if from: ☐ Form 4255 ☐ Form 8611	10
11	**Total tax.** Add lines 8 through 10. Enter here and on line 31, page 1	11

Schedule K   Other Information (See page 19 of instructions.)

		Yes	No
1	Check method of accounting: **a** ☐ Cash		
	b ☐ Accrual **c** ☐ Other (specify) ▶		
2	See page 21 of the instructions and enter the:		
a	Business activity code no. ▶		
b	Business activity ▶		
c	Product or service ▶		
3	At the end of the tax year, did the corporation own, directly or indirectly, 50% or more of the voting stock of a domestic corporation? (For rules of attribution, see section 267(c).)		
	If "Yes," attach a schedule showing: **(a)** name and employer identification number (EIN), **(b)** percentage owned, and **(c)** taxable income or (loss) before NOL and special deductions of such corporation for the tax year ending with or within your tax year.		
4	Is the corporation a subsidiary in an affiliated group or a parent-subsidiary controlled group?		
	If "Yes," enter name and EIN of the parent corporation ▶		
5	At the end of the tax year, did any individual, partnership, corporation, estate, or trust own, directly or indirectly, 50% or more of the corporation's voting stock? (For rules of attribution, see section 267(c).)		
	If "Yes," attach a schedule showing name and identifying number. (Do not include any information already entered in **4** above.) Enter percentage owned ▶		
6	During this tax year, did the corporation pay dividends (other than stock dividends and distributions in exchange for stock) in excess of the corporation's current and accumulated earnings and profits? (See sections 301 and 316.)		

		Yes	No
	If "Yes," file **Form 5452,** Corporate Report of Nondividend Distributions.		
	If this is a consolidated return, answer here for the parent corporation and on **Form 851,** Affiliations Schedule, for each subsidiary.		
7	At any time during the tax year, did one foreign person own, directly or indirectly, at least 25% of **(a)** the total voting power of all classes of stock of the corporation entitled to vote or **(b)** the total value of all classes of stock of the corporation?		
	If "Yes,"		
a	Enter percentage owned ▶		
b	Enter owner's country ▶		
c	The corporation may have to file **Form 5472,** Information Return of a 25% Foreign-Owned U.S. Corporation or a Foreign Corporation Engaged in a U.S. Trade or Business. Enter number of Forms 5472 attached ▶		
8	Check this box if the corporation issued publicly offered debt instruments with original issue discount . . ▶ ☐		
	If checked, the corporation may have to file **Form 8281,** Information Return for Publicly Offered Original Issue Discount Instruments.		
9	Enter the amount of tax-exempt interest received or accrued during the tax year ▶ $		
10	Enter the number of shareholders at the end of the tax year (if 75 or fewer) ▶		
11	If the corporation has an NOL for the tax year and is electing to forego the carryback period, check here ▶ ☐		
12	Enter the available NOL carryover from prior tax years (Do not reduce it by any deduction on line 29a.) ▶ $		

Note: *If the corporation, at any time during the tax year, had assets or operated a business in a foreign country or U.S. possession, it may be required to attach **Schedule N (Form 1120),** Foreign Operations of U.S. Corporations, to this return. See Schedule N for details.*

Form **1120** (2000)

Form 1120 (2000)   Page **4**

Schedule L — Balance Sheets per Books

		Beginning of tax year		End of tax year	
	Assets	**(a)**	**(b)**	**(c)**	**(d)**
1	Cash				
2a	Trade notes and accounts receivable				
b	Less allowance for bad debts	( )		( )	
3	Inventories				
4	U.S. government obligations				
5	Tax-exempt securities (see instructions)				
6	Other current assets (attach schedule)				
7	Loans to shareholders				
8	Mortgage and real estate loans				
9	Other investments (attach schedule)				
10a	Buildings and other depreciable assets				
b	Less accumulated depreciation	( )		( )	
11a	Depletable assets				
b	Less accumulated depletion	( )		( )	
12	Land (net of any amortization)				
13a	Intangible assets (amortizable only)				
b	Less accumulated amortization	( )		( )	
14	Other assets (attach schedule)				
15	Total assets				
	Liabilities and Shareholders' Equity				
16	Accounts payable				
17	Mortgages, notes, bonds payable in less than 1 year				
18	Other current liabilities (attach schedule)				
19	Loans from shareholders				
20	Mortgages, notes, bonds payable in 1 year or more				
21	Other liabilities (attach schedule)				
22	Capital stock: **a** Preferred stock				
	b Common stock				
23	Additional paid-in capital				
24	Retained earnings—Appropriated (attach schedule)				
25	Retained earnings—Unappropriated				
26	Adjustments to shareholders' equity (attach schedule)				
27	Less cost of treasury stock		( )		( )
28	Total liabilities and shareholders' equity				

Note: *The corporation is not required to complete Schedules M-1 and M-2 if the total assets on line 15, col. (d) of Schedule L are less than $25,000.*

Schedule M-1 — Reconciliation of Income (Loss) per Books With Income per Return (See page 20 of instructions.)

1	Net income (loss) per books		7	Income recorded on books this year not included on this return (itemize):	
2	Federal income tax			Tax-exempt interest $	
3	Excess of capital losses over capital gains			....	
4	Income subject to tax not recorded on books this year (itemize):		8	Deductions on this return not charged against book income this year (itemize):	
	....		a	Depreciation . . . $	
5	Expenses recorded on books this year not deducted on this return (itemize):		b	Contributions carryover $	
a	Depreciation . . . $			....	
b	Contributions carryover $			....	
c	Travel and entertainment $		9	Add lines 7 and 8	
	....		10	Income (line 28, page 1)—line 6 less line 9	
6	Add lines 1 through 5				

Schedule M-2 — Analysis of Unappropriated Retained Earnings per Books (Line 25, Schedule L)

1	Balance at beginning of year		5	Distributions: **a** Cash	
2	Net income (loss) per books			**b** Stock	
3	Other increases (itemize):			**c** Property	
	....		6	Other decreases (itemize):	
	....		7	Add lines 5 and 6	
4	Add lines 1, 2, and 3		8	Balance at end of year (line 4 less line 7)	

Form **1120** (2000)

Form **1120S**

Department of the Treasury
Internal Revenue Service

U.S. Income Tax Return for an S Corporation

▶ **Do not file this form unless the corporation has timely filed
Form 2553 to elect to be an S corporation.**
▶ **See separate instructions.**

OMB No. 1545-0130

2000

For calendar year 2000, or tax year beginning _____ , 2000, and ending _____ , 20 _____

A Effective date of election as an S corporation	Use IRS label. Other-wise, print or type.	Name	C Employer identification number
		Number, street, and room or suite no. (If a P.O. box, see page 11 of the instructions.)	D Date incorporated
B Business code no. (see pages 29–31)		City or town, state, and ZIP code	E Total assets (see page 11) $

F Check applicable boxes: (1) ☐ Initial return   (2) ☐ Final return   (3) ☐ Change in address   (4) ☐ Amended return
G Enter number of shareholders in the corporation at end of the tax year . . . . ▶

Caution: *Include* **only** *trade or business income and expenses on lines 1a through 21. See page 11 of the instructions for more information.*

Income

1a	Gross receipts or sales _____ **b** Less returns and allowances _____ **c** Bal▶	1c	
2	Cost of goods sold (Schedule A, line 8)	2	
3	Gross profit. Subtract line 2 from line 1c	3	
4	Net gain (loss) from Form 4797, Part II, line 18 *(attach Form 4797)*	4	
5	Other income (loss) *(attach schedule)*.	5	
6	**Total income (loss).** Combine lines 3 through 5 . . . . ▶	6	

Deductions (see page 12 of the instructions for limitations)

7	Compensation of officers	7	
8	Salaries and wages (less employment credits)	8	
9	Repairs and maintenance	9	
10	Bad debts	10	
11	Rents.	11	
12	Taxes and licenses	12	
13	Interest	13	
14a	Depreciation *(if required, attach Form 4562)* . . . . . . [14a]		
b	Depreciation claimed on Schedule A and elsewhere on return . [14b]		
c	Subtract line 14b from line 14a	14c	
15	Depletion **(Do not deduct oil and gas depletion.)**	15	
16	Advertising	16	
17	Pension, profit-sharing, etc., plans	17	
18	Employee benefit programs	18	
19	Other deductions *(attach schedule)*	19	
20	**Total deductions.** Add the amounts shown in the far right column for lines 7 through 19 . ▶	20	
21	Ordinary income (loss) from trade or business activities. Subtract line 20 from line 6. . . .	21	

Tax and Payments

22	**Tax: a** Excess net passive income tax *(attach schedule)* . . . [22a]		
b	Tax from Schedule D (Form 1120S) . . . . [22b]		
c	Add lines 22a and 22b (see page 15 of the instructions for additional taxes)	22c	
23	**Payments: a** 2000 estimated tax payments and amount applied from 1999 return [23a]		
b	Tax deposited with Form 7004. . . . . [23b]		
c	Credit for Federal tax paid on fuels *(attach Form 4136)* . . . [23c]		
d	Add lines 23a through 23c	23d	
24	Estimated tax penalty. Check if Form 2220 is attached . . . . ▶ ☐	24	
25	**Tax due.** If the total of lines 22c and 24 is larger than line 23d, enter amount owed. See page 4 of the instructions for depository method of payment . . . . ▶	25	
26	**Overpayment.** If line 23d is larger than the total of lines 22c and 24, enter amount overpaid ▶	26	
27	Enter amount of line 26 you want: **Credited to 2001 estimated tax** ▶ _____ **Refunded** ▶	27	

Sign Here

Under penalties of perjury, I declare that I have examined this return, including accompanying schedules and statements, and to the best of my knowledge and belief, it is true, correct, and complete. Declaration of preparer (other than taxpayer) is based on all information of which preparer has any knowledge.

▶ _____   _____   _____
    Signature of officer   Date   Title

Paid Preparer's Use Only

Preparer's signature ▶		Date	Check if self-employed ☐	Preparer's SSN or PTIN
Firm's name (or yours if self-employed), address, and ZIP code	▶		EIN	
			Phone no. ( )	

For Paperwork Reduction Act Notice, see the separate instructions.   Cat. No. 11510H   Form **1120S** (2000)

Form 1120S (2000)   **Page 2**

Schedule A   Cost of Goods Sold (see page 16 of the instructions)

1	Inventory at beginning of year	1
2	Purchases	2
3	Cost of labor	3
4	Additional section 263A costs (attach schedule)	4
5	Other costs (attach schedule)	5
6	**Total.** Add lines 1 through 5	6
7	Inventory at end of year	7
8	**Cost of goods sold.** Subtract line 7 from line 6. Enter here and on page 1, line 2	8

9a   Check all methods used for valuing closing inventory:

    (i) ☐ Cost as described in Regulations section 1.471-3

    (ii) ☐ Lower of cost or market as described in Regulations section 1.471-4

    (iii) ☐ Other (specify method used and attach explanation) ▶ ....

  b   Check if there was a writedown of "subnormal" goods as described in Regulations section 1.471-2(c)   ▶ ☐

  c   Check if the LIFO inventory method was adopted this tax year for any goods (if checked, attach Form 970)   ▶ ☐

  d   If the LIFO inventory method was used for this tax year, enter percentage (or amounts) of closing inventory computed under LIFO | 9d |

  e   Do the rules of section 263A (for property produced or acquired for resale) apply to the corporation?   ☐ Yes   ☐ No

  f   Was there any change in determining quantities, cost, or valuations between opening and closing inventory?   ☐ Yes   ☐ No
     If "Yes," attach explanation.

Schedule B   Other Information   Yes | No

1   Check method of accounting: **(a)** ☐ Cash   **(b)** ☐ Accrual   **(c)** ☐ Other (specify) ▶ ....

2   Refer to the list on pages 29 through 31 of the instructions and state the corporation's principal:

    (a) Business activity ▶ ....   **(b)** Product or service ▶ ....

3   Did the corporation at the end of the tax year own, directly or indirectly, 50% or more of the voting stock of a domestic corporation? (For rules of attribution, see section 267(c).) If "Yes," attach a schedule showing: **(a)** name, address, and employer identification number and **(b)** percentage owned.

4   Was the corporation a member of a controlled group subject to the provisions of section 1561?

5   Check this box if the corporation has filed or is required to file **Form 8264,** Application for Registration of a Tax Shelter   ▶ ☐

6   Check this box if the corporation issued publicly offered debt instruments with original issue discount   ▶ ☐

     If so, the corporation may have to file **Form 8281,** Information Return for Publicly Offered Original Issue Discount Instruments.

7   If the corporation: **(a)** filed its election to be an S corporation after 1986, **(b)** was a C corporation before it elected to be an S corporation **or** the corporation acquired an asset with a basis determined by reference to its basis (or the basis of any other property) in the hands of a C corporation, and **(c)** has net unrealized built-in gain (defined in section 1374(d)(1)) in excess of the net recognized built-in gain from prior years, enter the net unrealized built-in gain reduced by net recognized built-in gain from prior years (see page 17 of the instructions)   ▶ $ ....

8   Check this box if the corporation had accumulated earnings and profits at the close of the tax year (see page 18 of the instructions)   ▶ ☐

Note: If the corporation had assets or operated a business in a foreign country or U.S. possession, it may be required to attach **Schedule N (Form 1120),** Foreign Operations of U.S. Corporations, to this return. See Schedule N for details.

Schedule K   Shareholders' Shares of Income, Credits, Deductions, etc.

	(a) Pro rata share items		**(b)** Total amount
1	Ordinary income (loss) from trade or business activities (page 1, line 21)	1	
2	Net income (loss) from rental real estate activities (attach Form 8825)	2	
3a	Gross income from other rental activities	3a	
b	Expenses from other rental activities (attach schedule)	3b	
c	Net income (loss) from other rental activities. Subtract line 3b from line 3a	3c	
4	Portfolio income (loss):		
a	Interest income	4a	
b	Ordinary dividends	4b	
c	Royalty income	4c	
d	Net short-term capital gain (loss) (attach Schedule D (Form 1120S))	4d	
e	Net long-term capital gain (loss) (attach Schedule D (Form 1120S)):		
	(1) 28% rate gain (loss) ▶ .... (2) Total for year ▶	4e(2)	
f	Other portfolio income (loss) (attach schedule)	4f	
5	Net section 1231 gain (loss) (other than due to casualty or theft) (attach Form 4797)	5	
6	Other income (loss) (attach schedule)	6	

(Left margin label: Income (Loss))

Form 1120S (2000)   Page **3**

Schedule K	**Shareholders' Shares of Income, Credits, Deductions, etc.** (*continued*)		
	(a) Pro rata share items		**(b)** Total amount

Deductions

7	Charitable contributions (*attach schedule*)	7	
8	Section 179 expense deduction (*attach Form 4562*)	8	
9	Deductions related to portfolio income (loss) (itemize)	9	
10	Other deductions (*attach schedule*)	10	

Investment Interest

11a	Interest expense on investment debts	11a	
b (1)	Investment income included on lines 4a, 4b, 4c, and 4f above	11b(1)	
(2)	Investment expenses included on line 9 above	11b(2)	

Credits

12a	Credit for alcohol used as a fuel (*attach Form 6478*)	12a	
b	Low-income housing credit:		
(1)	From partnerships to which section 42(j)(5) applies for property placed in service before 1990	12b(1)	
(2)	Other than on line 12b(1) for property placed in service before 1990	12b(2)	
(3)	From partnerships to which section 42(j)(5) applies for property placed in service after 1989	12b(3)	
(4)	Other than on line 12b(3) for property placed in service after 1989	12b(4)	
c	Qualified rehabilitation expenditures related to rental real estate activities (*attach Form 3468*) .	12c	
d	Credits (other than credits shown on lines 12b and 12c) related to rental real estate activities	12d	
e	Credits related to other rental activities	12e	
13	Other credits	13	

Adjustments and Tax Preference Items

14a	Depreciation adjustment on property placed in service after 1986	14a	
b	Adjusted gain or loss	14b	
c	Depletion (other than oil and gas)	14c	
d (1)	Gross income from oil, gas, or geothermal properties	14d(1)	
(2)	Deductions allocable to oil, gas, or geothermal properties	14d(2)	
e	Other adjustments and tax preference items (*attach schedule*)	14e	

Foreign Taxes

15a	Name of foreign country or U.S. possession ▶ -------------------------------		
b	Gross income sourced at shareholder level	15b	
c	Foreign gross income sourced at corporate level:		
(1)	Passive	15c(1)	
(2)	Listed categories (*attach schedule*)	15c(2)	
(3)	General limitation	15c(3)	
d	Deductions allocated and apportioned at shareholder level:		
(1)	Interest expense	15d(1)	
(2)	Other	15d(2)	
e	Deductions allocated and apportioned at corporate level to foreign source income:		
(1)	Passive	15e(1)	
(2)	Listed categories (*attach schedule*)	15e(2)	
(3)	General limitation	15e(3)	
f	Total foreign taxes (check one): ▶ ☐ Paid ☐ Accrued	15f	
g	Reduction in taxes available for credit and gross income from all sources (*attach schedule*)	15g	

Other

16	Section 59(e)(2) expenditures: **a** Type ▶ ------------------------ **b** Amount ▶	16b	
17	Tax-exempt interest income	17	
18	Other tax-exempt income	18	
19	Nondeductible expenses	19	
20	Total property distributions (including cash) other than dividends reported on line 22 below	20	
21	Other items and amounts required to be reported separately to shareholders (*attach schedule*)		
22	Total dividend distributions paid from accumulated earnings and profits	22	
23	**Income (loss).** (Required only if Schedule M-1 must be completed.) Combine lines 1 through 6 in column (b). From the result, subtract the sum of lines 7 through 11a, 15f, and 16b .	23	

Form **1120S** (2000)

Form 1120S (2000)   Page **4**

Schedule L	**Balance Sheets per Books**	Beginning of tax year		End of tax year	
	Assets	(a)	(b)	(c)	(d)
1	Cash				
2a	Trade notes and accounts receivable . .				
b	Less allowance for bad debts				
3	Inventories				
4	U.S. Government obligations				
5	Tax-exempt securities				
6	Other current assets (attach schedule) .				
7	Loans to shareholders				
8	Mortgage and real estate loans . . .				
9	Other investments (attach schedule) . .				
10a	Buildings and other depreciable assets .				
b	Less accumulated depreciation . . .				
11a	Depletable assets				
b	Less accumulated depletion.				
12	Land (net of any amortization)				
13a	Intangible assets (amortizable only) . .				
b	Less accumulated amortization. . . .				
14	Other assets (attach schedule)				
15	Total assets				
	Liabilities and Shareholders' Equity				
16	Accounts payable				
17	Mortgages, notes, bonds payable in less than 1 year				
18	Other current liabilities (attach schedule) .				
19	Loans from shareholders.				
20	Mortgages, notes, bonds payable in 1 year or more				
21	Other liabilities (attach schedule) . . .				
22	Capital stock				
23	Additional paid-in capital.				
24	Retained earnings				
25	Adjustments to shareholders' equity (attach schedule)				
26	Less cost of treasury stock		( )		( )
27	Total liabilities and shareholders' equity . .				

Schedule M-1 **Reconciliation of Income (Loss) per Books With Income (Loss) per Return** (You are not required to complete this schedule if the total assets on line 15, column (d), of Schedule L are less than $25,000.)

1	Net income (loss) per books.		5	Income recorded on books this year not included on Schedule K, lines 1 through 6 (itemize):	
2	Income included on Schedule K, lines 1 through 6, not recorded on books this year (itemize):		a	Tax-exempt interest $	
	---			--	
3	Expenses recorded on books this year not included on Schedule K, lines 1 through 11a, 15f, and 16b (itemize):		6	Deductions included on Schedule K, lines 1 through 11a, 15f, and 16b, not charged against book income this year (itemize):	
a	Depreciation $		a	Depreciation $	
b	Travel and entertainment $			--	
	---		7	Add lines 5 and 6.	
4	Add lines 1 through 3.		8	Income (loss) (Schedule K, line 23). Line 4 less line 7	

Schedule M-2 **Analysis of Accumulated Adjustments Account, Other Adjustments Account, and Shareholders' Undistributed Taxable Income Previously Taxed** (see page 27 of the instructions)

		(a) Accumulated adjustments account	(b) Other adjustments account	(c) Shareholders' undistributed taxable income previously taxed
1	Balance at beginning of tax year . . .			
2	Ordinary income from page 1, line 21. .			
3	Other additions.			
4	Loss from page 1, line 21	( )		
5	Other reductions	( )	( )	
6	Combine lines 1 through 5			
7	Distributions other than dividend distributions.			
8	Balance at end of tax year. Subtract line 7 from line 6			

SCHEDULE K-1 (Form 1120S)	Shareholder's Share of Income, Credits, Deductions, etc.	OMB No. 1545-0130

SCHEDULE K-1
(Form 1120S)

Department of the Treasury
Internal Revenue Service

Shareholder's Share of Income, Credits, Deductions, etc.

▶ See separate instructions.

For calendar year 2000 or tax year

beginning _____ , 2000, and ending _____ , 20 ___

OMB No. 1545-0130

2000

Shareholder's identifying number ▶	Corporation's identifying number ▶
Shareholder's name, address, and ZIP code	Corporation's name, address, and ZIP code

A Shareholder's percentage of stock ownership for tax year (see instructions for Schedule K-1) . . . . ▶ _____ %

B Internal Revenue Service Center where corporation filed its return ▶ ------------------------------------

C Tax shelter registration number (see instructions for Schedule K-1) . . . . ▶ ------------------------------------

D Check applicable boxes: **(1)** ☐ Final K-1   **(2)** ☐ Amended K-1

		(a) Pro rata share items		(b) Amount	(c) Form 1040 filers enter the amount in column (b) on:
Income (Loss)	**1**	Ordinary income (loss) from trade or business activities . . .	**1**		See pages 4 and 5 of the Shareholder's Instructions for Schedule K-1 (Form 1120S).
	2	Net income (loss) from rental real estate activities	**2**		
	3	Net income (loss) from other rental activities	**3**		
	4	Portfolio income (loss):			
	a	Interest	**4a**		Sch. B, Part I, line 1
	b	Ordinary dividends	**4b**		Sch. B, Part II, line 5
	c	Royalties	**4c**		Sch. E, Part I, line 4
	d	Net short-term capital gain (loss).	**4d**		Sch. D, line 5, col. (f)
	e	Net long-term capital gain (loss):			
		(1) 28% rate gain (loss)	**4e(1)**		Sch. D, line 12, col. (g)
		(2) Total for year	**4e(2)**		Sch. D, line 12, col. (f)
	f	Other portfolio income (loss) (attach schedule)	**4f**		(Enter on applicable line of your return.)
	5	Net section 1231 gain (loss) (other than due to casualty or theft)	**5**		See Shareholder's Instructions for Schedule K-1 (Form 1120S).
	6	Other income (loss) (attach schedule)	**6**		(Enter on applicable line of your return.)
Deductions	**7**	Charitable contributions (attach schedule)	**7**		Sch. A, line 15 or 16
	8	Section 179 expense deduction	**8**		See page 6 of the Shareholder's Instructions for Schedule K-1 (Form 1120S).
	9	Deductions related to portfolio income (loss) (attach schedule) .	**9**		
	10	Other deductions (attach schedule)	**10**		
Investment Interest	**11a**	Interest expense on investment debts	**11a**		Form 4952, line 1
	b	**(1)** Investment income included on lines 4a, 4b, 4c, and 4f above	**11b(1)**		See Shareholder's Instructions for Schedule K-1 (Form 1120S).
		(2) Investment expenses included on line 9 above	**11b(2)**		
Credits	**12a**	Credit for alcohol used as fuel	**12a**		Form 6478, line 10
	b	Low-income housing credit:			
		(1) From section 42(j)(5) partnerships for property placed in service before 1990.	**12b(1)**		Form 8586, line 5
		(2) Other than on line 12b(1) for property placed in service before 1990	**12b(2)**		
		(3) From section 42(j)(5) partnerships for property placed in service after 1989	**12b(3)**		
		(4) Other than on line 12b(3) for property placed in service after 1989	**12b(4)**		
	c	Qualified rehabilitation expenditures related to rental real estate activities	**12c**		See page 7 of the Shareholder's Instructions for Schedule K-1 (Form 1120S).
	d	Credits (other than credits shown on lines 12b and 12c) related to rental real estate activities	**12d**		
	e	Credits related to other rental activities.	**12e**		
	13	Other credits	**13**		

For Paperwork Reduction Act Notice, see the Instructions for Form 1120S.   Cat. No. 11520D   **Schedule K-1 (Form 1120S) 2000**

Schedule K-1 (Form 1120S) (2000)

Page **2**

(a) Pro rata share items		(b) Amount	(c) Form 1040 filers enter the amount in column (b) on:
Adjustments and Tax Preference Items	**14a** Depreciation adjustment on property placed in service after 1986	**14a**	See page 7 of the Shareholder's Instructions for Schedule K-1 (Form 1120S) and Instructions for Form 6251
	b Adjusted gain or loss	**14b**	
	c Depletion (other than oil and gas)	**14c**	
	d (1) Gross income from oil, gas, or geothermal properties	**14d(1)**	
	(2) Deductions allocable to oil, gas, or geothermal properties	**14d(2)**	
	e Other adjustments and tax preference items (attach schedule)	**14e**	
Foreign Taxes	**15a** Name of foreign country or U.S. possession ▶		Form 1116, Part I
	b Gross income sourced at shareholder level	**15b**	
	c Foreign gross income sourced at corporate level:		
	(1) Passive	**15c(1)**	
	(2) Listed categories (attach schedule)	**15c(2)**	
	(3) General limitation	**15c(3)**	
	d Deductions allocated and apportioned at shareholder level:		
	(1) Interest expense	**15d(1)**	
	(2) Other	**15d(2)**	
	e Deductions allocated and apportioned at corporate level to foreign source income:		
	(1) Passive	**15e(1)**	
	(2) Listed categories (attach schedule)	**15e(2)**	
	(3) General limitation	**15e(3)**	
	f Total foreign taxes (check one): ▶ ☐ Paid ☐ Accrued	**15f**	Form 1116, Part II
	g Reduction in taxes available for credit and gross income from all sources (attach schedule)	**15g**	See Instructions for Form 1116
Other	**16** Section 59(e)(2) expenditures: a Type ▶		See Shareholder's Instructions for Schedule K-1 (Form 1120S).
	b Amount	**16b**	
	17 Tax-exempt interest income	**17**	Form 1040, line 8b
	18 Other tax-exempt income	**18**	See pages 7 and 8 of the Shareholder's Instructions for Schedule K-1 (Form 1120S).
	19 Nondeductible expenses	**19**	
	20 Property distributions (including cash) other than dividend distributions reported to you on Form 1099-DIV	**20**	
	21 Amount of loan repayments for "Loans From Shareholders"	**21**	
	22 Recapture of low-income housing credit:		Form 8611, line 8
	a From section 42(j)(5) partnerships	**22a**	
	b Other than on line 22a	**22b**	

Supplemental Information

23 Supplemental information required to be reported separately to each shareholder (attach additional schedules if more space is needed):

Form **2553**
(Rev. January 2001)

Department of the Treasury
Internal Revenue Service

Election by a Small Business Corporation

(Under section 1362 of the Internal Revenue Code)
► See Parts II and III on back and the separate instructions.
► The corporation may either send or fax this form to the IRS. See page 1 of the instructions.

OMB No. 1545-0146

Notes:
1. *This election to be an S corporation can be accepted only if all the tests are met under **Who May Elect** on page 1 of the instructions; all signatures in Parts I and III are originals (no photocopies); and the exact name and address of the corporation and other required form information are provided.*

2. *Do not file **Form 1120S**, U.S. Income Tax Return for an S Corporation, for any tax year before the year the election takes effect.*

3. *If the corporation was in existence before the effective date of this election, see **Taxes an S Corporation May Owe** on page 1 of the instructions.*

Part I   Election Information

Please Type or Print	Name of corporation (see instructions)	**A** Employer identification number
	Number, street, and room or suite no. (If a P.O. box, see instructions.)	**B** Date incorporated
	City or town, state, and ZIP code	**C** State of incorporation

D Election is to be effective for tax year beginning (month, day, year) . . . . ► / /

E Name and title of officer or legal representative who the IRS may call for more information

F Telephone number of officer or legal representative

(   )

G If the corporation changed its name or address after applying for the EIN shown in **A** above, check this box . . . . ► ☐

H If this election takes effect for the first tax year the corporation exists, enter month, day, and year of the **earliest** of the following: (1) date the corporation first had shareholders, (2) date the corporation first had assets, or (3) date the corporation began doing business . . . . ► / /

I Selected tax year: Annual return will be filed for tax year ending (month and day) ► -

If the tax year ends on any date other than December 31, except for an automatic 52-53-week tax year ending with reference to the month of December, you **must** complete Part II on the back. If the date you enter is the ending date of an automatic 52-53-week tax year, write "52-53-week year" to the right of the date. See Temporary Regulations section 1.441-2T(e)(3).

J Name and address of each shareholder; shareholder's spouse having a community property interest in the corporation's stock; and each tenant in common, joint tenant, and tenant by the entirety. (A husband and wife (and their estates) are counted as one shareholder in determining the number of shareholders without regard to the manner in which the stock is owned.)	**K** Shareholders' Consent Statement. Under penalties of perjury, we declare that we consent to the election of the above-named corporation to be an S corporation under section 1362(a) and that we have examined this consent statement, including accompanying schedules and statements, and to the best of our knowledge and belief, it is true, correct, and complete. We understand our consent is binding and may not be withdrawn after the corporation has made a valid election. (Shareholders sign and date below.)		**L** Stock owned		**M** Social security number or employer identification number (see instructions)	**N** Shareholder's tax year ends (month and day)
	Signature	Date	Number of shares	Dates acquired		

Under penalties of perjury, I declare that I have examined this election, including accompanying schedules and statements, and to the best of my knowledge and belief, it is true, correct, and complete.

Signature of officer ►   Title ►   Date ►

For Paperwork Reduction Act Notice, see page 4 of the instructions.   Cat. No. 18629R   Form **2553** (Rev. 1-2001)

Part II   Selection of Fiscal Tax Year (All corporations using this part must complete item O and item P, Q, or R.)

O   Check the applicable box to indicate whether the corporation is:

    1. ☐ A new corporation adopting the tax year entered in item I, Part I.

    2. ☐ An existing corporation retaining the tax year entered in item I, Part I.

    3. ☐ An existing corporation changing to the tax year entered in item I, Part I.

P   Complete item P if the corporation is using the expeditious approval provisions of Rev. Proc. 87-32, 1987-2 C.B. 396, to request **(1)** a natural business year (as defined in section 4.01(1) of Rev. Proc. 87-32) or **(2)** a year that satisfies the ownership tax year test in section 4.01(2) of Rev. Proc. 87-32. Check the applicable box below to indicate the representation statement the corporation is making as required under section 4 of Rev. Proc. 87-32.

    1. Natural Business Year ▶ ☐ I represent that the corporation is retaining or changing to a tax year that coincides with its natural business year as defined in section 4.01(1) of Rev. Proc. 87-32 and as verified by its satisfaction of the requirements of section 4.02(1) of Rev. Proc. 87-32. In addition, if the corporation is changing to a natural business year as defined in section 4.01(1), I further represent that such tax year results in less deferral of income to the owners than the corporation's present tax year. I also represent that the corporation is not described in section 3.01(2) of Rev. Proc. 87-32. (See instructions for additional information that must be attached.)

    2. Ownership Tax Year ▶ ☐ I represent that shareholders holding more than half of the shares of the stock (as of the first day of the tax year to which the request relates) of the corporation have the same tax year or are concurrently changing to the tax year that the corporation adopts, retains, or changes to per item I, Part I. I also represent that the corporation is not described in section 3.01(2) of Rev. Proc. 87-32.

Note: *If you do not use item P and the corporation wants a fiscal tax year, complete either item Q or R below. Item Q is used to request a fiscal tax year based on a business purpose and to make a back-up section 444 election. Item R is used to make a regular section 444 election.*

Q   Business Purpose—To request a fiscal tax year based on a business purpose, you must check box Q1 and pay a user fee. See instructions for details. You may also check box Q2 and/or box Q3.

    1. Check here ▶ ☐ if the fiscal year entered in item I, Part I, is requested under the provisions of section 6.03 of Rev. Proc. 87-32. Attach to Form 2553 a statement showing the business purpose for the requested fiscal year. See instructions for additional information that must be attached.

    2. Check here ▶ ☐ to show that the corporation intends to make a back-up section 444 election in the event the corporation's business purpose request is not approved by the IRS. (See instructions for more information.)

    3. Check here ▶ ☐ to show that the corporation agrees to adopt or change to a tax year ending December 31 if necessary for the IRS to accept this election for S corporation status in the event (1) the corporation's business purpose request is not approved and the corporation makes a back-up section 444 election, but is ultimately not qualified to make a section 444 election, or (2) the corporation's business purpose request is not approved and the corporation did not make a back-up section 444 election.

R   Section 444 Election—To make a section 444 election, you must check box R1 and you may also check box R2.

    1. Check here ▶ ☐ to show the corporation will make, if qualified, a section 444 election to have the fiscal tax year shown in item I, Part I. To make the election, you must complete **Form 8716,** Election To Have a Tax Year Other Than a Required Tax Year, and either attach it to Form 2553 or file it separately.

    2. Check here ▶ ☐ to show that the corporation agrees to adopt or change to a tax year ending December 31 if necessary for the IRS to accept this election for S corporation status in the event the corporation is ultimately not qualified to make a section 444 election.

Part III   Qualified Subchapter S Trust (QSST) Election Under Section 1361(d)(2)*

Income beneficiary's name and address	Social security number
Trust's name and address	Employer identification number

Date on which stock of the corporation was transferred to the trust (month, day, year) . . . . ▶   /   /

In order for the trust named above to be a QSST and thus a qualifying shareholder of the S corporation for which this Form 2553 is filed, I hereby make the election under section 1361(d)(2). Under penalties of perjury, I certify that the trust meets the definitional requirements of section 1361(d)(3) and that all other information provided in Part III is true, correct, and complete.

_____   _____

Signature of income beneficiary or signature and title of legal representative or other qualified person making the election   Date

*Use Part III to make the QSST election only if stock of the corporation has been transferred to the trust on or before the date on which the corporation makes its election to be an S corporation. The QSST election must be made and filed separately if stock of the corporation is transferred to the trust after the date on which the corporation makes the S election.

Form **4562**	**Depreciation and Amortization**	OMB No. 1545-0172
	(Including Information on Listed Property)	**2000**
Department of the Treasury Internal Revenue Service (99)	▶ See separate instructions. ▶ Attach this form to your return.	Attachment Sequence No. **67**

Name(s) shown on return	Business or activity to which this form relates	Identifying number

Part I   Election To Expense Certain Tangible Property (Section 179)
Note: If you have any "listed property," complete Part V before you complete Part I.

1	Maximum dollar limitation. If an enterprise zone business, see page 2 of the instructions	**1**	$20,000
2	Total cost of section 179 property placed in service. See page 2 of the instructions	**2**	
3	Threshold cost of section 179 property before reduction in limitation	**3**	$200,000
4	Reduction in limitation. Subtract line 3 from line 2. If zero or less, enter -0-	**4**	
5	Dollar limitation for tax year. Subtract line 4 from line 1. If zero or less, enter -0-. If married filing separately, see page 2 of the instructions	**5**	

(a) Description of property	(b) Cost (business use only)	(c) Elected cost
6		

7	Listed property. Enter amount from line 27.	**7**	
8	Total elected cost of section 179 property. Add amounts in column (c), lines 6 and 7	**8**	
9	Tentative deduction. Enter the smaller of line 5 or line 8	**9**	
10	Carryover of disallowed deduction from 1999. See page 3 of the instructions	**10**	
11	Business income limitation. Enter the smaller of business income (not less than zero) or line 5 (see instructions)	**11**	
12	Section 179 expense deduction. Add lines 9 and 10, but do not enter more than line 11	**12**	
13	Carryover of disallowed deduction to 2001. Add lines 9 and 10, less line 12 ▶	**13**	

Note: Do not use Part II or Part III below for listed property (automobiles, certain other vehicles, cellular telephones, certain computers, or property used for entertainment, recreation, or amusement). Instead, use Part V for listed property.

Part II   MACRS Depreciation for Assets Placed in Service Only During Your 2000 Tax Year (Do not include listed property.)

Section A—General Asset Account Election

14 If you are making the election under section 168(i)(4) to group any assets placed in service during the tax year into one or more general asset accounts, check this box. See page 3 of the instructions ▶ ☐

Section B—General Depreciation System (GDS) (See page 3 of the instructions.)

(a) Classification of property	(b) Month and year placed in service	(c) Basis for depreciation (business/investment use only—see instructions)	(d) Recovery period	(e) Convention	(f) Method	(g) Depreciation deduction
15a 3-year property						
b 5-year property						
c 7-year property						
d 10-year property						
e 15-year property						
f 20-year property						
g 25-year property			25 yrs.		S/L	
h Residential rental property			27.5 yrs.	MM	S/L	
			27.5 yrs.	MM	S/L	
i Nonresidential real property			39 yrs.	MM	S/L	
				MM	S/L	

Section C—Alternative Depreciation System (ADS) (See page 5 of the instructions.)

16a Class life					S/L	
b 12-year			12 yrs.		S/L	
c 40-year			40 yrs.	MM	S/L	

Part III   Other Depreciation (Do not include listed property.) (See page 5 of the instructions.)

17	GDS and ADS deductions for assets placed in service in tax years beginning before 2000	**17**	
18	Property subject to section 168(f)(1) election	**18**	
19	ACRS and other depreciation	**19**	

Part IV   Summary (See page 6 of the instructions.)

20	Listed property. Enter amount from line 26.	**20**	
21	**Total.** Add deductions from line 12, lines 15 and 16 in column (g), and lines 17 through 20. Enter here and on the appropriate lines of your return. Partnerships and S corporations—see instructions	**21**	
22	For assets shown above and placed in service during the current year, enter the portion of the basis attributable to section 263A costs	**22**	

For Paperwork Reduction Act Notice, see page 9 of the instructions.   Cat. No. 12906N   Form **4562** (2000)

Form 4562 (2000) Page **2**

Part V **Listed Property** (Include automobiles, certain other vehicles, cellular telephones, certain computers, and property used for entertainment, recreation, or amusement.)

Note: *For any vehicle for which you are using the standard mileage rate or deducting lease expense, complete **only** 23a, 23b, columns (a) through (c) of Section A, all of Section B, and Section C if applicable.*

Section A—Depreciation and Other Information (Caution: *See page 7 of the instructions for limits for passenger automobiles.***)**

23a Do you have evidence to support the business/investment use claimed? ☐ **Yes** ☐ **No** **23b** If "Yes," is the evidence written? ☐ **Yes** ☐ **No**

(a) Type of property (list vehicles first)	(b) Date placed in service	(c) Business/ investment use percentage	(d) Cost or other basis	(e) Basis for depreciation (business/investment use only)	(f) Recovery period	(g) Method/ Convention	(h) Depreciation deduction	(i) Elected section 179 cost
24 Property used more than 50% in a qualified business use (See page 6 of the instructions.):								
		%						
		%						
		%						
25 Property used 50% or less in a qualified business use (See page 6 of the instructions.):								
		%				S/L –		
		%				S/L –		
		%				S/L –		

26 Add amounts in column (h). Enter the total here and on line 20, page 1 . . . . . **26**

27 Add amounts in column (i). Enter the total here and on line 7, page 1 . . . . **27**

Section B—Information on Use of Vehicles

Complete this section for vehicles used by a sole proprietor, partner, or other "more than 5% owner," or related person.

If you provided vehicles to your employees, first answer the questions in Section C to see if you meet an exception to completing this section for those vehicles.

		(a) Vehicle 1	(b) Vehicle 2	(c) Vehicle 3	(d) Vehicle 4	(e) Vehicle 5	(f) Vehicle 6
28	Total business/investment miles driven during the year (**do not** include commuting miles— see page 1 of the instructions)						
29	Total commuting miles driven during the year						
30	Total other personal (noncommuting) miles driven						
31	Total miles driven during the year. Add lines 28 through 30.						

		Yes	No	Yes	No	Yes	No	Yes	No	Yes	No	Yes	No
32	Was the vehicle available for personal use during off-duty hours?												
33	Was the vehicle used primarily by a more than 5% owner or related person?												
34	Is another vehicle available for personal use?												

Section C—Questions for Employers Who Provide Vehicles for Use by Their Employees

Answer these questions to determine if you meet an exception to completing Section B for vehicles used by employees who **are not** more than 5% owners or related persons. See page 8 of the instructions.

		Yes	No
35	Do you maintain a written policy statement that prohibits all personal use of vehicles, including commuting, by your employees?		
36	Do you maintain a written policy statement that prohibits personal use of vehicles, except commuting, by your employees? See page 8 of the instructions for vehicles used by corporate officers, directors, or 1% or more owners		
37	Do you treat all use of vehicles by employees as personal use?		
38	Do you provide more than five vehicles to your employees, obtain information from your employees about the use of the vehicles, and retain the information received?		
39	Do you meet the requirements concerning qualified automobile demonstration use? See page 8 of the instructions . .		

Note: *If your answer to 35, 36, 37, 38, or 39 is "Yes," do not complete Section B for the covered vehicles.*

Part VI **Amortization**

(a) Description of costs	(b) Date amortization begins	(c) Amortizable amount	(d) Code section	(e) Amortization period or percentage	(f) Amortization for this year
40 Amortization of costs that begins during your 2000 tax year (See page 8 of the instructions.):					

41 Amortization of costs that began before 2000 . . . . **41**

42 **Total.** Add amounts in column (f). See page 9 of the instructions for where to report . . . **42**

Form **4562** (2000)

Form **4626**

Department of the Treasury
Internal Revenue Service

Alternative Minimum Tax—Corporations

▶ See separate instructions.
▶ Attach to the corporation's tax return.

OMB No. 1545-0175

2000

Name		Employer identification number

1	Taxable income or (loss) before net operating loss deduction	**1**	

2 **Adjustments and preferences:**

a	Depreciation of post-1986 property	**2a**	
b	Amortization of certified pollution control facilities	**2b**	
c	Amortization of mining exploration and development costs	**2c**	
d	Amortization of circulation expenditures (personal holding companies only) . .	**2d**	
e	Adjusted gain or loss	**2e**	
f	Long-term contracts	**2f**	
g	Installment sales	**2g**	
h	Merchant marine capital construction funds	**2h**	
i	Section 833(b) deduction (Blue Cross, Blue Shield, and similar type organizations only)	**2i**	
j	Tax shelter farm activities (personal service corporations only)	**2j**	
k	Passive activities (closely held corporations and personal service corporations only)	**2k**	
l	Loss limitations	**2l**	
m	Depletion	**2m**	
n	Tax-exempt interest from specified private activity bonds	**2n**	
o	Intangible drilling costs	**2o**	
p	Accelerated depreciation of real property (pre-1987)	**2p**	
q	Accelerated depreciation of leased personal property (pre-1987) (personal holding companies only)	**2q**	
r	Other adjustments	**2r**	
s	Combine lines 2a through 2r	**2s**	

3	Preadjustment alternative minimum taxable income (AMTI). Combine lines 1 and 2s	**3**	

4 **Adjusted current earnings (ACE) adjustment:**

a	Enter the corporation's ACE from line 10 of the worksheet on page 11 of the instructions	**4a**	
b	Subtract line 3 from line 4a. If line 3 exceeds line 4a, enter the difference as a negative amount (see examples on page 6 of the instructions)	**4b**	
c	Multiply line 4b by 75% (.75). Enter the result as a positive amount	**4c**	
d	Enter the excess, if any, of the corporation's total increases in AMTI from prior year ACE adjustments over its total reductions in AMTI from prior year ACE adjustments (see page 6 of the instructions). **Note:** *You **must** enter an amount on line 4d (even if line 4b is positive)*	**4d**	
e	ACE adjustment: • If you entered a positive number or zero on line 4b, enter the amount from line 4c here as a positive amount. • If you entered a negative number on line 4b, enter the smaller of line 4c or line 4d here as a negative amount.	**4e**	

5	Combine lines 3 and 4e. If zero or less, stop here; the corporation does not owe alternative minimum tax	**5**	
6	Alternative tax net operating loss deduction (see page 7 of the instructions)	**6**	
7	**Alternative minimum taxable income.** Subtract line 6 from line 5. If the corporation held a residual interest in a REMIC, see page 7 of the instructions	**7**	

For Paperwork Reduction Act Notice, see page 10 of separate instructions.   Cat. No. 12955I   Form **4626** (2000)

8   Enter the amount from line 7 (alternative minimum taxable income) **8**

9   **Exemption phase-out computation** (if line 8 is $310,000 or more, skip lines 9a and 9b and enter -0- on line 9c):

  a   Subtract $150,000 from line 8 (if you are completing this line for a member of a controlled group, see page 7 of the instructions). If zero or less, enter -0- . . **9a**

  b   Multiply line 9a by 25% (.25). **9b**

  c   Exemption. Subtract line 9b from $40,000 (if you are completing this line for a member of a controlled group, see page 7 of the instructions). If zero or less, enter -0- **9c**

10 Subtract line 9c from line 8. If zero or less, enter -0- **10**

11 Multiply line 10 by 20% (.20). **11**

12 Alternative minimum tax foreign tax credit. See page 7 of the instructions **12**

13 Tentative minimum tax. Subtract line 12 from line 11. . . . . **13**

14 Regular tax liability before all credits except the foreign tax credit and possessions tax credit . . . **14**

15 **Alternative minimum tax.** Subtract line 14 from line 13. If zero or less, enter -0-. Enter here and on Form 1120, Schedule J, line 4, or the appropriate line of the corporation's income tax return . . . **15**

Form **4626** (2000)

Form **4797**		**Sales of Business Property**	OMB No. 1545-0184

Form **4797**

Department of the Treasury
Internal Revenue Service   (99)

Sales of Business Property
(Also Involuntary Conversions and Recapture Amounts
Under Sections 179 and 280F(b)(2))
▶ Attach to your tax return.   ▶ See separate instructions.

OMB No. 1545-0184

2000

Attachment
Sequence No. **27**

Name(s) shown on return   Identifying number

1 Enter the gross proceeds from sales or exchanges reported to you for 2000 on Form(s) 1099-B or 1099-S (or substitute statement) that you are including on line 2, 10, or 20 (see instructions) . . . . | **1** |

Part I   Sales or Exchanges of Property Used in a Trade or Business and Involuntary Conversions From Other Than Casualty or Theft — Most Property Held More Than 1 Year (See instructions.)

(a) Description of property	**(b)** Date acquired (mo., day, yr.)	**(c)** Date sold (mo., day, yr.)	**(d)** Gross sales price	**(e)** Depreciation allowed or allowable since acquisition	**(f)** Cost or other basis, plus improvements and expense of sale	**(g)** Gain or (loss) Subtract (f) from the sum of (d) and (e)
2						

3 Gain, if any, from Form 4684, line 39 . . . . | **3** |
4 Section 1231 gain from installment sales from Form 6252, line 26 or 37 . . . . | **4** |
5 Section 1231 gain or (loss) from like-kind exchanges from Form 8824 . . . . | **5** |
6 Gain, if any, from line 32, from other than casualty or theft . . . . | **6** |

7 Combine lines 2 through 6. Enter the gain or (loss) here and on the appropriate line as follows: . . . . . . | **7** |

Partnerships (except electing large partnerships). Report the gain or (loss) following the instructions for Form 1065, Schedule K, line 6. Skip lines 8, 9, 11, and 12 below.

S corporations. Report the gain or (loss) following the instructions for Form 1120S, Schedule K, lines 5 and 6. Skip lines 8, 9, 11, and 12 below, unless line 7 is a gain and the S corporation is subject to the capital gains tax.

All others. If line 7 is zero or a loss, enter the amount from line 7 on line 11 below and skip lines 8 and 9. If line 7 is a gain and you did not have any prior year section 1231 losses, or they were recaptured in an earlier year, enter the gain from line 7 as a long-term capital gain on Schedule D and skip lines 8, 9, and 12 below.

8 Nonrecaptured net section 1231 losses from prior years (see instructions) . . . . | **8** |

9 Subtract line 8 from line 7. If zero or less, enter -0-. Also enter on the appropriate line as follows (see instructions): | **9** |

S corporations. Enter any gain from line 9 on Schedule D (Form 1120S), line 15, and skip lines 11 and 12 below.

All others. If line 9 is zero, enter the gain from line 7 on line 12 below. If line 9 is more than zero, enter the amount from line 8 on line 12 below, and enter the gain from line 9 as a long-term capital gain on Schedule D.

Part II   Ordinary Gains and Losses

10 Ordinary gains and losses not included on lines 11 through 17 (include property held 1 year or less):

11 Loss, if any, from line 7 . . . . | **11** (|) |
12 Gain, if any, from line 7 or amount from line 8, if applicable . . . . | **12** |
13 Gain, if any, from line 31 . . . . | **13** |
14 Net gain or (loss) from Form 4684, lines 31 and 38a . . . . | **14** |
15 Ordinary gain from installment sales from Form 6252, line 25 or 36 . . . . | **15** |
16 Ordinary gain or (loss) from like-kind exchanges from Form 8824 . . . . | **16** |
17 Recapture of section 179 expense deduction for partners and S corporation shareholders from property dispositions by partnerships and S corporations (see instructions) . . . . | **17** |
18 Combine lines 10 through 17. Enter the gain or (loss) here and on the appropriate line as follows: . . . . . | **18** |

a For all except individual returns: Enter the gain or (loss) from line 18 on the return being filed.

b For individual returns:

(1) If the loss on line 11 includes a loss from Form 4684, line 35, column (b)(ii), enter that part of the loss here. Enter the part of the loss from income-producing property on Schedule A (Form 1040), line 27, and the part of the loss from property used as an employee on Schedule A (Form 1040), line 22. Identify as from "Form 4797, line 18b(1)." See instructions . . . . | **18b(1)** |

(2) Redetermine the gain or (loss) on line 18 excluding the loss, if any, on line 18b(1). Enter here and on Form 1040, line 14 . . . . | **18b(2)** |

For Paperwork Reduction Act Notice, see page 7 of the instructions.   Cat. No. 13086I   Form **4797** (2000)

Form 4797 (2000)   Page **2**

Part III   Gain From Disposition of Property Under Sections 1245, 1250, 1252, 1254, and 1255

19   **(a)** Description of section 1245, 1250, 1252, 1254, or 1255 property:

	(b) Date acquired (mo., day, yr.)	**(c)** Date sold (mo., day, yr.)
A		
B		
C		
D		

These columns relate to the properties on lines 19A through 19D. ▶		Property A	Property B	Property C	Property D
20 Gross sales price (**Note:** *See line 1 before completing.*)	20				
21 Cost or other basis plus expense of sale	21				
22 Depreciation (or depletion) allowed or allowable	22				
23 Adjusted basis. Subtract line 22 from line 21	23				
24 Total gain. Subtract line 23 from line 20	24				
25 **If section 1245 property:**					
a Depreciation allowed or allowable from line 22	25a				
b Enter the **smaller** of line 24 or 25a	25b				
26 **If section 1250 property:** If straight line depreciation was used, enter -0- on line 26g, except for a corporation subject to section 291.					
a Additional depreciation after 1975 (see instructions)	26a				
b Applicable percentage multiplied by the **smaller** of line 24 or line 26a (see instructions)	26b				
c Subtract line 26a from line 24. If residential rental property or line 24 is not more than line 26a, skip lines 26d and 26e	26c				
d Additional depreciation after 1969 and before 1976	26d				
e Enter the **smaller** of line 26c or 26d	26e				
f Section 291 amount (corporations only)	26f				
g Add lines 26b, 26c, and 26f	26g				
27 **If section 1252 property:** Skip this section if you did not dispose of farmland or if this form is being completed for a partnership (other than an electing large partnership).					
a Soil, water, and land clearing expenses	27a				
b Line 27a multiplied by applicable percentage (see instructions)	27b				
c Enter the **smaller** of line 24 or 27b	27c				
28 **If section 1254 property:**					
a Intangible drilling and development costs, expenditures for development of mines and other natural deposits, and mining exploration costs (see instructions)	28a				
b Enter the **smaller** of line 24 or 28a	28b				
29 **If section 1255 property:**					
a Applicable percentage of payments excluded from income under section 126 (see instructions)	29a				
b Enter the **smaller** of line 24 or 29a (see instructions)	29b				

Summary of Part III Gains. Complete property columns A through D through line 29b before going to line 30.

30 Total gains for all properties. Add property columns A through D, line 24	30	
31 Add property columns A through D, lines 25b, 26g, 27c, 28b, and 29b. Enter here and on line 13	31	
32 Subtract line 31 from line 30. Enter the portion from casualty or theft on Form 4684, line 33. Enter the portion from other than casualty or theft on Form 4797, line 6	32	

Part IV   Recapture Amounts Under Sections 179 and 280F(b)(2) When Business Use Drops to 50% or Less (See instructions.)

		(a) Section 179	**(b)** Section 280F(b)(2)
33 Section 179 expense deduction or depreciation allowable in prior years	33		
34 Recomputed depreciation. See instructions	34		
35 Recapture amount. Subtract line 34 from line 33. See the instructions for where to report	35		

Form **4797** (2000)

Form **6251**

Department of the Treasury
Internal Revenue Service

Alternative Minimum Tax—Individuals

▶ See separate instructions.

▶ Attach to Form 1040 or Form 1040NR.

OMB No. 1545-0227

2000

Attachment
Sequence No. **32**

Name(s) shown on Form 1040 | Your social security number

Part I   Adjustments and Preferences

1	If you itemized deductions on Schedule A (Form 1040), go to line 2. Otherwise, enter your standard deduction from Form 1040, line 36, here and go to line 6	1
2	Medical and dental. Enter the smaller of Schedule A (Form 1040), line 4 **or** 2½% of Form 1040, line 34	2
3	Taxes. Enter the amount from Schedule A (Form 1040), line 9	3
4	Certain interest on a home mortgage **not** used to buy, build, or improve your home	4
5	Miscellaneous itemized deductions. Enter the amount from Schedule A (Form 1040), line 26	5
6	Refund of taxes. Enter any tax refund from Form 1040, line 10 or line 21	6 ( )
7	Investment interest. Enter difference between regular tax and AMT deduction	7
8	Post-1986 depreciation. Enter difference between regular tax and AMT depreciation	8
9	Adjusted gain or loss. Enter difference between AMT and regular tax gain or loss.	9
10	Incentive stock options. Enter excess of AMT income over regular tax income.	10
11	Passive activities. Enter difference between AMT and regular tax income or loss	11
12	Beneficiaries of estates and trusts. Enter the amount from Schedule K-1 (Form 1041), line 9 . . .	12
13	Tax-exempt interest from private activity bonds issued after 8/7/86	13
14	Other. Enter the amount, if any, for each item below and enter the total on line 14.	

a Circulation expenditures		**h** Loss limitations . . .		
b Depletion		**i** Mining costs		
c Depreciation (pre-1987) .		**j** Patron's adjustment . .		
d Installment sales . . .		**k** Pollution control facilities		
e Intangible drilling costs .		**l** Research and experimental		
f Large partnerships . .		**m** Section 1202 exclusion .		
g Long-term contracts . .		**n** Tax shelter farm activities		
		o Related adjustments .		14

15	Total Adjustments and Preferences. Combine lines 1 through 14 . . . . ▶	15

Part II   Alternative Minimum Taxable Income

16	Enter the amount from **Form 1040, line 37.** If less than zero, enter as a (loss) . . . . ▶	16
17	Net operating loss deduction, if any, from Form 1040, line 21. Enter as a positive amount	17
18	If Form 1040, line 34, is over $128,950 (over $64,475 if married filing separately), and you itemized deductions, enter the amount, if any, from line 9 of the worksheet for Schedule A (Form 1040), line 28	18 ( )
19	Combine lines 15 through 18 . . . . ▶	19
20	Alternative tax net operating loss deduction. See page 6 of the instructions	20
21	**Alternative Minimum Taxable Income.** Subtract line 20 from line 19. (If married filing separately and line 21 is more than $165,000, see page 7 of the instructions.) . . . . ▶	21

Part III   Exemption Amount and Alternative Minimum Tax

22	**Exemption Amount.** (If this form is for a child under age 14, see page 7 of the instructions.)

IF your filing status is . . .	AND line 21 is not over . . .	THEN enter on line 22 . . .	
Single or head of household	$112,500	$33,750	
Married filing jointly or qualifying widow(er) . .	150,000	45,000	} . .
Married filing separately	75,000	22,500	

If line 21 is **over** the amount shown above for your filing status, see page 7 of the instructions.

22

23	Subtract line 22 from line 21. If zero or less, enter -0- here and on lines 26 and 28 and stop here . ▶	23
24	If you reported capital gain distributions directly on Form 1040, line 13, **or** you completed Schedule D (Form 1040) and have an amount on line 25 or line 27 (or would have had an amount on either line if you had completed Part IV) (as refigured for the AMT, if necessary), go to Part IV of Form 6251 to figure line 24. **All others:** If line 23 is $175,000 or less ($87,500 or less if married filing separately), multiply line 23 by 26% (.26). Otherwise, multiply line 23 by 28% (.28) and subtract $3,500 ($1,750 if married filing separately) from the result . . . . ▶	24
25	Alternative minimum tax foreign tax credit. See page 7 of the instructions	25
26	Tentative minimum tax. Subtract line 25 from line 24 . . . . ▶	26
27	Enter your tax from Form 1040, line 40 (minus any tax from Form 4972 and any foreign tax credit from Form 1040, line 43)	27
28	**Alternative Minimum Tax.** Subtract line 27 from line 26. If zero or less, enter -0-. Enter here and on Form 1040, line 41 . . . . ▶	28

For Paperwork Reduction Act Notice, see page 8 of the instructions.   Cat. No. 13600G   Form **6251** (2000)

Form 6251 (2000)

Part IV   **Line 24 Computation Using Maximum Capital Gains Rates**

Caution: *If you **did not** complete Part IV of Schedule D (Form 1040), see page 8 of the instructions before you complete this part.*

29	Enter the amount from Form 6251, line 23		**29**
30	Enter the amount from Schedule D (Form 1040), line 27 (as refigured for the AMT, if necessary). See page 8 of the instructions. **30**		
31	Enter the amount from Schedule D (Form 1040), line 25 (as refigured for the AMT, if necessary). See page 8 of the instructions. **31**		
32	Add lines 30 and 31 . . . . **32**		
33	Enter the amount from Schedule D (Form 1040), line 22 (as refigured for the AMT, if necessary). See page 8 of the instructions **33**		
34	Enter the **smaller** of line 32 or line 33		**34**
35	Subtract line 34 from line 29. If zero or less, enter -0- . . . . ▶		**35**
36	If line 35 is $175,000 or less ($87,500 or less if married filing separately), multiply line 35 by 26% (.26). Otherwise, multiply line 35 by 28% (.28) and subtract $3,500 ($1,750 if married filing separately) from the result		**36**
37	Enter the amount from Schedule D (Form 1040), line 36 (as figured for the regular tax). See page 8 of the instructions **37**		
38	Enter the **smallest** of line 29, line 30, or line 37 . . . . ▶ **38**		
39	Multiply line 38 by 10% (.10)		**39**
40	Enter the **smaller** of line 29 or line 30 . . . . **40**		
41	Enter the amount from line 38 . . . . **41**		
42	Subtract line 41 from line 40 . . . . ▶ **42**		
43	Multiply line 42 by 20% (.20)		**43**

Note: *If line 31 is zero or blank, skip lines 44 through 47 and go to line 48.*

44	Enter the amount from line 29 . . . . **44**		
45	Add lines 35, 38, and 42 . . . . **45**		
46	Subtract line 45 from line 44 . . . . **46**		
47	Multiply line 46 by 25% (.25)		**47**
48	Add lines 36, 39, 43, and 47		**48**
49	If line 29 is $175,000 or less ($87,500 or less if married filing separately), multiply line 29 by 26% (.26). Otherwise, multiply line 29 by 28% (.28) and subtract $3,500 ($1,750 if married filing separately) from the result		**49**
50	Enter the **smaller** of line 48 or line 49 here and on line 24		**50**

Form **6251** (2000)

Form **8582**

Department of the Treasury
Internal Revenue Service

Passive Activity Loss Limitations

▶ See separate instructions.

▶ Attach to Form 1040 or Form 1041.

OMB No. 1545-1008

2000

Attachment
Sequence No. **88**

Name(s) shown on return

Identifying number

Part I   **2000 Passive Activity Loss**

Caution: *See the instructions for Worksheets 1 and 2 on page 8 before completing Part I.*

Rental Real Estate Activities With Active Participation (For the definition of active participation see **Active Participation in a Rental Real Estate Activity** on page 4 of the instructions.)

1a Activities with net income (enter the amount from Worksheet 1, column (a)).	**1a**		
b Activities with net loss (enter the amount from Worksheet 1, column (b)).	**1b** (	)	
c Prior years unallowed losses (enter the amount from Worksheet 1, column (c)).	**1c** (	)	
d Combine lines 1a, 1b, and 1c			**1d**

All Other Passive Activities

2a Activities with net income (enter the amount from Worksheet 2, column (a)).	**2a**		
b Activities with net loss (enter the amount from Worksheet 2, column (b)).	**2b** (	)	
c Prior years unallowed losses (enter the amount from Worksheet 2, column (c)).	**2c** (	)	
d Combine lines 2a, 2b, and 2c			**2d**

3 Combine lines 1d and 2d. If the result is net income or zero, all losses are allowed, including any prior year unallowed losses entered on line 1c or 2c. **Do not** complete Form 8582. Report the losses on the forms and schedules normally used.

If this line and line 1d are losses, go to Part II. Otherwise, enter -0- on line 9 and go to line 10 .   **3**

Part II   **Special Allowance for Rental Real Estate With Active Participation**

Note: *Enter all numbers in Part II as positive amounts. See page 8 for examples.*

Note: *If your filing status is married filing separately and you lived with your spouse at any time during the year, **do not** complete Part II. Instead, enter -0- on line 9 and go to line 10.*

4 Enter the **smaller** of the loss on line 1d or the loss on line 3		**4**
5 Enter $150,000. If married filing separately, see page 8	**5**	
6 Enter modified adjusted gross income, but not less than zero (see page 8)	**6**	

Note: *If line 6 is greater than or equal to line 5, skip lines 7 and 8, enter -0- on line 9, and go to line 10. Otherwise, go to line 7.*

7 Subtract line 6 from line 5	**7**	
8 Multiply line 7 by 50% (.5). **Do not** enter more than $25,000. If married filing separately, see page 9		**8**
9 Enter the **smaller** of line 4 or line 8		**9**

Part III   **Total Losses Allowed**

10 Add the income, if any, on lines 1a and 2a and enter the total		**10**
11 **Total losses allowed from all passive activities for 2000.** Add lines 9 and 10. See page 11 to find out how to report the losses on your tax return		**11**

For Paperwork Reduction Act Notice, see page 12 of the instructions.   Cat. No. 63704F   Form **8582** (2000)

Form 8582 (2000)

Page **2**

Caution: *The worksheets are not required to be filed with your tax return and may be detached before filing Form 8582. Keep a copy of the worksheets for your records.*

Worksheet 1—For Form 8582, Lines 1a, 1b, and 1c (See page 8.)

Name of activity	Current year		Prior years	Overall gain or loss	
	(a) Net income (line 1a)	(b) Net loss (line 1b)	(c) Unallowed loss (line 1c)	(d) Gain	(e) Loss
Total. Enter on Form 8582, lines 1a, 1b, and 1c. . . . . ▶					

Worksheet 2—For Form 8582, Lines 2a, 2b, and 2c (See page 8.)

Name of activity	Current year		Prior years	Overall gain or loss	
	(a) Net income (line 2a)	(b) Net loss (line 2b)	(c) Unallowed loss (line 2c)	(d) Gain	(e) Loss
Total. Enter on Form 8582, lines 2a, 2b, and 2c. . . . . ▶					

Worksheet 3—Use this worksheet if an amount is shown on Form 8582, line 9 (See page 9.)

Name of activity	Form or schedule to be reported on	(a) Loss	(b) Ratio	(c) Special allowance	(d) Subtract column (c) from column (a)
Total . . . . ▶			1.00		

Worksheet 4—Allocation of Unallowed Losses (See page 9.)

Name of activity	Form or schedule to be reported on	(a) Loss	(b) Ratio	(c) Unallowed loss
Total . . . . ▶			1.00	

Worksheet 5—Allowed Losses (See page 9.)

Name of activity	Form or schedule to be reported on	(a) Loss	(b) Unallowed loss	(c) Allowed loss
Total . . . . ▶				

Form **8582** (2000)

Worksheet 6—Activities With Losses Reported on Two or More Different Forms or Schedules (See page 10.)

Name of Activity:	(a)	(b)	(c) Ratio	(d) Unallowed loss	(e) Allowed loss
Form or Schedule To Be Reported on:					
1a Net loss plus prior year unallowed loss from form or schedule . ▶					
b Net income from form or schedule . . . . ▶					
c Subtract line 1b from line 1a. If zero or less, enter -0- ▶					
Form or Schedule To Be Reported on:					
1a Net loss plus prior year unallowed loss from form or schedule . ▶					
b Net income from form or schedule . . . . ▶					
c Subtract line 1b from line 1a. If zero or less, enter -0- ▶					
Form or Schedule To Be Reported on:					
1a Net loss plus prior year unallowed loss from form or schedule . ▶					
b Net income from form or schedule . . . . ▶					
c Subtract line 1b from line 1a. If zero or less, enter -0- ▶					
Total . . . . ▶			1.00		

Form **8832**
(December 1996)
Department of the Treasury
Internal Revenue Service

Entity Classification Election

OMB No. 1545-1516

Please Type or Print

Name of entity	Employer identification number (EIN)
Number, street, and room or suite no. If a P.O. box, see instructions.	
City or town, state, and ZIP code. If a foreign address, enter city, province or state, postal code and country.	

1 Type of election (see instructions):

a ☐ Initial classification by a newly-formed entity (or change in current classification of an existing entity to take effect on January 1, 1997)

b ☐ Change in current classification (to take effect later than January 1, 1997)

2 Form of entity (see instructions):

a ☐ A domestic eligible entity electing to be classified as an association taxable as a corporation.

b ☐ A domestic eligible entity electing to be classified as a partnership.

c ☐ A domestic eligible entity with a single owner electing to be disregarded as a separate entity.

d ☐ A foreign eligible entity electing to be classified as an association taxable as a corporation.

e ☐ A foreign eligible entity electing to be classified as a partnership.

f ☐ A foreign eligible entity with a single owner electing to be disregarded as a separate entity.

3 Election is to be effective beginning (month, day, year) (see instructions) . . . . ▶ ___ / ___ / ___

4 Name and title of person whom the IRS may call for more information

5 That person's telephone number

Consent Statement and Signature(s) (see instructions)

Under penalties of perjury, I (we) declare that I (we) consent to the election of the above-named entity to be classified as indicated above, and that I (we) have examined this consent statement, and to the best of my (our) knowledge and belief, it is true, correct, and complete. If I am an officer, manager, or member signing for all members of the entity, I further declare that I am authorized to execute this consent statement on their behalf.

Signature(s)	Date	Title

For Paperwork Reduction Act Notice, see page 2.

Cat. No. 22598R

Form **8832** (12-96)

Glossary of Key Terms

The key terms in this glossary have been defined to reflect their conventional use in the field of taxation. The definitions may therefore be incomplete for other purposes.

A

Accelerated cost recovery system (ACRS). A method in which the cost of tangible property is recovered over a prescribed period of time. Enacted by the Economic Recovery Tax Act (ERTA) of 1981 and substantially modified by the Tax Reform Act (TRA) of 1986 (the modified system is referred to as MACRS), the approach disregards salvage value, imposes a period of cost recovery that depends upon the classification of the asset into one of various recovery periods, and prescribes the applicable percentage of cost that can be deducted each year. § 168.

Accident and health insurance benefits. Employee fringe benefits provided by employers through the payment of health and accident insurance premiums or the establishment of employer-funded medical reimbursement plans. Employers generally are entitled to a deduction for such payments, whereas employees generally exclude such fringe benefits from gross income. §§ 105 and 106.

Accountable plan. An accountable plan is a type of expense reimbursement plan that requires an employee to render an adequate accounting to the employer and return any excess reimbursement or allowance. If the expense qualifies, it will be treated as a deduction *for* AGI.

Accounting income. The accountant's concept of income is generally based upon the realization principle. Financial accounting income may differ from taxable income (e.g., accelerated depreciation might be used for Federal income tax and straight-line depreciation for financial accounting purposes). Differences are included in a reconciliation of taxable and accounting income on Schedule M–1 of Form 1120 for corporations.

Accounting method. The method under which income and expenses are determined for tax purposes. Important accounting methods include the cash basis and the accrual basis. Special methods are available for the reporting of gain on installment sales, recognition of income on construction projects (the completed contract and percentage of completion methods), and the valuation of inventories (last-in, first-out and first-in, first-out). §§ 446–474.

Accounting period. The period of time, usually a year, used by a taxpayer for the determination of tax liability. Unless a fiscal year is chosen, taxpayers must determine and pay their income tax liability by using the calendar year (January 1 through December 31) as the period of measurement. An example of a fiscal year is July 1 through June 30. A change in accounting period (e.g., from a calendar year to a fiscal year) generally requires the consent of the IRS. Some new taxpayers, such as a newly formed corporation, are free to select either an initial calendar or a fiscal year without the consent of the IRS. §§ 441–444.

Accrual method. A method of accounting that reflects expenses incurred and income earned for any one tax year. In contrast to the cash basis of accounting, expenses need not be paid to be deductible, nor need income be received to be taxable. Unearned income (e.g., prepaid interest and rent) generally is taxed in the year of receipt regardless of the method of accounting used by the taxpayer. § 446(c)(2).

Accumulated adjustments account (AAA). An account that aggregates an S corporation's post-1982 income, loss, and deductions for the tax year (including nontaxable income and nondeductible losses and expenses). After the year-end income and expense adjustments are made, the account is reduced by distributions made during the tax year.

Accumulated earnings and profits. Net undistributed tax-basis earnings of a corporation aggregated from March 1, 1913, to the end of the prior tax year. Used to determine the amount of dividend income associated with a distribution to shareholders. § 316 and Reg. § 1.316–2.

Acquiescence. Agreement by the IRS on the results reached in certain judicial decisions; sometimes abbreviated *Acq.* or *A.*

Acquisition indebtedness. Debt incurred in acquiring, constructing, or substantially improving a qualified residence of the taxpayer. The interest on such loans is deductible as qualified residence interest. However, interest on such debt is deductible only on the portion of the indebtedness that does not exceed $1,000,000 ($500,000 for married persons filing separate returns). § 163(h)(3).

Active income. Active income includes wages, salary, commissions, bonuses, profits from a trade or business in which the taxpayer is a material participant, gain on the sale or other disposition of assets used in an active trade or business, and income from intangible property if the taxpayer's personal efforts significantly contributed to the creation of the property. The passive activity loss rules require classification of income and losses into three categories with active income being one of them.

Ad valorem tax.   A tax imposed on the value of property. The most common ad valorem tax is that imposed by states, counties, and cities on real estate. Ad valorem taxes can be imposed on personal property as well.

Additional depreciation.   The excess of the amount of depreciation actually deducted over the amount that would have been deducted had the straight-line method been used. § 1250(b).

Adjusted basis.   The cost or other basis of property reduced by depreciation allowed or allowable and increased by capital improvements. Other special adjustments are provided in § 1016 and the related Regulations.

Adjusted current earnings (ACE).   An adjustment in computing corporate alternative minimum taxable income (AMTI), computed at 75 percent of the excess of adjusted current earnings (ACE) over unadjusted AMTI. ACE computations reflect longer and slower cost recovery deductions and other restrictions on the timing of certain recognition events. Exempt interest, life insurance proceeds, and other receipts that are included in earnings and profits but not in taxable income also increase the ACE adjustment. If unadjusted AMTI exceeds ACE, the ACE adjustment is negative. The negative adjustment is limited to the aggregate of the positive adjustments under ACE for prior years, reduced by an previously claimed negative adjustments.

Adoption expenses credit.   A provision intended to assist taxpayers who incur nonrecurring costs directly associated with the adoption process such as legal costs, social service review costs, and transportation costs. Up to $5,000 ($6,000 for a child with special needs) of costs incurred to adopt an eligible child qualify for the credit. A taxpayer may claim the credit in the year qualifying expenses are paid or incurred if the expenses are paid during or after the year in which the adoption is finalized. For qualifying expenses paid or incurred in a tax year prior to the year the adoption is finalized, the credit must be claimed in the tax year following the tax year during which the expenses are paid or incurred. § 23.

Alimony and separate maintenance payments.   Alimony deductions result from the payment of a legal obligation arising from the termination of a marital relationship. Payments designated as alimony generally are included in the gross income of the recipient and are deductible *for* AGI by the payer.

Alternative depreciation system (ADS).   A cost recovery system that produces a smaller deduction than would be calculated under ACRS or MACRS. The alternative system must be used in certain instances and can be elected in other instances. § 168(g).

Alternative minimum tax (AMT).   The AMT is a fixed percentage of alternative minimum taxable income (AMTI).

AMTI generally starts with the taxpayer's adjusted gross income (for individuals) or taxable income (for other taxpayers). To this amount, the taxpayer (1) adds designated preference items (e.g., tax-exempt interest income on private activity bonds), (2) makes other specified adjustments (e.g., to reflect a longer, straight-line cost recovery deduction), (3) subtracts certain AMT itemized deductions for individuals (e.g., interest incurred on housing but not taxes paid), and (4) subtracts an exemption amount (e.g., $40,000 on an individual joint return). The taxpayer must pay the greater of the resulting AMT (reduced by only the foreign tax credit) or the regular income tax (reduced by all allowable tax credits). The AMT does not apply to certain small C corporations. AMT preferences and adjustments are assigned to partners and S corporation shareholders.

Alternative minimum taxable income (AMTI).   The base (prior to deducting the exemption amount) for computing a taxpayer's alternative minimum tax. This consists of the taxable income for the year modified for AMT adjustments and AMT preferences.

Amortization.   The tax deduction for the cost or other basis of an intangible asset over the asset's estimated useful life. Examples of amortizable intangibles include patents, copyrights, and leasehold interests. The intangible goodwill can be amortized for income tax purposes over a 15-year period.

Amount realized.   The amount received by a taxpayer upon the sale or exchange of property. Amount realized is the sum of the cash and the fair market value of any property or services received by the taxpayer, plus any related debt assumed by the buyer. Determining the amount realized is the starting point for arriving at realized gain or loss. § 1001(b).

Assignment of income.   A procedure whereby a taxpayer attempts to avoid the recognition of income by assigning to another the property that generates the income. Such a procedure will not avoid the recognition of income by the taxpayer making the assignment if it can be said that the income was earned at the point of the transfer. In this case, usually referred to as an anticipatory assignment of income, the income will be taxed to the person who earns it.

Assumption of liabilities.   In a corporate formation, corporate takeover, or asset purchase, the new owner often takes assets and agrees to assume preexisting debt. Such actions do not create boot received on the transaction for the new shareholder, unless there is no *bona fide* business purpose for the exchange, or the principal purpose of the debt assumption is the avoidance of tax liabilities. Gain is recognized to the extent that liabilities assumed exceed the aggregated bases of the transferred assets. § 357.

At-risk limitation.   Generally, a taxpayer can deduct losses related to a trade or business, S corporation, partnership, or investment asset only to the extent of the at-risk amount.

Automatic mileage method.   Automobile expenses are generally deductible only to the extent the automobile is used in business or for the production of income. Personal commuting expenses are not deductible. The taxpayer may deduct actual expenses (including depreciation and insurance), or the standard (automatic) mileage rate may be used (32.5 cents per mile for January, February, and March of 1999 and 31 cents per mile for the rest of 1999, 32.5 cents per mile for 2000, and 34.5 cents for 2001) during any one year. Automobile expenses incurred for medical purposes or in connection with job-related moving expenses are deductible to the extent of actual out-of-pocket expenses or at the rate of 12 cents per mile (14 cents for charitable activities).

B

Bad debts.   A deduction is permitted if a business account receivable subsequently becomes partially or completely worthless, providing the income arising from the debt previously was included in income. Available methods are the specific charge-off method and the reserve method. However, except for certain financial institutions, TRA of 1986 repealed the use of the reserve method for 1987 and thereafter. If the reserve method is used, partially or totally worthless accounts are charged to the reserve. A nonbusiness bad debt deduction is allowed as a short-term capital loss if the loan did not arise in connection with the creditor's trade or business activities. Loans between related parties (family members) generally are classified as nonbusiness. § 166.

Basis in partnership interest.   The acquisition cost of the partner's ownership interest in the partnership. Includes purchase price and associated debt acquired from other partners and in the course of the entity's trade or business.

Boot.   Cash or property of a type not included in the definition of a nontaxable exchange. The receipt of boot causes an otherwise nontaxable transfer to become taxable to the extent of the lesser of the fair market value of the boot or the realized gain on the transfer. For example, see transfers to controlled corporations under § 351(b) and like-kind exchanges under § 1031(b).

Brother-sister controlled group.   More than one corporation owned by the same shareholders. If, for example, Chris and Pat each own one-half of the stock in Wren Corporation and Redbird Corporation, Wren and Redbird form a brother-sister controlled group.

Built-in gains tax.   A penalty tax designed to discourage a shift of the incidence of taxation on unrealized gains from a C corporation to its shareholders, via an S election. Under this provision, any recognized gain during the first 10 years of S status generates a corporate-level tax on a base not to exceed the aggregate untaxed built-in gains brought into the S corporation upon its election from C corporation taxable years.

Business bad debt.   A tax deduction allowed for obligations obtained in connection with a trade or business that have become either partially or completely worthless. In contrast to nonbusiness bad debts, business bad debts are deductible as business expenses. § 166.

Buy-sell agreement.   An arrangement, particularly appropriate in the case of a closely held corporation or a partnership, whereby the surviving owners (shareholders or partners) or the entity agrees to purchase the interest of a withdrawing owner. The buy-sell agreement provides for an orderly disposition of an interest in a business and may aid in setting the value of the interest for death tax purposes.

C

C corporation.   A separate taxable entity, subject to the rules of Subchapter C of the Code. This business form may create a double taxation effect relative to its shareholders. The entity is subject to the regular corporate tax and a number of penalty taxes at the Federal level.

Cafeteria plan.   An employee benefit plan under which an employee is allowed to select from among a variety of employer-provided fringe benefits. Some of the benefits may be taxable, and some may be statutory nontaxable benefits (e.g., health and accident insurance and group term life insurance). The employee is taxed only on the taxable benefits selected. A cafeteria benefit plan is also referred to as a flexible benefit plan. § 125.

Capital account.   The financial accounting analog of a partner's tax basis in the entity.

Capital asset.   Broadly speaking, all assets are capital except those specifically excluded by the Code. Major categories of noncapital assets include property held for resale in the normal course of business (inventory), trade accounts and notes receivable, and depreciable property and real estate used in a trade or business (§ 1231 assets). § 1221.

Capital contribution.   Various means by which a shareholder makes additional funds available to the corporation (placed at the risk of the business), sometimes without the receipt of additional stock. If no stock is received, the contributions are added to the basis of the shareholder's existing stock investment and do not generate gross income to the corporation. § 118.

Capital gain.   The gain from the sale or exchange of a capital asset.

Capital gain property.   Property contributed to a charitable organization that, if sold rather than contributed, would have resulted in long-term capital gain to the donor.

Capital interest.   Usually, the percentage of the entity's net assets that a partner would receive on liquidation. Typically determined by the partner's capital sharing ratio.

Capital loss.   The loss from the sale or exchange of a capital asset.

Capital sharing ratio.   A partner's percentage ownership of the entity's capital.

Cash method.   See *cash receipts method.*

Cash receipts method.   A method of accounting that reflects deductions as paid and income as received in any one tax year.

However, deductions for prepaid expenses that benefit more than one tax year (e.g., prepaid rent and prepaid interest) usually must be spread over the period benefited rather than deducted in the year paid. For fixed assets, the cash basis taxpayer claims deductions through depreciation or amortization in the same manner as an accrual basis taxpayer. § 446(c)(1).

Casualty loss. A casualty is defined as "the complete or partial destruction of property resulting from an identifiable event of a sudden, unexpected or unusual nature" (e.g., floods, storms, fires, auto accidents). Individuals may deduct a casualty loss only if the loss is incurred in a trade or business or in a transaction entered into for profit or arises from fire, storm, shipwreck, or other casualty or from theft. Individuals usually deduct personal casualty losses as itemized deductions subject to a $100 nondeductible amount and to an annual floor equal to 10 percent of adjusted gross income that applies after the $100 per casualty floor has been applied. Special rules are provided for the netting of certain casualty gains and losses.

Charitable contributions. Contributions are deductible (subject to various restrictions and ceiling limitations) if made to qualified nonprofit charitable organizations. A cash basis taxpayer is entitled to a deduction solely in the year of payment. Accrual basis corporations may accrue contributions at year-end if payment is properly authorized before the end of the year and payment is made within two and one-half months after the end of the year. § 170.

Check-the-box regulation. A business entity can elect to be taxed as a partnership, S corporation, or C corporation by indicating its preference on the tax return. Legal structure and operations are irrelevant in this regard. Thus, by using the check-the-box rules prudently, an entity can select the most attractive tax results offered by the Code, without being bound by legal forms. Not available if the entity is incorporated under state law.

Child tax credit. A tax credit based solely on the number of qualifying children under age 17. The maximum credit available is $500 per child. A qualifying child must be claimed as a dependent on a parent's tax return in order to qualify for the credit. Taxpayers who qualify for the child tax credit may also qualify for a supplemental credit. The supplemental credit is treated as a component of the earned income credit and is therefore refundable. The credit is phased out for higher-income taxpayers. § 24.

Circuit Court of Appeals. Any of 13 Federal courts that consider tax matters appealed from the U.S. Tax Court, a U.S. District Court, or the U.S. Court of Federal Claims. Appeal from a U.S. Court of Appeals is to the U.S. Supreme Court by *Certiorari*.

Claim of right doctrine. A judicially imposed doctrine applicable to both cash and accrual basis taxpayers that holds that an amount is includible in income upon actual or constructive receipt if the taxpayer has an unrestricted claim to the payment. For the tax treatment of amounts repaid when previously included in income under the claim of right doctrine, see § 1341.

Closely held C corporation. A regular corporation (i.e., the S election is not in effect) for which more than 50 percent of the value of its outstanding stock is owned, directly or indirectly, by five or fewer individuals at any time during the tax year. The term is relevant in identifying C corporations that are subject to the passive activity loss provisions. § 469.

Collectibles. A special type of capital asset, the gain from which is taxed at a maximum rate of 28 percent if the holding period is more than one year. Examples include art, rugs, antiques, gems, metals, stamps, some coins and bullion, and alcoholic beverages held for investment.

Compensatory damages. Damages received or paid by the taxpayer can be classified as compensatory damages or as punitive damages. Compensatory damages are those paid to compensate one for harm caused by another. Compensatory damages are excludible from the recipient's gross income.

Completed contract method. A method of reporting gain or loss on certain long-term contracts. Under this method of accounting, gross income and expenses are recognized in the tax year in which the contract is completed. Limitations exist on a taxpayer's ability to use the completed contract method. Reg. § 1.451–3 and § 460.

Conduit concept. An approach assumed by the tax law in the treatment of certain entities and their owners. Specific tax characteristics pass through the entity without losing their identity. For example, items of income and expense, capital gains and losses, tax credits, etc., realized by a partnership pass through the partnership (a conduit) and are subject to taxation at the partner level. Also, in an S corporation, certain items pass through and are reported on the returns of the shareholders.

Constructive dividend. A taxable benefit derived by a shareholder from his or her corporation that is not actually called a dividend. Examples include unreasonable compensation, excessive rent payments, bargain purchases of corporate property, and shareholder use of corporate property. Constructive dividends generally are found in closely held corporations.

Constructive receipt. If income is unqualifiedly available although not physically in the taxpayer's possession, it is subject to the income tax. An example is accrued interest on a savings account. Under the constructive receipt of income concept, the interest is taxed to a depositor in the year available, rather than the year actually withdrawn. The fact that the depositor uses the cash basis of accounting for tax purposes is irrelevant. See Reg. § 1.451–2.

Contingent sales price. A sale or other disposition of property in which the aggregate selling price cannot be determined by the end of the tax year in which the sale or other disposition occurs. The term is relevant with respect to installment sales. § 453.

Control. Holding a specified level of stock ownership in a corporation. For § 351, the new shareholder(s) must hold at least 80 percent of the total combined voting power of all voting classes of stock and at least 80 percent of the shares of all nonvoting classes. Other tax provisions require different levels of control to bring about desired effects, such as 50 or 100 percent.

Controlled group. A controlled group of corporations is required to share the lower-level corporate tax rates and various other tax benefits among the members of the group. A controlled group may be either a brother-sister or a parent-subsidiary group.

Cost depletion. Depletion that is calculated based on the adjusted basis of the asset. The adjusted basis is divided by the expected recoverable units to determine the depletion per unit. The depletion per unit is multiplied by the units sold during the tax year to calculate cost depletion.

Cost recovery system. The system which provides for the write-off of the cost of an asset under ACRS or MACRS. The cost recovery system replaced the depreciation system as the method of writing off the cost of an asset for most capitalized assets placed in service after 1980 (after 1986 for MACRS).

Court of Federal Claims. A trial court (court of original jurisdiction) that decides litigation involving Federal tax matters. Appeal from this court is to the Court of Appeals for the Federal Circuit.

Court of original jurisdiction. The Federal courts are divided into courts of original jurisdiction and appellate courts. A dispute between a taxpayer and the IRS is first considered by a court of original jurisdiction (i.e., a trial court). The four Federal courts of original jurisdiction are the U.S. Tax Court, U.S. District Court, the Court of Federal Claims, and the Small Cases Division of the U.S. Tax Court.

Credit for child and dependent care expenses. A tax credit ranging from 20 percent to 30 percent of employment-related expenses (child and dependent care expenses) for amounts of up to $4,800 is available to individuals who are employed (or deemed to be employed) and maintain a household for a dependent child under age 13, disabled spouse, or disabled dependent. § 21.

Current earnings and profits. Net tax-basis earnings of a corporation aggregated during the current tax year. A corporate distribution is deemed to be first from the entity's current earnings and profits and then from accumulated earnings and profits. Shareholders recognize dividend income to the extent of the earnings and profits of the corporation. A dividend results to the extent of current earnings and profits, even if there is a larger negative balance in accumulated earnings and profits.

D

Death tax. A tax imposed on property transferred by the death of the owner.

De minimis **fringe.** Benefits provided to employees that are too insignificant to warrant the time and effort required to account for the benefits received by each employee and the value of those benefits. Such amounts are excludible from the employee's gross income. § 132.

Dependency exemption. The tax law provides an exemption for each individual taxpayer and an additional exemption for the taxpayer's spouse if a joint return is filed. An individual may also claim a dependency exemption for each dependent, provided certain tests are met. The amount of the personal and dependency exemptions is $2,900 in 2001 ($2,800 in 2000). The exemption is subject to phase-out once adjusted gross income exceeds certain statutory threshold amounts.

Depletion. The process by which the cost or other basis of a natural resource (e.g., an oil or gas interest) is recovered upon extraction and sale of the resource. The two ways to determine the depletion allowance are the cost and percentage (or statutory) methods. Under cost depletion, each unit of production sold is assigned a portion of the cost or other basis of the interest. This is determined by dividing the cost or other basis by the total units expected to be recovered. Under percentage (or statutory) depletion, the tax law provides a special percentage factor for different types of minerals and other natural resources. This percentage is multiplied by the gross income from the interest to arrive at the depletion allowance. §§ 613 and 613A.

Depreciation rules. The depreciation system that existed prior to the enactment of the Accelerated Cost Recovery System (ACRS). This system applies to depreciable assets placed in service prior to January 1, 1981, and to certain post-1980 assets that do not qualify for ACRS.

Determination letter. Upon the request of a taxpayer, an IRS District Director will comment on the tax status of a completed transaction. Determination letters frequently are used to clarify employee status, determine whether a retirement or profit sharing plan qualifies under the Code, and determine the tax-exempt status of certain nonprofit organizations.

Disabled access credit. A tax credit designed to encourage small businesses to make their facilities more accessible to disabled individuals. The credit is equal to 50 percent of the eligible expenditures that exceed $250 but do not exceed $10,250. Thus, the maximum amount for the credit is $5,000. The adjusted basis for depreciation is reduced by the amount of the credit. To qualify, the facility must have been placed in service before November 6, 1990. § 44.

Disaster area loss. A casualty sustained in an area designated as a disaster area by the President of the United States. In such an event, the disaster loss may be treated as having occurred in the taxable year immediately preceding the year in which the disaster actually occurred. Thus, immediate tax benefits are provided to victims of a disaster. § 165(i).

Disguised sale. When a partner contributes property to the entity and soon thereafter receives a distribution from the partnership, the transactions are collapsed, and the distribution is seen as a purchase of the asset by the partnership. § 707(a)(2)(B).

District Court. A Federal District Court is a trial court for purposes of litigating (among others) Federal tax matters. It is the only trial court where a jury trial can be obtained.

Dividends received deduction. A deduction allowed a shareholder that is a corporation for dividends received from a domestic corporation. The deduction usually is 70 percent of the dividends received, but it could be 80 or 100 percent depending upon the ownership percentage held by the recipient corporation. §§ 243–246.

Dollar value LIFO. An inventory technique that focuses on the dollars invested in the inventory rather than the particular items on hand each period. Each inventory item is assigned to a pool. A pool is a collection of similar items and is treated as a separate inventory. At the end of the period, each pool is valued in terms of prices at the time LIFO was adopted (base period prices), whether or not the particular items were actually on hand in the year LIFO was adopted, to compare with current prices to determine if there has been an increase or decrease in inventories.

E

Earned income credit. A tax credit designed to provide assistance to certain low-income individuals who generally have a qualifying child. This is a refundable credit. To receive the most beneficial treatment, the taxpayer must have qualifying children. However, it is possible to qualify for the credit without having a child. To calculate the credit for a taxpayer with one or more children for 2001, a statutory rate of 34 percent for one child (40 percent for two or more children) is multiplied by the earned income (subject to a statutory maximum of $7,140 with one qualifying child or $10,020 with two or more qualifying children). Once the earned income exceeds $13,090, the credit is phased out using a 15.98 percent rate for one qualifying child and a 21.06 percent rate for two qualifying children. For the qualifying taxpayer without children, the credit is calculated on a maximum earned income of $4,760 applying a 7.65 percent rate with the phase-out beginning at $5,950 applying the same rate.

Earnings and profits (E & P). Measures the economic capacity of a corporation to make a distribution to shareholders that is not a return of capital. Such a distribution results in dividend income to the shareholders to the extent of the corporation's current and accumulated earnings and profits.

Economic effect test. Requirements that must be met before a special allocation may be used by a partnership. The premise behind the test is that each partner who receives an allocation of income or loss from a partnership bears the economic benefit or burden of the allocation.

Economic income. The change in the taxpayer's net worth, as measured in terms of market values, plus the value of the assets the taxpayer consumed during the year. Because of the impracticality of this income model, it is not used for tax purposes.

Education expenses. Employees may deduct education expenses that are incurred either (1) to maintain or improve existing job-related skills or (2) to meet the express requirements of the employer or the requirements imposed by law to retain employment status. The expenses are not deductible if the education is required to meet the minimum educational standards for the taxpayer's job or if the education qualifies the individual for a new trade or business. Reg. § 1.162–5.

Educational savings bonds. U.S. Series EE bonds whose proceeds are used for qualified higher educational expenses for the taxpayer, the taxpayer's spouse, or a dependent. The interest may be excluded from gross income, provided the taxpayer's adjusted gross income does not exceed certain amounts. § 135.

e-file. The electronic filing of a tax return. The filing is either direct or indirect. As to direct, the taxpayer goes online using a computer and tax return preparation software. Indirect filing occurs when a taxpayer utilizes an authorized IRS e-file provider. The provider often is the tax return preparer.

Employment taxes. Employment taxes are those taxes that an employer must pay on account of its employees. Employment taxes include FICA (Federal Insurance Contributions Act) and FUTA (Federal Unemployment Tax Act) taxes. Employment taxes are paid to the IRS in addition to income tax withholdings at specified intervals. Such taxes can be levied on the employees, the employer, or both.

Entertainment expenses. These expenses are deductible only if they are directly related to or associated with a trade or business. Various restrictions and documentation requirements have been imposed upon the deductibility of entertainment expenses to prevent abuses by taxpayers. See, for example, the provision contained in § 274(n) that disallows 50 percent of entertainment expenses. § 274.

Entity concept. The theory of partnership taxation under which a partnership is treated as a separate and distinct entity from the partners and has its own tax attributes.

Estate tax. A tax imposed on the right to transfer property by death. Thus, an estate tax is levied on the decedent's estate and not on the heir receiving the property.

Estimated tax. The amount of tax (including alternative minimum tax and self-employment tax) a taxpayer expects to owe for the year after subtracting tax credits and income tax withheld. The estimated tax must be paid in installments at designated intervals (e.g. for the individual taxpayer, by April 15, June 15, September 15, and January 15 of the following year).

Excise tax. A tax on the manufacture, sale, or use of goods; on the carrying on of an occupation or activity; or on the transfer of property. Thus, the Federal estate and gift taxes are, theoretically, excise taxes.

F

Fair market value. The amount at which property would change hands between a willing buyer and a willing seller, neither being under any compulsion to buy or to sell, and both having reasonable knowledge of the relevant facts. Reg. §§ 1.1001–1(a) and 20.2031–1(b).

FICA tax. An abbreviation that stands for Federal Insurance Contributions Act, commonly referred to as the Social Security tax. The FICA tax is comprised of the Social Security tax (old age, survivors, and disability insurance) and the Medicare tax (hospital insurance) and is imposed on both employers and employees. The employer is responsible for withholding from the employee's wages the Social Security tax at a rate of 6.2 percent on a maximum wage base of $80,400 (for 2001) and the Medicare tax at a rate of 1.45 percent (no maximum wage base). The employer is required to match the employee's contribution.

Final Regulation. The U.S. Treasury Department Regulations (abbreviated Reg.) represent the position of the IRS as to how the Internal Revenue Code is to be interpreted. Their purpose is to provide taxpayers and IRS personnel with rules of general and specific application to the various provisions of the tax law. Regulations are published in the *Federal Register* and in all tax services.

Fiscal year. A fiscal year is a 12-month period ending on the last day of a month other than December. In certain circumstances, a taxpayer is permitted to elect a fiscal year instead of being required to use a calendar year.

Flexible spending plan. An employee benefit plan that allows the employee to take a reduction in salary in exchange for the employer paying benefits that can be provided by the employer without the employee being required to recognize income (e.g., medical and child care benefits).

Foreign tax credit. A U.S. citizen or resident who incurs or pays income taxes to a foreign country on income subject to U.S. tax may be able to claim some or all of these taxes as a credit against the U.S. income tax. §§ 27 and 901–905.

Franchise. An agreement that gives the transferee the right to distribute, sell, or provide goods, services, or facilities within a specified area. The cost of obtaining a franchise may be amortized over a statutory period of 15 years. In general, the franchisor's gain on the sale of franchise rights is an ordinary gain because the franchisor retains a significant power, right, or continuing interest in the subject of the franchise. §§ 197 and 1253.

Franchise tax. A tax levied on the right to do business in a state as a corporation. Although income considerations may come into play, the tax usually is based on the capitalization of the corporation.

Fruit and tree metaphor. The courts have held that an individual who earns income from property or services cannot assign that income to another. For example, a father cannot assign his earnings from commissions to his child and escape income tax on those amounts.

FUTA tax. An employment tax levied on employers. Jointly administered by the Federal and state governments, the tax provides funding for unemployment benefits. FUTA applies at a rate of 6.2 percent in 2001 on the first $7,000 of covered wages paid during the year for each employee. The Federal government allows a credit for FUTA paid (or allowed under a merit rating system) to the state. The credit cannot exceed 5.4 percent of the covered wages.

G

General business credit. The summation of various non-refundable business credits, including the tax credit for rehabilitation expenditures, business energy credit, welfare-to-work credit, work opportunity credit, research activities credit, low-income housing credit, and disabled access credit. The amount of general business credit that can be used to reduce the tax liability is limited to the taxpayer's net income tax reduced by the greater of (1) the tentative minimum tax or (2) 25 percent of the net regular tax liability that exceeds $25,000. Unused general business credits can be carried back 1 year and forward 20 years (back 3 years and forward 15 years for tax years beginning before January 1, 1998). § 38.

General partnership. A partnership that is owned by one or more general partners. Creditors of a general partnership can collect amounts owed them from both the partnership assets and the assets of the partners individually.

Gift. A transfer of property for less than adequate consideration. Gifts usually occur in a personal setting (such as between members of the same family). They are excluded from the income tax base but may be subject to a transfer tax.

Gift tax. A tax imposed on the transfer of property by gift. The tax is imposed upon the donor of a gift and is based on the fair market value of the property on the date of the gift.

Goodwill. The reputation and built-up business of a company. For accounting purposes, goodwill has no basis unless it is purchased. In the purchase of a business, goodwill generally is the difference between the purchase price and the fair market value of the assets acquired. Since acquired goodwill is a § 197 intangible asset, it is amortized for tax purposes over a 15-year period. Reg. § 1.167(a)–3.

Gross income. Income subject to the Federal income tax. Gross income does not include all economic income. That is, certain exclusions are allowed (e.g., interest on municipal bonds). For a manufacturing or merchandising business, gross income usually means gross profit (gross sales or gross receipts less cost of goods sold). § 61 and Reg. § 1.61–3(a).

Guaranteed payments. Payments made by a partnership to a partner for services rendered or for the use of capital to the extent that the payments are determined without regard to the income of the partnership. The payments are treated as though they were made to a nonpartner and thus are usually deductible by the entity.

G

Half-year convention. The half-year convention is a cost recovery convention that assumes all property is placed in service at mid-year and thus provides for a half-year's cost recovery for that year.

Head of household. An unmarried individual who maintains a household for another and satisfies certain conditions set forth in § 2(b). This status enables the taxpayer to use a set of income tax rates that are lower than those applicable to other unmarried individuals but higher than those applicable to surviving spouses and married persons filing a joint return.

Holding period. The period of time during which property has been held for income tax purposes. The holding period is significant in determining whether gain or loss from the sale or exchange of a capital asset is long term or short term. § 1223.

Home equity loans. Loans that utilize the personal residence of the taxpayer as security. The interest on such loans is deductible as qualified residence interest. However, interest is deductible only on the portion of the loan that does not exceed the lesser of (1) the fair market value of the residence, reduced by the acquisition indebtedness, or (2) $100,000 ($50,000 for married persons filing separate returns). A major benefit of a home equity loan is that there are no tracing rules regarding the use of the loan proceeds. § 163(h)(3).

HOPE scholarship credit. A tax credit for qualifying expenses paid for the first two years of postsecondary education. Room, board, and book costs are ineligible for the credit. The maximum credit available is $1,500 per year per student, computed as 100 percent of the first $1,000 of qualifying expenses, plus 50 percent of the second $1,000 of qualifying expenses. Eligible students include the taxpayer, taxpayer's spouse, and taxpayer's dependents. To qualify for the credit, a student must take at least one-half the full-time course load for at least one academic term at a qualifying educational institution. The credit is phased out for higher-income taxpayers. § 25A.

Hybrid method. A combination of the accrual and cash methods of accounting. That is, the taxpayer may account for some items of income on the accrual method (e.g., sales and cost of goods sold) and other items (e.g., interest income) on the cash method.

I

Implicit tax. A tax that is paid through higher prices or lower returns on tax-favored investments rather than being paid directly to the government (i.e., an explicit tax). The value added tax is an example of an implicit tax.

Imputed interest. For certain long-term sales of property, the IRS can convert some of the gain from the sale into interest income if the contract does not provide for a minimum rate of interest to be paid by the purchaser. The application of this procedure has the effect of forcing the seller to recognize less long-term capital gain and more ordinary income (interest income). § 483 and the related Regulations. In addition, interest income and interest expense are imputed (deemed to exist) on interest-free or below-market rate loans between certain related parties. §7872.

Income. For tax purposes, an increase in wealth that has been realized.

Independent contractor. A self-employed person as distinguished from one who is employed as an employee.

Individual retirement account (IRA). A type of retirement plan to which an individual with earned income can contribute a maximum of $2,000 ($2,000 each in the case of a married couple with a spousal IRA) per tax year. IRAs can be classified as traditional IRAs or Roth IRAs. With a traditional IRA, an individual can contribute and deduct a maximum of $2,000 per tax year. The deduction is a deduction *for* AGI. However, if the individual is an active participant in another qualified retirement plan, the deduction is phased out proportionally between certain AGI ranges (note that the phase-out limits the amount of the deduction and not the amount of the contribution). With a Roth IRA, an individual can contribute a maximum of $2,000 per tax year. No deduction is permitted. However, if a five-year holding period requirement is satisfied and if the distribution is a qualified distribution, the taxpayer can make tax-free withdrawals from a Roth IRA. The maximum annual contribution is phased out proportionally between certain AGI ranges. §§ 219 and 408A.

Inheritance tax. A tax imposed on the right to receive property from a decedent. Thus, theoretically, an inheritance tax is imposed on the heir. The Federal estate tax is imposed on the estate.

Inside basis. A partnership's basis in the assets it owns.

Installment method. A method of accounting enabling certain taxpayers to spread the recognition of gain on the sale of property over the collection period. Under this procedure, the seller arrives at the gain to be recognized by computing the gross profit percentage from the sale (the gain divided by the contract price) and applying it to each payment received. § 453.

Intangible drilling and development costs (IDC). Taxpayers may elect to expense or capitalize (subject to amortization) intangible drilling and development costs. However, ordinary income recapture provisions apply to oil and gas properties on a sale or other disposition if the expense method is elected. §§ 263(c) and 1254(a).

Interpretive Regulation. A Regulation issued by the Treasury Department that purports to explain the meaning of a particular Code Section. An interpretive Regulation is given less deference than a legislative Regulation.

Investment interest. Payment for the use of funds used to acquire assets that produce investment income. The deduction for investment interest is limited to net investment income for the tax year.

Involuntary conversion. The loss or destruction of property through theft, casualty, or condemnation. Any gain realized on an involuntary conversion can, at the taxpayer's election, be deferred for Federal income tax purposes if the owner reinvests the proceeds within a prescribed period of time in property that is similar or related in service or use. § 1033.

Itemized deductions. Personal and employee expenditures allowed by the Code as deductions from adjusted gross income. Examples include certain medical expenses, interest on home mortgages, state income taxes, and charitable contributions. Itemized deductions are reported on Schedule A of Form 1040. Certain miscellaneous itemized deductions are reduced by 2 percent of the taxpayer's adjusted gross income. In addition, a taxpayer whose adjusted gross income exceeds a certain level (indexed annually) must reduce the itemized deductions by 3 percent of the excess of adjusted gross income over that level. Medical, casualty and theft, and investment interest deductions are not subject to the 3 percent reduction. The 3 percent reduction may not reduce itemized deductions that are subject to the reduction to below 20 percent of their initial amount. §§ 63(d), 67, and 68.

K

Keogh plan. See *self-employment retirement plan.*

Kiddie tax. Passive income, such as interest and dividends, that is recognized by a child under age 14 is taxed to him or her at the rates that would have applied had the income been incurred by the child's parents, generally to the extent that the income exceeds $1,500. The additional tax is assessed regardless of the source of the income or the income's underlying property. If the child's parents are divorced, the custodial parent's rates are used. The parents' rates reflect any applicable alternative minimum tax and the phase-outs of lower tax brackets and other deductions. § 1(g).

L

Least aggregate deferral method. An algorithm set forth in the Regulations to determine the tax year for a partnership or S corporation with owners whose tax years differ. The tax year selected is the one that produces the least aggregate deferral of income for the owners.

Legislative Regulation. Some Code Sections give the Secretary of the Treasury or his delegate the authority to prescribe Regulations to carry out the details of administration or to otherwise complete the operating rules. Regulations issued pursuant to this type of authority truly possess the force and effect of law. In effect, Congress is almost delegating its legislative powers to the Treasury Department.

Lessee. One who rents property from another. In the case of real estate, the lessee is also known as the tenant.

Lessor. One who rents property to another. In the case of real estate, the lessor is also known as the landlord.

Letter ruling. The written response of the IRS to a taxpayer's request for interpretation of the revenue laws, with respect to a proposed transaction (e.g., concerning the tax-free status of a reorganization). Not to be relied on as precedent by other than the party who requested the ruling.

Life insurance proceeds. A specified sum (the face value or maturity value of the policy) paid to the designated beneficiary of the policy by the life insurance company upon the death of the insured.

Lifetime learning credit. A tax credit for qualifying expenses for taxpayers pursuing education beyond the first two years of postsecondary education. Individuals who are completing their last two years of undergraduate studies, pursuing graduate or professional degrees, or otherwise seeking new job skills or maintaining existing job skills are all eligible for the credit. Eligible individuals include the taxpayer, taxpayer's spouse, and taxpayer's dependents. The maximum credit is 20 percent of the first $5,000 ($10,000 beginning in 2003) of qualifying expenses and is computed per taxpayer. The credit is phased out for higher-income taxpayers. § 25A.

Like-kind exchange. An exchange of property held for productive use in a trade or business or for investment (except inventory and stocks and bonds) for other investment or trade or business property. Unless non-like-kind property (boot) is received, the exchange is fully nontaxable. § 1031.

Limited liability company (LLC). A form of entity allowed by all of the states. The entity is taxed as a partnership in which all members or owners of the LLC are treated much like limited partners. There are no restrictions on ownership, all members may participate in management, and none has personal liability for the entity's debts.

Limited liability partnership (LLP). A form of entity allowed by many of the states, where a general partnership registers with the state as an LLP. Owners are general partners, but a partner is not liable for any malpractice committed by other partners. The personal assets of the partners are at risk for the entity's contractual liabilities, such as accounts payable. The personal assets of a specific partner are at risk for his or her own professional malpractice and tort liability, and for malpractice and torts committed by those whom he or she supervises.

Limited partnership. A partnership in which some of the partners are limited partners. At least one of the partners in a limited partnership must be a general partner.

Listed property. The term listed property includes (1) any passenger automobile, (2) any other property used as a means of transportation, (3) any property of a type generally used for purposes of entertainment, recreation, or amusement (4) any computer or peripheral equipment (with an exception for exclusive business use), (5) any cellular telephone (or other similar telecommunications equipment), and (6) any other property of a type specified in the Regulations. If listed property is predominantly used for business, the taxpayer is allowed to use the statutory percentage method of cost recovery. Otherwise, the straight-line cost recovery method must be used. § 280F.

Long-term contract. A building, installation, construction, or manufacturing contract that is entered into but not completed within the same tax year. A manufacturing contract is a long-term contract only if the contract is to manufacture (1) a unique item not normally carried in finished goods inventory or (2) items that normally require more than 12 calendar months to complete. The two available methods to account for long-term contracts are the percentage of completion method and the completed contract method. The completed contract method can be used only in limited circumstances. § 460.

Long-term nonpersonal use capital assets. Includes investment property with a long-term holding period. Such property disposed of by casualty or theft may receive § 1231 treatment.

Lower of cost or market. An elective inventory method, whereby the taxpayer may value inventories at the lower of the taxpayer's actual cost or the current replacement cost of the goods. This method cannot be used in conjunction with the LIFO inventory method.

M

Majority interest partners. Partners who have more than a 50 percent interest in partnership profits and capital, counting only those partners who have the same taxable year, are referred to as majority interest partners. The term is of significance in determining the appropriate taxable year of a partnership. § 706(b).

Marriage penalty. The additional tax liability that results for a married couple when compared with what their tax liability would be if they were not married and filed separate returns.

Material participation. If an individual taxpayer materially participates in a nonrental trade or business activity, any loss from that activity is treated as an active loss that can be offset against active income. Material participation is achieved by meeting any one of seven tests provided in the Regulations. § 469(h).

Medical expenses. Medical expenses of an individual, spouse, and dependents are allowed as an itemized deduction to the extent that such amounts (less insurance reimbursements) exceed 7.5 percent of adjusted gross income. § 213.

Medical savings account. A plan available to employees of small firms (50 or fewer employees) with high-deductible health insurance. The employee can place money in the fund and then deduct the contributions (within limits) from gross income. If the employer contributes to the fund, the employee can exclude the contribution from gross income. Income earned from the fund and withdrawals for medical care are not subject to tax. §§ 106(b) and 220.

Mid-month convention. A cost recovery convention that assumes property is placed in service in the middle of the month that it is actually placed in service.

Mid-quarter convention. A cost recovery convention that assumes property placed in service during the year is placed in service at the middle of the quarter in which it is actually placed in service. The mid-quarter convention applies if more than 40 percent of the value of property (other than eligible real estate) is placed in service during the last quarter of the year.

Minimum tax credit (AMT). When a corporation pays an alternative minimum tax (AMT), a minimum tax credit is created on a dollar-for-dollar basis, to be applied against regular tax liabilities incurred in future years. The credit is carried forward indefinitely, but it is not carried back. The effect of the credit for corporate taxpayers alternating between the AMT and regular tax models is to make the AMT liabilities a prepayment of regular taxes. Noncorporate AMT taxpayers are allowed the credit only with respect to the elements of the AMT that reflect timing differences between the two tax models. § 53.

Miscellaneous itemized deductions. A special category of itemized deductions that includes such expenses as professional dues, tax return preparation fees, job-hunting costs, unreimbursed employee business expenses, and certain investment expenses. Such expenses are deductible only to the extent they exceed 2 percent of adjusted gross income. § 67.

Modified accelerated cost recovery system (MACRS). A method in which the cost of tangible property is recovered over a prescribed period of time. Enacted by the Economic Recovery Tax Act (ERTA) of 1981 and substantially modified by the Tax Reform Act (TRA) of 1986 (the modified system is referred to as MACRS), the approach disregards salvage value, imposes a period of cost recovery that depends upon the classification of the asset into one of various recovery periods, and prescribes the applicable percentage of cost that can be deducted each year. § 168.

Moving expenses. A deduction *for* AGI is permitted to employees and self-employed individuals provided certain tests are met. The taxpayer's new job must be at least 50 miles farther from the old residence than the old residence was from the former place of work. In addition, an employee must be employed on a full-time basis at the new location for 39 weeks in the 12-month period following the move. Deductible moving expenses include the cost of moving the household and personal effects, transportation, and lodging expenses during the move. The cost of meals during the move is not deductible. Qualified moving expenses that are paid (or reimbursed) by the employer can be excluded from the employee's gross income. In this case, the related deduction by the employee is not permitted. §§ 62(a)(15), 132(a)(6), and 217.

Multiple support agreement. To qualify for a dependency exemption, the support test must be satisfied. This requires that over 50 percent of the support of the potential dependent be provided by the taxpayer. Where no one person provides more than 50 percent of the support, a multiple support agreement enables a taxpayer to still qualify for the dependency exemption. Any person who contributed more than 10 percent of the support is entitled to claim the exemption if each person in the group who contributed more than 10 percent files a written consent (Form 2120). Each person who is a party to the multiple support agreement must meet all the other requirements for claiming the dependency exemption. § 152(c).

N

Net capital gain.   The excess of the net long-term capital gain for the tax year over the net short-term capital loss. The net capital gain of an individual taxpayer is eligible for the alternative tax. § 1222(11).

Net capital loss.   The excess of the losses from sales or exchanges of capital assets over the gains from sales or exchanges of such assets. Up to $3,000 per year of the net capital loss may be deductible by noncorporate taxpayers against ordinary income. The excess net capital loss carries over to future tax years. For corporate taxpayers, the net capital loss cannot be offset against ordinary income, but it can be carried back three years and forward five years to offset net capital gains. §§ 1211, 1212, and 1221(10).

Net investment income.   The excess of investment income over investment expenses. Investment expenses are those deductible expenses directly connected with the production of investment income. Investment expenses do not include investment interest. The deduction for investment interest for the tax year is limited to net investment income. § 163(d).

Net operating loss.   To mitigate the effect of the annual accounting period concept, § 172 allows taxpayers to use an excess loss of one year as a deduction for certain past or future years. In this regard, a carryback period of 2 years and a carryforward period of 20 years currently are allowed. For NOLs in tax years beginning before August 6, 1997, the carryback period is 3 years and the carryforward period is 15 years.

No-additional-cost services.   Services that the employer may provide the employee at no additional cost to the employer. Generally, the benefit is the ability to utilize the employer's excess capacity (e.g., vacant seats on an airliner). Such amounts are excludible from the recipient's gross income.

Nonaccountable plan.   An expense reimbursement plan that does not have an accountability feature. The result is that employee expenses must be claimed as deductions *from* AGI. An exception is moving expenses that are deductions *for* AGI.

Nonacquiescence.   Disagreement by the IRS on the result reached in certain judicial decisions. *Nonacq.* or *NA.*

Nonbusiness bad debt.   A bad debt loss that is not incurred in connection with a creditor's trade or business. The loss is classified as a short-term capital loss and is allowed only in the year the debt becomes entirely worthless. In addition to family loans, many investor losses are nonbusiness bad debts. § 166(d).

Nonrecourse debt.   Debt secured by the property that it is used to purchase. The purchaser of the property is not personally liable for the debt upon default. Rather, the creditor's recourse is to repossess the related property. Nonrecourse debt generally does not increase the purchaser's at-risk amount.

Nontaxable exchange.   A transaction in which realized gains or losses are not recognized. The recognition of gain or loss is postponed (deferred) until the property received in the nontaxable exchange is subsequently disposed of in a taxable transaction. Examples are § 1031 like-kind exchanges and § 1033 involuntary conversions.

O

Occupational tax.   A tax imposed on various trades or businesses. A license fee that enables a taxpayer to engage in a particular occupation.

Office-in-the-home expenses.   Employment and business-related expenses attributable to the use of a residence (e.g., den or office) are allowed only if the portion of the residence is exclusively used on a regular basis as a principal place of business of the taxpayer or as a place of business that is used by patients, clients, or customers. If the expenses are incurred by an employee, the use must be for the convenience of the employer as opposed to being merely appropriate and helpful. § 280A.

Options.   The sale or exchange of an option to buy or sell property results in capital gain or loss if the property is a capital asset. Generally, the closing of an option transaction results in short-term capital gain or loss to the writer of the call and the purchaser of the call option. § 1234.

Ordinary and necessary.   An ordinary expense is one that is common and accepted in the general industry or type of activity in which the taxpayer is engaged. It comprises one of the tests for the deductibility of expenses incurred or paid in connection with a trade or business; for the production or collection of income; for the management, conservation, or maintenance of property held for the production of income; or in connection with the determination, collection, or refund of any tax. §§ 162(a) and 212. A necessary expense is one that is appropriate and helpful in furthering the taxpayer's business or income-producing activity. §§ 162(a) and 212.

Ordinary income property.   Property contributed to a charitable organization that, if sold rather than contributed, would have resulted in other than long-term capital gain to the donor (i.e., ordinary income property and short-term capital gain property). Examples are inventory and capital assets held for less than the long-term holding period.

Organizational expenditures. Items incurred early in the life of a corporate entity, qualifying for a 60-month amortization under Federal tax law. Amortizable expenditures exclude those incurred to obtain capital (underwriting fees) or assets (subject to cost recovery). Typically, amortizable expenditures include legal and accounting fees and state incorporation payments. Such items must be incurred by the end of the entity's first tax year. § 248.

Original issue discount. The difference between the issue price of a debt obligation (e.g., a corporate bond) and the maturity value of the obligation when the issue price is *less than* the maturity value. OID represents interest and must be amortized over the life of the debt obligation using the effective interest method. The difference is not considered to be original issue discount for tax purposes when it is less than one-fourth of 1 percent of the redemption price at maturity multiplied by the number of years to maturity. §§ 1272 and 1273(a)(3).

Outside basis. A partner's basis in his or her partnership interest.

P

Parent-subsidiary controlled group. A controlled or affiliated group of corporations, where at least one corporation is at least 80 percent owned by one or more of the others. The affiliated group definition is more difficult to meet.

Passive investment income (PII). Gross receipts from royalties, certain rents, dividends, interest, annuities, and gains from the sale or exchange of stock and securities. With certain exceptions, if the passive investment income of an S corporation exceeds 25 percent of the corporation's gross receipts for three consecutive years, S status is lost.

Passive loss. Any loss from (1) activities in which the taxpayer does not materially participate or (2) rental activities (subject to certain exceptions). Net passive losses cannot be used to offset income from nonpassive sources. Rather, they are suspended until the taxpayer either generates net passive income (and a deduction of such losses is allowed) or disposes of the underlying property (at which time the loss deductions are allowed in full). One relief provision allows landlords who actively participate in the rental activities to deduct up to $25,000 of passive losses annually. However, a phase-out of the $25,000 amount commences when the landlord's AGI exceeds $100,000. Another relief provision applies for material participation in a real estate trade or business.

Patent. A patent is an intangible asset that may be amortized over a statutory 15-year period as a § 197 intangible. The sale of a patent usually results in favorable long-term capital gain treatment. §§ 197 and 1235.

Percentage depletion. Percentage depletion is depletion based on a statutory percentage applied to the gross income from the property. The taxpayer deducts the greater of cost depletion or percentage depletion. § 613.

Percentage of completion method. A method of reporting gain or loss on certain long-term contracts. Under this method of accounting, the gross contract price is included in income as the contract is completed. See § 460 and Reg. § 1.451–3.

Personal exemption. The tax law provides an exemption for each individual taxpayer and an additional exemption for the taxpayer's spouse if a joint return is filed. An individual may also claim a dependency exemption for each dependent, provided certain tests are met. The amount of the personal and dependency exemptions is $2,900 in 2001 ($2,800 in 2000). The exemption is subject to phase-out once adjusted gross income exceeds certain statutory threshold amounts.

Personal service corporation (PSC). A corporation whose principal activity is the performance of personal services (e.g., health, law, engineering, architecture, accounting, actuarial science, performing arts, or consulting) and where such services are substantially performed by the employee-owners. The 35 percent statutory income tax rate applies to PSCs.

Personalty. All property that is not attached to real estate (realty) and is movable. Examples of personalty are machinery, automobiles, clothing, household furnishings, inventory, and personal effects.

Points. Loan origination fees that may be deductible as interest by a buyer of property. A seller of property who pays points reduces the selling price by the amount of the points paid for the buyer. While the seller is not permitted to deduct this amount as interest, the buyer may do so.

Portfolio income. Income from interest, dividends, rentals, royalties, capital gains, or other investment sources. Net passive losses cannot be used to offset net portfolio income.

Precedent. A previously decided court decision that is recognized as authority for the disposition of future decisions.

Precontribution gain or loss. Partnerships allow for a variety of special allocations of gain or loss among the partners, but gain or loss that is "built in" on an asset contributed to the partnership is assigned specifically to the contributing partner. § 704(c)(1)(A).

Principal partner. A partner with a 5 percent or greater interest in partnership capital or profits. § 706(b)(3).

Private activity bond. Interest on state and local bonds is excludible from gross income. § 103. Certain such bonds are labeled private activity bonds. Although the interest on such bonds is excludible for regular income tax purposes, it is treated as a tax preference in calculating the AMT.

Procedural Regulation. A Regulation issued by the Treasury Department that is a housekeeping-type instruction indicating information that taxpayers should provide the IRS as well as information about the internal management and conduct of the IRS itself.

Profit and loss sharing ratios.   Specified in the partnership agreement and used to determine each partner's allocation of ordinary taxable income and separately stated items. Profits and losses can be shared in different ratios. The ratios can be changed by amending the partnership agreement. § 704(a).

Profits interest.   A partner's percentage allocation of partnership operating results, determined by the profit and loss sharing ratios.

Property.   Assets defined in the broadest legal sense. Property includes the unrealized receivables of a cash basis taxpayer, but not services rendered. § 351.

Property dividend.   Generally treated in the same manner as a cash distribution, measured by the fair market value of the property on the date of distribution. The portion of the distribution representing E & P is a dividend; any excess is treated as a return of capital. Distribution of appreciated property causes the distributing corporation to recognize gain. The distributing corporation does not recognize loss on property that has depreciated in value.

Proposed Regulation.   A Regulation issued by the Treasury Department in proposed, rather than final, form. The interval between the proposal of a Regulation and its finalization permits taxpayers and other interested parties to comment on the propriety of the proposal.

Proprietorship.   A business entity for which there is a single owner. The net profit of the entity is reported on the owner's Federal income tax return (Schedule C of Form 1040).

Punitive damages.   Damages received or paid by the taxpayer can be classified as compensatory damages or as punitive damages. Punitive damages are those awarded to punish the defendant for gross negligence or the intentional infliction of harm. Such damages are includible in gross income. § 104.

Q

Qualified employee discounts.   Discounts offered employees on merchandise or services that the employer ordinarily sells or provides to customers. The discounts must be generally available to all employees. In the case of property, the discount cannot exceed the employer's gross profit (the sales price cannot be less than the employer's cost). In the case of services, the discounts cannot exceed 20 percent of the normal sales price. § 132.

Qualified nonrecourse debt.   Debt issued on realty by a bank, retirement plan, or governmental agency. Included in the at risk amount by the investor. § 465(b)(6)

Qualified real property business indebtedness.   Indebtedness that was incurred or assumed by the taxpayer in connection with real property used in a trade or business and is secured by such real property. The taxpayer must not be a C corporation. For qualified real property business indebtedness, the taxpayer may elect to exclude some or all of the income realized from cancellation of debt on qualified real property. If the election is made, the basis of the property must be reduced by the amount excluded. The amount excluded cannot be greater than the excess of the principal amount of the outstanding debt over the fair market value (net of any other debt outstanding on the property) of the property securing the debt. § 108(c).

Qualified residence interest.   A term relevant in determining the amount of interest expense the individual taxpayer may deduct as an itemized deduction for what otherwise would be disallowed as a component of personal interest (consumer interest). Qualified residence interest consists of interest paid on qualified residences (principal residence and one other residence) of the taxpayer. Debt that qualifies as qualified residence interest is limited to $1 million of debt to acquire, construct, or substantially improve qualified residences (acquisition indebtedness) plus $100,000 of other debt secured by qualified residences (home equity indebtedness). The home equity indebtedness may not exceed the fair market value of a qualified residence reduced by the acquisition indebtedness for that residence. § 163(h)(3).

Qualified small business stock.   Stock in a qualified small business corporation, purchased as part of an original issue after August 10, 1993. The shareholder may exclude from gross income 50 percent of the realized gain on the sale of the stock, if he or she held the stock for more than five years. § 1202.

Qualified transportation fringes.   Transportation benefits provided by the employer to the employee. Such benefits include (1) transportation in a commuter highway vehicle between the employee's residence and the place of employment, (2) a transit pass, and (3) qualified parking. Qualified transportation fringes are excludible from the employee's gross income to the extent categories (1) and (2) above do not exceed $65 per month in 2001 and category (3) does not exceed $180 per month in 2001. These amounts are indexed annually for inflation. § 132.

R

Realized gain or loss.   The difference between the amount realized upon the sale or other disposition of property and the adjusted basis of the property. § 1001.

Realty.   Real estate.

Reasonableness requirement.   The Code includes a reasonableness requirement with respect to the deduction of salaries and other compensation for services. What constitutes reasonableness is a question of fact. If an expense is unreasonable, the amount that is classified as unreasonable is not allowed as a deduction. The question of reasonableness generally arises with respect to closely held corporations where there is no separation of ownership and management. § 162(a)(1).

Recognized gain or loss.   The portion of realized gain or loss subject to income taxation.

Recourse debt. Debt for which the lender may both foreclose on the property and assess a guarantor for any payments due under the loan. A lender may also make a claim against the assets of any general partner in a partnership to which debt is issued, without regard to whether the partner has guaranteed the debt.

Recovery of capital doctrine. When a taxable sale or exchange occurs, the seller may be permitted to recover his or her investment (or other adjusted basis) in the property before gain or loss is recognized.

Regular corporation. See *C corporation*.

Rehabilitation expenditures credit. A credit that is based on expenditures incurred to rehabilitate industrial and commercial buildings and certified historic structures. The credit is intended to discourage businesses from moving from older, economically distressed areas to newer locations and to encourage the preservation of historic structures. § 47.

Rehabilitation expenditures credit recapture. When property that qualifies for the rehabilitation expenditures credit is disposed of or ceases to be used in the trade or business of the taxpayer, some or all of the tax credit claimed on the property may be recaptured as additional tax liability. The amount of the recapture is the difference between the amount of the credit claimed originally and what should have been claimed in light of the length of time the property was actually held or used for qualifying purposes. § 50.

Related corporation. See *controlled group*.

Related-party transactions. Various Code Sections define related parties and often include a variety of persons within this (usually detrimental) category. Generally, related parties are accorded different tax treatment from that applicable to other taxpayers who enter into similar transactions. For instance, realized losses that are generated between related parties are not recognized in the year of the loss. However, these deferred losses can be used to offset recognized gains that occur upon the subsequent sale of the asset to a nonrelated party. Other uses of a related-party definition include the conversion of gain upon the sale of a depreciable asset into all ordinary income (§ 1239) and the identification of constructive ownership of stock relative to corporate distributions, redemptions, liquidations, reorganizations, and compensation.

Rental activity. Any activity where payments are received principally for the use of tangible property is a rental activity. Temporary Regulations provide that in certain circumstances activities involving rentals of real and personal property are not to be *treated* as rental activities. The Temporary Regulations list six exceptions.

Research activities credit. A tax credit whose purpose is to encourage research and development. It consists of two components: the incremental research activities credit and the basic research credit. The incremental research activities credit is equal to 20 percent of the excess qualified research expenditures over the base amount. The basic research credit is equal to 20 percent of the excess of basic research payments over the base amount. § 41.

Research and experimental expenditures. The Code provides three alternatives for the tax treatment of research and experimental expenditures. They may be expensed in the year paid or incurred, deferred subject to amortization, or capitalized. If the taxpayer does not elect to expense such costs or to defer them subject to amortization (over 60 months), the expenditures must be capitalized. § 174. Two types of research activities credits are available: the basic research credit and the incremental research activities credit. The rate for each type is 20 percent. § 41.

Reserve method. A method of accounting whereby an allowance is permitted for estimated uncollectible accounts. Actual write-offs are charged to the reserve, and recoveries of amounts previously written off are credited to the reserve. The Code permits only certain financial institutions to use the reserve method. § 166.

Residential rental real estate. Buildings for which at least 80 percent of the gross rents are from dwelling units (e.g., an apartment building). This type of building is distinguished from nonresidential (commercial or industrial) buildings in applying the recapture of depreciation provisions. The term also is relevant in distinguishing between buildings that are eligible for a 27.5-year life versus a 39-year life for MACRS purposes. Generally, residential buildings receive preferential treatment.

Revenue Procedure. A matter of procedural importance to both taxpayers and the IRS concerning the administration of the tax laws is issued as a Revenue Procedure (abbreviated Rev.Proc.). A Revenue Procedure is first published in an *Internal Revenue Bulletin* (I.R.B.) and later transferred to the appropriate *Cumulative Bulletin* (C.B.). Both the *Internal Revenue Bulletins* and the *Cumulative Bulletins* are published by the U.S. Government Printing Office.

Revenue Ruling. A Revenue Ruling (abbreviated Rev.Rul.) is issued by the National Office of the IRS to express an official interpretation of the tax law as applied to specific transactions. It is more limited in application than a Regulation. A Revenue Ruling is first published in an *Internal Revenue Bulletin* (I.R.B.) and later transferred to the appropriate *Cumulative Bulletin* (C.B.). Both the *Internal Revenue Bulletins* and the *Cumulative Bulletins* are published by the U.S. Government Printing Office.

S

S corporation. The designation for a small business corporation. See also *Subchapter S*.

Sale or exchange. A requirement for the recognition of capital gain or loss. Generally, the seller of property must receive money or relief from debt in order to have sold the property. An exchange involves the transfer of property for other property. Thus, collection of a debt is neither a sale nor an exchange. The term *sale or exchange* is not defined by the Code.

Sales tax. A state- or local-level tax on the retail sale of specified property. Generally, the purchaser pays the tax, but the seller collects it, as an agent for the government. Various taxing jurisdictions allow exemptions for purchases of specific items, including certain food, services, and manufacturing equipment. If the purchaser and seller are in different states, a use tax usually applies.

Schedule M–1. On the Form 1120, a reconciliation of book net income with Federal taxable income. Accounts for timing and permanent differences in the two computations, such as depreciation differences, exempt income, and nondeductible items.

Scholarships. Scholarships are generally excluded from the gross income of the recipient unless the payments are a disguised form of compensation for services rendered. However, the Code imposes restrictions on the exclusion. The recipient must be a degree candidate. The excluded amount is limited to amounts used for tuition, fees, books, supplies, and equipment required for courses of instruction. Amounts received for room and board are not eligible for the exclusion. § 117.

Section 179 expensing election. The ability to deduct a capital expenditure in the year an asset is placed in service rather than over the asset's useful life or cost recovery period. The annual ceiling on the deduction is $20,000 for 2000 and $24,000 for 2001. The ceiling amount is increased each year until it reaches $25,000 for 2003 and thereafter. However, the deduction is reduced dollar for dollar when § 179 property placed in service during the taxable year exceeds $200,000. In addition, the amount expensed under § 179 cannot exceed the aggregate amount of taxable income derived from the conduct of any trade or business by the taxpayer.

Section 1231 gains and losses. If the combined gains and losses from the taxable dispositions of § 1231 assets plus the net gain from business involuntary conversions (of both § 1231 assets and long-term capital assets) is a gain, the gains and losses are treated as long-term capital gains and losses. In arriving at § 1231 gains, however, the depreciation recapture provisions (e.g., §§ 1245 and 1250) are first applied to produce ordinary income. If the net result of the combination is a loss, the gains and losses from § 1231 assets are treated as ordinary gains and losses. § 1231(a).

Section 1231 lookback. In order for gain to be classified as § 1231 gain, the gain must survive the § 1231 lookback. To the extent of nonrecaptured § 1231 losses for the five prior tax years, the gain is classified as ordinary income. § 1231(c).

Section 1231 property. Depreciable assets and real estate used in trade or business and held for the required long-term holding period. Under certain circumstances, the classification also includes timber, coal, domestic iron ore, livestock (held for draft, breeding, dairy, or sporting purposes), and unharvested crops. § 1231(b).

Section 1245 property. Property that is subject to the recapture of depreciation under § 1245. For a definition of § 1245 property, see § 1245(a)(3).

Section 1245 recapture. Upon a taxable disposition of § 1245 property, all depreciation claimed on the property is recaptured as ordinary income (but not to exceed recognized gain from the disposition).

Section 1250 property. Real estate that is subject to the recapture of depreciation under § 1250. For a definition of § 1250 property, see § 1250(c).

Section 1250 recapture. Upon a taxable disposition of § 1250 property, some of the depreciation or cost recovery claimed on the property may be recaptured as ordinary income.

Securities. Generally, stock, debt, and other financial assets. To the extent securities other than the stock of the transferee corporation are received in a § 351 exchange, the new shareholder realizes a gain.

Self-employment retirement plan. A designation for retirement plans available to self-employed taxpayers. Also referred to as H.R. 10 and Keogh plans. Under such plans, a taxpayer may deduct each year up to either 20 percent of net earnings from self-employment or $35,000, whichever is less. If the plan is a profit sharing plan, the percentage is 13.043 percent.

Self-employment tax. In 2001, a tax of 12.4 percent is levied on individuals with net earnings from self-employment (up to $80,400) to provide Social Security benefits (i.e., the old age, survivors, and disability insurance portion) for such individuals. In addition, in 2001, a tax of 2.9 percent is levied on individuals with net earnings from self-employment (with no statutory ceiling) to provide Medicare benefits (i.e., the hospital insurance portion) for such individuals. If a self-employed individual also receives wages from an employer that are subject to FICA, the self-employment tax will be reduced if total income subject to Social Security is more than $80,400. A partial deduction is allowed in calculating the self-employment tax. Individuals with net earnings of $400 or more from self-employment are subject to this tax. §§ 1401 and 1402.

Separately stated item. Any item of a partnership or S corporation that might be taxed differently to any two owners of the entity. These amounts are not included in ordinary income of the entity, but are instead reported separately to the owners; tax consequences are determined at the owner level.

Short sale. A short sale occurs when a taxpayer sells borrowed property (usually stock) and repays the lender with substantially identical property either held on the date of the short sale or purchased after the sale. No gain or loss is recognized until the short sale is closed, and such gain or loss is generally short term. § 1233.

Short taxable year (short period). A tax year that is less than 12 months. A short taxable year may occur in the initial reporting period, in the final tax year, or when the taxpayer changes tax years.

Significant participation activity. There are seven tests to determine whether an individual has achieved material participation in an activity, one of which is based on more than

500 hours of participation in significant participation activities. A significant participation activity is one in which the individual's participation exceeds 100 hours during the year. Reg. § 1.469–5T.

Small business corporation. A corporation that satisfies the definition of § 1361(b), § 1244(c), or both. Satisfaction of § 1361(b) permits an S election, and satisfaction of § 1244 enables the shareholders of the corporation to claim an ordinary loss on the worthlessness of stock.

Small business stock. See *small business corporation.*

Small Cases Division of the U.S. Tax Court. Jurisdiction is limited to claims of $50,000 or less. There is no appeal from this court.

Special allocation. Any amount for which an agreement exists among the partners of a partnership outlining the method used for spreading the item among the partners.

Specific charge-off method. A method of accounting for bad debts in which a deduction is permitted only when an account becomes partially or completely worthless.

Standard deduction. The individual taxpayer can either itemize deductions or take the standard deduction. The amount of the standard deduction depends on the taxpayer's filing status (single, head of household, married filing jointly, surviving spouse, or married filing separately). For 2001, the amount of the standard deduction ranges from $3,800 (for married, filing separately) to $7,600 (for married, filing jointly). Additional standard deductions of either $900 (for married taxpayers) or $1,100 (for single taxpayers) are available if the taxpayer is either blind or age 65 or over. Limitations exist on the amount of the standard deduction of a taxpayer who is another taxpayer's dependent. The standard deduction amounts are adjusted for inflation each year. § 63(c).

Stock dividend. Not taxable if pro rata distributions of stock or stock rights on common stock. Section 305 governs the taxability of stock dividends and sets out five exceptions to the general rule that stock dividends are nontaxable.

Stock redemption. A corporation buys back its own stock from a specified shareholder. Typically, the corporation recognizes any realized gain on the noncash assets that it uses to effect a redemption, and the shareholder obtains a capital gain or loss upon receipt of the purchase price.

Subchapter S. Sections 1361–1379 of the Internal Revenue Code. An elective provision permitting certain small business corporations (§ 1361) and their shareholders (§ 1362) to elect to be treated for income tax purposes in accordance with the operating rules of §§ 1363–1379. S corporations usually avoid the corporate income tax, and corporate losses can be claimed by the shareholders.

Supreme Court. The highest appellate court or the court of last resort in the Federal court system and in most states. Only a small number of tax decisions of the U.S. Courts of Appeal are reviewed by the U.S. Supreme Court under its certiorari procedure. The Supreme Court usually grants certiorari to resolve a conflict among the Courts of Appeal (e.g.,

two or more appellate courts have assumed opposing positions on a particular issue) or when the tax issue is extremely important (e.g., size of the revenue loss to the Federal government).

Surviving spouse. When a husband or wife predeceases the other spouse, the survivor is known as a surviving spouse. Under certain conditions, a surviving spouse may be entitled to use the income tax rates in § 1(a) (those applicable to married persons filing a joint return) for the two years after the year of death of his or her spouse. § 2.

Syndication costs. Incurred in promoting and marketing partnership interests for sale to investors. Examples include legal and accounting fees, printing costs for prospectus and placement documents, and state registration fees. These items are capitalized by the partnership as incurred, with no amortization thereof allowed.

T

Tax avoidance. The minimization of one's tax liability by taking advantage of legally available tax planning opportunities. Tax avoidance can be contrasted with tax evasion, which entails the reduction of tax liability by illegal means.

Tax benefit rule. A provision that limits the recognition of income from the recovery of an expense or loss properly deducted in a prior tax year to the amount of the deduction that generated a tax saving. Assume that last year Gary had medical expenses of $3,000 and adjusted gross income of $30,000. Because of the 7.5 percent limitation, Gary could deduct only $750 of these expenses [$3,000 − (7.5% × $30,000)]. If, this year, Gary is reimbursed by his insurance company for $900 of these expenses, the tax benefit rule limits the amount of income from the reimbursement to $750 (the amount previously deducted with a tax saving). § 111.

Tax Court. The U.S. Tax Court is one of four trial courts of original jurisdiction that decides litigation involving Federal income, death, or gift taxes. It is the only trial court where the taxpayer must not first pay the deficiency assessed by the IRS. The Tax Court will not have jurisdiction over a case unless a statutory notice of deficiency (90-day letter) has been issued by the IRS and the taxpayer files the petition for hearing within the time prescribed.

Tax credits. Tax credits are amounts that directly reduce a taxpayer's tax liability. The tax benefit received from a tax credit is not dependent on the taxpayer's marginal tax rate, whereas the benefit of a tax deduction or exclusion is dependent on the taxpayer's tax bracket.

Tax evasion. The reduction of the taxpayer's tax liability through the use of illegal means. Tax evasion can be contrasted with tax avoidance, which entails the reduction of tax liability through the use of legal means.

Tax preference items. Various items that may result in the imposition of the alternative minimum tax. §§ 55–58.

Tax rate schedules. Rate schedules that are used by upper-income taxpayers and those not permitted to use the tax table. Separate rate schedules are provided for married individuals filing jointly, head of household, single taxpayers, estates and trusts, and married individuals filing separate returns. § 1.

Tax shelters. The typical tax shelter generated large losses in the early years of the activity. Investors would offset these losses against other types of income and, therefore, avoid paying income taxes on this income. These tax shelter investments could then be sold after a few years and produce capital gain income, which is taxed at a lower rate than ordinary income. The passive activity loss rules and the at-risk rules now limit tax shelter deductions.

Tax table. A tax table that is provided for taxpayers with less than $100,000 of taxable income. Separate columns are provided for single taxpayers, married taxpayers filing jointly, head of household, and married taxpayers filing separately. § 3.

Taxable year. The annual period over which income is measured for income tax purposes. Most individuals use a calendar year, but many businesses use a fiscal year based on the natural business year.

Technical advice memoranda (TAMs). TAMs are issued by the National Office of the IRS in response to questions raised by IRS field personnel during audits. They deal with completed rather than proposed transactions and are often requested for questions related to exempt organizations and employee plans.

Temporary Regulation. A Regulation issued by the Treasury Department in temporary form. When speed is critical, the Treasury Department issues Temporary Regulations that take effect immediately. These Regulations have the same authoritative value as Final Regulations and may be cited as precedent for three years. Temporary Regulations are also issued as proposed Regulations.

Theft loss. A loss from larceny, embezzlement, or robbery. It does not include misplacement of items.

Thin capitalization. When debt owed by a corporation to the shareholders becomes too large in relation to the corporation's capital structure (i.e., stock and shareholder equity), the IRS may contend that the corporation is thinly capitalized. In effect, this means that some or all of the debt is reclassified as equity. The immediate result is to disallow any interest deduction to the corporation on the reclassified debt. To the extent of the corporation's earnings and profits, interest payments and loan repayments on the reclassified debt are treated as dividends to the shareholders.

Transportation expenses. Transportation expenses for an employee include only the cost of transportation (taxi fares, automobile expenses, etc.) in the course of employment when the employee is not away from home in travel status. Commuting expenses are not deductible.

Travel expenses. Travel expenses include meals (generally subject to a 50 percent disallowance) and lodging and transportation expenses while away from home in the pursuit of a trade or business (including that of an employee).

U

Unearned income. Income received but not yet earned. Normally, such income is taxed when received, even for accrual basis taxpayers.

Uniform capitalization (UNICAP) rules. Under § 263A, the Regulations provide a set of rules that all taxpayers (regardless of the particular industry) can use to determine the items of cost (and means of allocating those costs) that must be capitalized with respect to the production of tangible property.

Unreasonable compensation. A deduction is allowed for "reasonable" salaries or other compensation for personal services actually rendered. To the extent compensation is "excessive" ("unreasonable"), no deduction is allowed. The problem of unreasonable compensation usually is limited to closely held corporations, where the motivation is to pay out profits in some form that is deductible to the corporation. Deductible compensation therefore becomes an attractive substitute for nondeductible dividends when the shareholders also are employed by the corporation.

Unrecaptured § 1250 gain (25 percent gain). Gain from the sale of depreciable real estate held more than one year. The gain is equal to or less than the depreciation taken on such property and is reduced by § 1245 and § 1250 gain.

Use tax. A sales tax that is collectible by the seller where the purchaser is domiciled in a different state.

V

Value added tax (VAT). A national sales tax that taxes the increment in value as goods move through the production process. A VAT is much used in other countries but has not yet been incorporated as part of the U.S. Federal tax structure.

W

Wash sale. A loss from the sale of stock or securities that is disallowed because the taxpayer, within 30 days before or after the sale, has acquired stock or securities substantially identical to those sold. § 1091.

Welfare-to-work credit. A tax credit available to employers hiring individuals who have been long-term recipients of family assistance welfare benefits. In general, long term recipients are those individuals who are certified by a designated local agency as being members of a family receiving assistance under a public aid program for at least an 18-month period ending on the hiring date. The welfare-to-work credit is available for qualified wages paid in the first two years of employment. The maximum credit is equal to $8,500 per qualified employee, computed as 35 percent of the first $10,000 of qualified wages paid in the first year of employment, plus 50 percent of the first $10,000 of qualified wages paid in the second year of employment. § 51A.

Wherewithal to pay.   This concept recognizes the inequity of taxing a transaction when the taxpayer lacks the means with which to pay the tax. Under it, there is a correlation between the imposition of the tax and the ability to pay the tax. It is particularly suited to situations in which the taxpayer's economic position has not changed significantly as a result of the transaction.

Work opportunity tax credit.   Employers are allowed a tax credit equal to 40 percent of the first $6,000 of wages (per eligible employee) for the first year of employment. Eligible employees include certain hard-to-employ individuals (e.g., qualified ex-felons, high-risk youth, food stamp recipients, and veterans). The employer's deduction for wages is reduced by the amount of the credit taken. For qualified summer youth employees, the 40 percent rate is applied to the first $3,000 of qualified wages. §§ 51 and 52.

Working condition fringe.   A type of fringe benefit received by the employee that is excludible from the employee's gross income. It consists of property or services provided (paid or reimbursed) by the employer for which the employee could take a tax deduction if the employee had paid for them. § 132.

Worthless securities.   A loss (usually capital) is allowed for a security that becomes worthless during the year. The loss is deemed to have occurred on the last day of the year. Special rules apply to securities of affiliated companies and small business stock. § 165.

Writ of Certiorari.   Appeal from a U.S. Court of Appeals to the U.S. Supreme Court is by Writ of Certiorari. The Supreme Court need not accept the appeal, and it usually does not (*cert. den.*) unless a conflict exists among the lower courts that must be resolved or a constitutional issue is involved.

Table of Code Sections Cited

[See Title 26 U.S.C.A.]

Table of Regulations Cited

Treasury Regulations

Table of Revenue Procedures and Revenue Rulings Cited

Table of Cases Cited

Present Value and Future Value Tables

Present Value of $1

N/R	4%	5%	6%	7%	8%	9%	10%	11%	12%	13%	14%
1	0.9615	0.9524	0.9434	0.9346	0.9259	0.9174	0.9091	0.9009	0.8929	0.8850	0.8772
2	0.9246	0.9070	0.8900	0.8734	0.8573	0.8417	0.8264	0.8116	0.7972	0.7831	0.7695
3	0.8890	0.8638	0.8396	0.8163	0.7938	0.7722	0.7513	0.7312	0.7118	0.6931	0.6750
4	0.8548	0.8227	0.7921	0.7629	0.7350	0.7084	0.6830	0.6587	0.6355	0.6133	0.5921
5	0.8219	0.7835	0.7473	0.7130	0.6806	0.6499	0.6209	0.5935	0.5674	0.5428	0.5194
6	0.7903	0.7462	0.7050	0.6663	0.6302	0.5963	0.5645	0.5346	0.5066	0.4803	0.4556
7	0.7599	0.7107	0.6651	0.6227	0.5835	0.5470	0.5132	0.4817	0.4523	0.4251	0.3996
8	0.7307	0.6768	0.6274	0.5820	0.5403	0.5019	0.4665	0.4339	0.4039	0.3762	0.3506
9	0.7026	0.6446	0.5919	0.5439	0.5002	0.4604	0.4241	0.3909	0.3606	0.3329	0.3075
10	0.6756	0.6139	0.5584	0.5083	0.4632	0.4224	0.3855	0.3522	0.3220	0.2946	0.2697
11	0.6496	0.5847	0.5268	0.4751	0.4289	0.3875	0.3505	0.3173	0.2875	0.2607	0.2366
12	0.6246	0.5568	0.4970	0.4440	0.3971	0.3555	0.3186	0.2858	0.2567	0.2307	0.2076
13	0.6006	0.5303	0.4688	0.4150	0.3677	0.3262	0.2897	0.2575	0.2292	0.2042	0.1821
14	0.5775	0.5051	0.4423	0.3878	0.3405	0.2992	0.2633	0.2320	0.2046	0.1807	0.1597
15	0.5553	0.4810	0.4173	0.3624	0.3152	0.2745	0.2394	0.2090	0.1827	0.1599	0.1401
16	0.5339	0.4581	0.3936	0.3387	0.2919	0.2519	0.2176	0.1883	0.1631	0.1415	0.1229
17	0.5134	0.4363	0.3714	0.3166	0.2703	0.2311	0.1978	0.1696	0.1456	0.1252	0.1078
18	0.4936	0.4155	0.3503	0.2959	0.2502	0.2120	0.1799	0.1528	0.1300	0.1108	0.0946
19	0.4746	0.3957	0.3305	0.2765	0.2317	0.1945	0.1635	0.1377	0.1161	0.0981	0.0829
20	0.4564	0.3769	0.3118	0.2584	0.2145	0.1784	0.1486	0.1240	0.1037	0.0868	0.0728

Present Value of an Ordinary Annuity of $1

N/R	4%	5%	6%	7%	8%	9%	10%	11%	12%	13%	14%
1	0.9615	0.9524	0.9434	0.9346	0.9259	0.9174	0.9091	0.9009	0.8929	0.8850	0.8772
2	1.8861	1.8594	1.8334	1.8080	1.7833	1.7591	1.7355	1.7125	1.6901	1.6681	1.6467
3	2.7751	2.7232	2.6730	2.6243	2.5771	2.5313	2.4869	2.4437	2.4018	2.3612	2.3216
4	3.6299	3.5460	3.4651	3.3872	3.3121	3.2397	3.1699	3.1024	3.0373	2.9745	2.9137
5	4.4518	4.3295	4.2124	4.1002	3.9927	3.8897	3.7908	3.6959	3.6048	3.5172	3.4331
6	5.2421	5.0757	4.9173	4.7665	4.6229	4.4859	4.3553	4.2305	4.1114	3.9975	3.8887
7	6.0021	5.7864	5.5824	5.3893	5.2064	5.0330	4.8684	4.7122	4.5638	4.4226	4.2883
8	6.7327	6.4632	6.2098	5.9713	5.7466	5.5348	5.3349	5.1461	4.9676	4.7988	4.6389
9	7.4353	7.1078	6.8017	6.5152	6.2469	5.9952	5.7590	5.5370	5.3282	5.1317	4.9464
10	8.1109	7.7217	7.3601	7.0236	6.7101	6.4177	6.1446	5.8892	5.6502	5.4262	5.2161
11	8.7605	8.3064	7.8869	7.4987	7.1390	6.8052	6.4951	6.2065	5.9377	5.6869	5.4527
12	9.3851	8.8633	8.3838	7.9427	7.5361	7.1607	6.8137	6.4924	6.1944	5.9176	5.6603
13	9.9856	9.3936	8.8527	8.3577	7.9038	7.4869	7.1034	6.7499	6.4235	6.1218	5.8424
14	10.5631	9.8986	9.2950	8.7455	8.2442	7.7862	7.3667	6.9819	6.6282	6.3025	6.0021
15	11.1184	10.3797	9.7122	9.1079	8.5595	8.0607	7.6061	7.1909	6.8109	6.4624	6.1422
16	11.6523	10.8378	10.1059	9.4466	8.8514	8.3126	7.8237	7.3792	6.9740	6.6039	6.2651
17	12.1657	11.2741	10.4773	9.7632	9.1216	8.5436	8.0216	7.5488	7.1196	6.7291	6.3729
18	12.6593	11.6896	10.8276	10.0591	9.3719	8.7556	8.2014	7.7016	7.2497	6.8399	6.4674
19	13.1339	12.0853	11.1581	10.3356	9.6036	8.9501	8.3649	7.8393	7.3658	6.9380	6.5504
20	13.5903	12.4622	11.4699	10.5940	9.8181	9.1285	8.5136	7.9633	7.4694	7.0248	6.6231

Future Value of $1

N/R	4%	5%	6%	7%	8%	9%	10%	11%	12%	13%	14%
1	1.0400	1.0500	1.0600	1.0700	1.0800	1.0900	1.1000	1.1100	1.1200	1.1300	1.1400
2	1.0816	1.1025	1.1236	1.1449	1.1664	1.1881	1.2100	1.2321	1.2544	1.2769	1.2996
3	1.1249	1.1576	1.1910	1.2250	1.2597	1.2950	1.3310	1.3676	1.4049	1.4429	1.4815
4	1.1699	1.2155	1.2625	1.3108	1.3605	1.4116	1.4641	1.5181	1.5735	1.6305	1.6890
5	1.2167	1.2763	1.3382	1.4026	1.4693	1.5386	1.6105	1.6851	1.7623	1.8424	1.9254
6	1.2653	1.3401	1.4185	1.5007	1.5869	1.6771	1.7716	1.8704	1.9738	2.0820	2.1950
7	1.3159	1.4071	1.5036	1.6058	1.7138	1.8280	1.9487	2.0762	2.2107	2.3526	2.5023
8	1.3686	1.4775	1.5938	1.7182	1.8509	1.9926	2.1436	2.3045	2.4760	2.6584	2.8526
9	1.4233	1.5513	1.6895	1.8385	1.9990	2.1719	2.3579	2.5580	2.7731	3.0040	3.2519
10	1.4802	1.6289	1.7908	1.9672	2.1589	2.3674	2.5937	2.8394	3.1058	3.3946	3.7072
11	1.5395	1.7103	1.8983	2.1049	2.3316	2.5804	2.8531	3.1518	3.4785	3.8359	4.2262
12	1.6010	1.7959	2.0122	2.2522	2.5182	2.8127	3.1384	3.4985	3.8960	4.3345	4.8179
13	1.6651	1.8856	2.1329	2.4098	2.7196	3.0658	3.4523	3.8833	4.3635	4.8980	5.4924
14	1.7317	1.9799	2.2609	2.5785	2.9372	3.3417	3.7975	4.3104	4.8871	5.5348	6.2613
15	1.8009	2.0789	2.3966	2.7590	3.1722	3.6425	4.1772	4.7846	5.4736	6.2543	7.1379
16	1.8730	2.1829	2.5404	2.9522	3.4259	3.9703	4.5950	5.3109	6.1304	7.0673	8.1372
17	1.9479	2.2920	2.6928	3.1588	3.7000	4.3276	5.0545	5.8951	6.8660	7.9861	9.2765
18	2.0258	2.4066	2.8543	3.3799	3.9960	4.7171	5.5599	6.5436	7.6900	9.0243	10.5752
19	2.1068	2.5270	3.0256	3.6165	4.3157	5.1417	6.1159	7.2633	8.6128	10.1974	12.0557
20	2.1911	2.6533	3.2071	3.8697	4.6610	5.6044	6.7275	8.0623	9.6463	11.5231	13.7435

Future Value of an Ordinary Annuity of $1

N/R	4%	5%	6%	7%	8%	9%	10%	11%	12%	13%	14%
1	1.0000	1.0000	1.0000	1.0000	1.0000	1.0000	1.0000	1.0000	1.0000	1.0000	1.0000
2	2.0400	2.0500	2.0600	2.0700	2.0800	2.0900	2.1000	2.1100	2.1200	2.1300	2.1400
3	3.1216	3.1525	3.1836	3.2149	3.2464	3.2781	3.3100	3.3421	3.3744	3.4069	3.4396
4	4.2465	4.3101	4.3746	4.4399	4.5061	4.5731	4.6410	4.7097	4.7793	4.8498	4.9211
5	5.4163	5.5256	5.6371	5.7507	5.8666	5.9847	6.1051	6.2278	6.3528	6.4803	6.6101
6	6.6330	6.8019	6.9753	7.1533	7.3359	7.5233	7.7156	7.9129	8.1152	8.3227	8.5355
7	7.8983	8.1420	8.3938	8.6540	8.9228	9.2004	9.4872	9.7833	10.0890	10.4047	10.7305
8	9.2142	9.5491	9.8975	10.2598	10.6366	11.0285	11.4359	11.8594	12.2997	12.7573	13.2328
9	10.5828	11.0266	11.4913	11.9780	12.4876	13.0210	13.5795	14.1640	14.7757	15.4157	16.0853
10	12.0061	12.5779	13.1808	13.8164	14.4866	15.1929	15.9374	16.7220	17.5487	18.4197	19.3373
11	13.4864	14.2068	14.9716	15.7836	16.6455	17.5603	18.5312	19.5614	20.6546	21.8143	23.0445
12	15.0258	15.9171	16.8699	17.8885	18.9771	20.1407	21.3843	22.7132	24.1331	25.6502	27.2707
13	16.6268	17.7130	18.8821	20.1406	21.4953	22.9534	24.5227	26.2116	28.0291	29.9847	32.0887
14	18.2919	19.5986	21.0151	22.5505	24.2149	26.0192	27.9750	30.0949	32.3926	34.8827	35.5811
15	20.0236	21.5786	23.2760	25.1290	27.1521	29.3609	31.7725	34.4054	37.2797	40.4175	43.8424
16	21.8245	23.6575	25.6725	27.8881	30.3243	33.0034	35.9497	39.1899	42.7533	46.6717	50.9804
17	23.6975	25.8404	28.2129	30.8402	33.7502	36.9737	40.5447	44.5008	48.8837	53.7391	59.1176
18	25.6454	28.1324	30.9057	33.9990	37.4502	41.3013	45.5992	50.3959	55.7497	61.7251	68.3941
19	27.6712	30.5390	33.7600	37.3790	41.4463	46.0185	51.1591	56.9395	63.4397	70.7494	78.9692
20	29.7781	33.0660	36.7856	40.9955	45.7620	51.1601	57.2750	64.2028	72.0524	80.9468	91.0249

AMT Formula for Individuals

Regular Taxable Income

Plus or minus:	Adjustments
Plus:	Tax preferences
Equals:	Alternative minimum taxable income
Minus:	Exemption
Equals:	Alternative minimum tax base
Times:	26% and 28% graduated rates
Equals:	Tentative minimum tax before foreign tax credit
Minus:	Alternative minimum tax foreign tax credit
Equals:	Tentative minimum tax
Minus:	Regular income tax liability
Equals:	Alternative minimum tax (if amount is positive)

AMT Formula for Corporations

Regular Taxable Income before NOL Deduction

Plus or minus:	Adjustments (except ACE adjustment)
Plus:	Tax preferences
Equals:	AMTI before ATNOL deduction and ACE adjustment
Plus or minus:	ACE adjustment
Equals:	Alternative minimum taxable income (AMTI) before ATNOL deduction
Minus:	ATNOL deduction (limited to 90% of AMTI before ATNOL deduction)
Equals:	Alternative minimum taxable income (AMTI)
Minus:	Exemption
Equals:	Alternative minimum tax base
Times:	20% rate
Equals:	AMT before AMT foreign tax credit
Minus:	AMT foreign tax credit (possibly limited to 90% of AMT before AMT foreign tax credit)
Equals:	Tentative minimum tax
Minus:	Regular income tax liability before credits minus regular foreign tax credit
Equals:	Alternative minimum tax (AMT) if positive

Tax Formula for Corporate Taxpayers

Income (broadly conceived)	$xxx,xxx
Less: Exclusions (income that is not subject to tax)	(xx,xxx)
Gross income..	$xxx,xxx
Less: Certain business deductions	(xx,xxx)
Taxable income	$xxx,xxx
Federal income tax (see Tax Rate Schedule inside front cover of text)..	$ xx,xxx
Less: Tax credits (including Federal income tax withheld and other prepayments of Federal income taxes).......................	(x,xxx)
Tax owed (or refund due)...	$ xx,xxx